Resolving Disputes

Resolving Disputes
Theory, Practice, and Law

Jay Folberg

University of San Francisco

Dwight Golann

Suffolk University

Lisa Kloppenberg

University of Dayton

Thomas Stipanowich

CPR Institute for Dispute Resolution

ASPEN

PUBLISHERS

111 Eighth Avenue, New York, NY 10011
www.aspenpublishers.com

© 2005 Aspen Publishers, Inc.
A Wolters Kluwer Company
www.aspenpublishers.com

Printed in the United States of America.

1 2 3 4 5 6 7 8 9 0

ISBN 0-7355-4020-9

Library of Congress Cataloging-in-Publication Data

Resolving disputes : theory, practice, and law / Jay Folberg . . . [et al.]. — 1st ed.
   p. cm.
  Includes bibliographical references and index.
  ISBN 0-7355-4020-9
  1. Dispute resolution (Law) — United States. 2. Compromise (Law) — United States. I.
Folberg, Jay, 1941–
  KF9084.R475 2005
  347.73'9 — dc22

                                          2005000047

About Aspen Publishers

Aspen Publishers, headquartered in New York City, is a leading information provider for attorneys, business professionals, and law students. Written by preeminent authorities, our products consist of analytical and practical information covering both U.S. and international topics. We publish in the full range of formats, including updated manuals, books, periodicals, CDs, and online products.

Our proprietary content is complemented by 2,500 legal databases, containing over 11 million documents, available through our Loislaw division. Aspen Publishers also offers a wide range of topical legal and business databases linked to Loislaw's primary material. Our mission is to provide accurate, timely, and authoritative content in easily accessible formats, supported by unmatched customer care.

To order any Aspen Publishers title, go to *www.aspenpublishers.com* or call 1-800-638-8437.

To reinstate your manual update service, call 1-800-638-8437.

For more information on Loislaw products, go to *www.loislaw.com* or call 1-800-364-2512.

For Customer Care issues, e-mail CustomerCare@aspenpublishers.com; call 1-800-234-1660; or fax 1-800-901-9075.

Aspen Publishers
A Wolters Kluwer Company

To my father, Lew Folberg, the pawn broker who taught me the
art of negotiation — J.F.

To my father, Herbert Goldberg, whose inventiveness in other fields has
inspired my work — D.G.

To my parents, Edwin and Angeline Kloppenberg,
and my first ADR teacher, the Honorable Dorothy Wright Nelson,
and my loving family — L.K.

To my wife, Sky, and my daughters, Laura and Sarah — all of whom,
in their various ways, contributed to this book — T.S.

SUMMARY OF CONTENTS

CONTENTS

CHAPTER 5
THE NEGOTIATION DANCE — STEP BY STEP   79

CHAPTER 6
GENDER AND CULTURAL CONSIDERATIONS   149

CHAPTER 7
THE ETHICAL NEGOTIATOR   165

PART II

MEDIATION	**221**

CHAPTER 9
MEDIATION — THE BIG PICTURE

223

CHAPTER 12
SPECIFIC APPLICATIONS   **355**

CHAPTER 17
THE LEGAL FRAMEWORK SUPPORTING
ARBITRATION   517

PART IV

MIXING, MATCHING, AND MOVING FORWARD   607

CHAPTER 19
MATCHING THE PROCESS TO THE DISPUTE   609

CHAPTER 20
"ICE BREAKERS," STEPPED CLAUSES, AND
CONFLICT MANAGEMENT SYSTEMS   619

PREFACE

The title of this book, *Resolving Disputes*, reflects the active role of lawyers in representing clients who retain us to conclude their disputes favorably. This text is based on three key assumptions: First, in order to represent clients effectively and craft successful outcomes, the next generation of lawyers must be able to use the full spectrum of dispute resolution options and match the appropriate process to the dispute. Second, new lawyers are much more likely to encounter dispute resolution processes as advocates or advisors to clients than as professional neutrals. Finally, a text on dispute resolution should be interesting to read and should bring together the latest and best writing on the use and limits of alternative dispute resolution (ADR).

Our book, therefore, has a different emphasis from that of other ADR texts. It is written from the perspective of a lawyer representing clients, rather than for someone negotiating for themselves, serving as a neutral, or seeking to reform our legal system. The text is practical, while grounded in theory. The material is lawyer focused, but enriched by interdisciplinary knowledge. The readings are current yet do not neglect historical roots or what appears on the horizon of practice.

Real-life and literary examples are provided to illustrate vividly the readings and pique interest. Ample questions are asked to provoke critical thinking about the readings and stimulate class discussion. Accompanying exercises and role-plays allow students to apply the readings and bring the material to life. Most of the exercises and role-plays are based on the types of disputes in which lawyers are most likely to find themselves — significant legal disputes, as opposed to neighborhood quarrels or personal conflicts. There is also a comprehensive bibliography to give readers access to a wide variety of writings by teachers and scholars in the field.

We begin the book with an overview of the disputing universe, including the phenomenon of the "vanishing trial." After an orientation to the full spectrum of dispute resolution and its context for lawyers, we study the lawyer's role in the four categories of alternatives to trial — negotiation, mediation, arbitration, and stepped or hybrid processes. In each section we cover theory, techniques, policy issues, ethics, and law.

The negotiation section starts with the nature of conflict and the role of perceptions. We emphasize negotiating as a professional agent for others, and analyze both distributive and integrative bargaining, with a step-by-step explanation and comparison. The negotiation process and outcome-enhancing skills are covered in detail from preparation to writing the agreement. Students are guided to explore issues of style, gender, and culture, and encouraged to negotiate within their comfort zone. A rich selection of readings is provided, and additional notes enhance the negotiation coverage, including game theory, decision analysis, and the use of computer software.

An inside look at the mediation of a prominent student death case and the Microsoft litigation introduces the mediation section. We consider the predominant styles of commercial mediation that lawyers are likely to experience, as well as other approaches such as transformative mediation. Our focus is on representing clients in mediation and using the power of the mediator to meet their needs. Separately we present specific application of mediation to several important categories of disputes, including family, employment, environmental, intellectual property, and criminal matters. Court-connected mediation and concerns about fairness are also covered.

In the arbitration materials we depart from the traditional emphasis exclusively on case decisions, while covering comprehensively the basics of arbitration for lawyers. We provide informative narratives and hands-on exercises that involve scenarios most often encountered by new lawyers. Legal issues are presented that arise in both domestic and international arbitration. The arbitration section offers what a lawyer needs to know to maximize clients' interests in drafting an agreement to arbitrate, as well as to advocate on their behalf. Concerns about the fairness of mandatory arbitration and other recent developments are also considered.

The book concludes with a synthesis of mixed and stepped processes. Hybrid combinations of negotiation, mediation, and arbitration are explored that allow clients to settle disputes more efficiently and lawyers to deal with barriers to resolution more effectively. Readers are provided with new and creative components to design dispute resolution programs for clients. Finally, we present evolving opportunities for using what has been learned in the course and discuss the challenges that lawyers are likely to encounter in preventing and resolving disputes.

We have deliberately chosen the most recent writings on ADR so teachers will not need to prepare supplements in order to assign entirely up-to-date material. Readings have been carefully selected and edited to keep the material interesting and lively. We also take advantage of new technology, and of students' increasing preference for electronic and video formats. Items that have traditionally gone into a paper appendix now appear on the book's Web site. This makes this book lighter and easier to carry without sacrificing depth. Readers can download a specific rule, law, or standard clause for discussion or study. An accompanying teaching DVD available to adopting professors shows various styles of negotiation and mediation, and techniques ranging from empathic listening to evaluation, as well as other learning examples coordinated with student role-plays.

A note about form: In order to focus discussion and conserve space, we have substantially edited the readings and have deleted most footnotes, references, and case citations. Deletions of material are shown by three dots, but omitted footnotes and other references are not indicated. The footnotes we have retained in excerpts carry their original number, while our own footnotes appear with either asterisks or sequential numbering, as appropriate.

This book is the culmination of our combined decades of teaching, practicing, and shaping dispute resolution in legal contexts. Although our acknowledgments follow, we are grateful to the many students and lawyers we have had the pleasure of teaching and from whom we have learned much about what they want in a dispute resolution text.

January 2005   J.F.
                                                                       D.G.
                                                                       L.K.
                                                                       T.S.

ACKNOWLEDGMENTS

This book, like ADR, has many mothers and fathers, as well as a supportive family too large to thank by name. We are most grateful to our past students who have inspired us and guided what we have selected here to present to the next generation of students. We are indebted to the many authors and publishers who have granted their permission for us to include and edit parts of their publications. We are thankful for the support and assistance we have received from the staffs of our respective institutions. Special thanks goes to the anonymous reviewers, whose comments on the draft text were incisive and extremely helpful in refining this book.

The genesis of this text was a fellowship from the Rockefeller Foundation that allowed then Dean Folberg to spend a heavenly month at the Foundation's Bellagio Center completing an outline of the contents and writing a publishing proposal. Our friend Laird Kirkpatrick helped shape the concept of this book and introduced our proposal to Aspen Publishers. Aspen Acquisition Editor Lynn Churchill was ever helpful and cheerful and Managing Editor Barbara Roth kept us on track and guided us along the way. We greatly appreciate the roles of Dean Kirkpatrick and the editors at Aspen for making this book a reality.

Jay Folberg particularly thanks University of San Francisco School of Law Dean Jeff Brand and Faculty Services Coordinator Julia Dunbar for their generosity in making precious resources available for this project, and Gabe Madway for his skillful word processing. The help of law students Allyson Ukishima, Ashley Schuh, and Michael Wilt was invaluable. The management, neutrals, and staff of JAMS have provided the model of ADR success and inspiration that demonstrate what professional ADR can accomplish.

Dwight Golann would like to recognize Frank Sander, whose encouragement and example brought him into the field of ADR. He would like also to thank Josh Cooper, Kathryn Karczewska, and Kerri Tasker for helpful critiques and research, and Sarah Swan and Marilyn Morehouse for typing the readings.

Lisa Kloppenberg expresses her thanks to her family—Mark, Kelly, Tim, and Nick Zunich—who supported this work with great patience, love, and generosity. She is grateful to her colleagues at the University of Dayton who understood the importance of this project. Finally, Dean Kloppenberg is indebted to the excellent effort of her student research assistants who lent their creativity, insights, and intelligence to strengthen this book: Barbara Hellman, Jennifer Holland, Justin Kudela, Jon Smallwood, and Betsy West Stuver.

Tom Stipanowich wishes to thank his colleagues at the CPR Institute for Dispute Resolution (now the International Institute for Conflict Prevention and Resolution) for their input and support, and the following law students for their excellent research assistance: Katja Modric (Columbia), Helen Sunderland (Washington), Laura Stipanowich (Virginia), and Mark Boyko (NYU). He particularly appreciates the support and understanding of his wife Sky and daughter Sarah, who missed him on many nights and weekends during the preparation of these materials.

We are grateful to the following sources for permission to publish excerpts of their work:

Aaron, Marjorie C., Mediation Practice Do's and Don'ts (2001). Reprinted with permission of the author.

Aaron, Marjorie, and David Hoffer, on Decision Analysis in Dwight Golann, Mediating Legal Disputes. Copyright © 1996 by Dwight Golann. Reprinted with permission.

Abramson, Harold, Mediation Representation: Advocating in a Problem-Solving Process. Copyright © 2004 by the National Institute for Trial Advocacy (NITA). Reprinted with permission from the National Institute for Trial Advocacy. Further reproduction is prohibited.

Adler, Robert S., and Elliot M. Silverstein, "When David Meets Goliath: Dealing with Power Differentials in Negotiations," 5 Harv. Negot. L. Rev. 1. Copyright © 2000. Reprinted with permission.

Ambrose, Stephen, Undaunted Courage: Meriwether Lewis, Thomas Jefferson and the Opening of the American West. Copyright © 1996 by Ambrose-Tubbs, Inc. Abridged by permission of Simon & Schuster Adult Publishing Group and Ambrose & Ambrose, Inc.

Arnold, Thomas, "Client Preparation for Mediation," 15 Corp. Couns. Q. 52 (April 1999). Copyright © 1999 by Tom Arnold, Esq. Reprinted with permission.

Arnold, Tom, "20 Common Errors in Mediation Advocacy," 13 Alternatives 69 (1995). Copyright © 1995. Reprinted with permission of John Wiley & Sons, Inc.

Bahadoran, Sina, "A Red Flag: Mediator Cultural Bias in Divorce Mediation," 18 Mass. Fam. L.J. 69. Copyright © 2000. Reprinted with permission of the author.

Berger, Marilyn, "Clark Clifford, Key Advisor to Four Presidents, Dies," New York Times, October 11, 1998. Copyright © 1998 by The New York Times Co. Reprinted with permission.

Bingham, Gail, "Mediators Are Making a Difference." This article originally appeared in AC Resolution 21 (Summer 2002). Reproduced by permission of the Association for Conflict Resolution (ACR). www.ACRnet.org.

Bingham, Lisa B., "A Breakthrough Mediation Program: REDRESS™ at the USPS." This article originally appeared in AC Resolution 34 (Spring 2002). Reproduced by permission of the Association for Conflict Resolution (ACR). www.ACRnet.org.

Birke, Richard, "Settlement Psychology: When Decision-Making Processes Fail," 18 Alternatives 203 (December 2000). Copyright © 2000. Reprinted with permission of John Wiley & Sons, Inc.

Birkoff, Juliana, and Robert Rack, with Judith M. Filner, "Points of View: Is Mediation Really a Profession?" 8 Disp. Resol. Mag. 10 (Fall 2001). Reprinted by permission.

Bowling, Daniel, and David Hoffman, "Bringing Peace into the Room: The Personal Qualities of the Mediator and Their Impact on the Mediation," 16 Negot. J. 5. Copyright © 2000 by Blackwell Publishers Ltd. Reprinted with permission.

Brazil, Wayne. This excerpt from "A Judge's Perspective on Lawyering and ADR" is reprinted from Into the 21st Century: Thought Pieces on

Lawyering, Problem Solving and ADR, 19 Alternatives (CPR Institute January 2001).

Brazil, Wayne D., "Why Should Courts Offer Non-Binding ADR Services?" 16 Alternatives 65 (May 1998). Copyright © 1998. Reprinted with permission of John Wiley & Sons, Inc.

Bryant, Ken, and Dana Curtis, Reframing. Reprinted with permission of the authors.

Bush, Robert Baruch, and Sally Ganong Pope, "Transformative Mediation: Principles and Practice in Divorce Mediation," from J. Folberg et al., eds., Divorce and Family Mediation. Copyright © 2004 by Guilford Press. Reprinted with permission of the Guilford Press.

Carlton, Jim, "Microsoft, Stac End Battle with Pact, A 'Win-Win' Cross-Licensing Agreement," Wall Street Journal, June 22, 1984. Copyright 1984 by Dow Jones & Co. Inc. Reproduced with permission of Dow Jones & Co. Inc.

Cole, Sarah Rudolph, "Incentives and Arbitration: The Case Against Enforcement of Executory Arbitration Agreements Between Employers and Employees," 64 UMKC L. Rev. 449 (Spring 1996). Copyright © 1996. Reprinted with permission.

Condlin, Robert, "Bargaining in the Dark: The Normative Incoherence of Lawyer Dispute Bargaining Role," 51 Md. L. Rev. 1, 71-72, 75-82, 84-85 (1992). Copyright © 1992 by Robert Condlin. Reprinted with permission.

Costantino, Cathy A., and Christina Sickles Merchant, Designing Conflict Management Systems. Copyright © 1996. Reprinted with permission of John Wiley & Sons, Inc.

CPR Institute for Dispute Resolution. © 2004 CPR Institute for Dispute Resolution, 366 Madison Avenue, New York, NY 10017-3122; (212) 949-6490, www.cpradr.org. This excerpt from CPR Corporate Policy Statement on Alternatives to Litigation reprinted with permission of CPR Institute. The CPR Institute is a nonprofit initiative of 500 general counsel of major corporations, leading law firms and prominent legal academics whose mission is to install alternative dispute resolution (ADR) into the mainstream of legal practice.

CPR Institute for Dispute Resolution. © 2004 CPR Institute for Dispute Resolution, 366 Madison Avenue, New York, NY 10017-3122; (212) 949-6490, www.cpradr.org. This excerpt from A Suitability Screen for Arbitration reprinted with permission of CPR Institute. The CPR Institute is a nonprofit initiative of 500 general counsel of major corporations, leading law firms and prominent legal academics whose mission is to install alternative dispute resolution (ADR) into the mainstream of legal practice.

Craver, Charles B. Excerpted from Effective Legal Negotiation and Settlement, 4th ed., with permission. Copyright 2001 Matthew Bender & Company, Inc., a member of the LexisNexis Group. All rights reserved.

Curtis, Dana, "Reconciliation and the Role of Empathy," in James Alfini and Eric Galton, ADR Personalities and Practice Tips, p. 53 (1998). Reprinted by permission.

Curtis, Dana, and John Toker, "Representing Clients in Appellate Mediation: The Last Frontier," 1 JAMS Alert 1 (December 2000).

Reprinted with permission. Copyright 2004 JAMS, The Resolution
Experts. All rights reserved.

Dawson, Roger. Reprinted, with permission of the publisher, from Secrets
of Power Negotiating, 2d ed. © 2001 Roger Dawson. Published by
Career Press, Franklin Lakes, NJ. All rights reserved.

Delgado, Richard, "ADR and the Dispossessed: Recent Books About the
Deformalization Movement," 13 Law & Soc. Inquiry 145. Copyright ©
1988 by The University of Chicago Press. Reprinted with permission.

Donahey, M. Scott, "The Asian Concept of Conciliator/Arbitrator: Is It
Translatable to the Western World?" 10 Foreign Investment L.J. 120
(1995). Reprinted with permission.

Dunnigan, Alana, "Comment—Restoring Power to the Powerless: The
Need to Reform California's Mandatory Mediation for Victims of
Domestic Violence," 37 U.S.F. L. Rev. 1031 (2003). Reprinted with
permission of the University of San Francisco Law Review.

Epstein, Lynn A., "Post-Settlement Malpractice: Undoing the Done Deal,"
46 Cath. U. L. Rev. 453. Copyright © 1997. Reprinted with permission.

Erickson, Stephen K., and Marilyn S. McKnight, The Practitioner's
Guide to Mediation: A Client-Centered Approach. Copyright ©
2001. Reprinted with permission of John Wiley & Sons, Inc.

Feinberg, Kenneth R. Using ADR to Resolve Disputes and Implement a
Settlement. This excerpt from "One-Stop Shopping: Using ADR to
Resolve Disputes and Implement a Settlement" is reprinted from
Into the 21st Century: Thought Pieces on Lawyering, Problem Solving
and ADR," 19 Alternatives (CPR Institute January 2001).

Fisher, Roger, "Negotiating Powers: Getting and Using Influence," 27 Am.
Behav. Sci. (November/December 1983). Reprinted by permission of
Sage Publications, Inc.

Flaherty, Francis, "Neutrals Deployed Several Kinds of ADR to Solve IBM-
Fujitsu Copyright Dispute," 5 Alternatives 187 (November 1987).
Copyright © 1987. Reprinted with permission of John Wiley & Sons,
Inc.

Folberg, Jay, "Divorce Mediation: The Emerging American Model," paper
presented at Fourth Annual Conference of the International Society
for Family Law, Harvard University (June 1982). From The Resolution
of Family Conflict, edited by John M. Eckelaar and Stanford Katz.
Reprinted with permission.

Fortier, L. Yves. This excerpt from "International 'E-Commercial' Dispute
Resolution" is reprinted from Into the 21st Century: Thought Pieces
on Lawyering, Problem Solving and ADR, 19 Alternatives (CPR
Institute January 2001).

Freedman, Lawrence, and Michael Prigoff, "Confidentiality in Mediation:
The Need for Protection," 2 J. Disp. Resol. 37. Copyright © 1986.
Reprinted with permission.

Golann, Dwight, "A Basic Mediative Strategy," in Mediating Legal Disputes.
Copyright © 1996 by Dwight Golann. Reprinted with permission.

Golann, Dwight, "Cognitive Barriers to Effective Negotiation," 6 ADR
Currents 6 (September 2001). Copyright © 2001 by American
Arbitration Association. Reprinted with permission.

Goldberg, Stephen B., Jeanne Brett, and William Ury, "Designing an
Effective Dispute Resolution System," adapted from Stephen B.

Laflin, James, and Robert Werth, "Unfinished Business: Another Look at
the Microsoft Mediation," 12 Cal. Tort Rep. 88 (April 2001). Reprinted
with permission.

Lax, David A., and James K. Sebenius. Reprinted with the permission of
the Free Press, a division of Simon & Schuster Adult Publishing Group,
from The Manager as Negotiator: Bargaining for Cooperation and
Competitive Gain by David A. Lax and James K. Sebenius. Copyright
© 1986 by David A. Lax and James K. Sebenius. All rights reserved.

Levin cartoon, © The New Yorker Collection 1982 Arnie Levin from car-
toonbank.com. All rights reserved.

Levinson, Conrad, Mark S.A. Smith, and Orvel Ray Wilson, Guerrilla
Negotiating: Unconventional Weapons and Tactics to Get What You
Want. Copyright © 1999. Reprinted with permission of John Wiley &
Sons, Inc.

Lewicki, Roy J., Bruce Barry, David M. Saunders, and John W. Minton,
Essentials of Negotiation, 3d ed., pp. 116-117. Copyright © 2004 by
the McGraw-Hill Companies, Inc. Reprinted with permission.

Lipsky, David A., and Ronald L. Seeber, "Patterns of ADR Use in
Corporate Disputes," Disp. Resol. J. 66 (February 1999). Reprinted
with permission of the Dispute Resolution Journal, a publication of
the American Arbitration Association.

Longan, Patrick, "Ethics in Settlement Negotiations: Foreword," 52 Mercer
L. Rev. 810-816. Copyright © 2001. Reprinted with permission.

Love, Lela, "The Top Ten Reasons Why Mediators Should Not Evaluate,"
24 Fla. St. U. L. Rev. Copyright © 1997. Reprinted with permission
from Florida State University Law Review.

Lowry, L. Randolph, "To Evaluate or Not—That Is Not the Question!"
2 Resolutions 2, 3 (Pepperdine University) (Winter 1997). Reprinted
with permission.

Lynch, Hon. Eugene, Douglas Young, Stephen Taylor, Jonathan Purver,
and James Davis III, The Settlement Agreement. Reprinted from
California Negotiation Handbook with permission. Copyright 1991
Matthew Bender & Company, Inc., a member of the LexisNexis
Group. All rights reserved.

McGuire, James E., "Certification: An Idea Whose Time Has Come," 10
Disp. Resol. Mag. 22 (Summer 2004). Reprinted by permission.

McGuire, James E., and Frank E.A. Sander, "Some Questions About 'The
Vanishing Trial,'"10 Disp. Resol. Mag. (Winter 2004). Copyright ©
2004 by the American Bar Association. Reprinted by permission.

Miller, Lee E., and Jessica Miller, A Woman's Guide to Successful
Negotiating, pp. 66-73 (2002). Reproduced with permission of the
McGraw-Hill Companies.

Milne, Ann L., "Mediation and Domestic Abuse," in J. Folberg et al., eds.,
Divorce and Family Mediation. Copyright © 2004 by Guilford Press.
Reprinted with permission of the Guilford Press.

Mnookin, Robert H., Scott R. Peppet, and Andrew S. Tulumello. Reprinted
by permission of the publisher from Beyond Winning: Negotiation to
Create Value in Deals and Disputes by Robert H. Mnookin, Scott R.
Peppet, and Andrew S. Tulumello, pp. 37-42, 282-286, Cambridge,
MA: The Belknap Press of Harvard University Press. Copyright ©
2000 by the President and Fellows of Harvard College.

Rummel, R.J., The Conflict Helix. Copyright © 1991 by Transaction Publishers. Reprinted with permission.

Salacuse, Jeswald, "Mediation in International Business." Copyright © Jacob Bercovitch. From Mediation in International Relations: Multiple Approaches to Conflict Management by Jacob Bercovitch. Reprinted with permission of Palgrave Macmillan.

Salem, Richard, "The Benefits of Empathic Listening" (2003). Reprinted from beyondintractability.org with permission of the Conflict Research Consortium, University of Colorado.

Saperstein, Guy T., Civil Warrior: Memoirs of a Civil Rights Attorney. Copyright 2003 by Guy T. Saperstein. Reprinted by permission of Berkeley Hills Books.

Scarlett, Helaine, and Dwight Golann, "Why Is It Hard for Lawyers to Deal with Emotional Issues?" 9 Disp. Resol. Mag. (Winter 2003). Copyright © 2003 by the American Bar Association. Reprinted by permission.

Schneider, Andrea Kupfer, "Perception, Reputation and Reality: An Empirical Study of Negotiation Skills," 6 Disp. Resol. Mag. (Summer 2000). Copyright © 2000 by the American Bar Association. Reprinted by permission.

Sebenius, James K., "Caveats for Cross-Border Negotiations," 18 Negot. J., 122-123, 126-131. Copyright © 2002 by Blackwell Publishers Ltd. Reprinted with permission.

Shell, G. Richard, "The Second Foundation: Your Goals and Expectations," in G. Richard Shell, Bargaining for Advantage. Copyright © 1999 by G. Richard Shell. Used by permission of Viking Penguin, a division of Penguin Group (USA) Inc.

Shell, G. Richard, "Step Four: Closing and Gaining Commitment," in G. Richard Shell, Bargaining for Advantage. Copyright © 1999 by G. Richard Shell. Used by permission of Viking Penguin, a division of Penguin Group (USA) Inc.

Singer, Linda R. This excerpt from "The Lawyer as Neutral" is reprinted from Into the 21st Century: Thought Pieces on Lawyering, Problem Solving and ADR, 19 Alternatives (CPR Institute January 2001).

Smith, Robert M., "Advocacy in Mediation: A Dozen Suggestions," 26 San Francisco Att'y 14 (June/July 2000). Copyright © 2000 by the Bar Association of San Francisco. Reprinted with permission.

Stipanowich, Thomas J., "The Multi-Door Contract and Other Possibilities," 13 Ohio St. J. on Disp. Resol. 303, 386-388. Copyright © 1998. Reprinted with permission.

Stipanowich, Thomas J., "ADR and the Vanishing Trial: The Growth and Impact of 'Alternative Dispute Resolution,'" 1 J. Empirical Legal Res. (2004). Reprinted by permission.

Stipanowich, Thomas J., and Craig A. McEwen, "Managing Corporate Disputing: Overcoming Barriers to the Effective Use of Mediation for Reducing the Cost and Time of Litigation," 14 Ohio St. J. on Disp. Resol. 1 (1998) as summarized in Thomas J. Stipanowich, "ADR and the Vanishing Trial: The Growth and Impact of 'Alternative Dispute Resolution,'" J. Empirical Legal Res. (2004).

Sumner, Ann Aven, "Is the Gummy Rule of Today Truly Better Than the Toothy Rule of Tomorrow? How Federal Rule 68 Should Be

Modified," 52 Duke L.J. 1055 (2003). Copyright © 2003. Reprinted with permission.

Technology Mediation Services, "Benefits of Mediating High Technology Disputes," www.technologymediation.com/hightech.htm. Copyright © 2004 by Technology Mediation Services. Reprinted with permission.

Thompson, Leigh L., The Mind and Heart of the Negotiator, 2d ed. © 2001. Reprinted by permission of Pearson Education, Inc., Upper Saddle River, NJ.

Uelmen, Gerald F., "Playing 'Godfather' " in Settlement Negotiations: The Ethics of Using Threats, California Litigation, pp. 3-8 (Fall 1990). Reprinted with permission.

Ukishima, Allyson, "Women and Legal Negotiation: Moving Beyond Gender Stereotypes and Adopting a 'Yin and Yang' Paradigm," University of San Francisco (Spring 2003). Reprinted with permission of the author.

Welsh, Nancy, and Barbara McAdoo, "Alternative Dispute Resolution in Minnesota—An Update on Rule 114," in Edward J. Bergman and John C. Bickerman, eds., Court-Annexed Mediation: Critical Perspectives on State and Federal Programs 203 (1998). Printed by permission of Pike & Fischer, Inc.

Wetlaufer, Gerald, "The Limits of Integrative Bargaining," 85 Geo. L.J. 369 (1996). Copyright © 1996. Reprinted with permission.

White, James J., "Pros and Cons of 'Getting to Yes'; Roger Fisher, Comments on White's Review," 34 J. Legal Educ. Copyright © 1984. Reprinted with permission.

Williams, Gerald. Reprinted from Gerald Williams, Legal Negotiation and Settlement (1983), with permission of Thomson West.

Williams, Gerald R., "Negotiation as a Healing Process," J. Disp. Resol. 1, 5-7, 42-46 (1996). Reprinted with permission of the author and the Journal of Dispute Resolution, University of Missouri-Columbia, Center for the Study of Dispute Resolution, 206 Hulston Hall, Columbia, MO 65211.

Wissler, Roselle, "To Evaluate or Facilitate? Parties' Perceptions of Mediation Affected by Mediator Style," 7 Disp. Resol. Mag. (Winter 2001). Copyright © 2001 by the American Bar Association. Reprinted by permission.

Wittenberg, Carol A., Susan T. Mackenzie, and Margaret L. Shaw, "Employment Disputes," in Dwight Golann, Mediating Legal Disputes. Copyright © 1996. Reprinted with permission of the author.

Zitrin, Richard A., and Carol M. Langford, in Richard Zitrin and Carol M. Langford, The Moral Compass of the American Lawyer. Copyright © 1999 by Richard A. Zitrin and Carol M. Langford. Used by permission of Ballantine Books, a division of Random House, Inc.

Resolving Disputes

CHAPTER
1

Dispute Resolution — What It's All About

"I found the old format much more exciting . . ."

It is a popular legend that the use of lawyers for dispute resolution evolved from the hiring of gladiators to fight the battles of those who retained them. Referring to lawyers as "modern-day gladiators" is, however, a misnomer. It is the parties who now directly bear most of the costs, risks, and injuries of legal combat. There have evolved multiple formats to resolve legal disputes, so today's lawyer when advising and representing clients must be familiar with available alternatives for dispute resolution and skillful in their use. The purpose of this course and this book is to provide you with the knowledge to counsel clients about the most appropriate process to resolve their dispute and to enhance your ability to represent them in the process chosen. The story about a carpenter with only a hammer and nails who has but one way to fix things is analogous to the limitations of a lawyer who only knows how to resolve disputes in court or a gladiator who only knows how to fight.

1

A. THE LANDSCAPE OF DISPUTES

Most of the disputes that your clients will seek your help to resolve will barely resemble the cases that you encountered in your first-year courses in law school. In place of a clearly defined contest between named parties over narrow issues, practicing lawyers typically deal with inchoate mixtures of grievances, emotions, and theories. Clients are usually clear about the heroes and villains in their disputes, but many of the other key facts are in doubt. Lacking a precise appellate record, attorneys typically work with, and must make decisions based upon, the fallible memories of clients and witnesses, as well as documents that are incomplete. In many situations attorneys must rely heavily on their experience and intuition to assess what their client's dispute is really about, and how it is likely to unfold.

The landscape of disputes that you will encounter in practice will depend on the path you choose. If you become a transactional lawyer, you will help clients to evaluate and structure potential deals, and then will be called upon to negotiate terms that give them the greatest advantages and least possible risk. Clients will respect you for your ability to steer them away from dangerous situations, but will value you most highly for positive skills — the ability to bring disparate parties together into productive agreements. Your ability to bargain well and be a problem solver will be crucial to your success as a deal maker.

If you become an inside counsel to a corporation or nonprofit organization, you will negotiate regularly as well, both with your counterparts in other entities and with colleagues in your own office. You may be surprised to learn that experienced corporate counsel often describe themselves not only as experienced negotiators, but also as "Mediators with a small 'm.'" What this means is that many inside counsel find that a major aspect of their work is to resolve disagreements and disputes between people within their company. Inside lawyers often find that they in fact have multiple "clients" in the form of different personalities and constituencies in their organization. Unless their constituencies can agree on a common course of action, it is very difficult for the attorney to produce a coherent legal policy or negotiate effectively with outsiders. Corporate counsel thus often find themselves playing the role of "honest broker," using meditative skills to forge a consensus among their multidimensional client.

Even if you assume the traditional role of civil litigator, the disputing landscape you encounter will bear little resemblance to the pinpointed issues and the neat body of appellate case law you studied. First, clients seldom know the precise issue that must be resolved, the opposing justification, or the remedies available. Second, most of the disputes that clients bring to litigators never become court cases. Good lawyers perform an important screening function, measuring their client's grievances against the requirements of the law and, perhaps even more critically, the client's larger interests.

Does the client have a viable legal theory? Will discovery produce factual evidence that supports a claim? Will the client be willing to persevere after his initial anger and frustration have died down, and does he have the resources to do so? Is it even in the client's best long-term interest to be involved in litigation? Is a court likely to side with him, and even if it does, will the potential defendant be able to satisfy a judgment? Just as very few screenplays ever become movies, the large majority of potential legal cases fall by the wayside long before they reach a courtroom!

Indeed, the rate of trial in the United States is miniscule. Of all civil cases that are filed in the federal court system, less than 2 percent actually reach trial. Statistics for most state courts are similar. This means that if a lawyer files a total of 100 cases in court, on average, she will never go to trial in 98 of them. Even if we allow for cases that are decided on the merits without a trial — for example through motions for summary judgment — *the vast majority of civil cases are never adjudicated on the merits*.

One important qualification needs to be noted when considering the relatively small number of cases going to trial. The possibility of going to trial has an impact on the dispute resolution decisions of litigants out of proportion to the actual frequency of trials. Their wish to avoid the "fire" of trial is a major factor in motivating parties to choose the "frying pan" of settlement. In other words, we bargain in the "shadow of the law." Decisions about whether, and on what terms, to settle a dispute are heavily influenced by predictions and concerns about what a court will do if an agreement is not reached. (See Mnookin and Kornhauser, 1979.)

B. DISPUTE RESOLUTION OPTIONS — THE SPECTRUM

As a practicing lawyer, you will have a wide variety of options to resolve your clients' disputes. They fall along a spectrum. At one end is direct negotiation. At the other end is a trial in court. Negotiation and trial are polar opposites. Parties who opt for trial have relatively little control over either the process or the outcome: The proceeding is a formal and public one, conducted under detailed procedural and evidentiary rules, with a judge in control. A third party — either a judge or jury — decides the outcome, and in doing so is bound to follow established legal principles. By contrast, negotiation gives parties maximum control over both the process and its outcome. Direct bargaining is an informal process, generally conducted in private and without set rules. Parties are free to agree to whatever outcomes they wish, subject to limits of contract law and public policy in enforcing their agreement.

In between direct negotiation and trial is a continuum of alternative dispute resolution (ADR) processes. The continuum moves from processes that have characteristics very similar to negotiation to ones that closely resemble a trial. The key characteristic that distinguishes negotiation-like processes from trial-like methods is whether a neutral party has the ability to impose a binding outcome on the participants. Proceedings in which the neutral can decide the result are all forms of adjudication. Processes that authorize the neutral to facilitate, persuade, even pressure parties — but not to impose a result on them — are all forms of assisted negotiation.

Mediators, for example, assist negotiators in reaching a settlement, but do not have the power to require disputants to reach agreement or impose a decision. For that reason, mediation and all of its variants are on the non-binding, assisted-negotiation side of the spectrum. By contrast, in traditional arbitration the neutral does have the power to decide the outcome, so

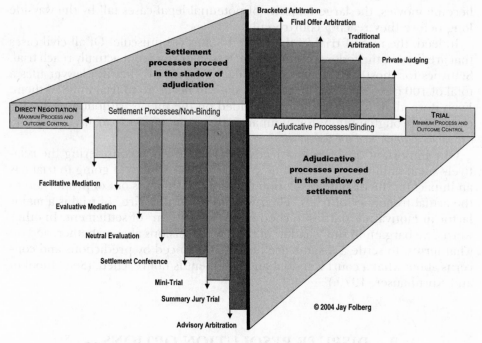

Figure 1.1
Dispute Resolution Spectrum

arbitration falls on the binding, adjudicative side of the spectrum. However, the terminology can be misleading. One example we will examine is a process known as advisory or judicial arbitration, which does not necessarily result in a binding decision. This is why we present dispute resolution processes as a spectrum of procedural shadings, with the central dividing characteristic or line being whether a neutral has authority to impose a binding outcome on the parties.

As we have noted, whenever a dispute involves a legal claim, the plaintiff can, at least in theory, obtain a binding decision from a court. The elephant in the closet of non-binding settlement efforts is the likely outcome if the dispute proceeds to trial. For this reason a "shadow of adjudication" extends across the non-binding side of the spectrum. Similarly, disputants can halt even a binding procedure by reaching agreement. Settlement negotiations, in effect, lurk in the closet of adjudication: We refer to this as the "shadow of settlement." A graphic presentation of the Dispute Resolution Spectrum is shown in Figure 1.1.

The process possibilities on the non-binding side of the spectrum are infinite, limited only by what the parties can create, agree upon, and afford. The spectrum displays the settlement processes and methods that are most often discussed in the literature and commonly used, now or in the recent past. They are arranged in descending order of process and outcome control, moving from free-flowing negotiation on the left toward processes that are more structured and judgmental. The processes are explained in more depth in the chapters that follow.

The variations of arbitration shown on the spectrum are discussed in the arbitration chapters of the book. A key element of arbitration, as compared with trial, is that it is a private process, defined by contract: The parties themselves can, within broad bounds, shape the process and set its rules. Parties can, for example, agree on maximum and minimum amounts that an arbitrator can award, known as "bracketed" arbitration. Alternatively, they can agree that the arbitrator must enter as her award either the terms proposed by the plaintiff or those submitted by the defendant, but cannot "split the difference" between them; this is known as "final offer" or "baseball" arbitration. Although parties can set the process rules and standards for the arbitrator's decision by contract, once they have agreed on a binding process, they are bound by their choices.

C. THE EVOLUTION OF DISPUTE RESOLUTION

The public, as well as most law students, think of dispute resolution primarily in terms of court trials. Access to courts to remedy wrongs and enforce legal rights is central to American democracy. We have fashioned a system of rules of procedure and evidence to ensure fair trials. We pride ourselves on having an independent judiciary composed of experienced and respected judges. We preserve the right to jury trials on common law claims. The judicial system provides for appellate review to ensure that the law is applied correctly and that procedural rules are properly followed. It is a complex and finely tuned system of public justice.

However, litigation with all of its procedural protections is slow, costly, and relatively inflexible. The process is also centered on lawyers, restricting the roles and expression of the disputing parties. The remedies available through adjudication are limited to what can be enforced through courts in combination with the police power of the state. Most commonly, a court judgment to resolve a dispute consists of ordering one party to pay money to another.

In part because of these limitations, alternatives to adjudication have long existed. Private negotiation of disputes and transactions has probably gone on literally since the beginning of human society, and third parties have helped people informally resolve conflicts since there were three people on earth. The early Quakers in the United States utilized mediation and arbitration as the principal means to resolve trade disputes and marital disagreements, and arbitration was used by merchants in pre-Revolutionary New York. Immigrants brought informal dispute resolution systems with them to the New World. Chinese immigrants, for example, set up the Chinese Benevolent Association to decide disputes between community and family members, and the American Jewish community reestablished its own dispute resolution forum, the Jewish Conciliation Board, in New York City. (See Folberg, 1983.)

Beginning in the 1960s the United States saw a flowering of interest in alternative forms of dispute resolution. The period was characterized by strife, conflict, and discontent on many fronts. The Vietnam War, civil rights struggles, student unrest, growing consumer awareness, examination of gender roles, and racial discrimination, all produced distrust of the status quo and more demand for court redress. Legislation created many new causes of action and reflected lower tolerance for perceived wrongs. Conflicts that in the past might have been resolved by deference, avoidance, or resignation were directed to the courts. Increased prosecution of drug related crimes, which have a

constitutionally based priority to speedy trial, also increased the demands on
the courts. Court resources were not increased proportionately and civil case
dockets became more backlogged.

Domestic relations case filings also soared. With the adoption of no-fault
divorce and the general increase in the divorce rate, court-connected family
mediation services proliferated, partly to conserve judicial resources and partly
to provide better outcomes for children. Parents more readily accepted a custody and visitation plan that they created with the help of a court mediator
than one imposed by a judge and filed fewer post divorce motions following
mediation. This served as an example of how courts could be more proactive in
managing their increasing case load by providing settlement services. (See
Folberg, 2003.)

At the same time community-based mediation programs grew up outside the
courts to resolve neighborhood disputes. Some legal service programs, as part
of the war on poverty, began experimenting with mediating and arbitrating
cases where neither party could afford lawyers. Business people, who could
afford lawyers but could not afford to wait for a court trial, increased their use
of private arbitration, particularly for time-sensitive cases such as disputes
involving ongoing construction projects. As all types of civil suits became
more complex and more expensive to prepare for trial, through extensive
motion practice and use of experts, interest in alternative forms of dispute
resolution increased.

Judges, motivated by a wish to relieve civil caseloads and reduce delay,
convened bench-bar committees to recommend alternative methods to resolve
cases. Local experimentation led to successes which were replicated and
refined in other jurisdictions. A rich array of court connected ADR processes
developed. Traditional settlement conferences conducted by judges were augmented and sometimes replaced by more innovative dispute resolution
options. Informal "settlement weeks" and case evaluation panels, both utilizing
volunteer lawyers, led to institutionalized programs, often imposed by statutes
and court rules that required litigants to engage in ADR.

Mediation of different types, often conducted for the court by lawyers in
their own offices, became the most popular form of court directed ADR. Some
courts hired full time staff to direct and manage cases in ADR programs. The
Alternative Dispute Resolution Act of 1998 requires all federal district courts to
establish an ADR program by local rule. Participation in some processes,
including early neutral evaluation and mediation, can be compelled in federal
courts, as in many state courts.

Although court ADR processes vary greatly, they share some common elements. Court ADR is intended to:

- relieve each attorney from being the one to initiate settlement discussions
- provide a stimulus or requirement for attorneys to explore settlement early
- promote or require involvement of key decision makers
- use attorneys as neutrals to augment judicial resources
- provide more flexibility than formal adjudication
- avoid involving the judge who will preside at trial

One perhaps unintended consequence of mandatory court connected ADR
programs, particularly mediation, has been to educate attorneys and business
executives about the positive potential of non-binding forms of ADR. Even

though most cases entered the court programs involuntarily, satisfaction rates were high. Occasional complaints about the quality of volunteer neutrals or bureaucratic restrictions could be remedied by having mutually respected neutrals serve for a fee privately outside the court. Corporate and insurance clients faced with long waits in court and increased litigation expenses, pushed for more use of private ADR. Plaintiffs' lawyers, reluctant at first, became more supportive of non-binding, voluntary forms of ADR when they realized that these could speed the collection of damages for clients in need and payment of their contingent fees. Greater efficiency, lower costs, more control, less risk, and improved outcomes were the driving forces for increased use of both court based and private ADR. The seeds were planted for what would later become a change in the legal culture regarding how disputes are resolved.

Existing private organizations providing ADR services had a growth spurt. The American Arbitration Association, which was arbitrating tens of thousands of cases in the 1980s, expanded and promoted the use of commercial mediation. The Center for Public Resources, now the CPR Institute for Dispute Resolution, supported primarily by corporate counsel and law firms to promote the use of appropriate dispute resolution, collected pledges from hundreds of major corporations and then law firms promising to use ADR to resolve disputes, rather than pursue litigation against one another. One private ADR provider organization founded in 1979 as Judicial Arbitration and Mediation Services, now JAMS, has grown to 22 offices nationwide. Local and regional groups of attorneys, as well as individual lawyers, retired judges and others, offer professional ADR services in every legal market. Listings of ADR neutral providers can be found in most telephone directories. Some law firms advertise their expertise in representing clients in ADR proceedings.

Whether due to the alternative dispute resolution movement or other factors, civil filings in some state courts have slowed, if not declined. In the Massachusetts court system, for instance, civil filings outside the family courts actually fell in the late 1990s, despite growth in both the state's population and economy. There has been a more dramatic decrease in both the percentage and actual number of cases going to trial in federal and state courts. The relationship between th   'ncrease in the percentage of filed cases being tried and the increased use of ADR in courts and privately is not clear.

The retirement of some judges to become well-paid private mediators and arbitrators, as well as other public policy concerns about the impact of ADR, resulted in the Chief Justice of the California Supreme Court appointing a task force to study the effects of ADR on the quality of justice. The task force found that the opportunity to serve as private ADR neutrals was only one of several possible causes of why judges might be retiring earlier. It also concluded that ADR, whether private, community, or court related, offered litigants and the public the benefit of greater choice, speed, savings, and satisfaction. (See Judicial Council of California, 1999.) The Task Force recommended several measures to educate the bench and the bar about the appropriate use of ADR and to gather more information on its effects. Based on a recommendation of the Task Force, California passed legislation creating court pilot programs to increase the use of early mediation and examine the results. In the reading that follows, one of this book's authors reviews some of the resulting data from the California pilot projects and then examines the profound acceptance and increased use of ADR by businesses and corporations.

THOMAS J. STIPANOWICH, ADR AND "THE VANISHING TRIAL": WHAT WE KNOW—AND WHAT WE DON'T

7-10, Disp. Resol. Mag. (Summer 2004)

Did a quarter-century of proliferating and widely disparate efforts to change the culture of conflict resolution—encompassing thousands of federal and state court, community, business and administrative agency initiatives promoting mediation, arbitration or other strategies; the spawning of new professional fields; and reforms in the education and training of lawyers and law students—transform the litigation experience of disputants, attorneys, and judges? . . . Here is a look at what we know—and don't know—about the relationship between ADR and litigation. . . .

ADR AND THE COURTS

A 2004 report published by the Judicial Council of California appears to have broken new ground in this regard, providing what may be the most enlightening examination of court-connected mediation ever conducted. A statute mandated Early Mediation Pilot Programs in four Superior Courts and required the Judicial Council to study these programs. The aim of the study was to assess the impact of the mediation programs in four distinctive areas: settlement/trial rate, disposition time, litigant/attorney satisfaction and costs for litigants and the court. To measure the overall effectiveness of the programs the research study used data provided by the courts' computerized case management system (CMS) and surveys of the parties, attorneys and judges. During the pilot period, nearly 8,000 cases were mediated in the programs. . . .

The California study produced a host of findings, including positive impacts on settlements and trial rate, disposition time, satisfaction and costs. Some salient points:

- In the San Diego and Los Angeles programs, the incidence of trial was 24 to 30 percent lower among cases in the mediation program group than those in the control group.
- All five pilot programs appeared to have resulted in reduced "disposition time" for cases and enhanced attorney perceptions of the services provided by the court and/or the litigation process.
- Additionally, four of the five pilot programs appear to have resulted in reduced numbers of motions or other pretrial court events.
- The data evidence significant reductions in litigant costs and attorney time resulting from the pilot programs: attorney estimates indicate that during 2000 and 2001, the programs may have saved in excess of $49 million in litigant costs and more than a quarter of a million attorney hours.

Within the 370+ pages of the report are important indicators of how program characteristics, the actions of courts, and local legal culture can cause wide variations in results. For example, whether a court-connected mediation program is officially "voluntary" or "mandatory," experiences, perceptions and results will vary considerably depending on the degree of judicial pressure to mediate, and the discretion judges show in determining which matters may be appropriately mediated. California's landmark study strongly supports the notion that court-connected mediation programs are capable of producing important benefits for courts, litigants and lawyers; it also reinforces the notion that much depends on the specific characteristics of a program, and the context within which it is established. The California data comes not a moment too soon; at least one of the court administrative centers connected to the pilot programs has already shut down for lack of funds.

BUSINESS AND CONFLICT MANAGEMENT

The rapid growth of federal and state court-connected ADR programs affected, and was paralleled by, initiatives to promote mediation and other alternatives to litigation in the world of business. Although there has been extensive research regarding ADR in some commercial sectors, such as the construction industry, empirical data on business experience has been relatively hard to find.

In 1997, a study of ADR use among Fortune 1,000 corporations was conducted by Cornell University. Based on responses from more than six hundred companies, the study concluded "that ADR processes are well established in corporate America, widespread in all industries and for nearly all types of disputes . . . [and] ADR practice is not haphazard or incidental but rather seems to be integral to a systematic, long-term change in the way corporations resolve disputes." A full 87% of responding companies reported some of use of mediation in the prior three years, and 80% reported using arbitration during the same period. Other forms of ADR, such as in-house grievance procedures, mini-trial, fact-finding, and ombudsman, were also used by some companies. Mediation was far and away the preferred ADR process, based on perceptions that it offers potential cost and time savings, enables parties to retain control over issue resolution, and is generally more satisfying both in term of process and outcomes. . . .

A more current look at corporate approaches to conflict management, albeit from a much more selective sample, is provided by a 2002 survey of corporate counsel conducted by The CPR Institute for Dispute Resolution. The survey collected responses from forty-three large companies regarding their use of mediation, arbitration and other approaches in different transactional and dispute settings, as well as other strategies and tools. Most of these companies have implemented procedures to provide an early assessment of the suitability of disputes for settlement, and conduct post-dispute review of dispute resolution with affected business units. . . . For many responding companies, the use of mediation, arbitration and other "ADR" approaches are facets of more extensive programs aimed at constructively managing conflict, including the appointment of an "ADR counsel" within the legal department; the use of standardized internal analyses to develop strategies for dispute resolution; written policies respecting settlement for inside or outside counsel, including expectations regarding the use of ADR in retainer agreements with outside counsel; making early settlement or mediation presumptive processes and requiring attorneys to justify proceeding to trial, informing business executives of ADR options; and charge-back of dispute resolution costs to responsible corporate departments. . . .

WHERE WE ARE NOW

The many-faceted "Quiet Revolution" in conflict management has resulted in many changes in the environment of court litigation, including the evolution of a wide range of process tools aimed at managing conflict. Although the evidence that court mediation programs reduce trial rates is mixed, there is substantial evidence that mediation often results in greater levels of satisfaction, reduced dispute resolution costs, shorter disposition times, and other benefits.

The great majority of corporations have some experience with ADR, with a number establishing programs aimed at resolving various kinds of disputes early, including multi-step systems addressing employee disputes.

As for litigation, while it has far from disappeared from the corporate world, it has changed shape. If fewer litigators are plying their trade in the court-house, more seem to be finding employment in business and other arbitration—and in mediated negotiation.

The increased use of ADR and the decrease in trials, although generally viewed positively, have raised policy concerns. Public court trials and appeals have the dual purposes of deciding the immediate dispute and providing standards for conduct and responsibility in similar circumstances. Trials and resulting appeals are the basis by which legal norms are articulated and one way the rule of law is maintained. Professor Deborah Hensler, a keen observer and researcher of the impact of ADR on the judicial system, states her concerns for the future of our public judicial values in light of the increased use of alternatives. The reading that follows is her conclusion from a lengthy and balanced article in which Professor Hensler traces the causes, origins, and effects of the increasing use of ADR.

DEBORAH R. HENSLER, OUR COURTS, OURSELVES: HOW THE ALTERNATIVE DISPUTE RESOLUTION MOVEMENT IS RESHAPING OUR LEGAL SYSTEM

108 Penn. St. L. Rev. 165, 195-197 (2003)

. . . Looking backwards, we may well come to view the dispute resolution move-ment as contributing to—if not creating—a profound change in our view of the justice system. With increasing barriers to litigating, fewer citizens will find their own way into court (although they may be brought there to answer crim-inal charges). Those who are not barred from using the courts by contractual agreement will increasingly find themselves shepherded outside the court-house to confidential conferences presided over by private neutrals in private venues. With little experience of public adjudication and little informa-tion available about the process or outcomes of dispute resolution, citizens' abilities to use the justice system effectively to achieve social change will dimin-ish markedly. Surrounded by a culture that celebrates social harmony and self-realization and disparages social conflict—whatever its causes or aims—citizens' tendencies to turn to the court as a vehicle for social transformation will diminish as well. Over the long run, all of the doors of the multi-door courthouse may swing outward.

Why should we care? If disputes are resolved efficiently in private, by private individuals and organizations, if conflict is avoided and citizens learn to seek compromise when disputes do arise, won't society be better off? Leaving aside the still unanswered question about whether private dispute resolution is, in fact, more efficient than public dispute resolution, and the considerable evidence that in most circumstances people already avoid conflict by compromising or "learning to live with" life's misfortunes and unfairness, I think the answer is "no." Owen Fiss, Judith Resnik, and others have written about the importance of public adjudication for the articulation of legal norms. I think there are also important political values that derive from widespread access to, and use of, the public justice system.

The public spectacle of civil litigation gives life to the "rule of law." To demonstrate that the law's authority can be mobilized by the least powerful as well as the most powerful in society, we need to observe employees and consumers successfully suing large corporations and government agencies, minority group members successfully suing majority group members, and persons engaged in unpopular activities establishing their legal rights to continue those activities.

Dispute resolution behind closed doors precludes such observation. In a democracy where many people are shut out of legislative power either because they are too few in number, or too dispersed to elect representatives, or because they do not have the financial resources to influence legislators, collective litigation in class or other mass form provides an alternative strategy for group action. Private individualized dispute resolution extinguishes the possibility of such collective litigation. Conciliation has much to recommend it. But the visible presence of institutionalized and legitimized conflict, channeled productively, teaches citizens that it is not always better to compromise and accept the status quo because, sometimes, great gains are to be had by peaceful contest.

NOTES AND QUESTIONS

1. Professor Hensler refers to "increasing barriers to litigating," and points to contractual agreements that bar lawsuits and require the arbitration of disputes arising under the contract. These contract provisions are used between businesses and, as she notes in her article, are increasingly imposed on consumers and employees. The rules of many courts also require parties to participate in non-binding ADR process as a precondition to getting a trial date. But ADR programs cannot bar citizens completely from access to court, a right guaranteed by virtually every state constitution. Are the concerns expressed by Professor Hensler about ADR diminishing citizens' abilities to use the justice system effectively to achieve social change limited to consumer and employee access to courts and the use of class actions? Do you share her concerns?

2. Lawyers are increasingly directing their clients to mediation and customized forms of arbitration. Efficiency and cost savings are only part of the motivation to choose ADR. Shaping the process by which disputes are resolved and, in non-binding processes, retaining control of the end

result also appeals to clients. The courts are limited in the remedies that can be imposed following a trial, but parties can be expansive and creative in fashioning a settlement in mediation or setting the framework for arbitration. However, endorsement of ADR is not unanimous. What are the downside risks of ADR to individual clients and lawyers?

3. There are many explanations of why the rate and number of trials is decreasing. We do not completely know the causes, but the success of ADR is, no doubt, a contributing factor. When parties in a dispute choose an alternative to trial or otherwise settle their case after initiating or responding to a lawsuit, are they defeating the purposes of our civil justice system? Does settlement sometimes thwart good public policy? Should we discourage settlements in certain cases in order to sustain the adjudication system and maintain a flow of trials? What is the critical mass of trials needed to maintain a healthy common law system of precedent and ensure the rule of law?

These questions are among those being pondered by lawyers, judges, and policy makers regarding what is referred to as "the vanishing trial." They are part of what you must consider in deciding whether society should endorse the extensive use of the alternative processes that you will encounter in this course. The statistics and the issues are discussed below by James McGuire and Professor Frank Sander, who fathered the concept of the multidoor, multi-process courthouse.

JAMES E. MCGUIRE AND FRANK E.A. SANDER, SOME QUESTIONS ABOUT "THE VANISHING TRIAL"

17-18, Disp. Resol. Mag. (Winter 2004)

The numbers are dramatic. As Professor Galanter notes . . . "In the federal courts, the percentage of civil cases reaching trial has fallen from 11 percent in 1962 to 1.8 percent in 2002." Despite a five-fold increase in the number of cases filed, the report documents an absolute decline in the number of civil cases tried. On the criminal side, the results are equally compelling — from 15 percent tried in 1962 to less than 5 percent in 2002. Preliminary data from state courts throughout the country show the same dramatic decline. Over a 25-year period with data from 22 states, the number of jury trials shows an absolute decline of more than 25 percent. Jury trials account for the disposition of less than 1 percent of filed cases.

However, the numbers do not tell us why and what it means for the future or how to fix it if one thinks it needs fixing. The decline in trials is a useful benchmark to document, but the question of why is complex. Complex questions will have complex answers and it is most likely that many forces must be factored in to account for this decline, some desirable and some perhaps less so.

At least two steps seem crucial in framing a constructive inquiry: identifying the stakeholders and their interests, and then asking whether those interests are being met. After all, if it ain't broke, don't fix it, and many dispute resolution professionals might welcome this research as evidence of progress, at least in part. Indeed, only where important interests or needs are not being met should we look for solutions to the "vanishing trial."

To this end, we offer the following initial sketch of issues.

STAKEHOLDERS AND THEIR INTERESTS

JUDGES AND JUDICIAL ADMINISTRATORS

To what extent have judges redefined their role? How do judges keep score? How are judges graded? Changes in rules and procedures, such as Rule 16 of the Federal Rules of Civil Procedure, serve to redefine the role of judge from adjudicator to case manager. Reporting requirements track the number and the length of time that cases have been on a judge's docket. Do these reporting requirements themselves influence the administrative discretionary tools used by judges to clear dockets by means other than trials?

CORPORATIONS AND GENERAL COUNSEL

In-house general counsel are gatekeepers for corporate litigation. Increasingly they control forum and process selection, and are less likely to defer to outside trial counsel for risk assessment and case management. Some of those preferences are reflected in the vibrant growth of organizations like the American Arbitration Association and the CPR Institute of Dispute Resolution, the latter of which is an organization created by major corporations to develop alternatives to traditional litigation. To what extent do global competitive pressures influence general counsel to opt out of trials that are seen as inherently risky and less efficient than other conflict management techniques?

LAWYERS AND LAW FIRMS

Lawyers in charge of litigation influence, and sometimes control, the decision of whether a matter will be settled or tried. What interests do they have to dispose of cases other than by trial? Trial lawyers became self-described "litigators" in the 1970s as discovery and motion practice mushroomed. Responsive to client concerns and interests, their clients may be expressing new preferences for alternatives to trials.

MEDIATORS, ARBITRATORS, AND THE ADR COMMUNITY

ADR may deserve both credit and blame for this phenomenon. To be sure, the resolution of disputes by means other than trial, such as mediation and arbitration, often produces better outcomes for disputing parties. But the ADR community's interest in diverting disputes to its processes must also be recognized, raising the question of whether it has helped swing the pendulum too far. Put another way, should the ADR community help identify ways to save for trial those disputes where trials serve valuable interest? To what extent should party autonomy be a factor in this determination?

ARE THE INTERESTS OF ALL BEING MET WITH FEWER TRIALS?

THE ROLE OF COURTS

Courts have at least two distinct functions: to resolve disputes and to articulate norms for the guidance of future disputants. We have learned in the past decades that not every dispute requires a Cadillac model for its effective resolution. Indeed, other processes, such as mediation, may be more efficient for certain cases, leaving the courts freer to handle the really complex and challenging cases. This calls for careful screening of cases so as to "fit the forum to the fuss." Do we have any evidence that the courts are less effective in articulating norms as a result of the "vanishing trial"? Does "vanishing trial" equal "vanishing precedent?"

WORKLOAD, ECONOMIC IMPLICATIONS

In view of the fivefold increase in cases filed and the fact that federal judges are hardly under worked, what would be the staffing implications if there hadn't been a drastic decline in the proportion of cases that are tried? Suppose the rate of trials in 2002 had dropped to 3.6 percent instead of 1.8 percent; that would mean twice as many trials as are being conducted now, necessitating a substantial increase in the number of judges, clerks, courtrooms and all the related judicial infrastructure. Is this feasible in the current climate, even if it were desirable?

THE INTERESTS OF PARTIES

If the parties to a dispute are the consumers of the justice system, it is also important to ask whether the consumers' interests are being met with, or frustrated by, fewer trials. Some preliminary studies on participant satisfaction with the mediation process suggests that parties are very satisfied with the process — that having "a day in court" really means "wanting to be heard." For these consumers, is the "vanishing trial" a bad thing? For criminal defendants, a different set of questions needs to be framed and answered. For example, it is generally acknowledged that defendants [who] insist on a trial can face much longer sentences than those who accept a plea bargain. Are these defendants being asked a fair price to exercise their right to trial?

THE PUBLIC INTEREST

The "vanishing trial" may also reflect a shift in perception of what is in the public interest. It may be that we collectively recognize that compromise may often be better than confrontation; that a more nuanced world view is superior to all-or-nothing, wrong-and-right approach to dispute resolution. Thus the question to ask is whether the public interest is better served by having fewer trials, or by having more trials? . . .

NOTE: CLIENT INTERVIEWING AND MATCHING THE PROCESS TO THE DISPUTE

Setting forth a spectrum, or menu, of dispute resolution possibilities does not in itself indicate which, if any, is most appropriate for a specific client in a particular dispute. If you understand the available process choices and how to match them with your clients' needs, or as Professor Sander states, "fit the forum to the fuss," you can provide a value-added service (Sander, 1994).

In order to effectively counsel and represent clients in resolving their disputes, you must know and understand their interests and goals. Only then can you match their needs to the most appropriate dispute resolution process. Client-centered interviewing is an important skill that shapes the attorney-client relationship and is the first step in helping clients resolve their dispute. Your questions during the initial interview must allow you to discover what the client wishes to achieve and why. Then you can intelligently explore the process of resolution most likely to fulfill the client's interests and goals within the available time and resource parameters.

This book, which surveys the spectrum of dispute resolution, does not offer a primer on client interviewing and counseling, although we do include readings on listening, questioning, and managing information, as well as on the role of perceptions and psychological factors. Separate courses in interviewing, counseling, and personal skills are offered at many law schools and most have clinics that provide opportunities to interview and work with clients. This course will provide the knowledge of dispute resolution that will enable you to help clients choose the most appropriate process, once you have learned their underlying needs.

Each process fills a need. A courtroom may be the best forum for resolving some cases. A private office where the parties have come voluntarily to conclude their dispute may be better in other cases. Litigation culminating in a trial is still the forum of choice when it is important to know what happened. The availability in litigation of evidentiary discovery and depositions, as well as the examination of witnesses at trial, is designed to find historical truth. Publicly exposing wrongdoing and gaining the satisfaction of vindication is also best achieved through a public trial. A court judgment is the surest path to state enforcement of a financial obligation and courts can compel specific performance in appropriate cases. Courts can provide provisional or interim relief while a lawsuit is pending, which more benign forms of ADR cannot. As discussed above, adjudication can, on appeal, establish precedent and shape rules of responsibility and future conduct, which may be important to some clients. Litigation can assist in organizing and rallying groups of people behind a principal or cause and in joining reluctant parties. The litigation process can also be used strategically in negotiations and the prospect of a trial often compels settlement. Of course the irony of all these advantages of litigation is that it can be a two-way street, where each reason for your client pursuing litigation can also be the reason the opposing side is doing so. The litigation curse is having a case in which your client, and the other side, absolutely know they are right!

An alternative to adjudication is a more appropriate choice when potential litigation costs are high relative to the amount in controversy or where the dispute is time sensitive. An ADR process is also likely to be appealing when standard adjudication remedies do not meet the disputants' real needs and interests. For example, sometimes the best resolution of an existing dispute is to make a deal that looks to the future. If the parties are entrepreneurial and creative, they may want more of a voice in shaping the final outcome, which they can better do outside a trial. Similarly, if the parties wish to limit their risk or qualify the decision, they will want to pursue an alternative to trial. If it is more important to the parties to have an active role in the process, rather than totally depend upon their lawyers, ADR will be more satisfying. If it is in the interests of the parties not to air their dispute in public, then the privacy afforded by ADR will be more desirable than a public trial. If the parties wish to preserve, or at least not worsen, their relationship, an alternative more gentle than a trial will be a better choice. Disputes over matters requiring special expertise may be better resolved by being able to choose the neutral with the necessary expertise.

Given the rapidly shrinking number of trials and changes in the legal culture supporting increased use of ADR, you are more likely in many jurisdictions to represent clients in mediation, or possibly arbitration, than in court. However, what lawyers do most often for clients is negotiate. So we start our study of dispute resolution processes in Part I with negotiation. Then, moving east along the ADR continuum, we take up mediation in Part II. Mediation is negotiation facilitated by a neutral. It often follows unsuccessful direct negotiation. Understanding the essentials of negotiation and obstacles to negotiated settlements is a key to successful mediation. The two topics are interrelated, and we take them in turn. Arbitration, presented in Part III, is next in our book's sequence. We conclude in Part IV with a more in-depth look at how to mix, match, and layer dispute resolution alternatives in order to more fully serve the needs of your clients.

PART
I

Negotiation

CHAPTER
2

Negotiation and Conflict — The Big Picture

A. INTRODUCTION TO NEGOTIATION

Negotiation is the process of communication used to get something we want when another person has control over whether or how we can get it. If we could have everything we wanted, materially and emotionally, without the concurrence of anyone else, there would be no need to negotiate. Because of our interdependence, there is a pervasive need to negotiate.

Everyone negotiates as part of modern life. However, because lawyers are paid to negotiate for others, we are considered professionals. A law student reading only casebooks might not know that the vast majority of disputes in which lawyers are involved are negotiated to a settlement without trial. Many major transactions are also the result of lawyer-negotiated agreements. Negotiation is at the core of what lawyers do in representing clients.

Most lawyers think they are skilled negotiators because they negotiate frequently. Negotiating frequently does not necessarily result in negotiating effectively. Unlike trial practice, negotiation is usually done in private without the opportunity to compare results or benefit from a critique. Those with whom you negotiate rarely give an honest assessment of how you did, and it is most often in their interest for you to believe you did well. Regardless of our intuitive ability, negotiation skills and results can be improved with analysis and understanding, as well as practice.

Lawyer negotiation occurs within the dynamics of settling a dispute or shaping a deal and is not always a tidy process that tracks a textbook diagram. Although certain types of negotiations may follow a pattern, not every negotiation will follow the same lineal staging, and each stage will not necessarily be completed in all negotiations. In this book we utilize a seven-stage model of negotiation for purposes of discussion and analysis, recognizing that the negotiation dance can be improvised to fit the situation. The seven stages are:

1. Preparation and Setting Goals
2. Initial Interaction and Offers
3. Exchanging and Refining Information
4. Bargaining
5. Moving Toward Closure

6.   Reaching Impasse or Agreement
7.   Finalizing the Agreement

Negotiation, whether settlement or deal-making, occurs because there are differences between what the parties want or how they perceive the situation. As a professional negotiator, you have an edge if you understand the nature of the differences or conflicts to be resolved, the psychology of negotiation, and the contrasting styles of bargaining. Therefore, in order to enhance your skills as a negotiator, we begin with the nature of conflict and the role of perceptions, as well as psychological traps. Next we look at the advantages and disadvantages of being more competitive or cooperative. We will then examine the stages of negotiation and the activities associated with each step, followed by consideration of gender and culture, ethics, and the role of law in negotiations.

B. CONFLICT IS WHAT WE MAKE IT

The Nature of Conflict and Disputes

Although conflict can cause distress and is usually viewed negatively, it can function in positive ways. Conflict may motivate people to take action and change their situations in ways that improve their lives and better fulfill their self-interests. Those in conflict who want to get it resolved may be forced to consider their role in creating the conflict and often gain insight about themselves and others. However, conflict can also create a crisis mentality that becomes destructive because people are driven to quickly relieve the anxiety they feel from the conflict. Lawyers can help create more constructive outcomes from conflicts or they can make a difficult situation worse. The ability to help clients better understand the conflict, reframe the issues, realistically analyze their interests, and how they can be negotiated, is an important lawyering skill.

Conflict is divided into two categories: interpersonal (differences that arise between individuals or groups) and intrapersonal (conflicts within ourselves). Interpersonal conflict is a situation in which the parties each want something that they perceive as incompatible, or at least inconsistent, with what the other wants. Because the parties in an interpersonal conflict cannot both have all that they want, their interests or goals are divergent. Although lawyers are retained to help resolve interpersonal conflicts between our clients and others, a client may also be conflicted internally about what it is they really want from an opponent. For example, does your client really want to return to the job from which she was fired or does she only want to restore her self-respect and get compensation? Does the father you represent in a divorce really want custody of the children or is he internally conflicted about the decision to divorce and trying to hold onto the marital relationship? Recognizing these two different types of conflict can be critical in achieving client goals.

It is also helpful to differentiate between a static conflict, where the positions are fixed and juxtaposed, and a dynamic or reactive conflict, in which the behavior of one party affects the subsequent behavior of the other party, which in turn affects the action of the first party, and so on. An automobile accident between strangers where the cause of the accident is at issue is a static conflict for purpose of establishing liability. However, many interpersonal conflicts are dynamic and occur in a context where one person's moves or behavior creates a countermove or reaction. This dynamic process of conflict can occur in all spheres of human interaction where there is an ongoing relation. Examples include conflicts and reactions between husband and wife, union and management, business competitors, and between nations.

Another distinction that can be particularly useful in negotiation and mediation is between the manifest conflict, which is overt or expressed, and the underlying conflict, which is implicit, hidden, or denied. Lawyers most often deal with manifest conflicts, which we refer to as disputes. A conflict may not become a dispute if it is not communicated in the form of a complaint or claim. What is communicated may be only a part of or symbol of the underlying conflict. The dispute between brothers over control of a family business seems safer to contest than the underlying conflict of who was the favored son or a better child. Indian tribes may actively dispute government fishing quotas, while the underlying conflict involves the more fundamental issue of outside control and alteration of Native American traditions. Residential development disputes may focus in court on specific environmental regulations or traffic issues, but the underlying conflict is about the changing character of the community. This dichotomy between the overt dispute and the hidden conflict can be viewed for purposes of negotiation as the presenting problem and the hidden agenda.

If the agreements reached in negotiation resolve only the presenting problems, they are less likely to last unless legally enforced. Surfacing the underlying conflict can clarify issues, focus objectives, generate new possibilities for settlement and ultimately improve relationships. Dealing with the underlying conflicts, however, may be emotionally painful and can stimulate internal conflict beyond the capacity of most lawyers to deal with it.

Outcomes of disputes are categorized as mutual loss (lose/lose), gain for one and loss for the other (lose/win), or mutual gain (win/win). Negotiation has a distinct advantage over trials in obtaining constructive outcomes because it allows resolution of dispute in the mutual gain or win/win mode. This win/win approach to negotiation has been popularized by Roger Fisher, William Ury, and Bruce Patton in their widely read book, *Getting to Yes: Negotiating Agreement Without Giving In* (1991).

The central theme of *Getting to Yes* is to focus on interests, not positions. Disputes cause people to lock in on positions. Positions are self-serving solutions to how the dispute should be resolved. This can lead to missed opportunities for mutual gain, particularly when negotiating a transaction or future relationship. A fixation on positions exacerbates conflict by concentrating on incompatible solutions rather than on complimentary or overlapping interests and creative ways to satisfy at least part of what each person wants. Lawyers who can help their clients engage in joint problem solving to mutually satisfy interests and optimize collective outcomes add value through their role in negotiation.

The excerpt that follows distinguishes conflict resolution, which denotes an end to the conflict through a change in underlying attitudes, from settlement based on a change in behaviors. Professor Rubin also differentiates cooperation from competition, emphasizes "relationship," and explains the important concepts of "enlightened self-interest" and "ripeness." Next, Gerald Williams discusses how a small percentage of grievances ripen into disputes, or "open conflicts," in which a claimant retains an attorney to negotiate. Professor Williams also identifies the stages a client must follow to move out of a conflict and heal from it. His original article, which you may find interesting, presents more detail than space allows here on the grieving and healing process related to conflicts. He suggests that lawyers must be sensitive to the "negotiation ritual" necessary to help clients through the pain often experienced with conflict.

JEFFREY Z. RUBIN, SOME WISE AND MISTAKEN ASSUMPTIONS ABOUT CONFLICT AND NEGOTIATION

in Negotiation Theory and Practice 3-10, Program on Negotiation Books (J.Z. Rubin and W. Breslin, eds., 1991)

For many years the attention of conflict researchers and theorists was directed to the laudable objective of conflict resolution. This term denotes as an outcome a state of attitude change that effectively brings an end to the conflict in question. In contrast, conflict settlement denotes outcomes in which the overt conflict has been brought to an end, even though the underlying bases may or may not have been addressed. . . . The gradual shift over the last years from a focus on resolution to a focus on settlement has had an important implication for the conflict field: It has increased the importance of understanding negotiation—which, after all, is a method of settling conflict rather than resolving it. The focus of negotiation is not attitude change per se, but an agreement to change behavior in ways that make settlement possible. Two people with underlying differences of beliefs or values (for example, over the issue of a woman's right to abortion or the existence of a higher deity) may come to change their views through discussion and an exchange of views, but it would be inappropriate and inaccurate to describe such an exchange as "negotiation."

Similarly, the shift from resolution to settlement of conflict has also increased the attention directed to the role of third parties in the conflict settlement process—individuals who are in some way external to a dispute and who, through identification of issues and judicious intervention, attempt to make it more likely that a conflict can be moved to settlement. . . .

COOPERATION, COMPETITION, AND ENLIGHTENED SELF-INTEREST

Required for effective conflict settlement is neither cooperation nor competition, but what may be referred to as "enlightened self interest." By this I simply mean a variation on what several conflict theorists have previously described as an "individualistic orientation"—an outlook in which the disputant is simply interested in doing well for himself or herself, without regard for anyone else, out neither to help nor hinder the other's efforts to obtain his or her goal. The added word "enlightened" refers to the acknowledgment by each side that the other is also likely to be pursuing a path of self interest—and that it may be possible for both to do well in the exchange. If there are ways in which I can move toward my objective in negotiation, while at the same time making it possible for you to approach your goal, then why not behave in ways that make both possible?

Notice that what I am describing here is neither pure individualism (where one side does not care at all about how the other is doing) nor pure cooperation (where each side cares deeply about helping the other to do well, likes and values the other side, etc.) — but an amalgam of the two. . . . I do not have to like or trust you in order to negotiate wisely with you. Nor do I have to be driven by the passion of a competitive desire to beat you. All that is necessary is for me to find some way of getting what I want — perhaps even more than I considered possible — by leaving the door open for you too to do well. "Trust" and "trustworthiness," concepts central to the development of cooperation, are no longer necessary — only the understanding of what the other person may want or need.

A number of anecdotes have emerged to make this point . . . Jack Sprat and his wife — one preferring lean, the other fat — can lick the platter clean if they understand their respective interests. The interesting thing about this conjugal pair is that, married though they may be, when it comes to dining preferences they are hardly interdependent at all. For Jack and his wife to "lick the platter clean" requires neither that the two love each other nor care about helping each other in every way possible; nor does it require that each be determined to get more of the platter's contents than the other. Instead, it is enlightened self interest that makes possible an optimal solution to the problem of resource distribution. . . .

THE IMPORTANCE OF "RELATIONSHIP" IN NEGOTIATION

Much of the negotiation analysis that has taken place over the last 25 years has focused on the "bottom line": who gets how much once an agreement has been reached. The emphasis has thus largely been an economic one, and this emphasis has been strengthened by the significant role of game theory and other mathematical or economic formulations.

This economic focus is being supplanted by a richer, and more accurate, portrayal of negotiation in terms not only of economic, but also of relational, considerations. As any visitor to the Turkish Bazaar in Istanbul will tell you, the purchase of an oriental carpet involves a great deal more than the exchange of money for an old rug. The emerging relationship between shopkeeper and customer is far more significant, weaving ever so naturally into the economic aspects of the transaction. . . .

Psychologists, sociologists, and anthropologists have long understood the importance of "relationship" in any interpersonal transaction, but only recently have conflict analysts begun to take this as seriously as it deserves. Although it seems convenient to distinguish negotiation in one time only exchanges (ones where you have no history of contact with the other party, come together for a "quickie," and then expect never to see the other again) from negotiation in ongoing relationships, this distinction is more illusory than real. Rarely does one negotiate in the absence of future consequences. Even if you and I meet once and once only, our reputations have a way of surviving the exchange, coloring the expectations that others will have of us in the future. . . .

THE ROLE OF "RIPENESS"

Although it is comforting to assume people can start negotiating any time they want, such is not the case. First of all, just as it takes two hands to clap, it takes two to negotiate. You may be ready to come to the table for serious discussion, but your counterpart may not. Unless you are both at the table (or connected by a telephone line or cable link), no agreement is possible.

Second, even if both of you are present at the same place, at the same time, one or both of you may not be sufficiently motivated to take the conflict seriously. It is tempting to sit back, do nothing, and hope that the mere passage of time will turn events to your advantage. People typically do not sit down to negotiate unless and until they have reached a point of "stalemate," where each no longer believes it possible to obtain what he or she wants through efforts at domination or coercion. It is only at this point, when the two sides grudgingly acknowledge the need for joint work if any agreement is to be reached, that negotiation can take place.

By "ripeness," then, I mean a stage of conflict in which all parties are ready to take their conflict seriously, and are willing to do whatever may be necessary to bring the conflict to a close. To pluck fruit from a tree before it is ripe is as problematic as waiting too long. There is a right time to negotiate, and the wise negotiator will attempt to seek out this point.

It is also possible, of course, to help "create" such a right time. One way of doing so entails the use of threat and coercion, as the two sides (either with or without the assistance of an outside intervenor) walk (or are led) to the edge of "lover's leap," stare into the abyss below, and contemplate the consequences of failing to reach agreement. The farther the drop—that is, the more terrible the consequences of failing to settle—the greater the pressure on each side to take the conflict seriously. There are at least two serious problems with such "coercive" means of creating a ripe conflict: First, as can be seen in the history of the arms race between the United States and the Soviet Union, it encourages further conflict escalation, as each side tries to "motivate" the other to settle by upping the ante a little bit at a time. Second, such escalatory moves invite a game of "chicken," in which each hopes that the other will be the first to succumb to coercion.

There is a second—and far better—way to create a situation that is ripe for settlement: namely, through the introduction of new opportunities for joint gain. If each side can be persuaded that there is more to gain than to lose through collaboration—that by working jointly, rewards can be harvested that stand to advance each side's respective agenda—then a basis for agreement can be established. . . .

GERALD R. WILLIAMS, NEGOTIATION AS A HEALING PROCESS

1996 J. Disp. Resol. 1, 5-7, 42-46 (1996)

HOW CONFLICTS ARISE

If we accept the proposition that people generally tend to avoid conflict rather than pursue it, we are led to a very intriguing question: how do conflicts arise? What distinguishes the situation that ends up on a lawyer's desk from all the other situations in which people are harmed but elect to deal with it by avoidance? In other words, what is the process by which grievances ripen into open conflicts? An important response to this question comes in an article by Felstiner, Abel, and Sarat, entitled "The Emergence and Transformation of Disputes: Naming, Blaming, and Claiming," 15 *L. & Soc. Rev.* 631 (1981). The authors suggest that this sequence of "naming, blaming, and claiming" describes the process by which harms or grievances become full scale conflicts. By naming, the authors mean, in part, that people must recognize they have been harmed. This is a problem where physical symptoms are delayed, as with exposure to slow-acting toxic substances. Except for cases of delayed recognition, however, the distinguishing factor is not awareness of the harm, but rather the victims' subjective reactions to it. For one reason or another, rather than accepting this particular harm as one of the risks of life and simply getting on with their lives, they feel this particular harm is too great, or is one harm too many, or for some other reason is "the straw that breaks the camel's back."

In the next step, blaming, aggrieved persons assign fault for the injury; they identify a wrongdoer and hold that person or institution responsible for the harm. Note, however, there is not yet a dispute. For the situation to ripen into a dispute, aggrieved parties must decide to assert themselves by making a claim upon the perceived wrongdoer and asking for an appropriate adjustment or other relief. This is called claiming. But, as the authors point out, even now there is no dispute. Presumably many problems are prevented from ripening into disputes by a satisfactory response to the claim. . . .

For the problem to mature into a dispute, the perceived wrongdoer must reject the claim or otherwise fail to give satisfaction. At this point, the aggrieved party is faced with the most difficult and fateful decision of all: whether to let go of the problem and get on with their lives (use exit or avoidance) or to "go public" by going to a lawyer or some other outside party or organization for assistance. The aggrieved person might file a complaint with a consumer-oriented organization, ask a respected third party to intervene, file a complaint in small claims court, submit the problem to a neighborhood dispute resolution center, or in some other fashion involve a third party. However, since the purpose of this article is to investigate the dynamics and purposes of legal negotiation, we will limit our discussion generally to situations in which the parties have retained lawyers to represent them. . . .

THE FIVE STEPS FOR RECOVERING FROM CONFLICT

I would like to propose a preliminary five-step model of the stages clients must generally move through in order to shift from being in a state of conflict to being healed from the conflict. The stages are: denial, acceptance, sacrifice, leaps of faith, and renewal. Just as researchers have found that getting into a conflict is a multi-step process that typically involves naming, blaming, claiming, rejection, and a decision to go public, even so, the task of getting out of a conflict requires the disputants to work their way through a multistage process. . . . [The author explains each of the five stages.]

From this perspective, we might even say that, in most instances, conflicts are meaningful; they have a purpose. Their purpose is to hold up a mirror so disputants may see themselves in a new light, an experience as painful as it is valuable. . . . Properly understood, then, conflicts serve as such a mirror. They expose the disputants' weaknesses; the areas in which they have been too much the victim, or too much the exploiter; their complexes, their unresolved angers, and their feelings of specialness and entitlement. Because it is so painful for disputants to see these parts of themselves exposed by their own involvement in the conflict, they need the protection and reinforcement, the containment and channeling, that the lawyer-client relationship provides, and they need the benefit of the full play of the negotiation process to help them gradually face what they see in the mirror and to come to terms with it.

This is why the negotiation ritual must be performed with such understanding and care. It is intended to help the disputants through an extremely painful and threatening process. . . .

NOTES AND QUESTIONS

1. Morton Deutsch, who pioneered the modern study of conflict resolution, distinguished manifest conflict from underlying conflict, as summarized in our introductory comments. (See Deutsch, 1973.) Rubin, a former student of Deutsch, separates settlement of the manifest conflict behaviors from the attitude changes necessary to bring an end to the underlying base of conflict. We noted a similar distinction between the presenting problem and the hidden agenda. Do you agree that settlement only of the manifest problem is unlikely to last? Why or why not? Is litigation limited only to the manifest or presenting issues? Is Rubin correct in indicating that negotiation is only a method of settling conflict rather than resolving it? Should the role of lawyers include assistance in resolving underlying conflicts or differences in hidden agendas?

2. Jeffrey Rubin in his excerpt introduces the concept of "enlightened self-interest," which is related to the "utility" theory that began with Jeremy Bentham in the late 1700s and underlies much of the current analysis of negotiation. How does enlightened self-interest, or utility theory, explain Rubin's conclusion that Mr. and Ms. Sprat could reach an "optimal solution" and "lick the platter clean?" Is Rubin correct in indicating that "trust" and "trustworthiness" are not relevant to reaching optimal solutions? Why or why not?

3. Just as it takes two or more people to have a conflict, so it takes two or more people to reach agreement. Ripeness of the conflict is critical for those involved to begin serious negotiation toward resolution. What do you think Rubin means when he suggests that new opportunities for joint gain create ripeness? How might this concept help lawyers get disputes resolved?

4. Many people have a negative view of conflict and try to avoid it. Do you? Was conflict viewed as negative in your family? During your childhood, how did your family deal with conflict? Will you try to model the same conflict process for your children? As a lawyer will you welcome representing clients who seek your help to resolve their conflicts? Why or why not?

CHAPTER
3

The Inner Negotiator — It's All in Our Heads

A. THE ROLE OF PERCEPTIONS

The core to understanding and mastering negotiation is to be aware that those in conflict and who want something from one another may see the situation differently. It is these differences that give root to the conflict and to the possibility of agreement. We assess conflict and evaluate a case or the worth of an item differently because of differing perceptions. Our individual perceptions determine how we view ourselves, others, and the world. No two views are exactly the same. We may selectively perceive or differ in our perceptions of:

facts	available resources
people	scarcity
interests	popularity
history	timing
fairness	market mechanisms
priorities	uses
relative power	costs
performance	applicable law or rules
abilities	likely outcomes

Our view of each of the above elements, as well as perceptions of other variables, may be a factor in how we determine the worth and reasonable price of an item or the value of a settlement. It is because of such differences in perceptions that people bet on horse races, wage war, and pursue lawsuits.

A classic Japanese story, on which the film *Rashomon* is based, illustrates the ancient literary awareness of the role of perceptions and how the truth through one person's eyes may be very different from another's, as seen through the prism of their own perceptions. Through divergent narratives, the story and the film explore how the power of perceptions may distort or enhance different people's memories of a single event, in this narrative the death of a Samurai warrior. Each tells the "truth," but perceives it very differently. The film, like the story, is unsettling because, as in much of life, no single truth emerges.

A more recent film, *The War of the Roses*, based on a book by Warren Adler, captures different truths as perceived by a divorcing couple. Early in the story,

Oliver and Barbara Rose each reveal to their own lawyer their perspective on the marriage and how their family home should be divided. Each see the marriage relationship and what's fair differently, as filtered through their own experience, values, and selectivity. Is there any doubt, based on such different perceptions, that the war between the Roses would follow?

WARREN ADLER, THE WAR OF THE ROSES
51-76, Stonehouse Press (1981)

[Oliver Rose's perception:] "She just upped and said, 'No more marriage.' Like her whole persona had been transformed. Maybe it's something chemical that happens as forty gets closer."

He had . . . been a good and loving husband. He had nearly offered "faithful" to complete the triad but that would have discounted his two episodes with hookers during conventions in San Francisco and Las Vegas when the children were small. My God, she had everything she could possibly want . . .

What confused him most was that he had not been warned. Not a sign. He hated to be taken by surprise.

"And the house?" Goldstein asked.

"I don't know. Say half the value. After all, we did it together. Half of everything is okay with me. . . ."

[Barbara Rose's perception:] "He's like some kind of animal. Almost invisible. He leaves early, before we get up, and comes home late, long after we've gone to bed. He doesn't take his meals at home. . . ."

"You think it's fair for me to have devoted nearly twenty years to his career, his needs, his wants, his desires, his security. I gave up my schooling for him. I had his children. And I devoted a hell of a lot more time to that house than he did. Besides, the house is all I have to show for it. I can't match his earning power. Hell, in a few years he'll be able to replace its value. I'll just have cash. Well, that's not good enough. I want the house. I want all of it. It's not only a house. It's a symbol of a life-style. And I intend to keep it that way. That's fair. . . ."

"It's my house. I worked my ass off for it," she said.

The following reading further develops the theme that conflict is subjective and flows from different perceptions in the minds of people. Rummel's "subjectivity principle" may help to explain the *War of the Roses* and many other conflicts that would otherwise defy understanding and resolution.

R.J. RUMMEL, THE CONFLICT HELIX
13-23, Transaction Publishers (1991)

THE SUBJECTIVITY PRINCIPLE

Perceived reality is your painting. You are the artist. You mix the colors, draw the lines, fix the focus, achieve the artistic balance. Reality disciplines your painting; it is your starting point. As the artist, you add here, leave out there; substitute color, simplify; and provide this reality with a point, a theme, a center of interest. You produce a thousand such paintings every moment. With unconscious artistry. Each a personal statement. Individualistic.

Now, most people realize that their perception of things can be wrong, that they may be mistaken. No doubt you have had disagreements with others on what you all saw or heard. And probably you have heard of eyewitnesses who widely disagree over the facts of a crime or accident. Some teachers who wish to dramatically illustrate such disagreement have staged mock fights or holdups in a classroom. A masked man rushes in, pointing some weapon at the teacher; demands his wallet; and with it hastily exits, leaving the class stunned. Then each member of the class is asked to write down what he saw and heard. Their versions usually differ widely.

But, of course, such are rapidly changing situations in which careful observation is difficult. Surely, you might think, if there were time to study a situation or event you would perceive it as others do. This is easy enough to test. Ask two people to describe in writing a furnished room, say your living room, or a car you may own. Then compare. You will find many similarities, but you should also find some important and interesting differences. Sometimes such differences result from error, inattentiveness. However, there is something more fundamental. Even attentive observers often will see things differently. And each can be correct.

There are a number of reasons for this. First, people may have different vantage points and their visual perspectives thus will differ. A round, flat object viewed from above will appear round, from an angle it will appear an ellipse, from the side a rectangle. This problem of perspective is acute in active, contact sports such as football or basketball. From the referee's line of sight there is no foul, but many spectators (especially the television audiences who see multiple angles and instant replays) know they saw an obvious violation.

But people can compare or change perspectives. Were this all, perception would not be a basic problem. The second reason for different perceptions is more fundamental. You endow what you sense with meaning. The outside world is an amorphous blend of a multitude of interwoven colors, lights, sounds, smells, tastes and material. You make sense of this complex by carving it into different concepts, such as table, chair, or boy. Learning a language is part of learning to perceive the world.

You also endow this reality with value. Thus what you perceive becomes good or bad, repulsive or attractive, dangerous or safe. You see a man running toward you with a knife as dangerous; a calm lake as peaceful, a child murderer as bad; a contribution to charity as good. And so on.

Cultures are systems of meanings laid onto reality; to become acculturated is to learn the language through which a culture gives the world unique shape and evaluation. A clear example of this is a cross, which to a Christian signifies the death of Jesus for mankind as well as the whole complex of values and beliefs bound up in the religion. Yet, to non–Christian cultures a cross may be meaningless: simply two pieces of wood connected at right angles. . . .

Besides varying perspectives and meanings, a third reason for different perceptions is that people have unique experiences and learning capacities, even when they share the same culture. Each person has his own background.

No two people learn alike. Moreover, people have different occupations, and each occupation emphasizes and ignores different aspects of reality. Simply by virtue of their separate occupational interests, the world will be perceived dissimilarly by a philosopher, priest, engineer, union worker, or lawyer.

Two people may perceive the same thing from the same perspective, therefore, but each through their diverse languages, evaluations, experience, and occupations, may perceive it differently and endow it with personal meaning. Dissimilar perspective, meaning, and experience together explain why your perception will often differ radically from others.

There is yet an even more basic reason: what you sense is unconsciously transformed within your mental field in order to maintain a psychological balance. This mental process is familiar to you. People often perceive what they want to perceive, what they ardently hope to see. Their minds go to great pains to extract from the world that which they put there. People tend to see things consistent with their beliefs. If you believe businesspeople, politicians, or bureaucrats are bad, you will tend to see their failings. If you like a person, you tend to see the good; hate him and you tend to see the worst. Some people are optimists, usually seeing a bottle half full; others are pessimists, seeing the same bottle half empty.

Your perception is thus the result of a complex transformation of amorphous sensory stimuli. At various stages your personal experience, beliefs, and character affect what you perceive. . . . Independent of the outside world's powers to force your perception, you have power to impose a perception on reality. You can hallucinate. You can magnify some things to fill your perception in spite of what else is happening. Think of the whisper of one's name.

What you perceive in reality is a balance between these two sets of powers: the outside world's powers to make you perceive specific things and your powers to impose a certain perception on the world. This is the most basic opposition, the most basic conflict. Its outcome is what you perceive reality to be. . . . The elements of The Subjectivity Principle are perception, mental field, and balance: your perception is a balance between the powers of your mental field and the outside world. It is a balance between the perception you tend to impose on the outside world and the strength of what is out there to force its own reality on you. It is a balance between what you unconsciously want to perceive and what you cannot help but perceive. . . .

This balance that envelopes your mental field changes with your interest and concentration. Its shape and extension will depend on your personality and experience. And, of course, your culture. No wonder, then, that you are likely to perceive things differently from others. Your perception is subjective and personal. Reality does not draw its picture on a clean slate—your mind. Nor is your mind a passive movie screen on which sensory stimuli impact, to create a moving picture of the world. Rather, your mind is an active agent of perception, creating and transforming reality, while at the same time being disciplined and sometimes dominated by it . . . .

You and I may perceive reality differently and we both may be right. We are simply viewing the same thing from different perspectives and each emphasizing a deferent aspect. Blind men feeling different parts of an elephant may each believe they are correct and the others wrong about their perception. Yet, all can be correct; all can have a different part of the truth.

———————————

NOTES AND QUESTIONS

Rummel's subjectivity principle explains how we process all the information and stimuli around us through the filters of our experience, needs, and biases. The complexity of our environment and our minds prevents us from taking it all in whole, so we focus selectively on some stimuli and ignore others. We develop shortcuts in our perceptual systems that allow us to function and process information more quickly and make timely decisions. These shortcuts, known as heuristics, can serve us well in allowing us to respond as needed. However, these mental shortcuts come at a risk that our selectivity can, on occasion, distort reality, as seen by others. It is the different ways we process information that can lead to conflict based on our different realities.

Jeffrey Rubin describes the conflict dynamics of "selective perception" and the nature of "self-fulfilling prophecies" as follows:

> Let us begin with selective perception. . . . In an escalating conflict, we tend to see what we want to see and to distort information to support our expectations. One way we do this is by selectively testing hypotheses. We form a hypothesis about the adversary such as, this person is nasty. Then we gather information to confirm our hypothesis and ignore information that does not support it. In selective perception we have only dealt with perceptions. When behavior is introduced, we have self-fulfilling prophecy, which connects attitudes and behaviors. I have an expectation of you that leads me to behave in a way that produces a response in you that confirms my expectation. My prophecy about the kind of person that you are is fulfilled. (Lavinia Hall, ed., *Negotiation: Strategies for Mutual Gain* (1993) 128-129)

1. Is the "subjectivity principle," as explained by Rummel, the same concept as "selective perception" and "self-fulfilling prophecies," as explained by Rubin?
2. Can you recall a conflict you have experienced that might be better understood in light of the subjectivity principle?
3. John Milton in *Paradise Lost* poetically stated "The mind is its own place, and in itself can make a heaven of hell, a hell of Heaven" (Milton, 1909, vol. 4. p. 96). In explaining his subjectivity principle, is Rummel just restating Milton?
4. If a conflict between people is the result of different perceptions, what might be of help in resolving the conflict?
5. Is there a connection between Rummel's subjectivity principle and the distinction made earlier between the manifest conflict and the underlying conflict? Can you articulate an explanation of manifest conflict or underlying conflict based on Rummel's subjectivity principle?
6. Is the conflict between Barbara and Oliver Rose really over their house or something else? If the division or ownership of the house is the manifest or presenting conflict, what is the underlying conflict or "hidden agenda?" Can lawyers negotiate what may be the underlying conflict regarding gender roles? Can they do something about each Rose's need for recognition of their contribution to the house and the marriage?

B. PSYCHOLOGICAL TRAPS AND PROFESSIONAL OBJECTIVITY

The study of perceptions and distortions in reasoning that immerse people in conflict, as well as psychological barriers to settlement, has allowed us to better understand clients' disputes. Lawyers in representing clients can provide professional objectivity in order to help overcome the perceptual errors that might affect the judgment of their clients. Although lawyers advocate on behalf of clients, they are removed from the partisan perspective that can create skewed distortions in their client's perception. This is because lawyers in negotiating against opponents may be professional adversaries but they do not have a direct stake in the outcomes, so they can maintain the clear thinking and rationality so important to successful outcomes. This is the common wisdom, but is it true?

In the articles that follow, the assumption of lawyers' objectivity is questioned. Lawyers may heighten partisan perceptions and fall into psychological traps that decrease their effectiveness in negotiating on behalf of clients. Although psychologists and other behavioral scientists have studied perceptual errors and cognitive biases for some time, the practical application of their findings to how lawyers negotiate is relatively new.

We can often recognize our client's partisan perceptions, but we are easily fooled by our own biases and distortions. By definition, what we believe, even if selective, is our reality. The longer we work with a client on a case or a deal, the more we share the same reality—distorted or not. We may be no more able than our clients to objectively analyze the strengths of their case or the weaknesses of the other side's case. It can be very helpful for you as a professional negotiator to understand some of the psychological factors likely to impact your assessment of the value of your client's case and that may influence how you negotiate. The articles that follow explain and apply the role of perception and the subjectivity principle, as well as other psychological concepts, to the lawyer's job in evaluating cases, discovery, and negotiating settlements.

DWIGHT GOLANN, COGNITIVE BARRIERS TO EFFECTIVE NEGOTIATION*

6 ADR Currents 6 (September 2001)

Students at Harvard are preparing to negotiate the settlement of a personal injury case. Before they begin, the students are told to make a private assessment of the plaintiff's chances of winning based on their confidential bargaining instructions. What the students don't know is that there is nothing confidential about their information: Representatives of the plaintiff and defendant have received exactly the same instructions. Since both sides have the same data, they should logically come out with the same answer—but this is not what occurs.

---

* The original article also provides practical ideas about how cognitive barriers might be overcome.

In fact, hundreds of law and business students told to negotiate for the plaintiff assessed her chances of winning at nearly 20% higher than did the students assigned to the defense. . . . When they were asked to estimate the damages that a jury would award the plaintiff if she did win, there was a similar disparity: Plaintiff bargainers estimated her damages at almost $100,000 higher than did the defense negotiators.

What caused these distortions? It was not that the negotiators were uninformed about the case, since they all had the same information. Nor was it due to their lack of experience: When I posed the same problem to experienced litigators in training to become mediators, a similar pattern emerged: Lawyers assigned to the plaintiff were consistently more optimistic than those assigned to the defense. Experiments in other settings also confirm the existence of an "advocacy effect" in case evaluation.

In real-life negotiations lawyers on opposing sides often arrive with sharply differing assessments of the odds of winning in court. . . . Even allowing for the inevitable "puffing" that occurs in bargaining, both sides honestly believe that they have a better than even chance of prevailing. These variances in perception obviously can affect the outcome of a negotiation, since bargainers who value a case differently will find it very hard to agree as to what constitutes a "fair" settlement. These and other hidden barriers to successful negotiation lie in the domain of cognitive psychology, the science of how people assimilate information and make decisions. This article focuses on four common cognitive obstacles that pose challenges even for experienced negotiators and mediators. . . .

SELECTIVE PERCEPTION

The first factor that explains the results at Harvard, as well as problems that arise in real-life bargaining, is that negotiators often miss key data in the case that would be apparent to an outsider. This phenomenon, known as "selective perception," happens in this way: Whenever we encounter a new problem, we must interpret a stream of unfamiliar, often conflicting data. We respond by instinctively forming a hypothesis about the situation, then organize what we later see and hear with the help of that image. The problem is that our hypothesis also operates as a filter, protecting us from conflicting data by automatically screening it out—which in turn reinforces the belief that our initial view was correct.

Selective perception is a universal phenomenon. Henry David Thoreau was probably thinking about it when he said, "We see only the world we look for." . . . Every piece of litigation involves a story, and lawyers usually hear only one version of that story from their client. Based on this data, they tend to form a hypothesis about the dispute. In many instances selective perception then takes over to "protect" both lawyers and clients from the dissonance of conflicting evidence. . . .

OPTIMISTIC OVERCONFIDENCE

Assessing the value of a legal case requires predicting events that are uncertain, for example, how an unknown jury will react to evidence that may or may not be admitted. These assessments are often unreliable. For one thing, people are consistently overconfident about their ability to assess uncertain data....

Why is this? The problem is that when we don't know something — even a fact that we aren't expected to have at our fingertips — either we are embarrassed to admit our ignorance or simply feel a competitive urge to be right. So we give a more precise answer than our knowledge can support: We are overconfident, in other words, about our ability to assess uncertainty.

There is a related problem. When people in an uncertain situation are asked to estimate the likelihood of a good or bad outcome, they consistently underestimate the chances of an unfavorable result. The reason, it appears, is that we like to believe that we are in control of events and thus able to bring about good results, even when we cannot.

These tendencies become even stronger when the person making the judgment acquires a personal stake in the outcome. In psychological experiments, for example, subjects who have wagered that a horse will win a race are typically more confident, both about their ability to handicap races and about the chance that their chosen horse will win, than are people who have not placed a bet.

How do these forces affect negotiations over lawsuits? Lawyers are often asked to estimate the likely outcome of court proceedings at a point when they have little basis for offering an accurate assessment. In such situations, to maintain their reputations as expert litigators and to avoid appearing ignorant to a client or another lawyer, they are likely to offer an overoptimistic estimate, and have more confidence in the correctness of their forecast than their knowledge supports. To make matters worst, both lawyers and clients "bet" on their cases by investing substantial amounts of time and money in them, thus accentuating the inherent tendency to err....

LOSS AVERSION

No one likes to lose, whether the issue is money or an abstract legal argument. Recent studies have made us aware, however, of just how strongly feelings of loss can affect bargaining decisions. The results of this research require modification of one of the pillars of modern negotiation — the search for "win-win" terms. Creating interest-based bargains is certainly valuable, but it turns out to be even more important that neither side in a negotiation feel that it has "lost."

To understand the impact of loss on bargaining, consider the following experiment: Students who had expected to attend a seminar without charge were told after they arrive that because of unexpected expenses, they would each have to pay $20. They could, however, spin a roulette wheel, with three chances in four of not having to pay the $20 and one chance of having to pay $100. These odds discouraged gambling: Since the average cost of spinning the wheel was $25, the smart choice was to pay the $20. However, a large majority of students chose to spin the wheel. Having expected to pay nothing, they apparently experienced the demand for $20 as an unwelcome loss, and were willing to take an unreasonable risk to avoid it.

This phenomenon, known as "loss aversion," affects legal bargaining because litigants usually enter negotiations with a clear view about what is the "right" settlement in their case. In effect, they carry a mental benchmark about the expected settlement value, a figure that is often distorted by optimistic overconfidence and includes recovery of their legal expenses. For example, the plaintiff in a case that is objectively valued at $75,000 may honestly believe that it is worth $90,000. Since he has had to pay $25,000 in legal expenses to pursue justice, the plaintiff may have a settlement benchmark of $115,000 in mind. The defendant, however, may well see the same case as being worth only $60,000, even before factoring his costs of defense. In situations like this one, no settlement is possible, either through direct negotiation or mediation, unless at least one party accepts an outcome that is significantly worse than his or her internal sense of what is fair. This inevitably produces strong feelings of loss. To avoid that loss, litigants often elect to spin the roulette wheel of litigation, even when the objective odds are against them. . . .

EXAMPLE

A corporation sued a supplier over an allegedly defective product. After a year of litigation, the plaintiff's vice president was discussing a defense settlement offer with his outside counsel. The offer made objective sense to the litigator in light of the company's damages and the objective risk of losing at trial, but the executive refused to consider it. He insisted that any recovery had to include not only damages, but also the nearly $50,000 that the company had paid in legal costs to bring the case. Indeed, perhaps because he felt responsible for the decision to sue, the executive seemed to care more about recovering the legal fees than the damages themselves. The company's lawyer was in a bind because she knew that there was no basis for seeking attorneys' fees in a breach-of-warranty case.

"You need to think about this like a hard-headed businessman," she argued. "At the point you came into my office, the defendant was offering you zero. You've made an investment in this case, and you're now being offered a return on it. How does the deal look — money in versus money out? What are the pros and cons of cashing out now, versus investing more and looking for a better payout later?"

After some resistance, the executive began to talk about what should be considered the "capital" in this situation, and gradually became less emotional. Eventually, with a few "sweeteners" that obscured the money terms, he decided to take the deal.

REACTIVE DEVALUATION

Imagine that you are defense counsel in a lawsuit. Your opponent is demanding that you pay $100,000 to settle, but appears sure that you will never agree. Now you decide to offer that sum. Is your adversary pleased? To the contrary, her first reaction is likely to be that she has undervalued the case: it must be worth more than $100,000, because you are the enemy and would never offer a fair deal.

We all have a tendency to reject offers made by anyone we see as an adversary, a phenomenon known as "reactive devaluation." Our instinctive response to an opponent's offer is reminiscent of Groucho Marx, who vowed never to join any club that would have him as a member. . . .

CONCLUSION

Advice about negotiation often focuses on conscious strategy and tactics. In fact, some of the most important factors affecting our judgments, and those of our negotiating partners, operate beneath the surface of our minds, outside our awareness. Knowing that these forces exist, and how to deal with them, will make you a more effective negotiator.

RICHARD BIRKE, SETTLEMENT PSYCHOLOGY: WHEN DECISION-MAKING PROCESSES FAIL

18 Alternatives 203 (December 2000)

[A]t each phase of the litigation/settlement process, pervasive psychological traps may impede lawyers' ability to make decisions that effectively maximize client values. This article describes a few of the most well-established psychological phenomena that occur during the litigation/settlement process.

WHY WE FORM INITIAL ESTIMATES THAT FAVOR OUR SIDE — AVAILABILITY AND ANCHORING

The most common way to form an estimate of the value of something unknown is to compare it to the value of something known. If a person wants to know what her house is worth, she may look to the price at which a similar house sold recently. So it is with litigation.

When clients describe cases and ask for estimates of strength and value, the lawyers try to recall cases that relate to the one described by the client. Unfortunately, the cases that come to mind do so because they are memorable and relatively unusual, not because they are run-of-the-mill. Thus, when a client describes his tort case against a restaurant, his lawyer is likely to flash for a moment on the McDonald's coffee cup case [multi-million dollar jury verdict for coffee being too hot]. When the client describes a sexual harassment claim, the lawyer might think of any of a number of such cases recently in the news. When the lawyer compares his or her client's case to a notorious case, he or she distorts its value as a result of the Availability heuristic. The attorney, like all people, doesn't have the memory to retain every bit of information that comes before him or her, so the mind selects the most vivid to remember. The vividness of the image or the ease with which it can be recalled distorts its representativeness. This is why people tend to believe, incorrectly, that there is more annual rainfall in Seattle than in northern Georgia, that shark attacks lead to more deaths than falling airplane parts, or that murder is more common than suicide.

Of course, a good lawyer understands that the case the client described is not the McDonald's coffee cup case. She understands that this client's case is probably worth less than that one, so she adjusts from the McDonald's verdict downward. The question is whether she adjusts far enough. Research suggests that she will not adjust sufficiently because of something called the Anchoring effect: that decision makers will become anchored on reference points with highly attenuated or even nonexistent links to the decision at hand. For example, people — many with legal training — have been asked questions such as, "What are the odds that the temperature in San Francisco is higher or lower today than 578 degrees?"

Of course, everyone says the odds are 100% that the temperature is lower than 578 degrees. But when they are then asked to estimate the true San Francisco temperature, their estimates are invariably higher than the true temperature. When asked the likelihood that the temperature is higher than 1,000 degrees below zero, they answer 100%. If then asked the true temperature, the distortion is toward the low side. Of course, these temperatures are absurdities and are entirely unrelated to the true temperature of any place on this planet. Nevertheless, they affect the responses given. Thus, when a lawyer recalls a notorious case like McDonald's Corp.'s for torts, Mitsubishi Motor Corp. or Baker & McKenzie for sexual harassment, or some locally notorious case after a client has begun to recount the facts of his case, rest assured that it has a distorting effect on the lawyer's initial case evaluation. When availability causes a case to pop to mind as comparable, the odds are that the mind will anchor on it and insufficiently adjust.

The best cure is to check base rates. Checking a database of awards in the local jurisdiction will yield a better estimate of case value than will reliance on experience and adjustment from seemingly comparable cases. Data always trumps intuition.

WHY WE THINK WE ALWAYS WIN — PERSPECTIVE BIASES AND POSITIVE ILLUSIONS

The mere fact that the client hires a particular lawyer often triggers a "bias of perspective" exacerbated by "positive illusions." . . . Perspective biases cause lawyers to overestimate the rightness of their side, and also to feel more confidence in their assessments. . . . Thus, when a client comes to his lawyer's office and tells his or her side of the case, the lawyer may know that there is another side of the story and may try to withhold evaluation until he or she hears it, but experiments indicate that the lawyer will form an opinion favorable to the client and be more confident in that opinion than the lawyer would be if he or she were not a partisan.

Perspective biases are reinforced by positive illusions — unrealistic optimism, exaggerated perceptions of personal control and inflated positive views of the self. For example, people tend to overestimate the probability that their predictions and answers to trivia questions are correct. There are a great many studies that indicate lawyer overconfidence. One study, conducted at a recent American Bar Association meeting, found that on average lawyers rated themselves in at least the top 80th percentile on such qualities as ability to predict the outcome of a case, honesty, negotiation skills and cooperativeness. This high degree of self-regard leads to an inflated sense of the value of a case.

These biases are difficult to correct, but if the goal is a realistic estimate of case value, lawyers should realize that their healthy self-images may lead to distorted images of how much a case is worth, and how likely they are to win. Finding a brutally honest colleague to act as "devil's advocate" may be a worthwhile investment of time. . . .

The next four principles, "Biased Assimilation," "Confirmation Bias," the "Certainty Effect," and the principle of "Commitment and Consistency," occur primarily during discovery.

WHY DISCOVERY MAKES US OVERCONFIDENT—BIASED ASSIMILATION AND CONFIRMATION BIASES

Operating in tandem, assimilation biases and confirmation biases distort both the search for information and the valuation of information found.

As the lawyer begins discovery, he or she has a theory of the case—a plan of attack or defense that is discussed with the client. As the attorney gathers cases and information, he or she sorts the information into three categories: helpful, harmful, or neutral. The psychology of biased assimilation suggests this lawyer will interpret cases and evidence in a way that supports the conclusion he or she wants, whether the information actually supports that conclusion or not. If the information is favorable, he or she will overweight its relevance and applicability. If the information is harmful, the attorney may concede that it is harmful but will underweight its harmful effects. If the information is neutral, he or she will tend to see it as marginally helpful.

Finally, if the information contains information that is part helpful and part harmful, the attorney will tend to overweight the helpful parts and under-weight the harmful parts, concluding that the information is of net positive value. This often causes a distortion in the valuation of the evidence. If both sides have done this, the case may be difficult to settle.

Moreover, experienced attorneys rarely start case research by canvassing the entire legal literature to determine the state of the law and the relative power of all of the related areas of law. It would be hard to justify billing too many hours doing general research. Instead, the lawyers try to go straight to research directly bearing on their clients' cases. They are biased and have incentives in favor of confirming that which they already believe to be true.

The same, of course, is true of lawyers processing cases. When they hope a proposition is true (e.g., a theory of liability or a defense), they will see supporting information as strong and negating information as weak. This is biased assimilation. Furthermore, because they tend to look for and find corroborating information first, their theories tend to be mentally reinforced. This is a confirmation bias.

In order to reduce the negative effects of these biases, it may make some sense to think about the "anti-thesis" before doing research. Ask yourself what the case looks like to the other client, and consider doing a little bit of research into their case-in-chief before starting your own. If you think about your research as rebutting their case (as opposed to building yours), you may retain a view of the case closer to the one that a neutral judge or juror might hold. If you can have such a neutral view, you will be more likely to settle earlier for an amount that would approximate an average verdict.

WHY WE SPEND TOO MUCH FOR INFORMATION—THE CERTAINTY EFFECT [AND COMMITMENT]

As attorneys approach the middle of the discovery process they face decisions whether to gather more information on a particular point or to spend the time and money on another aspect of the case or another case.

The certainty effect suggests that when people already have a great deal of information about an issue, they will spend more resources to establish that point than is warranted by the prospective value of the new information.

Studies of decision making have found that increasing the probability of winning a prize by a fixed amount, say 5%, has more impact on people when it changes the probability from 95% to 100%, than when it changes the probability from 25% to 30% or 65% to 70%. Stated another way, people are willing to pay a premium to change a high probability into a certainty. The certainty effect may cause lawyers who are "pretty sure" that they have uncovered all information to spend more in the search for information than is warranted by the value of the information uncovered. . . . Discovery exacerbates a tendency to escalate commitment to initial courses of action. The concept of "sunk costs" causes people who have invested in a course of action to make economically irrational choices to promote their desired outcome. . . .

WHY WE FAIL TO TREAT SIMILAR OFFERS IN SIMILAR WAYS — FRAMING

Not all offers are alike, but some only differ in the way that they are phrased. Empirical studies of attorneys suggest that particular phrasings, or "framings," can affect a lawyer's willingness to accept an offer. Experimental and real-world data demonstrate that losses have more impact on choices than do equivalent gains. For example, most people think that a 50% chance of gaining $100 is not sufficient to compensate for a 50% chance of losing $100. In fact, people typically need a 50% chance of gaining $200 or $300 to offset the 50% chance of losing $100.

The theory further asserts that decision makers are risk averse when faced with medium-to-high probability gains and risk seeking when faced with medium-to-high probability losses. By framing a settlement offer as a gain and the trial as a risk, the person making the offer may increase his chances of getting the offer accepted, relative to a framing in which the settlement is seen as partial compensation for a loss and a trial as a risky way to perhaps eliminate the whole loss. Furthermore, the tendency to think of gains and losses so differently may lead to a heightened aggressiveness when the bargaining is viewed as an attempt to minimize losses rather than maximize gains. . . .

HOW PEOPLE MANIPULATE EACH OTHER — TOOLS OF SOCIAL INFLUENCE

Notwithstanding the aforementioned obstacles, people do make deals. They manage, somehow, to persuade the other side to accept offers. They use tools of social influence. The psychological literature on topics related to persuasion is abundant — and as yet has been rarely adapted over to legal settings. A handful of the best-known tools of social influence are scarcity, authority, liking, social proof, and reciprocation. These are familiar, so the descriptions are brief.

Scarcity is the extra boost of desire one feels for something that will disappear after deadlines pass, opportunities disappear, or something becomes unavailable. Experience suggests that "exploding offers" are accepted more often than offers that ostensibly don't expire.

Authority captures the ways in which the trappings of authority promote certain behaviors. Stanley Milgrom's famous experiments showed that when an experimenter ordered subjects to administer painful electrical shocks to innocent people, that the subjects' willingness to cause pain in others was correlated with the trappings of authority of the experimenter. If the experimenter wore a white lab coat and other "scientific" emoluments, the subjects were more willing to obey the cruel commands. These experiments stand as a "shocking" reminder of the lengths to which people will go to please or placate someone perceived to be an authority figure. Liking is somewhat the opposite of reactive devaluation. Naturally, people think more kindly of offers made by people they like, but this may not always yield the best results for a client.

Social proof is the tendency to confirm the rightness of choices or actions by reference to observations of others in similar settings. People view a behavior as correct in a given situation to the degree that they see others performing it. Sometimes following the pack will yield a good result, but in other circumstances, this method of choice may result in a lemming-like march over a cliff.

Finally, the tendency to reciprocate should not be underestimated. Even uninvited favors and gifts leave people with a sense of indebtedness. In negotiation, there is a strong norm that the recipient of a concession from the other side should make a concession of her own, even if the initial offer from the other side was extreme and the concession not particularly meaningful. The tendency to reciprocate is not in itself problematic, but when the person on the receiving side reciprocates a relatively trivial concession with a more meaningful one, such as a significant reduction of an already-reasonable request, she may be committing a negotiation error. . . .

Lawyers, like all professionals, aspire to make rational decisions and to maximize their clients' outcomes. However, all decision makers, including lawyers, depart from the rational path to best outcomes. Fortunately, psychologists have shown that some of these departures are systematic, and by understanding that they exist and seeing how they operate, decision makers might be able to avoid or overcome the obstacles to best outcomes. For lawyers who settle the vast majority of the cases they handle on behalf of millions of people—many of whom are emotionally engaged in the conflict and rely on their lawyers for advice—this is an area of study of enormous importance. There are no simple answers for how to handle all of this psychology, but that is as it should be—the lawyer's mind is a complicated place.

NOTES AND QUESTIONS

Professor Birke goes on to list more psychological principles that may impact negotiations, including:

- Rejection of Offers and Later Cognitive Dissonance (Commitment Bias): It's harder to say "yes" if you've already said "no."
- False Uncertainty: People hesitate to make decisions when awaiting the outcome of a preliminary event, even where that preliminary event is irrelevant to the decision.
- False Consensus Bias (Projection): People believe that others think the way they do or have values similar to their own.

- Construal Biases: People think that others hold more extreme views than they do, and are unwilling to accept that others are moderates in a partisan situation.
- Concession Aversion (status quo bias): People don't value equal trades from a neutral perspective. They tend to overvalue what they give up relative to what they get, making equal trades difficult to effectuate.

Some of the "cognitive barriers" explained by Professor Golann and the "psychological traps" identified by Professor Birke are the same in their original articles and the duplication has been edited out. Other perceptual distortions they describe are similar, even if labeled differently. For example, Golann's "optimistic overconfidence" is very similar to Birke's "positive illusions." You may have noticed other similarities in their observations.

There are other perceptual distortions or cognitive biases. The most common is stereotyping, where we assign attributes to a person because they are part of a social, racial, or demographic group. A related mental shortcut can create a halo effect when we generalize about positive attributes of a person based on knowing only one attribute.

The psychological factors described by Golann and Birke may work against one another in making tactical decisions driving a negotiation. For example, as will be discussed later, there are differing views about the advantages and disadvantages of making the first offer in a negotiation. Several of the above perceptional elements come into play regarding first offers. Making the first offer, particularly if the values involved are uncertain or without ready reference comparisons, could take advantage of the anchoring bias set by your offer. However, reactive devaluation, which may be at a peak near the beginning of negotiations, may cause the other side to radically discount your first offer because of their suspicion.

Another psychological factor to consider is what Birke describes as the tendency to reciprocate concessions made by others. This tendency helps explain why negotiations often settle midway between the initial offer from each side. Following the first offer with a more extreme counteroffer may allow the party going second to influence the eventual midpoint. Although we will see that negotiation need not proceed in this extreme, hard-bargaining manner, attempts to manipulate perceptions and exploit cognitive errors may cut both ways and trigger conflicting reactive tendencies.

1. Does knowing about the potential of these perception biases and cognitive errors result in not being affected by them? How can they be overcome or neutralized?
2. If a lawyer is to follow a client's wishes regarding offers and acceptances, what is the lawyer's role if he or she is aware of the client's perception biases and cognitive distortions? Must the lawyer agree to an outcome acceptable to a client if the lawyer is aware that such acceptance is the result of a misperception or cognitive error?
3. How might you counter cognitive error and perceptual distortion that may result in your negotiating opponent rejecting a settlement that is otherwise acceptable? For example, the anchoring problem where your opponent is fixed on what you regard as an unrealistic outcome in another case, or the tendency of your opponent to reject your truly generous offer because of their suspicion of any offer coming from you?

CHAPTER
4

Negotiator Styles

A. COMPETITIVE AND COOPERATIVE NEGOTIATION

Negotiation can be viewed as a series of attempts to change the perceptions of an opponent to comply with either our own perceptions or with a targeted picture we desire them to see. The purpose for these behaviors is to shape the other side's perception that their case is weaker and worth less than they thought and that your case is stronger and more valuable than your opponent previously recognized. This approach to negotiation is generally categorized as positional or competitive.

Competitive negotiation is grounded on the assumption that there is a limited resource or fund to be distributed between competing parties. Each party postures about the dimensions of the issue or conflict, initiates a demand or a specific proposal for resolving the dispute, and bargains over that proposal or presents a counterproposal. Bargaining is accompanied by arguments and presentations to change perceptions of value. These arguments and negotiations may be informative, reasonable, and persuasive. Tactics to change an opponent's perception may also include distortion, manipulation, bullying, and dramatics. Incremental concessions are usually made that narrow the bargaining range. Finally, a compromise settlement may be agreed upon. This approach to negotiation centers on predetermined positions and maximizing individual gain. The underlying competitive concept that the parties are negotiating to somehow obtain or distribute between them a limited resource also lends itself to labeling this approach "distributive bargaining." Competitive negotiators tend to be more adversarial, but not all competitive negotiators manifest an adversarial persona. In other words, a cordial personal style may mask competitive tactics in negotiation.

Cooperative negotiation is marked by an effort to understand one another's perceptions and reexamine them together to arrive at a shared picture or a mutually acceptable valuation. This more cooperative approach, also referred to as interest-based negotiation or problem solving, involves parties in a collaborative endeavor to jointly meet each others' needs and satisfy interests. Rather than moving from positions to counterpositions to a compromise settlement, cooperative negotiators pursue a joint problem-solving approach to identify interests and reexamine valuations prior to considering specific solutions. After the interests are identified and prioritized, the negotiators search for a variety of alternatives that might best satisfy these interests. The parties can then create a solution from a combination of generated options. This approach to negotiation is frequently called "integrative bargaining" because of its emphasis on meeting multiple needs and on the efforts by the parties to expand and then integrate options so that a joint decision, with more benefits to all, can be achieved. This more collaborative approach does not necessarily produce a simple compromise between competing positions. It seeks creative settlement not bound by predetermined positions.

The line between competitive and cooperative negotiation is not always clear. (For now we use "competitive" to stand for positional, distributive, and adversarial; "cooperative" as synonymous with collaborative, integrative, and problem solving.) In practice, the two approaches may be mixed or sequenced, depending on the setting, subject, and personality of those negotiating. However, descriptions of cooperative and competitive styles, as well as distinctions between these two approaches, provide a beginning point for understanding the dynamics of negotiation.

NOTE: GAME THEORY AND THE PRISONERS' DILEMMA

In order to illustrate the distinction and tension between competitive and cooperative negotiation behavior, some teachers introduce game theory and use variations of a scored game known as the prisoners' dilemma. Chess players and lawyers make strategic decisions based on what they anticipate will be the response of others. Game theory combines mathematical and economic concepts to calculate and quantify what others are likely to do in response to what you do. It can provide valuable knowledge about the likely payoffs and risks of being cooperative or competitive. Classic game theory models assume that the players are economically rational and will behave in ways that maximize their quantifiable interests. It is more difficult to factor in psychological and emotional motivations, although newer theories at the intersection of economics and psychology have had some success with the combination.

The discipline of game theory was refined during World War II and applied to military tactics. Game theory was made more accessible for use by negotiators through the writing of a Harvard mathematician, Howard Raiffa, in his classic book, *The Art and Science of Negotiation* (1982). Professor Raiffa's most recent negotiation book, which includes application of game theory, is *Negotiation Analysis: The Science of Art and Collaborative Decision Making* (2002). A book specifically applying game theory to negotiation of legal disputes is Baird, Gertner, and Picker, *Game Theory and the Law* (1994). A short handbook for lawyers is Louis Kaplow and Steven Shavell, *Decision Analysis, Game Theory, and Information* (2004).

The prisoners' dilemma game demonstrates the potential benefits of cooperation, as well as the risk of getting sucked in and clobbered by the other side, who may not reciprocate your cooperation. References to prisoners' dilemma situations and the possibility of defection from past patterns of cooperation are common in negotiation literature and are referenced in some of the readings in this book, so we briefly explain the concept here.

The original prisoners' dilemma is a multiple round exercise in which players are instructed that two coconspirators in crime are caught and placed in separate rooms without being allowed to communicate with one another. They are separately told by the police that they will each be convicted of a lesser offense and serve one year in prison unless one of them testifies in convicting the other of a greater offense, which carries a penalty of five years. The testifying prisoner will then be released without serving time. However, if each testifies against the other, their five-year sentences will be reduced by one year, so each will then serve four years. They must each choose without knowing what the other prisoner will decide to do. Then, after finding out the result of their first round choices, they will each choose again until seven rounds are completed. Their cumulative years of incarceration for seven rounds will be their individual game score, with the lowest number being the best. If they are both silent for seven rounds, in effect cooperating with one another, each receives a total of seven years (1×7). If they each agree to testify all seven rounds, they will each receive 28 years (4×7). If one testifies each round and the other is silent, the testifier gets off free and the silent one receives 35 years in prison (5×7). If each is silent for six rounds and then one testifies, or defects, in the seventh round, the defector receives a seventh round score of zero, or 6 years total for all rounds, and the other gets 5 years for the last round, for a seven-round total of 11 ($6 \times 1 + 5$). In other words, it pays to obtain cooperation from the other player while you defect. The more times you defect, the better for you, unless the other player also defects and testifies, in which event you both end up with many years served. The paradox is that each player might optimize his individual outcome by defecting, but both are better off if they cooperate in silence than if they *both* defect.

The prisoners' dilemma game can serve as a metaphor for negotiation and life. Cooperation can be risky if you are not sure of the cooperation of others. If there is just one round to play, you are probably better off defecting. In multiple rounds, cooperation is safer than defecting, but defecting can provide quantitative rewards if only one person defects while others cooperate. Correct anticipation or prediction of the moves from others is one key to success. Gaining trust and then using that trust to your advantage when you betray it can score points. However, if defection and self-serving competition become the norm, all are worse off. Competitive negotiation tends to occur when the interaction is viewed as a single round and winning is valued more than an ongoing relationship. The more rounds with the same players, the more complex the decisions and the greater the opportunity for retaliation. Repeated interaction with anticipation of future dealings tends to produce more cooperation, as does concern about retaliation and your reputation among others with whom you might later negotiate. However, there is temptation to defect if you know it is the last round because the other player(s) cannot retaliate. (All of this may help explain why negotiation among attorneys who regularly interact together in a small town tends to be more cooperative than negotiation among attorneys in a big city who have less-frequent contact.)

The game does not directly factor in questions about the moral value or satisfaction of cooperation over competition (or visa versa), or the societal costs of rewarding defection or promoting crime. International tournaments have been structured around repetitive prisoners' dilemma games, and books have been written about the results with analogous lessons for real-life negotiation. (See Axelrod, 1984.)

Both competitive and cooperative negotiation are in use and should be understood. We begin with the competitive model.

1. Competitive Approach and Tactics

There is no shortage of advice about how to be a tough bargainer and how to get what you want in a negotiation. Check out the self-help and business advice sections of large booksellers for an array of titles on this subject. Although competitive negotiation may, at times, be advantageous and appropriate, many of these guides appear to assume that the opposing side is ignorant or gullible and will have no future opportunity to retaliate. Other books and articles catalogue "hardball" tactics in order to warn you of what you might encounter. These writings are premised on the theory that to be "forewarned is forearmed." The stages of negotiation with step-by-step suggestions of what is to be done in each stage is offered later in this volume. Here we present a sampling of tactics that will provide you a view of the competitive approach. The author of *Secrets of Power Negotiating* challenges the myth of "win-win" negotiation before sharing his adversarial secrets. The second excerpt describes more "old-school tactics" and offers "guerilla responses" to help neutralize them.

ROGER DAWSON, SECRETS OF POWER NEGOTIATING, 2ND EDITION
Career Press (2001) [the following are excerpted highlights from the book]

You have probably heard that the objective of a negotiation is to create a win-win solution. It is a creative way that both you and the other person can walk away from the negotiating table feeling that you've won. . . . Oh, sure! That could happen in the real world, but it doesn't happen enough to make the concept meaningful. Let's face it, when you're sitting down in a negotiation, chances are that the other side is out for the same thing as you are. There's not going to be a magical win-win solution. If they're buying, they want the lowest price and you want the highest price. If they're selling, they want the highest price and you want the lowest. They want to take money out of your pocket and put it right into theirs.

Power Negotiating takes a different position. It teaches you how to win at the negotiating table, but leave the other person feeling that he or she won . . . You play power Negotiating by a set of rules, just like the game of chess. The big difference between negotiating and chess is that, in negotiating, the other person doesn't have to know the rules. The other person will respond predictably to the moves that you make. . . .

[Chapter by chapter the author sets out the "gambits" of power negotiating and comments on them. He includes some gambits that he identifies as unethical in order to alert the reader and also has a section on "Negotiating Pressure Points," some of which are included on the following list.]

- **Ask For More Than You Expect to Get:** If you're asking for more than your maximum plausible position, imply some flexibility. If your initial position seems outrageous to the other person and your attitude is "take it or leave it," you may not even get the negotiations started. The other person's response may be, "Then we don't have anything to talk about." You can get away with an outrageous opening position if you imply some flexibility.

- **Never Say Yes to the First Offer:** The reason that you should never say yes to the first offer (or counteroffer) is that it automatically triggers two thoughts in the other person's mind . . . "I could have done better," and "something must be wrong."
- **Flinch at Proposals:** Power Negotiators know that you should always flinch — react with shock and surprise at the other side's proposals . . . They may not expect to get what they are asking for; however, if you do not show surprise you're communicating that it is a possibility.
- **Always Play Reluctant Seller:** Look out for the Reluctant Buyer. Playing this Gambit is a great way to squeeze the other side's negotiating range before the negotiation even starts.
- **Use the Vise Technique:** The Vise is another very effective negotiating Gambit and what it will accomplish will amaze you . . . Respond to a proposal or counter-proposal with the Vise Technique: "You'll have to do better than that."
- **Don't Let the Other Side Know You Have the Authority to Make a Decision:** Your higher authority should be a vague entity and not an individual . . . Leave your ego at home when you're negotiating. Don't let the other person trick you into admitting that you have authority.
- **Don't Fall into the Trap of Thinking That Splitting the Difference Is the Fair Thing to Do:** Splitting the difference doesn't mean down the middle, because you can do it more than once.
- **Always Ask for a Trade-Off:** The Trade-off Gambit tells you that anytime the other side asks you for a concession in the negotiations, you should automatically ask for something in return.
- **Good Guy/Bad Guy:** It's an effective way of putting more pressure on the other person without creating confrontation.
- **Nibbling:** Power Negotiators know that by using the Nibbling Gambit, you can get a little bit more even after you have agreed on everything. You can also get the other person to do things that she had refused to do earlier. It works because the other person's mind reverses itself after it has made a decision.
- **Taper Concessions:** The way that you make concessions can create a pattern of expectations in the other person's mind. Taper concessions to communicate that the other side is getting the best possible deal.
- **The Withdrawing an Offer Gambit:** The Withdrawing an Offer Gambit is a gamble, so use it only on someone who is grinding away on you. You can do it by backing off your last price concession or by withdrawing an offer to include freight, installation, training, or extended terms.
- **The Decoy:** The other side can use the Decoy Gambit to take your attention away from what is the real issue in the negotiation.
- **The Red Herring:** With the Red Herring, the other person makes a phony demand that he will withdraw, but only in exchange for a concession.
- **Cherry Picking:** Let's say that you're buying a piece of land in the country, and the seller is offering it for $100,000 with 20 percent down and the balance due over ten years with 10 percent interest added. You might ask the owner to quote his or her lowest price for an all-cash deal. He or she

might agree to $90,000 for all cash. Then you ask what the lowest interest rate would be for a 50 percent down transaction. The owner quotes you seven percent. Then you Cherry Pick the best features of both components of the deal and offer $90,000 with 20 percent down and the balance carried by the owner with seven percent interest added.

- **The Default:** The Default Gambit is one that involves a unilateral assumption that obviously works to the advantage of the side proposing it, such as the company that sends a payment check to a vendor after having deducted two and a half percent. Attached is a note that says, "All of our other vendors discount for payment within 15 days, so we assume you will too." . . . The Default Gambit preys on busy or lazy people: it assumes that rather than take action the other side will take the easy way out and let you get away with it.
- **Escalation:** Raising demands after both sides reach an agreement.
- **Time Pressure:** The rule in negotiating is that 80 percent of the concessions occur in the last 20 percent of time available.
- **Being Prepared to Walk Away:** Of all the negotiating pressure points, this one is the most powerful. It's projecting to the other side that you will walk away from the negotiations if you can't get what you want. If there's one thing that I can impress upon you that would make you a 10 times more powerful negotiator, it's this: Learn to develop walk-away power.
- **The Fait Accompli:** If you have ever sent someone a check for less than they're asking and marked the back of the check "Payment in full is acknowledged," you have used the Fait Accompli Gambit. It's when one negotiator simply assumes the other will accept the assumed settlement rather than go to the trouble of reopening the negotiations. It works on the principle that it's a lot easier to beg forgiveness than it is to get permission.
- **Ultimatums:** Ultimatums are very high-profile statements that tend to strike fear into inexperienced negotiators . . . An ultimatum is a powerful pressure point, but it has one major flaw as a gambit: If you say that you are going to shoot the first hostage at noon tomorrow, what had you better be prepared to do at noon tomorrow? Right. Shoot the first hostage. Because if 12:01 p.m. rolls around and you haven't done that, you have just lost all of your power in negotiation.

LEVINSON, SMITH, AND WILSON, GUERRILLA NEGOTIATING: UNCONVENTIONAL WEAPONS AND TACTICS TO GET WHAT YOU WANT

28-34, John Wiley & Sons (1999)

Your approach to the negotiation may be determined by the strategy of your counterpart. Most people have a particular strategy that they use in negotiations. These styles differ along a continuum ranging from total indifference to adamant insistence. In order to negotiate effectively, you must try to match the level of resistance you face. If you take a laissez-faire attitude toward your counterpart's hardball approach, you will lose. Recognize the style of negotiation being used by your opponent and adjust your counterstrategy accordingly.

WHATEVER

This person offers no resistance at all, and virtually gives up the negotiation even before it's begun. They concede to "whatever you want." This "have-it-your-way" approach may be appropriate when you have little or no investment in the outcome. It may also be a smoke screen that conceals a more aggressive, covert attack. You may feel uncomfortable making even legitimate requests. You may also reciprocate by giving in without asking for what you really need.

The guerrilla response to this strategy is to ask for more than you really want, more than you even feel comfortable requesting, "Well, in that case, I'll take it all." You may gain a windfall, or at least stimulate a more substantive discussion of the issues. Use this approach when dealing with customers who are dissatisfied and upset, and it really was your fault. Just ask, "What would you like me to do?" or "What would it take to make this right?" and wait for them to respond. Often the adjustment they ask for will be less than the one you would have offered . . .

WHATEVER'S FAIR

These negotiators take the position that "as long as it's fair" they will accept the outcome. But beware. They are asking you to define what constitutes "fair." Because you will want to be seen in a favorable light, viewed as being a "fair" person, you may be overly generous, compromise needlessly, or concede more than you really should. On the other hand, they too wish to be viewed as equitable, and they may be more interested in how you view them. Or they may simply be using an appeal to fairness as a smoke screen to rationalize an otherwise unfair position.

A successful negotiation is not necessarily fair. The guerrilla response to this strategy is to weigh the scales of "fairness" so that they tip at least slightly in your favor. In fact, the guerrilla's objective is to gain a fair advantage whenever possible, and then use that advantage to negotiate an equitable settlement. Otherwise you don't get the bargaining chips you will need later to trade for what you really want . . .

NICE GUY

These negotiators will try to ingratiate themselves to you and try to become your "friend," and then appeal to the relationship. They may appear to be very generous in the beginning, offering many small concessions so as to curry favor. They will appeal to your need to be loved and appreciated. They might say, "That's not a very friendly thing to do," when calling in their favors.

This style is often used as a counterpart to the Hardball in the classic game of White Hat, Black Hat. The glad-handing car salesman offers you a substantial discount, a handful of optional equipment, and an overly generous trade-in, only to have the deal shot down by the Hardball sales manager. Not wanting your new friend to get into trouble with his boss, you agree to pay a much higher price for the car.

The guerrilla response to the Nice Guy strategy is to maintain your perspective and keep your focus on the outcome you're seeking. Ask yourself, "How much history do I really have with this person? Is our relationship more valuable than what's at stake here?" In many negotiation situations, you'll never see this person again. . . .

WHINER

This approach appeals to your sympathy. While they commiserate about the weather, the traffic, and their business or financial woes, you're put off balance. After listening to their whining for a while, you may find yourself granting concessions out of pure condolence.

The guerrilla response to this strategy is to ask yourself, "Whose problem is this?" and then ask yourself, "Is this problem germane to the settlement?" If it's not your problem, don't try to fix it, and if it's not relevant to the negotiation, ignore it. . . .

STONEWALL

You may recognize this tactic as the one your spouse uses when annoyed with you. In this case, your counterpart becomes withdrawn and sullen, and may even refuse to talk. But this apparent retreat is tactically intended to apply pressure. You may become so uncomfortable with the silence that you back off from your position just to restart the conversation.

The guerrilla response to this strategy is to let them be quiet, but fill the dead airtime with something else. "Okay, let's put that aside for the time being," and change the subject. Keep the conversation open, but defer further negotiation as long as they continue the silent treatment.

Use the Stonewall approach when they demand detailed explanations of every point of your position. "I'm not discussing it!" is a fair negotiating position.

GUILT TRIP

This counterpart will set you up to be wrong, then take advantage of your vulnerability when you're feeling guilty for being so demanding. This is a one-way ticket to being taken.

The guerrilla responds by remaining objective. Refuse to let your emotions control you. Do you really have a reason to feel culpable? . . .

THE NIBBLER

The Nibbler will work out the best deal they can, then ask for "just one more thing," and then a little something else, then one more tiny thing. Just when you think you have an agreement, they balk and ask, "but what about . . ." They have pen in hand, ready to sign, and they ask, "This does include the extended warranty, doesn't it?" They are like a small leak that sinks a large boat.

Because they will ask for more and more and more until you say, "no!" the guerrilla response to this strategy is to just say "no," or at least say, "I'm sorry, but I can't. . . ." Or you can say, "I can do that, but only if you agree to write three recommendation letters and sign the contract now!" Asking for a substantial reciprocal concession usually stops the Nibbler. . . .

TIT-FOR-TAT

This negotiator uses a give-and-take approach, and will not offer a concession, not even a minor one, without demanding a reciprocal concession in exchange. They may be belligerent in their insistence.

The guerrilla response to this strategy is to keep your reciprocal concessions small, but be prepared to make a bunch of them. Brainstorm a long list of small concessions in advance so you'll be forearmed. . . .

RULE BOOK

This negotiator will focus on the form and format of the negotiation, placing great importance on the place and time, the shape of the table, or the formatting of the documents. They will cry "foul" and bring the negotiations to a halt if they feel that the rules are being broken. This preoccupation with the process is a ploy to distract you from the actual outcome, and you may make the mistake of granting real concessions in exchange for mere exceptions to protocol. Beware, because they will often structure the process so as to create every possible endemic advantage for themselves.

The guerrilla response to this strategy is to mentally separate the form from the substance of the negotiation. Ask questions concerning their reasons, and request explanations of their position. "I'm confused. Can you help me understand how a different table will move us toward an agreement?" You should be just as adamant about procedural issues as your adversary, but do not let the rules of the game keep you from playing to win.

HARDBALL

Stubborn, uncompromising, and belligerent, this counterpart is a negotiator's nightmare, because they're not really interested in negotiating at all. They want their own way, and they are unwilling or unable to consider an alternative position.

The guerrilla response to this strategy is to look for ways to satisfy their core issues, without giving in yourself. They're playing for as much as they can get, often to stroke their ego or to show that they're a tough negotiator. Often what they really need is a lot less than what they're asking for. Use the Hardball approach when you feel very strongly about the issues at hand, or when the requested concession runs counter to your moral or ethical values. . . .

Forewarned is forearmed. By recognizing these old-school tactics, you can neutralize them before you give up your advantage.

QUESTIONS

1. What ethical issues are raised by Dawson's listed tactics? Are any of these tactics unethical? Negotiation presents a fertile area for ethical transgressions, with relatively little guidance as to ethical limits. The ethics of negotiation are addressed in Chapter 7.

2. Is there a difference between hard, competitive negotiation and dirty bargaining tricks? If so, how would you distinguish them?
3. Are there any gambits or techniques that you could add to Dawson's list?
4. If the tactics listed by Dawson were used against you, what would you do? What is the best way not to be susceptible to such tactics? If any of these behaviors did produce an adverse result for your client, what would be your approach the next time you found yourself matched against this opponent?

In the book and film, *The Verdict*, Frank Galvin, a down-and-out alcoholic lawyer, represents a comatose client in a medical malpractice case against Boston's Catholic Archdiocese, which operates the defendant hospital. Because the case is significant and Galvin is Catholic, the Bishop personally negotiates with Galvin in an attempt to settle the claim. Consider the following negotiation dialogue from the book in light of what you have read about trying to change an opponent's perception, power negotiating, and guerrilla tactics. Also, although we do not separately address ethical issues until Chapter 7, do you see an ethical question raised by Galvin rejecting the Bishop's offer without first conferring with his client's family?

BARRY REED, THE VERDICT
8-11, Simon & Schuster (1980)

"I want to settle this matter of the lawsuit. I have releases here prepared by Monsignor O'Boyle. There's an agreement attached for a settlement of three hundred thousand dollars. I've been over this case with my staff, Frank, and this is a generous offer." There was an uncomfortable urgency in the Bishop's presentation. This was a distasteful duty. "It's really more than a compromise, you know. A compromise suggests retreat. This is nothing like that. This covers everything. It's fully adequate. Morally and legally. In fact, I'm amazed at the generosity of the insurance company." . . .

"You can't win this suit, you know, Frank. I am here as a friend. You will spend a lot of your time and a lot of our time, and in the end you'll lose. You have to. Think about it. You can afford to lose. You're one man. It's one man's destiny. We cannot afford to lose. We have two thousand years and eternity to protect. We have the immortal soul of the Church in our hands. How can we gamble with that? How can we afford to lose when we are losing so much? What is the fate of one man against the whole Church?"

"I have a client to protect."

"Protect your client, Frank. Protect that poor girl. I beg you. But fight us and you'll lose everything. Your case. Your client. Your license. Take the three hundred thousand dollars. For the sake of your client. For yourself. You won't do better. I promise you. There are things here at stake that are greater than you or me."

"I have an oath, Father. That may seem pretty thin measured against the fate of the Church, but I'm not fighting the Church. I'm fighting lousy medical care, I'm fighting for justice for one small girl who can no longer help herself."

"You are going to ruin your client, Francis. And yourself. Good Lord, man, I don't understand your hesitation. I swear I don't. When I walked into this room, you didn't have a future. I'm offering you one. You should be on your knees."

"Let me see the releases."

Galvin took the blue-backed papers and held them under the light. He did not read them for information. He knew what they would say. It was out of sheer wonder:

I, Karen M. Ross, duly appointed conservator of Deborah Ruth Rosen, in consideration of $300,000 in hand paid to me by St. Catherine Laboure Hospital . . .

The Bishop was right, thought Galvin. This would have been a famous victory. Yesterday. It was more than he had ever hoped to collect in the beginning. A great sum. And yet . . .

"Did Monsignor O'Boyle personally prepare these releases?"

"He did."

Galvin handed them back to the Bishop. "Please tell him that I said that he can personally shove them up his ass."

NOTE: RESPONSES TO COMPETITIVE HARDBALL AND DIFFICULT PEOPLE

Frank Galvin's response to the Bishop's offer is one way to deal with an opponent's use of power tactics. Predictably, telling the Bishop where his lawyer could file his proposed releases resulted in a lengthy trial and a large verdict. There are other ways to confront power plays and attempts at intimidation.

Many of the books and articles cataloging competitive negotiation tactics also prescribe competitive antidotes that could be used in response. Most of these reactive "hardball" tactics are either responses in kind or intended to notch the positioning up in a dance of "one-upmanship." The most effective countermove or response to sharp competitive tactics will depend on the context of the negotiation, your relationship with the other negotiators, your alternatives to continued negotiations, the strength of your own position, your goals in the negotiation, and the information available to you. The key to any effective response is being able to recognize aggressive and deceptive tactics and understanding their potential effect in distorting your perspective and masking the opposition's weaknesses.

There are alternatives to responding in kind to hardball tactics or ending the negotiation. The behavior can be recognized and labeled for what it is and then dismissed by making light of it, or you can just ignore it. You can be direct by making it clear that the tactic is not working and is interfering with either of you getting what you want out of a possible deal or settlement, and that it will not be tolerated. In effect, you can discuss and set ground rules for further negotiations. Hardball tactics are most commonly used in the absence of an ongoing relationship or friendship. Taking time to become friendlier before the bargaining begins or emphasizing the likely continuing contact or repeat plays following this negotiation may discourage hardball tactics — or may not.

The subject of responding to aggressive moves is related more generally to how we can best negotiate with people we consider difficult. Seminars and training programs are frequently offered to help us deal with "difficult people." The proliferation of these programs, including ones offered for attorneys, reflects the commonly experienced frustration most of us have had in trying to work or negotiate with others whom we perceive as being insensitive, obstinate, selfish, overly competitive, or generally unreasonable. It is an interesting paradox that experience with difficult people should be so common when few, if any, of us view ourselves as being difficult. Do you think the people you consider difficult believe themselves to be so? Studies show that opponents usually see us as more demanding and less reasonable than we view ourselves. (Thomas and Pondy, 1977.)

William Ury, in his book *Getting Past No: Negotiating with Difficult People* (1991), outlines problem behavior from difficult people in negotiations and offers five easy-to-remember countertactics, to which we have added our summary of his advice:

> **Stage One: Don't React — Go to the Balcony.** This means controlling your own behavior and distancing yourself from your natural impulses and emotions. Become an observer to an opponent's bad behavior rather than getting sucked in to the game.
>
> **Stage Two: Disarm Them — Step to Their Side.** Don't fight them, join them. Defuse anger, fear, and suspicion. Feel their pain and empathize, without agreeing to their demands or conceding.
>
> **Stage Three: Change the Game — Don't Reject . . . Reframe.** Ask questions to figure out what motivates the difficult behavior. Reshape the negotiation to address the issue you want to resolve and in the direction you want it to move.
>
> **Stage Four: Make It Easy To Say Yes — Build Them a Golden Bridge.** Make your devised outcome their idea, involve them in the solution, and help them "save face" and look good. Act more like a mediator than an adversary.
>
> **Stage Five: Make it Hard to Say No — Bring Them to Their Senses, Not Their Knees.** Now that you have made it easy for them to say yes, educate them so it is difficult to say no. Make it clear that their alternatives are worse than what you are offering.

2. Cooperative Approach

Cooperative negotiation involves parties in an effort to jointly meet each others' needs and satisfy interests. In their best-selling book *Getting to Yes*, Roger Fisher, William Ury, and Bruce Patton (1991) suggest that "you can change the game" (p. 9) and they prescribe a problem-solving, interest-based approach with suggested moves that they refer to as "principled" negotiation. *Getting to Yes* is recommended reading and familiar by now to many. The five basic elements of principled negotiation as listed by Fisher, Ury, and Patton are these:

1. **Separate the people from the problem.** The negotiators should focus on attacking the problem posed by the negotiations, not each other.
2. **Focus on interests not positions.** Distinguish positions, which are what you want, from interests, which are why you want them. Look for mutual or complementary interests that will make agreement possible.

3. **Invent options for mutual gain.** Even if the parties' interests differ, there may be bargaining outcomes that will advance the interests of both. The story is told of two sisters who are trying to decide which of them should get the only orange in the house. Once they realize that one sister wants to squeeze the orange for its juice, and the other wants to grate the rind to flavor a cake, a "win-win" agreement that furthers the interests of each becomes apparent.

4. **Insist on objective criteria.** Not all disputes and negotiations lend themselves to a "win-win" outcome. An insurance claim for damage to a car may create such a dispute, since each dollar paid by the insurance company is one dollar less for it. (Bargaining about issues of this nature is generally referred to as "zero-sum" bargaining.) Fisher, Ury, and Patton suggest that the parties first attempt to agree on objective criteria to determine the outcome. Thus, instead of negotiating over the value of a destroyed car, both parties might agree that the standard "blue book" price will determine the settlement amount. "Commit yourself to reaching a solution based on principle, not pressure."

5. **Know your Best Alternative to a Negotiated Agreement (BATNA).** The reason you negotiate with someone is to produce better results than you could obtain without negotiating. If you do not know the best you are likely to obtain without negotiating, you may accept an offer you should reject or may reject an offer better than you can otherwise get. Your BATNA is the measure to decide if you are better off agreeing to a negotiated outcome or pursuing your alternatives, whether it be a trial or a deal with someone else. Your BATNA is the basis of comparison to protect you from bad negotiating decisions and permits the exploration of imaginative solutions to satisfy your interests.

The negotiation concepts popularized by *Getting to Yes* have been widely taught and very influential. Nonetheless, some experienced negotiators believe the underlying theory and tactics espoused by Fisher, Ury, and Patton are naive and could set adherents to this approach up for failure. One frequently cited critic is James White, a well-respected professor and long-time teacher of negotiation. Professor White's review, excerpted next, is followed by comments from Professor Fisher.

JAMES J. WHITE, PROS AND CONS OF "GETTING TO YES"; ROGER FISHER, COMMENT ON WHITE'S REVIEW

34 J. Legal Educ. 115-124 (1984)

Getting to Yes is a puzzling book. On the one hand it offers a forceful and persuasive criticism of much traditional negotiating behavior. It suggests a variety of negotiating techniques that are both clever and likely to facilitate effective negotiation. On the other hand, the authors seem to deny the existence of a significant part of the negotiation process, and to oversimplify or explain away many of the most troublesome problems inherent in the art and practice of negotiation. The book is frequently naive, occasionally self-righteous, but often helpful . . .

Unfortunately the book's emphasis upon mutually profitable adjustment, on the "problem solving" aspect of bargaining, is also the book's weakness. It is a weakness because emphasis of this aspect of bargaining is done to almost total exclusion of the other aspect of bargaining, "distributional bargaining," where one for me is minus one for you . . . [S]ome would describe a typical negotiation as one in which the parties initially begin by cooperative or efficiency bargaining in which each gains something with each new adjustment without the other losing any significant benefit. Eventually, however, one comes to bargaining in which added benefits to one impose corresponding significant costs on the other . . .

One can concede the authors' thesis (that too many negotiators are incapable of engaging in problem solving or in finding adequate options for mutual gain), yet still maintain that the most demanding aspect of nearly every negotiation is the distributional one in which one seeks more at the expense of the other, my principal criticism of the book is that it seems to overlook the ultimate hard bargaining. Had the authors stated that they were dividing the negotiation process in two and were dealing with only part of it, that omission would be excusable. That is not what they have done. Rather they seem to assume that a clever negotiator can make any negotiation into problem solving . . . To my mind this is naive. By so distorting reality, they detract from their powerful and central thesis.

Chapter 5, entitled "Insist on Objective Criteria," is a particularly naive misperception or rejection of the guts of distributive negotiation. Here, as elsewhere, the authors draw a stark distinction between a negotiator who simply takes a position without explanation and sticks to it as a matter of "will," and the negotiator who is reasonable and insists upon "objective criteria." Of course the world is hardly as simple as the authors suggest. Every party who takes a position will have some rationale for that position; every able negotiator rationalizes every position that he takes. Rarely will an effective negotiator simply assert "X" as his price and insist that the other party meet it.

The suggestion that one can find objective criteria (as opposed to persuasive rationalizations) seems quite inaccurate . . . To say that there are objective criteria . . . in the case of a personal injury suit for a million dollars or an $800,000 judgment, is to ignore the true dynamics of the situation and to exaggerate the power of objective criteria. Any lawyer who has been involved in a personal injury suit will marvel at the capacity of an effective plaintiffs lawyer . . . to give the superficial appearance of certainty and objectivity to questions that are inherently imponderable . . . Their suggestion that the parties look to objective criteria to strengthen their cases is a useful technique used by every able negotiator. Occasionally it may do what they suggest: give an obvious answer on which all can agree. Most of the time it will do no more than give the superficial appearance of reasonableness and honesty to one party's position . . .

The author's consideration of "dirty tricks" in negotiation suffers from more of the same faults found in their treatment of objective criteria. At a superficial level I find their treatment of dirty tricks to be distasteful because it is so thoroughly self-righteous. The chapter is written as though there were one and only one definition of appropriate negotiating behavior . . . The authors seem not to perceive that between "full disclosure" and "deliberate deception" lies a continuum, not a yawning chasm. They seem to ignore the fact that in one sense the negotiator's role is at least passively to mislead his opponent about his settling point while at the same time to engage in ethical behavior.

Finally, because the book almost totally disregards distributive bargaining, it necessarily ignores a large number of factors that probably have a significant impact on the outcome of negotiations . . . There is evidence that the level of the first offer, and the pace and form of concessions all affect the outcome of negotiation, yet there is no consideration of those matters. Doubtless the authors can be forgiven for that. No book of 163 pages can be expected to deal with every aspect of negotiation. Yet this one suffers more than most, for implicitly if not explicitly, it seems to suggest that it is presenting the "true method." . . .

COMMENT BY ROGER FISHER

. . . White is more concerned with the way the world is, and I am more concerned with what intelligent people ought to do. One task is to teach the truth, to tell students the unpleasant facts of life, including how people typically negotiate. But I want a student to negotiate better than his or her father. I see my task as to give the best possible prescriptive advice, taking into account the way other human beings are likely to behave as well as one's own emotions and psychological state. . . .

The world is a rough place. It is also a place where, taken collectively, we are incompetent at resolving our differences in ways that efficiently and amicably serve our mutual interest. It is important that students learn about bluffing and hard bargaining, because they will certainly encounter it. It is also important that our students become more skillful and wise than most people in dealing with differences. Thus to some extent, White and I are emphasizing different aspects of what needs to be taught. . . .

The most fundamental difference between White's way of thinking and mine seems to concern the negotiation of distributional issues "where one for me is minus one for you." . . . By focusing on the substantive issues (where the parties' interests may be directly opposed), White overlooks the shared interest that the parties continue to have in the process for resolving that substantive difference. How to resolve the substantive difference is a shared problem. Both parties have an interest in identifying quickly and amicably a result acceptable to each, if one is possible. How to do so is a problem. A good solution to that process-problem requires joint action . . .

The guts of the negotiation problem, in my view, is not who gets the last dollar, but what is the best process for resolving that issue. It is certainly a mistake to assume that the only process available for resolving distributional questions is hard bargaining over positions. In my judgment it is also a mistake to assume that such hard bargaining is the best process for resolving differences efficiently and in the long-term interest of either side. . . .

White seems to find the concept of "raw power" useful for a negotiator. I do not. For a negotiator, the critical questions of power are (1) how to enhance one's ability to influence favorably a negotiator on the other side, and (2) how to use such ability as one has. My ability to exert influence depends upon the cumulative impact of several factors: skill and knowledge, the state of our relationship, the legitimacy of our respective interests, the elegance of a proposed solution, my willingness and ability to commit myself, and the relative attractiveness to each side of its best alternative. In advance of a negotiation I can work to enhance each of those elements . . .

Without knowing the particular subject matter of a negotiation or the identity of the people on the other side, what is the best advice one can give to a negotiator? People may prefer to ask different questions, but I have not yet heard better answers to the question on which we were and are working. . . .

Converting an apparent distributional negotiation to an integrative one and separating strong negative feelings about the people involved from the problem faced by both sides may not always succeed, but when it does, mutual gains can be created. Interests are not static and may change as events change, including the results of related litigation. Consider the distinction between positions and interests and the invention of options in the following dispute between Microsoft and Stac Electronics. What was the best alternative for each company if negotiations failed to produce an agreement?

JIM CARLTON, MICROSOFT, STAC END BATTLE WITH PACT, A "WIN-WIN" CROSS-LICENSING AGREEMENT
The Wall Street Journal, June 22, 1994

In a surprise ending to a bitter battle, Microsoft Corp. and Stac Electronics signed a broad cross-licensing agreement, settling their patent infringement dispute and giving Microsoft a 15% stake in Stac.

The move caught Wall Street off guard. Analysts had anticipated protracted legal appeals over a Los Angeles federal jury's verdict of $120 million against software behemoth Microsoft for using technology patented by little Stac. The same jury in February awarded $13.6 million against Stac for alleged use of Microsoft trade secrets. Moreover, Stac's chairman and chief executive officer, Gary Clow, had launched inflammatory attacks on Microsoft and its chairman, William Gates.

Under terms disclosed yesterday, both companies agreed to drop their claims in exchange for cross-licensing all of their existing patents, as well as future ones over the next five years. Those patents cover a technology that compresses software data on computer storage disks.

ROYALTIES OF $43 MILLION

The pact calls for Microsoft to pay Stac license royalties totaling $43 million over 43 months, while also investing $39.9 million for a 15% equity stake in Stac. . . .

The total $82.9 million outlay represents a victory for Microsoft, which had already charged $120 million for the jury award in its fiscal third quarter and now gets to credit much of the difference in the current period. Microsoft also comes out on top, analysts say, because it gets access to what they consider Stac's more reliable compression technology.

"Instead of a long and drawn out legal process, it's done and behind them," said Merrill Lynch analyst Stephen T. McClellan.

Stac also comes out ahead: It gets a significant cash infusion without a long appeals process to collect money from Microsoft. Indeed, Mr. Clow said the

$82.9 million being turned over by Microsoft represents more than Stac would have gotten had the $120 million been paid, today, since income taxes and Stac's own $13.6 million penalty would have whittled the final amount to about $64 million. Stac also gets an alliance with the most powerful player in the software industry.

"This demonstrates it is possible to do win-win deals," Mr. Clow said.

Mr. Clow's current demeanor is a dramatic turnabout from just a few weeks ago, when he appeared on CBS's "Eye to Eye With Connie Chung" to describe his competition against Microsoft Chairman Bill Gates as "like a knife fight." Mr. Gates, the subject of a profile on the show, walked out of an interview when Ms. Chung asked him about Mr. Clow's charges.

Yesterday, Mr. Clow backpedaled from his earlier criticisms, saying, "This is not personal. This [settlement] makes good business sense going forward. In doing battle . . . I gained a high degree of respect for Microsoft."

'MORE FUN THAN DISAGREEING'

Microsoft executives, too, expressed no hard feelings. "This is a lot more fun than disagreeing," said Michael Brown, Microsoft's vice president of finance.

Paul Maritz, a Microsoft senior vice president, said the company wanted to get the case over to end "any uncertainty in the minds of our customers" over Microsoft products that may have contained the offending compression code . . .

B.   A COMBINED APPROACH — CREATING VALUE AND CLAIMING VALUE

The distributional bargaining to which Professors White and Fisher refer occurs when the issue being negotiated is singular or all apparent possibilities of joint gain have been exhausted. Negotiation by a tourist over the cash price of a single item from a transient merchant at a bazaar is a simple example of a zero-sum game where a dollar more for the seller is a dollar less for the purchaser and no future relationship is anticipated. Where the possibility exists to go beyond a zero-sum situation and create additional value, such as in the Microsoft-Stac dispute reported above, a dilemma exists for negotiators between pursuing the cooperative moves to enhance the total value available jointly and competitive behavior to individually claim increased value and gain an advantage. Understanding this dichotomy of opportunities and the choice it presents creates a tension because after value is created through cooperation and sharing information about interests, value claiming is likely to occur and the information we shared could haunt us.

The next excerpt from an influential book by David Lax and James Sebenius identifies some of the sources of creating value in negotiation. It also introduces the "negotiator's dilemma," the tension that exists between the behaviors that tend to create value and those that individually claim the value that was jointly created. The authors promote open communication and sharing information to avoid leaving joint gains on the table. The critique by

Gerald Wetlaufer, which then follows, is more cautionary about buying into "win-win" negotiation and advises against sharing certain information, at least for the pecuniary reasons offered by Lax and Sebenius.

DAVID A. LAX AND JAMES K. SEBENIUS, THE MANAGER AS NEGOTIATOR: BARGAINING FOR COOPERATION AND COMPETITIVE GAIN

29-35, The Free Press (1986)

THE NEGOTIATOR'S DILEMMA: CREATING AND CLAIMING VALUE

We assume that each negotiator strives to advance his interests, whether they are narrowly conceived or include such concerns as improving the relationship, acting in accord with conceptions of equity, or furthering the welfare of others. Negotiators must learn, in part from each other, what is jointly possible and desirable. To do so requires some degree of cooperation. But, at the same time, they seek to advance their individual interests. This involves some degree of competition.

That negotiation includes cooperation and competition, common and conflicting interests, is nothing new. In fact, it is typically understood that these elements are both present and can be disentangled.

Deep down, however, some people believe that the elements of conflict are illusory, that meaningful communication will erase any such unfortunate misperceptions. Others see mainly competition and take the cooperative pieces to be minimal. Some overtly acknowledge the reality of each aspect but direct all their attention to one of them and wish, pretend, or act as if the other does not exist. Still others hold to a more balanced view that accepts both elements as significant but seeks to treat them separately . . . [W]e argue that all these approaches are flawed.

A deeper analysis shows that the competitive and cooperative elements are inextricably entwined. In practice, they cannot be separated. This bonding is fundamentally important to the analysis, structuring, and conduct of negotiation. There is a central, inescapable tension between cooperative moves to create value jointly and competitive moves to gain individual advantage. This tension affects virtually all tactical and strategic choice. Analysts must come to grips with it; negotiators must manage it. Neither denial nor discomfort will make it disappear.

WARRING CONCEPTIONS OF NEGOTIATION

Negotiators and analysts tend to fall into two groups that are guided by warring conceptions of the bargaining process. In the left-hand corner are the "value creators" and in the right-hand corner are the "value claimers."

VALUE CREATORS

Value creators tend to believe that, above all, successful negotiators must be inventive and cooperative enough to devise an agreement that yields considerable gain to each party, relative to no-agreement possibilities. Some speak about the need for replacing the "win-lose" image of negotiation with "win-win" negotiation, from which all parties presumably derive great value . . .

Communication and sharing information can help negotiators to create value jointly. Consider the case of a singer negotiating with the owner of an auditorium over payment for a proposed concert. They reached impasse over the size of the fee with the performer's demands exceeding the owner's highest offer. In fact, when the amount of the fixed payment was the issue, no possibility of agreement may have existed at all. The singer, however, based his demand on the expectation that the house would certainly be filled with fans while the owner projected only a half-capacity crowd. Ironically, this difference in their beliefs about attendance provided a way out. They reached a mutually acceptable arrangement in which the performer received a modest fixed fee plus a set percentage of the ticket receipts. The singer, given his beliefs, thus expected an adequate to fairly large payment; the concert hall owner was happy with the agreement because he only expected to pay a moderate fee. This "contingent" arrangement . . . permitted the concert to occur, leaving both parties feeling better off and fully willing to live with the outcome.

In addition to information sharing and honest communication, the drive to create value by discovering joint gains can require ingenuity and may benefit from a variety of techniques and attitudes. The parties can treat the negotiation as solving a joint problem; they can organize brainstorming sessions to invent creative solutions to their problems. They may succeed by putting familiar pieces of the problem together in ways that people had not previously seen, as well as by wholesale reformulations of the problem.

Roger Fisher and Bill Ury give an example that concerns the difficult Egyptian Israeli negotiations over where to draw a boundary in the Sinai. "This appeared to be an absolutely classic example of zero sum bargaining, in which each square mile lost to one party was the other side's gain. For years the negotiations proceeded inconclusively with proposed boundary lines drawn and redrawn on innumerable maps. On probing the real interests of the two sides, however, Egypt was found to care a great deal about sovereignty over the Sinai while Israel was heavily concerned with its security. As such, a creative solution could be devised to "unbundle" these different interests and give to each what it valued most. In the Sinai, this involved creating a demilitarized zone under the Egyptian flag. This had the effect of giving Egypt "sovereignty" and Israel "security." This situation exemplifies extremely common tendencies to assume that negotiators' interests are in direct opposition, a conviction that can sometimes be corrected by communicating, sharing information, and inventing solutions. . . .

We create value by finding joint gains for all negotiating parties. A joint gain represents an improvement from each party's point of view; one's gain need not be another's loss. An extremely simple example makes the point. Say that two young boys each have three pieces of fruit. Willy, who hates bananas and loves pears, has a banana and two oranges. Sam, who hates pears and loves bananas, has a pear and two apples. The first move is easy: they trade banana for pear and are both happier. But after making this deal, they realize that they can do still better. Though each has a taste both for apples and oranges, a second piece of the same fruit is less desirable than the first. So they also swap an apple for an orange. The banana pear exchange represents an improvement over the no trade alternative; the apple orange transaction that leaves each with three different kinds of fruit improves the original agreement—is a joint gain—for both boys.

The economist's analogy is simple: Creativity has expanded the size of the pie under negotiation. Value creators see the essence of negotiating as expanding the pie, as pursuing joint gains. This is aided by openness, clear communication, sharing information, creativity, an attitude of joint problem solving, and cultivating common interests.

VALUE CLAIMERS

Value claimers, on the other hand, tend to see this drive for joint gain as naive and weak minded. For them, negotiation is hard, tough bargaining. The object of negotiation is to convince the other guy that he wants what you have to offer much more than you want what he has; moreover, you have all the time in the world while he is up against pressing deadlines. To "win" at negotiating—and thus make the other fellow "lose"—one must start high, concede slowly, exaggerate the value of concessions, minimize the benefits of the other's concessions, conceal information, argue forcefully on behalf of principles that imply favorable settlements, make commitments to accept only highly favorable agreements, and be willing to outwait the other fellow.

The hardest of bargainers will threaten to walk away or to retaliate harshly if their one-sided demands are not met; they may ridicule, attack, and intimidate their adversaries. . . . At the heart of this adversarial approach is an image of a negotiation with a winner and a loser: "We are dividing a pie of fixed size and every slice I give to you is a slice I do not get; thus, I need to claim as much of the value as possible by giving you as little as possible."

A FUNDAMENTAL TENSION OF NEGOTIATION

Both of these images of negotiation are incomplete and inadequate. Value creating and value claiming are linked parts of negotiation. Both processes are present. No matter how much creative problem solving enlarges the pie, it must still be divided; value that has been created must be claimed. And, if the pie is not enlarged, there will be less to divide; there is more value to be claimed if one has helped create it first. An essential tension in negotiation exists between cooperative moves to create value and competitive moves to claim it.

[T]he concert hall owner may offer the singer a percentage of the gate combined with a fixed fee that is just barely high enough to induce the singer to sign the contract. Even when the parties to a potential agreement share strong common interests, one side may claim the lion's share of the value an agreement creates. . . .

THE TENSION AT THE TACTICAL LEVEL

The tension between cooperative moves to create value and competitive moves to claim it is greatly exacerbated by the interaction of the tactics used either to create or claim value.

First, tactics for claiming value (which we will call "claiming tactics") can impede its creation. Exaggerating the value of concessions and minimizing the benefit of others' concessions presents a distorted picture of one's relative preferences; thus, mutually beneficial trades may not be discovered. Making threats or commitments to highly favorable outcomes surely impedes hearing and understanding others' interests. Concealing information may also cause one to leave joint gains on the table. In fact, excessive use of tactics for claiming value may well sour the parties' relationship and reduce the trust between them. Such tactics may also evoke a variety of unhelpful interests. Conflict may escalate and make joint prospects less appealing and settlement less likely.

Second, approaches to creating value are vulnerable to tactics for claiming value. Revealing information about one's relative preferences is risky . . . The information that a negotiator would accept position A in return for a favorable resolution on a second issue can be exploited: "So, you'll accept A. Good, Now, let's move on to discuss the merits of the second issue." The willingness to make a new, creative offer can often be taken as a sign that its proposer is able and willing to make further concessions. Thus, such offers sometimes remain undisclosed. Even purely shared interests can be held hostage in exchange for concessions on other issues. Though a divorcing husband and wife may both prefer giving the wife custody of the child, the husband may "suddenly" develop strong parental instincts to extract concessions in alimony in return for giving the wife custody.

In tactical choices, each negotiator thus has reasons not to be open and cooperative. Each also has apparent incentives to try to claim value. Moves to claim value thus tend to drive out moves to create it. Yet, if both choose to claim value, by being dishonest or less than forthcoming about preferences, beliefs, or minimum requirements, they may miss mutually beneficial terms for agreement.

Indeed, the structure of many bargaining situations suggests that negotiators will tend to leave joint gains on the table or even reach impasses when mutually acceptable agreements are available.

GERALD B. WETLAUFER, THE LIMITS OF INTEGRATIVE BARGAINING

85 Georgetown L.J. 369, 370-372, 383-386 (1996)

It is now conventional wisdom that opportunities for integrative bargaining are widely available, that they are often unrecognized and unexploited, and that as a result both parties to negotiations and society as a whole are worse off than would otherwise have been the case. The failure to recognize and exploit these opportunities may reflect a failure of education, curable either by reading or by attending a course or seminar. It may reflect the "I'm right, you're wrong, and I can prove it" style of discourse associated with law school education and historically male modes of moral reasoning. Or it may be the result of the "negotiator's dilemma" in which the open and cooperative tactics thought appropriate to integrative bargaining are systematically exploited and driven out by the more combative tactics generally associated with distributive bargaining—starting high, conceding slowly, concealing and misrepresenting one's own interests, arguing coercively, threatening, and bluffing.

If the problem at hand is our failure to recognize and exploit opportunities for integrative bargaining, the solution, we are told, is to shift away from the tactics of distributive bargaining and toward the tactics appropriate to integrative bargaining: cooperation, openness, and truthtelling. Individual negotiators should embrace these tactics not because they are good or ethical, or because they will help to build a better society, but instead because they will promote the individual's immediate pecuniary self-interest. . . .

The proponents of integrative bargaining usually assert that opportunities for such bargaining are widely, if not universally, available. Lax and Sebenius, in the most important contribution yet made to our understanding of these matters, catalogue the opportunities for integrative bargaining. Their list includes differences between the parties in terms of (1) their interests, (2) their projections concerning possible future events (3) their willingness to accept risks, and (4) their time preferences regarding payment or performance . . . All four of these circumstances will sometimes, but only under certain further conditions and with certain important qualifications, afford opportunities for the parties to expand the pie through integrative bargaining. . . .

[The author next argues and attempts to demonstrate that the listed differences between negotiating parties rarely provide opportunities to lastingly expand the pie and create joint, integrative gains. He makes reference to the Lax and Sebenius example of a singer negotiating with the owner of an auditorium over payment for a proposed concert.]

Assume Ms. Singer will not sing for less than $14,000, and Mr. Owner, having taken account of his expenses and the number of seats he believes he can sell, cannot offer anything more than $10,000. As long as the parties seek to negotiate an agreement for a fixed dollar amount, there is no zone of agreement. That is to say, there is no dollar amount that is, as it must be for Ms. Singer, at or above $14,000 and is also, as it must be for Mr. Owner, at or below $10,000.

Assume further, however, that the two parties hold different expectations about the number of seats that will be sold and that both are willing to bet on their assessment. Ms. Singer is utterly confident that 10,000 tickets will be sold, while Mr. Owner — burned too often when he has tried to sell high culture to the burghers of his city — is equally certain that only 4000 tickets will be sold.

The integrative solution to this problem is to suggest a contingent agreement in which, for instance, Ms. Singer is paid $1.50 for every seat that is sold. From her perspective, such a contract is worth $15,000 ($1.50 per seat times 10,000 seats), which is $1000 better than (higher than) her $14,000 reservation price. From the perspective of Mr. Owner, the perceived cost of the agreement is $6000 ($1.50 per seat times 4000 seats), $4000 better than (lower than) his $10,000 reservation price. Through integrative bargaining and a contingent agreement, the parties can enter a contract that leaves them both better off than they otherwise would have been in the absence of this agreement. . . .

[However,] the uncertainty that created the opportunity for integrative bargaining will, in due course, be eliminated. When that uncertainty is eliminated and the contingency is removed, all of the parties' bets will have been won or lost. . . .

In the end, there will be a specific number of seats that are actually sold. If Ms. Singer is right and 10,000 seats are actually sold, then she will be paid $15,000 — $1000 better than her $14,000 reservation price. This time, though, Mr. Owner is also better off. Once he sold the first 4000 tickets, he recovered his costs as well as a reasonable profit. For every additional ticket sold, he earned pure profit. Although this profit must be split with Ms. Singer, Mr. Owner is still a great deal better off having sold 10,000 tickets than he would have been if he had sold only 4000. Of course, if Mr. Owner had proven right in his original judgment that they would only sell 4000 tickets, then he would have broken even, but Ms. Singer would have entered an agreement that turned out to be worth a great deal less than her reservation price. . . . Here, the uncertainty may be resolved in a way that is good for both parties—or in a way that is good for one party without being bad for the other. . . .

A final claim that can now be evaluated is that opportunities for integrative bargaining necessarily imply that it is in a negotiator's immediate pecuniary self-interest to engage in the tactics of cooperation, openness, truthtelling, honesty, and trust. First, I have demonstrated that opportunities for integrative bargaining, especially meaningful opportunities for integrative bargaining (e.g., where the pie may be made to expand and to stay expanded), exist within a narrower range of circumstances than sometimes has been claimed. Some of the differences cited by Lax and Sebenius simply do not create opportunities for integrative bargaining. Others, namely those involving different assessments regarding future events, create opportunities to expand the pie only if the parties are willing to bet on their projections. And even when the parties are willing to bet, there will be opportunities for integrative bargaining only some of the time and only in ways that will sometimes prove self-defeating in the sense that the pie may eventually return to its original size. If the pie shrinks back, one or both of the parties will be worse off than they had expected to be and, potentially worse off than they would have been had they not entered the agreement. Other circumstances named by Lax and Sebenius—multiple issues differently valued, differing projections concerning future events, differing time preferences, differing levels of risk aversion—sometimes offer opportunities for integrative bargaining but sometimes do not. Although the general claim is made that opportunities for integrative bargaining provide a reason, based solely on immediate pecuniary self-interest, to engage in openness and truthtelling, those opportunities are considerably less pervasive than has been announced. Thus, this argument for openness and truthtelling is, in that degree, narrower and less persuasive.

Second, even within the range of circumstances in which there are significant opportunities for integrative bargaining, the bargainer must almost always engage in distributive bargaining as well. Therefore, it is in the bargainer's self-interest not just to adopt the tactics of openness and truthtelling that are said to be appropriate to integrative bargaining, but somehow also to adopt the tactics of truth-hiding and dissimulation that are said to be appropriate in distributive bargaining. However we might manage these incompatible tactics, this situation presents at most a weak and highly qualified argument for openness and truthtelling. Moreover, the argument for openness and truthtelling is not an argument for openness and truthtelling with respect to everything, but instead, is limited to information useful in identifying and exploiting opportunities for integrative bargaining. Thus, an opportunity for integrative bargaining will present an occasion for a certain amount of truthtelling with respect to one's relative interest in various issues (or one's projections about the future or aversion to risk) without also presenting even a weak argument for truthtelling with respect to one's reservation price. . . .

If there is a general case for cooperation, openness, and truthtelling in negotiations, that case is multidimensional and parts of it are expressly ethical.

Certainly, because there are opportunities for integrative bargaining, a measure of openness and truthtelling is sometimes warranted as a matter of a negotiator's immediate pecuniary self-interest. Similarly, a negotiator's long-term pecuniary self-interest may sometimes be served by openness and truth-telling because of the costs that may be associated with a reputation for sharp dealing. But it is also true that a negotiator's pecuniary self-interest is, at best, only a portion of his true self-interest. Thus, it may be in his true self-interest to accept some pecuniary costs for the sake of living in a community in which cooperation, truthtelling, and ethical behavior are the norm. Moreover, Plato's Socrates may have been right when he argued that a person who has some combination of wealth and virtue may be happier and better off than a person who has more wealth but less virtue. . . .

We have, in certain respects, allowed ourselves to be dazzled and seduced by the possibilities of integrative or "win-win" bargaining. That, in turn, has led to a certain amount of overclaiming. The reason, I think, is that if we hold these possibilities in a certain light and squint our eyes just hard enough, they look for all the world like the Holy Grail of negotiations. They seem to offer that which we have wanted most to find. What they seem to offer—though in the end it is only an illusion—is the long-sought proof that cooperation, honesty, and good behavior will carry the day not because they are virtuous, not because they will benefit society as a whole, but because they are in everyone's individual and pecuniary self-interest. But however much we may want "honesty" to be "the best policy" in this strong sense, the discovery of integrative bargaining has not, at least so far, provided that long-sought proof.

Perhaps the time has finally come to consider the possibility that this proof will always elude us, for the simple reason that the world in which we live does not, in this particular way, conform to our wishes. Even if there is just the chance that this is so, and it looks much more like a certainty than a chance, it would be appropriate to acknowledge the ultimate insufficiency of under-standing self-interest in narrowly pecuniary terms. It would be appropriate to attend in a systematic way to the facts that, even when it is contrary to our pecuniary self-interest, relationships matter; that we care about our reputa-tions, not just for effectiveness but also for decency and good behavior: that we care about living in—and helping to create—communities in which pecuni-ary self-interest is not the only language that is spoken; and that Plato's Socrates may have gotten it right. And it would be appropriate to acknowledge the central importance of the ethical case against certain forms of competitive and self-interested behavior, especially those forms of behavior, central to the process of negotiations, that involve misrepresentations and other conduct that imposes harm upon others.

NOTE AND QUESTIONS

Lax and Sebenius (1986, p. 115) summarize the differences that can lead to joint gains and creation of value through negotiation as follows:

- Differences in relative valuation can lead to exchanges, directly or by "unbundling" differently valued interests.
- Differences in *forecasts* can lead to contingent agreements when the items under negotiation are uncertain and themselves subject to

different probability estimates, or when each party feels that it will fare well under and perhaps can influence a proposed contingent resolution procedure.

- Differences in *risk aversion* suggest insurance-like risk-sharing arrangements
- Differences in *time preference* can lead to altered patterns of payments or actions over time.
- Different *capabilities* can be combined.
- Other differences (evaluation criteria, precedent and substance, constituencies, organizational situation, conceptions of fairness, and so on) can be fashioned into joint gains.

You may recall that these "differences" relate to the role perceptions play in understanding conflict, as previously explained by Rummel in his excerpt on "The Subjectivity Principle." You will note that we have come full circle in connecting the cause of conflict — it's all in our heads, to a suggested approach for constructively resolving conflicts — recognize the different perceptions and trade on them.

1. Are the suggestions made by Lax and Sebenius for creating value by focusing on differences equally applicable to settlement of legal disputes as to deal-making negotiations? What differences on the above list could be utilized in settling a claim for damages by an injured driver against an insurance company?

2. Have you experienced situations where you were open and cooperative initially and then felt that you may have revealed too much or been too accommodating to get what you wanted for yourself? If in that same situation again, would you behave differently? Why or why not? What are the trade-offs?

3. Do the comments of Gerald Wetlaufer reflect the same concerns as those of James White? Is there any fundamental difference in their expressed view of "win-win" negotiation or in how negotiators should behave? If so, how do they differ?

4. Professor Wetlaufer concludes that being open and cooperative in negotiations may not benefit immediate pecuniary interests, but that relationships matter and that Plato may have been correct in teaching that virtue is more important than wealth. Even if we believe this is true when we negotiate for ourselves, as lawyers who negotiate for clients can we trade off a client's potential gain for our sense of virtue?

5. Do clients have a say in what information is voluntarily revealed and how cooperative they want their attorney to be in negotiating on their behalf?

6. Do the immediate pecuniary interests of the client and the longer-term interests of the attorney in maintaining good working relations with other lawyers or a reputation for "decency" create a conflict of interest between attorney and client?

7. Does an attorney's reputation for openness and cooperation present a particular attraction to a client willing to pay a premium for that attorney to engage in "hard bargaining" or sharp tactics in their behalf? (For an interesting real-life example, see David McKean and Douglas Frantz's book *Friends in High Places: The Rise and Fall of Clark Clifford*, 1995. A related story about Clark Clifford, as well as discussion of the above questions, is included in Chapter 7.)

NOTE: COOPERATION v. COMPETITIVENESS—WHO DECIDES?

If a client retains an attorney with a reputation for cooperation and instructs him during a negotiation to "defect" from his past cooperative pattern and to pursue competitive aggressive tactics, may the lawyer refuse? Generally clients get to choose the objective of negotiation and lawyers use their professional judgment in selecting the means of obtaining the client's objectives. Of course, it's not quite so simple. In matters of litigation, the lawyer owes the client an ethical obligation of zealous advocacy in pursuit of a client's interests. Some scholars interpret the ethical norms to mean, "the final authority on important issues of strategy rests with the client; and the client may discharge his lawyer at will, but the lawyer has only limited ability to withdraw from representation." (Gilson and Mnookin, 1995, p. 550.) Mnookin and Gilson believe that a lawyer who wishes to pursue a cooperative approach, with a sensitivity for long-term professional relationships with other attorneys, may not be able to do so in the litigation context, or at least that the client calls the negotiation shots. They also point out that the client can fire the lawyer at will if the lawyer seems more cooperative than the client wishes, but that ethical norms do not always allow the lawyer to quit if the client insists on a more aggressive strategy.

A different perspective is offered by Professor Robert J. Condlin, who points to practical norms that may differ from ethical norms for attorneys. He distinguishes between the reality of what lawyers do in negotiation and what the ethical rules appear to demand. The distinction according to Condlin is really between ends and means. Clients have control over the end result desired and lawyers choose the means. "Lawyers are persons in their own right, with moral and political rights and obligations of their own, and even though they must take direction from their clients, they need not do everything asked. For example, the duty of deference distinguishes between questions of ends and questions of means, and reserves to lawyers the tactical and technical decisions of how best to advance client objectives" (Condlin, 1992, p. 71).

According to Condlin, lawyers must be substantively competitive in negotiating for clients, but can choose their own personal style. As discussed earlier in this chapter, competitive attorneys can adopt a cordial and respectful persona in their negotiations, though this can be a fine and difficult distinction. Condlin refers to this tug between a client's wishes for the lawyers to defect from a pattern of cooperation and the lawyer's desire for long-term cooperation as the "bargainer's dilemma." Like the prisoner's dilemma, different negotiation tactics may be called for if the situation is viewed as a single- or multiple-round game. Clients tend to view litigation and some deals as a one-round game. Lawyers usually view their negotiation with other lawyers as unlimited multiple rounds, where any defect will bring future retaliation and a blemished reputation. Thus, the "bargainer's dilemma."

We will probe this dilemma in more depth when we examine the ethical constraints on lawyer negotiation in Chapter 7, The Ethical Negotiator. Articles by Professors Condlin and Mnookin (with coauthors Peppet and Tulumello) are presented there. In the meantime, please assume that lawyers, when negotiating for clients, do have a choice of being more cooperative or more competitive in their negotiation approach. Also recall that the choice of how to fulfill clients' interests is not completely bipolar. Cooperation may be the best way to fill the needs of all clients in negotiation when an integrative outcome is possible that allows each party to get some of what they want. In such situations, a competitive approach may eliminate the possibility of a win-win outcome that is otherwise available, however, it may produce an outcome most favorable for the client of a successful competitive negotiator.

C. CHOOSING AN EFFECTIVE APPROACH

1. *Negotiating Within Your Comfort Zone*

The previous sections refer to different approaches to negotiation. Being cooperative, collaborative, or competitive is, at least in part, a matter of choice. The choice you make depends on a number of factors. The subject of the negotiation, the interrelation between issues, the past or anticipated future relationship between the parties and between the attorneys, the customs and conventions where the negotiation occurs, the amount of time available, and the amount at stake may all influence your approach to negotiation. The biggest factor, however, is your own comfort zone formed by your personality and values. To the extent that how you negotiate is driven more by personality and values, it may be better described as a matter of style rather than approach. Behavioral style is more a function of who you are than what you choose to do. Choosing a style that does not fit your personality and values, if not a recipe for failure, is likely to make your work as a negotiator difficult and dissatisfying. In order to succeed as a professional and find satisfaction with what you are doing, you must negotiate within your personal comfort zone.

Defining our negotiating comfort zone is not always an easy task. It is a common desire to be liked rather than disliked. We know that we are more likely to be liked when we are cooperative and giving than when we are adversarial and taking. However, we also know that winners are admired and we want to be respected for vigorously representing our clients' interests and succeeding when we negotiate on their behalf. Law students without legal experience may share the view of attorneys popularized in movies and television series of hard-charging, aggressive lawyers. The dramatic, adversarial scenes popularly portrayed in jury trials may be transposed in our minds to all opposing lawyer interactions. As a result, many students have a latent fear that their preference for cooperation and friendliness will not serve them or their clients well in negotiation.

Other students may have enjoyed competition and winning in sports and other contests. We know that law students are a self-selected group of achievers that have succeeded, at least academically, and made it into law school through a competitive admissions process. Competition appears to be encouraged by the legal system, where cooperation and generosity may be viewed as a virtuous but less-valued quality. So it is understandable that some students are conflicted about whether negotiation should be approached as a professional game in which their competitive qualities are let loose and rewarded with success.

Mixed messages about lawyer competitiveness versus cooperation create tensions that are exasperated by ethical rules for lawyers. As you will read later in this book, the ethical standards require vigorous advocacy on behalf of clients and tolerate forms of deception in negotiation, while requiring lawyers to uphold the integrity of the profession and behave honestly.

As mentioned in the introduction, negotiation is usually done in private without opportunity to compare results. How lawyers behave in negotiation and what they do is not fully known. Personal experience can be extrapolated to form impressions that might be shared with others. However, as we know, the telling of what we experienced is filtered through the lens of our perception. Unless negotiations can be systematically observed on a grand scale, we will never know what really works best to produce desired negotiated outcomes. Indeed, the privacy and confidentiality surrounding most negotiations prevent those not party to negotiation from even knowing the negotiation outcome. So we must rely on self-reported accounts of success. Few lawyers ever "lose" a negotiation, or tell about it if they believe they did not do well. Spoken and written "war stories" of successful negotiations are not reliable descriptions of what typically occurs, or even of what occurred in the reported negotiation. (There appear to be no books on "How I Failed as a Negotiator.") These obstacles to the study and profiling of negotiations leave new lawyers little guidance on what is successful in negotiation and how to weigh the polar tensions they may feel in order to negotiate effectively within their comfort zone.

Two significant studies, reported in the excerpt that follows, help fill the void of information about how lawyers negotiate and which behaviors and styles are effective. Both studies are necessarily limited because they rely on attorneys responding to questionnaires and reporting their perceptions of effective and ineffective negotiation behavior by their opponents in recent negotiations. Nonetheless, both studies provide sources of information about how lawyers negotiate and what is considered effective, as well as ineffective. Because the studies were similar and conducted more than 20 years apart, we can obtain clues about changes over time in how attorneys negotiate.

The news from the studies is both good and bad. The good news for students struggling with the tension of deciding on their negotiation comfort zone and not knowing if what they are inclined to do is the right way to negotiate is that there is no one right way.

Both competitive and cooperative styles can be effective approaches to negotiation if done well and with integrity. Being an effective competitive negotiator does not require the use of tricks or deceit. Some competitive techniques can be legitimate ways to pursue negotiation goals, provided they are not carried to extremes. Being a cooperative negotiator need not be based on naiveté or being a pushover. Cooperative attorneys, who predominate in numbers and perceived effectiveness, are most successful when they are mindful of the interests they are pursuing and set limits on their cooperation.

Our experience in teaching negotiation is that the majority of law students are more comfortable being cooperative problem solvers than competitive adversaries. The studies indicate that although the percentage of attorneys who are adversarial has increased, about two-thirds of lawyer negotiators are classified as cooperative. Cooperative negotiators tend to be more effective. Their higher rating as more effective than adversarial negotiators has increased. Again, it should be noted that some adversarial attorneys are also rated as effective. Some admirable behaviors of negotiators (like preparation, a focus on the client's interests and high ethical standards) are shared by effective competitive and effective cooperative attorney negotiators.

The bad news is that the more recent study reported that adversarial negotiators, who are increasing in numbers, are becoming more extreme and unpleasant. The terms most frequently used to describe them are more negative than 20 years ago. This does not bode well for the legal profession or for clients, if the reports are accurate, because this group as a whole is less effective as negotiators than previously reported.

2. Effectiveness and Style

Professor Andrea Kupler Schneider describes her research on the effectiveness of negotiation styles, as well as the previous study by Professor Gerald Williams. She compares the results and states the lessons to be drawn.

ANDREA KUPFER SCHNEIDER, PERCEPTION, REPUTATION AND REALITY: AN EMPIRICAL STUDY OF NEGOTIATION SKILLS

6 Disp. Resol. Mag. 24-28, (Summer 2000)

This article examines perceptions of negotiation behavior based on an empirical survey of lawyers who were asked about their most recent negotiation experience. The data reveals several things. First, we can examine perceptions by attorneys' peers rather than the general public. Second, by comparing this data to similar data from 20 years ago, we can see how lawyers' perceptions of their peers have changed. Finally, we can outline the negotiation behaviors that appear to be highly valued by attorneys.

THE WILLIAMS STUDY

In 1976, law professor Gerald Williams undertook a study on lawyer negotiation styles by surveying 1,000 lawyers in the Phoenix area about their most recent negotiation experience. The first part of the survey asked for basic demographic information about the attorney filling out the survey and the attorney being evaluated on the other side. It did not ask for either attorney's name. Then the attorney was asked to rate the other side using three sets of scales. The first scale was a list of 75 adjectives on which attorneys were rated from zero (not characteristic) to five (highly characteristic). The second scale was a list of 43 bipolar adjective pairs from which attorneys could rate the other side from one (extremely characteristic of one end of the pole) to seven (extremely characteristic of the other end of the pole). The third scale was a list of 12 potential goals or objectives of the negotiation. The other attorney was rated from one to five on this last scale. After the adjective ratings, the attorney was asked to rate the general effectiveness of the attorney on the other side on a scale of one (ineffective) to nine (highly effective).

The methodology of the Williams study (and therefore of this new study) can be criticized for several reasons. First, the adjectives and other ratings scales

Table 1
Number of Lawyers Per Group by Perceived Effectiveness (1976)

	Ineffective	*Average*	*Effective*
Cooperative	7	84	133
Competitive	28	35	21

are subjective. Second, the determination of effectiveness is solely in the eye of the beholder as opposed to some objective measure. It is quite possible that respondents will reward negotiators like themselves with higher effectiveness ratings or punish negotiators different from themselves with lower effectiveness ratings. Finally, there could be some self-selection in terms of which lawyers actually return the survey. Recognizing these limitations, we can still use the information from these surveys to measure perceived negotiation behavior and perceived effectiveness.

Williams and his co-authors concluded that there were two primary styles of negotiation which they labeled "cooperative" and "competitive." A "cooperative" negotiator was ethical, fair and personable. A "competitive" negotiator was described as tough, egotistical and likely to use negotiation tactics. . . . Williams looked at the effectiveness of each style. Table 1 shows the results by style and effectiveness in the Williams study.

Close to 60 percent of all cooperative negotiators were considered effective by their peers. Only 25 percent of competitive negotiators were considered effective. As Williams concluded:

". . . [N]either pattern has an exclusive claim on effectiveness. Use of the cooperative pattern does not guarantee effectiveness, any more than does the use of the competitive pattern. . . . The higher proportion of cooperative attorneys who were rated effective does suggest it is more difficult to be an effective competitive negotiator than an effective cooperative."

THE NEW STUDY

It has been more than 20 years since Williams conducted his research. In the meantime, much has changed in the legal profession and in legal education. These changes include who is entering the law, the evolution of alternative dispute resolution and the growth of mega-law firms. This period also coincides with the decline in the reputation of the legal profession. How have these changes impacted how lawyers negotiate and how effective they are? To answer this question, I have added to Williams' study in the Milwaukee and Chicago legal communities with twice the number of lawyers. . . .

Of the 690 complete responses, 30 percent were from women. Interestingly, 17.8 percent discussed female negotiators. The ethnicity of respondents was overwhelmingly Caucasian (94.6 percent). The other 5.4 percent of lawyers were divided among African-American (3.1 percent), Asian (0.1 percent), Hispanic (1.3 percent), Native American (0.1 percent), and Other (0.8 percent). Fifty-seven percent of respondents practiced in Milwaukee and 43 percent practiced in Chicago. Finally, respondents came from a wide variety of practice areas: commercial (15.7 percent), corporate (6 percent), criminal (8.3 percent), family (12.3 percent), labor and employment (12.2 percent), personal injury (15.4 percent), property and real estate (11 percent) and other (19.1 percent).

STUDY RESULTS

I worked with statisticians at the Institute for Survey and Policy Research at the University of Wisconsin-Milwaukee to perform cluster analyses on the results. The first step was to divide negotiators into two groups as the Williams study had originally done. The lawyers divided into two clusters of approximately 64 percent and 36 percent. Given the adjectives listed, I labeled these clusters problem solving and adversarial. I labeled these clusters differently from Williams' original labels of competitive and cooperative for two reasons. First, I believe in the 20 years since the Williams study, the popular under-standing of "cooperative" has changed from the positive use by Williams to a more negative definition implying "wimpiness." Someone labeled "coop-erative" is more likely to be associated with soft-bargaining (roll-over-and-play-dead) than the positive adjectives actually used by Williams. Second, "problem-solving" and "adversarial" are labels more in current use in the negotiation literature. Table 2 is the list of the top 20 adjectives for each cluster. Problem-solving adjectives encompass several different elements of behavior. First, this negotiator is upstanding (ethical, trustworthy). Second, this negotiator is pleasant (personable, agreeable, sociable) and interested in the other side (fair-minded, communicative, perceptive, helpful). Third, this negotiator is flexible (accommodating, adaptable). Finally, this negotiator is prepared (experienced, rational, confident, realistic, astute, poised).

The adversarial adjectives offer a strong contrast. The adversarial negoti-ator is inflexible (stubborn, assertive, demanding, firm, tough, forceful) and

Table 2
Top 20 Adjectives Per Cluster

Problem-Solving Adjectives	*Adversarial Adjectives*
Ethical	Stubborn
Experienced	Headstrong
Personable	Arrogant
Rational	Assertive
Trustworthy	Irritating
Self-controlled	Argumentative
Confident	Egotistical
Agreeable	Confident
Realistic	Demanding
Accommodating	Quarrelsome
Sociable	Ambitious
Fair-minded	Experienced
Dignified	Firm
Communicative	Rough
Perceptive	Forceful
Adaptable	Suspicious
Astute about the law	Manipulative
Poised	Hostile
Careful	Masculine
Helpful	Evasive

Table 3
Number of Lawyers Per Group by Perceived Effectiveness (2000)

	Ineffective	*Average*	*Effective*
Problem-Solving	14	166	213
Adversarial	120	84	21

self-centered (headstrong, arrogant, egotistical). This negotiator likes to fight (irritating, argumentative, quarrelsome, hostile) and the method of fighting is questionable (suspicious, manipulative, evasive). Only two adjectives appear completely positive—confident and experienced—and these are the only two adjectives also cited for problem-solving negotiators. Thus we see very different approaches to negotiation.

The next step is a comparison of groups and effectiveness ratings. The survey asked each respondent to rate the other attorney's effectiveness as a negotiator compared to other attorneys with whom the respondent had negotiated. Lawyers were rated: ineffective, average, or effective (see Table 3).

Several items should stand out from these results. Respondents rated only 9 percent of their adversarial peers as effective. And only 9 percent of all effective lawyers were described as adversarial. Furthermore, 90 percent of lawyers seen as ineffective fell into the adversarial group. On the flip side of the analysis, 91 percent of lawyers seen as effective chose a problem-solving method of negotiation. More than 50 percent of problem-solving lawyers were perceived as effective and only 4 percent of these problem-solving lawyers were seen as ineffective.

Therefore, contrary to the popular (student) view that problem-solving behavior is risky, it is instead adversarial bargaining that is risky. A lawyer is much more likely to be perceived as effective when engaging in problem-solving behavior.

COMPARING THE STUDIES

After looking at the general results for the study, it is important to compare the behavioral traits of those negotiators perceived as effective. Have the characteristics of "effective" lawyers changed over the years? And since the two styles are so clearly different, what are the characteristics of effective problem-solvers and effective adversarials? Recognizing that the problem-solvers are generally perceived as more effective, nevertheless it is useful to understand what makes those attorneys in each style effective. . . .

Much of the list of adjectives remains the same, including the top five from the Williams study. The adjectives describe a negotiator who is both assertive (experienced, realistic, fair, astute, careful, wise) and empathetic (perceptive, communicative, accommodating, agreeable, adaptable). This mirrors what Professor Robert Mnookin and his co-authors have described as effective negotiation behavior. Furthermore, the effective problem-solver is also good (ethical, trustworthy) and offers enjoyable company (personable, sociable, poised). It should be no surprise this negotiator is seen as effective. . . .

The lack of change in the description of effective problem-solving offers some interesting insights. For example, despite the public perception of lawyers, it appears that close to two-thirds of lawyers continue to engage in non-adversarial modes of communication and that these same lawyers are perceived as highly effective compared to their peers. . . .

The competitive negotiator described by Williams was not nearly so unpleasant and negative. The top five adjectives describing the effectiveness competitive negotiator in the Williams study were: (1) convincing, (2) experienced, (3) perceptive, (4) rational, and (5) analytical. None of these adjectives have particularly negative connotations. In fact, perceptive even demonstrates some interest in the other side. Now the top five adjectives describing an effective adversarial negotiator are (1) egotistical, (2) demanding, (3) ambitious, (4) experienced, and (5) confident. Clearly things have changed for the worse when the most important description given to a lawyer is egotistical. The rest of the top 20 list is even more damning. Out of the entire list of adjectives, over half have negative connotations. Even their peers view these adversarial lawyers poorly as people despite their negotiation effectiveness.

Another interesting note is the lack of overlap between adjectives describing effective problem-solving behavior and adjectives describing effective adversarial behavior. In the Williams study, fully 14 of the top adjectives for the cooperative and competitive groups overlapped. This, of course, provided helpful advice to students that, regardless of which style they chose, these were the adjectives that were found to be effective. In this study only two adjectives overlap: experienced and confident. This lack of overlap suggests that the two negotiation styles have clearly diverged even more from one another in the last 24 years and that it has become more unlikely that a negotiator would move between these antithetical types of negotiation styles.

Finally, we can compare the effectiveness rating of Williams' two groups to this study. Compared to the Williams study, the percentage of problem-solving negotiators who were effective has dropped from 59 percent to 54 percent. The changes in the percentage of adversarial bargainers, however, is much more striking. In the Williams study, 25 percent of competitive negotiators were seen as effective, compared to 9 percent in this study. Alternatively, 33 percent of competitive negotiators were seen as ineffective in the Williams study while 53 percent were in this study.

In comparing general effectiveness of the lawyer population, the Williams study stated that 49 percent of the attorneys were considered effective, 38 percent were rated as average, and 12 percent were rated as ineffective. In contrast, only 38 percent of attorneys in this study were rated effective. As the vast majority of those attorneys who were considered ineffective were also adversarial negotiators (90 percent of ineffective lawyers were adversarial), we can hypothesize that the increase in ineffective lawyers (to 22 percent from 12 percent) comes from the increase in adversarial bargainers (to 36 percent from 27 percent).

LESSONS TO BE DRAWN

We can draw a few different lessons from this development in negotiation behavior. First, it looks as if the two predominant styles are growing further apart. While the problem-solving or cooperative group has remained much the same, the adversarial or competitive group is seen as growing more extreme and more negative. Second, as adversarial bargaining has become more extreme, it has also become far less effective. This is a key lesson for those hoping to become effective "Rambo" negotiators.

It appears that the declining public perception of lawyers is mirrored in how lawyers view each other. Fewer lawyers are viewed as effective by their peers and more lawyers are viewed negatively. Lawyers and popular culture are in accord in their perceptions and those perceptions are poor all around, at least as regards a significant minority of attorneys. . . .

What we can see in the preliminary results of this study is some interesting trends in terms of behavior and perceptions. A problem-solving approach to negotiation continues to be seen as effective by the legal community. The importance of developing this kind of reputation, particularly in smaller markets and within a practice area, has already been discussed. Furthermore, contrary to public perceptions, the majority of lawyers do engage in problem-solving behavior during a negotiation. On the other hand, the negative public perception of lawyers is matched by lawyers' own perceptions of the growing number and increased nastiness of adversarial lawyers. The good news is that the bar also increasingly views these adversarial lawyers as ineffective.

NOTES AND QUESTIONS

Professor Schneider provides more detail about her study and a more extensive analysis in her article *Shattering Negotiation Myths: Empirical Evidence on the Effectiveness of Negotiation Style* (2002).

1. Both the Schneider and Williams studies are based on perceptions of attorneys who chose to respond to survey questions about the effectiveness of their opponents. Is it problematic that attorneys who cooperated by responding to the surveys may tend to be more cooperative than those who did not respond and might rate as most effective those lawyers who manifest the same style as the person responding? In addition, as previously noted, we tend to perceive ourselves as being more reasonable and cooperative than an opponent thinks we are. (See Thomas and Pondy, 1977, pp. 1089-1102.) How might this affect the survey results?
2. Rather than impose their definitions of effectiveness, the researchers purposely left open the meaning of that key term so the respondents could themselves define negotiation effectiveness. What would be your definition of effectiveness for rating a negotiator?
3. Professor Williams, in his earlier study, found more commonality of qualities between effective competitive and effective cooperative negotiators than did Professor Schneider. He concluded that the most effective attorneys could switch between cooperative and competitive depending on their assessment of the circumstances. Many of the same effective qualities were utilized in either style. Professor Schneider's survey responses revealed fewer qualities in common between effective problem solvers and effective adversarial attorneys than did William's study. However, both effective problem solving and effective adversarial attorneys were reported as interested in the needs of their clients, acting consistently with those needs, maximizing settlement results, and representing their clients zealously

within the bounds of the law. They also shared being perceived as intelligent and taking satisfaction in being skillful. She concluded that effective negotiators, regardless of style, were assertive, smart, and prepared. Assuming you possess these qualities, can you envision situations where you would want to switch styles? What situations might trigger a switch for you?

4. What do you think accounts for the finding that adversarial negotiators are growing more extreme and negative and that, overall, fewer lawyers are viewed as effective by their peers?

5. Professor Schneider's respondents were over 30 percent women, compared to only 3 percent women in Professor Williams' original study. Do you believe this difference helps account for the significant increase in the percentage of negotiators that were perceived to be cooperative or problem-solving?

6. Because both studies surveyed perceived qualities and goals, is it possible that they underreported effective adversarial negotiators who were so successfully competitive they induced opponents to see them as cooperative when, in fact, they were not?

Negotiation style is subject to manipulation and may be deceiving. A negotiator who believes and lives by highly competitive values may be capable of employing a strategy of manifesting personal empathy, concern, friendliness, and warmth and appear to engage in problem-solving behavior. These characteristics can build trust for purposes of maximizing competitive gain. Have you known or seen anyone mask their purpose in this way, like a "wolf in sheep's clothing?" (Have you ever tried this?)

CHAPTER
5

The Negotiation Dance — Step by Step

A. NEGOTIATION STAGES AND APPROACHES

Negotiation, whether it be competitive, cooperative, or a mixed approach, can be viewed as occurring in stages. As stated in our introduction, although certain types of negotiations may follow a pattern, not every negotiation will follow the same lineal staging and each stage will not necessarily be completed in all negotiations. Lawyer negotiation occurs within the dynamics of settling a dispute or shaping a deal and is often not a tidy process. Breaking negotiation into stages is simply a way to help understand and analyze the process. Commentators list different stages, but all cover similar activities in varying configurations, in part depending on whether they have a more competitive or cooperative orientation. Listed below, for purposes of comparison, are the activities typically occurring in seven stages of competitive or cooperative negotiation. The activities within each stage can be mixed or alternated between competitive and cooperative, bearing in mind the warning that cooperation is commonly driven out by competitiveness. Note that in the early stage the activities and tasks within the competitive and cooperative approaches are more similar if not the same. Also, the labels "competitive" and "cooperative," like all one word descriptions, are too simple. Adversarial and problem-solving, positional and interest-based, or distributive and integrative may better capture the behavioral contrast. Although each pair of bipolar negotiation labels may signify nuanced differences, we will use them synonymously.

1. Negotiation Chart

© 2004 Jay Folberg

Stage	Competitive/adversarial approach	Cooperative/problem-solving approach
1. Preparation and Setting Goals	• Planning and research • Counseling client about negotiation • Assessing power of each party • Formulating positions and bottom lines • Setting goals	• Planning and research • Counseling client about negotiation • Assessing needs of each party • Formulating best alternative to negotiated agreement (BATNA) and reservation point • Setting goals

Stage	Competitive/adversarial approach	Cooperative/problem-solving approach
2. Initial Interaction and Offers	• Setting tone • Establishing credentials and authority • Making first demand or offer • Stating positions (often exaggerated)	• Setting tone • Establishing rapport and trust • Agreeing on agenda • Stating needs or interests
3. Exchanging and Refining Information	• Asking questions • Offering overstated or understated valuations • Informational bargaining • Formal discovery	• Asking questions • Sharing assessments or appraisals • Information exchange • Informal discovery (I'll show you mine, if you'll show me yours)
4. Bargaining	• Argument and persuasion • Making concessions • Forming coalitions and holding out	• Proposing principles • Applying principled criteria • Trading-off priorities and brainstorming
5. Moving Toward Closure	• Using power and threats • Creating time crisis • Evaluating offers	• Examining BATNAs • Agreeing on deadlines • Decision analysis
6. Reaching Impasse or Agreement	• Possible impasse • Compromising • Adding conditions	• Possible, but less likely, impasse • Reaching mutual decisions through joint problem solving • Creating alternative outcomes
7. Finalizing and Writing Agreements	• Preparing opposing drafts of agreement • Negotiating over drafts • Approval, ratification, and buy-in (as needed)	• Memorializing terms • Concurring on single text agreement • Approval, ratification, and buy-in (as needed)

NOTE AND QUESTIONS

Professor Williams in his article *Negotiation as a Healing Process,* part of which is excerpted in Chapter 2 on the Nature of Conflict and Disputes, refers to negotiation as a ritual. He goes on to say:

In law school we learn that no two cases are alike, and in our culture we assume that no two people are alike. We might surmise from this that no two negotiations are alike. Fortunately, this is only partially true. One of the defining characteristics of a ritual, including the ritual of negotiation, is that it provides an accepted structure for and sequencing of events. As a general proposition, then, we can say *the ritual of negotiation unfolds in predictable stages over time.* The predictability helps explain why so many lawyers lose patience with the process; it is highly repetitive, and thus not as stimulating as new adventures would be. This aspect of ritual is well captured by W. John Smith when he says, "*ritual* connotes . . . behavior that is formally organized into repeatable patterns. Perhaps the fundamental and pervasive function of these patterns is to facilitate orderly interactions between individuals." The point could not be more clear. Negotiation is a highly repetitive process. Without predictable patterns, the negotiators could not hope to achieve orderly interaction with each other. As Smith explains: "Ritual behavior facilitates interactions because it makes available information about the nature of events, and about the participants in them, that each participating individual must have to interact without generating chaos." The task now is to develop a working knowledge of the predictable stages of the negotiation process. (Williams, 1996, p. 33.)

1. Professor Williams' comment that the negotiation process is predictable seems to contradict other descriptions of the process. Can you offer any reconciliation of these views?
2. Have you found negotiations in which you were involved to be predictable in process? What types of negotiations are most likely to follow a ritualistic or predictable pattern? Might there be different negotiation rituals depending on what is being negotiated and the setting of the negotiation?
3. How might the stages of negotiation or the activities in each stage be combined or differ if the negotiations follow the creating and claiming approach suggested in the previous excerpt from Lax and Sebenius?
4. Can you think of how concurring on a single text agreement, listed on the chart as Stage 7 — "Finalization," might be taken up out of order and used in earlier stages to help formulate choices, bargain, and reach decisions? For a fascinating application of the one text procedure in reaching agreement between Israel and Egypt at Camp David, see Jimmy Carter's book *Keeping Faith: Memoirs of a President* (1982).

B.   GETTING READY TO NEGOTIATE

Like any demonstrated skill, watching a good negotiator or hearing about an effective negotiation can give the impression that it comes easily and that success is the result of intuitive ability, cleverness, and quick thinking. However, similar to trial practice, appellate advocacy, or any other disciplined endeavor, success in negotiation is in large part the result of planning, research, and preparation. The following excerpt provides a helpful blueprint for effective negotiation preparation that is likely to maximize results in most bargaining situations by refining your BATNA and reservation point, as well as by anticipating your opponent's bargaining zone.

1. *Preparation*

RUSSELL KOROBKIN, A POSITIVE THEORY OF LEGAL NEGOTIATION
88 Georgetown L.J. 1789, 1794-1800 (2000)

[The author posits two negotiation situations, one a potential transaction for the purchase by Esau of Jacob's catering business and the other a potential settlement of a suit by Goliath against David for battery.]

All observers of the negotiation process agree that painstaking preparation is critical to success at the bargaining table . . . "Internal" preparation refers to research that the negotiator does to set and adjust his own RP [reservation point or price]. "External" preparation refers to research that the negotiator does to estimate and manipulate the other party's RP.

1.   INTERNAL PREPARATION: ALTERNATIVES AND BATNAS

A negotiator cannot determine his RP without first understanding his substitutes for and the opportunity costs of reaching a negotiated agreement. This, of course, requires research. Esau cannot determine how much he is willing to pay for Jacob's business without investigating his other options. Most obviously, Esau will want to investigate what other catering companies are for sale in his area, their asking prices, and how they compare in quality and earning potential to Jacob's. He also might consider other types of businesses that are for sale. And he will likely consider the possibility of investing his money passively and working for someone else, rather than investing in a business.

Alternatives to reaching an agreement can be nearly limitless in transactional negotiations, and creativity in generating the list of alternatives is a critical skill to the negotiator. The panoply of alternatives is generally more circumscribed in dispute resolution negotiations. If Goliath fails to reach a settlement of some sort with David, he has the alternative of seeking an adjudicated outcome of the dispute and the alternative of dropping the suit. Most likely, he does not have the choice of suing someone else instead of David, in the same way that Esau has the choice of buying a business other than Jacob's.

After identifying the various alternatives to reaching a negotiated agreement, the negotiator needs to determine which alternative is most desirable. Fisher and his coauthors coined the appropriate term "BATNA"—"best alternative to a negotiated agreement"—to identify this choice. The identity and quality of a negotiator's BATNA is the primary input into his RP.

If the negotiator's BATNA and the subject of the negotiation are perfectly interchangeable, determining the reservation price is quite simple: The reservation price is merely the value of the BATNA. For example, if Esau's BATNA is buying another catering business for $190,000 that is identical to Jacob's in terms of quality, earnings potential, and all other factors that are important to Esau, then his RP is $190,000. If Jacob will sell for some amount less than that, Esau will be better off buying Jacob's company than he would be pursuing his best alternative. If Jacob demands more than $190,000, Esau is better off buying the alternative company and not reaching an agreement with Jacob.

In most circumstances, however, the subject of a negotiation and the negotiator's BATNA are not perfect substitutes. If Jacob's business is of higher quality, has a higher earnings potential, or is located closer to Esau's home, he would probably be willing to pay a premium for it over what he would pay for the alternative choice. For example, if the alternative business is selling for $190,000, Esau might determine he would be willing to pay up to a $10,000 premium over the alternative for Jacob's business and thus set his RP at $200,000. On the other hand, if Esau's BATNA is more desirable to him than Jacob's business, Esau will discount the value of his BATNA by the amount necessary to make the two alternatives equally desirable values for the money; perhaps he will set his RP at $180,000 in recognition that his BATNA is

$10,000 more desirable than Jacob's business, and Jacob's business would be equally desirable only at a $10,000 discount.

Assume Goliath determines that his BATNA is proceeding to trial. He will attempt to place a value on his BATNA by researching the facts of the case, the relevant legal precedent, and jury awards in similar cases, all as a means of estimating the expected value of litigating to a jury verdict. If Goliath's research leads to an estimate that he has a 75% chance of winning a jury verdict, and the likely verdict if he does prevail is $100,000, then using a simple expected value calculation ($100,000 × .75) would lead him to value his BATNA at $75,000.

For most plaintiffs, however, a settlement of a specified amount is preferable to a jury verdict with the same expected value, both because litigation entails additional costs and because most individuals are risk averse and therefore prefer a certain payment to a risky probability of payment with the same expected value. Goliath might determine, for example, that a $50,000 settlement would have the equivalent value to him of a jury verdict with an expected value of $75,000, because pursuing a jury verdict would entail greater tangible and intangible costs such as attorneys' fees, emotional strain, inconvenience, and the risk of losing the case altogether. If so, Goliath would set his RP at $50,000. On the other hand, it is possible that Goliath would find a $75,000 verdict more desirable than a $75,000 pretrial settlement. For example, perhaps Goliath would find additional value in having a jury of his peers publicly recognize the validity of his grievance against David. If Goliath believes that such psychic benefits of a jury verdict would make a verdict worth $10,000 more to him than a settlement of the same amount (after taking into account the added risks and costs of litigation), he would set his RP at $85,000.

The relationship between a party's BATNA and his RP can be generalized in the following way. A party's RP has two components: (1) the market value of his BATNA and (2) the difference to *him* between the value of his BATNA and the value of the subject of the negotiation. A seller sets his RP by calculating (1) and either *subtracting* (2) if the subject of the negotiation is more valuable than his BATNA (and therefore he is willing to accept less to reach an agreement) or *adding* (2) if the BATNA is more valuable than the subject of the negotiation (and therefore, he would demand more to reach an agreement and give up his BATNA). A buyer sets his RP by calculating (1) and either *adding* (2) if the subject of the negotiation is more valuable than his BATNA (and therefore he would pay a premium to reach an agreement) or *subtracting* (2) if his BATNA is more valuable than the subject of the negotiation (and therefore he would demand a discount to give up the BATNA).

Internal preparation serves two related purposes. By considering the value of obvious alternatives to reaching a negotiated agreement, the negotiator can accurately estimate his RP. This is of critical importance because without a precise and accurate estimation of his RP the negotiator cannot be sure to avoid the most basic negotiating mistake — agreeing to a deal when he would have been better off walking away from the table with no agreement.

By investigating an even wider range of alternatives to reaching agreement and by more thoroughly investigating the value of obvious alternatives, the negotiator can alter his RP in a way that will shift the bargaining zone to his advantage. Rather than just considering the asking price of other catering companies listed for sale in his town, Esau might contact catering companies that are not for sale to find out if their owners might consider selling under the right conditions. This could lead to the identification of a company similar to Jacob's that could be purchased for $175,000, which would have the effect of reducing Esau's RP to $175,000 and therefore shifting the bargaining zone lower. Goliath's attorney might conduct additional legal research, perhaps exploring other, more novel, theories of liability. If he determines that one or more alternative legal theories has a reasonable chance of success in court, Goliath might adjust upward his estimate of prevailing at trial—and therefore the value of his BATNA of trial—allowing him to adjust upward his RP.

2.   EXTERNAL PREPARATION: THE OPPONENT'S ALTERNATIVES AND BATNA

Internal preparation enables the negotiator to estimate his RP accurately and favorably. Of course, the bargaining zone is fixed by *both* parties' RPs. External preparation allows the negotiator to estimate his opponent's RP. If Esau is savvy, he will attempt to research Jacob's alternatives to a negotiated agreement as well as his own alternatives. For example, other caterers might know whether Jacob has had other offers for his business, how much the business might bring on the open market, or how anxious Jacob is to sell—all factors that will help Esau to accurately predict Jacob's RP and therefore pinpoint the low end of the bargaining zone. This information will also prepare Esau to attempt to persuade Jacob during the course of negotiations to lower his RP, a point discussed in detail below.

It is worth noting that in the litigation context both parties often have the same alternatives and the same BATNA. If plaintiff Goliath determines that his BATNA is going to trial, then defendant David's only alternative—and therefore his BATNA by default—is going to trial as well. In this circumstance, internal preparation and external preparation merge. For example, when Goliath's lawyer conducts legal research, he is attempting to simultaneously estimate the value of both parties' BATNAs. Of course, just because the parties have the same BATNA, they will not necessarily estimate the market value of it identically, much less arrive at identical RPs. Research suggests that an "egocentric bias" is likely to cause litigants to interpret material facts in a light favorable to their legal position, thus causing them to overestimate the expected value of an adjudicated outcome. Consequently, it is likely that, examining the same operative facts and legal precedent, plaintiff Goliath will place a higher value on the BATNA of trial than defendant David. This difference in perception often will be offset, however, by the fact that plaintiff Goliath is likely to set his RP, or the minimum settlement he will accept, below his perceived expected value of trial to account for the higher costs and higher risk associated with trial, while defendant David is likely to set his RP, or the maximum settlement he will agree to pay, above the expected value of trial for the same reasons. As long as the parties' preference for settlement rather than trial outweighs their egocentric biases, a bargaining zone will still exist, although it will be smaller than it would be if the parties agreed on the expected value of trial. Research also suggests that both parties are likely to be more risk averse when they are less confident in their prediction of the expected value of trial. In other words, the less confident the parties are in the value that they place on the BATNA of trial, the larger the bargaining zone between the RPs is likely to be.

Differential Value of Settlement vs. Trial Outweighs Egocentric Bias

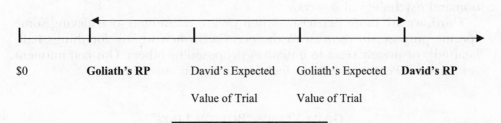

Bargaining Zone

| $0 | Goliath's RP | David's Expected Value of Trial | Goliath's Expected Value of Trial | David's RP |

2. Setting Goals

In addition to thinking through the least you can accept, or your reservation point, it is also helpful to formulate goals and set high expectations. Highs expectations lead to better outcomes, as discussed in this excerpt by Richard Shell.

G. RICHARD SHELL, BARGAINING FOR ADVANTAGE: NEGOTIATION STRATEGIES FOR REASONABLE PEOPLE

24-34, Viking (1999)

GOALS: YOU'LL NEVER HIT THE TARGET IF YOU DON'T AIM

In Lewis Carroll's Alice's Adventures in Wonderland, Alice finds herself at a cross-roads where a Cheshire Cat materializes. Alice asks the Cat, "Would you tell me please, which way I ought to go from here?" The Cat replies, "That depends a good deal on where you want to get to." "I don't much care where—"says Alice. "Then it doesn't matter which way you go," the Cat replies, cutting her off.

To become an effective negotiator, you must find out where you want to go—and why. That means committing yourself to specific, justifiable goals. It also means taking the time to transform your goals from simple targets into genuine—and appropriately high—expectations . . .

Our goals give us direction, but our expectations are what give weight and conviction to our statements at the bargaining table. We are most animated when we are striving to achieve what we feel we justly deserve.

Expectations in negotiation are a function of a number of factors, including our previous successes and failures in similar negotiations, prevailing market prices and standards, past practices, information about the other party's alternatives and frame of reference, our potential for a future relationship with the other side, and our basic personality . . .

The more time we spend preparing for a particular negotiation and the more information we gather that reinforces our belief that our goal is legitimate and achievable, the firmer the expectations grow . . .

Negotiations are no different from other areas of achievement. What you aim for often determines what you get. Why? The first reason is obvious: Your goals set the upper limit of what you will ask for. You mentally concede everything beyond your goal, so you seldom do better than that benchmark.

Second, research on goals reveals that they trigger powerful psychological "striving" mechanisms. Sports psychologists and educators alike confirm that setting specific goals motivates people, focusing and concentrating their attention and psychological powers.

Third, we are more persuasive when we are committed to achieving some specific purpose, in contrast to the occasions when we ask for things half-heartedly or merely react to initiatives proposed by others. Our commitment is infectious. People around us feel drawn toward our goals . . .

GOALS VERSUS "BOTTOM LINES"

Most negotiating books and experts emphasize the importance of having a "bottom line," "walkaway," or "reservation price" for negotiation. Indeed, the bottom line is a fundamental bargaining concept on which much of modern negotiation theory is built. It is the *minimum acceptable level* you require to say "yes" in a negotiation. By definition, if you cannot achieve your bottom line, you would rather seek another solution to your problem or wait until another opportunity comes your way. When two parties have bottom lines that permit an agreement at some point between them, theorists speak of there being a "positive bargaining zone." When the two bottom lines do not overlap, they speak of a "negative bargaining zone". . .

A well-framed goal is quite different from a bottom line. As I use the word, "goal" is your *highest legitimate expectation* of what you should achieve.

Researchers have discovered that humans have a limited capacity for maintaining focus in complex, stressful situations such as negotiations. Consequently, once a negotiation is under way, we gravitate toward the single focal point that has the psychological significance for us. Once most people set a firm bottom line in a negotiation, that becomes their dominant reference point as discussions proceed. They measure success or failure with reference to their bottom line, and it is very difficult to psychologically reorient themselves toward a more ambitious bargaining goal . . .

What is the practical effect of having your bottom line become your dominant reference point in a negotiation? Over a lifetime of negotiating, your results will tend to hover at a point just above this minimum acceptable level. For most reasonable people, the bottom line is the most natural focal point. Disappointment arises if we cannot get the other side to agree to meet our minimum requirements (usually established by our available alternatives or our needs away from the table), and satisfaction arises just above that level. Meanwhile, someone else who is more skilled at orienting himself toward ambitious goals will do much better. Not surprising, research shows that parties with higher (but still realistic) goals outperform those with more modest ones, all else being equal.

To avoid falling into the trap of letting our bottom line become our reference point, be aware of your absolute limits, but do not focus on them. Instead, work energetically on formulating your goals—and let your bottom line take care of itself . . .

Orient firmly toward your goal in the planning and initial stages of negotiation, then gradually re-orient toward a bottom line as that becomes necessary to close the deal. With experience, you should be able to keep both your goal and your bottom line in view at the same time without losing your goal focus.

Research suggests that the best negotiators have this ability. Meanwhile, during the actual negotiation, you should strive to determine what the other side's bottom line is as best you can — and not allow yourself to be too swayed by the other party's aspirations. If, in the end, you must make adjustments to your high expectations to close a deal, you can take care of that later.

If setting goals is so vital to effective preparation, how should you do it? Use the following simple steps:

1. Think carefully about what you really want — and remember that money is often a means, not an end.
2. Set an optimistic — but justifiable — target.
3. Be specific.
4. Get committed. Write down your goal and, if possible, discuss the goal with someone else.
5. Carry your goal with you into the negotiation.

SET AN OPTIMISTIC, JUSTIFIABLE TARGET

When you set goals, think boldly and optimistically about what you would like to see happen. Research has repeatedly shown that people who have higher expectations in negotiations perform better and get more than people who have modest or "I'll do my best" goals, provided they really believe in their targets . . .

Once you have thought about what an optimistic, challenging goal would look like, spend a few minutes permitting realism to dampen your expectations. *Optimistic goals are effective only if they are feasible; that is, only if you believe in them and they can be justified according to some standard or norm. . . .* [N]egotiation positions must usually be supported by some standard, benchmark, or precedent, or they lose their credibility . . .

COMMIT TO YOUR GOAL: WRITE IT DOWN AND TALK ABOUT IT

You goal is only as effective as your commitment to it. There are several simple things you can do that will increase your level of psychological attachment to your goal. First, as I suggested above, you should make sure it is justified and supported by solid arguments. You must believe in your goal to be committed to it.

Second, it helps if you spend just a few moments vividly imagining the way it would look or feel to achieve your goal. Visualization helps engage our mind more fully in the achievement process and also raises our level of self-confidence and commitment . . .

Third, psychologists and marketing professionals report that the act of writing a goal down engages our sense of commitment much more effectively than does the mere act of thinking about it. The act of writing makes a thought more "real" and objective, obligating us to follow up on it — at least in our own eyes.

QUESTIONS

1. Can you explain the difference between BATNA and RP?
2. Can you explain the difference between goals and expectations?

3. Does the advice to set high expectations only work if the other side does not follow the same advice? Will setting high expectations, particularly if done by both sides to a negotiation, likely lead to larger "negative bargaining zones," as explained by Shell, and thus more frequent impasse? Is there a way for two optimistic negotiators to deal with this and reach agreement?

4. If expectations in negotiation are, in part, a function of previous success and failures, as Shell suggests, how does a new lawyer set expectations? Would a client be well advised to seek out a lawyer who has had well-known recent success in trials and negotiations? Does this support the maxim that "success breeds success?" How might you leverage someone else's success with a similar case to your advantage in a negotiation?

For an in-depth scholarly discussion of the role of aspirations in settlement negotiations, see Korobkin (2002). Korobkin concludes that high aspirations may help negotiators reach better results, but at the cost of a greater risk of impasse and personal dissatisfaction in not fully achieving the expectations created by high aspirations.

3. Negotiation Preparation Checklist

The following checklist expands on the concepts developed in the previous excerpts and includes some points from the selections that follow. You may want to create a personal, comprehensive checklist to use in preparing for negotiations in both litigation and transactional settings. Using a checklist is a way to discipline your thinking so you may eventually not need the list. This checklist, although longer than one you might create, provides an inventory of helpful questions from which you can choose, depending on the case and the time available.

I. Information and Strategy

1. Information

- What information would be helpful to determine your opponent's needs, interests, and objectives?
- How can you best obtain this information?
- What questions will you ask to elicit such information?
- What information is the other side likely to seek?
- What are you willing to reveal and how do you plan to disclose it?
- What should you be careful to protect and how do you prevent disclosure?
- Are there any advantageous trades of information?

2. Alternatives

- What is your best alternative if no agreement is reached (BATNA)?
- Can you improve your BATNA or the way it is perceived?
- What is your worst alternative if no agreement is reached?
- What are your opponent's alternatives?
- How would you change how your opponent perceives alternatives?

- If an offered settlement is not accepted, are costs and attorney's fees triggered?

3.   Interests

- What are your client's interests and their relative importance?
- How will you go about advancing your client's interests?
- What are your opponent's interests?
- How does your opponent see your client's interests?
- How can you change your opponent's perspective about interests?

4.   Solutions and Positions

- What ideas do you have for a solution (based on what you know now)?
- Will you assert a position, and if so, what will it be?
- What is your opponent's current position or proposed solution?

5.   Principles and Standards

- What principles can you cite in support of your position?
- Which are most persuasive?
- What standards will they raise?
- What principles is your opponent likely to cite?

6.   Communication

- What theme or story will best present your case?
- What messages do you want to send?
- Are there any special issues to consider based on culture?
- Should you communicate prior to a negotiation meeting?

7.   Relationship

- Who should be at the table?
- Are there any relationship problems?
- Should you focus on some aspect of the relationship?
- Will there be a continuing relationship?
- Is there trust between you and your opponent?
- How can you build trust and credibility?

II.   Bargaining

1.   Process and Location

- Should you establish or follow an agenda?
- Are there applicable negotiation customs or rituals?
- What does your opponent expect?
- Can you negotiate over or influence the process?
- Where do you want to negotiate?

2. Expectations and Bottom Lines

- What goals and objectives do you hope to achieve?
- What is the best outcome you can realistically envision?
- What minimum terms are you willing to accept?
- What is your reservation or walkaway point?
- What are your opponent's goals and expectations?
- What value system will your opponent use in assessing his or her case?

3. Your Tactics

- What negotiation style or approach will you take?
- What factual or legal arguments do you have for each issue?
- Should you insist on any "preconditions"?
- What should be your first demand or offer?
- How will you support your demands and offers?
- How do you plan to move from your starting point to where you would like to end?

4. Your Opponent's Tactics

- What is the style of your opponent?
- What negotiation techniques do you expect your opponent to use? What pattern or moves do you anticipate? How will you counter those tactics?
- What factual or legal arguments does your opponent have for each issue? How should you challenge your opponent's claims? What counterarguments can you make?

5. Concessions

- What early concession will you make, if necessary?
- Do you have any easy "give-a-ways"?
- Are there any nonmonetary concessions you can give?
- Are there low-cost concessions of greater value to your opponent?
- What messages do you want to send with your concessions? What concessions do you anticipate receiving?

III. Settlement/Deal

- What terms will you insist upon?
- Do you have specific language to use in a final agreement?
- Are there terms and provisions you anticipate your opponent will insist upon?
- What legal requirements are there for an enforceable settlement or deal?
- Who must sign the agreement?
- Will there be time factors to consider?
- Is there any constituency or higher authority that must approve the agreement?
- Will you or your opponent insist that the settlement be confidential?
- Should the settlement/deal be publicized? If so, how?

NOTE: COMPUTER ASSISTED PREPARATION

The above preparation checklist, although lengthy, is incomplete. The questions to ask yourself in preparation will, in part, depend on your negotiation style and the subject of the negotiation. Many of the preparatory questions are interrelated, so the answer to one may influence others. Finally, after answering all of the questions, you must process the results to determine your strategy, BATNA, reservation point, first offer, and management of concession. Similarly, you will use the information generated from your preparation to anticipate what your opponent perceives, values, and will do during the negotiations.

Today's technology makes it possible to obtain and capture on a computer program the information necessary to prepare, generate options, value trade-offs, and anticipate the moves of a negotiation opponent. If computers can be used to research law, play chess (calculating the probable moves of an opponent and choosing the best move from all available options), engage in sophisticated market research, anticipate terrorist attacks, and plot wars, they should be of help in preparing for negotiations.

You are, no doubt, familiar with the capacity of the World Wide Web to provide information about your opponent, and for the people with whom you negotiate to learn about you. Knowing the background and experience of the attorneys and parties with whom you will negotiate can help you anticipate how they will negotiate, the value they might place on items of potential trade, their interests, and clues about their alternatives to a negotiated agreement. Knowing more about an opponent can also aid in establishing trust and rapport.

Another value of the Web is to help you calculate your BATNAs. Just as you may use the Web to comparative shop, you can find alternative ways to meet your interests, once identified, and the value of similar goods and services that might be the subject of your negotiation. You can better research jury awards for similar injuries and court decisions on questions that may have to be decided if your negotiation fails. Diligent computer research may reveal the outcome of similar negotiations from news and organizational sources.

What both sides to a negotiation previously had to guess at, and as a result probably perceived differently, can now be determined by a computer search. For example, the cost of replacing equipment or an object of art can quickly be determined by a search in a truly worldwide marketplace. Thus, the creation of objective criteria to propose for resolution of an anticipated issue can be easily researched and prepared in advance.

Commercially available software programs can now help you analyze the negotiation style that is most comfortable for you and determine the approach likely to be used by your negotiating counterpart, provided some questions can be answered about them. The programs can also assist you in designing concessions and assigning relative values to them. They collect input that is used to suggest the best opening offer and counteroffers. These programs can also formulate questions for you to ask during a negotiation and predict the actions of an opposing negotiator, along with recommended strategies for you to use. Finally, they can help you value and decide on outcomes once proposals emerge.

Although these programs are sophisticated with a type of built-in negotiation intelligence, like any productivity software, the quality of the result ultimately depends on the input you provide. If nothing else, a good negotiation software program can provide a guide for what you should do to be well prepared to negotiate and what the alternative approaches may be. They can also catalogue tactics you might not have considered and organize ideas and data helpful to you before commencing a negotiation.

At the time of this writing the most comprehensive and user-friendly negotiation software is Win Squared, Version 3, available at *http://www.winxwin.com*. In response to the user's answers to a wide range of questions, Win Squared offers graded techniques to aid in the negotiation and provides specific illustrations of their use. Negotiator Pro, Version 5, available at *http://www .negotiatorpro.com*, assesses negotiator styles based on responses to questions about each negotiator and then offers strategies of how to negotiate with the profiled personality type. A unique feature includes an international negotiation analysis where parties can learn about cultural differences. The Negotiator Assistant, *http://www.icasit.org/negotiator/*, focuses upon international negotiations between two parties. Based upon the answers to questions by category, the program computes a score and charts the parties' flexibility for successful negotiation. In the event that the flexibility score is low, the user may consult an impasse window specific to that category where tactics are offered to increase flexibility between the negotiating parties.

C. INITIAL INTERACTION AND OFFERS

1. *Trust and Rapport*

How we feel about those with whom we negotiate is a critical element to whether an agreement will be reached. Just as you may feel you can quickly "read" the character and trustworthiness of those you face, so others are forming a quick impression of you. The maxims that "you only get one chance to make a first impression" and "first impressions matter" need to be considered as you prepare for and commence a negotiation.

The impression you make on an opponent will probably be formed, in part, before you meet. If the negotiation is of significance you and your opponent will find out what you can about one another. Your reputation will precede you into the negotiation. In addition to informal inquiries among those with whom you have previously negotiated or had other professional contact, the Internet opens your public history, both accomplishments and mistakes, for all to see. So your preparation for a negotiation, in terms of the impression you make and whether you can be trusted, involves your entire professional life. Although a misimpression can be corrected, it is an uphill struggle because of what we know about self-fulfilling prophecies and the selective way we view evidence to support earlier impressions.

As the reading below informs us, trust is more likely to develop between negotiators if they see one another as similar. Similarity of backgrounds, experience, values, tastes, or group identity helps develop rapport and smoothes the way to trust. There is a delicate balance when opening a negotiation session between engaging in "small talk" that might establish a shared interest, affiliation, or acquaintance for the purpose of creating rapport, and getting to the point regarding the issues in dispute. However, providing the opportunity to establish a personal connection and the basis for trust is usually time well spent.

LEWICKI, SAUNDERS, BARRY, AND MINTON, ESSENTIALS OF NEGOTIATION, 3RD EDITION

116-117, McGraw-Hill/Irwin (2004)

TRUST

Although there is no guarantee that trust will lead to collaboration, there is plenty of evidence to suggest that mistrust inhibits collaboration. People who are interdependent but do not trust each other will act tentatively or defensively. Defensiveness usually means that they will not accept information at face value but instead will look for hidden, deceptive meanings. When people are defensive, they withdraw and withhold information. Defensive people also attack their opponent's statements and position, seeking to defeat their position rather than to work together. Either of these responses is likely to make the negotiator hesitant, cautious, and distrustful of the other, undermining the negotiation process.

Generating trust is a complex, uncertain process; it depends in part on how the parties behave and in part on the parties' personal characteristics. When people trust each other, they are more likely to share information, communicate accurately their needs, positions, and the facts of the situation. In contrast, when people do not trust each other, they are more likely to engage in positional bargaining, use threats, and commit themselves to tough positions. As with defensiveness, mistrust is likely to be reciprocated and to lead to unproductive negotiations. To develop trust effectively, each negotiator must believe that both she and the other party choose to behave in a cooperative manner; moreover, each must believe that this behavior is a signal of the other's honesty, openness, and a similar mutual commitment to a joint solution.

A number of key factors contribute to the development of trust between negotiators. First, people are more likely to trust someone they perceive as similar to them or as holding a positive attitude toward them. Second, people often trust those who depend on them: Being in a position to help or hurt someone (who can do the same in return) fosters mutual trust. Third, people are more likely to trust those who initiate cooperative, trusting behavior. Acting in a cooperative, trusting manner serves as an invitation to others, especially if the invitation is repeated despite initially contentious behavior from the opponent. Fourth, there is some evidence that giving a gift to the other negotiator may lead to increased trust. Finally, people are more likely to trust those who make concessions. The more other people's behavior communicates that they are holding firm in their fundamental commitment to their own needs at the same time as they are working toward a joint solution, the more negotiators are likely to find their conduct trustworthy, in the spirit of the best joint agreement.

Given that trust has to be built during the negotiation, tone-setting, and other opening moves are crucial. The more cooperative, open, and nonthreatening the opening statements and actions of a party are, the more trust and cooperation are engendered in the other party. Once a cooperative position is established, it is more likely to persist. If cooperative behavior can be established at the very beginning, there is a tendency for parties to lock in to this cycle and make it continue. Finally, opening moves not only help set the tone for the negotiation but also begin the momentum. The longer the cycle of trust and cooperation continues, the easier it would be to reestablish it should the cycle break down.

---

2. First Offers and Counteroffers

After negotiation starts, the negotiator is faced with deciding whether to make the first offer or inviting an offer from the other side. If choosing to make the first offer, should it be extreme, modestly favorable, exactly what you expect, or equitably calculated to be fair to all and maximize collective value? If the first offer is made by the other side, should you flinch, as recommended by Dawson, counteroffer immediately, or process the offer and come back with an exaggerated counteroffer or one closer to your reservation point? How does formulating the initial offer relate to what we have learned about perceptions, ripeness, anchoring, preparation, the role of expectations, and trust?

The negotiation guidebooks are full of advice on making offers, much of it contradictory. There appears to be consensus that in distributive negotiations, more extreme or aggressive offers result in more favorable outcomes. (However, an exaggerated offer can come before or after learning the other side's opening position.) This consensus appears to focus on distributive negotiation and doesn't provide guidance for encouraging integrative negotiation. The first selection below, which is based on extensive research of lawyer negotiators, weighs the advantages and disadvantages of three different opening strategies. The second excerpt by Leigh Thompson offers specific advice on how to begin with a first offer or an immediate counteroffer to a proposed offer.

GERALD R. WILLIAMS, LEGAL NEGOTIATION AND SETTLEMENT
73-77, West Publishing (1983)

[Professor Williams conducted pioneering empirical research, as described in Chapter 4 of this book, on styles of lawyer negotiation, which he designated competitive and cooperative. He then determined which strategies within each style were considered by peers and by systematic observation to be effective, average, and ineffective. This reading makes reference to and is based on his research.]

POSITIONING

The lawyers come forward with an opening position. At this early stage in the dispute, that is not as simple as it appears. The facts are not all in, the legal questions are not fully researched, and unforeseen developments loom on the horizon. In the face of these uncertainties, the negotiators must leave themselves a certain amount of latitude, yet they must come up with something. What they come up with is an opening position . . .

[T]here are essentially three strategies that can be used in framing an opening position. . . . [T]he negotiator may adopt the maximalist strategy of asking for more than he expects to obtain, he may adopt the equitable strategy of taking a position that is fair to both sides, or he may adopt the integrative strategy of searching for alternative solutions in the hope of finding the most attractive combination for all concerned. Each strategy has its own strengths and weaknesses.

MAXIMALIST POSITIONING

The arguments for maximalist positioning begin with the assumption that the opening position is a bargaining position, and that no matter how long the bargainer may deny it, he expects to come down from it to find agreement. Maximalist positioning has several advantages. It effectively hides the bargainer's real or minimum expectations, it eliminates the danger of committing to an overly modest evaluation of the case, it provides a cover for him while he seeks to learn his opponent's real position, and it will very likely lead the opponent to reduce his later expectations in the case. It also provides the negotiator with something to give up, with concessions he can make, in order to come to terms with the opponent. This last factor may be especially important when the opponent also opened high, and the negotiator is required to trade concessions in order to arrive at mutually agreeable terms . . . [T]he negotiator who makes high opening demands, has a high level of expectations, makes relatively small and infrequent concessions, and is perceptive and unyielding will fare better in the long run than his opponent.

The potential benefits of the maximalist position need to be weighed against its potential demerits, which are those of tough strategies generally. . . . The most important weakness is the increased risk of breakdown and throwback to trial. The competent opponent will prefer the extra burden of trial to the unreasonable demands and supporting tactics of the maximalist negotiator unless the opponent himself is equipped with an effective strategy for dealing with them.

We observe in the data that competitive attorneys at all levels of effectiveness are rated as making high opening demands. Yet, by definition, effective/competitives use the strategy effectively, and ineffective/competitives do not. We are forced to conclude that in the legal context the maximalist strategy does not consistently bring high returns for those who use it; only for those who use it effectively. For ineffective/competitive attorneys, at least, it is unsuccessful.

How high a demand can be without losing its effectiveness undoubtedly depends on several considerations. One is the nature of the remedy being sought. By their nature, contract damages are less inflatable than personal injury damages, for example, and the negotiator who multiplies his contract damages as he does his personal injury claims will undermine his own credibility. Another consideration is local custom. Specialized groups within the bar develop norms and customs that provide measures against which the reasonableness or extremism of a demand can be evaluated. So we see that not all high demands are the same. Some demands lack credibility on their face by their inappropriateness and lack of congruity in the context in which they are made. But the level of demands is not the sole factor. The data suggest that effective/competitive negotiators are able to establish the credibility and plausibility of high demands by convincing legal argumentation. Ineffective/competitives lack the skills to do so and in the absence of convincing support, their high demands suffer further losses of credibility.

Finally, it should be noted that how effective a high demand is will depend upon the opponent against whom the high demands are made. Experimental findings have demonstrated two possible effects. In cases where the opponent is unsure of the actual value of the case, high opening demands by the maximizing negotiator have the desired effect. The opponent, unsure of the value of the case, uses the maximizer's high opening demands as a standard against which to set his own goals in the case. However, when the opponent had evaluated the case and arrived at a judgment of its value, the opponent interpreted the maximizer's high opening demands as evidence of unreasonableness. In this latter case, we expect that the maximizer's credibility is diminished and the likelihood of breakdown and trial increased.

EQUITABLE POSITIONING

The equitable position is one calculated to be fair to both sides. Its most notable proponent is Bartos (1978). Bartos challenges the assumption of maximalist theorists that both sides to a negotiation are trying to maximize their own payoffs or benefits. He argues that a competing value is also operative; that negotiators feel a cooperative desire to arrive at a fair solution for both. In support of this argument, he cites not only humanistic literature defending equality as an essential ingredient of justice, but also anthropological and sociological studies confirming the widespread existence and operation in society of an egalitarian norm of reciprocity. Bartos has conducted numerous theoretical and experimental studies of negotiation which lead him to believe that the human desire to deal fairly with others, the equitable position, is preferable to toughness as a strategy. This is seen as the most economical and efficient method of conflict resolution. It minimizes the risk of deadlock and avoids the costs of delay occasioned by extreme bargaining positions. Bartos recommends that negotiators be scrupulously fair and that they avoid the temptation to take advantage of the opponent. He cautions that the equitable positioning requires trust, which he views as a positive and necessary attitude, but not naivete. Trust must be tempered with realism. It is out of trust that a negotiator makes concessions, but if the trust is not rewarded or returned in fair fashion, further concessions should be withheld until the opponent reciprocates.

As conceived by Bartos, then, equitable negotiators do not as a matter of practice open the negotiations with a statement specifying their final view of the ultimate fair solution. Rather, they open with a position that shows they are serious about finding agreement, and they trustingly work toward a mid-point between their reasonable opening position and the reasonable opening position of their opponent. Until both sides come forward with reasonable opening positions, Bartos considers the case unready for serious negotiation. It is not ripe.

Referring back now to the data on cooperative and competitive negotiators, we intuitively suspect that Bartos' equitable negotiator is a cooperative type, or that cooperative types embody the equitable position. This observation is borne out by the extremely high ratings received by cooperative attorneys on characteristics such as trustworthy, ethical, honest, and fair. Just as with our analysis of maximalist positioning by competitive attorneys, it must be pointed out that the use of equitable positioning by cooperative attorneys does not always bring satisfactory results. It is obviously satisfactory as used by effective/cooperatives, but it is just as obviously deficient when used by ineffective/cooperatives.

We must conclude that the positioning strategy, whether maximalist or equitable, does not guarantee success. Whichever one is used must be used with care and acumen or it will not be effective.

INTEGRATIVE POSITIONING

Integrative Positioning is more than an opening position. It describes an attitude or approach that carries through the other stages of the negotiation, and is an alternative to bargaining by positioning. The most effective advocates of this method for our purposes are Roger Fisher and William Ury, *Getting to Yes*. Among businesspeople, the method is seen as the art of problem solving.

The integrative negotiator views the case as presenting a number of alternative solutions, and he believes that chances for reaching agreement are enhanced by discovering the various alternatives, evaluating them in light of the interests of the parties, and seeking to arrange the alternatives in a package that yields maximum benefit to both parties. . . .

INALTERABLE COMMITMENT TO AN OPENING POSITION

The next element . . . relating to positioning is that each side seeks to establish the illusion that he is inalterably committed to his opening position. The purposes served by this tactic are several. It lends credibility to the demand, and particularly in the case of high opening demands, it gives time for the demand to have its effect on the hopes or expectations of the other side. It gives each negotiator time to make further evaluations of the value of the case and to gain information about what the other side is willing to accept. When the negotiators are ready to begin more serious negotiation, they are better informed and better able to bargain than when the extreme demands were established. As with the other elements of the negotiation process, however, this strategy can easily be overdone. It must be used with judgment, perceptiveness, and flexibility.

LEIGH THOMPSON, THE MIND AND HEART OF THE NEGOTIATOR, 2ND EDITION

40-41, Prentice Hall (2001)

MAKE THE FIRST OFFER

Folklore dictates that negotiators should let the opponent make the first offer. In fact, negotiators are at a pie-slicing advantage if they do make the first offer. In short, first offers act as an anchor point. First offers correlate at least .85 with final outcomes, suggesting they are very important! However, there are a number of factors to think about when making an opening offer. First and foremost, your opening offer should not give away any part of the bargaining zone; otherwise, you will be at a pie-slicing disadvantage. Second, many people worry that they will "insult" the other party if they open too high (if they are selling) or too low (if they are buying). However, the fear of insulting the other party and souring the negotiations is more apparent than real.

[Negotiators] tell us that when they are faced with an extreme opening offer from the other party, they are not insulted; instead, they prepare to make concessions.

There are distinct advantages associated with making the first offer in a negotiation. The first offer that falls within the bargaining zone can serve as a powerful focal point in negotiation . . . Making the first offer protects negotiators from falling prey to a similar anchoring effect when they hear the opponent's offer. Ideally, a negotiator's first offer acts as an anchor for the opponent's counteroffer.

One more thing about making the first offer: If you have made an offer to an opponent, then you should expect to receive some sort of counteroffer or response. Once you put an offer on the table, be patient. It is time for your opponent to respond. In certain situations, patience and silence can be important negotiation tools. Do not interpret silence on the other person's part to be a rejection of your offer. Many negotiators, especially those with a more urgent sense of time, tend to make premature concessions before their opponent has even had a chance to respond to their initial offer. Always wait to hear a response before making a further concession.

COUNTEROFFER IMMEDIATELY

If your opponent has made you an offer, then the ball is in your court. It is wise to make a counteroffer in a timely fashion. This does two things. First, it diminishes the prominence of the opponent's initial offer as an anchor point [in] the negotiation. Second, it signals a willingness to negotiate. It also helps to think about the opponent's BATNA when she makes you an offer. Above all, do not adjust your BATNA based upon your opponent's offer, and do not adjust your target. It is extremely important not to be "anchored" by the opponent's offer. The final outcome of a negotiation is often the midpoint between the first two offers on the table that are within the bargaining zone. Thus, if your first offer is within the bargaining zone, you have already given up precious bargaining ground. An effective counteroffer moves the focus away from the other party's offer as a reference point.

AVOID STATING RANGES

As noted in Chapter 2, we do not advise stating ranges. For example, employers often ask prospective employees to state a range in salary negotiations. Do not fall victim to this bargaining ploy. By stating a range, you are giving up precious bargaining ground. Your opponent will consider the lower end of the range as your target and negotiate down from there. A far better strategy is to respond to your opponent's request for a range by giving him or her several offers that would all be equally satisfying to you . . .

The advice to set high expectations and to make the first offer based on your aspirations can backfire. First, offers or demands should not be so extreme that your opponent walks out of the room. Even food and gifts may not prevent an impasse. Consider the following scene from a popular book and movie that chronicles the negotiation and trial of the claims of eight families in Woburn, Massachusetts, who sued the corporate owners of a tannery and chemical plants for cancer-related illnesses and deaths of their children.

JONATHAN HARR, A CIVIL ACTION
277-279, Vintage Books (1996)

After a few minutes, the lawyers took their assigned seats at the table. Schlichtmann began talking about how he and his partners took only a few select cases and worked to the exclusion of all else on those. (This was Schlichtmann's way of saying there was no stopping them.) He said he wanted a settlement that would provide for the economic security of the families, and for their medical bills in the future. The families, he continued, weren't in this case just for money. They wanted an acknowledgment of the companies' wrongdoing, Schlichtmann said, a full disclosure of all the dumping activities.

"Are you suggesting there hasn't been a full disclosure?" Facher asked. "No," said Schlichtmann, who was suggesting exactly that, but now made an effort to avoid confrontation. "But as part of a settlement, we want a disclosure that the judge will bless." Another condition of settlement, he added, was an agreement that the companies clean their land of the toxic wastes, and pay the costs for cleaning the aquifer.

None of the defense lawyers had touched any of the food or drink. As Schlichtmann spoke, he saw Facher reach for a bowl of mints on the table and slowly unwrap the foil from one. Facher popped the mint into his mouth and sucked on it, watching Schlichtmann watch him.

Schlichtmann talked for fifteen minutes. Then Gordon laid out the financial terms of the settlement: an annual payment of $1.5 million to each of the eight families for the next thirty years; $25 million to establish a research foundation that would investigate the links between hazardous wastes and illness; and another $25 million in cash.

Cheeseman and his partners took notes on legal pads as Gordon spoke. Facher examined the pen provided courtesy of the Four Seasons, but he did not write anything on his pad. Facher studied the gilt inscription on the pen. It looked like a good-quality pen. These figures, he thought, were preposterous. They meant that Schlichtmann did not want to settle the case, or else he was crazy. Maybe Schlichtmann simply wanted to go to trial. This opulent setting, and Schlichtmann sitting at the table flanked by his disciples like a Last Supper scene, annoyed Facher. Where was Schlichtmann getting the money for all this?

When Gordon finished, silence descended.

Finally Facher stopped studying the pen. He looked up, and said, "If I wasn't being polite, I'd tell you what you could do with this demand."

Cheeseman had added up Gordon's figures. By Cheeseman's calculations, Schlichtmann was asking a total of four hundred ten million over thirty years. "How much is that at present value?" Cheeseman asked Gordon.

Gordon replied that he would rather not say. "Your own structured-settlement people can tell you that."

Facher took a croissant from the plate in front of him, wrapped it in a napkin, and put it into his pocket. That and the mint he had consumed were the only items the defense lawyers had taken from the sumptuous banquet that Gordon had ordered.

Cheeseman and his partners asked a few more perfunctory questions about the terms of disclosure, which Schlichtmann answered. Facher had gone back to studying the pen. "Can I have this?" he said abruptly, looking at Schlichtmann.

Schlichtmann, appearing surprised, nodded. Facher put the pen into his breast pocket. "Nice pen," he said. "Thank you."

Then Facher got up, put on his coat, and walked out the door. Frederico, who had not uttered a word, followed him.

Cheeseman and his partners stood, too, and in a moment, they followed Facher.

Schlichtmann and his colleagues sat alone on their side of the table. Gordon looked at his watch. The meeting had lasted exactly thirty-seven minutes, he announced. "I guess we're going to trial," Gordon added.

Schlichtmann was surprised, but only for a moment. He looked at his colleagues and shrugged. "We're going to get a jury in two weeks," he said. "The pressure's on them."

Conway got up and paced the room and smoked a cigarette. He didn't feel like talking. There was nothing to discuss. They'd gotten nothing out of this so-called settlement conference, not even information from the other side. He put on his coat and, along with Crowley, walked up Tremont Street back to the office.

QUESTIONS

1. How did Schlichtmann go wrong? What advice offered by Shell about realism and justification for high demands and by Williams for an effective maximalist strategy might have been helpful for Schlichtmann in making his demand?
2. Might local custom and the experience of opposing counsel, as well as the evaluation done by the other side, all discussed by Williams, have been contributing factors to the defense walkout in the above scenes? What would you have done differently than Schlictmann in this situation?

D.   EXCHANGING AND REFINING INFORMATION

The task of finding out all that you can about the other side, their needs, their case, their BATNA, and other factors affecting their reservation point is a significant part of the preparation stage and pervades the entire negotiation process. Similarly, disclosing and managing information in your control that may shape their perceptions or that they want to know is also a continual part of the process. Exchanging and refining information are listed as a separate step only to emphasize their importance in the process and to recognize that there are points in the negotiation where information is expected to be exchanged formally or informally. This "stage" could just as well have been listed before initial interactions and offers. Exchanging and refining information is a dynamic that continually shapes expectations and effects negotiation and decision making. Information may be bargained before negotiating over outcomes.

A hallmark of effective negotiators, whether competitive or cooperative, is their ability to listen, their propensity to ask questions, and their desire to continually gather information. (As will be presented later, information is power in negotiations.)

1. Listening and Questioning

Lawyers are often characterized as good talkers, who love to argue. In court, being a "silver-tongued" attorney may be valued. In negotiations, as in conversations, being a good listener and knowing how to obtain information through the use of questions is more important than talking. This is true in interacting with clients when preparing to negotiate for them, as well as in negotiating. The old wisdom that "we were born with one tongue and two ears so that we can hear from others twice as much as we speak," is good advice for negotiators.

If you can learn what is in the brain and heart of an opponent, you can make a personal connection, satisfy their needs, and get what you want at the lowest possible cost. If you actively allow another to openly express themselves, they usually will tell you what you want to know. The more you talk, the less they can say, and the less you can listen and learn. You seldom learn anything new by speaking. The key lesson here is easy, talk less and listen more. When you do speak in a negotiation, do so in a way that elicits more information, directly or indirectly, or that helps shape the negotiation. Sometimes giving information is a way to get information, but know when and how to listen.

The most effective listening is active listening. Active listening is the opposite of deadpan, silent, passive listening. During active listening you focus your energy on what the speaker is communicating and provide responses that encourage the speaker to open up and say more. In active listening you hear not only the content, but also identify the emotion or sentiment expressed. You then briefly restate in your own words the feeling and some of the content you heard communicated so the speaker can confirm, clarify, or amplify. Most importantly, your response lets the speaker know you heard what they said and that you care about how they feel.

The following selection provides a guide for active listening and purposeful questioning when you are negotiating.

LEE E. MILLER AND JESSICA MILLER, A WOMAN'S GUIDE TO SUCCESSFUL NEGOTIATING

66-73, McGraw-Hill (2002)

ACTIVE LISTENING

There are numerous ways to encourage others to talk so you can find out what their real concerns are. These techniques are referred to as active listening and include the following:

REFLECT BACK

Restate what the other person has said in your own words. This ensures that you correctly understand what has been said, and it also shows the other person that you are trying to see things from their perspective. For example, if someone says, "I can't understand how you could come up with such an unworkable solution to our problem," you might paraphrase that by stating, "I guess we don't understand what your real needs are here."

CLARIFY

When something is not clear or you want a better understanding of what has been said, you can ask for clarification. For example, in response to the previous statement, you might say, "I don't understand. What do you mean by unworkable?" Or you could ask them to explain: "Why do you think it's unworkable?" In addition to giving you additional information, clarifying signals that you care about their concerns.

ENCOURAGE

Nod and smile, lean forward when others are talking, look them in the eye, and occasionally interject phrases such as "I see," "Go on," or "Really." This will encourage those who are speaking to expand upon what they are saying. The more they speak, the more information you will get. Again, by engaging in this behavior, you signal your willingness to listen and your interest in what is being said.

ACKNOWLEDGE EFFORT

Provide positive reinforcement when the speaker tries to work with you or says something you agree with. For example, you might respond by saying "I appreciate your efforts," or "That's a good point." This will encourage further efforts to find common ground with you.

RECOGNIZE FEELINGS

It often helps to address the feelings that people may be experiencing but not openly sharing. In response to the statement that "The proposal is unworkable," you could reply, "I see that you're frustrated with how the discussions are proceeding." Recognizing others' feelings often defuses anger and allows them to open up. This is frequently necessary before you can move on to problem solving.

SUMMARIZE

When you believe that you understand the other person's point of view, summarize your understanding of what has been said and ask whether your understanding is correct. Do the same when you reach an agreement on a particular issue. Summarizing helps to prevent misunderstandings, and you should use it continually throughout the course of negotiations. When done on an ongoing basis, it reinforces that the parties are making progress and encourages continued efforts toward reaching an agreement.

It doesn't do much good to listen, however, if you don't act on what you hear. Don't be afraid to stray from what you had planned to say if you get signals the other side is not receptive to the approach you are taking. Moreover, nothing works better than using what the other side says. You can achieve many of your objectives just by listening carefully to what is being said and agreeing to those points that are helpful. That is why it is always best to listen first.

PURPOSEFUL QUESTIONING

Good negotiators ask different types of questions for different reasons, from open-ended, information-gathering questions to focused questions intended to lead someone to a specific conclusion. The two primary reasons for asking questions during negotiations are to get information or to support your argument. How you ask a question will depend on what you are trying to achieve.

ASK OPEN-ENDED QUESTIONS

You should ask open-ended questions if your goal is to obtain information or to find out what the other person is thinking. Open-ended questions can't be answered with a yes or a no. They usually begin with "who," "what," "where," "when," "why," or "how," which allow for wide latitude as to responses. Their unstructured nature often enables you to find out what the real issues are and how you might satisfactorily resolve them. Open-ended questions such as "Tell me how you reached that conclusion" can also give you an insight into how someone else thinks.

Often, asking the right question at the right time can give you the information you need to completely turn around a negotiation. I recall one such situation. . . . I was practicing law, representing an executive who was taking a job with a new company and being asked to relocate from California to Connecticut. We had worked out the major issues — salary, bonus, stock options — to his satisfaction. The new company had a generous relocation policy, but it provided for only a 30-day temporary living allowance. My client's daughter was a senior in high school and he was not going to move his family until after she graduated. So he asked the company to pay his temporary living expenses for one year. The company representative insisted that they could not deviate from their relocation policy. My client was equally adamant and felt that if the company was taking such a bureaucratic approach to his request, it was probably not a place where he would want to work. Just when I thought the deal was about to fall through, I asked a question that allowed us to successfully conclude the negotiation. What was this brilliantly insightful question? It was simply "Why?" More specifically, I told the vice president of human resources that I couldn't understand why we were arguing about this issue. He explained that the relocation policy was written that way because the company had been burned by a senior executive who, after being paid temporary living expenses for well over a year, could not get his wife to move and rejoined his previous company. Having been embarrassed once, the vice president was not about to ask for another exception to the policy. Understanding his reasons for refusing our seemingly reasonable request enabled us to readily resolve the problem. We agreed that if my client did not move his family to Connecticut, he would repay the company for his temporary living expenses. This allowed the vice president to ask for and receive a modification to the relocation policy without the fear of looking foolish if things didn't work out. . . .

ADOPT THE COLUMBO TECHNIQUE

Acting as if you don't understand something is also a way of getting information. If you ask lots of questions and seem to need assistance, others feel a natural inclination to help. This is sometimes referred to as the Columbo technique, after the TV detective played by Peter Falk, who, by acting as if he did not understand anything, was always able to get the criminal to give him the information needed to crack the case. When you appear to be seeking help, others' defenses will drop, and they may unintentionally provide you with information that helps you make your case. For example, let's say you're looking to buy an antique table that's been advertised for $10,000. You meet with the owner and offer her $5,000. When she declines your offer, you say, "Even though I probably can't afford it, just so I know for the future, what would be a good price for a table like that?" You are now in a different position—no longer a serious buyer, but a neophyte collector seeking to tap her expertise. Although she might reply "$10,000," you are equally likely to get a more helpful response along the lines of, "You might get one for $8,500 if you're lucky." Whereupon you can ask, "If I can get that much cash together, would you consider selling it to me?" Be careful how and when you use this technique, though. Never overuse it. Limit this approach to people who would be expected to be more knowledgeable than you. Otherwise, it will undermine your credibility because people will begin to see what you are doing as disingenuous.

One purpose of asking open-ended questions is to keep the other side talking. The more someone talks, the more likely they are to provide valuable information. An added benefit is that it helps you develop a relationship with that person, which, in and of itself, is helpful. When you ask questions of others, people feel that you are working with them to find solutions, not negotiating against them.

ASK "WHY?"

As mentioned above, often the most useful question you can ask is "Why?" Asking why works particularly well as a response to statements such as, "We can't agree to that" or "That would be contrary to policy." When you ask, "Why can't you agree to that?" or "Why do you have that policy?," you are calling for a reasoned response. After you are given a reason, you can make a case that the reason is not applicable in this instance. Alternatively, you have an opportunity to satisfy the other side's objections.

REPEAT BACK IN QUESTION FORM

Another way to ask why is to use a variation on the reflecting back technique described above. Simply repeat what has just been said, but in question form . . . reflecting back the other side's own words when a proposal is not reasonable can be very effective. Similarly, when people make unqualified statements such as, "We never do that," a simple "Never?" will force them to either confirm that this is really the case, or, more likely, cause them to retreat to something like, "Except in very unusual circumstances." Once you get that kind of admission, you are well on your way to making your case because now you know what argument to make: that yours are unusual circumstances and require an exception to the normal practice. Once someone concedes that exceptions have been made in the past, it becomes much harder to claim that you don't deserve the same treatment.

ANSWER QUESTIONS WITH QUESTIONS

Sometimes you can answer a question with a question. If you don't want to respond to a particular question or you want to understand why someone is asking a particular question, you can respond by asking, "Well, what do you think?" If you do this too often you may appear evasive and argumentative, but using this approach sparingly can be effective.

ASK WHAT THEY WOULD DO

Finally, if you find yourself at an impasse, you can always ask what they would do if they were in your position. This can sometimes completely change the dynamics of the negotiations by forcing the other side to come up with a solution to the problem, rather than trying to convince you that there is no problem. In doing so, a solution may emerge that would be acceptable to you or could be made so with slight modification.

----

2. *Managing Information*

Effective negotiators also know how to manage information and thoughtfully determine when and what information to provide. Generally, it is advantageous to receive more information than you provide, but this is not an absolute. The distinction between managing information and purposely deceiving is a thin line and will be examined in the section on negotiation ethics.

The following selection provides advice and discusses issues regarding obtaining and providing information. Professor Nelken first focuses on managing and bargaining for information in distributive situations and then on the benefits and concerns of sharing information in more integrative negotiations. The separation between distributive and integrative negotiation is not always clear, so her comments may apply to both.

MELISSA L. NELKEN, UNDERSTANDING NEGOTIATION
68-71, Anderson Publishing (2001)

In the course of the negotiation, you will try to learn things about the other party's case, and about his perception of your case, that you don't know when the negotiation starts. He, of course, will do the same with you. Another important aspect of preparation, then, is deciding what you need to find out before you actually make a deal. Without considering what information you need to gather in the early stages of the negotiation, you will not be able to gauge how well the actual situation fits the assumptions you have made in preparing to negotiate. You may have overestimated how much the other party needs a deal with you, or underestimated the value he places on what you are selling. Only careful attention to gathering information will enable you to adjust your goals appropriately. In addition to what you want to learn, you also have to decide what information you are willing, or even eager, to divulge to the other party—for example, the large number of offers you have already received for the subject property—and what information you want to conceal—for example, the fact that none of those offers exceeds the price you paid for the property originally. Managing information is a central feature of distributive bargaining, and you have to plan to do it well.

A beginning negotiator often feels that she has to conceal as much as possible, that virtually anything she reveals will hurt her or be used against her. . . . [Y]ou are more likely to feel this way if you have not thought through your case and prepared how to present it in the best light that you realistically can. If you choose when and how you will reveal information, rather than anxiously concealing as much as possible, you gain a degree of control over the negotiation that you lack when you merely react to what your counterpart says or does. Increasing the amount of information you are prepared to reveal, and reducing the amount you feel you absolutely must conceal, will help you make a stronger case for your client. In addition, the more willing you are to share information that the other party considers useful, the more likely you are to learn what you need to know from your counterpart before you make a deal.

Using Outside Sources

As part of your preparation, you need to consult outside sources of information to help you understand the context of a given negotiation. You will need data about the subject of the negotiation—market prices, alternate sources of supply, industry standards, market factors affecting the company you are dealing with, and so on. In addition, information about the parties and their representatives from others who have negotiated with them in the past will be helpful in planning your strategy. You will also want to learn about any relevant negotiation conventions, for example, the convention in personal injury litigation that the plaintiff makes the first demand. . . .

Bargaining for Information

A central aspect of distributive bargaining is bargaining for information. In the course of planning, you have to make certain working assumptions about the motives and wishes of the other side, as well as about the factual context of the negotiation. In addition, we all have a tendency to "fill in" missing information in order to create a coherent picture of a situation. For a negotiator, it is imperative to separate out what you know to be true from what you merely believe to be true by testing your assumptions during the early stages of the negotiation. Otherwise, you risk making decisions based on inaccurate information and misunderstanding what the other side actually tells you. . . .

Many negotiators forget that they start with only a partial picture of the situation, and they push to "get down to numbers" before learning anything about the other side's point of view. Yet the relevant facts of a situation are not immutable; they are often dependent on your perspective. Knowing the other side's perspective is a valuable source of information about possibilities for settlement. The most obvious way to gather that information is by asking questions, especially about the reasons behind positions taken by the other party. Why does a deal have to be made today? How good are her alternatives to settlement with you? What is the basis for a particular offer? Asking questions allows you to test the assumptions that you bring to the negotiation about both parties' situations. Questions also permit you to gauge the firmness of stated positions by learning how well supported they are by facts. In addition, the information you gather can alert you to issues that are important (or unimportant) to your counterpart, opening up possibilities for an advantageous settlement if you value those issues differently.

In addition to asking questions, you have to learn to listen carefully to what the other party says, to look for verbal and nonverbal cues that either reinforce or contradict the surface message conveyed. If someone tells you that he wants $40,000–50,000 to settle, you can be sure that he will settle for $40,000, or less. If he starts a sentence by saying, "I'll be perfectly frank with you. . . . ," take whatever follows with a large grain of salt and test it against other things you have heard. Asking questions is only one way to gather information, and not always the most informative one. You also have to listen for what someone omits from an answer, for answers that are not answers or that deflect the question, for hesitations and vagueness in the responses that you get. There is no simple formula for what such things mean, but the more alert you are for ways in which you are not getting information in a straightforward way, the better able you will be to sort through the information that you get. . . .

One of the most effective and underutilized methods of bargaining for information is silence. Many inexperienced negotiators, especially lawyer-negotiators, think that they are paid to talk and are not comfortable sitting quietly. If you can teach yourself to do so, you will find that you often learn things that would never be revealed in response to a direct question. When silences occur, people tend to fill them in; and because the silence is unstructured, what they say is often more spontaneous than any answer to a question would be. Since you are interested in gathering new information in the course of the negotiation, it is useful to keep in mind that if you are talking, you probably aren't hearing anything you do not already know. Therefore, silence is truly golden. . . .

Sharing Information

All that has been said so far about integrative bargaining suggests that lawyers will only be able to do a good job if they share substantive information about their clients' needs and preferences and look for ways to make their differences work for them in the negotiation. According to Follett (1942, p. 36), "the first rule . . . for obtaining integration is to put your cards on the table, face the real issue, uncover the conflict, bring the whole thing into the open." This is a far cry from the bargaining for information that characterizes distributive negotiations, where each side seeks to learn as much as possible about the other while revealing as little as it can. The more straightforward and clear the negotiators' communications are, the fewer obstacles there will be to recognizing and capitalizing on opportunities for mutual gain. This means, first, that they must be clear about their clients' goals, even if they are open as to the means of reaching those goals. In addition, there must be sufficient trust between them so that both are willing to reveal their clients' true motivations. Such trust may be based on past experience, but it may also be developed in the course of a negotiation, as the negotiators exchange information and evaluate the information they have received. It does not have to be based on an assumption that the other side has your best interest at heart, but only that he is as interested as you are in uncovering ways that you can both do better through negotiation. Self-interest can keep both sides honest in the process, even where there might be a short-term gain from misrepresentation. Of course, the need to share information in order to optimize results creates risks for the negotiators as well. . . .

Flexibility, rather than rigid positions, is key to integrative bargaining, since the outcome will depend on fitting together the parties' needs as much as possible. When the negotiators share adequate information, they may end up redefining the conflict they are trying to resolve. For example, what seemed a specific problem about failure to fulfill the terms of a contract may turn out to be a more fundamental difficulty with the structure of the contract itself. A better outcome for both sides may result if the contract is renegotiated . . .

STRATEGIC USE OF INFORMATION

There is also anxiety because the amount of shared information needed for integrative bargaining to succeed may be more than a distributive bargainer wants to reveal. For example, a distributively-inclined buyer may prefer that his counterpart think that time of delivery, which he does not care much about, is very important to him, so that he can exact concessions on other aspects of the deal by "giving in" to a later delivery to accommodate the seller. Since it is hard to know in advance what issues will be most significant to the other side, it can be difficult to decide how much information to share and how to evaluate the quality of the information you receive about your counterpart's priorities. The fear of being taken advantage of often results in both sides' taking pre-emptive action focused on "winning" rather than on collaborating. Sometimes such strategies are effective; but they are also likely to impede or prevent what could be a fruitful search for joint gains.

QUESTIONS

1. The selection above on active listening and questioning by Miller and Miller is excerpted from their book written as a guide for women. Do you consider the advice given to be gender specific? Do you think men or women are generally better listeners? Why?
2. Are there times when active listening or responding to a question with a question should not be used? When would you find these techniques annoying or counterproductive?
3. The use of silence to elicit additional information after someone stops speaking can also be effective in situations other than negotiation. The silence should be accompanied by continued eye contact to convey an expectation or invitation for more information. Have you used this method with friends, a spouse or children? Do you think you are susceptible to this technique when used by others?

E. BARGAINING

Bargaining takes many forms and is not confined to a specific stage in the negotiation process. The term "bargaining" is more associated with the competitive/distributive approach. Phrases like "searching for solutions" and "problem solving" are frequently used to describe a more cooperative/integrative approach. However, at some point in any negotiation there must be movement from the differences that brought the parties to the table toward the agreement that will resolve the dispute or create a deal. Whether the movement results from arguments and persuasion or from proposed principles and criteria may be more a matter of semantics and tone than of real difference. For example, lawyers in negotiating a settlement of a lawsuit may agree, expressly or implicitly, that legal principles and precedent will be the criteria for settlement. Does this reduce the role of argument and attempts at persuasion regarding what case precedent is most analogous and applicable to the matter in dispute? Is trading off a lower priority to satisfy one more personally important not a form of concession?

1. Managing Concessions

Concessions are the compromises you make after your opening offer to move the negotiation forward. Usually the concessions you make are offered in return for those your negotiation opponent offers. Making concessions can be done strategically in recognition that the timing, amount, and nature of concessions is a form of communication by which you give and get information about priorities and reservation points. The pattern of concessions sends a message. By carefully considering what you want to communicate you can manage concessions to shape the message, particularly about how close you are to your reservation point. (Diminishing concessions signal you are close.) The flip side of anything that can be used strategically is that the strategy might be used by an opponent to manipulate you.

What follows is an exploration of concessions and their use as explained by a leading negotiation trainer.

THERON O'CONNOR, PLANNING AND EXECUTING AN EFFECTIVE CONCESSION STRATEGY
Bay Group International (2003)

Concessions and the Negotiating Process

Negotiation is the process for reaching an agreement—pure and simple. Well, maybe not so simple and maybe not so pure either. The process may be competitive; it may be collaborative; or, as in most cases, it may have significant elements of both. Negotiators typically aspire to maximize the satisfaction of their own interests and, at the same time, they must respond to the interests of and build a sustainable relationship with the other side. As with any process, negotiation is comprised of a number of moving parts which must be carefully managed and integrated—value must be anchored, framed and positioned; ambitious aspirations must be set; data must be handled in a disciplined way to ensure that only appropriate information is divulged to the other side and that the full range and depth of the other side's interests are uncovered; emotions and behavior must be rigorously controlled to both convey confidence and instill trust; and, finally, concessions typically have to be made in order to reach a meeting of the minds.

It is the concession piece of the negotiation process—the bargaining, the give-and-take, the "horse-trading," what the parties are willing to give up in order to reach an agreement—that will be discussed here. There are two principal sets of tasks to consider. The first is how to create the most advantageous negotiation context within which a concession strategy can be implemented. The techniques to establish a favorable negotiation context are discussed elsewhere in this volume. The second critical consideration is how to effectively handle the *execution* of the concession strategy or plan once the context has been established. This piece will focus upon the execution phase.

It should be noted that the many parts of the negotiation process are not strictly sequential. Rather, they occur and reoccur throughout the negotiation and must be attended to iteratively. That is particularly true of concession patterns. Often attention to concessions is mistakenly deferred until late in the game and concessions are used tactically, rather than strategically, as a closing tool.

PLANNING AND EXECUTING AN EFFECTIVE CONCESSION STRATEGY

Once a desirable negotiating context has been established, the concession strategy can be executed. Whether to concede, when to concede, what to concede, how to concede are among a number of important considerations to keep in mind in dealing with concessions. Skilled negotiators develop plans for managing the process of making concessions, and thereby exert more control over the negotiation process. Conceding without a plan can doom you to failure in negotiation.

Concessions Should Be Made Only as Required

Notwithstanding that a sophisticated concession strategy has been developed—replete with creative and cost effective negotiables—no concessions should be made unless they are demanded by the other side. If the other side is willing to accept the initial proposal, then there has probably been a failure to accurately gauge the unexpectedly high value perception of the other side and a failure to take a sufficiently ambitious opening position. That error ought not to be compounded by then freely granting concessions from the largesse that has been built into the plan. While this should go without saying, there is often the temptation to "throw something in" simply because it is unexpectedly still there.

Concessions Should Be Made Slowly and Reluctantly

At the early stages of the negotiation, the focus should be on continuing to shape and influence the value perception of the other side and continuing to uncover and evaluate their wants and needs. With the range of reason advantageously set, it is imperative to hold the line and show resolve with respect to the value proposition and opening position. Reluctance to make concessions early on tends to increase their value in the mind of the other negotiator when they are in fact granted. Care should be taken, however, not to communicate too aggressive and inflexible a stance.

Try Not to Be the First to Make a Concession

If possible, get the other party to move first. Take the time to test the resolve of the other side by asking for concessions and suggesting ways that interests might be satisfied by them. First concessions can carry strong signals as to the flexibility of the other negotiator and can help calibrate the distance between the party's positions. Do not hesitate to make a concession, however, if it seems necessary to keep the negotiation going.

Get Something in Return for Any Concession

Concessions should be made in the context of trades or exchanges rather than given simply to see if the other side's point of satisfaction might be found.

Demanding a concession in return both reinforces the value of what is being conceded and signals the resolve of the negotiator making the concession. It also helps to build the process of give and take and stimulate movement toward agreement.

First Concede Low Cost Negotiables That Represent High Value to the Other Side and Vice Versa

Having prioritized and ranked those things which might be offered to satisfy the wants and needs of the parties, it is important to evaluate each opportunity in terms of what might be offered that would be perceived to provide the highest possible value to the other side at the lowest cost. Likewise, in seeking concessions from the other side, it is important to seek concessions of high perceived value at comparatively low cost to them.

Use a Concession Pattern Designed to Leverage Fundamental Interests

Concession patterns communicate predictable messages to the other side. Holding firm and making one big concession at the end sends one message; making one large early concession and then holding firm sends another message. Making incremental but growing concessions sends one message; making incremental but diminishing concessions sends another message. Driving value early on and then executing a concession pattern of a large concession first and then progressively smaller ones often can be the most powerful pattern of all. It communicates resolve, then flexibility, and then diminishing returns moving toward closure.

CONCLUSION

It is critical to the ultimate success of the negotiation to deal with the concession process early on—even prior to initial contact—both to build the most advantageous context and to develop a strategy for execution of the concession plan. The context-building activities, anchoring, framing, positioning, setting high opening targets, discovering interests and negotiables, and managing emotions and behaviors, help to develop a robust value proposition and to stretch the range-of-reason within which an optimal outcome can be achieved.

Concession execution guidelines help to ensure that the negotiator will not give up too much too soon and that an appropriate balance will be maintained between self-interested competitiveness on the one hand and relational collaboration on the other. The concession execution guidelines are:

> *No Concession Unless Needed*
> *Get the Other Party to Make First Concession*
> *Concede Slowly and Reluctantly*
> *Get Something in Return*
> *Concede to High Value from Low Cost/Vice-Versa*
> *Use Advantageous Pattern*

Rigorous integration of both phases, building context and concession execution—from beginning to end—create the highest likelihood of successful negotiation.

2. *Value Creating Trades and Brainstorming*

Next, Mnookin, Peppet, and Tulumello propose a way to generate value-creating options and trade-offs as part of a problem-solving approach. This alternative to adversarial bargaining may create the risk of exploitation in the distributive aspects of negotiation. They acknowledge that the challenge of problem-solving negotiation is to recognize and manage the tension between value creation and later distribution of the created value, as explained in Chapter 4 by Lax and Sebenius. The helpful technique of brainstorming to generate more creative options based on different interests and values is described.

ROBERT H. MNOOKIN, SCOTT R. PEPPET, AND ANDREW S. TULUMELLO, BEYOND WINNING: NEGOTIATING TO CREATE VALUE IN DEALS AND DISPUTES

37-43, Harvard University Press (2000)

GENERATE VALUE-CREATING OPTIONS

Now ... look for value-creating trades. But this is not as easy as it might appear. Many negotiators jump into a negotiation process that inhibits value creation. One side suggests a solution and the other negotiator shoots it down. The second negotiator proposes an option, only to be told by the first why it can't work. After a few minutes of this, neither side is willing to propose anything but the most conventional solutions. This method mistakenly conflates two processes that should be engaged in separately: generating options and evaluating them.

It often helps to engage in some sort of brainstorming. The most effective brainstorming requires real freedom—however momentary—from practical constraints. . . . [There are two ground rules for brainstorming.]

- No evaluation
- No ownership

Premature evaluation inhibits creativity. We are all self-critical enough, and adding to our natural inhibitions only makes matters worse. When brainstorming, avoid the temptation to critique ideas as they are being generated. This includes avoiding even congratulatory comments about how great someone else's idea is, murmurs of approval, and backslapping. When you signal such approval, you send the implicit message that you're still judging each idea as it is generated—you're just keeping the *negative* comments to yourself. That does not encourage inventiveness. The goal is to liberate those at the table to suggest ideas. One person's idea may seem crazy, but it may prompt another person to suggest a solution that might otherwise have been overlooked. There will be time enough for evaluation. The idea behind brainstorming is that evaluation should be a separate activity, not mixed with the process of generating ideas.

The second ground rule of brainstorming is: *no ownership of ideas*. Those at the table should feel free to suggest anything they can think of, without fear that their ideas will be attributed to them or used against them. Avoid comments such as: "John, I'm surprised to hear you suggest that; I didn't think you believed that idea made much sense." John should be able to suggest an idea *without believing it*. Indeed, those at the table should feel free to suggest ideas that are not in their best interests, purely to stimulate discussion, without fear that others at the table will later take those ideas as offers.

In preparing for negotiations, brainstorming is often employed behind the table with colleagues in order to generate ideas. For many negotiators, however, it may feel very dangerous to engage in this activity with someone on the other side. Our own experience suggests, nevertheless, that by negotiating process clearly, brainstorming can also be productive across the table.

How do you convey these ground rules to the other side? You can get the point across without sounding dictatorial or rule-obsessed. Just explain what you're trying to achieve and then lead by example. . . . Generating these possible options may broaden the parties' thinking about the terms of their negotiated agreement.

Many of these options demonstrate that a negotiator's interests can often be met in a variety of ways. And often the simplest solution is to compensate one side by adjusting the price term . . . to accommodate the parties' needs and concerns. . . . In many deal-making situations, such "side-payments" can be an effective way to adjust the distributive consequences of value-creating moves. . . .

What happens to interest-based, collaborative problem-solving when you turn to distributive issues? Some negotiators act as if problem-solving has to be tossed overboard when the going gets tough. We could not disagree more. In our experience, it's when distributive issues are at the forefront that problem-solving skills are most desperately needed . . .

Sometimes, of course, you won't be able to find a solution that satisfies both sides. No matter how hard you try, you will continue to disagree about salary, the amount to be paid in a bonus, or some aspect of a dispute settlement. Norms may have helped move you closer together, but there's still a big gap between the two sides. What should you do?

Think about process. How can you design a process that would fairly resolve this impasse? In a dispute settlement, you might be able to hire a mediator to address the distributive issues that are still open. Is there anyone both sides trust enough to decide the issue? Could you put five possible agreements into a hat and pick one at random?

Procedural solutions can often rescue a distributive negotiation that has reached an impasse. They need not involve complicated alternative dispute resolution procedures that cost money and time. Instead, you can often come up with simple process solutions that will resolve a distributive deadlock and allow you to move forward.

CHANGING THE GAME

Not everyone approaches negotiation from a problem-solving perspective. The basic approach described in this chapter — with its emphasis on the sources of value creation and the importance of a problem-solving process — obviously departs from the norm of adversarial haggling. To be a problem-solver, a negotiator must often lead the way and change the game. . . .

CONCLUSION

The tension between value creation and value distribution exists in almost all negotiations. But as our teaching and consulting have shown us, many people tend to see a negotiation as purely one or the other. Some people see the world in zero-sum terms—as solely distributive. We work hard to demonstrate to people that there are nearly always opportunities to create value. Others believe that, with cooperation, the pie can be made so large that distributive questions will disappear. For these negotiators, we emphasize that there are always distributive issues to address.

Of course, some negotiations present many value-creating opportunities, while others are very distributive. Very distributive negotiations typically involve a one-shot dispute or single issue (such as price); fixed transaction costs; and parties with no continuing relationship. An example would be an accident victim's damage claim against an unknown or arm's-length insured driver. If both parties have fixed legal costs, the negotiation is essentially about how much one party will pay the other. A dollar more for the plaintiff means a dollar less for the defendant.

Other negotiations have many value-creating possibilities. If the parties value an ongoing relationship, they can both gain by pursuing this shared interest. If transaction costs are high relative to the amounts at stake, both parties may gain by designing an efficient negotiation process. If many issues or variables are involved, the parties may have different relative valuations and may thus be able to make trades.

The problem-solving approach we have suggested here will not make distributive issues go away or this first tension of negotiation disappear. But it does outline an approach that will help you find value-creating opportunities when they exist and resolve distributive issues efficiently and as a shared problem. . . .

----

3. Multiparty Bargaining—Coalitions and Holdouts

Legal disputes and transactions often involve multiple parties. The negotiation dynamic and trades then become more complex and there may be sub-bargaining within the more comprehensive negotiation. In a multiple party lawsuit, a plaintive must negotiate with the defendants and the defendants are likely to negotiate with each other. If there is also more than one plaintiff, negotiations occur on both sides of the table and across it. In multiple party transactions, there is a mix of complementary and competing interests that may require many negotiations within the larger negotiation context.

A key difference between two-party and multiparty bargaining is the formation of coalitions. A coalition forms when two or more parties discover that they have complementary interests or that they can form side deals. They can then leverage their combined bargaining strength against the others or reach a deal that leaves out another bargainer. It is the possibility of freezing someone out of participating in the deal that gives a coalition leverage. The more parties, the more possible alliances or coalitions. The bargaining gets both more extracted and complex as each party weighs their bargaining options with each of the other parties and the possible combinations. Bargaining can become very strategic. Because there are different payoffs possible with each combination and these are not immediately known, coalitions may dissolve and change before a final agreement is reached.

An example of a classic coalition arises when an injured driver sues another driver, the dealer who sold the other driver her car, the automobile manufacturer, and the auto repair shop, which last serviced the other driver's car. Although naturally allied in their defense against the injured plaintiff, because of joint and several liability, each defendant has individual interests that may motivate them to bargain separately with the plaintiff to form a coalition against the remaining defendants. So if the auto dealership bargains with the plaintiff to pay a limited amount that caps the dealer's liability and reduces its actual payout if the plaintiff recovers full damages from the other defendants, then a coalition of interests is formed against the remaining defendants. The settling defendant may agree to stay in the case to testify favorably and also avoid creating the "empty chair" defense. (This is known as a "Mary Carter" agreement and is discussed in Chapter 8. See *Abbot Ford, Inc. v. The Superior Court of Los Angeles County; Ford Motor Co.*, 43 Cal. 3d 858 (1987).) A similar coalition situation can occur in a breach of contract case or any other type of case involving multiple defendants or plaintiffs.

Another aspect of multiparty cases and transactions that can change the bargaining process is the prospect of one or more parties holding out from a settlement or deal knowing that the others want to close the deal and will pay proportionately more to bring in the holdout. A settlement requirement of unanimity among multiple parties in a negotiation increases the strategic motivation for one party to hold out for more and also increases the chance of a negotiation impasse. For example, one of four partners may hold out in negotiations to sell their business to a suitor unless the holdout is paid more than the other partners. One of several property owners may hold out until all other property owners have sold to a developer so he may demand more in order for the complete transaction to close. (For an analysis of the added complexities and obstacles to settlement created in multiparty situations, see Mnookin, 2003.)

Multiparty disputes and transactions, which create the prospect of coalitions and holdouts, complicate the bargaining phase and require more detailed analysis of the potential payoffs and negotiation leverage. Correctly anticipating the behaviors and moves of others in multiparty bargaining situations can be particularly valuable. A note in Chapter 2 explained the use of game theory to systematically assess the probable response of opponents in negotiation. Although more difficult to apply in multiparty negotiations, game theory can be a helpful tool worth the effort or cost of retaining an expert consultant.

Just as there may be a payoff for one seller in a multiple seller situation or one plaintiff in a multiparty claim who holds out to be the last to agree, there are situations where being the first defendant to settle is advantageous. Plaintiffs may, in effect, offer an attractive discount to the first to settle in order to obtain one defendant's cooperation and then leverage that agreement as pressure against the remaining defendants. The following excerpt illustrates the potential leverage created for the plaintiff by getting one of several defendants in a complex class action to settle early and the possible benefit to the first defendant to agree.

JOHN M. POSWALL, THE LAWYERS: CLASS OF '69
248-251, Jullundur Press (2003)

On Monday morning, Leon and Bishop did what appeared to be poor strategy in negotiations. They went to the turf of their opponent to talk settlement—into the luxurious 28th floor conference room of the largest defense law firm in Northern California. There, overlooking the San Francisco Bay, they met with the firm's senior litigation partner, Martin Crosby, Jr., flanked by his committee of defense attorneys representing the various levels of defendants. A number of corporate senior vice presidents were also in evidence, each being given careful deference by his representative attorney. Jack Merchant was absent. . . .

"We're all realists here," Crosby went on. "All professionals. Litigation is costly, even when we win. I'll be candid with you. I think class actions are legal blackmail and should be resisted forcefully. But my clients, our clients," he corrected himself, gesturing with his hands to the assembled group, "are willing to resolve the matter now to save the costs of litigation. Of course, if the matter proceeds, this offer will be withdrawn, and I can give you my personal assurance, Mr. Goldman, that we are prepared to spend whatever it takes to win." . . .

"We're prepared to pay your class of clients $1 million"—Crosby said $1 million very slowly to let it sink in—"for any real or imagined slight they have endured and," he looked at Leon closely, "$1 million in fees and costs to your firm for its efforts in this matter." . . .

"Marty"—he knew no one called Martin Crosby, Jr., anything but Mr. Crosby—"you invite me over here, threaten me, and then insult me and my clients, and conclude with offering me what amounts to a bribe to sell out my clients. I think I should report you to the State Bar." . . .

Leon smiled. . . . He stood up, leaned on the table with both hands, and spent a few seconds on each corporate vice president, after passing his eyes over their attorneys.

"Here's how it's going to be, gentleman. We will settle with each group separately. The first group will pay the least; the next a bit more; and so on. The last to settle will pay the most." . . .

"You should know that I met with Jack Merchant [a defense attorney not in the room] on Saturday and Sunday, and we have arrived at a settlement, signed last night, that includes all of the provisions I just outlined. The lenders group of defendants have agreed to pay $40 million in settlement with our guarantee that each remaining group will pay more."

He shifted his eyes around the room again. He sensed the shock bordering on panic.

"So gentlemen, I suggest each of you call me when you are ready."

He turned and walked to the door. . . .

F. MOVING TOWARD CLOSURE

1. The Role of Power and Commitment

Negotiation is often discussed in terms of power and how each side to a negotiation can use its power to move the negotiation in the direction it desires and get what it wants from the other side. Power comes from the mind of your negotiating opponents. If they believe that you can provide them what they want or deny it to them, then relative to them, you have power. Again, perception becomes reality for purposes of negotiation. What someone wants may be material or emotional. It may be a desire to gain something new or not to lose what they have. So, you have power if you control what your opponent wants, including peace of mind, looking good, or not being harmed — provided they think you will exercise your control.

Power is linked to commitment. If it is perceived that you are committed to do what another wants, or not do it, only if they give you what you want, then you have power to obtain what you want. A hostage taker has added power if one of several hostages is shot.

Power may be a factor from the beginning to the end of negotiation. However, the perception of power often changes during negotiations. Because power is in the mind of the perceiver, what is communicated verbally and nonverbally during the course of the negotiation determines how power is perceived at the time decisions must be made. Both parties will attempt to display or exercise the power they have over the other to move the negotiation to a successful closure. Each may communicate their power, or attempt to create a perception of power, by threats, displays of absolute commitment, or disclosure of better alternatives for themselves and worse alternatives for the opponent.

Getting to Yes did not place emphasis on negotiation power and was criticized for not addressing the topic more. In the article that follows, Roger Fisher takes up the subject of negotiating power and ties it to commitment. He defines power and expands the traditional concepts of power so that developing and using power is consistent with being a principled negotiator.

ROGER FISHER, "NEGOTIATING POWER: GETTING AND USING INFLUENCE," IN J. WILLIAM BRESLIN AND JEFFREY Z. RUBIN (EDS.), NEGOTIATION THEORY AND PRACTICE

127-128, 130-138, Program on Negotiation Books (1991)

Getting to YES (Fisher and Ury 1981) has been justly criticized as devoting insufficient attention to the issue of power. It is all very well, it is said, to tell people how they might jointly produce wise outcomes efficiently and amicably, but in the real world people don't behave that way; results are determined by power — by who is holding the cards, by who has more clout.

At the international level, negotiating power is typically equated with military power. The United States is urged to develop and deploy more nuclear missiles so that it can negotiate from a position of strength. Threats and warnings also play an important role in the popular concept of power, as do resolve and commitment. In the game of chicken, victory goes to the side that more successfully demonstrates that it will not yield.

There is obviously some merit in the notion that physical force, and an apparent willingness to use it, can affect the outcome of a negotiation. How does that square with the suggestion that negotiators ought to focus on the interests of the parties, on the generating of alternatives, and on objective standards to which both sides might defer? . . .

How Should We Define Negotiating Power?

If I have negotiating power, I have the ability to affect favorably someone else's decision. This being so, one can argue that my power depends upon someone else's perception of my strength, so it is what they *think* that matters, not what I actually have. The other side may be as much influenced by a row of cardboard tanks as by a battalion of real tanks. One can then say that negotiating power is all a matter of perception.

A general who commands a real tank battalion, however, is in a far stronger position than one in charge of a row of cardboard tanks. A false impression of power is extremely vulnerable, capable of being destroyed by a word. In order to avoid focusing our attention on how to deceive other people, it seems best at the outset to identify what constitutes "real" negotiating power — an ability to influence the decisions of others assuming they know the truth. We can then go on to recognize that, in addition, it will be possible at times to influence others through deception, through creating an illusion of power. Even for that purpose, we will need to know what illusion we wish to create. If we are bluffing, what are we bluffing about? . . .

Categories of Power

My ability to exert influence depends upon the combined total of a number of different factors. As a first approximation, the following six kinds of power appear to provide useful categories for generating prescriptive advice:

1. The power of skill and knowledge
2. The power of a good relationship
3. The power of a good alternative to negotiating
4. The power of an elegant solution
5. The power of legitimacy
6. The power of commitment. . . .

1. THE POWER OF SKILL AND KNOWLEDGE

All things being equal, a skilled negotiator is better able to influence the decision of others than is an unskilled negotiator. Strong evidence suggests that negotiating skills can be both learned and taught. One way to become a more powerful negotiator is to become a more skillful one. Some of these skills are those of dealing with people: the ability to listen, to become aware of the emotions and psychological concerns of others, to empathize, to be sensitive to their feelings and one's own, to speak different languages, to communicate clearly and effectively, to become integrated so that one's words and nonverbal behavior are congruent and reinforce each other, and so forth. . . .

The more skill one acquires, the more power one will have as a negotiator. These skills can be acquired at any time, often far in advance of any particular negotiation.

Knowledge also is power. Some knowledge is general and of use in many negotiations, such as familiarity with a wide range of procedural options and awareness of national or negotiating styles and cultural differences. A repertoire of examples, precedents, and illustrations can also add to one's persuasive abilities.

Knowledge relevant to a particular negotiation in which one is about to engage is even more powerful. The more information one can gather about the parties and issues in an upcoming negotiation, the stronger one's entering posture. . . .

2. THE POWER OF A GOOD RELATIONSHIP

The better a working relationship I establish in advance with those with whom I will be negotiating, the more powerful I am. A good working relationship does not necessarily imply approval of each other's conduct, though mutual respect and even mutual affection—when it exists—may help, the two most critical elements of a working relationship are, first, trust, and second, the ability to communicate easily and effectively.

Trust. Although I am likely to focus my attention in a given negotiation on the question of whether or not I can trust those on the other side, my power depends upon whether they can trust me. If over time I have been able to establish a well-deserved reputation for candor, honesty, integrity, and commitment to any promise I make, my capacity to exert influence is significantly enhanced.

Communication. The negotiation process is one of communication. If I am trying to persuade some people to change their minds, I want to know where their minds are; otherwise, I am shooting in the dark. If my messages are going to have their intended impact, they need to be understood as I would have them understood. . . .

3. THE POWER OF A GOOD ALTERNATIVE TO NEGOTIATION

To a significant extent, my power in a negotiation depends upon how well I can do for myself if I walk away. In *Getting to YES*, we urge a negotiator to develop and improve his "BATNA"—his Best Alternative To a Negotiated Agreement. One kind of preparation for negotiation that enhances one's negotiating power is to consider the alternatives to reaching agreement with this particular negotiating partner, to select the most promising, and to improve it to the extent possible. This alternative sets a floor. If I follow this practice, every negotiation will lead to a successful outcome in the sense that any result I accept is bound to be better than anything else I could do. . . . The better an alternative one can develop outside the negotiation, the greater one's power to affect favorably a negotiated outcome.

4. THE POWER OF AN ELEGANT SOLUTION

In any negotiation, there is a mélange of shared and conflicting interests. The parties face a problem. One way to influence the other side in a negotiation is to invent a good solution to that problem. The more complex the problem, the more influential an elegant answer. Too often, negotiators battle like litigators in court. Each side advances arguments for a result that would take care of its interests but would do nothing for the other side. The power of a mediator often comes from working out an ingenious solution that reconciles reasonably well the legitimate interests of both sides. Either negotiator has similar power to effect an agreement that takes care of some or most of the interests on the other side.

5. THE POWER OF LEGITIMACY

Each of us is subject to being persuaded by becoming convinced that a particular result ought to be accepted because it is fair; because the law requires it; because it is consistent with precedent, industry practice, or sound policy considerations; or because it is legitimate as measured by some other objective standard. I can substantially enhance my negotiating power by searching for and developing various objective criteria and potential standards of legitimacy, and by shaping proposed solutions so that they are legitimate in the eyes of the other side. . . .

To retain his power, a wise negotiator avoids advancing a proposition that is so extreme that it damages his credibility. He also avoids locking himself into the first principle he advances that he will lose face in disentangling himself from that principle and moving on to one that has a greater chance of persuading the other side. In advance of this process, a negotiator will want to have researched precedents, expert opinion, and other objective criteria, and to have worked on various theories of what ought to be done, so as to harness the power of legitimacy—a power to which each of us is vulnerable.

6. THE POWER OF COMMITMENT

There are two quite different kinds of commitments—affirmative and negative:

   (a) Affirmative commitments
      (1) An offer of what I am willing to agree to.
      (2) An offer of what, failing agreement, I am willing to do under certain conditions.
   (b) Negative commitments
      (1) A commitment that I am unwilling to make certain agreements (even though they would be better for me than no agreement).
      (2) A commitment or threat that, failing agreement, I will engage in certain negative conduct (even though to do so would be worse for me than a simple absence of agreement).

Every commitment involves a decision. Let's first look at affirmative commitments. An affirmative commitment is a decision about what one is willing to do. It is an offer. Every offer ties the negotiator's hands to some extent. It says, "This, I am willing to do." The offer may expire or later be withdrawn, but while open it carries some persuasive power. It is no longer just an idea or a possibility that the parties are discussing. Like a proposal of marriage or a job offer, it is operational. It says, "I am willing to do this. If you agree, we have a deal." . . .

A negative commitment is the most controversial and troublesome element of negotiating power. No doubt, by tying my own hands I may be able to influence you to accept something more favorable to me than you otherwise would. The theory is simple. For almost every potential agreement there is a range within which each of us is better off having an agreement than walking away. Suppose that you would be willing to pay $75,000 for my house if you had to; but for a price above that figure you would rather buy a different house. The best offer I have received from someone else is $62,000, and I will accept that offer unless you give me a better one. At any price between $62,000 and $75,000 we are both better off than if no agreement is reached. If you offer me $62,100, and so tie your hands by a negative commitment that you cannot raise your offer, presumably, I will accept it since it is better than $62,000. On the other hand, if I can commit myself not to drop the price below $75,000, you presumably will buy the house at that price. This logic may lead us to engage in a battle of negative commitments. Logic suggests that "victory" goes to the one who first and most convincingly ties his own hands at an appropriate figure. Other things being equal, an early and rigid negative commitment at the right point should prove persuasive.

Other things, however, are not likely to be equal.

The earlier I make a negative commitment—the earlier I announce a take-it-or-leave-it position—the less likely I am to have maximized the cumulative total of the various elements of my negotiating power.

The Power of Knowledge

I probably acted before knowing as much as I could have learned. The longer I postpone making a negative commitment, the more likely I am to know the best proposition to which to commit myself.

The Power of a Good Relationship

Being quick to advance a take-it-or-leave-it position is likely to prejudice a good working relationship and to damage the trust you might otherwise place in what I say. The more quickly I confront you with a rigid position on my part, the more likely I am to make you so angry that you will refuse an agreement you might otherwise accept.

The Power of a Good Alternative

There is a subtle but significant difference between communicating a warning of the course of action that I believe it will be in my interest to take should we fail to reach agreement (my BATNA), and locking myself in to precise terms that you must accept in order to avoid my taking that course of action. Extending a warning is not the same as making a negative commitment. . . .

The Power of an Elegant Solution

The early use of a negative commitment reduces the likelihood that the choice being considered by the other side is one that best meets its interests consistent with any given degree of meeting our interests. If we announce early in the negotiation process that we will accept no agreement other than Plan X, Plan X probably takes care of most of our interests. But it is quite likely that Plan X could be improved. With further study and time, it may be possible to modify Plan X so that it serves our interests even better at little or no cost to the interests of the other side.

Second, it may be possible to modify Plan X in ways that make it more attractive to the other side without in any way making it less attractive to us. To do so would not serve merely the other side but would serve us also by making it more likely that the other side will accept a plan that so well serves our interests.

The Power of Legitimacy

The most serious damage to negotiating power that results from an early negative commitment is likely to result from its damage to the influence that comes from legitimacy. Legitimacy depends upon both process and substance. As with an arbitrator, the legitimacy of a negotiator's decision depends upon having accorded the other side "due process." The persuasive power of my decision depends in part on my having fully heard your views, your suggestions, and your notions of what is fair before committing myself. And my decision will have increased persuasiveness for you to the extent that I am able to justify it by reference to objective standards of fairness that you have indicated you consider appropriate. That factor, again, urges me to withhold making any negative commitment until I fully understand your views on fairness. . . .

The Power of an Affirmative Commitment

Negative commitments are often made when no affirmative commitment is on the table. . . . To make a negative commitment either as to what we will not do or to impose harsh consequences unless the other side reaches agreement with us, without having previously made a firm and clear offer, substantially lessens our ability to exert influence. An offer may not be enough, but a threat is almost certainly not enough unless there is a "yesable" proposition on the table — a clear statement of the action desired and a commitment as to the favorable consequences which would follow.

CONCLUSION

This analysis of negotiating power suggests that in most cases it is a mistake to attempt to influence the other side by making a negative commitment of any kind . . . at the outset of the negotiations, and that it is a mistake to do so until one has first made the most of every other element of negotiating power.

This analysis also suggests that when as a last resort threats of other negative commitments are used, they should be so formulated as to complement and reinforce other elements of negotiating power, not undercut them. In particular, any statement to the effect that we have finally reached a take-it-or-leave-it position should be made in a way that is consistent with maintaining a good working relationship, and consistent with the concepts of legitimacy with which we are trying to persuade the other side. . . .

NOTE AND QUESTIONS

Getting to Yes is one of the world's best selling books and has been translated into every major language. Since its first publication in 1981, it has become the reference point for other writing on negotiation. Other writers either agree and expand on the concepts popularized by *Getting to Yes* or take issue with Fisher and Ury, as we have read in excerpts by James White and Roger Dawson. Roger Fisher has graciously responded to some of the criticisms of cooperative/principled negotiation by either conceding that *Getting to Yes* presents abbreviated concepts that need to be further expanded and specifically applied, or by elaborating on their principled theories and countering the criticisms.

1. Does the above essay by Professor Fisher on negotiating power depart from the principles of *Getting to Yes*? How is it consistent or inconsistent?
2. Does an affirmative commitment always create more power than a negative commitment or threat? When might threats be most effective? Are threats ever appropriate in negotiation? If so, when and under what circumstances?
3. Have you experienced or heard reports of threats that seemed irrational, but succeeded in getting the threatening party what they wanted?

NOTE: IRRATIONAL THREATS

The selections you have read are all premised on rational behavior to get what your client wants through negotiation. Expressed and implied threats can also be conveyed very powerfully when viewed as irrational. Nikita Khrushchev gained immense power when as premier of Russia, one of only two countries with a nuclear arsenal in the 1950s, he pounded his shoe on the table at the United Nations in an apparent fit of anger. An irrational, impulsive leader with his finger on the nuclear button had more power to get his way than a rational, restrained person, at least in the short run.

A commercial negotiator can exert persuasive power by threatening to end a negotiation where both sides will lose what they want, even if the result is irrational. The threat of going to trial over a small monetary dispute may seem irrational. However, if the commitment seems real and the means exist for the threat to proceed, the power of irrationality may prevail. The apparent irrationality may be explained by an absolute commitment to prevail, but it is no less effective. If in a game of "chicken" an opposing driver, headed toward you, removed his steering wheel and threw it out the window, would you get off the road? (See Schelling, 1960.)

Can you remember hearing about or experiencing irrational threats that helped the person threatening get what they wanted?

2. *Deadlines and Final Offers*

The well-known maxim that work expands to fill the time available applies to negotiation. Negotiations often continue until time runs out. As available time to conclude an agreement decreases, slow-moving or stalled negotiations seem to move toward closure. Concessions are offered and compromises are sometimes reached near the forced end of negotiations that would not be considered at the earlier stages. As Dawson noted in *Secrets of Power Negotiating*, quoted in Chapter 4, "the rule in negotiating is that 80 percent of the concessions occur in the last 20 percent of time available." More competitive negotiators will attempt to take advantage of any perceived need of the other side to conclude a deal, while hiding their own need for quick closure. However, creative solutions also materialize for more cooperative negotiators as available time comes to an end. Experienced cooperative negotiators will discuss their time constraints and agree on a deadline to conclude the negotiation.

The passage of time may be associated with costs or lost opportunities. Time is money in many situations. More often than not, both sides want to conclude an agreement as soon as practical. However, time and delay may be more costly for one side in a negotiation. An injured plaintiff may not be able to financially survive a protracted negotiation for payment of a claim, while the insurance company on the other side may benefit from delay if its claim reserves are earning interest. It is this type of asymmetrical time pressure that gives an advantage to one side and is subject to manipulation.

When it is to one party's favor to move to closure, particularly if they believe it is advantageous to prevent the other side from exploring other alternatives or opportunities, they will impose an accelerated deadline. The deadline may be linked to a concession or a desired sweetener in exchange for accelerating closure. ("Order now and receive a free set of 'Ginza' knives.") The deadline may be imposed to accept the entire last offer or end the negotiation. ("Accept this settlement amount by 5 p.m. or we go to trial.") This take-it-or-leave-it deadline proposal is referred to as an "exploding offer."

Deadlines can also be used to test if the other side is serious about settlement. Of course, any test can fail and the side imposing the deadline must be willing to live with the consequences. Consider the use of the bold and strategic deadline imposed by the plaintiff's attorney in a class action civil rights lawsuit brought by African American customers against Denny's restaurant chain.

GUY T. SAPERSTEIN, CIVIL WARRIOR: MEMOIRS OF A CIVIL RIGHTS ATTORNEY

384-386, Berkeley Hills Books (2003)

Tom Pfister showed up with the President of Denny's and began to present Denny's offer, as we sat and listened in our conference room. He explained what corrective action Denny's was willing to undertake, and, in some cases, had already undertaken. Much of that already was required under the agreement with the United States Department of Justice and we had no quarrel with the requirements of that agreement, except that it didn't go far enough. Then Tom addressed the damage issues, explaining that Denny's would donate $3 million to various civil rights groups. . . . I interrupted Tom before he finished, demanding, "Is that it? Is that all the money you're offering?" Tom said it was. So I said, "OK, I've heard enough," . . .

"You indicated Denny's is willing to donate $3 million to various civil rights groups. That is fine, but as far as I'm concerned, that is your client's charity. It has nothing to do with our lawsuit. We are not seeking charity, we are seeking damages for Denny's reprehensible behavior. You can give $3 million away to any group or groups you want, but you will get no credit from us for that. Frankly, I was astonished and angered at your money offer, as it bore no relation to the seriousness of our lawsuit. Your offer left me with the feeling that time spent in settlement negotiations with Denny's is time wasted. Therefore, I am going to tell you what Denny's has to do to maintain credibility with me. By 10 a.m. tomorrow morning, Denny's has to offer a *minimum* of $20 million to settle damage claims of the class. That $20 million offer which Denny's is going to make tomorrow morning will NOT settle this case. It is only Denny's down payment—a tangible expression of good faith that will allow Denny's to continue these discussions. In the end, Denny's will have to pay far more than $20 million to settle this case."

Tom and his cohort left the room. We went back to my office. The mood was heavy with gloom. No one said a word in support of what I had done; several attorneys quietly voiced negative opinions: "We overplayed our hand"; "They won't be back"; "It'll be a long time before we have settlement discussions again in this case." I responded, "We broke them today. Just watch."

I walked into the office the next morning around 9 a.m. Tom Pfister was sitting in our reception area, waiting for me. Tom, a former USC basketball player, and still trim and athletic, rose to his full height of about 6′ 3″, shook my hand, and said, "You've got your $20 million."

Negotiations in the above case continued until a settlement was reached that included the payment by Denny's of $54.4 million, reportedly the largest settlement in a public accommodations case in American history. This example also illustrates the power of commitment, the power of legitimacy, and the power of a good alternative, all explained by Roger Fisher in the previous selection. Guy Saperstein's power to successfully make this bold demand was enhanced by Denny's lawyers' awareness that Saperstein had tried and won a total of $250 million in a class action gender discrimination case against State Farm Insurance companies.

The following article explains the use of exploding offers and suggests a way to deal with them in select situations.

ROBERT J. ROBINSON, DEFUSING THE EXPLODING OFFER: THE FARPOINT GAMBIT

11 Negot. J. 277, 279-284 (1995)

WHY ARE EXPLODING OFFERS MADE?

It is not difficult to understand the thinking behind the use of exploding offers, in terms of the perceived advantage this affords the offeror. The ability to impose terms and back them up with a tight time limit may force the other side to capitulate or agree before it might otherwise have done so, increasing the value of the deal for the party making the offer. In many ways, the exploding offer is the ultimate hard bargaining tactic: Party A makes a final offer and then threateningly says, "And that's good until noon tomorrow. After that you can find another partner." In essence, the tactic defines an end to the negotiation process: An exploding offer is not only an offer in the traditional sense but is also the last offer. Rejection will automatically terminate the negotiation, and in some cases, the relationship as well. . . .

There is also another reason why the exploding offer is used. It can be a sign of offer weakness that might not be at all apparent to the recipient of the offer, but is almost always present. Negotiators who use exploding offers may perceive themselves to be at a disadvantage relative to their competitors. . . . Or they may have severe time or budget constraints. Once again, the function of the exploding offer can be either to force a quick acceptance by ending the negotiation (and thus avoiding the necessity of sweetening the deal to an unacceptably high level) or to restrict the ability of the recipient to comparison-shop, and therefore discover that the market was willing to pay at a significantly higher level.

DEALING WITH EXPLODING OFFERS: TRY BEING REASONABLE FIRST

In the tradition of *Getting to YES* (Fisher and Ury 1981), and *Getting Past No* (Ury 1991), there are a number of possibilities which exist for the individual faced with an exploding offer. Most of these involve getting away from positional stances, in order to explore underlying interests, and to look to create value via "principled negotiation" (Lax and Sebenius 1986). It is important to realize that exploding offers can be dealt with using these techniques, especially if there is some degree of goodwill in the interaction. An exploding offer is often made by a party who believes it stands to lose out in the negotiation, or is unsure of its power. Building trust and appealing to reason can go a long way toward addressing this underlying concern, resulting in the exploding aspect of the offer being withdrawn. . . .

The recipient of the exploding offer should also be prepared to make sensible counteroffers. He or she should be able to say when they *would* be in a position to accept, and to explain why this date makes sense (as opposed to choosing an equally arbitrary future time such as a week or ten days). . . . My first recommendation is, then, to engage in problem solving with respect to uncovering interests, generating and exploring options, moving to creative solutions, and emphasizing relationship issues. However, this can fail if the other party is unsympathetic, or locked into a positional or cynical stance. In such an instance, particularly if one feels that the other side is behaving in an ethically questionable fashion, I recommend the "Farpoint Gambit."

FIGHTING FIRE WITH FIRE: THE FARPOINT GAMBIT

While I always recommend first attempting a "principled" or integrative solution, I believe that when such tactics prove untenable, more assertive steps need to be taken. Doing this successfully depends on understanding where the power of the exploding offer resides. Exploding offers pivot on a credible, inviolable deadline. If the deadline is violated and the negotiation continues, the credibility of the explosion (the removal of the offer) is destroyed. And if the other side has depended on this threat as a central tactic, their entire position may collapse, putting the recipient of the initial offer in a very advantageous position. The technique I recommend, which I call the "Farpoint Gambit," is from the catalog of "hoist-them-by-their-own-petard" tools, which sometimes makes it particularly satisfying to employ.

The Farpoint Gambit derives from an episode of the science fiction television show, *Star Trek, the Next Generation*, in which the crew of the *Enterprise* (the spaceship from Earth) is put on trial by a powerful alien, "for the crimes of humanity." (The episode is called "*Encounter at Farpoint*," hence the name of the technique.) The alien creates a kangaroo court with himself as judge, and the captain of the *Enterprise* (Jean-Luc Picard), defends the human race. At a certain point, the alien judge becomes piqued by the captain's spirited defense, and says to the bailiff, "Bailiff, if the next word out of the defendant's mouth is anything but guilty, kill him!" He then turns to Picard and asks, "Defendant, how do you plead?" Picard thinks for a moment as the bailiff menacingly points a weapon at him, them firmly announces: "Guilty." As the courtroom gasps (and after an inevitable television commercial break), he adds, "Provisionally." This is essentially the Farpoint Gambit.

The alien has presented Picard with the ultimate coercive offer: Say you're guilty or I'll kill you. Obviously, Picard doesn't think he's guilty but he doesn't want to die. The power of the threat depends on getting Picard to admit that he's guilty—he does, but in such a way ("provisionally") that the alien judge is compelled to ask, "And what is the provision?" Picard then proceeds to talk his way out of the jam (as always happens with television heroes), and all is well. The point is that the alien is caught in his own trap: He's still arguing with Picard, who is still not guilty or dead. In the same way, an exploding offer can be defused by embracing it, using the Farpoint Gambit. . . .

The key is to make requests that are completely reasonable, but which will eventually result in the deadline being violated, due to the need for further clarification, or the lack of authority of the negotiator making the offer. Once the deadline passes, the credibility of the threat is destroyed, and successive attempts to set arbitrary deadlines can be dealt with in exactly the same way. The recipient of the offer can accept at his or her leisure, or reject the offer based on an unsatisfactory resolution of the provisions of the original acceptance.

The Farpoint Gambit also works by leveraging off fractures in the other side, or the imperfections in their informational strategies. . . . In such situations it is extremely easy to accept "pending satisfactory resolution of these issues," and then to continue to negotiate those and other issues.

The success of the Farpoint Gambit ultimately rests on the notion that the person receiving the exploding offer can eventually withdraw from the situation if no satisfactory resolution is forthcoming, without the offeror being able (or included) to sanction them for doing so. While this technique is about helping people get what they want from a coercive negotiating partner, it is not about helping people find a way to wriggle out of commitments given in good faith when they change their minds or get a better offer.

Inevitably, some negotiations, even those resuscitated by the Farpoint Gambit, are bound to fail. However, if conditions are attached to the acceptance — and these are not, by a reasonable assessment, met — then there really is not anything the company can do when the student withdraws, or the faculty candidate accepts an offer elsewhere, although possible reputational damage should still not be overlooked. It may be that each side has as much stake as the other, which will help to keep both reasonable — no organization wants to get the reputation for strong-arming prospective employees with techniques of dubious morality. In other cases, there may be actual legal provisions which allow the individual to withdraw within a specified time limit after accepting, such as in the case of signing an agreement to purchase a car.

The Farpoint Gambit has further advantage: It is nonescalative and non zero-sum in nature. Like the crew of the *Enterprise* in their endless quest for new frontiers, the Farpoint Gambit may force negotiators toward improved solutions at the "Pareto frontier" (see, e.g., Raiffa 1982). It moves the parties in the "right" direction, that is, toward one another rather than apart. In this sense, the Farpoint Gambit is not as dangerous as techniques that require one side to call the other's bluff, or see who can hold out the longest. In these latter cases, someone frequently wins, and someone loses. The Farpoint Gambit is about both sides being able to take care of underlying interests, and thus enable both to "win" and get what they want, with the offeror paying a fair price.

In Conclusion: When to Use — or Not Use — the Gambit

I would strongly caution against using the Farpoint Gambit as a routine technique to gain advantage. Nothing is more frustrating and unaccepting than someone who makes a habit of taking a deal, and who then continues to impose conditions or introduce new issues. Indeed, this is the flip side of the reprehensible lowballing technique employed by shady salespersons. In pondering this, I have come up with some guidelines for situations in which I believe it is legitimate to employ the Farpoint Gambit.

Ideally, I would make sure that all three of these conditions were present before I would feel completely comfortable in using this tactic:

- If the other side is perceived by the recipient of the exploding offer to be behaving unethically, and does not respond to appeals to reason;
- The recipient is truly interested in making a deal but needs more time to make a decision; and/or
- There genuinely are issues that need clarification, which would make the difference between accepting or rejecting the deal.

The Farpoint Gambit is a technique that should not be used lightly, in a spirit of deception, or with a lack of good faith. However, in situations where the individual is trapped by the hardball tactics of an offeror who relies on an exploding offer, the Farpoint Gambit offers a means whereby the pressure applied by the other side can be turned against them, much as a judo expert can use a foe's momentum to provide the energy which leads to the latter's own undoing. To be sure, this is itself a hardball tactic, and many might not feel comfortable using it. I offer the Farpoint Gambit as someone who has seen many friends, loved ones, and students put under enormous pressure, forced to make critical life decisions under unnecessarily difficult circumstances due to the callous use of power by people and institutions not operating in good faith.

NOTE: THE EFFECT OF SCARCITY AND DEADLINES

Moving to closure by imposing deadlines or making "exploding offers" may be a tactic in negotiation to take advantage of the effect of scarcity. The scarcity effect enhances the value of a desired item by making it appear less available or fleeting. We tend to pay more for something now if we believe it will not be available later. If something we want seems readily available, we tend to value it less and are less motivated to act decisively to obtain it. For example, a New Yorker may never visit the Statue of Liberty until she discovers she must move to the Midwest. The price of available Volkswagen convertibles was bid up when it was announced that no more would be made.

Scarcity is enhanced if we discover that others want what we want, particularly if the item is limited in quantity or unique. A common ploy to close a negotiation is to let it be known, directly or indirectly, that there is someone else interested in the deal if you do not accept it or that another offer is pending.

Introducing deadlines into a negotiation is a way to create a vanishing opportunity or scarcity. Deadlines may be imposed by one side in the form of a threat, or created by external factors (like the end of a tax year). Time limits or deadlines can also be agreed to between the negotiating parties. Mutually imposed deadlines help structure negotiations and ensure a finite conclusion. So deadlines can be used cooperatively in negotiations, as well as in a unilateral, threatening way. Of course, agreed-upon deadlines can be extended by agreement and unilateral deadlines may also be subject to negotiation.

3. Decision Tree Analysis

Moving toward closure by evaluating offers in light of probable BATNAs and making decisions about what is on the negotiation table may be aided by the use of decision tree analysis. Decision analysis provides a tool for making decisions in a rational, methodical, quantitative way, particularly in the face of uncertainty. Regularly taught in business schools to quantify strategic business choices, decision tree analysis has more recently been adopted within the legal community as an aid to decision making in complex litigation and in negotiations.

The first step in decision analysis is to convert a set of possible decisions into a graphic format: a decision tree graph. The decision tree displays possible decision choices and the probable consequences of each choice. The decision tree graph then leads to the next set of decision choices on a new limb of the tree and all of those probable outcomes. The decision maker works through the tree graph in sequence, one limb at a time, and makes decisions based on the most favorable probable outcomes expressed in quantitative sums. The process is both logical and intuitive.

When faced with a series of strategic choices, we intuitively go through a decision tree analysis in our head. For example, dealing with changes in the weather requires us to use a type of decision analysis on a daily basis. We listen to the weather report to know the probability of rain in order to make a decision about taking an umbrella. After knowing the percentage chance of rain, we then determine how far we have to walk in order to calculate the probable risk and degree of getting wet. Next we calculate the discomfort and damage depending on our attire. Each decision node is discounted or multiplied by the next to make a rational final choice. The higher the likelihood of rain, the less far the walk need be before deciding to carry an umbrella. The more casually we are dressed, the lower the need to take an umbrella.

Making decisions in litigation and business settings can become more complicated because of the number of choices, the number of possible consequences and their probability, and the impact of decisions at each stage on later choices. More than intuition may be needed to make a rational series of decisions and keep track of the probabilities along the way. Decision tree analysis can help with this task.

Decision tree analysis is also helpful because it requires that we and our clients write down all the explicit factors to be considered. This methodical process means we do not take mental shortcuts that leave out important points and considerations that should be factored into our clients' decisions. Going through a decision tree analysis with a client, in addition to promoting rationality, prevents misunderstandings and second guessing about strategic choices. The following example of a simple settle or go to trial evaluation illustrates the use of decision tree analysis in making decisions about reaching a settlement of pending litigation.

MARJORIE CORMAN AARON AND DAVID P. HOFFER, DECISION ANALYSIS AS A METHOD OF EVALUATING THE TRIAL ALTERNATIVE

In Golann, Mediating Legal Disputes, 312-317, Aspen (1996)

For legal disputes, decision analysis is used to value the parties' litigation alternatives—what will happen in litigation if the case does not settle. A decision tree used in litigation typically has two branches: *litigate* and *settle*. The settle branch may reflect the other side's most recent offer, or it may reflect the lawyer's estimate of what the adverse party might accept in settlement. The

litigate branch is generally an extended chance tree, whose branches represent
the different events that may transpire during litigation.

The following decision tree represents a situation in which a plaintiff must
decide whether to accept a settlement offer of $30,000 or proceed to trial with
a chance of recovering $100,000. Assume that you represent the plaintiff, with
whom you have a contingent fee arrangement in this lawsuit.

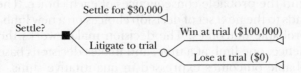

The plaintiff faces two choices—litigate or settle—which are represented by
branches emanating from the decision node at the left. If the plaintiff settles,
the inquiry is complete: he will get $30,000 and the dispute will be over. If he
chooses to litigate, there are two possible outcomes: win (a payoff of $100,000),
and lose (a payoff of $0). For the purposes of this example, all other uncer-
tainties associated with litigation have been ignored.

To make this decision intelligently, the plaintiff must assess how likely he is
to win if litigation is pursued. The $30,000 settlement offer may be inadequate
if the plaintiff has an excellent chance of winning $100,000. However, the offer
may be attractive if the chance is low.

Assume that, in the attorney's professional judgment, the plaintiff has a 60%
(.6) chance of winning at trial. This probability would be displayed beneath the
chance node labeled "win." Accordingly, it follows that a probability of 40% (.4)
would be displayed beneath the node labeled "lose."

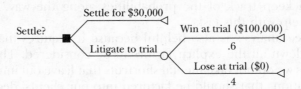

Litigation is apparently preferable to settlement (at least given the current
settlement offer) in this case because the probability of winning is more than
high enough to warrant gambling at trial. This evaluation is based on the
concept of *expected value* or *expected monetary value*. The expected value of a
node is defined as the sum of the products of the probabilities and the payoffs
of its branches.

In simple terms, the expected value of a course of action is the average value
of taking that course of action many times. If one were to try the identical case
one hundred times, and there is a 60% likelihood of a plaintiff's verdict,
approximately 60 trials would result in a plaintiff's verdict while 40 would
result in a defense verdict. The average recovery would be 60 victories multiplied by $100,000 per victory or $6,000,000, plus 40 losses multiplied by
$0 per loss, divided by 100 cases for an average recovery of $60,000. Thus,
the expected value associated with the litigate node is $60,000.

In this example, the plaintiff should not accept the settlement offer unless
other issues such as the need for immediate cash make immediate settlement

especially attractive, or unless the plaintiff simply cannot tolerate the risk of losing. However, the plaintiff should accept any settlement over $60,000. In reality, tolerance for risk and the value of current instead of future dollars would undoubtedly operate to make settlement a wise decision if the offer were "within range of" $60,000, albeit a bit lower . . .

It is important to remember that the outcome of any analysis is only as valuable as the input. One must consider carefully the numbers assigned to the range of predicted awards and associated costs at each terminal node. For example, where a party is paying for its attorney's time (not on a contingency fee), lower legal costs should be factored in at the terminal node where summary judgment is granted than at either the terminal nodes that follow trial. Depending on the level of precision required, one may design a rough-cut model, limiting the range of possibilities and making bold assumptions about damages. Or, one may develop a more refined tree, taking into account numerous possibilities (even if some have low probabilities) and assigning probabilities to different levels of damage awards.

Notwithstanding the inherent imprecision in assigning probabilities to events at trial, the process of designing a decision tree can itself assist in valuing litigation. Thinking through the hurdles to be surmounted in order to prevail can help each side organize its thinking. Furthermore, performing more advanced calculations . . . can identify those issues that have the greatest impact on case value, which can help focus negotiation strategy and research emphasis.

G. IMPASSE OR AGREEMENT

Once the negotiation has been moved toward closure through the use of power techniques or mutual assessment that what is on the table is better than no agreement, it is time to make decisions to conclude the negotiation. Specifics need to be agreed upon and the amounts to be paid or items exchanged must be decided. Small gaps or differences may still exist. Competitive negotiators may see this as the time to add new demands or conditions or test an opponent's resolve by threatening an impasse. More cooperative negotiations will see the need for joint problem solving and exploring the possibility of further improving the outcome for both sides. Several endgame moves or collaborative strategies are available to bring closure. When a basic agreement is reached, it may be advantageous for the participants, even if they have engaged in competitive negotiations to this point, to consider further trade-offs or timing issues that might enhance the interests of all.

1. Splitting the Difference and Dealing with Impasse

One deceptively simple concluding technique often used in both competitive and cooperative negotiations is "splitting the difference." The rationale for splitting the difference and a couple of caveats about agreeing to it are discussed in a book by Richard Shell under a category he refers to as "Softer Closing Tactics." Professor Shell also offers advice on what to do when the remaining gap causes the negotiation to reach impasse.

G. RICHARD SHELL, BARGAINING FOR ADVANTAGE: NEGOTIATION STRATEGIES FOR REASONABLE PEOPLE

189-195, Viking (1999)

... Perhaps the most frequently used closing technique is splitting the difference. Bargaining research tells us that the most likely settlement point in any given transaction is the midpoint between the two opening offers. People who instinctively prefer a compromise style like to cut through the whole bargaining process by getting the two opening numbers on the table and then splitting them right down the middle.

Even in cases in which the parties have gone through several rounds of bargaining, there often comes a time when one side or the other suggests that the parties meet halfway between their last position. In situations in which the relationship between the parties is important, this is a perfectly appropriate, smooth way to close.

Why is splitting the difference so popular? First, it appeals to our sense of fairness and reciprocity, thus, setting a good precedent for future dealings between the parties. ... Each side makes an equal concession simultaneously. What could be fairer than that?

Second, it is simple and easy to understand. It requires no elaborate justification or explanation. The other side sees exactly what you are doing.

Third, it is quick. For people who do not like to negotiate or are in a hurry, splitting the difference offers a way out of the potentially messy interpersonal conflict that looms whenever a negotiation occurs.

Splitting the difference is such a common closing tactic that it often seems rude and unreasonable to refuse, regardless of the situation. This is taking a good thing too far, however. There are at least two important situations in which I would hesitate to split the difference.

First, if you are in a pure Transaction situation, you should be careful that the midpoint being suggested is genuinely fair to your side. Experienced hagglers know that most deals end up halfway between the two opening offers, so they open aggressively. If you have opened at a reasonable price rather than an aggressive one, the midpoint is likely to favor the other party by a big margin. So don't split the difference at the end if there was a lack of balance at the beginning. Hold out for a fair price that achieves your goals.

A second time when splitting may be ill advised is in the early stages of Balanced Concerns bargaining. When a lot of money or an important principle is on the line and relationships matter, quick resort to a simple-minded closing gambit such as splitting may leave everyone worse off than necessary. It is nevertheless tempting to split because this tactic appears so transparently fair. ...

When the gap between offers is too wide to split, another friendly way to close is to obtain a neutral valuation or appraisal. ... If the parties cannot agree on a single appraiser, they can each pick one and agree to split the difference between the two numbers given by the experts.

WHAT HAPPENS IF NEGOTIATIONS BREAK DOWN?

The concession-making stage of bargaining sometimes ends with no deal rather than an agreement. The parties reach an impasse. In fact, a no deal result is sometimes the right answer. There are many reasons for bargaining breakdowns. In some cases, negotiators escalate their commitment to their prior positions and pride gets in the way of continuing with bargaining. . . .

In addition to escalation problems, sometimes the parties start too far apart to close the gap. Many times there are miscommunications, misunderstanding, and simple bad chemistry that the parties fail to overcome. Now what?

Accommodating people usually think that impasse is a bad thing. After all, people tend to get emotional when there is a bargaining breakdown, and interpersonal conflict usually bothers accommodators and avoiders.

But the truth is otherwise: Impasse can often be helpful. A Break in the negotiation causes parties to seriously reevaluate their expectations. They can return with clearer priorities and new solutions. And, as discussed above, walkouts are useful ways of signaling the issues of critical importance. Far from being anyone's fault, one party sometimes plans an impasse as part of its opening strategy — regardless of what the other side does.

That said, what can you do to get negotiations restarted once impasse occurs? I will touch on a few techniques below that I think work well.

JUMP-STARTING THE NEGOTIATION PROCESS

Perhaps the easiest way to overcome impasse is to leave yourself a back door through which to return to the table when you get up to leave it. "In light of the position you have taken," you might say as you pack your bags, "we are unable to continue negotiations at this time." An attentive opponent will pick up on your use of the words "at this time" and tactfully ask you later if the time has come to reinitiate talks. This back door also allows you to contact the other side at a later date without losing face.

If the other negotiator leaves in a genuine fit of anger, he may not be very careful about leaving a back door open. If so, you should consider how you can let him back in without unnecessary loss of face. You must, in one expert's phrase, build him a "golden bridge" across which to return to the table. Such bridges include "forgetting" that he made his ultimatum in the first place or recalling his last statement in a way that gives him an excuse for returning.

When miscommunication is the problem, a simple apology may be enough to get the parties back on track. If the relationship has deteriorated beyond apologies, changing negotiators or getting rid of intermediaries altogether may be necessary.

In America, the sport of professional baseball lost nearly two full seasons in the 1990s because of an impasse in negotiations between the players' union and the club owners. The team owners from the big cities wanted to limit the size of team payrolls. The team owners from smaller cities wanted the team owners from big cities to subsidize their franchises. The players wanted more money. It was a three-ring circus. The breakthrough came when the owners hired a new negotiator — a lawyer named Randy Levine — to represent them at the table. Levine acted in the role of mediator as much as advocate and brought a high degree of both credibility and creativity to the process that, according to one participant, "broke the dam of mistrust" that had built up between the parties. Another move that helped move the talks beyond impasse was getting all parties to agree to stop talking to the press and taking public positions that made it hard for them to compromise at the table. . . . [P]ublic commitments can help you stick to your goals, but there comes a time when it is in everyone's interest to get unstuck from their positions. In a high stakes negotiation such as a labor strike, this often means getting the parties out of the spotlight so they can work in private.

The worst impasses are the products of emotional escalation that builds on itself: My anger makes you angry, and your response makes me even angrier. . . . When people begin to fight over something, they tend to lose sight of the real issues. A deal is possible, but no one can make a move without losing face. What are the parties to do?

The solution to this sort of collision, in business deals as well as wars, is what I call the "one small step" procedure. One side needs to make a very small, visible move in the other side's direction, then wait for reciprocation. If the other party responds, the two can repeat the cycle again, and so on. Commentator Charles Osgood, writing about the Cold War in the early 1960s, created an acronym for this process: GRIT (Graduated and Reciprocated Initiatives in Tension Reduction).

Egypt's late prime minister, Anwar Sadat, used the "one small step" technique to deescalate the Arab-Israeli conflict when he flew to Jerusalem on November 19, 1977 and later met with Prime Minister Menachem Begin. By simply getting off a plane in Israel—a very small step indeed—Sadat demonstrated his willingness to recognize Israel's existence. This move eventually led to the Camp David peace accords and Israel's return of the Sinai Peninsula to Egypt.

An executive once told me a bargaining story that nicely sums up how the "one small step" process can work in everyday life. Two parties were in a complex business negotiation. Both were convinced that they had leverage, and both thought that the best arguments favored their own view of the deal. After a few rounds, neither side would make a move.

Finally one of the women at the table reached in her purse and pulled out a bag of M&M's. She opened the bag and poured the M&M's into a pile in the middle of the table.

"What are those for?" asked her counterparts.

"They are to keep score," she said.

Then she announced a small concession on the deal—and pulled an M&M out of the pile and put it on her side of the table.

"Now it's your turn," she said to the men sitting opposite.

Not to be outdone, her opponents put their heads together, came up with a concession of their own—and pulled out two M&M's. "Our concession was bigger than yours," they said.

The instigator of the process wisely let the other side win this little argument and then made another concession of her own, taking another M&M for herself.

It wasn't long before the parties were working closely together to close the final terms of the deal. Call this the M&M version of the GRIT process. Any similar mechanism that restarts the norm of reciprocity within the bargaining relationship will have a similar, helpful effect. Overall, when parties reach an impasse, it is usually because each sees the other's demands as leaving it below its legitimate expectations. Eventually, if the parties are to make any progress, they must change their frame of reference and begin seeing that they will be worse off with no deal than they would be accepting a deal that falls below their original expectations.

Sometimes this transition takes time. The impasse must be allowed to last long enough that one or both parties actually alter their expectations. A final agreement must be seen as a gain compared with available alternatives.

QUESTIONS

1. Have you ever "split the difference" in order to conclude a negotiation or sale? Looking back, was that the best way to close the deal? Are you now sure you were not manipulated into an outcome or price that was more favorable to the other side? Have you used this closing tactic to your advantage?
2. Do you agree with Shell that impasse can often be helpful? If so, when? Why would anyone plan an impasse as part of their negotiating strategy?
3. How might an apology get a negotiation back on track following an impasse? When is an apology most likely to be effective in moving stuck negotiations toward closure? Is an apology necessarily an admission of fault or responsibility? Can an apology be stated in a sincere way that rewards taking responsibility? If so, how can the apology be phrased? For a helpful and interesting discussion of the use of apology in negotiation and mediation, as well as the evidentiary use and protection of apologies, see O'Hara and Yarn (2002); see also Luskin and Curtis (2000) and Cohen (2000). See also our note in Chapter 10 on Apology and Mediation.

2.   *Packaging and Logrolling*

You should now be familiar with the concept that value is created through negotiation when what is received in trade is worth more to the recipient than to the provider. Differences in the value that negotiators place on multiple items or promises allow for integrated solutions that result in mutually beneficial agreements. You should also understand that the difference between overlapping reservation points, or "bottom lines," of negotiators creates a bargaining zone within which agreement is likely. Russell Korobkin, in the following selection, combines these concepts to explain how packaging, adding or subtracting items from the deal, and logrolling can expand the bargaining zone and help negotiators reach agreement. Although these practices are most often associated with problem-solving negotiation, packaging, trade-offs, and logrolling are frequently utilized by competitive negotiators at the end of the day. Effective negotiators, regardless of their general approach, will do what it takes to reach a settlement or complete a deal.

RUSSELL KOROBKIN, NEGOTIATION THEORY AND STRATEGY

130-133, Aspen (2002)

ADDING TO AND SUBTRACTING ISSUES FROM THE NEGOTIATION "PACKAGE"

Many negotiators enter a bargaining situation believing the subject of the negotiation is fixed. When Horace discusses with Sally the possibility of buying a Studebaker, both parties are likely to identify the subject of the negotiation as "Studebaker," with the only issue being how much money Horace will pay for it. When a plaintiff and defendant sit down to discuss settlement, both might define the subject of the negotiation as a release from liability issued by the plaintiff, with the only issue being how much the defendant will pay for this item. Negotiators with such a narrow view will miss out on opportunities to identify integrative solutions, because they fail to consider that the subject of the negotiation—or the "package" of items that will be transferred from seller to buyer if the negotiation succeeds—can be altered to the parties' mutual advantage.

Negotiators expand the bargaining zone by adding or subtracting issues from what they initially perceive to be the negotiation package. In the case of Horace and Sally, the bargaining zone was expanded when the negotiators added the issue of a warranty to what began as a negotiation over the issue of a Studebaker. Horace and Sally had opposing interests. Horace wanted to pay less money for the car, Sally wanted Horace to pay more money. Horace wanted a warranty, Sally preferred not to provide a warranty. But, importantly, Horace placed a relatively higher value on the warranty than did Sally, so adding the issue of the warranty to the negotiation package expanded the bargaining zone (and thus the cooperative surplus that could be created by the two ultimately striking a bargain) by increasing Horace's reservation price more than Sally's. If Sally and Horace had limited their view of what was included in the negotiation package to the Studebaker, they may have been able to divide the cooperative surplus that existed because Horace valued the car more than Sally did, but they would have missed out on the opportunity to expand the bargaining zone and increase the cooperative surplus created by their agreement.

Three additional points bear mentioning. First . . . adding an issue will only expand the bargaining zone when that issue is valued more by the buyer than by the seller. If Horace valued the warranty at only $100, and it would cost Sally $300 to provide the warranty, adding the issue of the warranty to the negotiation package would have had the opposite effect of reducing the bargaining zone.

Second, adding issues is an effective strategy when the parties have common interests, just as it is when the parties have opposing interests but differences in their preference structure. Recall the example of the home buyer who wanted the lovely chandelier and the seller who wanted to leave the chandelier with the house so as not to have to transport it. Assuming that the usual house transaction does not include chandeliers, by adding the chandelier to the negotiation package the parties could increase the bargaining zone by raising the buyer's reservation price and lowering the seller's.

Third, it is often the case that even more value can be created when the negotiators add more than one issue to a negotiation. Perhaps in addition to valuing a warranty more than it would cost Sally to provide one, Horace would find it extremely convenient to have the car delivered to his residence in the next town, and doing so would be only marginally inconvenient to Sally. By adding both issues to the negotiation, Horace's reservation price would increase by a much larger amount than it would if only one of the issues were added, while Sally's reservation price would increase by less than Horace's, making the bargaining zone larger than it otherwise would be. By merely taking time to consider what issues could be added to the negotiation package that the buyer would value more than the seller, negotiators can substantially improve their ability to find integrative solutions to bargaining problems.

It is reasonably intuitive for negotiators to think about adding issues of differential value to the parties as a way of creating value. It is less intuitive, but equally useful, for negotiators to think about how they can create value by subtracting issues. In general, subtracting issues creates value for the negotiators when a component of the package being negotiated is more valuable to the party that currently possesses it than to the other party. For example, perhaps Sally had advertised the Studebaker for sale with a car cover to protect it from the elements. If Horace has a garage for the car and Sally has other customers who would purchase the cover from her, it is possible than the cover is worth more to Sally than to Horace. In this case, the parties can create value by subtracting the cover from the bargain. With the cover subtracted, Horace's reservation price will decrease less than Sally's thus increasing the size of the bargaining zone.

Successful integrative negotiators can envision how apparently indivisible items can in fact be divided and unbundled so that value can be created by subtracting issues. To slightly alter the famous story recounted by Lax & Sebenius, suppose that Sister A is negotiating to purchase an orange from Sister B. Both place approximately the same value on the orange, so it is uncertain whether any bargain will be possible. Because the only issue under consideration is a single orange, it initially appears that there is nothing to subtract from the negotiation package without leaving the package completely empty. On further investigation, however, this analysis proves to be false. Suppose that Sister A wants the orange only to eat the fruit. Sister B is somewhat less enamored with the fruit, but she also wishes to use the peel to bake a cake. If the sisters redefine the subject of their bargain from "the orange" to "the fruit from the orange," Sister B's reservation price will fall while Sister A's remains approximately the same, insuring that a bargaining zone exists. In other words, value is created by dividing the issue of "orange" into two issues, "fruit" and "peel," and then subtracting the issue of "peel," which the seller values more than does the buyer, from the negotiation package.

To use another example, if Bonnie sues Clyde, a settlement need not necessarily be viewed as a single, indivisible item. Bonnie might have two or more causes of action. If she believes she is likely to prevail on the first, but not on the second, while Clyde thinks she might prevail on the second, but not on the first, their different predictions might form the basis of a negotiated agreement of the second cause of action. Essentially, value can be created by unbundling the claims and subtracting the first from the negotiation package.

LOGROLLING

"Logrolling" is a term often used to describe the practice of two or more legislators trading votes on bills that are of little importance to them in return for votes on bills that are very important to them. For example, a legislator from a rural district might agree to vote for a public transportation bill in return for a legislator from an urban district agreeing to vote for a farm subsidy bill. Logrolling creates value, because both legislators are much better off if both bills pass than if neither passes. The rural legislator strongly favors the farm bill and only moderately opposes the transportation bill, while the urban legislator strongly favors the transportation bill and only moderately opposes the farm bill. The concept is useful in thinking about how to create value in all types of bargaining situations, not just in negotiations between politicians. Conceptually, logrolling is just a slightly different perspective on the strategy of adding and subtracting issues. Many examples of successful integrative bargaining can be viewed through either conceptual framework. The negotiation between Sally and Horace can be understood as adding an issue (the warranty) that the buyer valued more than the seller, thus expanding the bargaining zone. Alternatively, it could be understood as an example of logrolling in which Sally traded the item of relatively more value to Horace (warranty) for something of relatively more value to Sally (a higher price for the car).

In practice, it is probably useful to think in terms of adding and subtracting issues when the negotiation package is open ended and malleable, and to think in terms of logrolling when the negotiation package contains multiple items that appear fairly well fixed. For example, if you are negotiating to buy a car, it is more useful to enter the negotiations thinking about how you might add issues of more value to the buyer and subtract issues of more value to the seller. If you are negotiating a property settlement between divorcing spouses who own a well-identified collection of assets, it might be more useful to think in terms of logrolling. For example, the wife gives the husband the motorcycle, which he loved to race, and the husband gives the wife the boat, because she loves to water ski. This trade would likely create more value than if the husband and wife randomly divided their possessions or used some other method of splitting them that did not take into account their different preferences.

Even when logrolling is a useful conceptual framework, however, it is important to remember that the set of relevant issues is rarely fixed and to consider carefully whether an even more integrative agreement could be designed by adding issues to or subtracting issues from the negotiation package. For example, we can conceptualize the divorce as the wife "buying" a divorce agreement from the husband (or vice versa) in return for relinquishing her claim to some jointly held assets. If the husband is handy and can maintain the boat with little trouble, and this would provide more value to the wife than would keeping the motorcycle, value can be created by adding the issue of "boat maintenance" to the package of goods the wife is bargaining to buy from the husband and subtracting the issue of "motorcycle."

H. FINALIZING AND WRITING THE AGREEMENT

After decisions are made about how the case will be settled or the deal will be structured, the work of the lawyer is not complete. The relief felt in reaching an agreement can induce negotiators to neglect the important task of how the agreement will be worded and how the remaining details will be determined. Issues of implementation and execution may remain to be determined. The old maxim that "the devil is in the details" is a warning to be heeded. A lack of clarity about the terms of the agreement can result in perceptual differences about what was decided and the unraveling of the agreement. Inattention to how the agreement is written can also put your client's interests at risk of intentional overreaching by the other side or unintentional differences of interpretation that do not favor your client. Not memorializing the agreement in writing as quickly as possible can lead to unnecessary expenses if more time is required to reconstruct exactly what was agreed or if legal uncertainty develops about the outcome. If you did well negotiating, the favorable result for your client can lead to buyer's remorse causing the other side to look for ways to change the nonfinalized terms or reject the not yet enforceable agreement.

A negotiated transaction is usually memorialized in the form of a written contract that incorporates the terms of the deal and follows general contract principals. An agreement to settle a claim or court case may have different characteristics and requirements. A release of claims, a dismissal or other disposition of the underlying lawsuit, enforceability by entry of judgment or liquidated damages, how and when money will be paid or performance of obligations will occur, costs, expenses, and tax aspects — all of these issues must be considered when writing an agreement to settle a lawsuit. Ambiguities must be avoided; a settlement document is written to resolve an existing dispute, not foster a future one.

It is also important to attend to the psychological and relationship aspects of closing the deal. Never celebrate a victory in the presence of an opponent. If you can leave the other side convinced they did well, there will be fewer questions regarding implementation of the agreement. The relationship is also strengthened if no one feels they were bested and if clients on both sides have reason to think they were well represented. (It is for this reason that a good negotiator on the other side will not give you an honest critique or tell you that you could have done better.) Even if the parties will not have an ongoing relationship, the attorneys may have future professional contact. There is value in the rapport that carries forward to future negotiations and great cost if an opponent feels compelled to "get even" at the next opportunity.

Both relationship and legal practicality issues involved in finalizing negotiated agreement, whether transactional or settlement, are addressed in the next selection. Then the following reading discusses the content and requirements for a written settlement of a case, including structured settlements.

CHARLES B. CRAVER, EFFECTIVE LEGAL NEGOTIATION AND SETTLEMENT, 4TH EDITION

212-218, Lexis (2001)

LEAVE OPPONENT WITH SENSE THEY GOT GOOD DEAL

As the overall terms are being finalized, negotiators should remember how important it is to leave their opponents with the feeling they got a good deal. If their adversaries are left with a good impression, they will be more likely to honor the accord and more likely to behave cooperatively when the parties interact in the future. Some advocates attempt to accomplish this objectively by making the final concession on a matter they do not highly value. Even a minimal position change at this point is likely to be appreciated by the other side. Others try to do it by congratulating their opponents on the mutually beneficial agreement achieved. Individuals must be careful, however, not to be too effusive. When negotiators lavish praise on their opponents at the conclusion of bargaining interactions, those individuals tend to become suspicious and think they got a poor deal.

TAKE TIME TO REVIEW AGREEMENT

When bargaining interactions are successfully concluded, many participants are anxious to terminate their sessions and return to other client matters. As a result, they fail to ensure a clear meeting of the minds. If both sides are not in complete agreement, subsequent misunderstandings may negate their bargaining efforts. To avoid later disagreements, the participants should take the time to review the specific terms agreed upon before they adjourn their discussions. In most instances they will encounter no difficulties and will merely reaffirm the provisions they have achieved.

ENDEAVOR TO DRAFT FINAL AGREEMENT

Once the Competitive/Distributive, Closing, and Cooperative/Integrative Stages have been completed and a final accord has been achieved, many negotiators are readily willing to permit opposing counsel to prepare the settlement agreement. While this may save them time and effort, it is a risky practice. It is unlikely that they and the opponent would employ identical language to memorialize the specific terms agreed upon. Each would probably use slightly different terminology to represent his or her own perception of the matter. To ensure that their client's particular interests are optimally protected, bargainers should always try to be the one to draft the operative document.

No competent attorney would ever contemplate the omission of terms actually agreed upon or the inclusion of items not covered by the parties' oral understanding. Either practice would be wholly unethical and would constitute fraud. Such disreputable behavior could subject the responsible practitioner and his or her client to substantial liability and untoward legal problems. Why then should lawyers insist upon the right to prepare the final accord? It is to allow them to draft a document that unambiguously reflects their perception of the overall agreement achieved by the parties.

Each provision should be carefully prepared to state precisely what the drafting party thinks was mutually agreed upon. When the resulting contract is then presented to the other party for execution, it is quite likely that it would be reluctant to propose alternative language, unless serious questions regarding the content of particular clauses were raised. Doubts tend to be resolved in favor of the proffered document. This approach best ensures that the final contract will most effectively protect the interests of the party who drafted it.

REVIEW OPPONENT'S DRAFT CAREFULLY

If negotiators are unable to prepare the ultimate agreement, they should be certain to review the terms of the document drafted by the other side before they permit their client to execute it. They should compare each provision with their notes and recollections of the interaction, to be positive that their understanding of the bargaining results is accurately represented. They should be certain that nothing agreed upon has been omitted and that nothing not agreed upon has been included. If drafters suggest that certain new terms are mere "boilerplate," reviewers should make sure those terms do not alter the fundamental substantive or procedural aspects of their agreement.

UNABASHED QUESTIONING OF DRAFTS

Agreement reviewers should not hesitate to question seemingly equivocal language that may cause future interpretive difficulties or challenge phrases that do not appear to describe precisely what they think was intended by the contracting parties. Since practitioners now use word processors to draft contractual documents, it is easy to accommodate additions, deletions, or modification. Bargainers should never permit opponents to make them feel guilty about changes they think should be made in finally prepared agreements. It is always appropriate for non-drafting parties to be certain that the final language truly reflects what has been achieved through the negotiation process. If the other side repeatedly objects to proposed modifications because of the additional work involved, the participant suggesting the necessary alterations can quickly and effectively silence those protestations by offering to accept responsibility for the final stages of the drafting process. It is amazing how expeditiously these remonstrations cease when such an easy solution to the problem is suggested!

TACT IN QUESTIONING

When negotiators reviewing draft agreements discover apparent discrepancies, they should contact their opponents and politely question the pertinent language. They should not assume deliberate opponent deception. It is always possible that the persons challenging the prepared terminology are mistaken and that the proposed terms actually reflect what was agreed upon. The reviewers may have forgotten modifications quickly accepted near the conclusion of the negotiation process. It is also possible that the drafting parties made honest mistakes that they would be happy to correct once they have examined their notes of the bargaining interaction. Even when document reviewers suspect intentional deception by drafting parties, they should still provide their opponents with a face-saving way out of the predicament. The best way to accomplish the desired result is to assume honest mistakes and give the drafters the opportunity to "correct" the erroneous provisions. If reviewers directly challenged opponent integrity, the dispute would probably escalate and endanger the entire accord.

VIGILANCE AGAINST UNDERHANDED TACTICS

In recent years, a few unscrupulous practitioners in the corporate area have decided to take advantage of the drafting stage of large documents to obtain benefits not attained during the negotiation process. They include provisions that were never agreed upon, or modify or omit terms that were jointly accepted. They attempt to accomplish their deceptive objective by providing their opponents with copies of the agreement at the eleventh hour, hoping that time pressure will induce their unsuspecting adversaries to review the final draft in a cursory manner. Lawyers who encounter this tactic should examine each clause of the draft agreement with care to be certain it represents the actual accord achieved. If necessary, they should completely redraft the improper provisions. If their proposed terms are rejected by opposing counsel, they should insist upon a session with the clients present to determine which draft represents the true intentions of the parties. When this type of meeting is proposed, deceitful drafters are likely to "correct" the "inadvertent misunderstandings" before the clients ever get together. If a client session were to occur and the other side enthusiastically supported the deceptive drafting practices of their attorneys, it would be appropriate for the deceived lawyers to recommend that their client do business with another party.

ADDRESSING UNFORESEEN AMBIGUITIES AND PROBLEMS

On some occasions, ambiguities or actual disagreements may be discerned during this stage. Negotiators should not allow these difficulties to destroy their previous progress. When good faith misunderstandings are found, the advocates should strive to resolve them before they terminate their current interaction. At the conclusion of the Closing or the Cooperative/Integrative Stage, the parties tend to be in a particularly accommodating frame of mind. They feel good about their bargaining achievements and are psychologically committed to a final accord. It is thus a propitious time to address newly discovered problems. If they do not deal with these issues now, they are likely to encounter greater difficulties when these questions arise at a later date.

WRITING AND SIGNING ITEMS AS SAFEGUARD

A few unscrupulous negotiators attempt to obtain a tactical advantage by deliberately creating "misunderstandings" as final agreements are being drafted. They hope to extract additional concessions from unsuspecting opponents as these seeming ambiguities are being resolved. Individuals who suspect that their adversaries may employ this tactic should insist on a careful review of the basic terms at the conclusion of the bargaining process. They should write out these items and have their opponents sign the draft to indicate their concurrence. This practice makes it difficult for adversaries to later create disingenuous "misunderstandings" that can be used to obtain unreciprocated benefits for their own side.

LYNCH, YOUNG, TAYLOR, PURVER, AND DAVIS, CALIFORNIA NEGOTIATION AND SETTLEMENT HANDBOOK, THE SETTLEMENT AGREEMENT*
Chapter 11, 5-12, 28-31, Bancroft-Whitney (1991)

A "GOOD" SETTLEMENT AGREEMENT

Often a negotiated settlement (usually an amount of money) triggers another set of negotiations, this time over the formal terms of the settlement agreement itself. Expect these additional negotiations, since a good settlement agreement must contain explicit terms for resolving competing claims, and thus must avoid vague or ambiguous language and unnecessary contingencies. If a contingency must be included in the agreement, take care to minimize risk of forfeiture. Terms should leave little to later interpretation.

Drafting an agreement is one of the most important steps in negotiating a settlement. A successful agreement reflects counsel's understanding of the client's needs and the strength of counsel's relationship with the client. In many ways, the client's future interests — to the extent the client has made

* Reprinted from California Negotiation Handbook with permission. Copyright 1991 Matthew Bender & Company, Inc., a member of the LexisNexis Group.

them known to counsel — depends on how carefully counsel drafts (or reviews) the settlement terms. . . .

RELEASE OF CLAIMS

The settlement agreement resolves the legal dispute between parties. Thus, the agreement should contain a clause mutually releasing parties from future legal claims, either in general or relating specifically to the present controversy. The release-of-claims clause can be broad or narrow, depending on the case, but every settlement agreement should contain some form of it. . . . In tort cases, the release clause usually releases defendant tortfeasor from all future claims by the injured party (and the party's heirs). It may release defendant from claims arising out of circumstances of the case, or more generally from all claims arising before the settlement date. If counsel represents a tortfeasor, it is essential to obtain such a release in the settlement document — otherwise the client could be exposed to future liability. Try to get the broadest release possible. Conversely, if counsel represents plaintiff, especially in a personal injury context where the full extent of injury and complications may not be known, try to grant the narrowest release possible so that damages not known at the time of settlement may be sought later, if necessary. . . .

A tortfeasor nearly always wants to establish that settling the case is not an admission of liability which could be used in actions by other parties. (This is a common feature, for example, in product liability settlements.) If terms of the settlement are beneficial to claimant, this type of release usually poses no problem.

In settlement agreements between businesses, it may not be desirable to release the other party from all claims arising before a certain date, since the business relationship may have ongoing problems and conflicts, and some future claims may not yet be apparent. A blanket release may not take into account realities of the continuing relationship, and so it may be better (if possible) to use a limited release.

TAX CONSIDERATIONS

Tax consequences of a settlement can affect all parties. For example, IRC §1 04(a)(2) provides that tort damages "on account of" personal injuries or sickness are not included in gross income. This exclusion extends equally to benefits received by suit or by agreement. It does not matter if money is received in a lump sum or in periodic payments. "Personal injuries" are not limited to injuries to the body — other tortious infringements of personal rights can qualify as well.

Tax consequences affect settlement of business disputes as well. For example, compensation for injury to capital is tax-free to the extent of the tax basis in the capital, but any excess will be treated as capital gain. ("Capital" in this context can include goodwill and other intangible interests.) Compensation for lost profits is fully taxable, as the profits themselves would have been.

Tax laws change often, and theft effect is often determined by fact-specific factors best analyzed by a tax expert. When in doubt, therefore, consult someone who can determine the tax consequences of a proposed settlement and (if necessary or advisable) recommend alternative proposals. . . .

LUMP-SUM SETTLEMENTS

The lump sum is the simplest and most common type of money settlement. Parties exchange legal claims for cash payments, and defendant is generally released from all claims in return. The advantages of this type of agreement are simplicity and finality. There is no need to monitor the continuing performance of parties or to obtain guarantees. All claims merge in the agreement. Parties no longer have to deal with each other and the matter is concluded.

STRUCTURED SETTLEMENTS — OVERVIEW

In a structured settlement, the amount recovered by plaintiff is paid over time in installments. Defendant funds payments by purchasing an annuity or bond, or by establishing a trust from which plaintiff receives periodic payments. . . .

A structured settlement may involve fixed payments for life, but the structure can be tailored to meet a variety of circumstances. Structured settlements are commonly used where damages are substantial or otherwise difficult to meet in one lump-sum payment, and in cases of catastrophic injury. . . .

ADVANTAGES AND DISADVANTAGES OF STRUCTURED SETTLEMENTS

Plaintiff benefits from a structured settlement because:

* Total amount of settlement may be greater than might otherwise be possible, since defendant is not forced to pay all at once;
* Stream of income is guaranteed; and
* If damages are for personal injury, payments received by plaintiff are not taxable as income.

Defendant benefits from a structured settlement because:

* Total payment can be spread over time;
* Defendant (or the insurer) has the use of unpaid money for a longer period of time; and
* If settlement is funded by an annuity, the up-front cost is less.

The principal disadvantages of a structured settlement flow to plaintiff who may prefer instead to invest money received from a lump-sum payment, rather than have the money invested for plaintiff by another party. Additionally, if plaintiff dies prior to payment of all benefits, the carrier generally inherits the remainder of the annuity, although payment to plaintiff can be guaranteed.

Contents of Settlement Agreement

In essence, a settlement agreement exchanges the release of a claim (on the part of plaintiff) for an undertaking (on the part of defendant). The settlement agreement is in the nature of a contract, and should be drafted according to contract principles.

Strictly speaking, several varieties of agreements may be utilized to resolve disputes, including accord and satisfaction, compromise and settlement, release, and novation. . . . In the present context, the word "settlement" is used in a broad sense and includes any consensual resolution of a dispute.

Ordinarily, a settlement agreement should include the following elements (though not necessarily in this order):

1. Identities and definitions. Recite identities of all parties to the agreement, including whether any party is acting in a representative or fiduciary capacity. Mention (if true) that each party is represented by counsel, and name the counsel. Recite authority of corporate officers to bind their corporations. Define any words used in a specialized or fact-specific sense.
2. Description of dispute. State the nature of the dispute, with sufficient specificity and reference to actual events to prevent misunderstanding. At a minimum, include a summary description of the dispute and reference to the case number (if an action has been filed). In some cases, a detailed description of the events at issue may be required.
3. Claims released. Define claims released by each party. It is customary to state that the release binds agents, representatives, heirs, assigns, and successors in interest. If a contract is involved, and settlement liquidates obligations under the contract, include a clause rescinding the contract by mutual consent and declaring it to have no more effect than if it had never existed.
4. Obligations and undertakings. Specify the obligations as assumed by each party, including any undertakings of confidentiality, undertakings to forbear from litigation and, if appropriate, full details of time, place, and manner of payment of money or other performance. Plaintiffs undertaking to file a dismissal with prejudice should be made explicit.
5. Consideration. State the consideration for each release and obligation, and an explicit acknowledgement of the mutuality of consideration and of its receipt. The technical requirements of various types of settlement should be recited as well — for example, in an accord and satisfaction, that tender of money is conditional on its acceptance in full discharge of the obligation.
6. Apportionment. A recital identifying which payments are for which claims may have important tax and insurance consequences. Recovery for some claims is tax-free to plaintiffs; also, it may be deductible by defendant. Much depends on what parties in their compromise agree payments are for. Similarly, given a choice, most defendants would prefer their payments to be for claims (e.g., negligence) for which their insurers must indemnify them. . . .
7. Disclaimer of liability. This purpose is served by a clause stating that the compromise is not an admission of liability of claims advanced.
8. Technical disposition of the litigation. The release should direct and authorize counsel for settling parties to do what is necessary to accomplish

procedural objectives. This usually means an agreement that the case be dismissed (i.e., that a request for dismissal be executed by plaintiff and filed by either party), but may include such things as an agreement that judgment be entered against a party on specified terms, an agreement not to oppose a motion for summary judgment or for judgment on the pleadings as to certain causes of action or defenses, and the like.

9. Disposition of any future litigation affected by the agreement. What exactly does the agreement bar? Is there a covenant not to sue? (If so, it should include a clause stating that the agreement may be pleaded as a defense and bar to future actions.) Perhaps most importantly, what claims merge in the agreement? Does it cover all claims between the parties, or all claims arising from certain circumstances, or all claims arising before a certain date, or all claims known before a certain date?

   Are concurrent actions affected? This portion of the agreement requires careful thought, care in drafting, and close collaboration with the client, whose special knowledge of circumstances can avoid costly errors in the merger clause. Where jurisdiction over further disputes (or venue, where jurisdiction is clear) may be an issue, one of the parties may wish to specify where such disputes will be litigated. Alternatively, a statement regarding where the agreement was negotiated and the law applicable to its terms may be inserted.

10. Enumeration of all contingencies. This is particularly important where performance of any portion of the settlement agreement is subject to prior satisfaction of another condition. It is sometimes useful to include a liquidated damages clause covering breach of obligations under the agreement. Such a clause might state that breach of the settlement agreement will constitute immediate and irreparable damage warranting equitable relief, including but not limited to specific performance.

11. Collateral items. These include responsibility for attorney fees, prejudgment interest, provision for payment in installments, and any other items which form part of the agreement.

12. Formal recitals such as an integration clause, a warranty of nonassignment of claims, a severability clause, a choice-of-law provision, a recital of joint preparation, a provision for counter part execution, a provision establishing jurisdiction and venue for any litigation for breach of the agreement, and so forth.

NOTE: RATIFICATION, BUY-IN, AND SINGLE TEXT AGREEMENTS

There are many situations where final authority to sign the agreement rests with someone not directly part of the negotiation. This can result in another opportunity to reopen negotiations to obtain approval of an absent authority and, in the process, for one side to "nibble" at what was thought to be an agreed deal. They might take advantage of asymmetrical timing needs or an opponent's investment in the anticipated outcome. Clarification of who has ultimate authority and whose signature is necessary to create an enforceable agreement should occur before the negotiation begins. (Some issues of enforcement and defenses are covered in Chapter 8.)

The settlement of some disputes or transactions requires ratification by a constituent group. The resolution of labor-management controversies may require ratification of union members. Some corporate issues may require a vote of stockholders. Disputes involving municipalities and other public bodies may rest upon final approval of elected councils or boards. Again, it is helpful to agree at the outset of negotiations on the approval/ratification process and on mechanisms to help ensure that those engaged in the negotiation have the confidence of the final decision makers. Good faith deposits or penalty provisions if approval is not forthcoming may help guard against last minute manipulations and disappointments.

The most effective way to ensure approval and ratification of "stakeholders" or interested parties not at the table is to involve in the negotiation those who hold final authority or to structure steps that require interim approval or endorsement along the way. If the stakeholder group becomes invested in the process and aware of the value being created, as well as the BATNAs involved and the concessions leading to the proposed agreement, its members are more inclined to concur with what they feel part of than if presented with an up or down vote on what appears to be a fait accompli. A gradual "buy-in" is more likely to result in endorsement than an after-the-fact request, even if a group process complicates the negotiation.

One method used by mediators can also be of help in direct negotiation, particularly when ratification may be required. The single text approach of building an agreement, by writing the provisions or sections together at the table and then circulating that section for approval before the next section is written, was made famous by President Jimmy Carter during the Camp David negotiations between Egypt and Israel. See Carter (1982). The resulting document grows section by section with the buy-in of all approving parties along the way. The completed agreement then reflects a joint effort that was grown to maturity by those who feel an ownership of what was built together. Of course, the pieces of an agreement are interrelated and final approval must await the completed document, so there is no guarantee that the end terms of a single text agreement will be accepted. However, using a single text approach and getting buy-in along the way makes it more likely that there will be concurrence on the cumulative final document that represents the resulting agreement.

CHAPTER
6

Gender and Cultural Considerations

A. MOVING BEYOND GENDER STEREOTYPES

Until recently, the issue of gender in negotiation was addressed as how well would women do bargaining in a male-dominated profession. Although this issue has not totally disappeared, it is no longer the central question. More than half of law students are women and the gender balance among attorneys will soon approach equanimity. If there is a male model of practice, it is not necessary that women strictly conform to it. Nor is it any longer necessary to ask whether women can succeed as negotiators. Experience and research has clearly answered that women can excel in all lawyering roles, including negotiation. We have seen that negotiation is increasingly approached as a process of problem solving and that what is perceived as effective negotiation draws upon a different set of qualities and skills than those typically associated with stereotyped male competitiveness. The game, as well as the players, have changed. In addition, the old stereotypes of gender-based behavior are also changing, but not forgotten.

The fact that women have taken their place at the negotiation table and that the results they obtain for clients are comparable to their male counterparts does not mean that gender does not matter. Questions remain about whether men tend to negotiate differently than women, whether negotiating with one of the other sex is different than when a negotiating opponent is of the same sex, and whether any differences can be used to advantage or disadvantage. There is also a question of whether men and women tend to communicate differently—whether we speak the same language. Knowing the answers to these questions is as important to men as to women, and perhaps even more important to clients choosing an attorney to represent them in resolving disputes and negotiating deals.

In considering matters of gender, as well as culture, it is important to note that there are no generic beings, no common man or woman. Every individual is unique, defined by genetic makeup, environment, and personal experience. Emphasizing gender differences detracts from considering women and men across culture, class, race, ethnicity, age, and sexual orientation. However, culture and perhaps chromosomes foster some male- and female-associated behaviors that identify us with our gender and set us apart. The phenomenon of selective perceptions, and its children, stereotyping and self-fulfilling prophecies, along with attribution errors, magnify these differences and create cognitive traps that shape and limit how we interact with those of the opposite sex when negotiating. The way to open these traps is to understand our individual uniqueness as well as our gender differences and work with them.

The following excerpt from a student negotiation class paper addresses the different communication styles of some men and women. The author then explains why female performance is undervalued and the importance of understanding sex stereotypes, before suggesting how women can use underestimation to their advantage.

ALLYSON UKISHIMA, WOMEN AND LEGAL NEGOTIATION: MOVING BEYOND GENDER STEREOTYPES AND ADOPTING A "YIN AND YANG" PARADIGM
USF Student Paper (Spring 2003)

COMMUNICATING IN DIFFERENT LANGUAGES

There may be communication styles and tendencies between genders that affect the way men and women negotiate. For example, men tend to interrupt more and use authoritative language during persuasive interactions, while women tend to use more disclaimers like "I think" and "you know," which are less forceful. Kolb & Coolidge elaborate on gender communication distinctions and conclude simply, "women speak differently":

> The female pattern of communication involves deference, relationship thinking in argument, and indirection . . . with many qualifiers to show flexibility and an opportunity for discussion. . . . Women's speech is more conforming and less powerful. . . . In mixed groups, they adopt a deferential posture and are less likely to advocate their positions. . . . There is a proclivity to be too revealing — to talk too much about their attitudes, beliefs, concerns . . . [as] [d]ialogue is central to a woman's model of problem solving. (Deborah M. Kolb & Gloria C. Coolidge, *Her Place At the Table: A Consideration of Gender Issues in Negotiation* (1988), 261-272)

Deborah Tannen distinguishes between two modes of conversation: "report-talk" and "rapport-talk." The primary function of report-talk (common to men) is to communicate information. Rapport-talk (common to women) focuses primarily on the interaction itself. According to Tannen, conversations for women are "negotiations for closeness in which people try to seek and give confirmation and support, and to reach consensus." Women may therefore perceive questions as being a respectful and undemanding way to let the other person know what they are thinking, while giving the listener the opportunity to agree or disagree.

Carol Gilligan presents a theory of moral development, which assumes that men and women think and speak differently when confronted with ethical dilemmas. Gilligan distinguishes a feminine "ethic of care" with a masculine "ethic of justice" and believes that these gender differences in moral perspective are due to contrasting images of self:

> My research suggests that men and women may speak different languages that they assume are the same, using similar words to encode disparate experiences of self and social relationships. Because these languages share an overlapping moral

vocabulary, they contain a propensity for systematic mistranslation, creating mis-understandings which impede communication and limit the potential for cooperation and care in relationships. (Carol Gilligan, *In a Different Voice: Psychological Theory and Women's Development* (1982), 173)

However, concepts of "justice" and "care" have not been proven to be gender specific. In an attempt to provide an empirically valid description of negotiation behavior of practicing attorneys, and identify effective negotiation characteristics, Lloyd Burton et al., conducted two studies. The authors hypothesized that the ethical and moral orientations of the men and women involved would show men to act more consistently with "justice," and women more consistently with "care." The authors' hypotheses were not proven. The results of the studies showed that both male and female attorneys considered "justice" and "care" to be necessary attributes to be an effective attorney, independent of gender.

ACHIEVEMENT ATTRIBUTION AND BIAS

Compared to men, female performance is highly undervalued—favorable results are too often overlooked and mistakes are too often noticed. Studies show that female work is less valued than identical work by men. While the achievements of men are usually attributed to intrinsic factors such as intelligence and hard work, women's achievements are attributed to extrinsic factors such as luck or others' actions.

Charles B. Craver, Research Professor at George Washington University School of Law, examined students in his legal negotiating course to see whether there were achievement differences between male and female law students. Craver hypothesized that there were "no meaningful differences" in the overall performance of male and female students. His 15-year collection of statistical results from class exercises confirmed his hypothesis.

However, Craver did recognize that females tended to fear being alienated from others for their competitive successes. The women were also more critical of other women who received exceptional bargaining results than they were of men who receive equal results. Interestingly, the males also admitted that they were uncomfortable when females received exceptional results when negotiating with them, and that some even preferred not to settle over the embarrassment of "losing" to females.

THE IMPORTANCE OF STUDYING GENDER STEREOTYPES

People come into negotiation with expectations about others and then in turn, fulfill those expectations. Therefore, people may selectively see only evidence that supports those stereotypes, which negatively impacts the negotiation. Yet, many experts such as Professor Kay Deaux criticize the existence of gender-based stereotypes and behavioral predictions:

Despite the persistence of stereotypes, the studies of social behavior suggest that there are relatively few characteristics in which men and women consistently differ. Men and women both seem to be capable of being aggressive, helpful, and alternately cooperative and competitive. In other words, there is little evidence that the nature of women and men is so inherently different that we are justified in making stereotyped generalizations. (Kay Deaux, *The Behavior of Women and Men* (1976), 144)

So why do we focus on such archaic traditions and uncertainties that further unwarranted assumptions? Menkel-Meadow emphasizes the importance of learning about the evolution of stereotypes to effectively teach students about negotiation.

> For some looking at the gender question, there is the hope of taking advantage of whatever gender-based attribute is thought to exist. . . . Others seek to "improve" their performances by learning to change behaviors, away from stereotypic notions of how they are expected to behave. For most of us with any sophistication about gender and negotiation, we know that as the conditions and situations of negotiated problems vary, so too will the salience and the expression of gender. Thus, the most effective pedagogy about gender and negotiation is to explore both when gender is or might be silent in a negotiation and when and how the significance of gender . . . might and does vary. . . . (Carrie Menkel-Meadow, *Teaching About Gender and Negotiation: Sex, Truths, and Videotape*, Negot. J. 16 (4) (2000), 358)

It is important to recognize that people do make choices with lasting consequences based upon assumptions that are reinforced in our society and cognitively engrained, particularly when that is the only information people have on which to base their decisions. Gender stereotypes play a major role in our understanding of others and are so prevalent in our society that it is often difficult to distinguish reality from falsity. In order to make intelligent decisions and move beyond such unfounded ignorances, we must look to the origin of gender stereotypes and how they have developed and evolved over time. By taking a retrospective approach, both male and female negotiators will have a better understanding about the persons with whom they are dealing, as well as questioning their own presumptions about others and making sure that they do not allow it to interfere with their negotiation interaction with others.

THE POWER OF UNDERESTIMATION

Both men and women underestimate women in male-dominated settings, particularly if the female is young. People tend not to expect women to be highly competitive or manipulative. This works to the advantage of the female negotiator. She can not only perform beyond her employers' or colleagues' expectations, but more importantly, she can also outsmart her opponents without their even realizing it. For example, if a male negotiator feels less intimidated by the young female negotiator, he may not fully engage his competitive skills and simply give her his "bottom line." The young female negotiator may then use that figure as the starting point for her negotiations.

Being underestimated can also be a great psychological motivator for women. Such offensive attitudes can act as a powerful catalyst to prove their opponent's wrong. From this vantage point, women can see how being underestimated can be a highly underrated advantage.

___

Several recent books provide guides for women on how to succeed at negotiating in a male-dominated environment. Some, in effect, educate women to negotiate more like men. Some advise women on how to take advantage of their feminine differences and qualities. Others rewrap traditional negotiation lessons in a package designed for the female market. *The Shadow Negotiation: How Women Can Master the Hidden Agendas That Determine Bargaining Process* is particularly insightful and helpful to women negotiators. Its general analysis and suggestions about negotiation and the shadow negotiation—the often determinative negotiation within a negotiation—provide a helpful guide for both men and women. The book draws upon some of the principles previously developed, including hidden agendas, the role of trust and rapport, and reciprocity of listening to demands and making concessions. However, the authors caution that a seemingly even playing field may slope against women.

DEBORAH M. KOLB AND JUDITH WILLIAMS, THE SHADOW NEGOTIATION: HOW WOMEN CAN MASTER THE HIDDEN AGENDAS THAT DETERMINE BARGAINING SUCCESS

20-26, Simon & Schuster (2000)

THE SHADOW NEGOTIATION

As we talked to women about what happens when they negotiate, we learned that a good idea alone rarely carries the day. Negotiations are not purely rational exercises in problem solving. They are more akin to conversations that are carried out simultaneously on two levels. First there is the discussion of substance—what the bargainers have to say about the problem itself. But then there is the interpersonal communication that takes place—what the talk encodes about their relationship. Yes, people bargain over issues, but they also negotiate how they are going to negotiate. All the time they are bargaining over issues, they are conducting a parallel negotiation in which they work out the terms of their relationship and their expectations. Even though they seldom address the subject directly, they decide between them whose interests and needs command attention, whose opinions matter, and how cooperative they are going to be in reaching an agreement. This interchange, often nonverbal and masked in the positions taken on issues, has a momentum all its own, quite apart from the substance of what is being discussed.

We call this parallel negotiation the *shadow negotiation*. This shadow negotiation takes place below the surface of any debate over problems. As bargainers try to turn the discussion of the problem to their advantage or persuade the other side to cooperate in resolving it, they make assumptions about each other, what the other person wants, his or her weaknesses, how he or she is likely to behave. They size each other up, poking here and there to find out where the give is. They test for flexibility, trying to gauge how strongly an individual feels about a certain point.

How you resolve the issues hinges on the actions you take in the shadow negotiation. If you don't move to direct the shadow negotiation, you can find the agreement tipping against you. The shadow negotiation is no place to be a passive observer. You can maneuver to put yourself in a good position or let others create a position for you. Your action — or inaction — here determines what takes place in the negotiation over problems.

Impressions count. Slight changes in positioning can cause a major shift in the dynamics within the shadow negotiation. You want to move into a position from which you can claim your place at the table. At the same time, you need to encourage your counterpart to collaborate with you in fashioning an agreement that works for both of you.

THE TWIN DEMANDS OF THE SHADOW NEGOTIATION: ADVOCACY AND CONNECTION

To hold your own in the shadow negotiation, you don't have to be brash or aggressive. You do need to be an advocate for your interests. Through strategic moves you position yourself in the shadow negotiation so that the other party takes your demands seriously. You also turn any attempts to put you on the defensive. In effect, your advocacy defines your claim to a place at the table. It tells the other side not only that you are going to be an active player, but that you will not and do not need to settle for less than you deserve.

Active positioning is critical to how you negotiate the issues. The impressions you create in the shadow negotiation determine how much give and take there will be over the issues. If you are unsure of yourself or doubt whether your demands are justified or legitimate, you will have a tough time convincing others to give them much weight. Bargainers are quick to ferret out points of weaknesses, where you are tentative or vulnerable. You must be ready to move in the shadow negotiation not just to promote your interests but to block any attempt to undermine your credibility.

The messages you send in the shadow negotiation establish your advocacy. But you cannot pay attention only to gaining an advantage for your demands and to how you are positioned in the negotiation conversation. Any good solution requires compromise, concessions, and creativity on both sides. Concentrate only on your agenda, promote it at the other party's expense, and she has little incentive to cooperate. Regard her as an enemy and pretty soon she starts acting like one — blind to the interests you share.

To find common ground, you have to work together, not against each other. This is where the *skills of connection* come into play. It takes sensitivity and responsive action to draw out what other people have on their minds in a negotiation. Often these hidden agendas are their real agendas. Unless bargainers are explicitly encouraged to talk about them, they will hesitate, fearing that any candor will be used against them. They don't want to tip their hand.

There is a pragmatic reason behind this attentiveness to relationship building in the shadow negotiation. Show the others involved that you value them and their ideas, and there is a good chance they will reciprocate. You'd be surprised how quickly they become more open in voicing the reasons for their demands *and* more receptive to listening to yours. But establishing a connection with the other party does a good deal more than facilitate equal airtime. When you each feel free to engage in an open exchange that flows both ways, you can confront the real issues rather than their proxies. Different perspectives surface and point to other, more creative ways of resolving the issues than either of you can contemplate on your own.

Advocacy and connection go hand in hand in successful negotiation, and you establish the terms of both in the shadow negotiation. Using strategic moves and turns, you create your own space in the conversation. You cannot let a need for responsive and open exchange hold your own interests hostage. You must lay the groundwork for dialogue with a forceful advocacy. The other person has to have something and someone to connect with for the skills of connection to work. But those skills hold a larger promise. They enable you to build a relationship across differences so that you are both committed to working collaboratively on a mutual solution.

WHAT DOES GENDER HAVE TO DO WITH NEGOTIATION?

Almost without exception, the women we interviewed could analyze a problem or a situation with great skill. Yet they stumbled in the shadow negotiation. The reason became clear the more we talked with them. Problems can be and often are gender neutral. But surprising things happen in negotiation. Unrecognized expectations and unwarranted assumptions come into play. And gender often sets them off.

Because we experience negotiation in such a personal way, we look for personal reasons why being a woman matters more at some times than at others. Something in the chemistry of this party negotiation, we figure, makes gender an issue. But even when we don't have a strong visceral reaction, gender colors our experience. Any negotiation is caught in a web of influence, social values, and informal codes of conduct. Social norms or standards that seem at first blush to have nothing to do with gender might generate troubling expectations about what we should and can do as women. Resources are often unevenly divided along gender lines. As a result, what appears to be a benign or even playing field might, in fact, slope against us.

GENDER FRAMEWORKS

To a great extent, how we see gender determines how we deal with its effects in the shadow negotiation. We can consider being a woman a hindrance in negotiation and take seriously Professor Higgins's exhortation in *My Fair Lady*: "Why can't a woman be more like a man?" Alternatively, we can celebrate our differences and adopt the approach of Sally Field and Dolly Parton in the movie *Steel Magnolias*. When Steel Magnolias negotiate, they tap feminine strengths to temper confrontational impulses and encourage collaborative exchange. Or we can focus on the social dynamic set in motion when common yardsticks used to measure performance don't fit a woman's experience.

PROFESSOR HIGGINS' ADVICE

For the Professor Higginses of this world, the gender glass is half empty for women. They are not, by nature, bad negotiators. Socialized to be mothers and caretakers, they have never been schooled in the art of hard-nosed bargaining.

They can, however, learn the "rules of the game." A woman need not fare badly in a salary negotiation or put in a double shift at home and at work. If she has not been able to argue her case for equal pay for equal work or prevent her colleagues from taking over her, she can study how to be more assertive, more strategic in her thinking, and less emotional.

The Professor Higgins approach is a remedial one. It assumes that individual deficiencies can be patched up with sufficient study and rigorous discipline: Passivity, for example, is a personal liability that can be corrected by training. The fault rests squarely on the particular woman's shoulders. She needs a "cure." Conveniently overlooked is the extent to which that cure will always be incomplete. No matter how hard a woman tries to learn the rules of the game, she will always play the game as a woman. Adopting aggressive behavior or a more "masculine" way of speaking in a negotiation can backfire. Instead of gaining her a voice and acceptance, it can provoke censure or backlash.

Remedial programs like these hold out a dubious promise: If you patch yourself up — fill in your obvious deficiencies and acquire the necessary skills — you can play the game as well as, or better than, many men. By recommending the wholesale assimilation of "good" masculine qualities, however foreign, advice like this encourages a woman to blame only herself when she is underpaid, overworked, or simply overlooked, invisible. The fault lies with her — in some inadequacy, in something she did or failed to do — not in the imbalances in the system itself.

THE STEEL MAGNOLIAS' ANSWER

Wait a minute, some critics say. Femininity is *not* an encumbrance. It gives a woman an edge, assets she can use to her advantage. Rather than lament the lack of assertive independence or competitive drive in women, why not celebrate an expressive, emotional, caring femininity? Women, through their capacity to mother and from their subordinate status at work, have developed not just coping mechanisms but real strengths. Empathy, an intuitive aptitude for collaboration, the ability to connect with others rather than to remain distanced as an independent actor, an instinctive feeling for "relationship" — these skills and inclinations carry an unrealized advantage in the new interconnected world of business. Women, it is suggested, build rapport and reach joint solutions more easily than men do precisely because they cooperate and empathize more naturally.

This thinking successfully challenges the notion that women are in some way deficient or inadequate. It runs into difficulty, however, when it assumes that a constellation of certain traits and qualities makes up the "female essence." This premise washes out differences among women. The problem is not that women do not have these special qualities. Many do. But others enjoy the challenge of competition; they are not by nature *only* concerned with others.

There is also some wishful thinking involved in declaring feminine attributes unqualified assets uniformly useful in negotiation. These "feminine" skills, far from being an advantage, can undermine a woman when she negotiates. If she is not careful, her attachment to relationship can be exploited and used against her. Of course, the helpful female colleague does not mind shouldering the lion's share of the work and ending up with none of the credit. Of course, a woman negotiating a severance package will sacrifice her financial interests to maintain cordial relations with her former employers. Taken to extremes, the feminine advantage does not gain a woman much credit when she negotiates.

While her empathetic male counterpart earns praise for his "people" skills, she is just acting like a woman. And if she is really successful, she is accused of being manipulative, of using feminine wiles to get her way. That is the flint behind the honey in Steel Magnolia's voice, the reason for the hint of the pejorative in the term's common usage.

There is a more damaging objection. Praise of the "feminine," when unqualified, makes it easy to discount or ignore the extent to which influence follows gender lines. As one commentator put it, an emphasis on women's special qualities of caring and nurturing amounts to a "setup to be shafted." In an unequal world, such critics argue, difference will always mean less and women will generally get less when they negotiate. In other words, the doubts women experience about their ability to do well often tell more about status, about bumping up against seemingly immovable walls and ceilings, about having less clout, than they reveal about underappreciated skills and abilities.

We are using the exaggerations of Professor Higgins and the Steel Magnolia for effect. They point to the extremes in the advice directed at women, but they also illustrate the extent to which we personalize the challenges gender creates in negotiation. On the one hand, it is our weakness and so we need to remedy it. On the other, it is *our* strength, but we must be wary in how we use it. But not all the challenges gender poses in negotiation are rooted in personal causes. However inclined we as individuals might be to view supposed differences as a handicap or a strength, a woman quite simply has to work harder than a man to get what she wants in a negotiation. When others automatically assume she will not push her own interests, they offer less, are more difficult to bring to the table, make unreasonable demands, and say no more freely. They might doubt her competence, her ability to be forceful and stand her ground under pressure. The power dynamics in the relationship or the organization might work against her. To counter this momentum, she might repudiate those qualities that have traditionally been associated with women — an ability to connect with other people, the capacity to listen. Empathy, she reasons, is not going to get her very far when she faces a hard bargaining situation — particularly when the other person interprets her concern as a sign that she will not put up much resistance. But being tough or hardnosed does not seem to solve the dilemma either.

THE YARDSTICK EXPLANATION

Gender is not a "woman's" problem — a question of whether women have deficiencies or special qualities. Although gender figures in most human relations, we deny its pervasiveness, preferring instead to see egalitarian gender neutrality in our relationships and in our organizations. Yet to a large extent, we still maintain implicit standards for behavior that can have a different impact on women than men. Standards generally reflect the experience of the people setting them. And, by and large, men do the setting in our society. As a result, their experience becomes the yardstick for measuring what is normal. And, in a masked exercise of power, that standard is then rather cavalierly assumed to be gender neutral. . . .

QUESTIONS

1. Do you agree that "being underestimated" can be a highly underrated advantage? Is the use of an opponent's underestimation of your negotiation savvy an acceptable manipulation? Will it create a trust or credibility deficit that might haunt you later?

2. Is the legal negotiation table still slanted against women? Does the fact that law schools are graduating approximately equal number of men and women mean that law practice is not a male-dominated field? What in the future might level or shift the balance?

3. Are female law students a self-selected group that do not reflect more general female negotiating characteristics identified with women? For a general report on gender differences in negotiation, see Babcock and Laschever (2003).

4. If relationships matter and effective negotiation results from connectiveness and problem solving skills, should men sign up for seminars on how to negotiate like a woman?

5. The above selection and the literature on gender and negotiation focuses on male perceptions of females and, to a lesser extent, on female perceptions of males. Isn't the perception that women have of women, and that men have of men, just as important in explaining our negotiation approaches and behaviors? Do you believe from what you have read and experienced that patterns between women negotiating with one another would be significantly different than negotiations between men? If so, how?

6. Might sexual orientation be a factor in negotiation style? What effect might sexual orientation have, and why?

7. Do you agree that "a woman quite simply has to work harder than a man to get what she wants at a negotiation"?

B. CULTURAL DIFFERENCES OR WHY THE WORLD IS NOT BORING

We tend to be most comfortable and trusting among people like ourselves and most fascinated with those who are different. Negotiating with people from other cultures can be challenging because trust and rapport affect negotiations, as do cultural values and traditions, which color what we perceive.

Cultural differences are difficult to discuss and apply to negotiation because the meaning of culture is elusive. Like highlighting gender, focusing on culture lends itself to stereotypes and creates a risk of substituting categorical norms for the uniqueness of individuals. Cultural considerations are so complex and ever changing in our globalized world that defining a person by identity to a single culture and using that identity to predict values or behavior is prone to error.

However, because it is helpful to have clues about how our negotiating counterparts perceive the world and perhaps value things differently than us, cultural variations should be considered. Sensitivity to cultural differences can assist in preparing for negotiations, interpreting behavior, and providing ideas for how impasse can be avoided and value might be created in a negotiation. Cultural awareness can also help us avoid unintended consequences of what we say and do, as well as alert us to what others may anticipate from us because of our own cultural identity.

Cultural classifications are similar to many conveniences in life that we use but wish we did not need. Like automatic home appliances, disposable products, computers, and other of life's shortcuts, we may wish we did not need them, but we cannot seem to live without them. We use culture as a label or shortcut about categories of people with whom we do not confidently identify. We know that there are shortcomings to this convenience, but we use it anyway. We know that no culture or grouping of people is monolithic or truly homogenous. Although a group of people may have some common characteristics, those characteristics are not distributed or shared uniformly. Even if we could be sure of the nature of a group, few people are part of only one cultural identity. So we can never be sure of which of several cultural influences will be most applicable. Will the culture of a person's national origin, ethnicity, religion, schooling, professional identity, or economic class predominate in a particular contextual situation? Finally, can we ever know if the culture of the last generation, when cultural norms for that group may have been identified or popularized, is the behavioral or value norms of that group today? We know that cultural generalizations, although convenient, are inherently unreliable. In constitutional parlance, they are necessarily underinclusive and overinclusive.

With all of these caveats, cultural considerations are of great interest because we feel we need all the help we can get in better understanding others. Travel guides feature a section on the culture you will encounter in another country. Sociologists and political scientists, among others, study the impact of culture. People regularly talk about cultural behavior. Most books on negotiation include advice on how to utilize cultural awareness and knowledge to improve negotiation results. The next article further explains both the value and shortcomings of using cultural categories. The perception errors referred to by Professor Sebenius, by now, should be familiar to you.

JAMES K. SEBENIUS, CAVEATS FOR CROSS-BORDER NEGOTIATIONS

18 Negot. J., 122-123, 126-131 (2002)

While some of the work on culture and negotiation is at best superficial, much of the relevant academic literature is well grounded and accompanied by careful statements as to its limits and the conditions under which it should apply. While holding on to the truth that some characteristics do systematically vary across national borders, however, there is often a general uneasiness about unwarranted use of purported cross-cultural insight. . . . My objective is to make analysts and negotiators more sophisticated consumers of this advice by suggesting four classes of caveat, each with a slightly tongue-in-check name that will, I hope, be usefully evocative.

1.   The John Wayne v. Charlie Chan Fallacy: Stereotyping National Cultures

Start with the obvious: All American negotiators are not like John Wayne and all Chinese negotiators are not like Charlie Chan. . . . In the face of such internal variation, we wisely caution ourselves against mindless stereotyping by nationality (as well as by gender, religion, race, profession, or age). Even so, in many situations it remains all-too-common to hear offhand remarks such as "all Chinese negotiators . . ." (as well as generalizations about "women . . ." or "engineers"). To combat this, a strong version of the anti-stereotyping prescription calls for ignoring nationality altogether in preparing for negotiation.

That advice is too strong. Nationality often does have a great deal to do with cultural characteristics, particularly in relatively homogeneous countries like Japan. The careful work of many researchers confirms significant associations between nationality and a range of traits and outcomes. . . . It would be foolish to throw away potentially valuable information. But what does information on a particular group's behavioral expectations or deeper cultural characteristics really convey? Typically, cultural descriptions are about central *tendencies* of populations that also exhibit considerable "within-group" variation. . . .

Inferences about individuals from central tendencies are often misleading or wrong. *You negotiate with individuals, not averages.*

But viewing the world without the aid of stereotypes is difficult. Forming stereotypes is a natural reflex that helps order the overflow of information that barrages people. Social psychologist Ellen Langer argues that a solution to the negative effects of stereotyping is "mindfulness," which she defines as a willingness to create new categories, an openness to new information, and an awareness that more than one perspective exists. Rather than straining against forming stereotypes, a more realistic strategy is to allow stereotypes room to change, multiply, and adapt to new information.

In sum, remember that "national traits" — as well as traits supposedly associated with gender, ethnicity, etc. — are *distributions* of characteristics across populations, not blanket descriptions applicable to each individual. Be very cautious about making inferences about characteristics of specific individuals from different groups — even where the groups are, on average, sharply different. Avoid stereotyping and the "prototypicality" error of assuming an individual will exhibit the most likely group characteristic. Even if U.S. negotiators are on average more impatient, deal-focused, and individually oriented than their Chinese counterparts, be careful not to help amplify that stereotype in the mind of the other side. . . .

2.   The Rosetta Stone Fallacy: Overattribution to National Culture

National culture clearly matters. But there is a tendency to see it as the Rosetta Stone, the indispensable key to describe, explain, and predict the behavior of the other side. Of course there are many possible "cultures" operating within a given individual. . . . National culture can be highly visible but, obviously, it is only one of many possible influences. For example, Jeswald Salacuse surveyed executives from a dozen countries to determine national tendencies on ten important bargaining characteristics, such as negotiating goal (contract v. relationship), orientation (win-win v. win-lose), formality level, communication style, risk-taking, etc. While his results showed significant national differences, he also analyzed the data according to profession and occupations of the respondents such as law, engineering, marketing, the military, diplomacy, accounting, etc. These categories, too, showed systematic association with different bargaining styles. Finally, Salacuse could also differentiate many of these characteristics by gender. Other extensive studies extend and elaborate analogous findings. Nationality often matters when considering someone's bargaining characteristics but so too does gender, ethnicity, functional specialty, etc. . . . [N]ational culture is but one of many "cultures" that can influence bargaining behavior. . . .

ATTRIBUTION BIAS

Cultural differences, often evident in surface behavior, are easy to see; richer contextual factors frequently are not. In unfamiliar cross-border settings, factors like strategic incompatibility, politics, or even individual personality are less likely to be "blamed" for undesirable outcomes. The powerful but unconscious tendency to overattribute behavior to culture, all too often clouds negotiators' vision of the full range of factors that can affect a negotiation. Psychologists have extensively documented this dynamic, a systematic tendency to focus on supposed characteristics of the person on the other side of the table, rather than on the economic or other powerful contextual factors. . . . The antidotes? First, remember that "culture" doesn't just mean nationality; instead there are many potentially influential "cultures" at work. Second, beyond "culture" are many other factors that have potential to affect negotiation behavior. Nationality can carry important information, but with many other cultures and many other factors at work, you should be careful not to treat your counterpart's passport as the Rosetta Stone.

3. THE "VISUAL FLYING RULES" AT NIGHT FALLACY: FALLING PREY TO POTENT PSYCHOLOGICAL BIASES

SELF-SERVING PERCEPTIONS OF OUR OWN SIDE

There is a powerful tendency, formally studied as "biased assimilation," for people to interpret information in negotiation self-servingly. For example, experiments give a number of people identical information about a pending court case but randomly assign them to the role of plaintiff or defendant. When each person is asked for his or her private assessment of the probability that the plaintiff will win, those assigned the role of plaintiff on average give much higher odds than those (randomly) assigned to the role of defendant (but, again, on the basis of identical information). People tend to "believe their own lines" or self-servingly interpret information. . . . And this tendency runs deep: Back in the 1950s, researchers conducted an experiment at a boy's camp, sponsoring a jelly bean hunt among the campers. After the hunt, the boys were shown an identical picture of a jar of jelly beans. Each boy evaluated the total number of beans in the jar according to whether he was told the jar belonged to his own team or to the other side. The same photograph was estimated to contain many more beans when it was presented as "your team's" and far fewer when it was alleged to be the "other side's."

PARTISIAN PERCEPTIONS OF THE OTHER SIDE

If our capacity to process information critical of our own side is flawed, it is even more the case for our assessments of the other side in a conflict or negotiation. In part, this stems from the in-group/out-group phenomenon. Persons from different cultures, especially on the opposite side of the bargaining table, are more readily identified as belonging to an out-group, or the Other. Once that labeling is in place, powerful perceptual dynamics kick in (beyond the tendencies toward stereotyping and overattribution). Robert Robinson describes extensive research over the last 40 years, documenting an unconscious mechanism that enhances "one's own side, portraying it as more talented, honest, and morally upright" while simultaneously vilifying the Other. This leads to a systematic exaggeration of the other side's position and the overestimation of the extent of the actual conflict. As a result, negotiators are often unduly pessimistic about their ability to find common ground, and can be unwilling to pursue it.

SELF-FULFILLING PROPHESIES

Such partisan perceptions hold the power to change reality by becoming self-fulfilling prophesies. The effects of labeling and stereotyping have been documented thoroughly to show that perceptions have the power to shape reality. . . . At the negotiating table, the same principle holds true: Clinging firmly to the idea that one's counterpart is stubborn, for example, is likely to yield intransigence on both sides, precluding the possibility of a compromise that might have occurred had the label of "obstinacy" not been so rigorously affixed.

In short, just as a pilot trying to navigate by visual flight rules at night or in a storm is prone to dangerous misjudgments, the psychology of perception in cross-cultural situations is rife with biases. Not only do we stereotype and over-attribute to nationality, we are also poor at interpreting information on our own situation, vulnerable to partisan perceptions of the other side, and likely to act in ways that become dangerously self-fulfilling.

4. ST. AUGUSTINE'S FALLACY: "WHEN IN ROME . . ."

Assume that you have undertaken a full analysis of the culture of the person you will meet on the other side of the bargaining table. St. Augustine gave the classic cross-cultural advice: When in Rome, do as the Romans do. While this admonition certainly has merit, it is not always good advice . . . much better options may be available. For example, learning that the Chinese, on average, are more hesitant than North Americans to take risks is only a first step. Clearly, a responsive strategy would not mimic this hesitancy, but effectively anticipate it.

Rather than learning to behave as the Romans do (while in Rome or elsewhere), strategies should accommodate the degree of cross-table understanding each side has of the other. For example, consider the best approach for a U.S. manager on his first visit to Japan dealing with a Yale-educated Japanese executive who has worked extensively in Europe and North America. Here it would be sensible to let the Japanese take the lead. If a negotiator is far more familiar with a counterpart's culture than vice versa, the best strategy might be to embrace the counterpart's negotiating "script." If both sides are equally "literate," an improvisational and mutually-accommodating approach might be most appropriate. A lower degree of familiarity dictates bringing in locally familiar expertise, perhaps on your side and perhaps even as a mediator.

A great deal depends on how familiar you are with "Roman" culture and how familiar your "Roman" counterpart is with your culture. And of course you want to avoid the previous fallacies as well. The nationalities across the table from each other may be Chinese and U.S., but both players may be regulars on the international business circuit, which has its own, increasingly global negotiating culture. Again, assess—etiquette, deeper traits, negotiation-specific expectations, and caveats; do not assume and project your assumption onto your counterpart.

In Conclusion

Cross-cultural negotiation analyses offer insight as to systematic differences in gestures and body language, etiquette and deportment, deeper behavioral traits, as well as organizational decision-making processes and forms of corporate and public governance. Accurately applying the very real insights from such studies can be challenging, but the difficulties perhaps lessened by thinking of four unlikely categories that themselves derive from cultures most dissimilar: John Wayne and Charlie Chan, the Rosetta Stone, VFR at night, and St. Augustine.

QUESTIONS

1. What is the dominant culture with which you identify? Is this the same culture that those who do not know you well would assume is your primary cultural group? Are there other cultural subgroups that help define who you are? Are there stereotypes that opposing negotiators may have about you based on the cultural group with which you are identified? Is there any way you can use those likely stereotypes to your advantage?

2. Does the downside of thinking about people as part of a cultural group outweigh the possible benefit of grouping people to help understand their values and anticipate their behavior? Would your answer have been different prior to the World Trade Center terrorism of September 11, 2001? If so, how?

3. Do you agree that "culture is the lens through which we make sense of the world?" If so, is there any doubt that people of different cultures will see the world so differently that world conflict is inevitable? Is conflict and how to deal with it culturally defined? For a comprehensive and instructive collection of provocative readings on both culture and gender as they relate to conflict, see Chew (2001).

4. Based on selection, training, and shared values, do lawyers constitute a cultural subgroup that helps others understand them and predict their behavior? Is your answer the same for doctors, accountants, and clergy?

CHAPTER
7

The Ethical Negotiator

A. DECEPTION v. DISCLOSURE

Lawyer is considered by many to be synonymous with liar. The 1997 movie, "Liar, Liar," featuring actor Jim Carey, was advertised by displaying the words "Lawyer, Lawyer" crossed out with "Liar, Liar" written over in red. This theme was repeated in the first scene of the film where the lawyer's son is asked in his kindergarten class what his father does for a living. He innocently tells the class that his father is a "liar." The public image of lawyers is also reflected in unflattering and prolific jokes. For example: "How do you know when a lawyer is lying? When his lips are moving."

Ethics codes forbid lawyers from lying in court, but permit in negotiation what the public would consider lying. Even if a lawyer would not deceive or lie in her own behalf when negotiating, the obligation to be a zealous advocate for clients confronts lawyers with the dilemma of deciding how far to go in gaining a negotiation advantage for clients by misstating or not revealing information.

Because negotiation occurs in private, usually without clients present, there is little check on what is said or not said in the negotiation, as well as what is communicated to clients. In addition, the ethics rules for negotiation are not precise, and sometimes contradictory, especially regarding what must be revealed to an opposing party. All of these elements result in constant and challenging choices facing attorneys in terms of ethics, morality, and negotiation effectiveness.

Ethics rules attempt to provide a guide for lawyers on how to balance their obligation to a client's interest and the integrity of the profession in a negotiation, but the specifics of applying the rules are elusive. Ethical limits can be found in each state's Rules of Professional Conduct or Code of Professional Responsibility and in its case and statutory law. The American Bar Association's Model Rules of Professional Conduct are the basis for most state ethics rules. The beginning point is Rule 4.1, which states that a lawyer shall not "knowingly (a) make a false statement of material fact or law to a third person; or (b) fail to disclose a material fact to a third person when disclosure is necessary to avoid assisting a criminal or fraudulent act by a client, unless disclosure is prohibited by Rule 1.6."

As you may recall, Rule 1.6 protects client confidences. An attorney who asks a client for bottom lines and other information that the client regards as confidential cannot, and pursuant to Rule 4.1 need not, reveal that information, unless the client authorizes the revelation. So, the confidence central to an attorney's obligation to a client severely restricts what can be disclosed in a negotiation.

Another serious limitation of knowing what should or should not be revealed is the qualification that only "material" facts must be revealed. The official comment to Rule 4.1 states that "under generally accepted conventions in negotiation, . . . estimates of price or value placed on the subject of the transaction" are not considered material, nor are "a party's intentions as to an acceptable settlement of a claim" covered by Rule 4.1's prohibitions against making false statements. (See Comment 2.)

The net effect of the ethical rules is that lawyers in negotiation can lie about some things, but not others. So, a lawyer can tell the other side that "this is a seven-figure case if it gets to a jury," even though she believes a verdict would not exceed $500,000, or that her client's bottom line is $100,000 when it is really $80,000. However, she cannot say her client sustained a broken neck, knowing he did not. Deception is still considered an acceptable aspect of negotiation, but only to a point. (See Chapter 8 for the limits imposed by contract law.) This creates a dilemma for the ethical negotiator and lends itself to a lot of debate and literature on the subject.

Richard Zitrin and Carol Langford have written extensively on legal ethics. In the excerpt below, from their popular book on the moral dilemmas confronting lawyers, they discuss issues raised by lawyers lying in negotiation and share their perspective. They also present a summary of interviews conducted on the topic. Patrick Longan, in his article, provides hypotheticals that highlight some of the ethical issues in negotiation. He analyzes the ABA Model Rules and opinions on point, but goes beyond these in urging consideration of both what is wise and most effective in the long run.

RICHARD ZITRIN AND CAROL M. LANGFORD, THE MORAL COMPASS OF THE AMERICAN LAWYER
163-168, Ballantine Books (1999)

Lawyers are perennially rated among the least beloved people in America. Perhaps the foremost reason is that almost everyone thinks they lie—from late-night talk show hosts performing monologues and reporters writing hit pieces to legal scholars, judges, and even lawyers themselves.

According to noted University of Pennsylvania ethics professor Geoffrey Hazard, lawyers, imbued with the adversary theorem, often seem like willing coconspirators in their clients' lies. "Shading the truth and telling lies occurs in almost every case, I am sure," says Professor Hazard. But we have created this adversarial system that encourages it. . . .

The adversary theorem raises at least two distinct issues about lawyers and lying. One is whether attorneys are ever justified in lying, or helping a client to lie. But this question can't be answered without addressing the first issue: defining what "lying" is. Are direct lies any worse than shading the truth, or simply remaining silent and leaving a false impression? Deciding if a lawyer is at fault for lying shouldn't turn on whether the lie is direct or indirect or spoken or silent, but rather on whether the circumstances permit something less than the truth.

Iowa law professor Gerald B. Wetlaufer thinks lawyers should both own up to the fact that they lie and do so under his broad definition: any effort "to create in some audience a belief at variance with one's own." Citing the *Randon House Dictionary*, which goes beyond direct falsehoods to define *lie* as "something intended or serving to convey a false impression," Wetlaufer argues that concealments and omissions are also lies. In a 1990 article he cataloged the ways in which lawyers lie — and fool themselves into believing either that they don't or that the lies don't count." Many sound all too familiar. We summarize:

- "*I didn't lie*," which includes "My statement was literally true" (though misleading), "I was speaking on a subject about which there is no absolute truth," and "I was merely putting matters in the best light."
- "*I lied, if you insist on calling it that, but it was . . .*": "ethically permissible" (and thus okay); "legal" (and thus okay); "just an omission"; or "ineffectual," because it was just a white lie or because it was simply not believed.
- "*I lied, but it was justified by the very nature of things*." This includes situations where lying is considered part of the rules of the game, such as negotiations, where most lawyers feel that candor defeats the very purpose of the exercise.
- "*I lied, but it was justified by the special ethics of lawyering*," especially the duties owed clients: loyalty, confidentiality, and, of course, zealous representation.
- "*The lie belongs to someone else*," usually the client, so that the lawyer is "just the messenger."
- "*I lied because my opponent acted badly*." This includes "self-defense," or "having to lie" before the opponent does, and lying to teach the opponent a lesson, or because bad behavior means the opponent has forfeited any right to candor.
- "*I lied, but it was justified by good consequences*," that is, justice triumphed. . . .

Are there occasions when lawyers *should* be permitted to lie? Can any of Professor Wetlaufer's colorful excuses become a justification? Most lawyers feel that when they are negotiating a case, it's impossible to be completely truthful and still engage in what Wetlaufer calls "strategic speaking." By its very nature, negotiation involves some measure of misleading the opponent, concealing one's true position, and — to use the poker parlance often adopted to describe the process — running a bluff. On one hand, the lawyer must be truthful; on the other hand, misleading the opponent, or at least allowing the opponent to be misled, seems a necessary part of the "game." Negotiation is not, and never will be, a matter of "putting all our cards on the table."

In 1975 Alvin B. Rubin, then a federal judge in Louisiana, wrote an article eloquently imploring "principled practitioners" to hold themselves to a simple ethics standard in negotiation: "The lawyer must act honestly and in good faith." He saw the adversary system as "means, not end," and argued that "client avarice and hostility neither control the lawyer's conscience nor measure his ethics." His article was widely reprinted, and it struck a chord with many lawyers. It began a debate on the ethics of negotiation that continues to this day. His complaint that there was no ethics rule requiring lawyers to be candid to opponents helped lead to a new, broader American Bar Association rule on lying. And his aphorisms — he also posited that "gamesmanship is not ethics" — received warm murmurs of support.

But Judge Rubin, possibly intentionally, set the bar too high. Most believe, as Michigan law professor James J. White said in an article aptly titled "Machiavelli and the Bar," that the "essence of negotiation" requires "even the most forthright, honest, and trustworthy negotiators" to actively mislead their opponents.

Some years ago the magazine *Inside Litigation* interviewed fifteen law professors, trial lawyers, and judges about how much they would lie in negotiating the settlement of a case. The group was asked whether it was acceptable to leave the other side with a false impression, so long as the lawyer didn't directly lie. Nine voted yes, making a distinction between "bald-faced lies" and misleading by silence, while only four voted no. And yet most of the group was familiar with a well-known Minnesota case from the early 1960s, *Spaulding v. Zimmerman*, 263 Minn. 346, 116 N.W.2d 704 (1961).

In *Spaulding*, a lawyer was defending the driver in a serious auto accident that injured the plaintiff, a young man in his late teens. The lawyer insisted that the plaintiff be examined by a doctor working for the defense. That doctor discovered something that the youth's own physician had missed: a life-threatening aortic aneurysm that could burst at any time, and had likely been caused by the accident. The defense lawyers said nothing, settling the case for less money than certainly would have been paid had the other side known of the aneurysm. Fortunately, the plaintiff learned of his condition later when taking an army physical and had corrective surgery.

Then he asked the court to reopen his settlement. Because the youth was still legally a minor, the judge had the power to set the settlement aside, which he did. But he refused to punish the defense lawyer, saying that the attorney had no obligation to reveal the aneurysm, even though his silence misled the youth in a way that jeopardized his life.

This case generated a great deal of comment in the legal community. Law professors wrote articles arguing that here was one case where surely a lawyer had a moral imperative to reveal the harm — and where lying by omission was just as serious as an affirmative lie. Yet one professor who had written extensively on the need to take personal responsibility in *Spaulding* voted for silence in the *Inside Litigation* poll because "it's not my job to do their job."

The magazine roundtable raised another important issue: May lawyers lie about whether they are authorized by their clients to settle a case for a particular amount? On this question, the group split straight down the middle. Several cited an exception to the ABA's ethics rule on lying — or what the rule calls making a "false statement of material fact" — that "estimates of price or value . . . and a party's intentions as to an acceptable settlement" are not ordinarily considered "statements of material fact." This language may reflect the practical reality that if lawyers had to tell the truth about their settlement positions, no negotiations would take place. But read literally, this comment is absurd. Nothing could be more "material" to a party than the value of the case.

Professor Wetlaufer pleads for lawyers to "stop kidding ourselves," call a lie a lie, and admit that lies can and do succeed. Wetlaufer believes that once lawyers accept this dose of realism, they could focus on lies that are not justified either "by the rules of the game or by our duties to our clients" and try to limit the circumstances in which lying is permitted. He argues that many lies are "impermissible" even if not directly forbidden by the rules.

Wetlaufer is right. Many lies—using his broad definition—are both unnecessary and wrong, even in negotiation. On the other hand, expecting lawyers to be completely candid with each other is neither realistic nor advisable. As long as any vestige of the adversary theorem remains, clients have the right to a lawyer to speak on their behalf, advocate their position, and look at the case from their point of view. Unless this concept is completely abandoned, lawyers will continue to advocate, and the cost will be a certain degree of candor.

It's interesting that the greatest consensus among the roundtable experts was that they reached one conclusion under a technical reading of the ethics rules—call it the "I-can-get-away-with-it" response—and another when they considered whether they personally would behave that way. The average practicing lawyer—in the field day in and out, closing deals, negotiating settlements, and, most likely, telling opposing counsel what he or she thinks the other side should hear in order to get the desired result—has little time for this distinction. As long as this lawyer expects the opposing counsel to play the negotiating game by I-can-get-away-with-it rules, the likelihood is that these rules will govern the game. . . .

PATRICK E. LONGAN, ETHICS IN SETTLEMENT NEGOTIATIONS: FOREWORD

52 Mercer L. Rev. 810-816 (2001)

There are two issues lurking within and behind . . . [Rule 4.1]. First, as to misrepresentations, comment two to Rule 4.1 contains a special qualification for statements in the context of settlement negotiations. It exempts from the requirements of Rule 4.1(a) certain statements that "under generally accepted conventions in negotiation" are not taken as statements of fact, such as the acceptability of a particular amount in settlement. In other words, there is room in negotiations for puffing and bluffing because those practices are what everyone involved expects. Second, the last phrase of Rule 4.1(b) appears to prohibit disclosure, even to prevent fraud, if Rule 1.6 would prohibit the disclosure. Rule 1.6 forbids disclosure of "information related to the representation of a client," absent client consent and with some very limited exceptions. The exception, therefore, threatens to swallow the rule about disclosure. . . .

A. THE LIMITS OF REPRESENTATIONS

. . . You represent the plaintiff in a breach of contract action. You are seeking lost profits. What can you say in negotiations about the lost profits if:

1. Your expert has come to no conclusion about their cause.
2. Your expert has told you the breach did not cause the lost profits.
3. Your expert has given you a range between $2,000,000 and $5,000,000 for the lost profits.
4. Your expert says the maximum lost profit is $2,000,000.
5. You do not have an expert; your client says the loss was $5,000,000.

It is common in negotiation for each side to emphasize the strength and persuasiveness of its evidence. On the other hand, each side in discovery has the opportunity to explore the other side's evidence. In this scenario, each side would be entitled to a report and a deposition of the other's testifying expert. Any statement about the expert would be a statement of fact. Because of the importance of expert testimony to this case, any statement of this sort would be material. The lawyer must be careful to tell only the truth to avoid violating Rule 4.1. Good lawyers, however, will test the assertions in discovery, consistent with the now-famous Russian proverb, "Trust, but verify."

Beyond the rules of ethics, however, it is proper to ask what the best strategy is for a lawyer in this negotiation. Here, any statement about the expert's conclusions probably will be the subject of discovery. If the statement is found to be false, the lawyer who made it will lose some credibility. That loss, which will likely survive the conclusion of this particular case and affect negotiations with the other lawyer in future cases, will cause these future negotiations to be more strained, more lengthy, and probably less fruitful. To the extent that the lawyer gains a reputation for untruthfulness as a result of statements about the expert, the lawyer may be impeding all his or her future negotiations. In other words, this hypothetical involves a happy situation in which it is both the right strategy and the smart strategy to tell the truth. . . .

In this breach of contract action, can you:

1. tell opposing counsel that you will not settle for less than $3.5 million when you have authority to settle for $2 million?
2. tell opposing counsel that five major buyers stopped buying from your client after the breach, knowing that they stopped buying for other reasons?

As discussed, comment 2 to Model Rule [4.1] defines statements about settlement authority not to be material. Technically, therefore, the lawyer should feel free to lie about his or her authority. Another strategy, however, and one that may be more effective in the long run, is simply to deflect any questions of authority with statements such as, "You know neither one of us can discuss our authority — let's talk about a fair settlement of this case." The reason a deflection may be more effective in the long run is the same reason exaggerations about the expert's conclusions may cause long term harm. You may be ethically permitted to lie about your authority, but if you do it, and the other lawyer catches you at it, he or she will not trust you again.

The misleading statement about the lost customers raises a persistent and subtle issue for lawyers about the use of language. The statement is literally true. These customers have left, and they did so at a time after the defendant's breach. The only reason the statement is made, however, is in the hope that the defendant will make the leap and conclude that the customers left because of the breach or, at least, that the plaintiff will attempt to prove that they did. The statement is, therefore, an intentionally misleading, sly use of language. It is reminiscent of former President Clinton's response to a question before the grand jury about his deposition testimony: "It depends on what the meaning of is is." The lawyer who engages in this type of deception is more clever, perhaps, than a straightforward liar, but the lawyer is no less worthy of condemnation.

Once again, however, we can rely on the power of reputation to deter lawyers (at least those who care about their reputations) from engaging in these tactics. Word gets around.

B. DISCLOSURE OF FACTUAL ERRORS

The second hypothetical concerned a duty to disclose facts when the other lawyer has made a settlement offer containing obvious mistakes:

> You represent the husband in a divorce action. You receive from opposing counsel a proposed property settlement with the following errors: (1) a transcription error that undervalues an asset; (2) an arithmetical error that undervalues an asset; (3) a valuation by purchase price of an asset when market value is much higher. All the errors work to your client's advantage. What, if anything, should you do about them?

To the extent that the first two errors are "scrivener's errors" (the other lawyer missed a typographical error or failed to add the numbers correctly), the lawyer has the duty to correct the mistakes. The third problem may raise more difficult issues because the error may come from opposing counsel's conscious but erroneous judgment about what valuation is best for his or her client. Can the lawyer in the hypothetical take advantage of his or her adversary's error in judgment?

The question is a species of a fundamental, recurring question in an adversarial system. The lawyer owes a primary duty of loyalty to the client. In most respects, the lawyer is not expected to be his or her brother's keeper. One answer to the particular ethical question presented is to say that it is not the interesting or important question. The client is not perpetrating a fraud or a crime by taking advantage of a bad lawyer on the other side. There is no duty to disclose under Rule 4.1.

Abiding by the rules of ethics, however, is necessary but not always sufficient for good lawyering. Ethically, the lawyer need not correct every misstep of opposing counsel. But sometimes correcting the mistake would be the wise thing to do. For example, if the mistakes involved in the proposal were fundamental mistakes, ones that under the law of contract the opposing party would provide grounds later to void the transaction, then the lawyer may best serve his or her client by alerting opposing counsel to the mistakes now. If the parties to the transaction will have a continuing relationship, such as shared responsibility for minor children, the best strategy might be to correct the mistakes and buy some trust, which may be sorely needed later. Here, as in many situations, ethics tells you the options available, but the lawyer must still exercise good judgment among the options.

C. DISCLOSURE OF LEGAL ERRORS

The final hypothetical . . . highlighted the fact that Model Rule 4.1 forbids a lawyer from making a material misrepresentation about the law. The hypothetical does so in the context of an interaction with a young lawyer who is operating under a mistake about the state of the law:

> You represent the defendant in a personal injury case. In negotiation with plaintiff's counsel (a young, relatively inexperienced lawyer), it becomes clear to you that this lawyer believes his or her client's potential recovery is limited by a tort reform statute. You know that this statute has been found unconstitutional by the state supreme court. May you, and should you, correct opposing counsel's mistake about the law?

Most practicing lawyers would not think twice about taking advantage of this younger lawyer. Again, the client is not perpetrating a fraud or a crime, and the client might be very happy to save some money because his or her adversary's lawyer is clueless. No rule of legal ethics requires the lawyer to be the opposing party's lawyer also. No rule requires that lawyers settle cases only on "fair" terms.

Again, however, the strictly ethical inquiry cannot end the discussion. For example, lawyers might find that taking advantage of the mistake in particular circumstances, such as a horrific injury to a young child, would be morally wrong although ethically permissible. The lawyer is free to counsel the client about nonlegal matters, such as the morality of leaving the injured child unable to obtain the life-long care the child needs. The lawyer is even free to seek to withdraw if assisting in a settlement under these circumstances would be repugnant to the lawyer. Here, as in the prior examples, the best lawyers consider all the circumstances and determine first whether the rules of ethics require a particular course of action and, if they do not, what under all the circumstances is the wisest choice. . . .

QUESTIONS

1. Assuming that a lawyer can lie about a client's bottom line and matters of value in negotiation without violating ethical rules, when might it be a good tactic and when not? What is the tactical advantage of candor? If there is reason to be candid when not ethically required, should it be selective candor depending on the situation, or is a uniform policy of candor more advantageous? Why?
2. Should the client have a say in what is revealed in the above hypotheticals? What if you disagree with your client? Must the client's wishes govern? (See the next section, Client Control v. Lawyer Integrity, for discussion of these issues.)
3. Zitrin and Langford in their book (p. 168) suggest that "instead of putting lawyers in the position of having to lie, as the rule does now, it could simply forbid lawyers from asking their opponents their ultimate positions on value." Would this be an effective, or at least preferable, solution to the dilemma between zealous representation and candor? Why or why not?
4. Is there any reason to behave differently toward people in negotiation than you would in other interactions? In other words, what distinguishes negotiation from interpersonal interactions generally? (For an interesting analysis of this question, see Cohen, 2001.)

5. There is much debate and also some case law on what is "a material fact" that must be revealed in a negotiation pursuant to Model Rule 4.1(a). For example, if you are representing a client injured in an automobile accident, need you reveal the client's death prior to finalizing settlement of a claim for his injuries? Why or why not? (See *Kentucky Bar Assn. v. Geisler*, 938 S.W. 2d 578 (K. 1997).)

6. Assuming that your client in the above question was alive at the initiation of the claim and the beginning of negotiation, the question raises an issue of what must be revealed when facts change or when what was revealed earlier is no longer true. This occurs frequently in the context of formal discovery. If a response to a question asked in formal discovery is no longer true, rules of civil procedure generally require an attorney to inform the opposing side of the change. (See FRCP Section 26(e).) If a fact material to a negotiation changes, is silence on the part of the knowing attorney a violation of Model Rule 4.1? Should the ethics rules governing attorneys permit silence when rules of procedure would require correction? Can you articulate a meaningful distinction? (See White, 1980.)

7. How does what Rule 4.1 requires of lawyers compare with what your personal moral values require of you? If your personal ethics are more restrictive than the rules that govern lawyer conduct, is there a risk that your interests might conflict with those of your client? (This topic is covered in the following section.)

B. CLIENT CONTROL v. LAWYER INTEGRITY (CONFLICTS OF INTEREST)

Ethical issues in negotiation are often compounded for lawyers because their interests are seldom in complete congruity with their client's interests. As noted earlier, when lawyers are employed to negotiate for principals, the interests in the timing, costs, trade-offs, goals, and relationships involved in a settlement may be different for the lawyer than for the client. However, lawyers work for clients and, at least to some extent, clients get to call the shots. ABA Model Rule 1.2(a) states that "A lawyer shall abide by a client's decisions concerning the objectives of representation . . . and shall consult with the client as to the means by which they are to be pursued. A lawyer shall abide by a client's decision whether to accept an offer of settlement of a matter." Under this rule, the decision to settle and under what terms is clearly the client's choice.

Earlier, in discussing cultural identities, we suggested that being a lawyer identifies you with what may be considered a cultural subgroup. Another way to view the relationship between lawyers is to analogize the relationship among lawyers as a "community." Whether viewed as a community or subculture, lawyers have long-term relationships with one another and repeatedly interact in ways that have their own norms of behavior and shared expectations. This may be in contrast to the relationship of clients to the legal/judicial system, which is likely to be a one-time occasion. A potential conflict exists between the client's interest in maximizing gain from a single transaction or settlement and a lawyer's longer term interest in maintaining credible and amicable relations with other lawyers. The gain from deceit and lying may benefit a client at the expense of the lawyer's relationship within the community.

A conflict may also exist between a client's personal economic needs, which drives her to value an attractive settlement offer more than societal interests, and a lawyer's ideals, which may focus more on broader policy concerns. This conflict can cut both ways if an idealistic client wants to reject a settlement on principle when the lawyer is coveting the immediate fee payoff.

Consider the following settlement situation and the conflicts it raises.

RICHARD ZITRIN AND CAROL M. LANGFORD, THE MORAL COMPASS OF THE AMERICAN LAWYER

183-207, Balantine Books (1999)

E.J. Boyette was a forty-eight-year-old computer programmer when he died, leaving a wife and five kids. Always active, Boyette had worked out three times a week, and on the weekends he rowed with a group of guys he knew from college. Shortly after his forty-seventh birthday he noticed that he was getting tired easily and was often short of breath. He made an appointment with his doctor, who referred him to a cardiologist. After extensive tests, the cardiologist recommended surgical placement of a new kind of heart valve from the Jones/Henning/Wharton Company that had been highly praised in all the medical journals.

At first everything seemed fine. Boyette was released from the hospital, started mild workouts, and had even begun dreaming of joining his rowing mates on the water again. But after three months Boyette's physical condition began deteriorating quickly. In another month he was dead. His widow consulted attorney Andrea Hardy, partner in a small firm that represents plaintiffs in injury cases. . . .

Now eighteen months later, after extensive discovery and a review of thousands of documents, Andrea and her paralegal have just found a memo that seems to show that the company knew its first-generation heart valves had design flaws that could cause some patients to get worse and even die. She and her paralegal can barely contain their excitement. They quickly draft a new and very specific demand for the other side to produce more documents, which Andrea believes will include the smoking gun she can use to prove that the manufacturer knew the heart valves were defective. . . .

On the appointed day for delivery, Andrea is surprised to find Burger himself [chief defense counsel] at her office. He asks if they can talk.

"Look," he says, "I'll hand over these documents in a minute. I think you know what's in them. But there's something I'd like you to consider. We'll offer you five million dollars right now to settle the case. There are just two conditions: the amount we pay must be secret, and the documents you've gotten from us must be returned. All of them, including copies." Andrea is dumbstruck. Until this moment Burger had maintained his client's innocence and never breathed a word about settlement. She knows $5 million is a lot more than she's likely to get for a case at trial, even with punishment damages. And the fee would easily be the largest her firm has ever received. She's sure the documents in George Burger's briefcase include the smoking gun she'd been looking for.

Andrea tells Burger that she'll have to review the documents and discuss things with her client before making a decision. "Fine," says Burger, "I'll give you a week." Later that day, with her paralegal and her law partners gathered around her, Andrea reads three memos from senior Jones/Henning/Wharton officials that conclusively prove that the manufacturer knew that the heart valve's design was defective before Mr. Boyette's valve was implanted. One memo summarizes 107 incidents in which the valve was considered a contributing cause in a patient's death. The other two discuss how the company should deal with the design flaw, eventually concluding that nothing should be done to take it off the market until a new product could be developed to replace it.

Andrea knows she must talk to Mr. Boyette's widow. But she ponders what to advise her about accepting Burger's offer. She loves her practice because she gets to expose dangerous products, not conceal them. She knows that if she agrees to keep the documents secret, other people with heart valves like Mr. Boyette's could be in danger, even die. But she also knows the guiding principle that her first duty is to her client, not the public at large. And the amount her client has been offered is enormous. . . .

She was not surprised when John Boyette called the next day to say that the family had met, discussed the offer, and decided to accept it.

QUESTIONS

1. Zitrin and Langford, after describing the $5 million Boyette secret settlement, discuss some state laws that ban secret settlements in order to prevent protection of public health and safety (see pp. 203-205). What are the arguments for and against statutory restrictions on secret settlements involving claims of defective products, fraud, and malpractice? Should lawyers be required to report such settlements? Why or why not? (See Doré, 1999; Zitrin, 1999.)

2. How do lawyers deal with this type of conflict or the more common one of the client's desire to have her lawyer shade the truth or conceal adverse bargaining information?

Both economic and ethical considerations may require lawyers to compromise their ideals and commitment to self-defined professional integrity. Preserving clients' confidences may prevent opposing lawyers from candidly discussing how their clients have instructed them to negotiate or giving warning that the other side should be cautious. Robert Condlin discusses below how the ethical conflict created by trying to get the most for your client can lead to unproductive behavior and ritualized aggression in negotiation that feeds the public's negative view of lawyers. Next, Mnookin, Peppet, and Tulumello provide examples and offer advice on how to grapple with the ethical dilemma of client short-term interests and lawyer longer term considerations, as well as how lawyers may in fact signal a warning to other lawyers without directly communicating confidential client information. We offer the example of Clark Clifford to illustrate the lawyer's ethical dilemma and the danger in selling his soul. Finally, Herbert Kritzer discusses how a contingent fee arrangement may create a conflict of interest for the lawyer or, at least, influence negotiation decisions.

ROBERT J. CONDLIN, BARGAINING IN THE DARK: THE NORMATIVE INCOHERENCE OF LAWYER DISPUTE BARGAINING ROLE

51 Md. L. Rev. 1, 71-72, 75-82, 84-85 (1992)

There is a contradiction in the prevailing understanding of lawyer dispute bargaining role, between what might be thought of as bargaining's practical norms and its ethical norms. The practical norms provide rules for maximizing long range client and lawyer returns. They tell lawyer bargainers to distribute resources efficiently, preserve bargaining relationships, and satisfy party interests in the aggregate. The ethical norms provide rules for representing clients competently and diligently. They tell lawyers to get the most they can for present clients, when so instructed, irrespective of the effects on resource distribution and future bargaining. Trying scrupulously to comply with both sets of norms, each for different reasons, lawyers frequently find themselves under contradictory commands, without meta norms to sort out the contradictions or rank order the commands, and thus, "in the dark" with respect to the central question of how they should act. This contradictory set of role commands has several effects, but one of the least salutary is that it seems to encourage the stylized adversarial maneuvering commonly associated with lawyers and dispute bargaining (e.g., exaggerated argument, insulting tone, routinized trading, circumspect and deceptive disclosure), which is now widely thought to make such bargaining inefficient, unpleasant, and unfair. If these effects are to be avoided, and bargaining role to be made more coherent, it is necessary that bargaining's ethical and practical norms be reconciled, or if that is too ambitious, at least their contradictions described in sufficient detail so that others may work on the problem. . . .

While lawyers may not take action that is frivolous (i.e., primarily to harass or maliciously to injure) or prohibited by law, they must use any legally available move or procedure helpful to a client's bargaining position. Among other things, this means that all forms of leverage must be exploited, inflated demands made, and private information obtained and used whenever any of these actions would advance the client's stated objectives, even if such action would jeopardize a lawyer's long-term, working relationship with her bargaining counterpart.

Lawyers also must show enthusiasm for the bargaining task. Once described as the obligation of zealous representation, and now expressed as the duty of diligence, this duty requires lawyers to act with "commitment and dedication to the interests of the client," and to "carry to a conclusion all matters undertaken" on the client's behalf. Lawyer bargainers, in other words, must develop and play out client-bargaining hands with energy and believability, and not undercut those efforts with a tone or attitude which indicates that their hearts are not in it, or that they do not believe what they say. Plausibility and sincerity are the most important attributes of effective bargaining maneuvers; the duty of competence requires the first, and the duty of diligence the second.

The duty of deference is concerned with which objectives are pursued, not how they are pursued. It makes client judgments supreme in disagreements with lawyers about which objectives to seek and, absent criminality or fraud, obligates lawyers to pursue all goals clients set. Deference is the centerpiece of lawyer-client relations and the feature of lawyer role that makes law practice a fiduciary enterprise. In bargaining, the main function of deference is to require that clients alone decide whether to accept or reject offers of settlement. . . .

When these duties are combined, as they must be, it may appear that lawyers are ethically obligated to be skillful, energetic, uncritical, and obedient instruments of selfish client ends, but the reality of lawyer dispute bargaining role is slightly less harsh. Lawyers are persons in their own right, with moral and political rights and obligations of their own, and even though they must take direction from their clients, they need not do everything asked. For example, the duty of deference distinguishes between questions of ends and questions of means, and reserves to lawyers the tactical and technical decisions of how best to advance client objectives. If a client asks a lawyer to use tactics that are repugnant, lawyers may refuse. Lawyers owe clients only substantive competitiveness; they may choose their own style. While clients should decide mixed questions such as how much expense to incur or how much harm to inflict, for the most part lawyers and clients divide bargaining decision responsibility along an ends-means line.

Similarly, as officers of the court and citizens of the community, lawyers have public responsibilities, to third parties and to the law, that clients may not trump. Lawyers may not lie for clients (though they may tell half truths and puff), either to adversaries or courts, or mislead opponents, either by act or omission, when to do so would be civilly actionable. In limited circumstances, occasionally present in bargaining, lawyers must correct adversary misapprehensions and remedy ignorance. They must bargain in good faith, not seek or agree to unconscionable settlements, and deal fairly with opponents by avoiding the use of force and fraud. These are limited obligations, imposed by law as much as by ethical rules, and while they prohibit few competitive maneuvers — there is still no obligation to make an adversary's factual case, correct analytical errors, or refuse any deal a court would enforce — they are supreme in their own realm. . . .

THE BARGAINER'S DILEMMA

Practical bargaining is cooperative bargaining. Clients do better, at least clients in the aggregate, when represented by lawyers who bargain cooperatively and are known to do so. Nevertheless, a particular client, valuing her own immediate return in an individual case more highly than the interests of clients in the aggregate (which may include the particular client's own future interests), may seek to trade on rather than contribute to her lawyer's history of cooperating. She may instruct the lawyer to defect when the adversary cooperates, and may ground this instruction on the lawyer's ethical obligations to be deferential and competent. This places the lawyer in a bind. Does she bargain ethically or practically? Does she reject the instruction and preserve her reputation for cooperating, so that she can secure better settlements, on average, for all of her clients, including those in the future? Or does she follow her client's instruction, exploit the adversary's reasonable but, as it will turn out, unwarranted cooperation, and plant the seeds of future retaliation?

The dilemma is serious, not necessarily because it is widespread — it may or may not be — but because lawyers seem to assume that it is the paradigm case. They see the defecting client as every client, and feel the pressure to bargain competitively across the board. Clients do not correct the assumption, some perhaps because they agree with it, others perhaps because they do not know that it has been made, and still others perhaps because they see legal representation as a technical process in which following the lawyer's lead is the proper (and safest) course. Whatever the reasons, the view that clients invariably want to compete has developed a life of its own, and is now treated as received wisdom in large parts of the profession. . . .

When a client asks a lawyer with a reputation for cooperating to defect on an adversary who also expected to cooperate, the lawyer's reputation for cooperating is likely to be jeopardized. She understandably will be reluctant to undercut this reputation because it allows her to coordinate activities and produce the largest aggregate returns over a bargaining career. This reluctance will make it difficult for the lawyer to make and carry out the decision to defect. Because lawyers may not represent clients when the lawyers' interests prevent them from considering and carrying out courses of action desired by clients, it may seem, at first glance, that a lawyer must either defect or refuse representation. Yet, a closer look at the Model Rules will show that they are more concerned with lawyer "income" and "business interests" specific to the particular representation than to the undifferentiated interest of doing well generally over time. The Rules try to make sure that lawyers do not exploit the influence provided by their clients' dependent circumstances to advance their own (the lawyers') interests by making favorable book deals, buying property at bargain prices, receiving gifts, unfairly appropriating resources held by clients, and the like. The Rules are less concerned with preventing lawyers from representing clients in ways that also maximize lawyer long range monetary return. In fact, if the latter was prohibited, representation would be denied to all but the most compliant clients. . . .

Seemingly trapped in a no-win situation, lawyers have made an interesting and clever, albeit probably unselfconscious, adaptation. Lawyer bargaining is not just adversarial; it is also stylized. It is adversarial because it is made up, in the main, of aggressive communication maneuvers such as argument, challenge, and demand. It is stylized because this aggressive maneuvering is carried out in a slightly exaggerated, somewhat predictable, and essentially impersonal fashion. Both dimensions are important to wriggling out of the dilemma of lawyer bargaining role. The adversarial part allows lawyers to believe that they have fought hard for their clients, and in the process that they have been deferential to client wishes and diligent in their pursuit. The stylized part allows them to preserve bargaining relationships with other lawyers by signaling, through a set of rhetorical conventions, that the aggressiveness is not personal, but is just part of the lawyer act. Behavior that is both adversarial and stylized is a lawyer's way of being (or believing she has been) both ethical and practical, of protecting her reputation for cooperating, while at the same time arguing zealously for the interests of her clients. It is an effort to walk a line between the important but conflicting normative pulls of bargaining's ethical and practical sides, complying minimally with each and not openly violating either. . . .

ROBERT H. MNOOKIN, SCOTT R. PEPPET, AND ANDREW S. TULUMELLO, BEYOND WINNING: NEGOTIATING TO CREATE VALUE IN DEALS AND DISPUTES

282-286, Harvard University Press (2000)

WHAT IF MY CLIENT WANTS ME TO MISLEAD THE OTHER SIDE?

Sometimes clients want their lawyers to lie, shade the truth, or withhold material information. Obviously, if a client proposes that you violate the codes of professional conduct or commit fraud, you should refuse and try to convince your client to take another approach. If the client rejects your counsel, you should withdraw. But what about cases that are less clear-cut, such as where the client asks you to do something that is not a clear violation of the rules but nevertheless makes you uncomfortable on professional or ethical grounds? What should you do then?

There are good reasons for a client to hire a reputable lawyer and then take advantage of the lawyer's reputation. To some extent, the profession permits clients to avoid tough ethical dilemmas. Imagine that Ed Burgess is about to negotiate a severance package with his employer, Mr. Jenks, who wants him to retire three years before Ed reaches age 65 and his current employment contract expires. There are no severance provisions. Ed would like to receive severance equal to a substantial portion of his current salary for the three-year period, and he would then expect to receive the full pension that he would have received had he worked until age 65. In arguing for the salary, Ed knows that Mr. Jenks will assume that Ed will have a hard time finding a new job; the market is tight and there aren't a lot of positions available in the area. Jenks is therefore likely to be fairly generous with Ed. In his last discussion with his boss, Ed talked at length about the hardships his family would have to endure if the company refused to pay a substantial yearly stipend.

Ed hasn't talked to Jenks in several weeks. He has, however, just received an offer from a competing firm for a good position as a senior analyst and advisor. Ed could earn approximately 75 percent of his previous salary, and he expects to accept this job *after* his severance package is negotiated. Ed knows that if he personally negotiates with Jenks, he will feel internal moral pressure to disclose this information, even if Jenks doesn't ask about his financial status. What might Ed do if he wants to squeeze Jenks for a large severance package? Hire a lawyer. Even if Ed discloses the investment advisor offer to his attorney, his lawyer cannot disclose that information to Jenks without authorization. A failure to disclose would probably not constitute fraud. (Of course, if Jenks asked Ed's lawyer directly about a competing offer, the lawyer would have to answer truthfully or not at all.)

One might question whether it is ethical for Ed to use an attorney in such a strategic manner. But he may prefer avoiding the more direct personal dilemmas raised in a face-to-face discussion with Jenks. Ed may even choose not to give his attorney this information at all. If he keeps the information completely private, then he may be able to avoid even discussing whether he has some sort of moral obligation to disclose.

SEEK TO UNDERSTAND THE CLIENT'S CHOICE

If a client is asking you to mislead the other side, the first step, as always, is to try to understand why. In what ways does this request make sense for the client? Put yourself in her shoes. If you were the client, would you propose the same thing that she's proposing?

By identifying the incentives that motivate your client to ask you to mislead the other side, you may be able to relate better to the client as you talk about his request. The key is to learn why the client thinks you should manipulate the truth. What does he see as the advantages? What does he see as the risks? What are the client's concerns? By listening and demonstrating understanding, you can often draw out the client to talk about the underlying choice of strategy.

RAISE YOUR CONCERNS EXPLICITLY

Lawyers also must learn to discuss ethical dilemmas explicitly. You can find yourself in a very uncomfortable situation if neither you nor your client is willing to discuss ethical conflicts. Learning to have such conversations productively is a critical skill.

If your client asks you to mislead the other side, you should negotiate with her and try to help her understand your views. You must explain that you don't want to violate established rules of professional responsibility, and that you don't want to do something that isn't in your client's best interests. You don't want to go against your personal beliefs, and you don't want to do something that hurts your reputation. By explaining your interests and perspective—while continuing to demonstrate understanding for the client's views—you can begin a conversation about the dilemma you face.

Ed's lawyer, for example, would want to explain that in the face of questioning by Mr. Jenks he would either have to tell the truth about a competing offer or refuse to answer a direct question. "That would probably give away the issue right there," Ed might say. "Couldn't you just say 'No, he has no other offers'?" "No," his lawyer might explain. "I can't lie about a material piece of information like that. And I've got to tell you, it would probably amount to fraud. Given that sooner or later he's going to find out whether you're working again, lying about it could cause serious problems later."

REMEMBER THAT YOUR REPUTATION IS A VALUABLE ASSET

Clients sometimes want to use a lawyer's reputation for honesty as a cover for their own unethical behavior. If a lawyer is known for telling the truth, this reputation can be a perfect smokescreen for throwing the other side off track. If your client persuades you to lie, however he may take advantage of your reputation for his own short-term gain, disregarding the long-term effect on your career and well-being.

We learned of a recent example in a divorce case. After discovering that his wife had hired an attorney, the husband hired an outstanding family lawyer—known in his community as an honorable problem-solver. The two lawyers had done many divorce cases together in the past and had built up a great deal of trust. Ordinarily they did not rely on formal discovery procedures, choosing instead to exchange information informally. This saved their clients a great deal of time and money.

The husband in this case insisted that his lawyer not disclose certain financial information to the other side unless forced to do so through formal discovery. The husband's lawyer faced a real ethical dilemma. When his colleague proposed that they informally exchange information as they had in the past, what was he to do? He knew that if he disclosed partially but withheld the information in question, it would go against his counterpart's clear expectation and would ultimately hurt his own reputation as an honest negotiator. At the same time, he was obligated to obey his client's wishes not to disclose the financial information.

Ultimately, he chose to refuse to engage in the informal information exchange process with the other attorney. This implicitly signaled, of course, that this divorce was unlike the others they had negotiated together before. Many lawyers had told us that in such situations they are likely to signal to the other side that the normal rules of play are suspended and that the baseline professional ethics rules are all that should be expected. One lawyer told of a case in which he entered the room where the negotiation was to occur, sat down across the table from a long-time colleague, and simply said "On guard." Both knew immediately that their normal collaborative rules of engagement were temporarily suspended.

Such signaling raises difficult ethical issues, of course. On the one hand, why should a client be able to gain distributive advantage by hiding behind his lawyer's reputation? Doesn't that disserve the attorney's other clients who rely on his problem-solving abilities? By refusing to engage in the informal discovery process that was based on trust, doesn't the lawyer merely give his client what the client would get from any other attorney that *didn't* have a reputation for honesty? On the other hand, is it ever legitimate for an attorney *not* to do something that would maximize the distributive benefit for a given client? If a lawyer's approach conflicts with his client's, would the best approach be simply to withdraw?

In our view, withdrawal is one possible solution. In practice, as we've discussed, however, lawyers *and clients* face real financial and logistical constraints that may make withdrawal unattractive. Once an attorney has worked with a client over time, the lawyer has built up a store of knowledge and experience relevant only to that client, and the client has invested time and money in educating his lawyer about the particulars of the case. Under such circumstances, rather than withdraw, it seems reasonable for an attorney to signal to the other side that for this negotiation they should not expect anything beyond what the formal discovery rules require.

The lesson we draw, however, is that lawyer-client preparation is essential. As a lawyer-client relationship begins, an attorney must be clear with his client about his problem-solving orientation and what that requires. If a lawyer is unambiguous about what he will and won't do, the client can make an informed choice about which lawyer to retain. Such ethical conflicts are thus much less likely to arise.

The story of Clark Clifford, a fabled Washington lawyer, illustrates how a client can benefit from an attorney's reputation for integrity when the client has something to hide and how an attorney must draw the line on how his credibility can be used for concealment.

MARILYN BERGER, CLARK CLIFFORD, KEY ADVISOR TO FOUR PRESIDENTS, DIES

New York Times, October 11, 1998

THE IMPORTANCE OF CREDIBILITY

In an interview in the mid-1980s Clifford said his concept of the practice of law "is that through the years you conduct yourself in such a manner that the staffs of the government agencies have confidence in your integrity and your credibility." . . .

It was precisely his reputation for integrity and credibility that led the group of Arab investors to seek Clifford's help in the late 1970s when they wanted to acquire an American bank. The Federal Reserve Board approved the takeover in 1981, reassured by Clifford that there would be no control by BCCI, which he also represented.

The fact that Clifford himself was to become chairman of the new bank provided further reassurance to the regulators. The bank, with Clifford as its chairman, was called First American Bankshares and became the largest in Washington.

Ten years later, Robert Morgenthau, the district attorney in New York City, disclosed that his office had found evidence that the parent company of Clifford's bank was secretly controlled by BCCI. The district attorney convened a grand jury to determine whether Clifford and his partner, Altman, had deliberately misled federal regulators when the two men assured them that BCCI would have no control.

Clifford's predicament worsened when it was disclosed that he had made about $6 million in profits from bank stock that he bought with an unsecured loan from BCCI. A New York grand jury handed up indictments, as did the Justice Department. Clifford's assets in New York, where he kept most of his investments, were frozen.

Clifford said the investigation caused him pain and anger. If the regulators had been deceived about any secret ownership by BCCI, he said, he too had been deceived. . . .

"It's easy to say I should have known, but a client tells his lawyer what the client wants the lawyer to know," Clifford said. "I have to admit that they came to me because of my standing and reputation. If you think that, then you'd understand better that I'd be the last person they'd divulge this stuff to. I gave them standing. Why would they jeopardize that? They know if they told me, I'd be out the door."

HERBERT M. KRITZER, FEE ARRANGEMENTS AND NEGOTIATION

21 L. & Socy. Rev. 341, 341-347 (1987)

My central argument is that discussions of the settlement process, and particularly of manipulations of that process, must consider the interests of *all* involved in litigation. Regular participants in litigation are well aware of this point. In my series of interviews with corporate lawyers and their clients in Toronto regarding the impact of fees and fee shifting a number of respondents mentioned the importance of taking into account the interest of the opposing lawyer. For example, a litigation partner in a firm with one hundred lawyers said, "If you can satisfy the lawyer [with regard to his fee], you'll be a lot closer to settlement." A lawyer for a large retailer similarly stated that to achieve settlement, "you need to provide an incentive for the [opposing] lawyer." Yet despite the evidence that litigation lawyers do not selflessly ignore their own interests, little attention has been paid to how these interests affect settlement and negotiation.

I am not suggesting that lawyers engage in questionable actions for financial gain. The argument is more subtle: Lawyers, like all of us, when forced to make a choice for which there is no definitive answer, will tend to select the option that is in their own interest. In other words, the financial incentives of their work will often influence the decisions, and it is not coincidental that they will personally benefit from these choices. Thus, although the plaintiffs' bar may truly believe that the contingent fee is the poor man's key to the courthouse door, this belief is shaped by the fact that the key to the courthouse also brings clients—and therefore a livelihood—to the plaintiffs' lawyers. Elsewhere I have pointed out that the relationship between lawyers and clients is shaped by professional, personal, and business considerations, the last, at their most basic, meaning income (and income streams.) But what is the significance of this type of analysis for settlement and negotiation? . . .

Contingent fee lawyers in cases with modest amounts at stake have an incentive to arrive quickly at a settlement, even if that settlement is not the best for the client. Whether this means that the fee arrangement directly affects the amount of time the lawyer spends on settlement negotiations (although I could in fact find no systematic difference in time spent on such activities between hourly and contingent fee lawyers), the same theoretical considerations apply to the content of the actual negotiation. Specifically, since the contingent fee lawyer is to receive a share of the ultimate recovery, she has an incentive to see to it that the recovery can in fact be shared.

A contingent fee lawyer who sought nonmonetary resolutions of her clients' cases, even if those resolutions were better from the clients' perspectives, would soon go out of business unless some alternate payment method were available for such settlements (e.g., fee shifting, whereby the defendant pays the plaintiff's attorney for his time, or a central fund, created by taxing contingent fees, from which the lawyer could receive compensation).

. . . Although lawyers are professionals who are concerned with the needs and interests of their clients, their behavior is nonetheless influenced (note the use of *influenced* rather than *determined*) by the forces of economic rationality or necessity or both, and this influence is felt as well in the lawyers' means of negotiating. If we want lawyers to consider actively what Menkel-Meadow calls the problem-solving approaches to negotiation, we must insure that their livelihood is not dependent upon adversary approaches to negotiation.

QUESTIONS

1. Professor Condlin states that "If a client asks a lawyer to use tactics that are repugnant, lawyers may refuse." He divides "bargaining decision

responsibilities along an end-means line." Is this a helpful distinction for you? If a client you represent in the sale of a business instructed you to make a first offer of $1,000,000 in order to eventually sell for his target of $500,000, can you refuse? If you do refuse, over the client's objection, is the representation necessarily ended? Can you make the first offer to opposing counsel with a wink and not be breaching a client confidence?

2. Is there a cleaner end-means line when representing an injured tort claimant than when representing a business person in a commercial transaction? Is an insurance company retaining a lawyer to defend a personal injury claim more likely to control the means of lawyer negotiating than is an injured plaintiff? Do different ethics rules apply to lawyers depending on who employs them?

3. There is no requirement that those wanting to settle a dispute or complete a transaction have to hire lawyers to negotiate for them. Could there be ethical and tactical advantages for a person to hire a lawyer when they do not wish to reveal "non-material" information? In the Mnookin et al. example of Ed Burgess hiring a lawyer to negotiate his severance package, is the lawyer acting unethically if he knows he is being retained to negotiate for Ed only so Ed will not have to reveal to his employer the consulting offer he received?

4. Should Clark Clifford have done his own investigation or "due diligence" of BCCI's ownership interest in First American Bankshares? Can you think of other situations where a client would have reason to lie to their attorney?

5. Do contingent fee arrangements create an attorney-client conflict of interest? Should they be considered unethical? Why or why not?

6. Would Kritzer's suggestion that contingent fees be replaced by a fee shifting method where the defendant pays the plaintiff's attorney for time spent or a tax on contingent fees to create a central lawyers' fee fund eliminate attorney-client conflicts of interest in settlement or create new ones? Would you support these "reforms"?

C. GOOD FAITH v. THREATS, EXPOSURE, AND COERCION

Although it can be hoped that lawyers will only be retained to negotiate when the client desires to reach an agreement and bargain in good faith, there may be occasions when settlement is not the goal or when compromise for purposes of agreement is not an option. On occasion a client may pursue negotiation for purposes of delay or distraction, to obtain information from a competitor, or to harass. As previously discussed, clients get to decide the purpose and objectives of negotiation, but lawyers can usually decline to represent a party or withdraw. Indeed, ethical rules may require the lawyer to withdraw if continued representation will result in violation of ethical rules. (See ABA Model Rule 1.16(a)(1).)

There is no general ethical duty to bargain in good faith, but if the parties have agreed by contract to negotiate in good faith before ending a business relationship or going to court, they may be held to their bargain. In some labor management disputes under the National Labor Relations Act, 29 U.S.C.A. 158(d), there may be a good faith negotiation requirement. Rules of court and court orders may also require "good faith" negotiation or mediation before a dispute will be heard.

Even if good faith in negotiation is not required by rules of legal ethics, ethical rules and contract law limit certain types of "bad faith" bargaining. A prohibition against bad faith negotiation is indicated by ABA Model Rule 4.4, which states:

> "*Respect for Rights of Third Persons*: In representing a client, a lawyer shall not use means that have no substantial purpose other than to embarrass, delay, or burden a third person, or use methods of obtaining evidence that violate the legal rights of such a person."

Tort law and criminal law may also restrict the use of threats, extortion, and some forms of coercion. However, threatening to file a civil lawsuit to resolve the matter in dispute when the lawyer has a good faith basis for the claim is not prohibited. Indeed, every legal negotiation carries, at least, an implicit threat that if agreement is not reached, further action will be taken or alternatives will be pursued. Adversarial negotiations and pressure from clients may tempt lawyers to go further and use threats of unrelated legal action or exposure of wrongdoing if negotiation demands are not met. The law, rather than ethical rules, may be used to decide when threatening exposure of wrongdoing or a ruinous lawsuit becomes criminal extortion, and also when lying becomes fraud.

A threat by a lawyer to punch an opponent in the nose if a demand is not met is clearly unethical and criminal. A threat to do something adverse to your opponent, even if not unlawful, only for the purpose of gaining an advantage in a negotiation, presents more challenging issues. For example, exposing or not exposing an opposing lawyer's unethical behavior in conjunction with a negotiation may place a lawyer between the proverbial "rock and a hard place." Power imbalances may also create questions of intimidation in the negotiation process, as might the otherwise legitimate threat of filing a class action against a modest-sized company if monetary demands are not met. In addition to being ethically risky, threats may jeopardize the enforceability of a settlement because of duress or other contract grounds for voiding or rescinding agreements.

The two articles that follow address some of these issues and are included to help you understand that even though the limits of what lawyers can do in negotiations are murky, tort, contract, and criminal law do impose outer limits on negotiation conduct and communications. The first article by Professor Uelmen regarding threats in negotiation is written for California lawyers, but is instructive for lawyers elsewhere. It also reminds us that ethics rules are not identical from state to state and that civil liability and criminal law limiting what lawyers may do in negotiations can vary, even if the red flags of caution are the same. The second article explains other negotiation constraints, particularly where there is unequal power.

GERALD F. UELMEN, PLAYING "GODFATHER" IN SETTLEMENT NEGOTIATIONS: THE ETHICS OF USING THREATS

Cal. Litigation 3-8 (Fall 1990)

In the course of negotiating a settlement, which of the following statements would be a breach of ethics for a California lawyer?

1. If you refuse this offer, I'll break both of your legs.
2. Just don't forget, my client knows where your daughter goes to school.
3. We can settle this case here and now, or we can just turn the whole matter over to the District Attorney's Office tomorrow.
4. Your unreasonableness in rejecting this offer can only be attributed to your conflict of interest in this case. I'm afraid this is a matter for the State Bar to look into. . . .

All four of the above statements could result in disciplinary action against the lawyer who made them. The first three could result in a criminal prosecution for extortion. A recent ruling of the California Supreme Court suggests broad immunity, however, from civil liability for all four statements—at least after a judicial proceeding has been initiated. Nonetheless, the use of threats to gain an advantage in settlement negotiations is fraught with substantial risks for lawyers who watch too many reruns of "The Godfather."

DISCIPLINARY ACTION

With respect to disciplinary action, our starting point is Rule 5-100 of the 1989 revision of the California Rules of Professional Conduct, which provides:

> A member of the State Bar shall not threaten to present criminal, administrative or disciplinary charges to obtain an advantage in a civil dispute . . .

. . . While threats of administrative or disciplinary charges have rarely appeared as the basis for lawyer discipline, threats of criminal charges are common grounds for disciplinary action, frequently in the context of collection matters.

The California rule resolves any doubts whether threats of administrative or disciplinary charges are proscribed. The prohibition of such threats is consistent with the absence of any mandatory duty on California lawyers to report misconduct by other lawyers. The new ABA Model Rules, by contrast, do impose reporting obligations. Model Rule 8.3 provides that a lawyer having knowledge of a violation of rules of professional conduct that "raises a substantial question" as to another lawyer's honesty, trustworthiness, or fitness as a lawyer must "inform the appropriate professional authority." While the ABA Model Rules do not incorporate the explicit prohibition of threats found in DR 7-105(a) [superseded], it has been widely assumed that threatening or filing criminal charges to gain an advantage in a civil matter would violate other provisions of the Model Rules. (Rules 3.1, 3.3, 3.4, 3.5, 3.8, 4.4, 8.4(b), and 8.4(e).) The addition of Rule 8.3, however, seems to undercut any expansion of this prohibition to administrative or disciplinary charges.

CRIMINAL LIABILITY

The starting point regarding criminal liability is California Penal Code Section 518, which defines the crime of extortion:

> Extortion is the obtaining of property from another with his consent, or the obtaining of an official act of a public officer, induced by a wrongful use of force or fear, or under color of official right.

Penal Code Section 519 defines wrongful use of fear to include a threat "to accuse the individual threatened, or any relative of his, or member of his family, of any crime . . ." Threats of physical violence, direct or indirect, are also encompassed. Our first two examples, since they are threats of criminal violence, would be grounds for attorney discipline pursuant to Section 6106 of the California Business and Professions Code, even though Rule 5-100 has no direct application.

Does a lawyer's threat of criminal prosecution qualify as extortion? That question was answered in *People v. Beggs*, 178 Cal. 79 (1918). Beggs was an attorney, representing a store owner who had been victimized by one of his employees. The employee was actually arrested and admitted having stolen two suites of clothes, worth less than $50. Learning the employee had $2,500 on deposit in bank accounts, Beggs threatened him that, unless he paid $2,000 to settle with his employer, he would be sent to prison for seven to ten years. The money was paid.

In upholding the attorney's conviction, the California Supreme Court made it quite clear that criminal liability did not depend on the amount extorted exceeding the lawful claim. Even assuming the employee had stolen $2,000, the threats of criminal prosecution would constitute extortion.

> It is the means employed which the law denounces, and though the purpose may be to collect a just indebtedness arising from and created by the criminal act for which the threat is to prosecute the wrongdoer, it is nevertheless within the statutory inhibition. The law does not contemplate the use of criminal process as a means of collecting a debt. 178 Cal. at 84. . . .

CIVIL LIABILITY

With respect to civil liability, our starting point is the decision of *Kinnamon v. Staiman & Snyder*, 66 Cal. App. 3d 893 (1977). There the court held that a cause of action for intentional infliction of emotional distress was stated in a complaint alleging that a lawyer made the following statement in a letter to the plaintiff who gave his client a check dishonored for insufficient funds:

> As you may be aware to issue a check with insufficient funds to cover said check is a misdemeanor. In addition to any civil remedies my client may have, we also plan to exercise our rights to file a criminal complaint against you for your action herein.

The court concluded that this threat met the requirement of "outrageous conduct" for the tort of intentional infliction of emotional distress because it was explicitly proscribed by then Rule 7-104 of the California Rules of Professional Conduct. . . .

Courts routinely rely on disciplinary rules as evidence of the standard of care required of attorneys. Likewise, the issue of "outrageousness" can certainly be illuminated by disciplinary rules. In fact, the reasoning of *Kinnamon* would equally support a conclusion that the use of a threat to bring disciplinary charges to gain an advantage in a civil action is also outrageous. . . .

ROBERT S. ADLER AND ELLIOT M. SILVERSTEIN, WHEN DAVID MEETS GOLIATH: DEALING WITH POWER DIFFERENTIALS IN NEGOTIATIONS

5 Harv. Negot. L. Rev. 1, 29-48 (2000)

... Although the superior bargaining power of one party, standing alone, does not generally provide the basis for invalidating an agreement, the law does set limits within which bargainers must operate. These limits apply both with respect to the terms that can be negotiated and to the methods one can use to influence an opponent to agree to the terms. They are premised on the assumption that at some point in the bargaining process, power advantages can produce inequities so pronounced that the law must step in to protect the weak. In negotiations involving power imbalances, most abuses arise when the stronger party, either through threats or other overt displays of power, intimidates the other into entering an agreement so one-sided that it offends reasonable sensibilities. Of course, not all bargaining abuses result from overt power displays. Some arise from shifting the balance of power by exploiting trust or employing deceit.

Depending on the nature of the abuse, the law may take different approaches — regulating modestly where "arm's length" conditions exist or expansively where a "special relationship" requires protection for particularly vulnerable individuals. Where special relationships exist, special protections apply.

A. Undue Influence

When a relationship of trust and dependency between two or more parties exists, the law typically polices the relationship closely and imposes especially stringent duties on the dominant parties. For example, although tort law generally imposes no obligations on citizens to assist those in danger, the courts take the opposite position when they determine that a special relationship exists. In those cases, the courts unhesitatingly find an affirmative duty to rescue.

Contract law imposes similar duties in the case of agreements involving undue influence in special relationships. Where one party — because of family position, business connection, legal authority or other circumstances — gains extraordinary trust from another party the courts will scrutinize any agreements between them with great care to ensure fairness. Common examples of special relationships include guardian-ward, trustee-beneficiary, agent-principal, spouses, parent-child, attorney-client, physician-patient, and clergy-parishioner. To treat negotiations in these settings as arm's length interactions would invite "unfair persuasion" by the dominant parties either through threats, deception, or misplaced trust. Accordingly, the law imposes special obligations on those who play the dominant role in such relationships, requiring them to exercise good faith and to make full disclosure of all critical facts when negotiating agreements with dependent parties. In determining whether a dominant party in a special relationship exerted undue influence, the courts generally look to the fairness of the contract, the availability of independent advice, and the vulnerability of the dependent party. An agreement entered into as a result of undue influence is voidable by the victim.

B. PROTECTIONS IN ARM'S LENGTH TRANSACTIONS

Under the "bargain theory" of contracts, parties negotiate at arm's length to exchange consideration. An arm's length transaction is one in which the parties stand in no special relationship with each other, owe each other no special duties, and each acts in his or her own interest. The vast majority of contracts fall within the arm's length category, which means that no special obligations of disclosure, fair dealing or good faith are generally required. This is not to suggest that parties are free to operate without rules, but it does mean that they are accorded substantial leeway in negotiating contracts. They certainly maintain the freedom to assume even foolish and shortsighted contractual obligations, so long as they do so knowingly and voluntarily. Once one of the parties acts in a patently abusive manner, however, the law does provide protection, as, for example, with fraud, duress, and unconscionability.

1. FRAUD

Negotiated agreements, to be binding, must be entered into by the parties in a knowing and voluntary manner. Lies undermine agreements by removing the "knowing" element from the bargain. That is, one induced by misrepresentations to purchase a relatively worthless item of personal property typically buys the product "voluntarily" — in fact, eagerly — with enthusiasm generated by the false promise of the product's value. The catch is that because of the defrauder's lies, the victim has unfairly lost the opportunity to "know" the precise nature of what he or she has bought. Lies of this nature clearly alter the normal contractual dynamic, unfairly shifting power from the victim to the defrauder. Because of the dramatic impact that fraud has on the power balance in negotiations, we necessarily review this doctrine.

In its classic formulation, common law fraud requires five elements: (1) a false representation of a material fact made by the defendant, (2) with knowledge or belief as to its falsity, (3) with an intent to induce the plaintiff to rely on the representations, (4) justifiable reliance on the misrepresentation by the plaintiff, and (5) damage or injury to the plaintiff by the reliance. Fraud entitles the victim to void the transaction and permits him or her to pursue restitution or tort damages. A false representation may be made in several ways — through a positive statement, through misleading conduct, or by concealing a fact that the defrauder has a duty to disclose. . . .

2. DURESS

Coercion, whether express or implied, takes many forms. One party, for example, might threaten to take its business elsewhere if its terms are not met. Another might threaten to file suit if its financial claims are not resolved. Still another might insist that it will no longer provide a discount or expedited delivery if a deal cannot be struck. These threats, designed to exert pressure on an opponent to secure his or her cooperation, generally fall into a category that the law would consider to be hard bargaining, but not illegal. At some point, however, coercion becomes objectionable. How does one distinguish between proper and improper behavior? Unfortunately, there is no clear dividing line. As various commentators and courts have stated, threats per se are acceptable; only wrongful threats are forbidden. What makes one threat "wrongful" and another not depends on the circumstances of each case. To constitute duress, threats must be of a particularly virulent nature. . . .

Threatened action need not be illegal — even acts otherwise legal may constitute duress if directed towards an improper goal. For example, a threat to bring a lawsuit — normally a legitimate form of coercion — becomes abusive if "made with the corrupt intent to coerce a transaction grossly unfair to the victim and not related to the subject of such proceedings." Similarly, a threat to release embarrassing, but true, information about another person, although abhorrent, would not constitute duress (in the form of blackmail) unless accompanied by an improper demand for financial or other favors.

Should negotiators with a decided power advantage feel inhibited from pushing for as hard a bargain as they can in light of the law of duress? Generally, no. Judging from the language in the courts' opinions, hard bargainers should have little to fear from the doctrine of duress. Nothing in the law of duress prevents negotiators from pushing to the limits of their bargaining power or from taking advantage of the economic vulnerabilities or bad luck of their opponents. Trouble arises only when a party makes threats that lapse into the illegal, immoral and unconscionable. Of greater impact on negotiators concerned about legal protections is the law of unconscionability, to which we now turn.

3.   UNCONSCIONABILITY

The doctrine of unconscionability functions to protect bargainers of lesser power from overreaching by dominant parties. Invoked in a variety of cases under the Uniform Commercial Code and elsewhere, the term has never been precisely defined, no doubt to provide greater flexibility in its use. . . .

What is an unconscionable contract? Given that the UCC drafters deliberately avoided an explicit definition, one cannot simply and easily capture the concept. At a minimum, an unconscionable contract is one "such as no man in his senses and not under delusion would make on the one hand and no honest and fair man would accept on the other." Unconscionability seeks to prevent two evils: (1) oppression and (2) unfair surprise. In a seminal analysis, Professor Arthur Allen Leff labeled these two concepts "substantive" and "procedural" unconscionability, respectively. Substantive unconscionability includes the actual terms of the agreement; procedural unconscionability refers to the bargaining process between the parties. . . .

Procedural unconscionability, what Professor Leff calls "bargaining naughtiness," arises when contracts involve the element of unfair surprise. This typically takes the form of terms hidden in a mass of contract language, terms hidden in small print, or on the back of an agreement where one would not think to look, or the like. Procedural unconscionability also assumes another, less clearly delineated form, that of "oppressive" tactics. When the dominant party uses high-pressure tactics in circumstances that result in unfair control of the situation, the courts will intercede. Although perhaps fully cognizant of the terms, the victim has to accept what the other party demands because of the victim's limited bargaining power. The abuse falls short of duress, but qualifies for judicial relief under the doctrine of unconscionability. . . .

Virtually all cases in which unconscionability arises as an issue involve significant disparities in bargaining power, but that, standing alone, rarely justifies a finding of unconscionability according to most courts and commentators. What draws judicial fire is when the party endowed with superior bargaining power imposes an extremely unfair and one-sided agreement on the weaker. In effect, the stronger party oppresses the weaker party through the application of brute power, thereby removing any real "choice" from the victim. Accordingly, inequality of bargaining power seems a generally necessary, but not sufficient, condition of unconscionability. . . .

How concerned should a negotiator be — especially one with superior bargaining power — that pursuing an advantage in a contract will result in a court ruling that the agreement is unconscionable? Our best answer: some, but not much. For the most part, the courts have taken a cautious approach to finding unconscionability in negotiated agreements. The vast majority of successful unconscionability claims involve poor, often unsophisticated, consumers challenging oppressive adhesion contracts foisted on them by retail merchants or credit sellers. . . . No doubt this reflects the general view that persons of greater sophistication suffer less contractual abuse and need less protection. . . .

QUESTIONS

1. If you become aware that an opposing lawyer is lying about a material fact, like the amount of medical damages incurred by a client, what do you do? Must you report the lie to the Bar? Should you first warn the lawyer or state your intent to report? Might this be considered a threat? Must you wait until after the negotiation is completed to report the ethical breach?
2. Suppose during a lawsuit you receive a copy of a letter from your opponent instructing one of their witnesses to lie under oath. May you use this letter in settlement negotiations? May you use the threat of a bar disciplinary proceeding or a criminal prosecution for obstruction of justice? In exchange for a favorable settlement, may you agree not to report the instructions the plaintiffs' lawyers had been giving? (See ABA Comm. on Ethics and Professional Responsibility, 1992.)
3. There is a generally recognized privilege for statements made in the course of judicial proceedings. If the threat of filing civil and criminal complaints for the dishonored check in *Kinnamon v. Staiman & Snyder*, cited by Professor Uelman, was made during the course of a civil proceeding, would it be privileged and, therefore, not actionable? (See *Silberg v. Anderson*, 50 Cal. 3d 205 (1990), holding that a letter with threats sent in the course of judicial proceedings is privileged.) If privilege does exist for communications made during lawsuits, would all four of Professor Uelman's threat examples be privileged, assuming they were made while negotiating settlement of a lawsuit? Would the threat of physical violence be distinguished?
4. The greatest power differentials in negotiation are associated with consumer cases and bargaining where one side is not represented by an attorney. Can undue influence and unconscionability in negotiations occur when all parties are represented by competent lawyers? By definition, if undue influence or unconscionability is found to void a settlement or transaction negotiated by lawyers, do incompetence and malpractice exist?

D. THE PUSH FOR ETHICS REFORM

The absence of a rule explicitly prohibiting deception by lawyers during negotiation has disturbed many who feel that a change in lawyer ethics is necessary to promote honesty and correct the lawyer-liar image. An array of proposals has been urged to formally change the Model Rules of Professional Conduct. Rule 4.1, which only prohibits lying about material facts, and Comment 2, which acknowledges and does not disapprove the use of deception about bottom lines and puffery about value. The rule would be easy to rewrite but the revisions could be difficult to sell and enforce. (For a specific proposal, see Alfini, 1999.)

For decades, there has been a debate within the Bar about prohibiting false statements of fact in negotiation, whether material or not. The American Bar Association (ABA), when drafting the Model Rules in the early 1980s, considered requiring that lawyers be "fair" in negotiations and not permit "unconscionable" agreements, but these requirements, following much debate, were rejected as untenable. For some, the ethics requirements should be enhanced to promote honesty and professional integrity. For others, requiring truthfulness in all matters relating to negotiation would be naive and undermine the enforceability of negotiated agreements, particularly when truthfulness regarding nonmaterial facts is not required of those who are not lawyers.

NOTE: GUIDELINES, COLLABORATIVE LAW, AND MINDFULNESS

The Litigation Section of the ABA has drafted a recent set of Ethics Guidelines for Settlement Negotiations, portions of which have been adopted by the ABA House of Delegates. Although the Guidelines do not change the ethics rules, they do suggest best practices and aspirational goals that go beyond the rules regarding honesty in negotiation. The ABA's Commission on Evaluation of the Rules of Professional Conduct, known as the "Ethics 2000 Commission," resulted in a slight change to Comment 2 of Rule 4.1. The official comment now states that "a party's intentions as to an acceptable settlement of a claim are *ordinarily* not in the category of facts" where candor can be expected.

A movement by some lawyers to adopt a nonadversarial approach and a higher morality in how they represent clients may have a more profound impact on lawyering ethics and the negotiation of disputes than would a change in ethics rules. The discontent with the practice of adversarial law, fueled in part by the tension created between the expectation of zealous representation and the desire for personal integrity, has caused some lawyers to explore other models of practice. These efforts have been thoughtful and courageous, as well as controversial. Individual lawyers have reshaped their practices by emphasizing aspects of representation that they find more comfortable and rewarding. We have previously covered the problem-solving approach in contrast to adversarial negotiations. This approach changes the practice paradigm and has implications for personal standards of professional integrity. (See Menkel-Meadow, 2000.)

Lawyers have formed regional groups of practitioners who pledge between them to abstain from some forms of practice and adhere to enhanced standards in their interactions. The most notable example is the collaborative law movement in domestic relations, where subscribing lawyers contract with clients about standards and limits of representation. A collaborative lawyer will not represent the client if the case goes to court and will not mislead another lawyer during negotiations. (For an explanation of the collaborative practice model, see Lawrence, 2003; Tesler, 2001.)

The basic elements of collaborative law, as explained by Pauline H. Tesler in 21 Alternatives (Jan. 2003) are:

- Each party is represented by separate counsel specially trained to provide effective collaborative representation.
- All parties and attorneys sign a binding participation agreement providing that the attorneys are retained solely to facilitate reasonable, efficient settlement of all issues (a "limited purpose" retention).
- The agreement commits all participants to good-faith negotiations, without the threat of or resort to litigation during the pendency of the collaborative process. All parties agree to provide early, voluntary, continuing disclosure of all information that a reasonable decision maker would need to make an informed decision about each issue in the dispute. If a party refuses to disclose information that counsel considers relevant and material to the dispute, collaborative counsel commit to withdraw and/or terminate the process. In other words, although collaborative lawyers remain bound by attorney-client privilege, they will not assist a client to participate in bad faith in the collaborative process or to misuse the process for undue advantage.
- Clients are free to terminate the process at any time and seek third-party dispute resolution, including litigation, but if any party does so, all attorneys are disqualified from participating in any way in nonconsensual third-party proceedings brought by any party to the dispute against any other party or parties.
- If the process is terminated and litigation follows, the collaborative agreement may give the court jurisdiction to make awards of attorneys' fees and costs against any party who has misused the collaborative process for delay, deception, or other bad-faith purposes. The collaborative lawyers, however, could not be witnesses in such proceedings.

Another developing concept that could influence how some lawyers negotiate is "mindfulness" in lawyering. Although too new to simply describe and pigeonhole, mindfulness derives from meditative qualities that put immediate demands in perspective regarding life as a whole. It focuses the practitioner on the big picture and not only on the discreet transaction of the moment. In this way mindfulness redirects the context of practice to the integrity of the person and the system rather than the immediate needs of the situation. Mindfulness focused on the bigger picture and on ethical decision making is not necessarily the opposite of adversarialness, but they may be difficult to reconcile.

A recent symposium issue of the Harvard Negotiation Law Review is dedicated to the values of meditation and mindfulness in the practice of alternative dispute resolution. One commentator, Professor Scott Peppet, takes on the logical extension of mindfulness, perhaps tongue-in-cheek, to reach an analogy between the mindful lawyer and a saint or holy man and then questions whether two saints could negotiate.

SCOTT R. PEPPET, MINDFULNESS IN THE LAW AND
ADR: CAN SAINTS NEGOTIATE?

7 Harv. Negot. L. Rev. 83, 86-87, 93-95, 2002

... [I]magine that, at the extreme, a diligent mindfulness practitioner might eventually reach a state of complete dedication to an ethical life. I will call this person a "saint" because she adopts a more conscientious stance toward her relations with the world and others than most of us will ever achieve. Our saint would also have to be sufficiently strong-willed to live up to her moral commitments. She must have developed herself to the point that the contingencies of her life — her history, attachments, psychology, and emotions — no longer lead her to act against these deeply-held beliefs. She is so mindful as to be somewhat frightening.

What sort of ethical commitments would our saint adopt? For the sake of argument, I will assert that at the very least such a person would commit to both honesty and fairness, resolving neither to deceive nor to take advantage of other human beings for her own ends and to respect and take others' interests into account. There is good reason to believe that a very mindful person would adopt such a saintly view of life. Even without turning extensively to religious doctrine, one can imagine that our saint would be consistently nonpartisan when it came to her own and others' interests. ...

Consider the negotiating standards of two holy men, one a willing buyer and the other a willing seller. If their personal commitments to holiness prevented them from making the slightest misrepresentation or from engaging in any abuse of their bargaining positions, how would the ultimate outcome of their negotiations differ from the outcome achieved by two lawyer negotiators? If deceit truly is inherent to negotiation, the outcome achieved by the holy men could not be defined as the product of a negotiation. ...

Not everyone agrees with this characterization, but it is certainly common. Perhaps the best example of this sort of thinking is, again, Model Rule 4.1's permission of misrepresentations about reservation price. According to the Rule's Comments, misleading statements of this sort are permitted because "under generally accepted conventions in negotiation, certain types of statements ordinarily are not taken as statements of material fact." Although the Rules do not say so explicitly, this Comment seems to imply that barring all types of misrepresentation would demand too much — it would make negotiation as we normally understand it impossible.

I disagree with this view, both as expressed in Steele's hypothetical and in the Comment to Model Rule 4.1. Although many negotiators may deceive and manipulate, I see nothing that requires one to do so, nor do I think that one can be effective only by doing so. Negotiation requires parties to manage different and sometimes conflicting interests to determine whether a jointly-created outcome can be found that is more satisfying than any self-help alternative. Two saints could honestly disclose their alternatives and reservation values, their interests and priorities, and still face a variety of challenging decisions regarding how best to maximize achievable joint gain and divide the pie. Even for the enlightened there would likely be no easy answer as to whether to give more of the economic surplus in a transaction to the person who needed it more, wanted it more, or deserved it more. Two saints might disagree about how to classify a used car in the "blue book" scheme, or about when an employment agreement should vest an executive's stock options. I see no reason to redescribe their interaction over these matters as something other than negotiation merely because they chose to avoid dishonesty or manipulation.

I must make one caveat, however. One can imagine a person who becomes so universal in her views — so detached from the particulars of her individual position — that she no longer values her own interests at all. Her only interest becomes to serve others' interests. Although it is difficult to imagine how two such people could interact (wouldn't they merely circle each other endlessly, each trying to help the other?), I think the introduction of even one such person into what would otherwise be a negotiation does require redescription of the interaction as something other than bargaining. In this extreme circumstance there would not be two people with differing or conflicting interests; only one with interests and another with a desire to serve. There would be nothing to negotiate about — person A would express needs and person B would satisfy them to the best of B's ability.

Finally, one might object that lawyers have a duty to compete. If a lawyer refuses to do so because of ethical commitments that include consideration of an opponent's interests, then even if we cannot redescribe that lawyer's interactions as something other than negotiation, perhaps we should simply decide that the person can no longer be a lawyer. Robert Condlin, for example, has written that lawyers "must use any legally available move or procedure helpful to a client's bargaining position. Among other things, this means that all forms of leverage must be exploited, inflated demands made, and private information obtained and used whenever any of these actions would advance the client's stated objectives. . . ." If negotiating lawyers will not play the game, they should be disqualified as players.

Although it opens yet another difficult line of argument, I think it unlikely that a saint, or even just a very reflective person, would decide, like Condlin, to prioritize client loyalty over the saint's already-discussed ethical commitments. As Riskin explains, mindfulness loosens one's attachments — one's loyalties. This is, again, what suggests that these practices might aid in adopting a more universal perspective on moral questions. It also suggests, however, that a loyalty-driven ethic, peculiar to one's particular duties to a particular client, will be relatively unpersuasive to our saint as compared to the basic obligations to honesty and fairness. . . .

QUESTIONS

1. Would a "saint" as described by Professor Peppet, who negotiates on behalf of a client, be subject to discipline by the Bar for failing to make the client's interests a priority and for not being a zealous advocate? Would you retain such a saint as your lawyer for purposes of negotiation?
2. What would Jim White, whose critique of *Getting to Yes* appeared in Chapter 4, have to say about the "mindful" practice of negotiation?
3. Would you change Rule 4.1 and the comments to it? If so, what would you change and why?
4. A corporate defendant may desire to restrict a plaintiff's lawyer from representing other plaintiffs with similar claims or may feel vulnerable to future

lawsuits based on information the plaintiff's lawyer obtained through discovery. As part of a negotiated settlement, the defendant in this situation may request that the plaintiff's attorney agree not to represent other plaintiffs with similar claims. Such a provision would contravene Model Rule 5.6, which provides, "A lawyer shall not participate in offering or making . . . an agreement in which a restriction on the lawyer's right to practice is part of the settlement. . . ." What do you think is the rationale and justification for this prohibition?

5. Is the "mirror test" the ultimate guide for negotiation ethics? That test takes into account your own values following a completed negotiation in asking "Can you look at yourself in the mirror and feel O.K.?"

CHAPTER
8

What's Law Got to Do with It?

LAW CAN MATTER

Most books on negotiation are devoid of material on how the law impacts negotiation and on the limitations and enforceability of settlement agreements. Therefore, students of negotiation may well ask "What's the law got to do with it?" There is considerable case law to guide negotiators and help avoid problems that arise after settlement. These problems may surface when enforcing negotiated agreements or being sued for malpractice for how you handled the negotiation or drafted the settlement agreement.

Previously discussed ethical responsibilities to disclose material facts during negotiations can lead to legal challenges to a settlement in some jurisdictions when such undisclosed or misrepresented facts were not discoverable by the other side. Questions about a lawyer's authority to represent parties' interests in settlement negotiations and lawyer's fees can lead to collateral litigation, particularly in class actions. (See, e.g., *Evans v. Jeff D.*, 475 U.S. 717, 106 S. Ct. 1531 (1986).) The drafting of settlement agreements, as an application of contract law, often creates subsequent litigation about what was negotiated and what was mutually intended as a settlement. The law relating to releases, confidentiality provisions, and promises to do something or not to do something in the future can be critical in fashioning a lasting negotiated settlement. The entire law school curriculum bears in some way on the process, substance, and outcomes of negotiations by lawyers.

We will focus on four areas where the law has shaped negotiation conduct. First, negotiated settlements can be encouraged by allocating attorney's fees and litigation costs based on the reasonableness of rejected settlement offers. The statutory and case law regarding offers of settlement and fee shifting is covered here. Second, strategic moves by lawyers to settle with only some of multiparty defendants have spawned appellate decisions about the consequences when some defendants settle and others do not. We will look at "Mary Carter" agreements, as these secret, selective settlements have become known. Third, because a settlement agreement is a contract, common law cases may limit the extent to which the settlement can be enforced if it is the result of fraud, misrepresentation, or duress. This chapter examines these common law limits to bargaining. Finally, lawyers must be aware that what they do or fail to do as negotiators for clients can lead to charges of professional malpractice.

197

We include material on potential claims by disappointed clients against their lawyers after the negotiation is concluded.

Other areas of law that significantly impact negotiations are not covered here, but should be noted. Insurance coverage issues and the role of insurance in paying settlement agreements loom in the background of tort negotiations and other lawsuit settlement negotiations. However, this topic cannot adequately be presented in a general negotiation or ADR survey course. Similarly, the tax aspects of settlements, which can influence negotiation tactics and outcomes, although mentioned in Chapter 5, must be saved for a more specialized course, but be aware that tax considerations can pervade negotiation discussions. Also there are distinct legal issues and possible reporting requirements regarding settlements when bankruptcy lurks in the shadows or when the negotiation may impact publicly traded securities of a company. Unique factors of which negotiators must be aware may also exist in domestic relations, environmental, and civil rights cases, particularly when courts must approve the settlement. Class actions also create settlement fairness issues and the need for court approval. What follows is intended to help familiarize you with just a few critical areas where the law does matter in lawyer negotiations and to help you spot red flags of caution.

A.   OFFERS OF SETTLEMENT AND FEE SHIFTING

The attorney's fees and costs of bringing or defending a lawsuit are a major factor in negotiating settlement of a dispute. Whether legal action is threatened or pending, each side must consider in its risk analysis the potential costs of court proceedings. Favorable verdicts must be discounted by the amount required to obtain them. Modest victories in court can be dwarfed by the costs expended, particularly for attorneys' fees. Anticipation of litigation costs effect reservation price calculations and can have a profound influence on negotiations.

In the United States the general rule is that each party pays its own legal expenses. This rule is modified by statute for some causes of action, like civil rights cases, or by predispute contractual agreements. In contrast to the "American rule," England and most of Europe impose costs on the losing party by awarding costs to the prevailing party. The "English rule," as this approach is known, tends to discourage litigation, particularly for those of limited means, by increasing the costs of losing. The leverage of increased costs on the loser increases the incentive for settlement. "Loser pays" legislative proposals in the United States have been favored by business defendants as part of "tort reform" to discourage frivolous lawsuits.

One problem with "loser pays" is defining who is the "loser." Is the person who obtains a verdict of $10,000, after bringing a lawsuit claiming damages of a million dollars and rejecting an offer of $100,000, the winner or loser? In order to more clearly define a court "win" for purposes of determining who pays the costs of suit, a modified loser pays approach is to allow a defendant to offer a judgment against itself for a designated amount. This offer, if unaccepted, then becomes the benchmark to decide who the winner is relative to the money put on the table before the trial begins. This approach, known as an "offer of judgment," is embodied in Federal Rule of Civil Procedure 68, which has many state counterparts and variants. Pursuant to this rule, a plaintiff who rejects the defendant's formal, unconditional settlement offer, made within a specified time prior to trial, and is awarded less than the offered amount, is responsible for the defendants court cost and fees incurred after the date of the offer. It is important to note that court costs and fees, as used in the rule, do not include actual attorney's fees, but may include certain discovery expenses from the time the offer is made, as well as statutory costs. The cost shifting mechanism of FRCP 68 is only available for defendants. Although the rule can only be invoked by defendants, it is thought to provide an incentive for more reasonable offers of settlement.

Offers of settlement "under the rule" can also be used strategically in negotiations and can be used to signal information in both directions. Consider the use of a cost shifting offer and counteroffer, as well as attorney-client decision making, in the following story of a medical malpractice case against "Dr. Wallace Bondurant—rich, influential and above the law—a selfish crusader determined to save his career from the courts, regardless of the consequences." (From the back cover of *Harmful Intent*.)

BAINE KERR, HARMFUL INTENT
73-77, Jove Books (2000)

He was stunned by the statutory offer of settlement. . . .

Not its amount, $60,000, insult-level, or the accompanying disparagement of Moss's case, or the tactic. Basteen presented the offer under the costs statute that provided that if not accepted within ten days all defense costs from that point forward would be assessed against the plaintiff and her attorney if she fared more poorly at trial. It was a standard Basteen ploy that forced plaintiff's lawyers to explain to clients the statute's mighty downsides, driving a wedge in their relationship and intimidating fainter hearts, colder feet, or weaker knees than Terry Winter's.

What blew Moss away was Bondurant's having authorized any settlement at all. . . .

To Bondurant, settlement implied an admission of professional unworthiness. Never would he authorize a dime.

But Basteen could not have faxed the offer without Bondurant's consent. Moss thought again of the look in his eyes at his office. The timing was also telling, eleven days before his deposition. What did he not want to talk about?

Moss was ethically required to run through with his client the offer and the risks of the statutory costs award if they did worse than sixty grand with a jury. . . .

"Terry. Bondurant wants to settle."

"Settle what?"

"Your case. He will pay you money if you dismiss your lawsuit against him."

It was a formulation that apparently had not occurred to her. "Is that good news?"

Moss explained the offer, the sixty thousand, the requirement of confidentiality, that the ball was in their court, he needed to respond, and quickly. He gave her the rap about the statute and potential defense costs award. "What do I tell him?"

"You're the lawyer."

"I can't make this call. Ethical rule. I make recommendation only. You have to decide. It needs to be an informed decision, so I explain the facts and the tactics, give you my opinion, and you tell me what to do."

"*I* tell *you* what to do?"

"I advise. You decide."

"You are shitting me." There was a period of contemplation that made Moss a little nervous. "You do all this work for which I'm paying nothing and I still call the shots?"

"Some shots. The big ones. I shit you not."

"Wow."

"But I'm not working for free, Terry. Payday comes at settlement time. One third plus costs are reimbursed, which would leave you barely half of this, maybe thirty-five thousand. So you need to reject it. It's an opener. There's much more money there."

"O.K. Tell him to stick to it."

"How about a counter?"

"I don't know. What do you think?"

"Something big, round, and fat."

"Tell him I'll walk away for a cool million. Hear that, girls?"

"My recommendation exactly."

NOTE: RULE 68 AND ITS EXPANSION

There are explicit and implicit requirements for making a Rule 68 offer of judgment. Failure to follow the requirements can defeat the recovery of costs and have adverse consequences. The principal requirements to invoke Federal Rule 68 and most of its state counterparts include

- The offer must be in writing.
- The offer must be served more than ten days before the trial begins (when the actual hearing commences), although the time requirement can vary state by state.
- The terms and amount of the offer must be clear.
- The acceptance must be in writing and unconditional.

Once an offer of judgment is made, it is irrevocable until the trial begins and it is then considered withdrawn and inadmissible as evidence at trial. Because the offer is treated as unconditional, there is no relief to a defendant for a unilateral mistake or misstated offer. On occasion this can result in a windfall for an accepting plaintiff. In *BMW of North America, Inc. v. Krathen*, 471 So. 2d 585 (1985), BMW offered a written settlement in the amount a purchaser paid for a new car claimed to be a "lemon." The plaintiff accepted the offer, which was silent about returning the car. The Florida Court of Appeals affirmed the trial court's ruling that the offer could not be clarified or withdrawn. The purchaser was entitled to keep the full amount offered for settlement and the car.

The important question of how a Rule 68 settlement offer effects a statutory right to attorney's fees was answered by the Supreme Court in *Marek v. Chesny*, 473 U.S. 1, 105 S. Ct. 3012 (1985). The plaintiff brought a civil rights cause of action pursuant to a federal statute that provides attorney fees if the plaintiff "prevails." The rejected Rule 68 offer of a lump sum judgment was more than plaintiff's eventual recovery of damages, but less than the total of damages added to recoverable fees, including attorney's fees, at the end of trial. The Court was asked to decide if the right to statutory attorney fees was lost when the judgment obtained for damages was less than the rejected Rule 68 offer. The majority held that post-offer costs and fees recovered were not part of the amount to be compared with the Rule 68 settlement offer and, therefore, plaintiff's attorneys fees were not recoverable.

Justice Brennan in his dissent in *Marek* noted that the Judicial Conference, which proposes the wording of the Federal Rules, and Congress has on multiple occasions considered amending Rule 68 to include attorney's fees and to make the same mechanism available to plaintiffs, as well as defendants. Congressional bills continue to propose expansion of Rule 68 to increase its impact on promoting settlement. This ongoing interest in amending Rule 68 is prompted, in part, by a sense that in its current form Rule 68 is not enough of an incentive in the negotiating process to make a meaningful difference in settlement rates and fails to shift enough expense risk to plaintiffs if they reject an offer. Although the frequency in which Rule 68 is invoked in negotiating lawsuit settlements is not regularly tracked, its incidence of use is thought to be relatively light.

On the other hand, increasing the economic incentive or coercion for plaintiffs to settle may diminish access to courts by less wealthy plaintiffs attempting to right wrongs or pursue public interest causes. This concern, along with the complexities of expanding Rule 68, has defeated attempts to broaden the Federal Rule. However, the beat goes on to promote more negotiated settlements by increasing settlement incentives and litigation disincentives. The issue is sometimes framed in terms of putting more "teeth" in Rule 68. Experimentation at the state level provides experience that may pave the way for change to Federal Rule 68.

QUESTIONS

1. Does the Court's holding in *Marek* defeat the incentive to bring civil rights rules as intended by Congress when it provided for recovery of plaintiffs' attorneys' fees?
2. Could some of the problems of determining if a Rule 68 offer was better than the outcome at trial be avoided by requiring that the final judgment if the case proceeds must be at least 25 percent greater than the total value of the offer of settlement? Would this approach be more fair to the plaintiff when confronted with deciding to accept or reject an offer of settlement? How might a requirement that the offer must be 25 percent greater than the trial outcome affect the negotiation dynamic? (A similar 25 percent margin of error proposal was part of a 1995 ABA task force package of suggested changes to Federal Rule 68. Some state statutes and court rules provide for a 10 percent differential.)
3. Earlier in "The Inner Negotiator" section of this book (Chapter 3) you read about risk adversity and the role of this concept in negotiation. Professor Ed Sherman suggests "that a well heeled defendant is less likely to be deterred from defending a weak suit by the threat of having to pay its

opponent's attorneys' fees than a plaintiff from prosecuting a possibly meritorious suit. Since plaintiffs are generally more risk adverse than defendants, a 'loser pays' rule impacts disproportionately on plaintiffs' access to the courts." (Sherman, 1998, p. 1863.) Is it convincing to you that well-heeled defendants are less risk adverse than less financially well off plaintiffs? Why might or might not this be correct?

4. You also read earlier about the tendency of parties and lawyers to be overly optimistic about the strength of their case and their chance of winning. If both sides in a case are confident about their chance of prevailing, does a "loser pays" rule promote or impede settlement? Are both sides likely to insist on more in their negotiations because each believes the other will have to pay all costs and fees following trial?

5. Do the statutes allowing attorney's fees to prevailing plaintiffs in civil rights, private attorney general, and environmental suits create ethical dilemmas for attorneys negotiating settlement of these cases? Often, attorneys negotiate the amount of statutorily allowed fees at the same time they seek substantive payments for their clients. The defendant may seek trade-offs of lower attorney's fees, or waiver of fees, in exchange for a higher payment to the client. This principal-agent conflict can pit client interests against those of the lawyer. The Supreme Court addressed this issue in *Evans v. Jeff D.*, 475 U.S. 717, and held that the plaintiff's waiver of statutory attorney fees to obtain a better settlement for his client would not be set aside and that the trial court could consider the propriety of such a trade-off on a case-by-case basis. Is the ethical dilemma greater for the plaintiff's attorney confronted with a coercive offer to waive or reduce fees to obtain a better settlement for her client or for the defendant's attorney whose client insists that the trade-off be proposed? Do you feel that such proposals for a fee waiver or reduction should be ethically prohibited?

The next article discusses the impact of "loser pays" rules on negotiation incentives and some state modifications to Rule 68 offers of settlement mechanisms.

ANNA AVEN SUMNER, IS THE GUMMY RULE OF TODAY TRULY BETTER THAN THE TOOTHY RULE OF TOMORROW? HOW FEDERAL RULE 68 SHOULD BE MODIFIED

52 Duke L.J. 1055 (2003)

INTRODUCTION

Federal Rule of Civil Procedure 68, the offer-of-judgment rule, has a portentous past and purpose, but it has never lived up to the hype surrounding its creation. Touted as a tool of settlement, the rule lacks the "teeth" necessary to effect settlements. The absence of any such teeth also means that the rule lacks the power to create disincentives for bringing frivolous suits — a second, complementary goal of the rule.

Despite these shortcomings, federal rulemakers have not amended the substance of Rule 68 since 1946. In contrast, state lawmakers have been more responsive to criticisms of the rule. Many states have either amended their respective versions of Federal Rule 68 or have completely rewritten the rule. Such state rules concerning attorney's fees may serve as useful models for amending Federal Rule 68 to better serve the rule's twin goals—those of encouraging settlement and deterring frivolous litigation. . . .

I. ATTORNEY'S FEES AND FEDERAL RULE 68

A. AN EXPLANATION OF ATTORNEY'S FEES UNDER OFFER-OF-JUDGMENT RULES

The most controversial of potential amendments to Rule 68, and perhaps the most necessary, would be the inclusion of attorney's fees, also referred to as "fee shifting," in the language of the rule, or the inclusion of attorney's fees in post-offer costs. In their most basic incarnations, statutes or procedural rules aimed at fee shifting require, under specified circumstances, the "loser" in a suit to pay the "winner's" attorney's fees. It is difficult to speak of fee-shifting rules in very specific terms without recourse to actual state statutes because the statutes vary in several respects, including the definition of "success," the inclusion of interest, and the "specified circumstances" under which fee shifting would occur.

Nonetheless, as a general example, suppose that, under a fee-shifting rule, A makes an offer of judgment to B for $10,000. B rejects this offer and recovers some amount less than $10,000, or fails to recover anything at trial. A would be considered the "winner." As the "winner," A would be entitled to recover from B all attorney's fees and costs A incurred in defending against the suit after its offer of judgment was made and rejected. If B does not pay immediately, A may be entitled to interest on the amount. The precise amount B must recover to avoid paying A's attorney fees depends upon the relevant statutory language.

If, on the other hand, after B's rejection, B recovers $10,000 or more at trial, two options are possible. First, each party might be responsible for its own attorney's fees. Alternatively, as a statutorily defined "loser," A might have to pay whatever attorney's fees and costs B incurred after A made the offer of judgment. Again, B may be entitled to interest of the costs and fees.

B. WHY IS INCLUDING ATTORNEY'S FEES A NECESSARY CHANGE TO THE RULE?

The two most logically appealing reasons to include attorney's fees in an offer-of-judgment rule are (1) to encourage parties to consider settlement carefully, and (2) to discourage frivolous litigation. Although encouraging settlement has long been an enunciated goal of offer-of-judgment rules, discouragement of frivolous litigation is less vocally supported. Perhaps if fears about this "penalty enhancement" justification for the addition of attorney's fees can be assuaged, an amendment including attorney's fees to Federal Rule 68 may be successful. . . .

II. STATE MODIFICATIONS PERMITTING INCLUSION OF ATTORNEY'S FEES

. . . Various states have adopted modified versions of Federal Rule 68 to include attorney's fees. These state rules provide models for improving

Federal Rule 68. This Note now turns to a discussion of the mechanics of the approaches that these states have taken.

A. THE EXPANSIVE EXTREME: ALASKA

Alaska has adopted an offer-of-judgment rule that supports the award of attorney's fees in virtually all circumstances. In Alaska's version of Federal Rule 68, if the judgment of the court is either 5 or 10 percent less favorable than the refused offer, the offeror is entitled to costs and "reasonable actual" post-offer attorney's fees. Attorney's fees, under the statute, are awarded according to when the offer was made. If the offer was made within sixty days of discovery, the offeror is entitled to have 75 percent of its attorney's fees paid. If the offer was made between sixty and ninety days after discovery, the offeror is entitled to have 50 percent of its attorney's fees paid. If the offer was made more than ninety days after discovery but at least ten days before the commencement of trial, the offeror is only entitled to have 30 percent of its attorney's fees paid. . . .

B. THE MIDDLE OF THE ROAD: CALIFORNIA AND NEVADA

Other states have embraced the middle road, permitting an award of attorney's fees only in cases of bad-faith actions of parties during litigation. California has adopted its rule explicitly in a state rule of civil procedure, while Nevada has generated similar results through case law interpreting a similar rule of civil procedure.

1. The California Framework

California's offer-of-judgment rule is section 998 of the Civil Procedure Code. Although the text of this rule differs greatly from that of Federal Rule 68, the relevant fee-shifting provision differs from the federal rule only in that it permits plaintiffs to make offers of judgment, and in that it applies equally to arbitration proceedings. To supplement section 998, California, in 1987, enacted as a pilot project Civil Procedure Code section 1021.1, a provision for discretionary awards of attorney's fees in conjunction with offers of judgment. Section 1021.1 initially applied to Riverside and San Bernadino counties. Subsequent extensions of the rule were applicable only to Riverside County. Together, these two sections create a possible model for amending Federal Rule 68. . . .

California courts have determined that inherent in any offer-of-judgment rule is the requirement that the offer not be token or in bad faith. A one-dollar offer of judgment, for instance, was found to have been made in bad faith, and, as such, no expert witness fees were awarded to the offering party, even though the offering party prevailed. This requirement of a good-faith offer of settlement has been applied when a nominal offer was as high as $15,001, in a case in which the ultimate judgment was for more than $1 million. Although the good-faith standard cannot be applied across the board, it appears that, at least in California, judicial discretion comfortably steps in and applies the standard as needed.

2. The Nevada Framework

Unlike California, Nevada's offer-of-judgment rule does not explicitly address the same concerns. On the face of the rule, when a party rejects an offer and fails to obtain a more favorable judgment, several penalties follow.

The first is that a party cannot recover "any costs or attorney's fees and shall not recover interest for the period after the service of the offer and before the judgment." Additionally, the offeree is bound to pay the offeror's post-offer costs from the time of the offer, and reasonable attorney's fees actually incurred by the offeror since the time of the offer. What the rule does not facially address is in what circumstances attorney's fees should be awarded under Nevada's Rule 68. Thus courts were left with the job of interpreting the rule to determine when attorney's fees were to be shifted.

The first case to address the appropriateness of an assessment of attorney's fees was *Beattie v. Thomas,* in which the Nevada Supreme Court enunciated four factors to guide the exercise of discretion for awarding attorney's fees: (1) whether the plaintiff's claim was brought in good faith; (2) whether the defendants' offer of judgment was reasonable and in good faith in both its timing and amount; (3) whether the plaintiff's decision to reject the offer and proceed to trial was grossly unreasonable or in bad faith; and (4) whether the fees sought by the offeror are reasonable and justified in amount. After weighing the foregoing factors, the district judge may, where warranted, award up to the full amount of fees requested. . . .

C. THE RESTRICTIVE EXTREME: ARIZONA

Arizona exemplifies the most restrictive approach to the modification of Federal Rule 68 by the imposition of attorney's fees, permitting an award of fees only if the parties agree to such fee shifting at the outset. First, attorney's fees, if contemplated by the parties, must be identified separately as a part of the offer. After an offer has been made, the offeree essentially has three different options. The first option, naturally, is to accept the offer in full. The second option is to permit the offer to lapse. If the offer is permitted to lapse, then and only then may an award of expert witness fees and double costs be permitted as sanctions, if the rejecting party recovers less than the offer. If the offer lapses, however, attorney's fees cannot be imposed. The third option is for the offeree to accept the offer in part. Partial acceptance of the offer occurs when the parties agree as to the monetary award for the causes of action asserted, but disagree as to whether attorney's fees should be awarded, and if awarded, disagree as to the specific amount. In such an instance, the parties may file the offer and acceptance thereof with the court, and apply to the court for a determination of whether or not an award of fees is appropriate, and if so, in what amount. . . .

B. MARY CARTER AGREEMENTS

Negotiation between a plaintiff and multiple defendants can get legally and ethically complex. When one or more of multiple defendants with joint and several liability settles with a plaintiff and the others do not, it is commonly referred to as a Mary Carter or sliding scale agreement. The settling defendant typically makes a deal with the plaintiff on the maximum amount that defendant will pay, regardless of the trial outcome or later settlement by plaintiffs with other defendants. The agreement also allows a decrease in the settling defendant's payment if the plaintiff obtains more from all defendants combined than the total amount of damages (sliding scale). In other words, the settling defendant caps his liability while potentially benefiting from plaintiffs success against the remaining defendants. It is possible that the settling defendant will pay nothing if plaintiff collects from the other defendants the full amount of damages (a "zero bottom" settlement.)

Mary Carter agreements are named after the Florida case of *Booth v. Mary Carter Paint Company*, 202 So. 2d 8 (Fla. App. 1967) in which the plaintiff, Booth, brought a negligence action against multiple defendants for the motor vehicle death of his wife. During settlement negotiations, the defense counsel for two of the defendants made a deal with the plaintiff, separately from Mary Carter Paint Company, also a defendant in the case, as to the maximum amount that they would pay. The signing defendants were not released of liability and remained in the case tried to a jury, which was unaware of the settlement agreement. Mary Carter Paint Company lost its post-trial objections to the secret settlement deal, which could have resulted in it paying the entire settlement (but did not). The Florida Court of Appeal confirmed the ruling and upheld the partial settlement agreement.

Mary Carter agreements typically involve four major features:

1. The plaintiff is guaranteed a certain amount of recovery.
2. The dollar liability of the settling defendant is limited to a maximum amount and may be reduced by plaintiff's recovery from other defendants.
3. The agreement between the settling defendant and the plaintiff is kept secret from the jury and often from the nonsettling defendants.
4. The settling defendant remains in the lawsuit.

Although a few states have banned Mary Carter agreements, most allow some form of this negotiated partial settlement, even if on a case-by-case basis or referred to by another name. In Arizona, this type of selective settlement is known as a "Gallagher covenant," from the case of *City of Tucson v. Gallagher*, 14 Ariz. App. 385, 483 P.2d 798 (1971). California relies on the wording of a state statute (CCP 877 and 877.6) to allow "sliding scale recovery agreements," provided the value of the settlement indicates it was entered in "good faith." As the California Supreme Court explained in *Abbot Ford, Inc. v. The Superior Court of Los Angeles County; Ford Motor Co.*, 43 Cal. 3d 858 (1987), the negotiated cap amount and other financial obligations must be within a reasonable range of the settling defendant's proportional share of comparative liability among tortfeasors.

One reason for the California requirement of "good faith" or proportionality of the settling defendant's obligation is that a Mary Carter agreement between a plaintiff and one of multiple defendants stops a codefendant/tortfeasor with joint and several liability from cross-complaining or suing the settling defendant for contribution. The plaintiff may want to keep secret from the jury that one of multiple defendants has settled or capped their payment to the defendant. This desire for secrecy is to avoid the "empty chair" defense, where the missing defendant will be blamed by the other defendants as the cause of plaintiff's loss. The plaintiff will prefer to keep the secretly settling defendant in the case and obtain favorable testimony from the settling defendant, who still appears to be adverse to the plaintiff, even though their interests are now aligned. This presents a policy question of whether the jury should know the new complimentary interests between the plaintiff and the settling defendant, who may pay less if the other nonsettling defendants are required to pay more. (See *Alcala Co., Inc. v. S. Ct.*, 49 Cal. 4th 1308, 1317, 57 Cal. 2d 349, 354 (1996).)

C. COMMON LAW LIMITS — FRAUD, MISREPRESENTATION, AND DURESS

A settlement agreement is usually drafted to bind the parties to each do something, like paying money, or refraining from actions, most often from pursuing a lawsuit. If there is not compliance with the settlement terms, the agreement can be enforced as a contract. Courts are called upon to enforce settlement agreements and, on occasion, to rescind them or declare their meaning. Defenses of fraud, misrepresentation, or duress may be invoked. Courts, in applying the common law when enforcing, or declining to enforce settlement agreements, in effect set limits on bargaining behavior. Those limits are discussed in the following article.

RUSSELL KOROBKIN, MICHAEL MOFFETT, AND NANCY WELSH, THE LAW OF BARGAINING

87 Marq. L. Rev. 839-842 (2004)

When a negotiated agreement results from false statements made during the bargaining process, the common law of tort and contract sometimes holds negotiators liable for damages or makes their resulting agreements subject to rescission.[1] The common law does not, however, amount to a blanket prohibition of all lying. Instead, the common law principles are subject to the caveats that false statements must be material, the opposing negotiator must rely on the false statements, and such reliance must be justified. Whether reliance is justified depends on the type of statement at issue and the statement's specificity. A seller's specific false claim ("this car gets 80 miles per gallon gas mileage") is actionable, but his more general claim ("this car gets good gas mileage") is probably not, because the latter statement is acknowledged as the type of "puffing" or "sales talk" on which no reasonable buyer would rely.

While it is often said that misrepresentations of fact are actionable but misrepresentations of opinion are not, this statement is not strictly accurate. Statements of opinions can be false, either because the speaker does not actually have the claimed opinion ("I think this Hyundai is the best car built in the world today") or because the statement implies facts that are untrue ("I think this Hyundai gets the best gas mileage of any car"). But statements of opinion are less likely to induce justified reliance than are statements of specific facts, especially when they are very general, such as a claim that an item is one of "good quality."[2]

---

1. See generally RESTATEMENT (SECOND) OF TORTS §525 (1986), RESTATEMENT (SECOND) OF CONTRACTS §164 (1982).
2. See Royal Bus. Machs., Inc. v. Lorraine Corp., 633 F.2d 34, 42 (7th Cir. 1980) (calling such statements "'puffing' to be expected in any sales transaction").

Whether reliance on a statement of fact or opinion is justified depends significantly on the context of the negotiation and whether the speaker has access to information that the recipient does not. A seller "aggressively" promoting his product whose stated opinions imply facts that are not true is less likely to find himself in legal difficulty if the veracity of his claims are easily investigated by an equally-knowledgeable buyer than if his customer is a consumer unable to evaluate the factual basis of the claims.[3] The case for liability is stronger still when the negotiator holds himself out as being particularly knowledgeable about the subject matter that the expressed opinion concerns.[4] Whether a false statement can be insulated from liability by a subsequent disclaimer depends on the strength and clarity of the disclaimer, as well as on the nature of the false statement. Again, the standard is whether the reasonable recipient of the information in total would rely on the statement at issue when deciding whether to enter into an agreement.[5]

It is universally recognized that a negotiator's false statements concerning how valuable an agreement is to her or the maximum she is willing to give up or exchange in order to seal an agreement (the negotiator's "reservation point," or "bottom line") are not actionable, again on the ground that such false statements are common and no reasonable negotiator would rely upon them. So an insurance adjuster who claimed that $900 was "all he could pay" to settle a claim is not liable for fraud, even if the statement was false.[6] The law is less settled regarding the status of false statements concerning the existence of outside alternatives for a negotiator. A false claim of an offer from a third-party is relevant because it implies a strong reservation point, so a negotiator might logically argue that such a claim is no more actionable than a claim as to the reservation point itself. But courts have occasionally ruled that false claims of a specific outside offer are actionable, on the ground that they are material to the negotiation and that the speaker has access to information that cannot be easily verified by the listener's independent investigation.[7]

The most inscrutable area of the law of deception concerns when a negotiator may be held legally liable for failing to disclose information that might weaken his bargaining position (rather than affirmatively asserting a false claim). The traditional laissez-faire rule of caveat emptor eroded in the twentieth century, with courts placing greater disclosure responsibility on negotiators. It is clear that any affirmative action taken to conceal a fact, including the statement of a "half-truth" that implies a false fact, will be treated as if it were an affirmative false statement. Beyond this point, however, the law becomes murky. Although the general rule is probably still that negotiators have no general disclosure obligation, some courts require bargainers (especially sellers) to disclose known material facts not easily discovered by the other party.[8]

3. See, e.g., Vulcan Metals Co. v. Simmons Mfg. Co., 248 F. 853 (2d Cir. 1918).
4. See Pacesetter Homes v. Brodkin, 85 Cal. Rptr. 39, 43 (Cal. Ct. App. 1970).
5. See, e.g., In re Trump, 7 F.3d 357, 369 (3d Cir. 1993) (finding that repeated warnings of risk meant that "no reasonable investor could believe anything but that the . . . bonds represented a rather risky, speculative investment," despite other optimistic claims about the financial stability of the issuer).
6. Morta v. Korea Ins. Corp. 840 F.2d 1452, 1456 (9th Cir. 1988).
7. See, e.g., Kabatchnick v. Hanover-Elm Bldg. Corp., 103 N.E.2d 692 (Mass. 1952) (falsely claiming a "bona fide offer from one Melvin Levine . . . of $10,000 per year"); Beavers v. Lamplighters Realty, 556 P.2d 1328 (Okla. 1976) (falsely claiming a prospective buyer was willing to pay the asking price for a house and would be delivering a check that same day).
8. See, e.g., Weintraub v. Krobatsch, 317 A.2d 68 (N.J. 1974) (sellers must disclose known insect infestation of house).

Just as the law places some limits on the use of deceptive behavior to seal a bargain, so too does it place some limits upon negotiators' ability to use superior bargaining power to coerce acquiescence with their demands. In general, negotiators may threaten to withhold their goods and services from those who will not agree to their terms. Courts can invoke the doctrine of duress, however, to protect parties who are the victims of a threat that is "improper" and have "no reasonable alternative" but to acquiesce to the other party's demand,[9] such as when one party procures an agreement through the threat of violence,[10] or through the threat to breach a prior agreement after using the relationship created by that agreement to place the victim in a position in which breach would cause noncompensable damage.[11] Judicial intervention is most likely when the bargaining parties' relationship was not arms-length. For example, the common law provides the defense of undue influence to negotiators who can show that they were dependent upon and thus vulnerable to the other, dominant negotiator.[12] . . .

D. NEGOTIATION MALPRACTICE

Client dissatisfaction, after the fact, with claim settlement and transactional agreements negotiated by their attorneys is not uncommon. An agreement that seemed appealing at the time it was obtained, when uncertainty, fear of the worse alternatives, and time pressure drove acceptance may, with hindsight, be unsatisfactory. A good negotiated result is attributed to a strong case and a resolute client; a marginal result, after the dynamics and trade-offs of the negotiation are forgotten, is attributed to poor representation.

The frequency of complaints filed against attorneys for malpractice in negotiations is not precisely known but is thought to be high, as noted by Professor Epstein in an article that follows. Even though there is a general requirement that clients must agree to a negotiated settlement or transaction before it becomes final, consent to the result is not a total barrier to a claim of malpractice. Clients have reason to rely on the professional expertise, skill, and integrity of the attorney negotiating in their behalf and may sue when that reliance is misplaced.

Malpractice is grounded in tort and requires proof of the classic tort elements:

- Duty to the plaintiff
- Breach of that duty
- Causation
- Damages

Proving causation and damages is difficult in claims of negotiation malpractice because, as we have presented throughout this text, there is no one right or

---

9. See RESTATEMENT (SECOND) OF CONTRACTS, §175(1) (1982).
10. See, e.g., Rubenstein v. Rubenstein, 120 A.2d 11 (N.J. 1956); RESTATEMENT (SECOND) CONTRACTS §176(1)(a) (1981).
11. See, e.g., Austin Instruments, Inc. v. Loral Corp., 272 N.E.2d 533 (N.Y. 1971).
12. See RESTATEMENT (SECOND) OF CONTRACTS §177 (1979).

sure way to negotiate. Damages can not be easily established by comparing a negotiated outcome to a trial result that did not occur or to another negotiation with all the same variables. Richard Posner, Chief Judge of the Seventh Circuit, stated the issue and the challenge succinctly:

> Proof of causation is often difficult in legal malpractice cases involving representation in litigation — the vast majority of such cases — because it is so difficult, yet vital, to estimate what difference a lawyer's negligence made in the actual outcome of a trial or other adversary proceeding. How many criminal defendants, required as they are to prove that their lawyer's ineffective assistance prejudiced them, succeed in overturning their convictions on this ground? Proof of causation is even more difficult in a negotiating situation, because while there is (at least we judges like to think there is) a correct outcome to most lawsuits, there is no "correct" outcome to a negotiation. Not only does much depend on the relative bargaining skills of the negotiators, on the likely consequences to each party if the negotiations fall through, and on luck, so that the element of the intangible and the unpredictable looms large; but there is no single "right" outcome in a bargaining situation even in principle. Every point within the range bounded by the lowest offer that one party will accept and the highest offer that the other party will make is a possible transaction or settlement point, and none of these points is "correct" or "incorrect." (*Nicolet Instrument Corp. v. Lindquest & Vennum*, 34 F.3d 453 (7th Cir. 1994))

Lawyers have both procedural and substantive duties when advising and representing clients in negotiations. Breach of the procedural duties, as well as the substantive ones, result in malpractice. The procedural duties reflect ethical responsibilities that lawyers have toward clients. These responsibilities were discussed earlier in Chapter 7, The Ethical Negotiator. Procedural requirements that are often the gravamen of malpractice claims against attorney negotiators include the following:

- Duty to communicate settlement offers to client (see ABA Model Rule 1.4(a))
- Duty to not exceed authority given by client in making or accepting offers (see ABA Model Rule 1.2(a))
- Duty to be diligent (see ABA Model Rule 1.3)
- Duty to reveal conflicts of interest (see ABA Model Rule 1.7) and not trade off clients' interests to cover up attorney error (see ABA Model Rule 1.7(2))

Substantively, lawyers owe their clients the duty to know the law and properly advise clients on how law and practice impact their situation. Accurate information is necessary for clients to make informed decisions about settlement. The test for purposes of malpractice is commonly stated as whether the attorney exercised that degree of skill, prudence, and diligence in investigating facts, legal research, and giving legal advice that lawyers of ordinary skill and capacity would in similar situations.

Only disappointed clients sue their lawyers. Domestic relations is an area of legal practice where client expectations are often unrealistically high, as are emotions. It is not unusual for clients to have second thoughts and be disappointed with a negotiated settlement. "Buyer's remorse" can lead to claims against lawyers following an accepted settlement, particularly in divorce. Consider the following malpractice case and the lessons you can learn from it.

ZIEGELHEIM v. APOLLO
128 N.J. 250, 607 A.2d 1298 (1992)

HANDLER, J.

... In September 1979, Mrs. Ziegelheim retained defendant, attorney Stephen Apollo, to represent her in her anticipated divorce action. Because this appeal relates to the trial court's granting of summary judgment against plaintiff, we assume for the purposes of our decision that all of the facts she alleges relating to Apollo's handling of her divorce are true. According to Mrs. Ziegelheim, she and Apollo met on several occasions to plan various aspects of her case. She told him about all of the marital and separate assets of which she was aware, and they discussed her suspicion the Mr. Ziegelheim was either concealing or dissipating certain other assets as well. In particular, Mrs. Ziegelheim told Apollo that she thought her husband had $500,000 hidden in the form of cash savings and bonds. Accordingly, she asked Apollo to make a thorough inquiry into her husband's assets, including cash, bonds, patents, stocks, pensions, life insurance, profit-sharing plans, and real estate. . . .

According to Mrs. Ziegelheim, Apollo failed to discover important information about her husband's assets before entering into settlement negotiations with Mr. Ziegelheim's attorney, Sheldon Liebowitz. Apollo hired an accountant who valued the marital estate at approximately $2,413,000. Mrs. Ziegelheim claims that the accountant substantially underestimated the estate because of several oversights by Apollo, including his failure to locate a bank vault owned by Mr. Ziegelheim; to locate or determine the value of his tax-free municipal bonds; to verify the value of his profit-sharing plan at Pilot Woodworking, a company in which he was the primary shareholder; to search for an estimated $500,000 in savings; to contact the United States Patent Office to verify the existence of certain patents he held; to inquire into a $1,000,000 life insurance policy naming an associate of his as the beneficiary; to verify the value of certain lakefront property; and to verify the value of his stock holdings. She alleges that had Apollo made a proper inquiry, it would have been apparent that the marital estate was worth approximately $2,562,000, or about $149,000 more than the accountant found. . . .

In sum, Mrs. Ziegelheim was to receive approximately $333,000 in alimony, $6,000 in contributions to insurance costs, and $324,000 in property, the last figure representing approximately fourteen percent of the value of the estate (as appraised by Apollo and the accountant). Mr. Ziegelheim was to receive approximately $2,088,000 in property, approximately eighty-six percent of the value of the estate.

When testifying before the court immediately after the settlement was read into the record, both Mrs. Ziegelheim and Mr. Ziegelheim stated that they understood the agreement, that they thought it was fair, and that they entered into it voluntarily. Mrs. Ziegelheim now asserts, however, that she accepted the agreement only after Apollo advised her that wives could expect to receive no more than ten to twenty percent of the marital estate if they went to trial. She claims that Apollo's estimate was unduly pessimistic and did not comport with the advice that a reasonably competent attorney would have given under the circumstances. Had she been advised competently, she says, she would not have accepted the settlement. . . .

The trial court ruled in favor of defendant on all counts. It noted that Mrs. Ziegelheim had stated on the record that she understood the settlement and its terms, that she thought the terms were fair, and that she had not been coerced into settling. . . .

In accepting a case, the lawyer agrees to pursue the goals of the client to the extent the law permits, even when the lawyer believes that the client's desires are unwise or ill-considered. At the same time, because the client's desires may be influenced in large measure by the advice the lawyer provides, the lawyer is obligated to give the client reasonable advice. As a legal matter progresses and circumstances change, the wishes of the client may change as well. Accordingly, the lawyer is obligated to keep the client informed of the status of the matter for which the lawyer has been retained, and is required to advise the client on the various legal and strategic issues that arise.

In this case, Mrs. Ziegelheim made several claims impugning Apollo's handling of her divorce, and the trial court dismissed all of them on Apollo's motion for summary judgment. As we explain, we believe that the trial court's rulings on several of her claims were erroneous. . . .

On Mrs. Ziegelheim's claim that Apollo negligently advised her with respect to her chances of winning a greater proportion of the marital estate if she proceeded to trial, we conclude, as did the Appellate Division, that there was a genuine dispute regarding the appropriate advice that an attorney should give in cases like hers. According to the expert retained by Mrs. Ziegelheim, women in her position—who are in relatively poor health, have little earning capacity, and have been wholly dependent on their husbands—often receive upwards of fifty percent of the marital estate. The expert said that Mrs. Ziegelheim's chances of winning such a large fraction of the estate had she gone to trial would have been especially good because the couple had enjoyed a high standard of living while they were together and because her husband's earning capacity was "tremendous" and would remain so for some time. Her expert's opinion was brought to the trial court's attention, as was the expert report of Mr. Ziegelheim. If plaintiff's expert's opinion were credited, as it should have been for purposes of summary judgment, then Apollo very well could have been found negligent in advising her that she could expect to win only ten to twenty percent of the marital estate.

Apollo urges us to adopt the rule enunciated by the Pennsylvania Supreme Court in *Muhammad v. Strassburger, McKenna, Messer, Shilobod and Gutnick*, 526 Pa. 541, 587 A.2d 1346 (1991), that a dissatisfied litigant may not recover from his or her attorney for malpractice in negotiating a settlement that the litigant has accepted unless the litigant can prove actual fraud on the part of the attorney. Under that rule, no cause of action can be made based on negligence or contract principles against an attorney for malpractice in negotiating a settlement. The Pennsylvania Supreme Court rationalized its severe rule by explaining that it had a "longstanding public policy which encourages settlements."

New Jersey, too, has a longstanding policy that encourages settlements, but we reject the rule espoused by the Pennsylvania Supreme Court. Although we encourage settlements, we recognize that litigants rely heavily on the professional advice of counsel when they decide whether to accept or reject offers of settlement, and we insist that the lawyers of our state advise clients with respect to settlements with the same skill, knowledge, and diligence with which they pursue all other legal tasks. Attorneys are supposed to know the likelihood of success for the types of cases they handle and they are supposed to know the range of possible awards in those cases.

As we noted in *Levine v. Wiss & Co*, 97 N.J. 242, 246, 478 A.2d 397 (1984), "One who undertakes to render services in the practice of a profession or trade is required to exercise the skill and knowledge normally possessed by members of that profession in good standing in similar communities." We have found in cases involving a great variety of professionals that deviation from accepted standards of professional care will result in liability for negligence. . . . Like most courts, we see no reason to apply a more lenient rule to lawyers who negotiate settlements. *After all, the negotiation of settlements is one of the most basic and most frequently undertaken tasks that lawyers perform* [emphasis is court's]. . . .

The fact that a party received a settlement that was "fair and equitable" does not mean necessarily that the party's attorney was competent or that the party would not have received a more favorable settlement had the party's incompetent attorney been competent. Thus, in this case, notwithstanding the family court's decision, Mrs. Ziegelheim still may proceed against Apollo in her negligence action.

Moreover, another aspect of the alleged professional incompetence that led to the improvident acceptance of the settlement was the attorney's own failure to discover hidden marital assets. When Mrs. Ziegelheim sought to reopen her divorce settlement, the family court denied her motion with the observation that "[a]mple opportunity existed for full discovery," and that "the parties had their own accountants as well as counsel." The court did not determine definitively that Mr. Ziegelheim had hidden no assets, but stated instead that it "suspected that everything to be known was known to the parties." The earlier ruling did not implicate the competence of counsel and, indeed, was premised on the presumptive competence of counsel. Hence, defendant cannot invoke that ruling now to bar a challenge to his competence. Mrs. Ziegelheim should have been allowed to prove that Apollo negligently failed to discover certain assets concealed by her former husband. . . .

In holding as we do today, we do not open the door to malpractice suits by any and every dissatisfied party to a settlement. Many such claims could be averted if settlements were explained as a matter of record in open court in proceedings reflecting the understanding and assent of the parties. Further, plaintiffs must allege particular facts in support of their claims of attorney incompetence and may not litigate complaints containing mere generalized assertions of malpractice. We are mindful that attorneys cannot be held liable simply because they are not successful in persuading an opposing party to accept certain terms. Similarly, we acknowledge that attorneys who pursue reasonable strategies in handling their cases and who render reasonable advice to their clients cannot be held liable for the failure of their strategies or for any unprofitable outcomes that result because their clients took their advice. The law demands that attorneys handle their cases with knowledge, skill, and diligence, but it does not demand that they be perfect or infallible, and it does not demand that they always secure optimum outcomes for their clients. . . .

QUESTIONS

1. The Supreme Court of New Jersey opinion in *Ziegelheim v. Apollo* states that "In holding as we do today we do not open the door to malpractice suits by

any and every dissatisfied party to a settlement." Does the New Jersey court, in reviewing the Summary Judgment for defendant and allowing the negligence action against the attorney to proceed, shut the door or, indeed, leave it open?

2. The court advises that "Many such claims could be averted if settlements were explained as a matter of record in open court in proceedings reflecting the understanding and assent of the parties." This advice may be practical in divorce cases, where the court is asked to approve and incorporate the marital settlement agreement into a court judgment, but is this cautionary step practical as a conclusion to most lawsuit and business settlements? Does this help explain why settlement agreements often do recite the facts, premises, and underlying reasons for the settlement?

3. Is the *Ziegelheim v. Apollo* case likely to be tried following this remand? If you represented defendant Apollo, how would you negotiate a final settlement of the Ziegelheim claim, and what amount would you anticipate it would take to conclude this matter?

The New Jersey Supreme Court in the Apollo case expressly rejects the reasoning of the Pennsylvania Supreme Court in *Muhammad v. Strassburger et al.*, which barred a client who accepted a negotiated settlement from suing his attorney in the absence of fraud. The Muhammad decision has been rejected by other courts, as illustrated by Apollo. In the following article, Professor Epstein explains why courts have rejected the *Muhammad* opinion reasoning and then contrasts malpractice actions arising from the negotiation process from other types of malpractice cases. She also offers advice on how to defend and avoid malpractice claims when clients initially accept the negotiated settlement.

LYNN A. EPSTEIN, POST-SETTLEMENT MALPRACTICE: UNDOING THE DONE DEAL

46 Cath. U. L. Rev. 453 (1997)

Clients voice their approval to mediators and judges as a settlement agreement is reached. A release is signed, the file is closed, and from the lawyer's perspective, another case ends. The settled case joins an overwhelming majority of civil cases that are resolved in pretrial settlement. Buried within this figure, however, is a more troubling statistic: Over twenty percent of civil cases will be resurrected in the form of malpractice actions initiated by dissatisfied clients. In those instances, and for various reasons substantiated by expert opinions, the client will charge that they could have received a better result in the settlement even though the client knowingly and willingly agreed to end the case.

In every state except Pennsylvania, a client is permitted to proceed with the theory that his attorney negligently negotiated an agreement despite the fact that the client consented to settlement. In *Muhammad v. Strassburger, McKenna, Messer, Shilobod & Gutnick*, the Pennsylvania Supreme Court determined that an attorney is immune from malpractice based on negligence where the client consented to settle. Court decisions after *Muhammad*, however, have uniformly rejected immunity for the attorney, permitting post-settlement malpractice actions to proceed in the same manner as the prototypical malpractice case.

This Article analyzes the Pennsylvania Supreme Court's decision to bar malpractice lawsuits based on settled cases. This Article then contrasts the opinion with the contradictory majority rule in other states. Next, this Article addresses the difference between mainstream malpractice actions and those malpractice actions arising from the negotiation of settled cases. . . .

MUHAMMAD AND ITS SUCCESSORS

Conventional wisdom dictates that attorneys settle cases effectively, as an estimated ninety-five percent of civil cases are resolved by settlement. Yet, an emerging trend of post-settlement malpractice claims threatens the integrity of the settlement negotiation process. While malpractice actions are on the rise, most attorneys reasonably believed they were insulated from liability because the client had consented to settlement, and because there was no affirmative wrongdoing by the attorney. Because so many factors influence a client's decision to settle, and because so many individuals, such as judges and mediators, are a part of the process, it would appear fundamentally unfair to hold the attorneys solely responsible for such malpractice claims. This is buttressed by a majority viewpoint which looks unfavorably upon malpractice claims that require the judiciary to infiltrate the negotiation process, a process traditionally viewed as immune from judicial scrutiny.

Balancing these competing interests, the Pennsylvania Supreme Court barred such malpractice actions to foster the negotiation and settlement process. In *Muhammad*, the Pennsylvania Supreme Court held that, absent fraud, an attorney is immune from suit by a former client dissatisfied with a settlement that the former client agreed to enter.

Pamela and Abdullah Muhammad sued the firm of Strassburger, McKenna, Messer, Shilobod, and Gutnick for malpractice arising from the settlement of an underlying medical malpractice suit. In the underlying action, the Muhammads sued the physicians and hospital that performed a circumcision on their son who died as a consequence of general anesthesia used during the procedure.

The Muhammads retained the Strassburger law firm. The physicians and hospital offered to settle the malpractice claim for $23,000, which was subsequently increased to $26,500 at the suggestion of the trial court. The Muhammads accepted the settlement offer. The Muhammads later grew dissatisfied with the amount received in settlement and instructed the Strassburger law firm to communicate this discontent to defense counsel. An evidentiary hearing ensued where the court upheld the settlement agreement, reasoning that the Muhammads agreed to the settlement amount and, thus, there existed a binding and enforceable contract.

Unable to reopen the medical malpractice proceeding, the Muhammads initiated a claim against the Strassburger law firm alleging legal malpractice, fraudulent misrepresentation, fraudulent concealment, nondisclosure, breach of contract, negligence, emotional distress, and breach of fiduciary duty. The court dismissed the fraud counts because the Muhammads had not pled fraud with specificity. Surprisingly, the court then barred the Muhammads from proceeding with their remaining negligence claim against the Strassburger firm, based on articulated public policy encouraging civil litigation settlement. In granting immunity, the court wrote:

> [W]e foreclose the ability of dissatisfied litigants to agree to a settlement and then file suit against their attorneys in the hope that they will recover additional monies. To permit otherwise results in unfairness to the attorneys who relied on their client's assent and unfairness to the litigants whose cases have not yet been tried. Additionally, it places an unnecessarily arduous burden on an overly taxed court system.

The court emphasized that this immunity extends to specific cases where a plaintiff agreed to settlement in the absence of fraud by the attorney. This is distinguished from the instance when a lawyer knowingly commits malpractice, conceals the wrongdoing, and convinces the client to settle in order to cover up the malpractice. According to the court, in this instance, the attorney's conduct is fraudulent and actionable. . . .

Muhammad has suffered widespread criticism and is uniformly rejected in every reported opinion reviewing post-settlement legal malpractice litigation . . . While most courts are expeditious in determining that an attorney is not absolutely immune from legal malpractice actions when the client consents to settlement, they are also uniform in expressing a desire to foster protection over the negotiation process.

COURSES OF ACTION FOR ATTORNEYS CONFRONTING POST-SETTLEMENT MALPRACTICE CLAIMS

A. THE CONTRIBUTORY/COMPARATIVE NEGLIGENCE DEFENSE

In a post-settlement malpractice action, an attorney should defend the action by claiming client contributory/comparative negligence. The defense should be presented by introducing evidence of the client's subjective reasons for settling the case.

The client contributory/comparative negligence defense is generally recognized in legal malpractice actions; however, some courts do not permit the issue to reach a jury. This reluctance is supported by the Restatement (Third) of Law Governing Lawyers, which asserts that the client contributory negligence defense is available in jurisdictions that recognize the same defense to general negligence actions. The Restatement cautions, however, that the lawyer/client relationship imposes fiduciary duties by which "clients are entitled to rely on their lawyers to act with competence, diligence, honesty, and loyalty." The lawyer/client relationship imposes numerous duties on the lawyer, while imposing few on the client. Yet, this cannot relieve clients from accepting responsibility for their own acts or omissions which result in unfavorable settlements.

Courts that permit the client comparative negligence defense, however, proceed with caution, premised on the view that attorneys should not be permitted to circumvent responsibility to former clients under the guise that the client should have known how to respond or act. Thus, even when a legal document contains simple English that needs no interpretation by a lawyer, the defense of client contributory negligence has been barred in certain jurisdictions. . . .

Courts should, however, permit the comparative negligence defense to proceed to the fact finder where the client settled a claim and now seeks to hold an attorney liable for malpractice committed in the negotiation of that settlement. In a majority of post-settlement malpractice claims, the former clients do not claim they did not understand the settlement agreement. Instead, this majority group freely admits they voluntarily entered into settlement, conceding they understood the agreement and abandoned their right to a trial. Only after settlement did these former clients contend there was "something else" their former lawyer should have done to secure a better result.

Although there will be cases where the client is genuinely aggrieved by a negligent attorney, the majority of post-settlement malpractice litigation arises from the client's own conduct. In those cases, the comparative fault defense should be considered by the fact finder.

While the comparative fault defense is available in the typical legal malpractice action, its use has been limited in post-settlement malpractice litigation. . . . [Courts] provide minimum guidelines to which an attorney should adhere in advising a client regarding settlement. . . . [T]he lawyer should hold an appreciation of (1) the relevant facts; (2) the present and future potential strengths and weaknesses of his case; (3) the likely costs, both objectively (monetarily) and subjectively (psychological disruption of business and family life) associated with proceeding further in the litigation; and (4) the likely outcome if the case were to proceed further.

Many cases of legal malpractice occur from "perceived" negligence by attorneys who fail to adhere to the [above] criteria. Common practice dictates that attorneys review the four factors in detail with their client prior to settlement. In post-settlement malpractice litigation analysis, courts tend to focus only on the result obtained (the settlement sum) to gauge the lawyer's liability exposure, ignoring the traditional factors preceding settlement. Hence, an attorney wishing to marshal an effective defense must take pre-settlement steps aimed to protect his client's interest. This will safeguard against subsequent malpractice claims within the framework developed by the courts.

B.   THE "RELEASE AND SETTLEMENT AGREEMENT": SOLIDIFYING THE DEAL

The "release and settlement agreement" is the final written document ending the litigation and, in many instances, the lawyer-client relationship. An historical review of related lawyer-client concern over apparent complications arising from contingency fee arrangements creates an additional post-settlement malpractice defense. To assure a client's comprehension of contingency fee contracts, many state bar associations require clients and attorneys to review and execute a "statement of client rights" which thoroughly explains the contingency fee agreement. This statement obligates the attorney to adhere to specific reporting and accounting requirements concerning fees throughout the client's case. It also provides the client with a remedy against unscrupulous attorneys.

Similar to the "statement of client rights," an attorney should be required to provide a client with a statement of the case before settlement. This statement would precisely articulate the ramifications of settlement and act as written confirmation of the attorney's work on the case. . . .

CONCLUSION

Post-settlement malpractice actions are quite unique. While the Pennsylvania Supreme Court effectively banned these lawsuits, providing former counsel immunity rather than engaging in the arduous analysis inherent to malpractice litigation, the better course of action is to permit attorneys to present the client comparative fault defense. This will allow an attorney to present evidence of the client's subjective reasons for settling the litigation. Additionally, through the use of a pre-settlement statement of the case form, attorneys will provide their clients sufficient information to adequately prepare for a successful negotiation and settlement process.

CONCLUDING NOTE

In the *Muhammad* case, Justice Larsen wrote a stinging dissent accusing the majority of creating a "LAWYER'S HOLIDAY" by barring malpractice against lawyers for negligence committed in the negotiation of civil settlements. He reasoned by comparison, "If a doctor is negligent in saving a human life, the doctor pays. If a priest is negligent in saving the spirit of a human, the priest pays. But if a lawyer is negligent in advising his client as to settlement, the client pays." Justice Larsen's dissent reflects the general view that most courts have taken in rejecting the Pennsylvania Supreme Court's protection of the negotiation process from claims of malpractice.

When negotiation malpractice cases do proceed to a jury trial, the jury is required to assess the negotiated outcome. The dilemma of evaluation confronted in these cases is "compared to what?" Most often the comparison is to the likely result if the negotiated claim proceeded to trial. This requires, in effect, a "trial within a trial." Although this approach is thought to apply an objective standard, it does not take into account the give and take of the negotiation process and the subjective, or nonmonetary interests, that may in reality have driven the negotiation. The "trial within a trial" approach reverts to a distributive negotiation model that launders out integrative aspects that favorably distinguished negotiation from trial.

Judging a negotiated outcome by an objective, monetary gauge fails to factor in the interest-based approach to which most of the new negotiation literature is directed. It raises the same concerns as does grading law students at the end of a negotiation course only on the quantitative, money results of a final negotiation role-play. As expressed by Epstein, ". . . every aspect of a negotiated settlement, particularly its conclusion, is a subjective evaluation premised on the client's needs and desires, coupled with the various influences that affect that client's ultimate desire to settle." (Epstein, *infra*, 463.) Gauging a lawyer's liability exposure only on the monetary result obtained can have a chilling effect on good integrative bargaining by attorneys.

Professor Epstein proposes that attorneys protect themselves from malpractice claims by regularly using a form entitled, "Pre-Settlement Statement of Client's Case," which the client is to sign before settlement. This form memorializes all the facts, assessments, and advice that were considered to decide upon settlement. The concluding sentence of the form states ". . . your attorney may use this document as a defense in a malpractice action if permitted by law." Although not a release per se, it is clearly intended to relieve the attorney of malpractice liability.

This "CYA" approach may or may not be effective protection, but is it the way you want to practice law? Each of us must ask how a precautionary approach with an eye ahead to defending malpractice claims will influence our relations with clients and impact our interaction with other attorneys. Will fear of malpractice hinder our nimbleness and creativity as negotiators? Was the *Muhammad* decision correct in its premise that opening up negotiation to after-the-fact legal scrutiny may impede negotiation and discourage settlement? If so, will judicial resources and client interests be adversely impacted?

As you consider these questions, please be aware that malpractice verdicts against lawyers for their good faith efforts in negotiating on behalf of clients appear to be rare. Keeping clients informed is the best prevention. Having read this book and studied the negotiation process has prepared you to be an effective negotiator with appreciative clients. Satisfied clients whose needs are met, including the need to know you have faithfully attended to their interests, do not sue their lawyers.

PART II

MEDIATION

CHAPTER
9

Mediation — The Big Picture

A. INTRODUCTION

1. The Process of Mediation

What Is Mediation?

Mediation is a process of assisted negotiation in which a neutral person helps people reach agreement. The process varies depending on the style of the mediator and the wishes of the participants. Mediation differs from direct negotiation in that it involves the participation of an impartial third party. The process also differs from adjudication in that it is consensual, informal, and usually private: The participants need not reach agreement, and the mediator has no power to impose an outcome.

In some contexts you may find that this definition does not fully apply. The process is sometimes not voluntary, as when a judge requires litigants to participate in mediation as a precondition to gaining access to a courtroom. In addition, mediators are not always entirely neutral; a corporate lawyer, for instance, can apply mediative techniques to help colleagues resolve an internal dispute, despite the fact that she is in favor of a particular outcome. Occasionally mediation is required to be open to the public, as when a dispute involves governmental entities subject to "open meeting" laws. And finally, a mediator's goal is not always to settle a specific legal dispute; the neutral may focus instead on helping disputants to improve their relationship.

There is an ongoing debate within the field about what "mediation" should be. To some degree, this results from the different goals that participants have for the process: Some focus only on settlement and seek to obtain the best possible monetary terms. Others seek to solve a problem or repair a relationship. Still other participants use mediation to change people's attitudes. As we will see, the increasing application of mediation to areas such as family and criminal law also raises serious questions of policy. We will focus primarily on "civil" mediation, involving legal disputes outside the area of collective bargaining, since that is the form that you are most likely to encounter in law practice. However, to give you a sense of what mediation may become, we also will present other perspectives on the process.

What Do Mediators Do?

Mediators apply a wide variety of techniques. Depending on the situation, a settlement-oriented mediator may use the following approaches, among others:

- Help litigants to design a process that assures the presence of key participants and focuses their attention on finding a constructive solution to a dispute.
- Allow the principals and their attorneys to present legal arguments, raise underlying concerns, and express their feelings directly to their opponents, as well as hear the other side's perspectives firsthand.
- Help participants to focus on their interests and identify imaginative settlement options.
- Moderate negotiations, coaching bargainers in effective techniques, translating communications, and reframing the disputants' positions and perceptions in constructive ways.
- Assist each side to assess the likely outcome if the case is litigated, and to consider the full costs of continuing the conflict.
- Work with the disputants to draft a durable agreement and, if necessary, to implement it.

What Is the Structure of Mediation?

Because mediation is informal, lawyers and clients have a great deal of freedom to modify the process to meet their needs. In practice, good neutrals and advocates vary their approach significantly to respond to the circumstances of particular cases. This said, a typical mediation of a legal dispute is likely to proceed through a series of stages.

Pre-mediation

Before the disputants meet to mediate, the neutral often has conversations with the lawyers, and sometimes also with the parties, to deal with issues such as who will attend the mediation and what information the mediator will receive beforehand. Lawyers can use these contacts to start to build a working relationship with the mediator and educate him about their client's perspective on the dispute and obstacles that have made direct negotiations difficult.

The Joint Session

Most mediations begin with a session in which the parties, counsel, and the mediator meet together. As we will see, the content and structure of a joint session can vary considerably, depending on the goals of the process. When mediation is focused on reaching a monetary settlement, the joint session is likely to be dominated by arguments of lawyers, perhaps followed by questions from the neutral. If, by contrast, the goal of the process is to find an interest-based solution or to repair a ruptured relationship, then the mediator is much more likely to encourage the parties themselves to speak, and to attempt to draw out underlying issues and emotions.

Private Caucusing, and No-Caucus Models

After disputants have exchanged perspectives, arguments, and questions, most civil mediators adjourn the joint session in order to meet with each side individually in private "caucuses." The purpose of caucusing is to permit disputants and counsel to talk candidly with the neutral. Keeping the parties separated, with communications channeled through the mediator, also allows the neutral to shape the disputants' dialogue in productive ways.

When the mediation process is focused on monetary bargaining, the participants usually spend most of their time separated, with the mediator shuttling back and forth between them. Occasionally, in extraordinarily contentious cases, parties may not meet at all. If, however, parties are interested in exploring an interest-based resolution or repairing a broken relationship, then the mediator is much more likely to encourage them to remain together so that they can work through difficult emotions, explore options, and learn to relate productively with each other. Mediators who handle family disputes often prefer to remain in joint session during the entire process, and some mediators are experimenting with no-caucus formats in general civil cases.

Moderated Discussions

Even when a mediation is conducted primarily through private caucusing, neutrals sometimes ask the disputants to meet with each other for specific purposes, for instance, to examine the tax issues in a business breakup or to deal with a difficult emotional issue in a tort case. And in almost every mediation, whether or not conducted through caucusing, the lawyers or parties meet at the end of the process to sign a memorandum of agreement or decide on future steps in the case.

Follow-up Contacts

Increasingly the mediation process is not limited to the specific occasions on which the mediator and disputants meet together. If a dispute is not resolved at a mediation session, then the neutral is likely to follow up with the lawyers or parties. Depending on the situation, the mediator may facilitate telephone or e-mail negotiations, or convene additional face-to-face sessions.

2. The Value of Mediation

Although litigants are sometimes compelled to enter mediation, the process can only be successful to the extent that disputants find it effective. What, in the eyes of parties and their lawyers, are the potential benefits of going to mediation? Consider the comments and data that follow.

a. Business Perspectives

In the late 1990s, researchers surveyed hundreds of major American corporations on their use of ADR. The following is a summary of what they found.

DAVID B. LIPSKY AND RONALD L. SEEBER, PATTERNS OF ADR USE IN CORPORATE DISPUTES

54 Disp. Resol. J. 66-71 (February 1999)

We asked respondents a range of questions designed to gauge the extent of ADR use [by large U.S. corporations.] Nearly all our respondents reported some experience with ADR, with an overwhelming 87% having used mediation and 80% having used arbitration at least once in the past three years . . . We conclude that ADR has made substantial inroads into the fabric of American business, with counsel overwhelmingly preferring mediation (63%); arbitration was a distant second (18%) . . . [N]early all corporations have experience with ADR, but a much smaller number of companies use mediation and arbitration frequently.

WHY DO CORPORATIONS USE ADR?

One of the more significant forces driving corporations toward ADR is the cost of litigation and the length of time needed to reach a settlement. All else being equal, ADR is widely considered cheaper and faster. . . .

Cost reduction may be the most widely cited reason for choosing ADR, but corporations report other reasons as well . . . We found that many of the answers related to the parties' desire to control their own destinies — to have some control over the path to resolution . . . The most often cited reason to use mediation (identified by 82% of the respondents) was that it allows the parties to resolve the dispute themselves. . . .

Eighty-one percent of those surveyed said that mediation provided a more satisfactory process than litigation, 67% said that it provided more satisfactory settlements, and 59% reported that it preserved good relationships. In sum, these responses indicate that mediation provides not just an alternative means to conventional dispute resolution but a superior process for reaching a resolution. . . .

Large corporations that have faced intense competitive pressures . . . appear more likely to have strong pro-ADR policies. Also, corporations that have adopted cutting-edge management strategies seem likelier to be pro-ADR. By contrast, smaller, more profitable corporations . . . are more likely to favor litigation.

BARRIERS TO THE USE OF ADR

When corporations use mediation frequently or very frequently, the dominant reason they do not use it is because opposing parties won't agree to it . . .

THE FUTURE OF ADR

In general, a large majority of the respondents in our survey believe that they are "likely" or "very likely" to use mediation in the future—38% and 46%, respectively. They were more cautious about the use of arbitration . . . If these projections are accurate, the use of ADR by U.S. corporations will grow significantly.

The trends noted in this article continue. A 2004 survey of corporate general counsel found that the respondents had mixed attitudes toward binding arbitration, but supported the use of mediation. Asked "What is your company's attitude toward nonbinding mediation clauses in its [domestic business] agreements?" the respondents gave these answers:

Strongly Favor	31%
Slightly Favor	29%
Neutral	25%
Slightly Disfavor	8%
Strongly Disfavor	7%

General counsel at large companies were the most likely to support mediation clauses, with 35% strongly favoring and only 1 percent strongly disfavoring their use. (For full survey results, see *Corporate Counsel Litigation Trends Survey Results* available at *www.fulbright.com*.) We will discuss the issues raised by mediation clauses in contracts, as well as those involved in creating a dispute-management program, in Chapters 20 and 21.

b. Viewpoints of Lawyers

Diane Gentile, Dayton

My practice is focused on employment law. These claims deal with one of the most important aspects of peoples' identity—their work. In addition, they often involve serious allegations of wrongdoing. Both sides in these disputes often have good reason to want a confidential solution. One example was a case I handled involving a worker and supervisor. Several years before the two had had a consensual intimate relationship, but the worker later accused her supervisor of sexual harassment. For the employer, the claim was a potential nightmare. The fact that the supervisor had at first denied the existence of the earlier relationship made it even more difficult. Moreover, because the employer was a nonprofit organization that depended in part on public funds, the potential for negative publicity could have crippled the organization. As soon as we received notice of the plaintiff's suit we suggested mediation. After nine hours of difficult discussions we had a resolution, and the organization's relief was limitless.

Mediation is effective in part because it allows the parties to talk about many things that will never be considered relevant by a court. When they are allowed to speak freely, often in private to a mediator offering a sympathetic ear, material just spills out, and afterward people are often much more willing to compromise. Mediation also allows for nonlegal relief, which is particularly important in employment cases: changes to a file to reflect a voluntary quit rather than termination, for example, or agreement on what the company will say to a future employer asking for a reference.

Mary Alexander, San Francisco, Former President, American Trial Lawyers Association

My practice focuses on personal injury cases, including auto accident, product liability, and defective design claims. Years ago we settled cases only on the courthouse steps, but courts in California now push parties to mediate long before trial. Often a case will not settle at court-ordered mediation, but the process gets lawyers talking and often leads to an agreement.

The single most useful service provided by mediators in my practice is to provide a reality check for clients. People often come into a lawyer's office with very real injuries, but unrealistic expectations about what they can obtain from the court system. They have heard somewhere about a large award and assume that it is typical, when in fact it is not. Clients are often in dire financial straits and physical pain, making it hard for them to listen to a lawyer's warnings about trial risk. When a mediator, especially a former judge, explains the realities of present-day juries—often in language that turns out to be very similar to what I had said earlier—it makes a real impression. Clients are able to become more realistic, and to accept a good offer when it appears. Even if the courts did not order it, I would elect to mediate almost every significant case.

Stephen Oleskey, Boston

I use mediation extensively in commercial cases to deal with a wide variety of obstacles. My goals depend on the nature of the situation. In one recent case, for example, the problem was anger: The parties had been talking off and on for two years, but both were so upset that they could not focus productively on settlement. At the same time, with several hundred million dollars at stake, neither side could bear the risk of a winner-take-all trial. Mediation created the context for a rational discussion of the merits and risks. In another case, we used mediation to get a group of corporate and political stakeholders to come to the same place and focus intensively on a case that some of them had not previously thought through. Occasionally, I've used a mediator to give a message to a client—or the other side's client—that was hard for a lawyer to deliver. In a few cases, it's been the way that the mediator has framed the discussions: her choice of what issues to focus on, or the statement that "We'll stay here until midnight if we have to, to get this done," that tells the parties that this is the time to make the difficult choices, put all their money on the table, and work out a deal if possible.

Katherine Gurun, Associate General Counsel, Bechtel Corporation

Our business involves complex construction and engineering projects. It is built around long-term relationships with suppliers and partners. Things inevitably go wrong—equipment fails, customers encounter financial problems, and so on. We have to resolve these issues, but in a way that keeps our relationships healthy. Mediation has become our most powerful and successful process for accomplishing this.

The flexibility of mediation is its most useful quality. In the disputes we encounter, the complex nature of the issues almost always requires several sessions, often spread over a period of months. During adjournments, people can confer with their organizations and the mediator can work on one or both sides. Overall, ADR has reduced our litigation costs phenomenally; just as important, it avoids the management distraction caused by formal litigation.

We also use mediation in international disputes. Here cultural differences are an important consideration. Many of our foreign partners are in mediation for the first time, and it's particularly important to find a neutral who "knows both sides of the fence." Asian executives seem especially comfortable with the mixture of joint and private meetings, because the structure accommodates their preference for conferring and reaching a consensus within the team at each point in the process. Europeans sometimes seem troubled by mediation's lack of formality, but I find that its adaptability is what makes the process so effective.

Paul Bland, Washington, D.C.

There are two major situations in which I find mediation helpful as a litigator for a public interest organization. The first is when we challenge widespread practices; for example, a group of HMOs flagrantly violating a statute. Inside counsel sometimes cannot believe that their organization has violated any law, simply because all of their peers are doing the same thing. In such cases I ask for mediation with a former judge or well-regarded private lawyer—someone who can convincingly tell the other lawyer that her client has a genuine problem.

Another indicator for mediation is when I suspect that defense counsel is not being candid with his own client. Many firms I encounter are completely ethical—they fight hard but fair. Some lawyers, however, seem to "milk" clients, playing on defendants' instinctive belief that they've done nothing wrong and billing them unnecessarily for a year or two. Mediation can be the best way to get the truth to an unrealistic client. I often have to work to get such cases into mediation. I have resorted to coming up to a defense counsel, in the presence of his client, and saying, "This looks like a perfect case for mediation." Or I might write to defense counsel and make an explicit request that he transmit the letter to his client. The hardest part of mediation is sometimes to get the other side into the process.

Patricia Lee Refo, Phoenix, Former Chair, ABA Section of Litigation

My caseload consists primarily of large commercial disputes. We use mediation in most of our cases—I sometimes joke that we lawyers have worked ourselves into a place where we can't settle cases by ourselves anymore! I don't believe that a bad settlement is better than a good trial. I am convinced, though, that in the right situation, a mediator can add a great deal of value.

Sometimes the problem is that both sides have the same facts, but they view them very differently. A mediator may not be able to convince a client to change his viewpoint, but she can make the client understand what the other side can do with the facts at trial. It's often the first time the client has heard the reaction of someone who comes to the case completely fresh.

There are also issues in business cases over which people become quite invested and emotional — for example, did someone violate an agreement in bad faith. Mediation allows clients to vent their feelings in private, making it easier for them to compromise later in the process. I recently encountered a mediator who said that he didn't "do venting." I find that aspect of the process often to be crucial, and I won't use neutrals who can't handle it. Mediators can also be helpful by "cutting to the chase," focusing on the few issues that will really matter at trial. This frees parties from arguing over every point, and moves them toward making settlement decisions.

Harry Mazadoorian, Connecticut

I've used mediative methods often in working out business relationships. Insurers, for example, often make investments in joint venture and partnership deals. It's impossible to predict the future, and as the project goes on and circumstances change, issues often arise about how the parties should share unexpected benefits and responsibilities. I remember one alternative energy venture that nearly broke down when money ran short and additional contributions were required from the participants. At first the lawyers focused on parsing the language of the contract, but as we talked I was able to persuade them to explore options that redistributed costs so that each partner could bear them most easily, and potential benefits in ways that they would be felt most strongly. Once the partners dropped their focus on legalese and looked instead at their specific needs, the conflict was quickly resolved. The greatest music to my ears in these situations was always to hear an executive say, "I just don't know how to get this done." I knew that if I could get the attention of high-level decision makers — ideally, get top people from both sides to sit down at lunch and commit to trying to work it out — success was nearly assured.

c. Is It Right for Every Dispute?

No one would argue that mediation is appropriate for every controversy. Even those who generally favor its use agree that mediation may not be effective in the following situations, among others:

- A disputant is not capable of negotiating effectively. This may occur, for example, because the person lacks legal counsel or is suffering from a personal impairment.
- One side in the controversy feels the need to establish a legal precedent. A party may need a judicial decision to use as a benchmark for settling similar cases.
- A litigant may require a court order to control the conduct of an adversary.

- One of the disputants is benefiting from the existence of the controversy. For example, a party may be using the litigation process to inflict pain on the other, or is maintaining a defense in court in order to delay making a payment for business reasons.
- A party needs formal discovery in order to evaluate the strength of its legal case.
- A crucial stakeholder refuses to join the process.

To some commentators, mediation is inherently unjust. They argue that the very informality of the process allows decision makers to express prejudice that is suppressed by more formal procedures, and permits case-by-case resolutions to siphon off pressure for law reform. Other critics concede that ADR may be useful generally, but sharply object to its application to specific areas such as divorce litigation. Some contend, for example, that by suggesting that legal standards are only one point of reference, ADR opens the way to the exploitation of unsophisticated parties. Such criticism is particularly strong in situations where participation in mediation is mandatory, as when parents in a dispute over child custody are required to go through ADR as a precondition to obtaining access to a court. Other writers have suggested that minorities tend to do less well in certain forms of mediation. Still another issue is whether ADR gives an advantage to "repeat players" such as corporations and insurers, who have the ability to direct business to favored neutrals. And some studies have called into question a basic premise of court-related mediation programs — that they reduce the duration of cases. All of these critiques raise significant policy issues, which are discussed in more depth in Chapters 13 and 14.

3. Examples of Mediation in Action

a. Death of a Student

Note: Confidentiality is one of the most important attributes of mediation. The facts in the following account that have not previously been published have been approved by attorneys for both parties.

In August 1997 Scott Krueger arrived for his freshman year at the Massachusetts Institute of Technology. Five weeks later, he was dead. In an incident that made national headlines, Krueger died of alcohol poisoning following an initiation event at a fraternity. Nearly two years later Krueger's parents sent MIT a demand letter stating their intent to sue. The letter alleged that MIT had caused their son's death by failing to address what they claimed were two longstanding campus problems: a housing arrangement that they said steered new students to seek rooms in fraternities, and what their lawyer called a culture of alcohol abuse at fraternities.

MIT's lawyers saw the case as one that could be won. An appellate court, they believed, would rule that a college is not legally responsible for an adult student's voluntary drinking. Moreover, under state law the university could not be required to pay more than $20,000 to the Kruegers (although that limit did not apply to claims against individual university administrators). MIT officials felt, however, that a narrowly-drawn legal response would not be in keeping with its values. They also recognized that there were aspects of the institution's policies and practices — including those covering student use of alcohol — that could have been better. MIT's president, Charles M. Vest, was prepared to accept responsibility for these shortcomings on behalf of the university, and felt a deep personal desire for his institution to reach a resolution with the Krueger family. MIT also recognized that defending the case in court would exact a tremendous emotional toll on all concerned. The Kruegers would be subjected to a hard-hitting assessment of their son's behavior leading up to his death, while MIT would be exposed to equally severe scrutiny of the Institute's culture and the actions of individual administrators. Full-blown litigation in a case of this magnitude was also sure to be expensive, with estimated defense costs well in excess of $1 million.

The question, as MIT saw it, was not whether to seek to engage the Kruegers in settlement discussions, but how. The university decided to forego a traditional legal response, and reply instead with a personal letter from President Vest to the Kruegers which noted the university's belief that it had strong legal defenses to their claims, but offered to mediate.

The Kruegers responded with intense distrust. Tortuous negotiations ensued. The parents eventually agreed to mediate, but only subject to certain conditions: At least one session would have to occur in Buffalo, where the Kruegers lived. MIT would have to offer a sincere apology for its conduct; without that, no sum of money would settle the case. There would be no confidentiality agreement to prevent the parents from talking publicly about the matter, while at the same time any settlement could not be exploited by MIT for public relations purposes. The Kruegers would have the right to select the mediator. And President Vest would have to appear personally at all the mediation sessions. The university agreed to most of the conditions and the mediation went forward.

MIT's lawyers believed that it was important that the Kruegers' lawyers and the mediator understand the strength of the university's defenses, but plaintiff counsel knew that subjecting the Kruegers to such a presentation would make settlement impossible. To resolve the dilemma, the lawyers bifurcated the process. The first day of the mediation, which the Kruegers would not attend, would focus on presentations by lawyers and would be held in Boston. One week later the mediation would resume at a conference center located a forty-minute drive outside Buffalo, this time with the Kruegers present. Their counsel selected that location so that "no one could leave easily." On the second day the Kruegers would personally meet President Vest, and the parties would begin to exchange settlement proposals.

Counsel had agreed that the mediator, Jeffrey Stern, should begin the day by having a private breakfast with Mr. and Mrs. Krueger and their lawyers. The Kruegers vented their anger, first to Stern and later to President Vest. "How could you do this?" they shouted at Vest, "You people killed our son!" They also challenged Vest on a point that bothered them terribly: Why, they asked him, had he come to their son's funeral but not sought them out personally to extend his condolences? Vest responded that he had consulted with people about whether or not to approach the Kruegers and was advised that, in light of their anger at the institution, it would be better not to do so. That advice was wrong, he said, and he regretted following it.

Vest went on to apologize for the university's role in what he described as a "terrible, terrible tragedy." "We failed you," he said, and then asked, "What can we do to make it right?" Mrs. Krueger cried out again at Vest, but at that point her husband turned to her and said, "The man apologized. What more is there to say?" Their counsel, Leo Boyle, later said that he felt that "There's a moment . . . where the back of the case is broken. You can feel it . . . And that was the moment this day." The mediator gradually channeled the discussion toward what the Kruegers wanted and the university could do.

Hard bargaining followed, much of it conducted though shuttle diplomacy by the mediator. In the end the parties reached agreement: MIT paid the Kruegers $4.75 million to settle their claims and contributed an additional $1.25 million to a scholarship fund that the family would administer. Perhaps equally important, President Vest offered the Kruegers a personal, unconditional apology on behalf of MIT that no court could have compelled and that would not have been believed if it were. At the conclusion of the process Vest and Mrs. Krueger hugged each other. For MIT the settlement, although expensive, made sense: It minimized the harm that contested litigation would have caused to the institution. And, most importantly, the university felt that it was the right thing to do.

What did the mediator contribute to the process? During the first day, Stern questioned both lawyers closely about the legal and factual issues, creating a foundation for realistic assessments of case value later in the process. The initial money offers put forth by each party were far apart, but the mediator put them into context so that neither side gave up in frustration. According to plaintiff counsel Brad Henry, Stern's greatest contribution was probably the way he responded to the Kruegers' feelings: "What he did most masterfully was to allow a lot of the emotion to be directed at him. He allowed it almost to boil over when it was just him with the Kruegers, but later he very deftly let it be redirected at President Vest and the university . . . He also prepared Charles Vest for the onslaught . . . Mediation can be like a funeral—especially with the death of a child. He mediated the emotional part of the case, and then let the rest unfold on its own."

QUESTIONS

1. What barriers appear to have made it difficult for the parties in the Krueger case to negotiate with each other directly?
2. What did the Kruegers obtain in mediation that they could not have won at trial?

b. United States et al. v. Microsoft Corporation

In one of the highest profile antitrust cases in American history, the Justice Department, later joined by several states, sued the Microsoft Corporation, arguing that it had monopolized certain markets in computer software. While the case was pending, judges twice ordered the parties into mediation processes, which are described in the following articles.

JAMES LAFLIN AND ROBERT WERTH, UNFINISHED BUSINESS: ANOTHER LOOK AT THE MICROSOFT MEDIATION: LESSONS FOR THE CIVIL LITIGATOR

12 Cal. Tort Rep. 88-92 (April 2001)

On November 18, 1999, twelve months into a case that was eventually to last eighteen, U.S. District Judge Thomas Penfield Jackson announced the appointment of Richard A. Posner, the Chief Judge of the Seventh Circuit Court of Appeals in Chicago, to serve as mediator in the Microsoft antitrust case . . . Posner was neither a practiced diplomat nor experienced mediator. However, he brought other credentials to the table. He had gained recognition as one of the most capable, influential members of the federal bench, and a recognized authority in the field of antitrust law. . . .

Posner's mission as a mediator was to induce Microsoft and the government to shed what he referred to as "emotionality" and come to a rational compromise. At the outset, the parties met for lunch at a private club, in what would turn out to be the only face-to-face meeting of the entire mediation process. In attendance were lawyers representing Microsoft, the Justice Department and three attorneys general representing the nineteen states who joined as plaintiffs in the suit. In describing the protocol, Posner indicated he would refrain from evaluating the strength of either side's case, "try to deflate unrealistic expectations" and keep all talks in confidence. Each side was asked "to make a detailed presentation of the facts and remedies it would consider." Posner promised to devote himself almost full time to the process.

To mitigate "emotionality" Judge Posner ordered separate meetings for at least the first month, the government each Monday, Microsoft each Tuesday. Two months later the process had evolved into a form of shuttle diplomacy interspersed with the judge's email inquiries seeking additional information. He began, in the words of one Microsoft negotiator, "growling at the other side, growling at us." After two months of work Posner outlined the first draft of a settlement proposal. Over the next several months, some nineteen draft proposals were exchanged via Posner, who edited them into his own language and emailed them either to Microsoft's General Counsel, or the chief of the Justice Department's Antitrust Division. Copies went to the chair of the association of the nineteen state attorneys general.

By mid-February, negotiations had stalled. Neither side believed that the other was open to a compromise, and both sides were often confused. At Microsoft, this was reflected by [General Counsel] Bill Neukum who said of Posner, "You keep asking yourself, 'Is he wearing his hat as a mediator, trying to motivate people to narrow their differences and come together, or is he speaking as the Chief Judge of the Seventh Circuit, who's an expert on antitrust law?'" Compounding this confusion, neither side could be sure whether, or which, terms contained in the successive draft proposals originated with Judge Posner or came directly from their adversary.

From late February 2000 through the end of March, Posner had extensive telephone conversions with Microsoft, sometimes with [Chairman William] Gates directly, and with Justice Department attorneys, in which successive draft agreements were negotiated and refined. In early March Gates seemed close to accepting the deal reflected in draft fourteen, which Posner forwarded to the Justice Department and the states. The states were given ten days to accept, or Posner would terminate the process. The state attorneys general made it clear that Joel Klein was not their spokesperson and responded separately to the proposal. The states were angry with both Posner and Klein. As one state official said, "Posner was more interested in dealing with Gates and Klein and didn't perceive that he had nineteen other parties to the lawsuit . . . He got enamored of talking to Gates. And he's not a mediator by training, and lacked basic mediation skills."

Posner was prepared to summon the parties to Chicago for direct face-to-face negotiations starting on March 24th. Their options would be to accept the basic terms contained in the most recent draft, or face termination of the mediation. More emails and telephone conversations between Posner and the two sides ensued. Meanwhile, the states had communicated their disapproval of parts of draft eighteen and added further conditions. Posner now realized he would have to negotiate with the nineteen state attorneys general to develop a single government proposal. Then, even if that could be accomplished, he would still have to negotiate the divide between the government stakeholders and Microsoft. That night he telephoned Microsoft and Klein and announced that his mediation effort was over.

The Microsoft case went to trial and the court found that Microsoft had violated antitrust laws. Judge Jackson ordered a breakup of the company, and Microsoft appealed. Several months later the Court of Appeals upheld some of the trial court's findings of antitrust violations, rejected others, and disapproved the court's breakup remedy. Criticizing the conduct of the trial judge, particularly his decision to talk privately with a reporter, the appeals court appointed a new judge to preside over the case. Other changes had occurred: While the appeal was pending, a new President had taken office and the Justice Department had announced that it would no longer seek a breakup of the company. Before resuming hearings, the second trial judge again referred the Microsoft case to mediation. The following article summarizes its results.

ERIC GREEN AND JONATHAN MARKS, HOW WE MEDIATED THE MICROSOFT CASE

The Boston Globe A23 (November 15, 2001)

Mediators never kiss and tell. But within the bounds of appropriate confidentiality, lessons can be learned from the three-week mediation marathon that led to Microsoft's settlements with the Department of Justice and at least nine states. Federal District Judge Colleen Kollar-Kotelly took over the case after the Court of Appeals partially affirmed the prior judge's findings that Microsoft had violated antitrust laws . . . Neither the mediation nor the settlements would have happened if Kollar-Kotelly had not acted to suspend litigation and order settlement negotiations. The judge's Sept. 28 mandate was blunt: "The Court expects that the parties will . . . engage in an all-out effort to settle these cases, meeting seven days a week and around the clock, acting reasonably to reach a fair resolution." The court gave the parties two weeks to negotiate on their own, ordering them to mediation if they couldn't reach agreement by then. The court bounded its "24/7" timetable by ordering the parties to complete mediation by Nov. 2 . . . Tight timetables command attention. In mediation, just as in negotiation, time used tends to expand to fit time available. A firm deadline gets the parties to focus. . . .

We are both mediators, with 40 years of combined experience . . . But we are not experts in the applicable law or the disputed technology. . . . Even had we had such expertise, our objective would not have been to try to craft our own settlement solution and sell its merits to the parties. We believed that the only chance of getting all or most parties to a settlement was for us to work intensively to help them create their own agreement. Our "job one" was to facilitate and assist in the gestation, birth, and maturing of such an agreement. We had to be advocates for settlement — optimistic and persistent — but not advocates for any particular settlement. . . .

Reaching a settlement required working with adversarial parties with very different views about a large number of technologically and legally complicated issues. When we arrived on the scene, the parties had begun exchanging drafts of possible settlement terms . . . After initial separate briefings, we moved the process into an extended series of joint meetings, involving representatives of the Antitrust Division, the state attorneys general and their staffs, and Microsoft. No party was left out of the negotiations. The bargaining table had three sides. . . .

Throughout most of the mediation the 19 states and the federal government worked as a combined "plaintiffs" team. We worked to ensure the right mix of people, at the table and in the background. The critical path primarily ran through managing and focusing across-the-table discussions and drafting by subject matter experts — lawyers and computer mavens — with knowledge of the technological and business complexities gained through working on the case since its inception. The critical path also required working with senior party-representatives who could make principled decisions about priorities and deal breakers.

[As a result of the mediation, Microsoft, the Justice Department, and ten state attorneys general reached agreement.] Even as settlement advocates we have no quarrel with the partial settlement that was achieved . . . Successful mediations are ones in which mediators and parties work to identify and overcome barriers to reaching agreement . . . Successful mediations are ones in which, settle or not, senior representatives of each party have made informed and intelligent decisions. The Microsoft mediation was successful.

Note: The remaining nine attorneys general filed objections to the settlement with the trial judge, but both the trial and appeals courts upheld its terms.

QUESTIONS

1. Consider the mediation of the student death case described above: What goals, other than avoiding litigation costs, did the university seem to have in proposing mediation?
2. What did the student's family appear to be seeking, other than maximizing the monetary settlement?

3. Neutrals reveal their own definition of mediation by the manner in which they practice it. Looking at the techniques that Judge Posner applied, what appeared to be his concept of how mediation should work?
4. How did mediators Green and Marks view the process?
5. Marks and Green emphasize the importance of deadlines. Could the judge have achieved the same settlement result by setting a firm trial date and ordering the parties to negotiate with each other directly?

B. GOALS AND STYLES

1. Goals for the Process

When you participate in mediation as an advocate, what will be your goals for the process? The answer may seem simple—to settle a legal dispute. But the question is often more complex. Many disputes involve issues, interests, and potential solutions that go beyond the legal issues that lawyers typically consider or the remedies that courts can grant. When a dispute arises from an important relationship, for example, repairing the rupture could be more significant to a client than how the current controversy is resolved. Sometimes, as well, lawyers are drawn into disputes in which the legal issues are relatively unimportant, as in the example of the corporate counsel in the "viewpoints" section who described managing bargaining between partners in a joint venture. The goals that you pursue in mediation thus may change greatly from one situation to another, and these differences will in turn influence your choice of a neutral and structure for the process. As a lawyer representing clients, you may have one or more of the following purposes in deciding to mediate.

Resolve a Legal Claim on the Best Possible Monetary Terms

When litigators enter mediation, their goal is usually to settle a legal dispute. Most trial lawyers take a narrow approach to the process: They discuss only the legally relevant facts and issues and set as their goal to obtain the highest (for the plaintiff) or lowest (for the defendant) possible monetary payment in return for ending the case. When litigators talk about mediation, they often reflect this perspective. One lawyer, for example, has said that "The effective advocate approaches mediation as if it were a trial . . . the overwhelming benefit of mediation is that it can reduce the cost of litigation" (Weinstein, 1996). Perhaps in response, commercial mediators often see their primary role as to facilitate distributive bargaining. One successful New England neutral, for example, has written that, "In the typical civil mediation, money is the primary (if not the only) issue" (Contuzzi, 2000), while a leading Southern mediator has said that, "The goal of resolution is always the same: allowing the parties to negotiate to a 'reasonable ballpark,' in which they, with the help of the mediator, identify 'home plate' based on what a jury will consider 'a reasonable verdict range'" (Max, 1999).

In the typical commercial dispute, then, litigants and their counsel are likely to enter the process assuming that it will focus primarily on legal arguments and principled/positional bargaining over money. Although this kind of negotiation often produces less-than-optimal results, a mediator can do a great deal to assist parties even when money is the only issue over which the disputants are willing to bargain.

Example: An inexperienced plaintiff's lawyer was representing an automobile accident victim in negotiations with the defendant's insurer. The victim had suffered broken bones, with out-of-pocket damages totaling $6,000. Requested by the defendant's adjuster to make a settlement demand, the plaintiff counsel asked for $1.2 million. The adjuster was incredulous: In her experience, plaintiff lawyers rarely demanded more than ten to fifteen times the "out-of-pockets." She refused to "dignify" the plaintiff's "wild number" with a response, and the result was a complete breakdown of talks.

The case went to mediation. In a private meeting with the plaintiff and his counsel, the mediator asked about their goals in the negotiation. The lawyer said that he was willing to be flexible, and the client indicated that he was seeking a much more modest amount than the $1.2 million demand might suggest. The neutral asked the plaintiff lawyer to make a new offer at a much lower level. She offered to tell the adjuster that the plaintiff had done this only to accommodate the mediator's request that both sides "cut to the chase," and that the plaintiff expected the defendant to respond in a similar vein. Three hours later the case settled at $27,500.

Develop a Broad, Interest-Based Resolution

As we have seen, parties to legal disputes often have interests that go far beyond money, and settlements that respond to these concerns can provide greater value to disputants than a purely monetary outcome. Some lawyers employ mediation to facilitate interest-based bargaining and obtain creative resolutions. One text for corporate attorneys, for example, emphasizes that "The process creates an opportunity to explore underlying business interests [and] offers the potential for a 'win-win' solution . . ." (Picker, 2003), while another describes the process as providing "a framework for parties to . . . privately reveal to the mediator in caucus sensitive interests that may assist the mediator to facilitate broad solutions" (CPR Institute, Scanlon ed., 1999).

Example: A company that processed hazardous chemical waste and one of its residential abutters had been embroiled for years in a series of disputes over the company's applications for licenses to expand its operations. They eventually agreed to mediate. Although the parties at first focused exclusively on the meaning of certain state hazardous waste regulations, the mediator noted that the abutter became most angry when he mentioned the company's practice of parking large trucks filled with waste on the street across from his house. The company insisted that such situations resulted from unpredictable traffic jams at the plant, but the abutter maintained that the problem showed the company's basic callousness about its neighbors' safety.

As he spoke with the parties, the mediator found that the company also wanted to end the practice, and could do so if it could widen its driveway to accommodate two trucks at a time. This was impossible because the driveway was wedged against the abutter's land. That land was not, however, being used. As part of an overall settlement, the mediator convinced the abutter to convey a narrow strip of his unused land to the company. The company in turn agreed to widen its driveway, thus solving the truck parking problem for everyone and increasing the value of the abutter's remaining land.

Repair the Parties' Ruptured Relationship

Attorneys sometimes enter mediation not so much to obtain specific terms of settlement as to repair the parties' relationship. When parties enter litigation they typically sever any prior connection between them, but many supporters of mediation believe, in the words of Professor Lon Fuller, that "mediation has as its primary goal the repair of the troubled relationship" (Fuller, 1971).

> *Example:* An Austrian company that marketed a process to stop soil erosion along river banks and a principal officer of its U.S. affiliate were in a dispute. The plaintiff was the founder of the company, who had trained the other protagonist, a young American woman, to create a subsidiary to sell his process in the United States. The woman modified the process in the belief that the original version would not fit the American market. This triggered a violent disagreement with the founder. Faced with the prospect of resolving the dispute or declaring bankruptcy, the shareholders and executives agreed to meet.
>
> The founder arrived at the mediation, and sat rigid and silent as others talked. When the mediator asked him to give his perspective on the situation, he refused: His position was stated in a letter that everyone had received. What else needed to be said? Still, the mediator asked if he would read the letter aloud in order to insure that everyone heard him clearly. As the founder began to read, feelings began to show under his stolid exterior. The woman responded angrily, and they began to argue. It seemed to be a classic daughter/mentee-grows-up-and-challenges-father/mentor situation. Eventually the two went to a corner and talked animatedly for more than an hour. Afterward, in a calmer atmosphere, the mediator led the principals through a discussion of the challenges facing the firm and how they might solve them. Under the leadership of a new CEO not linked to either of the protagonists, painful changes were agreed to and the company survived.

Change the Parties' Perspectives

In a still-broader view, the purpose of the mediation process is not to obtain any specific outcome. Instead its focus is to assist parties to transform their perspectives on the dispute and each other, a change that may or may not lead to an improvement in their relationship. Advocates of this perspective, known as "transformative" mediation, argue that the disputants should be allowed to take charge of the mediation process, with the mediator serving simply as a resource to facilitate their conversations. Professor Baruch Bush and Joseph Folger, for example, contrast transformative mediation with processes oriented toward problem solving, stating that

> a *transformative approach* to mediation, emphasizes mediation's capacity for fostering empowerment and recognition . . . Transformative mediators concentrate on empowering parties to define issues and decide settlement terms for themselves and on helping parties to better understand one another's perspectives. The effect of this approach is to avoid the directiveness associated with

problem-solving mediation. Equally important, transformative mediation helps parties recognize and exploit the opportunities for moral growth inherently presented by conflict. It aims at changing the parties themselves for the better, as human beings.

(Bush and Folger, 2004) This approach is described in more detail below.

Choices Among Potential Goals

Although a particular mediation can have more than a single purpose, one can think of possible goals for the process as falling along a continuum.

Potential Goals in Mediation

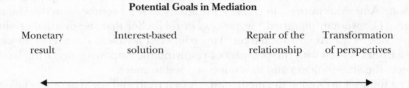

| Monetary result | Interest-based solution | Repair of the relationship | Transformation of perspectives |

How likely is it in practice that if an attorney seeks one of these goals, he will be able to achieve it — how often, in other words, can parties in a civil mediation expect to leave the process with a purely monetary settlement, an interest-based solution, or a relationship repair?

The answer will be heavily influenced by the nature of the case, the attitudes of clients and counsel, and the skills and goals of the mediator. Relationship repair in mediation is often not feasible: In most auto tort cases, for example, there is no prior relationship to revive. Even when a dispute does arise from a relationship, the parties often litigate bitterly before mediating, and in such situations repairing the relationship is very difficult. Sometimes, however, both sides recognize that it is in their interest to heal their rupture. This is most common in settings where the parties' past connection has been strong and their alternatives to relating are not attractive. One example of such a situation is a quarrel between a divorcing couple over how they will parent their children. Relationships can be important in commercial settings as well; partners in small businesses, like the Austrian-American venture described above, may have a strong interest in seeking a repair of a troubled relationship because neither is able to buy out the other, and continued conflict will destroy the enterprise. A study of mediations of larger civil disputes arising from relationships (excluding unionized labor and divorce cases) found the following:

Outcomes of Legal Mediation in "Relationship" Cases

Repair of relationship	Integrative term & money, but no repair	Money terms only	Impasse
17%	30%	27%	27%

In other words, when parties mediate a legal dispute arising from a significant prior relationship with a mediator open to imaginative solutions, there appears to be approximately a 15-20 percent chance that the process will culminate in a repair of the parties' relationship, a 30 percent chance of a settlement that has at least one significant integrative term[1] in addition to money, a 25-30 percent probability of a settlement consisting solely of a monetary payment, and a 25-30 percent likelihood of impasse. Interestingly, focusing only on those cases that settled, agreements with least one significant integrative term (either a relationship repair or another non-money term) totaled 47 percent, a much higher percentage than settlements consisting only of a monetary payment (27%) (Golann, 2002).

As a lawyer you are likely to encounter many situations in which your client's only stated goal is to end its relationship with an adversary on the best possible terms. The data suggests, however, that in cases that arise from a prior relationship, more often than not it is feasible to obtain an agreement that includes some term of significant value to the parties in addition to money, and that in a small but appreciable portion of cases it is possible to repair the parties' relationship.

QUESTIONS

1. In what kinds of legal cases would you expect the parties to have a weak or nonexistent prior relationship?
2. In what types of disputes are the parties likely to find it very difficult or costly to sever their connection?

2. Mediator Styles

a. Classifying Styles

It is possible to classify mediators according to the goals that they seek and the methods that they use to achieve them, and to show the results graphically. The following reading demonstrates how this can be done:

LEONARD L. RISKIN, RETIRING AND REPLACING THE GRID OF MEDIATOR ORIENTATIONS

21 Alternatives 69-74 (April 2003) and 12 Alternatives 111 (Summer 1994)

[A decade ago, there was] a vast and diverse array of processes . . . called mediation. Yet there was no accepted system for distinguishing among the various

---

1. Examples of integrative terms in business disputes included: an agreement among parties breaking up a partnership that one partner would have the exclusive use of certain billing software, or that the ex-partners would continue to share office space. In employment cases companies agreed to terms such as temporarily maintaining the health coverage of a departing employee, or changing records to reflect a voluntary quit rather than a termination, and employees sometimes agreed never to apply for employment with the company again. Releases of liability and confidentiality agreements were not counted as integrative terms in the survey because they were typically assented to as a matter of course.

approaches. As a result, there was great confusion in the field about what mediation is and what it should be . . . Looking back, I like to think about this confusion in terms of three gaps between mediation theory — that is, what the well-known writings and training programs, mainly those focusing on civil, non-labor mediation, said mediators did or should do — and mediation practice — that is, what mediators actually did.

First, mediation theory held that mediators don't evaluate, make predictions about what would happen in court, or tell parties what to do. In practice, however, many mediators evaluated and told people what to do. Second, mediation theory said that mediation was intended to address the parties' underlying interests or real needs, rather than, or in addition to, their legal claims. Quite commonly, however, mediations in civil disputes — especially those that were in the litigation process, or might be — were narrow and adversarial. The third disparity between theory and practice concerned self-determination. The "experts" touted mediation's potential for enhancing self-determination. Yet in practice, many mediation processes did not fulfill that promise.

These gaps between theory and practice produced a number of problems. The most salient problem concerned evaluation [— a mediator's decision to give an opinion as to the likely outcome of the case in adjudication, or to propose terms of settlement]: Sometimes parties went into a mediation thinking they were not going to get an evaluation, but got one nevertheless — without consenting to it or preparing for it. And sometimes the reverse happened: Parties who thought they would get an evaluation, because they were analogizing mediation to some judicial settlement conferences, didn't get one. Similarly, parties who entered a mediation thinking it would focus either broadly or narrowly often were surprised to find the opposite focus. And some mediators gave short shrift to party self-determination by exercising extensive control of the focus and even the outcome.

For all these reasons, great ambiguity suffused most conversations about mediation. In addition, many parties, potential parties, lawyers, and mediators did not recognize the existence of numerous choices about what would happen in a mediation and that someone would make those choices, either explicitly or implicitly. [To address these problems, I proposed a system for classifying mediator orientations.] It focused primarily on two of the gaps: evaluation by the mediator and problem-definition (which was my vehicle for addressing the tendency of many commercial mediators to focus on positions, in the form of claims of legal entitlements, rather than underlying interests) . . .

. . . The classification system [started] with two principal questions: 1. Does the mediator tend to define problems narrowly or broadly? 2. Does the mediator think she should evaluate — make assessments or predictions or proposals for agreements — or facilitate the parties' negotiation without evaluating? The answers reflect the mediator's beliefs about the nature and scope of mediation and her assumptions about the parties' expectations.

PROBLEM DEFINITION

Mediators with a narrow focus assume that the parties have come to them for help in solving a technical problem. The parties have defined this problem in advance through the positions they have asserted in negotiations or pleadings.

Often it involves a question such as, "Who pays how much to whom?" or "Who can use such-and-such property?" As framed, these questions rest on "win-lose" (or "distributive") assumptions. In other words, the participants must divide a limited resource; whatever one gains, the other must lose. The likely court outcome—along with uncertainty, delay and expense—drives much of the mediation process. Parties, seeking a compromise, will bargain adversarially, emphasizing positions over interests.

A mediator who starts with a broad orientation, on the other hand, assumes that the parties can benefit if the mediation goes beyond the narrow issues that normally define legal disputes. Important interests often lie beneath the positions that the participants assert. Accordingly, the mediator should help the participants understand and fulfill those interests—at least if they wish to do so.

THE MEDIATOR'S ROLE

The evaluative mediator assumes that the participants want and need the mediator to provide some directions as to the approximate grounds for settlement—based on law, industry practice, or technology. She also assumes that the mediator is qualified to give such direction by virtue of her experience, training, and objectivity.

The facilitative mediator assumes the parties are intelligent, able to work with their counterparts, and capable of understanding their situation better then either their lawyers or the mediator. So the parties may develop better solutions than any that the mediator might create. For these reasons, the facilitative mediator assumes that his principal mission is to enhance and clarify communications between the parties in order to help them decide what to do. The facilitative mediator believes it is inappropriate for the mediator to give his opinion, for at least two reasons. First, such opinions might impair the appearance of impartiality and thereby interfere with the mediator's ability to function. Second, the mediator might not know enough—about the details of the case or the relevant law, practices, or technology—to give an informed opinion.

Mediators usually have a predominant orientation, whether they know it or not, based on a combination of their personalities, experiences, education, and training. Thus, many retired judges, when they mediate, tend toward an evaluative-narrow orientation.

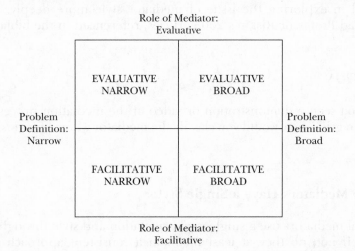

Yet mediators do not always behave consistently with the predominant orientations they express . . . In addition, many mediators will depart from their orientations to respond to the dynamics of the situation . . . [As an] example: an evaluative-narrow mediator may explore underlying interests (a technique normally associated with the broad orientation) after her accustomed narrow focus results in a deadlock. And a facilitative-broad mediator might use a mildly evaluative tactic as a last resort. For instance, he might toss out a figure that he thinks the parties might be willing to agree upon, while stating that the figure does not represent his prediction of what would happen in court . . . Many effective mediators are versatile and can move from quadrant to quadrant (and within a quadrant), as the dynamics of the situation dictate, to help parties settle disputes . . .

I appreciate the insight of Professor George Box: "All models are wrong. Some are useful." No graphic can capture the rich complexity of real life. Nevertheless, I hope that this grid will be useful.

Professor Riskin has since modified his grid by replacing the word "evaluative" with "directive" and "facilitative" with "elicitive" (the "broad" versus "narrow" continuum remains the same). He explains his reasons for doing so as follows.

> First, the terms "directive" and "elicitive" more closely approximate my goals for this continuum, which [is] to focus on the impact of the mediator's behavior on party self-determination. Second, the term "directive" is more general and abstract than "evaluative" and therefore may cover a wider range of mediator behaviors . . . Using the terms "directive" and "elicitive" also can help us recognize that mediators can direct (or push) the parties toward particular outcomes through "selective facilitation"—directing discussion of outcomes the mediator favors, while not promoting discussions of outcomes the mediator does not favor—without explicitly evaluating a particular outcome.

(Riskin, 2003d) Most writing on mediator styles continues to employ Riskin's evaluative-facilitative terminology. To avoid confusing the reader with inconsistent terms, therefore, we will use those terms in this book. Students interested in exploring the issue of mediator style more deeply, however, should read Professor Riskin's 2003 articles, referenced in the bibliography.

QUESTION

Have you seen a demonstration or video of the mediation process? Using the "Riskin grid," how would you classify the mediator whom you most recently observed?

b.   Do Mediators Have a Single Style?

Do legal mediators use a single goal orientation and style throughout their practice? If not, do they at least maintain a consistent approach during a single mediation? To investigate this issue, one of the authors asked several respected legal mediators to mediate a case in a roleplay format while being filmed. The experiment found, as Professor Riskin suggests, that good neutrals do not maintain a single orientation, but instead adapt their approach to fit the circumstances of a dispute. Indeed, neutrals typically changed their approach repeatedly during a single caucus meeting with a party. All of the mediators began in a broadly facilitative mode, asking about the parties' business and personal interests, but they were usually met with narrowly evaluative comments from the lawyers. In response, the mediators remained facilitative, but acceded to counsel's narrow subject-matter orientation. Periodically during the process, however, mediators would return to a "broad" orientation, asking about the client's interests and suggesting nonmonetary solutions.

This experiment confirms Riskin's observation that successful legal mediators are not consistently either facilitative or evaluative. The neutrals in the study did become increasingly evaluative over the course of each mediation, but their advice usually focused on the bargaining situation: They offered opinions, for instance, about how the other side was probably seeing the situation and what negotiating approach was most likely to be effective ("If you make that offer, I'm concerned that they will react by . . ."). As each of the filmed roleplays continued, the mediator became more willing to ask questions or make comments that suggested a view, or at least skepticism, about the disputants' legal arguments. However, when a neutral did make an evaluative comment about a legal issue, she almost always framed it in general terms ("The evidence on causation seems thin . . . I'm concerned that a court might . . ."). Overall, changes in the style of each mediator appeared to be determined much more by the personalities and tactics of the parties and lawyers than by tendencies of the neutral. Lawyer advocacy and client attitudes, in other words, counted for more than a mediator's preferred technique in determining what occurred during each mediation.

QUESTION

1. What type of mediator would you select if you were a lawyer representing the following clients?
    a. The family of the deceased MIT student.
    b. The chemical company in the abutter-chemical company case.
    c. The plaintiff in the "$1.2 million demand" personal injury mediation.

3. *Mediative Approaches and Techniques*

This section examines forms of mediation that you are likely to encounter in practice. As ADR has evolved, a wide variety of approaches to mediation have gained a measure of acceptance. Most lawyer-mediators focus on civil cases — that is, legal cases involving the kinds of tort, contract, property, and statutory claims that you have studied in law school, as opposed to domestic relations or collective bargaining disputes. We will refer to such neutrals as "commercial" mediators. Commercial mediators almost all use a caucus-based format, and the discussion tends to focus on legally relevant facts and issues and monetary offers. Mediators who specialize in mediating divorce and other disputes between family members, by contrast, usually avoid caucusing and place more emphasis on the parties' nonmonetary interests. The setting in which mediation occurs — for example, whether it is an all-day affair conducted by a private provider or a time-limited event ordered by a court — may also have a major impact on how the process unfolds. The readings below give a flavor of several models, beginning with commercial mediation and going on to processes that focus on transformation of perspectives, monetary issues, and relationship repair.

a. Commercial Mediation

Mediators who focus their practice on what we call commercial disputes tend to use similar methods to conduct the process. The following two readings describe these techniques.

DWIGHT GOLANN, A BASIC MEDIATIVE STRATEGY
Mediating Legal Disputes 39-59 (1996)

In order to be effective, a mediator needs to have a strategy. Your overall goal is to stimulate constructive negotiations. You have been called in, however, because the parties are unable to negotiate effectively on their own, and a general call to reasonableness will rarely be enough to resolve the situation. Some discussions of mediation list a variety of roles which a mediator can take on, ranging from translator to agent of reality to scapegoat. Simply to list a mediator's functions does not, however, help one to select the right approach at a specific point. If people are not negotiating effectively with each other, it is because they are being frustrated by one or more barriers. As you prepare for mediation, then, you should ask yourself two questions:

- What obstacles are preventing the parties from settling this dispute themselves?
- What strategy is most likely to overcome the barriers and help the parties negotiate?

Your understanding of what is keeping the parties apart will deepen over the course of a mediation, and the obstacles themselves may change as the process goes forward. Ideally, your strategy would be unique to each case; in practice, however, this may not be possible. Many mediators use a similar sequence of techniques to deal with the barriers that are most likely to be present and customize their approach as they go along.

This section sets forth a simple six-step strategy that works effectively in less complex situations. It assumes a number of factors, for example that the parties have agreed to mediate and that the right people are in the room. We suggest that you use the strategy set out here as a "default" framework, applying other approaches as your skills grow and circumstances demand it. The strategy is as follows:

A Basic Mediation Strategy

Problem	Responses
1. Lack of Focus	• Create a "settlement event."
	• Arrange for decision makers to attend.
	• Ensure that they have adequate information.
	• If necessary, propose deadlines.
2. Need to Vent Arguments and/or Emotions	• Provide disputants with a "day in court."
	• Help them to express their feelings.
	• Encourage participants to listen to opponents.
3. Positional Bargaining	• Ask for offers.
	• Clarify opponents' intentions and explain ambiguous moves.
	• Advise negotiators about the likely impact of tactics.
4. Hidden Nonlegal Issues	• Probe for psychological obstacles.
	• Seek out opportunities for gain.
	• Solicit ideas for addressing problems and exploiting opportunities.
	• Encourage candor and imaginative thinking.
5. Lack of Realism About Alternatives	• Reality test: Question legal and factual issues.
	• Lead disputants through a case analysis.
	• Bring out the monetary and other costs of conflict.
	• Challenge the litigants' views and point out neglected issues.
	• If necessary, offer a prediction of the likely outcome if the dispute is adjudicated.
6. Inability to Close	• Help participants to avoid bargaining confrontations.
	• Reframe their options and choices.
	• Play "confidential listener."
	• Find new issues to unfreeze impasse.
	• Offer a "mediator's proposal."

1. CREATE A SETTLEMENT EVENT

THE PROBLEM: PROCRASTINATION AND LACK OF FOCUS

Many cases don't settle as quickly as they could because the parties or their negotiators are unwilling to raise the topic of settlement. This may be due to tactical concerns — the fear of suggesting a lack of confidence in one's legal case, for instance, or of appearing overeager to bargain. Disputants also delay negotiations, however, because they are reluctant to confront unpleasant realities, such as problems that have arisen with their legal arguments. Another common cause of delay is that cases drop out of the daily consciousness ("off the radar screens") of the people whose decisions are needed to resolve them. When this occurs, settlement discussions may never begin, or go on unproductively for months or years.

THE RESPONSE: CREATE A SETTLEMENT EVENT

The very scheduling of a mediation is a powerful tactic for dealing with the barrier of procrastination. It creates a focus on the dispute by the key players, a mutual recognition that it is appropriate to compromise, and a sense of deadline ("If not now, when?"). This "focus" aspect is very significant. Simply by agreeing to mediate, each side sends the other a signal that it is willing to invest resources in exploring a settlement, and thus impliedly is ready to compromise. It is easier for each party to move because it has some assurance that its own painful concessions will be reciprocated.

Mediators can also work in advance to ensure that the right people participate in the process. Negotiators sometimes suggest mediation in order to get a key person on the other side, for example a CEO or plaintiff's counsel, to focus on the dispute. If necessary, the mediator can also create a "train is leaving the station" effect to prod a reluctant party to make a difficult decision. ("I think we should go as long as necessary — I'm not going to ask you to come back another day . . .") Mediators can either enhance or detract from the feeling of a "settlement event" by how they manage the process.

2. ALLOW THE PARTICIPANTS TO ARGUE AND VENT

THE PROBLEM: UNRESOLVED PROCESS AND EMOTIONAL NEEDS

If parties do not settle through direct negotiation, it may be because one or more of them want something other than the settlement terms they are discussing. In addition to money, for example, a litigant may be looking for an experience — the opportunity to appear before a neutral person, state his grievance to an adversary, and know that he has been heard. In addition to arguing substantive issues, participants often also want to express strong feelings about what happened. People enter litigation expecting to have the opportunity to speak out, only to learn that the legal process does not usually provide any hearing on the merits, and that their emotions are relevant only to the extent that they serve a strategic purpose. Until disputants feel adequately heard out, however, they are often unwilling to consider settling. Equally important, parties in legal conflicts frequently stop listening to each other except for the limited purpose of making their case. As a result, both sides often miss important data about the origins of the dispute and possibilities for settlement.

THE RESPONSE: AN OPPORTUNITY TO SPEAK AND FEEL HEARD

This aspect of the strategy has three elements: One is to give disputants some elements of a "day in court." The second is to provide a means for them to vent personal feelings. The third is to help each participant hear what the other is saying. The first aspect usually occurs primarily in joint session, while the second and third can happen either in joint session or during private caucuses.

Although mediation is not a court session and mediators are certainly not judges, they can give parties the opportunity during an opening session to present their legal case. Such presentations assist the settlement process in several ways. First, parties are able to see their lawyer argue their case or can do so themselves. In addition, each side hears a direct statement of the strengths of the other's case. The mediator, of course, will not decide the dispute and may never express an opinion about the merits, but the absence of a decision does not prevent the process from being effective. After such presentations and the discussions that follow, disputants often feel more ready to move on to settlement.

The experience of arguing the merits also facilitates the rest of the process, by focusing participants on the facts of the controversy and relevant principles. Through the way she moderates the opening session, the mediator also delivers a message that discussing issues and standards in a rational manner, rather than simply stating positions, is the most productive way to negotiate. Parties' knowledge that the mediator will be listening also encourages both sides to assess their facts and theories more carefully and edit out extreme contentions.

In addition to responding to participants' wish to argue legal issues, this aspect of the process often has an emotional component. The need to express strong feelings to one's adversaries or a neutral person is a very human one, felt by CEOs as much as by mail room clerks. Through their lawyers' presentations at the opening session, and perhaps by making comments themselves, parties can partially vent their feelings about the dispute and each other. This may also occur during caucuses. After they have experienced being heard out, disputants often gradually become less upset and angry, making it easier for them to consider settlement.

Novice mediators are often uncomfortable dealing with strong emotions, or worry about unleashing psychological issues with which they are not trained to deal. As a result, they often squelch emotional venting or even skip the opening session altogether. This is almost always a mistake. Unless a disputant appears to be dangerous or psychologically troubled, a mediator can achieve a great deal simply by allowing the parties to talk about their feelings and differences in a safe and controlled environment. The emotional and psychological aspects of mediation are discussed in more depth in Chapter 10.

3. MODERATE THE BARGAINING

THE PROBLEM: POSITIONAL TACTICS LEADING TO IMPASSE

Negotiators often have trouble reaching a settlement because they use a positional approach to bargaining and cannot successfully manage the resulting "dance" of numbers. One or both sides may, for example, try to claim value by locking themselves into a position, or bargainers may become angry as they feel that they are being pushed to make more than their fair share of concessions. The result often is an impasse.

THE RESPONSE: BECOME THE MODERATOR

When this kind of problem arises, a mediator can coach or advise each side, or lead them through the reciprocal steps needed to reach agreement. A mediator might begin by asking the party who last received a concession or who seems the least upset to make a new offer. (Techniques for moderating positional bargaining are discussed in the article "Mediating in the Dance for Dollars" below and in Chapter 10.)

Having restarted the process, a mediator can give a party advice about how a concession is likely to be received by the other side. She can also explore privately where each side intends to go ("I'll communicate that, but can you give me a private sense of what you'd be willing to do if they *did* make a six-figure offer?"). The mediator can then suggest a strategy to move toward a goal. Concurrently, she can remind the bargainers of the need to justify their positions with facts and arguments, and of the value of focusing on interests.

A mediator's presence helps positional negotiators make offers with less fear that they will be led down a slippery path to a one-sided compromise. In addition, by verifying for each side that their adversary is also "feeling pain," the neutral helps to overcome the tendency of disputants to devalue offers made by their opponent. Indeed, disputants often seem more sensitive to which side is losing more than to their own gains, and take surprising comfort from knowing that their opponent is feeling pain as well! Through such tactics, often mixed with continuing discussions of the merits and the consequences of failing to agree, a mediator can often orchestrate a pattern of reciprocal concessions that moves toward settlement.

4. PROBE FOR AND ADDRESS HIDDEN ISSUES

THE PROBLEM: DISREGARD OF HIDDEN COSTS OF
DISPUTING AND MISSED OPPORTUNITIES

Parties in legal disputes tend to view their situation through a narrow and often distorted lens: They focus almost exclusively on legal issues, even when the conflict appears to be driven primarily by other factors. Even as a mediator discusses litigation options and bargaining proposals, therefore, she should be thinking about what other issues may be keeping the parties apart. These might include the following:

Psychological and Emotional Issues

Parties often fall into impasse because of psychological or emotional factors. Those emotions, and the parties' inhibitions about expressing them, may be so strong that they will not raise the issue in joint session. Especially in business disputes, parties often appear at mediation with their "game faces on," presenting logical arguments while emotions boil underneath the surface. Simply giving disputants an opportunity to vent their feelings is not enough in these cases. Participants are so reluctant to mention emotions, or so unconscious of them, that they resist discussing feelings even in the privacy of a caucus.

Feelings of Loss

Lawsuits almost always impose losses on all of the parties. This is most clear when the parties shared a beneficial relationship, as is true of most contract cases and family disputes. But it is also true even in cases in which the parties had no past relationship, such as most auto accident claims: Simply being in a state of conflict can impose severe costs on litigants in the form of lost time and anxiety. These costs are usually not mentioned in negotiation because the legal system regards them as irrelevant. But they often leave disputants with the feeling that accepting even a rational settlement will involve a serious loss, and the phenomenon known as loss aversion then distorts their bargaining decisions.

Unexploited Opportunities for Gain

We know that repairing a relationship or satisfying other underlying interests is one of the rewards of effective bargaining. Litigators, however, often find it very difficult to identify and exploit opportunities for value creation, because they are conditioned by their roles as legal warriors to look only at remedies that a court can award, which are almost always restricted to money damages.

The Response: Identify and Address Hidden Issues

The next step in a mediator's basic strategy is thus to look for the hidden nonlegal issues that are contributing to the dispute or that that could be exploited for mutual gain, then foster a process that addresses them. The neutral should begin to do this even as he is carrying out other tasks. He should look for clues that a hidden issue is present, such as strong emotions, irrational arguments, or a past relationship between the parties. In most cases, the mediator should approach these issues in the privacy of the caucus. He can encourage the participants to address hidden issues in constructive ways or, if necessary, offer solutions himself.

5. TEST THE PARTIES' ALTERNATIVES. IF NECESSARY, EVALUATE THE ADJUDICATION OPTION

PROBLEM: LACK OF REALISM ABOUT THE OUTCOME IN ADJUDICATION

Legal disputes differ from other controversies in that one or more of the parties has the option to obtain a binding decision in adjudication. The issue of how an adjudicator will decide the case if it does not settle is usually treated by participants as a key factor in bargaining. Parties sometimes appreciate the weaknesses in their case, and even disputants who honestly disagree about the likely outcome in court may compromise in order to avoid the costs of litigation. In most cases, however, litigants suffer from "optimistic overconfidence," overestimating their chance of prevailing in adjudication. This makes it hard even for well-intentioned negotiators to reach an agreement that they both believe is fair.

THE RESPONSE: REALITY TEST

Mediators can help to solve merits-based problems by "reality testing" — that that is, by assisting each side to understand the weaknesses in its litigation option. Reality testing is a key part of most mediation strategies; the question is how best to go about it. At the outset mediators typically limit themselves to asking general questions that will draw out the parties' evidence and arguments. If, for instance, a party has emphasized its strength on liability issues but has avoided discussing the damage claims in a case, the neutral may ask about the neglected issue. Whenever possible, mediators should stress that their question has been raised by the other side; they, in other words are the bearer of the unwelcome question, but not its instigator.

Discussing the merits can help to narrow the gap between litigants for several reasons. First, it may genuinely change peoples' views about the strength of their case, or resolve disagreements between a client and lawyer. In addition, if a disputant is aware of a particular problem but has been hoping that the other side would not notice it, a mediator's question will signal that the weakness is apparent to its adversary or the neutral, and so also to a future judge or jury. Finally, even if a frank discussion does not shake a party's views, the process may convince it that compromise will be necessary and provide a face-saving excuse for what the party realizes it must do to settle.

There is a tension inherent in reality testing between being pointed enough to prompt decision makers to confront a problem, and being so tough that they conclude that the neutral has taken sides with their opponent. A mediator's questions should therefore progress gradually, from open-ended queries ("Have you thought about . . . ?") to more pointed comments ("They are resisting making a higher offer because they believe that you won't be able to establish causation . . . What can I tell them?")

If a diplomatic approach is not enough, a mediator should consider using "harder" reality testing. Hard testing is a matter of degree. It involves going beyond asking questions, even skeptical ones, to express the opinion that a participant's view of the case is not accurate, without however stating the mediator's own opinion on the issue. Examples include:

- "Perhaps you're right . . . Have you seen juries in this area award that level of damages? . . . Regularly?"
- "I'm having trouble following your argument on that issue. Give me a chance to think about it some more."

ALTERNATIVE RESPONSE: OFFER EVALUATIVE FEEDBACK

In some cases even reality testing will not be adequate. This can occur for a wide variety of reasons. For example, participants may be wedded to an unrealistic viewpoint, or may need a better approximation of a "day in court," or require explicit help from the mediator to justify a settlement to a superior. In such situations mediators have the option to go further, offering a specific opinion about how a court is likely to decide the entire case or a key issue in dispute. Evaluations can be structured in a variety of ways. Examples include:

- "I understand your argument on liability but, frankly, given the law in this state, I'd be concerned about whether you can get your emotional distress claim in."
- "My experience with Judge Jones is that she usually denies summary judgment in this kind of situation."
- "If the plaintiff prevails on liability, what I know of Houston juries suggests that they would value damages here at somewhere between $125 and $150,000."

Properly performed, a neutral evaluation can be helpful in producing an agreement, but one that is poorly done or badly timed can derail the settlement process. A deeper discussion of the appropriateness of evaluation in mediation appears in Chapter 10.

6. OFFER A SETTLEMENT PROPOSAL

THE PROBLEM: CLOSING THE FINAL GAP

Often even the combination of tactics described above will not produce agreement.

THE STRATEGY: PLAY CONFIDENTIAL LISTENER; IF NECESSARY, MAKE A "MEDIATOR'S PROPOSAL"

At this point, a mediator should press the parties more strongly. She can, for example, ask a party for a private indication of what they are willing to do to settle a case, distinct from the "public" position they are taking with the other side.

A slightly different approach is to play *confidential listener*. Here the mediator asks each side whether it is willing to tell the neutral privately the most that it would do to settle. Mediators ordinarily don't expect to be told a party's true "bottom line." Indeed, asking for a final position is often counterproductive, because it may lead a party to commit to unrealistic terms. Taking each side's statement with a grain of salt, the mediator can give both of them guidance about the gap between them.

Either as an alternative or a follow-up to confidential listener, mediators have the option of making a *mediator's proposal*. Here the mediator suggests a set of terms that he thinks may be acceptable to all of the disputants. In doing so, the neutral is not necessarily evaluating the merits of the case: More important than what might happen at some future trial is the mediator's practical assessment of what each side is willing to do at that moment to reach agreement. Equally important, the package should be presented as the *mediator's* proposal. Because of the phenomenon of reactive devaluation, any idea advanced by a party will be subject to suspicion, but the same terms coming from the mediator are likely to be received more positively. The process by which a mediator presents a proposal is crucial. The ground rules should be that:

- If all sides accept the proposal, they have an agreement.
- If a party rejects the proposal, it never learns whether its adversary would have accepted it.
- Thus litigants know that they will only have to make this difficult concession if it actually brings them a settlement, and that if the effort fails, their adversary will never know that they were willing to compromise further.

Because of these psychological factors, a mediator's proposal will often break an apparent impasse and produce agreement. Even if it doesn't, the proposal may prompt parties to rethink their positions and restart direct bargaining.

CONCLUSION

This six-step strategy can produce success in many situations. No limited strategy, however, can overcome all the subtle obstacles that prevent disputants

from settling. Experienced mediators therefore use these techniques as a foundation, modifying their approach to deal with the obstacles presented in
specific disputes.

Here are more specific suggestions about commercial mediation technique,
presented in the form of "do's" and "don'ts."

MARJORIE C. AARON, DO'S AND DON'TS OF MEDIATION PRACTICE

11 Disp. Resol. Mag. (Winter 2005)

PRELIMINARY MEETINGS AND TELEPHONE CONFERENCES

DO'S

In a preliminary meeting or telephone conference with one or all of the parties
and/or counsel,

do explore process options and interests. . . .

do probe the issue of authority. . . .

do in some complex, highly emotional, or very large stakes cases, . . . meet
privately with each party and their counsel before the mediation
session . . . Remember, unlike in a court or arbitration context, there is no
prohibition against a mediator contacting one or both parties separately to
discuss any question or issue in the case. . . .

do *really listen*, building trust and developing intuition. . . . Being a successful
mediator sometimes means having the nose and ear of a psychologist. You are
also making a personal connection with the people involved. At some point in
the process, you may be asking them to accept difficult suggestions. This is a lot
easier if they have grown to like and trust you.

DON'TS

don't accept the attorneys'/parties' suggestion regarding the process they
prefer ("Three hours will be enough . . . It's a simple case.") without asking
basic questions about the status of the dispute, the complexity of the issues, and
what is at stake.

don't accept the attorneys' assurances that they will have authority at the
mediation session. Probe further, particularly where an insurance company
holds the purse strings, to ensure that someone with true "worst case authority"
will be present. . . .

don't offer any opinion, or show skepticism or favor about the claims or
defenses raised in the case. . . .

INITIAL JOINT SESSION

At the initial joint session (there may well be other meetings between the
parties as the process continues), the mediator plays many roles: moderator,

master of ceremonies, evaluator, questioner, alter ego, persuader, deal maker. It is important that you:

DO'S

do set an appropriate tone with an opening statement. The degree of formality or informality of your statement will vary, but in just about every case, you should:

- Remind the parties and counsel of the confidentiality of the mediation process.
- Remind the parties that they own the process. Its outcome is theirs to determine . . . The mediator does not have the power to hand down a decision.
- Ask the parties and counsel to try to listen objectively to the other side's presentation. Suggest that rather than scribbling responses, they try to imagine how a jury listening for the first and only time would view the dispute.
- If appropriate, explain that you may help them to evaluate settlement options and the parties' alternatives to settlement. But *don't* raise the evaluation possibility in the joint session opening unless it is clear, based upon preliminary meetings or conferences, that it is likely to be necessary.

do develop an opening "patter" that fits your personality, your philosophy, and covers general process issues and questions, but be prepared to alter it to fit the parties, the chemistry, and the tone of the case. . . .

do listen and take notes during the presentations, even if you have heard it all before. . . .

do ask questions to focus the issues. You might use questions to demonstrate where the parties agree on the facts or the law, and the sources of disagreement. Ask questions gracefully, without indicating bias. Ask as if simply trying to understand. Make some effort to balance the questions directed at each side. . . .

do try to ask questions or comments that anticipate the reactions or feelings of the side listening to the presentation. Thus, if the speaking lawyer or party has said something outrageous or insulting, you might want to reframe or note that you understand this is an issue in dispute and that the other (listening) party would most likely disagree. . . .

do consider using active listening techniques from time to time, restating how you understand the party's perspective as expressed, but maintain neutrality in the process.

do make sure that all parties and counsel feel they have been given an opportunity to make all of their arguments and say their piece in the joint session.

DON'TS

don't act like a judge, or permit the parties or counsel to treat you like one.

don't allow cross-examination or disruptive interruptions or objections.

don't lose control of the proceeding, unless the parties have "taken over" to engage in real dialogue and problem solving.

don't indicate in any way that counsel could have done a better job of analyzing the case, advising their clients, or preparing for the mediation. . . .

don't, except in unusual circumstances, omit a joint session. . . .

don't interrupt the presentations too much. This is a judgment call. . . .

don't, by a question or statement in joint session, make one side's case stronger. This will buy you an enemy on the other side. In private session, you may point out how the other side's case could be even stronger and note that they will probably figure this out before trial.

PRIVATE CAUCUSES

DO'S

do start the private caucuses by asking the parties and counsel what they are thinking, and what they might want to say that they were not comfortable saying in the joint session.

do feel freer to empathize with each party's perspective, while still maintaining neutrality in the dispute. You can express your understanding of why the other side seems like the "bad guys" to them given the history or context . . . This is called manipulation, or perhaps the groundwork for effective manipulation. It is clearly part of the mediation process. . . .

do pay attention to the negotiation styles of all parties and counsel. . . .

do help the parties see that, whatever the past perceived injury or wrong, they are now faced with a decision problem that involves choices going forward. Can they find a settlement that serves their interests better than the alternatives?

do ask each party in private caucus how they believe the other sees the dispute, and what they think the other party would consider a fair settlement.

do ask how they evaluate the strengths and weaknesses of the other side's case, of their own case, if their analysis of the merits seems to be driving settlement positions . . . Try to get a sense of the settlement range that would be acceptable to both sides. . . .

do ask the parties to begin focusing on solution options, including but not limited to dollars. In some cases, you may suggest a number of options for them to think about and tinker with. Then it is your job to shuttle back and forth, trying to put a deal together.

do keep the numbers and the options rolling. Keep up the pressure and the momentum. If people must eat, it's generally best to order in.

don't allow the parties to dig in on a position or a number as a matter of ego. Turn it around: "It takes someone older and wiser to unlock this one . . ." Make the ego play the other way.

do wait to evaluate until you see no other way to achieve progress toward settlement . . . Make sure, before you evaluate, that the party would like to hear what you think of the case. . . .

do provide any evaluation *very, very gently*. Provide it in private session only. Couch your evaluation in terms of what an average jury might do . . . Don't argue . . . Try to prevent an unfavorable evaluation from turning a party or its counsel against you. . . .

do have patience. You will be in the fifth round of shuttle diplomacy and one of the parties will be arguing against your evaluation on the gravel issue. You must listen. You *cannot* say, "You simpleton. Didn't you hear what I said? Your gravel isn't worth beans." [B]e patient, and try to segue from the gravel issue to the question at hand.

DON'TS

don't ask for anyone's bottom line, at least not until the end of a long day, and certainly not in joint session . . . Most of the time, they won't tell you the truth and if they announce their (fake) bottom line, they may become entrenched. . . .

don't assume that you will be delivering an evaluation. An evaluation on the merits may be unnecessary and unhelpful. Explore all other paths to settlement first . . . Don't deliver an inconsistent evaluation (on the numbers) to both sides. It is always tempting to tell both sides they have a terrible case and find an easy settlement in the middle. That may settle one case, but it will quickly ruin your reputation as a mediator. . . .

don't lose momentum, or give up on the bidding. Too often, a party tells the mediator, "This is my final number, don't come back with anything else," and the mediator obeys. *Never* believe a number is final until the parties have walked out the door (threatening to walk out isn't good enough.). . . .

SETTLEMENT

do write up the deal then and there, no matter how tired and edgy people are, no matter if counsel would rather shake hands and go home with assurances that "We all have the same understanding." Drafting should be done with the assistance of both lawyers. . . .

do if possible, include a provision stating that the agreement is valid and enforceable. . . . Obtain signatures of all parties and, preferably, counsel as well.

do go home and relax. Have a fattening dessert. You've earned it. Contemplate a good mediation war story, concealing names and details to preserve confidentiality, of course!

QUESTIONS

1. What goals is a mediator using the "Basic Strategy" or the "Do's and Don'ts" approach seeking?
2. Using Professor Riskin's grid, how would you classify the style of a mediator applying this advice: Broad or narrow? Facilitative or evaluative?

b. Transformative Mediation

As we have mentioned, a very different kind of process, known as "transformative" mediation, does not seek to settle cases. Rather, its goal is to create a setting in which participants can, if they wish, change the way in which they view themselves and others in the dispute. The following reading describes the use of transformative techniques in family disputes, but it is applied in other areas as well. As you read, ask yourself:

- What appear to be the key differences in goals and techniques between transformative and commercial mediation?
- Are there any situations in which a transformative approach could be useful to you as a practicing lawyer?

ROBERT A. BARUCH BUSH AND SALLY GANONG POPE, TRANSFORMATIVE MEDIATION: PRINCIPLES AND PRACTICE IN DIVORCE MEDIATION

in Divorce and Family Mediation 53-71, Guilford Press
(J. Folberg et al., eds., 2004)

TRANSFORMATIVE CONFLICT THEORY: THE WHY AND WHAT OF TRANSFORMATIVE MEDIATION IN DIVORCE CASES

Why do parties come to divorce mediators, and what is it that mediators can do to best serve them? The parties themselves, as they enter mediation, give varied reasons for their choice, but most fall into the following categories. Saving money and time and avoiding the legal system are at the top of most lists. Reducing hostility and conflict for their own sake and the sake of their children, and developing effective parenting plans, are also important. One party may be more interested in the time-savings and the other in protection of the children. Most all, however, agree that staying out of the legal system is essential. Certainly, with few exceptions, all hope to achieve a fair divorce settlement agreement . . .

How then are we to understand the "why" of divorce mediation? In our view, all of the above descriptions of clients' goals express their desire to experience a different form of conflict interaction than they have experienced in their private negotiations and than they believe they would find in the legal system . . . Rather, they want to come out of the process feeling better about themselves and each other . . .

This conclusion is the result of insights from the fields of communication, developmental psychology and social psychology, among others. According to that view — what we call "transformative" theory — conflict is about peoples' interaction with one another as human beings. It is not primarily about problem-solving, about satisfaction of needs and interests. Certainly there are problems to be solved at the end of a marriage — the assets to be divided, the parenting plan to be created — and certainly parties want to solve those problems. The reality is, however, that they want to do so in a way that enhances their sense of their own competence and autonomy without taking advantage of the other. They want to feel proud of themselves for how they handled this life crisis, and this means making changes in the difficult conflict interaction that is going on between them, rather than simply coming up with the "right" answers to the specific problems.

. . . When we study perceptions of and attitudes towards conflict, we find that what most people find hardest about conflict is not that it frustrates their satisfaction of some interest or project, no matter how important, but rather that it leads and even forces them to behave toward themselves and others in ways that they find uncomfortable and even repellent. . . .

In sum, no matter how strong a person is, conflict propels them into relative weakness. No matter how saintly a person is, conflict propels them into self-absorption, self-centeredness . . . Before the conflict, there is some decent human interaction going on, whatever the context — between people in a family, a workplace, a community. Even divorcing couples were once engaged in some form of decent, even loving, human interaction. Then the conflict arises and, propelled by the vicious circle of disempowerment and demonization, what started as a decent interaction spirals down into one which is negative, destructive, alienating, and demonizing, on all sides . . .

Given this view of what conflict entails and "means" to parties, where does conflict intervention come into the picture? In particular, what are divorcing couples looking for when they seek the services of a mediator? One fundamental premise of the transformative model is that what bothers parties most about conflict is the interactional degeneration itself, and therefore what they most want from an intervener — even more than help in resolving specific issues — is help in reversing the downward spiral and restoring a more humane quality to their interaction. Perhaps no one can avoid the negative conflict spiral, but what can be done to reverse it?

[D]ivorcing parties often explain that they want to reach not simply agreement but "closure," to let go of their bitter conflict experience and move on with their lives. But if the negative conflict cycle is not reversed — if divorcing parties don't regenerate some sense of their own strength and some degree of understanding of the other — it is unlikely they can move on and be at peace with themselves, much less each other. In effect, without a change in the conflict interaction between them, parties are left disabled, even if an agreement on concrete issues has been reached . . .

But how do parties in conflict reverse the destructive conflict spiral? . . . The first part of an answer to this question is that the critical resource is the parties' own basic humanity: their essential strength, and their essential decency and compassion, as human beings . . . They move from weakness to strength, becoming (in more specific terms) calmer, clearer, more confident, more articulate and more decisive. They shift from self-absorption to responsiveness, becoming more attentive, open, trusting, and more responsive toward the other party . . . [T]hese dynamic shifts are called "Empowerment" and "Recognition." Moreover, there is also a reinforcing feedback effect . . . The stronger I become, the more open I am to you. The more open I am to you, the stronger you feel, the more open you become to me, and the stronger I feel . . . Why "conflict transformation"? Because as the parties make empowerment and recognition shifts, and as those shifts gradually reinforce in a virtuous circle, the interaction as a whole begins to turn the corner and regenerate . . .

What divorcing parties want from mediators, and what mediators can in fact provide — with proper focus and skills, as discussed below — is help and support for these small but critical shifts by each party . . . The mediator's primary goals are: (1) to foster Empowerment shifts, by supporting but never supplanting each party's deliberation and decision-making, at every point in the session where choices arise (regarding process or outcome); and (2) to foster Recognition shifts, by encouraging and supporting but never forcing each party's freely chosen efforts to achieve new understandings of the other's perspective. (Specific practices tied to these goals are discussed below.)

The transformative model does not ignore the significance of resolving specific issues; but it assumes that, if mediators do the job just described, the parties themselves will very likely make positive changes in their interaction and, as a result, find acceptable terms of resolution for themselves where such terms genuinely exist . . . The transformative model posits that this is the greatest value mediation offers to families in conflict: it can help people conduct conflict itself in a different way . . .

This is what we have learned from the parties that we have worked with and studied over all these years . . . The promise mediation offers is real . . . because wise mediators can support the parties' own work, create a space for that work to go on, and — most important — stay out of the parties' way . . .

TRANSLATING THEORY INTO PRACTICE: HOW DOES THE TRANSFORMATIVE MEDIATOR WORK?

ESSENTIAL SKILLS: LISTENING FOR EMPOWERMENT AND RECOGNITION OPPORTUNITIES

In order to notice the opportunities for supporting empowerment and recognition, the mediator pays close attention to the parties' own conversational cues in the immediate interactions between them — what they do and say. The mediator stays "in the moment" of the conversation between the parties. . . .

The mediator must know what these opportunities look and sound like: what she is listening and looking for. The following expressions are all examples of weakness or self-absorption. "What should I do?" shows that the party sees the mediator as the decision maker. "I'm really confused" shows confusion, uncertainty, lack of clarity. "I've had enough of this!!" expresses strong emotions and feelings and shows a sense of helplessness or frustration . . . A mediator listening in this way will not ignore or dismiss statements of this nature and will not view the parties as "resisting" or merely "venting." The statements will be seen and heard as opportunities . . . Once able to listen and observe, the mediator also needs to be able to enact supportive responses that assist the parties to make the shifts in the direction of empowerment and recognition and to do this without pushing, directing or having any agenda for the parties.

ESSENTIAL SKILLS: SUPPORTIVE RESPONSES

Reflection is a primary supportive response. In reflecting a party statement, the mediator simply says what she hears the party saying, using the party's own language, even (or especially) when the language is strong, loud, negative, or particularly expressive. The mediator will not soften the party's language or remove its "sting." The mediator . . . will simply acknowledge the anger by reflecting — saying what the mediator heard . . . Reflection is particularly helpful to assist a party to think through something that seems unclear or complex or to help a party who seems uncertain or ambiguous about what he is saying. It also may give the other party an opportunity to hear something she may not have heard or understood when it was being said.

In mediation conducted by a transformative mediator, the parties often begin talking directly to each other for extended lengths of time. Mediator participation in the discussion may be quite minimal for those periods, but the intense focus on listening by the mediator will continue . . .

Summarizing is often used when there have been long periods of party conversation, and the parties come to a natural break. It is also helpful when the parties don't know "where to go next" or say "We're stuck; we need some guidance here . . ." Like a reflection, a summary is inclusive. In the summary the mediator does not select from what has been said and does not drop any issues, and particularly does not drop intangible issues. The summary is not an educational monologue by the mediator and has no agenda or direction built into it . . .

Without any other skills, the mediator could effectively mediate in a supportive way with only listening, reflection and summary. *"Checking in,"* however, is an important and effective addition to the other essential skills and is frequently coupled with reflection and summary. Checking in may end a summary, when the mediator asks the parties "Where do you want to go from here?" . . . When there is a fork in the road, it is helpful for the mediator to point it out and ask the parties which road they want to take . . .

. . . There are other supportive responses. Silence is a natural response by parties to intense conversation . . . Eye contact, facial expression, and gestures are also part of the mediator's communication. Just looking at the other party when one party seems to be finished speaking may send the message that the mediator is asking the second party to speak . . .

All of the mediator responses—reflection, summary, checking-in—are used over and over again . . . The mediator cannot "try it out," but when the "going gets tough" abandon the approach. This approach to mediation requires courage—courage which comes from convictions. . . .

This section describes the "how" of transformative mediation. There are no other skills needed. Mediator personality and conversational style have an impact on how the responses are used, but consistency in the use of these responses will identify the transformative mediator. The mediator does not act differently in divorce mediation than in any other substantive area of practice . . .

ESSENTIAL SKILLS: AVOIDING DIRECTIVE RESPONSES

Using the essential skills of reflection, summary and checking in, the mediator "follows" or accompanies the parties . . . The transformative mediator is not the director of the discussion . . . He trusts the parties. He has confidence in them—that they know best—that they know what is right for themselves and their children. He will not attempt to substitute his judgment for theirs. He will not try to steer them in the direction of what he thinks is the best arrangement for them and their children. He will not decide what is fair for them. He respects and trusts the parties to make those decisions. The mediator is not trying "to get the parties to do anything." He is not trying to "get them" to talk to each other, to stop arguments for the sake of the children, or to stay out of court.

So, while intensely engaged in listening and observing and enacting supportive responses, the mediator constantly avoids or represses directive impulses . . . Trying to keep the parties "on track" or moving the discussion along interferes with the natural cycles of conversation of the parties. Pointing out common ground, such as "you both really care about your child" or "you both have fears about financial security," does not bring them together and actually obscures the real issues. The differences remain and the differences should not be downplayed in the attempt to find and stress the common ground. Probing for the "real, underlying issues" is leading, directive, and

disrespectful of the party choice about what to talk about. Following the parties
in their discussion will highlight all of the issues the parties choose to put out
on the table . . .

The skills employed by the transformative divorce mediator are simple to
describe: listening, reflection, summarizing, questions used to open doors, to
invite further discussion on a subject raised by the parties, and to "check in" on
what the parties want to do at a choice point in the discussion. . . . They are
difficult to employ. It is much easier to allow our directive impulses and positive goals for the parties steer us into leading and guiding the discussion and,
therefore, the outcomes. It is much more difficult to stay with the parties
through their cycles of conversation as they develop strength and understanding and become clear about what they want to do . . .

In the early 1990s the U.S. Postal Service was plagued by worker discontent.
The Postal Service is a unionized organization with over 800,000 employees.
At the time, the USPS was going through productivity pressures and was seen
by many employees as having an authoritarian, command-and-control management culture. But while employees were angry, many were not willing to
leave their job. They expressed their frustration by filing enormous numbers
of grievances under their union contract and complaints of discrimination with
the Equal Employment Opportunity Commission, causing major burdens and
distractions for Postal Service managers.

In 1994, as part of the settlement of a class action, the Postal Service created a
mediation program known as "REDRESS." The program was designed and
neutrals were trained based on the transformative model described above.
There is anecdotal evidence, however, that many USPS managers did not accept
all the premises of the transformative model, and sought to use the program for
the traditional purpose of resolving disputes. (Indeed, the word REDRESS
stands for "Resolve Employment Disputes, Reach Equitable Solutions
Swiftly.") The following article describes the results of the REDRESS program.

LISA B. BINGHAM, REDRESS™ AT THE USPS: A BREAKTHROUGH MEDIATION PROGRAM
1 AC Resolution 34 (Spring 2002)

Some have observed that getting federal agencies to use dispute resolution
instead of their traditional approaches to conflict is a battle against inertia, like
turning a big ship. Yet, the United States Postal Service (USPS), the largest
federal civilian employer and second largest civilian employer in the world,
implemented a national mediation program for employment disputes arising
out of claims of discrimination, named REDRESS™ . . . in just eighteen
months. Where there is a will, there is a way. Effective July 1999, every postal
employee in the country had access to outside neutral mediators. This award-
winning program . . . uses transformative techniques . . . and consists of the
following design features:

• Any employee who contacts the Equal Employment Opportunity (EEO)
counselor with an informal EEO complaint may request mediation. The

program is voluntary for complainants. Respondents, generally USPS supervisors and managers, are required to participate in one mediation session.

- Mediation is generally scheduled within two to three weeks of a request.
- The complainant and respondent may bring any representative they choose, including lawyers, union or professional association representatives, co-workers, friends, or family . . .
- Mediators do not evaluate the legal merits of or render opinions on the dispute. They do not press for particular settlements or recommend specific outcomes; any settlement is a function of the participants' mutual agreement.
- If there is no resolution, the complainant may return to the traditional EEO process, proceed with investigation, file a formal complaint, and proceed to an administrative hearing.
- At the formal complaint and administrative hearing stage, the complainant may again request mediation under REDRESS II, a new program implemented in 2001 using the same transformative model of mediation . . .
- From 70 to 75 percent of all employees offered the option to mediate participate in REDRESS.
- The USPS conducts approximately 11,500 REDRESS mediation sessions each year . . .
- Over 90% of all participants, including complainants, respondents, and their representatives, report they are satisfied or highly satisfied with the REDRESS process and mediators, and over 65% report they are satisfied or highly satisfied with the outcome of mediation. These rates have held steady throughout the period of the program.
- The REDRESS case closure rate is over 80% . . .
- After REDRESS, the annual rate at which employees filed formal EEO complaints dropped from a high of 14,000 to a low of slightly over 10,000.

REDRESS is now a permanent program at the USPS.

QUESTIONS

1. Why do you think that the U.S. Postal Service decided to use transformative mediation as the model for its program?
2. What would be your greatest concern about referring a client to such a process? Are there any steps you could take to minimize this concern?

c. "Pure Money" Mediation

The techniques described above can be used not only to bargain over money, but also to seek out solutions that meet the deeper interests of the parties. In many legal disputes, however, the only issue that the parties recognize, or at least that they are willing to negotiate over, is money. Even when disputants are open to discussing other issues, lawyers in mediation often spend much of their time exchanging offers couched primarily in monetary terms. In such situations, counsel may choose a mediator at least in part based on the neutral's ability to facilitate money bargaining, a process that is explored in the following reading.

J. MICHAEL KEATING, MEDIATING IN THE DANCE FOR DOLLARS

14 Alternatives 71-72 (September 1996)

Virtually every conflict involves a struggle over resources. Litigation, which characteristically transmutes wrongs into dollars, is full of "distributive" disputes . . . What does a mediator do when the dispute consists largely (if not solely) of a monetary demand and offer, with no future relationship at stake, as in personal injury and some contractual disputes? . . .

Even when parties are fully conscious of the need to reach some sort of accommodation, they are reluctant to begin bargaining: They worry about sending the wrong signal or being exploited by the other party. The mediator can provide both guidance and safety in these situations, principally through the use of the caucus. In an initial round of caucuses, a mediator will want to explore with parties the general nature of their demand or offer, gauge the flexibility of each party, and understand each party's level of sophistication about the negotiation. It is not even necessary to emerge from this first round of caucuses with a new offer or demand. You want to begin building empathy and trust with the parties, communicate your understanding of their positions and show you're dedicated to a fair bargaining process that will protect them from exploitation.

REASONABLE ANCHORS

The mediator needs to be endlessly patient in distributive bargaining. Resist the temptation to push immediately for settlement. Reasonable anchors rarely surface immediately. Especially useful in the quest for those anchors is your insistence that parties provide detailed justifications for their demands or offers, and for their rejections of the other side's offers or demands. Part of the mediator's task is to protect the bargaining process by making sure that concessions are responded to in a meaningful way. That can curb, or at least reduce, the fear of exploitation that often inhibits productive bargaining.

Initial concessions in distributive negotiation are usually the largest and tend to come most quickly. As the process continues, concessions shrink and take longer to elicit. Surprisingly, many negotiators seem oblivious to this pattern: They begin with piddling or insulting openings, discouraging the other party from serious bargaining and prolonging the negotiation process. The mediator needs to help the parties think through the likely impact of their initial concessions.

LENGTHY BARGAINING

. . . Many people aren't prepared for lengthy bargaining: They prefer to think that their first concession will bring the process to a quick end as the other party gratefully and immediately embraces the new offer. The mediator needs to educate participants about the pace of bargaining and orchestrate its progress. Even in distributive disputes, the mediator must look for ways to introduce integrative elements. The timing of payments, creating of a structured settlement, payment in kind of services, rebates or discounts, are all ways of maneuvering a seemingly inflexible distributive dispute . . . If the gap between the parties' positions is small, such a gambit may help close it.

One characteristic of a fierce distributive confrontation is the tendency of parties to demonize each other's motivations and behavior. A mediator has to take the venom out of the dialogue . . .

Many distributive negotiations involve a lump sum divisible into a variety of components. A personal injury case, for example, may include medical expenses, lost wages, pain and suffering, interest, and attorney's fees. Typically, each element is analyzed and subjected separately to the push and pull of bargaining. But parties may place widely different values on each component of the recovery; once such differences become evident, the smart mediator moves back to bargaining over the lump sum. That leaves the parties free to rationalize distribution. . . .

JOINT SESSION

While much of this bargaining process may best be executed in the caucus, if the parties remain significantly apart, the mediator ought to bring them back together in a joint session. The mediator then needs to help them rehearse their differences as calmly as possible, without interpersonal unpleasantness, so both sides understand the nature of (and reasons for) the remaining gap. This may be the most critical point in developing a mutually acceptable bargain. . . .

[Eventually] it is time for the mediator to put a range of numbers, somewhere near the mid-point of the difference between the parties, on the table. It is not the correctness of the range that counts. The aim here is simply to keep the parties' dialogue — their "dance for dollars" — alive. Ideally, the mediator should present the numbers not as an evaluation of what the case is worth, but as sums at which the parties might be able to settle. They may react with outrage, but meanwhile we want the dialogue to continue. . . .

Patience and optimism are always virtues in a mediator, but that's especially true in a distributive dispute. "No gap too wide" is the motto. Therefore, a party's description of a demand or offer is meaningless. I have watched many parties plummet through "bottom lines." The tactic, in the face of a solemn declaration of a party's bottom line, is simply to ignore it and move on . . . Mediation is just as relevant in distributive as in integrative situations. In both, the mediator's role is to navigate parties through what looks like stormy and unmanageable negotiation.

QUESTIONS

1. Which elements of the Basic Mediative Strategy set out above are not mentioned in Keating's "pure money" methodology?
2. What problems might arise if "pure dollar" methods are applied in a dispute that has significant nonmonetary aspects?

d. "No-Caucus" Approaches

Although commercial mediators typically employ a joint-session-followed-by-caucusing format, a growing number are experimenting with conducting all or most of the process in joint session. Transformative mediators use a no-caucus format almost exclusively. Domestic relations mediators typically also do most or all of their work with both parties present, in part to build a better working relationship between the spouses around issues such as parenting, and in part out of concern that caucusing would exacerbate the air of suspicion that often hangs over such disputes. Disputes arising from close business relationships have many of the characteristics of a family quarrel, and also may lend themselves to the use of a no-caucus format.

Some experts believe that no-caucus techniques should be used not only when a dispute involves a strong relationship, but whenever parties are seeking integrative terms of agreement. In the words of Professor Robert Mnookin, the no-caucus model:

> assumes [that] by working together with the parties and their counsel and avoiding separate meetings and shuttle diplomacy, where the mediator alone has information from both sides, mediation offers each party the best opportunity to deepen their own understanding, both of their own perspective and interests and those of the other side. Embracing conflict is often the best opportunity to create value.

(Friedman and Himmelstein, 2001) The following reading describes a no-caucus, relationship-based approach to mediating civil disputes.

STEPHEN K. ERICKSON AND MARILYN S. MCKNIGHT: THE PRACTITIONER'S GUIDE TO MEDIATION: A CLIENT-CENTERED APPROACH
23-44, Jossey-Bass (2001)

Client-centered mediation is closely tied to the work of the divorce mediators of the 1970s, who were the first to create a new mediation concept and apply it beyond labor negotiations to the intense and often bitter conflict of divorce and child custody battles. Their model differed from labor mediation by having mediation conducted with the clients meeting together (face to face), rather than by caucusing between the clients in separate rooms, and with the mediator acting in a less directive, non-coercive manner.

. . . Instead of asserting personal biases or opinions about what a necessary or fair solution is, the client-centered mediator creates a structured environment for the parties . . . This process is based upon the clients' sense of what is right, what is fair, and what will work for them . . . They may start out having very different ideas about fairness, but the process . . . motivates them to be more fair with each other than if they were in an adversarial environment. . . .

To many readers, this may sound like a naive and risky way to achieve fairness . . . The following are important characteristics of client-centered mediation. . . .

OPPORTUNITY VERSUS CONTEST

A client-centered mediator asks mutual, future-focused questions to help people in conflict begin to realize they have shared goals . . . The questions are designed to encourage a mutual response . . . If [the parties] have been in intense and bitter conflict for some period of time, the mediator may need to ask a series of small questions that leads them toward a realization of shared goals. . . .

CREATING A COOPERATIVE ENVIRONMENT

The client-centered mediator influences the participants' communication by encouraging the use of nonlegal, positive words that focus on the practical tasks at hand rather than negatively loaded legal words, allowing them to work together more easily . . . [For example, in a divorce case, b]y changing the labels from *custody* to *parenting*, and by asking a different question, the mediator helps participants in conflict over their children see that they have shared goals in building a future parenting arrangement as opposed to having a contest over who has been most unfit in the past . . . For civil and other types of mediation, the substitute words are:

- Foreclosure becomes loan workout
- Plaintiff or defendant becomes participant or party
- Problems become issues
- Illegal conduct becomes dispute, and
- Position becomes an option

BEING FUTURE FOCUSED

. . . Client-centered mediators create a future focus when establishing a cooperative setting. This is accomplished in the following two ways: Unlike the traditional labor-mediation process, the client-centered mediator does not ask for an opening statement. Formal opening statements tend to exaggerate the pain of the past or are used to stake out extreme positional demands. . . .

[I]n employment mediation [for example] the first question is often future-oriented: "Are the two of you interested in improving your relationship at work, or do you wish to discuss the terms of ending the employment relationship?" If they decide to improve their work relationship the next question might be, "What do you want to do to change the employment relationship in order for you to become comfortable and productive at work?" The legal adversarial question usually focuses on the past and asks, "What are the legal elements of a workplace law that have been breached and by whom?" . . .

Mediators do not balance power, but they help clients create a better use for their power. . . .

Example: A caucus-oriented mediator took on a case involving the dissolution of a design firm. One of the partners, whose specialty was marketing, had taken an inside position with a large client of the firm, while her partner, who focused on supervising the execution of projects, had decided to continue the business on her own. The two women remained friendly, but the situation had created tension around setting the terms of the remaining partner's buyout of her colleague's interest in the firm. The partner who handled production was anxious at the prospect of becoming solely responsible for the business and plainly felt some- what abandoned. Her marketing colleague, by contrast, tended to take an everything-will-work-out approach to life, and found it hard to credit her part- ner's concerns.

Although the mediator ordinarily used a caucus-based format, he decided in this case to keep the two women together throughout their discussions. He felt that with some assistance they could negotiate directly, and was concerned that if he held separate meetings it would be taken as a signal that their disagreements were more serious than they were. Most important, the partners themselves expressed a preference for face-to-face discussions. The mediation went forward in a joint-meeting format, although each party occasionally called the mediator and talked with him privately by telephone. The memo of agreement was written out and initialed in an ice cream shop located under the partnership's offices.

QUESTIONS

1.   What potential advantages would a no-caucus model provide, as compared to a caucus-based approach, in a typical commercial contract dispute? What drawbacks?
2.   Can a no-caucus model be effective when the disputants believe that the only issue in the case is money? If they insist on limiting bargaining to money?
3.   In the case example, the mediator had occasional private conversations with each party over the telephone. Although neither party appeared to feel excluded as a result, what concerns might a no-caucus mediator have about this technique?
4.   In terms of the "Riskin grid" described above, how would you chart the style of a mediator who uses the following techniques:
     a.   The "dance for dollars" approach outlined by Keating?
     b.   The "client-centered" process described by Erickson and McKnight?

4.   Is There More to Mediation Than Technique?

The discussion so far may give the impression that while mediators' styles vary widely, the differences revolve around choices of tactics. Mediation may, how- ever, involve subtle influences that are more important than any particular format or technique.

DANIEL BOWLING AND DAVID HOFFMAN, BRINGING PEACE INTO THE ROOM: THE PERSONAL QUALITIES OF THE MEDIATOR AND THEIR IMPACT ON THE MEDIATION
16 Negot. J. 5-21 (January 2000)

Empirical studies of the mediation process consistently show high rates of settlement, as well as high levels of participant satisfaction. These favorable results seem to occur regardless of mediation styles or the philosophical orientation of the individual mediator (e.g., evaluative vs. facilitative; transformative vs. problem-solving). Indeed, the history of mediation, as well as our own experience, shows that mediation sometimes works even when the mediator is untrained. Is there some aspect of the mediation process—wholly apart from technique or theory—that explains these results?

Some might say that mediation works because it provides a safe forum for airing grievances and venting emotion (that is, it gives people their "day in court"), and this can be done even with an unskilled mediator. Others might point to the use of active listening and reframing—skills that many people have, whether or not they have had any formal mediation training. Still others may focus on the use of caucusing and shuttle diplomacy—again, techniques that do not necessarily require specialized training.

We believe all of these techniques are important. We also believe that mediation training is vitally important. However, there is a dimension to the practice of mediation that has received insufficient attention: the combination of psychological, intellectual, and spiritual qualities that make a person who he or she is. We believe that those personal qualities have a direct impact on the mediation process and the outcome of the mediation. Indeed, this impact may be one of the most potent sources of the effectiveness of mediation . . . As mediators, we have noticed that, when we are feeling at peace with ourselves and the world around us, we are better able to bring peace into the room. Moreover, doing so, in our experience, has a significant impact on the mediation process. . . .

Our starting point is to reflect on how we ourselves developed as mediators. For us, and for many of our fellow mediators, the process seems to involve three major "stages." Although we describe these aspects of our development sequentially, for some mediators they may occur in a different order, overlap, or occur to some degree simultaneously.

First, as beginning mediators, we studied techniques [and] looked for opportunities to practice these skills. A period of apprenticeship ensued . . . The second stage of our development involved working toward a deeper understanding of how and why mediation works. In seeking an intellectual grasp of the mediation process, we hoped to find the tools with which to assess the effectiveness of various techniques . . . and better understand what we were doing, why we were doing it, and the meaning of the process for our clients. . . .

The third stage of our growth as mediators is the focus of this article, and we consider it to be the most challenging frontier of development. For us, the third aspect begins with the mediator's growing awareness of how his or her personal qualities—for better or worse—influence the mediation process . . . It is about being a mediator, rather than simply doing certain prescribed steps dictated by a particular mediation school or theory . . . More specifically, it is the mediator's being, as experienced by the parties, that sends the message. . . .

THE MEDIATOR'S "PRESENCE"

This brings us to the heart of our thesis—namely, that there are certain qualities that the mediator's presence brings to the mediation process that exert a powerful influence, and enhance the impact of the interventions employed by the mediator ... Central to this way of looking at mediation is the recognition that the mediator is not extrinsic to the conflict (any more than the therapist is wholly separate from the issues addressed in therapy). ...

SUBTLE INFLUENCES

If we accept the view that, notwithstanding impartiality, mediators are inevitably engaged in creating a relationship with the parties, a relationship in which their personal qualities will influence the parties' ability to negotiate successfully—we are led inevitably to the next question: What are the qualities in the mediator that will contribute to a successful relationship with the parties, one that will support reorganization of this conflict "system"? ...

In our work as mediators, integration comes in part from developing a strong identification with our role: the transition from feeling that "I am someone who mediates" to realizing that "I am a mediator"—from seeing mediation as work that we do to seeing it as an integral part of our identity ... [T]hese theories suggest that we as mediators "create" the conflict resolution process through our perception of the participants, the conflict, and our role in it as conflict resolvers ... Accordingly, who we are—i.e., the personal qualities we bring into the mediation room—begins to take on larger significance ... The effectiveness of our interventions often arises not from their forcefulness but instead from their authenticity. ...

IMPLICATIONS FOR MEDIATION PRACTICE

... Integration is a quality that we may never fully achieve but are continually developing. It is a quality which, we believe, mediators should foster because (1) it provides a model for the parties—bringing peace, if you will, into the room; and (2) by subtle means which are more easily described than understood, the "integrated" mediator's presence aligns the parties and mediation process in a more positive direction. ...

QUESTIONS

1. Are the qualities described in this article more compatible with some models of mediation you have read about than with others? Which ones?
2. Focusing on the two mediations in the *Microsoft* case, what quality did Judge Posner appear to "bring into the room"? Which did Green and Marks try to project?
3. Did it appear to matter that Posner conducted the process primarily by telephone and email, while Green and Marks met with the parties for long face-to-face sessions? Can a mediator communicate a "presence" to the parties without being physically present?

CHAPTER 10

A Deeper Examination of Method

This section delves more deeply into the mediation process, examining the techniques mediators use to assist persons in conflict. We organize the discussion around three topics: process skills, psychological and emotional forces, and barriers arising from disagreement over legal issues.

A. PROCESS SKILLS

Among the most important skills in a mediator's "toolbox" are the ability to:

- Listen
- Reframe communications
- Identify interests and develop options
- Manage positional bargaining

1. Listening

Most mediators would agree that of all the skills needed to be an effective neutral, the most important is to be a good listener. This is harder than it may seem, especially for those of us who are inclined by temperament and training to identify issues, discard irrelevancies, and make decisions quickly. It is often difficult, as we listen to clashing viewpoints, to restrain our instinctive wish to pass judgment upon them. Doing so requires us to put aside, if only temporarily, some of the important skills we have learned in law school in favor of a different approach to listening.

RICHARD SALEM, THE BENEFITS OF EMPATHIC LISTENING

Conflict Research Consortium, University of Colorado (2003)

Empathic listening (also called *active* listening or *reflective* listening) is a way of listening. Though useful for everyone involved in a conflict, the ability and willingness to listen with empathy is often what sets the mediator apart from others involved in the conflict.

How to Listen with Empathy

Empathy is the ability to project oneself into the personality of another person in order to better understand that person's emotions or feelings. Through empathic listening the listener lets the speaker know, "I understand your problem and how you feel about it, I am interested in what you are saying and I am not judging you." The listener unmistakably conveys this message through words and non-verbal behaviors, including body language. In so doing, the listener encourages the speaker to fully express herself or himself free of interruption, criticism, or being told what to do. It is neither advisable nor necessary for a mediator to agree with the speaker, even when asked to do so. It is usually sufficient to let the speaker know, "I understand you and I am interested in being a resource to help you resolve this problem." . . . [In the words of Madelyn Burley-Allen], a skilled listener:

- takes information from others while remaining non-judgmental and empathic,
- acknowledges the speaker in a way that invites the communication to continue, and
- provides a limited but encouraging response, carrying the speaker's idea one step forward.

Empathic Listening in Mediation

. . . Parties to volatile conflicts often feel that nobody on the other side is interested in what they have to say. The parties often have been talking at each other and past each other, but not with each other. Neither believes that their message has been listened to or understood. Nor do they feel respected. Locked into positions that they know the other will not accept, the parties tend to be close-minded, distrustful of each other, and often angry, frustrated, discouraged, or hurt.

When the mediator comes onto the scene, he or she continuously models good conflict-management behaviors, trying to create an environment where the parties in conflict will begin to listen to each other with clear heads. For many disputants, this may be the first time they have had an opportunity to fully present their story. During this process, the parties may hear things that they have not heard before, things that broaden their understanding of how the other party perceives the problem. This can open minds and create receptivity to new ideas that might lead to a settlement. In creating a trusting environment, it is the mediator's hope that some strands of trust will begin to connect the parties and replace the negative emotions that they brought to the table.

Mediator Nancy Ferrell . . . questions whether mediation can work if some measure of empathy is not developed between the parties. She describes a multi-issue case involving black students and members of a white fraternity that held an annual "black-face" party at a university in Oklahoma. At the outset, the student president of the fraternity was convinced that the annual tradition was harmless and inoffensive. It wasn't until the mediator created an opportunity for him to listen to the aggrieved parties at the table that he realized the extraordinary impact his fraternity's antics had on black students. Once he recognized the problem, a solution to that part of the conflict was only a step away. . . .

GUIDELINES FOR EMPATHIC LISTENING

Madelyn Burley-Allen offers these guidelines for empathic listening [the guidelines have been edited]:

1. *Be attentive.* Be interested. Be alert and not distracted.
2. *Be noncritical.* Allow the speaker to bounce ideas and feelings off you. Don't indicate your judgment.
3. *Indicate you are listening by:*
   - Making brief, noncommittal responses ("I see . . .").
   - Giving nonverbal acknowledgment, for example by nodding your head.
   - Inviting the speaker to say more: for example, "Tell me about it" or "I'd like to hear about that."
4. *Follow good listening ground rules:*
   - Don't interrupt.
   - Don't change the subject, or move in a new direction.
   - Don't rehearse a response in your own head.
   - Don't interrogate with continual questions.
   - Don't give advice.
   - Do reflect back to the speaker:
     - What you understand.
     - How you think the speaker feels.
5. *Don't let the speaker "hook" you emotionally.* Don't get angry or upset or allow yourself to get involved in an argument.

The ability to listen with empathy may be the most important attribute of interveners who succeed in gaining the trust and cooperation of parties to intractable conflicts and other disputes with high emotional content. . . .

DANA L. CURTIS, RECONCILIATION AND THE ROLE OF EMPATHY
ADR Personalities and Practice Tips 53-62 (1998)

. . . In some circles, empathy is criticized as being too "touchy-feely" or overly emotional to be useful or even relevant to a serious lawyer-mediator in commercial or civil mediation. It is thought to be the domain of the psychologist. In mediation courses, I've encountered initial resistance from judges, lawyers and law students based on empathy's undeserved bad reputation, only to have them embrace it and incorporate it immediately into their practice and personal relationships. They describe the experience in journals: "I watched with amazement what actually happens when people are really heard." . . .

EMPATHIZING WITH FEELINGS

Lawyers and law students in empathy training often shy away from empathizing with the speaker's feelings. One self-disclosing student—a litigator of 15 years—joked that he did not have problems identifying parties' feelings, as he had a broad range of them himself: hungry, sleepy, and angry. The obvious antidote is to start monitoring our own feelings and to attach words to them.

Another reason students shy away from feelings is that feelings often must be inferred, and they are afraid of making a mistake. Sometimes they do get it wrong. Either way, getting it wrong is not a problem. The speaker merely corrects the perception and moves on. What matters is that the mediator is listening attentively and trying to understand. . . .

WHAT WE DO INSTEAD OF EMPATHIZING

Some of us believe empathy is saying, "I understand." While it might be true that we understand, simply saying so does not demonstrate understanding. Another way of responding is with sympathy . . . A sympathetic response would be: "I am terribly sorry for your loss." An empathetic response, on the other hand, eliminates the mediator's feeling and focuses on the party's: "You're still deeply sad to have lost your spouse." Finally, particularly if a mediator wants the parties to empathize with each other, it is important to distinguish between empathy and agreement . . . By empathizing, we do not adopt the speaker's point of view; we simply demonstrate that we understand it. . . .

STEPHEN E. AMBROSE, UNDAUNTED COURAGE

361-362, Touchstone Books (1996)

Note: At the start of the 19th Century, acting on orders of President Thomas Jefferson, Meriwether Lewis and William Clark set out on an epic journey across the unexplored American continent. After reaching the Pacific coast and spending the winter, they began the long trip back to the eastern seaboard. The party reached the Bitterroot Mountains of Idaho, where they expected to recover horses that they had left with a local tribe. The horses were essential: without them, the party could not survive their trek through the arid mountains. Author Stephen Ambrose describes what happened next. The quotations are taken from Captain Lewis' journal of the expedition:

> That day, the Americans chanced on Chief Cut Nose with a party of six. Cut Nose had been off on a raid the previous fall, but Lewis had heard of him and knew he was regarded as a greater chief than Twisted Hair. The Indians and white men rode on together, and soon encountered Twisted Hair with a half-dozen warriors. It was Twisted Hair who had agreed to keep the Americans' horses through the winter—he had been promised two guns and ammunition as his reward . . . The captains were naturally delighted to see him. But he greeted the white men very coolly. Lewis found this "as unexpected as it was unaccountable."
>
> Twisted Hair turned to Cut Nose and began shouting and making angry gestures. Cut Nose answered in kind. This continued for some twenty minutes. The captains had no idea what was going on, but clearly they had to break it up. They

needed the friendship of both chiefs if they were to get through the next three weeks, and they needed their horses if they were to have any chance of getting over the mountains. . . .

. . . The chiefs departed for their respective camps, still angry with each other. An hour later, [the expedition's interpreter] returned from hunting. The captains invited Twisted Hair for a smoke. He accepted, and through [the interpreter] explained that . . . the previous fall he had collected the expedition's horses and taken charge of them. Cut Nose than returned from his war party and, according to Twisted Hair, asserted his primacy among the Nez Perce. He said Twisted Hair shouldn't have accepted the responsibility, that it was he, Cut Nose, who should be in charge. Twisted Hair said he got so sick of hearing this stuff that he paid no further attention to the horses, who consequently scattered. But most of them were around, many of them with Chief Broken Arm. . . .

The captains invited Cut Nose to join the campfire. He came and "told us in the presents (*sic*) of the Twisted Hair that he the twisted hair was a bad old man that he woar two faces." Cut Nose charged that Twisted Hair had never taken care of the horses but had allowed his young men to ride them and misuse them, and that was the reason Cut Nose and Broken Arm had forbidden him to retain responsibility for the animals. The captains said they would proceed to Broken Arm's camp in the morning, and see how many horses and saddles they could collect. This was satisfactory to Twisted Hair and Cut Nose, who had calmed down considerably after being allowed to tell their sides of the story. The next day, everyone moved to Broken Arm's lodge . . . There the expedition recovered twenty-one horses, about half the saddles, and some ammunition. . . .

QUESTIONS:

1. What was the "dispute" here?
2. Did either chief change his mind about who was at fault? If not, why was the meeting helpful?
3. If this encounter had been a modern mediation, what would one call the meeting hosted by Lewis and Clark?

Example: William Webster, a former federal judge who also served as Director of the CIA and FBI, later became a mediator. He was once asked to name the book that he had found most useful in his work as a neutral in complex corporate disputes. Webster's response: "When my wife and I had teenagers, I found Dr. Haim Ginnott's book, *Between Parent and Child*, very helpful . . . and I find it equally useful now." Dr. Ginnott emphasizes how important it is for parents to listen to children empathically, without expressing judgment on what they say. This, Judge Webster was suggesting, is one of the most important skills that a mediator can bring to a dispute — apparently as useful with angry CEOs as with upset children.

2. Reframing

The root of many disagreements is that two people see the same dispute in quite different ways. The "frame" that a person puts on a situation will influence, in particular whether he will see a proposal for settlement as a net loss or gain. This in turn will strongly affect his decision whether to settle. Helping disputants to reach agreement often requires finding a way to modify their perspectives, or frame, on a controversy, or at least to allow them to appreciate that an opponent honestly sees the same situation differently. One powerful technique for doing so is known as "reframing."

KEN BRYANT AND
DANA L. CURTIS, REFRAMING
(2004)

To "reframe" a statement (in mediation lingo) is to recast the statement in more neutral terms, giving the speaker, as well as his mediation partner(s), the chance to look at the problem differently, in a more positive way. The new statement offered by the mediator to accomplish this goal is the "reframe."

HOW IT WORKS

Let's assume for the moment that a mediation participant has made a statement using value-laden (negative) language. The statement is guaranteed to make the other party angry or defensive if simply left floating in air. The task and challenge for the attentive mediator is to quickly find a positive, constructive interpretation of the assertion. (It helps if you simply assume that every behavior, including a rude comment, is appropriate, given some context, or frame.)

Before you can restate or paraphrase, of course, you must be certain you have heard the original statement correctly, which involves a heavy dose of active listening. Your goal is to accurately reflect the message sent by the speaker, while simultaneously molding the statement into an aid for easier communication. In other words, the speaker must be comfortable that you heard what was said, the other party must not be offended by your restatement, *and* the new version (yours) should point the conversation in a constructive direction.

RESTATING THE MESSAGE

You might try restating the message by:

- Redirecting the thrust of the negative assertion, i.e., away from persons verbally attacked to problems inherent in the complaint.
- Narrowing or broadening the gist of the allegation by pinpointing a single problem, or generalizing the issues to include basic policy decisions.
- Forming a question: e.g., "Is there a specific issue you would like to work on? Is there another possible explanation for what happened?"
- Shifting the focus from problems to opportunities: "Recognizing that you feel the status quo is intolerable, do you have some ideas about what changes are needed?"
- Simplifying a complex statement of a dispute, by choosing a single issue which can be addressed immediately.

- Categorizing the speaker's concerns to be dealt with either on a "most important," "easiest to deal with first," or some other useful basis.
- Neutralizing the original statement by excising ad hominem attacks and generalizing the issues, while retaining the essential elements of the message.

It bears repeating: *Confirm the accuracy of your reframe*. You can confirm your reframe by simply asking, "Is that what you meant?" Or, "Have I expressed your concerns accurately?" Additional, and even more effective, confirmation can be obtained by using your powers of observation of the speaker's non-verbal communication. Check the body language: posture, facial expression, muscle tension, skin coloring, and breathing pattern. Remember, studies indicate that more than ninety-three per cent of human communication is non-verbal.

WHY REFRAME?

Your purpose is not only to change the harsh effect of the words used by the speaker, but also to create a new dynamic in the mediation. Reframes can change the focus of the speaker's statement, and the mediation, from

- Blame and guilt, to problem-solving
- Past to future
- Judgmental to non-judgmental
- Position to interest
- Ultimatum to aspiration

It probably goes without saying that reframing can, by lowering emotional temperature, increase the efficiency of the mediation process.

REFRAMING AS A JOKE

Consider that reframing is the essence of a good joke: What seems to be one thing suddenly shifts and becomes something else. Example: "What do Alexander the Great and Smokey the Bear have in common?" (Answer: their middle names). When you reframe a statement, you shift the speaker's perception, even if just a little. The shift can get creative juices flowing and enhance discussions of options for resolution.

"MEANING" REFRAME AND "CONTEXT" REFRAME

MEANING

There was a man who was compulsive about cleaning his house. He even dusted light bulbs. He made his family take their shoes off in their living room. His view of fulfillment as a father and husband was reflected in his home's cleanliness. The problem: He was driving his family crazy. The man was asked to visualize his living room rug, white and fluffy, not a spot anywhere. He was in seventh heaven. Then he was asked to realize that his vision meant he was totally alone, and that the people he cared for and loved were nowhere around. He ceased smiling, and felt terrible, until he was asked to visualize "a few footprints" on the carpet. Then, of course, he felt good again. This is a "meaning" reframe, where the stimulus in the world doesn't actually change, but the meaning does.

CONTEXT

A father complained that he and his wife hadn't done a very good job in raising their daughter, because the daughter was so stubborn. The father, a successful banker, acknowledged that he had acquired traits involving tenacity and a stubborn quality needed to protect himself. The father was asked to look at his daughter and to realize that he had taught her how to be stubborn and to stand up for herself, and that this gift might someday save her life. Imagine, he was asked, how valuable that quality will be when *his* daughter goes out on a date with a man who has bad intentions. This is a "context" reframe, demonstrating that every behavior in the world is appropriate in some context. Being stubborn may be judged bad in the context of a family, and becomes good in the context of banking and in the context of a man trying to take advantage of a young girl.

When faced with an assertion about the meaning of an event or a person's conduct, the mediator might ask, "What *else* might that conduct mean?" . . . A context reframe can be handled by asking, "Where would this behavior be *useful*? . . ."

Finding the appropriate reframe for negative or non-useful assertions during mediation is hard work and takes practice. No two circumstances will be the same. More often than not, you will not be quite sure if your reframe was useful. Sometimes you will know it was not. There is, however, no such thing as failure, only feedback. You will learn as you try different approaches, and your mediation partners will benefit from your dedication to improving your skills.

Perjury, or just hardball? During a mediation of a case arising from a failed partnership, the defendant's attorney argued vehemently that the plaintiff's lawyer had committed malpractice in drafting the partnership contract. This accusation inflamed the entire plaintiff side, requiring the mediation to be temporarily adjourned. A few days later the plaintiff lawyer produced a recently signed affidavit in which a key witness not only rebutted the defendant's version of events, but went on to say that the defense lawyer had told him that he would be given free legal counsel if he changed his story, arguably an incentive to perjure himself.

Defense counsel, told by the mediator about this in caucus, stood up and said angrily that he would not stand for being accused that way. The mediator replied that he thought the abetting-perjury innuendo was simply a "high inside fast-ball," thrown by the other side in response to the defense attorney's own "hardball" charge of malpractice. The defense lawyer, who did not really want to walk out, and did not mind being characterized as a tough player in front of his client, accepted the reframing of his adversary's accusation as a sports move and sat down. Both the perjury and malpractice issues tacitly dropped out of the case.

3. Identifying Interests and Developing Options

a. Interests

One of the key attractions of mediation is its ability to foster interest-based bargaining. How do mediators do this? Litigants rarely come to mediation ready to discuss their underlying concerns. Sometimes this is because they have focused only on the limited remedies available from a court, and sometimes because they fear that even mentioning an imaginative option will suggest that they lack confidence in their legal case or are willing to drop their demand for money. Mediators can advance the process of interest-identification in several ways.

Ask Specifically About Interests

It may seem obvious, but given the blinders with which many disputants approach negotiation, a mediator can often accomplish a good deal simply by looking actively for potential interests that can be addressed in settlement. A mediator may find it useful to think through these questions:

- What in my experience do people in this kind of situation really want?
- What seems to be motivating them to fight?
- What, apart from conventional legal remedies, might they find attractive in a settlement?

As one looks for interests, it is important to bear in mind that disputants on the same side of a case may have very different and even conflicting concerns. An executive, for instance, may be interested in resolving a controversy at minimal cost to her company, while a manager who attends the mediation is concerned about avoiding criticism of his division's performance, and the company's lawyer wishes to maintain a "warrior" reputation. Any proposal will be judged by the participants, consciously or not, in part by how well it achieves their personal objectives. In general, by designating a topic as relevant and asking about it, the neutral makes it easier for the participants to discuss how to satisfy underlying interests. Mediators should be careful to ask open-ended questions, avoid leading ones, and tolerate silence to draw out reluctant parties.

Listen for Clues

Asking is often not enough. Because disputants do not usually think in terms of their underlying interests, or are convinced that they are irrelevant to a legal dispute, mediators must listen carefully for clues about them. A small shift in posture or change in tone, for example, may indicate that a person is thinking about a matter that troubles her. Sometimes a mediator can gain insights indirectly, for example, when a disputant asks why his opponent is taking an illogical position.

Example: A failed businessman sued a bank that had foreclosed on his property, claiming that he had been misled by the bank's president during the transaction. As the mediator caucused with the defense, the attorney asked in an irritated tone why the plaintiff was bothering to press the suit, given that he had other creditors who would quickly seize any judgment he might obtain against the bank. In fact, the lender threatened to buy up these unsatisfied claims at a few cents on the dollar, which would put it in a position to recoup any money that it might eventually be ordered to pay the plaintiff.

The mediator was intrigued by this, and asked the plaintiff how he planned to deal with his other creditors. It turned out that the plaintiff was also attempting to resolve the debts, but did not have the resources to do so. A settlement was eventually reached by which the bank agreed to buy up the plaintiff's debts cheaply and then cancel them, in return for the plaintiff dropping his suit.

Suggest Needs and Give Examples

In addition to questions, a mediator can mention an interest that she thinks a party might have and ask about it. Or a neutral might tell a story in which satisfaction of a nonlegal interest was the key to a good settlement, and ask if a disputant can think of any items that could be included as "extras" in a resolution of the present case.

Ask Each Side to Describe the Other's Interests

Another option is to ask each side, perhaps as "homework" while the mediator is out of the room, to think about what their opponent might find valuable other than legal remedies. Such questions may feel less threatening to a litigant than being asked about his own needs and can produce interesting data, while also helping each side to understand the other's perspective.

Be Persistent

If a mediator asks about underlying interests he should not be surprised or offended to be rebuffed at first. Neutrals have to be persistent in order to draw out disputants on these topics. It is not unusual for a question about interests to be deflected at first, then welcomed later in the same process.

b. Options

One of the most difficult obstacles to creating value is the "negotiator's dilemma"—the basic tension that many bargainers feel between working with the other side to increase the overall value of a settlement, and competing to get the best possible share of the "settlement pie" for their own client. Plaintiffs, for example, often worry that if they even mention an interest-based option, it will be interpreted as a signal that they are willing to give up their demand for money. Parties also fear that "cement will set" around a tentative idea and prevent them from discarding it later on. Mediation can make this process both easier and more efficient.

Brainstorm in a Protective Setting

Parties often find it easier to generate options if a mediator designates a discussion as intended exclusively for "brainstorming" under a rule of "no commitment — no criticism." Private caucuses are the easiest forum in which parties can brainstorm. It is more difficult to create conditions of trust in joint meetings, but the greater resources and ease of communication that exist when parties are able to speak directly with each other can make joint sessions worthwhile, particularly in cases arising from a strong relationship.

Lower the Level of Pressure

The tension that accompanies many negotiations makes it hard for disputants to think creatively about options. To dissipate pressure it is sometimes helpful to change the setting, as by having people meet informally rather than around a conference table, distracting parties with a joke or anecdote, or adjourning in order to allow participants to recharge themselves psychologically.

Offer a Draft Proposal

A mediator can sometimes provoke a useful discussion of options by offering a draft proposal that he suspects will be rejected, but which has elements that respond to the parties' interests. The mediator can then invite each side to critique and improve on the draft. Focusing on a common proposal sometimes helps parties change their frame of reference.

Cite Models or Testimonials

Disputants may be uncomfortable with a new idea because they are afraid that it will not work, or that they will be criticized by someone outside the mediation for endorsing it. Mediators can reduce these concerns by citing examples of cases in which the concept has been successful. Such examples may also help participants anticipate problems of implementation.

Introduce New People

If disputants reach a genuine impasse, one option is to arrange for new people to come into the process. New players are less likely to feel locked into past proposals and, if they hold a higher position in their organizations, may have a broader perspective and more authority to act.

Present Ideas Anonymously

As we have seen, one of the most serious obstacles to creative thinking is parties' fear that mentioning an idea will be taken as a signal that they agree to it. A mediator can reduce this concern by offering to float a promising proposal as her own.

4.   Managing Positional Bargaining

One of the most common causes of impasse is positional bargaining. Positional negotiators are often reluctant even to make a first offer, for fear that they will be seen as overeager to settle. Or they start with an extreme position that the other side finds "insulting." Even when parties begin exchanging offers, the process often degenerates, as participants pressure each other to make concessions and become frustrated with their opponent's obduracy. A mediator faced with impasses created by positional bargaining has the following options.

Move the Parties into Principled or Interest-Based Bargaining

Ideally, a mediator would be able to encourage disputants to move to an interest-based or principled approach. By asking questions about the facts and principles behind each offer and probing for interests, a mediator can model constructive techniques and sometimes change the tenor of the discussion.

Reframe or Suppress Positional Tactics

A mediator can keep the sides in caucus and serve as the sole channel of communication between them. This allows the neutral to translate and reframe what each side says into more constructive wording and concepts. Mediators also sometimes edit out abrasive comments entirely, allowing parties to vent anger without offending each other.

Coach the Participants to Use More Effective Positional Methods

A mediator may also work to facilitate positional techniques. Many negotiators continue to use positional tactics despite a mediator's best efforts to refocus them. In such situations a neutral's practical choice is between facilitating the method the parties insist on using or giving up. Mediators can assist positional negotiators in several ways.

- Work with each party in caucus to select a starting offer that does not discourage the other.
- Tell one side that if it makes a relatively realistic proposal, the mediator will encourage the other to respond in the same spirit.
- Ask positional bargainers to explain the message behind their numbers, and then communicate it to the other side. ("They started at this level because they think that you are at your 'win' position in court, and felt that they should remain close to theirs. But if I could show them that you're open to compromise, then. . . ." or "I'm fairly sure that they'll go up. What I think this means is that they see this as a five-figure case.")

Minimize Emotional Reactions

By reassuring a party that its opponent is genuinely interested in reaching agreement, a mediator can reduce the anger, ego clashes, and other negative emotions that are often created by positional tactics. Sometimes a mediator can reduce a party's feeling that it is being unfairly forced to "give in" by stressing that the other side is feeling frustrated as well.

Moderate the Bargaining

Finally, a mediator may decide to intervene directly in the bargaining, becoming the "dance master" described in the "Dance for Dollars" reading in Chapter 9, and lead the parties toward agreement. A neutral could, for example, warn a party about the likely impact of its stance on the other side ("Unless you go to six figures, I'm concerned that they will . . .")

Distract the Parties

Finally, it may be effective to arrange for a temporary break or adjournment. Taking time off sometimes makes it easier for bargainers to move from entrenched positions, allowing both sides to tacitly "forget" that one of them has imposed an ultimatum. Indeed, a mediator can sometimes divert disputants from their fixation on existing positions simply by changing the subject.

B. EMOTIONAL AND PSYCHOLOGICAL FORCES

As the discussion of positional bargaining suggests, disputes often fail to settle because the people involved become emotionally at odds with each other. Disputants often do not volunteer information about such issues because they are embarrassed to do so, have been told that emotions are irrelevant to their case, or are not conscious that an issue exists. Still, personal clashes between participants, combined with forces generated by the dispute itself, are the primary obstacle to settlement in many cases. Indeed, some psychologists have commented that humans effectively "swim" in a "sea of emotions." In the context of disputes, this often means navigating through a mixture of emotional crosscurrents.

The judgment of disputants can be overwhelmed by a variety of strong feelings, ranging from guilt to frustration, sadness, and anger. Emotions may be provoked by the incident that gave rise to the dispute: An accident victim or employer charged with discrimination, for example, is likely to have intense feelings about his case. Even if the substance of a dispute is not inflammatory, people often become angry over events that occur during litigation; recall, for example, how upset the parents of the deceased MIT student became because the university president did not talk with them at the funeral.

Strong feelings can disrupt communication, produce irrational decision making, and create other obstacles to settlement.

Even disputants who are not in the grip of strong feelings are often subject to psychological influences that distort their decision making. We saw in the introductory chapter that people are subject to a variety of psychological forces known as "cognitive" conditions. These conditions can affect human judgment even when people are perfectly calm, but they tend to intensify when they fall into conflict. Mediators will often lead a disputant through a logical analysis of a bargaining issue or the value of a case, only to be frustrated when the party stubbornly refuses to accept the outcome. They may conclude that the disputant is not being candid, when the real obstacle is psychological in nature. We discuss below the how mediators can respond to emotional and cognitive forces in bargaining.

1. Strong Emotions

Mediators can contribute greatly to the process of settlement by dealing with emotional forces affecting the disputants. To do so, a neutral does not have to become a pseudotherapist or take on other inappropriate roles. Mediators must, however, be willing and able to manage expressions of strong feelings without becoming flustered or squelching them. The following responses may be effective in dealing with emotional issues:

- *Identify the issue*
- *Allow venting: Listen, acknowledge, empathize*
- *Trace the issue back to its source*
- *Arrange a response from the other side*
- *Treat continuing problems*
- *Circumvent persistently dysfunctional players*

Identify the Issue

Because of the "game-face" phenomenon described earlier, disputants often do not volunteer that an emotional issue exists unless it is an explicit part of their case (for example, a claim for emotional distress). A mediator's first task, therefore, is often to discover whether strong emotions are present. This may be obvious from a disputant's facial expression or body language, or the way in which disputants relate to each other. Often, however, mediator must ask questions to dig out emotional issues. Options include the following:

- *Open-ended questions.* (Many mediators begin their caucus discussions with a question such as "Is there anything you think I should know about, that you didn't feel comfortable mentioning in the opening session?")
- *Mildly prompting inquiries.* ("This must have been very difficult for you, Mr. Smith. . . .")
- *Leading questions.* ("You know, if I felt that I'd been fired because of my age, I'd be very angry . . . are you?").
- *References to similar events or personal experiences.* ("It's been my experience that when people have had this happen to them, they often feel. . . .")

- *Suggestions of possible responses.* ("Some people see being laid off as a chance to take it easy, others feel very low for quite a while, and some just get angry. I'm wondering how it was for you . . . ?) This approach may feel less threatening to listeners, because it allows them to adopt the possibility that feels most true or capable of being admitted. ("Well, I wasn't exactly angry, but I guess I felt misunderstood . . . and maybe even discriminated against!")
- *Inquiries to lawyers.* If a party is not willing to talk about an emotional issue, a mediator can sometimes gather information from his attorney.

Again, mediators must be willing to accept brush-offs at the outset, remembering that a question that is turned aside at first will often be answered later, as the participants become more comfortable with the neutral. The right approach, therefore, is to be both diplomatic and persistent.

Example: A mediator was attempting to settle a claim by an auto dealer that a banker had unfairly foreclosed on his loan and driven him into bankruptcy, then sold his property at a bargain price to a business associate. During the first caucus, when the mediator remarked to the plaintiff dealer how crushing the experience must have been, his lawyer interrupted saying, "Never mind that — I want to know what they'll offer to settle this thing!"

The mediator raised the emotional issue again during a second meeting a week later. This time the auto dealer hesitated and looked at his attorney. Gesturing expansively, the attorney said, "Joe, tell him how you felt when the bank foreclosed on you. . . ." A torrent of feelings about scheming lenders, the unfair way the public views car dealers, and other angry emotions poured out.

Allow Venting: Listen, Acknowledge, Empathize

Once an emotional issue has been identified, a mediator must decide how to deal with it. In some situations simply allowing the disputants to vent their feelings privately, and perhaps also to each other, is enough to clear the air. More often, however, a mediator will need to respond to what she has heard. The first-level response is simply to acknowledge the existence of the emotion. As we have discussed, mediators can go on to offer empathy to the person expressing it. One's reaction will vary depending on the nature of the issue; a lawyer's anger over an opponent's litigation tactics, for example, is very different from the feelings of a victim of sexual abuse.

It is worth stressing that one does not have to agree with a party's view of a situation in order to sympathize with his emotional reaction to it. Some mediators, especially those who come from careers as litigators and judges, may find it hard initially to focus on emotions. It may help to think of one's role as similar to that of a mourner at a funeral: You cannot change what has happened, but the very fact that you are present and showing concern provides solace to the bereaved.

Mediators need, however, to be careful to keep the issue of what happened separate from how a disputant feels about it. It often helps a party to express a difficult emotion and receive an acknowledgment or expression of empathy, but for a mediator to go further, to agree with the party's position on the merits, is neither required nor wise. Indeed, by characterizing the situation in terms of "if," a neutral can imply gently that there may be other ways of interpreting the underlying facts. ("If I felt that I'd been cheated by a business partner, I'd probably feel the same way you do," or "I can understand your frustration, given your belief that the company never tried to respond to your complaints. . . .")

Trace the Issue Back to Its Source

Sometimes identifying the issue and acknowledging or empathizing with the emotion is not enough: The person remains "stuck" in the feeling. When this occurs, it may help to trace the emotion back to the events that stimulated it. A mediator can, for instance, encourage a disputant to tell the story of how the situation developed. Telling one's story often has a calming effect and reduces the rigidity that some disputants adopt as a defensive posture. Also, by suggesting that the person once had different feelings about a situation, the mediator opens the possibility that the party's current state is not necessarily how she will feel in the future.

Arrange a Response

Even more can be accomplished with emotional issues when a mediator can bring an adversary into the process in a constructive way. A mediator may, for example, be able to persuade one party to listen to his opponent express feelings about a dispute, and then acknowledge that he has heard what was said. Disputants are sometimes able to go farther, to express empathy in the same manner as a neutral. In fact, as we discuss below, within the confidential setting of mediation neutrals can sometimes arrange for one person to express an apology or regret to another.

Treat Continuing Problems

Sometimes people are upset not by a past event, but by a party's present conduct. If, for example, one side is angry over what it sees as an opponent's improper negotiation tactics, the issue should be handled as a process problem. If, by contrast, the irritation is being caused by a condition outside the negotiation process, the mediator can approach it as a hidden substantive issue.

Example: A mediator was moderating discussions between a man and a woman who were breaking up their partnership. The mediator pushed to wrap up the case because he knew that the man was anxious to start a new job and the woman was pregnant. The woman partner, however, resisted scheduling efforts and then canceled a session at the last minute. The mediator learned from a friend that she had been diagnosed with a serious genetic problem that would affect her unborn child, and was agonizing over it.

Exploring the issue of scheduling gingerly with both partners, the mediator decided that it would make sense to delay the process. An adjournment would create additional issues, however, because the woman was upset that her partner was making efforts to collect their outstanding bills. The partner had meant this as a gesture of assistance, but the woman interpreted it as a maneuver to change the value of the remaining receivables and thus the sale price of the business. The mediator worked out an agreement by which the male partner would handle day-to-day finances under agreed criteria and there would be a two-week adjournment of the mediation.

Circumvent Persistently Dysfunctional Players

When it is impossible to calm or defuse a dysfunctional participant, the most effective approach may be to circumvent or even replace him. If, for instance, a manager representing a corporate defendant is too angry with the plaintiff to bargain effectively, the best strategy may be to invite a new person to join the process. The mediator might, for instance, ask the plaintiff lawyer to call in a higher level bargainer from her client's organization, then suggest that the defendant reciprocate. If the dysfunctional person cannot be circumvented or replaced, the mediator can separate the combatants into caucuses.

QUESTIONS

1. Why might it be easier for a mediator to identify and respond to an emotional obstacle than a lawyer in direct bargaining?
2. Which of the techniques described above could a lawyer apply directly with an angry opponent? Which could a lawyer apply with her own client?

A Note on Apology in Mediation: One of the potentials of mediation is that it can stimulate disputants to offer apologies. In part this is because the process is confidential, making it possible for a party to apologize without concern that his gesture will be thrown back at him if the case does not settle. In part it is because of the atmosphere created by mediation—what Daniel Bowling and David Hoffman referred to as a mediator's "presence in the room." This said, mediators in commercial cases report that it is very unusual for a litigant to apologize. When it occurs, however, an expression of regret can have an major impact. Consider this example.

A famous singer wanted to refurbish an old mansion she had just purchased. She decided to hire a well-known contractor who specialized in restorations, draw her vision of what she wanted, and have the contractor execute it. The contractor gave her a price of several hundred thousand dollars for the job. She agreed, and work began. The project, however, rapidly spun out of control. Changes were made, expenses mushroomed, and the eventual cost ran well over a million dollars. The singer refused to pay the final bill and the contractor sued. The parties agreed to mediate.

Each side sat rather stiffly at a conference table and the mediator asked the attorneys to make statements. After the singer's lawyer had summarized her legal arguments, the singer asked to speak. Looking directly at the contractor, she said that she had realized that she bore some of the responsibility for what had happened: She had very much wanted to realize a vision for her new home, but had made a mistake in deciding not to use an architect. She felt that while the contractor could have done a better job of explaining the cost of the changes in the project, part of the fault for the misunderstandings was hers.

As the singer spoke, the contractor visibly relaxed. He responded that he had tried to do his best, but was willing to work to find a fair solution. After a day of hard bargaining, the case settled.

For a discussion of the impact of apology in mediation, and legal issues that an apology may raise, see the articles by Professor Jonathan Cohen and Deborah Levi referenced in the bibliography.

In practice, lawyers and other professionals often find it difficult to deal with emotional issues. As you read the following dialogue, ask yourself if any of the comments might describe your own reaction to an intensely emotional situation.

HELAINE S. GOLANN AND DWIGHT GOLANN, WHY IS IT HARD FOR LAWYERS TO DEAL WITH EMOTIONAL ISSUES?

9 Disp. Resol. Mag. 26-29 (Winter 2003)

Lawyer: The fact is, I sometimes don't feel that I'm being professional when I work with emotions. It's not what lawyers do.

Psychologist: That's interesting—What *does* make you feel as if you're acting like a professional?

L: Dealing with facts and arguments, analyzing issues, generating strategies and, most important, solving problems. . . .

P: Well, those are clearly professional activities, and they are often invaluable to clients. My only concern would be not to rush into them too soon. In an emotional situation—and people who feel that they've been hurt or treated unfairly are often quite emotional—people *can't really listen until they feel they've been heard.* You might think that you can predict their story because you have heard so many similar ones, but even if you are right, they won't feel heard until they've told it. In fact they may need to review the story with you in order to hear it themselves and become open to different ways of resolving the problem. Rushing to analyze can get in the way of disputants figuring out what is important to them.

L: I do remember one fairly dramatic instance of that from when I was in law practice. It was a tort case brought against a state trooper. The trooper had been chasing a drunk driver on a rainy night, when he went through a stop sign and accidentally hit another motorist. The driver, a high school student, was killed. His family sued the state and I supervised the defense. After two years of litigation we made a substantial settlement offer, but the family refused to discuss it. They said that they wanted to meet the trooper first. We were suspicious. Everyone had been deposed; what was the point? But eventually we agreed.

It was quite a session. The mother of the student read a poem describing what she hoped her son would have accomplished had he lived. His sisters also spoke about who their brother had been. The trooper said he wanted to say something too. He told the family that he didn't feel that he'd driven negligently, but he did feel awful about what had happened. He had three sons himself and had thought about how he would feel if one of them were killed. He had asked to be assigned to desk work, he told the family, because he could no longer do high-speed chases. As the participants walked out, one of the children turned to the trooper. "It's been three years since my brother died," she said, "and now I feel he's finally had a funeral." Two weeks later, they accepted our offer.

I have to say, though, that we agreed to the meeting only because the other side insisted on it. Not many cases are so openly emotional. Litigants usually don't come in asking for a chance to tell their story.

P: That's an unusual and deeply touching example, and yes, you're right that clients are rarely so clear about their emotions and what they need to do to resolve them. Litigants need you to assure them that dealing with emotions is a valid and potentially productive way to spend time, and even then they may initially resist.

I sometimes think of people in this situation as being like a tightly-closed fist: One option is to help them strike with that fist. Another is to counsel them about their chances of winning the fight. But it could be even more useful to help them uncurl their fist, so that they can grasp other possibilities. Strategizing with "closed fist" clients who don't know what they feel or why they feel it is often unproductive. The issues they present are often only a smokescreen for other, more important concerns. Lawyers or mediators who charge ahead to focus on legal or bargaining issues may find themselves going off in a direction that the client may later resist or even sabotage. . . .

L: I think it's sitting without doing anything that often strikes us lawyers as meaningless.

P: OK, I'm hearing how important it is to feel that you are *doing something specific* in order to feel like a responsible professional. It's true that usually more is needed than silence; we need to find a way for lawyers to experience listening, and even encouraging the expression of emotions, as an active, professional activity in and of itself. . . .

L: Another problem is that lawyers often feel lost in long discussions about emotions — they seem directionless.

P: It's true that exploring emotional territory makes it difficult to have a clear agenda. Your questions and interventions need to be guided by what emerges as important to the client as she tells her story. Early in my training as a psychologist, for example, I was assigned to interview a client. The session occurred in a special room fitted out with a one-way mirror and a telephone. Behind the mirror was my professor, also with a phone, and the rest of my class. A patient came in and we began to talk, but he only wanted to discuss his hobby, which was scuba diving.

After about twenty minutes of listening to his adventures while diving, I began to worry about demonstrating my therapeutic skills and interrupted the client to ask what had led him to make the appointment. Immediately the phone rang. I picked it up. It was, of course, my professor. He had one question: "*So . . . what's the matter with scuba diving?*" I took the hint and began to listen more closely to the diving talk. Almost immediately it became clear that he was talking about some complex issues, for example, his anxiety over sharing an air tank with his girlfriend. Was it something about her, about their relationship, or was it more about him and past relationships that had compromised his ability to trust? All I needed to do was reflect the questions I began to hear in his story to help him begin to formulate his own answers.

Years later, the part of me that wanted to say, "Why don't you just get a second tank and let's move on to talking about something *important*?" still occasionally rears its head. I can cringe as I review a session and recognize that I failed to hear something that was essential to my client because I was too caught up in trying to be "helpful."

Shutting up and listening can be as hard for psychologists as for other professionals, but equally rewarding.

L: Actually, many of us became lawyers to avoid dealing with these messy emotional issues. I've sometimes said that hearing people out is like "draining pus from an infected wound."

P: Ugh — I can understand why you wouldn't be enthusiastic about doing it. That metaphor also helps me understand why I've rarely heard "venting" described by lawyers as anything more than a necessary evil, to be gotten out of the way as quickly as possible. But allowing people to vent emotions doesn't have to be distasteful, and it does have a purpose and goal — it's just that *you* are not the one setting the goal. It might help to imagine a litigant's experience as a dark room filled with noxious fumes; "venting" is an opportunity to open the windows, release the blinding smoke and let in fresh air so your client can think more clearly.

L: Are you saying that venting moves inevitably toward clarity?

P: Not necessarily . . . Active listening stays focused on encouraging the client to tell her story fully, but it also offers opportunities for lawyers to use their organizational skills to bring clarity. You might summarize with a statement such as "As I listen to you, I think I'm hearing at least three separate issues here. Please correct me if I'm wrong." By separating and listing the concerns in this way, you are demonstrating your attempt to understand their perspective (including their feelings), but also are introducing clarity and perhaps facilitating movement. Of course, when you ask if you are getting it right, you also have to be prepared to hear that you've got it all wrong!

L: Many of us worry that if we start to let parties express emotions, the situation will blow up. It'll be like uncapping a volcano — lava everywhere! And people will get burned.

P: In fact, no one can cap an emotional "volcano," and even if you could, it might not be a wise course. The pressure is there and denying it may fuel it further. If you don't drain emotional pressures off, they will find their own escape routes — often to fuel more arguments and hardened positions.

If you want to think of emotional release as a volcano erupting, think of your job as allowing the lava to escape, while at the same time channeling it away from the "village" and into a safe area. There are ways to channel flows of feelings so that they do not disrupt the process of settlement or your relationship with the parties. Just by modeling respectful listening yourself and establishing ground rules for how people express themselves, you can channel emotional "lava." Perhaps the most important rule I enforce in working with families is to ask each participant to focus on his own experience, feelings and wishes, without accusing or analyzing the motives of the other side.

L: Again, as I think about it, the more usual problem is that most parties come to mediation with "game faces on." They act as if there is no emotional issue, when I suspect they are simmering inside.

P: Yes, in therapy, too, clamming up is by far the more common and challenging response to emotional turbulence. The listening techniques we've been discussing are the most effective ways I've found to get at buried emotions.

L: The final obstacle is litigators — the people who usually hire legal mediators. One might fairly ask: If the lawyers don't want to get into an emotional issue, how can we do it without offending them?

P: I wonder if you're reading them right? A major problem may be that a litigator's role as an advocate armored for battle often makes it hard for her to explore a client's mixed feelings. I think a mediator could make himself quite valuable as someone prepared to handle the messy emotions that some attorneys don't feel in a position to confront, yet know are preventing a resolution of the dispute. . . .

QUESTION

Do you think that any of these factors might lead you to avoid dealing with intense emotions in a dispute? Which seem most significant?

2. Cognitive Effects

As we have seen, cognitive forces often prevent persons from making good decisions even when they feel perfectly calm. Some conditions impair a disputant's ability to assess the merits of a case, while others affect a bargainer's ability to negotiate well. We will discuss each in turn.

a. Forces Affecting Assessment of the Merits

Selective Perception

We have learned that once people adopt a certain view of a situation, they are affected by the phenomenon of "cognitive dissonance"—that is, they unconsciously seek to maintain a consistent picture of the world, and find it psychologically difficult to consider data that contradict their viewpoint. To avoid such dissonance, the mind unconsciously screens out conflicting information, leaving people with a false sense of certainty. Lawyers fall into this trap when they listen to a client's version of the facts and form a viewpoint about what occurred, then disregard conflicting evidence that later comes to light. Mediators use several techniques to minimize the distortions caused by selective perception. They can:

- Ask the parties to state their cases directly to each other, so that each side hears an unfiltered statement of its opponent's views.
- Ask each party to assume the role of a neutral judge or juror as he listens, imagine that he is hearing the case for the first time, and ask himself how the other side's version would sound to someone who did not know what had "really" happened.
- Review the facts and arguments with each side in private, gently questioning them about apparent gaps.
- Emphasize missing facts and issues visually, for instance with colored markers on a flip chart.

Optimistic Overconfidence

We have also seen that humans consistently overestimate their ability to assess matters about which they are unsure, and are likely to be overoptimistic about their chances of prevailing in an uncertain situation. They also become even more confident about their ability to assess uncertainty when they have made a personal investment in the outcome. Thus, for example, people who place a bet on a horse are more sure than those who do not that their steed will win. These forces tend to distort the judgment of litigants and their lawyers, who must assess the outcome of an uncertain "race"—the likelihood that they will prevail at trial — and regularly place large "bets on their horses," in the form of the time and money they invest in their cases. To combat optimistic overconfidence a mediator can:

- Encourage an information exchange that provides disputants with new data about their case. The less uncertainty in a situation, the less likely it is that humans will overstate their ability to estimate it. People, it seems, are willing to admit to having *some* doubt about their predictions.
- Distance bettors from their "horses," by making a case seem less unique: For example, a mediator might place the claim among a group of similar ones (e.g., all soft-tissue injuries) and ask about trial results for the group. By doing so, a neutral can help participants see that they are treating their own case as an exception to the general pattern of outcomes. A mediator might then ask the parties what is truly exceptional about the case.

b.   Influences on Bargaining Decisions

Cognitive barriers also affect how parties behave in the bargaining process. Among these are reactive devaluation, loss aversion, and the attraction to certainty and familiar risks.

Reactive Devaluation

We know that people tend to react negatively to any offer or information that is presented by an adversary, perceiving ominous overtones in what an outsider would view as an innocent gesture. To lessen this effect, a mediator can:

- Discuss the merits of a settlement option in the abstract, before the listener knows whether an opponent has proposed or endorsed it.
- Offer a proposal as the mediator's idea.
- Diminish the negative impact of an adversary's proposal by offering an opinion that in the mediator's view, it may have advantages for the listener.

Loss Aversion

We have also seen that disputants tend to develop a perception about the "right" outcome in a case, regardless of its objective merit, and then take unreasonable risks to avoid what they see as a "loss" compared to that standard. To minimize the impact of loss aversion, a mediator can:

- Work to reframe a situation, so that a settlement proposal does not appear a loss.
- Use charts and other visual techniques to help disputants break away from a past loss benchmark. If a disputant is being unduly influenced by the money he has spent on a case, for example, the mediator might distinguish past — unrecoverable — legal costs from future expenses that can be avoided through settling by placing each in a different column or contrasting colors.
- Look for new terms that will distract parties from their "loss/gain" calculations.

Example: It is said, perhaps apocryphally, that Henry Kissinger ascribed his success in bringing about agreements between Arabs and Israelis to "making the deal so complicated that no one could tell who was winning." In essence, it seems, Kissinger used complex proposals to prevent the parties from comparing his settlement proposals with their initial goals, and thus seeing them as a loss.

Attraction to Certainty and Familiar Risks

We have seen that disputants are willing to pay a premium to achieve certainty, and are likely to shy away from a result that contains even a minor degree of risk. People also prefer to assume familiar risks rather than strange ones. People find it easier, for example, to take on a commonplace risk like jaywalking across a busy street than an unusual one like walking along a cliff, although the consequence is the same in either case — death — and the familiar risk is actually greater than the strange one.

Mediators encounter this premium for certainty whenever they work to close the final gap in a case or advocate a less-than-airtight resolution. Neutrals confront parties' preference for familiar risks whenever a settlement requires a party to bear a risk that it sees as unusual. In response mediators can:

- Analyze less-than-certain proposals carefully, so that listeners understand that while a risk exists, it is minor in objective terms.
- Reframe unusual risks in familiar terms ("This is really just like giving a warranty . . .")
- When a settlement does provide certainty, use this as a lever to persuade parties to settle. Disputants are more likely, for example, to agree to a painful concession if a mediator can assure them that doing so will bring them complete peace. ("If you can just take this last step, you will never have to hear about this case again.")

QUESTIONS

1. Have cognitive factors affected the bargaining in an exercise you have done in this course?
2. Have you ever encountered such a reaction in real life?

C. EVALUATIVE BARRIERS

Litigators tend to assume that if they cannot settle a case, it is because the other side has misevaluated its chances of prevailing on the merits. When this occurs, one or both parties may ask the mediator to give an opinion as to who is likely to win in court. Legal issues are not the only topics on which disputants ask mediators' advice; participants may also request a mediator's opinion about what offer they should make, or how to respond to an opponent's tactics. One of the strongest ways in which mediators give bargaining advice is to suggest specific terms of settlement. For example, neutrals sometimes offer a "mediator's proposal," discussed in Chapter 9, to both sides on a take-it-or-leave-it basis. Even when parties do not ask a mediator to give an opinion about legal issues or the bargaining situation, neutrals, especially in the commercial arena, often offer advice on their own initiative.

The issue of mediator advice is controversial. Commercial mediators tend to think that offering evaluative advice is part of what they have been hired to do, and that in the right circumstances advice can be very helpful. Mediators almost always offer advice in the belief that it will facilitate the settlement process. Such advice may, however, interfere with one of the core values of mediation—the right of parties to self-determination, to make their own decisions about how to proceed and whether to settle. This section deals with some of the ways in which mediators give advice and evaluate, and the issues that these techniques present.

1. Lack of Information

One of the most common reasons people misevaluate legal cases is that they lack key information about the situation. Mediators are frequently surprised to discover how little disputants know about each other's legal claims and defenses, and how ignorant they are about each other's attitude toward settlement, even after years of litigation. In part this is because lawyers work to conceal data from each other. When the principals in a case attend a deposition, for example, they are typically cautioned to say as little as possible. Similarly, disputants are often reluctant to mention the idea of settlement for fear of showing weakness. As a result, mediators can often make significant progress toward agreement simply by encouraging parties to exchange information with each other.

> *Example:* A sales manager fired by a software company sued his former employer and its chief executive for violating his employment contract. The case remained in pretrial discovery for years and then, as trial approached, went to mediation. When the neutral caucused with the parties, it quickly became apparent that a major component of the manager's claims involved lost stock options in the company. The plaintiff, however, had never been able to obtain the internal financial reports needed to value his options. He assumed that the company was concealing assets and intended to go public in the near future, an event that would make the options very valuable.
>
> Questioned about this in caucus, the company's CEO said that he had ordered the data withheld from the plaintiff because "It's none of his business." In fact, the company was only marginally profitable and the plaintiff's options were virtually worthless. The mediator suggested to the CEO that if there really was no pot of gold, he could help to settle the case by letting the plaintiff know this. The parties agreed to review the financial data together, and within an hour a settlement was worked out. Among its terms were verification of the company's financial representations and termination of the stock options.

Exchanges of Information

Mediators can greatly assist disputants to trade relevant information. Litigants are usually more forthcoming in the context of mediation because they feel some hope of settling the case, want to cooperate with the neutral, and trust the mediator to referee the process. The special confidentiality protections that apply in mediation also encourage disputants to share data.

Access to Internal Data

Mediators can sometimes help bargainers obtain data from their own side. This may be necessary, for example, because the litigation contact for a corporate party does not see the case as a priority or does not have the influence needed to obtain relevant information.

Information About Other Issues

For understandable reasons, litigators tend to seek out data that may be useful at trial and often slight their clients' nonlitigation interests. In a dispute about the direction of a family-owned business, for example, discovery might not be sought on issues such as the future income needs of relatives or the majority's ability to buy out a minority interest. Mediation can provide a vehicle to develop additional data that help the parties to understand the value of their nonlitigation alternatives.

2. Disagreement About the Likely Outcome in Adjudication

The "Dispute Resolution Spectrum" that appears in Chapter One sets forth two distinct forms of mediation: facilitative and evaluative. Almost no one would argue that mediators should employ evaluation as a first resort, and processes that rely primarily on evaluation, such as early neutral evaluation and advisory arbitration, have declined greatly in popularity. Still, the discussion of commercial mediation has assumed that it is appropriate, in some circumstances at least, for a mediator to offer litigants a prediction as to the likely outcome of the case in adjudication. Indeed, in commercial mediation there is often no clear dividing line between the facilitative and evaluative phases of the process. However, a significant number of neutrals, particularly transformative mediators and persons with a background in family or neighborhood mediation, believe that evaluation should not be part of the mediation process at all. Consider the following perspectives on this issue.

a. Should Mediators Evaluate?

LELA P. LOVE, THE TOP TEN REASONS WHY MEDIATORS SHOULD NOT EVALUATE
24 Fla. St. U. L. Rev. 937-948 (1997)

... The debate over whether mediators should "evaluate" revolves around the confusion over what constitutes evaluation and an "evaluative" mediator ... An "evaluative" mediator gives advice, makes assessments, states opinions — including opinions on the likely court outcome, proposes a fair or workable resolution to an issue or the dispute, or presses the parties to accept a particular resolution. The ten reasons that follow demonstrate that those activities are inconsistent with the role of a mediator.

1. *The Roles and Related Tasks of Evaluators and Facilitators Are at Odds*

Evaluating, assessing, and deciding for others is radically different than helping others evaluate, assess, and decide for themselves. Judges, arbitrators, neutral experts, and advisors are evaluators. Their role is to make decisions and give opinions. To do so, they use predetermined criteria to evaluate evidence and arguments presented by adverse parties. The tasks of evaluators include: finding "the facts" by properly weighing evidence; judging credibility and allocating the burden of proof; determining and applying the relevant law, rule, or custom to the particular situation; and making an award or rendering an opinion. The adverse parties have expressly asked the evaluator — judge, arbitrator, or expert — to decide the issue or resolve the conflict.

In contrast, the role of mediators is to assist disputing parties in making their own decisions and evaluating their own situations. A mediator "facilitate[s] communications, promotes understanding, focuses the parties on their interests, and seeks creative problem-solving to enable the parties to reach their own agreement." Mediators push disputing parties to question their assumptions, reconsider their positions, and listen to each other's perspectives, stories, and arguments. They urge the parties to consider relevant law, weigh their own values, principles, and priorities, and develop an optimal outcome. In so doing, mediators facilitate evaluation by the parties.

These differences between evaluators and facilitators mean that each uses different skills and techniques, and each requires different competencies, training norms, and ethical guidelines to perform their respective functions. Further, the evaluative tasks of determining facts, applying law or custom, and delivering an opinion not only divert the mediator away from facilitation, but also can compromise the mediator's neutrality — both in actuality and in the eyes of the parties — because the mediator will be favoring one side in his or her judgment.

Endeavors are more likely to succeed when the goal is clear and simple and not at war with other objectives. Any task, whether it is the performance of an Olympic athlete, the advocacy of an attorney, or the negotiation assistance provided by a mediator, requires a clear and bright focus and the development of appropriate strategies, skills, and power. In most cases, should the athlete or the attorney or the mediator divert their focus to another task, it will diminish their capacity to achieve their primary goal. "No one can serve two masters." Mediators cannot effectively facilitate when they are evaluating.

2. *Evaluation promotes positioning and polarization, which are antithetical to the goals of mediation* . . .

3. *Ethical codes caution mediators — and other neutrals — against assuming additional roles* . . .

4. *If mediators evaluate legal claims and defenses, they must be lawyers; eliminating non-lawyers will weaken the field* . . .

5. *There are insufficient protections against incorrect mediator evaluations* . . .

L. RANDOLPH LOWRY, TO EVALUATE OR NOT—THAT IS NOT THE QUESTION!
2 Resolutions 2-3 (Pepperdine University) (Winter 1997)

One of the joys of the mediation field is the spirit of debate that takes place regarding approaches to the process. Notable in recent years has been the debate over "evaluation"—the mediator providing an opinion about the case, a perspective on a party's position, or even suggesting an appropriate outcome . . . I want to suggest that perhaps the question is wrong. In many cases it is not a question as to whether or not evaluation will take place, but more accurately, when and how it does so.

Let me attempt to state the case. First of all, I would contend that all mediators are at least involved in internal "evaluation," in the sense of making judgments on the information presented . . . It is the basis on which decisions are made regarding the process, the people and the resolution of the problem. Even "facilitative" mediators exercise evaluative judgment internally while deciding how to reframe issues or which areas of questioning to pursue with the objective of bringing the parties to an agreement. . . .

If one concedes the reality that evaluation takes place, then the question changes to whether or not the door is open to reveal the evaluation to the parties . . . My strong sense is that mediators not only evaluate internally, but also express some sense of that evaluation during the mediation process. What we argue about, or *should* argue about, is how the evaluation is expressed. . . .

First, evaluation ought to take place at a time when its influence will be greatest. Evaluation is not a tool for the mediator to demonstrate competence. It is not a technique allowing the mediator to manipulate a case in such a way that it comes out as he or she designates. Rather, evaluation is a tool to move parties from positions that have resulted in impasse to positions that are consistent with each other so that a settlement can take place. . . .

Second, the style of evaluation may be critical. . . .

Third, the nature of the evaluation is somewhat affected by the type of relationship the mediator wishes to establish with those involved in the mediation . . . While a relationship is important for some, it is not important for others.

Fourth, there may be a strong connection between the nature of evaluation and the type of claim involved in the mediation process. For instance, a claim in which the alternative is extraordinarily clear may allow the mediator greater confidence and promote more willingness to be evaluative. In cases where there is no clear external alternative . . . a basis for evaluation may not exist.

Fifth, the method of evaluation may make a difference as well. For instance, if the case turns on the dollar amount of a damage award, one option would be for the mediator simply to state [her opinion] . . . An alternative would be to arrive at the same place through a series of questions . . . For instance, in a personal injury case one might ask,

- "What is the jury verdict range for these kinds of cases?"
- "What is the settlement range for these kinds of cases?"
- "Does the existence of a particular fact increase or decrease the likelihood of being at the top of that settlement range?"
- "If that fact has that influence, does it not then affect the real settlement range?"
- "If that is the real settlement range, does it not seem reasonable to lower your demand so that you . . . attract . . . the insurance company to meet you there . . . ?"

Such questioning can be expressed in an almost indicting spirit or . . . in the spirit of one . . . seeking to understand and massage the process in such a way that parties can come together. In any event, the mediator has never made a statement as to his or her opinion directly, but has reflected it in questions.

While others debate [the] abstract question of whether there is a place for evaluation in mediation, I invite you to join me in a more pragmatic examination of when and how some level of evaluation should be manifested.

QUESTIONS

1. Do Professor Lowry's arguments answer any of Professor Love's concerns? Which are not addressed?
2. The Supreme Court of Virginia has adopted the following rule for court mediators:

   The mediator may offer legal information if all parties are present, or separately if they consent, and shall inform unrepresented parties or those parties who are not accompanied by legal counsel about the importance of reviewing the mediator's legal information with legal counsel. Also, the mediator may offer evaluation of strengths and weakness of positions only if such evaluation is incidental to the facilitative role and does not interfere with the mediator's impartiality or the self-determination of the parties.

Does this rule respond to Professor Love's concerns about evaluation? Which ones?

b. How Should Evaluation Be Done?

Assuming that a mediator does evaluate the merits, how should it be carried out? Professor Lowry's article addresses this issue, but other points arise as well. One key issue is what substantive standard to apply to an evaluation. There are several possible criteria.

- A mediator can offer a *prediction of what will happen* if a particular issue or the entire matter is adjudicated. Here the mediator is not saying how she personally would decide the issue, but rather is assessing how a judge, jury, or arbitrator in that jurisdiction, with all *their* quirks and foibles, is likely to respond. The mediator may stress that she is simply offering a "weather forecast" about the atmosphere in some future courtroom, not advocating rain. This is the classic form of evaluation.

- Alternatively, a mediator can give an *expert judgment about what happened or a personal view of what is fair*. In effect the neutral is assuming the role of advisory arbitrator in the case. This is the most dangerous form of evaluation because the loser is likely to feel, with some justification, that the neutral has taken sides against him. In any case, the mediator's personal view of a case is usually irrelevant, since she is disqualified from sitting in judgment on it.

- Finally, a mediator may not evaluate the legal merits at all, but instead *assess the bargaining situation*. Here the neutral is giving an estimate of what each side needs to do in order to get an agreement, given the state of mind of the other party. A neutral might, for instance, say, "Given how they are feeling, my sense is that you'll need to go to six figures if you want a deal tonight."

Will a disputant's reaction to an evaluation differ depending on what issue the mediator evaluates, or the reasons the neutral gives for the opinion? Consider the following survey of parties' reactions to evaluation in court-connected mediation programs.

ROSELLE P. WISSLER, TO EVALUATE OR FACILITATE? PARTIES' PERCEPTIONS OF MEDIATION AFFECTED BY MEDIATOR STYLE
7 Disp. Resol. Mag. 35 (Winter 2001)

Some commentators have argued that if a mediator evaluates the merits of a case instead of using a more purely facilitative approach, the parties will feel that the mediator is less neutral. The parties will also have less opportunity to participate in the mediation process and to determine its outcome, will not gain a better understanding of the other side's position and their own interests, and will be less satisfied with mediation. Four recent studies of mediation in civil and domestic relations cases provide the opportunity to empirically test the effect of mediator style on parties' perceptions. . . .

One of the studies involved 708 general jurisdiction civil trial cases mediated by court-employed attorney-mediators in three Ohio courts. A second study of civil cases involved 698 cases mediated by volunteer attorney-mediators during Settlement Week in four different Ohio courts. The third and fourth studies involved domestic relations cases . . . mediated in 13 Maine courts [and] six Ohio courts . . . In this article, I report findings that occurred in [two] or more of the studies. No consistent differences were observed in the pattern of findings between the studies of civil cases and the studies of domestic relations cases.

When the mediator evaluated the merits of the case, no negative effects on parties' perceptions of mediation or the mediator were observed in any of the studies. Instead . . . parties were more likely to say that the mediation process was fair and the mediator understood their views. They were also more likely to say that they had enough opportunity to express their views, had input in determining the outcome, were satisfied with the outcome and gained a better understanding of their own interests. Importantly, parties who reported that the mediator evaluated the case did not feel more pressure to settle. In contrast, when the mediator recommended a particular settlement, parties were *less* likely to say that the mediation process was fair and the mediator was neutral [and] parties were more likely to feel pressured to settle. . . .

When the mediator suggested possible options for settlement, parties were more likely to say that the mediation process was fair and that the mediator was neutral and understood their view. By far the strongest and most consistently positive effects on parties' perceptions were observed when the mediator encouraged the parties to express their feelings and summarized what they said . . . (These actions were examined only in the domestic relations studies.)

In summary, if the mediators evaluated the merits of the case and even made some suggestions about possible settlements, the parties had more favorable perceptions of mediation with virtually no negative repercussions, as long as the mediators did not recommend a specific settlement. . . .

QUESTIONS

1. According to Professor Wissler, which kinds of evaluation are likely to lead to negative reactions from litigants and which are not? Assuming that parties do not object to certain forms of evaluation, does this answer Professor Love's concerns?

2. Imagine that you are the defense counsel in the student death case described in Chapter 9. Can you imagine circumstances in which you would want the mediator to give an evaluation? If so, what issue would you wish to be evaluated?

3. Now assume that you are counsel for the plaintiffs in the same case. How, if at all, might an evaluation be useful to your side?

4. If you agree with Professor Love, how would you want a mediator to respond to a situation in which you and your opposing counsel disagreed vehemently about the likely outcome at trial, and you thought the other lawyer was being unrealistic? What if your own client appeared to be unrealistically optimistic about her chances of winning in court?

PROBLEMS

Read the following exchanges, taken from the mediation of a commercial breach of warranty case. The plaintiff entered the mediation with a demand of $1.5 million, based on "hard" damages of about $250,000, a controversial argument to an additional $250,000 in "soft" damages, and a claim that the defendant was subject to treble damages under an unfair business practices statute. The defense has made no offer of settlement. The mediator has formed an initial impression that the plaintiff will face significant obstacles in proving liability, will find it difficult to establish damages beyond the

$250,000 in "hard" claims, and has little to no chance of winning its treble damages claim. As to each exchange, ask yourself:

- Is the mediator performing an "evaluation," or merely "reality testing"?
- What issues are being evaluated or tested?
- Is the mediator acting in a manner likely to incur resentment?

a. A Caucus Meeting with the Defense

Mediator: Well, all right, you heard the frustration from the plaintiff side, and you said you were surprised by it. What I'm hearing from (the vice president of the plaintiff company) is that he feels that there has never been a dialogue, acknowledgment of their difficulties and, most importantly to them, I guess, an offer of cash to settle this dispute. I'm hearing from you that you are not willing to make a specific settlement offer at this point. If you can't authorize me to bring back a specific number to the plaintiff . . . what I'd like to have is a feel for the range that you are in that I could communicate to them, so that they would have a sense of where things are going. . . .

Defense counsel: We will respond if they come down to a range of reasonableness, but their demand of $1.5 million is just in the stratosphere. I know that you're experienced, and I'm going to rely on you to digest what our view of the damages are and speak to them and maybe tell them what the real world is like: A million five is just *not* the real world.

Mediator: Well . . . What if the plaintiff were willing at this point to accept an amount that would allow them to recoup their out of pocket costs, and were perhaps looking for a little bit extra to put away in case their soft damages become a reality: Would you think that was a more reasonable place for them to be?

Defense counsel: Well, that would be a more reasonable place for them to *start,* and then we have to discount that number for the risk that they won't be able to prove liability at all. . . .

b. Meeting with the Plaintiff

Plaintiff counsel: The bottom line is—*what is their bottom line?* What's their offer? That's what we have been trying to get at for two years.

Mediator: I think there is a number that they would pay, which maybe will turn out to be a number that you would accept. But they haven't told me what it is yet. I don't think you're going to find out what they'll pay unless you get past this impasse. I see you as being at an impasse so far because they see you as "up in the clouds," and because you see them as completely recalcitrant "stones" who won't offer a thing. In fact, I don't see them as stones refusing to deal—I think they *will* deal. But they want to have some confidence that they are in the right universe with you, and if I can give them that confidence, then we'll get a number out of them . . . A better indication of what you're really looking for is what I need. . . .

c. Second Meeting with the Defense

Mediator: What is it going to cost to try this case?
Defense counsel: Oh, about $25,000.
Mediator: Wow, that's a bargain . . . You really think you can do it for that?
Counsel: Most of the discovery is done, and my rates are reasonable . . .

Mediator: Well, you're going to need an expert . . . They'll get an expert . . . It'll get expensive. . . .

d.   Meeting with the Defense Late in the Process

Inside counsel: You don't have to do this now, but if at some point if you could explain to me if you think we are being too optimistic about our chances at trial . . . I just don't see very much risk here.

Mediator: Well, I think the following . . . So far, the court has been willing to accept the plaintiff's case on their "res ipsa" theory that incidents of this type just don't occur without somebody being negligent. It looks as if the judge will let the case go to the jury on that theory. As a result, I think you run the risk that the jury will seize the appealing simplicity of the plaintiff's argument, and if it does it will find against you.

You have a credible, viable defense, and I think that this significantly reduces the likelihood that the plaintiff will prevail. But the likelihood that the other side will win on liability, given their res ipsa argument, is probably at least 50-50, and maybe better than that . . .

CHAPTER
11

Representing Clients in Mediation

A. INTRODUCTION

This chapter focuses on the lawyer's role in mediation. We have described how the mediation process can facilitate disputants' ability to communicate and bargain with each other. We will now explore how advocates can use the process to best advantage.

1. Identifying Goals

The first important issue to decide at the outset is what goal your client wants to achieve in a case. Is the client seeking the best possible monetary outcome? An imaginative solution? Repair of a troubled relationship? Your goals in mediation will strongly influence the approach you take to the process and how you relate to the mediator.

Disputants' goals in mediation vary widely. An organization that advocates the use of ADR in business disputes stresses that "Mediation provides a framework for parties to . . . achieve remedies that may be outside the scope of the judicial process . . . maintain privacy . . . preserve or minimize damage to relationships and reduce the costs and delay of dispute resolution" (CPR Institute, 1999). By contrast, San Francisco tort lawyer Guy Kornblum describes mediation as "an opportunity—a time for you, as the legal representative of your client, to avoid putting your client through the litigation 'mill' . . . and get results . . . It is a means of essentially 'selling' your client's lawsuit to a buyer, who buys off the expense and exposure of an ongoing lawsuit. The client has the money to begin the life restructuring process and has avoided the pressures and uncertainties of litigation. . . ."

If you see your objective as solving a problem or repairing a relationship, you will be inclined to treat the mediator almost as a member of your team. You will reveal interests and solicit the neutral's advice about how to achieve them. If the focus is on relationship repair, both the lawyer and mediator may gradually withdraw as the process progresses, so as to give the parties an opportunity to regain the ability to communicate positively. If, however, your goal is to obtain the best possible monetary settlement, your relationship with the mediator will be more complex. You can continue to take advantage of the neutral's knowledge, for example, by asking about hidden obstacles. And as long as you employ genuinely principled bargaining techniques, you will be able to work together cooperatively. At the point, however, that you begin to compete with the other side for the best possible terms, your goal and that of the neutral will diverge, because the mediator cannot take sides. Indeed, competitive bargainers talk about "spinning" a mediator to advance their client's objectives.

Legal mediators have significant power, whether or not they decide to use it. Although mediators cannot compel parties to settle, they can greatly influence the *process* of bargaining, opening opportunities for advocates to mold the process to their clients' needs. We believe that whatever their goals, lawyers can use the mediation process to advantage by approaching it actively and keeping in mind its special characteristics.

QUESTIONS

1. Which of these concepts of mediation goals felt most appropriate when you began this course? Has your perspective changed?
2. When you enter practice, what goals do you think your clients will wish to achieve through mediation? If in a particular case your view of the appropriate goal differs from your client's, how might you deal with the issue?

2. An Overview of Strategy

Over time we believe that more lawyers and parties will come to view bargaining primarily as a method of problem solving. At present, however, most attorneys who use mediation are litigators who see the process mainly as a way to settle cases through money bargaining. To prepare for what you are likely to encounter in practice, we will examine how counsel should approach a mediation process that includes interest-based elements, but is dominated by competitive bargaining over money. To provide you with tools to adapt to the future, however, we will also discuss how to represent a client in a process focused on problem solving.

a. Problem-Solving Approaches

HAROLD ABRAMSON, MEDIATION REPRESENTATION: ADVOCATING IN A PROBLEM-SOLVING PROCESS
1-3, NITA (2004)

The mediation process is indisputably different from other dispute resolution processes. Therefore, the strategies and techniques that have proven so effective in settlement conferences, arbitrations, and judicial trials do not work optimally in mediation. You need a different representation approach . . . Instead of advocating as a zealous adversary, you should advocate as a zealous problem-solver. . . .

[I]n mediation there is no third party decisionmaker, only a third party facilitator. The third party is not even the primary audience. The primary audience is the other side, who is surely not neutral and can often be quite hostile. In this different representational setting, the adversarial approach is less effective, if not self-defeating. Many sophisticated and experienced litigators realize that mediation calls for a different approach, but they still muddle through mediation sessions. They are learning on the job. . . .

As a problem-solver . . . you do more than just try to settle the dispute. You creatively search for solutions that go beyond the traditional ones based on rights, obligations, and precedent. Rather than settling for win-lose outcomes, you search for solutions that can benefit both sides. To creatively problem-solve in mediation, you develop a collaborative relationship with the other side and the mediator, and participate throughout the mediation process in a way that is likely to result in solutions that are enduring as well as inventive. . . .

You should be a constant problem-solver. It is relatively easy to engage in simple problem-solving moves such as responding to a demand with the question "why?" in order to bring to the surface the other party's interests. But it is much more difficult to stick to this approach throughout the mediation process, especially when faced with an adversarial, positional opponent. Trust the problem-solving approach. And, when the other side engages in adversarial tactics—a frequent occurrence in practice—you should react with problem-solving responses, responses that might even convert the other side into a problem-solver.

Also strive to create a problem-solving process when your mediator does not. Your mediator may fail to follow this approach (even though he professes to foster one) because he lacks the depth of experience or training to tenaciously maintain a consistent approach throughout the mediation process. Or, your mediator may candidly disclose his practice of deliberately switching tactics based on the needs of the parties—a philosophy that . . . undermines the problem-solving approach.

Finally, for the skeptics who think that problem-solving does not work for most legal cases because they are primarily about money, I offer three responses. First, the endless debate about whether or not legal disputes are primarily about money is distracting. Whether a dispute is largely about money varies from case to case. You have little chance of discovering whether your client's dispute is about more than money if you approach the dispute as if it is only about money. Such a preconceived view, backed by a narrowly focused adversarial strategy, will likely blind you to other parties' needs and inventive solutions. . . .

Second, if the dispute or any remaining issues at the end of the day turn out to be predominately about money, then at least you will have followed a representation approach that may have created a hospitable environment for dealing with the money issues. A hospitable environment can even be beneficial when there is no expectation of a continuing relationship between the disputing parties. Third, the problem-solving approach provides a framework for resolving money issues. . . .

In short, the problem-solving approach provides a comprehensive and coherent approach to representation that can guide you throughout the mediation process. By sticking to this approach, you will be prepared to deal with the myriad of unanticipated challenges that inevitably arise as mediation unfolds.

b. Commercial Mediation Processes

Most litigators approach what we call "commercial" mediation in a predominantly adversarial frame of mind. We begin with a reading that focuses on some errors that this mind-set can produce. Inherent in this listing, however, are messages about what lawyers can do to be effective in mediation. As you read, ask yourself:

- Have you made any of these mistakes in a roleplay exercise? Can you imagine making them in a real case?
- How do Tom Arnold's assumptions about the nature of mediation differ from those of Professor Abramson?

TOM ARNOLD, TWENTY COMMON ERRORS IN MEDIATION ADVOCACY
13 Alternatives 69 (1995)

Trial lawyers who are unaccustomed to being mediation advocates often miss important opportunities. Here are twenty common errors, and ways to correct them.

PROBLEM: WRONG CLIENT IN THE ROOM

CEOs settle more cases than vice presidents, house counsel, or other agents. Why? For one thing, they don't need to worry about criticism back at the office. Any lesser agent, even with explicit "authority," typically must please a constituency which was not a participant in the give and take of the mediation. That makes it hard to settle cases.

A client's personality also can be a factor. A "Rambo" who is highly self-confident, aggressive, critical, unforgiving, or self-righteous doesn't tend to be conciliatory. The best peace-makers show patience, creativity and sometimes tolerance for the mistakes of others. Of course, it also helps to know the subject.

PROBLEM: WRONG LAWYER IN THE ROOM

Many capable trial lawyers are so confident that they can persuade a jury of anything (after all, they've done it before) that they discount the importance of preserving relationships, as well as the common exorbitant costs and emotional drain of litigation. They can smell a "win" in the court room, and so approach mediation with a measure of ambivalence. Transactional lawyers, in contrast, having less confidence in their trial outcome, sometimes are better mediation counsel. At a minimum, parties should look for sensitive, flexible, understanding people who will do their homework, no matter what their job experience. Good preparation makes for more and better settlements. A lawyer who won't prepare is the wrong lawyer. Good mediation lawyers also should be good risk evaluators and not averse to making reasonable risk assumptions.

PROBLEM: WRONG MEDIATOR IN THE ROOM

Some mediators are generous about lending their conference rooms, but bring nothing to the table. Some of them determine their view of the case and like an arbitrator urge the parties to accept that view without exploring likely win-win alternatives. The best mediators can work within a range of styles described by Leonard L. Riskin. As Mr. Riskin described them, these styles fall along a continuum from being totally facilitative, to offering an evaluation of the case, to being highly directive and adjudicative. Ideally, mediators should fit the mediation style to the case and the parties before them, often moving from style to style as a mediation progresses, relatively more facilitative at the beginning and more instructive or directive as the end comes into view. Masters of the questioning process can render valuable services whether or not they have relevant substantive expertise.

When do the parties need an expert? When do they want an evaluative mediator, or someone of relevant technical experience who can cast meaningful lights and shadows on the merits of the case and alternative settlements? It may not always be possible to know and evaluate a mediator and fit the choice of mediator to your case. But the wrong mediator may fail to get a settlement another mediator might have finessed.

PROBLEM: WRONG CASE

Almost every type of case, from antitrust or patent infringement to unfair competition and employment disputes, is a likely candidate for mediation. Occasionally, cases don't fit the mold, not because of the substance of the dispute, but because one or both parties want to set a precedent. For example, a franchisor that needs a legal precedent construing a key clause that is found in 3,000 franchise agreements might not want to submit the case to mediation. Likewise, an infringement suit early in the life of an uncertain patent might be better resolved in court; getting the Federal Circuit stamp of validity could generate industry respect not obtainable from ADR.

PROBLEM: OMITTING CLIENT PREPARATION

Lawyers should educate their clients about the process and the likely questions the mediator will ask. At the same time, they need to understand that the other party (rather than the mediator) should be the focus of each side's presentation. [*Note:* Tom Arnold gives more detailed advice about client preparation later in this chapter.]

PROBLEM: NOT LETTING A CLIENT OPEN FOR HERSELF

At least as often as not, letting the properly coached client do most or even all of the opening, and tell the story in her own words, works much better than lengthy openings by the lawyer.

PROBLEM: ADDRESSING THE MEDIATOR INSTEAD OF THE OTHER SIDE

Most lawyers open the mediation with a statement directed at the mediator, comparable to opening statements to a judge or jury. Highly adversarial in tone, it overlooks the interests of the other side that gave rise to the dispute. Why is this strategy a mistake? The "judge" or "jury" you should be trying to persuade in mediation is not so much the mediator as the adversary. If you want to make the other party sympathetic to your cause, most often at least it is best not to hurt him. For the same reason, plenary sessions should demonstrate your client's humanity, respect, warmth, apologies, and sympathy. Stay away from inflammatory issues, which are better addressed by the mediator in private caucuses with the other side.

PROBLEM: MAKING THE LAWYER THE CENTER OF THE PROCESS

Unless the client is highly unappealing or inarticulate, the client should be the center of the process. The company representative for the other side may not have attended depositions, so is unaware of the impact your client could have on a judge or jury if the mediation fails. People pay more attention to appealing plaintiffs, so show them off.

Prepare the client to speak and be spoken to by the mediator and the adversary. He should be able to explain why he feels the way he does, why he is or is not responsible, and why any damages he *caused* are great or only peanuts. But he should also consider extending empathy to the other party.

PROBLEM: FAILURE TO USE ADVOCACY TOOLS EFFECTIVELY

You'll want to prepare your materials for maximum persuasive impact. Exhibits, charts, and copies of relevant cases or contracts with key phrases highlighted can be valuable visual aids. A ninety-second video showing one or more key witnesses in depositions making important admissions, followed by a readable-sized copy of an important document with some relevant language underlined, can pack a punch.

PROBLEM: TIMING MISTAKES

Get and give critical discovery, but don't spend exorbitant time or sums in discovery and trial prep before seeking mediation. Mediation can identify what's truly necessary discovery and avoid unnecessary discovery.

One of my own war stories: With a mediation under way and both parties relying on their perception of the views of a certain neutral vice president who had no interest in the case, I leaned over, picked up the phone, called the vice president, introduced myself as the mediator, and asked whether he could give us a deposition the following morning. "No," said he, "I've got a board meeting at 10:00." "How about 7:30 a.m., with a one-hour limit?" I asked. "It really is pretty important that this decision not be delayed." The parties took the deposition and settled the case before the 10:00 board meeting.

PROBLEM: FAILURE TO LISTEN TO THE OTHER SIDE

Many lawyers and clients seem incapable of giving open-minded attention to what the other side is saying. That could cost a settlement.

PROBLEM: FAILURE TO IDENTIFY PERCEPTIONS AND MOTIVATIONS

Seek first to understand, only then to be understood. [B]rainstorm to determine the other party's motivations and perceptions. Prepare a chart summarizing how your adversary sees the issues: Part of preparing for mediation is to understand your adversary's perceptions and motivations, perhaps even listing them in chart form. Here is an example, taken from a recent technology dispute:

Plaintiff's Perceptions:	*Defendant's Perceptions:*
Defendant entered the business because of my sound analysis of the market, my good judgment and convictions about the technology.	I entered the business based on my own independent analysis of the market and the appropriate technology that was different from plaintiff's. . . .
Defendant used me by pretending to be interested in doing business with me.	Plaintiff misled me with exaggerated claims that turned out to be false.
Defendant made a low-ball offer for my valuable technology. Another company paid me my asking price.	I made plaintiff a fair offer; I later paid less for alternative technology that was better.

PROBLEM: HURTING, HUMILIATING, THREATENING, OR COMMANDING

Don't poison the well from which you must drink to get a settlement. That means you don't hurt, humiliate, or ridicule the other folks. Avoid pejoratives like "malingerer," "fraud," "cheat," "crook," or "liar." You can be strong on what your evidence will be and still be a decent human being. All settlements are based upon trust to some degree. If you anger the other side, they won't trust you. This inhibits settlement.

The same can be said for threats, like a threat to get the other lawyer's license revoked for pursuing such a frivolous cause, or for his grossly inaccurate pleadings. Ultimatums destroy the process and destroy credibility. Yes, there is a time in mediation to walk out—whether or not you plan to return. But a series of ultimatums, or even one ultimatum, most often is counterproductive.

PROBLEM: THE BACKWARDS STEP

A party who offered to pay $300,000 before the mediation, but comes to the mediation table willing to offer only $200,000, injures its own credibility and engenders bad feelings from the other side. Without some clear and dramatic reasons for the reduction in the offer, it can be hard to overcome the damage done.

The backwards step is a powerful card to play at the right time—a walk away without yet walking out. But powerful devices are also dangerous. There are few productive occasions to use this one, and they tend to come late in a mediation. A rule of thumb: Unless you're an expert negotiator, don't do it.

PROBLEM: TOO MANY PEOPLE

Advisors — people to whom the decision-maker must display respect and courtesy, people who feel that since they are there they must put in their two bits worth — all delay mediation immeasurably. A caucus that with only one lawyer and vice president would take twenty minutes, with five people could take an hour and twenty minutes. What could have been a one-day mediation stretches to two or three.

This is one context in which I use the "one martini lunch." Once I think that everyone present understands all the issues, I will send principals who have been respectful out to negotiate alone. Most come back within three hours with an oral expression of settlement. Of course, the next step is to brush up on details they overlooked, draw up a written agreement and get it signed. But usually those finishing touches don't ruin the deal.

PROBLEM: CLOSING TOO FAST

A party who opens at $1 million and moves immediately to $500,000 gives the impression of having more to give. Rightly or wrongly, the other side probably will not accept the $500,000 offer because they expect more give. By contrast, moving from $1 million to $750,000, $600,000, $575,000, $560,000, $550,000, sends no message of yield below $500,000, and may induce a $500,000 proposal that can be accepted. The "dance" is part of communication. Skip the dance, lose the communication, and risk losing settlement at your own figure.

PROBLEM: FAILURE TO TRULY CLOSE

Unless parties have strong reasons to "sleep on" their agreement, to further evaluate the deal, or to check on possibly forgotten details, it is better to get some sort of enforceable contract written and signed before the parties separate. Too often, when left to think overnight and draft tomorrow, the parties think of new ideas that delay or prevent closing.

PROBLEM: BREACHING CONFIDENTIALITY

Sometimes parties to mediation unthinkingly, or irresponsibly, disclose in open court information revealed confidentially in a mediation. When information is highly sensitive, consider keeping it confidential with the mediator. Or if revealed to the adversary in a mediation where the case did not settle, consider moving before the trial begins for an order in limine to bind both sides to the confidentiality agreement.

PROBLEM: LACK OF PATIENCE AND PERSEVERANCE

The mediation "dance" takes time. Good mediation advocates have patience and perseverance.

PROBLEM: MISUNDERSTANDING CONFLICT

A dispute is a problem to be solved together, not a combat to be won.

QUESTIONS

1. Have you made any of Arnold's errors in an exercise in this course?
2. Which errors might you make in an actual case?
3. Can you recast Arnold's "errors" as statements about how to be effective in mediation?

B. ENTERING THE PROCESS

1. Whether to Mediate

The first strategy issue in mediation advocacy is whether to mediate at all. Although we have emphasized what mediation can contribute to bargaining efforts, it is not appropriate for every case or at every stage of a dispute. Arnold, for example, suggests that mediation may not make sense if one side would benefit greatly from obtaining a precedent to set a pattern for future disputes — and, of course, is confident that it will get a favorable one. In the reading that follows, John Cooley gives other criteria for whether or not to mediate.

JOHN COOLEY, MEDIATION ADVOCACY
38-39, NITA (2002)

[The following are] some situational indicators favorable to a mediated settlement of a dispute. The presence of only one of these indicators (and the absence of any unfavorable indicators) may be sufficient to trigger scheduling of mediation.

- The parties and counsel are agreeable to participating in the mediation process and desire a prompt settlement.
- The parties will have to maintain a direct or indirect relationship after resolution of a dispute.
- Sufficient discovery has occurred to make settlement discussions meaningful.
- The parties desire to minimize litigation costs.
- In addition to or instead of damages, the parties desire a remedy that is non-monetary or one that the court cannot provide.
- The parties wish to avoid establishing a judicial precedent or a judgment. . . .

- The parties or their lawyers have difficulty initiating negotiations with the other side, lack adequate negotiation skills, or are deadlocked. . . .
- The parties have differing appraisals of the facts of a case.
- Resolution requires complex trade-offs.
- The parties want the matter settled confidentially.

[By contrast, the] presence of one of these indicators could be a sufficient basis to decline using mediation to resolve a particular dispute.

- A party cannot effectively represent its best interests and will not be represented by counsel at the mediation sessions.
- The parties have a history of acting in bad faith in negotiations.
- A party seeks to establish legal precedent or a judgment with preclusive effect.
- Significant parties are unwilling to mediate.
- The parties are engaged in a dispute directly affecting the public interest, and the government is not represented.
- A party is threatening to press criminal charges.
- One or more parties stand to gain from a strategy of delay.
- A party needs more formal discovery to obtain necessary information. . . .
- The parties have rigid assessments of the law applicable in the case and desire the court to decide who is right and who is wrong, legally.
- A third party neutral needs to make an immediate decision to protect the interests of a disputant or of the public.

It is worth bearing in mind that Cooley's factors apply mainly to decisions about whether to use mediation for the purpose of settling a dispute. Lawyers sometimes elect to mediate for other reasons, such as to set up an efficient discovery plan or to improve the parties' overall relationship. The fact that a settlement does not appear realistic at a certain point, in other words, is not always a reason to reject mediation.

2. When to Mediate

Assuming that mediation is appropriate, when is the right time to undertake it? Sometimes there is no choice: Parties may be required to mediate by a contract clause or court rule, and in such circumstances the issue of timing is academic. If a disputant does have a choice, however, the issue is an important one. To answer the question you and your client must again consider your goals for the process. If your primary objective is to solve a problem or restore a relationship, it is usually best to mediate as soon as possible. If not, the parties' positions are likely to harden and they may replace the relationship with new ones, making a repair nearly impossible.

If relationships are not a priority, then the issue of timing is more complex. By delaying mediation an advocate may be able to improve his client's bargaining position, for instance, by winning a round in court. But in doing so the client will incur costs, and its opponent may react in kind. As we know, the American legal system does not ordinarily allow litigants to recover their legal expenses and makes no provision for the nonlegal costs of conflict. As a result, parties must "swallow" any expenses that they incur in an effort to improve their bargaining position. The phenomenon of loss aversion then becomes an even greater obstacle to agreement.

Disputants tend to enter legal mediation at particular points along the litigation continuum, in particular when they face either a sharp increase in cost or the risk of a significant loss in adjudication. Natural points for mediation are before a legal case is filed, before the start of costly discovery, before a significant court ruling, and just before trial.

Before a Formal Legal Action Is Filed

A supplier and customer involved in a dispute over the quality of goods supplied under a contract, for example, may opt to mediate in order to minimize the damage to a profitable relationship and avoid the expense of hiring outside law firms. Alternatively, a discharged employee may decide to mediate before filing a charge of discrimination with a state agency in order to avoid the inflamed feelings that often result from such a step. Whenever disputants decide to enter mediation before filing a law suit they accept a trade-off: Each side has less information about the case, but also has avoided the cost of litigating to obtain it. Parties appear to be electing to enter mediation before filing suit with increasing frequency; this is what occurred, for instance, in the student death case described in Chapter 9.

After Preliminary Discovery

Parties may file suit and undertake some discovery, for example, an exchange of documents, but enter mediation at the point they face more costly and adversarial processes such as depositions. In essence, the parties' common wish to avoid a higher level of conflict serves as a "settlement event." Thus Jeffrey Senger of the U.S. Justice Department has written that:

> One approach . . . is to follow the 80-20 rule: 80 percent of the relevant information that parties learn from discovery often comes from the first 20 percent of the money they spend. Tracking down the last, difficult-to-obtain data is the most expensive part of discovery . . . If parties conduct initial core discovery, they may find all they need to know in order to resolve the case appropriately. Following this approach, parties can agree to take abbreviated depositions of the key witnesses and then proceed to ADR. If necessary, they also may serve certain essential interrogatories and requests for production of vital documents. Often this will give them everything they need to determine their negotiation position with reasonable accuracy. . . . (Senger, 2004)

"In the Shadow" of a Significant Ruling

Parties sometimes elect to mediate when they are approaching a significant stage in the court process, such as a motion for summary judgment. In such situations, each side knows that its bargaining position will either improve or deteriorate, depending on the court's decision. One might think that if one side were willing to mediate because it fears a loss, its opponent would refuse in hope of obtaining a gain. As we have seen, however, humans are generally more sensitive to losing than to winning, and as a result both parties in a case are often motivated to mediate at the point they face the risk of a significant loss in adjudication.

Shortly Before Trial

This has been the traditional point at which to pursue settlement, either through direct bargaining or mediation, for several reasons. First, as trial approaches, attorneys must prepare intensively, imposing higher costs on them or their clients. Second, trial represents the ultimate win-or-lose event, triggering feelings of loss aversion. Finally, there are cultural assumptions about the "right" time to broach settlement: In the legal community, this used to mean that mentioning mediation early in a case was considered a sign of weakness, while raising the issue on the eve of trial was acceptable, an assumption that no longer appears to be true.

3. How to Initiate the Process

In the past, lawyers were often reluctant to propose mediation, out of concern that an adversary would see it as a sign of weakness. That attitude has largely disappeared — as one litigator remarked in Chapter 9, many lawyers now find it easier to propose mediation than to suggest direct negotiation. Lawyers have several options for initiating the process.

Point out That Settlement Discussions Are Inevitable

Given the phenomenon of the "vanishing" civil trial described in Chapter 1, settlement discussions are nearly inevitable at some point. You like to litigate — it's what you do for a living. But given that the parties will be talking settlement sooner or later in any event, why not do it now and save everyone the distraction and expense of litigation?

Rely on a Policy

If a lawyer represents an organization that has a uniform policy of exploring ADR early in every dispute (see, for example, the "CPR Pledge" at the beginning of Chapter 19), she can cite the policy as the reason for suggesting mediation. More than 4,000 companies have signed this pledge, and 1,500 law firms have signed a commitment to explore ADR with their clients in appropriate cases. For the text of both pledges, see *www.cpradr.org*.

Cite a Rule

Some court systems require counsel to discuss ADR or to make a good faith effort at settlement in every case. Even if no judicial mandate exists, lawyers may consider contacting an ADR administrator or clerk of court, and ask that the judge in the case suggest mediation to both sides.

Invite a Third Party to Do It

Another way to have a third party play "matchmaker" is to ask a private neutral to approach an adversary and advocate mediation. Although the opponent will probably know that opposing counsel initiated the contact, this allows lawyers to avoid the burden of "selling" the process to a reluctant adversary.

So far we have assumed that the issue is to persuade one's opponent to mediate. In some situations, though, the major obstacle is one's own client. In the words of litigator David Stern:

> There are no hard and fast rules as to when that perfect moment has arrived to mediate, [but] one point is clear. Before you begin, recognize that the first obstacle to starting the dialogue early may well be your own client, particularly if you have not represented him in the past. He may wonder if you lack confidence in yourself or the case if you push for settlement too early. On the other hand, if you don't mention settlement to the more sophisticated client, he may well wonder whether you are looking to "milk" a case that will likely never be tried. As such, begin with the adversary only after you have reached a consensus with your own client. . . . (Stern, 1998)

C. STRUCTURING THE MEDIATION

How mediation is structured is often crucial to its success. In each case an advocate must think about the following issues.

1. Selecting a Mediator

The most important issue in arranging for mediation, apart perhaps from agreeing on who will attend the process, is to select the right neutral. We have seen that mediators vary in characteristics such as the breadth or narrowness of their approach, substantive expertise, and willingness to use facilitative or evaluative techniques. When selecting a legal mediator you will typically be able to choose among former or practicing litigators, transactional lawyers, and ex-judges, as well as professionals in fields ranging from psychotherapy to civil engineering. Your goal should be to select a neutral with qualities that match the needs of your case.

One approach is to think about what barriers are making it difficult to negotiate directly with the other side. The answer will give you an insight into what qualities a neutral will need in order to help you overcome them. If, for example, the key problem is that your opponent has an abrasive or insulting manner, then a mediator with strong process skills may be the best choice. If your own client needs "cover" to justify a compromise to an outsider, then an evaluative neutral may be helpful. If the parties are very angry or need to repair their relationship, then a neutral with skills in counseling may be what is called for. In many situations more than one barrier exists, calling for a mediator with a blend of abilities.

DAVID S. ROSS, STRATEGIC CONSIDERATIONS IN CHOOSING A MEDIATOR: A MEDIATOR'S PERSPECTIVE
2 J. Alt. Disp. Res. in Empl. 7 (Spring 2000)

Because the mediation process is only as effective as the mediator who manages it, choosing the right mediator is critical. The mediator selection process demands a thoughtful balancing of many criteria, including:

- Mediation experience
- Mediation process skills
- Substantive expertise
- Reputation for neutrality
- Creativity
- Strong interpersonal skills and an ability to connect with people, and
- The ability to help parties reach agreement

Since every case is different, it makes sense to prioritize these criteria based on the needs of the case and parties. . . .

SUBSTANTIVE EXPERTISE

People often ask whether they should choose a mediator with substantive expertise or one with strong process skills. A short answer is "both." A longer answer is that in most employment disputes, process skills count as much or more than substantive expertise. However, more mediators are specializing in specific substantive areas [such as] employment law, so parties now can more easily choose a mediator with both substantive expertise and process skills.

REFERENCES

Participants should take the time to speak directly with individuals—ideally both lawyers and principals—who have worked with a proposed mediator to learn their candid assessment of the mediator's strengths and weaknesses, mediation style, and overall effectiveness. Most mediators provide references upon request. If they do not, then press the mediator to do so.

OPPOSING COUNSEL'S RECOMMENDATIONS

What should you do if opposing counsel proposes a mediator? There may be a strong instinct to reject such a proposal. My experience suggests that sophisticated lawyers should seriously consider mediators proposed by opposing counsel, honestly hashing out the advantages and disadvantages of various candidates. . . .

Attorneys should consult with their clients when choosing a mediator . . . Encouraging client participation in the mediator selection process empowers clients. Finally, and perhaps most importantly, it builds trust in the attorney-client relationship and in the mediation process, promoting a sense of shared responsibility in making mediation work.

Assuming you have identified the skills you want in a mediator, how can you determine whether a particular candidate possesses them? Common sources include recommendations from colleagues, references, and the opposing party's suggestions. In addition, companies and law firms that engage regularly in mediation sometimes create private data banks with information about their experience with various neutrals. Some organizations and government agencies develop rosters of mediators who are approved to handle their cases. Mediators also provide prospective clients with information. Such documents typically emphasize the neutral's qualifications, but advocates may be able to read between the lines to identify potential gaps as well. In addition most mediators are willing to talk informally with attorneys who express interest in hiring them.

> *Example:* In the student death case described in Chapter 9, counsel for both sides gave careful thought to selecting the mediator. Defense counsel decided to allow the Kruegers to select the neutral. In part this was because the Kruegers insisted on the right to do so, and in part because the defense respected the plaintiff counsel's ability to choose wisely. The Kruegers selected a mediator who regularly handled personal injury cases for claimants, but they had other concerns as well. It was important that the mediator be willing to work with counsel to customize the process, and that he or she be respected by the defense. Plaintiff counsel also knew that the discussions would be extremely emotional — in the course of the process both the lawyers and parties found themselves in tears — and it was therefore crucial that the mediator have the ability to absorb and manage intense anger and grief. The mediator's final qualification was unique: Counsel learned that he had once lost a college-age son himself.

QUESTIONS

1. Texas mediator Eric Galton has suggested that transactional lawyers are better advocates in mediation because "they negotiate better, more creatively and are more acutely aware of business solutions which may be advantageous to their clients."
   a. Assuming that this is true, what types of legal disputes would a transactional lawyer be best suited to mediate?
   b. What might you sacrifice by selecting a transactional lawyer rather than a litigator as your mediator?
2. The other side in a case proposes as a mediator someone with whom they have mediated more than a dozen times. What should you do in response?

3. If you wished to propose a mediator with whom you had worked repeatedly, what would be the best way to do so?
4. You represent a party in an exercise assigned by your teacher. You have agreed to mediate, and are now in the process of selecting a neutral. What qualities would you look for in a mediator for your case? If you can obtain biographies of mediators in your area, review some and prioritize the candidates in terms of attractiveness.

2. Ensuring the Presence of Necessary Participants

We know that mediation is an intensely personal process. As a result, the presence of the right people is perhaps the single most important factor in its success. Who these people are in a particular case will depend again on your objectives.

- If the primary goal is to repair a personal relationship, then the presence of the principals themselves, to talk out their problems and regain the ability to relate productively to each other, is usually essential.
- If the parties' relationship is attenuated, as, for example, in the case of a rent dispute between a corporate landlord and a former commercial tenant, the presence of principals may be less important.
- If the objective is to work out an imaginative solution, then it is important that the participants be capable of thinking "outside the box" and know enough about the parties' interests to identify and flesh out useful options. Working out a novel solution to a business dispute, for instance, may require executives rather than lawyers.
- If the only goal is to settle a legal claim on the best possible monetary terms, as is true in many negligence cases, then the primary concern is probably that the bargainers arrive at the table with sufficient authority.

JERRY SPOLTER, A MEDIATOR'S TIP: TALK TO ME!
The Recorder 4 (March 8, 2000)

This may come as a surprise to even the most seasoned mediation participants, but there is nothing wrong with communicating ex parte with a mediator or prospective mediator. In fact, it's usually the smart and right thing to do to secure the best result for your client. So don't be bashful. Talk to your mediator.

A recent mediation session I conducted highlights what can happen when you leave your mediator in the dark. Everything went great for about five hours . . . The joint session was textbook material, with lots of helpful information exchanged; the private caucuses peeled away postured "positions" to reveal the parties' real interests. And then it happened: Although the physician accused of malpractice was in the room, the doc wouldn't make a move until his personal attorney gave the OK.

Unfortunately, the personal attorney was on a chairlift in the Sierra with a dead battery in her cell phone. And since this was a malpractice case requiring the doc's consent, "my" mediation was suddenly in trouble. To make matters worse, the doc's insurance representative had to consult two "invisible-hierarchy" decision-makers to discuss increasing authority.

If only I had received a "heads up" beforehand, we could have resolved the authority problems in advance and taken advantage of the momentum we had generated that day to settle the case. (Instead, the parties are now scurrying around trying to acquire the necessary authority to put Humpty-Dumpty back together again.) . . .

There is a good deal that lawyers can do beforehand to ensure that the right people are at a mediation.

Parties

If the parties are individuals, then they should be personally present. Corporations and other organizations, however, must act through agents. Some corporate representatives are positively harmful to the settlement process: An example would be an executive who had a personal stake in defending the decision at issue in the dispute. Others may lack the right kind of expertise: An outside litigator, for instance, might be a good representative in a process that turned on the trial value of a claim, but wrong for a mediation that focused on resolving an employee's grievance and bringing her back to work.

When parties are represented by agents, and especially when a nonparty such as an insurer is involved, advocates face a challenge to ensure that the people who come to the table have the authority to make the decisions needed to resolve the case. Negotiators routinely claim to have "full authority," but in practice their ability to agree is usually limited. Bargainers may arrive at mediation with:

- "best-case" authority (the ability to accept the terms their side believes that their opponent *ought* to accept),
- "reasonable" authority (their estimate of what the opponent at the end of the day *will* agree to), or
- "worst-case" authority (the ability to agree, if necessary, to an outcome very close to the other side's *actual* offer going into mediation).

In practice disputants usually conceal or misrepresent their authority, for fear that it will be taken as their "bottom line." It is often useful, however, to touch on the issue with an opposing negotiator, and perhaps to ask about his role in the organization, in order to estimate his ability to make decisions.

Advisors and Stakeholders

People other than parties may also play key roles in decision making at mediation. A husband, for instance, may look to his wife for advice, or a company may be unable to make a deal without permission from its insurer. There is no easy way to resolve this issue. Wise lawyers know that they may need to bargain for the presence of the right person, and that the mediator can help with the process. In asking a neutral for assistance in securing the presence of key decision makers, lawyers benefit from several forces. First, having agreed to mediate, disputants usually feel an interest in establishing a good relationship with the mediator. Mediators, too, acquire a stake in the process, and have a bias toward inclusion. Better, a typical legal mediator will think to ask for the presence of a person who later proves unnecessary than to find oneself lacking a key decision maker at crunch time. Advocates can take advantage of their opponent's wish to humor a mediator and the neutral's own investment in the process by agreeing to mediate, and then enlisting the neutral's help to shape the field of bargaining.

> *Example:* A high-tech company was suing a former employee who had left and then recruited her software team to join her at a competitor. For technical reasons the new employer was not a party to the litigation, although it had agreed to indemnify the employee for any liability in the matter. The plaintiff company and the employee agreed to mediate, but the competitor's general counsel refused to attend, arguing that her company was not a party. In response, the plaintiff lawyer first agreed to mediate and then lobbied the mediator to secure the presence of the missing lawyer. He began his effort by stressing to the mediator how important the general counsel would be to the success of "our" process. The general counsel eventually agreed to join all sessions of the mediation by conference call, and her presence proved crucial to reaching agreement.

QUESTIONS

1. Neutrals come to mediation from very different careers. What background might make a mediator either more or less willing to take active steps to bring the right people into the process?
2. How could you test for this quality when selecting a neutral?

3. *Drafting an Agreement to Mediate*

Lawyers who undertake private mediation processes usually enter into written agreements that set out the ground rules for the process, and court-affiliated programs typically deal with such issues through a combination of agreements and program rules. Attorneys can deal with the following issues through a mediation agreement.

- Who are the parties?
- What rules of confidentiality will apply and who will be bound by them?
- Who will pay the cost of mediation?
- Under what conditions can the mediator evaluate legal issues in the case?
- How can a party terminate its participation?
- Can the mediator be called to testify in a later proceeding?
- Is the mediator liable for wrongful or negligent acts?
- What will be the status of ongoing litigation while the mediation occurs?

Examples of typical mediation agreements appear on the Web site.

4. *Influencing the Format*

Mediation can occur in a wide variety of formats. The parties, for example, can choose to meet entirely in joint session or rely heavily on caucusing. They can bargain with each other directly or through attorneys. The best format for a particular case again depends on your overall goal.

- In a case focused on relationship repair, you will probably want the clients to have as much opportunity as possible to communicate directly. It may make sense, for instance, to arrange for the principals to talk without counsel present, or perhaps to remain in joint session throughout the process.
- In a highly emotional case it may be important for a party to meet with the mediator ahead of time to begin venting, and to carefully structure the party's interactions with the other side.
- In complex cases it may be necessary to arrange for enough time for each side to present a lengthy opening statement, perhaps supported by computerized exhibits or comments from an expert.

These issues are discussed in more detail below. For now, it is important to bear in mind that experienced advocates often ask for changes in the usual format of commercial mediation. If you see a reason to vary the format, you should alert the mediator to this before the process begins.

D. PREPARING TO MEDIATE

Once advocates have agreed on an overall structure for a mediation, they should focus on their participation in the process. This requires planning not only what the lawyer will do, but also the roles of the client and other members of the team. Preparation includes at least three areas: developing a negotiation plan, exchanging information, and coaching clients about what to do and say.

1. *Developing a Negotiating Plan*

Texts often speak of the art of "mediation advocacy," but you now know that the process consists primarily of informal negotiation. Lawyers usually make an opening statement at the outset of the process, and this is a form of advocacy, but the rest of the mediation is typically taken up with discussions and bargaining. You should therefore plan for mediation in much the same way that you would for a direct negotiation. You will wish, for example, to consider each side's alternatives to agreement, the principles that you can cite and those that your opponent will rely on, the parties' underlying interests, and potential options for settlement. If your primary goal is to obtain the best possible monetary outcome, your plan will be similar to that of a competitive bargainer. If you see the purpose of the process as solving a common problem, then you are likely to focus on the parties' interests and ways to address them. Whatever your goal, however, you will need to modify your approach to bargaining in order to take advantage of the special aspects of mediation. The readings below look at mediation planning from several perspectives.

A Mediator's Perspective

What constitutes a "winning" strategy in mediation, and is it possible that the other advocate could play a role in achieving it? Consider this advice from a commercial mediator.

JEFFREY G. KICHAVEN, HOW ADVOCACY FITS IN EFFECTIVE MEDIATION
17 Alternatives 60 (1999)

Clients and attorneys generally have one of two conceptions of what it means to win in mediation. Some define winning as "clobbering the other side." Others see it as "the satisfaction of our own needs," regardless of whether the other side suffers along the way. In the litigation context, and in many others, clients often start out in a "clobbering" mode. They may believe they have been "done wrong," and want revenge. And more revenge. And more.

This is a serious problem for lawyers. Such a client is almost never satisfied with the result, with the process, or with counsel's performance, because the other side, no matter how badly clobbered, rarely has suffered enough. A vengeful client . . . has a hard time planning, in advance, the specific result to be achieved or the goal against which success or failure will be measured. No matter what happens to the other side, it could always have been worse! These clients believe that their attorneys have failed them. Yet the lawyers have done all that they can. Far better is the situation in which the client focuses on the satisfaction of his or her own needs. This client is better able to give clear instructions and if this client's own goals are satisfied, it doesn't matter very much whether the other side suffers a lot, a little, or even at all.

Mediation has an important role in the pursuit of this second concept of the win . . . In the hands of skilled mediators and counsel, the process can be designed to minimize the incentives to clobber and enhance the likelihood that the parties will engage in goal-oriented, client-satisfying negotiation.

In mediation after mediation, clients and lawyers come to change their negotiating tune. The desire for revenge is trumped by a desire for finality: A desire to eliminate the newly perceived enhanced risks of continued litigation; to eliminate the certainty of the mental, emotional and financial drains of conflict; and to get on with one's career and life with a "bird in the hand" settlement . . . The key to all this, however, is profoundly counterintuitive. In mediation, your effectiveness as an advocate will vary in direct proportion to that of opposing counsel, not the inverse proportion you might expect in the generally "clobbering" mode of traditional litigation.

In this sense, you and opposing counsel have become each other's best friends. You have given each other's clients what you often cannot give your own: The means by which one can achieve a balanced perspective . . . with the craving to clobber taking a back seat. Let's face it: It's tough for a lawyer to break bad news to his or her own client. It's tough on clients, too, to go beyond denial, even when that bad news is broken with candor and compassion. Yet in virtually every unsettled case, bad news needs to be broken and accepted. In some cases, it's the other side that needs it. In others, it's your side. In most cases, there's plenty of bad news to go around.

In mediation, you and opposing counsel have found uniquely qualified messengers to deliver this essential communication—each other. The mediator works along with you to make sure that the bad news is not only delivered to your client, but also received. Effective mediation advocates, therefore, must be able to hold both conceptions of "the win" in mind simultaneously, side by side, each in its appropriate place, each conception taking the forefront when appropriate.

QUESTION

What could you do as an advocate to enhance the likelihood that the other side's arguments would help to educate your own unrealistic client?

A Litigator's Viewpoint

The following suggestions about preparation come from a litigator.

ROBERT M. SMITH, ADVOCACY IN MEDIATION: A DOZEN SUGGESTIONS
26 San Francisco Att'y 14 (June/July 2000)

Your strongest ally, if you can make him or her an ally, is the mediator. It is the mediator's neutral voice that is most powerful in carrying your argument to the other side. This is true even if the mediator asks a lawyer to put on the chalkboard the strongest points of the case, then unveils the board to the other side.

The mediator knows you—indeed, everyone—are trying to manipulate, or con, him or her. Manipulation is as much a given as the coffee machine. But often—perhaps usually—the mediator is aware of the con. Good advocates know when to stop the con, show some trust, and make a straighter, and more reasonable, argument. Honesty can buy an advantage.

PLAY THE ODDS

When you go to a commercial mediation, there is, statistically, close to an eighty-five percent chance of settling the case. This means you should probably prepare as if the mediation session will be the last step in the case, and prepare your client accordingly. To tell the client, for example, that we are all just going through the motions and then find yourself in serious end-game bargaining is not prudent.

BLACK-TIE AFFAIR

Often—we all know this—lawsuits bobble along like a play in search of a theater; they need a defining event before both parties and lawyers get serious.

Mediation is an event — probably the event. If the mediator is effective, every-one will focus on the matter in a way that they haven't before.

THE ART OF SCRIBBLING

This is the time to do your best brief. Mediators read them — they get paid to. And this may be all they know about the case before you troop in. The mediator is likely to ensure that the parties, as well as the lawyers, see the brief and consider your most forceful arguments, or what a neutral sees as your most forceful arguments. It may be worth considering their impact on the plaintiff or the defendant when sections are pointed out to them.

SHARING CAN BE BEAUTIFUL

You might consider whether you want to give a copy of the brief to the other side, as well as to the mediator. But you can give only a portion of the brief to the other side — or the whole brief, with only a secret annex going to the mediator (for instance, "I think the claims rep was himself a party to a similar squabble two years ago"). The process is what you make of it. Flexible, it bends to your imaginative sculpting.

WE DON'T ACCEPT CASH HERE

Some have pointed out the power of an apology, appropriately timed and tendered. But advocacy may also involve asking for a non-economic concession — even one you know you likely won't get; it may put other demands in a new, or reframed, perspective.

ABOUT REFRAMING

Once discussions have foundered, the mediator knows that . . . the parties are not likely to move on their own. It is up to the mediator to step back and find a new perspective or approach. You should anticipate the possible reframing, or you may not like the suddenly unfamiliar perspective. Be reframed, not hung.

A LAS CINCO DE LA TARDE

"At five in the afternoon" is a repetitive line in a poem by Federica Garcia Lorca. It has to with a death, not mediation. But I sometimes think of it when discussions bog down after hours of negotiation because it is about five in the afternoon that the role of poetic imagination is sometimes called into play in mediations. You hope the mediator did not lose his or her imagination in the second year of law school; part of what you are paying for is creativity. But when the clock strikes — or beeps — in a soundless room, your own imagina-tive suggestion may prove sublime advocacy.

A Problem-Solving Approach

The following reading is addressed to problem-solving advocates, but many of the points apply to other forms of mediation as well.

HAROLD ABRAMSON, MEDIATION REPRESENTATION: ADVOCATING IN A PROBLEM-SOLVING PROCESS

221-222, NITA (2004)

[*Note:* Professor Abramson recommends that advocates begin their preparation by analyzing the overall nature of the dispute, doing any necessary research, and resolving issues of structure such as who will attend. Having done this, lawyers should prepare for the actual process of mediation by considering the following issues.]

. . . Identify three components of the mediation representation formula: interests, impediments, and ways the mediator might contribute to resolving the dispute.

1. *Goal: Identify Interests to Meet: Your Client's*
   Goal: Identify Interests to Accommodate: The Other Side's
2. *Goal: Identify Impediments to Overcome* . . .
3. *Identify Mediator's Possible Contributions to Resolving the Dispute*

A. APPROACHES TO DISPUTE

You want the mediator to use the following approaches [select among the options for each item]:

- Manage the process by primarily facilitating, primarily evaluating, or following a transformative approach.
- View the problem broadly or narrowly.
- Involve the clients actively or restrictively.
- Use caucuses extensively, selectively, or not at all.

B. USEFUL TECHNIQUES

You want the mediator to use his or her techniques to [select one or more]:

- Facilitate the negotiation of a problem-solving process.
- Promote communication through questioning and listening techniques.
- Deal with the emotional dimensions of the dispute.
- Clarify statements and issues through framing and reframing.
- Generate options for settlement (e.g., brainstorming).
- Separate process of inventing settlement options from selecting them.
- Deal with power inequalities.
- Overcome the impediments to settlement.

- Overcome the chronic impediment of clashing views of the court outcome.
- Close any final gaps (consider your preferred methods for closing gaps).
- Deal with _____ . . . .

QUESTIONS

1. Assume that you are a competitive advocate in your most recent roleplay, or in a specific exercise assigned by your teacher. Your goal is to get the best possible money outcome for your client. How would you answer the questions on Professor Abramson's checklist?
2. Now assume that you have a problem-solving orientation. How would your answers change?

2.   Exchanging Information

One of the key aspects of any negotiation is exchanging information, and one of mediation's effects is to enhance the flow of data between the parties. This process often begins well before disputants actually meet to mediate. As an advocate, you will need to think about two types of information:

- What data does your client need to make a good settlement decision?
- What information will help your adversary to agree to the outcome you are seeking?

If necessary, you should be prepared to enlist the mediator's help in persuading the other side to provide you with data. The neutral may also be able to help you explain to your own client why in this context it is a good idea to give an opponent some "free discovery."

What information is relevant depends again on your goals. If the process turns on money, then legal evidence and arguments are likely to be key. If your purpose is to repair a relationship, knowing the "why" behind a disputed action will be important. If the objective is to create a new business arrangement, then financial data may be more useful. As a rule, negotiations that focus on imaginative options require a broader base of information than discussions that revolve solely around money.

a.   Exchanging Data with the Other Party

Disputants usually need less data to mediate effectively than they would require to try the same case. Still, especially if parties mediate early in a dispute, one side may lack information that is necessary to make an informed decision. Without that data the party may not be able to assess the value of its litigation alternative or determine whether an imaginative option is viable. An insurance adjuster, for example, may not be able to obtain the authority needed to settle a claim without documents verifying the plaintiff's medical expenses, while a plaintiff lawyer might be unable to accept a reasonable settlement offer without assurances that there is no "smoking gun" in the defendant's files.

In litigation there is ordinarily no reason for a party to show its hand to an adversary, but in mediation disputants know that providing information will increase their chances of reaping a good settlement. Equally important, they know that the mediator is present to help ensure that the exchange will be mutual. As a result, parties in mediation often provide each other with surprising amounts of information.

Example: A large computer manufacturer asserted a claim against its chip supplier, arguing that the chips had an unreasonably high rate of failure, requiring the manufacturer to make expensive repairs to servers in the field. The parties agreed that the problem existed, and that it was caused by defects in the compound used to finish the chips. The chip maker had bought the compound from a reputable supplier and had no way to foresee the problem. Still, the computer manufacturer asserted a right to be compensated for its costs, relying on a document whose interpretation the chip maker hotly disputed.

Inside counsel for the two companies agreed to meet informally to mediate the claim. When they exchanged mediation briefs, however, it quickly became apparent that the manufacturer's $15 million claim was both unclear — the chip maker could not understand how losses had reached such a level — and impossible for the chip maker to satisfy — it would go bankrupt if it had to pay such an amount.

With the mediator's assistance, the parties agreed to postpone the mediation for a month and exchange data. The manufacturer agreed to supply documents verifying its damage claim and the chip maker undertook to provide information about its financial situation. The chip maker also volunteered data about products under development, so that the manufacturer could consider taking part of a settlement in the form of discounts on future purchases.

QUESTIONS

1. What types of data gathered before mediation might help an advocate avoid the "twenty common errors" described earlier in the chapter by Tom Arnold?
2. Assume that you are the lawyer in an exercise assigned by your teacher. What additional information, beyond the facts stated in the problem instructions, would you want in order to mediate well? What data might the other attorney ask for?

b. Educating the Mediator

In small cases and court-connected programs, neutrals sometimes arrive at mediation knowing almost nothing about the dispute. In privately conducted mediations, however, lawyers typically make an effort to orient, and begin to persuade, the neutral in advance. Pre-mediation communications can take at least three forms: written statements, joint meetings, and private conversations.

Written Statements

Parties commonly give a mediator written statements, sometimes called mediation "briefs" or "submissions," to read in advance. As they prepare their statements, advocates should consider:

- Is it better to prepare a statement or use an existing document? A customized document has obvious advantages, but particularly in smaller cases it is appropriate to use an existing document or pleading that summarizes the party's views.
- Is it preferable to submit the statement on an ex parte basis or exchange it with opposing counsel? Mediators usually prefer that lawyers exchange statements, so that they are free to discuss the points one side makes with the other. Even if you exchange statements, however, you are ordinarily free to write or call the neutral to discuss sensitive issues privately.

What should be in the mediation statement? A mediator is likely to be interested in knowing, among other points:

- How did the dispute arise?
- What are the key factual and legal issues?
- What nonlegal concerns are present?
- What barriers have made direct bargaining difficult?
- What is the status of any legal proceedings? Is there a history of bargaining?
- Who are the key decision makers in the dispute?

Organizational Discussions

In complex cases mediators often schedule joint meetings with counsel to discuss organizational questions, such as who will be present at the mediation. Such meetings usually occur by conference call, but they are sometimes convened in person. Organizational meetings are typically limited to lawyers, but clients and experts may occasionally participate as well.

Private Conversations

Mediators sometimes take the initiative to talk with advocates before a mediation session. Such conversations typically occur over the telephone, but may occur in person. Mediators use these private conversations to ask about hidden obstacles, fill factual gaps, or simply listen to disputants vent.

Attorneys often do not ask for a pre-mediation conversation with the neutral, or if they do, devote it primarily to repeating legal points made in their written statements. This is usually a mistake. Apart from the fact that the mediator may already have read the briefs, lawyers will have a chance to make their legal arguments during the process itself. At this stage many mediators want to know about issues that typically do not appear in the briefs, such as what hidden issues may be present, what the participants are like, and what might be done to resolve the case. Pre-mediation private conversations provide an exceptional opportunity for advocates to shape a mediator's "take" on a dispute, focusing on obstacles, interests, and perhaps the shape of a potential solution.

Another alternative is for a lawyer and client to meet personally with the neutral before the "formal" process begins. An advocate might seek out a meeting for these reasons, among others:

- To build a relationship with a neutral.
- To permit a client to begin the process of working through his emotions without antagonizing an opposing party, or to allow the client to get to know the mediator.
- To present sensitive data or proposals.
- To allow the mediator to meet with a key witness or decision maker who will not be present at the mediation itself.

For example, in the student death case described in Chapter 9, plaintiff counsel arranged for the student's parents to have breakfast with the mediator before the mediation session began. The purpose of the encounter, which had been cleared with the defense, was to allow the plaintiffs to begin to get to know the neutral, and also to let them start the process of expressing their anger and sorrow over their son's death before they met with representatives of the university.

QUESTIONS

1. You are representing a party in an exercise assigned by your teacher. What might be helpful for you or your client to tell the mediator in a private conversation before the process begins?
2. You have sent your mediation statement to your adversary and the mediator. The other side now sends its confidential statement to the mediator alone. What can you do in response? How might you have avoided this problem?

3.   Preparing the Client

Mediation is in essence a process of negotiation, but it varies in significant ways from direct bargaining, requiring different preparation of clients. Attorneys usually conduct negotiations outside their clients' presence, often without even meeting face-to-face. In mediation, by contrast, both attorneys and clients are ordinarily physically present and the mediator has direct conversations with them. In addition, in the typical caucus-based mediation, disputants spend much of their time isolated from each other, interacting with and through the neutral rather than directly with their opponents. Because of these structural differences, lawyers need to cover the following topics, in addition to the issues they would address when preparing for a direct negotiation.

- How the mediation process will differ from negotiations to which the client is accustomed.
    - The background, personality, and likely approach of the mediator, including potential changes in style, for example, from an empathic to evaluative approach.
    - The likely format of the process and potential variations, for instance, the possibility that the client will be invited to meet privately with the other principal.

- The confidentiality rules that will apply to the process, as well as possible gaps and exceptions. (Confidentiality issues are discussed in Chapter 14.)
- What role the client should play in the process. In particular,
  - What questions the client should expect from the mediator.
  - What the client should expect the other side to say and do.
  - How the lawyer and client should coordinate. The client should be aware, for instance, that she can ask the mediator to leave the room so that she and her lawyer can talk privately.
- What role the lawyer will play in the process. Advocates should be sure the client understands that while their overall goal—getting the best possible outcome for the client—will remain the same, they will adapt their tactics to the special nature of mediation. In particular,
  - The attorney will probably take a different tone than she would in a courtroom or direct bargaining session. The presence of the mediator may call for a more conciliatory stance.
  - The lawyer may also "pull punches" in order not to antagonize the other side while they explore a possible deal, and may not mention some evidence in order to save it for trial.

The following article gives more specific advice about how to prepare for mediation.

THOMAS ARNOLD, CLIENT PREPARATION FOR MEDIATION
15 Corporate Counsel Q. 52 (April 1999)

In adjudicative processes (both arbitration and court trials), it is common for the advocacy to be an attack upon the good faith, integrity, and alleged wrongs of the other . . . Necessarily that attack angers the other party, stirs up animosity, and interferes with any settlement effort.

In mediation the intent is to move the parties together, to treat the dispute as a problem to be solved together by respectful partners rather than a combat to be won. It is not the neutral but the other *party* and counsel that are the critical persons to be persuaded. So you don't hurt or disparage them: You seek out, you court, their good will and understanding. From this and other differences between mediation and adjudicative processes, you will see that advocacy and exhibit preparation . . . are poles apart as between mediation and adjudication. In this paper I list key client and some lawyer preparation pointers for mediation.

WHO REPRESENTS THE CLIENT?

Who is the choice client representative for this mediation? A bellicose, unforgiving, inflexible, arrogant, and/or big-risk-taking personality? A wet rag personality who might give away the store? A person whose concessions at the mediation inherently imply criticism of his own prior actions, or his boss's prior actions? A temperate-mannered somebody who knows the subject matter, knows the values of the likely trade-outs? An open-minded person with quiet courage but no arrogance? Merely discussing these considerations and what available person is the best client representative with the client contact . . . becomes importantly educational . . . as to how (s)he should undertake to conduct him/herself. . . .

First Impression

Upon arrival at the mediation, [the client should be cautioned to] be friendly and respectful, and attempt to build trust with the adversaries. Most settlements involve some degree of trust between client to client, client to counsel, counsel to counsel . . . so it is important to start developing trust at the first opportunity. . . .

Confidentiality

Acquaint the client with the rules and realities of confidentiality. Emphasize what not to say in plenary session, and that it's okay simply to decline to answer some questions. Only some, not all, disclosures in mediation are confidential . . . Once learned in a mediation, . . . information can still be discovered by regular discovery processes and used, even though it may not be attributed to the . . . mediation.

Consider Strengths and Weaknesses

Counsel in a preparation session should have the client write down all of the weaknesses and strengths in his/her case, and discuss and evaluate each with counsel. It is important that counsel strain hard to be objective. . . .

Don't Argue

The client should be cautioned not to argue with the other party or try hard to "win" the . . . case. The stock in trade in most legal negotiation is the other party's (and your own) risk of a substantial loss at important expense. But arguing hard and aggressively to get an admission . . . is usually counterproductive. Just be sure the other party truly knows their risks. . . .

Know Which Questions to Answer

The client should be advised to answer questions from the other lawyer without exaggeration, honestly, carefully, and correctly. And he or she should also know which questions to quietly, simply decline to answer. Some lawyers try to use mediation as if it were primarily a discovery tool. You must make material disclosures for the process to work, but you don't have to tell the other side everything (for example, information subject to the attorney-client privilege). . . .

BECOME FAMILIAR WITH "THE DANCE"

Plan with the client how you might handle the first . . . rounds of offers and counter-offers to convey subliminal messages. Plan not to be disturbed by an outlandish initial offer by the other party, but to turn it to . . . advantage by showing how ridiculous it is. . . .

CONSIDER SPEAKING OUT

When the parties can understand the issues, as is usual in commercial and many other disputes, encourage them to speak up during the mediation and participate in the negotiation.

END THE BATTLE WITHIN THE CAMP

Within a "party" there often are many constituencies . . . with different interests or viewpoints, for example, a partner, the vice-president . . . , the union, the board, the marketing manager. They may be represented at the mediation by one, two, or three persons, or some of them by no one . . . Not infrequently, the most important and destructive disputes are between constituencies on the same side. In multi-faction situations, counsel and the client business representatives at the mediation must each be sure to address all internal disputes before they face the other side.

DON'T LOOK LIKE A KLUTZ

This goes for you and the client, but the client is more likely to need the reminder. It is important to show the client off in the mediation as someone who would be an appealing witness in any court process, should mediation fail. People pay more to, and accept less from, a party with jury appeal.

BE PREPARED FOR DOWN TIME

There is often some idle time during mediation, while the other party meets with the mediator in private caucus, so the client should bring work or reading material. . . .

PLAN FOR A LONG SESSION

Let the client know that it will be necessary to make sure work and children are taken care of all day — until 7:30 in the evening or later, if need be. It is a good idea to talk to the mediator in advance about termination times. Some mediators like the pressure of late hours and work on past midnight if there is even a little movement in parties' positions; some quit at 6:00 p.m. no matter what is going on.

BOW OUT GRACEFULLY

Advise your client that when the process ends, you should each shake hands with your opposite number and say "Thank you," even if there's no settlement. Many settlements follow shortly after a mediation, when the right flavor is left in the mouth of an adversary.

CONCLUSION

By their very nature . . . , mediation processes depart fundamentally from the adversarial nature of litigation. But in at least one respect, they do resemble litigation: They call for very careful, thoughtful, thorough preparation. . . .

QUESTIONS

1. What aspects of the mediation process do you think a typical auto accident plaintiff is unlikely to understand? What might a business executive find surprising about mediation in a contract case?
2. Arnold's underlying theme is that a lawyer needs to prepare a client differently for mediation than for litigation. Which of his suggestions would you *not* follow if you were preparing a client for an adversarial hearing in court?
3. Any advice must be adapted to the needs of specific situations: As one example, Arnold advises that clients be told to assume an "empathetic" role. In what kinds of disputes would empathy be likely to be productive? Are there situations in which it might be the wrong emotion to show?
4. Which aspects of Arnold's advice are unique to mediation, as opposed to points that apply equally to direct negotiation?

E.   THE LAWYER'S ROLE AT THE MEDIATION SESSION

We now turn to the point in the mediation process at which the parties and mediator convene together to talk and bargain. This is what many lawyers think of as the "actual" mediation, although by now you know that effective advocacy begins before the parties meet in person. We have seen that commercial mediation tends to follow a joint-session-plus-caucusing format, while family and problem-solving mediators are much more likely to keep disputants together.

There is relatively little written about advocacy outside commercial mediation. This may be due to the fact that in the traditional family-mediation format counsel are available for consultation, but do not participate directly in the mediation session. "No-caucus" and "transformative" mediation also emphasize direct party-to-party communication, with lawyers either staying away or playing only a subsidiary role. We will therefore discuss advocacy in the context of civil, nonfamily cases, in which lawyers are more likely to play significant roles.

1. Joint Meetings

a. The Opening Session

(1) Should There Be an Opening Session?

Most mediators prefer to begin the process with an opening session that is attended by all the disputants. Lawyers, however, regularly suggest to mediators that the parties dispense with this stage and go directly into caucuses. Each side already knows the other's arguments, they say — What benefit could there be to repeating them? Or, they warn, the session will simply inflame their clients. Moreover, time is limited: Why not cut right to the chase?

There is often some truth to each of these concerns. Still, however repetitive or uncomfortable an opening session may appear, you should be extremely reluctant to ask that it be entirely omitted. An adversary's comments may offend your client (and vice versa), but the experience of speaking directly to an opponent often helps disputants to let go of emotions that would otherwise impair their decisionmaking later in the process. Allowing a party to listen directly to an adversary's evidence and arguments can also help to bring reality to later discussions, giving each side a better appreciation of what they will face if the case does not settle. And after a time, even angry listeners usually become calmer. Mediators find that it is almost always useful to hold at least one joint meeting early in the process.

> *Example:* Lawyers in a large construction dispute decided to mediate. Their pre-mediation statements set out the facts of the dispute thoroughly, and the mediator was experienced in such cases. Stressing that their clients were sophisticated executives, both lawyers asked the mediator to "cut to the chase," skipping the opening session and going directly into caucusing. Reluctantly, she agreed. After several hours, however, the parties fell into impasse.
>
> The mediator decided to convene a joint session in the middle of the process. For more than an hour and a half the principals argued angrily about why their side would prevail if the matter had to be arbitrated. They then returned to their caucuses and made the compromises needed to settle.

If you do have a particular reason for avoiding a joint meeting, raise this with your mediator in advance. Before doing so, however, carefully examine the pros and cons. Remember that you have the option to request that an opening session be restructured, and consider options that fall between cancellation and the "usual format." You might, for example, ask that the session be focused on presentations by experts or comments by executives.

QUESTION

Can you think of any type of dispute in which an early joint meeting is likely to be counterproductive? What format would you advocate using instead?

(2) What Role Will You Take in the Session?

You may have a variety of goals for a joint meeting. Even if your objective is solely to get the best possible monetary outcome, you will usually not want to exchange offers during the opening session. Too often, offers made directly by one side to another are "reactively devalued." (One exception to this is when one party wants to make a complex proposal that the mediator will have difficulty explaining, or that requires back-and-forth discussion to flesh out.) Instead, your strategy should be to create the conditions for successful bargaining later in the process. You can do this in several ways.

Foster a Working Relationship.   Advocates and clients can use an opening session, and perhaps also the casual conversation that often occurs as people assemble, to foster a better working relationship with an opponent. This does not necessarily mean repairing a past connection, although that might be desirable. Instead the goal is typically more modest—to create a basis for the parties to bargain effectively later on. Disputants can do this, for example, by demonstrating that they are serious about settlement and are willing to make principled compromises to reach one. Alternatively, a lawyer can use an opening session to help an emotional or angry participant, like the contractors in the above example, work through difficult feelings.

Gather Information.   Lawyers can also use the opening session to gather information. In a joint meeting, unlike discovery or court proceedings, disputants can talk informally with each other. Attorneys and clients also have the opportunity to observe the lawyer and witnesses for the other side, and perhaps also the chance to speak directly with the opposing principal. (The other side, of course, will have the same opportunity to "size up" you and your client.)

Focus the Discussion on Key Issues.   Skilled lawyers use the opening session to focus discussion on the issues most helpful to their case or that create a platform for effective bargaining. If, for example, an advocate wants to emphasize the evidence (or lack of it) supporting the damage claims in a case, she can alert the mediator beforehand that this issue is significant to her client and then focus attention on it through her comments. If the attorney's primary goal is to explore an interest-based solution, she can use the opening session to send signals about this as well—or prime the mediator to raise the issue as his own idea. Neither side can control the agenda of an opening session, but attorneys who take the initiative can influence the content of such discussions significantly.

Persuade an Opponent.   Finally, lawyers use the opening session to persuade their opponents to compromise. They focus their advocacy on the opposing decision maker, knowing that they will have other chances to talk with the mediator but the opening session may be their only opportunity to speak directly to the other party. The goal will usually be to convince the other side that it is in its own best interest to compromise. Opponents are more likely to do so if they believe that:

- You are serious about seeking a settlement.
- You are open to options that will advance their interests.
- If discussions fail, you have a good alternative to settlement.
- You are willing to compromise, but will accept impasse sooner than agree to an unfair result.

(3) What Role Will Your Client Take?

Most lawyers are inclined to take the lead in the opening session, treating it as a kind of informal pretrial hearing. As we have already noted, however, clients can play crucial roles in these meetings as well.

Should the Client Speak in the Opening Session? As a general rule, clients should be active in joint meetings. Opponents tend to "tune out" what an opposing attorney says, but they are usually very interested in hearing from the opposing principal. Mediators also seek out contact with parties and therefore pay especially close attention to what they say. For these reasons, statements from principals are likely to have a greater impact than the same words spoken by an attorney. By participating effectively in a joint session, parties can significantly affect how opponents view them as witnesses, future partners, or negotiators.

- In personal injury and employment cases, in which the plaintiff's pain and suffering or emotional distress is often an important element of the claim, a plaintiff who can persuasively describe how he has suffered increases the settlement value of the claim. In general, whenever a person is likely to be a significant witness in a future adjudication, his presentation in mediation is likely to affect the other side's estimate of the value of the case at the bargaining table.
- When parties wish to repair a relationship, as in some business cases, or the principals cannot avoid relating with each other, which is true of many cases involving children, one party's participation in mediation can significantly affect the other side's willingness to settle on terms that maintain a working relationship. Again, statements made by one party directly to another almost always have greater impact than comments made through a lawyer or mediator.
- Parties can often articulate their interests more persuasively if they speak themselves.
- If one side doubts an opponent's commitment to settling, he may be able to dispel those concerns in the opening session.

All this assumes, of course, that a client presents himself positively. If a party is obnoxious, inarticulate, or unattractive, then his participation will lower an opponent's opinion of his case and hurt his bargaining objectives. In such situations the client should remain silent if possible.

How Should the Client Present Herself? In the course of preparing a client, advocates should again stress that mediation is an informal process which combines discussion with bargaining, and the party should therefore speak in a conversational tone. In general, speakers should focus on the person who seems to be the key decision maker or, perhaps, the most persuadable listener.

If the speaker is focusing on background facts that are familiar to the other side, she should address the neutral. If the issue involves past incidents between the principals, or the party is attempting to explain a misunderstanding, to apologize, or to empathize with an adversary, she should speak directly to the concerned person. If the purpose is to show the client's effectiveness as a witness, then it is appropriate to address both the other side and the mediator.

If, however, the speaker has decided that it is necessary to make an accusation, for example, that the other side has committed fraud, listeners will probably feel less "assaulted" and find it easier to listen if the speaker directs such comments toward the neutral. Finally, mediators with backgrounds as judges sometimes prefer that participants use a "settlement conference" format and speak directly to them.

QUESTION

You represent a company that vacated commercial space because of dissatisfaction with the condition of the building. Your client is being sued by a corporate landlord for rent due under the lease. Both sides have agreed to mediate. Apart from the basic issue of liability, which you see as a 50–50 proposition, you believe that the landlord ignored its responsibility to maintain the building, and as a result would not be awarded much even if it did establish a technical violation of the lease. How can you best use the opening session to make the landlord aware of its risk at trial?

b.   Other Joint Formats

We have seen that commercial mediation typically relies on extensive private caucusing. The caucus format can be useful, but it also imposes significant limitations. Advocates should not let themselves fall into caucusing as a matter of routine without thinking about whether other formats might be more effective. Caucusing is most useful when disputants want to focus primarily on legal issues and monetary offers, or when they are too emotional, inarticulate, or unskilled in bargaining to interact effectively.

If, however, parties wish to repair a relationship or work out inventive solutions, direct discussions, perhaps moderated by the mediator, are often more effective because they allow the people who are most concerned or knowledgeable about a situation to talk directly with each other. Even when a case is "only about money," it may be useful for representatives of each side to talk directly in order to resolve emotional issues, address complex factual issues, or deal with misunderstandings. The flexible nature of mediation allows participants to change its structure on an ad hoc basis. Again, this creates opportunities for sophisticated counsel to use the process to advantage. Consider this example.

Example: A manufacturer and a trucking company had a productive relationship for more than a decade, with the trucker distributing the manufacturer's products throughout the southern United States. Then their relationship somehow went sour. The manufacturer eventually sued the trucking company, claiming that it had fraudulently inflated its costs by overstating mileage and had padded its bills for loading. After two years of angry litigation the parties agreed to mediate.

The mediation process began with an unusual twist, however. The plaintiff's lawyer contacted the mediator ahead of time to suggest that he ask the defense to dispense with the usual opening statements by lawyers, and instead have the two CEOs meet privately with each other. The mediator contacted defense counsel, who agreed, subject to the neutral being present during the conversation.

At the outset the two executives and the mediator retired to a room, leaving the lawyers behind. The manufacturer's CEO opened the discussion by retracing the companies' initial good relationship and their later problems. He suggested that the breakdown had been provoked in part by a wayward manager, whom he had hired away from the trucker but had recently let go for poor performance. The executive then made a settlement offer. The defendant's CEO thanked him, and said that he needed to run it by his lawyers. The parties then engaged in several hours of tough but productive bargaining, reducing their initial $900,000 gap to $30,000 — a demand of $300,000 against an offer of $270,000. At that point, however, the defense dug in and refused to make another offer.

As the mediator searched for ways to break the impasse, the defendant CEO suddenly pulled a quarter out of his pocket. "See this?" he asked. "You check — It's an honest quarter. I'll flip him for it!" "For what?" said the neutral. "The 30," he replied. "Let's see if he's got the ****s to flip for it!" The mediator looked at the trucker's lawyer: Was this serious? The attorney shrugged his shoulders; "It's OK with me. Why don't you take Jim down and present it to them. But you should do the talking; Jim's feeling really frustrated by all this." Why not? the mediator thought — it was better than anything he had to suggest.

The neutral led the defendant CEO into the plaintiff's conference room and, with a smile, said, "Jim has an idea to break the deadlock. It's kind of . . . unusual, but you might want to listen to it." In a calm voice and without anatomical references, the CEO repeated his coin-toss offer. The plaintiff executive grinned. "OK," he said, "But you didn't answer my last move, so the real spread is 50, between my 320 (his last offer before dropping to $300,000) and your 270." They argued over what should be the outcomes for the flip, showing some exasperation but also bits of humor. When the discussion stalled, the mediator suggested options to keep it going ("Why not give the 20 to charity?"), but in the end they could not agree and the defendant CEO walked out. As he left, the mediator followed him down the hall. "Suppose I could get him to drop to a flat 290," he asked. "Would that do it?" As it turned out, it would.

In this example both sides' initiatives proved important to settlement. The plaintiff lawyer's proposal that the mediation begin with a principals-only meeting created an informal connection between the executives that helped them to get over difficult points later on. And the defendant CEO's idea of a coin toss (which the mediator later learned had been suggested by his lawyer) was key to shaking the parties out of their impasse.

As this example demonstrates, even in a process in which the parties are separated in caucuses, lawyers can advance their client's interests by arranging meetings of subgroups of disputants. The mediator will usually be present to moderate such sessions, but this is not always true: In a case described later, the plaintiff's inside counsel asked to meet privately with the defendant's CEO, outside the presence of both the lawyers and the neutral. Good mediators readily agree to adjourn from caucusing in order to allow people to talk directly with each other. Effective lawyers are not afraid to ask a mediator to vary the usual format of the process. They understand that mediation is inherently a fluid process, and that mediators are working for the parties, not the other way around.

2. Caucusing

Because caucusing is so common in civil mediation outside the family law area, attorneys and mediators whom you encounter in practice are likely to expect to spend most of the time in caucuses. As a result, you will need either to take action in advance to obtain modifications in the caucus format, or to plan to reap the greatest advantage from using it.

To make the best use of caucuses, you will have to prepare in two ways. First, you will need to adapt your direct bargaining tactics to the special structure of caucusing, and second, you will need to deal with the mediator differently from the way you respond to opponents. If, for example, opposing counsel asks your client a question, you would ordinarily feel free to cut him off or step in and answer the question yourself. But if a mediator asks your client the same question in the privacy of a caucus, the considerations are quite different. You may be more willing to have your client answer a mediator's question. But even if you are reluctant, you may let the client respond in order not to offend the neutral. The nature of caucusing typically changes over the course of a mediation, and we will therefore discuss early and later caucusing separately.

a. Early Caucuses

During the early caucuses of a mediation, you are likely to have some or all of the following goals:

* Relationships:
  * Develop a good working relationship with the mediator.
  * Not harm, and perhaps improve, your relationship with the other side.
* Legal issues:
  * Focus the participants' attention on your issues.
  * Gather data needed to bargain and provide the other side with information it will need to move in your direction.
  * Persuade the other party and the neutral that you have a good alternative to settling.
* Interests:
  * Identify nonlegal barriers that have made settlement difficult.
  * Focus the mediator on your interests and identify the key concerns of the other side.
* Bargaining:
  * Start the process of exchanging options.
  * Encourage the mediator to pursue interest-based options as well as money offers.

Of these possible goals, we will focus on two: using mediation to facilitate exchanges of information and to initiate bargaining.

(1) Exchanging Information and Arguments

Sophisticated negotiators often spend a good deal of time exchanging information and feeling each other out before making explicit offers. Because legal mediation is at heart a process of negotiation, it is not surprising that good advocates and mediators use caucusing to facilitate the flow of information. A lawyer might, for example, tell a mediator what she wishes the neutral to stress to an opponent as well as questions that she needs answered.

Neutrals, for their part, understand that disputants often come to mediation without data that they need to make settlement decisions, and that good lawyers will work to get points across to an adversary through them. Indeed, to the extent that a party's "questions" are implicit arguments, mediators are often willing to transmit them to encourage the listener to reassess the value of its case. To understand how counsel uses mediation to convey questions and arguments, consider the following.

A few years ago one of the authors filmed a series of roleplays in which professional mediators and litigators tried to settle a case. The experiment was based on a manufacturer's claim against a supplier for selling a defective product. The manufacturer also sued the supplier's insurer, alleging that the insurer had acted in bad faith by refusing to make an offer to settle the claim, and asked for treble damages for this alleged violation. The insurer's counsel argued that his client had based its decision on the report of an independent expert, which appeared to be a convincing defense to the allegation of bad faith. Still the treble-damages claim hung over the case, inflating the plaintiff's monetary demands and discouraging the defense from making a serious settlement offer. Toward the end of the defense's first caucus meeting with the mediator, defense counsel decided to highlight this issue:

Defendant's inside counsel: We hope you'll raise with them that we see the crux of settlement as hinging on the fact that we don't see any evidence to support their case on treble damages . . . .

Mediator: But if they do have evidence, that might influence your bargaining position?

Counsel (smiling):   Yes, and if they don't, we hope it influences theirs. . . .

The mediator got the message, and raised the issue during his meeting with the plaintiff side.

Mediator: Suppose an outside expert reports that she found nothing in the insured's product that could have caused the damage, and the insurer then denies the claim on that basis. If all that is true and the expert is credible . . . How would you then get the insurer into the case?

Plaintiff counsel: Well . . . It's a problem, no question about it. . . .

Mediator: What percentage chance would you place on the bad faith claim?

Counsel: Twenty-five percent. . . .

At the conclusion of this discussion the plaintiff team agreed to discount the bad faith claim heavily. What the defense counsel obtained by making this request of the mediator was to focus his discussion with the plaintiff on her preferred issue. She also benefited from the inclination of plaintiff counsel to be candid with the neutral.

PROBLEM

You represent the defense in the mediation of an employment discrimination case. A typical plaintiff's claim for damages in such a case consists of lost wages, out-of-pocket expenses, and emotional distress. Of these, the item that is often the largest, and the most subject to dispute, is emotional distress. Here the plaintiff is demanding $200,000 in damages for emotional distress, but you think it is highly unlikely that he will recover more than a modest amount, because he never sought medical care for the condition. Also, there are no egregious facts, such as being ordered out of the building by a guard, that a fact finder would think likely to trigger serious distress.

You are in the first round of caucusing. The mediator is coming in to meet with you and your client, and will then meet with the plaintiff. Outline how you would raise the distress issue with the mediator.

(2)   Initiating Bargaining

Depending on the circumstances, an advocate in mediation may decide to focus either on money bargaining or creative solutions. The format allows lawyers to advance either of these goals.

Interest-Based Bargaining.   We know that interest-based bargaining is desirable. One practical problem for advocates, however, is that even when they wish to explore nonmonetary terms, they are often reluctant to do so, for fear of signaling that their client is not committed to its monetary position. This is particularly true of plaintiffs because they are typically the ones seeking damages. Defense lawyers, by contrast, tend to be receptive to imaginative terms, because they see them as a substitute for paying money.

Mediation can allow a lawyer to have it both ways. He can press "publicly" — in communications sent through the mediator or made in joint session — for the best possible money outcome, while "privately" — through a pre-mediation talk or caucus discussion — asking the neutral to explore nonmonetary options.

> *Example:* A large manufacturer sued a supplier of chemicals, alleging that the defendant's product was defective and had caused an unacceptable rate of failure in its products. The supplier was interested in restoring its business relationship with the manufacturer. Not only had the relationship been a source of substantial profit, the supplier knew that if the manufacturer resumed using its products it could not continue to denigrate the defendant's reputation.
>
> Because the plaintiff knew that the quality failure had been a one-time event, it was not necessarily opposed to this. Still, it was wary of talking about a new relationship because it badly needed a cash infusion, and feared that the defense would seize on a "win-win" solution involving providing products at a discount so as to avoid offering money. To deal with this problem, the manufacturer's lawyer continued to press for large money payment but at the same time indicated to the mediator privately that her client would not object to a new contract as long as it was not a substitute for a cash payment.

A "Hard" Bargaining Strategy.   One rarely mentioned aspect of mediation is that it offers protection to parties who opt for a competitive approach, as well as to negotiators pursuing creative solutions. Indeed, the mediation process allows counsel to take tougher stands than would be possible in direct negotiation. Because mediation is more complicated to arrange than an ordinary bargaining session, participants are more reluctant to walk out in response to an "insulting" proposal. More important, a mediator will "scrape the other side off the ceiling" when they erupt at an opponent's stubbornness. Lawyers sometimes take advantage of this dynamic to play "tough cop," knowing that good mediators will instinctively take on a "good-cop" role in order to keep the process alive.

> *Example:* A manufacturer was in a dispute with its insurer over the insurer's refusal to pay nearly a billion dollars in claims against the manufacturer. The parties agreed to go to mediation. The insurer's CEO prepped intensively for the process, planning to have a point-by-point discussion of the merits with the manufacturer's representatives. When the parties convened in joint session and the CEO tried to discuss the case, however, the plaintiff's inside counsel said that he wasn't interested. He had listened carefully to his litigation team's analysis, he said, and saw no point in having a debate. The lawyer went on to say that he would not make any concessions at all on the claim until the insurer agreed to pay the full amount that he believed was due under an "incontestable" section of the policy. That amount, counsel said, was slightly under 130 million dollars.
>
> The mediation was held in a conference room at an airport, and in a direct negotiation, the insurer's team would very likely have been on the next flight out. The manufacturer's lawyer knew, however, that the mediator would respond to his tactic by cajoling, even begging, the CEO to ignore his opponent's obnoxiousness, look at the big picture, examine the legal risks — and put up a very large amount of money. And that is exactly what happened. After hours of talking, the CEO strode into the manufacturer's conference room, wrote "100" on the board, and walked out. Now it was the neutral's job to convince the plaintiff team that although a hundred million dollars might seem paltry in light of its claim, from the insurer's perspective it was a huge step forward. To counter reactive devaluation, he stressed that the right way to assess the offer was to count up from zero, rather than down from the original demand.
>
> Months later the case settled. The turning point came when the manufacturer's counsel — the same lawyer who had refused to discuss the merits with the CEO — intervened to make an unusual request. He asked the mediator to invite the executive to meet him in the lobby of the hotel where the mediation was being held. As the neutral and the lawyers sat in conference rooms, reading newspapers and speculating about what might be going on, the two key players sat down over coffee and cut a deal.

As these examples illustrate, sophisticated counsel can use mediation to enhance both cooperative and competitive bargaining strategies. They can privately encourage a mediator to raise creative options while adhering to a monetary demand, or pursue a genuinely competitive strategy secure in the knowledge that their mediator will work to keep the process from falling apart. Good advocates should also keep in mind that the mediator will be interpreting their position and viewpoint to the other side, and offer suggestions to the neutral about what they want her to say in the other room.

b. Later Caucuses

As caucusing progresses, the tactics of the disputants and the mediator are likely to evolve. Advocates will continue to probe for information, explore interests, and argue the merits, but as the process continues these aspects usually become less dominant. For one thing, the parties will cover issues repeatedly, making continued discussion seem repetitive. As a result, during the later stages of a mediation focused on monetary demands, caucuses are likely to become progressively shorter as both sides focus on bargaining. In a creative process, parties often shift their attention gradually from identifying and communicating interests to devising options to satisfy them. In an interest-based process, later caucuses are likely to remain relatively long, but their focus is likely to be on crafting terms to produce the best possible "fit" of the parties' concerns.

Mediators are also more likely to express opinions as mediation continues. In part this is because as they gather more information, mediators become increasingly confident about their assessment of the participants and the obstacles to agreement. Parties also typically become more receptive to a mediator's advice; they realize that the mediator has genuinely listened to their concerns, and from the answers she brings back after each round of caucusing know that mediator has communicated their views clearly to the other side. Competitive bargainers in particular are likely to become more receptive to a mediator's advice as they realize that they are approaching an impasse. As mediators become more active in the process, advocates should consider modifying their own tactics in response.

(1)   Facilitating Bargaining

One option is to ask the mediator to assess the emotional "temperature" in the other room, or predict how a counterpart is likely to react to a proposal. Lawyers can also seek to take advantage of the mediator's special status in order to enhance the effectiveness of their offers.

Obtaining Information.   One of the paradoxes of mediation is how mediators are expected to treat information that they gather during private caucuses. On the one hand, caucus discussions are confidential. On the other hand, one of mediation's key purposes is to foster better communication, and as long as the parties are separated in caucuses, this can only happen if the mediator conveys information between them. How can an advocate take advantage of this seeming contradiction?

In practice most lawyers in mediation designate very few facts as confidential and appear to expect a mediator to reveal at least some of what they say in private caucus. For example, a plaintiff lawyer might tell a mediator, "$500,000 is as low as we'll go at this point. You can tell them 500." The attorney knows that the neutral will interpret this to mean that she can tell the other side that the plaintiff is reducing his demand to $500,000, and also that the plaintiff will probably willing to go further ("at this point") if the defendant makes an appropriate response.

Experienced lawyers know, in other words, that while mediators will not report sensitive data to the other camp, they will usually feel some license to go beyond simply repeating what a party says and convey its general intentions and signals. Unless instructed otherwise, a mediator will convey this information as her own impression, not attributing it to the speaker. The result resembles the way government officials sometimes float trial balloons to the press on a "background" basis. This approach has two advantages. First, the listener may be left a bit unsure as to what signal has been given, giving the sender leeway either to reinforce or back away from the signal in light of the response. Second, the fact that the mediator is the one making the interpretation makes it appear less manipulative, and therefore less subject to reactive devaluation, than if the lawyer had given the signal directly.

The implication here is that advocates should consider what questions they wish to ask a mediator about the other side's state of mind, and think about what the neutral is likely to tell the other side about their own team. If, for instance, a plaintiff seems agitated during an opening session, defense counsel might later ask the mediator, "Has Smith calmed down?" or "If his lawyer recommends a deal, do you think he'll listen?" Alternatively, a lawyer might ask a mediator to collect specific information, such as whether the other side has retained an expert. Lawyers can also ask mediators to explore an adversary's reaction to a potential deal without disclosing their own interest in it.

Questions about what the other side is thinking pose tricky ethical and practical issues for mediators because of the paradox mentioned above. But that does not mean that counsel should not ask them. Lawyers should be aware, however, that if they ask a neutral for information about their opponent, the neutral may interpret this as permission to provide the other side with the same kind of data about the questioner. As in direct bargaining, in other words, information exchange is often a two-way street. That does not mean, however, that asking questions is not helpful, and mediation can amplify the effectiveness of doing so. To take advantage of the mediator's ability to gather and convey information during the caucusing process:

- Ask the mediator questions about the other side's current attitude and intentions.
- Discuss with the mediator what she will say to your opponent about you.
- Use the mediator as a sounding board as to how a potential offer will be received.

QUESTIONS

You are in the late afternoon of a mediation of a commercial contract dispute. You and your client have become very frustrated with the slow pace of the bargaining and the defendant's lack of realism. You began with an offer of $5 million, and your most recent proposal was $2.75 million, with a final "bottom-line" target of $1.9 million. The defense opened with an offer of $200,000 and has been inching up, their last move being only from $650,000 to $700,000.

1. In a private conversation while the mediator is out of the room, your client tells you that he is willing to drop to $2.5 million, but that unless the defendant's next offer "hits seven figures" (i.e., $1,000,000) he's inclined to pack up and leave. How might the mediator help you? What should you and/or your client say to the neutral?
2. Assume that the mediator comes back 30 minutes later with a defense offer of $900,000. What should you do now?

Using a Mediator's Neutrality. As we have seen, mediators have a key advantage that is not available even to the best advocate: the simple fact that they are seen by disputants as neutral. Although the phenomenon of reactive devaluation makes humans instinctively suspect anything that is proposed by an opponent, mediators can potentially deliver bargainers from its impact. Take, for example, a situation in which a defendant is stubbornly clinging to an offer of $75,000. The mediator could say to the plaintiff, "You know,

I think that if we could ever get them up to $100,000, it would be worth serious consideration . . . What do you think?" By phrasing the issue in this way, the neutral has done two things. First, she has presented the offer as hypothetical—it is not yet "cursed" by the fact that the defendant is actually willing to make it. Second, she has tentatively endorsed its reasonableness. If the plaintiff buys into the potential offer, the mediator will have partially "inoculated" it against being devalued if it materializes.

Good lawyers instinctively work to take advantage of the mediator's neutral status. In one of the roleplays in the experiment described above, for instance, defense counsel's initial response to a high plaintiff demand was to propose that his client provide the plaintiff with future product at a discounted price, but no actual cash. In making this offer counsel, while pretending to be imaginative, was in fact offering no money in order to deflate the plaintiff's expectations. At the same time, however, he tried to induce the mediator to take responsibility for his proposal.

Mediator: I've told you that the plaintiff is willing to move significantly from their opening demand. This isn't just the mediator reading tea leaves—they gave me explicit permission to tell you that . . . But if I go back now and say, "They're willing to give you a discount but . . . *that's it*," we will have a big problem and a short afternoon, I think . . . But I could be wrong.

Outside counsel: David, we need you to be more . . . *creative* than that. The challenge is going to be to sell [the plaintiff's vice president] on the idea that he can go to his father-in-law with this offer and look like a hero rather than a bum . . .

Mediator: That's going to be a hard sell . . . But Steve, if that's the way you think is the best way to move this forward, then I'll try it.

Outside counsel: No, I don't think that *those* words are the best way, and I don't think that's the way you would phrase it. I'm confident that you would say to them that you decided after talking to us that it wasn't fruitful to talk in terms of how many dollars we would give them to settle—that *you* came up with the suggestion for a discount program . . .

Mediator: Well . . . I'll phrase it however I'm going to phrase it.

In this instance, defense counsel was not able to persuade the mediator to take responsibility for his proposal, probably because the mediator was justifiably concerned that he would seriously damage his credibility if he endorsed an offer that the plaintiff saw as unfair. But the lawyer was not bashful about asking, and in the end he got an excellent result for his client.

> *Example:* A federal government lawyer was willing to settle a weak claim against an insolvent bank for a few cents on the dollar. He was concerned, however, that his agency superiors might refuse to approve the deal. To deal with this, the lawyer asked the mediator to prepare a written case evaluation that he could use as "cover" for his decision to compromise. To avoid the evaluation being used against him if the settlement were not approved, he secured the agreement of bank counsel that the mediator would provide the written evaluation only to the government.

Counsel can take advantage of a mediator's perceived neutrality by:

- Asking a mediator to deliver unwelcome information to the other side.
- Suggesting that a mediator offer a party's proposal or argument as his own.
- Requesting a neutral to certify the fairness of a proposal, either to the other side or to an outside constituency.

Using a Mediator to Carry Out Uncomfortable Tasks.   Mediators are freer to use unorthodox tactics to solve bargaining impasses because they needn't worry about maintaining a judge's reserve or showing a litigator's resolve. Attorneys can take advantage of this by asking mediators to take on difficult tasks.

> *Example:* Two brothers were fighting over the business empire of their deceased uncle. Following years of inconclusive court proceedings, the two agreed to mediate. The parties went through a difficult first day, in part because the mediator encountered ambivalence from the plaintiff: He would make a decision, then backpedal after the neutral left the room. The defendant's lawyer became angry over this, and the mediator hinted at what was happening.
>
> The defense counsel told the mediator that the plaintiff couldn't decide anything without first talking to his wife. Unfortunately, the wife was not at the mediation; to alleviate the family's dire financial needs she had taken a job as a bookkeeper at a local store. "Why don't you go talk to her before we meet tomorrow?" the lawyer suggested. With the assent of the plaintiff's attorney, the mediator agreed to do just that.
>
> Early the next morning the neutral drove out to the store, walked down to the basement, and amid boxes of auto parts sat down to talk with the plaintiff's wife. After listening to a tearful story of betrayal and sacrifice, he suggested that she accompany him to the mediation — it was her family's future that was being discussed, after all. She agreed and rode with the mediator to the mediation site. In the ensuing hours the wife proved to be more decisive than her husband, and also better with numbers. The case settled, but absent an outside-the-box suggestion from counsel, and a mediator's freedom to respond to it, the process would almost certainly have foundered.

> *Example:* In yet another case, a defense lawyer berated a mediator in front of his client for "mistakenly" communicating a concession to the other side — a move that counsel in fact had told the neutral to make, but that his client had apparently balked at accepting. The mediator apologized for the misunderstanding, but the offer broke the deadlock . . . and the lawyer later complimented the neutral for his effectiveness.

Mediators can take on a wide variety of unusual roles to support the settlement process. They might range from counseling a distraught litigant, to delivering a "hard sell" to a stubborn executive, to acting as the scapegoat for a difficult compromise. If a mediator does not see the need or seems reluctant to take on such a role, however, counsel should take the initiative to ask.

QUESTIONS

1. Is there any reason that you as an advocate would feel reluctant to ask a mediator to take the kinds of initiatives described above?
2. What kind of background would make a neutral more likely to take such initiatives? Less open to doing so?

(2)   Impasse-Breaking Techniques

Each of the techniques described above can assist an advocate to achieve more than might be possible through direct negotiation. Suppose, however, that despite a lawyer's best efforts the bargaining process hits an impasse. The reasons can be complex. Negotiations may become stalled because of a process issue such as lack of authority, psychological factors such as loss aversion, merits-based problems like misevaluation of the chances of winning in court, or other obstacles. Impasses occur most frequently when negotiators focus narrowly on monetary solutions, but they are possible even during interest-based bargaining. Two parties may agree, for example, that it would be desirable to restore their business relationship, but reach a stalemate trying to decide how to share the costs and rewards of the new arrangement. When an impasse does occur, advocates can often take advantage of a mediator's assistance to resolve it.

Ask the Mediator for Advice.   Mediators are experienced negotiators. More importantly, they have a unique opportunity to observe and talk candidly with both sides and, at least until the end of the process, are not under pressure to express an opinion themselves. As the process goes on, they often acquire a great deal of information about each party's state of mind, approach to bargaining, and priorities for settlement. A mediator will not help one side obtain an advantage over an opponent, and settlement-oriented neutrals do have an interest in seeing each side compromise as much as possible. But when the negotiation process bogs down, advocates should consider asking the mediator for advice about how to restart it. Lawyers can also use a mediator to educate an unsophisticated or emotional client, or to present difficult truths about what is achievable and what it is not. Possible questions for the mediator are:

- What seems to be the obstacle here? What can we do to resolve it?
- Would a gesture toward the other side help?
- Is a new combination of terms likely to get a positive response?
- Are other process options available?

Retry an Earlier Step.   Many of the interventions discussed in Chapters 9 and 10 can be useful at the end of the process as well as early on. The concept of returning to a tactic may seem strange — after all, if a particular approach wasn't successful when the participants were fresh, why should it be productive when everyone is tired and frustrated? Necessity, however, can be the mother of invention, in mediation as elsewhere. For example, would a brainstorming session produce new ideas? Does a review of disputed facts appear capable of helping? A party who rejected an option early in the process may become more open to advice as time goes on. As a result, the fact that a particular step has been taken earlier in the process, either with or without success, does not mean that it cannot be used again.

Arrange a Discussion Among a Subset of Participants.   A variant of retrying a prior technique is to go to a different format. You will recall, for example, that in the "hundred-million-dollar offer" case, the same lawyer who during the opening session had flatly refused to discuss the legal merits with the defendant's CEO, asked weeks later to talk with him privately — and resolved the case. In the "$30,000 coin-toss" mediation, defense counsel asked the mediator to arrange for his client to meet for a second time with the plaintiff's executive, an encounter that led to a solution.

Most common is for a person on one team to talk with her counterpart on the other side: VPs with VPs, experts with experts, and so on. Such discussions can produce genuine insights. Even when this does not occur, however, a new exchange may provide a party with an excuse — a "fig leaf," one might say — to take a step that it knows is necessary to revive the process. By demanding a meeting, even an inconclusive one, a bargainer can feel that she has sent a signal that concessions will not be easily obtained.

Make a Hypothetical Offer.   Counsel who will not make a unilateral concession will sometimes authorize a mediator to make an offer in a hypothetical, or "if . . . then," format. The motivation can be to test the waters, probe the other side's flexibility, and/or ensure that a potential move will be reciprocated. For instance, a lawyer might say to the mediator, "Given the other side's refusal to go below 250, I cannot see us going beyond 100. However, you could tell them that you think you could get us to 125 if they would respond by breaking 200."

The hypothetical formula gains added impact if it is presented as a final resolution of the case rather than simply as a new move. By proposing an actual settlement, bargainers take advantage of the "certainty effect" described in Chapter 10 — the fact that disputants will often make a special effort to obtain complete peace. An advocate wishing to take this approach might say, "You can tell them that if they could only get to 150, you have some optimism that you could convince my client to go there — but only if it would settle the case, once and for all." Such hypotheticals can sometimes short-circuit impasses caused by positional bargaining.

Ask the Mediator to Intervene.   If other steps are not effective, lawyers can ask a mediator to intervene directly in the process. Good mediators will delay doing so for as long as possible, knowing that disputants may be alienated by the perception that the neutral is "taking over" the process, or because the mediator wants to avoid control for philosophical reasons. Still, many commercial mediators will intervene actively in a case when the bargaining process appears to be seriously stalled.

If an advocate wants a mediator to adopt a restrained role in the face of impasse, she should make her preference known early in the process. Alternatively, if a lawyer wants the neutral to become more active, she should say so. We discuss below three of the most common interventions used by mediators to resolve impasses — confidential listener, evaluation of the merits, and a mediator's proposal. We also suggest ways in which lawyers can use each tactic to best advantage.

Confidential Listener.   Sometimes each side in mediation will refuse to move to a reasonable position until its adversary has done so. The result is an "After you, Alphonse . . . No you, Gaston . . ." effect in which both sides remain stuck, but the mediator is fairly sure that each would be willing to compromise further. In such situations a mediator may offer to play "confidential listener." This involves asking each side to disclose to him privately how far it would go to settle the case. The mediator can then make a judgment about the real gap between the parties.

At one time participants in mediation tended to assume that unless the parties' confidential positions were identical or very close, the mediation would end. This put considerable pressure on each party to give the mediator its "last and best offer." In modern practice, however, both lawyers and mediators are likely to assume that the purpose of the confidential listener technique is for the neutral to form a better estimate of the actual gap between the parties. People now appear to approach confidential listener on the assumption that the mediator will not end the process even in the face of a large gap.

The first question about the confidential listener technique is whether you wish the mediator to use it. If so, you should suggest it; if not, you should ask the neutral to hold off. Sophisticated lawyers sometimes ask, for example, that a mediator delay doing so for a time, so that the parties can continue to exchange offers. The next question is how to use the technique to best effect. Lawyers should keep in mind that at this point they are in what amounts to a three-sided negotiation, with their opponent and with the mediator. The neutral, one must remember, is not on anyone's side: Her goal is simply to obtain a settlement.

Mediators usually do not expect the tactic to settle a case, although they would be delighted if it did. Rather, their goal is to get a more realistic offer from each side. Once both sides have given their response, the neutral usually gives the litigants an assessment of the situation; for example, "You're still a considerable distance apart, but I think it's worth continuing." In addition, some neutrals will ask the parties for permission to disclose their confidential responses on a mutual basis, so that both can form a better estimate of the distance between them.

What should you as an advocate tell a mediator who is playing confidential listener? Unless you are in a situation in which a mediator states explicitly that she wants each side's true bottom-line number *and* you believe that she really means it—that unless the parties' positions either touch or come very close, the mediator will terminate the mediation—it is not wise to give your client's actual final terms. Doing so will place you at a disadvantage in the next stage of the process, in which the parties are asked to continue to bargain, and may lead your client to dig prematurely into an unrealistic position. For these reasons, experienced mediators often avoid asking litigants for a bottom-line number at all. Professor-mediator Marjorie Aaron's practice, for instance, is to ask disputants instead for their "next-to-last number"; this sends a signal that she does not want a "final" offer.

For a competitive bargainer, the challenge in the confidential listener process is to make an offer high or low enough to set up a favorable compromise, but realistic enough to motivate the other participants to continue. A principled bargainer, by contrast, will gravitate toward a proposal that is solidly based on neutral criteria, but may also leave some room to move. A cooperative bargainer will be inclined to answer the mediator honestly and to consult with the neutral about steps to keep the process alive. Parties can also sometimes couple a response with an indication of their intentions. The explanation can be either for the mediator's private information ("Our number is $100,000. That's as far as we're willing to go at this point. Let's see what they come back with") or for the other side ("Tell them $100,000 is as far as we're willing to go until they move down to six figures").

One final point: If a neutral does ask flat out for your "bottom line," how should you respond? If you are cooperative and fully trust the neutral, you can answer with complete candor. In other situations, you may want to adopt this response, suggested by litigator David Stern:

> Based on what we currently know about the case and taking into account the arguments, we believe that the offer we have made is the best we could make.

Obviously, we would like to pay less and [they] would like to receive more, but what we might like is not the issue. If you can give me a principled reason why my client should consider paying more, we will consider it; otherwise, we don't believe that any further adjustments are warranted.

[By this response,] you are conveying at least two messages. First, you are flexible. Second, your flexibility is based on principle — meaning the value of the case — not demands, extortion or other extraneous factors. With this response, you have left the door open for dialogue and you have moved the dialogue to the plane of principle rather than petulance (Stern 1998).

Evaluation.   If shuttle diplomacy fails, lawyers often ask mediators to evaluate the legal merits of a case. As was pointed out in Chapter 10, evaluation is a controversial technique but can be useful, not only with opponents but also with clients. Whenever, for example, an advocate stops a mediator in the hall and suggests that she give his client her "thoughts" about the case, the neutral knows that she is being enlisted in the difficult task of client education and management.

In the large majority of situations, evaluation will focus on the legal issues in the case — who is likely to prevail in court, what the damages are likely to be, and similar issues. It is possible, however, to have a mediator evaluate broader issues as well. If, for example, a disputant is suspicious that its adversary will not carry out a proposed settlement, the mediator could assess the risk on the basis of his discussions with the opponent or his experience in other cases.

Before requesting a mediator's evaluation on a legal issue, an attorney should ask himself two basic questions. First, is the primary obstacle to settling this case really a disagreement about the outcome in court, or some other issue that evaluation can address? As we have seen, the real barriers to settlement often lie in issues other than the legal merits. Second, if a mediator does evaluate the merits, is the advocate confident that the result will be helpful — that is, will he get the opinion he wants?

Once a lawyer has decided to seek an evaluation, the next issue is how to structure it to maximize the chances of a helpful result. The first issue is what data the mediator will consider. Bear in mind that a mediator's views about a case are usually based solely on the briefs and documents she sees, augmented by personal observations of the people present at the mediation. This has two implications:

- Like trial, mediation has a "primacy" effect: Evidence and people whom the mediator actually observes tend to be more vivid, and thus have more impact on her decisionmaking, than data that the neutral merely hears about. Actual documents and face-to-face encounters with potential witnesses are thus likely to have much more impact on a mediator's opinion than evidence summarized in a brief.
- There is also a "melding" effect: When a mediator cannot personally observe a witness, she must place the person in a category ("nurse," "retired accountant," etc.), then make an assumption about how a fact finder would react to a typical member of that group.

As a result, if you want a mediator to give full weight to a witness or a piece of evidence, you should make a special effort to place it directly in front of the neutral. In a construction case, for example, you might ask the mediator to visit the site so that she has a vivid image of the project when she evaluates legal claims arising from it. You may also want to have a mediator meet a key witness. In mediation, unlike a court proceeding, you can arrange for a private meeting without incurring an obligation to expose the witness to your opponent.

You should also take care to ensure that the mediator takes the time required to give your evidence adequate consideration. Don't assume, for example, that a mediator will read every document you give her. Mediators often receive thick piles of paper that they must review without knowing what will turn out to be relevant later in the process. If a neutral is busy or concerned about keeping down costs, she is likely to skim through voluminous materials and wait for the parties to tell her what is important. In addition, mediators are often reluctant to take long breaks in the midst of mediation to review evidence, for fear of losing momentum. If you have documents that are important to a mediator's evaluation, tell the neutral what you would like her to focus on, provide a highlighted copy of the key passages, and ask her to examine the evidence carefully before opining. A mediator assisted in this way is less like to jump to an erroneous conclusion.

A second crucial question is what, exactly, you want evaluated. Don't simply say "the case." Ten years ago mediators routinely provided global opinions about the likely outcome if a dispute were adjudicated. Increasingly, however, mediators think of evaluation simply as a means to jump-start a stalled negotiation — more like filling a "pothole" in which the "settlement bus" has gotten stuck than building a road to a predetermined destination. Often a prediction limited to a single issue is enough to put the parties back on the path to settlement. The question then is: What specific aspect of the case do you want evaluated?

Finally, as discussed in Chapter 10, you should not expect every evaluation to take the form of an explicit opinion. Good mediators see evaluation as a spectrum of interventions rather than a single event. They rely on pointed questions, raised eyebrows, and other "shadow" techniques, much more than explicit statements, to nudge negotiations back on track. When an advocate hears a mediator make such comments, he should realize that the evaluation process is under way, but in a form less likely to provoke resentment than an explicit conclusion.

Mediator's Proposal.   In this method, discussed as part of the "basic meditative strategy" for commercial mediators in Chapter 9, the neutral suggests a set of terms to both parties under the ground rule that each litigant must tell the mediator privately whether it will agree to the proposal if the other side does so. If both say yes, there is a settlement. But if either party rejects the proposal, it never learns whether its opponent was willing to agree. Parties thus know that they can achieve complete peace by saying yes, but that if the effort fails, their bargaining position will not be compromised.

In formulating a proposal, mediators typically try to "balance the pain" that each party will have to bear in order to accept it (although some neutrals base the proposal solely on their estimate of the likely outcome in adjudication — see Contuzzi, 2000). One concern is that mediator's proposals have a take-it-or-leave-it quality: Once made, a proposal will tend to "set in cement," in the sense that both parties will resist agreeing to terms less favorable than the neutral has recommended. As a result, if a mediator proposes terms that are even minimally acceptable to a party in light of the costs of litigation, it will feel significant pressure to accept it.

However, a mediator's proposal has some major advantages. For one thing, it allows a party to test a potential settlement without indicating to the other side that it is willing to compromise. In addition, the technique often works — parties often will go to great lengths to accept a proposal because it holds out the promise of settling the dispute, while at the same time protecting their bargaining positions. If, however, an advocate believes that he can induce the other side to accept terms more favorable than those the mediator will propose, it is usually not in his client's interest to have one made. Advocates might also wish to talk with the mediator about what standard he will use in setting the terms: balancing the pain, predicting the outcome in court, or something else?

If the Mediation Session Ends Without Agreement.   If a case does not settle at the mediation session, what should an advocate do? One option is to try again later. A mediator's task is to keep working for settlement until the parties tell him unequivocally to stop, and he sees no plausible way to change anyone's mind.

This was brought home by a comment made by defense counsel to one of the authors at the end of a long case. The mediator had continued to work after each attorney had told him privately that the case could not settle. Finally, however, the parties did reach agreement. As the mediator went over the terms, defense counsel suddenly exclaimed, "They kept beating you up and you just kept going. You were like . . . like . . . the *Energizer Bunny*!" At first, the mediator found the idea of being compared to a drum-beating pink rodent a bit insulting. But as he thought more about it, the comparison was apt. A mediator's job is to keep advocating settlement until the parties tell him unequivocally to stop, and he sees no plausible way to change anyone's mind.

The corollary is that if a neutral does not appear ready to take the initiative, a good advocate will prod her to do so. Neutrals' spirits, like those of other humans, occasionally flag, and some have a narrow conception of their role. A polite reminder that you are counting on a mediator to pull a settlement out of her hat will often encourage the neutral to make further efforts. Consider this example, related by mediator Benjamin Picker:

> An inventor sued a company for patent infringement. The company hired a large law firm to represent it. It was aware, however, that litigation costs in such a case could easily exceed one million dollars, and in the meantime its business strategy would be in limbo. The company therefore decided to explore settlement, and designated a separate lawyer in the firm as "settlement counsel," responsible for seeking an agreement while his colleagues focused on litigating. The lawyer suggested early mediation. The plaintiff agreed, and the parties selected a retired judge as mediator.
>
> At the end of the first day of mediation, notwithstanding a defense offer of several million dollars, the mediator indicated that the parties were far apart and recommended that the process end. Settlement counsel suggested, however, that the mediator instead ask the plaintiff to think about how he would spend the millions of dollars that were on the table, and adjourn the process for a week. The hope was that loss aversion would set in, making the plaintiff reluctant to risk money that was already "his." At the second session, the parties reached agreement.

QUESTIONS

1. Parties are mediating a dispute concerning the amount due from a commercial real estate developer to a building contractor under a "cost-plus" contract. You represent the developer. The contract provides that the contractor will be reimbursed for its reasonable costs plus a 10 percent profit. The project is complete and all issues have been resolved except one: The contractor has demanded that the developer pay for the cost of benefits in a tax-sheltered retirement plan accrued by the contractor's employees while they were working on the project. Your client believes that the contract, which is silent on the issue, does not call for reimbursement of employee expenses other than wages and usual fringe benefits such as medical care. The mediation proceeds through an opening session and a lengthy series of caucuses. The law and facts relevant to the issue are exhaustively discussed, but the parties see no reasonable prospect of agreeing on the merits. You privately evaluate the likely outcome in court at a $650,000 verdict for the contractor, with a high verdict of $1 million and a low of zero. You also expect the future defense costs in the case to be roughly $75,000. Your client is reluctantly prepared to offer up to $600,000, and if absolutely necessary would go to a maximum of $700,000. He has no interest in working with this contractor again. During the afternoon the process gradually focuses on exchanges of money offers. The offers are as follows:

Contractor's demand:	Developer's offer:
$1.5 million	$100,000
$1.3 million	$200,000
$1.25 million	$250,000
$1.2 million (with difficulty)	$275,000
Remains at $1.2 million	Defendant refuses to "bid against myself"

   a. Assuming that the only term at issue is money, what should the developer do?
   b. Suppose that your client sees a possibility of using the contractor to do about $200,000 worth of work on another property. What process would you recommend?

2. You represent the plaintiff in an employment dispute. It is five in the afternoon and you have been mediating for nearly eight hours. You began with a demand of $1.5 million, and in response the defendant offered $25,000. After laborious bargaining, you have dropped to $400,000. You need at least $350,000 in a cash settlement, but could conceivably go to $200,000 if your client were offered a good job back at the company. Unfortunately, the defendant is only at $100,000, having moved there from a prior offer of $85,000. Your client is feeling very frustrated and has told the mediator this. The mediator has gone back to the defense and returned:
   a. Assume that the defendant suggests that the mediator play "confidential listener" and you agree. What should you tell the mediator?
   b. Assume instead that the defense suggests a "mediator's proposal." Should you agree?

If Negotiations Fail.   Sometimes settlement is genuinely unachievable. Even in such situations, a mediator can be of use, by helping counsel design an efficient process of adjudication. A mediator might, for example, facilitate negotiations over a discovery plan. Or the neutral could broker an agreement on an expedited hearing process, perhaps coupled with "bracketed" or "final offer" arbitration (described in Chapter 19). To take advantage of mediation even when settlement is not possible:

- Ask the mediator to contact the parties periodically to urge further negotiations.
- Ask the mediator to facilitate agreement on an efficient process of adjudication.

How should an advocate leave an unsuccessful mediation process? Litigator David Stern offers the following advice:

> At some point, hours or days after you have started, the mediation process will end. If it ends with an agreement, that is fine. But if you can't reach agreement, accept that as well. Parties and lawyers often get desperate as the mediation nears conclusion, but the dispute remains unsettled. It is possible, but exceedingly unlikely, that the mediation is the last chance to settle the case. More likely, there will be multiple opportunities—at deposition, at court-ordered settlement conferences, before trial, during trial, even after trial and appeal—to settle. As such, do not despair or let your client despair if you walk away without a deal. Not all cases should be settled, and almost none should be settled on any available terms. Most will eventually settle one way or another, so if you can't settle at the mediation, ask yourself what benefits you can achieve before you part ways.
>
> Occasionally, you can agree to keep talking. Sometimes that dialogue will depend on one side or the other developing more information. Or it might depend on how well a witness does at a deposition or whether a particular motion is granted or denied. Search for partial agreements if feasible, or part company respectfully, so that the possibility of future negotiation remains open. In all likelihood, settlement will eventually occur and both you and your client will benefit if you keep that probability in mind.

F.   CONCLUSION

Too often attorneys treat the mediation process simply as a safe place in which to conduct positional bargaining, trading arguments and offers until they reach impasse. At that point mediators take over the process by making settlement recommendations or offering evaluations. We hope you appreciate that whatever approach you take to bargaining, the mediation process has a great deal to offer. Lawyers who approach mediation actively, looking at the mediator as a consultant, resource, and potential ally, use the process to best effect and are able to obtain optimal outcomes for their clients.

CHAPTER
12

Specific Applications

Mediation is used in a wide variety of subject areas. From its traditional roots in family, union, and construction disputes, it has expanded to employment, environmental, high-tech, and even criminal cases. The application of mediation to specialized fields raises issues of process design, and also poses the question of whether the process is appropriate for every kind of dispute. The following readings explore these issues.

A. FAMILY DISPUTES

1. What Is Unique About Family Mediation?

Family disputes involve several factors that make them different from other civil cases. Among them are:

Intense Emotions

Marriage is perhaps the most intimate relationship that human beings can enter. People often define themselves around being a husband or wife, and divorce thus strikes at the very heart of their sense of identity and self-worth. This is likely to provoke feelings more intense than those found in almost any other kind of conflict. Marital discord can also trigger deep and sometimes irrational emotions that stem from each spouse's own childhood.

Continuing Relationships

Ordinarily when people fall into disagreement, they have the option to separate from each other. But if a couple has children they usually cannot completely dissociate, even when they divorce. Instead ex-spouses remain connected to each other in their roles as parents, often for many years. Divorced parents must find ways to share their children's physical presence, financial responsibility for their expenses, commitment to teaching and socializing the child, and a variety of other tasks. People often find it difficult to cooperate on these issues even when they are happily married. If both parties seek custody, or if a spouse decides to use children as a weapon in the marital conflict, the difficulties created by an unwelcome parenting relationship will multiply.

Impact On, and Participation By, Children

While children are young, parents can usually enforce decisions about their upbringing. This raises a concern that a spouse who is desperate to escape a marriage or not thinking clearly may sacrifice a child's best interests to his own. For teenagers a different problem arises. Older children often have strong wishes about where they want to live and how they want to lead their lives. They can become third-party players in disputes over custody and visitation, rejecting agreements that have been worked out by their parents and further complicating the process of settling such cases.

Physical or Emotional Abuse

In domestic conflicts, unlike most civil disputes, there is a real possibility that criminal acts, in the form of physical or emotional abuse, will occur. Even when victims do not complain, society has a strong interest in preventing such acts and in protecting an abused spouse from giving away rights. This issue is especially acute in states that require couples to engage in mediation as a precondition to gaining access to court, an issue discussed in Chapter 13.

Lack of Legal Counsel

Despite the fact that family disputes involve some of people's most basic rights, divorcing spouses are less likely than most litigants to obtain legal advice. Business disputants typically have the resources to obtain counsel, and in personal injury cases contingent fees and insurance can provide access to lawyers. Family disputes, however, involve disagreements between individuals who often have neither assets nor insurance to cover legal costs. There is a serious risk that participants in family mediation will not get good legal advice, making it difficult for them to negotiate effectively and putting the mediator in an awkward position as well.

Although these factors greatly complicate the use of mediation in family cases, the consequences of litigating such disputes can be horrific: Legal proceedings are often deeply destructive, creating rather than healing emotional scars. They can also exhaust a family's financial resources at the very time that its expenses are increasing because of the need to establish a second household. Legal battles over custody and visitation, in particular, often have a severe impact on children. For these reasons, as the use of mediation grew, family disputes were among the first areas to which it was applied. Today, most states have statutes and policies governing family mediation and mandate that parties involved in disputes over child custody or visitation go to mediation before entering a courtroom.

As we have seen, the process of family mediation differs from traditional civil or commercial mediation in several respects. The parties generally remain together throughout the process rather than separating into private caucuses. Attorneys are ordinarily not present, although parties may consult them between sessions. Because many couples have issues around custody and visitation, there is more need for the process to be interest based and future oriented. Family mediations often are not one-day affairs, but rather extend over a period of weeks or months. Finally, perhaps due to the strong emotional issues present in such cases, most family mediators have in the past been mental health professionals, although the proportion of attorney-mediators in the field is increasing.

2. The Process

Given the special characteristics of family disputes, it is not surprising that the process differs from general civil mediation. The following is an edited transcript of a mediation session that occurred at the outset of a divorce case. As you read it, think about these questions:

QUESTIONS

1. How does this process differ from examples you have seen of commercial mediation?
2. What might have happened in this case if the parties had not gone to mediation?
3. Some commentators criticize this mediator's technique as overly directive, even occasionally manipulative. They see him as sometimes maneuvering disputants into going in a certain direction, rather than giving them the ability to make decisions for themselves. Do you see any evidence of this in the transcript?
4. Like many mediators in this field, John Haynes was not a lawyer, instead holding a doctorate in the social sciences. Do you think his background has any impact on how he mediates?

JOHN HAYNES, MEDIATING DIVORCE: CASEBOOK OF STRATEGIES FOR SUCCESSFUL FAMILY NEGOTIATIONS

50-95, Jossey-Bass (1989)

TRANSCRIPT AND ANNOTATIONS*

Mediator: [Your] counsel has asked you to come today to see if we can work out an agreement that is appropriate for both of you and in the best interest of Sarah and Daniel. I wonder if you could tell me a little bit about what's happened in the last month.[1] Perhaps if I could ask you to begin, Debbie, in terms of where the children are living currently and what the arrangements are.[2] Then we can see what differences there are between you and see where we go from there.

---

*Note: The footnotes set out the mediator's comments as he reviewed the transcript after the session. They contain the mediator's reconstruction of the reasons he made certain interventions, and his assessment of what the disputants were feeling at the time.

1. I open with this information question about the events of the last month to focus on what is current and avoid drifting into the past and the marriage. The body language of the couple throughout the session is very revealing. Michael is very closed when I talk to Debbie and tends to open when I talk to him. Debbie looks away from Michael and down on the floor when Michael says something she does not like. Michael frequently turns away from both Debbie and the mediator, gazing at the wall.

2. A focused question, directed at Debbie, is designed to limit the amount of space for a marital fight to develop. This future-oriented question sets the agenda for the session.

Debbie: Well, the children are with me in the matrimonial home. Michael left a month ago, and I have let him see the children on several occasions.[3] But the children aren't happy seeing their father. They said they don't want to see him. They are very unhappy about the separation.[4] When they come home, they're very upset. They're crying, and it takes me hours to settle them down. I just don't know how they're going to cope with this.

Mediator: So they're currently living in the family home with you, and they're spending time with their dad.[5] Michael, what is your feeling?

Michael: I think that Debra's a little . . . ah . . . she doesn't have a grasp on the situation. I've seen these kids now five times over the past month. They are happy to come with me; we have a good time. We've done a lot of things together; they enjoy being with me. They're obviously at strain, because when I was living at home they were seeing me daily, constantly . . . I don't think that Debra is helping them at all. I'm having a great difficulty in coming back and watching her dissemble. When I bring the kids back home, she starts. . . .

Mediator: How old are the children?[6]

Michael: Five and seven.

Mediator: Five and seven, and the older one is . . .

Michael: Daniel.

Mediator: Daniel is seven and Sarah is five. Okay. It's not unusual for them to have this tension and lots of crying when they go back and forth . . . So it's perfectly possible for them to have a good time when they're with you, Michael, but also express real concerns and reservations when they're with you, Debbie. That's not an unusual situation. Let me just see now what's the difference between you. What is it that brings you here?

Michael: Well, the difference basically is this: Debra says that I can be a part-time parent and I can see my kids every second weekend from Saturday morning until Sunday night, if I see them alone and so long as she maintains control over it.

Mediator: What does Michael want?

Michael: These are my children. I am one-half of their parents. I want the kids half-time. When we were living together, I was spending most of the time with the children.

Mediator: So you'd like to have the children spend half of the time with you and half the time with Debbie.[7]

Michael: I think so. I don't see that it's inappropriate in our circumstance.

Debbie: I don't think he wants to see the children. I think he's using that.[8]

Mediator: What do you want, Debbie? . . .

Debbie: I want him to come back. My children are devastated. I'm devastated . . . We had plans for us and for our children, and he's destroyed that. He's giving me no reason. All of a sudden, after fifteen years of marriage, he says that's it, I can't stand it

---

3. "I have let" indicates that Debbie believes she has the power in the situation. If Michael agrees with this assessment, it will provide me with some power-balancing information.

4. Debbie's complaint about Michael is diffuse as she stakes out a tough opening position, defining the problem as the children's unhappiness, which can be solved only by a change in Michael's behavior, as defined by Debbie.

5. This summary of the factual content makes no comment on Debbie's charges, so as not to solidify her position. If the mediator comments or argues with her about this, she will have to defend her position and thereby become more "wedded" to it.

6. As Michael continues his complaints, I cut through the "feelings" with a factual (closed) question on a different subject. This process interruption breaks the cycle Michael is about to launch.

7. The summary of Michael's proposal reframes it, to help Debbie hear that under his proposal she would also have them half of the time. She probably heard only that he wanted them. By pointing out the "half-full glass," the mediator facilitates the bargaining.

8. Debbie ignores the reframing of Michael's statement.

any more. And I think you should know he's seeing someone else, and he's exposing our children to that other person. . . .[9]

Mediator: Help me understand, Debbie, what it is you are looking for me to do . . .

Debbie: Well, I'm here because I don't want to go through the court system. If we're going to separate, I don't want a lawyer or judge shoving an agreement down my throat.

Mediator: That's wise. So, what you want me to do is mediate . . . ?

Debbie: Yes.

Mediator: . . . I'm not going to work with you to get back together.[10] If you want to do that, there are other people competent at doing that. That's not my area. . . . What I'm going to do is to help you define the problem between the two of you, see what options there are to solve that problem, and help you solve that problem in a way that's mutually acceptable to you, and in the best interests of Sarah and Daniel. . . .

Mediator (To Michael): So you'd like to have them. Right? You'd like to have them half of the time.[11]

Michael: Yes.

Mediator: Debbie, if you were to structure the arrangement for the parenting, how would you structure it?[12]

Debbie: Well, I think the children need a home . . . And I don't think he's prepared to give them the proper kind of a home. . . .

Mediator: . . . That's an issue; we will deal with it because it's obviously an issue between you. But assuming that was not an issue, then how much time would you want Sarah and Daniel to spend with their daddy?

Debbie: The children love their father, and I don't want to keep the children away from their father. I suppose if we could sort out other problems, I would want him to see them as much as he could and as much as their schedules would allow.[13]

Michael: . . . She's misrepresenting me to the children on a constant basis. She tells them that I'm sick, she tells them that I'm depressed, she tells them that poor daddy doesn't know what he's doing, poor daddy has a mean friend, poor daddy has a friend who's taking your daddy away from you.

Mediator: It's very, very hard when you get divorced, isn't it? To deal with all of the emotions and all of the things that happen.[14]

Michael: She's a professional woman, she's a smart lady. I have a lot of respect for her. She moves in those circles, she knows what she's doing. . . .

Debbie: Well, I don't see how the children can live one week here and one week there. I think it will be too hard on them. I don't think he's being fair to them. He's the one that broke up this family. . . .

Mediator: Are there any other problems?

Debbie: I don't think they should be exposed to this woman.[15]

9. Debbie sends two messages: She wants Michael back, and he is seeing another woman. I develop a hypothesis that the fight is over the other woman and devise questions to test my hypothesis.

10. I clarify my role, disclaiming responsibility for repairing the marriage.

11. The restatement of the content of Michael's proposal is designed to redirect the discussion and to emphasize "half."

12. Debbie is asked for the first position statement. Given their respective positions and the fact that hers is unlikely to be supported by community norms, I decide to look for the first concession from her.

13. Debbie makes the first significant move, acknowledging Michael's father role. She picks up my language, moving from the spousal to the parenting designation.

14. I let Michael ventilate . . . I empathize with Michael . . . to re-engage him in the process.

15. I continue probing until all the issues are on the table. This helps to test my hypothesis and determine the order of priority of the issues. Debbie restates an untenable demand, confirming my hypothesis.

Mediator: Okay . . . you're living with somebody, Michael?

Michael: No. I have a relationship with a woman I've come to know over the last period of time. And I can honestly say this isn't the reason that I left. The reason I left is that I was sitting at home and dying, waiting to die in that house. I was sitting at home looking after the kids. Mommy's got a meeting. Mommy's at the hospital . . . They need their mother, they love their mother. But . . . all of a sudden I'm a bad bastard. . . .

Mediator: I'm hearing Debbie say that. I'm also hearing her say they love their father and they need their father and she would like to work it out so they could be with their father.[16] That's what I'm hearing on two levels . . . and those are the issues that we need to focus on and get some agreement on. . . . What would you like?[17]

Debbie: Well, I don't think he should be sleeping—letting his girl friend sleep overnight, and sleeping in the same bedroom with her with our children in the house. I don't think it's right.

Mediator: Let me ask you now: A question, if . . . excuse me just one second, but what is her name?

Michael: Jocelyn.

Mediator: Jocelyn. If Jocelyn is not sleeping over, would you feel comfortable working out some arrangement for the children?[18]

Debbie: I'd feel more comfortable. I'd be more comfortable, as well, if he had a house not too far from ours, so the children could go back and forth on their bicycles . . .

Michael: Tell him about what sort of car I should drive. Tell him about where I should take the kids on the afternoons. Tell him about . . .

Mediator: And you, Michael, would like to make your own decisions about these issues?

Michael: Of course. This is ridiculous. . . .

Mediator: Okay, so you've been living apart for a month. You're both angry with each other, and that's perfectly legitimate, and that's perfectly normal, too . . . Although, interestingly enough, so far today I've not heard any serious differences emerge between you as father and mother. There's a lot as wife and husband—there you're way apart—but not as mother and father. I'm wondering now where you want to go. . . .

Debbie: He's a good father. He's been a good father. I can't deny that. The children love him and he loves the children.

Mediator: In the short run, Michael, could you agree that Jocelyn would not sleep over when the kids are with you?

Michael: What's the short run?

Mediator: Two months . . . Give the children a sort of chance to settle in.

Michael: I can live with that. I don't know if Jocelyn can, but I can live with that. . . .

Mediator: All right. Debbie, if, for the next two months, when the children were with Michael . . . she's not sleeping over, . . . how would you then feel about sharing the parenting? . . .

Debbie: Well, I want the children to see their dad, but why does she have to be along? . . .

16. Michael moves from talking to me to talking directly to Debbie. Therefore, I permit him to continue . . . even though he begins to ventilate. Michael sends a message to Debbie that she will not be displaced. The mediator considers this directional information, indicating where Michael might move in the negotiations.

17. I am using a particularly gentle tone of voice as I pursue this line of questions and providing Debbie with a face-saving way out.

18. A reframing into a future goal, not a current impediment, in an effort to decouple the issue from Jocelyn.

Mediator: There's a lot of work to be done by all of us in terms of working out all of the details . . . I'm wondering if we could move for just the next two months, in a sense of trying to get a little space for both of you as we think through all of the issues.

Debbie: Well, maybe if he would agree not to hold her hand and kiss her in front of the children — that's just his friend, that's what he's told them . . .

Mediator: Okay, so you're saying that if Michael would agree not to be physically affectionate with Jocelyn while the children are there, you'll feel comfortable moving off your position and sharing time for the children with both of you.

Debbie: I'm not saying fifty-fifty, but . . . I'd try.

Michael: I'll live with it.

Mediator: All right. Let's then do that for the next few weeks. Let's review it along the way, and let's get back together next week to talk about some of the other issues that are going on between you, so that we can try to get the children clearly out of the middle of your fight as spouses. Okay?

Debbie: Thanks.

The Mediator's Concluding Thoughts

It could be argued that Michael lost in this settlement. He did not achieve the 50-50 shared parenting he sought, and he did give up his girlfriend when the children slept over. It could also be argued that I had a major role in shaping the agreement. These observations are true — in the short run. Note, however, that I sought the agreement only for a couple of months; it was not a permanent agreement. I did not make a moral judgment about Jocelyn's sleeping with Michael; I made a practical one. Debbie was incapable of dealing with her displacement by Jocelyn as wife, and her possible displacement by Jocelyn as mother, while she was still dealing with her loss of Michael . . . What this couple needed was a brief respite from the battle, to give them a chance to organize their lives for the next two months . . . Mediation is situational . . . The agreement provided them with a breathing space in which to collect themselves and sort out the more serious emotional issues.

3.   Policy Issues

The special characteristics of family disputes raise important policy issues. The paper that follows offers a viewpoint on several of these questions. As you read it, ask yourself:

QUESTIONS

1.   Should family mediation be barred or restricted when one or both participants do not have a lawyer?
2.   Does this depend whether the case arises in a court system that requires divorcing parents to mediate disputes over custody and visitation?
3.   Are there any steps that could alleviate your concerns?

JAY FOLBERG, DIVORCE MEDIATION:
THE EMERGING AMERICAN MODEL
Paper presented at Fourth Annual Conference of the
International Society for Family Law,
Harvard University (June 1982)

ISSUES RELATING TO DIVORCE MEDIATION

The very elements that make divorce mediation so appealing compared to the adversarial model also create its dangers and raise substantial issues not yet resolved. Because mediation distinguishes itself as an approach that recognizes divorce and family disputes as both matters of the heart and of the law, there exist issues of how emotional feelings are to be weighed against and blended with legal rights and obligations and what are appropriate subjects for mediation. Because mediation is conducted in private and is less hemmed-in by rules of procedure, substantive law, and precedent, there will remain the question of whether the process is fair and the terms of a mediated agreement are just. This concern for a fair and just result has particular applicability to custody and child support provisions because mediated bargaining occurs between parents, and children are rarely present or independently represented during mediation.

Because mediation represents an "alternative" to the adversarial system, it lacks the precise and perfected checks and balances that are the principal benefit of the adversary process. The purposeful "a-legal" character of mediation creates a constant risk of overreaching and dominance by the more knowledgeable, powerful, or less emotional party. Some argue that the "a-legal" character of divorce mediation requires all the more careful court scrutiny before mediated agreements are approved and incorporated into a decree. Others argue against court review of mediated agreements. They reason that if the parties have utilized mediation to reach agreement, there is no need for the expense, delay, and imposition of a judge's values — all features of the judicial review process. Questions about the enforceability of agreements to mediate as well as the enforceability of mediated agreements cannot long be avoided.

FAIRNESS

In considering whether mediated settlements will be fair and just, we must ask "compared to what"? We know that the great majority of divorce cases currently go by default. The default may be a result of ignorance, guilt, or a total sense of powerlessness. The default may also be a result of an agreement between the parties on distributional questions, eliminating the need for an appearance. The question persists in our present dispute resolution system of whether such agreements are the result of unequal bargaining power due to different levels of experience, patterns of dominance, the greater emotional need of one divorcing party to get out of the marriage, or a greater desire on the part of one of the parties to avoid the expense and uncertainty of litigation. The present "adversarial" approach does not require the adverse parties to be represented, nor does it impose a mediator or "audience" to point out these imbalances and assure that they are recognized by the parties, as mediation should attempt to do. Pro se divorce is increasingly popular and sanctioned by our present system in which there need be no professional intervention prior to court review. Mediation, at least, provides a knowledgeable third party to help the couple evaluate their relative positions so that they may make reasoned decisions with minimal judicial intrusion.

The most common pattern of legal representation in divorce is for one party to retain an attorney for advice and preparation of the documents. The other party will often negotiate directly with the moving party's attorney or retain an attorney to do so without filing an appearance. If a second attorney has not been retained, the unrepresented party will often consult with an attorney to determine whether the proposed settlement is "fair enough" not to contest and if all necessary items have been covered or discussed. The reviewing attorney serves as a check, informing the client of any other options to the suggested terms and whether the points of agreement fall within acceptable legal norms. The likelihood of a different court outcome than the proposed agreement is weighed against the financial, time, and emotional expenses of further negotiation or litigation.

A similar pattern of independent legal consultation could, and should, be utilized for review of mediated agreements. Current mediation practice, influenced by ethical restraints, is to urge or require that each divorcing party seek independent legal counsel to review the proposed agreement before it is signed. Though the criteria for independent attorney review of a proposed mediated agreement are not clear, the purpose of the review is no less clear than it is under the present "fair enough" practice. The initial mediated agreement is formed in a cooperative environment with the assistance of a neutral person who serves as a check against intimidation and overreaching. Independent legal review by an attorney for one spouse pursuant to a "fair enough" standard should assure at least as great a fairness safeguard as the common reality of our present adversary system. When both parties to the mediation obtain independent legal review, as they should be encouraged to do, there is a double-check of what is fair enough. In some complex cases, other professional review, such as that of a CPA, may be necessary for still another opinion and double-check. . . .

PROTECTION OF CHILDREN

When divorce involves minor children, some argue that the state has a responsibility for the children beyond encouraging the speedy, private settlement of disputes between parents. The state, however, under the well-developed doctrine of parens patriae has a responsibility for the welfare of children *only when parents cannot agree or cannot adequately provide for them.* Divorce mediation begins with the premise that parents love their children and are best able to decide how, within their resources, they will care for them. . . .

A mediated agreement is much more likely than a judicial decision to match the parents' capacity and desires with the child's needs. Whether the parents' decision is the result of reasoned analysis or is influenced by depression, guilt, spite, or selfishness, it is preferable to an imposed decision that is more likely to impede cooperation and stability for the child. In any event, a resolution negotiated by attorneys, reviewed by a court, or litigated before a court, is no more likely than a mediated settlement to disclose which outcomes are the result of depression, spite, guilt, or selfishness. . . .

The principal protection that the mediator can offer the child is to ensure that the parents consider all factors that can be developed between them relative to the child's needs and their abilities to meet those needs. The mediator should be prepared to ask probing and difficult questions and to help inform the parents of available alternatives. The mediator's ethical commitment, however, is to the process of parental self-determination and not to any given outcome. . . .

THE CONTINUING ROLE OF COURTS AND ATTORNEYS

Increased use of divorce mediation does not remove the courts from the divorce process and would not entirely eliminate adversarial proceedings. We know that some cases cannot be settled or mediated. There must be a fair and credible forum with procedural safeguards and rules to assure the peaceful resolution of disputes for parties who are unable to recognize the benefits that may come from a less coercive process. The threat of court litigation, with all of the human and material expense that it requires, may be the very element that will help some parties cut through their egocentric nearsightedness to see that their self-interests, as well as the interest of the family, may be promoted through mediation rather than a court fight. . . .

CONCLUSION

Divorce mediation has been touted as a replacement for the adversary system and a way of making divorce less painful. Though it should be available as an alternative for those who choose to use it, it is not a panacea that will create love where there is hate, nor will it totally eliminate the role of the adversary system in divorce. It may, however, reduce acrimony and post-divorce litigation by promoting cooperation. It may also lessen the burden of the courts in deciding many cases that can be diverted to less hostile and less costly procedures. . . .

B. EMPLOYMENT CASES

One of the fastest growing areas of mediation practice is employment disputes. These range from contract claims by terminated executives to discrimination charges lodged by hourly employees. In the excerpt that follows, practicing mediators analyze the special issues likely to arise in such cases.

CAROL A. WITTENBERG, SUSAN T. MACKENZIE, AND MARGARET L. SHAW, EMPLOYMENT DISPUTES

in D. Golann, Mediating Legal Disputes 441-456 (1996)

The use of mediation to resolve employment disputes is on the rise. Increasingly, federal district courts are referring discrimination cases to mediation, and administrative agencies charged with enforcing anti-discrimination laws are also experimenting with mediation programs. Mediation is well-suited to resolving employment disputes for a number of reasons.

EMOTIONALITY

Employment disputes usually involve highly emotional issues. It is said that loss of one's job is the third most stressful life event, next only to the death of a loved one and divorce. Whether one's livelihood is at stake, as in a wrongful termination case, or the issue involves a professional relationship that has gone awry, as in a sexual harassment claim, the dispute occurs in a charged atmosphere. A mediator can help parties vent their anger and frustrations in a nonjudgmental setting that allows them to feel that their positions have been heard and to move on to a more productive, problem-solving viewpoint.

One of us, for example, had the experience of being asked by a plaintiff after several hours of mediation if a one-on-one meeting with the mediator was possible, and counsel agreed. After telling the mediator that she reminded her of a former boss who had been an important mentor, the plaintiff talked about how upset the case had made her. She also talked about how much the negotiations over dollars were leaving her feeling disassociated from the process, and from what she was personally looking to accomplish. The mediator was able to help the plaintiff identify her feelings, think through what she really wanted out of a resolution, and work within the process to accomplish that result. The case settled shortly after their caucus.

CONFIDENTIALITY

The privacy and confidentiality that mediation affords may be especially important to employees and employers alike. For example, in many of the sexual harassment cases that we mediate a primary focus of the claimant is to have an unpleasant situation stop, stop quickly, and stop permanently. Individual respondents, unless they are looking for vindication, may also want to put the incident behind them and get on with their lives, while employers, for their part, are almost always interested in confidentiality. This is particularly true in discrimination cases, since publicity about claims can affect a company's reputation in the marketplace. Employers are also concerned that without confidentiality, settlements will create precedents or "benchmarks" for future plaintiffs, or encourage "me-too" complaints.

CREATIVITY OF OUTCOMES

Mediation's creativity is particularly important in employment disputes, where the impact of the controversy can have profound effects on the parties' lives. We find that in many of the litigated disputes we mediate, non-legal and non-monetary issues are as significant a barrier to resolution as the financial and legal aspects of the case. For example, in one age discrimination claim we mediated, the settlement called for the employee to retain his employment status without pay for a two-year period, so as to vest certain benefits afforded retirees. In a gender discrimination case, the terms involved keeping the employee on the payroll for a period of time with a new title to assist her in securing alternative employment. In a breach of contract case involving a senior executive, part of the settlement involved a guaranteed loan to invest in a new business.

COST SAVINGS

Practical considerations also make mediation of employment disputes an attractive alternative to litigation. The process is likely to be much less expensive than litigation, or even arbitration. One attorney who frequently represents plaintiffs in discrimination cases observed that, as of the mid-1990s, the litigation cost of a discrimination claim to individual claimants was roughly $25,000, as compared to $1,000 to $3,000 for mediation. A study in the early 1990s estimated the cost to defend a single discrimination claim at $81,000, a figure that is now almost certainly much higher.

Note also that the monetary cost of litigation does not take into account the indirect, personal, and emotional costs of a court proceeding to all parties. All workplaces have informal information channels; we often hear from individual mediation participants about the disruptive effects of the case on fellow employees. For instance, at one company with which we worked speculation was rampant about who would be let go or reassigned in the event the case resulted in the reinstatement of a discharged employee.

SPEED

Mediation is also likely to be significantly faster than litigation. This is of particular importance in the employment context, given the dramatic increase in anti-discrimination claims. In our experience, mediation of a routine employment case involving an individual claimant generally can be concluded in one or sometimes two days. Although some parties are unable to reach complete closure in the mediation sessions, often additional follow-up telephone conferences with one or both parties will bring about a settlement. An evaluation of the EEOC's pilot mediation program, for instance, showed that mediation resolved charges of discrimination less expensively and more quickly than traditional methods, with closure in an average of 67 days as opposed to 294 days in the regular administrative process.

QUESTIONS

Are there disadvantages to mediation in the context of employment disputes? Of course there are, although we believe that some of the "dangers" are often overemphasized. Some employers are concerned that the availability of mediation will encourage frivolous complaints. Others are concerned that mediation simply adds a layer of time and expense when a case does not settle. Certain attorneys have also expressed a concern that an opposing party might merely be using mediation as a form of discovery. There are, of course, specific cases that are inappropriate for mediation, cases that upon analysis are without any apparent merit and call for the employer to take a firm stance.

CHALLENGES FOR THE MEDIATOR

There are some distinctive characteristics of employment cases that can challenge a mediator and require special approaches.

DISPARITY IN RESOURCES

While parties in other kinds of cases may have unequal resources, in employment disputes a lack of parity can make it difficult even to get the parties to the table. Employment claimants are often out of work, or face an uncertain employment future. They may balk at the added expense of a mediator, particularly when the outcome is uncertain. While some employers will agree to pay the entire mediation bill as an inducement to a plaintiff to participate, others are concerned that without some financial investment a plaintiff will not participate in the process wholeheartedly. In these circumstances, we have found several approaches effective. If, for example, the employer is worried about the employee's investment in the process, the mediator can explore the nature of that concern and determine whether verbal representations by the claimant or claimant's lawyer might allay them. As an alternative, a mediator can suggest having the employer assume most of the cost, while requiring the employee to pay something toward it.

TIMING

The timing of mediation can affect both the process and its outcome. Where it is attempted shortly after a claim has been raised, the claimant may need extra help in getting beyond feelings of anger or outrage, while an individual manager or subject of a claim may feel betrayed. If little or no discovery has occurred, the lack of information about the facts on the part of one or both parties can hamper productive negotiations. At the other extreme, when a case has already been in litigation for an extended period of time, positions can become hardened and the parties even more determined to stop at nothing short of what they perceive to be "justice."

For instance, in one case we handled, an age discrimination claim referred by a court, the plaintiff's attorney had done little investigation prior to the mediation and thus was unaware of circumstances that called into question the plaintiff's integrity during his final year of employment. Assisting the attorney to become more realistic about the chances for a recovery at trial became the challenge of this mediation. In another case that involved a sexual harassment claim, outside counsel for the employer, who had recommended mediation, was unaware of some of the conduct of the individual manager who was the subject of the allegations. That case required us to mediate between the employer and the manager, the individual manager and the claimant, and the claimant and the corporate entity as well.

IMBALANCES OF POWER

In certain employment disputes, such as those involving sexual harassment claims, a perceived or real imbalance in the power relationship between the parties may itself constitute an impediment to settlement. We have found that as a general proposition, particularly in dealing with an individual who feels at a power disadvantage in mediation, movement is better accomplished by pulling rather than by pushing. For example, in one case where the facts underlying the claim were perhaps unconscionable but not legally actionable, helping the claimant to recognize the benefits of moving forward with her life was more effective than trying to convince her that she had a weak case.

When an issue of power imbalance is articulated or apparent, it is helpful to take the time to consult with the parties before the "real" mediation begins in order to structure the process. We typically discuss, for example, whether the complainant or the attorney wants to make an opening statement. We have observed that complainants who prepare a statement for the initial joint session tend to feel a sense of control and dignity in the process that is not otherwise possible. At times, having a family member or close friend attend a session is helpful. We also attempt to establish in advance whether it will be necessary to keep the complainant and individual respondent apart at least initially. We routinely schedule premediation conference calls with all persons involved in the case to work through these kinds of issues.

DESIRE FOR REVENGE

Complainants who feel they have been wronged will sometimes look for a way to make the employer or the individual charged with harassing or discriminatory behavior "pay." Such a focus on revenge can present a major obstacle to settlement. There is no simple way to deal with this in mediation. Sometimes, particularly in cases where the complaint has already prompted the employer to take preventive measures, explaining the full impact that the complaint has already had on workplace policies or on the careers of others can help the complainant change to a posture more conducive to resolution. Another approach may be to have the individual respondent contribute out of his or her own pocket to a financial settlement.

NEGOTIATION BY NUMBERS

In some employment mediations, one or both parties may become fixed on a settlement figure and refuse to budge. Finding a new framework for analysis that appears objectively fair can help parties stuck on numbers save face and ultimately agree on a different figure to settle the case.

NONLEGAL AND PERSONAL ISSUES

At times both parties will fail to realize that a nonlegal problem is the root cause of an employment dispute. For example in one case we handled, a personality conflict between the head of accounting and his most senior employee had festered for years. The working relationship between the two had deteriorated to the point that they routinely hurled racial and sexual epithets at one another. At that point, management could see no alternative to dismissing one or both of them. With the mediator's assistance, each party was able to shift focus from placing blame on the other to recognizing their mutual interest in continuing to be employed, and mutually acceptable procedures for personal interaction in the office were identified and reduced to writing. During the mediation, the parties also came to recognize that a contributing, if not overriding, cause of the deterioration of their relationship was an outstanding loan from the department head to the bookkeeper. While the department head had treated the loan as forgiven years ago, in reality the bookkeeper's failure to repay it had continued to bother the department head. The resolution included a repayment schedule for the loan.

"OUTSIDE" BARRIERS TO RESOLUTION

In some employment cases, the real barrier to resolution may be an individual who is not a direct party to the dispute. For instance, in one case we mediated involving a disability claim by an airline manager, it became clear that his spouse, who was also present, was so angered by what she perceived as unconscionable treatment that she urged rejection of all settlement offers as insulting. The mediator dealt with this situation by recognizing the spouse's feelings and helping her understand that her anger was fueled at least in part by resentment over the amount of time her spouse had spent on his job rather than with his family. The spouse was also given an opportunity to air her position directly to the corporate representatives. Once she had done this, she was able to reorient her focus from the past to the future, and the elements of a mutually acceptable package fell into place.

QUESTIONS

1. What style would you look for in an employment mediator?
2. Would a caucus or no-caucus model be more likely to be effective in such cases?

3. You may remember that the U.S. Postal Service has used a form of trans-formative mediation in employee disputes. Why do you think that two styles as different as conventional commercial and transformative media-tion have each enjoyed success in this area?

4. The U.S. Equal Employment Opportunity Commission, in an effort to address lengthy delays in processing complaints, has adopted a policy of active and early promotion of mediation of all employment claims filed with the Commission. Do you see any dangers in the EEOC policy? Any advantages for parties?

C. PUBLIC AND ENVIRONMENTAL CONTROVERSIES

GAIL BINGHAM, THE ENVIRONMENT IN THE BALANCE: MEDIATORS ARE MAKING A DIFFERENCE

2 AC Resolution 21 (Summer 2002)

[T]he number and magnitude of environmental disputes is rising, and finding solutions only gets more difficult . . . there are many reasons why environmental and other public policy disputes are difficult to resolve . . . For a mediation process to be successful, it must be designed with these challenges in mind.

MULTIPLE FORUMS/CHANGING INCENTIVES

Frequently, the same or related [environmental] issues may be the subjects of simultaneous action at different levels of government and in one or more admin-istrative, legislative, or judicial forums. Disputing parties may have different advantages in different forums, creating conflicting views about the best process to use. A mediated negotiation is just one more choice among competing forums.

MULTIPLE PARTIES/ISSUES

Because environmental disputes typically affect large numbers of interested parties and involve a multiplicity of issues, organizing the negotiation process may prove to be extremely difficult. Sometimes coalitions can be formed, allowing several parties to be represented by one negotiator. At other times, one must design ways to have conversation in large groups. . . .

INSTITUTIONAL DYNAMICS

Environmental and resource management conflicts are more often played out between organizations or groups than between individuals. Therefore, the individuals at the table must get proposals ratified by others who are not participating directly. . . .

COMPLEX SCIENTIFIC AND TECHNICAL ISSUES

[P]arties to environmental disputes are often confronted with large volumes of information that require broad-based expertise and may be subject to honest differences of opinion. . . .

INEQUALITY OF RESOURCES

Mediation processes are resource intensive in the sense that the parties take the time to negotiate with one another up front, and need funds for travel expenses, information collection, evaluation, and expert advice. While government agencies and private corporations are generally well funded and represented by paid staff, other parties may lack the necessary financial and technical resources. . . .

PUBLIC/POLITICAL DIMENSION
Environmental disputes generally involve public issues, addressed in public forums, with laws, governmental institutions, and the media all playing a significant role. Any mediation process must therefore respond with sensitivity to the press and open meeting laws and must attempt to arrive at outcomes that can withstand public scrutiny. . . .

QUESTIONS

1. What qualities would you look for in selecting a mediator for an environmental dispute, as compared with an employment case?
2. Would the Basic Mediative Strategy described in Chapter 9 need to be modified to deal with an environmental controversy? In what respects?

D. INTELLECTUAL PROPERTY DISPUTES

TECHNOLOGY MEDIATION SERVICES, HIGH TECH AND INTELLECTUAL PROPERTY DISPUTES
www.technologymediation.com/hightech (2004)

ABOUT MEDIATING INTELLECTUAL PROPERTY DISPUTES

Mediation is not just for simple contractual disputes. Indeed, complex intellectual property matters may be resolved best through mediation. An intellectual property dispute may be especially ripe for mediation if any of the following factors exist.

ONE OR BOTH PARTIES MAY HAVE AN INTEREST IN COST CONTROL
Most intellectual property matters are expensive to litigate. It is not unusual for a patent infringement dispute to cost each side well over $1 million through trial, and such cases are often appealed, adding more to the cost. Moreover, they often are settled via business agreements. Much of the cost of extensive discovery, trial preparation, voluminous exhibits, expert witness testimony, and diverted executive time can be spared by using mediation at an early stage to craft an appropriate settlement.

A BUSINESS RESOLUTION MAY SOLVE THE LEGAL DISPUTE
A mediator can help the parties craft a variety of business arrangements, such as licensing (or cross-licensing) agreements, joint ventures, distributor agreements, usage phase-out agreements, etc., which may lay the groundwork for future business. A mediated agreement may extend well beyond the subject matter of the pending lawsuit and accommodate larger business interests.

THE DECISION MAKER MAY MISUNDERSTAND THE LAW OR TECHNOLOGY

If the judge, jury or arbitrator may have trouble understanding intellectual property law issues such as prior art or doctrine of equivalents, or the underlying technology, it may be best to avoid the possibility of being handed a "poor" decision. The parties can keep control of the outcome by mediating, rather than relinquishing the decision to a third party.

THE DEFENDANT MAY FEEL DISADVANTAGED IN THE FORUM CHOSEN BY THE PLAINTIFF

In complex intellectual property matters, a defendant may need lots of time (and money) to prepare its defense and cross-claims alleging invalidity of the patent, trademark, or copyright. If time is short, such as in investigations before the U.S. International Trade Commission, or in federal courts such as the "rocket docket" of the Eastern District of Virginia, it may be better to settle a dispute than to defend under such constraints. Similarly, a defendant may prefer not to defend in a jury trial in the plaintiff's "home" court, or in a jurisdiction with precedent favorable to the plaintiff. Mediation offers a sensible way to end the dispute before it's too late.

THE USEFUL LIFE OF THE SUBJECT MATTER MAY BE DEPLETED BEFORE THE LITIGATION IS OVER

Many "hot" products or technologies are covered by patents, trademarks or copyrights, and by virtue of their appeal become subject to infringement. But how good is a favorable judicial decision if the patented technology already has been superceded by another patent, or if last season's most popular toy now sits on the shelf, or if some other copyrighted software game now heads the "top 10" sales list? Mediation can resolve the dispute quickly, while the product is still commercially viable.

ONE OR BOTH PARTIES ARE CONCERNED ABOUT DISCLOSURE OF CONFIDENTIAL INFORMATION

Many intellectual property disputes, particularly alleged trade secret misappropriation, involve confidential business and technical information. Mediation avoids disclosure of such sensitive information, to the public and to your adversary. Everything said in mediation is protected as confidential settlement discussions, and cannot be introduced in litigation or disclosed in public. Additionally, a party can disclose certain information in confidence to the mediator, who will not transmit it to the opponent.

WHY USE A TECHNOLOGY MEDIATOR INSTEAD OF A GENERAL MEDIATOR?

Disputes that involve specialized industries or complex technology benefit from having a mediator that understands the context in which the dispute arose, and/or the technology involved. A mediator knowledgeable about high tech businesses and their problems can delve right into the issues, without expending a lot of time learning about them. In patent, trademark or copyright disputes, it is useful to use a mediator experienced in intellectual property law, who will be familiar with the legal and factual issues related to, e.g., prior art, doctrine of equivalents, and likelihood of confusion. The mediator will know who needs to be included in the mediated settlement.

The mediator will have a real-world context for the parties' positions, and won't be easily persuaded by a party's legal bluster or alleged inability to comply with a standard request. Moreover, prior experience will enable the mediator to make suggestions to facilitate resolution, or to offer a realistic evaluation of the parties' chances of success outside of mediation.

QUESTIONS

1. Given the advantages of mediation in this area, why do you think that every high-technology dispute that cannot be settled through direct negotiation is not mediated?
2. If you were counsel to a company that had a claim against a competitor for infringement of a biotech patent and wished to try mediation, but the only available mediators had either strong process skills or extensive technical knowledge, but not both, which type of mediator would you choose? Is there a way to obtain the presence of both qualities?

E.   CRIMINAL MATTERS

One of the most controversial uses of mediation is in criminal cases. The vast majority of criminal charges, ranging from small misdemeanors to capital cases, are plea bargained—that is, negotiated by prosecutors and defense counsel—rather than tried. Mediation has not, however, been used with any frequency to assist the process of plea bargaining. At the same time, the use of mediation is expanding in other areas of the criminal justice system, raising both exciting possibilities and troubling issues of justice.

QUESTIONS

1. As prosecutors and defense counsel negotiate plea bargains in criminal cases, what obstacles might they encounter? Could mediation be useful in overcoming these obstacles?
2. Why do you think lawyers in the criminal justice system so rarely use mediation to help work out plea bargains?

1.   Potential Charges

CHRISTOPHER COOPER, POLICE MEDIATORS: RETHINKING THE ROLE OF LAW ENFORCEMENT IN THE NEW MILLENNIUM
7 Disp. Resol. Mag. 17 (Fall 2000)

In the 21st century, it is time for new and fresh police strategies. One such strategy is mediation of interpersonal disputes by patrol police officers . . . The patrol police officer is often the first person to respond to many of American society's interpersonal squabbles, including disputes between neighbors, siblings, and customers and merchants. Many of these disputes are marked by flared tempers or chaos . . . Mediation by a patrol officer need not be carried out in an office. It can be conducted on a basketball court or in a parking lot, for example. It can be done standing up or sitting down . . .

For calls-for-service involving an interpersonal dispute in which there are no grounds to arrest or to cite a party for a law violation, mediation by a police officer often is a sensible approach . . . When police officers apply this approach to conflict, citizens make fewer repeat calls-for-service, including 911 calls . . . Whereas poor conflict resolution skills and unsystematic approaches by an officer can escalate disputes, using a systematic dispute resolution process such as mediation is less likely to have such a negative effect. . . .

Poor relations, particularly between people of color and police, are at epidemic levels throughout the United States. The relationship is strained in part by police who act as arbitrators in situations in which citizens have a legitimate expectation that they should be empowered to help themselves . . . It makes good sense to provide police officers with the professional skills they need to empower others . . . Mediation by patrol officers champions community policing objectives by providing . . . self-empowerment to citizens, who should expect contemporary law enforcement officers to function as a police service, rather than a police force.

QUESTION

Does the use of informal mediative techniques by police officers pose any dangers?

2. Victim-Offender Cases

Although mediation is rarely applied early in the criminal process, it does appear to be taking root at a different phase—post-sentencing encounters between victims and offenders. Here the issue is not the defendant's guilt, but rather how he and the victim will deal with what has happened. As we have seen, mediation can be used to help people change their perspectives and even to restore ruptured relationships. In the criminal context, however, such efforts are much more controversial. As you read this article, ask yourself:

QUESTIONS

1. For what purpose is mediation being used here?
2. Should the process be applied at all in such situations?

MARTY PRICE, PERSONALIZING CRIME: MEDIATION PRODUCES RESTORATIVE JUSTICE FOR VICTIMS AND OFFENDERS
7 Disp. Resol. Mag. 8-11 (Fall 2000)

Our traditional criminal justice system is a system of retributive justice—a system of institutionalized vengeance. The system is based on the belief that justice is accomplished by assigning blame and administering pain. If you do the crime, you do the time, then you've paid your debt to society and justice has been done. But justice for whom? . . .

Because our society defines justice in terms of guilt and punishment, crime victims often seek the most severe possible punishment for their offenders. Victims believe this will bring them justice, but it often leaves them feeling empty and unsatisfied. Retribution cannot restore their losses, answer their questions, relieve their fears, help them make sense of their tragedy or heal their wounds. And punishment cannot mend the torn fabric of the community that has been violated . . .

FOCUS ON INDIVIDUALS, HEALING

Restorative justice has emerged as a social movement for justice reform. Virtually every state is implementing restorative justice at state, regional and/or local levels . . . Instead of viewing crime as a violation of law, restorative justice emphasizes one fundamental fact: crime damages people, communities, and relationships.

Retributive justice asks three questions: who did it, what laws were broken and what should be done to punish or treat the offender? Contrast a restorative justice inquiry, in which three very different questions receive primary emphasis. First, what is the nature of the harm resulting from the crime? Second, what needs to be done to "make it right" or repair the harm? Third, who is responsible for the repair? . . .

As the most common application of restorative justice principles, VOM [victim-offender mediation] programs warrant examination in detail. These programs bring offenders face to face with the victims of their crimes with the assistance of a trained mediator, usually a community volunteer. Victim participation is voluntary in most programs.

In mediation, crime is personalized as offenders learn the human consequences of their actions, and victims have the opportunity to speak their minds and their feelings to the one who most ought to hear them, contributing to the victim's healing. Victims get answers to haunting questions that only the offender can answer. The most commonly asked questions are "Why did you do this to me? Was this my fault? Could I have prevented this? Were you stalking or watching me?" Victims commonly report a new peace of mind, even when the answers to their questions were worse than they had feared.

Offenders take meaningful responsibility for their actions by mediating a restitution agreement with the victim to restore the victim's losses in whatever [way is] possible. Restitution may be monetary or symbolic; it may consist of work for the victim, community service, or other actions that contribute to a sense of justice between the victim and offender.

FULFILLING RESTITUTION

. . . There are now more than 300 programs in the United States and Canada and more than 700 in England, Germany, Scandinavia, Eastern Europe, Australia, and New Zealand. Remarkably consistent statistics from a cross-section of the North American programs show that about two-thirds of the cases referred resulted in a face-to-face mediation. More than 95 percent of the cases mediated resulted in a written restitution agreement. More than 90 percent of those restitution agreements are completed within one year. In contrast, the rate of payment of court-ordered restitution is typically only from

20 to 30 percent. Recent research has shown that juvenile offenders who participate in VOM subsequently commit fewer and less serious offenses than their counterparts in the traditional juvenile justice system . . .

CAREFUL PREPARATION REQUIRED

Mediation is not appropriate for every crime, every victim, or every offender, Individual, preliminary meetings between mediator and victim, mediator and offender permit careful screening and assessment according to established criteria . . . At their best, mediation sessions focus upon dialogue rather than the restitution agreement (or settlement), facilitating empathy and understanding between victim and offender. Ground rules help assure safety and respect. Victims typically speak first, explaining the impact of the crime and asking questions of the offender. Offenders acknowledge and describe their participation in the offense, usually offering an explanation and/or apology. The victim's losses are discussed. Surprisingly, a dialogue-focused (rather than settlement-driven) approach produces the highest rates of agreement and compliance.

Agreements that the victim and offender make together reflect justice that is meaningful to them, not limited by narrow legal definitions. [T]he overwhelming majority of participants — both victims and offenders — have reported in post-mediation interviews and questionnaires that they obtained a just and satisfying result. Victims who feared re-victimization by the offender before the mediation typically report that this fear is now gone.

Forgiveness is not a focus of VOM, but the process provides an open space in which participants may address issues of forgiveness if they wish. Forgiveness is a process, not a goal, and it must occur according to the victim's own timing, if at all. For some victims, forgiveness may never be appropriate. Restorative justice requires an offender who is willing to admit responsibility and remorse to the victim. . . .

DIFFERENT CONCEPT OF NEUTRALITY

Neutrality, as understood in the mediation of civil disputes, requires that the mediator not take sides with either party. Judgments of right and wrong are not within the mediator's role. The mediation of most crime situations, however, presents a unique set of circumstances for a mediator and the concept of neutrality must be different. In the majority of criminal cases, the parties come to VOM as a wronged person and a wrongdoer, with a power imbalance that is appropriate to this relationship. The mediator balances power only to ensure full and meaningful participation by all parties . . . The mediator is neutral toward the individuals, respecting both as valuable human beings and favoring neither, but the mediator is not neutral regarding the wrong . . .

Most victim-offender programs limit their service to juvenile offenses, crimes against property, and minor assaults, but a growing number of experienced programs have found that a face-to-face encounter can be invaluable even in heinous crimes. A number of programs have now mediated violent assaults, including rapes, and mediations have taken place between murderers and the families of their victims. Mediation has been helpful in repairing the lives of surviving family members and the offender in drunk-driving fatalities. In severe crime mediations, case development may take a year or more before the mediation can take place . . . In cases of severely violent crime, VOM has not been a substitute for a prison sentence, and prison terms have seldom been reduced following mediation. . . .

WHAT CAN WE LEARN?

What can attorneys and other dispute resolution professionals learn from the philosophy and successes of restorative justice? Our system, which settles most cases without trial, does so with adversarial assumptions as its foundation. Each attorney is expected to maximize her client's win at the expense of the other attorney's client's loss. In the majority of cases, the clients of both attorneys (and often the attorneys, as well) feel like losers in the settlement. . . .

Our system of money damages and financial settlements for losses and injuries has a faulty assumption at its core. We give lip service to the truth that "no amount of money can right this wrong," then we conclude that the only available measure of amends is the dollar! In contrast, a basic principle of restorative justice is that a wrong creates a singular kind of relationship — an obligation to personally right that wrong . . . The most important lesson learned from restorative justice practice may be the realization that the key to justice is found not in laws but in the recognition and honoring of human relationships.

QUESTIONS

1. If you were designing a VOM program, what types of cases would be the most likely candidates for inclusion?
2. Criminal prosecutions serve important public functions. Which of these functions may not be fulfilled when cases go into a VOM program?

F.   INTERNATIONAL MEDIATION

Until now we have discussed mediation almost entirely as an American phenomenon. In fact, however, people across the world have turned to third parties to assist them in resolving disputes. International mediation is best known in the context of disputes involving nation-states. Theodore Roosevelt, for example, won the Nobel Peace Prize for his work as mediator of peace talks between Russia and Japan, and Jimmy Carter is remembered for facilitating the Camp David accords between Egypt and Israel. Mediation has also produced settlements between warring factions in Northern Ireland, Bosnia, and other regions.

Mediation is not nearly as well established in private international disputes. But the growth of legal mediation in the United States and the rapid rise of world trade raise questions: Do other countries use mediation in their legal systems — for example, do British courts use mediation to resolve lawsuits? How often is mediation applied in disputes between citizens of different nations? Are there significant differences between mediation as practiced in international disputes and the processes we have described in the preceding chapters?

1.   Foreign Legal Systems

The use of mediation in legal disputes varies greatly from country to country. As a result, no single statement about its prevalence is possible. In countries with common-law legal systems, particularly Canada, Great Britain, and Australia, mediation has become quite popular. England, for instance, has mandated that certain types of civil cases go through mediation before proceeding to trial.

In the civil-law countries of continental Europe, there is growing interest, but to date mediation has not yet been applied other than in isolated cases and specialized areas such as family law. The same is true of most of the rest of the world. Some suggest that because civil law systems do not allow extensive motion practice or discovery, parties are not as motivated by the need to avoid legal expense as in the American legal system. Overcrowded court dockets appear to be the primary impetus for experimentation with mediation in civil law countries. In Italy, for example, the fact that a typical case requires approximately 10 years to proceed from filing to final judgment has stimulated business interest in mediation. The process is also being explored as a method to reduce delay in Russia and some eastern European countries.

2. *International Legal Disputes*

Mediation can also be used to resolve disputes between citizens of different countries. Parties to international contracts are understandably reluctant to litigate in a foreign court system, and typically specify that disputes will be resolved by arbitration, a topic discussed in Chapter 16. Although international business contracts rarely refer explicitly to mediation, international arbitrators have long followed the custom of seeking to "conciliate" cases. The following readings explore the different forms that these processes can take in an international business deal, and what they mean when implemented by neutrals of different cultures. . . .

JESWALD SALACUSE, MEDIATION IN INTERNATIONAL BUSINESS

in J. Bercovitch, Studies in International Mediation 213-224 (2002)

. . . THE INTERNATIONAL DEAL: A CONTINUING NEGOTIATION

All international transactions are the product of negotiation — the result of *deal-making* — among the parties. Although lawyers like to think that negotiations end when the participants agree on all the details and sign the contract, this view hardly ever reflects reality. In truth, an international deal is a *continuing negotiation* between the parties to the transaction as they seek to adjust their relationship to the rapidly changing international environment . . . in which they must work. . . .

In the life of any international deal, one may therefore identify three distinct stages when conflict may arise and the parties rely on negotiation and conflict resolution to achieve their goals: *deal-making, deal-managing,* and *deal-mending*. Within the context of each of these three kinds of negotiation, one should ask to what extent third parties, whether called mediators or something else, may assist the parties to make, manage, and mend productive international business relationships. . . .

DEAL-MAKING MEDIATION

The usual model of an international business negotiation is that of representatives of two companies from different countries sitting across a table in face-to-face discussions to shape the terms of a commercial contract. While many transactions take place in that manner, many others require the services of one or more third parties to facilitate the deal-making process. These individuals are not usually referred to as "mediators." They instead carry a variety of other labels: consultant, adviser, agent, broker, investment banker, among others. . . .

Although it could be argued that consultants and advisors should not be considered mediators since they are not independent of the parties, a close examination of their roles . . . reveals that they exercise a mediator's functions . . . [I]n most cases, one of the principal assets of deal-making mediators is the fact that they are known and accepted by the other side in the deal.

DEAL-MAKING MEDIATION IN HOLLYWOOD

The acquisition in 1991 by Matsushita Electric Industrial Company of Japan, one of the world's largest electronics manufacturers, of MCA, one of the United States' biggest entertainment companies, for over $6 billion illustrates the use of mediators in the deal-making process. Matsushita had determined that its future growth was dependent upon obtaining a source of films, television programs, and music—what it termed "software"—to complement its consumer electronic "hardware" products. Matsushita knew that it could find such a source of software within the U.S. entertainment industry, but it also recognized that it was virtually ignorant of that industry and its practices. For Matsushita executives, embarking on their Hollywood expedition may have felt almost interplanetary. . . . They therefore engaged Michael Ovitz, the founder and head of Creative Artists Agency, one of the most powerful talent agencies in Hollywood, to guide them on their journey.

After forming a team to assist in the task, Ovitz . . . first extensively briefed the Japanese over several months, sometimes in secret meetings in Hawaii, on the nature of the U.S. entertainment industry, and he then proceeded to propose three possible candidates for acquisition, one of which was MCA. Ultimately, Matsushita chose MCA, but it was Ovitz, not Matsushita executives, who initiated conversations with the MCA leadership, men whom Ovitz knew well. Indeed, Ovitz assumed the task of actually conducting the negotiations for Matsushita. At one point in the discussions, he moved constantly between the Japanese team of executives in one suite of offices in New York City and the MCA team in another building, a process which one observer described as "shuttle diplomacy" . . . Although Matsushita may have considered Ovitz to be their agent in the talks, Ovitz seems to have considered himself to be both a representative of Matsushita and a mediator between the two sides.

Because of the vast cultural and temperamental differences between the Japanese and American companies, Ovitz's strategy was to limit the actual interactions of the two parties to a bare minimum . . . He was not only concerned by the vast differences in culture between the two companies but also by the greatly differing personalities in their top managements. The Japanese executives, reserved and somewhat self-effacing, placed a high value on the appearance if not the reality of modesty, while MCA's president was an extremely assertive and volatile personality. Like any mediator, Ovitz's own interests may also have influenced his choice of strategy. His status in the entertainment industry would only be heightened by making a giant new entrant into Hollywood dependent on him and by the public image that he had been the key to arranging one of the biggest deals in the industry's history. . . .

. . . Eventually the talks stalled over the issue of price, and meetings between the two sides ceased. At this point, a second deal-making mediator entered the scene to make a crucial contribution. At the start of the negotiation, Matsushita and Sony together had engaged Robert Strauss, a politically powerful Washington lawyer who had been at various times U.S. Ambassador to the Soviet Union and U.S. Trade Representative, as "counselor to the transaction." Strauss, a member of the MCA board of directors and a close friend of its chairman, was also friendly with the Matsushita leadership and did legal and lobbying work in Washington for the Japanese company . . . Strauss' close relationship to the two sides allowed him to act as a trusted conduit of communication who facilitated a meeting between the top MCA and Matsushita executives . . . [H]e apparently gained an understanding of the pricing parameters acceptable to each side and then communicated them to the other party . . . In the end, as a result of that meeting, the two sides reached an agreement by which Matsushita acquired MCA.

[A]lthough Matsushita did succeed in purchasing MCA, the acquisition proved to be troubling and ultimately a disastrous financial loss for the Japanese company. One may ask whether Ovitz' strategy of keeping the two sides apart during negotiations so that they did not come to know one another contributed to this unfortunate result. It prevented the two sides from truly understanding the vast gulf which separated them and therefore from realizing the enormity and perhaps impossibility of the task of merging two such different organizations into a single coordinated and profitable enterprise.

OTHER DEAL-MAKING MEDIATORS

An opposite mediating approach from that employed by Ovitz is the use of consultants to begin building a relationship between the parties *before* they have signed a contract and indeed before they have actually begun negotiations. When some companies contemplate long-term relationships . . . they may hire a consultant to develop and guide a program of relationship building, which might include joint workshops, get-acquainted sessions, and retreats, all of which take place before the parties actually sit down to negotiate the terms of their contract. . . .

. . . Sometimes persons involved in the negotiation because of their technical expertise or specialized knowledge, may assume a mediating function and thus help the parties reach agreement. For example . . . local lawyers or accountants engaged by a foreign party to advise on law or accounting practices in connection with an international negotiation may assume a mediating role in the deal-making process by serving as a conduit between the parties, by suggesting approaches that meet the other side's cultural practices [or] by explaining why one party is behaving in a particular way. . . .

DEAL-MANAGING MEDIATION

Once the deal has been signed, consultants, lawyers, and advisers may continue their association with one or both parties and informally assist as mediators

in managing conflict that may arise in the execution of the transaction
. . . Once top management of the two sides have reached an understanding,
they may have to serve as mediators with their subordinates to get them to
change behavior and attitudes with respect to interactions at the operational
level. . . .

DEAL-MENDING MEDIATION

The parties to an international business relationship may encounter a wide
variety of conflicts that seem irreconcilable . . . A poor developing country may
stop paying its loan to a foreign bank. Partners in an international joint venture may disagree violently over the use of accumulated profits and therefore
plunge their enterprise into a state of paralysis. Here then would seem ideal
situations in which mediation by a third party could help in settling conflict. In
fact, mediation is relatively uncommon once severe international business conflicts break out. To understand why, one must first understand the basic
structure of international business dispute settlement.

INTERNATIONAL COMMERCIAL ARBITRATION

Nearly all international business contracts today provide that any disputes that
may arise in the future between the parties are to be resolved by international
commercial arbitration . . . Thus in the background of virtually all international business disputes is the prospect of binding arbitration if the parties,
alone or with the help of a third person, are unable to resolve the conflict
themselves.

Arbitrating a dispute is not, however, a painless, inexpensive, quick solution.
Like litigation in the courts, it is costly, may take years to conclude, and invariably results in a final rupture of the parties' business relationship . . .
[Arbitrators sometimes seek to play a mediating role. Their usual strategy]
is to give the parties a realistic evaluation of what they will receive or be
required to pay in any final arbitration award.

MEDIATION IN INTERNATIONAL BUSINESS DISPUTES

Traditionally, companies engaged in an international business dispute have
not actively sought the help of mediators . . . With increasing recognition of
the disadvantages of arbitration, some companies are beginning to turn to
more explicit forms of mediation to resolve business disputes.

CONCILIATION

One type of deal-mending mediation used occasionally in international business is *conciliation* . . . While the conciliator has broad discretion to conduct the
process, in practice he or she will invite both sides to state their views of the
dispute and will then make a report proposing an appropriate settlement. The
parties may reject the report and proceed to arbitration, or they may accept it.

In many cases, they will use it as a basis for a negotiated settlement.
Conciliation is thus a kind of non-binding arbitration. Its function is predic-
tive. It tends to be rights-based . . . Conciliators do not usually adopt a
problem-solving or relationship-building approach . . . The process is confidential and completely voluntary . . . Thus far few disputants in international
business avail themselves of conciliation. . . .

M. SCOTT DONAHEY, THE ASIAN CONCEPT OF CONCILIATOR/ARBITRATOR: IS IT TRANSLATABLE TO THE WESTERN WORLD?

10 Foreign Investment Law J. 120-128 (1995)

In various Asian countries, there is a profound societal and philosophical preference for agreed solutions.[1] Rather than a cultural bias toward "equality" in relationships, there exists an intellectual and social predisposition towards a natural hierarchy which governs conduct in interpersonal relations. Asian cultures frequently seek a "harmonious" solution, one which tends to preserve the relationship, rather than one which, while arguably factually and legally "correct," may severely damage the relationship of the parties involved.

Where the Westerner will segregate the function of facilitator from that of decision-maker, the Asian will make no clear distinction. The Westerner seeks an arbiter that is unconnected to the parties to the dispute, one whose mind has not been predisposed by previous knowledge of the dispute or the facts which underlie it, a judge who is prepared to "let the chips fall where they may." On the other hand, many Asians seek a moderator who is familiar with the parties and their dispute, who will not only end their state of disputation but assist the parties in reaching an agreed solution, or, failing that, will find a position which will not only be one that terminates their dispute, but one that will allow the parties to resume their relationship with as little loss of "face" as possible. Thus, the distinction between the function of the arbitrator and that of the conciliator is blurred.

Clearly, as there is increased interaction in the forms of tourism and trade between the Western world and Asia, differences between the two cultures have diminished and will continue to diminish. We in the West tend to view this process as one in which the Asian countries are influenced by our economic and political systems and become more "Westernized." Our western pride and predispositions often do not permit us to recognize the degree to which we have been influenced and changed by the Asian cultures with which we have come in closer contact. . . .

Within the Confucian tradition, there is a concept known as "li," which concerns the social norms of behavior within the five natural status relationships: emperor and subject, father and son, husband and wife, brother and brother, or friend and friend. *Li* is intended to be persuasive, not compulsive and legalistic, a concept which governs good conduct and is above legal concepts in societal importance. The governing legal concept, "fa," is compulsive and punitive. While having the advantage of legal enforceability, *fa* is traditionally below *li* in importance. The Chinese have always considered the resort to litigation as the last step, signifying that the relationship between the disputing parties can no longer be harmonized. Resort to litigation results in loss of face, and discussion and compromise are always to be preferred. Over time the concepts of *fa* and *li* have become fused, and the concept of maintaining the relationship and, therefore, face, has become part of the Chinese legal system. . . .

---

1. The author recognizes that the generalizations in which he engages tend to explain away the complexities and vast difference that exist in any nation or culture and are inherently suspect. Nevertheless, such generalizations are often necessary when comparing one cultural system to another.

Adjudication is an act-oriented process. . . . In contrast, since conciliation/mediation is a "person-oriented" one, it is non-adversarial and set in a warm and friendly air of informality unbound by technical rules of procedure. Furthermore, while the nature of the adjudicative process requires that evidence and arguments presented by one party be made in the presence of the adverse litigant, separate conferences with the parties have been found to be an effective tool of conciliation. It is less important, in conciliation proceedings, to be accurate in finding the truth of the issues than to know what values are held by the parties so that a "trade-off" may be effected that will restore the disrupted harmonious relationship.

In Japan, as well, permitting a relationship to fall into a state of disharmony is culturally unacceptable: "In Japan . . . the existence of a dispute may itself cause a loss of 'face,' and submission of a dispute to a third party may carry with it some sense of failure." . . . Thus, if there is one principle which can be said to lead to the combining of the role of arbitrator with that of conciliator it is that of preserving the harmonious relationship between the parties to the dispute. This principle is one that is frequently cited by Western arbitral institutions in promoting the use of commercial arbitration over litigation. . . .

Perhaps the foremost proponent of the practice of combining the role of conciliator and arbitrator . . . is the People's Republic of China. While no written rules have ever sanctioned or even described the practice, Chinese arbitrators and practitioners both practice and espouse the combination of mediation and conciliation: Arbitration and conciliation are interrelated and complementary with one another. They are not antagonistic and do not exclude each other. . . .

It is important to understand that the Chinese combination of arbitration and conciliation occurs during the ongoing process of arbitration. The arbitrator, after taking some evidence and hearing some witnesses, might attempt to conciliate the differences and, if efforts at conciliation fail, return to the receipt of evidence and the hearing of witnesses, ready to attempt conciliation again at an opportune time during the course of the proceedings . . . [I]it is unclear whether parties convey information to the arbitrators/conciliators in confidence during the conciliation phase, and, if so, how it is maintained . . . This is different from the way that other Asian nations combine the functions of arbitrator and conciliator. . . .

The traditional Western view is that the conciliation process should be separate from the arbitration process and that the same persons who act as conciliators should not act as arbitrators in the same dispute . . . However, the traditional Western view is changing, largely due to the influence of Asian cultures . . . A combined conciliation and arbitration process offers significant advantages in reaching an agreed settlement and in preserving existing commercial relations between the parties. It is a system that apparently has worked well in Asia, and we in the West should not shrink from its use. . . .

QUESTIONS

1. What approach would you expect from an Asian conciliator: Facilitative or evaluative? Narrow or broad?
2. You are involved in an arbitration of a business contract dispute on behalf of an American computer manufacturer who contracted with a Chinese firm to produce silicon chips, paid for and installed the chips in its products, and

has since found out that they are unreliable, leading to serious repair costs and lost profits. Your client believes that the Chinese partner failed to comply with the quality requirements because it overstated its expertise in the area and simply did not understand them. The contract gives you the right to recover your damages, but it is not clear how you would enforce an award in arbitration against the supplier. If you know that the chair of the arbitration panel is a Chinese attorney,

   a. What, if anything, would you say to the neutral about the possibility of conciliation before the process begins?
   b. What instructions would you give your client about how to act during conciliation?

G.   ON-LINE MEDIATION

One potential development in mediation does not involve a new subject area, but rather the use of technology to enhance its impact. Mediators already use conference calls to allow people to talk without meeting in person. Law firms and businesses employ video conferencing to bring people together visually, and nothing prevents mediators from doing so as well. The most novel application of technology to mediation, however, is in small disputes where it is impractical for disputants to meet face-to-face. In such cases, e-mail and other computer-assisted techniques might be used to conduct the process electronically — that is, to engage in "on-line" mediation.

So far, on-line mediation has proven less popular than its proponents had hoped. One reason is that the very fact of meeting face-to-face is an important aspect of mediation. In part, physical presence matters because so much of communication between people occurs through their tone of voice, facial gestures, and body language. Although disputants separated in caucuses cannot exchange such information, they communicate directly with the mediator, and most neutrals consider the ability to talk face-to-face with a party crucial to their effectiveness. Electronic communication thus eliminates one of the most important qualities of classic mediation.

There is also the psychological reality that meeting in person forces disputants to go through trouble and expense — clearing schedules, traveling to a site, hiring a neutral, and remaining isolated for hours. Requiring parties to attend in person thus forces them to confirm that they take the process seriously, demonstrates to each side that their opponent is equally committed to the process, and marks mediation as a "settlement event."

Perhaps as a result of these factors, efforts by private companies to establish e-mail or computer-based settlement systems have been largely unsuccessful, and even video conferencing in high-end cases appears to be quite infrequent. The vast majority of mediations continue to involve face-to-face meetings between the disputants and a neutral.

One exception is a process used by one of the most successful Internet companies, eBay, to resolve customer complaints arising from its system of facilitating sales. The eBay system relies heavily on mediation conducted by a panel of neutrals over the Internet. Because, however, mediation constitutes only one stage of the eBay system, we deal with it as part of the discussion of multistage ADR systems in Chapter 21.

CHAPTER

13

Court-Connected Mediation and Fairness Concerns

Much of the early impetus for applying ADR to civil litigation came from judges concerned about overloaded dockets. It is not surprising, therefore, that courts throughout the United States have established dispute resolution programs. Legislators have supported court-sponsored ADR; Congress, for example, has required every federal district court in the nation to implement a dispute resolution program (ADR Act of 1998, 28 U.S.C. sec. 651(b)). Modern ADR programs cover general civil litigation as well as special categories such as family, small claims, and even criminal cases. Programs are most common at the trial level, but exist in appellate courts as well. Although some court programs offer litigants a choice of ADR processes, mediation has become by far the most popular form of court-connected dispute resolution.

The primary reason that courts have embraced mediation is to relieve their dockets of unwanted cases. In the words of one Texas judge, "I am interested in mediation because the cases settle earlier, and that gives me more time to be a judge, to spend that time I can gain to improving the quality of justice in my court." Although their primary motivation is usually to reduce backlogs, courts divert cases to mediation for other reasons as well. Some cases involve complex continuing relationships, such as disputes between parents over the custody and visitation rights to their children. Adjudication is often ineffective to resolve such disputes, because it focuses on the past rather than the future and addresses only the presenting problem rather than underlying conflicts. Litigating such controversies is also beyond the financial means of many individuals, and such cases often require continuing supervision that can drain court resources.

Courts also sometimes promote mediation to divert cases that judges do not want to hear and court personnel do not wish to process. Family and neighborhood disputes, for example, often provoke raw emotions that defy rational analysis. These and other categories of cases, such as small claims and prisoners' rights suits, also frequently involve pro se litigants who place extra burdens on court staff.

Court-connected mediation thus raises important policy issues, which involve not simply designing programs to yield the greatest benefit to the system, but also to ensure fundamental fairness for participants. Fairness issues arise most pointedly in the context of court-sponsored mediation, especially when courts require litigants to engage in the process. However, such problems can appear in private mediations as well, particularly when disputes involve allegations of criminal conduct or parties from different cultures. The second part of this chapter deals with the troubling question of how to ensure fairness for all who participate in the mediation process.

A. COURT-CONNECTED MEDIATION

1. Issues of Program Design

a. What Goals Should a Program Seek to Achieve?

What should be the purpose of a court-connected mediation program? Although many judges have embraced court-connected mediation as a means to reduce delay, the evidence that it does so is conflicting. A study of six federal court programs that used mediation as one ADR technique, for example, did not find statistically significant evidence that the programs reduced the duration of cases. On the other hand, a study of five other courts did find significant reductions in the length of cases due to the use of mediation. (Compare Kakalik et al., 1996, with Stienstra et al., 1997.) Similar variations appear in empirical studies of state court programs. Abstracts of these and other studies of court-related ADR programs can be found at *www.caadrs.org*.

The differences in study results may be due to the great variations in how individual courts design and implement their programs. Some courts, for example, do not send cases to mediation until after the completion of discovery, which greatly reduces the possibility of cutting cost and delay. One federal court, for example, requires parties to appear at mediation for only one hour per case, much too little time to apply many of the techniques described in this book. Given these variations, it is not surprising that results are mixed. But even if court-sponsored mediation does not consistently reduce the duration of cases, there may be other reasons to support its use.

WAYNE D. BRAZIL, WHY SHOULD COURTS OFFER NON-BINDING ADR SERVICES?

16 Alternatives 65 (1998)

[T]here is no one method of procedure that works best for resolving . . . every kind of dispute. . . . In some cases, the parties' dominating concern will be with trying to establish the truth. They will want to use the process that is most likely to generate historically accurate factfinding, regardless of other considerations . . . Traditional adversarial litigation may well best meet the needs of such parties.

But for parties to whom other values or interests loom larger, other processes are likely to deliver more valued service — and are more likely to result in consensual disposition . . . To some parties, relationship-building . . . may be of prime importance . . . In some cases, what the parties care most about are feelings . . . In some disputes, it is the quality and character of communication that matters most — or that holds the most promise of delivering constructive solutions. . . .

It follows that if our judicial system is to be responsive to the full range of interests and needs that cases filed in our courts implicate, then the system cannot offer only one dispute resolution method. . . .

One role of public courts in a democratic society is to try to assure that it is not only the wealthy or the big case litigants who have access to appropriate and effective dispute resolution processes. Poor litigants, and parties to cases without substantial economic value, should not be relegated by our judicial system to the often-slow and disproportionately expensive procedures of traditional adversarial litigation. To force poor people and small cases into that system can be tantamount to denying them access to any system at all. . . .

A related consideration supporting court sponsorship of ADR begins with the observation that some litigants and lawyers might have greater confidence in the integrity of an ADR process and the neutral when the ADR services are provided or sponsored by a court than when they are provided in a wholly private setting. When the service provider is a public court, for example, there is no occasion for the concerns that have surfaced about the possible influence . . . of large companies that are current or potential sources of considerable repeat business. . . .

[In addition,] active participation in designing and implementing ADR programs provides courts with opportunities to gain insight that they can use to improve their handling of traditional litigation . . . [A] thoughtfully monitored ADR program can develop . . . insights into negotiation dynamics that can be shared with judges who host settlement conferences, enhancing the skills . . . that judges can bring to their work as settlement facilitators. . . .

Unhappily, there is a risk that courts could be tempted to permit institutional selfishness to infect the thinking that drives their program design. Some judges and judicial administrators, for example, might be attracted to ADR only or primarily as a docket reduction tool, [posing] serious threats to fairness or other values that ADR should be promoting. There also is a risk that some judges and administrators could try to use ADR programs as dumping grounds for categories of cases that are deemed unpopular, unimportant, annoying, or difficult.

QUESTIONS

1. Would a traditional judge disagree with any of the arguments that Judge Brazil makes for court-connected mediation? Which ones?
2. Brazil promotes mediation as a means of securing justice for poor people. Others, however, have raised concerns that ADR provides "second-class justice" to the disadvantaged. What aspects of the process is each side focusing on?

b. How Will Services Be Provided?

The goals of promoting settlement and exploring litigants' deeper interests are not necessarily contradictory, but varying goals are likely to lead to different program designs. A program focused on stimulating settlements at minimal cost, on the one hand, might set up short sessions, rely on volunteer neutrals, and encourage participants to "cut to the chase." A program whose goal was to address parties' underlying interests, on the other hand, would be more likely to use a broad range of techniques and carefully trained mediators, likely increasing its cost.

One key issue is who will mediate court-sponsored cases. Most court programs rely on panels made up of lawyer, and occasionally non-lawyer, neutrals with limited training and experience. This approach allows courts to offer ADR services at low cost and build support for mediation in the private bar. The services themselves, however, vary widely in quality. A second option is to create a roster of professional neutrals. Such panels are more consistently competent than volunteer groups, because the participants have been tested by the market. Professionals, however, are likely to charge for their services. Some courts reduce costs by requiring professionals to contribute their initial time on each case without charge or to work at reduced rates. Finally, some courts, particularly in the federal and family court systems, use full-time employees as mediators. These neutrals may be lawyers, magistrates, or senior judges, and may have the advantage of having received special training and being able to devote substantial time to each case. However, this design requires the court to bear the entire cost of providing neutrals, and may make it difficult for litigants to avoid a mediator they consider ineffective.

Cases in court-connected programs are typically selected either by the litigants or by judges or court screeners. As noted, courts vary widely as to when they order or permit cases to go into mediation. Empirical research has not resolved which approach is more effective, but the general trend is to mediate disputes earlier in their lives.

2. Models of Court-Connected Mediation Programs

a. Trial Court

Almost every state has a mediation option or requirement in its civil court system. To give you a sense of the forms these programs can take and the obstacles to their implementation, we provide descriptions of three state programs.

NANCY A. WELSH AND BARBARA MCADOO, ALTERNATIVE DISPUTE RESOLUTION IN MINNESOTA—AN UPDATE ON RULE 114

in Court-Annexed Mediation: Critical Perspectives on State and Federal Programs 203-212 (1998)

When Rule 114 [requiring litigants to engage in mediation in most state civil cases] arrived on the Minnesota legal scene in July, 1994, it took many attorneys by complete surprise . . . Today, largely as a result of Rule 114, nearly 80 percent of Minnesota's attorneys report that they are using ADR to help resolve their civil cases filed in trial courts, and a majority of the state's attorneys indicate that they would continue to use ADR even if Rule 114 were repealed. . . .

RULE 114'S UNIQUE APPROACH

[T]he ADR Task Force struggled mightily with the question of whether or not to make ADR *mandatory* in all civil cases. The experience of other jurisdictions was instructive. In those jurisdictions where ADR was totally voluntary, parties used ADR rarely or not at all. In jurisdictions that made ADR mandatory for certain classes of cases, there was not always a good "match" between a case and the ADR process used to attempt resolution of the case.

Therefore, the ADR Task Force recommended an approach which institutionalizes *consideration of ADR* in every case. Basically, early in the life of a case, attorneys and parties are required to think and talk about ADR. They are given overwhelming discretion and creative freedom in selecting an ADR process, the ADR neutral, and the timing of the ADR process. And, to ensure that attorneys and parties take advantage of this window of opportunity, Rule 114 and its enabling legislation supply judges with a "stick." Simply, judges have the authority to order parties into non-binding ADR processes against their will. This provision has helped to ensure that attorneys and parties actively investigate and select ADR processes. . . .

Generally, the court exercises this discretion within the first 90 days after a case has been filed. However, the Rule provides the court with the authority to issue an order for non-binding ADR at any time, upon its own initiative or pursuant to a party's motion. . . .

AN INFRASTRUCTURE OF QUALIFIED ADR NEUTRALS

. . . The Rule also recognizes the need to ensure that *qualified* neutrals are available to support the creative and appropriate application of Rule 114 . . . [Neutrals selected by parties] tend to be lawyers and litigators, and, most importantly, to have substantive experience in the field of law related to the case. . . .

PAYING FOR ADR

When Rule 114 was being developed, it was very clear that Minnesota's judicial system could not assume responsibility for paying for ADR services . . . The Rule provides that the parties will pay for the services of an ADR neutral. . . .

ON-GOING EVALUATION AND MONITORING

This is an area of concern for Minnesota. [T]here is no on-going monitoring or required party evaluation process to assure the quality of the ADR neutrals. . . .

EFFECT OF RULE 114 ON THE USE OF ADR PROCESSES

Recent research indicates that Rule 114 has had a dramatic effect in increasing the use of ADR in Minnesota's courts. The overwhelming majority of the attorneys who responded to the Rule 114 Questionnaire — more than 80% — reported that they had used an ADR process for their civil cases in the past two years. . . .

MIKE AMIS ET AL., THE TEXAS ADR EXPERIENCE

in Court-Annexed Mediation: Critical Perspectives on State and Federal Programs 369, 376-378 (1998)

THE DALLAS EXPERIENCE

Court-annexed mediation seemed to take off in Dallas County in 1989. Now, nine years later, on any given day, dozens of cases are being mediated in the county, with the use of mediation having spread to all civil, family, and probate courts. Virtually all types of cases have proven to be appropriate, from the large, complex commercial or injury case to the neighborhood dispute . . . Overcrowded dockets, Rambo litigation, with widespread client dissatisfaction, particularly in the business sector, paved the way for a new day: Our existing jury system was wonderful when it worked, but it was not functioning very well. The courts were overburdened, and no settlement system was in place. . . .

It is our belief that the transformation which took place in Dallas can occur in any community with certain fundamental elements in place . . . [A rule] that provides for court-ordered mediation, giving counsel an opportunity to reasonably object, is crucial . . . Our experience is that busy lawyers, perhaps worried that suggesting mediation will be construed as a sign of weakness, need a mandatory referral, the proverbial "two by four on the head of the donkey to gain attention." The mandatory orders, in turn, paved the way for voluntary efforts; attorneys, with credibility, can advise their clients that the Order is coming. . . .

TODAY

The ripple effect of the [many] lawyers trained in mediation skills serves to change the litigation landscape for the better . . . Some attorneys now have participated in hundreds of mediations as advocates. Experienced mediators are currently serving on the bench . . . Dallas has a mature court-annexed mediation system. . . .

SHARON PRESS, FLORIDA'S COURT-CONNECTED STATE MEDIATION PROGRAM

in Court-Annexed Mediation: Critical Perspectives on State and Federal Programs 55-59 (1998)

Mediation is on the rise in Florida. Statistics of court-connected mediation programs from 1988 to 1996 indicated an increase from approximately 10,000 cases to more than 74,000 documented cases mediated annually . . .

In 1997 . . . Florida had 12 Citizen Dispute Settlement Center programs, 34 county programs, 23 family programs, 13 circuit programs, 12 dependency mediation programs, and one appellate mediation program. . . . In toto, we estimate that more than 100,000 cases are diverted from the traditional court process to mediation each year . . . [This figure does not include private mediations that are scheduled without court involvement.]

Currently, there is a trend in Florida toward greater freedom of choice. Although courts still retain the authority to mandate that parties attend mediation, more parties, through their attorneys, are selecting mediation before receiving a court order. . . .

QUESTIONS

1. What appear to be the key differences among the court programs described above?
2. Regarding the Texas comment about applying a "two by four on the head of the donkey": Who is the donkey? Is there any downside to this approach to encouraging use of mediation?
3. A court that has mandated parties to participate in ADR for several years has asked you whether, as a matter of policy, it should now drop the requirement. What would you recommend? What are the arguments pro and con?

b. Appellate

DANA CURTIS AND JOHN TOKER, REPRESENTING CLIENTS IN APPELLATE MEDIATION: THE LAST FRONTIER

1 JAMS Alert No. 3, 1 (December 2000)

These days mediation of disputes in trial courts is commonplace. Yet mediation of appeals is relatively rare, even though each circuit of the U.S. Court of Appeals has long maintained staffs of mediators and some state appellate courts have mediation programs. [In] the Ninth Circuit, the eight full-time . . . mediators helped parties settle over 600 cases last year. [And more] than forty percent of cases sent to mediation in [a California state court appellate program] have settled.

. . . The introduction of mediation into the appellate process requires appellate lawyers to take on the role of counselor in the broadest sense. Lawyers must analyze cases not only from a *legal* viewpoint, but also from a *human* and *business* perspective. They need to help their clients make good decisions regarding not only whether, but also how, to proceed. The consideration of mediation should be part of that process. . . .

The similarities between mediation of appellate cases and other matters far exceed the differences. Nevertheless, understanding the distinctions will help you do a better job of representing your clients in appellate mediation.

1. *There's already a winner and a loser.* As counsel for the appellant, it may be that you have not considered mediation of appeals because it doesn't occur

to you that the respondent, as the victor, would be willing to accept a compromise instead of an appellate decision. There are a number of reasons why a respondent may be willing to accept a compromise instead of [a] decision. Essentially, they boil down to a five little words: risk, cost, time, life, and gain.

Risk   Appellate courts can be unpredictable, even in cases that seem open and shut. Appeals from judgments entered as a matter of law, such as summary judgments . . . are particularly risky because the appellate court reviews these appeals de novo. The reversal rate in these cases is approximately 30 percent . . .

Cost   Appeals can be very expensive. A five-day trial can translate into a $30,000 appeal with transcript production and briefing. If the appellate court reverses the judgment, the case may be remanded to the trial court for further costly proceedings. A reasonable compromise may be in the best interest of all parties.

Time   It likely is in the interest of a respondent to have a judgment satisfied sooner rather than later . . .

Life   There comes a time for many litigants . . . when they just want to end the pain and get on with their lives.

Gain   Mediation offers creative solutions outside of the litigation box. . . .

2. *The participants may be less optimistic about resolution.* Generally, parties in appellate mediation have had a number of failed negotiations and are therefore more discouraged about settlement than they were at the beginning of the dispute. And they also suffer from the skepticism discussed above, that is, why would the winner want to sit down at the mediation table?

3. *Paradoxically, the law and evaluation of the legal issues by the mediator may not be as important to settlement as it was before trial* . . . Mediator evaluation of the merits of the case may not play an important role as it does in other litigated cases [because] parties have already had an evaluation by a judge or a jury, and at least one of them is not convinced it was right.

4. *The relationships between the parties may be more strained.* A contested trial court proceeding that has been resolved in favor of one of the parties never *enhances* the relationships between them. If they were antagonistic before litigation, parties often are bitter enemies by the time of the appeal. In selecting a mediator for an appeal, you'll need to consider the mediator's ability to manage high conflict and create a positive environment for problem solving.

5. *Lawyers and clients both have problems with cognitive dissonance* between their negotiating positions before and after the trial court decision. Failing to settle earlier for a greater/lesser amount before the court decision may make it more difficult for the client to enter into a settlement that differs greatly from the earlier offer or demand. You may also struggle with your failure to have settled for more/less before the decision . . . If you can't put aside the previous settlement proposal, and your regret at having passed it up, you may not be able to advise your client rationally. . . .

B. IS MEDIATION FAIR?

The most troubling critique of mediation is not that it is ineffective, but rather that it can be unfair or even harmful to some of the people who enter the process. Regardless of its other attributes, some argue, mediation should be avoided because its very virtue — informalism — results in vulnerable parties receiving worse treatment than they would in traditional litigation.

Issues of fairness can arise even when disputants voluntarily elect to go to private mediation; some of these concerns are discussed in Chapter 14. Problems of fairness are particularly acute, however, when mediation occurs in the context of a court. First, the very fact that a mediation program is affiliated with a court may lead litigants to believe that the justice system has endorsed the quality of what occurs. In addition, many courts now require litigants to participate in mediation as a precondition to obtaining access to a judge. Making mediation mandatory raises especially serious concerns about its quality. The readings below explore the issue of fairness in the mediation process.

1. A Critique of Process

RICHARD DELGADO, ADR AND THE
DISPOSSESSED: RECENT BOOKS
ABOUT THE DEFORMALIZATION MOVEMENT

13 Law & Soc. Inquiry 145-154 (1988)

Early writing on Alternative Dispute Resolution (ADR) . . . was almost uniformly congratulatory. The movement appealed both to the technocratic-managerial instincts of the right and moderate center, as well as to the desire of many on the political left to avoid the polarization, contentiousness, and all-or-nothing character of formal, in-court justice. Drawing support from across the spectrum, the ADR movement grew rapidly. More recent writings about ADR have been more nuanced. Several respected writers have criticized the politics of ADR or questioned its ability to deliver the promised benefits. At the same time, the proponents' claims have become more modest and less global. . . .

Many of ADR's claims rest on user satisfaction surveys. Yet . . . satisfaction is a measure of the discrepancy between what a disputant expects and what he or she gets. Since ADR frequently draws only on those who want informality, it is not surprising that they are satisfied when they receive it . . . When, due to subtle or not-so-subtle pressures, unwilling disputants are brought before a deformalized forum, the forum typically cools out their expectations long before a result is reached. . . .

There are only a handful of basic ways in which our society responds to insoluble social problems — ones that, like blacks' demands for justice, women's claims for comparable worth, consumers' demands for well-made, reasonably priced goods, workers' demands for a larger share of the industrial pie, and everyone's desire for a safe, nonpolluted environment, cannot be solved at an acceptable cost.

If those agitating for reform are aroused and united, we cannot dismiss their problem as a nonproblem or the claimants as nonpersons (as we once did with slaves or do today with children and the insane). That would simply inflame them further. The only solution is to seem to be addressing the problem, but without doing anything that threatens the status quo too drastically. . . .

[One] approach is to enlarge the problem—to concede its existence but insist that it is much broader than most realize, that its solution entails expanding the context and taking account of a multitude of factors . . . When "the problem" is transformed into something so complex and multifaceted that no simple legal formula can encompass it, it is also likely that no single remedy—such as an injunction or damages—can solve it. Instead, we must strive to avoid simplistic win-lose thinking and look for creative solutions that maximize many variables at once. Equally important, . . . [s]ince dozens, perhaps hundreds, of details are relevant to a case's resolution, the likelihood that identical cases will recur is remote. Therefore, we can dispense with stare decisis, the rule of law, written opinions, and judicial review. . . .

The movement toward alternative dispute resolution illustrates [this] approach . . . It is an excellent way of seeming to be doing something about intractable social problems while actually doing relatively little . . . [P]roblems are not faced, responsibility is diffused, grievants are cooled out, while everyone leaves thinking something positive has been done.

Some grievances will not succumb to burial. They will retain their sharp edges despite being embedded in a mass of extraneous detail. The grievant will decline ADR's demand for peace, for compromise, and insist that his or her problem be dealt with in accord with justice. In disputes of this type—ones that retain their initial polarity—a second problem with ADR emerges. . . .

Formal adjudication contains a multitude of rules and practices the effect, and sometimes intent, of which is to constrain bias and prejudice. These range from rules dealing with disqualification of judges and jurors for bias, to rules that protect the jury from prejudicial influence . . . Moreover, studies indicate that simply becoming a member of a jury has a fairness-inducing effect on jurors, causing them to display a greater degree of impartiality and fairness than they ordinarily do in daily life. . . .

. . . [P]rejudice is widespread in American society—surveys and polls indicate that most Americans harbor some degree of prejudice toward members of groups other than their own . . . The expression of prejudice is far from simple, however, and certainly not automatic . . . The formalities of a court trial are calculated to check prejudice. The trappings of formality—the flags, black robes, the rituals—remind the participants that trials are occasions on which the higher values of the American Creed are to preponderate, rather than the less noble values we embrace during times of intimacy . . . [They] also encourage minority-race persons to press their claims more forthrightly. . . .

. . . ADR can, by expanding disputes beyond recognition, cause them to lose their urgency and sharp edges. When ADR cannot avoid dealing with sharply contested claims, its structureless setting and absence of formal rules increase the likelihood of an outcome colored by prejudice, with the result that the haves once again come out ahead. . . .

QUESTIONS

1. In what types of cases does it seem most likely that the concerns set out by Professor Delgado may arise?
2. Are there categories of disputes in which they are unlikely to occur?

2. Issues of Gender, Ethnicity, and Culture

MICHELE HERMANN, NEW MEXICO RESEARCH EXAMINES IMPACT OF GENDER AND ETHNICITY IN MEDIATION
1 Disp. Resol. Mag. 10-11 (Fall 1994)

Professors and students from the University of New Mexico Schools of Law and Sociology are collaborating on a research project ... to study the effects of race and gender on mediation and adjudication of cases in Albuquerque's small claims court. This court, the Bernalillo County Metropolitan Court, is a non-record court with jurisdiction to hear civil cases in which the amount in controversy is $5,000 or less. All three judges are male; one is African American, one is Hispanic American, and one is European American ... The court contracts with a local mediation center to operate the court's mediation program, under which all civil filings are screened ... and about one-third of the cases are referred to mediation.

The research project randomly assigned more than 600 cases to either adjudication or mediation, and tracked both the case results and the participants' reactions ... The study sought to evaluate results in mediation and adjudication by using two measures: (1) an objective formula for outcome ... , and (2) subjective measures of satisfaction. ...

Perhaps the most startling finding is that in the objective outcomes of both adjudicated and mediated cases, disputants of color fared worse than did white disputants. These disparate results were more extreme in mediated than in adjudicated cases. An ethnic-minority plaintiff could be predicted to receive eighteen cents on the dollar less than a white plaintiff in mediation, while an ethnic-minority respondent could be predicted to pay twenty cents on the dollar more. When examining how the ethnicity of the co-mediators affected outcomes, the study found that when there were two mediators of color, the negative impact of the disputant's ethnicity disappeared. The ethnicity of the mediators did not change the objective outcomes of white disputants' cases.

The negative outcomes found for ethnic minority participants were not replicated when the data were analyzed for gender. For the most part, neither the gender of the claimant nor that of the respondent had a statistically significant effect on monetary outcomes in either adjudicated or mediated cases, except that female respondents did better in mediation than male respondents, paying less than their male counterparts.

The examination of procedural and substantive satisfaction produced interesting contrasts to the objective outcome analysis. Despite their disparately poorer outcomes, ethnic minority disputants were more likely to express satisfaction with mediation than were white disputants. Female disputants, on the other hand, were more likely to express satisfaction with adjudication. Indeed, white female respondents, who had the most favorable objective outcomes in mediation, reported the lowest level of satisfaction. Furthermore, compared to other mediation respondents, white women were less likely to see the mediation process as fair and unbiased. Women of color, on the other hand, reported the highest level of satisfaction with mediation, despite their tendency to fare the worst in objective outcomes as either claimants or respondents.

The evidence that disputants of color fare significantly worse in mediation than do white participants raises important questions about whether the traditional mediation process is appropriate in disputes involving ethnic minorities, as well as members of other groups who are traditionally disempowered in American society. . . .

It is far from clear, however, that bias, prejudice, and cultural blindness are the only explanation for the results of the UNM study. The underlying effects may be considerably more complex . . . Similarly, the fact that white women fare well in small claims mediation does not dispel the concerns raised by scholars . . . about gender bias in other forums, such as family court. . . . In the meantime, mediation and other dispute resolution programs need to pay serious attention to the potential impact of power imbalances between and among parties who are in dispute, and should not assume that mediator neutrality will guarantee fairness.

QUESTIONS

1. If the conclusions of the New Mexico study are correct, can you think of any steps or safeguards that might reduce the risk of disparate results in small claims mediation? In the mediation of family disputes?
2. Can you suggest any reason why minorities might be more satisfied with mediation, despite receiving less favorable results?

SINA BAHADORAN, A RED FLAG:
MEDIATOR CULTURAL BIAS IN DIVORCE MEDIATION
18 Mass. Fam. L.J. 69-73 (2000)

Scenario One: An American wife and her Albanian husband are participating in divorce mediation. The couple shares a four-year-old daughter. During mediation, the wife alleges that her husband sometimes acts inappropriately with their daughter—one time fondling her genitalia. The mediator asks the husband about the wife's allegation and the husband responds that it is true.

Scenario Two: An American man and his Danish wife are involved in a divorce mediation. The couple share a 14-month-old son. During mediation, the husband alleges that on several occasions his wife left their son outside in his stroller, while she went into diners to have lunch.

Scenario Three: An American woman and her Iraqi husband are participating in divorce mediation. The couple shares a nine-year-old daughter. During mediation, the wife accuses the husband of being violent and aggressive with their daughter. The wife also expresses fear over her husband's renewed interest in Islam.

In each of the above scenarios a mediator, as currently trained, would be unprepared to adequately handle these situations. In other words, mediation would be inappropriate. Scenario One is based on the incident involving Sadri Krasniqi of Plano, Texas. After fondling his daughter during a basketball match, Krasniqi was charged with sexual abuse and lost custody of his daughter. Eventually, five years later, charges against him were dropped after the prosecutors became aware that the idea of parent-child sex is so unimaginable in Albania that parental fondling is acceptable behavior.

Scenario Two is based on the case of Annette Sorenson, a Danish woman who left her 14 month old daughter outside while she went into a diner to have lunch. Sorensen was jailed and charged with child endangerment. Only later was she freed after authorities learned that "parking," or leaving children in their strollers outside of stores, is common behavior in Denmark.

Scenario Three is a fictitious situation where the foreign spouse would be just as disadvantaged as in the first two scenarios, not because of *actual* cultural differences, but rather because of *perceived* cultural stereotypes. . . .

AMERICAN COLLECTIVE UNCONSCIOUS: CULTURAL MYTHS AND STEREOTYPES

. . . A non-American spouse entering divorce mediation will face a great many cultural myths and stereotypes . . . The cultural myths that surround people of various ethnicity and nationality vary greatly, but all are unified by a common theme: cultural inferiority.

. . . Parent-child suicide, religious fanaticism, barbarity, laziness, wife beating, forced marriage, and female genital mutilation are just some of the images associated with non-European immigrants . . . Arab Muslims are seen as irrational beings, incapable of achieving cultural or intellectual success . . . With Asian cultures, the myths take on a different quality. Asians are often seen as the "model minority." . . . Although intended to be complimentary to Asian-Americans, the "praise" can go too far. Most Asians are seen as being fungible . . . In contrast to the "model" minority status associated with Asians, Latinos are often relegated to the bottom of the minority hierarchy: laziness, alcoholism, criminality, and gang culture are just a few of the myths . . . [G]iven the cultural myths and stereotypes that pervade the American collective unconscious, the informal nature of mediation creates an atmosphere that is particularly prone to bias. . . .

POWER AND DANGER OF NARRATIVE IN MEDIATION

Much of the power of mediation comes from its opportunity for divorcing spouses to tell their own stories. Each spouse is the director, producer, and actor . . . Despite the benefits of the narrative style, it is also at the center of the problems with mediation. Mediation is essentially a struggle between two opposing narratives. The prevailing narrative sets the context for all of the subsequent descriptions. Minority spouses will have more negative cultural myths aligned against them and will be disadvantaged in their ability to compete for narrative preeminence. . . .

Imagine a scenario where the Iraqi husband and his American wife are seeking mediation for their divorce. The couple has a nine-year-old daughter and is in a heated disagreement as to custody. One portion of the mediation revolves around an incident where the husband smacked their daughter's hand for misbehaving. In the wife's description, she will assign her husband the role of the violent, strict middle-easterner and herself and her daughter as the innocent victims of his rage. The husband will try and reconfigure the wife's "primary narrative." He will explain that the young girl had repeatedly misbehaved and that he lightly slapped her hand after several previous admonitions. In his narrative, the husband will assign himself the role of the "good" loving father and his wife as the unresponsive, distant mother who allows their daughter to be spoiled.

. . . The conversational narrative in this case is created from fragments of larger cultural stereotypes . . . Each spouse will attempt to manipulate the conversation by relying on as many positive cultural stereotypes about their identity group and negative ones about their spouse as possible . . . The mediator sits in the middle of the competing stories as they circle around her. She must choose one . . . Her choice will not be explicit, but she will offer more credence to one narrative over the other. The mediator enters meditation with his or her own selected conscious and unconscious cultural stereotypes. As the mediator listens to each spouse's perception of reality, she filters all of the narratives through her own individual (experiential) and cultural (identity group) filter. The effects of the narratives will be greater if they are of a subliminal rather than overt nature. . . .

QUESTIONS

These articles raise difficult questions about how to ensure the quality of mediation, not simply in court-connected programs but in private processes as well.

1. Do you think that such myths are widespread enough to pose a serious problem in mediation?
2. Assume that you are the lawyer for a client from another culture who is involved in a parenting dispute that is going to mediation. How might you monitor whether your mediator is allowing stereotypes to influence his approach to the case?

3.   Should Mediation Be Used in Domestic Violence Cases?

One of the most controversial issues in mediation is whether the process has any place in cases in which violent acts may have occurred. This issue arises most often in the context of domestic disputes. The first reading argues against the use of mediation in such cases, focusing in particular on California, where parents are required to mediate disputes over child custody or visitation as a precondition to gaining access to a court hearing. As you read the piece, ask yourself whether the same arguments apply in systems where parties can ask the court to be exempted from mediation.

ALANA DUNNIGAN, COMMENT — RESTORING
POWER TO THE POWERLESS: THE NEED TO
REFORM CALIFORNIA'S MANDATORY
MEDIATION FOR VICTIMS OF DOMESTIC VIOLENCE

37 U.S.F. L. Rev. 1031-1053 (2003)

Forty-three states and the District of Columbia have legislation regulating family mediation . . . [E]leven states uniformly order mandatory mediation. [Most such state] programs are discretionary and provide exemptions . . . States vary as to what is required for an exemption . . . California is the only state that utilizes mandatory mediation without any exemptions.

DOMESTIC VIOLENCE AND ITS EFFECTS

Although domestic violence against women is "as old as recorded history," it took hundreds of years for it to be treated as a crime . . . American courts in the 1800s allowed a man to beat his wife, and followed the "rule of thumb," whereby a husband could beat his wife with any stick as long as it was no thicker than his own thumb. It was not until the latter half of the twentieth century that society awakened to the problem of domestic violence and responded with protective laws and programs.

[S]tatistics show that the violence increases when women leave their abusers. According to one study of domestic homicides, 75% of the victims had ended or stated an intention to end the relationship at the time of their death . . . [S]ome scholars describe the patterns of an abusive relationship as a "culture of battering." The "culture of battering" includes three primary elements: the abuse itself (physical, emotional, sexual, etc.); the systematic pattern of domination and control the batterer exerts over his victim; and the coping strategies, including hiding, denying and minimizing the abuse, which a battered woman employs to reduce the psychological impact of the abuse. . . .

MANDATORY MEDIATION INVOLVING DOMESTIC VIOLENCE UNDERMINES THE PRINCIPLES AND GOALS OF MEDIATION

Effective mediation is premised upon voluntary participation, equal bargaining power, and confidentiality. However, these principles, along with the premise of mediation as a self-determining and empowering process, are undermined in the context of mandatory mediation involving domestic violence.

VOLUNTARINESS

. . . The belief that, due to the voluntary nature of their participation, the parties are more likely to invest emotionally in the success of their personally formulated agreements is not applicable if the parties are forced to mediate . . . These problems . . . have a much greater detrimental impact when the state is forcing a victim of domestic violence to mediate, because it reinforces her lack of power and lack of control, which have already been beaten into her.

EQUAL BARGAINING POWER

More problematic, however, is the premise of effective mediation based upon parties with equal bargaining power fairly negotiating with each other. Commentators have recognized that . . . mediation "lacks the precise and perfected checks and balances that are the principal benefit of the adversary process," and thus, "mediation creates a constant risk of overreaching and dominance by the more knowledgeable, powerful or less emotional party." This risk is at its greatest in situations with domestic violence victims. . . .

THE BATTERER'S PSYCHOLOGICAL ADVANTAGE: THE VICTIM'S FEAR AND DENIAL ARE NOT ASSUAGED BY SEPARATE MEETINGS

A battered woman has significant fears, including the fear of revenge by her partner and the fear that he will take the children. Taking into consideration her perspective of powerlessness and the reticent, accommodating stance she has adopted through the cycle of violence, coupled with her fears of retaliation and kidnapping, it is likely that mediation negotiations will indirectly coerce a battered woman into a less desirable agreement.

[Many programs] seek to offset these problems by providing for separate meetings for the parties. According to the California Rules of Court, [for example,] these separate sessions "must protect the confidentiality of each party's times of arrival, departure, and meeting with Family Court Services." Separate meetings may provide for the battered woman's immediate safety and offset some pressure and coercion she might feel in the direct presence of the batterer, but the victim's fears of retaliation and kidnapping, and her reluctance to assert her wishes, cannot be expected to dissipate suddenly once she is out of the abuser's presence. [This] is like trying to argue that a victim of domestic violence no longer fears her batterer when he leaves the house . . . As one researcher stresses, "It's vital to understand that battering is *not* a series of isolated blow-ups. It is a *process of deliberate intimidation intended to coerce the victim to do the will of the victimizer*" (emphasis in original). . . .

. . . Furthermore, there is a significant risk of the victim's denial that she is abused. The separate meetings may not take place immediately, or at all, if the battered woman never alleges domestic violence. . . .

[The author also strongly critiques California's "recommending" or "evaluative" model of court-sponsored mediation, which gives individual judges the authority to have neutrals in unsuccessful mediations make recommendations to the court on unresolved issues, drawing on what they have learned during the process.]

MANDATORY MEDIATION UNDERMINES THE BEST INTERESTS OF THE CHILD

Mediation allows a batterer who has not been held accountable for his behavior, and who may not even be identified as an abuser, to simply sit down and freely negotiate with his victim for control of the children. . . . As he achieves the custody arrangement that will best suit his abusive needs, there is no attorney, no judge, and no therapist to intervene and demand what is best for the children. It is in this sense that mandatory mediation is fundamentally contradictory and detrimentally inconsistent with legislation aiming to protect the child . . . Between 50 and 70% of men who abuse their female partners also abuse their children . . . Additionally, 25 to 33% of men who batter their wives also sexually abuse their children. . . .

STIFLING THE SCREAMS OF PROGRESS: THE PRIVATIZATION OF DOMESTIC VIOLENCE THROUGH MEDIATION

Allowing victims of domestic violence to pursue adjudication rather than medi-ation is essential. On a practical level, battered women are in a disadvantaged position from the moment the State forces them to sit down at the bargaining table and negotiate with their abusers. . . . On an ideological level, battered women individually and as a group are ultimately disadvantaged by mandatory mediation because it stifles the progress of domestic violence issues and does nothing to empower or vindicate the victims in the long term. In mediation, "the emphasis is not on who is right or who is wrong." . . . While not everyone will want to pursue litigation or even be able to afford it, to take away that option is disempowering to victims and stifling to the progress of the battered women's movement. . . .

QUESTIONS

Bearing in mind that Ms. Dunnigan's arguments are presented in the con-text of the California system, in which there is no option to seek an exemption from mediation in domestic disputes and mediators sometimes make recom-mendations to the court about unresolved issues:

1.   Would any of her concerns be alleviated by a system that allowed disputants to ask for exemptions from mediation?
2.   What procedural guarantees would be needed to make such an exemption option effective?
3.   To what extent are these concerns less severe in systems where mediators are forbidden from communicating with courts, other than to say whether or not a settlement has been reached?

The following article presents a different view of the use of mediation in domestic violence cases.

ANN L. MILNE, MEDIATION AND DOMESTIC ABUSE

in Divorce and Family Mediation 304-331, Guilford Press (J. Folberg et al., eds., 2004)

There are nearly 6 million incidents of physical assault against women reported every year, and 76% of these are perpetrated by current or former husbands, cohabiting partners, or dates . . . Changes in the law and the increased media attention given to domestic abuse have sensitized the public to this formerly private issue. In contrast, the use of mediation has increased significantly as a less-public forum to resolve disputes between former spouses. Courts in at least 38 states have mandated that parents be referred to mediation when they are disputing custody or parental access schedules.

. . . The juxtaposition of strengthened court and legal interventions in domestic abuse cases with the expanded use of mediation has resulted in considerable controversy . . . Current arguments about the use of mediation in domestic abuse cases . . . do not focus so much on the mediation process itself, but rather on the nature of domestic abuse and the concerns endemic to these cases. *Mediators should take these public policy concerns seriously.* . . .

IN SUPPORT

Most mediation proponents agree with the following guidelines:

- Some cases involving domestic abuse are inappropriate for mediation.
- Screening is necessary to determine which cases are appropriate.
- Mediators must be well trained in the dynamics of domestic abuse.
- Participation in the mediation process must be safe, fair, and voluntary.
- Victims of abuse should not be required to mediate.

Given these guidelines, proponents of making mediation available in cases of domestic abuse generally start with the argument of the "BATMA": What is the couple's "best alternative to a *mediated* agreement" . . . In short, if mediation is not used, then what? It is argued by both social science experts and legal scholars that mediation is more appropriate and effective than the adversarial process, even in cases of domestic abuse. Some have said that the adversarial process exacerbates the dynamics between partners when abuse is a factor by escalating the conflict and reinforcing the power and control differential and the win/lose aspects of the relationship . . . Few judges and lawyers have expertise in the subject of domestic abuse, whereas many mediators have had training in it. . . .

REFRAMING THE DEBATE

. . . As in any conflict, the framing of the issues is critical in order to adequately address [these concerns]. Rather than framing the question, *Should mediation be used in cases involving domestic abuse?*, a more useful framing of the issue would be: *What process can we develop that will best help individuals who have been involved in an abusive relationship address the issues between them, so that they can move on with their lives without violence and without the need for ongoing court and legal interventions?* . . .

When providing mediation to batterers and victims, the following are excluded from the list of topics to be addressed:

We are not mediating whether or not the abuse occurred . . .
We are not mediating reconciliation . . .
We are not mediating fault and blame . . .

> We are not mediating punishment and consequences . . .
> We are not mediating dropping of charges, protective orders, or res-
>   training orders. ("Do this, then she will drop the abuse charges").
> We are not mediating contingencies or leveraging of issues . . .
> We are not mediating court orders.
> We are not mediating threshold issues.

With the above procedural ground rules in place, the following areas can be effectively mediated:

TERMS OF LIVING APART

Matters such as establishing a date for moving out, determining who is going to live where, division of household accessories, establishing a parenting sched-ule, and payment of household expenses are all day-to-day living arrangements that parties may need to address. The judge often does not have the time to take up each of these individual issues, and paying lawyers to negotiate them can be too costly for many. . . .

PROPERTY DIVISION

Mediation can be a very helpful process for dividing up personal possessions such as furnishings, household supplies, photographs, books, tools, and all the other sundry things that family members need to manage their daily lives.

FINANCIAL SUPPORT . . .

USE OF CLOTHING AND TOYS . . .

ACTIVITIES WITH THE CHILDREN

Mediation can be a very useful forum in which to share information about what activities the children would enjoy as well as to resolve disputes regarding activities of which a parent disapproves. Is it OK to take the children hunting? To a friend's home? To the corner tavern? . . .

SCHOOL CONTACT

Is it OK for a parent to stop by the school to say hello to a child or to chat with the teacher? . . . Will both parents participate in children's sporting and other school events? . . .

CHILD-CARE ARRANGEMENTS

How will child-care decisions be made? . . . If a parent is called away from home, will the other parent be given the first opportunity to babysit? . . .

RESEARCH FINDINGS

Quantitative longitudinal research on the impact of mediation in cases of domestic abuse is lacking . . . [S]tudies found that mediation was associ-ated with a greater reduction in physical, verbal, and emotional abuse than lawyer-assisted settlement . . . For the growing unrepresented or pro se popu-lation of litigants, mediation may be the only consumer support available, short of litigation. Outcome studies on the impact of precluding mediation would be very illuminating.

"CONFESSIONS OF A MEDIATOR"

I have been a mediator for more than 30 years and have worked in both a court-connected setting and a private practice. Over time I have come to several personal conclusions and observations about my own practices when mediating cases involving allegations or instances of domestic abuse:

I AM FAR MORE CONTROLLING OF THE PROCESS

Whereas I normally espouse a mildly directive, facilitative style, when I am mediating in a case known to me to include allegations or instances of domestic abuse, I often find that I must be far more controlling of the process . . . At the same time, I need to avoid becoming enmeshed in an arm-wrestling contest with the batterer, who may attempt to take over the process. . . .

JUDGMENT IS IMPORTANT

The role of the mediator is typically described as that of a nonjudgmental neutral party . . . However, when mediating in cases of possible or known domestic abuse, . . . [t]he mediator must continually reevaluate whether this case is appropriate for mediation and whether he or she has the skills needed to work effectively with this couple.

FORGET THE BALANCING ACT

Terms such as *maintaining balance, power balancing*, and *level playing field* are often used when describing the mediation process. However, when mediating in a case involving issues of domestic abuse, I find that I am "off-balance" much of the time because I am challenged to keep control of the process.

THE PROCESS IS LESS COLLABORATIVE AND MORE OF A FACILITATED NEGOTIATION

. . . The parties focus more on their separate interests and solutions rather than the mutual interests that I tend to focus on when abuse is not a factor.

SHORT-TERM AGREEMENTS

One of the incentives to using mediation in cases involving concerns about domestic abuse is the ability to put in place agreements of a short-term nature and revisit and revise them as needs dictate. Predictability and steadfastness are not often present with these couples. Putting together agreements or court orders that apply over the long haul is often counter-productive. . . .

NEED FOR RELIABLE RESOURCES

The need to establish a scaffolding of support can be very important when mediating in domestic abuse cases. The support of the parties' attorneys, victim and batterer advocates, counselors, and a safety plan can all work together to facilitate the success of the mediation process.

WATCH YOUR LANGUAGE

Colloquialisms that I use in everyday speech can often take on unintended meanings with domestic abuse partners. Using expressions such as "Can you live with that?," "It strikes me that . . . ," or "Please cut that out," would be insensitive and inappropriate with couples who have abuse issues. . . .

SWEAT EQUITY IS A FACT OF LIFE

I usually tell my mediation students that I know something is wrong when I am working harder than the clients. I have found that, when mediating in cases where abuse concerns have been raised, my skills are challenged, there is a level of stress not found with non-abuse cases, and I work *hard* to ensure that the mediation process is serving the interests and safety of both parties.

CONCLUSIONS

The question of whether or not mediation is appropriate in cases of domestic abuse must be reframed to focus on finding an answer to the question of what kind of system we could design that would provide a safe and secure decision-making process for spouses and parents in dispute. Although a traditional mediation process may not offer the protection necessary in domestic abuse cases, dismissing mediation outright may also be a mistake. The development of hybrid mediation models that embody the self-determination principles of the mediation process while also addressing power, control, coercion, and safety issues must be the goal.

QUESTIONS

1. Does Milne's model accommodate Dunnigan's concerns? Overall, which approach seems most appropriate?
2. Assuming Milne's model could work in the right circumstances, is it practical to implement in court programs? What assurances would you need in order to support such a program in your local family court?
3. If you favor excluding cases involving allegations of abuse from court programs, would you also favor barring such cases from going to private mediation voluntarily?

CHAPTER
14

Law and Ethics

A. CONFIDENTIALITY

One of the key attractions of mediation for many clients and lawyers is that the process is confidential. Participants in mediation routinely sign agreements in which they pledge not to disclose to outsiders anything communicated during the process. In addition, states and the federal government have given mediation varying levels of confidentiality protection. Sometimes, however, participants in mediation seek to disclose, or outsiders attempt to discover, what occurred during the process.

Disputes over mediation confidentiality arise in two different ways. First, litigants sometimes attempt to take confidential information from the mediation process and use it in another context, such as in court. ("Isn't it true that in mediation you admitted that . . . ?"). A second type of confidentiality case arises from a party's allegation that the mediation process itself went awry ("Your Honor, the defendant failed to participate in the process in good faith, as the court's rules require. . . .") To understand how confidentiality issues can present themselves, consider the following problems.

PROBLEM

You represent a St. Louis company, Bates, Inc. Bates is a "headhunter" firm that fills executive positions for corporations. A year ago Bates contracted with a Chicago software consultant, Alpha Websites, to develop a Web site for Bates. A key goal for Bates was that its clients be able to advertise openings without revealing their identity, and that candidates be able to input personal data online in confidence. One function of the new software was thus to screen out conflicting requests (e.g., an executive applying for an opening at a company where he is currently working). The site was to be developed over six months for a total fee of $150,000.

Bates reports that the transaction was a disaster. The developer took nearly a year to deliver the site, and the security provisions proved to be porous. Clients complained that candidates could determine who was advertising, and some people found themselves applying to their current employer, causing embarrassment for all concerned. Bates estimates that it lost at least a million dollars in business as a result of the Web site problems.

You filed suit against Alpha in federal court in Illinois, and a few months later accepted an invitation from Alpha's counsel to go to mediation. The mediation was governed by a confidentiality agreement. After several hours of mediation you deadlocked, with your client at $350,000 and Alpha at $50,000. In an effort to break the impasse, the mediator offered both sides a tentative opinion that while Bates had a good case on the contract, the site was now up and running fairly smoothly, and that given the language of the contract he did not think the court would grant a recovery on the lost profits claim. He recommended a settlement at $125,000. You declined this proposal, feeling that the evaluation was unrealistic and that the neutral was "bending" his evaluation to produce a number that Alpha would accept.

Three months later, you are called into a status conference with the judge presiding over the case. He asks both sides if they have explored settlement. You mention the unsuccessful mediation. The judge asks if the mediator gave an evaluation of the case. You say that the discussions were confidential, but the Alpha lawyer says, "Yes, Judge. Do you want to know what it was?" The judge nods affirmatively.

a. What should you do?
b. How should you respond if Alpha seeks to mention the mediator's evaluation at trial?

PROBLEM

Assume that at a settlement conference in the Bates-Alpha case, the presiding judge suggests that the litigants participate in mediation. Bates is willing but Alpha declines. The judge says that in his experience mediation is often beneficial, and exercises his authority to order the parties to mediate. Rules of the court's mediation program require that participants mediate "in good faith" and bring with them "full settlement authority." Three weeks later Bates and Alpha appear before a court-appointed mediator. Bates is represented by its CFO and outside counsel, Alpha by an associate from its outside law firm. In its opening statement Bates indicates that while it believes strongly in its case, it is willing to consider a reasonable compromise. Alpha argues that there is no basis for liability and that Bates' damage claims are wildly inflated.

After four hours of mediation Bates, which entered the mediation demanding $750,000, has dropped to $450,000. Alpha, which had made no offer before the mediation, offers $5,000, then $10,000, and then refuses to move further. In a caucus discussion with the mediator, Alpha's counsel reveals that she has no authority to go beyond $15,000, since that is all the company thinks the claim is worth, and that any offer above $100,000 would have to be approved by the defendant's board of directors. Bates does not know about this conversation, but tells the neutral that it strongly suspects that Alpha never gave its negotiator "real" settlement authority.

A week later, Bates files a motion for sanctions with the judge, charging that Alpha's conduct at mediation violated the court's ADR program rules. Bates subpoenas the mediator to testify at the hearing on its motion.

a. How should Alpha respond to Bates' claim that it violated program rules?
b. How should it respond to the mediator subpoena?

1. How Important Is Confidentiality to Mediation?

LAWRENCE R. FREEDMAN AND MICHAEL L. PRIGOFF, CONFIDENTIALITY IN MEDIATION: THE NEED FOR PROTECTION

2 Ohio St. J. Disp. Resol. 37-38 (1986)

. . . Confidentiality is vital to mediation for a number of reasons:

Effective mediation requires candor . . . Mediators must be able to draw out baseline positions and interests, which would be impossible if the parties were constantly looking over their shoulders. Mediation often reveals deep-seated feelings on sensitive issues. Compromise negotiations often require the admission of facts which disputants would never otherwise concede. Confidentiality insures that parties will voluntarily enter the process and further enables them to participate effectively and successfully.

Fairness to the disputants requires confidentiality. The safeguards present in legal proceedings, qualified counsel and specific rules of evidence and procedure, for example, are absent in mediation . . . Subsequent use of information generated at these proceedings could therefore be unfairly prejudicial, particularly if one party is more sophisticated than the other. Mediation thus could be used as a discovery device against legally naive persons if the mediation communications were not inadmissible in subsequent judicial actions. . . .

The mediator must remain neutral in fact and in perception. The potential of the mediator to be an adversary in a subsequent legal proceeding would curtail the disputants' freedom to confide during the mediation. Court testimony by a mediator, no matter how carefully presented, will inevitably be characterized so as to favor one side or the other. This would destroy a mediator's efficacy as an impartial broker.

Privacy is an incentive for many to choose mediation. Whether it be protection of trade secrets or simply a disinclination to "air one's dirty laundry" in the neighborhood, the option presented by the mediator to settle disputes quietly and informally is often a primary motivator for parties choosing this process.

Mediators and mediation programs need protection against distraction and harassment. Fledgling community programs need all of their limited resources for the "business at hand." Frequent subpoenas can encumber staff time, and dissuade volunteers from participating as mediators. . . .

There is virtual unanimity that some degree of confidentiality is appropriate in most mediations, but commentators do not agree on how strong the protection should be. In particular, some question whether mediation requires a legal privilege. Consider the following perspective.

SCOTT H. HUGHES, A CLOSER LOOK: THE CASE FOR A MEDIATION CONFIDENTIALITY PRIVILEGE STILL HAS NOT BEEN MADE

5 Disp. Resol. Mag. 14-15 (Winter 1998)

Consider the case of the manipulating minister: At a small women's college, a minister with the campus ministry seduces a naive young coed into a sexual relationship. When she attempts to break off the relationship, the minister responds with harassment. She subsequently sinks into a deep depression and drops out after her first semester. Several months later, she confides in her sister, who promptly relays the sordid tale to their mother.

The family's attorney files suit and commences discovery, from which she learns about an earlier incident involving the same minister while at the college's sister institution. Finding that the previous dispute had been settled through mediation, the attorney issues a subpoena for the mediator and his notes. During a caucus with the mediator, it seems, the minister stated that his supervisors had been aware of his illicit urges for some time. The mediator, joined by the church and the minister, seeks to quash the subpoena by asserting the privilege contained in the state mediation act. Does the need to encourage settlement outweigh the victim's rights to this information? I think not.

[Or] consider the case of the disputant in duress: During a mediation, one party complains of chest pains and fatigue, only to be told by the mediator that he cannot leave the mediation session until a settlement has been reached. The disputant subsequently signs a settlement, but tries to have it set aside during a subsequent action for specific performance. The adverse party contends that the mediation privilege prohibits an examination of the communications that took place during mediation, preventing the assertion of such a defense. Mediation privileges would foreclose disputants from raising this or many other contract defenses. . . .

Over the past two decades we have witnessed a vast proliferation of mediation statutes throughout the United States, many of which contain privileges shielding the mediator and/or the parties from the disclosure of events that take place during mediation, thus shrouding mediation proceedings in a veil of secrecy . . . Before rushing to create another privilege that may preclude the law's traditional right to "every person's evidence," we should take at least one more close look at the social and legal cost of such a privilege. If that important step is taken, it will become apparent that the benefit of the mediation privilege does not justify its cost.

To begin with, it should be noted that there is almost no empirical support for mediation privileges. For example, no data exists to show a difference in growth rates or overall use of mediation services between jurisdictions with privileges and those without such protections, or from within any jurisdiction before and after the creation of a privilege . . . Moreover, there is no empirical work to demonstrate a connection between privileges and the ultimate success of mediation. Although parties may have an expectation of privacy, no showing has been made that fulfilling this expectation is crucial to the outcome of mediation. . . .

[T]o assess the overall value of mediation privileges, it is important to weigh any gains that would be attributable to mediation against their cost. Privileges sacrifice potentially important evidence for subsequent legal proceedings and restrict public access to information that may be necessary to a democratic society. Of course, finely detailed exceptions to a mediation privilege could be crafted that would help overcome many problems. However, numerous exceptions could well lead to an unpredictable privilege that would be more detrimental than no privilege at all.

Until [an] empirical connection can be made, the arguments in favor of mediation privileges should not overcome the historical presumption favoring the availability of "every person's evidence."

QUESTIONS

1. Who do you find more persuasive: Freedman and Prigoff, or Hughes?
2. In the absence of a mediation privilege, what can a lawyer do to increase the likelihood that mediation communications will be kept confidential?
3. The introduction to Chapter 9 lists several ways in which a mediator can facilitate settlement, including:
   - Helping to ensure the presence of key decision makers at the table.
   - Allowing disputants to present arguments, interests, and feelings directly to their opponent.
   - Moderating negotiations, coaching bargainers, and reframing positions.
   - Assisting each side to reassess its litigation option.
   - Helping participants to focus on their underlying interests.

For which of these functions is the assurance of confidentiality most significant?

2. Sources of Mediation Confidentiality

There are five primary sources of rules governing confidentiality in mediation:

- Rules of evidence
- Privileges
- Rules adopted by courts and ADR programs
- Confidentiality agreements
- Positive disclosure obligations

Rules of Evidence

Virtually every jurisdiction has adopted a rule of evidence to protect the confidentiality of settlement discussions. The key federal provision is Federal Rule of Evidence (FRE) 408.[1] About two-thirds of the states have evidentiary rules patterned on FRE 408. The first point to note about Rule 408 is that it is a rule of evidence, not a guarantee of confidentiality. Rule 408 is intended to limit what litigants can offer in evidence in a court proceeding, not what parties or observers can disclose in any other context. Rule 408 does not, for example, apply to discovery depositions, nor does it limit what a person

---

1. The text of the rule is as follows:

Rule 408. Compromise and Offers to Compromise. Evidence of (1) furnishing or offering or promising to furnish, or (2) accepting or offering or promising to accept, a valuable consideration in compromising or attempting to compromise a claim which was disputed as to either validity or amount, is not admissible to prove liability for or invalidity of the claim or its amount. Evidence of conduct or statements made in compromise negotiations is likewise not admissible. This rule does not require the exclusion of any evidence otherwise discoverable merely because it is presented in the course of compromise negotiations. This rule also does not require exclusion when the evidence is offered for another purpose, such as proving bias or prejudice of a witness, negativing a contention of undue delay, or proving an effort to obstruct a criminal investigation or prosecution.

can say in a conversation or a media interview. In addition, FRE 408 and its counterparts typically apply only to court proceedings. They may therefore not be effective in less-formal forums such as administrative hearings and arbitrations; whether a mediation conversation will be admissible in another forum will depend on its rules and the approach of the presiding officer.

Even in court, Rule 408 may not prevent information about settlement discussions from being disclosed. The rule and its state counterparts cover only evidence that a person offered or agreed to accept "valuable consideration" to compromise a claim, not everything said in settlement discussions. Thus, for example, the rule does not protect trade secrets from being disclosed unless they are part of an offer to settle. Indeed, even an offer of compromise is not necessarily sacrosanct under Rule 408, because the rule has many exceptions. The rule applies, for example, only if an offer of compromise is introduced for the purpose of proving a party's "liability for or invalidity of the claim or its amount." Confidential data that is offered for another purpose is not protected by the rule. A litigant might, for instance, avoid Rule 408 by arguing that evidence of an offer is being offered to show that a witness is biased, or that a party did not bargain in good faith.

Other uncertainties arise from the fact that only the person against whom evidence is being offered can make a Rule 408 objection. The rule, in other words, is designed to prevent a party from being shot in court with a "gun" that it provided to the other side during settlement discussions, not to help non-parties or mediators keep discussions confidential. Finally, a rule of evidence can often be hard to enforce, since parties who evade it ordinarily risk at most a judicial reprimand.

Statutes and Privileges

In light of the inherent weaknesses of evidentiary rules, almost every state, as well as the federal government, has created some form of confidentiality protection for mediation. States can create confidentiality rules by statute, and courts can do so as a matter of common law. Twenty-five states now have statutes that apply generally to mediation, and most of the rest have laws that cover the use of mediation in specific types of cases or programs, such as environmental disputes or court-connected programs. A Massachusetts statute, for instance, states that any communication during a mediation, as well as the mediator's work product, "shall be confidential" and inadmissible in adjudication. California statutes similarly provide that the mediation process shall be "confidential." (See Mass. G.L. c. 233, §23C; Cal. Code §§1115-1128.) To say that a process is confidential, however, does not necessarily fix the extent of protection: For example, a statute may simply establish an evidentiary rule akin to FRE 408, or may bar participants from disclosing mediation communications outside of court as well.

Of the twenty-five states with general statutes, most have created formal legal "privileges." Although the term "privilege" can have different meanings, it usually means not only that a communication is inadmissible in evidence, but also that it cannot be disclosed outside of court. In addition, a violation of a privilege carries potentially greater penalties than does noncompliance with a rule of evidence: A person injured by a violation of a privilege can usually sue

the offender for damages. To understand the level of protection in any particular setting, however, a lawyer needs to consider the following issues:

- What privilege applies to the process?
- What aspects of the process does it cover?
- Who can invoke the privilege?
- Is it subject to any exceptions or exclusions?

What privilege applies? Courts almost always apply their own rules of evidence,
but this is not true of privileges. Thus, if a mediation takes place in State A, but the
case later goes to trial in State B, choice of law principles will often determine
which state's mediation privilege is applied. Indeed, Professor Ellen Deason
has commented that "Mediation confidentiality would make an ideal poster
child for the shortcomings of choice-of-law" (Deason, 2002b).

There is no general federal mediation privilege, although a few federal
courts have recognized a mediation privilege as a matter of common law,
and federal trial courts are mandated to provide confidentiality protection
for their mediation programs (28 U.S.C. §652(d)). As a result, when a case
is tried in federal court, an *Erie v. Tompkins* issue may arise: Should the court
view the mediation privilege of the state in which it sits as a "substantive" legal
standard that must be applied in the case, or as a "procedural" rule that it can
disregard? The absence of a federal privilege of general application makes it
hard to predict how confidential communications will be treated in federal
proceedings.

What aspects of the process are covered? The coverage of some statutes is narrow
or poorly defined. A particular state's privilege may, for example, apply only to
the mediation session itself, not to conversations and e-mails between counsel
and the neutral before and after the "formal" mediation.

Who holds the privilege? Only persons designated as "holders" of a privilege are
entitled to invoke it. Typically the parties to a case hold the privilege and thus
can prevent disclosures about the mediation process. The mediator, however,
may not be entitled to use the privilege as a shield, just as lawyers are not usually
permitted to invoke the attorney-client privilege unless their client elects to do
so. Thus if a neutral is called to testify about what occurred during a mediation,
she may well have to ask a party to protect her from testifying. This is not always
true, however: California, for example, requires the mediator's as well as the
parties' consent for anyone to testify as to the content of a mediation and
bars testimony from mediators (Cal. Evid. Code §§1122, 703.5.)

Is the privilege qualified or absolute? What exceptions apply? Some states have
adopted mediation privileges that are absolute, meaning that they contain no
stated exceptions. Other privilege laws allow or even require mediators to
breach confidentiality in certain situations, for example, to report evidence
of a felony, threats of harm to children, perjury, and other matters. Even when
privileges are absolute on their face, courts sometimes create exceptions as a
matter of common law.

Rules Adopted by Courts and ADR Programs

Mediations often take place under the auspices of a court or other program
and are therefore subject to the rules promulgated by the sponsor. These rules

typically provide that the mediation process will be confidential, although they may not specify what is meant by that term. In one sense, a party's incentive to comply with the rules of a court-affiliated program is strong, because litigants may be concerned that if they violate a rule they will incur the wrath of the judge who will hear their case. This is not to say, however, that a party will have a legal cause of action or other remedy if another litigant violates a confidentiality rule.

Mediation Agreements

Mediation agreements offer the best opportunity for a lawyer to tailor confidentiality protections to the needs of particular cases. An agreement is a contract, however, and thus is subject to the limitations inherent in any contractual undertaking. First, agreements bind only those who enter into them, not nonparties. In the case of mediation, this means that outsiders to the process, such as third-party litigants, are not constrained by the parties' mediation agreement. Second, if a breach does occur, a party's only remedy is usually to sue for monetary damages, if any can be proved. Even in the unusual situation in which a litigant knows of an impending violation and is able to seek a court order to prevent it, a judge may refuse to enforce the obligation out of concern that a contract not to provide evidence in court violates public policy. This said, however, practicing neutrals report few, if any, complaints from parties who sign a confidentiality agreement that their opponent later violated it.

Positive Disclosure Obligations

Public policy sometimes weighs against secrecy concerning settlement negotiations. Many states, concerned that secret settlements have operated to hide serious social problems—for example, that confidential agreements settling individual sexual abuse and toxic tort cases have delayed authorities from discovering the extent of these problems—have considered statutes that would bar courts from ordering certain kinds of settlements to be sealed. Some states also have decisional law or statutes that require persons who become aware of certain offenses to report them to authorities. Thus, for example, some jurisdictions require therapists to report potential harm that they learn about from clients (see *Tarasoff v. Regents of University of Cal.*, 17 Cal. 3d 425 (1976)), and many states require mediators to report instances of child abuse. Finally, both individual states and the federal government have enacted "sunshine laws," which require that certain meetings involving government officials be open to the public. As a result, when environmental and regulatory issues are mediated, the process may have to be open to outside observers.

3. Examples from Practice

As we have discussed, most attempts to breach the confidentiality of mediation occur either because a litigant seeks to use admissions or other information revealed in mediation to its advantage in court, or because a participant in mediation alleges that the process itself was defective. We consider each category in turn.

a. Use of Mediation Information in Litigation

ROJAS v. SUPERIOR COURT OF LOS ANGELES COUNTY
33 Cal. 4th 407 (2004)

CHIN, J.:

We granted review in this case to consider the scope of Evidence Code Sec. 1119(b), which provides: "No writing . . . that is prepared for the purpose of, in the course of, or pursuant to, a mediation . . . is admissible or subject to discovery. . . ." In a divided decision, a majority of the Court of Appeal held that application of this statute is governed by the same principles that govern application of the work product privilege. . . . We conclude that the Court of Appeal's interpretation . . . is contrary to both the statutory language and the Legislature's intent. We therefore reverse the . . . judgment.

FACTUAL BACKGROUND

Julie Coffin is the owner of an apartment complex in Los Angeles that includes three buildings and a total of 192 units. In 1996, Coffin sued the contractors and subcontractors who built the complex . . . alleging that water leakage due to construction defects had produced toxic molds and other microbes on the property . . . In April 1999, the litigation settled as a result of mediation. . . .

In August 1999, several hundred tenants of the apartment complex filed the action now before us against [Coffin and] numerous . . . entities that participated in development or construction of the complex. Tenants alleged that defective construction had allowed water to circulate and microbes to infest the complex, causing numerous health problems. They also alleged that all defendants had conspired to conceal the defects and that they (Tenants) had not become aware of the defects until April 1999. Tenants served [a] request for production of all photographs . . . taken . . . during the underlying action . . . Coffin asserted that, under section 1119, the requested documents were not discoverable. . . .

On March 7, 2002, Judge Mohr denied Tenants' motion . . . explaining: "The plaintiffs say that they need these photos and there's no other evidence of the conditions as they were at that time and in those places, and defendants are saying these photographs were created for mediation purposes. . . . They're clearly protected by the mediation privilege. This is a very difficult decision . . . because it could well be that there's no other way for the plaintiffs to get this particular material. On the other hand, the mediation privilege is an important one, . . . and if courts start dispensing with it by using the . . . test governing the work product privilege, . . . you may have people less willing to mediate."

DISCUSSION

As we recently explained, implementing alternatives to judicial dispute resolution has been a strong legislative policy since at least 1986. Mediation is one of the alternatives the Legislature has sought to implement . . . One of the fundamental ways the Legislature has sought to encourage mediation is by enacting several mediation confidentiality provisions. [C]onfidentiality is essential to effective mediation because it promotes a candid and informal exchange regarding events in the past. This frank exchange is achieved only if participants know that what is said in the mediation will not be used to their detriment through later court proceedings and other adjudicatory processes.

The particular confidentiality provision at issue here is section 1119(b), which provides: "No writing . . . that is prepared for the purpose of, in the course of, or pursuant to, a mediation or a mediation consultation, is admissible or subject to discovery, and disclosure of the writing shall not be compelled, in any arbitration, administrative adjudication, civil action, or other noncriminal proceeding . . ." The Court of Appeal's holding directly conflicts with the plain language of these provisions. . . . [Section 1120 of the Code] does not, as the Court of Appeal held, support a contrary conclusion. As noted above, section 1120(a), provides that "[e]vidence otherwise admissible or subject to discovery outside of a mediation . . . shall not be or become inadmissible or protected from disclosure solely by reason of its introduction or use in a mediation. . . ." Read together, sections 1119 and 1120 establish that a party cannot secure protection for a writing — including a photograph, a witness statement, or an analysis of a test sample — that was not "prepared for the purpose of, in the course of, or pursuant to, a mediation" simply by using or introducing it in a mediation. [The statutory scheme] prevents parties from using a mediation as a pretext to shield materials from disclosure.

The Court of Appeal's holding is also inconsistent with the relevant legislative history . . . [The California Law Reform Commission], in making its recommendation regarding mediation confidentiality, . . . chose language expressly designed to give a mediation participant who takes a photograph for purpose of the mediation "control over whether it is used" in subsequent litigation, even where "another photo" cannot be taken because, for example, "a building has been razed or an injury has healed." The Legislature adopted the Commission's recommendation and enacted the mediation confidentiality provisions in substantially the form the Commission proposed . . . The Court of Appeal's conclusion that photographs and videotapes taken for purposes of mediation are not protected under section 1119 is inconsistent with this legislative history. . . . More broadly, the Court of Appeal's construction is inconsistent with the overall purpose of the mediation confidentiality provisions. . . .

For all of the above reasons, we conclude that the Court of Appeal erred in holding that photographs, videotapes, witness statements, and "raw test data" from physical samples collected at the complex — such as reports describing the existence or amount of mold spores in a sample — that were "prepared for the purpose of, in the course of, or pursuant to, [the] mediation" in the underlying action are not protected under section 1119.

The Court of Appeal also erred in holding that, although section 1119's protection applies to so-called derivative material "that is prepared for the purpose of, in the course of, or pursuant to, a mediation" — such as charts, diagrams, information compilations, and expert opinions and reports — such material is nevertheless discoverable "upon a showing of good cause."

[T]he Legislature did expressly enact other exceptions to section 1119's protection, [such as for] settlement agreements made or prepared "in the course of, or pursuant to, a mediation." Under [maxims] of statutory construction,

if exemptions are specified in a statute, we may not imply additional exemptions unless there is a clear legislative intent to the contrary. Here, there is no
evidence of a legislative intent supporting the "good cause" exception the
Court of Appeal majority read into the statute. [A]s Judge Mohr observed,
"the mediation privilege is an important one, and if courts start dispensing
with it by using the . . . test governing the work-product privilege, . . . you may
have people less willing to mediate." The judgment of the Court of Appeal is
reversed.

QUESTIONS

1. The California Supreme Court in *Rojas* refused to allow judicially created
   exceptions to the state's mediation privilege statute. Suppose, however,
   that you were a legislator. Would you support a law giving materials prepared for mediation absolute protection, or the narrower protection
   available under the "work product doctrine" that governs materials lawyers
   create in preparation for trial? Why?
2. Can you think of any other situations in which the interest in mediation
   confidentiality should give way to the needs of the justice system or other
   social needs?

One of the strongest arguments for allowing a party to disclose information
that has been revealed by an opponent during mediation in a subsequent
proceeding involves criminal law enforcement. The following case illustrates
how the issue can arise.

BYRD v. THE STATE
367 S.E.2d 300 (Ga. App. 1988)

[Byrd was accused of stealing property from Graddy. He participated in pretrial mediation and agreed to pay $800 in restitution. Byrd failed to make the
payments required by the mediated settlement, criminal charges were rein-
stated, and he was convicted. Byrd appealed on the ground that statements he
had made during mediation were introduced against him at trial.]

BEASLEY, J. . . . Appellant alleges error [by the trial court] in allowing evidence concerning a mediation proceeding . . . [T]he parties were directed to
the Neighborhood Justice Center of Atlanta, Inc., by the state court before
which the criminal charge was first pending. The purpose was to facilitate a
civil settlement for the dispute by way of the mediation process provided by
that agency. The criminal charge, brought by warrant, remained pending, to
await the outcome of the settlement efforts. If they were successful, the state
court would entertain dismissal of the criminal charges. If not, the latter would
proceed. After about eight months elapsed without appellant's compliance
with the mediated agreement, he was indicted and bound over to superior
court for trial.

By allowing this alternative dispute resolution effort to be evidenced in the
subsequent criminal trial, the trial court's ruling eliminates its usefulness. For

ho criminal defendant will agree to "work things out" and compromise his position if he knows that any inference of responsibility arising from what he says and does in the mediation process will be admissible as an admission of guilt in the criminal proceeding which will eventualize if mediation fails ... Federal Rule of Criminal Procedure 11(e)(6) ... protects statements and conduct made in negotiations and plea bargains in criminal cases except in very limited circumstances. ...

In the instant case, as is standard in these referrals, defendant's mediation-related statements and actions were not made with any warning of rights against self-incrimination, and yet they were prompted by court action itself creating a close procedural tie. A serious Fifth and Fourteenth Amendments *Miranda* problem is created by the admission of the objected-to evidence. This differs from the situation in *Williams v. State*, 342 S.E.2d 703 (Ga. App. 1986), in which a privately-negotiated agreement, not instigated at court direction during criminal proceedings, was ruled admissible.

Just as a withdrawn plea of guilty "shall not be admissible as evidence against [a defendant] at his trial," so too must be the words and actions which defendant undertakes in an effort to comply with the court's direction that mediation be pursued to resolve the pending criminal matter.

A new trial is required because we cannot conclude that the inadmissible evidence did not contribute to reaching the verdict ... Judgment reversed.

SOGNIER, JUDGE, dissenting:

I respectfully dissent. "Any statement or conduct of a person, indicating a consciousness of guilt, where such person is, at the time or thereafter, charged with or suspected of the crime, is admissible against him upon his trial for committing it." ... The mediation proceedings in this case occurred while appellant was under criminal charges, and his conduct in signing a mediation agreement acknowledging his liability is conduct indicating a consciousness of guilt. Hence, under the rule ... the evidence was admissible as bearing on appellant's guilt or innocence. Accordingly, I would affirm appellant's conviction. ...

QUESTIONS

1. Do you agree with the majority or the dissent in *Byrd*? Does it make a difference that Byrd failed to comply with the agreement he made in mediation?

2. Would it be better policy to give a *Miranda* warning to all defendants in such mediations, then to permit the use of any statements that they make?

3. The court says that an admission by someone in Byrd's situation differs from one made by a party in a private mediation process. Should a defendant's admissions during a non-court-sponsored process be admissible?

4. If a defendant cannot be "hoist with his own petard," by using statements he makes in mediation against him, is it also improper to invade confidentiality when it is the defendant who asks for disclosure? In one case a defendant charged with attempted murder claimed that he had acted in self-defense. As part of his defense, he sought to introduce into evidence threatening statements made by the alleged victim during the mediation of an earlier altercation between them. Should defendants be barred from using such evidence? (See *State v. Castellano*, 400 So. 2d 480 (Fla. App. 1984).)

PROBLEM

Assume that you are counsel for the defendant Alpha in the Alpha-Bates case at the start of this chapter. In the course of mediation you argued that Bates should accept a reasonable settlement, because as a practical matter your client could never pay a six-figure judgment. In response to a request for substantiation, you provided the mediator with an asset-liability statement for Alpha. The mediation failed and the parties returned to court. Two days later Bates moves for a $250,000 attachment against Alpha's bank account, including with its motion copies of the asset-liability statement that your client provided in mediation.

a. How should you respond on behalf of Alpha?
b. Is there anything that you could do, before or during the process, that would make such an event less likely?

PROBLEM

Seven years ago you represented a young man, James Connor, who said that he had been sexually abused ten years before by the minister of his church. The abuse occurred when your client was 12 years old, during outings of the church's youth group. It appeared to be a difficult case to prove because of the absence of objective evidence and the time that had elapsed since the incidents, but you gave notice of your intent to sue the minister and the church official who oversaw his work. Shortly afterwards the church agreed to mediate the matter. In the course of the mediation, the supervisory official offered your client a heartfelt apology and swore that this kind of abuse would never happen again. The church made what you thought was a good monetary offer; however, it was conditional on Connor signing a confidentiality clause that barred him from ever discussing the case. Connor decided to accept the offer and the settlement was finalized.

Over the past month your local newspaper has published a series of dramatic stories alleging a widespread pattern of sexual abuse by clergy. One of the stories said that the same minister who abused your client had been sued several other times, and that two months after the settlement in your case the church had transferred him to a different community where he continued his pattern of abuse. Connor has just called you: He is outraged by the stories, and even more so by the church's violation of its promise to him. He wants to talk to a reporter about what happened in his case, including the promise he was given in mediation.

a. What advice should you give to Connor? What are the potential consequences of his talking with the reporter?
b. Assume that your client has said nothing yet, but that a lawyer has subpoenaed him to testify at a deposition in another case brought against the same minister. The lawyer plans to ask about what occurred during Connor's mediation. What advice should you give Connor?
c. If Connor refuses to answer questions at the deposition and the lawyer seeks a court order compelling him to testify, how should the court rule?

b. Supervisory Intrusions into the Process

To this point we have focused on the confidentiality issues that arise when a litigant discloses confidential mediation information for an ulterior purpose — usually to advance its case in court. The other major category of confidentiality disputes involves claims that the mediation process itself went awry. In these situations a litigant is typically alleging either that mediation was thwarted because an opponent did not participate in good faith, or that the process itself was badly flawed, making a resulting settlement invalid. This second type of claim poses a conflict between a court's need to gather evidence in order to determine what happened in mediation, and the general interest in preserving the confidentiality of the process. In the following case, a judge grapples with these issues.

QUESTIONS

As you read the *Olam* case, consider these questions:

1. Are you persuaded by the judge's decision? What factors seem most significant to it?
2. If you were a lawyer practicing in the court that decided *Olam*, would the decision affect the advice you gave to clients about what to say or do during mediation?
3. Would the decision affect your willingness to recommend that a client enter the court's mediation program?

OLAM v. CONGRESS MORTGAGE CO.
68 F. Supp. 2d 1110 (N.D. Cal. 1999)

BRAZIL, UNITED STATES MAGISTRATE JUDGE:

The court addresses in this opinion several difficult issues about the relationship between a court-sponsored voluntary mediation and subsequent proceedings whose purpose is to determine whether the parties entered an enforceable agreement at the close of the mediation session. As we explain below, the parties participated in a lengthy mediation that was hosted by this court's ADR Program Counsel — an employee of the court who is both a lawyer and an ADR professional. At the end of the mediation (after midnight), the parties signed a "Memorandum of Understanding" (MOU) that states that it is "intended as a binding document itself . . ." Contending that the consent she apparently gave was not legally valid, plaintiff has taken the position that the MOU is not enforceable. She has not complied with its terms. Defendants have filed a motion to enforce the MOU as a binding contract. One of the principal issues with which the court wrestles, below, is whether evidence about what occurred during the mediation proceedings, including testimony from the mediator, may be used to help resolve this dispute. . . .

FACTS

The events in the real world out of which the current dispute arises began unfolding in 1992, when Ms. Olam applied for and received a loan from Congress Mortgage in the amount of $187,000. The 1992 loan is secured by two single-family homes located in San Francisco and owned by Ms. Olam. Eventually she defaulted. Thereafter, Congress Mortgage initiated foreclosure proceedings. [Mrs. Olam later sued the mortgage company, alleging violations of state and federal consumer laws, and the case went through discovery.]

At the final pretrial conference, the court asked plaintiff's counsel whether there was any meaningful possibility that a mediation would be useful. [Both sides subsequently agreed to mediate.] The mediation continued throughout the day and well into the evening. Sometime around 10:00 p.m. [the mediator and counsel went into another room] to type up what they believed were the essential terms of a binding settlement agreement. At approximately 1:00 a.m., when the mediation concluded, Ms. Olam and her lawyer, and [the defendant] signed the MOU.

[Later on the same day, counsel confirmed the settlement with the court.] At approximately 1:45 p.m. [that day], plaintiff telephoned my chambers. She was referred to the mediator . . . [M]ore than seven months after the mediation, defendants filed a Motion to Enforce the Original Settlement . . . Ms. Olam, through [a] new attorney, filed her "Opposition" to the defendants' motion to enforce. [One ground] for opposition was that at the time she affixed her name to the MOU (at the end of the mediation) the plaintiff was incapable (intellectually, emotionally, and physically) of giving legally viable consent. Specifically, Ms. Olam contended that at the time she gave her apparent consent she was subjected to "undue influence" as that term is defined by California law.

[P]laintiff alleges that at the time she signed the MOU she was suffering from physical pain and emotional distress that rendered her incapable of exercising her own free will. She alleges that after the mediation began during the morning of September 9, she was left *alone* in a room *all* day and into the early hours of September 10, while all the other mediation participants conversed in a nearby room. She claims that she did not understand the mediation process. In addition, she asserts that she felt pressured to sign the MOU — and that her physical and emotional distress rendered her unduly susceptible to this pressure. As a result, she says, she signed the MOU against her will and without reading and/or understanding its terms.

[The court determined that California law, rather than federal law, governed the issue of mediation confidentiality.] California has offered for some time a set of strong statutory protections for mediation communications. If anything, those state law protections might be stronger than the [federal] protections offered through the relevant local rule of the Northern District of California or through any federal common law mediation privilege that might have been emerging when the mediation took place in this case.

As we noted earlier, the plaintiff and the defendants have expressly waived confidentiality protections conferred by [California law.] Both the plaintiff and the defendants have indicated, clearly and on advice of counsel, that they want the court to consider evidence about what occurred during the mediation, including testimony directly from the mediator. . . .

THE MEDIATOR'S PRIVILEGE

[U]nder California law, a waiver of the mediation privilege by the parties is not a sufficient basis for a court to permit or order a mediator to testify. Rather, an independent determination must be made before testimony from a mediator should be permitted or ordered.

. . . First, I acknowledge squarely that a decision to require a mediator to give evidence, even *in camera* or under seal, about what occurred during a mediation threatens values underlying the mediation privileges. [T]he California legislature adopted these privileges in the belief that without the promise of confidentiality it would be appreciably more difficult to achieve the goals of mediation programs. While this court has no occasion or power to quarrel with these generally applicable pronouncements of state policy, we observe that they appear to have appreciably less force when, as here, the parties to the mediation have waived confidentiality protections, indeed have asked the court to compel the mediator to testify — so that justice can be done.

. . . [O]rdering mediators to participate in proceedings arising out of mediations imposes economic and psychic burdens that could make some people reluctant to agree to serve as a mediator, especially in programs where that service is pro bono or poorly compensated. This is not a matter of time and money only. Good mediators are likely to feel violated by being compelled to give evidence that could be used against a party with whom they tried to establish a relationship of trust during a mediation . . . These are not inconsequential matters.

. . . But the level of harm to that interest likely varies, at least in some measure, with the perception within the community of mediators and litigants about how likely it is that any given mediation will be followed at some point by an order compelling the neutral to offer evidence about what occurred during the session . . . [T]his case represents the first time that I have been called upon to address these kinds of questions in the more than fifteen years that I have been responsible for ADR programs in this court. [M]y partially educated guess is that the likelihood that a mediator or the parties in any given case need fear that the mediator would later be constrained to testify is extraordinarily small.

The magnitude of the risk to values underlying the mediation privilege that can be created by ordering a mediator to testify also can vary with the nature of the testimony that is sought. [E]vidence about what words a party to the mediation uttered, what statements or admissions that party made . . . could be particularly threatening to the spirit and methods that some people believe are important both to the philosophy and the success of some mediation processes.

[W]e turn to the other side of the balance. The interests that are likely to be advanced by compelling the mediator to testify in this case are of considerable importance. Moreover, as we shall see, some of those interests parallel and reinforce the objectives the legislature sought to advance by providing for confidentiality in mediation. The first interest we identify is the interest in doing justice. Here is what we mean. For reasons described below, the mediator is positioned in this case to offer what could be crucial, certainly very probative, evidence about the central factual issues in this matter. There is a strong possibility that his testimony will greatly improve the court's ability to determine reliably what the pertinent historical facts actually were [and to do justice.]

. . . In sum, it is clear that refusing even to determine what the mediator's testimony would be, in the circumstances here presented, threatens values of great significance.

[The Court decided that the mediator's testimony might be sufficiently important to justify an *in camera* exploration of what he would say. After the hearing, the Court decided] that testimony from the mediator would be crucial to the court's capacity to do its job.

THE EVIDENTIARY HEARING

The court held the evidentiary hearing. We heard testimony and considered documentary evidence about Ms. Olam's medical conditions, the events of September 9-10 . . . and various post-mediation events related to the purported settlement. All the participants in the mediation testified, as did the physician who was treating plaintiff during the pertinent period. We took [the mediator's] testimony.

CONCLUSION

Because plaintiff has failed to prove either of the necessary elements of undue influence, and because she has established no other grounds to escape the contract she signed . . . the court GRANTS defendants' Motion to Enforce the settlement contract that is memorialized in the MOU.

QUESTIONS

Recall that in *Rojas v. Superior Court*, the California Supreme Court rejected a litigant's effort to intrude into the mediation process for purposes of discovery.

1. Which is more likely to promote effective mediation, the approach adopted by the court in *Rojas* or the one favored by the *Olam* judge?
2. Would the *Rojas* decision make you, as a California lawyer, more or less likely to advise clients to participate in mediation?

4. Confidentiality in Caucusing

So far we have discussed confidentiality only in terms of disclosures that are made to persons outside the mediation process. In caucus-based mediation, however, there is an additional layer of privacy: Mediators typically reassure disputants that if they request that information disclosed in a caucus be held in confidence, the mediator will not disclose it to their opponent. As we noted in Chapter 9, however, mediators are also supposed to facilitate communication between the parties. What is the appropriate balance between confidentiality and communication in caucus-based mediation? Consider how you would respond to the following situations, gathered from actual cases by Professor Marjorie Aaron.

PROBLEM

You are plaintiff's counsel in the mediation of a commercial contract case. After hours of bargaining, the parties are stuck, with the plaintiff at $240,000 and the defendant at $90,000. The mediator proposes to play "confidential listener," and asks for the absolute lowest dollar number that you would accept to settle the case. The mediator also asks you for a "public" offer that he can convey to the other side. You tell the mediator that your client will never accept less than $150,000 to settle, and authorize him to communicate to the other side a new demand of $225,000.

When the mediator conveys the $225,000 figure, the other side expresses frustration. "They've hardly moved at all," says counsel. "It looks like they won't go any lower than $200,000 to settle, and we're just not going to go that high. The very most this case is worth is 150. We'd be prepared to go to $100,000 at this point, but it's probably a waste of time. I hate playing games — what will it take? Should we just pack up and leave?"

a.   The mediator says to the defense, "I think I can get them to 150, if I can tell them that that will truly settle it — Are you saying that 150 would do it?" Has he broken his pledge of confidentiality to you?

b.   Suppose you had told the mediator that your bottom line was $175,000, but the mediator suspects from observations of your client's body language that she would in fact go as low as $150,000. Can the mediator say "They're hanging tough at 225, but I'm willing to work to get them to 150. If I can do that, will it settle the case?" Does it depend on whether the mediator "read" your client's intentions correctly?

PROBLEM

It is the mediation of a discrimination case and you are representing the complainant. After the legal arguments have been aired in joint session, the mediator moves both sides into private caucusing. The mediator spends a great deal of time with you and your client, who is decidedly "dug in" and unwilling to see any weakness in her case or the need to lower her settlement expectations. Although you are well known as a zealous advocate, in this case you see reasons to reach a reasonable settlement. In a hallway conversation you indicate to the mediator that you are aware of the problems in the case and support his efforts to bring your client into a zone of reality.

In the mediator's caucus with the defense side, counsel expresses frustration at the lack of progress. "I bet the problem is the lawyer here. I've litigated with her before," he complains. "She is just hell-bent on getting a high number. This is a political cause for her, but we're not going to cave to meet her agenda." His anger toward you seems to be driving his resistance to further movement.

What if anything can the mediator appropriately say about your or your client's attitude toward the case?

5.   The Current State of Confidentiality Protection and Proposals for Change

The Current State of Protection

How serious is the problem of mediation confidentiality in practice? From the discussion above and the varying responses of courts, it is plain that significant gaps and ambiguities exist in mediation's "confidentiality safety net." But while reported cases dealing with confidentiality issues exist, they appear to represent only a tiny fraction of all disputes that are mediated. Private mediators report, for instance, that they rarely hear parties complain about breaches of confidentiality. Similarly, the judge in *Olam* commented that in more than 15 years he had spent supervising the Northern District of California's mediation program, this was the first case in which parties had ever sought a mediator's testimony.

Why do disputes over confidentiality arise in such a small percentage of mediated cases? The large majority of cases that go to mediation reach an agreement, and even those that do not settle are very unlikely ever to go to trial. If a case is never adjudicated, then the parties have less reason to breach confidentiality in order to bolster their arguments. It also appears that when people enter into a clear commitment to keep information confidential, they consistently honor their agreements, either as a matter of morality or because they are afraid of the possible consequences of a violation. The remedies for confidentiality violations may be uncertain, but as Professor Ellen Deason has observed, disputants' "*perception* of confidentiality is [what is] of central importance" (Deason, 2002a). Also, as we have seen, when the mediation process focuses on distributive bargaining, disputants are less likely to reveal significant confidences in the first place. Finally, we should bear in mind that to the extent that mediation brings a sense of peace to a situation, as was suggested in Chapter 9, the process itself may induce participants to treat rules with respect. Whatever the cause, parties' compliance with confidentiality obligations appears to be higher than a purely tactical analysis would suggest.

Reported cases involving confidentiality arise largely in the context of court-connected mediation. This may be because parties are often compelled to participate in court programs, while they usually enter private mediation voluntarily. A person unhappy to be in a process is probably less willing to respect its rules. Also, litigants are probably more apt to complain, and judges to impose sanctions, when a problem arises in a court-affiliated process.

A Potential Response: The Uniform Mediation Act

What level of protection should be given to confidentiality in mediation? Assuming that confidentiality is necessary, the lack of uniformity among jurisdictions, and the resulting uncertainty about what rule will apply to a given mediation, may be retarding the growth of the field. One possibility is for the states, and ideally also the federal courts, to adopt a uniform mediation confidentiality statute. To this end, the National Conference of Commissioners on Uniform State Laws has proposed a Uniform Mediation Act ("UMA") for adoption by the states. (The complete text of the UMA appears on the Web site.) If the UMA is enacted on a widespread basis, confidentiality rules will become more uniform from one state to another, and the likelihood that federal courts will develop a uniform rule may also increase.

The UMA does not provide an absolute guarantee of confidentiality, however. Section 4(a) of the Act creates a "privilege" for communications made during mediation. But in addition to allowing the participants in a mediation to waive confidentiality, Sections 5 and 6(a) of the UMA permit a court to order disclosure as to:

- Agreements signed by all parties,
- Documents required to be kept open to the public,
- Threats to commit bodily injury or crimes of violence,
- Plans to commit or conceal an ongoing crime,
- Information needed for a mediator to respond to claims or charges against him, and
- Situations involving child abuse and neglect.

Section 6(b) of the UMA creates an additional exception to confidentiality in situations where a tribunal finds that a party has shown that

- Evidence is not otherwise available,
- There is a need for the evidence that substantially outweighs the interest in protecting confidentiality, and
- The mediation communication is sought or offered in a court proceeding involving a felony or litigation over a contract reached in mediation (but in the latter situation the mediator cannot be compelled to testify).

Perhaps the most controversial aspect of the UMA is that it is not a classic privilege like the one that exists between a lawyer and client. Rather, it only protects confidentiality in adjudicatory proceedings. A communication that falls within the UMA would not be "subject to discovery or admissible in evidence" in a legal proceeding (§4(a)). However, nothing in the statute prevents a disputant from disclosing such a communication outside of court, for example, in a conversation with a friend or to the media. (See comments to UMA §8.) For this reason, it is more accurate to think of the UMA as a more-precise version of FRE 408 than as a classic legal privilege. Disputants who wish to prevent extra-judicial disclosures in a UMA jurisdiction would have to rely on private agreements.

The UMA has provoked sharp disagreement within the mediation community. Some commentators argue that its provisions are inadequate, while others consider them excessive: One example is Professor Hughes' article above. In addition, some mediators and lawyers who practice in states that already have strong mediation confidentiality rules object to "watering down" their existing protections in the interest of national uniformity. As of this writing, it is not clear whether the UMA will be widely adopted.

B. ENFORCEMENT OF PARTICIPATION IN MEDIATION

1. *Agreements to Mediate*

Parties entering into relationships, particularly ones that are lengthy or complex, are increasingly likely to include a clause obligating them to mediate any dispute that may arise as a result of their interactions. Businesses entering into commercial supply contracts or divorcing parents with young children, for instance, can expect to encounter changes in circumstances over the term of their agreement and may wish to create a process to address them. Agreements to mediate are also required by law in some states: Arizona and Washington, for example, require divorcing parents who seek court approval of certain kinds of child custody and visitation arrangements to include ADR provisions in their plans.

The first question raised by an agreement to mediate is what it obligates the parties to do. For instance, what constitutes "good faith bargaining" and what does it mean to come to mediation with "full settlement authority"? A party who does not wish to mediate might also assert contractual defenses such as lack of assent or misrepresentation. It seems most likely that such defenses will be raised by consumers, who are increasingly subject to compulsory ADR clauses imposed through adhesion contracts. Such issues arise most often in the context of arbitration (discussed in Chapter 18). However, a mediation clause that imposed serious costs on consumers could also raise serious questions.

There have been few reported cases concerning compliance with private agreements to mediate. This may reflect the fact that parties who contract to mediate usually carry out their obligation. The presence of an ADR clause may also prompt disputants to enter into direct negotiations, making mediation unnecessary. Even when a disputant does not wish to mediate, it may conclude that it is easier to comply with the obligation than to litigate over it, or a party confronted with an opponent who refuses to mediate may conclude that a compelled process would be meaningless.

QUESTIONS

In the early 1990s a large California bank instituted a multistep ADR program for many of its customers. The program required consumers to mediate any dispute they might have with the bank. Under the program, professional mediators would be provided through either of two prominent ADR organizations. Many of these mediators charged hundreds of dollars per hour for their time. Consumers were obligated to pay half of the cost of mediation, although the program allowed them to apply for an exemption from the payment obligation. The plan also stated that neither party could leave mediation until the mediator had made a finding that there was "no possibility of resolution without pursuing the adjudicatory phase."

1. If you were a customer with a claim against the bank, would you challenge this program? What grounds might there be to do so?
2. Is the program likely to create practical problems for the mediators in it?

2. Mandates to Mediate

a. Issues of Authority

Many court systems, impressed with the potential of mediation, have decided to make participation in the process mandatory. Courts sometimes do so in the belief that disputants and counsel are unfamiliar with the benefits of mediation and need to be compelled to "try some." This was, for instance, the motivation of the Texas court rule described in Chapter 13. Other courts impose such requirements out of concern that the parties most in need of mediation—or those most likely to consume judicial resources unnecessarily—will not enter the process voluntarily. Thus many states require parents involved in a child visitation or custody dispute to mediate before seeking orders from a court.

Early in the development of court-connected mediation, commentators were concerned that it might be unconstitutional for a court to order parties into ADR—for example, that such a requirement might interfere with provisions in many state constitutions that give citizens a right to free access to justice. Courts, however, have upheld mediation mandates against arguments that they violate constitutional guarantees, probably because participation in mediation is inherently no more burdensome than other steps in the litigation process, such as compelled appearance at a deposition (see Golann, 1989).

The fact that mandatory ADR is constitutional, however, does not mean that a particular court has the authority to order it. Courts ordinarily derive their authority from specific sources, such as constitutional provisions and statutes. Many federal courts, for example, base orders compelling litigants to mediate on formal plans and court rules adopted pursuant to the Civil Justice Reform Act of 1990, 28 U.S.C. §§471-482, or the ADR Act of 1998, 28 U.S.C. §§651-658. The 1998 Act, in particular, bars federal courts from forcing parties to arbitrate but not to mediate, which has been interpreted to mean that federal courts may adopt rules providing for mandatory mediation.

Can a federal court that has not adopted a rule pursuant to these statutes nevertheless order parties to mediate as a matter of "inherent judicial power"? On the one hand, the Seventh Circuit Court of Appeals has ruled that a federal court can use its inherent power to force parties to attend a pretrial settlement conference. (See *Heileman Brewing Co. v. Joseph Oat Corp.*, 871 F.2d 648, 650 (7th Cir. 1989) (en banc).) On the other hand, both the Sixth and Seventh Circuits have ruled that federal courts cannot rely on inherent powers to force litigants to engage in so-called "summary jury trials," an ADR process that involves an abbreviated trial to a jury with a non-binding verdict, usually followed by mediation (described in Chapter 19). (See *In re NLO, Inc.*, 5 F.3d 154 (6th Cir. 1993); *Strandell v. Jackson County*, 838 F.2d 884 (7th Cir. 1987).)

The First Circuit Court of Appeals, in the case of *In re: Atlantic Pipe Corp.*, 304 F.3d 135 (1st Cir. 2002), confronted the issue of whether a federal district court may use its inherent powers to order a party in a civil case to participate in and pay for mediation. The case involved a complex construction dispute with many parties. The Court of Appeals confirmed the inherent power of a trial judge to order mediation over a party's objection, to require the objector to pay part of the cost of the process, and to name as a mediator a private neutral nominated by one of the parties. The court expressed concern, however, over the lack of any restriction over the extent of the process, particularly in light of the mediator's quoted rate of $9,000 per day, and remanded the case to the trial court for further orders.

QUESTION

Assume you are a law clerk to the trial judge in *Atlantic Pipe*. What conditions might you add to the mediation order to meet the First Circuit's concerns?

b. Good-Faith Bargaining Requirements

If a court has the power to order disputants to mediate, should it require them to satisfy any minimum standard of conduct? If the adoption of rules is any guide, the answer is plainly yes. Professor John Lande has found that at least 22 states have "good-faith bargaining" requirements for mediation, and that 21 or more federal district courts and 17 state courts have local rules imposing such duties on disputants, usually in connection with a court ADR program. The problem is that virtually none of these rules defines what constitutes "good faith" in mediation, or its absence. According to Professor Lande, the reported cases on good-faith obligations break down as follows:

- Failure to attend mediation at all.
- Failure to send a representative with adequate settlement authority.
- Failure to submit required memoranda or documents.
- Failure to make a suitable offer or otherwise participate in bargaining.
- Failure to sign an agreement.

In practice courts have found it easiest to sanction objective conduct, such as a party's failure to appear or file a statement. Judges have found it much more difficult to determine whether a party has made a "suitable offer" or sent a representative with "adequate settlement authority." There are only a few cases in which sanctions based on subjective conclusions about misconduct in mediation have been upheld on appeal (Lande, 2002).

Attempts to regulate parties' conduct during mediation raise difficult issues. To begin with, a court would have to define what it meant by "good faith." In many cases the court would also have to take evidence about what had been said or done during the mediation process itself, raising serious issues of confidentiality. Assuming that enforcement were feasible, many argue that good-faith bargaining requirements are in inherent conflict with a key value of mediation. In the words of the leading ethical code for mediators, "Self determination is the fundamental principle of mediation . . . Any party may withdraw from mediation at any time." (See Joint Standard I, on Web site.) If parties have the unfettered right to make their own decisions about mediating, however, how can any specific level of participation in the process be required? At the same time, if parties are ordered to mediation by a court and one party expends substantial resources to comply, should its adversary be permitted to nullify the process by failing to prepare or refusing to bargain? The following problems illustrate the challenge.

QUESTIONS

1. Consider again the problem at the start of this section in which Alpha's counsel offered $10,000 in response to the plaintiff lowering its demand from $750,000 to $450,000.
   a. If applicable rules require that the parties "bargain in good faith," has Alpha complied?
   b. Does anything else that Alpha did or failed to do in that process strike you as "bad faith"?

2. Consider the situation of defense counsel in the following California case:
    A court-appointed master ordered the parties to engage in a five-day medi-
    ation process of a complex construction defect claim. Knowing that such
    claims necessary involve expert testimony, the neutral instructed each side
    to bring its experts to the process. The neutral's charges and the plaintiff's
    cost for assembling its experts for mediation totaled nearly $25,000.
    Defense counsel, however, arrived 30 minutes late for the first session
    and appeared alone. Asked about his failure to bring his client or his
    experts, he said, "I'm here, you can talk to me." (See *Foxgate Homeowner's
    Association, Inc., v. Bramlea California, Inc., et al.*, 25 P.3d 1117 (Cal. 2001).)
    a. Did the defense counsel's actions in this mediation constitute bad faith?
    b. The mediator in *Foxgate* reported to the court that defense counsel
        took this approach because he believed that his pending motion for
        partial summary judgment would substantially reduce the value of the
        plaintiff's claims. Does this justify the lawyer's strategy?
    c. The neutral also reported that in his opinion, the defendant had suffi-
        cient time to present the motion before the mediation but had not
        done so. Does this change your opinion?

In response to the difficulty of defining and enforcing "good faith" requirements, some have argued that such rules should be discarded. Professor
Lande, for example, warns that

> Sanctioning bad faith in mediation actually may stimulate adversarial and dis-
> honest conduct . . . [I]t might also encourage surface bargaining . . . Because
> mediators are not supposed to force people to settle, participants who are deter-
> mined not to settle can wait until the mediator gives up . . . Similarly, tough
> mediation participants could use good-faith requirements offensively to intimi-
> date opposing parties . . . [I]nnocent participants may have legitimate fears
> about risking sanctions when they face an aggressive opponent . . . [In addition,
> a] good-faith requirement gives mediators too much authority . . . to direct the
> outcome in mediation. . . .

He has proposed that litigants be provided instead with education about the
value of interest-based processes, and that courts limit themselves to enforcing
objective standards of conduct, such as a requirement that parties appear at
mediation for a minimum period of time (Lande, 2002).

PROBLEM

Two companies are in mediation. In the underlying lawsuit, the plaintiff has
alleged that the defendant knowingly violated a franchise agreement. The
"hard" damages in the case, computed on the basis of the franchisee's minimum purchase requirements, are about $100,000. However, the plaintiff has
also claimed $500,000 in lost profits and made an initial settlement demand of
$600,000. It appears to the franchisee's lawyer that her client has about a 50-50
chance of being found liable under the contract and having to pay the hard
damages, but that the risk that her client will be liable for lost profits is virtually

nil. Applying a 50 percent risk factor to the hard damages, the defense assesses the value of the case at $50,000. The parties agree to mediate.

In a first caucus meeting with the mediator, the plaintiff's lawyer says that while its demand is "negotiable," it will not make any concessions until the defense puts a "significant offer" on the table. The defense informs the neutral that she will not make any offer at this point because the plaintiff is "on another planet." She tells the mediator that it's his job first to bring the plaintiff into a zone of reality, and $600K is not it. The mediation agreement commits the parties to "engage in good-faith bargaining." Is either the plaintiff or the defendant violating its obligation?

3. Enforcement of Mediated Settlements

Mediation is a voluntary process, but if it is successful then the parties usually enter into a binding contract—a settlement agreement. Even settlements, however, may provoke new controversies over issues such as the following:

- Did the parties actually reach a final agreement? If so, what were its terms?
- Should the agreement be invalidated on grounds such as duress, mistake, unconscionability, or lack of authority?

a. The Existence of an Agreement

Good practice calls for parties who settle in mediation to memorialize their agreements in writing. To ensure that this occurs, mediation texts counsel neutrals, however late the hour or strong the parties' wish to depart, to push the disputants to sign a memorandum that summarizes the settlement before they leave. Sometimes, however, the parties do not execute an agreement, or it is later attacked as incomplete.

Most courts test mediated settlements by the standards that apply to contracts generally. If an agreement is oral, the first issue is whether it complies with the applicable statute of frauds. Courts in several states have held oral mediated settlements to be enforceable contracts, and although there are few reported cases, it appears that federal common law also permits enforcement of oral settlements. Where a court has refused to enforce an oral agreement reached in mediation, it has usually been due to procedural rules that go beyond the requirements of contract law. Florida, Washington, and Texas, for example, mandate that pending court cases may be settled only through a written document signed by the parties or their counsel (Cole, McEwen, and Rogers, 2001).

As we have seen, virtually every state has rules intended to guarantee the confidentiality of mediation. Some state privilege laws contain explicit exceptions that permit the introduction of evidence of oral settlements, and other statutes, although absolute on their face, have been interpreted to permit such testimony. In many states, however, it is not clear whether disputants may testify about the existence of an oral settlement, or whether the mediator can be called as a witness on the issue. Sections 4(a) and 6(a) of the Uniform Mediation Act prevent participants from testifying about agreements reached in mediation, but exempt agreements that are signed and in writing or electronically recorded from the restriction. The net effect of the UMA is thus to bar enforcement of purely oral settlements.

b. Grounds for Invalidation

Suppose, following a successful mediation process, that the lawyers draw up a settlement agreement and the parties sign it. Is that enough to ensure that a settlement will be enforced? Generally the answer is yes, but not always. Again there are potential concerns. Some of these are formal in nature. First, settlement agreements must contain the essential terms of the parties' bargain. Where, for example, a settlement provides that "the parties shall exchange mutual releases," a court would probably find the language sufficient to form a binding agreement. If, however, a settlement states that a defendant will make payments "in installments" but does not specify a schedule, a challenge would be more likely to succeed. In addition, some jurisdictions impose special requirements on mediated agreements. A California statute, for instance, requires that for evidence of a mediated agreement to be admissible over objection, the document must either state that it is admissible or intended to be enforceable, or words to that effect, or be offered to show illegality (Cal. Evid. Code §1123). A few jurisdictions also require that mediated settlements of pending litigation be approved by a court.

The most serious basis for invalidating mediated settlements is a substantive one: That the process of mediation itself was so deficient that any resulting agreement is invalid. On the one hand, the presence of a neutral person would seem to make it less likely that a "bad" settlement would result. On the other hand, aspects of the process that are intended to push litigants to confront unpleasant realities may also create stress that inhibits good decision making. An example is the *Olam* case, above, in which a consumer who remained in mediation for many hours and agreed to a late-night settlement later claimed that she did so under duress.

QUESTIONS

1. Is the UMA provision allowing the introduction of evidence about written or recorded settlements, but not oral ones, justified? Why or why not?
2. Do you agree with the California law requiring that mediated agreements, but not directly negotiated ones, state that they are admissible or intended to be enforceable in order to be introduced into evidence?
3. Are there particular circumstances in which a mediated settlement should be subject to special scrutiny?
4. When a mediated agreement is challenged on grounds such as duress or misrepresentation, should the court apply a different standard than it would to a settlement reached through direct negotiation? Why or why not?

CHRISTIAN COOPER v. MELODIE AUSTIN
750 So. 2d 711-715 (Fla. App. 2000)

HARRIS, J.

Cooper appeals a final judgment which adopted a mediation agreement Cooper alleges was obtained by extortion and was the basis for [a] contempt citation . . . During the course of a lengthy mediation, it is undisputed that the wife sent Cooper the following note:

> If you can't agree to this, the kids will take what information they have to whomever to have you arrested, etc. Although I would get no money if you were in jail — you wouldn't also be living freely as if you did nothing wrong.[2]

Relatively soon thereafter, the parties "settled" their property matters.

. . . In the midst of extended negotiations before the mediator, the wife sent the husband a note that constituted classic extortion. However, the wife convinced the [trial] judge that the note was merely a "wake-up" call and did not influence the agreement subsequently reached. The court relied on two established facts to reach this conclusion. First, the husband did not immediately accede to the wife's demands but continued to negotiate for a period thereafter. Second, the husband did not seek relief from the extortionate agreement until after his efforts to reconcile with the wife failed. Even accepting these facts as true, we cannot agree that they negate the effect of extortion when reviewing the remainder of the record.

The husband testified, without contradiction, that the result of the mediated agreement was that the wife received $128,000 in marital assets while the husband received $10,000 . . . This grossly unequal distribution speaks volumes about the effect of the extortionate note sent by the wife. . . .

In this case, the wife's "wake-up call," which demanded the husband either give in to her demands or go to jail, was clearly extortionate and her presentation of the extorted agreement to the court was a fraud on the court making the trial court an instrument of her extortion. Mrs. Cooper should not profit from her actions. Nor should this Court, or any court, ignore them.

GRIFFIN, J., dissenting.

This is not the first time an appellate court has been unable to overcome the urge to trump factual findings of a trial judge with which the panel violently disagrees, nor will it be the last. But it is awkward when it happens . . . *How*, the majority asks incredulously, could the trial judge have allowed himself to be hoodwinked in this fashion? After reading the transcript of the hearing, it is clear to me that Judge Hammond simply did not believe Mr. Cooper. This is important because there are only three items of evidence to support Mr. Cooper's claim of duress: (1) the threat; (2) the apparent uneven distribution of assets; and (3) Mr. Cooper's testimony that the reason he entered into the agreement was because of the threat.

The lower court so much as said it did not find Mr. Cooper to be credible. First of all, Mr. Cooper, who has a bachelor's degree and a master's degree in business, both from Duke University . . . testified repeatedly that he had no idea of the value of the marital assets. [T]he evidence, in fact, showed that he had a very good idea of what the marital assets were. . . .

---

2. [Footnote to court opinion] The crime threatened to be reported by the wife was Cooper's photographing a nude, underage girl. Cooper, who had experienced firsthand the law's disapproval of this practice on an earlier occasion, was aware that in going through his property, the wife's children had found a photograph taken by him of a young woman who indeed looked underage. It was not until shortly before this action for relief from judgment was filed that Cooper tracked down the woman and verified she was "of age" at the time the photograph was taken.

There was direct conflict between Mr. and Mrs. Cooper concerning Mr. Cooper's response to her threat. She testified that his response was that he was not scared, that the kids did not "have anything" and that he knew that he "owed it to her to put her through school." . . . As the lower court succinctly said: "The former husband knew that the photographs in his possession were not illegal."

There is also the fact that Mr. Cooper, his free will forborne due to his "fear of arrest," continued to negotiate the agreement for another two and one-half hours [securing substantial changes in the terms of a promissory note to the wife] . . . The fact that he received all of the benefits of the mediation agreement as adopted by the Final Judgment, made all alimony payments . . . , received back all of the personal property he was concerned about, [and] continued his pursuit of the Former Wife are not the actions of a man who was subject to extortion, coercion or duress . . . We should affirm.

QUESTION

If Mr. Cooper's counsel thought that his client might be feeling extorted during the mediation, what should he have done?

C. CERTIFICATION AND LICENSING

There is a continuing debate about whether mediators should be either certified or licensed. Licensing is an official act carried out by a government agency, whereas certification can be done by an official organization such as a court program, or a private entity (e.g., a professional association). The two options have different implications. Licensing would be more restrictive, since only persons who obtained the license could mediate the types of cases covered by it (e.g., family disputes). Certification has less effect: It restricts neutrals from working in settings in which the certification is required (e.g., a court mediation panel), but not from mediating in general.

Mediation licensing does not exist: There is no equivalent to bar membership for neutrals. Even a child can act as a mediator — and many students do, in fact, mediate peer disputes in school. This reflects the history of mediation, which was fueled in large measure by frustration with the conventional legal system and peoples' wish to find new ways to approach disputes. The idea of creating licensing systems for mediators, with the need for agencies to administer them, strikes many in the field as antithetical to their basic values. There is also concern that regulation of ADR would stifle its creativity. Finally, there is little empirical evidence that licensing or certification is needed, leading many to say, "If it ain't broke, don't fix it!"

Most of the court systems and private organizations that offer mediation do, however, impose standards for admittance to their panels. The effect is that certification standards have become widespread. Certification standards generally apply only to mediators who wish to join programs or organizations, however, not to private mediators who simply "hang out a shingle." There is also no national or, in many cases, even statewide uniformity in the standards for mediator certification. The following articles discuss whether a wider and more consistent system for certifying mediators should be created.

JULIANA BIRKOFF AND ROBERT RACK, WITH JUDITH M. FILNER, POINTS OF VIEW: IS MEDIATION REALLY A PROFESSION?

8 Disp. Resol. Mag. 10-21 (Fall 2001)

[T]here has been a push for quality assurance by developing credential programs for mediators. Skeptics have said that the drive toward credentials comes from the desire of some practitioners to reduce competition. Others have urged resistance to this impetus to create qualifications, claiming it is elitist and exclusionary. Some further assert that creating qualifications will limit the diversity of the field. Advocates, however, perceive a need and responsibility to protect consumers from incompetent mediators, to enhance the credibility and status of the field, and to address the need for agencies, courts, and other referral sources to assure the quality of the services provided.

Skeptics and advocates alike puzzle over how qualifications can be related to performance, whether credential programs assure quality, and whether or not the field of mediation is sufficiently mature to define what mediation is, what mediators do, and what they have to know to serve competently. While the discussion continues, various states and agencies are, in fact, establishing qualifications and standards. And, the field is maturing . . . The interview that follows . . . frames the quality assurance discussion.

JMF: So . . . is mediation a profession?

JB: Yes, I think mediation is a profession or is becoming a profession. When I began my research, I did not expect to find [this]. . . .

BR: I certainly think most mediators are professional in the sense that they are committed to their work . . . But I think mediation is bigger than a profession and I resist the temptation to try to capture and contain it. We've seen mediation explode in use throughout society . . . I see it as a broad social movement. . . .

JMF: . . . If mediation is a profession, how do we, as a field, as practitioners, as program directors, assure quality or address issues of quality practice?

JB: Credentialing is a way that professionals try to define what they do and distinguish it from what other professions or occupations do. For me, it is not so important to look at credentialing. Rather, it is important to look at the body of knowledge that a mediator uses to do the work, to practice. . . .

BR: . . . I see the heart of good mediation as skillfully facilitating communication and effectively infusing strained relationships with goodwill. The most essential "knowledge" for a mediator seems to me to be an understanding of human nature and human behavior, especially under stress and in conflict. That knowledge can be largely intuitive, and developed through experience. We may one day have such a precise understanding of human behavior that we can write it down and require mediators to commit it to memory, like biology, laws, and accounting rules for doctors, lawyers, and accountants. And we might then be able to measure a mediator's ability to apply that knowledge. But I doubt that will happen anytime soon.

JB: Let me clarify; mediators do not develop their unique knowledge by studying literature. This is why so few mediators find that going to M.S. or Ph.D. programs improves their skills as mediators. Mediators develop their knowledge by doing the work. . . .

BR: The first thing I look for in new mediator candidates is a kind of life stance — an inclination to see the validity in apparently conflicting points of view and to seek synthesis, rather than domination by anyone of those views. The second thing I look for is experience that demonstrates a skillful articulation of that inclination . . . So I'd say that mediation is a life skill first . . . Daniel Bowling and David Hoffman published an article in . . . which they concluded that a mediator's mere "presence" is a major ingredient in the mediation dynamic . . . I completely agree. Now, how do we "credentialize" that?

JB: While I understand where Bob is coming from, it sounds like he believes that being artistic and creative has no place in a profession . . . Professional knowing is not only tacit theory but also the intuition, skill, and experience of trained and talented individuals who know how to apply that knowledge. . . .

JMF: One of the reasons mediators talk about assuring quality is that there is poor practice out there. . . .

JB: I guess I would ask what proof exists, besides rumors and anecdotes, that there is a need to protect the public. This is often an argument that beginning professions use to protect their insecure control of their work . . . However, I do believe that the mediation organizations should promote standards of practice and require a commitment from members to abide by the standards of practice.

BR: I agree with almost everything Juliana has said. If participants understand the very basics of mediation, it's really pretty hard for a mediator to do much harm . . . I believe the focus and responsibility for resolution should remain on the parties and there already is a tendency for many disputants to hand over that responsibility to the mediator. I hate to give any more authority or stature to the mediator than is absolutely necessary. . . .

JMF: Finally, I see a strong, albeit disorganized and informal, move toward credentialing. . . .

JB: It is significant that people are representing themselves as professional mediators . . . This says more about the ways we as a society judge the effectiveness of lawyers and therapists than it does about the benefits of having a conflict resolution profession.

BR: I understand the disdain for charlatans, the frustration over not being able to do anything about incompetent people in our field, and the feeling of responsibility for assuring quality. It's just that we have no reason at this time to believe we know how to legislate for the selection of good mediators and the screening out of bad ones. . . .

        . . . There are things that can be done to advance the quality ball without legislating requirements for everyone. First, let's . . . let [private associations] experiment with qualifications and see if they can find some that really make a difference . . . This field is still hot and is still evolving rapidly. My vote remains that we not try to freeze it with mandatory qualifications or performance standards until we know it will make a significant and positive difference.

JAMES E. MCGUIRE, CERTIFICATION: AN IDEA WHOSE TIME HAS COME

10 Disp. Resol. Mag. 22-23 (Summer 2004)

Is mediation a profession? If it is, what are the requirements to be a professional mediator? Who should do the certifying? These seemingly simple questions have been part of the mediation dialogue in the United States for more than 25 years. . . .

WHY CERTIFY ANY MEDIATOR?

Mediators not only want to be competent, they want to be perceived as competent. Currently, mediators do so by collecting credentials: training programs taken, panels joined, articles written, and for those with actual experience, number of cases mediated. While not ensuring competence, credentialing creates a competitive advantage for a mediator.

In order to secure the credential of participating on a panel, taking the sponsor's training course is often a prerequisite. Training programs can be a major source of revenue for the sponsor and a significant burden for potential mediators. Moreover, multiple, repetitive, mandatory entry-level training programs exist within most states and practice areas. Certification may provide an answer to the frustration these duplicative requirements present. . . .

As legislators begin to codify mediation confidentiality . . . some are asking the basic hard questions: Who are these mediators? How do they get trained? What safeguards exist to ensure that the mediators are trustworthy? An additional reason for considering voluntary mediator certification is recognition that if mediators do not create a certification process, others will and it may not be as voluntary or nuanced and flexible as the field would desire. . . .

HOW TO BECOME CERTIFIED

The exact contours of a certification program will be determined through the current collaborative process between [the Association for Conflict Resolution, many of whose members are not lawyers, and the American Bar Association.] A likely model is [a] two-step process . . . : preparation and submission of a "portfolio," which, if accepted, qualifies the applicant to sit for an examination to become a certified mediator. The portfolio is a paper submission documenting 100 hours of training and relevant course work, including a minimum of 80 hours in mediation process skills. The portfolio must also document at least 100 hours as an active mediator within the last five years. Letters of recommendation, evidence of professional liability insurance, and disclosure of disciplinary matters complete the portfolio requirements.

A candidate with an acceptable portfolio would then take a written examination. The examination itself would be prepared by an independent professional. The exam is intended to test awareness of mediation principles, approaches, and relevant techniques. [T]here is likely to be no provision for reviewing an actual demonstration of mediation skills. Such live evaluations are difficult to develop and expensive to administer. This is especially true where the goal is to avoid having certification itself become an economic barrier to entry into the mediation field.

WHO CERTIFIES?

The development and successful implementation of certification standards is most likely to succeed if it is a multiorganizational effort . . . [N]either lawyers nor the ABA "own" the mediator certification process . . . Though there can be no guarantee of success, any other approach may well be a guarantee of failure.

QUESTIONS

1. Assume that you wish to become a mediator and can meet the qualifications described by James McGuire. Would you favor having your state adopt a credentialing program like the one outlined in his article, or the "hands-off" approach advocated by Rack and Birkoff?
2. Most mediators of legal cases are selected by lawyers. In such situations, who would a credentialing requirement protect?
3. What is gained or lost if regulation of mediators is limited to certification, rather than a licensing system like bar membership?

D. ETHICAL ISSUES

Lawyers may engage in mediation either as advocates or as neutrals. Some attorneys play both roles, maintaining an active law practice and also accepting assignments as a mediator. The ethical issues for each role are different, and we will discuss them in turn.

1. *Advocates in Mediation*

We have seen that advocates in mediation act primarily as negotiators. The rule that governs lawyers as negotiators is ABA Model Rule 4.1, which does not mention mediation. The ABA has proposed changes to the Model Rules through its Ethics 2000 (or "E2K") Commission. The E2K Report suggests that "tribunal" be defined to include arbitrators. (See E2K Report, Rules 1.0(m), 3.3, on Web site.) As a result, lawyers would have the same duty of truthfulness toward arbitrators as toward judges.

The E2K Report does not, however, create any new ethical duties for lawyers regarding mediators. The effect of the current rules and the Report is that attorneys need be no more truthful with mediators than with opponents in direct negotiation. Dean Alfini has criticized the E2K Report for having left mediation in an ethical "black hole" between formal adjudication and ordinary bargaining (Alfini, 2001), and Professor Cooley has written that "As long as there are not uniform ethical standards defining truthfulness in mediation, lawyer-mediators and mediation advocates will have the unfettered capacity to practice their showmanship and produce their 'magic' effects by any method they wish"(Cooley, 1997).

Although the canons of ethics say nothing on the subject, other rules may apply to a lawyer in mediation. For one thing, many court-connected ADR programs impose standards of conduct on participants, such as the obligation to mediate in good faith. Lawyers who engage in private mediation also often sign agreements that commit them to higher standards of conduct, for example, the obligation to appear with full settlement authority. Finally, as we saw in the context of direct bargaining, advocates often choose voluntarily to observe standards of conduct higher than the minimum requirements of the Model Rules. Lawyers may do so because their personal values call for a cooperative approach to bargaining, or for practical reasons such as the wish to maintain good professional relationships within their community. Some of the special issues that can arise for advocates in mediation are discussed below.

a.   Candor Toward the Mediator

Bargaining in mediation is unique because it is often three-sided. At times disputants are negotiating directly with their opponent, using the mediator simply as a better channel of communication ("Tell them that we won't move into six figures until. . . ."). Attorneys in a competitive bargaining situation, however, must often also bargain with the neutral. Here are two examples:

Mediator: "I understand that your current offer is $10,000, but can you give me a private indication of where you'd be willing to go if the plaintiff dropped its demand significantly?"
Lawyer: "Well, if they drop to six figures, I would recommend . . . "

. . .

Mediator: "I am going to ask each side to tell me confidentially how far they would go to get a final settlement in this matter . . ."
Lawyer: "The absolute bottom dollar we can take in this case is . . ."

Should lawyers be more candid with a mediator than with an adverse party? While there is no legal obligation to bargain differently, there are practical reasons why an advocate might do so. First, if mediators adopt a cooperative approach, disputants might feel a natural inclination to reciprocate. A lawyer might also opt to treat a mediator differently in the hope that she would exercise her influence over the process to his client's benefit.

PROBLEM

You represent the employer in a bitterly contested case involving an executive fired from a Silicon Valley company. The parties have bargained fiercely for several hours. For the past hour they have been at an impasse. The mediator now offers to make a mediator's proposal in an effort to break the deadlock. You ask for a few minutes to confer privately with your client, the company's CEO. After batting the idea back and forth the CEO says, "Well, I don't know if we can live with that, but let's say 'yes' and see if the plaintiff bites. Nothing's final until it's signed anyway." You fear that the CEO is simply testing the waters and will renege if the employee accepts the deal.

a.   Can you indicate that your client assents to the proposal? Would doing so violate the Model Rules?
b.   Suppose that the CEO's tactic will achieve his goal, but will impair your credibility with the mediator in future cases. Does this change the analysis?
c.   Under the law of confidentiality in your jurisdiction, can anyone be compelled to testify concerning your client's response to the mediator's proposal?

PROBLEM

Assume the same facts as in the earlier problem, except that the CEO thinks that the plaintiff's entire case is bogus. He does not authorize you to make any settlement offer, but instead tells you to go to mediation "just to see where they're coming from." The president will be available by telephone, but he has given no indication that he will authorize you to make an actual offer.

a. If the mediation agreement commits the parties to bargain in "good faith," have you or he violated it?
b. Do you owe the mediator any obligation to disclose your situation?
c. Does this approach create any risks for your client?

b. The Duty to Maintain Confidentiality

As we have seen, one of the hallmarks of mediation is confidentiality. Sometimes, however, this obligation comes into conflict with what counsel believes, or claims to believe, is a higher duty. What then should a lawyer do? Consider the following situation.

PROBLEM

Hurricane George devastated much of Puerto Rico, and HUD stepped in to repair the damage. It awarded reconstruction funds to several towns, including Los Baños. Unfortunately, the mayor of Los Baños appears to have run a kickback scheme with several local contractors, possibly including Bravo Contracting, which had received HUD funds and is supposedly a major contributor to the mayor's political party. HUD yanked the contract from Bravo and awarded it to your client, Lone Star Construction, which completed the work. Los Baños, Bravo, and Lone Star are now fighting over the contract payment. At HUD's urging, they agreed to mediate.

The parties signed a standard mediation agreement, like the commercial example on the Web site, which includes a confidentiality clause, and prepared mediation statements. Your statement included an appendix setting forth information about Lone Star's costs and the profit margin on its bids, which could be of great advantage to a competitor. You filed the appendix under a stipulation that it would be given to HUD and the Los Baños representatives, but not to anyone at Bravo.

You arrive in San Juan the day prior to the mediation and find a message to call the HUD representative immediately. You are told that the lawyers for Los Baños have turned your mediation submission, including the appendix, over to Bravo and the local district attorney's office, alleging that it reveals criminal fraud by Lone Star.

QUESTIONS

1. Did the Los Baños lawyers violate their confidentiality obligation by giving the mediation materials to Bravo and the DA?
2. How should you respond?

c. The Duty to Advise Clients About ADR

An increasing number of jurisdictions require lawyers to advise clients about the nature of alternative dispute resolution and its potential use in their dispute. For example, Colorado (via the bar association), Arkansas (by statute), and Ohio, New Jersey, and Massachusetts (through court rules), each require attorneys to give such advice. Several federal and state courts have adopted similar rules. Thus the Colorado Bar's Code of Ethics states that lawyers should "advise the client of alternative forms of dispute resolution that might reasonably be pursued to attempt to resolve the legal dispute or to reach the legal objective sought." Comments to the ABA's Ethics E2K proposals concerning advice to clients also mention ADR, stating that "In general, a lawyer is not expected to give advice until asked by the client . . . [W]hen a matter is likely to involve litigation, it may be necessary . . . to inform the client of forms of dispute resolution that might constitute reasonable alternatives to litigation. . . ." (E2K Report, Comments to Rule 2.1).

QUESTIONS

1. What, in practical terms, does the Colorado rule require a lawyer to do? Draft the key points you would mention about ADR if you were meeting with a secretary at a local manufacturing company who had just retained you to sue the company for sexual harassment that created a hostile work environment, forcing her to leave her job.
2. Could a lawyer comply with the Colorado rule by giving a one-sentence definition of mediation and simply saying that it would be a waste of time in this particular case? If so, what is the value of the rule?

2. Concerns for Mediators

There is no empirical evidence that mediators often engage in misconduct. Professor Michael Moffit has observed that "Despite the thousands, if not millions of disputants who have received mediation services, instances of legal complaints against mediators are extraordinarily rare." His exhaustive survey yielded only one reported case in the past quarter century in which a verdict had been entered against a mediator for improper conduct, and that result was overturned on appeal. Many mediators operate under civil immunity conferred either by court rules or clauses in mediation agreements, and even if a mediator is not immune from suit, it is likely to be difficult as a practical matter to prove a causal connection between mediator misconduct and an ascertainable monetary loss (Moffit, 2003b).

Even allegations of mediator misconduct are very unusual. In Florida during the late 1990s, for example, state courts were sending more than 100,000 cases per year to mediation. Florida maintains a board to investigate complaints against court-certified mediators, but over its first eight years of operation the Board received a total of only 49 complaints (Press, 1998). The cost of mediator malpractice insurance is also very low. As of 2004, the largest insurer of mediators was offering a million-dollar liability policy in most states for a yearly premium of approximately $500. Such rates could not be offered if there were a significant number of claims requiring a defense. Formal complaints against mediators thus appear to be extremely infrequent — although this is admittedly only a minimal measure of ethical behavior.

Several ADR organizations have promulgated codes that are intended to guide mediators in resolving ethical issues. However, unless a mediator participates in a mediation panel affiliated with a court or some other organized program, the absence of licensing means that he will not be subject to any binding rules of ethics akin to the canons of ethics for lawyers. In the interest of advancing the field, and recognizing the value of self-regulation as a way to avoid bureaucratic controls, several organizations have drafted voluntary ethical standards for mediators. The best known are the Standards of Conduct for Mediators ("Model Standards") promulgated by the American Arbitration Association, the American Bar Association, and what is now the Association for Conflict Resolution. The Uniform Mediation Act also sets out ethical requirements for disclosure of conflicts of interest, and individual states and programs have promulgated rules that incorporate ethical norms. The Model Standards, the UMA, and other prominent ethical standards for mediators appear on the Web site. Please review the Model Standards and Section 9 of the UMA, and then consider the following issues.

QUESTIONS

1. Any standard of conduct embodies a vision of what the mediation process should be. Can you classify the vision implicit in the Model Standards in terms of mediator styles — broad or narrow? Facilitative or evaluative?
2. Do the Model Standards appear to discourage any particular approach to mediation?

The Model Standards embody core values of mediation, such as party self-determination, mediator impartiality, and the maintenance of confidentiality, and for that reason are relatively noncontroversial. The fact that rules are widely accepted does not mean, however, that they are easy to apply in practice. Most ethical codes are clear as to what a mediator must do in egregious situations, such as when he discovers that a case involves a family member or close friend. Good mediators, however, have little difficulty deciding how to behave in such cases. Far more difficult are situations in which two ethical principles, valid in themselves, come into conflict, and there appears to be no way to satisfy both of them fully. To understand how this can occur, consider the following problems.

a. Issues of Fairness

We noted in Chapter 13 that the most serious issues of fairness in mediation arise in the context of court-connected programs that require litigants to engage in mediation under an official imprimatur. Even when mediation processes are wholly private and voluntary, however, neutrals can encounter difficult issues of fairness. The most serious problems involve pro se disputants. Such cases present a tension between Sections I, II, and VI of the Model Standards.

PROBLEM

In a private mediation of a divorce case, the husband appears without a lawyer and the wife has counsel. As the process goes forward, the husband becomes progressively more upset, sometimes making illogical arguments and reversing decisions that he had previously made. The mediator suggests to the husband that the mediation be adjourned so that he can rest and consult a lawyer, but the husband expresses a strong wish to "get it over with." He tells the mediator privately that "outside factors" make it important that he resolve the case quickly. The husband will not explain what they are, but the mediator suspects that he has formed a new relationship and is anxious to get out of his old one.

The wife's counsel, sensing this, drives a very hard bargain, demanding that she receive 50 percent more alimony than court guidelines would suggest and three-quarters of the marital estate. The process continues for several hours. The husband becomes increasingly upset but refuses to stop. At one point, late in the afternoon during a private caucus, he says to the mediator in an agitated tone, "This can't go on any longer! I guess I've got to take their offer."

a. What provisions of the Model Standards apply to this situation?
b. How should the mediator respond? Is there a problem if the husband signs an agreement?

PROBLEM

A volunteer mediator is handling landlord-tenant cases in a community mediation program. A case is referred over by a court clerk. The defendant is a tenant facing eviction who is proceeding pro se. The landlord is a corporation represented by counsel. The tenant seems to have little understanding of what will happen in court if he does not settle. At one point shortly before lunch, the landlord offers a "final deal": He will allow the tenant two more month's occupancy, provided that all past rent is paid, the future rent is put into escrow, and the tenant agrees now to the entry of judgment for eviction at the end of the two months. The landlord's representative states that if the plaintiff does not accept the offer by 2 p.m., he will go back to court and ask the judge to rule on his request that the tenant be ordered to vacate the premises within seven days.

The tenant is unsure what to do, and in a private caucus asks the mediator, "Are they right about the law here? What do you recommend?" The mediator privately believes that if the tenant offers to pay rent into escrow, it is very likely that the court will give him at least six months to move, although for a judge to grant the landlord's request is not completely inconceivable.

a. Which of the Model Standards apply here? What do they counsel the mediator to do?
b. Does it make any difference that this case was referred by a court?

b. Questions of Competence

Mediators sometimes encounter cases in areas in which they have not practiced or previously mediated — indeed, if their practices expand then such situations are quite likely. What obligation does a mediator have to disclose her lack of expertise to disputants? Article IV of the Joint Standards and Section 9 of the UMA each deal with this issue. Consider this situation.

PROBLEM

You are a litigator with 10 years' experience who occasionally acts as a mediator. You have handled a total of 15 mediations as a neutral and participated in dozens more as an advocate. You have been asked to mediate a bitter employment dispute involving an employee who says that she was sexually harassed by her supervisor and that management knew of the problem but "swept it under the rug." You do not handle employment cases and have never mediated one, but you do read the summaries of decided cases that are printed in your local legal newspaper, and these include reports of court decisions in employment cases among others.

a. Do the Model Standards or the UMA require you to make any disclosure?
b. Draft an outline of what, if anything, you would tell the parties about your background.

c. "Repeat Player" Concerns

In order to be successful as a mediator one must have clients, and busy neutrals rely on repeat business. One national organization of mediators estimates, for example, that approximately two-thirds of the revenue of their leading panelists comes from cases submitted by lawyers who have selected the neutral three or more times during the past 12 months. When does repeat business create unhealthy dependence? Mediator David Geronemus comments that:

> [F]ull-time mediators need to be careful on a variety of fronts as they face the continuous need to generate new cases to keep their dockets full . . . Good mediators undoubtedly will have repeat business. And we need to engage in marketing activities. But unless we are careful to fulfill our disclosure obligations, and to make sure that no one client becomes too large a share of our practice, parties will lose confidence in the process (Geronemus, 2001).

Sections II and III of the Model Standards and Section 9 of the UMA may apply to a mediator in such situations; other standards may apply to advocates.

PROBLEM

You are an advocate preparing for your first mediation with mediator Jones, who retired about one year ago from a major law firm. He has an excellent reputation as a litigator and did well with a small personal injury case that you mediated with him six months ago. You ran into Jones on the street a few weeks ago and he mentioned his interest in doing another case with you. A long-term client, a casualty insurer, has come to you seeking to mediate a major tort case. You recommended Jones as a possibility, and it appears that he is acceptable to the plaintiff's counsel. As you are preparing to call Jones to make final arrangements, your contact at the insurer calls and says, "Tell him we're a major player in the market. If he does a good job on this one, we'll think strongly about sending him more cases."

a.   Under the Model Rules of Professional Conduct for lawyers or the sample mediation agreement, is it improper for you to pass along this comment to Jones? Why or why not?
b.   If you say something to the mediator, how will you phrase it? If not, will you say anything to the adjuster?

PROBLEM

You practice as a litigator in a small firm and are representing a plaintiff in an automobile tort case. The defendant is insured by a major insurance company. Given the market power of your adversary, you are concerned that the mediator might be less than fully neutral. Is there anything that you can do to alleviate your concern? Is there any risk to your proposed course of action?

d.   Differences Between Attorney and Client

At times a mediator is dealing with people who are on the same side of a dispute, but have widely divergent viewpoints. An attorney, for example, may not appear to be "on the same page" as her client about the risks of litigation or whether to take an offer. Ethical standards for both lawyers and mediators state that in such situations the client's wishes govern; however, parties often hire lawyers precisely because they have more experience and better judgment in highly charged situations, and many lawyers report that their clients sometimes become too emotional to recognize a good offer when it appears. And, it must be noted, mediators know that attorneys rather than clients are their primary source of referrals. Sections I, II, III, and VI of the Model Rules may apply to such situations. Consider the following problem.

PROBLEM

Two parties have gone through nine hours of difficult mediation in a product liability case. The plaintiffs have alleged that their infant daughter died because of defects in a baby carriage manufactured by the defendant. The plaintiff couple is represented by experienced counsel and has held up well to the stress of the process. The maker of the carriage is represented by its CFO and outside counsel. The mediator's impression is that the CFO is being unrealistic about the company's legal exposure. The mediator has tried to bring other company officials into the case, but without success.

At 6 p.m. the mediator brings another offer to the defense, which is promptly rejected. At this point the neutral says to the defense team that while he's willing to keep talking, they appear to be close to deadlock and it may make sense to adjourn for the day. As the neutral leaves the room, defense counsel says she's going to the restroom. In a private conversation in the hallway, she asks the mediator to "bring down the hammer" on her client. The CFO, she says, has a visceral dislike of the plaintiff's lawyer. He is letting his determination to beat the other guy lead him into a position that is against the company's best interests.

The neutral respects counsel's reputation as an advocate and privately agrees with her assessment of the situation. On his return that he asks the defense team if it would be helpful for him to give his impressions of how a court would view the case if it had to be tried. The defense lawyer promptly responds that they would welcome his thoughts. The mediator delivers a hard-hitting evaluation that represents his honest assessment, and emphasizes some jury sympathy factors that he believes the CFO is ignoring. The CFO does not directly respond to the mediator's comments, but appears to be a bit taken aback. The bargaining process resumes, and the disputants continue without a dinner break, munching on fast food. At 9:30 p.m., after several lengthy caucuses, the CFO agrees to essentially the same proposal that the mediator had brought to it at 6 p.m.

a.   Did the lawyer act unethically in saying what she did to the mediator?
b.   Did the mediator act improperly in his response? Why or why not?

e. Questionable Conduct by Litigants

Ethical standards instruct mediators to support the parties' right to self-determination. But what should a mediator do when parties attempt to "create value" through an agreement that appears to be immoral, or of dubious legality? Family mediators may confront this problem when two spouses reach a tortured visitation agreement that is acceptable to them, but appears to the mediator to create serious difficulties for their young children. In commercial mediation the problem is more likely to arise when disputants create value for themselves by appearing to cheat an outsider, often the Internal Revenue Service. Mediators may not be asked to contribute ideas to the solution, but they are typically called on to carry proposals back and forth, advocate their acceptance, and act as scribes for memoranda that memorialize them. Several provisions of the Model Standards may apply in such cases. Consider the following example.

PROBLEM

A terminated executive has been mediating with his former employer for 10 hours. After fierce bargaining in which the mediator has used her entire "bag of tricks," the defense has come painfully to a final offer of $180,000, but the plaintiff refuses to accept less than $200,000. A key issue, from the plaintiff's perspective, is that he needs to come out of the process with $100,000 in the bank, net of his attorney's one-third contingency fee. Since the primary claim is for lost pay, however, any settlement will be treated by the company as back pay and therefore will be subject to tax withholding. The effect is that the plaintiff would net only about $70,000, well below his minimum requirement. The plaintiff also has asserted a vague claim for emotional distress, but federal law bars plaintiffs from receiving settlement money tax free unless an injury was physical in nature. "Mere" emotional distress is not sufficient to avoid a tax bite.

Suddenly the plaintiff attorney asks the mediator to take an idea to the defense: In a spell of depression caused by the firing, he now remembers, the plaintiff suffered from erectile dysfunction. Counsel didn't make it an explicit part of the claim because of the embarrassment factor, but it's there and it was a physical injury. The lawyer, with his client's approval, proposes allocating most of the settlement to this injury, allowing the plaintiff to receive his $100,000.

a. Is there a problem for the mediator with presenting this idea to the defense?

b. Assume that the mediator does so. Defense counsel laughs and says that this is the first she's heard about this malady. However, if the plaintiff says that he's dysfunctional, that's his problem. She says the proposal is OK with her client, as long as the plaintiff certifies the condition and assumes any risk that the IRS will contest it. The lawyers ask you to write down the terms they dictate summarizing the deal. Does this pose a problem for you as the mediator?

3. Combining Practice as an Advocate and a Mediator

Experienced lawyers increasingly seek to combine their practices as litigators with work as mediators. There are pluses and minuses to such a combination. Experienced attorneys find it refreshing to take on new roles, and if a lawyer is thinking of changing careers, such an approach allows him to explore a neutral's role without "quitting his day job." Even if an attorney decides to continue to practice law, experience as a mediator is likely to enhance his effectiveness as an advocate in the process.

Conflicts of Interest

One major issue for lawyers who alternate between the roles of advocate and neutral is the potential for conflicts of interest — the possibility that a party in a mediated case will be a past or future legal client of the mediator-lawyer. This is a particular concern in large law firms, where a lawyer-neutral's partners may be concerned that a single modestly compensated mediation will disqualify the entire firm from representing the party in a much more lucrative matter.

Standards for neutrals call for disclosure in such situations. Model Standard III requires disclosure of "all actual and potential conflicts that are reasonably known to the mediator and could reasonably be seen as raising a question about impartiality." If the facts "cast serious doubt on the integrity of the process," the Standards require a mediator to recuse herself. The UMA relies on disclosure: Section 9(a) requires a neutral "to make an inquiry that is reasonable under the circumstances to determine whether there are any known facts that a reasonable individual would consider likely to affect the impartiality of the mediator [including] an existing or past relationship with a mediation party or foreseeable participant . . ." and disclose any such facts if they exist. The UMA does not impose disqualification on the lawyer or her firm, but Section 9(d) does bar violators from asserting the mediation privilege.

The ABA's E2K Report deals explicitly with conflicts between roles, stating that that "a lawyer shall not represent anyone in connection with a

14. Law and Ethics

matter in which the lawyer participated personally and substantially as a . . . mediator . . ." The rule goes on to provide that "If a lawyer is disqualified . . . , no lawyer in a firm with which that [lawyer-mediator] is associated may know-ingly undertake or continue representation in that matter unless" the lawyer-mediator is screened from knowledge or fees associated with the case, and the parties to the mediation are notified of the situation (E2K Report, §1.12 (a,c)). The issue is also addressed by other codes of ethics, in particular the CPR-Georgetown rules (on Web site).

QUESTION

A lawyer-mediator has no current or past attorney-client relationship with the parties in a case she is mediating, but she knows that lawyers in another department of her firm have approached the defendant in the case about serving as outside counsel. The firm has never received a case from the defen-dant, but hopes to represent it in the future.

a. What do the above standards require of the lawyer?
b. Must she disqualify herself as mediator? If she mediates the case, is her firm disqualified from representing the party as counsel?

Role Confusion

The very fact that a mediator is an attorney may lead pro se litigants to believe that the neutral will provide them with legal advice. The E2K Report proposed the following rule to deal with this issue:

> Rule 2.4(b) . . . A lawyer serving as a third-party neutral shall inform unrepre-sented parties that the lawyer is not representing them. When the lawyer knows or reasonably should know that a party does not understand the lawyer's role in the matter, the lawyer shall explain the difference between the lawyer's role as a third-party neutral and a lawyer's role as one who represents a client.
>
> Comment: . . . Where appropriate, the lawyer should inform unrepresented parties of the important differences between the lawyer's role as third-party neu-tral and a lawyer's role as a client representative, including the inapplicability of the attorney-client evidentiary privilege. . . .

QUESTIONS

1. In what kinds of cases is the danger of confusion between the role of counsel and mediator likely to be greatest?
2. Assume that you are a lawyer who has agreed to mediate a dispute between a quarry and neighbors who are complaining about noise and dust from its operations. The company is represented by its business manager, the neighbors by a committee of three laypeople. Draft a statement that you could make to the participants to explain your role. When and how would you deliver it?

The role of a mediator is inherently ambiguous, and ethical standards that apply to the role tend to be stated in general terms, leaving even conscientious neutrals in doubt about what they should do in a particular situation. This is especially true when the ethical principles applicable to a given situation appear to conflict. We hope to have convinced you that being an ethical mediator or lawyer is a process of continuing self-examination rather than a matter of learning a set of rules, and that you will continue to ask these questions for the rest of your professional life.

E.   CONCLUSION: MEDIATIVE SKILLS AS PART OF A LEGAL CAREER

It is tempting to look at the mediation process solely from the perspective of a neutral, but you now know that lawyers are much more likely to enter the process as advocates than as mediators. This is particularly true for young lawyers who are in the process of establishing their reputation in the legal community. The fact that an attorney does not embark on a full-time career as a mediator does not, however, mean that she will not benefit greatly from having meditative skills.

The ability to mediate is helpful to lawyers in a wide variety of settings. Transactional lawyers often find themselves called on to pull together multi-sided deals, where the ability to resolve disagreements and form coalitions with other participants is crucial to success. Similarly, attorneys for organizations ranging from corporate boards to community groups often find that their "client" consists of individuals with differing views. To represent such an organization effectively, an inside lawyer must be able to bring his diverse constituencies to a consensus on a common course of action. Even litigators can benefit from studying mediation: In a world in which the vast majority of legal cases are settled, the ability to negotiate well is a crucial aspect of a trial lawyer's toolbox of skills. By learning what mediators do, litigators can better understand when to invoke mediation and how to advocate most effectively for clients in the process. Mediation, and meditative skills, are useful to both lawyers and their clients.

PART
III

Arbitration

CHAPTER
15

Arbitration — The Big Picture

Knowledgeable attorneys understand the term "arbitration" to refer to any process in which a private third party neutral renders a judgment, or "award," regarding a dispute after hearing evidence and argument, like a judge. "Arbitration" comprehends a wide variety of procedures, similar in varying degrees to litigation and usually intended as a partial or complete substitute for court trial.

Look again at Professor Folberg's "Dispute Resolution Spectrum" on page 4 in Chapter 1. Several forms of arbitration are referenced in the chart — but most types are listed on the right side of the spectrum, among "Adjudicative Processes/Binding." This placement emphasizes two essential characteristics of most arbitration procedures: They are adversary *adjudicative* procedures analogous to court trial, and they result in a judgment that is *binding*.

Typically, lawyers act as advocates for parties in arbitration in much the same way they do in trial court. They make oral arguments at hearings, present documentary and testimonial evidence, and prepare briefs for the arbitrators, who act as neutral decision makers. When the lawyers' work is done, the parties and lawyers await a judgment from the arbitrators, an award that is difficult to alter. Hence, arbitration processes are of a fundamentally different character from negotiation, mediation, and other processes on the left side of the Dispute Resolution Spectrum.

In most kinds of arbitration, moreover, the parties agree that the arbitrator's award will be mutually binding and enforceable in a court of law. "Binding arbitration" is our primary focus in Part III. We will explore the many aspects of "traditional arbitration," and touch briefly upon recently developed variants in the Dispute Resolution Spectrum such as "Bracketed Arbitration" and "Final Offer Arbitration."

On the left-hand side of the Dispute Resolution Spectrum, under the heading of "Settlement Processes/Non-binding" is "Advisory Arbitration." This refers to processes, common in federal and state court programs, where the arbitrator's judgment, or award, takes the form of a non-binding advisory opinion; the latter is not enforceable in a court of law. Such non-binding processes are beyond the scope of Part III, but we will touch briefly on the subject of non-binding or advisory arbitration in court ADR programs in Chapter 16 and Part IV, Chapter 19.

Although it is not made clear by the Dispute Resolution Spectrum, it makes a big difference whether parties come to arbitration as the result of a court order or by a mutual agreement. In the United States, lawyers are most often involved with arbitration pursuant to a private agreement between two or more parties. It is this kind of arbitration—binding arbitration by agreement—that is the essential focus of Chapters 15-18.

What kinds of disputes may find their way into binding arbitration under the terms of an agreement? The answer may surprise you. Consider the following examples of disputes that have been the subject of arbitration:

- A dispute involving the design and construction of a major league baseball stadium;
- A controversy between U.S financial institutions and the Government of Iran;
- A fight over the valuation and distribution of assets among entities and individuals in the wake of a corporate dissolution;
- A disagreement over the quality of textiles manufactured by one company for another;
- A dispute over liability and damages resulting from delays in the arrival of a cargo ship in San Francisco;
- A claim of fraud by an investor against her securities broker;
- The controversy over the disqualification of an Olympic skater;
- A claim for employment discrimination and intentional infliction of emotional distress by an employee against his employer;
- A dispute aired on TV as entertainment, like The People's Court.

For a compendium of arbitration and dispute resolution approaches, see Stipanowich (2001).

A.   A BRIEF HISTORY OF ARBITRATION

Arbitration has a long and venerable history, having been used by many cultures in a variety of contexts over the centuries. In Biblical times, King Solomon was famous for his wisdom as an arbitrator. Archaeologists have found papyrus documenting arbitration among Phoenician grain traders. In England, arbitration was recognized as part of the judicial system as early as 1281. Many Native American tribes turned to wise elders to resolve disputes.

Binding arbitration has long been an attractive alternative for commercial parties, for whom courts were often too slow and cumbersome, too expensive, too inflexible in remedy-making, and lacking in familiarity with business practices. In medieval times, merchant courts dispensed speedy justice for traders at commercial fairs. In the American colonies, arbitration among merchants was common, since it proved more efficient and effective than the courts during that period. Our first president, George Washington, served as an arbiter of private disputes before the Revolution, and incorporated the following provision in his will:

> I hope and trust, that no disputes will arise concerning [the devises in this will]; but if, contrary to expectation, of the usual technical terms, or because too much

or too little has been said on any of the Devises to be consonant with law, My Will and direction expressly is, that

- all disputes (if unhappily any should arise) shall be decided by three impartial and intelligent men, known for their probity and understanding.
- two to be chosen by the disputants—each having a choice of one—and the third by those two.
- Which three men thus chosen, shall, unfettered by Law, or legal constructions; declare their Sense of the Testator's intention;
- and such decision is, to all intents and purposes to be as binding on the Parties as if it had been given in the Supreme Court of the United States (Nordham, 1982).

The New York Chamber of Commerce has provided for the use of arbitration beginning with its inception in 1768, and the New York Stock Exchange established arbitration as a dispute resolution mechanism in its 1817 constitution. By the middle of the twentieth century, dozens of industry and trade associations were sponsoring private arbitration programs for business-to-business disputes. Binding arbitration also became a fixture in arbitration of rights and interests under collective bargaining agreements between unions and employers.

Today, arbitration remains an important alternative to court litigation of business disputes. A 1997 survey by the Cornell School of Industrial and Labor Relations and the Center for Prevention and Early Resolution of Conflict showed widespread use of arbitration among Fortune 1000 corporations. In international business relationships, binding arbitration provides a critical substitute for litigation in any of the partners' national courts.

In recent years, binding arbitration agreements have become a feature of many contracts between employers and individual employees, as well as contracts for consumer goods and services. These developments reflect, among other things, an important shift in prevailing judicial attitudes toward arbitration, as courts that were once skeptical of binding arbitration have embraced it as an effective dispute resolution option, in large part because of legislative approval and encouragement of arbitration. This evolution, the implications for employees and consumers, and the variety of responses to concerns about the fairness of arbitration in such settings, will be addressed in Chapter 18.

B. ARBITRATION VS. LITIGATION

According to a recent study of conflict resolution among leading corporations, business lawyers choose arbitration over litigation in a public forum for a variety of reasons: in order to achieve a speedy resolution; to avoid the costs and delays of litigation; to forgo extensive discovery; to escape the glare of a public proceeding; to avoid the publication of a legal precedent; to choose a decision maker with pertinent business or legal expertise; or to achieve a more satisfactory or more durable resolution. Arbitration may or may not achieve these anticipated benefits. Much hinges on key choices made by attorneys at the time of drafting and during the course of the arbitration process—choices that should be informed by the particular needs and goals of their clients.

Relative Speed and Economy

As compared to litigation, arbitration has traditionally been touted as a more efficient, speedy, and inexpensive path to justice. There is no question that in certain jurisdictions, private arbitration may be a welcome alternative to waiting one's turn on a crowded civil docket. There is empirical evidence indicating that in some categories of cases, especially those that do not involve high stakes, arbitration is often speedier than court trial. See, e.g., Stipanowich (1988) (summarizing survey of U.S. construction lawyers). Arbitration sometimes avoids, and often attenuates, time-consuming (and costly) procedural steps such as pretrial motion practice and discovery. And due to relatively strict limits on judicial review of arbitration awards, the likelihood of lengthy postarbitration appellate practice is low.

However, depending on the scope or complexity of the issues, the nature of agreed-upon procedures, and the process management skills of the arbitrator(s), arbitration may end up being just as lengthy or as costly as litigation. High stakes may induce lawyers to introduce more extensive procedural elements into the process, including discovery analogous to that available in court, and to require the services of multiple arbitrators whose often busy schedules must be coordinated. In some cases, lawyers have even tried to establish procedures for expanded judicial review of arbitration awards—sometimes with disastrous results. Indeed, many business attorneys now say that arbitration is often too much like litigation; a 2002 survey of leading commercial arbitrators supports the same conclusion.

Privacy and the Avoidance of Precedent

Arbitration typically involves proceedings that are not open to the public, and privacy is a major concern for many parties who utilize the arbitration process. Extremely sensitive business and personal documents, including those detailing financial information, are foreclosed from the public, and witnesses are also shielded from public scrutiny during arbitration. In the case where special protection is desired, however, for financial data, intellectual property or other proprietary information, the normal confidentiality provisions in arbitration agreements may not be sufficient, and special arrangements may be necessary. Arbitration awards are not made public. Moreover, the law places major obstacles in the way of parties seeking court testimony by arbitrators regarding the process or their decision.

Additionally, arbitration awards do not establish precedent in most circumstances. In most arbitral proceedings, the absence of a public award and published reasoning accompanying awards ensures that awards in one dispute are not used as precedent in similar situations. As discussed below, arbitrators traditionally have only issued written decisions that are publically available in special areas such as labor law and domain name disputes. Even there, the awards do not function as a strict form of precedent. Thus, arbitration is a desirable dispute resolution option if one party wants to avoid a precedent. If, on the other hand, a client seeks to establish a new precedent affecting other pending or future disputes, arbitration may be less attractive.

Choice of Expert Decision Maker(s)

Arbitration allows parties to select their own decision makers; they have the freedom to choose an expert in pertinent fields including law, business and finance, accounting, engineering, technology, and other areas. In some cases, a panel of arbitrators may bring to the table complementary knowledge, skill, and experience. For example, an arbitration panel selected to resolve a complex construction dispute might consist of a lawyer familiar with construction contracts and disputes, an architect or engineer, and a contractor or construction manager. In a large or complex case, the ability of an arbitrator (or chair of an arbitration panel) to manage a dispute resolution process may be of paramount significance.

Of course, the practice of choosing decision makers with related professional background and expertise enhances the likelihood that those chosen will have connections to the parties or will already have formed perspectives on issues at the heart of the dispute. For this reason, as explored later, arbitration agreements, statutes, and ethical codes routinely require arbitrators to disclose relationships to the parties and, their counsel, as well as other information that might indicate a conflict of interest.

Informality, Arbitral Flexibility, Finality

Another trademark of arbitration is its informality. The atmosphere tends to be less formal and intimidating than a court proceeding; arbitrations frequently take place in an attorney's conference room. Moreover, the rules of evidence and procedure are usually somewhat flexible, allowing the parties to submit certain kinds of evidence that would not be considered in court. For clients frustrated by the sometimes technical constraints of formal rules of evidence and the cost of formal procedures, this can be a benefit. However, an attorney must make her client aware that this relaxation of the rules also means that parties in an arbitration process may not receive all of the formal procedural opportunities and protections of litigation. For example, hearsay may be more widely admitted than in court, even if arbitrators give it less weight. On the one hand, proceedings may be truncated, foreclosing certain avenues of evidence or testimony (although an arbitrator's refusal to hear material evidence is grounds for reversal of award under federal and state law). On the other hand, some arbitrators tend to be very expansive in their admission of evidence, leading to the complaint that the proceeding resembles a "fishing expedition." Again, much hinges on the choice of arbitrator(s) and other decisions made by attorneys in defining the process.

In arriving at a final decision, arbitrators typically have broad flexibility. The law recognizes that their awards will not be measured against judicial precedent, and courts have sometimes spoken of the ability of arbitrators to rely on their own notions of fairness and equity to tailor a remedy appropriate to the circumstances. On the one hand, in some forms of arbitration, including many forms of commercial and labor arbitration, the emphasis was and is on "fact-dominated rough justice. Equity, not law, is the order of the day . . ." (Brunet, 2002). In high stakes commercial cases, on the other hand, lawyers often dominate the process; advocates and arbitrators often place considerable emphasis on legal issues and legal precedents. Nevertheless, based on the principle that in choosing arbitration parties bargain for the determination of the arbitrator, and not the court, modern law places stringent limits on judicial review of arbitral awards, and restricts the ability of parties to overturn awards on the basis of errors of fact or law.

Arbitration awards are, in fact, more ironclad than jury verdicts or trial court judgments, since appeal is limited to very narrow grounds. Courts give great deference to arbitrators and allow very few avenues of redress. This finality may be one of the greatest advantages of arbitration for many clients who want to get a dispute behind them and move on with new business, but it can also be a serious disadvantage for parties that are displeased with a ruling or believe that the integrity of the process was compromised, or where a dispute presents important or novel legal issues. Lawyers sometimes express concern about the possibility that arbitral awards will be undisciplined by legal or other norms, resulting in unpredictable and unforeseen outcomes. "Compromise arbitration awards, and awards based upon equity, benefit parties who ignore the law and punish firms who seek to comply with substantive law" (Brunet, 2002). The complaint is often made, with some justification, that some arbitrators too often "split the baby" in order to avoid hard decisions on the merits.

Concerns regarding rigorous application of precedent and the danger of an extreme or seemingly irrational award may cause counsel to conclude that arbitration is an unacceptable option for a particular dispute. Alternatively, attorneys may use arbitrator selection; guidelines, standards, or limits for decision making; or other means to reduce the risk of a "knucklehead" award.

Flexibility and Choice

When all is said and done, it may be that the greatest potential benefit of arbitration is the flexibility afforded participants in crafting a private system of justice tailored to fit the needs of their specific dispute. However, this places a premium on the ability of counsel to provide effective guidance in making process choices. Parties often choose an administered process where arbitral institutions help with the various stages of arbitration. Forms of administrative support include selection of arbitrators, scheduling, and handling fees and expenses. Some parties forgo administrative support, opting for a non-administered arbitration to minimize costs.

Limitations and Concerns

While binding arbitration is often perceived as preferable to going to court, it is nearly always more formal, time consuming, and expensive than unassisted negotiation or mediation — and cedes final decision-making authority to a third party. And although it is sometimes said that arbitration may help to reduce friction between the parties and lay the groundwork for future relations, its impact is very often as negative as litigation. It is, after all, a backward-looking, adversarial process in which the parties take a back seat to their lawyers and to a third-party decision maker who will impose a judgment.

For these reasons, arbitration is increasingly viewed as a last resort among ADR processes, to be employed only after negotiation and/or mediation have failed. Today, business lawyers often advise clients to attempt negotiation and mediation even after they have agreed to arbitrate, and, if appropriate, to continue such settlement attempts during the arbitral process. The growing use of dispute resolution processes incorporating multiple approaches or strategies is explored in Part IV.

Finally, serious issues of fairness and unequal bargaining power arise in disputes involving consumers who entered into predispute arbitration contracts. There are concerns over the elimination of an aggrieved party's right to a trial by jury, as well as arbitration's impact on class action disputes. Fairness issues also arise in employment disputes, when employees find they are bound to assert any claims against an employer through arbitration because of the employment agreement they signed before any disputes arose. Consumers or employees may find themselves in a "take it or leave it" position because all jobs in a given industry or all similar products can only be obtained by signing nearly identical arbitration clauses. In such circumstances, the secrecy provided by the arbitral process, plus participants' real or perceived lack of control over designing the dispute resolution process and choosing the arbitration provider or arbitrators, can foster suspicion, anger, and less incentive to comply with an arbitral award. In some jurisdictions, these concerns generated a backlash against arbitration in the 1990s and encouraged legislatures or others to attempt to alter arbitration processes to protect less-powerful parties. These concerns also prompted some judges to review arbitral awards more closely, undermining the finality of the process, arguably one of arbitration's more appreciated benefits. These and other responses to the concerns about the use and fairness of arbitration in certain settings will be explored in more detail in Chapter 18.

PROBLEM 1: CHOOSING ARBITRATION: A DIGITAL DOWNLOAD CONTRACT

Your client, MDM, is an entertainment production company. One of the many television shows the company produces is a popular series entitled, "Starscape." The series is shown exclusively on a cable network, which airs the show in a small but expanding number of U.S. markets. Starscape has enjoyed relatively high ratings and has a strong following of loyal and enthusiastic fans.

The Fandom Company (Fandom) owns and administers a Web site called "ScapePlace.com." On this site, visitors can find transcripts of interviews with Starscape cast members as well as airdates and other things of interest to fans of the show. Users can log on to the site after a brief, and free, registration process.

Now that Starscape is about to enter its third season, MDM is negotiating a contract with Fandom allowing Fandom to host video files of Starscape episodes on its "ScapePlace" site. Fandom is interested in hosting the files, as it would mean a huge increase in traffic to the ScapePlace site. ScapePlace, like many other such sites, makes its profit by providing advertising space. The more visitors, the more money advertisers will be willing to pay to place their banners on the site.

MDM also anticipates benefits from the arrangement. Its marketing people believe that allowing Fandom to distribute episodes of Starscape to people who access the ScapePlace site would increase the show's following beyond that which the limited cable market could provide. MDM hopes the increased interest in the show will put pressure on the network to expand the number of markets airing the series, as well as increase the interest in the season boxed sets of "Starscape" MDM plans on releasing early next year.

MDM plans to include in the contract numerous limitations and conditions relating to the quality of the video files Fandom can provide. For example, the contract will prohibit Fandom from hosting video captures of seasons one and two of "Starscape" that are larger than 80 Mb. The clarity of an 80 Mb video file would be enough for a viewer to enjoy the episode in a two-inch box on their computer monitor, but would not be of a high enough quality to compete with the soon to be released DVDs.

QUESTION

1. Suppose you are discussing with your client MDM the possibility of including an arbitration provision in the dispute-resolution clause of the proposed contract with Fandom. What, if any, aspects of this scenario suggest that MDM may want to propose an arbitration provision? What aspects might make arbitration less appealing than litigation? Use the following suitability guidelines to help you evaluate your answers:

A "SUITABILITY SCREEN" FOR ARBITRATION
(Copyright 2004, The CPR Institute for Dispute Resolution, Reprinted with permission of The CPR Institute, with adaptations)

The CPR Institute for Dispute Resolution, a New York-based non-profit organization comprised of leading in-house lawyers and outside corporate counsel, judges, scholars, and thinkers about ADR, publishes an ADR Suitability Screen for the guidance of lawyers and clients considering the use of mediation, arbitration, and other ADR options. The following set of questions, adapted from that document, provides a starting point for counsel advising clients about whether to arbitrate or to litigate.

1. Does a party seek to secure a decision in a public setting?
   ___ a) no
   ___ b) yes

2. Does a party want to prevent the specter of a massive or unpredictable jury award?
   ___ a) yes
   ___ b) no

3. Is the establishment of precedent or articulation of public policy an important goal for either party?
   ___ a) no
   ___ b) yes

4. Is a vital corporate interest or "bet the company" case involved that requires the full panoply of procedural protections afforded by a court, including full appellate rights?
   ___ a) no
   ___ b) yes

5. Is there a need for continuing court supervision of the case or parties?
   __ a) no
   __ b) yes

6. Is the selection of the decision maker an important objective for either party?
   __ a) yes
   __ b) no

7. Does the case require an understanding of complex or technical factual issues?
   __ a) yes
   __ b) no

8. Is the ability to have some degree of control over case-scheduling issues an important objective for either party?
   __ a) yes
   __ b) no

9. Is the ability to conduct full discovery an important objective for either party?
   __ a) no
   __ b) yes

10. Does either party (or both) seek to retain unabridged appellate rights?
    __ a) no
    __ b) yes

———————

As the authors of the Suitability Screen explain, the number and importance of (a) responses argue in favor of arbitration, while responses in the (b) category may encourage parties to consider going to court.

2. Note, the decision to include arbitration in the agreement is one that is made at the outset, before conflict actually arises. How do you suppose that lawyers and developers of arbitration procedures address this issue?

CONCLUSION

The next chapter presents an overview of the arbitration process and briefly examines several key practice issues for lawyers advising clients about arbitration and those preparing to be effective advocates in arbitration. We will canvass the various routes by which parties arrive at arbitration; basic considerations for attorneys drafting arbitration agreements; the selection of qualified arbitrators; the management of information exchange and discovery; and other aspects of the arbitration process, including the unique challenges and benefits of those arbitrations set on an international stage.

CHAPTER
16

Arbitration Agreements, Procedures, and Awards

A. A MYRIAD OF CHOICES: THE ROLE OF COUNSEL IN ARBITRATION

In the modern environment arbitration deals with a much broader range of conflict than in the "old days," including big cases involving complex legal issues. While parties may see the virtues of a private substitute for court trial in many different kinds of cases, the nature of that private alternative will vary with the circumstances. Arbitration may mean anything from a rudimentary, expedited, non-lawyered process involving a quality determination by a technical expert to a much more formal proceeding with many of the trappings of court trial (Stipanowich and Kaskell, 2001).

Much of the material in this chapter is adapted from this source, a report by the CPR Institute for Dispute Resolution Commission on the Future of Arbitration.[1] The wide-ranging report, by a commission of more than 50 experienced counsel, aimed to address common complaints about arbitration by business clients. The report began with the observation that arbitration processes must be carefully tailored to the varying needs and expectations of users — and that lawyers must be well informed regarding the many choices that arbitration presents. By introducing you to key issues surrounding arbitration, we hope to provide you with the knowledge and skills needed in order to fulfill the promise and avoid the pitfalls of arbitration for your clients. In the course of this discussion, considerable emphasis will be placed on various standards that govern or provide guidance for arbitration proceedings, arbitrators, and advocates. These include published procedures, policies, and guidelines of national and international institutions supporting or sponsoring arbitration, which offer primary and often controlling information for attorneys.

Although arbitration is generally a creature of contract, it is critical to have a structure for the judicial enforcement and facilitation of agreements to arbitrate and the enforcement of arbitration awards. Lawyers must therefore understand the interplay of federal arbitration law and state statutes

---

1. Another important source for the chapters on arbitration is Macneil, Speidel, and Stipanowich (1997).

on arbitration in the United States, and the role of international treaties in arbitration of cross-border disputes. While legal topics surrounding modern arbitration will be treated further in Chapter 17, we will occasionally address the impact of arbitration law on the practice exercises in this chapter. And, although ethical issues are pervasive in arbitration, in this chapter we introduce you to the topic by addressing arbitrators' biases, disclosure requirements, and neutrality issues.

B. LEGALLY MANDATED ARBITRATION; AGREEMENTS TO ARBITRATE

Arbitration Pursuant to Statute or Court Rule

Parties can be required by statute or court rule to participate in arbitration in certain instances. In recent decades, this option has grown increasingly popular with judges and legislatures as some court systems struggle with delays. The law sometimes requires advisory arbitration or non-binding arbitration of certain types of disputes, such as lawsuits involving medical malpractice claims and civil claims filed in courts of a lesser monetary amount (e.g., suits involving less than $25,000 or $50,000 in damages). See Chapter 13.A above. Typically, volunteer lawyers serve as neutrals in these proceedings. The arbitrations are "mandatory" only in the sense that arbitration is a precondition to litigation. The arbitral awards issued are usually not binding in such situations, and parties retain rights of access to the courts and a jury trial. However, if the party insisting on litigation does not improve on the arbitration award at trial, that party may be required to pay the opponent's expenses in some states, including California and Michigan. Keep in mind that court-annexed arbitration is quite different than the private arbitration pursuant to party agreement discussed throughout this Part. Indeed, some of the benefits of arbitration—most notably, its finality—would not apply to advisory or non-binding arbitration.

Executory Agreements to Arbitrate

Occasionally, parties agree to submit a dispute to arbitration after it has arisen. These agreements are called *submission agreements*. Much more commonly, however, lawyers are involved with arbitration pursuant to a provision in a commercial, labor, or other contract that binds the parties to arbitrate some or all future disputes as part of the initial contract. Such clauses, known as *executory agreements to arbitrate*, have long been a standard feature of collective bargaining agreements between unions and employers, as well as construction and other kinds of commercial contracts. Today, they are also widely used in contracts relating to employment, insurance, health care, retail sales, banking, professional services (including legal services), real estate agreements, repair services, utility services, and myriad other transactions.

You may be the attorney responsible for considering whether to incorporate an arbitration provision in a client's contract. That decision is often complicated by the fact no disputes have actually arisen; the decision to use arbitration must be based on experience and educated guesses. Today, a contract drafter should also consider whether arbitration should be preceded by other strategies for resolving disputes, such as stepped negotiation or mediation. These options, and the growing use of multistep or "hybrid" approaches, will be explored in Chapters 19 and 20. Other choices remain. How broad should the arbitration agreement be? Is it necessary to have the administrative support of a third party institution? How should arbitrators be selected? What level of "due process" — discovery, prehearing practice, evidentiary rules — is appropriate? These and other considerations for drafters will be treated in the following pages, as will issues confronting lawyers who serve as advocates for parties in the arbitration process.

Executory agreements to arbitrate future disputes have generated controversy when incorporated as boilerplate in some kinds of standardized contracts, such as those involving employees or consumers. Since such terms typically purport to waive the right to go to court in favor of private adjudication through arbitration, they raise legitimate concerns about the fairness of the alternative system. We first explore the typical contract formation and the steps of the process before returning to these intriguing issues in Chapter 18.

QUESTIONS

1. *Basic Executory Provisions*. Arbitration provisions come in all shapes and sizes. Most, however, tend to be relatively concise and straightforward. Consider the following model arbitration clause, which is recommended by a major provider of arbitration services for inclusion in contracts:

   > Any controversy or claim arising out of or relating to this contract, or the breach thereof, shall be settled by arbitration administered by the American Arbitration Association in accordance with its [insert type of rules] Arbitration Rules [including the Emergency Interim Relief Procedures], and judgment on the award rendered by the arbitrator(s) may be entered in any court having jurisdiction thereof.[2]

   What key functions are served by this provision? Notice that the parties can select from arbitration rules for various types of disputes (e.g., commercial, construction, labor, patent, financial planning, and wireless Internet).

2. *Submission Agreements*. As noted above, sometimes parties agree to submit existing disputes to arbitration. A basic template for such an agreement would look something like this:

   > We, the undersigned parties, hereby agree to submit to arbitration the following controversy:_____.

---

2. *http://www.adr.org/index2.1.jsp?JSPssid=15727&JSPsrc=upload\LIVESITE\Rules_Procedures\ ADR_Guides\clausebook.html.*

> We agree that the arbitration will be conducted in accordance with the Commercial Arbitration Procedures of the ACME Dispute Resolution Association, as modified below.
>
> We further agree that a judgment of any court having jurisdiction may be entered upon the award.

What are the potential advantages of making the decision to arbitrate after disputes have arisen? Why do you suppose that far fewer arbitrations are conducted pursuant to the terms of submission agreements than predispute executory agreements in contracts?

C. DRAFTING ARBITRATION AGREEMENTS: ARBITRATION PROCEDURES, ARBITRATION INSTITUTIONS

Standard Institutional Procedures

Today, many if not most arbitrations are conducted under the rules or procedures of various for-profit or non-profit national or international institutions that provide guidance or support for arbitration proceedings. Such institutions include the International Chamber of Commerce (ICC), the London Court of International Arbitration (LCIA), the American Arbitration Association (AAA) and its International Dispute Resolution Center (IDRC), the CPR Institute for Dispute Resolution (CPR), Judicial Arbitration and Mediation Services (JAMS), and other organizations.

These institutions promulgate rules governing arbitral procedures, which often run to many pages of text and thus are typically incorporated only by reference in the agreement to arbitrate. Arbitration procedures vary among institutions, and by subject matter: in the United States there are literally dozens of different arbitration rules for different trade groups or practice areas, including securities disputes, construction matters, commercial disputes, and small claims. Some organizations publish different sets of rules to handle cases of varying size or complexity. For example, as long as a claim or counterclaim in arbitration does not exceed $75,000, AAA will use its Expedited Procedures,[3] unless the parties or AAA do not deem it otherwise necessary.

Arbitration procedures, which have tended to become longer and more detailed in recent years, usually address most or all of the following: the filing of an arbitration demand (or joint submission) and other pleadings, what constitutes "notice" for procedural purposes, methods of choosing arbitrators (including procedures for challenging appointees), prearbitration conferences, elements of the hearing, arbitral awards and remedies, and procedures for publication or clarification of awards.

---

3. *http://www.adr.org/index2.1.jsp?JSPssid=15747&JSPsrc=upload\LIVESITE\Rules_Procedures\ National_International\..\..\focusArea\commercial\AAA235current.htm#ExpeditedProc.*

Even if parties elect not to make reference to such procedures in favor of an "ad hoc" approach to arbitration, drafters who fail to consult institutional rules or other models for guidance do so at their peril. In addition to publishing arbitration procedures, "arbitration institutions" also (1) maintain lists or panels of arbitrators, (2) provide some level of administrative support for arbitration proceedings, and (3) in some cases, support mediation and other processes as well as arbitration. When it comes to arbitration, therefore, familiarity with applicable rules, and with the organizations that publish them, is as essential for drafters and advocates as is familiarity with the procedural and evidentiary rules that apply in courts.

Panels of Arbitrators

By incorporating an institution's arbitral procedures in their agreement, parties have probably indicated their mutual intent to rely upon certain services of the "provider" institution, although they can alter provider rules by agreement. This includes, most notably, the institution's panel of arbitrators. The makeup of the latter, which varies from institution to institution, is a critical point of comparison.

In a particular case, the institutional role may involve providing names of candidates from which the parties may choose arbitrators, administering a process for determining and resolving conflicts of interest, and replacing arbitrators if necessary. Some arbitration organizations collect and distribute arbitrator fees; a few share fees with the arbitrators.

Some arbitral institutions also publish or adhere to ethical rules for the guidance of arbitrators. The leading U.S. standard is the *Code of Ethics for Arbitrators in Commercial Disputes*. Originally developed in 1977, the Code was recently updated by a joint effort of the American Bar Association, the AAA, and CPR. The Code of Ethics is used extensively by commercial arbitrators in the United States, and is occasionally referenced in court opinions. Its precepts, such as those governing arbitrator disclosure of conflicts of interest, may parallel legal principles under federal and state arbitration law or provisions of institutional arbitration procedures.

However, the Code is not intended to have legal consequences, but only guides the behavior of the arbitrator. And, unlike rules of professional conduct for lawyers, there is no general mechanism for policing infractions of the Code by arbitrators.

Administrative Support

There are considerable differences in the level of administrative support provided by arbitral institutions, and in related administrative costs. Some procedures contemplate limited institutional support—such as helping parties with the selection of arbitrators where necessary. Many rules, however, envision institutional involvement in some or all of the following activities: transmitting communications between parties and arbitrators, handling fees and expenses, scheduling and setting locations for hearings, putting arbitration awards in final form, and even conducting a substantive review of the award before publication.

Other Services

Some but not all institutions sponsoring arbitration services also provide media-tion and other services. Today, as arbitration is less and less likely to "stand alone" as a dispute resolution approach, multifaceted institutional support may be critical in situations involving multistep ADR processes such as the ones discussed in Chapter 20.

Ad hoc Arbitration vs. Arbitration Supported by an Institution

Should attorneys incorporate institutional rules or develop "ad hoc" arrange-ments under which the parties conduct arbitration without institutional support? The answer depends on the circumstances.

Using established procedures reduces the possibility that disputes will arise regarding *the procedures themselves*. An experienced, independent organization may be able to help the parties avoid common problems that they did not anticipate when drafting an arbitration agreement themselves. In cases where counsel or clients lack experience with the arbitration process, an administra-tive structure may provide comfort and guidance. Where hostility or lack of trust hinders the working relationship between parties or between counsel, the administrative structure may be necessary to promote a smoother and more efficient process. For example, it is important in most cases to have a default procedure for arbitrator selection and other functions in the event a party fails to comply with procedures. Finally, consistent with the consensual character of arbitration, institutional procedures may be modified in important ways by agreement of the parties where necessary.

However, institutional involvement usually entails costs that should be weighed against benefits provided. In some cases, moreover, there may be questions about the quality of an institution's administrative services, or delays resulting from institutional efforts.

A non-administered, or "self-administered" arbitration avoids adminis-trative costs and offers great potential flexibility in the structuring and management of the arbitration process, but must be approached with care. The sophistication and working relationship of parties and their counsel are the primary factors to consider in choosing administered or non-administered arbitration. Parties with more experience may choose little or no administra-tion on the grounds that some or all of those functions may be unnecessary, or will be assumed by the arbitrators. Parties opting for non-administered arbi-tration need to put great importance on selecting an experienced arbitrator or chair (for a panel) because this individual will often assume administrative responsibilities. Thus, one factor in deciding whether to use non-administered arbitration is the availability to the parties of an experienced, efficient arbi-trator who can shepherd the parties through the process. Parties should also depend on appropriate models in structuring their rules, such as the UNCITRAL Model Rules in the international sphere, and CPR Rules for Non-Administered Arbitration of Business Disputes.[4]

4. *http://www.cpradr.org/*.

PROBLEM 1: SELECTING ARBITRATION PROCEDURES; ARBITRATION INSTITUTIONS

Review the hypothetical scenario presented by Problem 1, Chapter 15. Assume that after discussing the matter with your client, MDM, there is a strong inclination to incorporate an arbitration agreement in the contract currently being negotiated between MDM and Fandom. Your client informs you that the parties have no prior relationship, and that the Fandom people are, in the opinion of your client's business people, "typical dot.com types, crossed with obsessive TV fan types" — not your typical business partners. Their lawyer is a relatively sophisticated corporate lawyer, but probably knows little about arbitration or other forms of ADR.

In order to help you in rendering advice to the client, your senior partner has encouraged you to review the JAMS Comprehensive Arbitration Rules and Procedures as well as the CPR Institute's (CPR) Rules for Non-Administered Arbitration of Business Disputes, and to consult their Web sites.

QUESTIONS

1. Compare and contrast the JAMS procedures with the CPR procedures. What kinds of (or level of) administration is contemplated by each set of procedures? If an ad hoc approach, or an approach with minimal administration, is desired, which if any of the procedures would be most suitable?
2. Can you develop a reasonable argument for the incorporation of one or the other set of procedures in the arbitration agreement, addressing the particular circumstances set forth above for MDM and in the initial scenario? What other questions might you ask your client?

D. SCOPE OF THE ARBITRATION AGREEMENT

An important issue for every drafter is the scope of the arbitration agreement — in other words, what disputes related to the contract and parties' relationship will be subject to arbitration? Under the law, only those issues that the parties have agreed to arbitrate will be subject to the process.

As noted earlier, it is the common practice of drafters to use language of extreme breadth in describing the scope of the agreement. Broad provisions can minimize the likelihood of court disputes over what is arbitrable, especially since courts enforcing arbitration agreements under the Federal Arbitration Act [hereinafter FAA] and similar state statutes interpret these now-familiar, essentially ubiquitous terms with a presumption in favor of arbitration.

Sometimes, however, attorneys may believe they have sound reasons for limiting what is arbitrable to specific issues. They may wish to reserve issues of particular size, complexity, or subject matter for the public forum, either because they are uncomfortable with the perceived risks of arbitration or because they believe a court may provide more suitable relief, such as a preliminary injunction or temporary restraining order. Attorneys must be aware that great care is required in the drafting of arbitration provisions, since they may result in controversies about whether the dispute that has arisen is arbitrable.

PROBLEM 2: SCOPE ISSUES IN ARBITRATION

Building on the fact pattern in Problems 1 of Chapters 15 and 16, assume MDM and Fandom included in their contract the following arbitration provision:

> Any dispute arising out of any of the terms or conditions of the contract and involving more than $1,000,000 are subject to resolution through arbitration administered by the American Arbitration Association.

Once the contract was in place, Fandom began uploading 80Mb video files of seasons one and two "Starscape" episodes on ScapePlace.com. Six months into the contract, MDM discovered that Fandom had begun uploading high-quality 450Mb videos of season three episodes to ScapePlace.com. In total, seven such video files of "Starscape" had been made available on the site. Outraged, MDM asked you, its attorney, to initiate immediate legal action.

You immediately notified Fandom of MDM's intention to arbitrate, and shortly thereafter filed a demand with the AAA, alleging that Fandom had frustrated the contract's purpose, and that Fandom had distributed the season three video files without MDM's permission and in violation of MDM's copyright and in breach of contract. On behalf of MDM, you requested compensatory damages for copyright violations and breach of contract totaling $1 million for each third season episode of "Starscape" uploaded to ScapePlace.com, as well as $5 million in punitive damages. You also sought interim relief in the form of a preliminary injunction to prevent Fandom from continuing to display the season three episodes.

QUESTIONS

1. Do you see any potential procedural defenses that Fandom might raise in response to your arbitration demand? If you had drafted the arbitration clause for MDM, would you advise your client to use different language in its arbitration clauses in the future? If not, why not? If so, what language would you suggest adding or removing?
2. Assume that the arbitration procedures of the AAA Commercial Arbitration Rules and Mediation Procedures (Including Procedures for Large, Complex Commercial Disputes) apply. If Fandom decides not to submit voluntarily to arbitration, who would decide the question of whether certain issues are within the scope of the arbitration clause—the court or the arbitrator(s)?

E.   SELECTING THE ARBITRATOR(S)

It has been said that the selection of the arbitrator(s) is the single most important decision confronting parties in arbitration, since in many respects "the arbitrator *is* the process." Judicial review of arbitral awards is exceptionally limited, making the choice of arbitrators critical for two reasons: They will likely provide the only review of the case's merits, and arbitrators will have primary control over the process itself. The necessary attributes of arbitrators will vary according to particular circumstances and the party's interests, needs, and priorities. Nevertheless, fairness and open-mindedness is critical to the reality and perception of due process, and arbitration law recognizes the basic entitlement of parties to be judged impartially and independently. Therefore, where an arbitrator actively refuses to hear evidence from a particular party or clearly reveals a closed mind toward that party's case in the course of hearings, that party has grounds to request that a court overturn, or vacate, the resulting award.

In selecting their own decision maker(s), moreover, parties to arbitration frequently seek out those with specialized commercial, legal, or technical knowledge, training, and experience. The assumption is that such grounding reduces the amount of time that will be required to explain issues in dispute to the arbitrators and enhances the likelihood that the outcomes will be more in keeping with pertinent business, legal, or technical standards. This approach contrasts with the realities of most public tribunals: Judges tend to be generalists, steeped in legal traditions and focused on application of legal standards; jurors may be chosen precisely because they *lack* pertinent expertise.

Of course, there is frequently a tension between expertise and impartiality. Besides the fact that arbitrators may bring to the hearing room a point of view that is conditioned by their experience, they are often of the same business or professional community as the parties. While this may only enhance their acceptability as arbitrators, such relationships might also give rise to potential conflicts of interest. As we will see, arbitration procedures, and the law of arbitration, tend to address this concern through the mechanism of arbitrator disclosure. (We will return to this fascinating and much-litigated topic shortly.)

Particularly in large or complex cases, arbitrators must have strong case management skills. They, or at least the designated chair of the tribunal, should be able to run arbitration proceedings efficiently and attentively, and act decisively when necessary. Foresight, planning, diligence, and dedication are normally required to achieve a quick and efficient resolution — which is what arbitrating parties should expect in the absence of a mutual agreement to the contrary. Unfortunately, judging by the experiences of arbitrating parties, these goals are often not achieved in big arbitrations. One of the authors of this text was counsel in commercial arbitrations involving complex disputes, which extended over several years with months elapsing between hearings. The length of the processes and delays between hearings were in large part the fault of the arbitrators, whose efforts in scheduling hearings and controlling the timeline proved ineffective.

Sources of Information About Arbitrators

It is imperative for counsel to conduct a thorough, independent investigation of potential arbitrators; this may mean examining their professional qualifications, education, training, arbitration experience, fees, and even published awards and writings. Most sponsoring organizations offer updated arbitrators' biographies, as well as information on the identification, training, and evaluation of listed arbitrators. They may also provide information on potential arbitrators' possible conflicts of interest, availability, and fee schedules.

In important cases, counsel sometimes seek to arrange a joint interview with the arbitrator in which both sides ask questions of the arbitrator in person or by telephone. Candidates may be asked about their background, relevant professional experience, including experience with the issues of the particular dispute, the availability of the candidate to oversee the dispute, and what the candidate's personal expertise and style is in handling disputes. Moreover, the parties and their counsel often clear up potential conflicts of interest during this interview.

One fast and efficient means of accumulating information about candidates is through the use of the Internet. Some professional, trade, and Internet groups provide arbitrator biographies and links to their publications. Public, private, and governmental alternative dispute resolution organizations and alternative dispute resolution resources can also be accessed. In some cases, awards that have been written by arbitrators may be found by using an arbitrator's name, company, or firm using LexisNexis, Westlaw, and other search engines.

The Number of Arbitrators

Another consideration for parties is the number of arbitrators who will be employed to adjudicate the dispute. The two most common scenarios are using a single arbitrator or a panel of three arbitrators to issue a decision. Why do you suppose two-member panels are generally avoided?

Generally, arbitration procedures establish guidelines for the use of arbitration panels. As a rule, for relatively low-dollar disputes, or where it is vital to limit the cost of the arbitration, a single arbitrator is preferable. If cost is less of a factor, then a panel of three arbitrators can offer distinct advantages. Some lawyers advance the rationale that the decision of a three-member panel is more authoritative, especially if the award is unanimous. Further, it is thought, a panel of three arbitrators is less likely to hand down irrational or arbitrary awards because the arbitrators can "check" each other. Finally, a three-member panel can provide a unique mix of experience and perspectives. Differing expertise may be complementary: for instance, an arbitrator familiar with construction disputes states,

> "I've appreciated the way arbitrators with different backgrounds complement each other. Construction professionals understand the way things go together, the dynamics of the job site, and relevant cost implications. Experienced construction lawyers place these realities in the legal framework of statute, common law and contract. In the best case, each arbitrator brings something to the table, and relies on the other arbitrators."

When choosing a panel, measures must be taken to identify the panel's chair. Sometimes the panel chair is selected by the arbitration organization; other times, the arbitrators agree on a chair. The chair normally acts as the panel's voice and is primarily responsible for managing the arbitration proceedings. Chairs may have to arrange the meeting times and locations for the parties. Sometimes, they solely run several or all of the prehearing conferences. They should be counted on to facilitate a sense of teamwork and effective communication among panel members. In addition to supervising the work of the panelists, the chair is expected to keep in close contact with the appropriate arbitration organization. Under AAA rules, for instance, the chair should coordinate with the AAA case administrator regarding issues such as fee deposits, scheduling, hearing location, physical surroundings, availability of equipment, and storage of documents. The chair is also responsible for reassuring the arbitration organization that all panelists are conforming their behavior to the Code of Ethics.

Selection Processes

There are several different methods of selecting arbitrators. In some cases the parties identify them by name in the agreement, or set forth experiential or professional qualifications in the arbitration provision. Most commonly, however, selection occurs after a dispute has arisen. The parties may jointly agree on the arbitrator(s), or delegate an arbitration institution or other third party to make the selection(s) for them. Many institutional arbitration procedures contemplate a "list selection" process, in which parties identify and rank suitable candidates from lists provided by the institution; the latter selects those mutually acceptable candidates based on highest overall rankings. In some cases, the failure of the parties to agree upon one or more arbitrators requires the institution to select an arbitrator. One popular approach in the United States and in international arbitration is the "tripartite panel"—a panel of three arbitrators in which each party designates one panelist, and the two party-designees (or "party arbitrators") agree upon a third, who then chairs the panel. This seemingly straightforward and balanced approach appears to have much to recommend it. As we will see, however, there has been considerable concern regarding the role of party arbitrators and their relationships with those who appointed them.

QUESTIONS

1. Consider the pros and cons of each of the following approaches:
   a. identifying one or more arbitrators in the original MDM/Fandom contract;
   b. setting out experiential or professional qualifications for one or more arbitrators in the contract;
   c. agreeing to a "tripartite" approach in which each party picks an arbitrator, and the party arbitrators pick a third;
   d. relying on a "list selection" process supervised by an arbitral institution.
2. Now review the related MDM/Fandom dispute scenario. If the arbitration provisions of the AAA Commercial Arbitration Rules and Mediation Procedures (Including Procedures for Large, Complex Commercial Disputes) are applicable, would there be a single arbitrator or arbitration panel? How would the selection process work, assuming the parties had no other selection agreement? Under the AAA procedures, how are the arbitrators' fees paid, and how are communications between the parties and the arbitrators handled?

F. ARBITRATOR DISCLOSURE AND CHALLENGES

As discussed above, the selection of private decision makers with ties to the same business or professional community as the parties or their counsel involves a tension between two principles: party autonomy in selecting arbitrators of their choice, on the one hand, and concepts of judicial fairness, independence and impartiality, on the other. In order to reconcile the potential conflict between these principles, arbitrators are expected to make a timely disclosure of facts that may raise conflict-of-interest concerns, including relationships with counsel, the parties, witnesses, or the issues in dispute. Armed with this information, parties may make a knowledgeable choice about a candidate's suitability for the role of arbitrator, and accede to or, alternatively, deny or challenge their appointment. The concept of arbitrator disclosure — and related guidelines for arbitrators, parties and counsel, arbitral institutions, and courts — are embodied in institutional arbitration procedures, ethical guidelines for arbitrators, and federal and state arbitration law. Some of the basic guidelines will be touched on below.

Institutional Procedures for Disclosure and Challenge

A key element of most institutional arbitration procedures is the procedure for arbitrator disclosure and challenge. Under the AAA Commercial Arbitration Rules and Mediation Procedures, for example, upon appointment arbitrators must "disclose to the AAA any circumstance likely to affect impartiality or independence, including bias or any financial or personal interest in the result of the arbitration or any past or present relationship with the parties or their representatives." Upon a showing of arbitrator partiality, the AAA will inform the parties of the situation, and conclusively rule on any objections the parties make to the continued appointment of the allegedly biased arbitrator. Under the CPR Rules, "[a]ny arbitrator may be challenged if circumstances exist or arise that give rise to justifiable doubt regarding that arbitrator's independence or impartiality . . . If neither agreed disqualification nor voluntary withdrawal occurs, the challenge shall be decided by CPR."

Ethical Standards

The *Code of Ethics for Arbitrators in Commercial Disputes* (1977) contains numerous admonitions to arbitrators regarding the fairness and integrity of the arbitration process. Among other things, Canon II requires arbitrators, before they accept appointment, to "disclose any interest or relationship likely to affect impartiality or which might create an appearance of partiality or bias." The obligation is a continuing one, and requires disclosure to all parties and to other appointed arbitrators. The Canon proceeds to identify courses of action for an arbitrator, including withdrawal in appropriate circumstances.

Judicial Decisions Under Federal and State Arbitration Law

Disclosure standards under arbitration procedures and ethical rules are reinforced by case law interpreting federal and state arbitration statutes. In light of strong policies supporting the finality of arbitration awards, courts are hesitant to allow parties who are disappointed by an award to use a claim of bias as a way to undermine the finality of arbitration. However, an arbitrator's failure to disclose actual or perceived conflicts of interest may result in judicial over-turning, or vacation, of a subsequent arbitration award.

COMMONWEALTH COATINGS CORP. v. CASUALTY CO.
393 U.S. 145 (1968)

At issue in this case is the question whether elementary requirements of impartiality taken for granted in every judicial proceeding are suspended when the parties agree to resolve a dispute through arbitration.

[Commonwealth Coatings Corporation was a painting subcontractor who sued the Casualty Co., surety for the prime contractor, to recover money alleged to be due for a painting job. The contract between the parties contained an arbitration clause that provided for each party to select one arbitrator for a tripartite panel, with those arbitrators then selecting the panel's chair. The panel's chair conducted a large amount of business in Puerto Rico, and the prime contractor being sued in this case was one of his regular customers. While this relationship between the prime contractor and the chair of the arbitration panel was irregular at times, the prime contractor's patronage was repeated and significant, involving fees of about $12,000 over a period of four or five years. The relationship even went so far as to include the rendering of services, albeit over a year since the commencement of this suit, on the very projects involved in this lawsuit. The relationship between the chair and the prime contractor was not disclosed by either party until after an arbitration award had been granted. Petitioner challenged the award on this ground, among others, but the District Court refused to set aside the award. The Court of Appeals affirmed and the Supreme Court then granted certiorari.]

JUSTICE BLACK delivered the opinion of the Court.

In 1925 Congress enacted the United States Arbitration Act, 9 U.S.C. §§1-14, which sets out a comprehensive plan for arbitration of controversies coming under its terms, and both sides here assume that this Federal Act governs this case. Section 10, quoted below, sets out the conditions upon which awards can be vacated.[1] The two courts below held, however, that §10 could not be construed in such a way as to justify vacating the award in this case. We disagree

---

1. "In either of the following cases the United States court in and for the district wherein the award was made may make an order vacating the award upon the application of any party to the arbitration —

"(a) Where the award was procured by corruption, fraud, or undue means.
"(b) Where there was evident partiality or corruption in the arbitrators, or either of them.
"(c) Where the arbitrators were guilty of misconduct in refusing to postpone the hearing, upon sufficient cause shown, or in refusing to hear evidence pertinent and material to the controversy; or of any other misbehavior by which the rights of any party have been prejudiced.
"(d) Where the arbitrators exceeded their powers, or so imperfectly executed them that a mutual, final, and definite award upon the subject matter submitted was not made.
"(e) Where an award is vacated and the time within which the agreement required the award to be made has not expired the court may, in its discretion, direct a rehearing by the arbitrators."

and reverse. Section 10 does authorize vacation of an award where it was "procured by corruption, fraud, or undue means" or "[w]here there was evident partiality . . . in the arbitrators." These provisions show a desire of Congress to provide not merely for any arbitration but for an impartial one. It is true that petitioner does not charge before us that the third arbitrator was actually guilty of fraud or bias in deciding this case, and we have no reason, apart from the undisclosed business relationship, to suspect him of any improper motives. But neither this arbitrator nor the prime contractor gave to petitioner even an intimation of the close financial relations that had existed between them for a period of years. We have no doubt that if a litigant could show that a foreman of a jury or a judge in a court of justice had, unknown to the litigant, any such relationship, the judgment would be subject to challenge. This is shown beyond doubt by *Tumey v. Ohio*, 273 U.S. 510 (1927), where this Court held that a conviction could not stand because a small part of the judge's income consisted of court fees collected from convicted defendants. Although in *Tumey* it appeared the amount of the judge's compensation actually depended on whether he decided for one side or the other, that is too small a distinction to allow this manifest violation of the strict morality and fairness Congress would have expected on the part of the arbitrator and the other party in this case. Nor should it be at all relevant, as the Court of Appeals apparently thought it was here, that "[t]he payments received were a very small part of [the arbitrator's] income. . . ." 382 F.2d at 1011. For in *Tumey* the Court held that a decision should be set aside where there is "the slightest pecuniary interest" on the part of the judge, and specifically rejected the State's contention that the compensation involved there was "so small that it is not to be regarded as likely to influence improperly a judicial officer in the discharge of his duty. . . ." 273 U.S. at 524. Since in the case of courts this is a constitutional principle, we can see no basis for refusing to find the same concept in the broad statutory language that governs arbitration proceedings and provides that an award can be set aside on the basis of "evident partiality" or the use of "undue means." See also *Rogers v. Schering Corp.*, 165 F. Supp. 295, 301 (D.C.N.J. 1958). It is true that arbitrators cannot sever all their ties with the business world, since they are not expected to get all their income from their work deciding cases, but we should, if anything, be even more scrupulous to safeguard the impartiality of arbitrators than judges, since the former have completely free rein to decide the law as well as the facts and are not subject to appellate review. We can perceive no way in which the effectiveness of the arbitration process will be hampered by the simple requirement that arbitrators disclose to the parties any dealings that might create an impression of possible bias.

While not controlling in this case, [section] 18 of the Rules of the American Arbitration Association, in effect at the time of this arbitration, is highly significant. It provided as follows:

> "Section 18. Disclosure by Arbitrator of Disqualification — At the time of receiving his notice of appointment, the prospective Arbitrator is requested to disclose any circumstances likely to create a presumption of bias or which he believes might disqualify him as an impartial Arbitrator. Upon receipt of such information, the Tribunal Clerk shall immediately disclose it to the parties, who if willing to proceed under the circumstances disclosed, shall, in writing, so advise the Tribunal Clerk. If either party declines to waive the presumptive disqualification, the vacancy thus created shall be filled in accordance with the applicable provisions of this Rule."

And based on the same principle as this Arbitration Association rule is that part of the 33d Canon of Judicial Ethics which provides:

Section 33. Social Relations.

" . . . [A judge] should, however, in pending or prospective litigation before him be particularly [393 U.S. 145, 150] careful to avoid such action as may reasonably tend to awaken the suspicion that his social or business relations or friendships, constitute an element in influencing his judicial conduct."

This rule of arbitration and this canon of judicial ethics rest on the premise that any tribunal permitted by law to try cases and controversies not only must be unbiased but also must avoid even the appearance of bias. We cannot believe that it was the purpose of Congress to authorize litigants to submit their cases and controversies to arbitration boards that might reasonably be thought biased against one litigant and favorable to another.

Reversed.

Justice WHITE, with whom Justice MARSHALL joins, concurring.

While I am glad to join my Brother BLACK's opinion in this case, I desire to make these additional remarks. The Court does not decide today that arbitrators are to be held to the standards of judicial decorum of Article III judges, or indeed of any judges. It is often because they are men of affairs, not apart from but of the marketplace, that they are effective in their adjudicatory function. *Cf. United Steelworkers v. Warrior & Gulf Navigation Co.*, 363 U.S. 574 (1960). This does not mean the judiciary must overlook outright chicanery in giving effect to their awards; that would be an abdication of our responsibility. But it does mean that arbitrators are not automatically disqualified by a business relationship with the parties before them if both parties are informed of the relationship in advance, or if they are unaware of the facts but the relationship is trivial. I see no reason automatically to disqualify the best informed and most capable potential arbitrators.

The arbitration process functions best when an amicable and trusting atmosphere is preserved and there is voluntary compliance with the decree, without need for judicial enforcement. This end is best served by establishing an atmosphere of frankness at the outset, through disclosure by the arbitrator of any financial transactions which he has had or is negotiating with either of the parties. In many cases the arbitrator might believe the business relationship to be so insubstantial that to make a point of revealing it would suggest he is indeed easily swayed, and perhaps a partisan of that party.[2] But if the law requires the disclosure, no such imputation can arise. And it is far better that the relationship be disclosed at the outset, when the parties are free to reject the arbitrator or accept him with knowledge of the relationship and continuing faith in his objectivity, than to have the relationship come to light after the arbitration, when a suspicious or disgruntled party can seize on it as a pretext for invalidating the award. The judiciary should minimize its role in arbitration as judge of the arbitrator's impartiality. That role is best consigned to the parties, who are the architects of their own arbitration

---

2. In fact, the District Court found — on the basis of the record and petitioner's admissions — that the arbitrator in this case was entirely fair and impartial. I do not read the majority opinion as questioning this finding in any way.

process, and are far better informed of the prevailing ethical standards and reputations within their business.

Justice FORTAS, with whom Justice HARLAN and Justice STEWART join, dissenting.

. . . The facts in this case do not lend themselves to the Court's ruling. The Court sets aside the arbitration award despite the fact that the award is unanimous and no claim is made of actual partiality, unfairness, bias, or fraud. . . . The third arbitrator was not asked about business connections with either party. Petitioner's complaint is that he failed to volunteer information about professional services rendered by him to the other party to the contract, the most recent of which were performed over a year before the arbitration. Both courts below held, and petitioner concedes, that the third arbitrator was innocent of any actual partiality, or bias, or improper motive. There is no suggestion of concealment as distinguished from the innocent failure to volunteer information.

The third arbitrator is a leading and respected consulting engineer who has performed services for "most of the contractors in Puerto Rico." He was well known to petitioner's counsel and they were personal friends. Petitioner's counsel candidly admitted that if he had been told about the arbitrator's prior relationship "I don't think I would have objected because I know Mr. Capacete [the arbitrator]." . . .

The Court nevertheless orders that the arbitration award be set aside. It uses this singularly inappropriate case to announce a per se rule that in my judgment has no basis in the applicable statute or jurisprudential principles: that, regardless of the agreement between the parties, if an arbitrator has any prior business relationship with one of the parties of which he fails to inform the other party, however innocently, the arbitration award is always subject to being set aside. This is so even where the award is unanimous; where there is no suggestion that the nondisclosure indicates partiality or bias; and where it is conceded that there was in fact no irregularity, unfairness, bias, or partiality. Until the decision today, it has not been the law that an arbitrator's failure to disclose a prior business relationship with one of the parties will compel the setting aside of an arbitration award regardless of the circumstances. . . .

Arbitration is essentially consensual and practical. The United States Arbitration Act is obviously designed to protect the integrity of the process with a minimum of insistence upon set formulae and rules. The Court applies to this process rules applicable to judges and not to a system characterized by dealing on faith and reputation for reliability. Such formalism is not contemplated by the Act nor is it warranted in a case where no claim is made of partiality, of unfairness, or of misconduct in any degree.

NOTES

1. *Judicial decisions on nondisclosure*. Arbitrator nondisclosure is one of the most commonly cited grounds for a motion to vacate an arbitration award. Yet, despite the outcome in *Commonwealth Coatings*, relatively few court decisions have overturned awards on the basis of undisclosed relationships or facts. For example, the Seventh Circuit refused to find arbitrator bias in

Merit Insurance Company v. Leatherby Insurance Company, 714 F.2d 763 (1983). The arbitrator did not disclose a prior business relationship with an opposing party. The arbitrator had ended the business relationship 14 years before the dispute; their relationship was characterized as "distant and impersonal"; and they never socialized together. The court stated that it "d[id] not want to encourage the losing party to every arbitration to conduct a background investigation of each of the arbitrators in an effort to uncover evidence of a former relationship with the adversary. This would only increase the cost and undermine the finality of arbitration."

There are, however, notable exceptions. In *University Commons-Urbana, Ltd. v. Universal Constructors Inc.*, 304 F.3d 1331 (11th Cir. 2002), the court found that an arbitrator's general and speculative statements regarding relationships with parties or counsel are insufficient disclosure with respect to specific concurrent relationships or connections, at least those involving financial interests. An arbitrator is obligated to reveal those facts which would lead a reasonable person to believe that a potential conflict exists.

Decisions regarding arbitrator nondisclosure, reflected in the differences of opinion among Supreme Court justices in *Commonwealth Coatings*, have relied on a number of different standards under federal and state law. A few decisions were based on some variant of the "appearance of bias" test enunciated by Justice Black. More, however, have applied a more rigorous standard akin to Justice White's analysis.

QUESTIONS

1. You are representing the Batman Co. in arbitration proceedings with Joker, Inc. Batman is in the business of making high-tech uniforms and weapons. Batman Co. and Joker, Inc. have a contract to sell and buy certain amounts of both products each month. The contract includes an arbitration clause for any disputes concerning the contract. Recently Joker, Inc. has refused to purchase the 100 night vision goggles monthly, as required in the contract. The two companies proceeded to arbitration. Three arbitrators were mutually selected for the arbitration panel through a list selection process. Before hearings commence, the parties exchange witness lists. The chair of the arbitration panel reveals that she has current business dealings with a key witness for Joker, Inc. You and your client are very concerned about the connection. What procedural options does your client have? For the purpose of this discussion, assume that the JAMS comprehensive procedures are applicable.

2. a. Suppose instead that the information regarding the relationship between the arbitrator and the witness in Problem 1 was not revealed until after the arbitration panel published its award, which was favorable to Joker, Inc. What options exist under the law?

    b. Recently, the Uniform Arbitration Act (UAA), which served as the template for the arbitration law of most U.S. states, was revised by the National Conference of Commissioners on Uniform State Laws (NCCUSL). Among other things, the revised uniform statute now sets forth affirmative guidelines for arbitrator disclosure. Only a handful of States have adopted the Revised UAA (RUAA). Among other things, the RUAA now sets forth affirmative guidelines for arbitrator disclosures. How, if at all, does Section 12 of the RUAA affect your analysis in this problem?

   c. Considering the Revised UAA, could Batman Co. sue the arbitrator for failing to disclose the relationship?

3.   If, instead, you were the arbitrator here, what would your ethical responsibilities be under the *Code of Ethics for Arbitrators in Commercial Disputes*? Please note that the Code of Ethics was modified in 2004.

G.   THE PROBLEM OF PARTY ARBITRATORS

Tripartite arbitration panels are a common feature of the landscape. The concept—each party picking an arbitrator, and the two "party arbitrators" agreeing on a third arbitrator—is seemingly straightforward and inherently fair. Such arrangements, however, often bring unanticipated results and not a little litigation. As the following case reveals, the issue inevitably comes down to the precise role of party arbitrators and their obligation of disclosure.

DELTA MINE HOLDING CO. v. AFC COAL PROPERTIES, INC.
280 F.3d 815 (8th Cir. 2001), *cert. denied*, 123 S. Ct. 87 (2002)

Delta Mine entered into a long-term lease for the mining of coal on two parcels of AFC property, the Williamson County property and the Saline County property. The contract provided Delta Mine the ability to terminate the leases when all "Economically Recoverable Coal" had been mined and further provided that disputes over the termination provision would be subject to arbitration conducted by a tripartite panel. Per the contract, each party was to select an arbitrator with the two selected arbitrators choosing the panel's chair, in accordance with the applicable rules of the AAA. Paragraph 8.3 of the contract provided that "each of the arbitrators . . . shall be a professional mining engineer, or firm of professional mining engineers," and that the third or neutral arbitrator may not be "an officer, employee or shareholder of, attorney or auditor to, or otherwise interested in" either party or the matter to be arbitrated.

In November 1995, Delta Mine invoked the termination provision in each lease and AFC objected, and arbitration ensued. For both arbitrations, Delta Mine chose as its party arbitrator Alan Stagg, a mining engineer, and AFC designated mining engineer Paul Jones. Together, Stagg and Jones selected John Wilson to chair the panel for the Williamson County arbitration and Eugene Kitts to chair the panel for the Saline County arbitration. Both Wilson and Kitts were also mining engineers.

The two arbitration panels held a joint organizational meeting on November 24, 1997, attended by the four arbitrators, the parties, and their attorneys. At the suggestion of arbitrator Jones, each arbitrator briefly described his background. Stagg stated that he had maintained a client consulting relationship with Delta Mine's predecessors since 1981, that he had never worked with Delta Mine's law firm, and that he had previously met the neutral arbitrators. The neutral arbitrators overruled AFC's objection to joint proceedings, concluding that the two panels would hold a joint hearing on common issues, followed by separate hearings on issues unique to each arbitration. Over AFC's strenuous objection, arbitrator Kitts ruled "that the two partial panel members [Stagg and Jones] should be in a position to ask the pertinent questions of the witnesses, rather than having it turn into a more formal judicial [proceeding] with cross-examinations and so forth."

On March 31, 1998, after deposing Delta Mine witnesses, AFC's counsel wrote the arbitrators complaining that Delta Mine's party arbitrator, Alan Stagg, had been present at Delta Mine's witness preparation and strategy sessions and was acting as Delta Mine's expert in preparing witnesses for depositions and the hearings. AFC expressed concern "whether an arbitrator who invests himself deeply in the preparation of a case, and then becomes the chief interrogator for his side at the hearing, can be reasonably expected to judge a case on its merits as called for by the *Code of Ethics for Arbitrators in Commercial Disputes*." AFC concluded by requesting "a brief postponement of perhaps a few weeks, to a convenient date in May, to allow each side a reasonable opportunity to prepare."

On April 13, 1998, the two panels responded. In a letter ruling signed by each of the four, the arbitrators rescheduled the hearings to the first week in May. As a "compromise" between AFC's request for full attorney cross-examination of witnesses and the arbitrators' intent "that this arbitration should not become a formal judicial exercise," the panels ruled that only the arbitrators would be permitted to question witnesses during the presentation of their testimony, but the panels would receive follow-up questions, comments, and requests for clarification from counsel following each witness's presentation. (As the hearings later progressed, AFC's counsel was permitted to cross-examine Delta Mine's witnesses.)

The April 13 letter ruling did not address AFC's concern over Stagg's role in assisting Delta Mine with the preparation of its case. However, on April 8, AFC's party arbitrator, Paul Jones, had sent AFC's attorneys a long memorandum describing a two-hour meeting of the arbitrators. Jones reported:

ROLE OF PARTY ARBITRATOR AT HEARING:

It was the opinion or expectation of the two Neutral Arbitrators that each Party Arbitrator would serve to question witnesses to bring out issues which were not clear in the witness presentations. To do this, the Neutrals expect the Party Arbitrator to be adequately briefed to know where the testimony is going and to be able to ask questions for clarification, etc. They did not seem "taken back" by Alan Stagg's attendance at the prep sessions. . . .

[JONES] COMMENTS :

Gentlemen, I know you are not happy with the results of today's meeting but I am certainly willing to do what I can to make the hearing effective for your position. . . . I would suggest if you could FedEx to me (home delivery Saturday) as much material regarding the depositions, your expert witness concepts, etc. as possible. I can then spend this weekend and early next week reviewing the material. . . . If [the hearing] is not delayed, we need to discuss ASAP when I might be briefed on your side of the issues so that I can do a decent job in raising questions at the hearings.

Following the hearings, the two panels began their separate deliberations. In the district court, AFC conducted a thorough discovery of party arbitrator Stagg, but neither party conducted discovery of party arbitrator Jones or the neutral arbitrators. Thus, the record provides a substantial but incomplete picture of the deliberations. We know that each neutral arbitrator discussed the issues with Stagg and Jones, prepared a draft award and circulated it to the party arbitrators for comment, and after further deliberations prepared the final award. Neutral arbitrator Wilson ruled that Delta Mine was entitled to terminate the Williamson County lease under the Economically Recoverable Coal provision but awarded AFC an offset based upon amounts Delta Mine had received from its coal customer for future mining royalties. Party arbitrator Stagg concurred in the termination ruling but dissented from the offset award, while party arbitrator Jones dissented from the termination ruling but concurred in the offset award. In the other arbitration, neutral arbitrator Kitts ruled that Delta Mine was entitled to terminate the Saline County lease. Arbitrator Stagg concurred in this award; arbitrator Jones dissented.

AFC then petitioned the district court to vacate both awards. Delta Mine petitioned to confirm the Saline County award and to modify the Williamson County award. The district court vacated both awards based upon the following misconduct by Delta Mine's party arbitrator Stagg:

- Stagg's failure to fully disclose his substantial and ongoing relationship with Delta Mine and its attorneys, including his consulting relationship in these proceedings.
- The substantial role played by Stagg and his firm in helping Delta Mine prepare for the arbitration hearings, including Stagg's participation in a mock arbitration held days before the hearings.
- Stagg's disclosure of the ongoing panel deliberations to Delta Mine and his communications with Delta Mine and its attorneys concerning "how to sway the arbitrators to rule in Delta Mine's favor."

Accepting AFC's view of the legal issues, the district court discussed at length how Stagg's conduct violated the Code of Ethics and then asserted in conclusory fashion that such misconduct justified vacating the awards under §10(a) of the Federal Arbitration Act. On appeal, Delta Mine argues that the district court erred in placing undue emphasis on the Code of Ethics and in applying the statutory grounds for vacating arbitration awards found in §10(a) of the Act.

Judge LOKEN delivered the opinion of the court.

Though arbitration has been present in America as a form of dispute resolution since the eighteenth century, the Federal Arbitration Act of 1925 firmly established a "national policy favoring arbitration." *Southland Corp. v. Keating*, 465 U.S. 1, 10, 104 S. Ct. 852, 79 L. Ed. 2d 1 (1984). Under that Act, "the grounds for challenging an arbitration award are narrowly limited, reflecting the voluntary contractual nature of commercial arbitration." As relevant to this case, §10(a) of the Act authorizes a reviewing court to vacate an arbitration award:

1. Where the award was procured by corruption, fraud, or undue means.
2. Where there was evident partiality or corruption in the arbitrators, or either of them.
3. Where the arbitrators were guilty of . . . any other misbehavior by which the rights of any party have been prejudiced.

In this case, the lease agreements provided that arbitration proceedings shall "comply with the then applicable rules of the American Arbitration Association." However, the district court focused on whether party arbitrator Stagg violated the Code of Ethics, not the AAA's Commercial Arbitration Rules. The Code of Ethics provides that it "does not form a part of the arbitration rules of the American Arbitration Association," nor does it "establish new or additional grounds for judicial review of arbitration awards." It is well-settled that only the statutory grounds in §10(a) of the Act justify vacating an award; arbitration rules and ethical codes "do not have the force of law." *Merit Ins. Co. v. Leatherby Ins. Co.*, 714 F.2d 673, 680 (7th Cir. 1983). Thus, the district court erred in placing primary emphasis on whether party arbitrator Stagg violated various provisions of the Code of Ethics. "Unless there is a specific [statutory] ground for vacating an award, it must be confirmed." We therefore focus exclusively on those statutory grounds.

1. SECTION 10(a)(2) — "EVIDENT PARTIALITY"

The district court ruled that Stagg's ongoing consulting relationship with Delta Mine and its attorneys, his participation in the pre-hearing preparation of Delta Mine's case, and his communications with Delta Mine and its attorneys during the panels' deliberations constituted "evident partiality" requiring that the awards be vacated under §10(a)(2). In one sense, the district court's ruling was factually accurate — Stagg was obviously partial, and his conduct during the course of the arbitrations was clearly inconsistent with the impartiality required of a neutral arbitrator in numerous cases such as the Supreme Court's *Commonwealth Coatings* decision. But whether we view the ruling as a finding of fact or a conclusion of law, it cannot be upheld because the court committed three errors of law in applying §10(a)(2):

FIRST

AFC waived this contention by failing to raise it to the arbitrators. AFC learned of Stagg's ongoing participation in the preparation of Delta Mine's case well before the hearings. AFC expressed concern to the arbitrators, but only in the context of requesting a delay in the hearings (which was granted). AFC did not request Stagg's removal. Even when a neutral arbitrator is challenged for evident partiality, the issue is deemed waived unless the objecting party raised it to the arbitration panel.

SECOND

Had AFC timely requested Stagg's removal on the ground of evident partiality, the request would have been denied as contrary to the parties' agreements to arbitrate. "Generally, partisan arbitrators are permissible." *ATSA of Cal., Inc. v. Continental Ins. Co.*, 754 F.2d 1394, 1395 (9th Cir. 1985). Here, the lease agreements authorized the selection of a party arbitrator who is "an officer, employee or shareholder of, attorney or auditor to, or otherwise interested in, either of the Parties or the matter to be arbitrated." In other words, the arbitration agreements expressly contemplated the selection of partial arbitrators — persons with substantial financial interests in and duties of loyalty to one party. "The parties to an arbitration choose their method of dispute resolution, and can ask no more impartiality than inheres in the method they have chosen." *Merit Ins.*, 714 F.2d at 679.

AFC counters by arguing, without citation to pertinent authority, that party arbitrator Stagg's failure to fully disclose the extent of his relationship with Delta Mine and its attorneys constitutes evident partiality for purposes of §10(a)(2). We disagree. At the organizational meeting, Stagg disclosed that "I've had a client consultant relationship with [Delta Mine's predecessor] since probably 1981, '82, somewhere in there." AFC should have assumed that Stagg had the same degree of "evident partiality" as an officer, employee, or attorney of Delta Mine, persons the lease agreements expressly authorized to be party arbitrators. Moreover, because the leases authorized the selection of partial party arbitrators, Stagg would have perceived no apparent need to disclose more than his long-standing "client consultant relationship," absent a direction from the neutral arbitrators to do so.

THIRD

AFC failed to show that Stagg's "evident partiality" had a prejudicial impact on the arbitration awards. When a neutral arbitrator fails to disclose a relationship with one party that casts significant doubt on the arbitrator's impartiality, as in *Commonwealth Coatings*, it is appropriate to assume that the concealed partiality prejudicially tainted the award. But where the parties have expressly agreed to select partial party arbitrators, the award should be confirmed unless the objecting party proves that the party arbitrator's partiality prejudicially affected the award.

In this case, AFC failed to show that the neutral arbitrators were deceived or misled by party arbitrator Stagg's partiality. During the initial organizational meeting, neutral arbitrator Kitts referred to the party arbitrators as "partial."[2] The neutral arbitrators ruled that the party arbitrators, not the parties' attorneys, would question witnesses at the hearings. When AFC complained that party arbitrator Stagg was participating in the preparation of Delta Mine's case, the neutral arbitrators were not "taken back" because they wanted the party arbitrators fully prepared to question witnesses at the hearings. During deliberations, the neutral arbitrators dealt with the party arbitrators as advocates for their respective positions, precisely as one would expect from the terms of the agreements to arbitrate. So long as the neutral arbitrators were not deceived — an issue AFC did not pursue in the district court — there was nothing insidious about this process. As Judge Posner observed in *IDS Life Ins.*, 266 F.3d at 651, "Arbitration is customized, not off-the-rack, dispute resolution."

Nor did AFC prove that its ability to prepare and present its case was prejudiced by Stagg's role as a partial party arbitrator. AFC knew from the agreements to arbitrate that the party arbitrators would be partial in the conflict-of-interest sense of that word. At the organizational meeting, AFC learned that the party arbitrators would question witnesses at the hearings. Weeks before the hearings, AFC learned that Stagg was helping Delta Mine prepare its case. Thus, AFC had ample time to prepare its party arbitrator to play a comparable role.

---

2. The Commercial Arbitration Rules provide that, absent an agreement to the contrary, party-appointed arbitrators are presumed to be non-neutral. See American Arbitration Association, *Commercial Arbitration Rules* §12 (1996). [Editor's note: The AAA Rules have since been changed to require independent and impartial party appointees, unless the parties agree otherwise.]

2. SECTIONS 10(a)(1) AND (3) — "UNDUE MEANS" AND "MISBEHAVIOR"

The district court also ruled that the awards must be vacated because Stagg's conduct before the hearings and during deliberations constituted "undue means" and "misbehavior by which [AFC's rights were] prejudiced" within the meaning of §§10(a)(1) and (3). A party seeking vacation of an award on either of these grounds must demonstrate that the conduct influenced the outcome of the arbitration. Once again, AFC failed to sustain its burden on this issue.

AFC argues that Stagg disclosed to Delta Mine the substance of the panel's deliberations and the neutral arbitrators' draft decisions, and obtained input from Delta Mine before responding to neutral arbitrator Wilson's proposed offset. But there is no evidence that this was contrary to what the neutral arbitrators expected and encouraged, and there is considerable evidence that party arbitrator Jones knew the role Stagg was playing and had equal access to his client and to the neutral arbitrators, for example, on the offset issue. We know that the neutral arbitrators' final awards were consistent with their draft decisions, so Stagg failed to dissuade arbitrator Wilson from award-ing AFC an offset in the Williamson County award. AFC failed to satisfy its substantial burden to "demonstrate that the conduct influenced the outcome of the arbitration."

3. AFC'S ALTERNATIVE GROUNDS

AFC argues that the awards should be vacated because the arbitrators improp-erly consolidated two separate arbitrations, disallowed cross-examination of witnesses, refused to hear new evidence, ignored key lease provisions, and issued awards that are irrational on their face. Having carefully reviewed the arbitration records, we conclude these contentions are without merit. Arbitration awards should be construed, whenever possible, so as to uphold their validity. "A contrary course would be a substitution of the judgment of the chancellor in place of the judges chosen by the parties, and would make an award the commencement, not the end, of litigation." *Burchell v. Marsh*, 58 U.S. (17 How.) 344, 349, 15 L. Ed. 96 (1854). The arbitrators' rulings were well within their procedural discretion, their analysis drew its essence from the lease agreements, and we are satisfied that the awards were not "completely irrational" and did not "evidence[ ] a manifest disregard for the law." *Kiernan*, 137 F.3d at 594.

4. DELTA MINE'S PETITION TO MODIFY

Delta Mine argues that the Williamson County award must be modified because neutral arbitrator Wilson exceeded his authority by including an offset in favor of AFC. Although an arbitration award may be modified to eliminate mistakes affecting the merits of the controversy "[w]here the arbitrators have awarded upon a matter not submitted to them," 9 U.S.C. §11, we are satisfied the offset was fairly within the controversy submitted to the Williamson County panel. We decline Delta Mine's further invitation "to invade the province of the panel and re-adjudicate this [portion of the] dispute on its merits."

III. CONCLUSION

. . . It may be that many professional neutral arbitrators, if presented with this situation, would have required fuller initial disclosures by the party arbitrators and would have established clearer and better articulated procedural ground rules for the pre-hearing preparations and the post-hearing deliberations. But consistent with the agreements to arbitrate, the neutral arbitrators in this case were mining engineers, not professional arbitrators. Each announced at the organizational meeting that he had not previously served as a neutral arbitrator. Because arbitration is a matter of contract, we neither endorse nor condemn this mode of proceeding (though the litigation it has produced is certainly unfortunate). . . .

QUESTIONS

1. In describing standards for party arbitrators, in what specific ways does the Eighth Circuit part ways with standards established under *Commonwealth Coatings* and its progeny?
2. To what extent does *Delta Mine Holding* reinforce—or undermine—the following policies associated with arbitration: party autonomy, finality of award, and respect for the integrity of the arbitration as an adjudication process?

PROBLEM 3: ARBITRATOR DISCLOSURE AND CHALLENGE — PARTY ARBITRATORS

1. You still represent Batman Co. in arbitration proceedings with Joker, Inc. Each party selected an arbitrator, and the party arbitrators selected a third individual to serve as chair of the panel. You determine that Joker, Inc.'s arbitrator is assisting in the preparation of Joker, Inc.'s case, and you and your client are very concerned about the situation. What procedural options does your client possess? For the purpose of this discussion, assume that the CPR procedures are applicable.
2. Suppose instead that the information regarding the relationship between the arbitrator and the witness was not revealed until after the arbitration panel published its award, which was favorable to Joker, Inc. What options do you have under the law?
3. What would be the result under Section 12 of the recently revised Uniform Arbitration Act (RUAA)?

H. THE ARBITRATION PROCESS

Arbitration typically involves several procedural stages, although specific features may vary considerably depending on the party's agreement, including incorporated institutional procedural rules (such as, for example, those of the AAA, CPR, or JAMS). The process nearly always begins with initial and responsive filings and the appointment of arbitrators. Some form of preliminary planning, including a prehearing conference, is likely to occur, perhaps followed by information exchange or discovery.

Then comes some form of hearing. Usually each side will present an opening statement, followed by introductory evidence, examination and cross-examination of witnesses, testimony under oath, and closing statements and arguments. Depending on the complexity of the matter and number of parties involved, a hearing could last less than a day or hearings could extend over a long period of time, at the convenience of parties and arbitrators. Scheduling hearings in complex cases can sometimes delay arbitral proceedings, particularly with a panel of highly sought-after neutrals. The hearing is less formal than a court trial, and may be held around a conference table. Unless otherwise agreed, the formal rules of evidence and civil procedure do not apply and thus hearsay or other testimony inadmissible in court may be considered by arbitrators. Arbitrators normally have plenary authority over all aspects of the hearing; leading institutional arbitration procedures give arbitrators wide discretion on whether to allow in various evidence. Many arbitrators err on the side of admitting evidence so as to ensure finality of an arbitral award, since Section 10(c) of the FAA provides for judicial vacatur of an arbitral award where an arbitrator is "guilty of misconduct . . . in refusing to hear evidence pertinent and material to the controversy." Federal Arbitration Act, 9 U.S.C. §10(c) (West Supp. 1994).

Arbitration hearings offer a greater degree of privacy and confidentiality than the courthouse. There is often no stenographer present to take a record, and arbitrators have authority to bar nonessential persons from the hearing room. In some cases, additional confidentiality protections are established by the agreement of the parties or by arbitral order.

The attorney's role during the arbitration process is similar in many respects to preparing and presenting a case in litigation. There are analogues to the familiar incidents of trial process, including the filing of pleadings, interviewing and preparing witnesses, the development of a direct case (including the preparation of exhibits, demonstrative evidence, a trial notebook, etc.), and some, perhaps extensive, information exchange, and discovery. The attorney should normally be prepared to make opening and closing arguments, to prepare briefs on factual or legal issues, and perhaps to file a dispositive motion or even an appeal from an arbitration award.

Experienced advocates and arbitrators warn that arbitration before experienced arbitrators is not a forum for the strutting and posturing employed by some lawyers in civil trials. Moreover, attorneys should remember that because their panel of adjudicators may bring significant expertise to the table, they may find extensive explication or foundation-laying unnecessary or even offensive. Arbitrators may also engage in extensive interrogation of witnesses.

Arbitration concludes with arbitrator deliberations leading to the rendition of an award. The form of the award will vary depending on the parties' agreement and applicable rules; there may or may not be a published rationale or opinion along with the award. The issuance of a "bare" award, limited to a straightforward declaration of the panel's grant or denial of relief, has long been viewed as a bulwark against judicial intrusion into the realm of the arbitrator.

PROBLEM 4: THE ARBITRATION PROCESS

Assume you are an arbitrator in a commercial dispute concerning a breach of warranty in connection with the sale of an office park. For the purpose of answering the following questions, assume the AAA procedures are applicable.

1. Just after your appointment, the defendant seeks to file a counterclaim for monies owed against the plaintiff. Who determines whether the counterclaim should be heard?
2. After reviewing the initial pleadings of the parties, you realize that you have very little information on the factual and legal issues. How might you go about getting more information about the parties' positions? What other information might you seek, how and when?
3. Suppose one party seeks to avoid the expense and inconvenience of an oral hearing, and rely entirely on submissions of written documents, briefs, etc. Is it within your authority to direct a "paper hearing"?
4. You are confronted with a prehearing motion by the defendant to dismiss on the basis that the plaintiff's claim is not cognizable in law, and is barred by applicable statutes of limitations. How will you respond to this motion? See, e.g., *Schlessinger v. Rosenfeld, Meyer & Susman*, 47 Cal. Rptr. 2d 650 (Cal. Ct. App. 1995).
5. You would like to permit the statement of several witnesses that are redundant of other testimony to be introduced by affidavit. Is this permissible?
6. The night before the first day of four consecutive days of scheduled hearings, your office receives a call and fax from an attorney for one of the parties informing you that they will be unable to attend the proceedings that week. The explanation is that the client has been called away "on personal business." You learn of the communication the following morning, right before the hearing is scheduled to begin in your office. Meanwhile, the other party has appeared for the hearing. What is the appropriate course of action?
7. The case centers on a valuation question, and each of the parties has hired an accountant to address the key issues. You would like to put them on the stand at the same time, ask them questions simultaneously, and even permit them to question one another. Can you do this? Could you appoint your own expert and have the parties pay the cost?
8. After several days of hearings, the plaintiff announces that it has concluded the presentation of its case. You are convinced that the plaintiff has not proved its case, but believe that it is likely that the information exists to support its case. Is it appropriate, and within your authority, to direct the parties to provide additional information on the key issues?

I.   INFORMATION EXCHANGE AND DISCOVERY

Greater likelihood of discovery. For many years, a popular understanding was that there was "no discovery in arbitration." In recent years, however, that reality has changed. Counsel for parties in arbitration often agree to mutual information exchange, with or without arbitrator supervision. Moreover, leading arbitration procedures, some state statutes and judicial decisions constructing the FAA and state law have made clear that some form of arbitrator-supervised discovery is often a feature of arbitration processes. According to the CPR Commission on Arbitration, in private proceedings as in public forums, fundamental fairness often requires a sharing of information, and it is generally fairer and more efficient to have a consensual or supervised information exchange prior to hearings. Indeed, in large, complex commercial cases, discovery is very likely.

The Commission's report goes on to explain, however, that discovery in arbitration is usually more limited than that contemplated by civil procedural rules. This reflects the normal expectation that arbitration offers a speedier and more efficient path to resolution, and that cost/benefit considerations will temper the normal broad relevance standard in litigation.[6] For example, CPR Rule 11 states that "the Tribunal may require and facilitate such discovery as it shall determine appropriate to the circumstances, taking into account the needs of the parties and the desirability of making discovery expeditious and cost-effective." The accompanying commentary explains that as contemplated by the CPR procedures, "[a]rbitration is not for the litigator who will 'leave no stone unturned.'" Most often, arbitrators will seek to restrict discovery to categories of information, such as documents, that speak to the primary issues in dispute. Requests for admission and interrogatories are relatively rare. Unless the parties have otherwise agreed, arbitrators often demand justification for the taking of depositions. For example, the AAA Optional Procedures for Large, Complex Commercial Disputes (AAA Commercial Procedures) §L-5(b) (Jan. 1, 1999), provide that arbitrators can "upon good cause shown . . . order the conduct of the deposition of . . . such persons who may possess information . . . necessary to determination of [the case]." Arbitrators in larger or high stakes disputes often permit depositions in order to preserve testimony or save time at the hearing.

Often, experienced arbitrators initially seek to facilitate agreement among the parties regarding the nature and scope of discovery rather than adjudicate multiple discovery disputes. Competent arbitrators help set and enforce strict time limits for information exchange, which can expedite the discovery process. An arbitrator may draw an adverse inference if a party refuses to comply with a discovery order.

Arbitral Summonses and Subpoenas

The FAA and most state arbitration statutes do not specifically address the subject of arbitration-related discovery. However, the FAA and corresponding

---

6. Fed. R. Civ. P.26(5)(b) (2002) (" . . . the scope of discovery is as follows: Parties may obtain discovery regarding any matter, not privileged, that is relevant to the claim or defense of any party, including the existence, description, nature, custody, condition and location of any books, documents or other tangible things and the identity and location of persons having knowledge of any discoverable matter. For good cause, the court may order discovery of any matter relevant to the subject matter involved in the action. Relevant information need not be admissible at the time of trial if the discovery appears reasonably calculated to lead to the discovery of admissible evidence.").

state laws give arbitrators authority to issue summons or subpoenas to parties or nonparties, and provide for their judicial enforcement. FAA §7, for example, states that arbitrators may "summon in writing any person to attend before them or any of them as a witness and in a proper case to bring with him or them any book, record, document, or paper which may be deemed material as evidence in the case." This language, with its reference to "attend [ing] before [one or more arbitrators]" fails to establish a clear predicate for ordering a party to appear at a deposition. Indeed, the section goes on to require subpoenas issued by arbitrators to be directed and served "in the same manner as subpoenas to appear and testify before the court." While some courts have interpreted the section to permit deposition subpoenas, others have held to the contrary. *Compare Meadows Indemnity Co. v. Nutmeg Insur. Co.*, 157 F.R.D. 45 (M.D. Tenn. 1994) *with COMSAT Corp. v. National Science Foundation*, 190 F.3d 269 (4th Cir. 1999).

Some courts question whether a party's agreement gives arbitrators subpoena power over nonparty witnesses. Generally, the subpoena power of arbitrators is supported by court enforcement as long as information being requested is relevant and material, and subject to territorial limits on the arbitral subpoena power. Recent revisions to the UAA have attempted to directly address these and other concerns through specific provisions for arbitrator-supervised discovery, including depositions.

QUESTIONS

1. Again returning to the MDM/Fandom scenario described in earlier exercises, suppose that at the time you file an arbitration demand, you discover that Fandom's CEO, Will Gates, is severely ill. What steps would you follow to try to preserve Mr. Gates' testimony in arbitration? Assume the JAMS rules apply.
2. Alternatively, you consider asking a court to order a deposition of Mr. Gates pending the commencement of arbitration. What is the likelihood that a court will direct Mr. Gates to attend a deposition? See Macneil, Speidel, and Stipanowich (1997).
3. Many people do not like the loss of confidentiality regarding their personal or business finances. Suppose MDM sought confidential documents from Fandom that would reveal the profits earned from advertising since they began hosting the 450Mb files. Is the arbitrator likely to require Fandom to disclose this information to MDM? Why or why not?
4. What steps would you advise Fandom take if it wanted to keep this information from being used in any future litigation proceedings? See *A.T. v. State Farm Mut. Auto. Ins. Co.*, 989 P.2d 219 (Colo. Ct. App. 1999) (holding that records disclosed at an arbitration hearing were permitted to be used at a later, unrelated trial because the party did not request a protective order and did not enter into a confidentiality agreement with insurance company); but see *Group Health Plan, Inc. v. BJC Health Systems, Inc.*, 30 S.W.3d 198 (Mo. Ct. App. 2000) (holding that confidentiality agreement signed by parties in an earlier arbitration proceeding was enough to prevent documents from being disclosed in a new arbitration proceeding).

J. ARBITRATION AWARDS, ARBITRAL REMEDIES: THE BROAD REMEDIAL AUTHORITY OF ARBITRATORS

DAVID COMPANY v. JIM MILLER CONSTRUCTION, INC.
444 N.W.2d 836 (Minn. 1989)

[Miller Construction Co. contracted with David Co. to construct townhouses in two phases on property owned by David Co. After phase one was complete, a dispute between the parties regarding defective workmanship arose. Following arbitration of the dispute, the arbitrators, as part of their award, ordered the general contractor (Miller) to purchase the real property on which the subject buildings had been erected. The issue presented to the court is whether in so doing the arbitrators exceeded their powers. A divided court of appeals panel affirmed a district court order which had affirmed the award. The Minnesota Supreme Court now hears Miller's appeal.]

KELLEY, Justice.

The construction contract at issue was entitled "General Conditions of the Contract for Construction." It included an arbitration clause by which the parties agreed that "[a]ll claims, disputes and other matters in question . . . arising out of, or relating to, the contract documents or the breach thereof . . ." would be subject to arbitration with the exception of claims waived by the making of final payment . . .

Shortly after the commencement of construction on Phase I of the project, construction problems began to surface and thereafter continued throughout construction. David Company attributed the recurrence of these problems to Miller's inadequate supervision of subcontractors and its tolerance of poor workmanship by them. Primarily because of those problems, completion of construction on Phase I was delayed beyond the contract completion date of May 1984 to October of that year. David Company claimed this delay not only caused it to lose sales of the units and to incur additional interest and other expense, but, in addition, left it with shoddily constructed units which were unmarketable as the luxury-type units originally contemplated by the project.

David Company was aware of numerous construction deficiencies, knew they had not been rectified, and that Phase I completion had been delayed for months, when it made final payment to Miller on Phase I in November 1984. Miller argues that the final payment constituted waiver under subparagraphs 9.9.4 and 9.9.5 of the contract. In response, David Company claims it made the payment reluctantly and only after it had been induced to do so by Miller's reaffirmation of its contractual and other legal obligations to remedy all construction deficiencies in its work.

Shortly after making final payment, David Company learned of additional previously unknown extensive and serious construction defects. Moreover, further nonconformities with contract requirements and building code violations emerged. After Miller refused to correct the newly discovered deficiencies, David Company filed its Demand for Arbitration with the American Arbitration Association. In its Demand it alleged breach of contract, negligence and misrepresentation. For relief it requested "compensation for damages in excess of $250,000, including damages which continue to accrue, plus costs, disbursements, attorney fees and interest." It likewise expressly reserved the right to later amend the demand.

A building contractor and two professional engineers were selected by the parties to arbitrate the dispute. The arbitrators heard evidence presented by the parties over a span of three days, heard submissions of counsel for each party, and physically visited the project site to inspect and evaluate the quality of construction. Evidence presented to the arbitrators revealed numerous and serious construction defects and deficiencies . . . resulting in rescission demands from owners to whom David had sold units prior to completion, and [rendering] the unsold units, in a practical sense, unmarketable absent extensive and costly repairs.

During the course of his closing argument before the arbitration panel, one of David Company's attorneys, while highlighting the numerous and substantial items of shabby workmanship, observed that his client, and, perhaps as well, vendees who had purchased the units, might be saddled with contingent future liabilities under statutory warranties. He noted that Miller was not only a building contractor, but, as well a developer and owner of real estate thereby implying that, as such, Miller might well better bear that risk than could the respondents. Thereupon, the arbitrators suggested to the parties that they might consider an award resulting in Miller ending up with the project and the property on which it was located in exchange for a cash payment to David Company. Miller's counsel promptly objected on the ground that to so structure an award, the arbitrators would exceed the power granted to them. Nonetheless, David Company's lawyers prepared an itemized "sell back" option claiming $884,476 in damages. . . . The arbitrators' award incorporated the "sell back" option. Alternatively, in the event David Company was unable to convey the property free of liens within 45 days, the award provided for a monetary damages award of $497,925 to be paid to David Company. David Company chose to exercise the "sell back" option, and pursuant thereto, made timely tender of performance. When Miller refused to perform by making the payment as required by the arbitrators' award, David Company commenced an action in district court to confirm the award. . . .

Before this court Miller contends that the arbitrators exceeded their powers within the meaning of Minn. Stat. §572.19.1(3) (1988) when they ordered it to purchase real property from David Company when an alternative damage award was likewise made because: (a) the compelled purchase violated strong public policy as codified by the statute of frauds, and, (b) the order for compelled purchase of real estate was not authorized by either the contract between the parties nor the submittal. Miller further asserts that the arbitrators exceeded their powers by inclusion in the purchase figure that was part of the ultimate award, certain claims which, pursuant to the contract documents, Miller claims had been waived by David Company when it made final payment of Phase I of the project in October 1984.

We first address the claim that the arbitrators did exceed their powers. Because David Company's Demand for Arbitration claimed relief for negligence, breach of contract and misrepresentation, all of which arose out of, or were relevant to, the contract documents, the issue raised here relates not to the question of arbitrability, but rather to the question of whether the arbitrators exceeded their powers in structuring a remedy. If they did, of course, their award may be vacated (Minn. Stat. §572.19, subd. 1(3)). While the parties, either by contract or by written submission circumscribing the arbitrator's authority, may limit the arbitrator's authority, absent such consensual limitations, the arbitrators are the final judges of both the facts and the law concerning the merits. *State v. Berthiaume*, 259 N.W.2d 904, 910 (Minn. 1977). Moreover, an award will not be vacated merely because the court may believe the arbitrators erred.

The innovative and unique remedy structured by the arbitrators in the instant case, unlike the customary award ordering payment of monetary damages, may be considered equitable in nature. However, merely because the relief granted is equitable in nature does not, by itself, preclude arbitrators from employing it when otherwise appropriate. Indeed, it appears that our statute contemplates "equitable" as well as "legal" remedies in that it provides that upon confirmation of an award, a "judgment or *decree*" shall be entered. Minn. Stat. §572.21 (1988). No prior holdings of this court which involved comparable types of awards in construction disputes have been brought to our attention. However, in the area of labor relations although an agreement itself contained no provision relative to the scope of the authority of the arbitrators to structure a remedy, we observed that "we defer to the arbitrator's discretion, preserving the flexibility which commends arbitration as an effective means of resolving labor disputes." *Children's Hosp. v. Minnesota Nurses Ass'n*, 265 N.W.2d 649 (Minn. 1978) (a case where arbitrators "mandated" collective bargaining — arguably an equitable remedy — as an alternative in their award). . . .

Our cases as well as those from other jurisdictions . . . reveal the emergence of a general trend of courts, in the absence of limiting language in the contract itself, to accord judicial deference and afford flexibility to arbitrators to fashion awards comporting with the circumstances out of which the disputes arose. Recognition by us in this case that arbitration awards of an equitable nature may be appropriately fashioned would be entirely consistent with this court's long tradition of favoring the use of arbitration in dispute resolution and rejecting challenges to its employment, which, if granted, would limit, rather than expand, its utility. Thus, we hold that merely because the novel relief structured by the arbitrators in this case may have been equitable in nature does not support appellant's claim that they thereby exceeded their authority. Nonetheless, the power exercised in fashioning the award must have its genesis either from the underlying contract, the arbitration clause itself, or the submission. . . .

In the instant case the basis for the award cannot be found in the submission. The original demand sought "compensation for damages in excess of $250,000" (later increased to $598,622.45). Prior to the close of the final arguments before the arbitrators, never did David amend its submission demand to seek relief of the nature provided in the award. Rather, it was one of the arbitrators who, after argument, suggested the "sell back" option. When he did so, appellant promptly voiced its objection. Neither expressly nor tacitly did Miller agree that the submission be expanded to authorize a remedy of this type. Nor, with the exception of the arbitration clause itself in the "General Conditions of the Contract for Construction," does the underlying contract provide any basis for the remedy formulated by the arbitrators. Accordingly, the basis, if any, for the award which was fashioned must depend upon construction of the contract's arbitration clause . . .

The scope of the arbitration clause is extremely broad. It authorizes arbitrators to decide "[a]ll claims, disputes and other matters in question . . . relating to, the Contract . . . or the breach thereof. . . ." No provision in the arbitration clause expressly or implicitly limits the arbitrators to structuring only a remedy calling for the payment of a monetary award nor does any provision expressly authorize, or prohibit, arbitrators from formulating remedies that are equitable in nature. However, in conformity with our long established policy favoring expansion of the arbitration remedy, we conclude that implicit in the exceedingly broad powers which were granted by the parties to the arbitrators to decide "[a]ll claims, disputes, and other matters in question" is a grant of authority to structure an award which is commensurate with the extent, the pervasiveness, and nature of the poor workmanship resulting in construction deficiencies of such patent magnitude which existed. The appellant, and the dissenter in the court of appeals' opinion, argue that the arbitration clause should be more restrictively construed to limit the type of relief to the more traditional monetary award. While it may be correct to surmise that initially neither party specifically contemplated that in case of dispute between them this type of an equitable award might ensue from arbitration, yet both, neither of whom were inexperienced in construction projects of this nature, knew that the project involved the construction of luxury style residential townhomes for immediate resale to third parties, and each were undoubtedly aware of the potential future warranty liability to vendees and subvendees. Nonetheless, the parties executed a contract containing an arbitration clause affording to arbitrators wide and virtually unlimited latitude to fashion a remedy. By their agreement, either initially or in the submission, the parties could have limited the arbitrators' authority. See, e.g., *Metropolitan Waste Control*, 308 Minn. at 385, 242 N.W.2d at 830. They failed to do so. We decline to judicially restrict the powers of the arbitrators which the parties themselves have so broadly granted to them. Nor, in our opinion, does the fact that the arbitrators were able to make an alternative monetary award have relevance to the determination of the scope of the powers delegated to them. By fashioning the award, the arbitrators not only acted within the scope of the broad grant of authority in fashioning the "sell back" option, but also placed the obligation on Miller, the party responsible for the gross construction deficiencies, to remedy them and bear the risk of potential future warranty liabilities . . .

[The court then went on to address Miller's claims that the arbitration award violated the Statute of Frauds, and that David Co. had waived its right to collect damages by rendering final payment to Miller.]

Accordingly, because we hold that the award structured by the arbitrators was within the powers granted to them by the arbitration clause of the general contract; that the award did not do violence to the underlying policy of the Statute of Frauds; and that the award did not include items which were "waived" by final payment, we *affirm*.

QUESTIONS

1. How does the remedy-making power of arbitrators as described by the Minnesota Supreme Court in *David Co.* differ from that of a civil court? Would a court have been able to render similar relief had the case been brought in court?

2. Why is the court so deferential to the arbitrators?

3. What specific elements of the arbitration agreement reinforced the court's conclusion regarding the breadth of the arbitrators' authority? Could the parties have limited the scope of their remedial power by a specific statement in the agreement?

4. Do you believe the makeup of the panel of arbitrators had anything to do with the nature of the final arbitration award? What if the panel had consisted of three attorneys? Three laypersons without pertinent knowledge or experience?

Provisional Remedies

In some instances, irreparable injury will occur to one or more parties if the arbitrator does not act quickly to address a situation and render a final award. Many providers' rules allow the arbitrator equitable discretion to grant interim remedies, such as preserving the condition of perishable goods or taking appropriate security measures or even monetary relief. In some circumstances, institutions such as the AAA allow for the appointment of a single emergency arbitrator, a quick hearing, and emergency monetary relief, pending the formation of an arbitration panel. Additionally, the FAA and state arbitration statutes grant implied power to arbitrators to provide interim remedies. Most broad-form commercial arbitration agreements allow arbitrators the authority, for instance, to direct a posting of a bond as security for claims, or order the creation of an escrow account.

Courts may also grant limited provisional relief to parties in certain situations. If the need for an immediate order for relief must be satisfied before an arbitrator can be appointed, a court may order relief. Courts, however, are hesitant to interfere if the parties have an arbitral agreement. Only a court is able to exercise a contempt power to enforce the preservation of assets or to ensure continuing performance. Arbitrators lack such a contempt power, even though they are able to issue sanctions against one or more parties. Therefore, if a party secures interim relief, an arbitrator's order should be given to the court as an interim award subject to confirmation under the relevant state or federal arbitration law. These court powers are also reflected in the pending revisions to the Uniform Arbitration Act (UAA). The relationship between the arbitral forum and courts is explored in more detail in Chapter 17.

Damages

Damages are an extremely important issue in arbitration for a variety of reasons. One reason many parties may choose arbitration is to avoid the risk of facing a large, unpredictable, or unreasonable jury award. Under administrative rules, the arbitrator has great freedom in determining awards and damage amounts. For example, the AAA rules allow for "any remedy which the arbitrator deems just or equitable within the scope of the agreement." This freedom from the limited statutory remedies a trial court can offer is certainly one of the hallmarks of arbitration, but it can also raise problems.

Final Offer Arbitration

As noted earlier, options exist for parties to create their own arbitration rules. One popular variant parties have adopted is "final offer arbitration," often termed "baseball arbitration" because of its importance in major league baseball salary dispute resolution. It is also used in commercial cases and can be adapted for other disputes. Final offer arbitration requires that each party submit its "final offer" to the arbitrator after making appropriate submissions on the merits of the dispute. The arbitrator then chooses the most fair and reasonable offer, considering all of the facts and arguments presented. The arbitrator is not permitted to compose what he regards as a better or more just solution. He must choose one party's final offer. In contrast, with conventional arbitration, an arbitrator can select either party's position on some or all of the pending issues. Arbitrators choose a compromise point between the parties' positions and value estimations. In final offer arbitration, the arbitrator's discretion is limited because the parties themselves create the only two possible awards.

A "final offer arbitration" procedure has been used in major league baseball salary arbitrations with great success for nearly 25 years and has become a familiar example of arbitration for baseball fans. See Abrams (1998). The hope in "final offer arbitration" is that the parties will partake in good faith negotiations to facilitate a reasonable settlement. The risk of a complete loss if the arbitrator chooses the other party's offer encourages both parties to engage in prearbitration negotiations and to produce final offers closer to the other party's final offer. "Under baseball's salary arbitration scheme, a neutral arbitrator selects either the final demand of the eligible player or the final offer of the employing [baseball team]. . . . A greedy player who sets his demand too high or a stingy club that makes an offer too low is likely to lose. . . ." *Pennsylvania Environmental Defense Foundation (P.E.D.F.) v. Canon-McMillan School Dist.*, 152 F.3d 228, 239 (3d Cir. 1998) (Garth, J. dissenting), citing Abrams (1998).

Typically, final offer arbitration saves both parties money and time compared to litigation or conventional arbitration. Other advantages are the avoidance of considerable paperwork and the confidential nature of the proceedings. "Baseball's salary arbitration saves time and money over conventional negotiations by providing structure to salary negotiations and imposing strict timing requirements for filing, submission of final offers, the hearing, and the arbitrator's decision. Because the arbitrator does not issue a written decision, further costs are eliminated" (Meth, 1998).

Bracketed Arbitration, etc.

Other variants designed to encourage reasonableness and minimize exposure on awards include "bracketed (high-low)" and "incentive" arbitration. In bracketed (high-low) arbitration, parties agree in advance to limit the amount of recovery and loss. If the arbitrator's award falls within the identified range, it is binding on the parties. Alternatively, incentive arbitration is not binding, but penalties are imposed on parties who reject the award (*The ABCs of ADR: A Dispute Resolution Glossary*, 1995).

K. ARBITRATION AWARDS AND JUDICIAL REVIEW

Form of Awards

Traditionally, arbitration awards have tended to be issued without an accompanying rationale or explanation. For example, in the MDM/Fandom dispute described above, an arbitrator might review papers and hold hearings over several days, and a few weeks later issue a typical, single-sentence award:

"Fandom shall pay MDM $175,000 in damages in connection with the parties contract dated June 12, 2002."

As MDM's lawyer, you might be terribly disappointed in the amount of the award, reasoning that if the arbitrator ruled in MDM's favor, damages under $1 million make no sense as a matter of contract law or in terms of fairness. Fandom's lawyer might also be upset because the award does not acknowledge its counterclaims. Nevertheless, both parties have little recourse. Even if courts were willing to scrutinize arbitral awards closely, the arbitrator's conclusion is not supported by any legal or equitable reasoning.

The AAA has long advised commercial arbitrators not to explain their awards because written reasoning gives parties possible grounds for appeal based on their dissatisfaction with the outcome, undermining the advantage of arbitration as a prompt and final method of dispute resolution. Writing a rationale may also take time and complicate the deliberation process, especially when there are three arbitrators.

If parties to a dispute agree that some statement of explanation is appropriate, however, it is their prerogative to so direct the arbitrators. Written awards explaining in detail the rationale behind an arbitrator's decision have been standard for many years in the areas of labor relations and international commercial arbitration. Today, commercial arbitration agreements in business contracts often call for arbitrators to reveal their reasoning. Under AAA rules, the arbitrator(s) are advised to accommodate such a request, and the CPR rules make written opinion the default option for arbitrators, unless the parties agree otherwise. While the drawbacks to written, reasoned awards mentioned above are valid, their benefits are becoming more apparent — especially in high-stakes cases. For one thing, obvious errors can be brought to the arbitrator's attention rapidly. Moreover, requiring arbitrators to write out their thought process can lead to a more complete analysis of the issues involved. Parties are more likely to feel that they were, if not "victorious," at least heard on the matter. Finally, as we will see in Chapter 17, lack of a written opinion can be very detrimental to a party who seeks judicial review of the decision. While written opinions by arbitrators do not function like judicial precedent, they may in some cases provide some insights into an arbitrator's leanings, experience, and qualifications. Of course, the outcome and reasoning in one arbitral decision might be limited by the factual circumstances and evidence presented, providing little indication of how that arbitrator would rule in the next situation, or with a different panel of arbitrators.

Although it is becoming more common for parties and administering organizations to require written opinions, lawyers are less likely to advise clients to seek written opinions in disputes where the stakes are smaller because parties usually will bear the expense of the additional time arbitrators devote to rendering more detailed written opinions. Written opinions may be most valuable where a novel issue is presented, where a case is quite complex or where significant amounts of money are at stake, or where there is a special need for the adjudicator's rationale — such as, for example, where an award may serve as a basis for damages in a separate adjudication involving a third party.

Judicial Review Under Arbitration Statutes

In order to ensure the finality of arbitral awards, consistent with the agreement of the parties, while promoting fundamental fairness of process, the FAA and corresponding state arbitration statutes contemplate very limited avenues of appeal and forms of redress from arbitral awards. Judicial scrutiny is generally restricted to due process considerations. For example, FAA §10 empowers courts to overturn, or vacate, an award

- where the award was procured by corruption, fraud or undue means;
- where there was evident partiality or corruption in one or more arbitrators;
- where the arbitrators were guilty of misconduct in refusing to postpone the hearing upon sufficient cause shown, or in refusing to hear evidence pertinent and material to the controversy, or of any other misbehavior by which the rights of any party have been prejudiced; or
- where the arbitrators exceeded their powers, or so imperfectly executed them, that a mutual, final, and definite award upon the subject matter was not made.

There is no provision authorizing vacatur of award for errors of law or fact, leading at least one court to suggest that the process under the FAA "ought not to be called review at all." *UHC Management Co. v. Computer Services Corp.*, 148 F.3d 992 (1998). As explored in Chapter 17, however, over time federal and state courts have enunciated additional standards for review and vacatur of arbitration awards. These "nonstatutory" grounds — "manifest disregard of the law," "irrationality," "arbitrariness and capriciousness," "public policy" — vary from jurisdiction to jurisdiction, but in one way or the other they all open the door, however slightly, to some judicial review or oversight of the subject matter or the merits of the case.

In recent years, a few lawyers have assisted in the drafting of contractual provisions for expanded judicial review of arbitrators' factual or legal determinations. Besides inspiring a fundamental legal debate resulting in conflicting federal and state court decisions, such arrangements raise a host of serious practical concerns. These and other issues associated with judicial review will be explored in Chapters 17 and 18.

Private Appellate Processes

In light of concerns associated with expanded judicial review of awards, some attorneys have counseled clients to opt for an appellate arbitration process. Some providers offer an optional appellate arbitration procedure; the CPR Institute, for example, not only offers appellate rules, but also an appellate arbitration panel of former federal judges. The JAMS appellate procedure is adopted as a part of consensual arbitration procedures in about 10 percent of cases filed, although it is actually resorted to in very few cases. Those favoring private appeal may view it as a salutary alternative to judicial review, both in terms of cost- and time-saving, while providing meaningful oversight of the arbitral award. Some believe private procedures can alleviate the need to challenge an award in court, while enhancing confidence in the arbitration process. Others argue that appeal to a private panel may only add to the time and expense of finally resolving a dispute. Better, some say, to concentrate on the first arbitral proceeding and "getting it right the first time around."

QUESTIONS

Suppose your business client, Micron, is in the process of forming a contract with Dall Computers to install Micron 2005 software in every computer Dall makes. Micron is inclined to include an arbitration provision in the contract, but is concerned about the risk of an extreme or irrational award in arbitration. Advise Micron regarding the pros and cons of each of the following options:

a. Employ a panel of three arbitrators for disputes involving larger stakes;
b. Direct the arbitrators to follow certain legal standards in reaching a decision;
c. Direct the arbitrators to provide a written rationale for their award;
d. Agree that the parties will attempt to establish a range (a minimum and a maximum) for the arbitrators' award;
e. Agree that the arbitrators will not be empowered to consider claims for punitive or exemplary damages, or to make such awards;
f. Agree to expanded judicial review of arbitration awards;
g. Agree to appellate arbitration.

Can Arbitrators Award Punitive or Exemplary Damages?

Of all current issues respecting arbitral awards and remedies, the rendition of awards of punitive or exemplary damages is among the most controversial. Let us compare two seminal decisions on the subject.

GARRITY v. LYLE STUART, INC.
40 N.Y.2d 354 (N.Y. 1976)

[Garrity, an author, sought to confirm an arbitration award granting her $45,000 in compensatory damages and $7,500 in punitive damages against her publishing company Lyle Stuart, Inc., defendant. The trial court confirmed the award, and a divided appellate court affirmed. Lyle Stuart then appealed.]

Chief Judge BREITEL.
Plaintiff is the author of two books published by defendant. While the publishing agreements between the parties contained broad arbitration clauses, neither of the agreements provided for the imposition of punitive damages in

the event of breach. A dispute arose between the parties and in December, 1971 plaintiff author brought an action for damages alleging fraudulent inducement, "gross" underpayment of royalties, and various "malicious" acts designed to harass her. That action is still pending.

In March, 1974, plaintiff brought a new action alleging that defendant had wrongfully withheld an additional $45,000 in royalties. Defendant moved for a stay pending arbitration, which was granted, and plaintiff demanded arbitration. The demand requested the $45,000 withheld royalties and punitive damages for defendant's alleged "malicious" withholding of royalties, which plaintiff contended was done to coerce her into withdrawing the 1971 action. Defendant appeared at the arbitration hearing and raised objections concerning plaintiff's standing and the conduct of the arbitration hearing. Upon rejection of these objections by the arbitrators, defendant walked out.

After hearing testimony, and considering an "informal memorandum" on punitive damages submitted by plaintiff at their request, the arbitrators awarded plaintiff both compensatory and punitive damages. On plaintiff's motion to confirm the award, defendant objected upon the ground that the award of punitive damages was beyond the scope of the arbitrators' authority. Arbitrators generally are not bound by principles of substantive law or rules of evidence, and thus error of law or fact will not justify vacatur of an award. It is also true that arbitrators generally are free to fashion the remedy appropriate to the wrong, if they find one, but an authentic remedy is compensatory and measured by the harm caused and how it may be corrected. These broad principles are tolerable so long as arbitrators are not thereby empowered to ride roughshod over strong policies in the law which control coercive private conduct and confine to the State and its courts the infliction of punitive sanctions on wrongdoers.

The court will vacate an award enforcing an illegal agreement or one violative of public policy. Since enforcement of an award of punitive damages as a purely private remedy would violate public policy, an arbitrator's award which imposes punitive damages, even though agreed upon by the parties, should be vacated. *Matter of Associated Gen. Contrs., N.Y. State Chapter (Savin Bros.)* (36 N.Y.2d 957) is inapposite. That case did not involve an award of punitive damages. Instead, the court permitted enforcement of an arbitration award of treble liquidated damages, amounting to a penalty, assessed however in accordance with the express terms of a trade association membership agreement. The court held that the public policy against permitting the awarding of penalties was not of "such magnitude as to call for judicial intrusion" (*Id.* at 959). In the instant case, however, there was no provision in the agreements permitting arbitrators to award liquidated damages or penalties. Indeed, the subject apparently had never ever been considered.

The prohibition against an arbitrator awarding punitive damages is based on strong public policy indeed. At law, on the civil side, in the absence of statute, punitive damages are available only in a limited number of instances (see *Walker v Sheldon*, 10 N.Y.2d 401, 404). As was stated in *Walker v Sheldon (supra):* "[p]unitive or exemplary damages have been allowed in cases where the wrong complained of is morally culpable, or is actuated by evil and reprehensible motives, not only to punish the defendant but to deter him, as well as others who might otherwise be so prompted, from indulging in similar conduct in the future." It is a social exemplary "remedy," not a private compensatory remedy.

It has always been held that punitive damages are not available for mere breach of contract, for in such a case only a private wrong, and not a public right, is involved. Even if the so-called "malicious" breach here involved would permit of the imposition of punitive damages by a court or jury, it was not the province of arbitrators to do so. Punitive sanctions are reserved to the State, surely a public policy "of such magnitude as to call for judicial intrusion" (*Matter of Associated Gen. Contrs., N.Y. State Chapter [Savin Bros.]*, 36 N.Y.2d 957, 959, supra.). The evil of permitting an arbitrator whose selection is often restricted or manipulatable by the party in a superior bargaining position, to award punitive damages is that it displaces the court and the jury, and therefore the State, as the engine for imposing a social sanction. As was so wisely observed by Judge, then Mr. Justice, Bergan in *Matter of Publishers' Assn. of N.Y. City (Newspaper Union)* (280 App. Div. 500, 503, *supra*):

> "The trouble with an arbitration admitting a power to grant unlimited damages by way of punishment is that if the court treated such an award in the way arbitration awards are usually treated, and followed the award to the letter, it would amount to an unlimited draft upon judicial power. In the usual case, the court stops only to inquire if the award is authorized by the contract; is complete and final on its face; and if the proceeding was fairly conducted.
>
> Actual damage is measurable against some objective standard—The number of pounds, or days, or gallons or yards; but punitive damages take their shape from the subjective criteria involved in attitudes toward correction and reform, and courts do not accept readily the delegation of that kind of power. Where punitive damages have been allowed for those torts which are still regarded somewhat as public penal wrongs as well as actionable private wrongs, they have had rather close judicial supervision. If the usual rules were followed there would be no effective judicial supervision over punitive awards in arbitration. . . ."

Parties to arbitration agree to the substitution of a private tribunal for purposes of deciding their disputes without the expense, delay and rigidities of traditional courts. If arbitrators were allowed to impose punitive damages, the usefulness of arbitration would be destroyed. It would become a trap for the unwary given the eminently desirable freedom from judicial overview of law and facts. It would mean that the scope of determination by arbitrators, by the license to award punitive damages, would be both unpredictable and uncontrollable. It would lead to a Shylock principle of doing business without a Portia-like escape from the vise of a logic foreign to arbitration law.

In imposing penal sanctions in private arrangements, a tradition of the rule of law in organized society is violated. One purpose of the rule of law is to require that the use of coercion be controlled by the State. In a highly developed commercial and economic society the use of private force is not the danger, but the uncontrolled use of coercive economic sanctions in private arrangements. For centuries the power to punish has been a monopoly of the State, and not that of any private individual. The day is long past since barbaric man achieved redress by private punitive measures.

The parties never agreed or, for that matter, even considered punitive damages as a possible sanction for breach of the agreement (see dissenting opinion below by Mr. Justice Capozzoli, 48 A.D.2d 814). Here there is no pretense of agreement, although plaintiff author argues feebly that the issue of punitive damages was "waived" by failure to object originally to the demands for punitive damages, but only later to the award. The law does not and should not permit private persons to submit themselves to punitive sanctions of the order reserved to the State. The freedom of contract does not embrace the freedom to punish, even by contract. On this view, there was no power to waive the limitations on privately assessed punitive damages and, of course, no power to agree to them by the failure to object to the demand for arbitration (*Cf. Brooklyn Sav. Bank v. O'Neil*, 324 U.S. 697, 704, *aff'g* 293 N.Y. 666 ["waiver" of right "charged or colored with the public interest" is ineffective]; *see generally*, 6A Corbin, Contracts, §1515, pp. 728-732 [e.g., "waiver" of defenses to an usurious agreement is ineffective]).

Under common-law principles, there is eventual supervision of jury awards of punitive damages, in the singularly rare cases where it is permitted, by the trial court's power to change awards and by the Appellate Division's power to modify such awards (*see Walker v. Sheldon*, 10 N.Y.2d 401, 405, n.3, *supra*). That the award of punitive damages in this case was quite modest is immaterial. Such a happenstance is not one on which to base a rule.

Accordingly, the order of the Appellate Division should be modified, without costs, to vacate so much of the award which imposes punitive damages, and otherwise *affirmed*.

WILLOUGHBY ROOFING v. KAJIMA INTL.

598 F. Supp. 353 (N.D. Ala. 1984), *aff'd*,
76 F.2d 269 (11th Cir. 1985)

[Willoughby Roofing & Supply Company ("Willoughby Roofing"), filed suit against Kajima International, Inc. ("Kajima"), seeking compensatory and punitive damages for breach of contract, fraud, misrepresentation, and breach of the duty of good faith and fair dealing. These claims arose from a contract between the parties whereby the subcontractor Willoughby Roofing was to construct and install a roof on a building for Kajima, the general contractor. After accepting Willoughby Roofing's bid on the project, Kajima substantially altered the specifications and plans for the job and added new specifications which would have substantially increased the cost for Willoughby Roofing to complete the project. Understandably, Willoughby Roofing then sought to renegotiate their price or to submit a new bid. Kajima refused, canceled the contract, and hired another subcontractor.

Willoughby Roofing filed suit and Kajima removed the case to the district court, where it then filed a motion to stay the proceedings pending arbitration. This motion was based upon the arbitration clause of the contract between the parties which was quite broad and which evinced an intent of the parties to vest the arbitrators with authority to decide virtually any claim that could arise in relation to the contract and its performance.

The court granted Kajima's request for a stay. The arbitration panel awarded Willoughby Roofing $150,000 in unspecified damages. Kajima first objected by claiming that the arbitrators had awarded punitive damages and that to do so was beyond their authority. The court ordered the award to be resubmitted to the arbitration panel for clarification. The panel did so but Kajima was unhappy with the outcome and now seeks an order vacating the award on two separate grounds: (1) the contract between the parties does not authorize the arbitrators to award punitive damages; and (2) even if the contract does authorize the arbitrators to make such an award, public policy prohibits them from doing so.]

LYNNE, Senior District Judge.

I.

The contention that the arbitration clause involved in this case is not broad enough to empower the arbitration panel to award punitive damages is one that must fail. As the defendant has candidly admitted, "it would have been difficult, if not impossible, for the parties to have drafted a *broader* arbitration provision." Moreover, the arbitration clause incorporates by reference the Construction Industry Arbitration Rules. Rule 43 of those rules provides that:

> The arbitrator may grant *any remedy or relief* which is just and equitable and within the terms of the agreement of the parties (emphasis supplied).

When the extremely broad arbitration clause is read in light of the equally broad grant of remedial power in Rule 43, it is clear that the parties by their contract have authorized the arbitrators to award punitive damages. The contract purports to place no limits on the remedial authority of the arbitrators, nor should one be implied to exclude the authority to award punitive damages. The parties certainly had the power to limit the arbitrator's ability to fashion appropriate remedies, but they chose not to do so. As defendants have conceded, strong federal policy requires a liberal construction of arbitration agreements, not a strict one. In resolving questions pertaining to the arbitrator's authority, courts must broadly construe the agreement and resolve all doubts in favor of the arbitrator's authority. This is particularly true with respect to the remedial authority of arbitrators, for it is essential that arbitrators have a great deal of flexibility in fashioning remedies if the national policy favoring the settlement of disputes by arbitration is to have any real substance. Accordingly, federal policy places a heavy burden upon those claiming that arbitrators' awards exceed their authority.

In the present case, the award of punitive damages is neither explicitly nor implicitly prohibited by the agreement. Indeed, it was all but expressly authorized. Although the defendant has cited certain labor cases which lend some support to the theory that an arbitrator has no power to award punitive damages absent express authority,[1] this Court is convinced that such a restrictive presumption is contrary to the overriding principle under the Federal Arbitration Act that "any doubts concerning the scope of arbitrable issues," as well as any doubts concerning the scope of the arbitrators' remedial authority, are to be resolved in favor of the arbitrators' authority as a matter of federal law and policy. Only in the presence of "clear and express exclusions" could it be said that the arbitrators lacked authority under the contract to consider the plaintiff's claims for punitive damages. . . .

II.

This brings us to the defendant's second contention. Does public policy prohibit the parties to a contract from vesting an arbitration panel with authority

---

1. In truth, none of these cases actually involved factual findings or allegations sufficient to support the award of punitive damages under applicable substantive law. The case *sub judice* is decidedly different in this respect.

to consider their claims for punitive damages for fraud in the inducement or performance of the contract? The Court thinks not. It is true, as Kajima points out, that certain state courts have held that under the law of those states arbitrators cannot award punitive damages even if the parties authorize them to do so. Decisions such as those, however, deal only with the powers of arbitrators under state law and state public policy. Federal law and federal policy under the Federal Arbitration Act apply to the arbitration provision in the case *sub judice*, since that provision is part of a written contract evidencing a transaction in interstate commerce. 9 U.S.C. §2 et seq. Even if Alabama law and policy were deemed consistent with that of New York and Indiana, it would not control the issue presented here, despite the stipulation contained in the contract that Alabama law would generally be deemed to govern the agreement. "Although the parties to a contract can agree that a certain state's law will govern the resolution of issues submitted to arbitration (i.e., plaintiff's entitlement to punitive damages, assuming [a certain state's substantive] law applies), federal law governs the categories of claims subject to arbitration" and the "resolution of issues concerning the arbitration provision's interpretation, construction, validity, revocability, *and enforceability*." *Willis v. Shearson/American Express, Inc.*, 569 F. Supp. 821, 823-824 (M.D.N.C. 1983) (emphasis supplied). . . .

Southland Corp. v. Keating firmly establishes that it is the "federal substantive law" of arbitrability that governs questions such as the one presented here. 104 S. Ct. at 859. Therefore, if federal policy allows enforcement of an arbitration provision vesting the arbitrators with the authority to award punitive damages, then such a provision remains enforceable despite contrary state law or policy.

It is clear that federal policy does not prohibit the award of punitive damages by arbitrators if the parties' agreement is found to confer upon them the authority to make such an award. *Willis v. Shearson/American Express*, 569 F. Supp. at 824. Even the cases cited by Kajima in support of its contention that as a matter of contract construction, arbitrators do not have the authority to award punitive damages unless that authority is expressly conferred in the contract, are cases that clearly stand for the proposition that such an award is entirely consistent with federal policy whenever the agreement of the parties encompasses it. . . .

This Court agrees that there is no public policy bar which prevents arbitrators from considering claims for punitive damages. The Supreme Court has emphasized that the arbitration process can be a viable method of dispute resolution only if "it serves as a vehicle for handling any and all disputes that arise under the agreement," and only if the arbitrators are given a great deal of flexibility in the fashioning of appropriate remedies. . . . To deny arbitrators the full range of remedial tools generally available under the law would be to hamstring arbitrators and to lessen the value and efficiency of arbitration as an alternative method of dispute resolution. This would not sit well with the strong federal policy favoring arbitration.

The defendant insists, however, that because an award of punitive damages serves not only to punish the present wrongdoer for willful or wanton misconduct, but also to deter others in society at large, the power to award them should not be wielded by anyone other than a judge or jury. The defendant raises the spectre of overly partial arbiters manipulated by the party in a superior bargaining position, who may award punitive damages out of bias and prejudice. . . . If corruption or evident partiality in fact surfaces, naturally an award of punitive damages emanating from such circumstances should be set aside. Clearly, however, the possibility of an occasional abuse of power is no grounds for an absolute bar on the award of punitive damages by arbitrators.

Kajima also complains that to allow arbitrators to hear and decide claims for punitive damages is to displace the court and jury as an engine for imposing a social sanction designed more to punish and deter than to compensate. Of course, the argument that it is unfair to allow an arbitrator to displace a court and jury is one that has been sounded before. Not only litigants but state courts as well have questioned the ability of arbitrators to properly dispense justice. Many state courts have therefore declared contractual agreements to submit all disputes to arbitration to be totally unenforceable as a matter of public policy because they "defeat the jurisdiction of the courts." But Congress has enunciated a broad and pervasive federal policy that overrides all such arguments. That policy, embodied in the Arbitration Act, mandates that whenever a written contract evidencing a transaction in interstate commerce contains an arbitration provision, that provision must be given effect by state and federal courts alike, and that "any doubts concerning the scope of arbitrable issues should be resolved in favor of arbitration." Indeed, the very purpose of the Act was to overrule long-standing judicial precedents which declared agreements to submit justiciable controversies to arbitration to be contrary to public policy as displacing the functions of the courts. *Southland v. Keating*, 104 S. Ct. at 859, 860. There is no reason to believe that the Act's mandate of enforceability did not extend to agreements to arbitrate issues of punitive damages. Nor is there reason to believe that the purposes of punitive awards — punishment of the present wrongdoer and deterrence of others who might otherwise engage in similar conduct — will not be furthered by arbitral awards every bit as much as by formal judicial awards. Indeed, an arbitrator steeped in the practice of a given trade is often better equipped than a judge not only to decide what behavior so transgresses the limits of acceptable commercial practice in that trade as to warrant a punitive award, but also to determine the amount of punitive damages needed to (1) adequately deter others in the trade from engaging in similar misconduct, and (2) punish the particular defendant in accordance with the magnitude of his misdeed.

The wisdom of allowing arbitrators to consider and resolve issues of punitive damages becomes all the more plain when we consider the practical effect of a contrary result. Defendant urges that merely by agreeing to arbitration, a plaintiff has automatically forfeited his right to punitive damages because arbitrators are prohibited by public policy from awarding such damages. Thus, by entering an arbitration agreement the plaintiff has contractually waived his right to punitive damages. Yet, not only would such a mandatory result seriously undermine the value and sufficiency of the arbitral process as a method of dispute resolution, it would also constitute a total frustration of the public policies and purposes served by punitive damage awards. Merely by agreeing to arbitrate a defendant could escape the monetary sanction of punitive damages that the law would otherwise impose upon him for gross and malicious conduct. Both the policies of deterrence and of punishment would be completely thwarted in a broad range of commercial transactions involving agreements to arbitrate. Moreover, granting such automatic immunity could well encourage grossly unjustified conduct in certain cases by making it more economically feasible. Surely that would be a much more serious distortion of public policy than vesting the authority to award such damages in an impartial and experienced arbiter.

Even if the plaintiff who has agreed to arbitration is not deemed to have automatically waived his right to be heard on the issue of punitive damages, the practical effect of a bar on the arbitrability of such issues would be unsatisfactory. In essence, where tort and contract claims are mixed and punitive damages are sought, to follow the *Garrity* rule in these circumstances would require two trials — one before the arbitrator and then "a separate judicial trial on essentially the same facts — obviously a wasteful exercise. This would undermine the chief advantages and purposes of arbitration — to relieve congestion in the courts and to achieve a quick, inexpensive, and binding resolution of all disputes that arise between the parties to an agreement. . . .

Of course, where the parties expressly exclude certain claims or issues from their agreement to arbitrate, a certain amount of repetitiveness and the attendant failure to promote judicial economy may have to be tolerated. But otherwise, the principles of arbitral flexibility, judicial deference to an arbitrator's superior knowledge of a given business, and extreme skepticism of judicial intrusion into the disputes parties have agreed to arbitrate all militate in favor of the simpler, more efficient and less costly option of allowing the arbitrator to handle "any and all disputes that arise under the agreement," including claims for punitive damages.

CONCLUSION

. . . If parties to an arbitration agreement desire to exclude the issue of punitive damages from the consideration of an arbitrator and reserve it for judicial hearing, they are free to specify that in their contract. Otherwise, the strong federal policies favoring arbitrability of issues and remedial flexibility of arbitrators will govern. Those principles are dispositive of this case.

QUESTIONS

1. What assumptions about the role of binding arbitration, the character and background of arbitrators, and their agendas, underlie each of these two decisions? What assumptions are made regarding the ability of courts to oversee arbitral awards?
2. In 1995, the Supreme Court recognized that arbitrators can award punitive damages. *Mastrobuono v. Shearson Lehman Hutton, Inc.*, 115 S. Ct. 1212 (1995). The New York courts have since made clear that *Garrity* is no longer controlling authority under the law of that state. Although punitive or exemplary damages are very rarely awarded in commercial arbitration cases, they are frequently sought in employment and securities brokerage disputes. Has Judge Breitel's specter of unbridled awards raised its head? What, if any, oversight should courts have of arbitral awards of punitive damages? See *Sawtelle v. Waddell & Reed*, No. 2330 (N.Y. App. Div. 1st Dep't. 2003) (overturning judgment affirming $25 million punitive damages award against brokerage firm on the ground that it was grossly disproportionate to the harm suffered by the plaintiff, a mutual funds broker, and thus "arbitrary and irrational" under New York law).

3. Should parties be able to avoid punitive or exemplary damages by contract? Since it is generally within the power of the parties to arbitration agreements to include or exclude particular claims or controversies as they see fit, isn't it possible to structure an arbitration provision that functions as a partial or complete predispute waiver of claims for punitive damages? One commentator suggests that remedy-stripping arbitration clauses may be limited as a practical matter because they raise preclusion problems. See Schwartz (2003). Could the parties agree to exclude an arbitral award of punitive damages after a dispute has arisen? What are the difficulties of securing such an agreement? See Stipanowich (1997).

L. THE REGULATED CONTEXT OF LABOR ARBITRATION

This chapter concludes by exploring briefly three specific contexts in which arbitration is frequently used: for resolving labor disputes, securities claims, and international business disputes. Labor arbitration is a highly detailed and regulated field, beyond the scope of this text. We offer only a brief synopsis here, as this area is often covered in a specialized "Labor" or "Employment" Law course.

Labor arbitration is somewhat unique and is governed by particular law and procedures. Labor arbitration arises under the collective bargaining agreements between employers and the unions representing the employees. This area of the law is one in which the federal government predominates due to a history of congressional involvement designed to keep the economy running as smoothly as possible while parties to labor agreements resolve disputes. Additionally, both management and union leaders sought systems for addressing inevitable disputes safely and efficiently. As noted earlier, modern American mediation arose in response to the rise of organized labor. Until the expansion of arbitration to employment and consumer disputes in recent decades, labor disputes were one of the most common subjects for arbitration. Labor arbitration is most often statutorily mandated, and procedures for progressive dispute resolution are set out in federal law and contractual agreements between unionized employees and management. Parties to labor arbitrations frequently select nonlawyers as arbitrators and labor arbitrators issue opinions that are published, although they do not serve as binding precedent.

As noted above, early common law developed in U.S. courts rejected the enforceability of executory agreements to arbitrate. For 35 years after enactment of the FAA, the Court construed it so narrowly that it was not even mentioned in the majority opinions of any of the key labor arbitration law cases handed down by the Supreme Court in 1957 and 1960 (Hayford, 2000a).

The dormancy of the FAA, along with the widespread hostility of the judiciary toward commercial arbitration at the time, propelled the Supreme Court to quarantine the law of labor arbitration from the remainder of arbitration law. The Court's search for a legal doctrine that would preserve the central role labor arbitration had assumed in the labor-management relations sphere led it to

§301(a) of the Labor Management Relations Act. Therein the Court perceived congressional sanction for the invention of a new body of federal common law to govern the labor arbitration process. The Supreme Court's decision to forsake the FAA and the traditional law of commercial arbitration resulted in the traditional belief that labor arbitration is special—a process apart—that merits legal treatment separate from commercial arbitration.

Hayford (2000b).

M. LESSONS FROM SECURITIES ARBITRATION

Since the U.S. Supreme Court paved the way for broad enforceability of arbitration provisions in contracts between investors and securities brokers in *Shearson/American Express v. McMahon*, 482 U.S. 220 (1987) (holding that claims under RICO and the Securities and Exchange Act of 1934 Act are subject to arbitration), out-of-court dispute resolution has virtually displaced court litigation as a means of resolving disputes in the arena of investor/broker disputes.[7] A growing number of investor-claimants have found themselves before tribunals of the National Association of Securities Dealers (NASD), the New York Stock Exchange, and other self-regulatory organizations of the securities industry. Composite figures for the NASD and other securities regulatory organizations (SROs) reflect important growth in case filings during the past two decades, from 830 filings in 1980 to more than 9,000 in 2002. The tremendous growth of the investor base and recent market reverses have added new momentum to the long-term trend. Equally impressive is the growth of investor/broker mediation under the auspices of recently established programs at the NASD and the NYSE. (More than 2,500 matters were submitted to mediation in 2002.)

Judicial encouragement of securities arbitration is founded in part on the perceived benefits of the alternative for both industry members and customers, including reduced costs and speedier results (Perino, 2002). As in the employment arena, the arbitration system has made it possible to try smaller cases that might never have seen the inside of a courtroom. At the same time, the costs associated with arbitration hearings, including administrative costs and arbitrator fees, can in some cases be an obstacle.

Investor/broker arbitration and mediation are regulated more extensively than any other form of out-of-court dispute resolution. The Securities & Exchange Commission (SEC) oversees the practices and policies of all SRO arbitration programs, conducting audits and passing upon changes to arbitration procedures; the General Accounting Office also conducts occasional reviews. The Securities Industry Conference on Arbitration (SICA), established two decades ago at the behest of the SEC, provides a forum for debate on policy and procedural issues among representatives of SROs, the securities industry, and representatives of the investing public. (See generally Katsoris, 1996.) SICA produced the original Uniform Code of Arbitration, the model (and

---

7. This subsection is adapted from Stipanowich (2004).

minimum standard) for all current SRO arbitration procedures; it continues to review and revise provisions of the Code and offer guidance regarding parallel SRO rules.

Securities arbitration has come to share more and more features with traditional court trial, including increased emphasis on prehearing discovery and the availability of punitive damages. Moreover, the growth of securities arbitration has stimulated the establishment of the Public Investors Arbitration Bar Association (PIABA)—an organization of "repeat players" in securities arbitration, who are among the most active representatives of the investing public. PIABA holds conferences, publishes educational materials, and lobbies the SEC and other regulatory bodies on behalf of its constituency. And, while arbitration is not a system of precedents, there are also published decisions in the securities arena. Reflecting endless rounds of debates over the rights of investors and the needs of brokers, the NASD and New York Stock Exchange Arbitration Rules have become increasingly lengthy and detailed. Here, again, anecdotal evidence supports the notion that the litigation model has had considerable impact on private arbitration. In 1996, concerns regarding the growing cost and complexity of securities arbitration procedures led to a set of proposals for the reform of NASD arbitration. See *Report of the Arbitration Policy Task Force to the Board of Governors National Association of Securities Dealers, Inc.* (Jan. 1996). See also *Perino Report*. It is no surprise that, as in the court system, mediation has become an increasingly popular alternative.

N.   INTERNATIONAL ARBITRATION—THE CHALLENGE OF GLOBAL DISPUTES

As we have seen, arbitration offers various benefits and concerns, the impact of which are magnified in the international arena, where litigation can be extremely lengthy and complex. Today, economies and markets are more global than ever, with companies routinely doing business abroad. It can be essential to the success of a business to foster positive continuing relationships with organizations in other parts of the world. Because international relationships may be costly and difficult to develop, maintaining them will be of the utmost importance. Attorneys involved with corporate or commercial law will often handle disputes that extend beyond the United States. When disputes do arise in the international realm, management and settlement of disputes becomes extremely critical.

The next problem depicts an international dispute settled by means of arbitration. It concerns a dispute at the Olympic Games employing a fast-track, unique arbitral process, which conveys the potential value of arbitration for international disputes. As the following account will demonstrate, several aspects of arbitration make it particularly effective in the international sphere, where litigation can be especially lengthy and involve the courts of several countries. The questions at the end of this chapter will pertain to this example, so it will be useful for you to keep the scenario in mind as you read through the material on international arbitration.

INTERNATIONAL ARBITRATION: A DISPUTE OF OLYMPIC PROPORTIONS

During the 2002 Olympic Winter Games in Salt Lake City, Utah, referees issued controversial rulings in several sporting events. Perhaps the most memorable controversies occurred in the rough and tumble short-track skating events. Combining elements of speed skating and roller derby, the events included pushing, cutting off competitors at turns, and several disqualifications. On February 20, 2002, the final of the men's 1500-meter race was held, and many Americans cheered for Apollo Anton Ohno, an aggressive young skater who had qualified for the final despite sustaining an injury requiring six stitches in an earlier race during the Salt Lake games. He competed against a strong field, including Korea's most acclaimed short-track skater, Kim Dong-Sung. The skaters raced around the track at incredible speeds. Heading into the final lap, Kim was the only skater Ohno needed to pass to win gold. Kim cut off Ohno and crossed the finish line just ahead of him. The referee ruled immediately, however, that Kim was disqualified because he had illegally blocked Ohno during the final lap. While many American fans rejoiced and the Salt Lake City crowd cheered, a "firestorm of protest" was set off around the globe. Ohno received death threats and an Italian skater declared he should be shot. The U.S. Olympic Committee's server crashed after it received over 16,000 e-mails protesting the disqualification.

Korean officials immediately protested, but Chief Referee James Hewish of Australia refused to overturn the disqualification. The next day, Korean officials pursued their claims within speed skating's governing body. When that group confirmed the referee's decision as final, the Korean Olympic Committee appealed to the Court of Arbitration for Sport (CAS), the final and exclusive dispute resolution board for the Olympic games. As a condition of participating in the games, all athletes and organizations must sign entry forms agreeing to binding arbitration before the CAS. On the evening of February 22, the CAS held a hearing. Judge R.S. Pathak of India headed the Salt Lake arbitral pool, which involved nine arbitrators, each from a different country. The International Council of Arbitration for Sport had selected the arbitrators before the start of the games for their expertise in arbitration and sports law. Each arbitrator signed a declaration attesting to his independence before the games began.

Late in the evening on February 22, Kim's disqualification appeal was heard by a panel of three arbitrators; a British lawyer served as President and the other members were from Switzerland and Finland. During the arbitration proceeding, panelists called the referee and his four assistants as witnesses. Other interested parties were summoned, including the Korean Skating Union and the Olympic Committees of the United States, Canada, China, Italy, and France. An American attorney represented the Korean committee, which had to establish that the referees acted with bad faith or arbitrarily. All parties agreed that the panelists could not attempt to "second guess" decisions made by referees on technical "field of play" issues. The grievant's attorney cited the controversy surrounding the earlier men's 1,000-meter race when Ohno, who was leading, wiped out in the final turn and brought down three other skaters with him. Additionally, counsel argued that U.S. media pressure and local audience pressure in Ohno's favor influenced the referees.

The arbitrators could review a videotape of the race, even though the head referee did not have instant replay review at the time of the race, but declined to do so because this would be closer to a technical "field of play" review than an examination of bad faith or illegitimate decision making. Instead, the arbitrators heard from three assistant referees (from the United States, Norway, and England) that they had independently observed the Korean skater's "cross-tracking" infraction, noted that disqualification was the appropriate penalty, and reported this to the head referee at the conclusion of the race. The arbitrators, finding the witnesses honest and straightforward, ruled in favor of Ohno retaining the gold medal. On February 23, only three days after the race, the arbitrators issued a nine-page "Final Award" upholding the disqualification.[9]

Thus, within a few days of the hotly contested disqualification, a binding decision was issued at the games. The panelists heard testimony from the referees involved in the dispute and listened to attorney presentations. The grievants and respondents were given their "day in court" before an expert panel, which rendered justice much more swiftly and with less expense than litigation. Unlike many domestic commercial arbitrations, the panel issued a full written opinion canvassing the facts, issues, and reasoning behind its decision. Although many of Kim's fans were likely distressed by the result, the multinational character of the CAS panelists arguably provided a more neutral forum for all parties than either a Korean or U.S. judge or jury. Because all participants had agreed to arbitration in advance, there was no need for the potential jurisdictional jockeying, delay, and enforcement difficulties that often accompany international litigation.

Substantive and procedural differences in the legal systems of different countries can lead to a lengthy resolution process. Language and cultural barriers will tend to impede party communications and may be difficult to overcome. Parties may also be wary of impartiality of the "home country" and have legitimate concerns regarding the independence of a judiciary. These issues may seriously limit the effectiveness of the courts on an international level. These considerations favor arbitration as a means of resolution for global disputes. Using arbitration sometimes allows the parties a greater opportunity to select a neutral forum that is readily accessible to each party. Accordingly, a basic understanding of the roots of international arbitration, as well as an understanding of the unique requirements involved in drafting an international arbitration agreement, is imperative to providing a client a fundamentally fair hearing.

1.   The Foundations of International Arbitration

Fundamental to international arbitration is knowledge and understanding of the treaties ratified in two separate conventions on the subject. These

---

9. For more information regarding the ensuing events, including contentions between Ohno and Kim Dong-Sung, who would meet again in the 500-meter event, see *http://www.sltrib2002.com/ Main/Story.asp?VOL=02232002&NUM=713987&OPT2=STR*.

conventions are commonly known as the New York Convention and the Panama Convention. The New York Convention is the popular name given to the 1958 Convention on the Recognition and Enforcement of Foreign Arbitral Awards, while the Panama Convention refers to the Inter-American Convention on International Arbitration. The New York Convention has been ratified by over 120 countries, including the United States, Japan, China, Russia, and most of the countries in Europe and Latin America. The Panama Convention is restricted to countries of the Western Hemisphere. Both of the treaties provide for enforcement of arbitration awards and agreements with little judicial intervention. These treaties will generally only apply to awards that are made in another signatory state and disputes arising from commercial relationships, since most international arbitration centers on commercial disputes.

As you might expect, these conventions are not the end of the line; national and state statutes also need to be considered. The domestic arbitration law of any country will play an important role because the terms of an international arbitration agreement need to be consistent with the law of the place of arbitration, even if the nation has ratified one of the conventions. The New York Convention incorporates various provisions of the FAA. Thus, portions of this statute will often be applicable even though the arbitration might involve a foreign nation. Another item to be considered is The United Nations Committee on International Trade Law's (UNCITRAL) model law on arbitration and rules for arbitration. The number of institutions that offer international arbitration procedures is expanding. Many foreign countries and U.S. states have adopted international arbitration laws modeled after UNCITRAL's model code.

Many administrative organizations offer guidance on international arbitration. AAA and CPR offer rules and procedures for international arbitration. The International Chamber of Commerce (ICC), the London Court of International Arbitration (LCIA), the Stockholm Chamber of Commerce (SCC), and the Commercial Arbitration and Meditation Center for the Americas (CAMCA) are other agencies that are available to offer guidance on international arbitration. The China International Economic and Trade Arbitration Commission (CIETAC) is an international commercial arbitration institution which resolves contractual or noncontractual economic and trade disputes involving Chinese citizens and entities.[10] If parties wish to use an agency they would probably decide on one based on the location of the parties and the nature of the dispute. All of these organizations have been modifying their rules to make international arbitration more efficient. They are especially helpful in overcoming difficulties caused by vague arbitration agreements, strict timelines, and arbitrator selection issues.

2. Drafting International Arbitration Agreements

In drafting arbitration provisions or agreements to be used in an international setting, an attorney must certainly consider all the same basic issues that were considered previously for domestic disputes. However, certain issues that have a greater impact in an international setting must be given extra attention and

10. *http://www.cietac.org.cn.*

care. Certainly, administrative procedures may be adopted or consulted for guidance, or an attorney may draft procedures. An attorney who lacks experience in international arbitration should seriously consider seeking the help of an administering agency, or at the very least, consult its procedures.

As in domestic arbitration, when drafting an international arbitration provision or agreement a good place to start is a model agreement. Below are two different model clauses provided by institutions sponsoring international arbitration:

The London Court of International Arbitration (LCIA) suggests that the following clause be used by parties wishing to have future disputes resolved through arbitration:

> Any dispute arising out of or in connection with this contract, including any question regarding its existence, validity, or termination, shall be referred to and finally resolved by arbitration under the LCIA Rules, which Rules are deemed to be incorporated by reference into this clause.
>
> The number of arbitrators shall be [one/three].
>
> The seat, or legal place, of arbitration shall be [City and/or Country].
>
> The language to be used in the arbitral proceedings shall be [   ].
>
> The governing law of the contract shall be the substantive law of [   ].[11]

The International Chamber of Commerce provides the following model clause to be used in international disputes:

> All disputes arising out of or in connection with the present contract shall be finally settled under the Rules of Arbitration of the ICC by one or more arbitrators appointed in accordance with the said Rules.[12]

Obviously, these are quite similar to the model domestic provisions. The difference is the language indicating that the dispute is in an international setting. The two different clauses simply select different procedural rules for an arbitration. Beyond this, it will be important to give careful attention to the governing law, language of the hearing, time limitations imposed, and arbitrator selection, as all have particularly unique and important roles in drafting arbitration agreements for global disputes.

3. Governing Law

It is important to agree on the substantive law to govern an arbitration agreement and the arbitration itself. The purpose of choosing a governing law is to provide predictability. Choice of law has important implications for arbitrator selection and procedural matters as well as questions of enforceability and

11. More information about LCIA can be found on its Web site located at *http://www.lcia arbitration.com/arb/uk.htm*.
12. More information about the ICC, including its rules and other model clauses, can be found at *http://www.iccwbo.org/court/english/arbitration/model_clause.asp*.

interpretation of contracts, the effect of bankruptcy, and many other issues. The attorneys who are drafting the agreement and those likely to handle any arbitration should be familiar with the governing law. It is generally advisable to exclude conflict of law rules that would call for application of the law of another jurisdiction. Often neither party will agree to use the law of the country of the other party, and it may be necessary to agree to employ the law of a third country. It is advisable to consult an attorney familiar with the latter to be sure it is a wise choice for a particular transaction.

Like domestic arbitration, international arbitrators are free to abandon the technicalities of law and instead substitute their sense of basic fairness in resolving disputes between parties. However, international arbitrators are usually required to issue written opinions explaining the reasoning behind their decisions. These opinions do not create a strict system of precedent, but may serve to constrain some arbitrators and the facts of a situation may receive less privacy. International arbitrators are also more likely to look to solutions fashioned in other international arbitration disputes. This too has impacted the decision-making process of international arbitrators, albeit in the form of a self-imposed system rather than in the sense of formal, binding precedent.

4. *Language of the Proceedings*

Particularly when the parties to an arbitration agreement speak different languages, it is important to specify the language of the arbitration. The latter should be one in which counsel, party-appointed arbitrator, and presiding arbitrator are completely fluent.

It is rarely advisable to agree to use more than one language in arbitration. It is dangerous to have a case decided on translations of briefs and interpretations of oral arguments and witness testimony. Confirming the quality of written translations and oral interpretation is difficult. Deadlines for briefs and other written submissions must take into account the time necessary for translation. Using more than one language also creates special logistical issues. Finally, the use of multiple languages tends to increase the cost of arbitration.

If parties insist on using more than one language, it is best to negotiate a place of arbitration and an appointing authority that will increase the likelihood that the presiding arbitrator's first language will be the preferred language of party and counsel. CIETAC's list of arbitrators includes a significant number of "foreign" arbitrators, but many are from Hong Kong, Macau, and Taiwan, so the opportunity to have an English-speaking arbitrator in this instance may be quite limited. CIETAC is working to expand its roster of English-speaking neutrals as more U.S.-based entities do business in China.

In the absence of specific agreement by the parties, institutional rules concerning the language of arbitration vary, but all place some degree of emphasis on the language of the arbitration agreement itself. The ICC Rules authorize the arbitrators to make the determination, with due regard to all circumstances "including the language of the contract." The CPR Rules and the AAA Rules presume that the language of the "documents containing the arbitration agreement" will control, but give the arbitrators discretion to determine otherwise in appropriate circumstances.

5. *Selection of Arbitrators*

Perhaps the most important issue in international arbitration is the selection of the arbitrators. This is especially true since international arbitration is generally over commercial disputes. For international arbitration, this is usually a two-step process. International arbitration often employs the use of a three-arbitrator panel, so the selection process involves unilaterally selecting the arbitrator your party wants to use and then agreeing with the opposing party and appointing authority to name the chair of the panel. While each step is critically important, different considerations apply to each.

How should one go about deciding whom to select as a party-nominated arbitrator? However an adversary may behave, counsel should take care not to expose a client to any imputation that it failed to respect the neutrality of the tribunal. At the same time, it is logical to exercise the choice of the arbitrator in the manner most likely to help that party's chances of a favorable outcome. This presents a difficult balancing act.

The first step in this process is to define the characteristics the appointing party would like to see in an arbitrator, with a view to how the presiding arbitrator is to be chosen and the characteristics that process is expected to produce. The nominee should be an individual that is likely to relate well to the presiding arbitrator, who will realistically be the one to make the ultimate decision. Thus, for example, if one anticipates that the process for selecting the presiding arbitrator is likely to result in the selection of a professor from the German-speaking cantons of Switzerland, a party's interest may be better served by selecting a German arbitrator, or at least a German-speaking arbitrator, than selecting an arbitrator from its own country, who may have a more difficult time communicating with the presiding arbitrator. Ideally, a party's nominee should be someone who understands the party's legal culture and perspectives as well as that of the presiding arbitrator. Such an individual may help the presiding arbitrator better understand the legal arguments advanced by a party.

If one expects the presiding arbitrator to be a lawyer, it may be important to make a reasoned guess about whether the presiding arbitrator comes from a common law or civil law background. The civil law/common law divide is one of the great traps for the unwary in international arbitration. It remains true that process analysis, proof, and legal reasoning differs across the common law/civil law divide, and that it is often easier for those with common legal traditions to communicate. Thus, if the presiding arbitrator and the party-appointed arbitrator share this characteristic, it may be much easier for them to communicate. Further, just as in domestic arbitration, one should consider the kinds of professional qualifications that may give an arbitrator a helpful perspective on legal, business, or technical issues in dispute. Likewise, a situation may call for the most effective arbitrator to be a nonlawyer, such as an engineer or accountant.

After the desirable characteristics have been established, the next step is to find a person to fit the mold. This is commonly done through interviews and considering whether the arbitrator to be nominated comes from within "The Club," a small number of people who have served as arbitrators in international cases.

With regard to selecting the presiding arbitrator, it is best to reach an agreement with the opposing party on who should serve as the presiding arbitrator. The approach guarantees that a party will have at least some input into the choice of the arbitrator, as opposed to letting an appointing authority or administering organization choose the arbitrator. If agreement cannot be reached, it is best to include the process by which the chair shall be selected in the agreement to arbitrate itself, in an effort to promote predictability and methodical, unbiased selection.

Maintaining the trust of the parties, and also that of the governments involved, is critically important to resolving international disputes. One need only look to the world news to see examples of global disputes that depict a strong sense of nationalism and posturing of various countries on the international stage. The need for flexibility and the ability to delicately weave a solution that can be sensitive to these concerns of political loyalty while still providing all involved with a viable solution is most evident when one looks to Northern Ireland's "Good Friday Agreement" or even the fledgling peace talks between Palestine and Israel. Thus, arbitration in the international context is becoming an increasingly valuable means of dispute resolution as our involvement in international commercial and political development continues to expand.

QUESTIONS

To answer the following questions, you will need to review the Olympic International Arbitration scenario at the outset of this section.

1. Is arbitration the best mechanism to resolve this dispute? Why or why not?
2. What are some significant differences between this arbitral process and the one described in Problem 4? Why would the processes differ?
3. How might the skating dispute scenario differ if the participants had not signed an arbitration agreement prior to the Olympic Games?
4. Would you consider the use of arbitration in an international context to be as appropriate in commercial settings as it might be in political/cultural scenarios such as the Olympic Games? What are the differences between the two situations? Are the goals of the parties in resolving the dispute the same regardless of the context?

Conclusion

Arbitration is an increasingly popular method of dispute resolution, both internationally and domestically, particularly for commercial parties who desire an efficient and flexible method of resolving disputes. The next chapter examines the statutes and case law governing arbitration, which demonstrate how modern courts and legislatures have supported arbitration within the United States, making it a fairly effective and popular option for many types of disputes.

CHAPTER
17

The Legal Framework Supporting Arbitration

A. INTRODUCTION: HISTORICAL SHIFTS IN JUDICIAL AND LEGISLATIVE SUPPORT FOR ARBITRATION

As noted earlier, arbitration has been a popular dispute resolution choice throughout history in many cultures. But its use has waxed and waned over time in the United States, reflecting power struggles between advocates of arbitration and those who were suspicious of its potential to supplant court adjudication and interfere with the law governing contractual relations. On the one hand, English and American colonial courts guarded their power "jealously" and were quite hostile to arbitration agreements, readily allowing parties to evade their agreements to arbitrate or, if they had to proceed to arbitration, get unsatisfactory awards revoked. H.R. Rep. No. 96, 68th Cong., 1st Sess. 1-2 (1924). On the other hand, merchants favored arbitration because they could select their own decision makers and rules. At the behest of increasingly powerful business interests, state legislatures actively attempted to reverse this hostility and encourage arbitration in the nineteenth century. In 1925 Congress enacted the Federal Arbitration Act (FAA). Business-to-business disputes were the most common type subject to arbitration in the decades following enactment of the FAA, and after World War II, arbitration became a popular method of resolving labor and construction disputes. Nevertheless, courts remained hostile to arbitrators resolving statutory claims outside the labor relations context, where Congress had developed a specified framework for arbitration of labor disputes to prevent violence, delayed resolution of problems, and the resultant disruption of business. Judges were suspicious that arbitration would be too different from adjudication and less loyal to law. Aristotle once explained that "the arbitrator sees equity, the juror the law; indeed that is why an arbitrator is found—that equity might prevail" (Stipanowich, 2001). Moreover, the Supreme Court viewed public judgments rendered by federal trial courts as desirable mechanisms of social regulation on statutory matters, emphasizing their effect in shaping the conduct of non-parties. Finally, judges were skeptical that parties had knowingly and voluntarily waived their rights to the judicial forum for statutory claims like federal securities laws. See, e.g., *Wilko v. Swan*, 346 U.S. 427 (1953); see also Resnik (1995).

During the 1980s, however, the Supreme Court reinterpreted congressional intent, finding that the FAA created a broad national policy favoring arbitration when parties choose it. In a number of cases, the Court emphasized that, "[b]y agreeing to arbitrate a statutory claim, a party does not forgo the substantive rights afforded by the statute; it only submits to their resolution in an arbitral, rather than judicial, forum." *Mitsubishi Motors Corp. v. Solar Chrysler-Plymouth, Inc.*, 473 U.S. 614, 628 (1985). The Court reasoned that the arbitral forum provided distinct advantages for many parties: "It trades the procedures and opportunity for review of the courtroom for the simplicity, informality, and expedition of arbitration."

Following the Supreme Court's lead, many other federal and state courts have been quite respectful of arbitration as a dispute resolution option, even for statutory claims alleging employment discrimination, consumer fraud, or securities law violations. Despite the controversies surrounding its use in consumer and employment agreements, discussed in Chapter 18 below, most courts have heartily endorsed arbitration and shown arbitrators great deference. One federal judge's remarks about why courts should welcome arbitration rather than be suspicious of it typified the tone and sentiments of many American jurists at the close of the twentieth century:

> Access to the courts now is neither affordable nor expeditious. In many federal district courts and state courts, years pass before an aggrieved party can even have the proverbial day in court. In the meantime, the process grinds along, inflicting staggering legal expenses on the parties. Except for the very rich (and very poor, in some circumstances), we have simply priced the court system beyond the reach of most citizens, because the cost of litigation far exceeds the value of the decision itself. Indeed, even the most resourceful parties often decline to pursue legal rights, simply because quickly accepting or paying a sum of money in settlement of any claim often costs far less than determining in court the merit of that claim. In short, our current legal system for resolving disputes is losing the respect of the public and is rapidly approaching failure.

Bright v. Norshipco & Norfolk Shipbuilding & Drydock Corp., 951 F. Supp. 95, 98 (E.D. Va. 1997). See also *Gilmer v. Interstate/Johnson Lane Corp.*, 500 U.S. 20 (1991). Thus, in addition to relieving crowded court dockets, arbitrators can offer a better, private system of justice today, in the eyes of many judges and legislators. While the backlash against predispute arbitration clauses explored in Chapter 18 tempers this enthusiasm for arbitration in consumer and employment cases, the remainder of this chapter details the legal framework used by courts, as they interpret federal and state legislation. In general, modern courts, relying in large part on the FAA, have developed a legal framework that undergirds the work of arbitrators, honoring party choice to use arbitration rather than the courts and giving effect to important arbitration attributes, including efficiency and finality.

B. ELEMENTS OF MODERN ARBITRATION LAW

Common law developed in England and early colonial practice in the United States supplied two doctrines that courts used frequently to undermine parties' agreements to arbitrate: revocation and unenforceability. Basically, those courts would allow a party to revoke its earlier consent to arbitration once a dispute arose and would frequently refuse to enforce arbitral awards if parties sought to undo the awards in court. To counter these doctrines when parties had clearly agreed to arbitration, Congress in the Federal Arbitration Act instructed judges to treat written agreements to arbitrate like other valid contracts. Although this bare-bones Act is short and straightforward, it has become a powerful tool to support agreements to arbitrate, allowing courts to compel parties to proceed with arbitration and stay (i.e., put on hold) related litigation. After Congress adopted the Federal Arbitration Act, most states adopted similar statutes, giving courts broad powers to support and enforce arbitral awards. Today an overwhelming majority of states have arbitration statutes based on the Uniform Arbitration Act. In 2000, the Revised Uniform Arbitration Act (RUAA) was approved, and it is covered more fully in Chapter 18.[13] Thus far, only a handful of States have adopted the RUAA. Because the Supreme Court has construed the FAA so broadly in recent decades, however, the role of state arbitration statutes has been greatly minimized in comparison to the role of the FAA, as you will observe when we canvass preemption materials below. In sum, modern precedents make agreements to arbitrate fully enforceable in both federal and state courts.

It's worthwhile to read the entire Act. The following road map examines its major provisions, illustrating how courts are under a directive to cooperate with arbitration agreements. They must assist parties by enforcing agreements to arbitrate and support the arbitrators in exercising the powers granted to them by Congress and the parties' agreements.

A QUICK TOUR OF THE FEDERAL ARBITRATION ACT

- Section 1 provides that the Federal Arbitration Act (FAA) applies to:
    all contracts affecting commerce
    but not to employment contracts for certain categories of workers
    engaged in interstate commerce

The Supreme Court has broadly construed "commerce" to mean most economic transactions in our modern national (and global) economy. Indeed, it will be difficult to find purely intrastate—as opposed to interstate—commercial transactions, and the FAA will thus apply to most parties' disputes. Several cases exploring the breadth of this provision are included below. See, *infra, Citizens Bank v. Alafabco, Inc.*, 123 S. Ct. 2037 (2003); *Allied-Bruce Terminix Companies v. Dobson*, 513 U.S. 265 (1995).

In *Circuit City Stores v. Adams*, 532 U.S. 105 (2001), the Court held that Section 1 exempts from the FAA only employment contracts of transportation

---

13. The original Uniform Arbitration Act (UAA) was adopted by the National Commissioners on Uniform State Laws in 1955. A revised and updated version was approved in 2000.

workers. The FAA thus applies to employees generally, even if their work involves interstate commerce.

- Section 2 states that written contracts to arbitrate are:
  valid, irrevocable, and enforceable
  except on "such grounds as exist at law or in equity for the revocation of any contract."

This section expressly counters the common law's hostility toward arbitration, reversing the doctrines of revocation and unenforceability and putting arbitration contracts on equal footing will all other types of contracts. It also makes clear that parties can raise standard state law contract defenses to challenge an arbitration clause. We will canvass some of the most commonly raised defenses in the next chapter.

- Section 3 of the FAA provides that if one party to an arbitration contract sues, the court *shall* stay the trial [i.e., court proceedings on the same controversy] until the arbitration is completed.

This has been broadly construed so that all court proceedings, including pretrial phases, are stopped until the arbitration is concluded. The Act thus tries to avoid the duplicative proceedings and potentially conflicting outcomes, which could occur if arbitrators and courts both conducted proceedings on the same matter simultaneously.

- Section 4 provides that if a party refuses to arbitrate, the opposing side can sue in federal court for an order to compel the party to participate in arbitration. Section 6 states that any application to compel arbitration shall be heard as a motion, and the court shall proceed summarily to determine whether a written agreement to arbitrate affecting commerce exists.

These sections attempt to ensure expeditious resolution of the question by mandating that courts issue orders to compel arbitration if an agreement to arbitrate is present. These provisions make it relatively easy for a lawyer to go to federal or state court, file a petition, and get a fairly speedy resolution of the issue, backed by the contempt power of the court. To underscore the presumption in favor of courts not interfering with the progress of arbitration if any arbitration agreement is found, the Act provides that appellate courts can conduct interlocutory review of certain anti-arbitration rulings by a trial court (e.g., orders enjoining or stopping arbitration proceedings). Such interlocutory review is extremely rare; appellate courts generally try not to interfere with ongoing trial court proceedings and parties must await a final judgment before appealing. In contrast, the FAA declares that appellate courts are not allowed to review orders of trial courts *upholding* arbitration (e.g., orders refusing to enjoin arbitrations) on an interlocutory basis. This underscores the idea that courts should strive hard to avoid interfering with arbitral proceedings.

- Section 5 of the FAA provides that if the parties fail to agree on an arbitrator, the court may appoint one.

This power is rarely exercised, as most parties opt into administered systems where rules for selecting arbitrators are clear or the parties agree to their own methods of selection. Nevertheless, this provision is an important fallback option for a party in the event that another party attempts to evade or slow arbitration proceedings by refusing to cooperate in selecting arbitrators.

- Section 7 grants arbitrators power to issue subpoenas for witnesses to appear before them and bring material evidence. If a witness refuses, the court may compel attendance or hold the person in contempt of court.

As noted earlier, arbitrators call on nonparties to provide critical evidence in arbitral proceedings. (This provision makes no reference to subpoenas for prehearing discovery, and most witnesses appear at actual hearings.) This power, like the subpoena power trial courts possess under the Federal Rules of Civil Procedure and state analogs, make arbitration and litigation good alternatives to negotiation and mediation when a party is dependent on securing material evidence from the opposing party or nonparty witnesses to prove its claims. As explained earlier, the scope of discovery is generally not as broad in arbitration as litigation, resulting in less expansive discovery material and testimony as well as less expense for adjudicating most claims.

- Section 9 provides that a victorious party in arbitration may petition a court to enter the arbitration award as a court judgment, if the parties have provided for this option in their agreement. If such a petition is filed within a year of the award being issued, the court *must* grant judgment unless it modifies or vacates the award (on the limited grounds described in sections 10-11 of the FAA). Once a party secures a court judgment, it can execute on that judgment just as if it had won a victory at trial.

While most students do not learn much about enforcing judgments during law school, this provision can make a great deal of practical difference. With a negotiated settlement or mediation agreement, enforcing compliance can sometimes become difficult. On the other hand, a party who secures an arbitral award and has it entered as a judgment has access to the court's authority and processes for enforcement, including garnishing of wages, postjudgment discovery of assets, etc. Thus, although most arbitration clauses are brief, it is common to include language providing for entry of judgment in court of any arbitral award rendered.

Finally, some of the most important sections of the FAA provide narrow grounds for judicial review of arbitral awards. We will proceed through these grounds for appeal separately below, providing illustrative cases. For now, it is important for you to understand that judicial review of arbitral rulings and awards is *extremely limited*, buttressing arbitration as a final, efficient, cost-effective dispute resolution option.

C. JUDICIAL REVIEW OF ARBITRAL AWARDS

If a claim does proceed to arbitration and arbitrators render an award, it is very difficult to get that award altered by resort to judicial review. It is rare for a court to engage in close scrutiny of an arbitrator's work and even rarer for a judge to overturn or alter an arbitral award. Under the FAA, federal and state courts are afforded review of arbitrators' decisions only in certain narrow circumstances. Most of the categories for altering awards concern procedural mistakes an arbitrator might make or a process flaw (e.g., a mathematical error, and evident bias or prejudicial misbehavior by arbitrators), which do not extend to the *merits* of arbitrators' decisions. Examining the two sections allowing judges to vacate or modify arbitral awards, set out in their entirety here, will help you understand why courts are so deferential to arbitral awards.

§10. Same; vacation; grounds; rehearing

(a) In any of the following cases the United States court in and for the district wherein the award was made may make an order vacating the award upon the application of any party to the arbitration—

(1) where the award was procured by corruption, fraud, or undue means;

(2) where there was evident partiality or corruption in the arbitrators, or either of them;

(3) where the arbitrators were guilty of misconduct in refusing to postpone the hearing, upon sufficient cause shown, or in refusing to hear evidence pertinent and material to the controversy; or of any other misbehavior by which the rights of any party have been prejudiced; or

(4) where the arbitrators exceeded their powers, or so imperfectly executed them that a mutual, final, and definite award upon the subject matter submitted was not made.

(b) If an award is vacated and the time within which the agreement required the award to be made has not expired, the court may, in its discretion, direct a rehearing by the arbitrators.

(c) The United States district court for the district wherein an award was made that was issued pursuant to section 580 of title 5 may make an order vacating the award upon the application of a person, other than a party to the arbitration, who is adversely affected or aggrieved by the award, if the use of arbitration or the award is clearly inconsistent with the factors set forth in section 572 of title 5.

§11. Same; modification or correction; grounds; order

In either of the following cases the United States court in and for the district wherein the award was made may make an order modifying or correcting the award upon the application of any party to the arbitration—

(a) Where there was an evident material miscalculation of figures or an evident material mistake in the description of any person, thing, or property referred to in the award.

(b) Where the arbitrators have awarded upon a matter not submitted to them, unless it is a matter not affecting the merits of the decision upon the matter submitted.

(c) Where the award is imperfect in matter of form not affecting the merits of the controversy.

The order may modify and correct the award, so as to effect the intent thereof and promote justice between the parties.

As you will notice, most of the grounds for modifying or correcting an award involve obvious mistakes that can be easily remedied without a judge delving into the merits of the claims and defenses reviewed by the arbitrator(s). While the FAA contains a few broad phrases in the judicial review sections, courts have construed those grounds for review narrowly. In fact, it is hard to over-state how deferential courts are toward arbitrators. Judicial review in this context is fairly meaningless compared to the other forms of judicial review you have encountered in your legal studies. You will recall that substantial deference for a "lower" tribunal's factual findings and procedural decisions is already built into our legal system. For example, appellate courts typically review trial courts' findings on legal issues de novo, but they overturn trial courts' factual findings only if they are clearly erroneous and revise procedural choices only if the lower court abused its discretion. This deference toward factual findings is magnified in the arbitration context so that reviewing courts merely inquire as to whether the arbitrators interpreted the contract. As one prominent jurist summarized:

> [T]he question for decision by a federal court asked to set aside an arbitration award . . . is not whether the arbitrator or arbitrators erred in interpreting the contract; it is not whether they clearly erred in interpreting the contract; it is not whether they grossly erred in interpreting the contract; it is whether they interpreted the contract.

Hill v. Norfolk and Western Ry. Co., 814 F.2d 1192, 1194 (7th Cir. 1987) (Hon. Richard Posner). Thus, even if a judge would interpreted the contract differently herself, she is not supposed to substitute her judgment for that of the arbitrator(s).

Moreover, as a practical matter, a court is hampered in reviewing the merits of an arbitrator's ruling because written reasoning to support the decision is frequently withheld, making it quite difficult to review an arbitrator's rulings pertaining to the making of the agreement to arbitrate or the merits of the underlying dispute. In international commercial arbitration and labor relations arbitration, arbitrators typically do provide reasoning to support their decisions. While these rulings are not used as precedent in entirely the same way that court decisions are, they nevertheless provide a basis for parties to familiarize themselves with an arbitrator's work and give a court more assurance that the award was supported by actual contractual interpretation. Outside of those two discreet areas of arbitration, however, awards are often not accompanied by written opinions.

1. FAA Grounds for Review

Thus, it is not surprising that few arbitration awards are challenged in court. Of those challenges, very few succeed. Resort to courts is more frequent in complex business disputes where significant amounts of money are at stake. But even in such cases judicial review is rare and judicial alteration of arbitrators' decisions is even rarer. It is not easy to find judicial rulings overturning arbitral awards under the FAA, but the examples provided below illustrate the types of situations in which courts may countenance being less deferential to arbitral rulings. Each of these rulings was influenced by the specific circumstances and evidence presented to the judge, and there is no guarantee that other judges would be willing to overturn arbitral rulings on the same facts.

Clear Evidence of Perjury

One court vacated an arbitral award under the FAA when it found that an expert witness whose testimony influenced an arbitral award had committed perjury.[14] The circumstances were unusual in that there was very clear evidence of perjury, which the aggrieved party could not discover until after the arbitration proceedings ended. In most cases where claims of perjury or improper evidence are raised after arbitrators have ruled, courts find that they do not need to "reopen" proceedings and hear such "new" evidence.[15] Instead, they emphasize finality, giving parties and lawyers incentives to present all evidentiary problems, including claims of perjured testimony, to the arbitrators themselves.

Failure to Hear Evidence

Arbitrators have some incentive to err on the side of allowing evidence to be heard and are granted broad discretion under most administered systems as to defining what constitutes relevant information. Most courts are very deferential to arbitrators' evidentiary determinations, but occasionally a court will vacate an arbitral award when an evidentiary ruling prejudiced one party. For example, one court found that an employer's administrative assistant was a crucial witness for the employer/party, but the arbitrator refused to postpone hearings after the assistant was hospitalized. This was no fake claim of illness; the court noted that she was noticeably ill in the presence of the arbitrators. *Tempo Shain Corp. v. Bertek, Incorp.*, 120 F.3d 16 (2d Cir. 1997).

Arbitrator Bias

One court found "evident partiality" under the FAA when a father served as arbitrator in a dispute in which his son was the officer of the international union that was a party to the arbitration. *Morelite Construction Corp. v. New York City District Counsel Carpenters Benefits Fund*, 478 F.2d 79 (2d Cir. 1984). However, research reveals many more cases in which courts declined to find evident partiality, even when parties had former business relationships with arbitrators and failed to disclose those connections. As some Supreme Court Justices noted in *Commonwealth Coatings*, excerpted in Chapter 16 above, parties sometimes value the expertise and connections arbitrators bring to their role. They may be chosen in part because of their immersion in an industry and reputation. With such experience, arbitrators often bring a web of connections to persons and companies within their industry. Courts are often reluctant to closely scrutinize claims of arbitrator bias and make decisions regarding what type of connections evidence bias. Thus, to prove evident

---

14. *Bonar v. Dean Witter Reynolds, Inc.*, 835 F.2d 1378 (Fla. 1988) (finding perjury of investors' purported expert witness required vacation of punitive damages portion of arbitration award against securities broker where broker clearly proved expert's perjury, that it could not have discovered expert's perjury before or during arbitration hearing, and that expert's testimony influenced arbitrators on central issue of broker's negligent supervision).

15. See, e.g., *Terk Technologies Corp. v. Dockery*, E.D. Mich. 2000, 86 F. Supp. 2d. 706, *aff'd* 3 Fed. Appx. 459, 2001 WL 128317 (arbitration award was not procured by fraud, even if party agreed to arbitration only after witness gave perjured testimony, where witness' testimony was not considered by arbitrators).

partiality, a party and its lawyer generally need to show a very close, undisclosed relationship between a purportedly neutral arbitrator and a party.

2. Judicial Expansion of Grounds for Review

In addition to the statutory grounds for review included in the FAA and state analogs, courts have infrequently recognized nonstatutory grounds for reviewing arbitral awards. For example, in rare instances a court might determine that an award was rendered in manifest disregard of the law. In one case, a federal appellate court concluded that, given overwhelming evidence that an employee was fired because of his age, the parties' concurrence that the arbitrators were correctly advised of the applicable legal principles, and the fact that the arbitrators did not explain their award, the award was in manifest disregard of the law. *Halligan v. Piper Jaffray, Inc.*, 148 F.3d 197 (2d Cir. 1998). In unusual circumstances, courts might vacate awards as being "arbitrary and capricious" or irrational. See, e.g., *Ainsworth v. Skurnick*, 960 F.2d 939 (11th Cir. 1992) (district court upheld the decision of an arbitration panel finding Skurnick negligent, but vacated the arbitration judgment as being in manifest disregard of the law for failing to provide for mandatory damages under Florida law, rendering the panel's denial of damages arbitrary or capricious); *Swift Indust. v. Botany Indust.*, 466 F.2d 1125 (3d Cir. 1972) (two companies disputed who owed the IRS taxes connected to a corporation's sale; the lower court affirmed the arbitration panel's award as to the fees but vacated the award of a cash bond on the ground that a bond was not requested; the arbitration agreement did not provide for any security nor did it include the authority of the arbitrator to award a $6 million cash bond to cover liability not yet incurred).

Some parties have attempted to expand the grounds of judicial review of arbitral awards by contract. For example, in *Lapine Technology Corp. v. Kyocera Corp.*, 130 F.3d 884, 887 (9th Cir. 1997), the parties expressly provided grounds for judicial review beyond those available under the FAA, including court modification or vacatur if arbitrators made findings not supported by substantial evidence or made erroneous legal conclusions. The federal circuits have split on whether to permit this expansion of judicial review by contract, with some honoring contractual autonomy and others finding that expansion of review would undercut the proarbitration policy of the FAA, as interpreted by the Court in recent decades. See Moses (2004).

As noted earlier, arbitrators have significant discretion in determining damages. Parties, by contract, can limit or specify the amount or types of damages that can be awarded in arbitration. Courts, however, will be reluctant to scrutinize closely the amount of damages awarded by arbitrators. Parties can contract for more extensive review of arbitral rulings by setting up another tier of review (e.g., other arbitrators, retired judges, or any trusted neutral). Most parties are unlikely to opt for such appellate review, because of its expense and its potential to undermine the finality of the arbitration proceedings. Nevertheless, in a complex business dispute or in a case involving a novel claim, such review may be an important safeguard and provide some negotiating leverage after arbitrators issue their decision.

Now that you have explored the limited nature of judicial review of arbitral decisions, you understand the importance of threshold challenges to the scope of arbitral proceedings. Once arbitration begins, it will be difficult to get courts to intervene or review what happens in arbitration. Thus, the issues canvassed in the remainder of this chapter include important methods by which parties and their lawyers, when appropriate, can attempt to avoid arbitration or limit its scope.

D. ARBITRABILITY

In the overwhelming majority of cases, it is clear that the parties have agreed to arbitrate and that the agreement covers *all* disputes relating to a particular contractual relationship, given the breadth of standard arbitration clauses. In some instances, however, a party seeks to challenge the validity or scope of an arbitration clause on the grounds that arbitrators "exceeded their powers" or decided a matter not submitted to them. These threshold jurisdictional questions of (a) whether there was an agreement to arbitrate and (b) what topics the agreement covers are termed "arbitrability" issues. If the parties opted in to administered rules, those arbitrability issues will most likely be resolved by the arbitrator(s). The CPR Rules, for example, provide:

> The Tribunal shall have the power to hear and determine challenges to its jurisdiction . . . It shall have the power to determine the existence, validity or scope of the contract . . . and/or the arbitration clause itself . . .

Such rules discourage parties from resorting to court, which can delay and disrupt the arbitration proceedings. If the parties have opted in to such rules or otherwise agreed that arbitrators should resolve arbitrability questions, courts will find "clear and unmistakable" evidence that jurisdictional questions belong to the arbitrator(s) and honor those preferences.

If courts do not find a clear agreement to let arbitrators handle arbitrability issues, however, then courts have jurisdiction to hear those threshold challenges under the FAA and prevailing state arbitration law. In the following case, the Supreme Court explains how arbitrability determinations should proceed.

FIRST OPTIONS OF CHICAGO, INC. v. KAPLAN
514 U.S. 938 (1995)

[First Options of Chicago, Inc., a firm that clears stock trades on the Philadelphia Stock Exchange, entered into a "workout" agreement, embodied in four documents, which governed the "working out" of debts owed by Manuel Kaplan, Carol Kaplan, and their investment company ("MKI"). The Kaplans and MKI lost money in the October 1987 stock market crash and in 1989. First Options sought arbitration after its demands for payment were not satisfied. MKI, which had signed the only workout document containing an arbitration agreement, submitted to arbitration, but the Kaplans, who had not signed that document, objected. The arbitrators ruled in First Options' favor. The District Court confirmed the award, but the Court of Appeals reversed, finding that the dispute was not arbitrable.]

JUSTICE BREYER delivered the opinion for a unanimous Court.
... The first question — the standard of review applied to an arbitrator's decision about arbitrability — is a narrow one. To understand just how narrow, consider three types of disagreements present in this case. First, the Kaplans and First Options disagree about whether the Kaplans are personally liable for MKI's debt to First Options. That disagreement makes up the *merits* of the dispute. Second, they disagree about whether they agreed to arbitrate the merits. That disagreement is about the *arbitrability* of the dispute. Third, they disagree about *who should have the primary power to decide the second matter*. Does that power belong primarily to the arbitrators (because the court reviews their arbitrability decision deferentially) or to the court (because the court makes up its mind about arbitrability independently)? We consider here only this third question.

Although the question is a narrow one, it has a certain practical importance. That is because a party who has not agreed to arbitrate will normally have a right to a court's decision about the merits of its dispute (say, as here, its obligation under a contract). But, where the party has agreed to arbitrate, he or she, in effect, has relinquished much of that right's practical value. The party still can ask a court to review the arbitrator's decision, but the court will set that decision aside only in very unusual circumstances ... Hence, who — court or arbitrator — has the primary authority to decide whether a party has agreed to arbitrate can make a critical difference to a party resisting arbitration.

We believe the answer to the "who" question (i.e., the standard-of-review question) is fairly simple. Just as the arbitrability of the merits of a dispute depends upon whether the parties agreed to arbitrate that dispute ... so the question "who has the primary power to decide arbitrability" turns upon what the parties agreed about *that* matter. Did the parties agree to submit the arbitrability question itself to arbitration? If so, then the court's standard for reviewing the arbitrator's decision about *that* matter should not differ from the standard courts apply when they review any other matter that parties have agreed to arbitrate ... That is to say, the court should give considerable leeway to the arbitrator, setting aside his or her decision only in certain narrow circumstances ... If, on the other hand, the parties did *not* agree to submit the arbitrability question itself to arbitration, then the court should decide that question just as it would decide any other question that the parties did not submit to arbitration, namely, independently. These two answers flow inexorably from the fact that arbitration is simply a matter of contract between the parties; it is a way to resolve those disputes — but only those disputes — that the parties have agreed to submit to arbitration. ...

We agree with First Options, therefore, that a court must defer to an arbitrator's arbitrability decision when the parties submitted that matter to arbitration. Nevertheless, that conclusion does not help First Options win this case. That is because a fair and complete answer to the standard-of-review question requires a word about how a court should decide whether the parties have agreed to submit the arbitrability issue to arbitration. ...

When deciding whether the parties agreed to arbitrate a certain matter (including arbitrability), courts generally (though with a qualification we discuss below) should apply ordinary state-law principles that govern the formation of contracts. ... The relevant state law here, for example, would require the court to see whether the parties objectively revealed an intent to submit the arbitrability issue to arbitration ...

This Court, however, has . . . added an important qualification . . . : Courts should not assume that the parties agreed to arbitrate arbitrability unless there is "clear and unmistakable" evidence that they did so. . . . In this manner the law treats silence or ambiguity about the question "*who* (primarily) should decide arbitrability" differently from the way it treats silence or ambiguity about the question "*whether* a particular merits-related dispute is arbitrable because it is within the scope of a valid arbitration agreement"—for in respect to this latter question the law reverses the presumption. . . . The latter question arises when the parties have a contract that provides for arbitration of some issues. In such circumstances, the parties likely gave at least some thought to the scope of arbitration. And, given the law's permissive policies in respect to arbitration . . . one can understand why the law would insist upon clarity before concluding that the parties did *not* want to arbitrate a related matter. . . . On the other hand, the former question—the "who (primarily) should decide arbitrability" question—is rather arcane. A party often might not focus upon that question or upon the significance of having arbitrators decide the scope of their own powers. . . . And, given the principle that a party can be forced to arbitrate only those issues it specifically has agreed to submit to arbitration, one can understand why courts might hesitate to interpret silence or ambiguity on the "who should decide arbitrability" point as giving the arbitrators that power, for doing so might too often force unwilling parties to arbitrate a matter they reasonably would have thought a judge, not an arbitrator, would decide. . . .

On the record before us, First Options cannot show that the Kaplans clearly agreed to have the arbitrators decide (i.e., to arbitrate) the question of arbitrability. . . . We conclude that, because the Kaplans did not clearly agree to submit the question of arbitrability to arbitration, the Court of Appeals was correct in finding that the arbitrability of the Kaplan/First Options dispute was subject to independent review by the courts. The judgment of the Court of Appeals is *affirmed*.

QUESTIONS

1. The Court describes three possible levels of decision-making in *First Options*: "First, the Kaplans and First Options disagree about whether the Kaplans are personally liable for MKI's debt to First Options . . . Second, they disagree about whether they agreed to arbitrate the merits . . . Third, they disagree about *who should have the primary power to decide the second matter*." What, if anything, did the Court determine as to each of the three issues? What was the next procedural step for the parties after the Court rendered its decision?
2. Identify the two countervailing presumptions the Court discusses in *First Options*. When does each apply?
3. Why does the law treat silence in a contract differently when it concerns who should decide arbitrability versus whether a particular issue is arbitrable? Do you agree with this reasoning? In the following case the Court faces another example of silence in an arbitration agreement about an important procedural and remedial question.

GREEN TREE FINANCIAL CORP. v. BAZZLE
123 S. Ct. 2402 (2003)

[Five homeowners brought class actions in South Carolina state courts against Green Tree Financial Corp. ("Green Tree") in connection with a home improvement loan and loans for mobile homes. State appellate courts affirmed class certification and awards in two separate actions against Green Tree. The South Carolina Supreme Court consolidated the appeals and affirmed that the class action arbitration was legally permissible.]

JUSTICE BREYER announced the judgment of the Court and delivered an opinion, in which Justices SCALIA, SOUTER, and GINSBURG join.

This case concerns contracts between a commercial lender and its customers, each of which contains a clause providing for arbitration of all contract-related disputes. The Supreme Court of South Carolina held (1) that the arbitration clauses are silent as to whether arbitration might take the form of class arbitration, and (2) that, in that circumstance, South Carolina law interprets the contracts as permitting class arbitration ... We granted certiorari to determine whether this holding is consistent with the Federal Arbitration Act ...

We are faced at the outset with a problem concerning the contracts' silence. Are the contracts in fact silent, or do they forbid class arbitration as petitioner Green Tree Financial Corp. contends? Given the South Carolina Supreme Court's holding, it is important to resolve that question. But we cannot do so, not simply because it is a matter of state law, but also because it is a matter for the arbitrator to decide.

[Lynn and Burt Bazzle and Green Tree entered into a contract provided that]:

> "All disputes, claims, or controversies arising from or relating to this contract or the relationships which result from this contract ... *shall be resolved by binding arbitration by one arbitrator selected by us with consent of you*. This arbitration contract is made pursuant to a transaction in interstate commerce, and shall be governed by the Federal Arbitration Act.... THE PARTIES VOLUNTARILY AND KNOWINGLY WAIVE ANY RIGHT THEY HAVE TO A JURY TRIAL, EITHER PURSUANT TO ARBITRATION UNDER THIS CLAUSE OR PURSUANT TO COURT ACTION BY US (AS PROVIDED HEREIN). ... The parties agree and understand that the arbitrator shall have all powers provided by the law and the contract. These powers shall include all legal and equitable remedies, including, but not limited to, money damages, declaratory relief, and injunctive relief." ...

[Other class members signed similar agreements with Green Tree.]

In April 1997, the Bazzles asked the court to certify their claims as a class action. Green Tree sought to stay the court proceedings and compel arbitration. On January 5, 1998, the court both (1) certified a class action and (2) entered an order compelling arbitration.... Green Tree then selected an arbitrator with the Bazzles' consent. And the arbitrator, administering the proceeding as a class arbitration, eventually awarded the class $10,935,000 in statutory damages, along with attorney's fees. The trial court confirmed the award ... and Green Tree appealed to the South Carolina Court of Appeals claiming, among other things, that class arbitration was legally impermissible. ...

The South Carolina Supreme Court's determination that the contracts are silent in respect to class arbitration raises a preliminary question. Green Tree argued . . . that the contracts are not silent—that they forbid class arbitration. . . . Whether Green Tree is right about the contracts themselves presents a disputed issue of contract interpretation. . . . [Three of the dissenting Justices argue] that the contracts say that disputes "shall be resolved . . . by one arbitrator selected by us [Green Tree] with consent of you [Green Tree's customer]." . . . [and they conclude] that class arbitration is clearly inconsistent with this requirement. After all, class arbitration involves an arbitration, not simply between Green Tree and a *named customer*, but also between Green Tree and *other* (represented) customers, all taking place before the arbitrator chosen to arbitrate the initial, *named customer*'s dispute.

We do not believe, however, that the contracts' language is as clear . . . The class arbitrator *was* "selected by" Green Tree "with consent of" Green Tree's customers, the named plaintiffs. And insofar as the other class members agreed to proceed in class arbitration, they consented as well. Of course, Green Tree did *not* independently select *this* arbitrator to arbitrate its disputes with the *other* class members. But whether the contracts contain this additional requirement is a question that the literal terms of the contracts do not decide . . . Do the contracts forbid class arbitration? Given the broad authority the contracts elsewhere bestow upon the arbitrator, (. . . "all powers," including certain equitable powers "provided by the law and the contract"), the answer to this question is not completely obvious.

At the same time, we cannot automatically accept the South Carolina Supreme Court's resolution of this contract-interpretation question. Under the terms of the parties' contracts, the question—whether the agreement forbids class arbitration—is for the arbitrator to decide. The parties agreed to submit to the arbitrator "*all* disputes, claims, or controversies arising from or relating to this contract or the relationships which result from this contract." . . . And the dispute about what the arbitration contract in each case means . . . is a dispute "relating to this contract" and the resulting "relationships." Hence the parties seem to have agreed that an arbitrator, not a judge, would answer the relevant question. . . . And if there is doubt about that matter—about the " 'scope of arbitrable issues' "—we should resolve that doubt " 'in favor of arbitration.' " . . .

In certain limited circumstances, courts assume that the parties intended courts, not arbitrators, to decide a particular arbitration-related matter (in the absence of "clear and unmistakable" evidence to the contrary). . . . These limited instances typically involve matters of a kind that "contracting parties would likely have expected a court" to decide. . . . The question here—whether the contracts forbid class arbitration—does not fall into this narrow exception. It concerns neither the validity of the arbitration clause nor its applicability to the underlying dispute between the parties. Unlike *First Options*, the question is not whether the parties wanted a judge or an arbitrator to decide *whether they agreed to arbitrate a matter*. . . . Rather the relevant question here is what *kind of arbitration proceeding* the parties agreed to. . . . It concerns contract interpretation and arbitration procedures. Arbitrators are well situated to answer that question. Given these considerations, along with the arbitration contracts' sweeping language concerning the scope of the questions committed to arbitration, this matter of contract interpretation should be for the arbitrator, not the courts, to decide. . . .

The judgment of the South Carolina Supreme Court is *vacated*, and the case is *remanded* [to the arbitrator] for further proceedings.

Justice STEVENS, concurring in the judgment and dissenting in part.

The parties agreed that South Carolina law would govern their arbitration agreement. The Supreme Court of South Carolina has held as a matter of state law that class-action arbitrations are permissible if not prohibited by the applicable arbitration agreement, and that the agreement between these parties is silent on the issue. . . . There is nothing in the [FAA] that precludes either of these determinations by the Supreme Court of South Carolina. Arguably the interpretation of the parties' agreement should have been made in the first instance by the arbitrator, rather than the court. . . . Because the decision to conduct a class-action arbitration was correct as a matter of law, and because petitioner has merely challenged the merits of that decision without claiming that it was made by the wrong decision maker, there is no need to remand the case to correct that possible error.

Chief Justice REHNQUIST, with whom Justices O'CONNOR and KENNEDY join, dissenting:

The parties entered into a contract with an arbitration clause that is governed by the Federal Arbitration Act . . . The Supreme Court of South Carolina held that arbitration under the contract could proceed as a class action even though the contract does not by its terms permit class-action arbitration. . . . This determination is one for the courts, not for the arbitrator, and the holding of the Supreme Court of South Carolina contravenes the terms of the contract and is therefore pre-empted by the FAA. . . .

While the observation of the Supreme Court of South Carolina that the agreement of the parties was silent as to the availability of class-wide arbitration is literally true, the imposition of class-wide arbitration contravenes [the contract's provision about the consent of each party to the arbitrator selected]. . . . [P]etitioner had the contractual right to choose an arbitrator for each dispute with the other 3,734 individual class members . . . Petitioner may well have chosen different arbitrators for some or all of these other disputes; indeed, it would have been reasonable for petitioner to do so, in order to avoid concentrating all of the risk of substantial damages awards in the hands of a single arbitrator. . . . [T]he FAA does not prohibit parties from choosing to proceed on a class-wide basis. Here, however, the parties simply did not so choose. . . .

NOTES AND QUESTIONS

1. This ruling is unusual in the Court's modern FAA interpretation in that it is closely divided. Justice Stevens provides the critical fifth vote, but only concurs in the judgment. He refuses to join in the plurality's reasoning. How does his approach diverge from that of the plurality opinion?
2. The Chief Justice's opinion, for three members of the Court, finds that the parties did not agree to authorize a class-wide arbitration through the individual arbitration contracts. Which interpretation most likely evidences the parties' intent? What do you draw on to support your

conclusion? Were you surprised that the Supreme Court sent the case back to the arbitrators?

3. Although the three dissenting Justices conclude that the FAA preempts (or bars) the conclusion of the South Carolina court, they do so merely because they view the judgment as in conflict with their interpretation of the contract. They do not state that the FAA prohibits class-wide arbitration if permitted by state law. Instead, they expressly leave that option open for contracting parties. "[T]he FAA does not prohibit parties from choosing to proceed on a class-wide basis. Here, however, the parties simply did not so choose." What are some potential advantages and disadvantages of class-wide arbitration in these circumstances?

4. Justice Thomas separately dissented and did not join the Chief Justice's opinion. He would have affirmed the South Carolina Supreme Court's judgment because he does not believe that the FAA applies to state court proceedings. Thus, it cannot be a ground for preempting South Carolina's interpretation of a private arbitration agreement. (See *infra*, Chapter 17.H for cases on FAA preemption of state law.) Other Justices have espoused this view in earlier decisions, but most have now agreed (albeit reluctantly) with Court precedents applying the FAA to both state and federal courts. See, e.g., *Allied-Bruce Terminix Companies v. Dobson*, 513 U.S. 265, 283 (1995) (O'Connor, J., concurring) ("I continue to believe that Congress never intended the [FAA] to apply to state courts. . . . Were we writing on a clean slate, I would adhere to that view . . . But . . . more than 10 years have passed since [precedent establishing otherwise] and parties have undoubtedly made contracts in reliance on the Court's interpretation. . . . After reflection, I am persuaded by considerations of *stare decisis* . . .").

5. As you may recall from other courses, federal courts, including the Supreme Court, are restricted in construing state law. Federal courts must defer to state court interpretation of state substantive law. See *Erie v. Tompkins*, 58 S. Ct. 817 (1938). Because much of what arbitrators do is construe state contract law, federal judges have two reasons to be very deferential in reviewing arbitral decisions: for the general reasons supporting deference to arbitrators discussed earlier, and to honor the *Erie* principle.

E. "PROCEDURAL" ARBITRABILITY

How broadly should arbitrability questions be defined? When a court inquires into arbitrability issues, it may be difficult to refrain from becoming involved with the merits of the contract dispute. Given the enthusiasm of state and federal law for arbitration, this can be a difficult line for judges to walk. Judges are often cognizant of what the Supreme Court has called the "liberal federal policy favoring arbitration agreements." *Moses H. Cone Memorial Hosp. v. Mercury Constr. Corp.*, 460 U.S. 1, 24-25 (1983). Thus, "procedural" questions which grow out of a dispute, even if they bear on its final disposition, are presumptively for the arbitrator, *not* for the judge, to decide. *Green Tree Financial Corp. v. Bazzle*, No. 123 S. Ct. 2402 (2003). While an inquiry into arbitrability can delay arbitration proceedings and make dispute resolution more expensive, it serves as an important judicial safeguard on arbitration and the underlying contracting process. Given that judicial examination of the merits of any dispute sent to arbitration is extremely limited, this check at the outset may make agreements to arbitrate more palatable to courts and fairer for parties.

In *Howsam v. Dean Witter Reynolds, Inc.*, 123 S. Ct. 588, 592 (2003), the Supreme Court noted that "one might call any potentially dispositive gateway question a 'question of arbitrability,' for its answer will determine whether the underlying controversy will proceed to arbitration on the merits." The Court's unanimous opinion concluded, however, that it has defined arbitrability much more narrowly, finding the "phrase applicable in the kind of narrow circumstance where contracting parties would likely have expected a court to have decided the gateway matter." This rather circular inquiry into parties' intent after a dispute has arisen can generate confusion, but the *Howsam* Court gave a few examples. A court should decide whether an arbitration contract binds parties who did not sign the agreement and whether an arbitration agreement survives a corporate merger to bind the resulting entity. However, the Court did not find procedural matters such as whether required grievance procedures were completed prior to arbitration, or whether a party had waived its right to arbitrate, to be questions of arbitrability.

In *Howsam*, for example, Karen Howsam chose to arbitrate a dispute that arose with her brokerage firm under the National Association of Securities Dealers' ("NASD") Code of Arbitration Procedure. The Code provides that a dispute must be submitted to arbitration within six years of the occurrence or event giving rise to the dispute. The Supreme Court held that an NASD arbitrator, not a court, should apply the six-year limit to the underlying dispute to see if Ms. Howsam's arbitration submission was timely. Although the federal circuit courts had split previously on whether an arbitrator or court should determine this issue, the Court reasoned that what constitutes a question of arbitrability — presumed to be within the court's control absent party agreement to the contrary — should be narrowly construed. The Court emphasized the comparative expertise of the NASD arbitrators in construing their own time limits, and expressed hope that this outcome would advance goals of both arbitration systems and judicial systems by "secur[ing] a fair and expeditious resolution of the underlying controversy."

In sum, parties can always agree expressly that arbitrators should handle certain types of threshold questions. Under the FAA and state arbitration laws, courts give great deference to arbitrators to handle procedural matters. With the typical, broadly framed clause, arbitrators will determine any procedural questions that arise in connection with an arbitration agreement, whether they are phrased as *procedural* arbitrability questions or simply deemed not to fall into the category of "arbitrability" questions.

F. SEPARABILITY

The separability doctrine is an important limit on the authority of courts to consider the enforceability of arbitration agreements. In *Prima Paint Corp. v.*

Flood & Conklin Mfg. Co., 388 U.S. 395 (1967), a party who had signed a contract with a broad arbitration clause claimed that the entire contract was induced by fraud. The Supreme Court had to determine whether the arbitration clause should be considered separately from the underlying contract.

PRIMA PAINT CORP. v. FLOOD & CONKLIN MFG. CO.
388 U.S. 395 (1967)

[In 1964, Prima Paint purchased Flood & Conklin's ("F&C") paint business and entered into a consulting agreement with the chairman of F&C. Soon Prima Paint stopped making payments under the agreements, charging that F&C had breached both agreements by fraudulently representing that it was solvent when it intended to file for bankruptcy. F&C served a notice of intent to arbitrate. Three days before its answer to the notice was due, Prima Paint filed a lawsuit in the federal court in New York, seeking to rescind the consulting agreement as fraudulently induced. The court had subject matter jurisdiction because the parties were from New Jersey and Maryland and the dispute met the amount in controversy requirement of the diversity statute.]

JUSTICE FORTAS delivered the opinion of the Court.

This case presents the question whether the federal court or an arbitrator is to resolve a claim of "fraud in the inducement," under a contract governed by the [FAA] where there is no evidence that the contracting parties intended to withhold that issue from arbitration.

... [T]he parties agreed to a broad arbitration clause, which read in part: "Any controversy or claim arising out of or relating to this Agreement, or the breach thereof, shall be settled by arbitration in the City of New York, in accordance with the rules then obtaining of the American Arbitration Association. . . ." . . .

Having determined that the contract in question is within the coverage of the Arbitration Act [because the underlying transaction involved interstate commerce], we turn to the central issue in this case: whether a claim of fraud in the inducement of the entire contract is to be resolved by the federal court, or whether the matter is to be referred to the arbitrators. The courts of appeals have differed in their approach to this question. The view of the Court of Appeals for the Second Circuit . . . is that—*except where the parties otherwise intend*—arbitration clauses as a matter of federal law are "separable" from the contracts in which they are embedded, and that where no claim is made that fraud was directed to the arbitration clause itself, a broad arbitration clause will be held to encompass arbitration of the claim that the contract itself was induced by fraud. . . . The Court of Appeals for the First Circuit, on the other hand, has taken the view that the question of "severability" is one of state law, and that where a State regards such a clause as inseparable a claim of fraud in the inducement must be decided by the court . . . [Under the FAA], we think that Congress has provided an explicit answer. That answer is to be found in §4 of the Act, which provides a remedy to a party seeking to compel compliance with an arbitration agreement. Under §4 . . . , the federal court is instructed to order arbitration to proceed once it is satisfied that "the making of the agreement for arbitration or the failure to comply [with the arbitration agreement] is not in issue." Accordingly, if the claim is fraud in the inducement of the arbitration clause itself — an issue which goes to the "making" of the agreement to arbitrate — the federal court may proceed to adjudicate it. But the statutory language does not permit the federal court to consider claims of fraud in the inducement of the contract generally.... We hold, therefore ... that a federal court may consider only issues relating to the making and performance of the agreement to arbitrate. In so concluding, we not only honor the plain meaning of the statute but also the unmistakably clear congressional purpose that the arbitration procedure, when selected by the parties to a contract, be speedy and not subject to delay and obstruction in the courts.

[The Court further concluded that such a rule was constitutionally permissible.]

... Accordingly, the decision below dismissing Prima Paint's appeal is *affirmed*.

Justice BLACK, with whom Justice DOUGLAS and STEWART join, dissenting:

The Court here holds that the [FAA] ... compels a party to a contract containing a written arbitration provision to carry out his "arbitration agreement" even though a court might, after a fair trial, hold the entire contract — including the arbitration agreement — void because of fraud in the inducement. The Court holds, what is to me fantastic, that the legal issue of a contract's voidness because of fraud is to be decided by persons designated to arbitrate factual controversies arising out of a valid contract between the parties. And the arbitrators who the Court holds are to adjudicate the legal validity of the contract need not even be lawyers, and in all probability will be nonlawyers, wholly unqualified to decide legal issues, and even if qualified to apply the law, not bound to do so. I am by no means sure that thus forcing a person to forgo his opportunity to try his legal issues in the courts where, unlike the situation in arbitration, he may have a jury trial and right to appeal, is not a denial of due process of law. I am satisfied, however, that Congress did not impose any such procedures in the [FAA]. And I am fully satisfied that a reasonable and fair reading of that Act's language and history shows that both Congress and the framers of the Act were at great pains to emphasize that nonlawyers designated to adjust and arbitrate factual controversies arising out of valid contracts would not trespass upon the courts' prerogative to decide the legal question of whether any legal contract exists upon which to base an arbitration....

NOTES AND QUESTIONS

1. As the dissenters point out, the Court's holding means that arbitrators will often resolve rather arcane contractual and jurisdictional issues. This could be viewed as a positive or negative development, depending on your client's claim and the quality of the arbitrators selected. What are some of the positive and negative aspects of leaving such technicalities to arbitrators?

2. Courts look to state contract law to interpret parties' agreements, and most states recognize some form of the separability doctrine. The Uniform

Arbitration Act also incorporates this principle. A comment on the practical impact of the separability doctrine:

There was a time not so long ago when courts would single out a clause of a business contract calling for arbitration of any disputes under that contract for the specific purpose of striking the arbitration clause down. Now, the tables have effectively turned: Courts will enforce a commercial arbitration agreement under federal or state law even if there are allegations that the contract of which it is a part is unenforceable, so long as there are no valid defenses to the arbitration agreement itself (such as a misrepresentation of the nature or content of that arbitration agreement, or unconscionable arbitration procedures). That's a relatively rare case in the commercial world.

Under the typical broadly framed arbitration provision . . . virtually any defense relating to the overall contract—material breach, mutual mistake, fraud—you name it—is a matter for the arbitrators to decide. Some people have problems with the separability concept because it means that arbitrators determine the viability and enforceability of the contract under which they are empowered. On the other hand, the separability principle substantially reduces the likelihood of a party running to court to challenge an arbitration agreement on the eve of arbitration.

Stipanowich and Kaskell (2001) (quoting member of the CPR Commission on the Future of Arbitration).

3. Outside of the business-to-business context, courts might be more willing to examine circumstances more closely (i.e., be less concerned about violating the separability doctrine) to conclude that the arbitration agreement itself was a product of misrepresentation or was unconscionable because of the disparate bargaining power of the parties (see Chapter 18).

G.   THE "PUBLIC POLICY" LIMITATION

Until recently, it was thought that the role of arbitration should be primarily confined to the interpretation of contracts. While arbitration was common for "private law" conflicts involving common law issues, it was not deemed amenable for resolving "public law" issues (i.e., rights created by the legislature, including federal antitrust or civil rights claims). "Less than twenty years ago, the concept of arbitrating federally created rights . . . was virtually unthinkable" (Offenkrantz, 1997). Certainly this was true in commercial arbitration, where arbitration in U.S. legal circles originated. It was also the case in labor arbitration, where the primary responsibility of the arbitrator has always been to interpret the collective bargaining agreement between the unions and the employer. Many arbitrators are not lawyers, and it was thought inappropriate to have them consider complex statutory claims, particularly when any legal decision they reached was not subject to a more public court process and appellate review.

An illustration of judicial unwillingness to allow arbitration of statutory claims is *Wilko v. Swan*, 346 U.S. 427 (1953). Although the FAA had been in existence since 1925, the *Wilko* Court held that an agreement to arbitrate disputes arising under the Securities Act of 1933 was unenforceable, because the Act prohibited waiver of "compliance with any provision of this title," which the court interpreted as including the right to a judicial forum to resolve any disputes. The Court noted that arbitrators do not receive "judicial instruction on the law," "their award may be made without explanation of their reasons and without a complete record," and "the arbitrators' conception of the legal meaning of . . . statutory requirements" is not subject to judicial review. As Professor Judith Resnik summarizes:

> Three assumptions, central to *Wilko*, were key to its intellectual framework. First, arbitration was assumed to be something *different* from and less loyal to law than adjudication. Second, public judgments rendered by federal trial courts on factual questions, such as the claim of fraudulent inducement of a client by a firm to purchase stock, in individual cases, were viewed as desirable *mechanisms* of social regulation. Third, the judiciary viewed with skepticism the agreements of parties; parties' agreements were *insufficient*, in and of themselves, to valorize all the decisions embodied in those agreements.

Resnik (1995). For nearly 30 years, this reasoning served as "public policy" limitation on submitting federal statutory claims to arbitration. However, the attitude of the Supreme Court toward arbitration of federal statutory claims shifted dramatically in the mid-1980s. Consider the following cases.

MITSUBISHI MOTORS CORP. v. SOLER CHRYSLER-PLYMOUTH, INC.

473 U.S. 614 (1985)

[Mitsubishi, an auto manufacturer, brought an action in federal court against one of its dealers (Soler), to compel arbitration of a variety of claims for breach of contract. The contract contained a clause requiring arbitration by the Japan Commercial Arbitration Association of all disputes arising under the contract. Soler filed an answer and counterclaim alleging violation of the Sherman Antitrust Act as well as other causes of action. The district court ordered arbitration of most of the claims, including the federal antitrust issues. The Court of Appeals reversed the order compelling arbitration of the antitrust claim, relying on *American Safety Equipment Corp. v. J.P. Maguire & Co.*, 391 F.2d 821 (2d Cir. 1968), which held that rights conferred by the antitrust laws are inappropriate for arbitration.]

JUSTICE BLACKMUN delivered the opinion of the Court.

. . . [W]e find no warrant in the Arbitration Act for implying in every contract within its ken a presumption against arbitration of statutory claims. . . .

By agreeing to arbitrate a statutory claim, a party does not forgo the substantive rights afforded by the statute; it only submits to their resolution in an arbitral, rather than a judicial, forum. It trades the procedures and opportunity for review of the courtroom for the simplicity, informality, and expedition of arbitration (emphasis added). We must assume that if Congress intended the substantive protection afforded by a given statute to include protection against waiver of the right to a judicial forum, that intention will be deducible from text or legislative history.

Having made the bargain to arbitrate, the party should be held to it unless Congress itself has evinced an intention to preclude a waiver of judicial remedies for the statutory rights at issue. Nothing, in the meantime, prevents a party from excluding statutory claims from the scope of an agreement to arbitrate. . . .

We now turn to consider whether Soler's antitrust claims are nonarbitrable even though it has agreed to arbitrate them. In holding that they are not, the Court of Appeals followed the decision of the Second Circuit in *American Safety Equipment Corp. v. J.P. Maguire & Co.*, 391 F.2d 821 (1968). Notwithstanding the absence of any explicit support for such an exception in either the Sherman Act or the Federal Arbitration Act, the Second Circuit there reasoned that "the pervasive public interest in enforcement of the antitrust laws, and the nature of the claims that arise in such cases, combine to make . . . antitrust claims . . . inappropriate for arbitration." . . .

At the outset, we confess to some skepticism of certain aspects of the *American Safety* doctrine. As distilled by the First Circuit, the doctrine comprises four ingredients. First, private parties play a pivotal role in aiding governmental enforcement of the antitrust laws by means of the private action for treble damages. Second, "the strong possibility that contracts which generate antitrust disputes may be contracts of adhesion militates against automatic forum determination by contract." Third, antitrust issues, prone to complication, require sophisticated legal and economic analysis, and thus are "ill-adapted to strengths of the arbitral process, i.e., expedition, minimal requirements of written rationale, simplicity, resort to basic concepts of common sense and simple equity." Finally, just as "issues of war and peace are too important to be vested in the generals, . . . decisions as to antitrust regulation of business are too important to be lodged in arbitrators chosen from the business community — particularly those from a foreign community that has had no experience with or exposure to our law and values."

Initially, we find the second concern unjustified. The mere appearance of an antitrust dispute does not alone warrant invalidation of the selected forum on the undemonstrated assumption that the arbitration clause is tainted. A party resisting arbitration of course may attack directly the validity of the agreement to arbitrate . . . But absent such a showing — and none was attempted here — there is no basis for assuming the forum inadequate or its selection unfair.

Next, potential complexity should not suffice to ward off arbitration. We might well have some doubt that even the courts following *American Safety* subscribe fully to the view that antitrust matters are inherently insusceptible to resolution by arbitration, as these same courts have agreed that an undertaking to arbitrate antitrust claims entered into *after* the dispute arises is acceptable. And the vertical restraints which most frequently give birth to antitrust claims covered by an arbitration agreement will not often occasion the monstrous proceedings that have given antitrust litigation an image of intractability. In any event, adaptability and access to expertise are hallmarks of arbitration. The anticipated subject matter of the dispute may be taken into account when the arbitrators are appointed, and arbitral rules typically provide for the participation of experts either employed by the parties or appointed by the tribunal. Moreover, it is often a judgment that streamlined proceedings and expeditious results will best serve their needs that causes parties to agree to arbitrate their disputes; it is typically a desire to keep the effort and expense required to resolve a dispute within manageable bounds that prompts them mutually to forgo access to judicial remedies. In sum, the factor of potential complexity alone does not persuade us that an arbitral tribunal could not properly handle an antitrust matter. . . .

For similar reasons, we also reject the proposition that an arbitration panel will pose too great a danger of innate hostility to the constraints on business conduct that antitrust law imposes. International arbitrators frequently are drawn from the legal as well as the business community; where the dispute has an important legal component, the parties and the arbitral body with whose assistance they have agreed to settle their dispute can be expected to select arbitrators accordingly. We decline to indulge the presumption that the parties and arbitral body conducting a proceeding will be unable or unwilling to retain competent, conscientious, and impartial arbitrators. . . .

We are left, then, with the core of the *American Safety* doctrine — the fundamental importance to American democratic capitalism of the regime of the antitrust laws. As the Court of Appeals pointed out:

"'A claim under the antitrust laws is not merely a private matter. The Sherman Act is designed to promote the national interest in a competitive economy; thus, the plaintiff asserting his rights under the Act has been likened to a private attorney-general who protects the public's interest.'" 723 F.2d at 168, quoting *American Safety*, 391 F.2d at 826.

The treble-damages provision wielded by the private litigant is a chief tool in the antitrust enforcement scheme, posing a crucial deterrent to potential violators.

The importance of the private damages remedy, however, does not compel the conclusion that it may not be sought outside an American court. . . . Having permitted the arbitration to go forward, the national courts of the United States will have the opportunity at the award-enforcement stage to ensure that the legitimate interest in the enforcement of the antitrust laws has been addressed. . . .

The judgment of the Court of Appeals is affirmed in part and reversed in part, and the cases are remanded for further proceedings consistent with this opinion.

Justice STEVENS filed a dissenting opinion.

. . . This Court agrees with the Court of Appeals' interpretation of the scope of the arbitration clause, but disagrees with its conclusion that the clause is unenforceable insofar as it purports to cover an antitrust claim against a Japanese company. This Court's holding rests almost exclusively on the federal policy favoring arbitration of commercial disputes and vague notions of international comity arising from the fact that the automobiles involved here were manufactured in Japan. . . . The plain language [of the FAA] encompasses Soler's claims that arise out of its contract with Mitsubishi, but does not encompass a claim arising under federal law, or indeed one that arises under its distributor agreement with Chrysler. Nothing in the text of the 1925 Act, nor its legislative history, suggests that Congress intended to authorize the arbitration of any statutory claims. . . .[11]

---

11. In his dissent in [*Prima Paint, supra*], Justice Black quoted the following commentary written shortly after the statute was passed:

"Not all questions arising out of contracts ought to be arbitrated. It is a remedy peculiarly suited to the disposition of the ordinary disputes between merchants as to questions of

Until today all of our cases enforcing agreements to arbitrate under the [FAA] have involved contract claims . . . [T]his is the first time the Court has considered the question whether a standard arbitration clause referring to claims arising out of or relating to a contract should be construed to cover statutory claims that have only an indirect relationship to the contract. In my opinion, neither the Congress that enacted the Arbitration Act in 1925, nor the many parties who have agreed to such standard clauses, could have anticipated the Court's answer to that question. . . .

"Arbitral procedures, while well suited to the resolution of contractual disputes, make arbitration a comparatively inappropriate forum for the final resolution of rights created by [statute]. This conclusion rests first on the special role of the arbitrator, whose task is to effectuate the intent of the parties rather than the requirements of enacted legislation . . . [T]he specialized competence of arbitrators pertains to the law of the shop, not the law of the land . . ." (quoting *Alexander v. Gardner-Denver*, 415 U.S. 36, 56–57 (1974)).

[T]he informal procedures which make arbitration so desirable in the context of contractual disputes are inadequate to develop a record for appellate review of statutory questions. Such review is essential on matters of statutory interpretation in order to assure consistent application of important public rights.[14] . . . "Finally, not only are arbitral procedures less protective of individual statutory rights than are judicial procedures, but arbitrators very often are powerless to grant the aggrieved employees as broad a range of relief." . . .

The Sherman and Clayton Acts reflect Congress' appraisal of the value of economic freedom; they guarantee the vitality of the entrepreneurial spirit. Questions arising under these Acts are among the most important in public law. . . . The provision for mandatory treble damages—unique in federal law when the statute was enacted—provides a special incentive to the private enforcement of the statute. . . .

There are . . . several unusual features of the antitrust enforcement scheme that unequivocally require rejection of any thought that Congress would tolerate private arbitration of antitrust claims in lieu of the statutory remedies that it fashioned. . . .

In view of the history of antitrust enforcement in the United States, it is not surprising that all of the federal courts that have considered the question have uniformly and unhesitatingly concluded that agreements to arbitrate federal antitrust issues are not enforceable. . . .

This Court would be well advised to endorse the collective wisdom of the distinguished judges of the Courts of Appeals who have unanimously concluded that the statutory remedies fashioned by Congress for the enforcement of the antitrust laws render an agreement to arbitrate antitrust disputes unenforceable . . . Despotic decision making of this kind is fine for parties who are willing to agree in advance to settle for a best approximation of

---

fact—quantity, quality, time of delivery, compliance with terms of payment, excuses for non-performance, and the like. It has a place also in the determination of the simpler questions of law—the questions of law which arise out of these daily relations between merchants as to the passage of title, the existence of warranties . . ." Cohen & Dayton, *The New Federal Arbitration Law*, 12 Va. L. Rev. 265, 281 (1926).

14. "Moreover, the factfinding process in arbitration usually is not equivalent to judicial factfinding. The record of the arbitration proceedings is not as complete; the usual rules of evidence do not apply; and rights and procedures common to civil trials, such as discovery, compulsory process, cross-examination, and testimony under oath, are often severely limited or unavailable."

the correct result in order to resolve quickly and inexpensively any contractual dispute that may arise in an ongoing commercial relationship. Such informality, however, is simply unacceptable when every error may have devastating consequences for important businesses in our national economy and may undermine their ability to compete in world markets. Instead of "muffling a grievance in the cloakroom of arbitration," the public interest in free competitive markets would be better served by having the issues resolved "in the light of impartial public court adjudication."

NOTES AND QUESTIONS

1.   This case involved an antitrust claim arising in the international context. Would the result be different if the case had involved a wholly domestic dispute where a party sought to compel arbitration of an antitrust claim? Is the *American Safety* doctrine, which holds that domestic antitrust claims are not subject to arbitration, still good law? How does the increasingly global nature of commerce influence your thinking about the assumptions of the Justices in *Mitsubishi*?

2.   Who would the arbitrators be in this dispute? They would likely be Japanese. They *might* be lawyers. How familiar would they be with, and supportive of, U.S. antitrust law? If the parties agreed in advance to use what Justice Stevens termed "despotic" decision makers (arbitrators), why should U.S. courts be concerned?

3.   Two years after *Mitsubishi* the Court held that statutory claims arising under the Racketeer Influenced and Corrupt Organizations Act (RICO) are subject to mandatory arbitration. See *Shearson/American Express, Inc. v. McMahon*, 482 U.S. 220 (1987) (finding no basis for concluding that Congress intended to prevent enforcement of agreements to arbitrate RICO claims and concluding that a RICO claim can be effectively vindicated in an arbitral forum).

4.   *Shearson/American Express v. McMahon* also held that claims under the Securities Act of 1934 are subject to mandatory arbitration, rejecting the reasoning of *Wilko v. Swan*, 346 U.S. 427 (1953), which held that claims arising under the Securities Act of 1933 were not subject to mandatory arbitration. Not suprisingly, the Court overruled *Wilko* two years later in *Rodriguez de Quijas v. Shearson/American Express, Inc.*, 490 U.S. 477 (1989). The following case narrowed the so-called "public policy" limitation further.

GILMER v. INTERSTATE/JOHNSON LANE CORP.
500 U.S. 20 (1991)

[Robert Gilmer was employed by defendant as a Manager of Financial Services, which required him to register as a securities representative with the New York Stock Exchange (NYSE). His registration application provided that he agreed to arbitrate "any dispute, claim or controversy" arising between him and his employer. After Interstate terminated Gilmer's employment in 1987, at which time Gilmer was 62 years of age, he filed an action in federal court under the Age Discrimination in Employment Act (ADEA). Interstate filed a motion to compel arbitration pursuant to the NYSE rules. The Fourth Circuit ruled in favor of Interstate that the dispute should be resolved by arbitration.]

JUSTICE WHITE delivered the opinion of the Court.

... Congress enacted the ADEA in 1967 "to promote employment of older persons based on their ability rather than age; to prohibit arbitrary age discrimination in employment; [and] to help employers and workers find ways of meeting problems arising from the impact of age on employment." To achieve those goals, the ADEA, among other things, makes it unlawful for an employer "to fail or refuse to hire or to discharge any individual or otherwise discriminate against any individual with respect to his compensation, terms, conditions, or privileges of employment, because of such individual's age." ...

As Gilmer contends, the ADEA is designed not only to address individual grievances, but also to further important social policies. We do not perceive any inherent inconsistency between those policies, however, and enforcing agreements to arbitrate age discrimination claims. It is true that arbitration focuses on specific disputes between the parties involved. The same can be said, however, of judicial resolution of claims. Both of these dispute resolution mechanisms nevertheless also can further broader social purposes. ...

We also are unpersuaded by the argument that arbitration will undermine the role of the EEOC in enforcing the ADEA. An individual ADEA claimant subject to an arbitration agreement will still be free to file a charge with the EEOC, even though the claimant is not able to institute a private judicial action. ...

Gilmer also argues that compulsory arbitration is improper because it deprives claimants of the judicial forum provided for by the ADEA. Congress, however, did not explicitly preclude arbitration or other nonjudicial resolution of claims, even in its recent amendments to the ADEA ... Moreover, Gilmer's argument ignores the ADEA's flexible approach to resolution of claims. The EEOC, for example, is directed to pursue "informal methods of conciliation, conference, and persuasion," which suggests that out-of-court dispute resolution, such as arbitration, is consistent with the statutory scheme established by Congress. ...

In arguing that arbitration is inconsistent with the ADEA, Gilmer also raises a host of challenges to the adequacy of arbitration procedures. Initially, we note that in our recent arbitration cases we have already rejected most of these arguments as insufficient to preclude arbitration of statutory claims. ...

Gilmer first speculates that arbitration panels will be biased. However, "[w]e decline to indulge the presumption that the parties and arbitral body conducting a proceeding will be unable or unwilling to retain competent, conscientious and impartial arbitrators." ...

Gilmer also complains that the discovery allowed in arbitration is more limited than in the federal courts, which he contends will make it difficult to prove discrimination. It is unlikely, however, that age discrimination claims require more extensive discovery than other claims that we have found to be arbitrable, such as RICO and antitrust claims. ...

A further alleged deficiency of arbitration is that arbitrators often will not issue written opinions, resulting, Gilmer contends, in a lack of public knowledge of employers' discriminatory policies, an inability to obtain effective appellate review, and a stifling of the development of the law. The NYSE rules, however, do require that all arbitration awards be in writing, and that the awards contain the names of the parties, a summary of the issues in controversy, and a description of the award issued. In addition, the award decisions are made available to the public. Furthermore, judicial decisions addressing ADEA claims will continue to be issued because it is unlikely that all or even most ADEA claimants will be subject to arbitration agreements. Finally, Gilmer's concerns apply equally to settlements of ADEA claims, which, as noted above, are clearly allowed. . . .

It is also argued that arbitration procedures cannot adequately further the purposes of the ADEA because they do not provide for broad equitable relief and class actions. As the court below noted, however, arbitrators do have the power to fashion equitable relief. Indeed, the NYSE rules applicable here do not restrict the types of relief an arbitrator may award, but merely refer to "damages and/or other relief." But "even if the arbitration could not go forward as a class action or class relief could not be granted by the arbitrator, the fact that the [ADEA] provides for the possibility of bringing a collective action does not mean that individual attempts at conciliation were intended to be barred." *Nicholson v. CPC Int'l Inc.*, 877 F.2d 221, 241 (CA3 1989) (Becker, J., dissenting). Finally, it should be remembered that arbitration agreements will not preclude the *EEOC* from bringing actions seeking class-wide and equitable relief.

An additional reason advanced by Gilmer for refusing to enforce arbitration agreements relating to ADEA claims is his contention that there often will be unequal bargaining power between employers and employees. Mere inequality in bargaining power, however, is not a sufficient reason to hold that arbitration agreements are never enforceable in the employment context. Relationships between securities dealers and investors, for example, may involve unequal bargaining power, but we nevertheless held in *Rodriguez de Quijas* and *McMahon* that agreements to arbitrate in that context are enforceable. As discussed above, the FAA's purpose was to place arbitration agreements on the same footing as other contracts. Thus, arbitration agreements are enforceable "save upon such grounds as exist at law or in equity for the revocation of any contract." 9 U.S.C. §2. "Of course, courts should remain attuned to well-supported claims that the agreement to arbitrate resulted from the sort of fraud or overwhelming economic power that would provide grounds 'for the revocation of any contract.'" *Mitsubishi*, 473 U.S. at 627, 105 S. Ct. at 3354. There is no indication in this case, however, that Gilmer, an experienced businessman, was coerced or defrauded into agreeing to the arbitration clause in his registration application. As with the claimed procedural inadequacies discussed above, this claim of unequal bargaining power is best left for resolution in specific cases. . . .

We conclude that Gilmer has not met his burden of showing that Congress, in enacting the ADEA, intended to preclude arbitration of claims under that Act. Accordingly, the judgment of the Court of Appeals is *Affirmed*.

Justice STEVENS filed a dissenting opinion.

. . . There is little dispute that the primary concern animating the FAA was the perceived need by the business community to overturn the common-law rule that denied specific enforcement of agreements to arbitrate in contracts between business entities. . . . At the [legislative hearing regarding the FAA], Senator Walsh stated:

> "The trouble about the matter is that a great many of these contracts that are entered into are really not [voluntary] things at all. Take an insurance policy;

there is a blank in it. You can take that or you can leave it. . . . It is the same with a good many contracts of employment. A man says, 'These are our terms. All right, take it or leave it.' Well, there is nothing for the man to do except to sign it; and then he surrenders his right to have his case tried by the court, and has to have it tried before a tribunal in which he has no confidence at all." . . .

Not only would I find that the FAA does not apply to employment-related disputes between employers and employees in general [based on construction of section 1 of the Act], but also I would hold that compulsory arbitration conflicts with the congressional purpose animating the ADEA . . . [A]uthorizing the courts to issue broad injunctive relief is the cornerstone to eliminating discrimination in society. . . . Because commercial arbitration is typically limited to a specific dispute between the particular parties and because the available remedies in arbitral forums do not provide for class-wide injunctive relief, . . . an essential purpose of the ADEA is frustrated by compulsory arbitration of employment discrimination claims. Moreover, as Chief Justice Burger explained:

"Plainly, it would not comport with the congressional objectives behind a statute seeking to enforce civil rights protected by Title VII to allow the very forces that had practiced discrimination to contract away the right to enforce civil rights in the courts. For federal courts to defer to arbitral decisions reached by the same combination of forces that had long perpetuated discrimination would have made the foxes guardians of the chickens."

NOTES AND QUESTIONS

1. Did Congress intend the FAA to apply to employment disputes such as Gilmer's ADEA claim? The FAA provides in Section 1 that "nothing herein contained shall apply to contracts of seamen, railroad employees, or any other class of workers engaged in foreign or interstate commerce." Doesn't this mean that arbitration clauses cannot bind employees whose work involves interstate commerce, as Gilmer's surely did? The Court refused to address the question in *Gilmer* but resolved it 10 years later in *Circuit City Stores v. Adams*, 532 U.S. 105 (2001). There the Court held that section 1 exempts from the FAA only employment contracts of transportation work-ers, not contracts of employees generally even though their work may involve interstate commerce.

2. Doesn't the *Gilmer* decision conflict with *Alexander v. Gardner-Denver Co.*, 415 U.S. 36 (1974), which held that even though an employment dispute has been arbitrated pursuant to a collective bargaining agreement the employee is not precluded from filing a subsequent lawsuit for employ-ment discrimination under Title VII? Doesn't this suggest that an employee's statutory rights against discrimination in employment are not subject to mandatory arbitration? The Court in *Gilmer* distinguished the *Alexander* case on three grounds: (1) The arbitration clause in *Alexander* authorized arbitration only of claims under the collective bargaining agree-ment, not statutory claims; (2) the claimant in *Alexander* was represented by his union in the arbitration proceeding rather than proceeding individu-ally; and (3) *Alexander* was not decided under the FAA.

3. What role does the EEOC have in pursuing ADEA claims in light of the *Gilmer* decision? Can administrative or class relief be sought in addition to individual arbitration of Mr. Gilmer's claims?
4. What changed between *Wilko* and *Gilmer* about the Supreme Court's assumptions animating the public policy limitation on arbitration of federal statutory claims? Why do you find the majority or dissent persuasive in *Gilmer*? Would it make any difference to know that Mr. Gilmer eventually was awarded $200,000 in arbitration? The cases in Chapter 18 develop further the arguments over parties' relative lack of bargaining power, fraud, adhesion, and unconscionability.

H. PREEMPTION OF STATE LAW BY THE FEDERAL ARBITRATION ACT

One further consideration in applying the FAA is the preemption law developed by courts in examining the complex interplay of federal and state law in the arbitration field. In the 1980s and 1990s, the Supreme Court spent a significant portion of its time and effort determining controversies about the scope and force of the Federal Arbitration Act, as it construed the FAA broadly to cover arbitration of statutory claims and displaced the traditional role of state law in this area. These decisions conflict with what the Court has done during the same period in many other areas of law, as it delegated more power to States and reined in the role of federal law.[16] Two commentators explain why the Court, in this series of "bold" decisions, rewrote the law governing arbitration:

> The Court's aggression has been the product of two worthy but overindulged impulses. One impulse has been to encourage international trade by enforcing dispute resolution provisions in international commercial contracts. The second has been to conserve scarce judicial resources by encouraging citizens to resolve disputes by private means.

Carrington and Haagen (1996).

Moreover, the Court has expressed strong unanimity in many of these rulings, and frequently issued *per curiam* decisions. The agreement among the Justices in interpreting the FAA contrasts sharply with its 5-4 rulings in many areas of constitutional law, including other federalism decisions. The Court may reason that, in interpreting congressional intent, it can — at least in theory — rely on Congress to revise the FAA if the Court misconstrues its scope and import.

As noted above, most States adopted versions of the Uniform Arbitration Act after Congress enacted the FAA. However, the operational scope of these statutes is now significantly qualified by the following Supreme Court decision.

---

16. Kloppenberg (2001) and Noonan (2002).

SOUTHLAND CORP. v. KEATING
465 U.S. 1 (1984)

[The Southland Corporation, which is the franchisor of 7-Eleven convenience stores, had an arbitration clause in its standard franchise agreements requiring arbitration of "any controversy or claim arising out of or relating to this agreement." Keating, a franchisee, filed a class action against Southland on behalf of approximately 800 California franchisees alleging fraud, oral misrepresentations, breach of contract, breach of fiduciary duty, and violation of the disclosure requirements of the California Franchise Investment Law. Southland petitioned the Superior Court to compel arbitration of all claims. The trial court granted the petition and compelled arbitration, except with respect to claims based on the California Franchise Investment Law which provided as follows: "Any condition, stipulation or provision purporting to bind any person acquiring any franchise to waive compliance with any provision of this law or any rule or order hereunder is void." The California Supreme Court agreed with the trial court that the claims under the state statute were not arbitrable, and the decision was appealed to the United States Supreme Court.]

Chief JUSTICE BURGER delivered the opinion of the Court.

[We noted probable jurisdiction to consider] (a) whether the California Franchise Investment Law, which invalidates certain arbitration agreements covered by the Federal Arbitration Act, violates the Supremacy Clause. . . .

In enacting §2 of the federal Act, Congress declared a national policy favoring arbitration and withdrew the power of the states to require a judicial forum for the resolution of claims which the contracting parties agreed to resolve by arbitration. The Federal Arbitration Act provides:

> "A written provision in any maritime transaction or a contract evidencing a transaction involving commerce to settle by arbitration a controversy thereafter arising out of such contract or transaction, or the refusal to perform the whole or any part thereof, or an agreement in writing to submit to arbitration an existing controversy arising out of such a contract, transaction, or refusal, shall be valid, irrevocable, and enforceable, save upon such grounds as exist at law or in equity for the revocation of any contract." 9 U.S.C. §2 (1976).

Congress has thus mandated the enforcement of arbitration agreements.

We discern only two limitations on the enforceability of arbitration provisions governed by the Federal Arbitration Act: they must be part of a written maritime contract or a contract "evidencing a transaction involving commerce" and such clauses may be revoked upon "grounds as exist at law or in equity for the revocation of any contract." We see nothing in the Act indicating that the broad principle of enforceability is subject to any additional limitations under State law. . . .

At least since 1824 Congress' authority under the Commerce Clause has been held plenary. *Gibbons v. Ogden*, 22 U.S. 1 (1824). In the words of Chief Justice Marshall, the authority of Congress is "the power to regulate; that is, to prescribe the rule by which commerce is to be governed." Id. The statements of the Court in *Prima Paint* (388 U.S. 420) that the Arbitration Act was an exercise of the Commerce Clause power clearly implied that the substantive rules of the Act were to apply in state as well as federal courts. . . .

Although the legislative history is not without ambiguities, there are strong indications that Congress had in mind something more than making arbitration agreements enforceable only in the federal courts. The House Report plainly suggests the more comprehensive objectives:

> "The purpose of this bill is to make valid and enforceable agreements for arbitration contained *in contracts involving interstate commerce* or within the jurisdiction or admiralty, *or* which may be the subject of litigation in the Federal courts." H.R. Rep. No. 96, 68th Cong., 1st Sess. 1 (1924) (Emphasis added.).

This broader purpose can also be inferred from the reality that Congress would be less likely to address a problem whose impact was confined to federal courts than a problem of large significance in the field of commerce. The Arbitration Act sought to "overcome the rule of equity, that equity will not specifically enforce any arbitration agreement." Hearing on S. 4214 Before a Subcomm. of the Senate Comm. on the Judiciary, 67th Cong., 4th Sess. 6 (1923) ("Senate Hearing") (remarks of Sen. Walsh). The House Report accompanying the bill stated:

> "[t]he need for the law arises from . . . the jealousy of the English courts for their own jurisdiction. . . . This jealousy survived for so [long] a period that the principle became firmly embedded in the English common law and was adopted with it by the American courts. The courts have felt that the precedent was too strongly fixed to be overturned without legislative enactment. . . ." H.R. Rep. No. 96, *supra*, 1-2 (1924).

Surely this makes clear that the House Report contemplated a broad reach of the Act, unencumbered by state law constraints. . . .

The problems Congress faced were therefore twofold: the old common law hostility toward arbitration, and the failure of state arbitration statutes to mandate enforcement of arbitration agreements. To confine the scope of the Act to arbitrations sought to be enforced in federal courts would frustrate what we believe Congress intended to be a broad enactment appropriate in scope to meet the large problems Congress was addressing. . . .

In creating a substantive rule applicable in state as well as federal courts, Congress intended to foreclose state legislative attempts to undercut the enforceability of arbitration agreements. We hold that §31512 of the California Franchise Investment Law violates the Supremacy Clause. . . . The judgment of the California Supreme Court denying enforcement of the arbitration agreement is reversed. . . .

Justice O'CONNOR with whom Justice REHNQUIST joins, dissenting.

Section 2 of the Federal Arbitration Act (FAA) provides that a written arbitration agreement "shall be valid, irrevocable, and enforceable, save upon such grounds as exist at law or in equity for the revocation of any contract." Section 2 does not, on its face, identify which judicial forums are bound by its requirements or what procedures govern its enforcement. The FAA deals with these matters in §§3 and 4. Section 3 provides:

> "If any suit or proceeding be brought *in any of the courts of the United States* upon any issue referable to arbitration . . . the court . . . shall on application of one of the parties stay the trial of the action until such arbitration has been had in accordance with the terms of the agreement . . ."

Section 4 specifies that a party aggrieved by another's refusal to arbitrate "may petition *any United States district court* which, save for such agreement, would have jurisdiction under Title 28 . . . for an order directing that such arbitration proceed in the manner provided for in such agreement. . . ."

Today, the Court takes the facial silence of §2 as a license to declare that state as well as federal courts must apply §2. In addition, though this is not spelled out in the opinion, the Court holds that in enforcing this newly discovered federal right state courts must follow procedures specified in §3. The Court's decision is impelled by an understandable desire to encourage the use of arbitration, but it utterly fails to recognize the clear congressional intent underlying the FAA. Congress intended to require federal, not state, courts to respect arbitration agreements. . . . One rarely finds a legislative history as unambiguous as the FAA's. That history establishes conclusively that the 1925 Congress viewed the FAA as a procedural statute, applicable only in federal courts, derived, Congress believed, largely from the federal power to control the jurisdiction of the federal courts. . . .

If characterizing the FAA as procedural was not enough, the draftsmen of the Act, the House Report, and the early commentators all flatly stated that the Act was intended to affect only federal court proceedings. Mr. Cohen, the American Bar Association member who drafted the bill, assured two congressional subcommittees in joint hearings:

> "Nor can it be said that the Congress of the United States, *directing its own courts* . . . , would infringe upon the provinces or prerogatives of the States. . . . [T]he question of the enforcement relates to the law of remedies and not to substantive law. The rule must be changed for the jurisdiction in which the agreement is sought to be enforced. . . . There is no disposition therefore by means of the Federal bludgeon to force an individual State into an unwilling submission to arbitration enforcement." [Additional discussion of legislative history is omitted.]

Today's decision is unfaithful to congressional intent, unnecessary, and, in light of the FAA's antecedents and the intervening contraction of federal power, inexplicable. Although arbitration is a worthy alternative to litigation, today's exercise in judicial revisionism goes too far. I respectfully dissent.

NOTES AND QUESTIONS

1. The majority opinion concludes that the FAA is a substantive law based on the power of Congress under the Commerce Clause to regulate interstate commerce, and therefore it applies in both federal and state courts. The dissent argues that it is a procedural statute based upon congressional power under Article III to establish and regulate federal courts and therefore applies only in federal proceedings. Who has the better of the argument? This is a complicated area of constitutional and statutory law; if these issues intrigue you, we recommend *Constitutional Law: Principles and Policies* by Erwin Chemerinsky (2002).

2. In another part of its opinion, the majority expressed concern that interpreting the FAA to apply only in federal courts and not state courts would

"encourage and reward forum shopping." Justice O'Connor responded to this concern as follows:

> Because the FAA makes the federal courts equally accessible to both parties to a dispute, no forum shopping would be possible even if we gave the FAA a construction faithful to the congressional intent. In controversies involving incomplete diversity of citizenship there is simply no access to federal court and therefore no possibility of forum shopping. In controversies *with* complete diversity of citizenship the FAA grants federal court access equally to both parties; no party can gain any advantage by forum shopping. Even when the party resisting arbitration initiates an action in state court, the opposing party can invoke FAA §4 and promptly secure a federal court order to compel arbitration.

3. Assume the majority is right that §2 of the FAA, which makes arbitration clauses "valid, irrevocable and enforceable," creates a substantive right which state courts must enforce. Does this mean state courts are required to apply the enforcement mechanisms of the FAA, which include compelling arbitration and staying judicial proceedings? The majority apparently concluded the answer was "yes," but Justice O'Connor thought not:

> [A]bsent specific direction from Congress the state courts have always been permitted to apply their own reasonable procedures when enforcing federal rights. Before we undertake to read a set of complex and mandatory procedures into §2's brief and general language, we should at a minimum allow state courts and legislatures a chance to develop their own methods for enforcing the new federal rights. Some might choose to award compensatory or punitive damages for the violation of an arbitration agreement; some might award litigation costs to the party who remained willing to arbitrate; some might affirm the "validity and enforceability" of arbitration agreements in other ways. Any of these approaches could vindicate §2 rights in a manner fully consonant with the language and background of that provision.

4. *Southland* concludes that the enactment of the FAA was an exercise of congressional power under the Commerce Clause. How broad an exercise of that power was intended? Consider the following case.

ALLIED-BRUCE TERMINIX COMPANIES v. DOBSON
513 U.S. 265 (1995)

[The plaintiffs, Mr. and Mrs. G. William Dobson, purchased a house which had been subject to a lifetime "Termite Protection Plan" provided by Allied-Bruce Terminix. After the purchase they found the house to be severely infested with termites. They filed a lawsuit against defendant Allied-Bruce in Alabama state court. Defendant asked the court for a stay, citing the fact that the "Termite Protection Plan" contained an arbitration clause providing for arbitration of "any controversy or claim . . . arising out of or relating to the interpretation, performance or breach of any provision of this agreement." The Alabama court refused to grant the stay on the basis of a state statute making predispute arbitration agreements invalid and unenforceable. The Alabama court found the FAA inapplicable because the connection between the termite contract and interstate commerce was too slight. Despite some interstate activities (e.g., Allied-Bruce was a multistate firm and shipped treatment and repair material from out of state), the court found that the parties "contemplated" a transaction that was primarily local and not "substantially" interstate. . . . The court took the view that the FAA applied only if at the time the parties entered a contract they "contemplated substantial interstate activity."]

Justice Breyer delivered the opinion of the Court.

This case concerns the reach of §2 of the Federal Arbitration Act. That section makes enforceable a written arbitration provision in "a contract *evidencing* a transaction *involving* commerce."9 U.S.C. §2 (emphasis added). Should we read this phrase broadly, extending the Act's reach to the limits of Congress' Commerce Clause power? Or, do the two italicized words — "involving" and "evidencing" — significantly restrict the Act's application? We conclude that the broader reading of the Act is the correct one, and we reverse a State Supreme Court judgment to the contrary. . . .

After examining the statute's language, background, and structure, we conclude that the word "involving" is broad and is indeed the functional equivalent of "affecting." For one thing, such an interpretation, linguistically speaking, is permissible. The dictionary finds instances in which "involve" and "affect" sometimes can mean about the same thing. For another, the Act's legislative history, to the extent that it is informative, indicates an expansive congressional intent. . . . Further, this Court has previously described the Act's reach expansively as coinciding with that of the Commerce Clause. . . .

Finally, a broad interpretation of this language is consistent with the Act's basic purpose, to put arbitration provisions on " 'the same footing' " as a contract's other terms. Conversely, a narrower interpretation is not consistent with the Act's purpose, for (unless unreasonably narrowed to the flow of commerce) such an interpretation would create a new, unfamiliar test lying somewhere in a no man's land between "in commerce" and "affecting commerce," thereby unnecessarily complicating the law and breeding litigation from a statute that seeks to avoid it. We recognize arguments to the contrary: The pre-New Deal Congress that passed the Act in 1925 might well have thought the Commerce Clause did not stretch as far as has turned out to be the case. But, it is not unusual for this Court in similar circumstances to ask whether the scope of a statute should expand along with the expansion of the Commerce Clause power itself, and to answer the question affirmatively — as, for the reasons set forth above, we do here. . . .

Section 2 applies where there is "a contract *evidencing a transaction* involving commerce." The second interpretive question focuses on the italicized words. Does "evidencing a transaction" mean only that the transaction (that the contract "evidences") must turn out, *in fact*, to have involved interstate commerce? Or, does it mean more?

Many years ago, Second Circuit Chief Judge Lumbard said that the phrase meant considerably more. He wrote:

"The significant question . . . is not whether, in carrying out the terms of the contract, the parties *did* cross state lines, but whether, *at the time they entered into it* and accepted the arbitration clause, they *contemplated* substantial interstate activity. Cogent evidence regarding their state of mind at the time would be the terms of the contract, and if it, on its face, evidences interstate traffic . . . , the contract should come within §2. In addition, evidence as to how the parties expected the contract to be performed and how it was performed is relevant to whether substantial interstate activity was contemplated." *Metro Industrial Painting Corp. v. Terminal Constr. Co.*, 287 F.2d 382, 387 (CA2 1961) (concurring opinion).

The Supreme Court of Alabama and several other courts have followed this view, known as the "contemplation of the parties" test.

We find the interpretive choice difficult, but for several reasons we conclude that the first interpretation ("commerce in fact") is more faithful to the statute than the second ("contemplation of the parties"). First, the "contemplation of the parties" interpretation, when viewed in terms of the statute's basic purpose, seems anomalous. That interpretation invites litigation about what was, or was not, "contemplated." Why would Congress intend a test that risks the very kind of costs and delay through litigation (about the circumstances of contract formation) that Congress wrote the Act to help the parties avoid?

Moreover, that interpretation too often would turn the validity of an arbitration clause on what, from the perspective of the statute's basic purpose, seems happenstance, namely, whether the parties happened to think to insert a reference to interstate commerce in the document or happened to mention it in an initial conversation. After all, parties to a sales contract with an arbitration clause might naturally think about the goods sold, or about arbitration, but why should they naturally think about an interstate commerce connection?

Further, that interpretation fits awkwardly with the rest of §2. That section, for example, permits parties to agree to submit to arbitration "an existing controversy arising out of" a contract made earlier. Why would Congress want to risk nonenforceability of this *later* arbitration agreement (even if fully connected with interstate commerce) simply because the parties did not properly "contemplate" (or write about) the interstate aspects of the earlier contract? The first interpretation, requiring only that the "transaction" *in fact* involve interstate commerce, avoids this anomaly, as it avoids the other anomalous effects growing out of the "contemplation of the parties" test.

Second, the statute's language permits the "commerce in fact" interpretation. . . .

Third, the basic practical argument underlying the "contemplation of the parties" test was, in Chief Judge Lumbard's words, the need to "be cautious in construing the act lest we excessively encroach on the powers which Congressional policy, if not the Constitution, would reserve to the states." The practical force of this argument has diminished in light of this Court's later holdings that the Act does displace state law to the contrary. See *Southland Corp. v. Keating*. . . .

The parties do not contest that the transaction in this case, in fact, involved interstate commerce. In addition to the multistate nature of Terminix and Allied-Bruce, the termite-treating and house-repairing material used by Allied-Bruce in its (allegedly inadequate) efforts to carry out the terms of the Plan, came from outside Alabama. Consequently, the judgment of the Supreme Court of Alabama is reversed, and the case is remanded for further proceedings not inconsistent with this opinion.

Justice O'CONNOR, concurring.

I agree with the Court's construction of §2 of the Federal Arbitration Act. As applied in federal courts, the Court's interpretation comports fully with my understanding of congressional intent. A more restrictive definition of "evidencing" and "involving" would doubtless foster prearbitration litigation that would frustrate the very purpose of the statute. As applied in state courts, however, the effect of a broad formulation of §2 is more troublesome. The reading of §2 adopted today will displace many state statutes carefully calibrated to protect consumers, see, e.g., Mont. Code Ann. §27-5-114(2)(b) (1993) (refusing to enforce arbitration clauses in consumer contracts where the consideration is $5,000 or less), and state procedural requirements aimed at ensuring knowing and voluntary consent, see, e.g., S.C. Code Ann. §15-48-10(a) (Supp. 1993) (requiring that notice of arbitration provision be prominently placed on first page of contract). I have long adhered to the view, discussed below, that Congress designed the Federal Arbitration Act to apply only in federal courts. But if we are to apply the Act in state courts, it makes little sense to read §2 differently in that context. In the end, my agreement with the Court's construction of §2 rests largely on the wisdom of maintaining a uniform standard.

I continue to believe that Congress never intended the Federal Arbitration Act to apply in state courts, and that this Court has strayed far afield in giving the Act so broad a compass . . . Yet, over the past decade, the Court has abandoned all pretense of ascertaining congressional intent with respect to the Federal Arbitration Act, building instead, case by case, an edifice of its own creation. I have no doubt that Congress could enact, in the first instance, a federal arbitration statute that displaces most state arbitration laws. But I also have no doubt that, in 1925, Congress enacted no such statute.

Were we writing on a clean slate, I would adhere to that view and affirm the Alabama court's decision. But, as the Court points out, more than 10 years have passed since *Southland*, several subsequent cases have built upon its reasoning, and parties have undoubtedly made contracts in reliance on the Court's interpretation of the Act in the interim. After reflection, I am persuaded by considerations of *stare decisis*, which we have said "have special force in the area of statutory interpretation," to acquiesce in today's judgment. Though wrong, *Southland* has not proved unworkable, and, as always, "Congress remains free to alter what we have done."

Today's decision caps this Court's effort to expand the Federal Arbitration Act. Although each decision has built logically upon the decisions preceding it, the initial building block in *Southland* laid a faulty foundation. I acquiesce in today's judgment because there is no "special justification" to overrule *Southland*. *It remains now for Congress to correct this interpretation if it wishes to preserve state autonomy in state courts.*

NOTES AND QUESTIONS

1. Justice Breyer gives the FAA the broadest possible interpretation, holding that it can extend to any contracts involving matters "affecting" interstate commerce. How broad a scope is that? See *Wickard v. Filburn*, 317 U.S. 111 (1942) (giving an expansive interpretation to Commerce Clause); but see *United States v. Lopez*, 514 U.S. 549 (1995) (holding unconstitutional a federal statute prohibiting carrying of a gun within 1,000 feet of a school on grounds that it exceeded congressional authority under the Commerce Clause).

2. In *Citizen's Bank v. Alafabco, Inc.*, 123 S. Ct. 2037 (2003), the Court again construed the "commerce" requirement in the FAA broadly. There, residents of Alabama entered into debt restructuring agreements providing for arbitration. Although all parties were Alabama residents, one of the parties had engaged in business throughout the southeastern United States using loans related to the agreements. The debt was secured by goods that contained out-of-state parts and raw materials. After *Allied Bruce* and *Citizen's Bank*, what scope of operation is left for state arbitration statutes? What disputes can be viewed as involving matters that are purely intrastate?

3. In her concurring opinion, Justice O'Connor points out that the Court's broad interpretation of the FAA means that it will override statutory protections that have been enacted by state legislatures to protect their citizens from unknowing waiver of their rights by signing arbitration clauses. Consider the following case.

DOCTOR'S ASSOCIATES, INC. v. CASAROTTO
517 U.S. 681 (1996)

JUSTICE GINSBURG delivered the opinion of the Court.

This case concerns a standard form franchise agreement for the operation of a Subway sandwich shop in Montana. When a dispute arose between parties to the agreement, franchisee Paul Casarotto sued franchisor Doctor's Associates, Inc. (DAI), and DAI's Montana development agent, Nick Lombardi, in a Montana state court. DAI and Lombardi sought to stop the litigation pending arbitration pursuant to the arbitration clause set out on page nine of the franchise agreement.

The Federal Arbitration Act (FAA or Act) declares written provisions for arbitration "valid, irrevocable, and enforceable, save upon such grounds as exist at law or in equity for the revocation of any contract." 9 U.S.C. §2. Montana law, however, declares an arbitration clause unenforceable unless "[n]otice that [the] contract is subject to arbitration" is "typed in underlined capital letters on the first page of the contract." Mont. Code Ann. §27-5-114(4) (1995). The question here presented is whether Montana's law is compatible with the federal Act. We hold that Montana's first-page notice requirement, which governs not "any contract," but specifically and solely contracts "subject to arbitration," conflicts with the FAA and is therefore displaced by the federal measure. . . .

Section 2 of the FAA provides that written arbitration agreements "shall be valid, irrevocable, and enforceable, save upon such grounds as exist at law or in equity for the revocation of *any* contract." 9 U.S.C. §2 (emphasis added). . . . [S]tate law may be applied "*if* that law arose to govern issues concerning the validity, revocability, and enforceability of contracts generally." Thus, generally applicable contract defenses, such as fraud, duress, or unconscionability, may be applied to invalidate arbitration agreements without contravening §2.

Courts may not, however, invalidate arbitration agreements under state laws applicable *only* to arbitration provisions. By enacting §2, we have several times said, Congress precluded States from singling out arbitration provisions for suspect status, requiring instead that such provisions be placed "upon the same footing as other contracts." Montana's §27-5-114(4) directly conflicts with §2 of the FAA because the State's law conditions the enforceability of arbitration agreements on compliance with a special notice requirement not applicable to contracts generally. The FAA thus displaces the Montana statute with respect to arbitration agreements covered by the Act. . . .

For the reasons stated, the judgment of the Supreme Court of Montana is *reversed*, and the case is remanded for further proceedings not inconsistent with this opinion.

NOTES AND QUESTIONS

1. Do you think decisions such as *Doctor's Associates* might create occasional tensions between state judges and federal judges, at least in states that have developed special protections for consumers with respect to arbitration clauses? Consider the specially concurring opinion of Justice Trieweiler in the decision below of the Montana Supreme Court:

   > To those federal judges who consider forced arbitration as the panacea for their "heavy case loads" and who consider the reluctance of state courts to buy into the arbitration program as a sign of intellectual inadequacy, I would like to explain a few things.
   >
   > In Montana, we are reasonably civilized and have a sophisticated system of justice which has evolved over time and which we continue to develop for the primary purpose of assuring fairness to those people who are subject to its authority. . . .
   >
   > What I would like the people in the federal judiciary, especially at the appellate level, to understand is that due to their misinterpretation of congressional intent when it enacted the Federal Arbitration Act, and due to their naive assumption that arbitration provisions and choice of law provisions are knowingly bargained for, all of these procedural safeguards and substantive laws are easily avoided by any party with enough leverage to stick a choice of law and an arbitration provision in its pre-printed contract and require the party with inferior bargaining power to sign it. . . .
   >
   > [I]f the Federal Arbitration Act is to be interpreted as broadly as some of the decisions from our federal courts would suggest, then it presents a serious issue regarding separation of powers. What these interpretations do, in effect, is permit a few major corporations to draft contracts regarding their relationship with others that immunizes them from accountability under the laws of the states where they do business, and by the courts in those states.
   >
   > These insidious erosions of state authority and the judicial process threaten to undermine the rule of law as we know it.
   >
   > Nothing in our jurisprudence appears more intellectually detached from reality and arrogant than the lament of federal judges who see this system of imposed arbitration as "therapy for their crowded dockets." These decisions have perverted the purpose of the FAA from one to accomplish judicial neutrality, to one of open hostility to any legislative effort to assure that unsophisticated parties to contracts of adhesion at least understand the rights they are giving up.

   268 Mont. 369, 384-385, 886 P.2d 931, 940-941(1994).

2.   Would the result in *Doctor's Associates* be different if the franchise agreement had provided that the agreement was to be governed by Montana law? See *Volt Information Sciences, Inc. v. Stanford*, 489 U.S. 468 (1989) (holding that where an arbitration agreement contained a choice-of-law clause providing that the contract was to be governed by the law of California, it was proper for a federal district judge to apply a California statute authorizing a stay of the arbitration proceeding pending resolution of related litigation between a party to the arbitration agreement and third parties not bound by it; even though such a state statute conflicts with the FAA, it is proper to apply state law where the parties have specified that state law controls). The majority in *Doctor's Associates* suggested that *Volt* is limited to state procedural rules regulating arbitration. The majority distinguished *Volt* as follows:

> *Volt* involved an arbitration agreement that incorporated state procedural rules, one of which, on the facts of that case, called for arbitration to be stayed pending the resolution of a related judicial proceeding. The state rule examined in *Volt* determined only the efficient order of proceedings; it did not affect the enforceability of the arbitration agreement itself. . . . Applying [the Montana notice requirement], in contrast, would not enforce the arbitration clause in the contract between DAI and Casarotto; instead, Montana's first-page notice requirement would invalidate the clause. (517 U.S. at 688.)

I.   ENFORCEMENT OF AGREEMENTS

Because arbitration is a creature of contract, parties need a valid and enforceable agreement to arbitrate. As the FAA makes clear in Section 2, standard state law contract defenses can be raised to challenge arbitration agreements, including failure of consideration, no "meeting of the minds," mutual mistake, fraud, adhesion, etc. If the parties have signed a broad arbitration clause, arbitrators will hear and rule on such defenses, and the parties will have minimal recourse to judicial review of the merits of an arbitrator's ruling. The most commonly litigated contract defenses in recent years are the fairness issues associated with the increased use of arbitration to resolve disputes arising out of employment contracts and consumer transactions, explored in the next chapter.

CHAPTER
18

Fairness in Arbitration: Developments in Employment and Consumer Contexts

A. INTRODUCTION

Private dispute resolution is more than ever a fact of everyday life. Increasingly, we see binding arbitration clauses in transactions such as banking, credit card agreements, insurance policies, and sales of consumer goods. Very often people sign contracts that contain boilerplate arbitration clauses without focusing on those clauses. This has created a good deal of controversy in recent years as to the fairness of these boilerplate clauses, especially when the person signing the contract is frequently not aware of the entire package of what she is agreeing to by consenting to binding arbitration. A private arbitration process may well fall short of parties' reasonable expectations of fairness and have a dramatic impact on consumers' or employees' substantive rights and remedies.

The range of concerns raised by arbitration agreements in consumer or employment transactions include awareness of the arbitration agreement and of waiver of the right to trial; access to information about the arbitration program; the independence and impartiality of decision makers, and of the administering institution, if any; the quality of the process and the competence of arbitrators; the cost, location, and time frame of arbitration; the right to representation; the fundamental fairness of hearings; access to information (discovery); the nature of arbitral remedies, including the availability of punitive damages in cases where they would be available in court; the availability of class actions; the scope of judicial review of arbitration awards; and the availability of binding precedents for the future guidance of actors in various arenas. This chapter draws extensively on Thomas J. Stipanowich, *Contract and Conflict Management*, 2001 Wis. L. Rev. 831, to address these critical issues challenging modern arbitration.

These concerns have prompted responses at several different levels. Some arbitration institutions and other groups have responded by promulgating rules that are designed to regulate arbitration and ADR procedures in special contexts. The consensual efforts of broad-based groups representing affected public and private interests have produced several due process standards or protocols for employment and consumer arbitration and mediation. Judicial scrutiny of arbitration provisions in adhesive contracts is increasing, as are calls for federal legislation. Thus, while arbitration existed as a creature of contract traditionally, it has become more closely linked to the judicial process as courts and legislatures more willingly scrutinize the process and outcomes of arbitration. In this chapter the current landscape of conflict management in adhesion settings will be examined and different approaches to addressing fairness will be explored. We will see the themes of systemic, procedural, and outcome fairness play out against the backdrop of strong federal policies favoring the enforcement of arbitration agreements and past and present legislative, judicial, institutional, and "community" efforts to address the foregoing concerns.

B. PERCEPTIONS OF FAIRNESS

1. Fairness in Entering into Arbitration Agreements

Concerns about fairness in arbitration may often arise due to a lack of transparency in the arbitration process and a lack of an understanding about how the process works. Even a relatively sophisticated attorney may not have more than a general idea of how arbitration will proceed without knowing what particular arbitration rules are governing the process. Modern dispute resolution procedures often run to dozens of provisions covering many pages, similar to rules of procedure in the courts. Therefore the governing documents and provisions are usually only incorporated by reference in the contract, and are not always easy to locate.

This concern about understanding the arbitration process is only magnified for the consumer who first becomes aware of what arbitration is when he realizes he must submit to arbitration because of an agreement he signed with his bank or a credit card company. Many consumers are unaware that by signing agreements with arbitration clauses, they are agreeing to forgo rights to trials and fuller judicial review. These concerns have prompted a variety of academic commentary, state legislative measures, and court decisions addressing the enforceability, formation, and contents of arbitration agreements. Given the growing use of arbitration, courts and legislatures have been attempting to make arbitration a more "user-friendly" process for the legal and nonlegal communities alike.

Some legislatures, members of the judiciary, and arbitration providers have attempted to make the problematic "grey areas" less troublesome by more clearly defining issues, but—as with many legal issues—clarification is never as easy as one would wish. For example, legislatures and courts have stated that an illusory arbitration agreement will not be enforceable. An agreement is illusory if it is subject to change by one party absent the consent of the other party. The following cases show two different perspectives about what constitutes consent to arbitrate a dispute that may arise in the future between parties.

AMERICAN HERITAGE LIFE INS. CO. v. ORR
294 F.3d 702 (5th Cir. 2002)

[John Orr and others ("Appellants") obtained consumer loans from Republic Finance. When they entered into loan agreements with Republic, they were also sold disability life insurance to insure against the risks of sickness and death. American Heritage was the insurer for these policies. At the loan closings Appellants and Republic Finance signed an arbitration agreement, to which American Heritage was not a signatory. Appellants later filed suit in a state court alleging among other things that American Heritage conspired with Republic to sell unnecessary insurance at inflated rates. American Heritage brought suit in a U.S. District Court, seeking to compel arbitration. The District Court held, among other things, that Appellants did not offer suffi- cient evidence to support a jury trial demand for resolution of the factual issues. It issued an order compelling arbitration, which also stayed the state court proceedings filed by Appellants. Appellants then appealed to the 5th Circuit.]

Judge LITTLE delivered the opinion of the court:
. . . Appellants maintain that under §§2 & 4 of the FAA, they are entitled to a trial by jury on the issue of arbitrability. . . .

1. Right to a Jury Trial Under §4 of the FAA

Appellants contend that they deserve a jury trial on the question of the validity of the Agreements. Specifically, by alleging that the Agreements are unconscionable, the products of unequal bargaining power between the par- ties, lacking mutuality of obligation between the parties, and failing to result in a meeting of the minds, Appellants argue that they have put the "making" of the Agreements in issue, thereby complying with §4 of the FAA. The district court held, however, that the issues raised by Appellants relate to enforceability of the Agreements, but do not impact the "making of the arbitration" agree- ment. We agree with the district court's holding and rationale.

Although the FAA permits parties to demand a jury trial to resolve factual issues surrounding the making of an arbitration agreement, or the failure, neglect, or refusal to perform the agreement, it is well-established that "[a] party to an arbitration agreement cannot obtain a jury trial merely by demanding one." . . .

. . . In the instant case, Appellants submitted evidence in the form of affida- vits that claim, *inter alia*, that Appellees did not explain the Agreements to Appellants or that Appellants did not realize that they were waiving a trial by jury. The affidavits proffered by Appellants, however, amount to nothing more than hollow, bald assertions that do not approach fraud in the "making" of the Agreements. . . . Furthermore, Appellants' affidavits fail to identify any misrep- resentation by Appellees peculiar to the Agreements, which forecloses Appellants' ability to state a claim of fraud in the inducement. . . . Other than their self-serving affidavits, Appellants have not submitted a whisper of evidence to support the conclusion that a jury trial is warranted under §4 of the FAA. Raising issues of the Agreements' procedural or substantive uncon- scionability, as Appellants have in the instant case, is not the equivalent of questioning the "making" of an arbitration agreement. . . . Under §4 of the FAA and [precedent], therefore, Appellants have not met their burden to show their entitlement to a jury trial.

2.   The Seventh Amendment Right to a Trial by Jury

Next, Appellants claim that by forcing them to submit their claims to an arbitrator, the district court deprived them of their Seventh Amendment right to a trial by jury. Appellants suggest that the waiver of a constitutional right should be closely scrutinized, and that a waiver of jury trial rights must be clearly and unmistakably expressed.

Appellants' argument is without foundation. First, we point out that Appellants agreed to submit to arbitration because they assented to the terms of the Agreements, which contained the following clause, located just above the signature lines:

THE PARTIES UNDERSTAND THAT BY SIGNING THIS ARBITRATION AGREEMENT, THEY ARE LIMITING ANY RIGHT TO PUNITIVE DAMAGES AND GIVING UP THE RIGHT TO A TRIAL IN COURT, BOTH WITH AND WITHOUT A JURY.

Therefore, by agreeing to arbitration, Appellants have necessarily waived the following: (1) their right to a judicial forum; and (2) their corresponding right to a jury trial. . . .

The Seventh Amendment right to a trial by jury is limited by a valid arbitration provision that waives the right to resolve a dispute through litigation in a judicial forum. . . . Here, Appellants agreed to resolve their disputes with Appellees through arbitration, and they did so in clear and unmistakable, capitalized and boldfaced words which expressly waived their right to a jury trial as well. Thus, Appellants validly waived their rights to a judicial forum, including the corollary right to a trial by jury. . . .

For the foregoing reasons, the district court's order compelling arbitration, staying the state court proceedings, and closing the case is AFFIRMED.

PENN v. RYAN'S FAMILY STEAK HOUSES, INC.
269 F.3d 753 (7th Cir. 2001)

[Craig Penn was fired from Ryan's Family Steak Houses, where he had worked as a server from 1996 until 1998. He subsequently filed suit under the Americans with Disabilities Act (ADA), alleging retaliation for complaints about harassment. Ryan's then filed a motion in a federal district court seeking to stay the litigation and compel arbitration. The court found that the arbitration agreement Penn had signed when applying for his job allowed for the creation of an arbitration panel that would favor Ryan's and thus denied Ryan's motion. Ryan's brought an appeal in the Seventh Circuit Court of Appeals.]

DIANE P. WOOD, Circuit Judge:
. . . Arbitration has become a common tool in resolving employment disputes in recent years, and employers are increasingly requiring employees to sign contracts obligating them to arbitrate disputes as a condition of employment. . . .

The Supreme Court has repeatedly counseled that the FAA leaves no room for judicial hostility to arbitration proceedings and that courts should not presume, absent concrete proof to the contrary, that arbitration systems will be unfair or biased. . . . In this appeal, Ryan's argues that the district court violated these principles when it determined that the EDS system [EDS was a company which Ryan's had entered into a contract with to provide a forum for arbitration disputes] was inherently biased against employees. While the district court was correct to recognize that at some point an arbitral procedure may become so biased (perhaps because of "evident partiality" of the arbitrators, perhaps for another reason) that an award would not be entitled to recognition and enforcement, we are concerned that the district court placed too much weight on certain specifics of this system that, in and of themselves, do not distinguish it from many others that have passed muster . . . The court placed little weight on the safeguards that EDS had built into its system, particularly the unwritten rules that LaCoste, who is charged with interpreting the EDS Rules, described in his affidavit. Ultimately, though, we need not resolve whether the EDS system is so deeply flawed that it should be rejected on its face . . . as opposed to compelling its use in arbitrations and evaluating the enforceability of particular awards. In this case, we find that regardless of the merit of EDS's system, Penn never entered into an enforceable contract to participate in it. . . .

. . . Because Indiana was the situs of all relevant events in this dispute, we apply that state's law in analyzing the contract question. . . . The threshold question in this case, therefore, is whether the arbitration agreement that Penn signed amounted to an enforceable contract under Indiana law.

The existence of a valid Indiana contract depends on mutuality of obligation. "[T]here can be no contract unless both parties are bound." . . . An illusory promise, one which "by its terms makes performance entirely optional with the promisor," cannot form the basis for a valid contract, . . . because "a contract is unenforceable if it fails to obligate [one party] to do anything." . . .

As we have already observed, this case differs from the typical case in which an employer and employee agree to arbitrate their disputes because of the complicated three-party [Penn, Ryan's, and EDS] approach by which Ryan's sought to bind Penn to arbitration. Although Penn obviously was motivated to sign the arbitration agreement because Ryan's otherwise would not have considered him for employment, the contract that Penn signed underscores that it is between Penn and EDS and that Ryan's is *not* a party to the contract. (We add for the sake of completeness that if the Penn-EDS contract is not valid, then the claim Ryan's has to third-party beneficiary status also falls by the wayside.) The first question is therefore whether the Penn EDS contract contains mutual promises and commitments by each party to the other.

We conclude that it does not; to the contrary, the arbitration agreement between EDS and Penn contains only an unascertainable, illusory promise on the part of EDS. The agreement is clear enough as to what Penn is promising: he agrees that he will bring any employment-related dispute that he has with Ryan's in the EDS arbitration forum and not in state or federal court. The agreement restates this proposition several times in various ways, and goes into some detail as to the types of disputes that are covered by the agreement and the duration of Penn's obligation. In marked contrast to the specificity of Penn's obligation is the language describing the consideration EDS is obligated to provide Penn in return: EDS commits itself only "to provide an arbitration forum, Rules and Procedures, and a hearing and decision based on any claim or dispute" that the employee might raise. Nothing in the contract provides any details about the nature of the forum that EDS will provide or sets standards with which EDS must comply; EDS could fulfill its promise by providing Penn and Ryan's with a coin toss. Although Penn was given the EDS Rules along with the contract he signed, and we will assume that the Rules form part of the contract, adding the Rules to the mix does nothing to make EDS's commitment more concrete, because the Rules specifically give EDS the sole, unilateral discretion to modify or amend them. The contract is therefore hopelessly vague and uncertain as to the obligation EDS has undertaken. For all practical purposes, EDS's promise under this contract "makes performance entirely optional with the promisor." . . .

This is not the end of our inquiry. Indiana law does not require that both promises of obligation be contained in the contract at issue. It is also permissible to incorporate such contract terms by reference in a separate contemporaneous document. . . . Thus, we may also search other agreements to locate a promise that binds EDS . . . The only other contract involving EDS here is its contract with Ryan's, which hypothetically could contain a promise to take some action in this contract that would have the effect of binding it with respect to Penn. But the EDS Ryan's contract also does nothing to limit EDS's ability to amend its procedures, reinforcing our opinion that its promise to Penn is unenforceable and illusory. The fact that EDS and Ryan's may cancel their agreement with ten days' notice also does nothing to inspire our confidence that EDS is incurring any real detriment here.

The last place we can look for some mutuality of obligation is in the employment application Penn submitted to Ryan's. Mutuality can be imposed not only through a detriment to the promisor but also through a benefit to the promisee. . . . The application twice states that all applicants must sign the arbitration contract with EDS in order to be considered for employment with Ryan's. Perhaps, then, this benefit could be seen as consideration for Penn's agreement to arbitrate.

We have several problems with such an approach. First, despite a careful search, we find no support in Indiana law for the proposition that a benefit received from a third party, as opposed to a benefit received from the other contracting party in a contemporaneous document, can be sufficient to create mutuality. . . . Second, even if such an approach were possible, the two agreements do not seem to relate to the same basic subject matter. . . . Third, while an offer of employment may constitute consideration for a separate agreement . . . the defendants provide no evidence that any Indiana court has ever held that a mere promise to consider an application for employment would provide consideration for a separate contract. Finally, we note that the parties could have solved their consideration problem entirely simply by making Ryan's a party to the contract. . . . While this may be a formal distinction, the fact remains that EDS and Ryan's affirmatively chose to structure their transaction this way. Contracts are in part about formalism, and courts do not simply rewrite them to provide the necessary elements of initial contract formation. . . . Therefore, we find that any promises Ryan's made to induce Penn to enter the contract with EDS did not create an enforceable contract between those parties.

For these reasons, we hold that the arbitration agreement between Penn and EDS is not enforceable. Given this holding, we need not decide whether this circuit should adopt the Ninth Circuit's "knowing and voluntary waiver" standard for evaluating the enforceability of arbitration agreements in the employment context, although we question the continued validity of such an approach in light of the *Circuit City* decision.

The decision of the district court is Affirmed, and the case is remanded for further proceedings.

HARLINGTON WOOD, JR., Circuit Judge, concurring.

I completely agree with the careful and thoughtful analysis of the foregoing opinion and the result reached, and only write separately to note a few practical considerations to put this in perspective. It was an unfair situation from its inception. Penn was being hired as a waiter in a chain restaurant, not as a corporate executive. His employment was only to be "at will." Likely a substantial share of his income would be from tips. The agreement, the rules, the relationships between the parties, and the ramifications of the arbitration arrangement have now reached this court to sort out. Above his signature this agreement states that Penn signed it "knowingly and voluntarily." We doubt it could have been "knowingly" in view of its complexities, or even "voluntarily." Had he questioned its meaning and its complexities, it is doubtful Penn would have been hired. However, the agreement provided that Penn had the right to consult an attorney, but even if Penn could have afforded an attorney, the appearance of any attorney on the scene would doubtless have foreclosed any job opportunity. In Ryan's eyes, Penn would look like a troublemaker. If he wanted the waiter's job, he would be trapped in an unfair situation until a court could unravel it.

NOTES AND QUESTIONS

1. Notice the importance of contract law in the *Penn* case and how the principles of contract law apply to entering into an arbitration agreement. You may remember from your Contracts course that one of the key principles to forming a valid contract is mutual assent; this principle is often an important issue for courts examining the validity of arbitration clauses. Do the holdings in *American* and *Penn* conflict? Clearly Mr. Penn was aware, or should have been aware, that he was consenting to arbitration. The court points out that the arbitration clause was directly above the signature line. Which approach do you agree with? Why?

2. The court in *Penn* states that there is no support in Indiana contract law that a benefit, "received from a third party, as opposed to a benefit received from the other contracting party in a contemporaneous document, can be sufficient to create mutuality." What do you think the outcome of the *American* case would have been if Indiana law governed, considering that it was American (a third party) who was seeking to enforce the arbitration agreement against Mr. Orr?

3. From these cases can you discern the difference between the "making" of an arbitration agreement and the "enforceability" of an arbitration agreement? The court in *American* states that although there were issues relating to the enforceability of the agreement, no issue existed as to the making of the agreement and therefore the case should proceed to arbitration. Even if no issues existed as to the making of the agreement, does the court's

resolution of the problem create excess litigation for the parties? Now they will be forced to go to arbitration before a court addresses the issue of whether the decision by the arbitrator will be enforceable. Does the *Penn* approach of addressing both issues simultaneously seem more appropriate?

4. As canvassed in Chapter 17, arbitrability issues can be quite complex. In 1995, the Supreme Court stated in *First Options*, 514 U.S. 938 (1995), that if the issue of arbitrability is supposed to be submitted to the arbitrator, pursuant to the arbitration agreement, then the courts should give great leeway to the arbitrator's determination on issues of arbitrability. What are the essential differences between the Fifth Circuit's decision in *American*, which follows the reasoning of the Supreme Court in *First Options*, and the Seventh Circuit's decision in *Penn*? Why does Orr have to submit to arbitration while Penn does not, even though both signed documents with language about arbitration?

5. Commentators have explored a wide variety of concerns about the growth of predispute arbitration clauses, including the foreclosure of access to juries and judges, restriction of remedies (e.g., class-wide relief), and process failures (arbitral bias, cost, etc.). See, e.g., Bingham (2003), Sternlight (1996, 2002), and Stone (1996). Why do you think courts persist in upholding arbitration agreements so readily in light of serious concerns and the suspicions that predispute arbitration clauses foster? See, e.g., Ware (2003).

―――――――――――

Another area where courts have split and cases are difficult to reconcile concerns figuring out when arbitration clauses will be deemed invalid due to *unconscionability*. What constitutes an unconscionable arbitration clause varies widely from state to state and court to court. Generally, the more suspect (i.e., ambiguous) terms an arbitration clause contains, the more likely it is to be rendered unenforceable because it is so unfair as to be unconscionable. See, e.g., *Harper v. J.D. Byrider of Canton*, 148 Ohio App. 3d 122 (Ohio 9th Dist. 2002) (an arbitration contract was not unconscionable solely because it was on a preprinted sales agreement); but see *Geiger v. Ryan's Family Steakhouses, Inc.*, 134 F. Supp. 2d 985 (S.D. Ind. 2001) (finding that an arbitration agreement that allowed the employer to select the arbitration panel, forced the employees to pay one-half or more of the cost of arbitration, and limited discovery to one deposition, was impermissible).

Suspect terms in an arbitration agreement are not the only item that may lead a court to invalidate an arbitration clause as unconscionable. Another common factor that courts and legislatures have looked to in determining the unconscionability of an arbitration clause is whether the challenging party was aware of the clause. Concerns of unfairness and surprise arise not only between a large company and the private consumer, but also between large companies doing business with each other. The sales agreements in business-to-business agreements often fall under the Uniform Commercial Code. U.C.C. section 2-207, which provides that if a new term is inserted into the contract that materially alters the contract, then that term will be null and void, is a direct result of the drafters' efforts to address the realities of boilerplate contractual provisions in the "battle of the forms." In 1978, for example, the New York Court of Appeals, applying U.C.C. 2-207(2)(b), ruled that an inclusion of an arbitration agreement without the consent of all parties materially alters a contract for the sale of goods and therefore does not become part of the contract. *In re* arbitration between *Marlene Indus. v. Carnac Textiles*, 380 N.E.2d 239 (N.Y. 1978).

When both parties unquestionably have agreed to arbitration and the only dispute is the scope of the arbitration agreement, however, there is a presumption of resolving all disputes in favor of arbitration. In contrast, when one party states it was unaware that it had agreed to an arbitration clause, the opposite presumption may apply. Thus, if a party is actually surprised to learn it had signed an arbitration clause, often there is a presumption against arbitration, and all doubts are to be resolved against requiring a party to waive its right to a judicial forum.

Typically the party who asserts surprise is the private individual in a consumer or employment setting or the company with less bargaining power in a business-to-business dispute. Generally these parties signed an agreement, often without reading it completely; they did not draft the written agreement. Often a private individual will claim her due process rights are being violated because she was never aware she was giving up a right of access to the courts and perhaps to a jury trial. See generally Schwartz (1997). However, an arbitration clause will not be unconscionable solely because it is contained in a preprinted sales agreement that the buyer may not have fully read, as the following case demonstrates.

HARPER v. J.D. BYRIDER OF CANTON
772 N.E.2d 190 (Ohio App. 9th Dist. 2002)

[Jason W. Harper purchased a 1996 Ford Escort from J.D. Byrider for $13,017.64. At the time of purchase, the odometer read 50,305 miles. Subsequently, Harper believed that the odometer had been rolled back and the mileage misrepresented. After Harper filed suit against J.D. Byrider, the defendant filed a motion for a stay so that the case could be referred to arbitration pursuant to the terms of the sales agreement. The state trial court denied J.D. Byrider's motion, finding that the arbitration clause in the sales agreement was adhesive and unconscionable.]

PER CURIAM:

. . . J.D. Byrider claims that the trial court erred when it denied the motion for stay after concluding that the arbitration clause in the sales agreement with Harper was adhesive and unconscionable. This court agrees.

The Ohio Supreme Court has stated:

"Ohio and federal courts encourage arbitration to settle disputes. . . . Our General Assembly also favors arbitration. . . . [citing Ohio statutory provisions similar to FAA provisions on compelling arbitration and staying litigation] . . .

To defeat a motion for stay to compel arbitration, "a party must demonstrate that the arbitration provision itself in the contract at issue, and not merely the contract in general, was fraudulently induced." . . .

"A claim of fraud in the inducement arises when a party is induced to enter into an agreement through fraud or misrepresentation. The fraud relates not to the nature or purport of the contract, but to the facts inducing its execution. . . . In order to prove fraud in the inducement, a plaintiff must prove that the defendant made a knowing, material misrepresentation with the intent of inducing the plaintiff's reliance, and that the plaintiff relied upon that misrepresentation to her detriment. . . .

The trial court concluded that the arbitration clause was unconscionable because (1) the clause was in a preprinted form, lessening Harper's bargaining power without input on the contract's construction; (2) the unsupported rumination that a "true 'meeting of the minds'" may not have occurred; and (3) the predicate language — "IN ORDER TO COMPLETE THE PURCHASE" — to the arbitration clause evinced a condition precedent to finalizing the sale.

The trial court is mistaken. The record is bereft of Harper's absence of meaningful choice, i.e., that he was unable to purchase an analogous motor vehicle from another dealership without an arbitration clause. The record is devoid of a claim that the arbitration clause was concealed or misrepresented. Preprinted forms are a fact of commercial life and do not serve to demonstrate prima facie unconscionability with regard to arbitration clauses. . . . This court concludes that a preprinted sales agreement which contains an arbitration clause as a condition precedent to the final sale, without more, fails to demonstrate unconscionability of the arbitration clause. Accordingly, the trial court abused its discretion.

Judgment *reversed and cause remanded.*

CARR, Judge, dissenting:
I respectfully dissent. The Ohio Supreme Court has recognized that arbitration clauses that arise in sales agreements between consumers and retailers are subject to considerable skepticism upon review because of the disparity in the bargaining positions between the parties:

> "In the situation presented here, the arbitration clause, contained in a consumer credit agreement with some aspects of an adhesion contract, necessarily engenders more reservations than an arbitration clause in a different setting, such as in a collective bargaining agreement, a commercial contract between two businesses, or a brokerage agreement. See, generally, 1 *Domke on Commercial Arbitration* (Rev. Ed. 1997), 17-18, Section 5.09. . . .
> ". . . [T]he presumption in favor of arbitration should be substantially weaker in a case such as this, when there are strong indications that the contract at issue is an adhesion contract, and the arbitration clause itself appears to be adhesive in nature. In this situation, there arises considerable doubt that any true agreement ever existed to submit disputes to arbitration." . . .

In *Williams*, the court reviewed all the circumstances surrounding the agreement, taking special note of the requirement that the borrower had to prepay a substantial fee even to get access to an arbitration before endorsing the trial court's conclusion that the contract at issue was an adhesion contract that vitiated the arbitration clause. . . .

QUESTIONS

1. The court concluded that because Mr. Harper could have purchased a similar automobile at another dealership without the arbitration clause, the clause was not unconscionable. What if all the dealers in the area had arbitration clauses in their agreements? Would a court require more than that to find an arbitration clause unconscionable?

2. How is this arbitration clause different, if at all, from an arbitration clause in an employment agreement? Isn't it much easier to shop around for cars than jobs, depending on your specialty?

3. Increasingly, contracts for medical services provide that all disputes arising out of the contract will be arbitrated. Should a patient injured by medical malpractice be bound to arbitration? See, e.g., *Engalla v. Permanente*, 15 Cal. 4th 951 (1997). Does it make a difference whether the patient is in a large city with a choice of specialists and health care plans or in an area where his choices for particular medical services are greatly limited?

4. The Ohio appellate court in *J.D. Byrider* reviews the trial court's decision under an "abuse of discretion" standard. Thus, the court examined whether the trial court's attitude was "unreasonable, arbitrary, or unconscionable." Is it surprising that the appellate court felt the arbitration clause was so conclusively not part of an adhesion contract or unconscionable that the trial court was acting unreasonably and unconscionably in finding otherwise?

A recent Second Circuit Court of Appeals case shows that, unlike the typical scenario illustrated by *J.D. Byrider*, it is not always the consumer who claims that an arbitration clause violates her rights. In *Perpetual Securities, Inc. v. Tang*, Perpetual Securities brought an action in federal district court seeking to vacate an arbitration award in the customer's favor. 290 F.3d 132 (2d Cir. 2002). The crux of Perpetual's claim was that its due process rights had been violated because the National Association of Securities Dealers (NASD) — of which Perpetual was a member — requires its members to submit to compulsory arbitration of all disputes with customers. Perpetual claimed that its due process rights were violated only after the arbitration panel ruled in favor of the customer. The Second Circuit held, among other things, that because the NASD was a private actor, the federal courts did not have jurisdiction to vacate the arbitration award. Thus, even large businesses with greater bargaining power than individual consumers will sometimes perceive arbitration clauses to be unfair, at least when the arbitration fails to go in their favor.

Courts' mixed rulings on fairness issues will likely lead to increased litigation over arbitral clauses, removing some of the efficiency, finality, and freedom from court processes that arbitration promises. The rulings in this area are hard to reconcile, in part because they are based on varying state contract law and in part because the judicial decisions are quite dependent on the facts in a given situation. Additionally, many judges are trying to strike the right balance between upholding the federal and state laws promoting arbitration and reining in some of the more egregious examples of unfairness. As noted in Chapter 17, state laws designed to single out arbitration clauses from other contractual clauses, even if meant to protect consumers from arbitral abuses, are preempted by the Federal Arbitration Act. See, e.g., *Cassarotto v. Doctor's Associates*, 517 U.S. 861 (1996). Moreover, because most arbitration clauses implicate interstate commerce under the FAA, even if they involve only a local grocer and customer (see, for example, *Terminix v. Allied Bruce*, 513 U.S. 265 (1995)), the national policy favoring arbitration applies. There is no bright-line test in this emerging body of law as to when an arbitration clause will be considered unconscionable, or when a party's due process rights will be considered infringed upon by an arbitration agreement. However, courts are often reluctant to counteract the strong presumption in favor of arbitration when parties have signed a written contract providing for arbitration, unless it is unquestionably clear that the arbitration clause is unfair and unreasonable.

2. *Procedural Fairness in Arbitration*

It is worth reviewing some of the advantages of arbitration you have learned throughout Part III and distinguishing the consumer and employment contexts from the business-to-business and international agreements in which arbitration has long been popular. Where unequal bargaining power exists, some of the favorable attributes of arbitration may appear to be one-sided advantages. An agreement to arbitrate often effectively eliminates the ability to use the public justice system. Thus, for a company producing defective products, arbitration may be a mechanism to shield the company from consolidated consumer efforts (e.g., class action lawsuits), avoid potentially large jury awards, disfavorable judicial precedent, and media attention. Cf. *Green Tree v. Bazzle*, 123 S. Ct. 2402 (2003). Instead, the company will be able to handle each claim on a case-by-case basis in the relative privacy of an arbitral proceeding. Of course, consumers still have recourse to the media, legislatures, and consumer protection groups. Not all documents shared in arbitration are guaranteed confidentiality in future proceedings, but it will often be difficult for an individual consumer or employee to expend time and resources pursuing justice in these situations. And many may choose not to pursue redress if the prospect of a large damages award is removed.

Moreover, in some respects, arbitrators are more powerful than judges. While a judge decides the law, it is common for a jury to evaluate the facts and render a verdict. In contrast, an arbitrator evaluates the facts, contractual expectations, legal claims and defenses, and equitable considerations. An arbitrator is not bound by precedent and quite often a decision is rendered without a written opinion. Arbitrators control the arbitral process and have significant discretion over evidence allowed, timing, and other important choices.

An individual forced to submit to arbitration may be unfamiliar with the process, while the party who drafted the arbitration clause may be a repeat player who is familiar with the process and with particular arbitrators. Although in one sense an arbitrator is like a judge without a robe, that lack of a robe can sometimes be a cause for concern. In the judicial system a party is not able to choose the person who adjudicates her case, as parties can in arbitration. Thus, while businesses may look for commercial or technical expertise in an arbitrator, consumers may be wary of the perceived bias borne of experience as an "insider." Additionally, a judge's salary is regulated by the legislature and limits are placed on fees that judges can earn related to their judicial work. No entity regulates the fees that arbitrators receive. This becomes an especially prominent cause for concern when certain companies continue to give repeat business to the same arbitrators, and it is those very same companies that provide all or a large part of the arbitrators' fees. Sometimes an entity requiring arbitration agreements as a condition of employment or of doing business controls the arbitral process itself, as demonstrated by the *Hooters* excerpt below. While the FAA Act provides that a court may overturn an arbitration award if an arbitrator engages in "evident partiality," this is not easy to prove and is rarely found. 9 U.S.C. §10(a)(2); see Chapter 17.C *supra*. Clearly, these concerns are real and call into question the viability of arbitration when significant gaps in bargaining power exist between parties entering arbitral agreements.

Nevertheless, arbitration still retains many advantages for consumers and employees. As we considered earlier, arbitration is considerably different than mediation. It is more complex, costly, and time consuming. It is more dominated by lawyers and the arbitrator, who has a very final say. In contrast, when mediation functions effectively, each party retains control over the disposition of a dispute and has an active role in resolving it. A negotiated settlement of claims may also be a good option for an aggrieved employee or consumer who can afford a skilled attorney. But if mediation and negotiation efforts fail, or are repudiated by the more powerful party, arbitration may be a better choice than litigation for many consumers and employees. In many instances, it is still cheaper and quicker than litigation. While the process may be unfamiliar for many parties, it is relatively straightforward. Ideally, each party has the opportunity to tell its side of the story to a neutral, who decides a fair resolution. Witnesses can be called; documents can be subpoenaed. Litigation against a large company can entail a significant drain on a person's resources. Even if the individual prevails at the trial court level, damage awards can be tied up for years on appeal or reduced by appellate courts. In contrast, an arbitrator's award is essentially final and there is little room for appeal. Arbitrators frequently issue compromise awards, giving something to each side. Thus, in one study of securities arbitrations, complaining consumers received awards in over half of the arbitrations, although the awards were somewhat smaller than what they might have received in court.[17] Their lawyers' fees were likely not as high, either. A number of courts have upheld arbitration in the consumer and employment contexts, reasoning that the party with lesser bargaining power still gains advantages by agreeing to arbitrate, rather than litigate, claims against a more powerful party. See, e.g., *Gilmer*, 500 U.S. 20 (1991).

---

17. One study found that individuals prevail at least slightly more often in arbitration than litigation, and that monetary relief for individuals is slightly higher in arbitration than in lawsuits. See Delikat and Kleiner (2003).

When the arbitral process selected by one party, however, is not a fair and balanced system, those advantages dissipate. One of the leading cases invalidating an arbitration agreement because of an unfair process follows.

HOOTERS OF AMERICA, INC. v. PHILLIPS
173 F.3d 933 (4th Cir. 1999)

[Annette R. Phillips alleges that she was sexually harassed while working as a bartender at a Hooters restaurant in Myrtle Beach, South Carolina. After quitting her job, Phillips threatened to bring a suit against Hooters ("HOMB") under Title VII. Arguing that Phillips had agreed to arbitrate employment-related disputes, Hooters preemptively filed suit to compel arbitration under section 9 of the FAA. She responded, asserting individual and class counterclaims against HOMB. The federal district court refused to compel arbitration, finding the agreement unconscionable and void for reasons of public policy.]

WILKINSON, Chief Judge:
    . . . This agreement arose in 1994 during the implementation of Hooters' alternative dispute resolution program. As part of that program, the company conditioned eligibility for raises, transfers, and promotions upon an employee signing an "Agreement to arbitrate employment-related disputes." The agreement provides that Hooters and the employee each agree to arbitrate all disputes arising out of employment, including "any claim of discrimination, sexual harassment, retaliation, or wrongful discharge, whether arising under federal or state law." The agreement further states that:

> The employee and the company agree to resolve any claims pursuant to the company's rules and procedures for alternative resolution of employment-related disputes, as promulgated by the company from time to time ("the rules"). Company will make available or provide a copy of the rules upon written request of the employee.

The employees of HOMB were initially given a copy of this agreement at an all-staff meeting held on November 20, 1994. HOMB's general manager, Gene Fulcher, told the employees to review the agreement for five days and that they would then be asked to accept or reject the agreement. No employee, however, was given a copy of Hooters' arbitration rules and procedures. Phillips signed the agreement on November 25, 1994. When her personnel file was updated in April 1995, Phillips again signed the agreement. . . .
    Pre-dispute agreements to arbitrate Title VII claims are thus valid and enforceable. The question remains whether a binding arbitration agreement between Phillips and Hooters exists and compels Phillips to submit her Title VII claims to arbitration. . . . "It [i]s for the court, not the arbitrator, to decide in the first instance whether the dispute [i]s to be resolved through arbitration." . . . In so deciding, we "'engage in a limited review to ensure that the dispute is arbitral—i.e., that a valid agreement to arbitrate exists between the parties and that the specific dispute falls within the substantive scope of that agreement.'" . . .
    . . . The judicial inquiry, while highly circumscribed, is not focused solely on an examination for contractual formation defects such as lack of mutual assent

and want of consideration. . . . Courts also can investigate the existence of "such grounds as exist at law or in equity for the revocation of any contract." 9 U.S.C. §2. . . . In this case, the challenge goes to the validity of the arbitration agreement itself. Hooters materially breached the arbitration agreement by promulgating rules so egregiously unfair as to constitute a complete default of its contractual obligation to draft arbitration rules and to do so in good faith. . . .

The Hooters rules when taken as a whole . . . are so one-sided that their only possible purpose is to undermine the neutrality of the proceeding. The rules require the employee to provide the company notice of her claim at the outset, including "the nature of the Claim" and "the specific act(s) or omissions(s) which are the basis of the Claim." Rule 6-2(1), (2). Hooters, on the other hand, is not required to file any responsive pleadings or to notice its defenses. Additionally, at the time of filing this notice, the employee must provide the company with a list of all fact witnesses with a brief summary of the facts known to each. Rule 6-2(5). The company, however, is not required to reciprocate.

The Hooters rules also provide a mechanism for selecting a panel of three arbitrators that is crafted to ensure a biased decision maker. Rule 8. The employee and Hooters each select an arbitrator, and the two arbitrators in turn select a third. Good enough, except that the employee's arbitrator and the third arbitrator must be selected from a list of arbitrators created exclusively by Hooters. This gives Hooters control over the entire panel and places no limits whatsoever on whom Hooters can put on the list. Under the rules, Hooters is free to devise lists of partial arbitrators who have existing relationships, financial or familial, with Hooters and its management. In fact, the rules do not even prohibit Hooters from placing its managers themselves on the list. Further, nothing in the rules restricts Hooters from punishing arbitrators who rule against the company by removing them from the list. Given the unrestricted control that one party (Hooters) has over the panel, the selection of an impartial decision maker would be a surprising result.

Nor is fairness to be found once the proceedings are begun. Although Hooters may expand the scope of arbitration to any matter, "whether related or not to the Employee's Claim," the employee cannot raise "any matter not included in the Notice of Claim." Rules 4-2, 8-9. Similarly, Hooters is permitted to move for summary dismissal of employee claims before a hearing is held whereas the employee is not permitted to seek summary judgment. Rule 14-4. Hooters, but not the employee, may record the arbitration hearing "by audio or videotaping or by verbatim transcription." Rule 18-1. The rules also grant Hooters the right to bring suit in court to vacate or modify an arbitral award when it can show, by a preponderance of the evidence, that the panel exceeded its authority. Rule 21-4. No such right is granted to the employee.

In addition, the rules provide that upon 30 days notice Hooters, but not the employee, may cancel the agreement to arbitrate. Rule 23-1. Moreover, Hooters reserves the right to modify the rules, "in whole or in part," whenever it wishes and "without notice" to the employee. Rule 24-1. Nothing in the rules even prohibits Hooters from changing the rules in the middle of an arbitration proceeding.

If by odd chance the unfairness of these rules were not apparent on their face, leading arbitration experts have decried their one-sidedness. George Friedman, senior vice president of the American Arbitration Association (AAA), testified that the system established by the Hooters rules so deviated from minimum due process standards that the Association would refuse to arbitrate under those rules. [other expert testimony omitted] . . . In a similar vein, two major arbitration associations have filed amicus briefs with this court. The National Academy of Arbitrators stated that the Hooters rules "violate fundamental concepts of fairness . . . and the integrity of the arbitration process." Likewise, the Society of Professionals in Dispute Resolution noted that "[i]t would be hard to imagine a more unfair method of selecting a panel of arbitrators." It characterized the Hooters arbitration system as "deficient to the point of illegitimacy" and "so one-sided, it is hard to believe that it was even intended to be fair."

We hold that the promulgation of so many biased rules—especially the scheme whereby one party to the proceeding so controls the arbitral panel—breaches the contract entered into by the parties. The parties agreed to submit their claims to arbitration—a system whereby disputes are fairly resolved by an impartial third party. Hooters by contract took on the obligation of establishing such a system. By creating a sham system unworthy even of the name of arbitration, Hooters completely failed in performing its contractual duty.

Moreover, Hooters had a duty to perform its obligations in good faith. . . . Good faith "emphasizes faithfulness to an agreed common purpose and consistency with the justified expectations of the other party." Restatement (Second) of Contracts §205 cmt. a. Bad faith includes the "evasion of the spirit of the bargain" and an "abuse of a power to specify terms." *Id.* §205 cmt. d. By agreeing to settle disputes in arbitration, Phillips agreed to the prompt and economical resolution of her claims. She could legitimately expect that arbitration would not entail procedures so wholly one-sided as to present a stacked deck. Thus we conclude that the Hooters rules also violate the contractual obligation of good faith.

Given Hooters' breaches of the arbitration agreement and Phillips' desire not to be bound by it, we hold that rescission is the proper remedy. Generally, "rescission will not be granted for a minor or casual breach of a contract, but only for those breaches which defeat the object of the contracting parties." . . . As we have explained, Hooters' breach is by no means insubstantial; its performance under the contract was so egregious that the result was hardly recognizable as arbitration at all. We therefore permit Phillips to cancel the agreement and thus Hooters' suit to compel arbitration must fail. . . .

We respect fully the Supreme Court's pronouncement that "questions of arbitrability must be addressed with a healthy regard for the federal policy favoring arbitration." *Moses H. Cone*, 460 U.S. at 24. Our decision should not be misread: We are not holding that the agreement before us is unenforceable because the arbitral proceedings are too abbreviated. An arbitral forum need not replicate the judicial forum. "[W]e are well past the time when judicial suspicion of the desirability of arbitration and of the competence of arbitral tribunals inhibited the development of arbitration as an alternative means of dispute resolution." . . . Nor should our decision be misunderstood as permitting a full-scale assault on the fairness of proceedings before the matter is submitted to arbitration. Generally, objections to the nature of arbitral proceedings are for the arbitrator to decide in the first instance. Only after arbitration may a party then raise such challenges if they meet the narrow grounds set out in 9 U.S.C. §10 for vacating an arbitral award. In the case before us, we only reach the content of the arbitration rules because their promulgation was the duty of one party under the contract. The material breach of this duty warranting rescission is an issue of substantive arbitrability and thus is reviewable before arbitration. . . . This case, however, is the exception that proves the rule: fairness objections should generally be made to the arbitrator, subject only to limited post-arbitration judicial review as set forth in section 10 of the FAA.

By promulgating this system of warped rules, Hooters so skewed the process in its favor that Phillips has been denied arbitration in any meaningful sense of the word. To uphold the promulgation of this aberrational scheme under the heading of arbitration would undermine, not advance, the federal policy favoring alternative dispute resolution. This we refuse to do. . . .

AFFIRMED and REMANDED.

NOTES AND QUESTIONS

1. Are there other possible grounds on which the court could have held that Ms. Phillips should not be required to arbitrate? Is it fair that a company can condition raises, transfers, and promotions on a current employee's assenting to binding arbitration? Does it make a difference if the agreements are only applied to new employees? Why do you think the court fails to even address the assent issue?

2. Considering the court's statements that it is up to the judges to determine if an arbitration clause is valid, but up to the arbitrator to determine if the procedural aspects of arbitration are fair, at least initially, why not just force this case to go to arbitration first? If the system HOMB created operated in an unfair manner in Ms. Phillips' case or if the system produced an unfair result, could the court vacate the award on appeal? Does the court create too broad an opening for litigation relating to the fairness of procedural designs of particular arbitration processes?

3. The court says that HOMB's breach of the duties under the contract made the issue one of substantive arbitrability, reviewable before arbitration. Would the court have engaged in review of Ms. Phillips' unconscionability claim if HOMB had opted into an administered rules system (e.g., JAMS, CPR, AAA)?

4. If you were advising a restaurant chain, what advice would you give if it sought to establish an arbitral process for settling disputes between the chain and its employees? Considering all the cases discussed in this chapter thus far, how would you resolve issues of fairness concerning the formation of the agreement and the administration of the process? What procedural aspects would be the riskiest for your client? The next case may provide you with further insights into fair process formation.

ENGALLA v. PERMANENTE MEDICAL GROUP, INC.
15 Cal. 4th 951 (1997)

[Plaintiffs in this case were the surviving family of Wilfredo Engalla, who through his employer was enrolled in Kaiser's health maintenance organization. Part of the standard insurance agreement contained an arbitration clause providing for binding arbitration of disputes related to Kaiser's services.

Alleging that Kaiser had lost X-rays, failed to follow its physician's recommendations, and otherwise negligently failed to diagnose his cancer until it was inoperable, Mr. Engalla initiated arbitration. Although Kaiser represented that an arbitration within its self-administered program would reach a hearing within several months' time, the final arbitrator was not even selected until more than five months after the service of Mr. Engalla's claim. Mr. Engalla died before an arbitral hearing could be held. After his death, his family initiated a medical malpractice action in superior court.]

MOSK, J.:

. . . The arbitration clause contained in the Service Agreement . . . provides that each side "shall" designate a party arbitrator within 30 days of service of the claim and that the 2 party arbitrators "shall" designate a third, neutral arbitrator within 30 days thereafter. . . . The arbitration program is designed, written, mandated, and administered by Kaiser. It does not . . . employ or contract with any independent person or entity to provide such administrative services, or any oversight or evaluation of the arbitration program or its performance. Rather, administrative functions are performed by outside counsel retained to defend Kaiser in an adversarial capacity. . . . The fact that Kaiser has designed and administers its arbitration program from an adversarial perspective is not disclosed to Kaiser members or subscribers . . . [In materials distributed to Kaiser members,] Kaiser represented that an arbitration in its program would reach a hearing within several months' time, and that its members would find the arbitration process to be a fair approach to protecting their rights. [The opinion recounts in detail multiple requests from Mr. Engalla's counsel for expeditious processing of the claim due to his terminal condition. It details delays on the part of the lawyers for Kaiser in the selection of arbitrators so that the final, neutral arbitrator was not appointed until more than five months after the service of Mr. Engalla's claim, well beyond the representations made by Kaiser, and shortly before his death.] . . .

The Engallas claim fraud in the inducement of the arbitration agreement and therefore that "[g]rounds exist for the revocation of the agreement" [under California law]. As has been pointed out . . . "Offers are 'revoked.' . . . Contracts are extinguished by rescission." . . . Fraud is one of the grounds on which a contract can be rescinded. In order to defeat a petition to compel arbitration, the parties opposing a petition to compel must show that the asserted fraud claim goes specifically " 'to the "making" of the agreement to arbitrate,' " rather than to the making of the contract in general . . .

The Engallas claim that Engalla was fraudulently induced to enter the arbitration agreement — in essence a claim of promissory fraud. " 'Promissory fraud' is a subspecies of fraud and deceit. A promise to do something necessarily implies the intention to perform; hence, where a promise is made without such intention, there is an implied misrepresentation of fact that may be actionable fraud. . . ."

Here the Engallas claim (1) that Kaiser misrepresented its arbitration agreement in that it entered into the agreement knowing that, at the very least, there was a likelihood its agents would breach the part of the agreement providing for the timely appointment of arbitrators and the expeditious progress towards an arbitration hearing; (2) that Kaiser employed the above misrepresentation in order to induce reliance on the part of Engalla and his employer; (3) that

Engalla relied on these misrepresentations to his detriment. The trial court found evidence supporting those claims. . . .

First, evidence of misrepresentation is plain. "[F]alse representations made recklessly and without regard for their truth in order to induce action by another are the equivalent of misrepresentations knowingly and intentionally uttered." As recounted above, section 8.B. of the arbitration agreement provides that party arbitrators "shall" be chosen within 30 days and neutral arbitrators within 60 days, and that the arbitration hearing "shall" be held "within a reasonable time thereafter." Although Kaiser correctly argues that these contractual representations did not bind it to appoint a neutral arbitrator within 60 days, since the appointment of that arbitrator is a bilateral decision that depends on agreements of the parties, Kaiser's contractual representations were at the very least commitments to exercise good faith and reasonable diligence to have the arbitrators appointed within the specified time. This good faith duty is underscored by Kaiser's contractual assumption of the duty to administer the health service plan as a fiduciary.

Here there are facts to support the Engallas' allegation that Kaiser entered into the arbitration agreement with knowledge that it would not comply with its own contractual timelines, or with at least a reckless indifference as to whether its agents would use reasonable diligence and good faith to comply with them. As discussed, a survey of Kaiser arbitrations between 1984 and 1986 submitted into evidence showed that a neutral arbitrator was appointed within 60 days in only 1 percent of the cases, with only 3 percent appointed within 180 days, and that on average the neutral arbitrator was appointed 674 days—almost 2 years—after the demand for arbitration. Regardless of when Kaiser became aware of these precise statistics, which were part of a 1989 study, the depositions of two of Kaiser's in-house attorneys demonstrate that Kaiser was aware soon after it began its arbitration program that its contractual deadlines were not being met, and that severe delay was endemic to the program. Kaiser nonetheless persisted in its contractual promises of expeditiousness.

Kaiser now argues that most of these delays were caused by the claimants themselves and their attorneys, who procrastinated in the selection of a neutral arbitrator. But Kaiser's counterexplanation is without any statistical support, and is based solely on anecdotal evidence related by Kaiser officials. Moreover, the explanation appears implausible in view of the sheer pervasiveness of the delays. While it is theoretically possible that 99 percent of plaintiffs' attorneys did not seek a rapid arbitration, a more reasonable inference, in light of common experience, is that in at least some cases Kaiser's defense attorneys were partly or wholly responsible for the delays, and Kaiser's former general counsel conceded as much in deposition testimony. It is, after all, the defense which often benefits from delay, thereby preserving the status quo to its advantage until the time when memories fade and claims are abandoned. Indeed, the present case illustrates why Kaiser's counsel may sometimes find it advantageous to delay the selection of a neutral arbitrator. There is also evidence that Kaiser kept extensive records on the arbitrators it had used, and may have delayed the selection process in order to ensure that it would obtain the arbitrators it thought would best serve its interests. Thus, it is a reasonable inference from the documentary record before us that Kaiser's contractual representations of expeditiousness were made with knowledge of their likely falsity, and in fact concealed an unofficial policy or practice of delay.

The systemwide nature of Kaiser's delay comes into clearer focus when it is contrasted with other arbitration systems. As the Engallas point out, many large institutional users of arbitration, including most health maintenance organizations (HMO's), avoid the potential problems of delay in the selection of arbitrators by contracting with neutral third party organizations, such as the American Arbitration Association (AAA). These organizations will then assume responsibility for administering the claim from the time the arbitration demand is filed, and will ensure the arbitrator or arbitrators are chosen in a timely manner. Though Kaiser is not obliged by law to adopt any particular form of arbitration, the record shows that it did not attempt to create within its own organization any office that would neutrally administer the arbitration program, but instead entrusted such administration to outside counsel retained to act as advocates on its behalf. In other words, there is evidence that Kaiser established a self-administered arbitration system in which delay for its own benefit and convenience was an inherent part, despite express and implied contractual representations to the contrary. . . .

We turn then to the Engallas' unconscionability argument. We have required that "contractual arrangement[s] for the nonjudicial resolution of disputes" must possess "'minimum levels of integrity.'" Thus, in *Graham v. Scissor-Tail, Inc.*, we held that an arbitration agreement that called for the selection of an arbitrator affiliated with one of the parties to the contract was unconscionable . . . In addition to the general doctrine of unconscionability derived from contract law, HMO's such as Kaiser are regulated by the Knox-Keene Health Care Service Plan Act, which provides among other things that all contracts made in connection with a health service plan be "fair, reasonable, and consistent with the objectives" of that statute. HMO's are therefore especially obligated not to impose contracts on their subscribers that are one-sided and lacking in fundamental fairness.

In determining whether a contract term is unconscionable, we first consider whether the contract between Kaiser and Engalla was one of adhesion. In [*Madden*], we held that an agreement between Kaiser and a state employee was not a true contract of adhesion, although Kaiser's health plan was offered to state employees "on a 'take it or leave it' basis without opportunity for individual bargaining." We reasoned that the Kaiser contract was not adhesive because (1) it "represents the product of negotiation between two parties, Kaiser and the [State Employees Retirement System], possessing parity of bargaining strength" and (2) the state employee could choose from among a number of different health plans, and thus was not confronted with the choice typical of a contract of adhesion of "either adher [ing] to the standardized agreement or forego[ing] the needed service." We also found that the arbitration clause in question was not, unlike the unconscionable clauses in adhesion contracts, a term that limits the liability or obligations of a stronger party, but rather "could prove helpful to all parties."

The present agreement, which was also offered to Engalla on a "take it or leave it" basis, has more of the characteristics of an adhesion contract than the one considered in *Madden*. First, although Oliver Tire [Engella's employer] is a corporation of considerable size, it has had only a small number of employees enrolled in Kaiser, and did not have the strength to bargain with Kaiser to alter the terms of the contract. Second, Engalla did have one other health plan from which to choose, but not several plans as was the case in *Madden*. Finally, unlike in *Madden*, the Engallas do not claim that the arbitration clause itself is unconscionable, but that the arbitration program Kaiser established was biased against them.

Nonetheless, although the present contract has some of the attributes of adhesion, it did not, *on its face*, lack " 'minimum levels of integrity.' " The unfairness that is the substance of the Engallas' unconscionability argument comes essentially to this: The Engallas contend that Kaiser has established a system of arbitration inherently unfair to claimants, because the method of selecting neutral arbitrators is biased. They claim that Kaiser has an unfair advantage as a "repeat player" in arbitration, possessing information on arbitrators that the Engallas themselves lacked. They also argue that Kaiser, under its arbitration system, has sought to maximize this advantage by reserving for itself an unlimited right to veto arbitrators proposed by the other party. This method is in contrast to arbitration programs run by neutral, third party arbitration organizations such as the AAA, which give parties a very limited ability to veto arbitrators from its preselected panels.

Yet none of these features of Kaiser's arbitration program renders the arbitration agreement per se unconscionable . . . The alleged problem with Kaiser's arbitration in this case was not any defect or one-sidedness in its contractual provisions, but rather in the gap between its contractual representations and the actual workings of its arbitration program. It is the doctrines of fraud and waiver, rather than of unconscionability, that most appropriately address this discrepancy between the contractual representation and the reality. Thus, viewing the arbitration agreement on its face, we cannot say it is unconscionable.

[REVERSED and REMANDED to the trial court for a determination of the Engalla's waiver claim. The Engallas argued that arbitration should not be compelled because of Kaiser's conduct.]

BROWN, J., dissenting:

. . . Almost lost in the majority's exhaustive procedural summary is one key fact — namely, the arbitration process was already underway by the time the plaintiffs unilaterally withdrew . . . The reason the Engallas withdrew from the arbitration was that Kaiser declined to stipulate that Mrs. Engalla's separate loss of consortium claim survived her husband's death. It is this unilateral withdrawal from a pending arbitration that the majority's decision validates. . . .

In evaluating both the Engallas' fraudulent inducement claim and their waiver claim, the majority focuses on Kaiser's *performance* during the course of the aborted private arbitration. According to the majority, the sine qua non of successful fraudulent inducement and waiver claims is unreasonable or bad faith delay by Kaiser. . . .

Although the majority's desire to penalize Kaiser's obduracy is understandable, the consequences of validating a party's unilateral withdrawal from a pending arbitration based on the conduct of its arbitration adversary will reverberate far beyond the bad facts of the instant case. In stark contrast to the legislative response, which enhances the procedures for *keeping* a case in private arbitration . . . , the majority expands the procedures for *removing* a case from arbitration. . . .

In this case, having previously submitted their dispute to private arbitration and having already completed the arbitrator selection process, the Engallas should have sought relief for Kaiser's dilatory conduct in the pending arbitration. For example, the Engallas could have presented their fraud and waiver claims directly to the arbitrators and requested that they not enforce the arbitration provision. Likewise, the Engallas could have requested that the arbitrators sanction Kaiser's dilatory conduct by deeming Mrs. Engalla's separate loss of consortium claim to have survived her husband's death [describing broad remedial powers of arbitrators]. In fact, at oral argument, the Engallas' counsel conceded that this case could likely have remained in private arbitration if Mrs. Engalla's economic loss had been ameliorated.

The one thing the Engallas should not be permitted to do, however, is to circumvent the arbitrators altogether. The consequences of validating a party's unilateral withdrawal from a pending arbitration will be dramatic. Jurisdictional disputes will inevitably arise. Suppose, for example, that following the Engallas' unilateral withdrawal, Kaiser had elected to continue to pursue the pending arbitration and that the arbitrators had ultimately entered a default judgment in favor of Kaiser. Would that default judgment have been valid? Would the same have been true if the trial court had simultaneously entered a default judgment in favor of the Engallas in the pending litigation?

In addition, . . . other parties to pending arbitrations will doubtlessly engage in the same conduct. Counsel's answer to this dilemma was that this court should "trust the trial courts." The majority's answer is to "emphasize . . . that the delay must be substantial, unreasonable, and in spite of the claimant's own reasonable diligence" and not "the result of reasonable and good faith disagreements between the parties."

Neither answer is satisfactory. Under the majority's holding, which has all the precision of a "SCUD" missile, the resolution of fraudulent inducement and waiver claims will necessarily entail fact-intensive, case-by-case determinations. The disruptive, time-consuming nature of these determinations is well illustrated by the facts of the present case, in which "[t]he Engallas ultimately had five months to complete discovery [on the petition to compel arbitration], during which time thirteen motions were filed and more than a dozen depositions were taken." Even assuming that the trial courts ultimately resolve all future claims correctly, the interim disruption to pending arbitrations will be simply intolerable.

Great cases like hard cases make bad law. For great cases are called great, not by reason of their real importance in shaping the law of the future, but because of some accident of immediate overwhelming interest which appeals to the feelings and distorts the judgment. These immediate interests exercise a kind of hydraulic pressure which makes what previously was clear seem doubtful, and before which even well settled principles of law will bend." Although legislators, practitioners, and courts have all expressed concern that disparities in bargaining power may affect the procedural fairness of consumer arbitration agreements, this case amply demonstrates why any solutions should come from the Legislature, whose ability to craft precise exceptions is far superior to that of this court.

However well-intentioned the majority and however deserving its intended target, today's holding pokes a hole in the barrier separating private arbitrations and the courts. Unfortunately, like any such breach, this hole will eventually cause the dam to burst. Ironically, the tool the majority uses to puncture its hole is the observation that "those who enter into arbitration agreements expect that their dispute will be resolved without necessity for any contact with the courts." Because I suspect that parties to private arbitrations will be having quite a bit more contact with the courts than they ever bargained for, I dissent.

NOTES AND QUESTIONS

1. The California Supreme Court stated that Kaiser Permanente contractually promised an expeditious arbitral process, but that on average it took almost two years after a demand for arbitration for the final arbitrator of a three-person panel to be chosen. Although this delay may seem clearly unreasonable, the ruling raises yet more questions regarding arbitration that courts will likely have to decide. If you had to advise a client today, what constitutes an "unreasonable delay" in arbitration?
2. Compare the court's approach in *Engalla* with that in *Hooters*. Would it have been easier for the court to not require arbitration because of unconscionability (as was the case in *Hooters*) as opposed to fraud?
3. The dissent states that although Kaiser's process did have unreasonable delays, the issues regarding delay should have been first brought up with the arbitrator since the arbitration had already begun. Judge Brown believes that the majority has essentially created more problems than it solved because now parties will find it easier to circumvent arbitrators in favor of the courts during the arbitral proceeding. Can you think of better solutions to address the delay problem?
4. Note that after this case the AAA passed a resolution asking its arbitrators to refrain from medical malpractice arbitration. Does this suggest that medical malpractice arbitration is necessarily unworkable? Is the majority missing the fact that medical malpractice actions are inherently long and drawn out in the judicial system as well as in the arbitral system?

Other elements of judicial due process—the ability to obtain necessary information in the hands of another party, the ability to confront and question witnesses, and the opportunity to challenge positions and join issues in an open hearing before the decision makers—may also assume critical dimensions when courts examine arbitral processes. So, too, may the right to effective legal representation. The absence of such elements, either because they are not provided for or because procedures were ignored, can effectively undermine perceptions that a process is fundamentally fair.

What suffices as adjudicative "due process" hinges heavily on circumstances. As in the court system, small claims may permit—or require—the use of processes that place a premium on efficiency and expedition, even to the point of dispensing with many of the incidents of traditional court proceedings and permitting judges to rule "from the hip." Procedural concerns may be much further attenuated if a consumer retains the option to go to court, as in "lemon law" programs and other procedures that require consumers to submit to arbitration but permit a de novo hearing in court if they are dissatisfied with the arbitration award. Likewise, some private conflict resolution programs for employees or consumers give the latter an option of pursuing a remedy in arbitration or proceeding to court. However, the Uniform Code of Arbitration and National Association of Securities Dealers arbitration rules reveal a procedural system that has adopted many of the features of courtroom litigation. Although the process may provide greater due process protections, the more it resembles litigation, the greater the likelihood of increasing cost and delay for the parties.

ARMENDARIZ v. FOUNDATION HEALTH PSYCHCARE SERVICE, INC.

24 Cal. 4th 83 (Cal. S. Ct. 2000)

MOSK, J.

In this case, we consider a number of issues related to the validity of a mandatory employment arbitration agreement, i.e., an agreement by an employee to arbitrate wrongful termination or employment discrimination claims rather than filing suit in court, which an employer imposes on a prospective or current employee as a condition of employment. The employees in this case claim that employees may not be compelled to arbitrate antidiscrimination claims brought under the California Fair Employment and Housing Act (FEHA) (Gov. Code, §2900 et seq.) We conclude that such claims are in fact arbitrable if the arbitration permits an employee to vindicate his or her statutory rights. As explained, in order for such vindication to occur, the arbitration must meet certain minimum requirements, including neutrality of the arbitrator, the provision of adequate discovery, a written decision that will permit a limited form of judicial review, and limitations on the costs of arbitration.

The employees further claim that several provisions of the arbitration agreement are unconscionable, both because they fail to meet these minimum requirements and because the arbitration agreement is not bilateral. We conclude that the agreement possesses a damages limitation that is contrary to public policy, and that it is unconscionably unilateral.

Finally, the employees contend that the presence of these unconscionable provisions renders the entire arbitration agreement unenforceable. The employer argues that even if some of the provisions are unconscionable or contrary to public policy, the proper remedy is to strike or restrict those clauses pursuant [the California Civil Code], and to enforce the rest of the arbitration agreement. The trial court chose the employees' preferred solution of refusing to enforce the arbitration agreement, but the Court of Appeal sided with the employer and enforced the agreement minus the one provision it found unconscionable. We conclude, for reasons explained below, that the arbitration agreement is unenforceable and that therefore the Court of Appeal's judgment must be reversed.

I.   STATEMENT OF FACTS AND PROCEDURAL ISSUES

Marybeth Armendariz and Dolores Olague-Rodgers (hereafter the employees) filed a complaint for wrongful termination against their former employer, Foundation Health Psychcare Services, Inc. (hereafter the employer) ... In July and August of 1995, the employer hired the employees in the "Provider Relations Group" and they were later given supervisory positions ... On June 20, 1996, they were informed that their positions were being eliminated and that they were being terminated. During their year of employment, they claim that their supervisors and coworkers engaged in sexually based harassment and discrimination. The employees alleged that they were "terminated . . . because of their perceived and/or actual sexual orientation (heterosexual)."

Both employees had filled out and signed employment application forms, which included an arbitration clause pertaining to any future claim of wrongful termination. Later, they executed a separate employment arbitration agreement, containing the same arbitration clause. The clause states in full: "I agree as a condition of my employment, that in the event my employment is terminated, and I contend that such termination was wrongful or otherwise in violation of the conditions of employment or was in violation of any express or implied condition, term or covenant of employment, whether founded in fact or in law, including but not limited to the covenant of good faith and fair dealing, or otherwise in violation of any of my rights, I and Employer agree to submit any such matter to binding arbitration pursuant to the provisions of [the California Code of Civil Procedure]. I and Employer further expressly agree that in any such arbitration, my exclusive remedies for violation of the terms, conditions or covenants of employment shall be limited to a sum equal to the wages I would have earned from the date of any discharge until the date of the arbitration award. I understand that I shall not be entitled to any other remedy, at law or in equity, including but not limited to reinstatement and/or injunctive relief."

The employees' complaint against the employer alleges a cause of action for violation of the FEHA and three additional causes of action for wrongful termination based on tort and contract theories of recovery. The complaint sought general damages, punitive damages, injunctive relief, and the recovery of attorney fees and costs of suit.

The employer countered by filing a motion for an order to compel arbitration . . .

II. DISCUSSION

A. ARBITRABILITY OF FEHA CLAIMS

. . . We therefore conclude that nothing in the 1991 Act prohibits mandatory employment arbitration agreements that encompass state and federal antidiscrimination claims.

B. THE APPLICABILITY OF THE FAA AND THE CAA
[CALIFORNIA ARBITRATION ACT]

. . . Whether the FAA applies to employment contracts presents a substantial question, but one we need not decide here. California law, like federal law, favors enforcement of valid arbitration agreements. . . . We find nothing in the language or the legislative history of the FEHA that suggests it was intended to prohibit arbitration, and the employees cite us to none. To be sure, the FEHA provides critically important protections against discrimination. But the imperative to enforce such protections does not, as a general matter, inherently conflict with arbitration. Assuming an adequate arbitral forum, we agree with the Supreme Court that "[b]y agreeing to arbitrate a statutory claim, a party does not forgo the substantive rights afforded by the statute; it only submits to their resolution in an arbitral, rather than a judicial, forum." (*Mitsubishi Motors v. Soler Chrysler-Plymouth*, 473 U.S. 614, 628 (1985).)

In short, even assuming that the FAA does not apply to employment contracts, our inquiry into the enforceability of the arbitration agreement at issue in this case entails the same inquiry under the CAA as the FAA: Are there reasons, based on general contract law principles, for refusing to enforce the present arbitration agreement? . . .

C.   ARBITRATION OF FEHA CLAIMS

The United States Supreme Court's dictum that a party, in agreeing to arbitrate a statutory claim, "does not forgo the substantive rights afforded by the statute [but] only submits to their resolution in an arbitral . . . forum" (*Mitsubishi Motors, supra*, 473 U.S. at p.628) is as much prescriptive as it is descriptive. That is, it sets a standard by which arbitration agreements and practices are to be measured, and disallows forms of arbitration that in fact compel claimants to forfeit certain substantive statutory rights.

Of course, certain statutory rights can be waived. But arbitration agreements that encompass unwaivable statutory rights must be subject to particular scrutiny. This unwaivability derives from two statutes that are themselves derived from public policy. First, Civil Code section 1668 states: "All contracts which have for their object, directly or indirectly, to exempt anyone from responsibility for his own fraud, or willful injury to the person or property of another, or violation of law, whether willful or negligent, are against the policy of the law." "Agreements whose object, directly or indirectly, is to exempt [their] parties from violation of the law are against public policy and may not be enforced." Second, Civil Code section 3513 states, "Anyone may waive the advantage of a law intended solely for his benefit. But a law established for a public reason cannot be contravened by a private agreement."

There is no question that the statutory rights established by the FEHA are "for a public reason." . . . It is indisputable that an employment contract that required employees to waive their rights under the FEHA to redress sexual harassment or discrimination would be contrary to public policy and unlawful.

. . . The employees argue that arbitration contains a number of shortcomings that will prevent the vindication of their rights under the FEHA. In determining whether arbitration is considered an adequate forum for securing an employee's rights under FEHA, we begin with the extensive discussion of this question in *Cole v. Burns Intern. Security Services*, 105 F.3d 1465 (D.C. Cir. 1997) [323 App. D.C. 133] (*Cole*), in the context of Title VII claims. In that case, the employee, a security guard, filed Title VII claims against his former employer alleging racial discrimination and harassment. He had signed an arbitration form committing himself to arbitrate such claims.

The court began its analysis by acknowledging the difficulties inherent in arbitrating employees' statutory rights, difficulties not present in arbitrating disputes arising from employee rights under collective bargaining agreements. "The reasons for this hesitation to extend arbitral jurisprudence from the collective bargaining context are well-founded. The fundamental distinction between contractual rights, which are created, defined, and subject to modification by the same private parties participating in arbitration, and statutory rights, which are created, defined, and subject to modification only by Congress and the courts, suggests the need for a public, rather than private, mechanism of enforcement for statutory rights." (*Cole, supra*, 105 F.3d at p.1476.) Although *Gilmer, supra*, 500 U.S. 20, as discussed above, had held that statutory employment rights outside of the collective bargaining context are arbitrable, the *Cole* court recognized that *Gilmer*, both explicitly and implicitly, placed limits on the arbitration of such rights. . . .

Based on *Gilmer, supra*, 500 U.S. 20, and on the basic principle of nonwaivability of statutory civil rights in the workplace, the *Cole* court formulated five minimum requirements for the lawful arbitration of such rights pursuant to a mandatory employment arbitration agreement. Such an arbitration agreement is lawful if it "(1) provides for neutral arbitrators, (2) provides for more than minimal discovery, (3) requires a written award, (4) provides for all of the types of relief that would otherwise be available in court, and (5) does not require employees to pay either unreasonable costs or any arbitrators' fees or expenses as a condition of access to the arbitration forum . . ."

Except for the neutral arbitrator requirement, which we have held is essential to ensuring the integrity of the arbitration process, and is not at issue in this case, the employees claim that the present arbitration agreement fails to measure up to the *Cole* requirements enumerated above. We consider below the validity of those requirements and whether they are met by the employer's arbitration agreement.

1. Limitation of Remedies

The principle that an arbitration agreement may not limit statutorily imposed remedies such as punitive damages and attorney fees appears to be undisputed. . . . The employer does not contest that the damages limitation would be unlawful if applied to statutory claims, but instead contends that the limitation applies only to contract claims, pointing to the language in the penultimate sentence that refers to "my exclusive remedy for violation of the terms, conditions or covenants of employment. . . ." Both the trial court and the Court of Appeals correctly rejected this interpretation. While the above quoted language is susceptible to the employer's interpretation, the final sentence — "I understand that I shall not be entitled to any other remedy. . . ." — makes clear that the damages limitation was all-encompassing. We conclude this damages limitation is contrary to public policy and unlawful.

2. Adequate Discovery

The employees argue that employers typically have in their possession many of the documents relevant for bringing an employment discrimination case, as well as having in their employ many of the relevant witnesses. The denial of adequate discovery in arbitration proceedings leads to the de facto frustration of the employee's statutory rights.

. . . [A]lthough the employees are correct that they are entitled to sufficient discovery as a means of vindicating their sexual discrimination claims, we hold that the employer, by agreeing to arbitrate the FEHA claim, has already impliedly consented to such discovery. Therefore, lack of discovery is not grounds for holding a FEHA claim inarbitrable.

3. Written Arbitration Award and Judicial Review

The employees argue that lack of judicial review of arbitration awards makes the vindication of FEHA rights in arbitration illusory . . . Arbitration, they argue, cannot be an adequate means of resolving a FEHA claim if the arbitrator is essentially free to disregard the law.

As the United States Supreme Court has stated: "[A]lthough judicial scrutiny of arbitration awards necessarily is limited, such review is sufficient to ensure that arbitrators comply with the requirements of the statute" at issue. (*Shearson/ American Express Inc. v. McMahon*, 482 U.S. 220, 232 (1987).) . . . We are not faced in this case with a petition to confirm an arbitration award, and therefore have no occasion to articulate precisely what standard of judicial review is "sufficient to ensure that arbitrators comply with the requirements of [a] statute." All we hold today is that in order for such judicial review to be successfully accomplished, an arbitrator in a FEHA case must issue a written arbitration decision that will reveal, however briefly, the essential findings and conclusions on which the award is based. While such written findings and conclusions are not required under the CAA, nothing in the present arbitration agreement precludes such written findings, and to the extent it applies to FEHA claims the agreement must be interpreted to provide for such findings. In all other respects, the employees' claim that they are unable to vindicate their FEHA rights because of inadequate judicial review of an arbitration award is premature.

4. Employee Not to Pay Unreasonable Costs and Arbitration Fees

The employees point to the fact that the agreement is governed by Code of Civil Procedure section 1284.2, which provides that "each party to the arbitration shall pay his pro rata share of the expenses and fees of the neutral arbitrator, together with other expenses of the arbitration incurred or approved by the neutral arbitrator. . . ." They argue that requiring them to share the often substantial costs of arbitrators and arbitration effectively prevents them from vindicating their FEHA rights.

. . . [After extensive review of other decisions on this topic, the court concluded that] when an employer imposes mandatory arbitration as a condition of employment, the arbitration agreement or arbitration process cannot generally require the employee to bear any type of expense that the employee would not be required to bear if he or she were free to bring the action in court. This rule will ensure that employees bringing FEHA claims will not be deterred by costs greater than the usual costs incurred during litigation, costs that are essentially imposed on an employee by the employer.

Three principal objections have been raised to imposing the forum costs of arbitration on the employer. The first is that such a system will compromise the neutrality of the arbitrator. (*Cole, supra*, 105 F.3d at p.1485.) As the *Cole* court recognized, however, it is not the fact that the employer may pay an arbitrator that is most likely to induce bias, but rather the fact that the employer is a "repeat player" in the arbitration system that is more likely to be a source of business for the arbitrator. Furthermore, as the *Cole* court recognized, there are sufficient institutional safeguards, such as scrutiny by the plaintiff's bar and appointing agencies like the AAA, to protect against corrupt arbitrators.

The second objection is that although employees may have large forum costs, the cost of arbitration is generally smaller than litigation, so that the employee will realize a net benefit from arbitration. Although it is true that the costs of arbitration are on average smaller than those of litigation, it is also true that amount awarded is on average smaller as well. (*See* David S. Schwartz, *Enforcing Small Print to Protect Big Business: Employee and Consumer Rights Claims in an Age of Compelled Arbitration*, 1997 Wis. L. Rev. 33, 60-61.) The payment of large, fixed, forum costs, especially in the face of expected meager awards, serves as a significant deterrent to the pursuit of FEHA claims.

... Moreover, the above rule is fair, inasmuch as it places the cost of arbitration on the party that imposes it. Unlike the employee, the employer is in a position to perform a cost/benefit calculus and decide whether arbitration is, overall, the most economical forum. Nor would this rule necessarily present an employer with a choice between paying all the forum costs of arbitration or forgoing arbitration altogether and defending itself in court. There is a third alternative. Because this proposed rule would only apply to mandatory predispute employment arbitration agreements, and because in many instances arbitration will be considered an efficient means of resolving a dispute both for the employer and the employee, the employer seeking to avoid both payment of all forum costs and litigation can attempt to negotiate postdispute arbitration agreements with its aggrieved employees.

The third objection to requiring the employer to shoulder most of the costs of arbitration is that it appears contrary to statute . . . We do not believe the FEHA contemplates that employees may be compelled to resolve their antidiscrimination claims in a forum in which they must pay for what is the equivalent of the judge's time and the rental of the courtroom.

D.   UNCONSCIONABILITY OF THE ARBITRATION AGREEMENT

1. *General Principles of Unconscionability*

. . . "[U]nconscionability has both a 'procedural' and a 'substantive' element," the former focusing on " 'oppression' " or " 'surprise' " due to unequal bargaining power, the latter on " 'overly harsh' " or " 'one-sided' " results. "The prevailing view is that [procedural and substantive unconscionability] must both be present in order for a court to exercise its discretion to refuse to enforce a contract or clause under the doctrine of unconscionability. But they need not be present in the same degree." "Essentially a sliding scale is invoked which disregards the regularity of the procedural process of the contract formation, that creates the terms, in proportion to the greater harshness or unreasonableness of the substantive terms themselves." In other words, the more substantively oppressive the contract term, the less evidence of procedural unconscionability is required to come to the conclusion that the term is unenforceable, and vice versa.

2. *Unconscionability and Mandatory Employment Arbitration*

Applying the above principles to this case, we first determine whether the arbitration agreement is adhesive. There is little dispute that it is. It was imposed on employees as a condition of employment and there was no opportunity to negotiate.

Moreover, in the case of preemployment arbitration contracts, the economic pressure exerted by employers on all but the most sought-after employees may be particularly acute, for the arbitration agreement stands between the employee and necessary employment, and few employees are in a position to refuse a job because of an arbitration requirement. While arbitration may have its advantages in terms of greater expedition, informality, and lower cost, it also has, from the employee's point of view, potential disadvantages: waiver of a right to a jury trial, limited discovery, and limited judicial review. Various studies show that arbitration is advantageous to employers not only because it reduces the costs of litigation, but also because it reduces the size of the award that an employee is likely to get, particularly if the employer is a "repeat player" in the arbitration system. (Lisa B. Bingham, *Employment Arbitration: The Repeat Player Effect*, 1 Empl. Rts. & Emplmt. Pol'y J. 189 (1997).) . . . It is perhaps for this reason that it is almost invariably the employer who seeks to compel arbitration.

. . . We conclude that [other decisions] are correct in requiring this "modicum of bilaterality" in an arbitration agreement. Given the disadvantages that may exist for plaintiffs arbitrating disputes, it is unfairly one-sided for an employer with superior bargaining power to impose arbitration on the employee as plaintiff but not to accept such limitations when it seeks to prosecute a claim against the employee, without at least some reasonable justification for such one-sidedness based on "business realities." As has been recognized unconscionability turns not only on a "one-sided" result, but also on an absence of "justification" for it. If the arbitration system established by the employer is indeed fair, then the employer as well as the employee should be willing to submit claims to arbitration. Without reasonable justification for this lack of mutuality, arbitration appears less as a forum for neutral dispute resolution and more as a means of maximizing employer advantage. Arbitration was not intended for this purpose. (*See Engalla, supra,* 15 Cal. 4th at p. 976.)

The employer cites a number of cases that have held that a lack of mutuality in an arbitration agreement does not render the contract illusory as long as the employer agrees to be bound by the arbitration of employment disputes. (*Michalski v. Circuit City Stores, Inc.,* 177 F.3d 634 (7th Cir. 1999); *Johnson v. Circuit City Stores,* 148 F.3d 373, 378 (4th Cir. 1998).) We agree that such lack of mutuality does not render the contract illusory, i.e., lacking in mutual consideration. We conclude, rather, that in the context of an arbitration agreement imposed by the employer on the employee, such a one-sided term is unconscionable.

A contrary conclusion was reached by the Alabama Supreme Court in *Ex Parte McNaughton,* 728 So. 2d 592, 598-599 (Ala. 1998). In that case, the employer required the employee to submit claims to arbitration, but expressly reserved for itself a choice of the arbitral or judicial forum . . .

We disagree that enforcing "a modicum of bilaterality" in arbitration agreements singles out arbitration for suspect status. . . . We agree . . . that the ordinary principles of unconscionability may manifest themselves in forms peculiar to the arbitration context. One such form is an agreement requiring arbitration only for the claims of the weaker party but a choice of forums for the claims of the stronger party. The application of this principle to arbitration does not disfavor arbitration. It is no disparagement of arbitration to acknowledge that it has, as noted, both advantages and disadvantages. The perceived advantages of the judicial forum for plaintiffs include the availability of discovery and the fact that courts and juries are viewed as more likely to adhere to the law and less likely than arbitrators to "split the difference" between the two sides, thereby lowering damages awards for plaintiffs. An employer may accordingly consider a court to be a forum superior to arbitration when it comes to vindicating its own contractual and statutory rights, or may consider it advantageous to have a choice of arbitration or litigation when determining how best to pursue a claim against an employee. It does not disfavor arbitration to hold that an employer may not impose a system of arbitration on an employee that seeks to maximize the advantages and minimize the disadvantages of arbitration for itself at the employee's expense. On the contrary, a unilateral arbitration agreement imposed by the employer without reasonable justification reflects the very mistrust of arbitration that has been repudiated by the United States Supreme Court in *Doctors' Associates, Inc. v. Casarotto, supra*, 517 U.S. 681, and other cases. We emphasize that if an employer does have reasonable justification for the arrangement — i.e., a justification grounded in something other than the employer's desire to maximize its advantage based on the perceived superiority of the judicial forum — such an agreement would not be unconscionable. Without such justification, we must assume that it is.

Applying these principles to the present case, we note the arbitration agreement was limited in scope to employee claims regarding wrongful termination.

. . . The arbitration agreement in this case lacks mutuality in this sense because it requires the arbitration of employee — but not employer — claims arising out of a wrongful termination. An employee terminated for stealing trade secrets, for example, must arbitrate his or her wrongful termination claim under the agreement while the employer has no corresponding obligation to arbitrate its trade secrets claim against the employee.

The unconscionable one-sidedness of the arbitration agreement is compounded in this case by the fact that it does not permit the full recovery of damages for employees, while placing no such restriction on the employer. . . .

E. SEVERABILITY OF UNCONSCIONABLE PROVISIONS

The employees contend that the presence of various unconscionable provisions or provisions contrary to public policy leads to the conclusion that the arbitration agreement as a whole cannot be enforced.

. . . In this case, two factors weigh against severance of the unlawful provisions. First, the arbitration agreement contains more than one unlawful provision; it has both an unlawful damages provision and an unconscionably unilateral arbitration clause. Such multiple defects indicate a systematic effort to impose arbitration on an employee not simply as an alternative to litigation, but as an inferior forum that works to the employer's advantage. In other words, given the multiple unlawful provisions, the trial court did not abuse its discretion in concluding that the arbitration agreement is permeated by an unlawful purpose.

III. DISPOSITION

The judgment of the Court of Appeal upholding the employer's petition to compel arbitration is *reversed*, and the cause is *remanded* to the Court of Appeal with directions to affirm the judgment of the trial court.

BROWN, J., concurring:

Although I agree with most of the majority's reasoning, I write separately on the issue of apportioning arbitral costs. The majority takes the simple approach: where the employer imposes mandatory arbitration and the employee asserts a statutory claim, the employer must bear all costs "unique to arbitration." Simplicity, however, is not a proxy for correctness. As explained below, I do not

believe that the possible imposition of arbitration forum costs automatically
undermines an employee's statutory rights. Accordingly, I see no reason to
adopt the majority's preemptive approach. Instead, the issue of apportionment
is better left to the arbitrator, and any problems with the arbitrator's decision
should be resolved at the judicial review stage.

. . . "[A]rbitration is often far more affordable to plaintiffs and defendants
alike than is pursuing a claim in court." Because employees may incur fewer
costs and attorney fees in arbitration than in court, the potential imposition of
arbitration forum costs does not automatically render the arbitral forum more
expensive than — and therefore inferior to — the judicial forum.

The majority's approach also ignores the unique circumstances of each case.
Not all arbitrations are costly, and not all employees are unable to afford the
unique costs of arbitration. . . .

As long as the mandatory arbitration agreement does not require the
employee to front the arbitration forum costs or to pay a certain share of
these costs, apportionment should be left to the arbitrator. When apportioning
costs, the arbitrator should consider the magnitude of the costs unique to arbitration, the ability of the employee to pay a share of these costs, and the overall
expense of the arbitration as compared to a court proceeding. Ultimately, any
apportionment should ensure that the costs imposed on the employee, if known
at the onset of litigation, would not have deterred her from enforcing her
statutory rights or stopped her from effectively vindicating these rights.

If the employee feels that the arbitrator's apportionment of costs is unreasonable, then she can raise the issue during judicial review of the arbitration
award.

NOTES AND QUESTIONS

1. Does the California Supreme Court, relying on state contract law, constrain
   parties' autonomy too much in *Armendariz*, or is the structure developed to
   guide arbitrations appropriate? Why or why not?
2. If you were advising an employer bound by California law after *Armendariz*,
   what issues relating to the arbitration clause and the arbitration process do
   you need to consider?

The following example is illustrative of the kinds of problems that can arise
out of the growing use of predispute arbitration clauses. It involves a discrimination claim by an employee who consented to such a clause as a condition
of employment before any dispute arose. While this example shows why these
clauses have the potential to create a backlash against arbitration, it also provides an opportunity to formulate possible methods of reducing or eliminating
fairness problems in arbitration. Consider this problem in light of what has
been discussed thus far and then answer the questions at the end of the problem. Then compare your resolution of the issues with those suggested by the
various protocols and statutes discussed in the following section.

PROBLEM 1: EQUAL OPPORTUNITY IN ARBITRATION[18]

Sarah Miller, a 21-year-old junior at the local university with aspirations for medical school, was employed as a waitress at Mom & Pop's Barbeque Restaurant, earning minimum wage. On the date of hiring, Sarah signed the employment contract typically signed by all new employees. The contract contained an arbitration clause that required Sarah to arbitrate any dispute related to her employment in lieu of going to court. The clause required that Sarah split the cost of the arbitration, and gave the restaurant the sole power to select the arbitrator and craft the proceeding.

Unbeknownst to the restaurant, Sarah had a history of sporadic, epileptic seizures that occurred intermittently throughout her life. Sarah regulated her condition with medication, and it had been three years since her last seizure. One busy, rainy Saturday afternoon at work, Sarah suffered a seizure that lasted 20 seconds. She left the restaurant early that day but returned to work the following day and continued to work thereafter. Over the next three weeks Sarah missed three days with the flu and six days because of office visits to the physician treating her seizures. Sarah's physician was trying a variety of treatments for her seizures, and needed to see Sarah often to monitor their effectiveness. After three weeks the restaurant fired Sarah because she was missing too much time from work. Sarah met with the manager of the restaurant in an attempt to explain her situation and a heated debate ensued, ending with Sarah threatening to take the restaurant to court.

Sarah contacted an attorney, who set up an initial consultation and told Sarah to bring her employment contract. After the attorney read through the contract, he informed Sarah that it contained an arbitration clause. The attorney told Sarah that since she was the plaintiff, she was expected to bear the burden of proof, either in litigation or arbitration. After explaining the rest of the arbitration process to Sarah, the attorney advised her that arbitration would still be cheaper and more efficient than litigation.

Sarah knew she was in financial trouble. She could barely scrape up the $60 needed to pay the attorney, much less come up with the several thousand dollars to split the cost of hiring the arbitrator. She figured the restaurant could come up with the money fairly easily. Sarah, short on cash, attempted to obtain relevant information from the restaurant through her own "discovery" process. The restaurant flatly refused to disclose any information to her.

Sarah and the restaurant met with the chosen arbitrator for a preliminary meeting in which the arbitrator explained his previous arbitration experience. The manager, fully aware of the arbitration clause in Sarah's employment contract and familiar with many local arbitrators, selected one known for very business-friendly rulings. The arbitrator was a member of a nationally known arbitration provider organization, which supplied biographies to the disputants. Sarah discovered at the initial meeting, however, that the selected arbitrator's biography had not been updated to reflect that he had also served as general counsel to several large restaurant chains in the area. The restaurant objected, stating that this arbitrator was necessary because of past experience with the restaurant industry. Shocked and dismayed, Sarah asked the arbitrator

---

18. This fictional account was developed from certain actual events, as reported in *EEOC v. Waffle H., Inc.*, 122 S. Ct. 754 (2002) and Walsh (2001).

to recuse himself. The arbitrator declined, assuring Sarah that despite any appearance of impropriety, there was no actual conflict of interest. The arbitrator then proceeded to set the date of the arbitration.

Sarah, suspicious that the restaurant was trying to take advantage of her, deemed the entire process unfair and refused to show up for the meeting. She was already indebted several thousand dollars from splitting the costs with the restaurant from the first arbitration meeting. The arbitrator denied Sarah's ADA claim due to her failure to appear, reasoning that Sarah had rested her case by not showing up for the proceeding. He ordered Sarah to pay the restaurant's legal bills and 75 percent of the cost of the arbitration. This amounted to approximately $5,000.

Sarah is extremely frustrated and would like to correct the situation. Since she is short on cash, she only wants to pursue an appeal if there is a strong argument for her position. She also wonders what options she could pursue.

QUESTIONS

1. If Sarah comes to you following this award and tells you about her situation, how would you advise her? Do you think a court would vacate this award? Is this agreement unconscionable? Why or why not?

2. Did the restaurant have any distinct advantages that made the process unfair? Would it have made a difference in your analysis if the arbitrator recused himself, as Sarah requested?

3. Consider the possibility that a third party could bring a law suit on Sarah's behalf. In *EEOC v. Waffle H., Inc.*, 122 S. Ct. 754 (2002), the Supreme Court held that the Equal Employment Opportunity Commission (EEOC) could bring an action under the Americans with Disabilities Act and seek victim specific relief such as back pay and reinstatement despite the fact that an employee signed an enforceable arbitration agreement. The Court found that the EEOC could bring an action on an employee's behalf because it was not a party to the arbitration agreement and thus could not be bound by it. How does this ruling undermine the policy favoring arbitration to resolve disputes when a contract so provides? Why would the Supreme Court allow this? How effective is the option of pursuing EEOC action? See Matthews (1997) (discussing EEOC processes and substantial backlog).

C. DIFFERENT APPROACHES TO ADDRESSING FAIRNESS

Many persons and organizations have begun to address the fairness issues raised by the use of arbitration clauses in consumer and employment disputes. Government entities and private organizations have authored proposals for reform. This chapter examines some of those reforms and the impact they are having on the arbitral process. Some state legislatures, for example, have expressed concern about fairness in the administration of arbitration programs. Concern for balance and fairness in the structuring of consumer arbitration is reflected in the typical state "lemon law" program. Take, for example, Maine's law, which provides that all manufacturers submit to state-certified new car arbitration if arbitration is requested by the consumer within two years from the date of original delivery of a new car to the consumer or during the first 18,000 miles, whichever comes first. Me. Rev. Stat. Ann. 10, §1169 (West 1997). This state-certified arbitration panel consists of one or more neutral arbitrators selected by the Department of the Attorney General. The Attorney General's office is responsible for administering the proceedings under such rules as will "promote fairness and efficiency." This state regulation of arbitration increases the chances that a private individual engaging in arbitration for the first time may look upon the process with some sense of fairness because of its structured independent administration. However, it is likely that some consumers will view government administration as skeptically as opting into the largely unknown rules of a private arbitration provider. The California legislature recently enacted ethics strictures governing "mandatory arbitration." See Folberg (2003).

A much-scrutinized example of consumer arbitration involves programs governing the resolution of disputes between investors and securities brokers. Here, concerns about the fair administration of the arbitration process prompted the Securities and Exchange Commission to create the Securities Industry Conference on Arbitration (SICA). SICA has been the primary instrument for the development, implementation, and monitoring of uniform policies and procedures governing securities arbitration. Thus, SICA is attempting to accomplish for securities arbitration what the Consumer Due Process Protocol, discussed below, is doing for other consumer disputes.

Before we examine the protocols suggested for establishing fair arbitral processes to resolve consumer and employment disputes — issued by private dispute resolution providers — Professor Sarah Rudolph Cole articulates some of the main criticisms of arbitration in the employment context, most of which would also apply to the consumer context.

SARAH RUDOLPH COLE, INCENTIVES AND ARBITRATION: THE CASE AGAINST ENFORCEMENT OF EXECUTORY ARBITRATION AGREEMENTS BETWEEN EMPLOYERS AND EMPLOYEES

64 UMKC L. Rev. 449 (Spring 1996)

. . . To ensure the continued success and viability of the alternative dispute resolution (ADR) movement, courts confronted with challenged executory arbitration agreements must learn to separate those cases where it is appropriate to enforce an executory agreement to arbitrate from those where the agreement should be overridden and the dispute resolved using alternative methods. Failure to limit the types of disputes that may be arbitrated is likely to discredit arbitration as a legitimate means for resolving disputes. As challenges to the fairness of arbitral proceedings increase, litigants who might otherwise welcome the use of arbitration may reject it as ill-advised because they are fearful that arbitration will result in a restriction of their basic rights.

This increasing suspicion of arbitration may be traced to the courts' willingness to enforce executory arbitration agreements without regard to the parties' disparate negotiating incentives. . . . In such a setting, the arbitral agreement is suspect because the employer, like a merchant or a labor union, is a "repeat player." The employee, by contrast, is a one-shot player. An analysis of the interactions between these types of people and entities demonstrates that repeat players will have a distinct and systematic advantage in interactions with one-shot players. As a result, agreements between one-shot and repeat players should only be enforced where the incentives and ability of the parties to negotiate is similar.

A repeat player is an individual or organization who repeatedly interacts with a particular institution or engages in certain behaviors, for example, commercial transactions or dispute resolution. Representative repeat players include merchants as well as large organizations such as securities firms or insurance companies. By contrast, a lack of organization and sophistication characterizes the one-shot player. The one-shot player will usually have few opportunities to negotiate agreements and even fewer opportunities to litigate a claim. In essence, the one-shot player's limited exposure to contracts and the legal system are the defining aspects of his nature.

Typically, a repeat player will have greater experience and expertise in both contract negotiation and dispute resolution than will a one-shot player. Because the repeat player more frequently engages in these activities, he will have a greater understanding of both processes. Moreover, economies of scale favor the repeat player over the one-shot player; the repeat player typically has lower start-up costs in each separate negotiation and is in a better position to draft the agreement. While this, in itself, may not be problematic — the repeat player may be able to structure an agreement that provides benefits to both parties — it does provide the opportunity for abuse. In drafting the agreement, the repeat player may attempt to garner the lion's share of the potential benefits for himself. . . .

Further aggravating circumstances increase the repeat player's opportunity for undetected exploitation of his superior position. One-shot players, such as employees, improperly value the inclusion of an arbitration agreement in their employment agreement. Employees suffer from judgmental bias as a result of their personal experiences. That is, they systematically ignore or deemphasize the likelihood that a low probability event will occur because the event has never affected them. In the employment context, this judgmental bias causes employees to misapprehend the risk that they will engage in litigation with their employer. This informational problem leads employees to demand lower wages and fewer benefits than they might if they were fully cognizant of the risks present in the proposed arbitral agreement.

Obviously, many of these problems could be eliminated if employees could make fully-informed job choices. Unfortunately, imperfect information and constraints on employee mobility prevent this outcome. In the employment setting, neither the employer nor the employee need suffer. There are a number of legitimate ways in which employers can reduce their litigation expenses and, at the same time, avoid placing their employees in a disadvantageous position. For example, the employer could describe arbitration at the time the dispute arises and allow the employee to choose to proceed with arbitration or litigation at that time. Alternatively, the employer could continue to include the arbitration agreement in the employment contract, but permit a disgruntled employee to opt out of the process at the time the dispute arises. Both alternatives would allow employers to reduce costs while avoiding inequity.

QUESTIONS

1. Note carefully the distinction between a "one-shot" and "repeat" player. The cases in the previous section often dealt with courts trying to ensure that procedures were not unfair to the "one-shot" player, although courts will not always find in favor of the party with less negotiating power. In *J.D. Byrider*, 148 Ohio App. 3d 122 (Ohio 9th Dist. 2002), the court found against the plaintiff, reasoning in part that he had other car dealers from whom he could buy a car without signing an arbitration agreement. Do you think courts would consider the ability of employees to "shop around" for different employers in a similar light? Would a court's view of the ability to shop around change when the economy was in a slump and unemployment was high?

2. In the following section you will read about the development of the Consumer and Employment Due Process Protocols. These Protocols were essentially various suggestions for reform in consumer and employment arbitration clauses and processes. As you read about them, you may want to draw on the earlier Negotiation materials as you consider the problem of disparate negotiating power between "one-shot" and "repeat" players. Do the Protocols address these problems in an adequate manner?

1. Development of the Protocols

"Arbitration is simply a matter of contract between parties; it is a way to resolve disputes — but only those disputes — that the parties have agreed to submit to arbitration." *First Options of Chicago, Inc. v. Kaplan*, 514 U.S. 938, 943 (1995). Although arbitration may have originally been a creature of contract used as a simple, efficient means of resolving disputes, due process issues and the growing use of arbitration between disputants with disparate negotiating power have raised new concerns.

In response to these concerns, *A Due Process Protocol for Mediation and Arbitration of Statutory Disputes Arising Out of the Employment Relationship* was one of the first attempts to resolve the problems arising from mandated arbitration of statutory claims. 91 Daily Lab. Rep. (BNA) A-8, E-11 (May 11, 1995). The Protocol, which was adopted by AAA and JAMS, was geared specifically to deal with issues of due process for one-shot disputants in employment arbitration. The Protocol attempted to address these problems by recommending that certain procedural and substantive aspects of litigation be employed in arbitration. For example, the Protocol recommends allowing employees to be represented by an attorney, having the employer reimburse the employee for attorney's fees, encouraging the use of pretrial discovery, and allowing the arbitrator to provide any type of relief that would be similar to that available in a court proceeding. These recommendations would in many situations give an employee a greater sense of fairness, preserving some protections available in litigation and further reducing the cost of arbitration. Nevertheless, if a party is unsatisfied with the outcome of an arbitration, the party may often feel that the process was unfair simply because the party had no choice about the dispute resolution option. Thus, even reformation of the arbitral process may not yield significant satisfaction for some parties. The recent movement away from arbitration and toward mediation by employers may suggest that some employers also view the transformation of arbitration into a process more closely resembling litigation as not worth the high expenses entailed or benefits garnered (Brennan, 1999). Alternatively, perhaps employers are simply becoming more knowledgeable about the benefits of mediation for resolving employer-employee disputes. See Chapter 12, Section B above.

The Employment Protocol was the primary model for the 1998 *Due Process Protocol for Mediation and Arbitration of Consumer Disputes*, a statement of 15 principles to "establish clear benchmarks for conflict resolution processes involving consumers," embodying consumers' "fundamental reasonable expectation" of a fair process. The Consumer Protocol is a major step beyond the Employment Protocol in several respects. In addition to requiring an independent administration of ADR if participation is mandated by a predispute agreement, the Protocol sets forth many elements of a "fundamentally fair process," including: (1) provision of "full and accurate information regarding Consumer ADR programs," (2) independent and impartial neutrals, and (3) the right of parties "to seek relief in a small claims court for disputes or claims within the scope of its jurisdiction."

The principles of the Consumer Protocol address many of the problems observed in the cases above regarding the perceived unfairness sometimes associated with binding arbitration. By providing for a full disclosure of information about consumer arbitration programs, the consumer is aware of what rights they are surrendering by agreeing to submit to the process. This helps to prevent problems with unconscionability of arbitration clauses in contracts, removing a ground of challenge that could to a great extent undermine arbitration as a quick and efficient resolution of disputes. The ability to resolve some issues in small claims courts may assuage the consumer by allowing them to feel that a public airing of the dispute before an independent judiciary remains an option. Many small claims courts in the United States offer mediation or settlement services for parties.

The Protocols have greatly influenced arbitration because prominent arbitration providers have chosen to abide by them and promulgated corresponding rules. Critics remain concerned, however, that providers' adherence to the Protocols is voluntary and that the Protocols may be insufficient to guarantee fairness in some circumstances.

> Although the protocols have had an impact on arbitration, they do not have the force of law. They were developed by task forces and advisory committees composed of various groups, including the arbitration industry, interested in the resolution of disputes concerning employment, consumer, and health care issues. The effectiveness of the protocols thus lies in the voluntary agreement by arbitrators and arbitration service providers to require adherence to the procedures called for in the protocols for the administration and conduct of an arbitration proceeding. By voluntarily agreeing to adhere to the requirements of the protocols, those providing arbitration services have essentially agreed to regulate themselves. As a self-regulatory effort, the protocols seek to infuse arbitration with certain due process protections, thereby filling the procedural gap that was created when the United States Supreme Court endorsed the use of arbitration for the resolution of statutory claims. They also seek to encourage and promote the use of alternative dispute resolution for certain disputes. By committing itself

to ensuring that due process protections are provided, the arbitration industry's decision to regulate itself may have helped to legitimize the prevalent and growing use of pre-dispute arbitration clauses in contracts of adhesion. It may also have been instrumental in fending off more direct government regulation of the arbitration industry and in maintaining the favored status the Supreme Court has bestowed upon arbitration.

Harding (2004). In addition to directly influencing the AAA's consumer ADR procedures, the development of the Protocol is likely to spur other ADR providers to issue their own consumer dispute standards. The Employment Protocol and Consumer Protocol took serious steps to address some of the perceived unfairnesses associated with arbitration in the 1990s, and the Revised Uniform Arbitration Act (discussed below) would develop what the Protocols had begun.

A recent study compared randomly selected arbitrated cases under the AAA National Rules for Resolution of Employment Disputes in 1999-2000 with state court trial outcomes reported by the Civil Trial Court Network (see Eisenberg and Hill, 2003-2004). Researchers concluded that higher paid employees pursuing non-civil rights employment claims, the group most likely to be able to afford representation to go to court and therefore most represented in state court trials, won more frequently in arbitration than at trial. The authors found no statistically significant difference in median or mean awards in trial and arbitration. Moreover, the evidence indicated that the mean and median times to resolution were much shorter in arbitration than in litigation. They also observed that some pro-employee arbitration awards would probably have ended up as pro-employer summary judgments in litigation, since courts are significantly more likely than arbitrators to dismiss claims prior to trial on the merits. The authors considered it important that the AAA adheres to the Employment Due Process Protocol. Recent research by Professor Bingham supports the conclusion that the imposition of community due process standards in private arbitration has positive implications for employees.[19]

QUESTIONS

1. Although the Protocols have been developed to resolve issues of procedural and substantive fairness that surround arbitration, have they gone too far in altering arbitration? Do they appear to be creating processes that resemble litigation too closely? Is the trade-off of an increased perception of fairness worth the loss of speed, low cost, and simplicity for the parties?

2. When arbitration is mandated by statute, issues of due process and fairness, at least with regards to entering into an arbitral agreement, may be less weighty. Certainly, government-mandated arbitration reduces party autonomy, but at least the dispute resolution process is required by law rather than a result of the superior bargaining power of the repeat

---

19. See generally Bingham and Sharaf (2004).

player party. Do you think all fairness concerns are alleviated when the government, rather than private parties, effectively controls choices about dispute resolution?

2. *The Revised Uniform Arbitration Act*

Although the Revised Uniform Arbitration Act (RUAA) has not yet been adopted widely, it is worth examining as a guide to potential problems under the current law governing most arbitrations. The drafters of the RUAA wanted to resolve, among other things, the problems associated with due process and arbitration. But rather than impose specific due process limitations on adhesion agreements, they included a lengthy Reporter's comment discussing the need for judicial scrutiny of adhesion contracts. The approach gives courts flexibility to treat each arbitration agreement on its own terms and to police fairness in a way that does not strait jacket the broad realm of arbitration agreements. Of course, the discretion given to courts is likely to result in a lack of predictability for those who wish to employ arbitration clauses.

Under the RUAA, as with its predecessor, the courts are responsible for enforcing arbitration agreements, or refusing enforcement via "a ground that exists at law or in equity for the revocation of a contract." The FAA contains similar language. While courts may not invalidate arbitration agreements within the scope of the FAA when state laws single out arbitration agreements for special requirements (see, e.g., *Doctor's Associates*, 517 U.S. 861 (1996)), courts can rely on generally applicable contract defenses such as fraud, duress, unconscionability, or reasonable expectations to invalidate arbitration agreements.

Rather than focus on the arbitration agreements themselves, the RUAA is limited solely to the arbitral process. The RUAA includes a number of provisions that a party could not waive, and some which a party could waive only after the dispute arose. Specifically, the RUAA prohibits parties from waiving a court's power to confirm, modify, or vacate awards, as well as a court's power to award reasonable costs. Thus, the RUAA provides more safeguards for parties who have entered arbitration, but deprives them of some contracting autonomy and the ability to make the process less subject to judicial intervention. Moreover, judges retain discretion to reach differing analyses as they examine arbitral awards. In seeking to create a more uniform and fair process, the RUAA curtails many of the attractive qualities that lead people to arbitration. Stephen Hayford, one of the drafters of the RUAA, responds to some of those criticisms in the excerpt below.

STEPHEN HAYFORD, A RESPONSE TO RUAA CRITICS
Disp. Resol. Mag. (Summer 2002)

From day one, the RUAA Drafting Committee of the National Conference of Commissioners for Uniform State Laws ("NCCUSL") took as its charge the creation of a model for modern state arbitration statutes that would advance the state of the practice of arbitration and help make arbitration a truly fair and viable substitute for traditional litigation in a court of law for anyone involved in the process. The drafters sought to do so by building on, and working within, the bounds of the strong pro-arbitration public policy of the Federal Arbitration Act ("FAA"). They took great care to ensure that the framework created for state legislative action would comport with the federalism scheme reflected in the Supreme Court's unwavering view of the FAA as a preemptive statute that voids state law efforts to limit the enforceability of otherwise valid arbitration agreements. State arbitration legislation that ignores this imperative will be of no effect.

The option of simply outlawing pre-dispute agreements to arbitrate in adhesion contracts with consumers and employees was not really available to the RUAA Drafting Committee. The Committee deliberately weighed the concerns raised by the imposition of adhesion arbitration agreements on employees, consumers and others by commercial entities with superior economic strength. However, it was evident that the option of rendering these "take it or leave it" arbitration agreements unenforceable was unavailable because the strong pro-arbitration public policy identified by the Supreme Court as residing within Sections 1 and 2 of the FAA would block the way.

Critics of the RUAA are doing no favor for the consumers and employees who reside in their state when they suggest passage of [legislation modeled on the RUAA] . . . will . . . lead only to expensive and futile litigation. . . . The route taken by the Drafting Committee was to try to assure a fair and effective process to any party that might find itself in arbitration, like it or not. . . . Professor Cole, however, claims that in fact the RUAA offers little assurance to employees or consumers that the adhesion arbitration agreements they are obliged to sign will provide them with an adequate forum for vindicating their statutory rights. She cites four rights that may be waived under the RUAA: the right to punitive damages, the right to attorneys' fees, the right to pursue class actions and the right to meaningful judicial review of an unfavorable arbitration result . . .

The Drafting Committee recognized that the law of unconscionability is available to protect the party that has less bargaining power from seriously unfair provisions in an arbitration agreement contained in a contract of adhesion—which may include the waiver of punitive damages and/or attorneys' fees. Section 4(a) governs all waivers or modifications of provisions of the RUAA and allows them only "to the extent permitted by law." Section 4(a) thus contemplates the application of unconscionability and other generally applicable contract defenses such as a statute prohibiting any waiver of the opportunity to seek punitive damages, not one limited to arbitration. . . .

The Supreme Court has made clear that "generalized" claims that arbitration is an inadequate substitute for traditional litigation in the courts will not suffice to prevent the enforcement of adhesion employment arbitration agreements. The RUAA was drafted in a manner intended, not to invalidate arbitration agreements—which could not be done in any case—but generally to assure, together with the law of unconscionability, that claimants in arbitration will have the same rights and remedies they would be afforded in a court of law. It is this very scenario that the Supreme Court contemplates with its "equal footing" rule and its reliance on the common law of contracts. . . .

Professor Cole complains further that, in its futile attempt to protect the interests of consumers and employees by imposing certain procedural requirements on all arbitration agreements, the RUAA mistakenly treats arbitration as a "one size fits all dispute resolution mechanism . . . that can and should be regulated using a uniform approach, regardless of the participants' negotiating incentives." She also asserts that, by codifying these procedural protections, the RUAA inordinately judicializes commercial arbitration. Nothing could be further from the truth.

Modern arbitration has, to a degree, become judicialized, that is, it has come somewhat to resemble litigation in court. However, to the extent this phenomenon has occurred, it has been driven by users of the system — the parties and the advocates who represent their interests. Judicialization cannot be said to have resulted from the RUAA.

In setting a baseline for a fair and efficient arbitration process, the RUAA clarifies and codifies the case law of the states and makes choices where competing positions have evolved. It embraces the consensus view of which issues are to be decided by a court and which are to be decided by an arbitrator. It confirms arbitrator power to conduct preliminary conferences and grant dispositive motions.

The RUAA leaves discovery to the parties and the arbitrator, under the guiding principle that it is to be "fair, efficient and cost effective." The RUAA confirms arbitrator power to require discovery from a third party, and it provides a streamlined mechanism for acquiring evidence from another state with less than the traditional need to obtain judicial assistance.

The RUAA leaves it to the parties to agree on whether to permit consolidation. In the absence of agreement, it permits a court to consolidate arbitrations that have some common parties and issues, as well as risk of inconsistent results, if a balancing of interests favors arbitration, and substantial rights are not abrogated.

Unlike the UAA, the RUAA permits arbitrators to award attorneys' fees, without party agreement, if the parties have not forbidden them and such fees could be awarded in court. Similarly, unless parties agree to the contrary, the RUAA confirms arbitrator power to award punitive damages if they could be awarded in court, but it requires that they be set forth separate from compensatory damages and that the basis in law and in fact for awarding them be noted in the award.

In general the RUAA is a default statute, the provisions of which can be waived or modified by the parties. However, the parties cannot waive basic elements of the process, such as the applicability of the RUAA and the non-waiver clause, the validity of the parties' agreement, the power of an arbitrator to provide preliminary relief, and immunity for the arbitrator and the provider. Nor may the parties change the means of access to and use of the judicial system in aid of arbitration, or eliminate the fundamental mechanisms needed to ensure a fair and effective procedure, such as the power to subpoena documents, the means of acquiring and preserving testimony, reasonable notice, neutral arbitrator disclosure of interests and relationships, and the right to representation. Finally, as noted above, the RUAA provides inalienable minimum grounds for vacatur or modification of an award if the process fails.

Together with the law of unconscionability these provisions will assure due process in the context of adhesion arbitration agreements by guarding against unfair terms. They will have little or no effect on typical ad hoc commercial arbitrations or arbitrations administered by leading providers of arbitration services such as the American Arbitration Association, JAMS and the National Arbitration Forum. These institutions will continue to operate under their own rules, and they support the RUAA, as do numerous Sections of the American Bar Association and its House of Delegates, and many other organizations. . . .

The drafters of the RUAA chose not to propose to the states approaches that would be preempted. Instead, they created a balanced template for modern arbitration that provides default standards, subject to modification by the parties under the law of unconscionability, intended to make arbitration a viable substitute for traditional litigation in court. For that, neither they nor the RUAA they produced can be faulted.

QUESTIONS

1. Who has the better of the argument? Which of the critics' arguments do you find most persuasive? Does your analysis differ depending on whether it is an employee or consumer who is involved in arbitration?
2. What impact, if any, is the RUAA likely to have on the arbitration law set out above?

The following excerpt from *Cole v. Burns International Security Services*, written by Judge Harry Edwards, should help you reflect on these controversies. The case involved the enforcement of an arbitration claim of employment discrimination pursuant to Title VII of the Civil Rights Act of 1964 under the AAA Employment Rules. Accepting the Supreme Court's decision in *Gilmer v. Interstate/Johnson Lane Corp.*, 500 U.S. 20 (1991), as a qualified mandate for arbitration as a condition of employment, Judge Edwards set forth a number of "minimal standards of procedural fairness" for employees entering into binding arbitration of statutory discrimination claims. In the conclusion of the ruling, excerpted below, he offers a thoughtful discourse on binding employment arbitration.

COLE v. BURNS INTERNATIONAL SECURITY SERVICES
105 F.3d 1465 (D.C. Cir. 1997)

HARRY T. EDWARDS, Chief Judge:

. . . We acknowledge the concerns that have been raised regarding arbitration's ability to vindicate employees' statutory rights. However, for all of arbitration's shortcomings, the process, if fairly conducted, is not necessarily inferior to litigation as a mechanism for the resolution of employment disputes. As the Dunlop Commission recognized:

> [L]itigation has become a less-than-ideal method of resolving employees' public law claims. . . . employees bringing public law claims in court must endure long waiting periods as governing agencies and the overburdened court system struggle to find time to properly investigate and hear the complaint. Moreover, the average profile of employee litigants . . . indicates that lower-wage workers may not fare as well as higher-wage professionals in the litigation system; lower-wage workers are less able to afford the time required to pursue a court complaint, and

are less likely to receive large monetary relief from juries. Finally, the litigation model of dispute resolution seems to be dominated by "ex-employee" complainants, indicating that the litigation system is less useful to employees who need redress for legitimate complaints, but also wish to remain in their current jobs . . .

Arbitration also offers employees a guarantee that there will be a hearing on the merits of their claims; no such guarantee exists in litigation where relatively few employees survive the procedural hurdles necessary to take a case to trial in the federal courts.

As a result, it is perhaps misguided to mourn the Supreme Court's endorsement of the arbitration of complex and important public law claims. Arbitrators, however, must be mindful that the Court's endorsement has been based on the assumption that "competent, conscientious, and impartial arbitrators" will be available to decide these cases. . . . Therefore, arbitrators must step up to the challenges presented by the resolution of statutory issues and must be vigilant to protect the important rights embodied in the laws entrusted to their care.

Greater reliance on private process to protect public rights imposes a professional obligation on arbitrators to handle statutory issues only if they are prepared to fully protect the rights of statutory grievants. . . . To meet that obligation, arbitrators must educate themselves about the law. . . . They must follow precedent and must adopt an attitude of judicial restraint when entering undefined areas of the law. . . . Arbitrators must actively ensure that the record is adequately developed and that procedural fairness is provided. . . . And appointing agencies like AAA must be certain that only persons who are able to satisfy these criteria are added to arbitrator-panel lists. For if arbitrators and agencies do not meet these obligations, the courts will have no choice but to intercede.

---

3. Magnuson-Moss Warranty Act

One attempt by the federal government to encourage the use of ADR can be seen in the Magnuson-Moss Warranty Act, enacted in 1975 in response to address increasing consumer protection concerns. 15 U.S.C. §§2301-2312 (2004). The Act takes a unique approach in that it allows warrantors to require that consumers enter into alternative dispute resolution if a dispute arises, but it specifies that the ADR be non-binding, and that the consumer be able to assert claims in court if ADR is unsuccessful. The Act is an attempt to encourage the increased use of ADR in common situations while at the same time decreasing the public's hesitation for entering into these nonjudicial fora for fear of an unfair process or result. The Act attempts to provide common ground and fair process for resolving certain types of consumer disputes, as can be seen from the floor remarks of the Act's sponsor:

First, the bill provides the consumer with an economically feasible private right of action so that when a warrantor breaches his warranty or service contract obligations, the consumer can have effective redress. Reasonable attorney's fees and expenses are provided for the successful consumer litigant, and the bill is further refined so as to place minimum extra burden on the courts by requiring as a prerequisite to suit that the purchaser give the [warrantor] reasonable opportunity to settle the dispute out of court, including the use of a fair and formal dispute settlement mechanism. . . . (119 Cong. Rec. 972 (1973) (statement of Rep. Moss))

After the enactment of the Magnuson-Moss Act, every federal court which had a Magnuson-Moss case come before it concluded that the Act vested a non-waivable right of court access and thus that the Act precluded binding arbitration. One of the first and most prominent cases dealing with the Act was *Wilson v. Waverlee Homes Inc.*, in which a federal district court held that the Act makes clear that the "informal dispute resolution procedures" allowed by the Act "are a prerequisite, not a bar, to relief in court." 954 F. Supp. 1530, 1537 (M.D. Ala. 1997), *aff'd* 127 F.3d 40 (11th Cir. 1997). This holding was followed by many other courts in the years that followed. As late as 2000, in *Pitchford v. Oakwood Mobile Homes, Inc.*, a federal district court in Virginia held that the clear intent behind the implementation of Magnuson-Moss was to encourage ADR without stripping parties of their access to the judicial system. 124 F. Supp. 2d 958 (W.D. Va. 2000).

In light of Supreme Court decisions in the 1980s and 1990s expanding the scope of the FAA, the validity of that interpretation of the Magnuson-Moss Act is likely to be questioned. The following case, from a federal circuit which had previously ruled that the Act prevented binding arbitration in warranty agreements, summarizes the controversy well.

DAVIS v. SOUTHERN ENERGY HOMES, INC.
305 F.3d 1268 (11th Cir. 2002)

[In October 1999, Michael Shane Davis and Heather N. Davis purchased a manufactured home constructed by Southern Energy Homes, Inc. ("Southern"). When the Davises purchased the home, they signed a binding arbitration agreement contained within the home's written warranty. They later discovered multiple defects in the home and notified Southern of the problems. After Southern failed to correct the defects to their satisfaction, the Davises filed suit in a state trial court in Alabama, asserting claims for breach of express and implied warranties, violations of the Magnuson-Moss Warranty-Trade Commission Act ("MMWA"), negligent and wanton repair, and fraud. Southern removed the case to federal court and moved to compel arbitration. The district court denied Southern's motion, reasoning that the MMWA prohibits binding arbitration. Southern appealed the denial of the motion to the Eleventh Circuit.]

DUBINA, Circuit Judge:

The important question presented in this appeal is whether the Magnuson-Moss Warranty Act permits or prohibits the enforcement of pre-dispute binding arbitration clauses within written warranties. We hold that the Magnuson-Moss Warranty Act permits binding arbitration and that a written warranty claim arising under the Magnuson-Moss Warranty Act may be subject to a valid pre-dispute binding arbitration agreement. . . .

In this appeal, Southern argues that, based upon the strong federal policy of enforcing valid arbitration agreements under the Federal Arbitration Act ("FAA"), the Davises must submit their written warranty claims to binding arbitration rather than file suit for breach of warranty. To support this argument, Southern notes that the Supreme Court continually enforces binding arbitration agreements of statutory claims and argues that the MMWA is similar to these other statutes because nothing in the MMWA's text, legislative history, or underlying purposes evinces that Congress intended to preclude binding arbitration of written warranty claims. Southern also asserts that the Federal Trade Commission's ("FTC") regulations and interpretations, which prohibit binding arbitration of MMWA claims, are unreasonable, and thus, we should accord them no deference.

The Davises, conversely, assert that arbitration is an improper forum for MMWA claims and that the Act's language, legislative history, and underlying purposes compel a conclusion that dispute settlement procedures cannot be binding under the MMWA. The Davises argue that §2310(a) of the MMWA, which states that consumers must resort to a warrantor's informal dispute settlement mechanism *before* commencing a civil action, necessarily implies that the decision of any informal settlement procedure may not be binding. . . .

Congress passed the MMWA in 1975 in response to an increasing number of consumer complaints regarding the inadequacy of warranties on consumer goods. . . . In order to advance these goals, §2310(d) of the MMWA provides a statutory private right of action to consumers "damaged by the failure of a supplier, warrantor, or service contractor to comply with any obligation under this chapter, or under a written warranty, implied warranty, or service contract. . . ." . . . Consumers may sue for a MMWA violation in either state or federal court. . . .

In order to encourage settlements by means other than civil lawsuits, §2310(a) allows a warrantor to include a provision for an informal dispute settlement mechanism in a warranty. . . . Although the MMWA does not define "informal dispute settlement procedure," it does provide that if a warrantor incorporates a §2310(a) informal dispute settlement procedure into the warranty, the provision must comply with the minimum requirements that the FTC prescribes. . . . If the informal dispute settlement procedure properly complies with the FTC's minimum requirements, and if the written warranty requires that the consumer "resort to such procedure before pursuing any legal remedy under this section respecting such warranty, the consumer may not commence a civil action . . . under subsection (d) of this section unless he initially resorts to such procedure. . . ." . . .

Congress enacted the FAA in 1925 to reverse the longstanding judicial hostility towards arbitration and "to place arbitration agreements on the same footing as other contracts." . . . The Supreme Court has interpreted §2 of the FAA as "a congressional declaration of a liberal federal policy favoring arbitration agreements." . . .

Generally, a court should enforce an arbitration agreement according to its terms, and no exception exists for a cause of action founded on statutory rights. . . . In every statutory right case that the Supreme Court has considered, it has upheld binding arbitration if the statute creating the right did not *explicitly* preclude arbitration. . . . Thus, unless Congress has clearly expressed an intention to preclude arbitration of the statutory claim, a party is bound by its agreement to arbitrate. . . .

The MMWA's text does not expressly prohibit arbitration and, in fact, fails to directly mention either binding arbitration or the FAA. Nevertheless, the Davises argue that the MMWA reserves strictly a judicial forum for consumers by providing a private right of action for consumers. The Supreme Court, however, has held that a statute's provision for a private right of action alone is inadequate to show that Congress intended to prohibit arbitration. . . . As the Fifth Circuit recently recognized, "binding arbitration generally is understood to be a *substitute* for filing a lawsuit, not a prerequisite." . . . Furthermore, the fact that the MMWA grants a judicial forum with concurrent jurisdiction in state and federal courts for MMWA claims is insufficient evidence that Congress intended to preclude binding arbitration. . . .

The second factor the Supreme Court instructs us to examine in determining Congress' intent to preclude the application of the FAA is the MMWA's legislative history. . . . Like the MMWA's text, its legislative history only addresses "internal dispute settlement procedures;" it never directly addresses the role of binding arbitration or the FAA. In trying to show that Congress intended to bar binding arbitration, the Davises rely on the MMWA's House Report, which notes that "[a]n adverse decision in any informal dispute settlement proceeding would not be a bar to a civil action on the warranty involved in the proceeding." . . . The Davises argue that Congress considered all methods of dispute resolution, including arbitration, before allowing warrantors to pursue only informal, non-binding settlement procedures. After a thorough reading of the MMWA's legislative history, we disagree. . . .

The Davises have proved only that the MMWA's legislative history is ambiguous at most. When considering a preliminary draft of the MMWA, the Senate reflected that "it is Congress' intent that warrantors of consumer products cooperate with government and private agencies to establish informal dispute settlement mechanisms that take care of consumer grievances without the aid of litigation *or formal arbitration*." . . . As the Fifth Circuit concluded, "there is still no evidence that Congress intended binding arbitration to be considered an informal dispute settlement procedure. Therefore the fact that any informal dispute settlement procedure must be non-binding, does not imply that Congress meant to preclude binding arbitration, which is of a different nature." . . . Thus, given the absence of any meaningful legislative history barring binding arbitration, coupled with the unquestionable federal policy favoring arbitration, we conclude that Congress did not express a clear intent in the MMWA's legislative history to bar binding arbitration agreements in written warranties.

[Finally, we] examine the purposes of the MMWA to determine whether the MMWA and the FAA conflict. . . . The MMWA expressly states three purposes: "to improve the adequacy of information available to consumers, prevent deception, and improve competition in the marketing of consumer products." . . . These purposes are not in conflict with the FAA. In fact, the Supreme Court has repeatedly enforced arbitration of statutory claims where the underlying purpose of the statutes is to protect and inform consumers. . . . Consumers can adequately vindicate their rights arising under the MMWA and written warranties in an arbitral forum. . . . Thus, we conclude that the MMWA's consumer protection goals do not conflict with the FAA.

The MMWA's legislative history also indicates that Congress was concerned with addressing the unequal bargaining power between warrantors and consumers with the enactment of the MMWA, thus creating another possible purpose. Unequal bargaining power alone, however, is not a sufficient reason to never enforce an arbitration agreement of a statutory claim. . . . Inequality in bargaining power is a procedural question that courts should analyze on a case by case basis. . . . REVERSED and REMANDED.

QUESTIONS

1. Almost all federal cases interpreting the MMWA prior to *Davis* held that the Act precluded binding arbitration. Frequently, those courts relied on the Act's distinction between "more formal" binding arbitration and the informal dispute resolution that the Act explicitly regulates. In contrast, the Michigan Supreme Court reached the same outcome as the *Davis* court, finding that the MMWA does not preclude enforcement of binding arbitration agreements in *Abela v. General Motors*, 469 Mich. 603, 677 N.W.2d 325 (2004). Which approach do you think the U.S. Supreme Court would adopt? Why?

2. The MMWA, as the court recognizes, fails to mention binding arbitration or the FAA. Did the Eleventh Circuit approach this ambiguity correctly? The court was constrained in part by the Supreme Court's test for determining congressional intent set out in *Shearson/American Express, Inc. v. McMahon*, 482 U.S. 220 (1987). In reviewing the text, legislative history, and the existence of any "inherent conflict between arbitration" and the statute's purpose, courts must be mindful of the federal policy favoring arbitration, and the party opposing arbitration bears the burden of showing that Congress intended to preclude arbitration. *Id.* at 226-227.

3. Is the judiciary usurping the power of the legislature in such rulings? Congress did not amend the MMWA during the 1980s or 1990s to address the Supreme Court's precedents favoring arbitration. Congress may have relied on the court decisions now conflicting with *Davis*. What avenues does Congress have if it does indeed disagree with the outcome in *Davis*?

CONCLUSION

These important fairness issues are likely to remain incompletely resolved and thus critical for lawyers, dispute resolution providers, legislatures, and courts in the coming years. Fairness concerns increase the risk that arbitration agreements and awards will be subject to greater legislative and judicial scrutiny, with the resultant increase in cost, delay, and uncertainty for the parties. As noted previously, the concerns canvassed above may spur more entities — including repeat players — to experiment with mediation, negotiation, and hybrid forms of dispute resolution.

> Questions of fairness and assent still form important considerations for drafters and advocates. The concerns are most frequently voiced about the systems, procedures and employment contracts. Although fairness issues have led some to advocate legislation proscribing the use of such provisions in various kinds of transactions, a variety of other statutory, judicial, and regulatory approaches have been or could be employed. In addition, efforts have been made to establish

community standards for due process in private dispute resolution. Moreover, negotiation, mediation, and other approaches can facilitate the resolution of most issues and conflicts short of arbitration and other forms of adjudication (Stipanowich, 2001).

While arbitration remains an attractive dispute resolution choice in many circumstances and reforms are likely to continue, it is not without its drawbacks and complications, at least for some parties in some contexts. Our exploration of ADR processes would not be complete without a review of an important emerging phenomenon: the inclusion of stepped, hybrid processes of dispute resolution in arbitration contracts and other agreements.

PART
IV

Mixing, Matching, and Moving Forward

CHAPTER
19

Matching the Process to the Dispute

THE BIG PICTURE

The prior chapters of this book have explored the roles lawyers play in the context of various discrete conflict resolution approaches: negotiation, mediation, and arbitration. The final four chapters offer different forms of synthesis. These include an examination of ways in which multiple conflict resolution approaches have been integrated in multifaceted court programs (Chapter 19) or multi-step dispute resolution systems (Chapter 20), the growing use of "hybrid" approaches like "Med-Arb" in which a single neutral plays multiple roles (Chapter 21), and a glimpse at online dispute resolution (ODR) and other developments and trends that may represent the future of ADR and conflict management (Chapter 22).

It is not surprising that legal counselors, experiencing the benefits and limitations of various approaches to conflict resolution, have tried to synthesize their experience and find creative ways of matching a given dispute with the process most appropriate to achieving their clients' goals. Chapter 19 briefly examines several ADR processes that evolved alongside mediation to provide multiple "doors" to resolution of disputes in federal and state courts. These include procedures such as minitrial, summary jury trial, and non-binding arbitration which provide a foretaste of the courtroom through abbreviated best-case presentations by advocates—not for the purpose of adjudication on the merits, but to promote settlement.

Chapter 20 looks at multi-step conflict resolution or conflict management programs that offer new opportunities for lawyers to serve as creative problem solvers, but require particularly careful crafting and implementation. These developments began with wide acceptance of "ice breaker" clauses that commit a company or law firm to attempt to resolve problems out of court. Today, more and more attorneys in the United States and abroad are drafting contractual provisions that incorporate two or three process elements—so-called "Stepped ADR Processes"—and advising clients how to implement them. Such provisions nearly always place primary emphasis on negotiation, mediation, and other approaches that give parties control over the process and permit them to address underlying interests and relationships. If these steps fail, however, stepped ADR clauses typically require the parties to adjudicate their dispute—either through court litigation or through binding arbitration.

Chapter 21 examines the growing tendency of many lawyers — contrary to the prevailing wisdom of the past — to structure "hybrid" procedures in which a neutral may be called upon to play multiple roles in a single dispute. In "Med-Arb," for example, if mediation fails to bring about settlement, the mediator switches hats and arbitrates the dispute to a final award. Such processes, however, raise a number of legal, practical, and ethical concerns that we will explore.

Chapter 22, our final chapter, deals with important themes on the cutting edge of ADR and conflict management. It examines opportunities for lawyers to apply a mediator's skills "upstream" in deal mediation and so-called "part-nering" between participants in a long-term relationship before conflicts have an opportunity to arise. An even more visible new frontier is the world of the Internet, which affords disputants unique opportunities to resolve conflicts speedily, economically, and efficiently. (Our foray into the eBay negotiation and mediation process will provide a firsthand introduction to this new dispute resolution "environment.")

We conclude with essays by two leaders in the field — one assessing the future of lawyers in neutral roles, and another offering an ambitious vision of a society transformed by the values inherent in the Quiet Revolution in constructive conflict management.

A.   NEW "DOORS" FOR RESOLVING DISPUTES AT THE COURTHOUSE

In their search for appropriate ways of resolving disputes, modern lawyers have experimented with many different variations on the fundamental process elements (negotiation, mediation, arbitration) described in this book. One primary arena for experimentation is the public justice system.

Many date the modern era of conflict resolution to the 1976 Pound Conference, at which Chief Justice Warren Burger and other leaders of bench and bar sounded a clarion call for more appropriate, less-costly alternatives to traditional litigation. No presentation was more influential than that of Professor Frank Sander, who called for "a flexible mechanism that serves to sort out the large general question from the repetitive application of settled principle" (Sander, 1976). Sander's proposed solution was a "multi-door courthouse" incor-porating three notions: (1) a choice of several discrete approaches to conflict resolution, (2) a mechanism for channeling disputes into specific processes, and (3) sufficient information about a given dispute to facilitate a rational pairing of problem and process (or, as Sander would say, "fitting the form to the fuss").

In the quarter century following Sander's call for a multi-door courthouse, the judiciary came to acknowledge the value of programmed third-party inter-vention in conflict. Federal and state court-connected programs centered upon mediated negotiation, non-binding or advisory arbitration, early neutral evalua-tion, and other processes are now ubiquitous. See Plapinger and Stienstra (1996).

Look once again at Professor Folberg's "Dispute Resolution Spectrum" in Chapter 1, pages 79-80. On the left-hand side of the chart, under the heading of "Settlement Processes," a number of process alternatives are listed. Nearly all of these except Direct Negotiation evolved in whole or in part through court programs. Some of these, Direct Negotiation, Facilitative Mediation, and Evaluative Mediation, are very familiar to you from prior chapters. Others—Neutral Evaluation, Settlement Conference, Mini-Trial (Minitrial), Summary Jury Trial, and Advisory Arbitration—have not yet been discussed.

In the following pages, we will briefly explore these latter options (except the Settlement Conference, which is a common element of courses on civil procedure). As you read about these processes, consider why—from the standpoint of degree of party control over process and outcome, degree of formality, place in the "chronology" of litigation or adjudication, or similarity to court trial—Professor Folberg placed them as he did in the "spectrum" of non-binding processes.

B. SIMULATING ADJUDICATION AND STIMULATING SETTLEMENT: EARLY NEUTRAL EVALUATION, MINITRIAL, SUMMARY JURY TRIAL, AND NON-BINDING (ADVISORY) ARBITRATION

Mediation is far and away the most widely used of ADR approaches in court-connected programs. However, courts have also employed several other processes with discrete aims, such as providing an objective judgment of matters in controversy and/or providing a forecast of the result at trial, thereby enhancing the likelihood of settlement and avoiding full-blown adjudication.

ROBERT J. NIEMIC ET AL., DESCRIPTIONS OF THE PRINCIPAL COURT-BASED ADR PROCESSES

Guide to Judicial Management of Cases in ADR 128-135 (Federal Judicial Center, 2001)

[This excerpt from a current guidebook on federal court ADR summarizes various processes now in use in federal district court ADR programs. The authors' order of discussion reflects the relative frequency of use of different processes, from most-widely used to least-widely used. References to the most popular court-connected process, mediation, are deleted in light of its extensive treatment in Part II of this book.]

1. Advisory or Non-Binding Arbitration

Unlike mediation, arbitration is an adjudicatory, rights-based process. In federal court-based arbitration, one or three arbitrators hear adversarial presentations, usually in summary form, by each side to the litigation and then issue a nonbinding "award," or decision, on the merits. Witnesses may or may not be called, but exhibits are often submitted to the arbitrators. At a party's request and cost, the hearing may be held on the record. Either party may reject the arbitration award and request a trial de novo in the district court. Arbitration is a fairly formal process, in many ways resembling an expedited court trial. . . .

[Under a 1988 federal statute ten district courts were authorized] to implement arbitration programs where litigant participation is presumptively mandatory. Eligible cases, which are defined by specific objective case characteristics such as nature of suit, are generally automatically referred to arbitration by court order once the suit is filed. Certain types of cases are excluded from mandatory arbitration, such as cases involving violations of constitutional rights or damage claims in excess of a specified dollar amount. In all mandatory arbitration programs, the parties are provided an avenue for seeking exemption from the referral to arbitration. . . .

Several of [the ten courts that were authorized to implement mandatory programs] . . . have amended their processes to make them voluntary; one has dropped the program altogether. . . . The ADR Act [of 1998] authorizes voluntary arbitration for all district courts. Among other provisions, referral to arbitration requires party consent, the action may not be based on alleged violations of constitutional rights, jurisdiction may not be based on an alleged deprivation of civil or elective franchise rights, and the relief sought must consist of money damages not in excess of $150,000. The ADR Act does not alter any arbitration program established under the 1988 Act.

2. Early Neutral Evaluation

Early neutral evaluation (ENE) is a nonbinding process designed to improve case planning and settlement prospects by giving litigants an early advisory evaluation of the case. Like mediation, ENE is thought to be widely applicable to many types of civil cases, including complex disputes.

In ENE, a neutral evaluator, usually a private attorney with expertise in the subject matter of the dispute, holds a confidential session with the parties and counsel early in the litigation—generally before much discovery has taken place—to hear both sides of the case. The evaluator then helps the parties clarify issues and evidence, identifies strengths and weaknesses of the parties' positions, and gives the parties a nonbinding assessment of the values or merits of the case. Depending on the goals of the program, the evaluator also may mediate settlement discussions or offer case management assistance, such as developing a discovery plan.

The process was originally designed to improve attorneys' pretrial practices and knowledge of their cases by forcing them and their clients to conduct core investigative and analytical work early, to communicate directly across party lines, to expose each side to the other's case, and to consider the wisdom of early settlement.

In some district courts with ENE programs, the ENE sessions occur later, rather than earlier, in the case. Although the term "*early* neutral evaluation" is less apt in such circumstances, the key feature of the process—evaluation of the case by a neutral—remains the same.

3. Summary Jury Trial

The summary jury trial is a non-binding ADR process designed to promote settlement in trial-ready cases. A judge presides over the trial, where attorneys for each party present the case to a jury, generally without calling witnesses but relying instead on the submission of exhibits. After this abbreviated trial, the jury deliberates and then delivers an advisory verdict. After receiving the jury's advisory verdict, the parties may use it as a basis for subsequent settlement negotiations or proceed to trial.

A summary jury trial is typically used after discovery is complete. Depending on the structure of the process, it can involve both facilitated negotiations, which can occur throughout the planning, hearing, deliberation, and post-verdict phases, and outcome prediction, that is, an advisory verdict. Part or all of the case may be submitted to the jury. The jurors are chosen from the court's regular venire; some judges tell the jurors at the outset that their role is advisory, but others wait until a verdict has been given.

Some judges use this process only for protracted cases where the predicted length of a full trial justifies the substantial resources required by a summary jury trial. Other judges use it for routine civil litigation where litigants differ significantly about the likely jury outcome. The format of this ADR process is determined by the individual judge more than in most ADR procedures. A variant of the summary jury trial is the summary bench trial, where a judge, rather than a jury, issues the advisory opinion.

4. Minitrial

The minitrial is a flexible, non-binding ADR process used primarily out of court. A few federal judges have developed their own versions of the minitrial, which is generally reserved for large cases.

In a typical court-based minitrial, each side presents a shortened version of its case to party representatives who have settlement authority — for example, the senior executives of corporate parties. The hearing is informal, with no witnesses and with relaxed rules of evidence and procedure. A judge or non-judicial neutral may preside over the one-day or two-day hearing. Following the hearing, the client representatives meet, with or without the neutral presider, to negotiate a settlement. . . .

ROBERT J. NIEMIC ET AL., MATCHING THE ADR PROCESS TO THE CASE
Guide to Judicial Management of Cases in ADR 38-47
(Federal Judicial Center, 2001)

Although it is difficult to generalize, certain types of cases are usually seen as more suitable than others to particular kinds of ADR processes. Below we identify the types of cases typically viewed as suitable for each of the major types of court-based ADR. . . .

1. MEDIATION

Mediation is considered appropriate for most kinds of civil cases, and in some district courts, referral to mediation is routine in most general civil cases. In some other courts, use of the process is targeted at specific kinds of disputes or is determined by the judge on a case-by-case basis. Most courts exclude certain categories of cases from mediation, such as cases involving a pro se party, prisoner civil rights cases, and Social Security cases. . . .

2. NON-BINDING OR ADVISORY ARBITRATION

. . . [E]xamples of cases traditionally considered appropriate for voluntary arbitration:

- Cases involving small money damages claims, and
- Cases in which technical or scientific questions are involved and an arbitrator with expertise in the field would be beneficial to resolution and is available to serve as arbitrator.

Cases that are traditionally considered inappropriate for voluntary arbitration include:

- Cases exempted by statute or local rules;
- Cases in which the parties want help in improving communications, finding common ground, or arriving at a creative solution to the dispute;
- Cases in which equitable relief is sought;
- Cases involving complex or novel legal issues;
- Cases where legal issues predominate over factual issues;
- Class actions; and
- Administrative agency appeals . . .

3. EARLY NEUTRAL EVALUATION (ENE)

Like mediation, ENE is generally thought to be applicable to civil cases of varying kinds and complexity. Some courts select cases for ENE according to case type; types of cases targeted include not only routine cases, but also more complex cases, such as fraud, antitrust, banking, environmental, copyright, patent, trademark, and labor/employment cases. . . .

Listed below are examples of kinds of cases generally considered appropriate for ENE:

- Cases in which subject matter expertise may be helpful in narrowing issues or simplifying them at trial;
- Cases in which issues raised in papers filed in the case indicate that one or more of the attorneys in the case are inexperienced or poorly prepared;
- Cases in which a party refuses to confront the weaknesses in its case and has unrealistic expectations regarding the amount of damages involved;
- Cases with complex legal issues;

- Cases involving multiple parties with diverse interests and numerous cross-claims, as opposed to merely multiple defendants with the same or similar interests; and
- Cases in which discovery will be substantial.

Examples of cases generally considered inappropriate for ENE include the following:

- Class actions;
- Cases in which there are significant personal or emotional barriers to settlement that might better be addressed in mediation;
- Cases in which the decision will turn primarily on the credibility of witness testimony; and
- Cases needing substantial discovery before an evaluation can be made.

4. SUMMARY JURY TRIAL

Because the summary jury trial (SJT) is a resource-intensive ADR process, it is most often used for fairly large cases that would involve long jury trials. Generally, the more complex and potentially protracted a case is, the greater the potential that a summary jury trial will result in reduced costs for the parties when compared with traditional litigation. Some proponents of the process believe, however, that it also can be used effectively in cases expected to have short trials. The process has been used in a wide variety of cases expected to have short trials.

In considering whether to use a summary jury trial, the decision may turn more on case-specific dynamics than on the substantive legal aspects of the controversy. . . . In addition, a practice committee in the Second Circuit advised that, to ensure a more-effective summary jury trial, the parties should have completed or have nearly completed discovery. . . .

NOTES AND QUESTIONS

1. *Benefits, Limitations of Summary Jury Trial.* Based on what you know about summary jury trial, what more might you guess about the cases that are generally considered appropriate for, or inappropriate for, the process? The strongest advocate for the SJT was Judge Thomas Lambros, who successfully utilized the process in a wide range of cases. See Lambros (1984).
2. *Concerns About Summary Jury Trial.* You are a lawyer representing a client in federal court, and are on the eve of trial. You were diligent in conducting discovery and feel fully prepared to go to trial, but were surprised that opposing counsel sought almost no discovery and doubt that she will effectively present her case at trial. At today's pretrial conference, the judge informed both parties that she intends to conduct a summary jury trial of the case before a full trial on the merits, suggesting that she believes it will stimulate settlement and avoid weeks of trial. You are concerned about

having to reveal the product of your discovery and trial preparations through the process. What are your options? See *Strandell v. Jackson County, Illinois*, 838 F.2d 884 (7th Cir. 1988). The Manual for Complex Litigation, Third advises that "[b]ecause of the time and expense involved, and because the process is less likely to be productive with unwilling parties, it is not advisable to hold an SJT without the parties' consent." *Manual for Complex Litigation* §23.152 (3d ed. 1995).

3. *The Waxing and Waning of Minitrial.* As noted in the excerpt above, Minitrial, or mini-trial, evolved primarily as a private process outside the courts. In the 1980s, the CPR Institute for Dispute Resolution and other organizations promoting ADR in the business arena touted the benefits of Minitrial. The process is unique in that it postures key decision makers from each party as members of a panel hearing "best shot" presentations of evidence and arguments by advocates for each side for each party to the controversy — thus potentially laying a foundation for mutual discussions aimed at settlement which would follow immediately upon the conclusion of the "hearing." In the typical minitrial proceeding, principals of each party sit on either side of a neutral third-party referee or minitrial "judge" who supervises the process. As lawyers for the parties present rigorously abbreviated cases, with summaries of best evidence (including, perhaps, videotapes of key witnesses) and arguments, the principles and the referee act as inquisitors, probing the main elements of each party's case. At the conclusion of the presentations, the principals have the opportunity to negotiate face-to-face, perhaps with the assistance of the neutral. The latter may at some point be called upon to offer a non-binding advisory opinion regarding a resolution of the controversy. An excellent and extremely realistic depiction of a minitrial is provided by the CPR Institute's videotape, *Out of Court: The Minitrial* (1987), and accompanying procedures and guidelines produced by CPR.

   Minitrial has been successfully employed to settle numerous commercial cases, including some very large ones. See ABA Sub-Committee on Alternative Means of Dispute Resolution, *The Effectiveness of the Mini-Trial in Resolving Complex Commercial Disputes: A Survey* (1986). However, it is not widely used today, largely because the format has often proven to be quite costly. Moreover, where minitrial is not used until the conclusion of discovery, the possibility of deriving significant cost savings is substantially diminished. Today, whether or not they are so-described, abbreviated minitrial formats are sometimes employed in the context of mediation.

4. *Real Time ADR on the "Big Dig."* The Boston Central Artery/Tunnel Project, better known as the "Big Dig," is the nation's largest construction project. It is also the premier application of a "real time" dispute resolution system called the Dispute Review Board, or "DRB." The typical Artery/Tunnel construction contract calls for a DRB made up of two neutral technical panelists (such as construction engineers with specialties in excavation) and a panel chair with significant dispute resolution experience. Panelists are appointed at project start-up, permitting them to become familiar with project personnel, technical aspects, and progress. DRB operating rules minimize formality and attempt to cut out all vestiges of legal hearing process, such as lawyer argument and examination of witnesses, and maximize the flexibility of the panel to control the gathering of information. At the conclusion of the inquisitorial process, the panel deliberates and

produces a recommendation, complete with supporting rationale, for the project director. The DRB system has been a great success in getting disputes resolved short of the courthouse. What are the potential benefits of such a system? What limitations?

5. *The Evolution of the Multi-Door Courthouse Concept.* A number of federal and state court programs here and abroad have attempted to provide a smorgasbord of ADR choices for parties. However, for a variety of reasons most court programs have tended to emphasize only one or two processes. As discussed in Chapter 22, the most promising evocations of the spirit of Sander's vision for a dynamic program matching ADR process to the issues at hand are court programs in which magistrates or special masters have been given wide discretion as process architects and case managers. See Stipanowich (1998).

CHAPTER
20

"Ice Breakers," Stepped Clauses, and Conflict Management Systems

The developments described in Chapter 19 paralleled (and to some extent prefigured) a growing body of experience with approaches incorporating a series of discrete dispute resolution "steps." Such stepped ADR "systems" often begin with simple, straightforward, and informal approaches (such as face-to-face negotiation of a business issue, or a confidential "hotline" for employee grievances), and, if necessary, provide parties with a series of additional strategies for addressing conflict up to and including arbitration or litigation. Stepped approaches are well established in commercial and employment settings in the United States and are becoming increasingly common in international business transactions.

A. GENERAL COMMITMENTS, "ICE BREAKER" CLAUSES

The first step many organizations took to implement an ADR system was to make a general commitment to employ ADR before litigation by signing what might be called an "ice breaker" clause. Lawyers often voiced concern that if they raised the possibility of settlement, it would be taken by adversaries, and even by their own clients, as a signal that they did not believe in their cases and were overanxious to settle. One way to overcome this barrier, it was thought, would be for corporations and law firms to adopt a uniform policy of exploiting ADR in every dispute. Lawyers could then tell both clients and opposing counsel that they were mentioning settlement as a matter of policy and not because of concern about any particular case.

The first and most influential of such clauses was created by the CPR Institute of Dispute Resolution. The current text is set forth below:

CPR Corporate Policy Statement
on
Alternatives to Litigation

(COMPANY NAME)

We recognize that for many disputes there is a less expensive, more effective method of resolution than the traditional lawsuit. Alternative dispute resolution (ADR) procedures involve collaborative techniques which can often spare businesses the high costs of litigation.

In recognition of the foregoing, we subscribe to the following statements of principle on behalf of our company and its domestic subsidiaries:*

In the event of a business dispute between our company and another company which has made or will then make a similar statement, we are prepared to explore with that other party resolution of the dispute through negotiation or ADR techniques before pursuing full-scale litigation. If either party believes that the dispute is not suitable for ADR techniques, or if such techniques do not produce results satisfactory to the disputants, either party may proceed with litigation.

_____

CHIEF EXECUTIVE OFFICER

_____

CHIEF LEGAL OFFICER

_____

DATE

Forms of this Policy Statement, often referred to as the "CPR Pledge," have been adopted by several thousand companies and their subsidiaries. A similar Policy Statement for law firms has been signed on behalf of more than 1,500 of the world's largest law firms and legal practices.

QUESTIONS

1. Does the foregoing commitment appear to be legally binding?
2. Why do you suppose so many corporate counsel signed the document on behalf of their companies or law firms? Can you see any potential limitations of this approach?

B.   STEPPED DISPUTE RESOLUTION PROGRAMS

1.   *General Principles for Design and Implementation*

a.   Design

STEPHEN B. GOLDBERG, JEANNE M. BRETT, & WILLIAM L. URY, DESIGNING AN EFFECTIVE DISPUTE RESOLUTION SYSTEM

Adapted from Stephen B. Goldberg et al., in John Wilkinson et al., Donovan Leisure Newton & Irvine ADR Practice Book, 253-265 (1997 supp.)

In 1987, IBM and Fujitsu, in settling a number of disputes arising out of IBM's charge that Fujitsu had improperly used IBM software, agreed to set up a technical facility under the direction of a neutral expert. In that facility, Fujitsu could examine certain categories of IBM software and choose those it wished to use. IBM was entitled to compensation for any software used by Fujitsu. Disputes about appropriate use were to be resolved by the neutral expert; disputes about compensation were to be resolved by arbitration prior to Fujitsu's use of the software in question.

In 1986, two oil companies that were about to engage in a joint venture agreed that all disputes arising out of the joint venture would be submitted to a partnership committee. Disputes not resolved by the partnership committee were to be referred to two senior executives, one from each company, both uninvolved in the joint venture. The executives' task was to study the problem and, in consultation with their companies, negotiate a settlement. If they were unsuccessful, the dispute was to be sent to final and binding arbitration.

Why did the corporations in these two examples set up elaborate dispute resolution systems? Why didn't Fujitsu and IBM simply agree on a monetary settlement of their disputes? Why didn't the two oil companies simply provide that any dispute between them would be resolved by arbitration?

The answer is clear. More and more companies are realizing that if they are involved in a long-term relationship—buyer-seller, client-service provider, joint venture, or market leader-follower (like IBM and Fujitsu)—disputes between them are inevitable. It is not enough to settle one of those disputes, as IBM and Fujitsu might have done, because many more are likely to arise. It is not enough to agree on a single dispute resolution procedure, as the oil companies might have done, because a procedure that is satisfactory for one dispute may not be satisfactory for all disputes, and a procedure that is satisfactory at one stage of a dispute may not be satisfactory at another stage of the same dispute.

The task for parties who can reasonably anticipate a stream of disputes between them is thus to go beyond settling those disputes one at a time and to go beyond selecting one procedure to resolve all disputes. Their goal should be to design a comprehensive and effective dispute resolution system which contains effective procedures arranged in an appropriate sequence. In addition, the people using the system should possess the skills, motivation, and resources they need to make those procedures function effectively.

Interests, Rights, and Power

In seeking to resolve a dispute, parties may focus on their interests, their rights, or their power. *Interests* are the needs, desires, concerns, or fears that underlie what the parties say they want: the positions they take in a dispute. If the parties focus on interests, the procedure they will use, at least initially, is interests-based negotiation, in which a dispute is treated as a problem to be resolved by reconciling the parties' underlying interests . . .

[For parties with an ongoing relationship, an approach to dispute resolution which focuses on interests is better than one which focuses on rights, which in turn is better than one which focuses on power. What does *better* mean? That is determined by four criteria: satisfaction with outcome, effect on the relationship, recurrence of disputes, and transaction costs.]

Research shows that reconciling interests tends to produce higher satisfaction with outcomes, better relationships, and less recurrence of disputes than does determining who is right or more powerful. . . . If the parties are more satisfied, their relationship benefits and disputes are less likely to recur. Determining who is right or more powerful, with the emphasis on winning and losing, typically makes the relationship more strained if it does not completely destroy it. . . . The transaction costs—time, money, and emotional energy—involved in reconciling interests through negotiation can be great. . . . Still, the transaction costs of interest-based negotiation pale in comparison with those of a rights or power battle.

Despite the general advantages of resolving disputes by procedures that focus on the parties' interests, resolving all disputes in this fashion is not possible. In some disputes, though fewer than is often supposed, interests are so opposed that agreement is not possible. In others, the parties' perceptions of who is right or more powerful are so different that they cannot establish a range within which to negotiate a resolution of their competing interests. A rights procedure may be needed to clarify their rights before an interests-based resolution can be sought. . . .

In sum, the general principle is not that *all* disputes should be resolved by focusing on interests, but that *most* should. The problem is that rights and power procedures are often used when they are not necessary. A procedure that should be the last resort too often becomes the first resort. The task of those designing a dispute resolution system, typically the parties' attorneys, is not to eliminate rights and power procedures but to limit their use to those situations in which they are necessary. It is also to provide low-cost ways to determine rights or power for those disputes that cannot be resolved by focusing on interests alone. . . .

Diagnosis

[The authors explain that dispute systems design may occur when parties are about to enter into a relationship, or midstream, perhaps after efforts to resolve disputes have proved unsuccessful.]

Learning what kinds of disputes occur and with whom is the designers' first diagnostic task. . . . If the disputes tend to have a strong emotional element, the designer should consider methods to vent emotions. If the disputes involving purely legal or technical issues, such as the extent to which Fujitsu may use IBM software, a low-cost rights procedure may be appropriate. . . . [T]he designers will also focus on the causes of those disputes. Sometimes identifying causes can suggest ways to prevent similar disputes in the future.

The designers' next diagnostic task is to determine how many disputes are currently being handled and why. If the parties are relying substantially upon rights and power contests, rather than resolving their disputes through interests-based negotiation, there may not be a convenient or well-understood procedure for encouraging negotiations. . . .

Design: Six Principles

Principle 1: Building in Consultation Before, Feedback After   When one party to a relationship is considering action that will affect the other, it should at least notify, and ideally consult, the other before taking that action. (*Notification* refers simply to an announcement in advance of the intended action; *consultation* goes further and offers an opportunity to discuss the proposed action before it takes place.) Notification and consultation can prevent disputes that arise through sheer misunderstanding. They can also reduce the anger and unthinking opposition that often result when decisions are made unilaterally. They further serve to identify points of difference that may be more easily resolved before action is taken than after.

Sophisticated parties seek not only to avoid disputes but also to learn from them. At some manufacturing companies, lawyers, and managers regularly analyze consumer complaints to determine what changes in product design might reduce the likelihood of similar disputes in the future. Wise designers build into the system procedures for postdispute analysis and feedback.

Principle 2: Put the Focus on Interests In order to encourage the interests-based resolution of disputes, an increasing number of contract clauses explicitly provide for negotiation as the first step in resolving a dispute between competing businesses. These clauses typically designate who will participate in the negotiation, when it must begin and end, and what happens if it is unsuccessful. They often provide for a multistep procedure in which a dispute that is not successfully resolved at one step is then negotiated at a higher step by different negotiators. [The authors also recommend providing negotiation skills training within the organization, including joint negotiations training for parties who will be negotiating with each other in the future.]

Principle 3: Build in "Loop-Backs" to Negotiation Sometimes interests-based negotiations fail because the parties' perceptions of who is right or who is more powerful are so different that, when interests clash, they cannot establish a range within which to negotiate. At the same time, resort to a full-blown rights or power contest would be costly, not only in financial terms but also in relational terms. Thus, the wise designer will build into the system procedures for providing the parties with information about who would prevail in the event of a contest, without the necessity of their actually engaging in such a contest. Because such procedures are designed to encourage the parties to return to negotiation, they are called *loop-back* procedures. [The authors provide examples such as mediator predictions of the outcome of a case, as well as the use of minitrial and summary jury trial.]

Principle 4: Provide Low-Cost Rights and Power Backups In some disputes interests are so opposed that agreement is not possible. Still, resort to a full-blown court battle would have damaging financial and relational consequences. Thus, an effective dispute resolution system will contain procedures for final and binding resolution of disputes through low-cost alternatives to litigation. Among these procedures are conventional arbitration, expedited arbitration, final-offer arbitration and Med-Arb. . . .

Principle 5: Arrange Procedures in a Low-to-High Cost Sequence The first four design principles — consultation before, feedback after; put the focus on interests; build in loop-backs to negotiation; provide low-cost rights and power backups — suggest a fifth. Create a sequence of procedures that is based on

these principles. The following is a menu of procedures to draw on in designing such a sequence:

1. Prevention procedures:
   — Notification and consultation
   — Postdispute analysis and feedback

2. Interests-based procedures
   — Negotiation
   — Mediation

3. Loop-back procedures
   — Advisory arbitration
   — Minitrial
   — Summary jury trial
   — Cooling-off period

4. Low-cost backup procedures
   — Conventional arbitration
   — Expedited arbitration
   — Med-Arb
   — Final offer arbitration

*Principle 6: Provide Disputants with the Necessary Motivation, Skills, and
Resources*   A final principle cuts across all others. Providing appropriate procedures is important, but insufficient if the parties lack the motivation, skills
and resources to use those procedures effectively. For example, two companies
entering into a long-term buyer-seller relationship set up a three-step negotiation procedure in which the first-step negotiators were the managers involved
in any dispute, the second-step negotiators were their immediate supervisors,
and the third-step negotiators were vice presidents from each corporation.
Although both corporations hoped that most disputes would be resolved at
step one, the results were just the opposite. After the first few months, nearly
all disputes went to steps two and three for resolution. The reason?
Investigation disclosed that the first few settlements reached at step one were
carefully scrutinized and strongly criticized by a high-ranking officer at one of
the companies. As a result, managers at that company decided that the wisest
course of action for them was simply to go through the motions of attempting
to negotiate a settlement, rather than to try to reach agreement. They would
then blame the resulting impasse on the other party's intransigence. In that
way, they were able to avoid the criticism from corporate higher-ups.
    The moral is clear: If the goal of the parties is to encourage negotiated
settlements, the negotiators must be motivated to settle. At one corporation,
this is done by providing positive feedback to all managers who negotiate step-
one settlements. The terms of the settlement are discussed with the manager,
but all comments that might be viewed as critical are directed toward improving future settlements, not criticizing the subject settlement. Good settlements
are reflected in positive evaluations; bad settlements are ignored.
Management's philosophy is clear: in the long run, the cost of a few bad
step-one settlements will be outweighed by the increased step-one settlement

rate resulting from a corps of managers who are genuinely motivated to negotiate settlements at step one. . . .

---

b. Implementation

Attorneys for institutions, or representatives of key "stakeholders," who will participate in and be affected by conflict management programs (such as employees of a company) may also be involved in strategies for implementation of such programs within the organization. As two experienced "workplace" conflict management system designers explain, the scale of organizational change implicated in such programs demands careful planning and consideration of the needs, expectations, and concerns of the stakeholders. This excerpt, which picks up where the earlier Goldberg, Brett, and Ury excerpt ends, summarizes the various strategies that may be necessary to a successful "rollout."

CATHY A. COSTANTINO AND CHRISTINA SICKLES MERCHANT, IMPLEMENTING A NEW CONFLICT MANAGEMENT SYSTEM

Adapted from Designing Conflict Management Systems (1996), Chs. 2, 9-12

THE IMPORTANCE OF A PILOT PROGRAM

After organizational assessment and design, and the start-up of training and educational efforts, the organization's leadership and ADR design team now face a choice: should they introduce ADR broadly on a large scale and permanent basis in multiple programs or should they test an experimental design in a given dispute arena? . . . Pilot testing, where ADR is introduced on a limited, experimental basis in particular programs, affords the design team, the organization's leadership, and its particular stakeholders with the opportunity to test out the reliability of their information, their design and their planning—with relatively low cost and low risk . . . Successful pilots can give ADR early, favorable publicity resulting in added credibility within the organization, rather than the reputation of being a mistake, inadequate, or "just another gimmick." . . .

[The ADR design team should ask several questions before selecting a target for the pilot program.] Are there sufficient numbers of disputes to test success? . . . Are there sufficient resources (time, staff, money) to allocate to the pilot? . . . Are the results of the pilot measurable and easily evaluated? . . . Is the area of the pilot important to the rest of the organization? . . . If the answers to most of these questions are affirmative, the critical factors for a successful pilot have probably been met.

With the selection of the target, the actual details of the pilot design and attendant implementation now begin. . . . [Ten general guidelines to steer the pilot's successful implementation: (1) Look at similar programs in similar organizations; (2) Design according to the problems; (3) Check the design with experienced neutrals; (4) Determine case selection criteria; (5) Identify goals and process for evaluating results; (6) Notify, prepare, and educate participants; (7) Acquire neutral practitioners; (8) Determine how costs will be met; (9) Identify incentives to use ADR; and (10) Develop information exchange and case procedures.] In addition, the ADR design team and

ADR pilot project coordinator need to identify the information necessary to close a dispute (whether it settles or not) and to develop any necessary evaluation documents. The forms to be completed upon the resolution of the dispute or to signal a dispute's exit out of the ADR process are prepared in advance of the pilot's start-up. This facilitates case tracking and ongoing measurement of the progress of the cases in the pilot. . . .

BROADER IMPLEMENTATION

Once the pilot has been completed and evaluated, it is time to roll out the ADR approach on a wider scale. . . . Because the pilot has (ideally) gone well and achieved its goals as measured against the baseline data, there is a tendency to simply take the pilot design and graft it onto another section of the organization's conflict management system. This can be a mistake and may result in the new system rejecting the grafted pilot. . . . Here, the "4-T's" approach to organization-wide implementation can help: [*tout* the pilot program and its success, *test* its utility in other areas of the organization, *tailor* it as necessary, and bring together a *team* of representatives from all parts of the organization to facilitate further implementation.]

EVALUATION

Implementation efforts alone are not enough to assure the use of and satisfaction with the revised conflict management system. Once the system is implemented, the next stage, and the last one of the organization's first pass through the ADR design cycle, is evaluation. The purpose of the evaluation stage is to determine whether the revised system is working and if it is addressing the issues raised on the organization-wide assessment. . . . [T]he formal evaluation stage takes a determined look at what has actually been learned and achieved so far in the management of conflict by the organization and its members.

USE OF INCENTIVES AND REWARDS

Where incentives (both individual and organizational) to use new ADR processes and procedures are maximized and constraints are minimized, the likelihood that stakeholders will try out the new system is increased. . . . [For organizational, or inside, stakeholders these incentives might include: recognition for efforts to promote and apply the ADR system, the chance to be part of a team, the chance to create new initiatives, achievement of the established organizational mission, increased efficiency or effectiveness, and economics. For external stakeholders: positive publicity, increased access to organizational leaders and operations, and improved relations with the organization.]

DEALING WITH RESISTANCE

It is human nature to fear the unknown, and the introduction of any new system, including a conflict management system, encourages this emotion to emerge. Most individuals do not like change, in part because of their fear that it will lead to a loss of some kind (usually of control). . . . [It can be] useful to group the sources of resistance and types of constraints into three broad categories: personality, politics, and practice. . . . [W]hat is most important is the ability of the ADR design team to be open to data and to the more subtle hints and guesses about what is truly going on organizationally when the team senses resistance and constraints. . . . In addition, ADR design team members need to be aware of their own "stuff" — discomfort, resentment, or defensiveness when resistance emerges, which can block important signals about the need for action.

By anticipating resistance and constraints as organizational responses to change in the conflict management system, planning for them, and naming these behaviors, the ADR design team can move into the tension and work with these concerns rather than block them or deny their existence. . . .

---

2. *Examples of Stepped Programs or Systems*

a. Commercial Relationships

The design principles articulated by Goldberg, Brett, and Ury were put into practice in whole or in part by many organizations. Many companies have created "stepped" dispute resolution programs or systems and written them into their business contracts.

Stepped systems have long been in use in the field of construction disputes. A notable example is the program developed by British Columbia Hydro (BC Hydro), which oversees a broad ranges of construction projects. Frustrated with its inability to handle construction project claims and concerned with expanding contract verbiage, BC Hydro established an ADR program that begins with face-to-face negotiation and progresses, if necessary, through the following formal steps: an initial decision on claims and controversies by a BC Hydro project representative, a review of the initial decision by a "standing neutral" (appointed for the specific purpose of addressing such claims during the life of the construction project), and, ultimately, binding arbitration. In the first three years of operation, BC Hydro used the system in 119 contracts involving $55 million in construction costs. Forty-seven disputed claims were processed through the system; all but 12 were negotiated face-to-face. Only two reached the "standing neutral," and all were settled without the need for binding arbitration (Stipanowich, 1998).

In some industries, companies have entered into collective agreements embracing the principles set forth above. For example, the American Chemistry Council has created its own stepped dispute resolution system for corporations in the chemical industry. Signatories to the Chemical Industry Dispute Resolution Commitment agree to "commit that any dispute arising hereafter between our company, including its subsidiaries, and another company in the chemical industry which has made a similar commitment, will be resolved in the manner stated below." The document continues:

A. PROCEDURES

1. Negotiation

When a dispute has arisen between our company and another signatory and negotiations between the regularly responsible persons have reached an impasse, other executives having authority to settle the matter . . . shall confer in a good faith effort to resolve the dispute. The General Counsel of the companies shall arrange the conference and may participate in it.

2. Mediation

If the parties have not resolved the dispute within 30 days of their first contact pursuant to paragraph A.1., they will attempt in good faith to resolve the dispute by mediation in accordance with the CPR Procedure for Chemical Industry Dispute Resolution . . .

3. *Adjudication*

If the mediation procedure fails to result in resolution of the dispute within 60 days of selection of a mediator, any party may unilaterally terminate the procedure and pursue other remedies. Either party may propose submission of the dispute to arbitration . . . or to a private judicial procedure, but no party is obligated to agree to any such procedure. . . .

CONTRACTUAL DISPUTE RESOLUTION PROVISIONS

Signatories are encouraged to include dispute resolution provisions in their contracts. The above procedures notwithstanding, if a dispute relates to a matter which is subject to a contractual dispute resolution provision (including without limitation an agreement among co-defendants in a litigation), and if such provision is in conflict with those set forth above, such contractual provision will govern.

The above commitment is entered into in consideration of similar commitments by other companies in the chemical industry and shall become operative when signed by ten companies. After two years from the date thereof, this commitment may be terminated on 90 days written notice to CPR, without affecting any case then pending.

QUESTIONS

1.   In what ways does this document differ from the previously discussed CPR Policy Statement?
2.   What are the pros and cons of the Chemical Industry approach?

b.   Employment Programs

The first stepped dispute resolution systems were created in the context of collective bargaining agreements between companies and unions. With the rise of protective legislation and the modern labor movement, unions and management recognized that they were in long-term relationships from which they could not escape. Both labor and management saw a need for systems that could handle the inevitable disputes that would arise under collective bargaining agreements efficiently, without triggering retaliatory actions by either side. The solution was to create grievance systems defined by contract. Originally such systems consisted simply of arbitration, but over time negotiators developed more complex and efficient systems that featured a series of steps.

A typical labor grievance procedure might consist of the following three steps:

1.   an initial conference between the grievant employee, a union steward, and an employer representative;
2.   a second conference attended by an officer or representative of the employer and the union shop committee or a union representative;
3.   binding arbitration.

The unionized sector of the American economy has shrunk, and most Americans now work in a nonunion environment. At the same time, there has been an enormous growth in legislation to protect the rights of individual workers: civil rights statutes that bar job discrimination on the basis of race, disability, and other factors, as well as individual laws that provide medical benefits, family leave, and other protections. Not surprisingly, employees began to file legal claims against employers with unprecedented frequency.

Some of these new lawsuits addressed serious problems in the workplace, but others did not. Regardless of their intrinsic merit, the rapid increase in employee lawsuits imposed serious costs on American companies and their shareholders. In 2000, for example, the estimated average cost of defending an individual employment lawsuit was $92,000, and the cost of defending a class action was $496,000 (Stallworth et al., 2001).

There are also significant costs and related barriers for employees seeking legal redress. One survey of employee advocates determined that responding lawyers accepted only 5 percent of the employment discrimination cases of prospective clients seeking representation. The lawyers required, on average, minimum provable damages of $60,000 to $65,000, a retainer of $3,000 to $3,500, and a 35 percent contingency fee (Howard, 1995).

In an effort to respond to employee grievances and avoid the cost, disruption and risk inherent in court litigation, many American companies have adopted dispute resolution systems for their employees.

Although these programs vary widely in detail, they include some of the most advanced applications of the systems approach advocated by Goldberg, Brett, and Ury. Some also benefited from the implementation strategies advocated by Costantino and Merchant. The most successful employment conflict resolution programs do more than just resolve individual disputes; they are important, integrated components of an organization's entire personnel policy and operations. Well implemented, these systems set the tone for employee-employer relations and the company's commitment to its employees.

At the same time, concerns about fairness and transparency require that such programs be designed and implemented with care. Where employees' access to the courts and/or to class actions are affected (as by provisions for binding arbitration that are established as a condition of employment), due process and other issues discussed at length in Chapter 18 are implicated.

Keep these issues in mind as you read the following excerpt, which summarizes the goals underlying the evolution of employment conflict management systems from a management perspective and compares several different employment programs.

PETER PHILLIPS, HOW COMPANIES MANAGE EMPLOYMENT DISPUTES

5-7, 8-13, CPR Institute for Dispute Resolution (2003)

The case for establishing an employment dispute management program is, by this time, broadly recognized. Employment dispute resolution programs lend consistency and therefore manageability to the handling of employment workplace disputes. When neutrally applied and administered, they enhance employee confidence and morale. . . . Approached systematically, the interests of the employee and employer predominate over the individual employee's or supervisor's concern that his or her conduct be vindicated.

A systematic, managerial approach to employment disputes also encourages early assessment of conflicts in the workplace to determine at an early juncture such important issues as the extent of company legal exposure, the likelihood that the employee complaint is well-grounded, and ways in which company procedures or supervisory skills might be improved. . . .

There are, of course, employment disputes to which ADR may be inappropriate or precluded. Certain employee claims, such as those involving workers compensation, pension benefits or unemployment insurance, often are expressly excluded from an ADR program by statute. Employers frequently want to reserve access to judicial process in order to prevent the immediate harm that can flow from breaches of non-compete agreements or unauthorized use of trade secrets or other proprietary information. . . . [Recall that employees may also have strong reasons for wanting to preserve the right to go to court to vindicate their rights. See Chapter 18.]

Because quantification of system performance is vital to the management of any system, one should consider what "benchmarks" might be useful to measure system success. These may include:

> *Cycle Time*: How many days, or person-hours, elapse between the initiation of the employment dispute process and the resolution of the issue? . . .
>
> *Legal Costs*: Over a period of time, how much money was spent on legal fees to address employee disputes?
>
> *Rate of Litigation:* Has the number of private and governmental charges been reduced? . . .
>
> *EEOC [Equal Employment Opportunity Commission] Charges:* Has the rate of charges brought before state and federal employment agencies changed?
>
> *Utilization:* Over a period of time, have more or fewer employees availed themselves of the program?

Rate of Resolution at Various Levels: Over a period of time, have issues been resolved more frequently at lower (i.e., less expensive) levels of management? . . .

User Satisfaction: Are employees and other stakeholders satisfied by the process and the outcome of disputes taken through the program? Would they recommend that their peers use it?

[The author explains that institutional employment conflict management systems often include (1) internal efforts at resolution through discussion, negotiation, peer review, ombuds facilities or other advisory and facilitative techniques; (2) intervention by a third-party neutral using non-adjudicative tools such as voluntary mediation or neutral merits evaluation; and (3) adjudication in the form of binding arbitration. These elements vary considerably in detail, however, as the following examples reveal:]

ALCOA offers a program for disputes that cannot be resolved informally and directly that is a classic three-step structure: a review of the problem by senior management; then non-binding mediation; and finally binding arbitration. The program is voluntary—employees may choose to ignore the program and sue if they wish—and is offered to employees after a dispute has arisen rather than as a condition of employment. But an employee who chooses the dispute resolution program waives access to [the courts.] . . .

Johnson & Johnson's "Common Ground" Program is mandatory but does not culminate in arbitration. The three parts of the program are "Open Door," "Facilitation," and "Mediation." "Open Door" encourages employees to discuss problems with their supervisor, their supervisor's boss, human resources personnel, or with "whatever level of management is necessary to resolve the issue." Although no documentation is needed to commence this stage, "Open Door" must be attempted before moving on to the next stage. "Facilitation" involves a designated individual who will ensure that all options of communication have been exhausted. "Mediation" introduces a trained neutral to assist the parties in reaching a mutually acceptable resolution. Employees are notified that, "if none of these steps resolves your dispute with the Company, you are free to pursue legal action in court." . . .

CIGNA offers employees a mandatory program that comprises an "internal" and an "external" component. The employee must choose between two internal processes: the "Speak Easy Process" and the "Peer Review Process"—either, but not both. The Speak Easy Process consists of Phase I—where an employee discusses the problem with a manager/supervisor—and Phase II—a review of issues with an Employee Relations Speak Easy Consultant. The Peer Review Process has three steps: Step I with the supervisor/manager, Step II with the next higher level of management, and Step III with either the head of the division or a Peer Review Panel of five trained specialists including supervisors and exempt and nonexempt employees. Decisions of the Peer Review Board are binding on the company. Complainants dissatisfied with these processes are required to request arbitration, if the issue would otherwise be heard in court. Employees seeking arbitration may request mediation first, which the company may agree to at its discretion. . . .

The U.S. Air Force offers a wide variety of ADR tools, including facilitation, mediation, early neutral evaluation, and access to ombuds, in its Employment ADR Program for nonmilitary employees. As a federal agency the Air Force is prohibited from engaging in binding arbitration unless it is agreed to as part of a negotiated grievance procedure in a collective bargaining agreement. Facilitation, the most used technique, is offered on an ad hoc basis in various nationwide installations, with central guidance in the form of "best practices." Air Force personnel are trained in interest-based negotiation for this purpose. Mediation, the second most-used technique, is conducted pursuant to standard practices for intake, ethical standards, and treatment of settlement agreements, by a uniformly trained corps of practitioners. Notwithstanding a requirement that all Air Force installations have a champion and system for resolution of workplace disputes, and that the Air Force has a number of agreements with labor unions that provide for the use of ADR as an option prior to undertaking other dispute resolution procedures, the agency takes the position that all ADR use is voluntary. . . .

In Shell's "RESOLVE" program, employees are first offered "Early Workplace Resolution," which may involve a meeting with the person complained of, assistance from a supervisor, or intervention by Human Resources or upper management. Next, employees are offered a toll-free hotline to the "Shell Ombuds," who can "confidentially answer questions, offer support and advice, or refer [the complainant] to internal or external processes and resources, as needed." The third step is mandatory mediation, and the fourth step is optional, voluntary arbitration. Thus there is no waiver of any legal right by employees.

Under the program, "External Mediation" (that is, involving a neutral from outside the company) of an employee's claim is required before proceeding to arbitration (at the unilateral election of the employee), or to litigation on either an individual or class basis. If the conflict is not satisfactorily resolved through External Mediation and the conflict involves a legally protected right, an employee may request arbitration or proceed to litigation. . . .

[Further insights into the goals and evolution of the RESOLVE program are provided by an interview conducted by the author with the ombudsperson who administered the program.[1]]

QUESTION: Did any particular event or concern give rise to the decision to go ahead and do this program?
ANSWER: [T]here were at least two precipitating events, one internal and one external. [The new president of the company] brought a vision to bring to Shell a new way of doing business, with a heavy emphasis on employees. And how we resolved conflicts was a part of that. The issue was kind of on the periphery and never came into play until a race discrimination suit was filed by Texaco employees. . . . that made national headlines. . . . So Shell, heeding the warning of what happened at Texaco, decided that now was the time to go forward with this . . . dispute resolution system which eventually became known as RESOLVE. . . .
Q: What were the metrics that the program was designed to address?
A: There were none. The orders did not include anything like, "You must reduce the number of lawsuits or EEO claims by 'x' factor." There were none. The president at the time . . . would probably say he was looking for something kind of immeasurable.
    . . . Shell was a traditional command-and-control culture. [The president] wanted to change that. This was a conflict-averse culture. People raised issues at

1. Interview with Wilbur Hicks, Shell Oil Company, Jan. 14, 2002.

their own peril. [He] wanted to change that. He felt that knowing what was on people's minds, knowing what conflicts they dealt with, would help the business. Not only their workplace problems, but problems they face in doing their jobs — if we knew what those are, if we can figure them out and let people have the tools to solve their own problems, this can only help the business. . . .

Q: One consequence of that, I guess, might be lower turnover?

A: Absolutely. We have made investments in these employees and they have all this valuable information; and if they feel that they can't solve their own problems, they'll look for a workplace where they can. And there are many corporations that are developing that model. . . . We do a report from time to time about what's going on in the program, usually what kind of issues come forward — and, by the way, the number of lawsuits is down substantially. We kind of say that as an aside, but I know that to many people in the company, that's what they're looking for. Now with the changing economic situation [*Note*: The interview was conducted during a recession], the pendulum has swung back more to a concern for the business proposition: What is the bottom line here? . . . And clearly our business proposition is that we do save the company money.

We're getting these things earlier in the process, when the emotions haven't ratcheted up. Big lawsuits drag on and on and people perceive that the company is resisting and holding out and they become more and more angry, so the price of resolving it goes higher and higher. . . .

Q: What about the legal assistance plan? What did you accomplish by it?

A: We gained another incentive to solve problems early. If the employees could have access to good legal advice of their own choosing, paid for by the company, that would give the company a heads-up in terms of solving the problem. Now the counterargument was that people would just abuse this. The first thing that they would do would be to get a lawyer. We would have lawsuits on our hands. But the reality has been nothing near that. Very few employees have used this legal assistance program, and those that do so, do it after they're in the process. Where there has been an issue and a lawyer has raised that to the company's attention, the company has paid serious attention. . . By the same token, where there has *not* been an issue, better that the person's own lawyer say that, than the company. It really worked out to the benefit of everybody. I know we haven't spent much at all on this legal assistance program over five years. And the benefits have just been enormous. That has been the experience across the board with all the companies with legal assistance programs.

QUESTIONS

1. Does it appear that Shell adhered to the basic principles espoused by Goldberg, Brett, and Ury in creating and implementing the RESOLVE Program? Can you tell whether they adopted any of the precepts advocated by Costantino and Merchant for implementation?

2. In Chapter 18, we analyzed the current debate over provisions requiring employees to submit to mandatory binding arbitration of employment-related claims and controversies as a condition of employment — issues that are often of paramount importance to legal counselors in this environment. In what ways did Shell and other companies

described above try to address concerns associated with such provisions? Did they succeed?

3. The Director of Maryland-based Giant Food's Fair Employment Practices Program reports that the company mediates most EEOC claims and cases filed in the courts. Beforehand, her office uses various approaches to respond to and resolve workplace disputes early. Of 800 internal workplace complaints filed in 2002, only 20 resulted in formal complaints; of the latter, 90 percent were resolved through settlement. See *The Use of Alternative Dispute Resolution (ADR) in Maryland Business: A Benchmarking Study* by the Maryland Mediation and Conflict Resolution Office (2004). Do you think this should be taken as a sign of success? Why or why not?

4. Some well-known institutional employment mediation programs make use of mediators who are themselves employees of the institution. Is it possible to have a workable, reliable mediation program under such circumstances? What concerns must be addressed, and how?

5. Even where litigation is imminent and numerous parties are involved, ADR may provide an avenue to constructive resolution of the issues. For example, in *Kosen v. American Express Financial Advisors, Inc.* (Civ. Action No. 1: ___ 02CV0082 (D.D.C. 2002)), a group of 15 women who worked as financial advisors for American Express filed a class action lawsuit against the latter alleging a systematic practice of denying equal employment opportunities to women. The next day they filed a proposed consent decree.

Before filing the complaint and consent decree, plaintiffs and defendants retained a private mediator who facilitated negotiations leading to the consent decree. During the period of mediation, defendants turned over to plaintiffs data and other information about the makeup of and practices in their workplace, and counsel for the plaintiffs retained a consultant to conduct a statistical analysis of the data. The consent decree, approved by the court on June 16, 2002, provided for a settlement fund of $31 million. Class counsel together received $10.85 million, or 35 percent of the total amount. The decree also provided for various injunctive relief measures, including the creation of a central database for distribution of leads and client accounts, establishment of objective criteria for assignment of client accounts, and implementation of a diversity training program. At the parties' request, the court appointed a private attorney as special master to oversee implementation of the decree (Green, 2003).

c. Mass Claims Programs

No discussion of the evolution of conflict management systems is complete without a brief reference to the development of ADR programs to handle multitudes of individual claims pursuant to court settlements of class actions or mass claims. Below, the Special Master charged with designing and implementing the program for resolution of claims by September 11th victims and their families summarizes the nature and utility of such programs.

KENNETH R. FEINBERG, ONE-STOP SHOPPING: USING ADR TO RESOLVE DISPUTES AND IMPLEMENT A SETTLEMENT

19 *Alternatives* 59 (January 2001)

One curious feature of ADR is how often it is associated only with the resolution of an underlying dispute. Once mediation or some other form of ADR is effective in settling the dispute among the parties, it often disappears from the radar screen. When it comes to ADR, the visibility of any particular technique often begins and ends with news concerning its effectiveness in settling a major source of disagreement among the parties. What is usually ignored is the role of ADR after the underlying dispute is resolved; all too often there is little or no followup when it comes to the role ADR plays in implementing a settlement, in making sure that the terms and conditions of the settlement are satisfied in an efficient and fair manner.

The role of ADR in post-settlement implementation is most apparent in large class actions involving mass torts, major insurance policy settlements and consumer litigation. In these and other similar complex and protracted litigations, a comprehensive settlement involves literally thousands of individual plaintiff claimants, all demanding their fair share of allocated settlement proceeds. To the public and many ADR commentators, an aggregate settlement has in fact been achieved. But fundamental questions remain: Which claimants will receive the benefits of the comprehensive settlement? How much they will receive and based upon what terms and conditions? It is in resolving these questions that ADR plays an additional creative and important role.

First, the ADR neutral may play an important role after a settlement is reached by fashioning an allocation formula for distribution of proceeds to eligible claimants. Plaintiff's lawyers may welcome such an initiative, thereby avoiding potential conflict of interest problems in the allocation of limited funds among their various clients. The defendants also may support this initiative, eager to make sure that the settlement is successful and fair when it comes to eligibility criteria and the distribution of monies to the population of plaintiff claimants. In mass tort cases such as Agent Orange and silicone breast implants, as well as asbestos and DES litigation, and in some "vanishing premium" insurance settlements, the role of the neutral in fashioning and implementing settlement terms and conditions loomed large in the ultimate success of the settlement initiative.

Second, even in those cases where comprehensive settlement terms and conditions are negotiated up front by the litigating parties themselves, ADR may still play a critically important role in the settlement's implementation. Mediation or arbitration may become available to those individual claimants who challenge their allocated share of the aggregate award. Convinced that they are entitled to more of the proceeds, or that they have been unfairly placed on the wrong level of an allocation matrix, individual claimants may avail themselves of mediation or arbitration in an effort to improve their respective award.

In the mass tort heart valve and Dalkon Shield settlements, for example, the availability of ADR processes to assist individual claimants who honestly believed that they were wronged by their allocated award, went a long way in convincing the courts (and the claimants themselves) of the ultimate fairness of the settlement. At the same time, the availability of such ADR processes at the "back end" implementation stage of a comprehensive mass settlement, helps minimize the likelihood that individual claimants will opt-out of the deal and decide to litigate (thus threatening the comprehensiveness of the settlement itself).

All too often, the public and consumers of ADR services fail to recognize the value of alternative dispute resolution in providing "one-stop shopping" for the litigants themselves. Not only can ADR be used effectively to help resolve the underlying dispute among the parties, but it also can become a valuable tool in assuring effective implementation of a settlement, maximizing the likelihood that all parties will comply with the deal and will view the settlement as fair, just, and equitable.

---

3. Drafting a Multi-Step Clause

As more and more attorneys have acquired experience with multi-step dispute resolution systems, it has reinforced a growing awareness that reliance on standard contract boilerplate, like that offered by many institutional providers of dispute resolution services, may not result in a conflict resolution approach that is most appropriate for a particular transaction or dispute. One former corporate house counsel warns, "The dispute resolution process . . . imposed on a client by using a boilerplate clause may permanently sour them on ADR when they experience just as many — or worse — problems than they did in the courts. In fact, they may be subjected to the worst of both worlds and end up spending inordinate time in court and in ADR and unhappy with the lawyer that suggested ADR" (Trantina, 2001). Attorneys are encouraged to take a proactive role in tailoring a dispute resolution process to a client's particular needs and goals. One checklist of drafting considerations includes the following:

- Take time to understand the client's needs, including the nature of probable or potentially significant disputes, the nature of underlying business relationships, and the client's concerns and expectations regarding conflict resolution [cf. Goldberg, Brett, and Ury];
- Be aware of the changing legal environment surrounding ADR, and consider drafting choices to avoid pitfalls and address key issues;
- Beware of standard templates or provisions that were designed for different situations;
- Develop and use an up-to-date "drafting issues checklist" — perhaps initially relying on a published checklist and revising it;
- Understand the differences between institutional procedures before deciding which to incorporate.

Given the importance of this preparation, it is a matter of concern that as the pivotal players in the development of approaches to resolving conflict, lawyers have often failed to move beyond traditional "liti-gotiation" approaches. As observed in a 2003 study, "[W]hile attorneys may be trained in representing parties in disputes, most have not been specifically trained in ADR techniques and processes" [Maryland Mediation and Conflict Resolution Office, 2004]. Of particular concern is the relative ignorance of ADR and conflict management options among those who have the responsibility to negotiate and draft contracts. While "trial lawyers" have often had experience with mediation and other approaches, corporate transactional counsel tend to have little or no experience with these choices—and are reluctant or unable to incorporate discussions about dispute resolution in commercial contract negotiations. As one senior lawyer at a leading Boston law firm fretted,

> As an advocate who is a member of a good-sized law firm, I found one of the problems was that many of these ADR issues were addressed by my transactional corporate partners, who didn't like me tinkering with the ADR provisions at the end of the deals so they couldn't close the transaction. Unfortunately, the clauses they used were often taken out of form books and not really discussed between the parties.

Stipanowich and Kaskell (2001). Thus, opportunities to incorporate lessons learned from a company's or department's negotiation, mediation, or arbitration experiences are often foregone. Among other things, our investigations into corporate disputing must help us to understand how to effectively channel feedback into the negotiating and drafting process. The CPR Institute recently made an effort to inform and educate corporate counsel and business persons by assembling guidelines for drafters. See Scanlon (2003).

4.   *Enforcement of Contractual Provisions Involving Multi-Step ADR*

The growing use of multi-step clauses has confronted federal and state courts with questions relating to a party's failure to comply with contract directives to participate in negotiation or mediation prior to arbitration. Judicial responses vary. (As you have seen, courts sometimes refuse to enforce such clauses.) As you read the following cases, consider the extent to which each succeeds in (1) fulfilling the apparent intent of the contracting parties and (2) promoting the policies underlying the Federal Arbitration Act.

WELBORN CLINIC v. MEDQUIST, INC.

301 F.3d 634 (7th Cir. 2002)

. . . To create the medical records necessary for patient care, a medical facility must transcribe the reports, notes, and summaries dictated by health care professionals. In December 1998, Welborn, which historically had transcribed in-house, entered into a written contract with The MRC Group, Inc., under which MRC agreed to perform all transcription services on behalf of Welborn at a charge of 13.2 cents per line transcribed. The form contract was supplied by MRC. Under the heading "Payments and Charges" the contract included §3.5, labeled "Dispute Resolution," which provided in its entirety:

> In the event that any invoice amount is disputed by Client, Client shall deliver written notice of such disputed amount to Vendor within ten (10) days of receipt

of the invoice by Client. Vendor shall promptly deliver to Client any backup or other information which supports the correctness of such disputed amount. Upon receipt of such information, Client shall have ten (10) days in which to examine such information and to pay to Vendor any portion of such disputed amount which Client, in its sole discretion, has determined to be substantiated. Thereafter, if any dispute still remains with respect to any amount, Vendor and Client shall immediately enter into good faith negotiations to resolve it. In the event the parties are unable to resolve such dispute within ten (10) days of entering into negotiations, the dispute shall be settled by arbitration in accordance with the commercial arbitration rules of the American Arbitration Association. Such arbitration shall be conducted in the State of Ohio. The decision reached through arbitration shall be final and binding on both parties.

Soon thereafter, MedQuist acquired MRC and succeeded to all its rights and obligations under the contract.

MedQuist began performing under the contract on March 23, 1999. Almost immediately, Welborn challenged the methods MedQuist was using to count the number of lines transcribed and to calculate its charges. Welborn believed both that MedQuist was inflating its line count and that it had misrepresented key elements of its counting and billing practices before entering into the contract. This prompted Welborn to initiate the dispute resolution procedure by delivering written notice of its disputes to Med-Quist and requesting backup information. MedQuist refused to provide any backup. When Welborn subsequently withheld payment of the disputed invoices in October 1999, MedQuist stopped performing under the contract and refused to return any medical records it had in its possession. After several rounds of squabbling, Welborn exercised its right to cancel the contract.

On May 3, 2000, Welborn filed a complaint in the district court [demanding that] MedQuist return Welborn's medical records. At a pretrial conference, MedQuist agreed to turn over those records and then moved to dismiss the complaint and compel arbitration. The district court granted MedQuist's motion in its entirety. Welborn appeals, claiming [among other things] that MedQuist waived its right to arbitration through its pre-litigation conduct . . .

Like any other contractual right, the right to arbitrate a claim may be waived. . . . We will find waiver when "based on all the circumstances, the party against whom the waiver is to be enforced has acted inconsistently with the right to arbitrate." . . . Welborn contends that MedQuist has waived its right to arbitrate through a series of delay tactics and its refusal to participate in informal dispute resolution.

[As to MedQuist's delay in providing records, the court concluded that:] even strong-arm tactics like the withholding of important medical records while demanding payment are not automatically enough to constitute an implied waiver of the agreement's arbitration provision.

Welborn also argues that MedQuist's failure to follow the explicit steps of §3.5 dictates that it cannot now move for arbitration. Since MedQuist did not promptly deliver to Welborn any backup information to support the correctness of its disputed amounts or enter into good-faith negotiations with Welborn, Welborn argues, it should not now be permitted to jump ahead to arbitration, the final step in the dispute resolution process.

The district court found that the other steps listed in §3.5 were not conditions precedent to arbitration. As MedQuist points out, breach of a contract containing an arbitration clause does not amount to a waiver of arbitration. . . . While it is certainly true that an ordinary breach cannot constitute a rejection of arbitration, Needham and its progeny do not speak to the specific situation where the party seeking arbitration has allegedly breached a part of the arbitration clause itself. . . . Based on the pleadings, MedQuist here failed to pursue any form of negotiation between the parties but instead jumped straight to arbitration.

In the labor context, Congress has voiced a strong preference for nonjudicial resolution of employment disputes. . . . Here too it has expressed through the Federal Arbitration Act a strong presumption in favor of alternative dispute resolution. . . . In a close case, this may make all the difference. . . . If there is a condition precedent, it must be met before a court may compel arbitration. On the other hand, a party cannot avoid arbitration because of the other party's failure to comply with the negotiation steps of a grievance procedure as long as that other party acted in good faith to preserve its right to arbitration. . . . In St. John, the party resisting arbitration argued that its opponent had failed to meet the technical requirements of an arbitration provision by failing to bargain, to provide written demand for arbitration within specified time limits, or to supply the names of arbitrators. The court construed the agreement in favor of arbitration, finding that the defendant need only act in good faith in moving for arbitration; the failure to meet time limits or other technical provisions would not forfeit the right. *Id.* at 1163-1164.

Based on Indiana law and the general presumption in favor of arbitration, we find that the time limits and requirements to provide backup in this case were not conditions precedent to MedQuist's contractual right to compel arbitration and that MedQuist has not waived this right. Indeed, the purpose of §3.5 is undoubtedly to encourage successful negotiations so that neither litigation nor arbitration will be necessary, not to prefer the courts to an arbitrator if informal discussions break down.

KEMIRON ATLANTIC, INC. v. AGUAKEM INT'L
290 F.3d 1287 (11th Cir. 2002)

This interlocutory appeal arises from a civil action filed by Kemiron Atlantic, Inc. ("Kemiron"), against Aguakem International, Inc. ("Aguakem"). . . . Kemiron produces ferric sulfate and Aguakem sells and distributes the substance. Both parties entered into a requirements contract, entitled "Exclusive Purchase and Sale Agreement" (hereinafter "Agreement") on June 2, 1995. Kemiron agreed to supply Aguakem with ferric sulfate, and, in return, Aguakem promised to pay for the material. The contract provided, however, that if any dispute arose from the agreement between the two companies, the matter would be resolved according to section 25 of the Agreement. Section 25, entitled "Dispute Resolution," provided as follows:

> The parties, convinced that a large part of the litigation arising from the nonfulfillment of contracts and agreements is caused by a failure to reduce the essential terms and conditions to writing, and much of the remainder of the litigation in connection with written contracts is caused by weaknesses of various kinds in such written documents, have endeavored to use every care and caution in the preparation of this instrument, knowing nevertheless that a relationship of this character may pose new problems from time to time requiring subsequent resolution and agreement. It shall therefore be the aim and intention of the

parties, and in their mutual interests, to provide practical and dignified means for friendly resolution of any differences in interpretation of this Agreement or the settlement of disputes of any kind that may arise between the parties.

To this end, it is mutually agreed that the parties shall be free to bring any and all such matters to the attention of the other at any time without prejudicing their harmonious relationship and operations hereunder, and that the offices of either party shall be available at all times for the prompt and effective adjustment of any and all such differences, either by mail, telephone, or personal meeting under friendly and courteous circumstances.

In the event that a dispute cannot be settled between the parties, the matter shall be mediated within fifteen (15) days after receipt of notice by either party that the other party requests the mediation of a dispute pursuant to this paragraph. If the parties are unable to select a mediator, the Florida Mediation Group shall select a mediator. The parties agree to use their best efforts to mediate a dispute.

In the event that the dispute cannot be settled through mediation, the parties shall submit the matter to arbitration within ten (10) days after receipt of notice by either party. The arbitration shall be conducted in accordance with the Commercial Arbitration Rules of the American Arbitration Association then in effect. The parties shall each select an arbitrator and the two arbitrators thus selected shall select a third arbitrator. These three arbitrators shall constitute the arbitration panel. It is understood that a judgment or award rendered, which may include an award of damages, may be entered in any court having jurisdiction thereof.

On October 13, 2000, Kemiron made a demand on Aguakem for payment. On November 30, 2000, Aguakem sent Kemiron a notice acknowledging that it owed some of the money, but not all. A payment was not included with the notice. Kemiron presented Aguakem with another demand on April 5, 2001. Aguakem did not respond. Kemiron terminated the Agreement with Aguakem on May 3, 2001.

On May 15, 2001, Kemiron then brought this suit. On July 5, 2001, Aguakem filed, among other matters, a motion to stay the proceeding pending arbitration, pursuant to the Federal Arbitration Act ("FAA"), 9 U.S.C. §§1 et seq.

On October 1, 2001, the district court held an evidentiary hearing on Aguakem's motion to stay the proceeding pending arbitration; the presidents of both Kemiron and Aguakem testified and both parties presented exhibits. Kemiron's President, Lawrence Hjersted, testified that he did not receive any notice or indication from Jorge Unanue, President of Aguakem, that Unanue wanted to mediate the dispute at hand. Unanue admitted that "I didn't — have not given notice per the agreement terms, no" when questioned by the district court. . . .

The court decided the motion on the record after the end of the hearing, and in a written order entered seven days later. The court ruled that, in order for there to be a duty to arbitrate, the parties "must first mediate their dispute and then one party must give notice of their desire to arbitrate the dispute." The court subsequently found that neither party gave notice to mediate or arbitrate, and consequently, the duty to arbitrate was not triggered. . . .

II

A

. . . In this case, the district court denied Aguakem's petition to stay the action pending arbitration on the ground that Aguakem did not perform the steps necessary, as spelled out in the contract, to trigger arbitration. We review this legal conclusion de novo. . . .

B

The appellant contends that Sections 2 and 3 of the FAA, in addition to the FAA's general policy encouraging arbitration, require the district court to stay the proceedings and direct the parties to enter into arbitration. . . . Section 3 of the FAA provides for proceedings to be stayed in district courts when an issue in the proceeding "is referable to arbitration." . . . We disagree with the appellant that the FAA requires the district court to stay the proceedings pending arbitration. Although there is an arbitration agreement between the parties, it is conditioned by the plain language of section 25 of the Agreement, which prescribes what must take place before arbitration. Specifically, the parties had to request mediation and "the matter shall be mediated within fifteen (15) days after receipt of notice by either party that the other party requests mediation." Moreover, the Agreement states that, if the dispute "cannot be settled through mediation, the parties shall submit the matter to arbitration within ten (10) days after receipt of notice by either party."

Thus, under the plain language of the contract, to invoke the arbitration provision, either party must take two steps: first, Aguakem or Kemiron must request mediation and provide notice of the request to the other party. If the mediation subsequently fails, arbitration still cannot take place. The aggrieved party must then take a second step, by providing additional notice, under the terms of the contract, that they wish to pursue arbitration. Then, and only then, is the arbitration provision triggered.

The FAA's policy in favor of arbitration does not operate without regard to the wishes of the contracting parties. See *Mastrobuono*, 514 U.S. at 57, 115 S. Ct. at 1216. Here, the parties agreed to conditions precedent before arbitration can take place and, by placing those conditions in the contract, the parties clearly intended to make arbitration a dispute resolution mechanism of last resort. Unanue told the court that he did not give any notice to Kemiron that he wanted to mediate the disagreement over the ferric sulfate payment. Hjersted testified that Unanue failed to provide any notice or indication that Aguakem wanted a mediation with respect to the payment dispute. Thus, neither party met the first condition required to invoke the arbitration clause in the Agreement. In fact, the record reveals that Aguakem still has not demanded any mediation or arbitration. Because neither party requested mediation, the arbitration provision has not been activated and the FAA does not apply.

For the foregoing reasons, the decision of the district court is AFFIRMED.

QUESTIONS

1. To what extent are each of the foregoing decisions consistent with recent Supreme Court decisions respecting arbitrability, and the relative spheres of courts and arbitrators in addressing procedural issues, under *First Options* and *Howsam*, both discussed in Chapter 17?
2. As a drafter, what might you do to avoid having these kinds of issues end up in court?

PROBLEM

You are working with the general counsel of the Springfield Power Association (SPA), a regional utility that is finalizing a five-year contract with NatLee Coal Company (NatLee) to furnish SPA's requirements of coal for power generation. SPA's general counsel suggests she would prefer a multi-step dispute resolution clause, and sends you "a great provision" that was furnished by a speaker at a recent meeting of the Springfield Bar Association's ADR Committee:

DISPUTE RESOLUTION

Before submitting any dispute between the parties to binding arbitration, they will first follow the informal and escalating procedures set forth as stated herein:

(A) The complaining party's representative will notify the other party's representative in writing of the problem, and both parties will exercise good faith efforts to resolve the matter as quickly as possible.

(B) In the event the matter is not resolved ten days after the delivery of the written notice, the complaining party must request a meeting between the senior representatives of each party to resolve the controversy. The meeting shall take place within five days.

(C) In the event the meeting between the senior representatives does not resolve the issue in a timely fashion, they shall mediate in good faith before a mutually acceptable mediator within 10 days.

(D) If the parties are unable to resolve the dispute through these procedures, they may ask the mediator to submit a non-binding award in order to promote settlement.

BINDING ARBITRATION

If none of the steps above are successful in resolving the dispute, the parties shall submit the matter to binding arbitration <u>within two weeks</u>. Each party shall select an arbitrator, and these two appointed arbitrators shall pick a third.

She realizes this provision is "rather rough" and would like you to critique it and offer suggestions. She warns you that it may be necessary for her company to obtain relief rather quickly in some cases—perhaps through a temporary injunction. (She added the language that would require the institution of arbitration within two weeks after other options were exhausted.) She also wants to keep the costs of dispute resolution down if possible. (The situation is complicated because the requirements contract is a long-distance transaction; NatLee's operations are 750 miles away.) She welcomes any pertinent questions that might assist in finalizing the arrangement.

CONCLUSION

As the foregoing reveals, much time and thought has been given to the development of appropriate conflict resolution processes for specific situations, including multi-stepped or multi-faceted programs. As we will see in the next chapter, experimentation with dispute resolution processes has also included mechanisms calling upon neutrals to act in different capacities, or "wear multiple hats." Although such approaches may afford particular benefits to parties, they must be approached with care.

CHAPTER
21

When Neutrals Wear Multiple Hats: Med-Arb and Arb-Med

A. EXPERIMENTATION WITH MIXED ROLES

Disputing parties have experimented with formats in which a single person plays more than one neutral role in a dispute. Typically the neutral plays these roles in succession, but in some formats the roles are mixed. In a common format known as "Med-Arb," a single individual acts as mediator and, if the negotiations fail to achieve settlement, assumes the role of arbitrator. The following account describes an early, notable example of how appointed arbitrators "changed hats" to help craft a remarkable resolution to a complex, high-profile intellectual property dispute.

FRANCIS FLAHERTY, NEUTRALS DEPLOYED SEVERAL KINDS OF ADR TO SOLVE IBM-FUJITSU COPYRIGHT DISPUTE
5 Alternatives 187 (November 1987)

During the late 1970s and early 1980s, a dispute arose between IBM and Fujitsu over software copyright. Prior to 1980, the year that Congress passed the Computer Software Act, few thought that copyright protection extended to this intellectual property. The right to protection confirmed, IBM lodged a formal complaint against Fujitsu in October 1982, necessitating a settlement agreement between the companies that took eight months to negotiate. Unfortunately, the 1983 accord was poorly drafted and collapsed not long after its adoption.

IBM and Fujitsu continued to negotiate for a solution to the dispute, but no resolution was forthcoming. The parties at last turned to the ADR clause in the 1983 accord, which mandated a two-part ADR procedure: negotiation and arbitration. Basically, the parties agreed to attempt negotiation between themselves and, should that fail to resolve the issue in 60 days, then submit the dispute to binding arbitration. Each side nominated an arbitrator — IBM choosing retired railroad executive and computer expert John Jones and Fujitsu nominating Stanford Law Professor Robert Mnookin. A third arbitrator, Donald A. MacDonald, was nominated by these two.

Although the neutrals began the case in conventional arbitration fashion, they soon resolved to conduct a mini-trial. Arbitrators *and* executives from both parties listened to arguments from both sides relating to Fujitsu's alleged violation of IBM's rights under the 1983 agreement, following the recitations with negotiations. The mini-trial took place between June and July 1986; it was unsuccessful.

At this point in time, MacDonald resigned, leaving Jones and Mnookin to resolve the case. They decided to engage the parties in mediation, with themselves acting as mediators. Unlike the mini-trial, the mediation attempt was successful at reaching a solution to the dispute. Two documents resulted from the mediation strategy, the "1986 Agreement," settling all IBM's intellectual property claims with respect to Fujitsu programs, and the "Washington Agreement," a framework for the resolution of all other issues. This agreement provided the foundation for the Order detailing the neutrals' two-fold solution to the dispute.

First, the neutrals called for Fujitsu to pay a sum for the past and future use of an agreed-upon list of software items. The second part of the solution, a "Secured Facility Regime," dictates a process by which each of the two companies may, under elaborate safeguards and for a fee, observe the software of the other and make use of the technology in their own products. This agreement makes use of another ADR approach: preventative law. Professor Mnookin summarized the benefits of this scheme:

> "The Secured Facility regime provides a unique advantage as a means of settling complicated issues in evolving technological and legal fields. In the past, IBM could never know exactly how Fujitsu was using IBM programming material. In order to determine if some violation of its rights may have occurred, IBM had to wait until after the public release of a Fujitsu program and then conduct an elaborate technical examination of the program. Then, if it chose to pursue a claim, it was extremely expensive and time-consuming.
>
> "Meanwhile, of course, the Fujitsu program at issue was already in the marketplace. Even the threat that IBM might at some point pursue a claim would create a potential problem for both Fujitsu and for the Fujitsu customers using a new Fujitsu program.
>
> "The Secured Facility exposes and resolves disagreements before public release of software. The determination made in the facility as to what goes on the survey sheet is the final word on what material of one company can be used by the other company. Once that sheet leaves the facility, the issue is settled. IBM can be assured that only the material allowed by the instructions is being shared. Fujitsu can be assured that IBM will not make a claim with respect to the use of that material at some date in the future. And customers who license Fujitsu operating system software can be assured that no future controversy will disrupt their use of these programs."

Mini-trial, arbitration, mediation, and preventative law were not the only ADR approaches utilized by the neutrals. They described in their award a Secured Facility supervisor, "an experienced, unbiased, and qualified person or firm . . . with relevant programming experience," to serve as an expert factfinder under the direction of the neutrals. The neutrals themselves were to serve as monitors or "special masters," overseeing the resolution of the dispute and aiding the parties in resolving further disputes.

Although ADR institutions and commentators have expressed concerns about neutrals wearing "multiple hats," the reality is that a significant percentage of active arbitrators and mediators sometimes end up serving roles very different from the one to which they were initially appointed. Recently a group of 128 commercial and employment mediators were queried about how frequently they end up changing hats. They responded as follows:

When initially appointed as a mediator, I have arbitrated issues at the request of the parties when mediation failed to resolve them:

Always	Often	About half the time	Occasionally	Never
1	3	0	45	78

I have mediated issues at the request of the parties even though I was initially appointed as arbitrator:

Always	Often	About half the time	Occasionally	Never
1	3	3	46	69

Attorneys representing clients in mediation or arbitration are likely to be confronted with the option of employing a neutral in multiple roles, either as a matter of initial planning or midway through the course of an ADR process. Therefore, it is critical to understand relevant practical, legal, and ethical concerns. See Stipanowich (2001).

B. CONCERNS ABOUT MED-ARB

Some neutrals regularly employ Med-Arb to resolve contractual disputes, and some institutional sponsors of ADR are now offering Med-Arb procedures. Advocates of such approaches argue that having a single neutral serve in both roles avoids the necessity of having to educate two separate neutrals, saving time and money. They also reason that if the parties are aware that their mediator will render a final and binding decision if disputes are not settled, they may be encouraged to resolve the issues in mediation.

Despite the arguments put forward in favor of Med-Arb, many generally disfavor a mixing of such roles, for the following reasons:

First, it is argued that the roles of mediator and arbitrator are fundamentally incompatible: The arbitrator's interaction with the parties is confined to adversary hearings in which parties present evidence and contest opposing evidence, while mediation usually involves extensive confidential ex parte communications with individual parties. Parties, who know their mediator will decide should mediation fail, may be less candid in communicating with the mediator, undermining a primary goal of the process. Moreover, there is always the possibility that the mediator-turned-arbitrator's view of the issues has been affected by information imparted confidentially in ex parte discussions — information that may not be directly relevant to the issues contested in arbitration, and never subjected to cross-examination or rebuttal. Another concern is that the "big stick" wielded by a mediator-arbitrator will undermine party self-determination and prevent a negotiated settlement from expressing the free will of the parties—especially if the intervener "telegraphs" her own views of the issues in dispute. Finally, many mediators have little or no experience conducting an arbitration hearing, and may not be competent to take on the other role or to address the foregoing concerns. In any event, parties who want a neutral to serve in mixed roles must be very clear about the resolution of the foregoing issues and should address pertinent waiver issues (such as parties' waiver of the right to challenge any resulting arbitration award on grounds of ex parte contact). Otherwise, the arrangement may set the stage for a motion to disqualify an arbitrator or vacate a resulting arbitration award.

The latter difficulty is exemplified by *Township of Aberdeen v. Patrolmen's Benevolent Ass'n*, 669 A.2d 291 (N.J. S. Ct., App. Div. 1996), a decision under New Jersey law regarding a Med/Arb arrangement in a public employment contract. When negotiations over a new collective bargaining agreement between the township and the police officers' union reached an impasse, the union petitioned for the initiation of arbitration under the state's Compulsory Interest Arbitration Act. Prior to the start of hearings, the parties agreed to have the arbitrator attempt to mediate the dispute. When mediated settlement negotiations fell apart, the case went to arbitration. The arbitrator rendered an award in favor of the union, largely on the basis of the township's shifting positions during mediation. Although the interest arbitration statute and implementing regulations permitted Med/Arb, the court struck down the award on the basis that the arbitrator had improperly relied on information gained during the course of mediation and not presented in the arbitration hearing. The court reasoned that "parties should feel free to negotiate without fear that what they say and do will later be used against them," and that "[m]ediation would be a hollow practice if the parties' negotiating tactics could be used against them by the arbitrator in rendering the final decision." For the same reason that "it would be unthinkable for a trial court to base its decision on information disclosed in pretrial settlement negotiations," mediated negotiations preceding arbitration should be protected.

With these concerns in mind, consider your approach to the following scenarios based on real cases.

QUESTIONS

1. ExGen Corporation, a major multinational corporation, filed suit in federal court against Sosumi, Inc., a supplier of components for ExGen's new manufacturing process, alleging $8 million in damages resulting from delays in the delivery of components. Liability was not contested, but there was a dispute as to damages. When discovery was nearly concluded, the parties were strongly encouraged by the court to mediate the disputes.

   You are selected to be the mediator. After two lengthy days of bargaining, including extensive ex parte discussions with both parties, you have engendered some movement on both sides. The parties are still about $1.8 million apart—ExGen demands about $4.8 million and Sosumi is offering $3.0 million. There does not appear to be an opportunity for avoiding impasse by expanding the pie through collateral business arrangements, etc.

   A. Faced with the possibility that there will be no settlement, you are considering a recommendation to the parties to consider submitting the dispute to an abbreviated "baseball arbitration" process in which the arbitrator picks between the final numbers. How should you handle this situation?

B. Suppose you go ahead and invite the parties to discuss whether to use this process and jointly advise you as to their mutual decision. You are somewhat surprised when the parties' attorneys notify you that they have agreed to such a process, and want *you* to be the arbitrator. What will you do?

C. What if the parties also tell you that after discussing the matter, they want you to decide the matter without a hearing, but on the basis of memoranda that each party will submit to you in confidence?

2. Assume you have resolved some but not all the issues in a complex commercial dispute between ExGen and Sosumi. The parties indicate that they desire to arbitrate, but have reached no agreement on the nature of the agreement or the selection of arbitrators. Can you help design an arbitration process?

3. You are designated as chair of a panel of arbitrators in a significant commercial case. During a break in the initial prehearing conference with the parties, all three arbitrators share the sense that the circumstances might lend themselves to mediated negotiation.

A. Should you raise the issue with the parties? If so, how?

B. What if the parties discuss the matter and ask that you mediate the dispute?

4. You have been appointed to arbitrate various issues associated with a corporate "divorce." The parties have agreed that the proceeding will be bifurcated. The initial series of sessions will address the valuation of assets; after the rendition of the initial partial award, a second set of sessions will consider allegations of breach of contract, fraud, etc., among the parties.

After several sessions, the parties jointly inform you that they have discussed settlement of the valuation issue and believe it would be productive to mediate. Given your familiarity with the issues and their comfort with you as a neutral, they seek your participation as mediator. What will you do?

C. ARB-MED

Although not as popular as Med-Arb, another process involves neutrals acting as arbitrators and then switching to the mediator's hat. In "Arb-Med," a neutral initially acts as sole arbitrator, or as a member of an arbitration panel, avoiding all ex parte contact with the parties during hearings, deliberations, and rendition of a final award. Once the award is signed by the arbitrator(s), it is sealed pending mediation of the dispute. The arbitrator-turned-mediator is free to engage in ex parte discussions with the parties and to help them settle the case, but may not disclose the contents of the award. The parties, meanwhile, know that the award will be published in the event mediation fails to produce a settlement.

QUESTIONS

1. Does Arb-Med avoid any of the practical, legal, and ethical issues raised by Med-Arb?
2. Does it lack any of the potential advantages of Med-Arb?

D. THE NEED FOR PRECISION IN STRUCTURING NEUTRAL ROLES

Efforts to structure a suitable, workable, and enforceable ADR agreement are sometimes undermined by a lack of precision. Such issue may be particularly acute when a single individual is assigned multiple roles, or where the neutral's role may be characterized in more than one way.

These concerns are illustrated by *Ex parte Industrial Technologies*, 707 So. 2d 234 (Ala. 1997), a case in which a bank filed suit on a promissory note, and the defendants counterclaimed for conversion of certain equipment taken by the bank during collection efforts. Prior to trial, the parties agreed to refer the matter to out-of-court process (described as "mediation or arbitration") with a retired circuit judge, Snodgrass, as "mediator/arbitrator." After a period of settlement negotiations supervised by the latter, the parties announced to Snodgrass their "stipulation of agreement" acknowledging the conversion of the equipment, calling for appraisers to determine fair market value of the detained property, and for Snodgrass to determine the interest factor to be used in computing the rental value of the property during the detention period.

Snodgrass subsequently issued an "order" directing the bank to pay both rental value during the detention and the value of the equipment at the time of detention, less salvage value at the time of return. The defendants/counterclaimants sought to enforce the outcome, which they termed a "binding arbitration order"; but the bank responded that the proceeding was merely a mediation without binding results. The Alabama Supreme Court determined that both the parties' agreement and the subsequent process were fatally flawed. First of all, it was impossible to determine the precise character of the process agreed to by the parties, but rather only that the parties apparently intended for the judge to determine damages based upon a mutually agreeable formula. Unfortunately, the court concluded, there was never a meeting of the minds as to whether Snodgrass was empowered to award damages over and above the rental value. While the lack of precision in tailoring the original ADR agreement might have been overcome by the participants during the subsequent negotiation and drafting of the "stipulation of agreement," they merely exacerbated their earlier mistakes.

QUESTION

The borrower in the Snodgrass case has approached you. It wants to know how in the future it should draft an ADR clause so as to avoid the problems identified by the court. What suggestions can you offer? (We *will return* to the subject of ADR processes involving multiple steps in Chapter 22.)

CHAPTER
22

Looking Ahead: Opportunities and Challenges in ADR and Conflict Management

We conclude these materials with a look at important opportunities and challenges confronting lawyers as problem solvers today and in the future. After more than a quarter century of diverse and proliferating efforts aimed at developing and employing different, hopefully more appropriate and effective ways of managing conflict, we have a much better understanding of the dynamics of conflict and a much broader variety of tools to bring to bear in different settings.

Legal counselors now have the opportunity to approach the litigation experience in a wholly new way, with more satisfactory results for those they represent. As advisors to organizations, they are ideally poised to bring about a wholesale change in the culture of disputing. Understanding the role and value of mediators in enhancing relationships and facilitating the resolution of active conflict, they may pioneer applications of interventions "upstream," such as the mediation of deals and the facilitation of long-term relationships. In the Internet and other modern technologies, they have unprecedented tools for realizing the goals of efficiency and economy in resolving disputes, even in long-distance transactions. As neutrals, and as consumers of dispute resolution services, they must face the challenges of an expanding and increasingly competitive field, including the spectres of fragmentation, standardization, and regulation. And as citizens, they are equipped to play a leading role in creating a society transformed by the same principles that we have learned to apply in the resolution of individual disputes.

A. CHANGING ROLES, CHANGING CULTURES

1. Changing Views of Lawyering in the Litigation Landscape

Throughout this book, we have underlined the primary role played by judges in reordering the landscape of litigation. One of these, the Honorable Dorothy Nelson of the U.S. Court of Appeals for the Ninth Circuit, has said,

Lawyers and other ADR providers can expand the parties' tools for dealing with the psychological, social and economic dynamics that accompany and sometimes drive litigation. Their roles should be that of constructive problem solvers and peacemakers rather than zealous advocates. The approach in each case should be tailored to the context in which it evolves with particular attention to the cultural forces that are at work.

Nelson (2001).

Another creative force in the judicial ranks is Wayne Brazil, who as U.S. magistrate judge in California's Northern District since 1984 pioneered one of the nation's most innovative multifaceted court-connected ADR programs. Here, Magistrate Brazil considers all of the ways in which, with a different mind-set, today's attorneys may dramatically alter the litigation experience for the benefit of those they represent.

HON. WAYNE BRAZIL, A JUDGE'S PERSPECTIVE ON LAWYERING AND ADR

19 Alternatives 44 (January 2001)

I choose . . . to examine a specific case—to search in the social wreckage it represents for lessons about lawyering and ADR—lessons that may apply broadly, from lawyering for the little guy(s) to lawyering in self-perceived cynicism for the largest of economic stakes.

The case is *Anderson v. Cryovac Inc.*, also known as *Anderson v. W.R. Grace, Co. and Beatrice Foods*, but best known, simply, as "A Civil Action." Made famous by a book and movie, this litigation pitted 33 individual plaintiffs against large corporations. The plaintiffs alleged that the defendants had contaminated the local public water supply—and that contamination was responsible for the deaths of five children and for serious injuries and illnesses suffered by other children and by adults.

My interest here is not in how the case was litigated, but on how it wasn't lawyered. With the benefit of hindsight, disengagement, and the considerable developments in ADR since the mid-1980s (when the case was tried), I would like to use this case to make an argument about what really good, really pro- fessionally responsible lawyering should be all about—and to show how essential a problem solving spirit, aided by ADR processes, is to lawyering that aspires to deem itself "the highest quality."

Many of the plaintiffs in "A Civil Action" had suffered in the most severe of ways—physically and emotionally. They felt confused, alone, and betrayed— even though they weren't sure by whom. Some probably felt, at some level, guilty and responsible for the terrible things that their children and they had suffered. They remained both afraid and angry. They wanted answers. Why did this happen? Who was really responsible? Can anything be done about the present and the future? They wanted help dealing with the consequences of their tragedies. They wanted restoration of and to their community.

Lawyers with insufficient vision might say that the plaintiffs were naive to think that they could achieve these kinds of ends through the legal system. Certainly the system as it was actually used by the lawyers who handled the case, traditionally and narrowly over a period of eight years, delivered precious little toward these ends. The transaction costs (not counting a dime of settlement money) were well above $15 million. But the huge investment of money and time yielded a judgment and a settlement that brought no answers to the biggest questions, no emotional healing, no restoration of community, no repair of severely damaged good will, and addressed only modestly the plaintiffs' need to respond financially to the consequences of their injuries (each plaintiff received through settlement about $100,000).

Really good lawyers, however, would have understood that in the aftermath of the tragedy there was an opportunity to build — to use ADR to create new, long-range value of great significance. What could have been?

Let's look at the situation primarily through the eyes of the defendant corporations. Even if the only value that really mattered to the defendants was profit, a good lawyer would have counseled them to move in a very different direction — and to use ADR to do so.

The defendants knew that the U.S. Environmental Protection Agency had designated the accused area as a Superfund site and had been investigating the extent and sources of the obvious contamination for some time before the lawsuit was filed. The defendants knew that they were required by law to cooperate fully with the EPA investigation. The defendants knew that there was a substantial possibility that the EPA would order them to contribute toward the cost of clean up. The defendants knew that the U.S. Geological Survey also was studying contamination in the area. And the defendants should have known that if they were not truthful with federal authorities, the U.S. Department of Justice might well intervene. In fact, the Justice Department ultimately indicted one of the corporate defendants for just such untruthfulness — and that defendant ultimately pled guilty.

The defendants also could foresee that a case like this would generate a great deal of press coverage (as it did), and that the defendants would not be favored in the sympathy slant (77% of people polled in surveys taken as the trial date approached believed that the corporate defendants were responsible for the deaths of the children). Moreover, two of the three companies that ended up being pulled into the case knew they would remain in the community — that they would employ local workers, work with local politicians, and need local services.

Given these circumstances, a good lawyer would have counseled his or her client to use an ADR process early in the pretrial period — well before most of the litigation transaction costs were incurred and before the litigation process further alienated the plaintiffs and rigidified their positions. The goal would be to use ADR to explore what was most important to the plaintiffs themselves (as opposed to their lawyers), to de-demonize the defendants, and to reach out to the plaintiffs in a constructive and civic spirit that might make it possible to work out a settlement that would simultaneously save the defendants money and yield potentially huge public relations benefits.

A good lawyer would have urged each corporate defendant to send its chairman or its CEO to the ADR session — to demonstrate graphically that the company understood the gravity of the losses that plaintiffs had suffered. This was a big case — economically, "politically," and emotionally. Direct participation by the highest level corporate officers was fully justified (by financial considerations alone) and would have improved the odds, considerably, that the companies' presentations would elicit favorable responses from the plaintiffs.

A good lawyer would have advised the representative of the company to begin the neutraled ADR session by listening to the plaintiffs — actively, openly, and sympathetically. After listening, the CEO or chairman would seek an opportunity to speak directly to the plaintiffs (in the presence of their lawyers and the neutral) and would communicate, gently, the following messages and proposals.

He would begin by telling the plaintiffs how sorry he and his company were about what had happened to them. Then he would say that he really doesn't understand what the causes were of these tragedies — but that he wants to. He would explain that the scientists who advise him do not think that chemicals from his operations reached the wells or caused the illnesses, and he would emphasize that he and his staff never would have permitted the operations to proceed if he had known that they would cause such effects. But he would concede that no one knows enough about the sources of these kinds of illnesses to be completely sure — so one of his goals will be to support the effort to learn from these tragedies.

He would propose doing that in two ways. One would be to cooperate fully with the EPA and all other governmental agencies who are investigating these matters. He would promise that his company would open its records and provide the authorities promptly with all the information and other forms of assistance they might seek. The second way his company (along with the other defendants) would support the search for answers would be to contribute several million dollars directly to support research into the possibility that there are environmental causes of leukemia.

In making these proposals, the spokesman for the company would emphasize that many of the company's valued and longtime employees live here — so it is partly on their behalf that he wants to help find out why this happened. But the spokesman also would emphasize that the company wants to be a responsible and valued member of this community — and thus wants to identify with certainty any aspects of its operations that might cause harm to any other members of the community.

Next, the CEO or chairman would commit the company to contribute its full fair share to the cost of cleaning up the contaminated area. He would say that even though it is not clear that the contamination that has been found caused the cancer, it is clear that the contamination is a legitimate source of concern and must be removed. So the company, the spokesman would say, stands ready to pay (toward the cost of the cleanup) whatever share the government scientists conclude is appropriate. The company representative also would say that the company would do everything it can to speed up the process of making that determination and to press for completion of the cleanup work on as fast a timetable as possible.

To evidence the company's good faith, the representative then would say that none of the commitments just described are contingent on the case settling. The company intends to go forward with them — including the commitment to support the cancer research, even if the parties cannot reach an agreement that would end the litigation.

Finally, the spokesman, on behalf of the defendants as a group, would offer money to help the plaintiffs meet the needs they face. The spokesman would start by acknowledging that no amount of money could adequately compensate for the personal losses that have been suffered — but also that the tragedies have had real and damaging consequences that require resources. The defendants collectively would like to provide some of those resources — and toward that end they are offering the plaintiffs, as a group, $10 million.

Making a package of proposals like this early in the pretrial period would have encouraged a perception that defendants were sincerely sorry about the plaintiffs' losses and wanted not only to act responsibly, but also as real members of a shared community. The likelihood that the plaintiffs would not have responded positively to such an offer is quite small. Good lawyers for them would have encouraged acceptance.

With acceptance of this offer, the defendants would have saved considerable money. They also would have generated considerable positive press and good will — and avoided the years of bad press (to say nothing of the criminal indictment) that accompanied the protracted litigation. Moreover, they would have distinguished themselves from their competitors — encouraging investors to perceive them as possessing especially acute business judgment — and so worthy of investment confidence.

It is clear that there is a very real chance that a scenario like the one described here could have occurred. That real possibility demonstrates, contrary to a high visibility suggestion to the contrary, that statesmanship actually can have a great deal to do with good lawyering. Breadth of solution-vision can be an essential tool even in pursuing narrow client interests. And a lawyer who cannot help his or her client explore problem-solving solutions simply cannot be considered a wise counselor.

QUESTION

Do you think Magistrate Brazil's admonitions are realistic? What barriers might there be — on the defendants' side, the plaintiffs' side, or elsewhere — to successsfully executing the scenario he contemplates?

2. Changing the Corporate Culture

Cathy Costantino and Christina Merchant have observed that organizations historically have failed to view the management of conflict systematically. "Rather, conflict in organizations is viewed and managed in a piecemeal, ad hoc fashion as isolated events, which are sometimes grouped by category if the risk exposure is great enough but that are rarely examined in the aggregate to reveal patterns and systemic issues. In a sense, most organizations regard disputes as 'local' events." See Costantino and Merchant (1996). Their work in the field of systems design and implementation, briefly summarized earlier in Chapter 21, envisions a process of bringing about cultural change in the corporation.

There is evidence that a few corporations have moved beyond piecemeal approaches, including ad hoc applications of ADR, to embrace a new way of managing conflict. The following excerpt summarizes one scholar's research into corporate disputing, with emphasis on his description of developments at an unnamed large company he designated "MOD."

CRAIG A. MCEWEN, MANAGING CORPORATE DISPUTING AT "MOD"[2]

In a groundbreaking study, Professor Craig McEwen closely examined the way six large companies managed business-to-business disputes and concluded

---

2. Craig A. McEwen, *Managing Corporate Disputing: Overcoming Barriers to the Effective Use of Mediation for Reducing the Cost and Time of Litigation*, 14 Ohio St. J. on Disp. Resol. 1 (1998) as summarized in Thomas J. Stipanowich, *ADR and the "Vanishing Trial: The Growth Impact of "Alternative Dispute Resolution"* 1 J. EMPIRICAL LEGAL RES. 843, 883-885 (2004).

that whether or not a company employs mediation may be less important than the extent to which mediation is employed in the context of a systematic approach to the "management of disputing." Interviews with business leaders and senior corporate counsel and a study of roughly 170 disputes led McEwen to identify four major factors preventing faster and less costly resolution of disputes: contentious and competitive corporate cultures, the personal emotional investment of business managers in disputes, "misaligned incentives" such as hourly billing arrangements for outside counsel, and the professional legal culture that expects full information (and thus, discovery) before deciding how to dispose of the case.

While several of the companies used mediation (some quite often), and all were concerned about litigation costs and had tried to address such concerns, one company (which he designated "MOD") distinguished itself by embracing an overall strategy for achieving corporate goals through thoughtful dispute management. Motivated by a company-wide effort to define efficiency and quality management in measurable ways, MOD's general counsel and several other key attorneys moved beyond the traditional "case-by-case client service role" and assumed the role of managers of the disputing process. The MOD legal division developed a clear organizational mission — "to maximize prompt and favorable settlements," measured by the shortness of dispute resolution, "favorable outcomes, cost savings, and client satisfaction." The program that evolved from these initial determinations included:

- redesign of the dispute resolution approach, including early case evaluation by inside and outside counsel to achieve earlier and less costly settlement in "Stage 1" (prior to discovery);
- examination of "patterns of disputing" in different business units, and efforts to train business managers about how to achieve the objectives of earlier settlements and fewer lawsuits;
- the use of "wise advisors" — high-level individuals without personal involvement in disputes who could promote reasonable outcomes;
- changed billing practices, including billing business units directly for outside counsel fees;
- encouraging lawyers and business people to learn about, understand, and apply the principles underlying mediation and interest-based negotiation;
- periodic measurements of favorable outcomes and other benchmarks of success.

Thus, "the lawyers at MOD went well beyond the more typical, reactive and case-centered roles of other corporate counsel by taking on leadership as managers of the disputing process" and achieved a greater level of success in altering the cost and timing of disputes as well as the quality of outcomes. In other words, instead of incorporating mediation into the traditional "litigotiation" culture of their company, the MOD legal department set about changing the whole culture of conflict management — employing mediation in the context of a systemic approach built on a clearly defined corporate objective aimed at speedy and low-cost resolution through settlement and preserved business relationships. The principles underlying mediation, including active listening and understanding and responding to interests were integrated into the evaluative and negotiating efforts of lawyers and business persons.

QUESTIONS

1. How does the approach undertaken by "MOD" lawyers in their organization compare with the role(s) implicitly described in your law school courses and casebooks?
2. A recent review of empirical studies on corporate conflict management suggests that MOD's proactive approach remains exceptional. Why do you suppose that is the case?

B. "RELATIONAL" ADR AND CONFLICT MANAGEMENT

1. "Deal Mediation"

You now understand, as many practicing lawyers do, the potentially significant role that a mediator can play in resolving disputes, enhancing communication, and even transforming relationships. It should therefore come as no surprise that some have theorized about—and in some cases implemented—intervention strategies that apply these same principles at points "upstream" from active disputes.

In the following article, one scholar asks a simple question: Could third-party mediators be helpful in deals, just as they are in disputes? He posits a potential role for mediators in helping the parties to overcome psychological, emotional, and relational barriers to reaching an agreement.

SCOTT R. PEPPET, CONTRACT FORMATION IN IMPERFECT MARKETS: SHOULD WE USE MEDIATORS IN DEALS?

38 Ohio St. J. on Disp. Resol. 283 (2004)

[M]any of the same barriers to negotiation that plague litigation settlement exist in commercial transactions, particularly during the closing stage of a deal when lawyers attempt to negotiate terms and conditions. [A] transactional mediator could help lawyers and clients to overcome such barriers. By a "transactional mediator," the author means an impartial person or entity that intervenes in a transactional negotiation pre-closing to facilitate the creation of a durable and efficient contract.

In one experiment, for example, small teams of experienced executives were given detailed information about two simulated companies. They were then assigned to represent one company or the other and asked to evaluate the companies and negotiate a merger. Although agreement was possible, only nine of the twenty-one pairings reached agreement. In addition, the executives disagreed wildly about the relevant valuations-selling prices ranged from $3.3 million to $16.5 million. This suggests that occasionally transacting parties fail to "close the deal" because of strategic posturing. [Moreover], as in litigation, transacting parties may fail to find Pareto-efficient agreements. . . . Information asymmetries and strategic posturing may lead to inefficiencies. . . . Interestingly, the researcher in this corporate acquisitions experiment re-ran the simulation offering each negotiating pair the service of a trained mediator, but not requiring that they use the mediator. Those executives that made use of the mediator reached more efficient contracts than those that did not. . . . [M]ediators should theoretically be able to help merging companies resolve disagreements over "social issues," such as how to name the post-merger corporation, how to resolve status and position questions (e.g., who will be CEO), and where to locate the new company's headquarters.

Howard Raiffa also suggests that a mediator might serve as a "contract embellisher" in transactions. [A]t the start of bargaining a mediator could privately interview each party about its needs, priorities, and perceptions. The mediator would lock away that information and the parties would be left alone to negotiate a deal. At the conclusion of their negotiation, but prior to closing the deal, the intervenor would return [. . .] try to use his private information about the parties' interests to craft a superior deal. He would then show his substitute agreement to each party privately. If both sides agreed that the mediator's suggestion was superior to their own contract, the substitution would be made. There would be no haggling about the terms of the mediator's proposal — it would be a take-it-or-leave-it situation.

[U]nder what market conditions the argument that "mediators add value by mitigating adverse selection" will hold? In a bilateral monopoly, there is only one seller and only one buyer. In other words, there is no market to establish a market price. There are no external bargaining alternatives that will drive the price towards the seller's marginal cost (or reservation price). [T]he outcome of bilateral monopoly bargaining depends on the negotiators' ability to wield bargaining power and invoke procedural and substantive norms of bargaining to their advantage. [A] competitive market, by contrast, . . . will discipline negotiators to bargain reasonably. . . .

[However,] a complex deal often takes on bilateral monopoly characteristics at certain stages of the deal's life cycle. [A]dverse selection problems may arise at any of four stages of a transaction — matching, pricing, closing, and renegotiation — but they are likely to increase in intensity as a transaction progresses towards closing and renegotiation.

In complex transactions, lawyers, accountants, bankers, and other agents are generally brought in to assist in the closing stage. Lawyers in particular are needed to draft legal language for an acquisition agreement or other contract. As the closing stage progresses, due diligence may not eliminate all uncertainties about the company or assets in question [and] [l]awyers will therefore bargain over contract language to shift the risks associated with these remaining uncertainties.

A lawyer-mediator might prevent the parties' lawyers from blowing up the deal unnecessarily, and, perhaps more importantly, from reaching an inefficient set of contract terms. Although the bargaining about a single contract term may be largely distributive contracting attorneys can generally create value by trading between terms. For example, if a contract contains ten legal provisions (A, B, . . . , J), parties X and Y will value those terms differently. If X finds term A extremely important and Y term B, they can create joint gains by allocating the risk in term A as X prefers and the risk in term B as Y prefers. And so on.

Empirical analysis of contracts shows that parties often do not trade risk in complex — yet value-creating — ways. Instead, in many domains contracts are simpler than one might expect. Various explanations have been offered for this simplicity, including behavioral explanations and the network effects

theory. Another, less-explored, explanation is that the threat of strategic behavior prevents parties from complex contracting. To create a tailored term
requires disclosing information about one's interests and preferences. This,
again, permits exploitation. In the absence of trust, parties may resort to a
standard term to minimize this risk.

A mediator might help the parties to overcome these strategic difficulties,
thereby permitting more complex contracting. Again, a mediator can solicit
and compare information from each side, potentially finding value-creating
trades. The mediator might test the viability of various packages of trades of
legal terms, asking each side in confidence which of several sets of terms the
party would accept, but not revealing the origin of the various packages. In this
way, the mediator can surmount the adverse selection problems that might otherwise prevent tailoring contract language during the deal's closing stage. . . .

[Besides helping the parties to overcome strategic barriers to transactions,
mediators can also help them to overcome psychological barriers.] A neutral is
in an ideal position to identify self-serving assessments by one or both parties.
At a substantive level, if the neutral has sufficient expertise she can check each
side's assumptions about "what's fair" and keep the parties from locking in to
diverging stories about how a transaction should be priced or closed.
Moreover, the mediator may be able to offer a neutral assessment or fair
proposal that the parties will adopt. [. . .] At a procedural or process level,
a neutral can also help the parties avoid spinning very biased interpretations of
how their bargaining is unfolding.

Negotiating parties must constantly assess information received from the
other side. Research has shown, however, that negotiators [. . .] sometimes
overly devalue an opponent's proposal or concession merely because their
opponent made it. This phenomenon is known as "reactive devaluation."
[A] neutral can help parties to overcome reactive devaluation in transactional
bargaining by either adding noise to the parties' communication or proposing
solutions of her own. Adding noise may be as simple as raising Party A's
proposed solution privately with Party B without telling B that the idea
came from Party A. If B assumes that the idea originated with the neutral,
B may be more willing to consider it on the merits.

A neutral may be less susceptible to the endowment effect than a partisan
agent, and therefore able to help parties to overcome it. For example, a neutral
may be able to provide both sides with market information against which they
can test their (biased) evaluations. This is particularly plausible vis-à-vis the
legal terms and conditions in a contract. A lawyer-neutral might be familiar
with the legal norms in a given context and be able to point the parties towards
compromise legal language. Rather than start with a standard form or with a
first draft, which would typically become the original endowment against which
the parties compared, the neutral could manage the negotiation process so
that the parties instead would work collaboratively to build a contract draft
from framework through to completion.

In addition to managing information exchange and helping parties to overcome these cognitive and social psychological biases, a neutral can help parties
to manage emotional and relational difficulties in their negotiations. This may
facilitate trust and permit more efficient outcomes.

. . . [N]egotiation breakdowns occur in transactional bargaining, sometimes
to the detriment of both parties. To some extent, agents such as investment
bankers and lawyers already serve to mediate emotional conflicts during

mergers, acquisitions, and other transactions. A neutral sometimes has an advantage over an agent in this regard, however. An agent may naturally take his client's perspective as given and discount the likelihood that the other side has a valid interpretation of events or more benign intentions than the client understands. A neutral positioned between two parties can often help them to gain such perspective. In strategic situations it is easy to assume that when the other bargainer "starts high" or "holds out," they do so because they intend to harm you or to treat you unfairly. Bargainers are less likely to attribute such actions to the exigencies of circumstance. By screening some overly opportunistic offers and at times sending fuzzy rather than clear information between the parties, a mediator can blunt such emotions and thereby keep the negotiations on track. Over time, avoiding emotional disagreements may help the parties to establish trust. This not only leads to more amiable negotiations, but also has serious substantive benefits. If the parties trust each other they may be better positioned to find value-creating solutions to their substantive differences. They may be able to rely more on informal agreements rather than contractual obligations and may be more flexible in the face of unexpected bumps in the road. Perhaps most importantly, they may avoid the destructive cycle of misattributions that can lead parties to "blow up" a deal or reach a Pareto-inefficient agreement.

QUESTION

Why do you suppose deal mediation is not prevalent?

2. *Partnering*

Long-term relationships involving significant financial stakes may justify more deliberate conflict management efforts that go beyond traditional ADR. For example, many public and private owners of major construction projects have found it advantageous to reduce the likelihood of major disputes by establishing a good working relationship at the outset, and set the pattern for more successful interaction throughout the project. They often employ "partnering" — a program of facilitated, structured workshops involving specific relational objectives — with contractors, design professionals, and other persons involved in the project before work begins and as it goes forward. See *Dispute Prevention Through Partnering*, CPR Institute For Dispute Resolution MAPP Series (1998).

Effective partnering permits parties to clarify and prioritize goals and expectations, anticipate critical performance problems, enhance communications among key personnel, and establish a blueprint for resolving conflict at the earliest possible time.

Most discussions of partnering at the project level focus on a facilitated workshop conducted at the beginning of a construction project. Participants include representatives of the owner, the contractor, and other "stakeholders" — individuals closely affiliated with the project as well as key decision makers higher in the organization, including legal counsel for the project. A typical multiday partnering session might begin with training and exercises focusing on interpersonal communication, "disputing" styles, and management of conflict. The agenda also includes discussion of the project mission, the specific performance objectives and expectations of companies and individuals, and, in some cases, the development of a specific dispute resolution process for handling conflict on the project. The initial partnering session often concludes with the signing of a project charter setting forth the team's mission and specific goals—a document that may be displayed prominently at the project site.

To be effective, partnering must involve far more than a discrete event in the life of a project; it must permeate and become an integral part of project relationships. While the inaugural workshop is often described as the "centerpiece" of partnering, it must reflect a commitment of the highest levels of management that is transmitted through the ranks to the level of field personnel. It must also amount to something more than a simplistic drill—a feelgood exercise that results in collective intonation of general platitudes—and business as usual during performance of the contract. Successful partnering is, after all, about addressing the real needs of team members and reinforcing the values of reciprocity, solidarity, and trust, which must animate successful partnerings. It is therefore essential that the workshop treat real project planning issues, allowing project participants to state their respective requirements in frank and specific terms, and to model the behaviors that will sustain those ends in the long term. Thus, a workshop agenda might involve detailed treatment of the roles and responsibilities of all members of the project team, and their respective plans and expectations for the entire project.

The initial partnering conference is also the ideal platform for exploration of a structure for long-term governance of the relationship, including a variegated conflict resolution scheme. The result might be a conflict resolution system that places initial emphasis on informal, face-to-face problem solving, and integrative bargaining, followed by settlement-oriented interventions (mediation, non-binding evaluation, dispute review boards) and, ultimately, adjudication (often some form of binding arbitration). Of course, such efforts come face-to-face with the natural tendencies of new partners to bask in the sunshine of a dawning relationship and avoid addressing the sharp realities of the future. Yet if not in the conducive environment of partnering, where?

Partnering concepts are readily adaptable to other commercial arenas involving long-term performance and a high potential for disputes, such as joint ventures involving technology sharing or development.

QUESTIONS

Why do you suppose relatively few lawyers have participated in, let alone proposed, partnering processes? Should proposing partnering be within a lawyer's role as counselor to a client who is getting ready to enter into a long-term contractual relationship? Why or why not?

3. Dynamic Conflict Management in Public and Private Settings

a. The Creative Role of Magistrates and Special Masters

As discussed in Chapter 19, Professor Frank Sander's seminal 1976 concept paper, *Varieties of Dispute Processing*, The Pound Conference, 70 F.R.D. 111

(1976), spoke of the need for "a flexible mechanism that serves to sort out the large general question from the repetitive application of settled principle." *Id.* at 119. Sander's solution was a "multi-door courthouse" incorporating three notions: (1) a choice of several discrete approaches to conflict resolution, (2) a mechanism for channeling disputes into specific processes, and (3) sufficient information about a given dispute to facilitate a rational pairing of problem and process.

However, Sander's template for a "multi-door courthouse," with a clerk directing entrants to different "doors," has not been widely embraced in the form he envisioned. Nevertheless, the three elements underlying his original proposal may be even better served by the role of magistrate judges, who play a key case management role in many federal district court programs. Among other things, their function is to explore a range of conflict resolution strategies, to tailor methods to the issues and hand, and to respond dynamically to the circumstances of the case and the needs of the parties. As compared to Sander's "screening clerk," magistrates may bring into play greater preparation, broader discretion and coercive authority, and a greater understanding of the circumstances of the case and the requirements of the parties. Their continuing participation, coupled with an opportunity for appropriate evaluation by users of the program, enhances the likelihood of developing an institutional memory regarding ADR options and related case management issues.

Special masters and other court-appointed neutrals may also perform tasks that transcend their more traditional focus on fact-finding and evaluating or facilitating resolution of substantive issues. Some courts now utilize special masters for all aspects of pretrial case management, usually with the deliberate intention of preparing a case for mediation or other intervention. Like magistrate judges, court-appointed neutrals often function as "process architects."

b. The Dispute Resolution Adviser[2]

While much has been done to enhance the ability of courts to dynamically respond to the dispute resolution requirements of individual cases, there is even more room for innovation in the realm of private contracts in long-term relationships. In some notable circumstances, "partnering" approaches have been combined with truly innovative efforts aimed at providing parties with a highly tailored yet flexible and dynamic conflict management process — moving beyond the confines of contractual dispute resolution provisions to address particular, unanticipated needs and changing circumstances.

A system put in place on a Hong Kong construction project represented a quantum leap in the evolution of contractual dispute systems. The contract for the renovation of Queen Mary Hospital, a venerable 56-year-old edifice, required performing intricate demolition and construction services while keeping the hospital and operating theatres operational — a complex and challenging theme likely to prove a hotbed of conflict. The project owner, the Hong Kong Government's Architectural Services Department (ASD), desirous of strict budget control, required a system that would identify and

---

2. Adapted from Stipanowich (1998).

resolve disputes in the shortest possible time and prior to the completion of the project. ASD retained the services of an international team of consultants to develop an appropriate dispute resolution system for the project.

The result was a report setting forth specific recommendations for project organization and administration aimed at avoiding or minimizing areas of dispute. These included tight time frames for job site decision making and handling of claims, and the establishment of a flexible, dynamic dispute resolution system centered upon the figure of a Dispute Resolution Adviser (DRA). The resulting agreement called for joint appointment of a neutral, a construction expert possessing dispute resolution skills, as the DRA at the time the construction contract commenced. A default mechanism was established for independent appointment of a DRA should the parties fail to agree on an appointee. The DRA's fees were to be shared equally between the owner and the general contractor.

The DRA's first function was to meet with job participants to explain and build support for a cooperative approach to problem solving on the project. Among other things, the DRA was to discuss basic rules of communication and attitudinal changes necessary to avoid adversarial positions. Thereafter, the DRA was to make monthly visits to the site for the purpose of consulting with project participants on the status of the job and facilitating discussions respecting any conflicts. The DRA was given considerable flexibility in managing such discussions. In the event of a formal challenge to a project decision, the parties were given four weeks to negotiate pertinent issues (with or without the assistance of the DRA). In the event the problem remained unresolved, a party's written notice of dispute would trigger a more formal stage of dispute resolution in which the DRA had freedom to employ any of several methods of dispute resolution.

If assisted site-level negotiations failed, the DRA was to prepare a report identifying the key issues in dispute, the positions of the parties, and the perceived barriers to settlement and making either a recommendation for settlement or a non-binding evaluation of the dispute. The report would be used by senior off-site representatives of the parties to further negotiations, perhaps assisted by the DRA. Should matters not be resolved within 14 days of the issuance of the DRA's report, the DRA would set into motion a short-form arbitration procedure or other mutually acceptable means recommended by the DRA. The arbitrator would be appointed by the parties; failing their agreement, the DRA would make the selection.

The DRA procedure worked well. Despite the usual problems and several hundred owner-directed changes [to the construction project], no disputes reached the stage of non-binding evaluation. The DRA system has since been applied on at least one other hospital project for the same owner.

The planners of Queen Mary Hospital and their able consultants came to recognize that in the relational sphere, conflict resolution is properly approached not as an event or set-piece intervention, but as a process inextricably intertwined with the relationships that evolve along with the physical design, procurement, and construction of the building. Their solution embraces a number of the following elements that might be the hallmarks of a contractual conflict management system:

1. a comprehensive *program* that commences with the contractual relationship(s) and extends throughout the life of the relationship(s);

2. the *active involvement of key contract participants* in "partnering," in initial program design and, ultimately, in the resolution of conflict;
3. the establishment of a *variegated conflict resolution scheme* that incorporates a series or selection of strategies consistent with the parties' goals; and
4. an *independent adviser* who, either alone or as part of a larger team or organization, advises, models, teaches, facilitates, and provides the human backbone for the entire program.

QUESTIONS

1. How does the Dispute Resolution Adviser concept differ from traditional ADR approaches you have encountered in this book?
2. When, if ever, might you consider counseling a client to adopt this approach?

C. ONLINE DISPUTE RESOLUTION (ODR)

1. The Advent of ODR

No treatment of evolving approaches in conflict resolution can ignore the advent of online dispute resolution, or ODR. See Katsh and Rivkin (2001).

The Internet affords extraordinary opportunities for resolving disputes over long distances efficiently and at minimal cost, and it is only a matter of time before the new electronic media revolutionize our approaches to resolving disputes, along with most other aspects of modern life.

One harbinger of what is to come is SquareTrade's office of Online Dispute Resolution Services, which has achieved some prominence as the mechanism for online negotiation and mediation of disputes between buyers and sellers on eBay. Since February 2000, SquareTrade's growing range of applications (including eBay, Yahoo!, Google, the Federal Trade Commission's *www. econsumer.gov* program, and the California Association of Realtors) has resulted in the handling of over 1.5 million disputes online (with participants representing 120 different countries), at a current rate of approximately 80,000 new online case filings a month. SquareTrade claims success rates of over 80 percent when both parties participate in online mediation, and over 98 percent follow-through on settlement agreements. More than 80 percent of buyers and sellers report satisfaction with their experience.

ODR is still in its infancy, but will come to the fore as new generations of lawyers and potential users accustom themselves to performing all kinds of tasks online. Ultimately, the concept of interaction in a virtual reality will likely transform many of our concepts of negotiating and adjudication, and even our notions of "in-court" and "out-of-court."

What follows are two perspectives on ODR—that of one of its most experienced advocates, and that of a long-time, internationally renowned lawyer/arbitrator.

COLIN RULE, ONLINE DISPUTE RESOLUTION

Adapted from Online Dispute Resolution for Business: B2B, Ecommerce, Consumer, Employment, Insurance, and Other Commercial Conflicts (2002)

Dispute resolution and information technology have combined into an important new tool, a new system, a new way of doing business which is more efficient, more cost effective, and much more flexible than traditional approaches. The tool is called Online Dispute Resolution, and it combines the efficiency of alternative dispute resolution with the power of the Internet to save businesses money, time, and frustration.

Online dispute resolution is not tied to geography, so disputants can reach resolution even if they are located on different continents. ODR can move to resolve matters before they escalate, so that disputants can quickly resolve the matter and get back to business. ODR is not tied to particular bodies of law, so there is no need for each side to retain expensive legal counsel to learn the legal structure of the other side's country. ODR can be priced much more reasonably than legal options, and even less than the cost of a single plane ticket. ODR can also leverage expertise from skilled neutrals around the world, ensuring that the participants will get a fair hearing, from someone who has knowledge and experience in the matter at hand. ODR enables businesses, governments, and consumers to achieve the best resolution possible in the shortest amount of time.

These advantages apply to all kinds of disputes. Intellectual property disputes, insurance claims, and B2B and B2C e-commerce matters are all good fits with the power of ODR. Some disputes are over more abstract issues not related to monetary payments, like privacy or workplace conflict. For example, ICANN (the Internet Corporation for Assigned Names and Numbers) faced monumental problems when they decided to build a global process to handle domain name disputes. What courts should govern the matter? What laws should apply? No one country has the jurisdiction over domain names, it is a truly international system. ICANN solved the problem by creating a global domain name dispute resolution process, the UDRP, administered by a variety of ODR providers. Over the past three years this process has resolved thousands of disputes all over the world, none of which have ever been appealed in a courtroom. Soon similar ODR systems will be created for a wide variety of areas, such as insurance, commerce, privacy, government, workplace, and finance.

[T]he rapid growth in online-only disputes has cast the shortcomings of court litigation in even starker contrast. Legal systems are tied to geography almost by definition. In the U.S., lawyers are only admitted to the bar on a state-by-state basis, facing penalties if they even offer legal advice to clients in other states. Enforcement of court decisions involves jails and policemen that also only operate in a particular geographic area.

It is obvious that transaction partners who meet on the web can take little comfort from the redress options provided in the face-to-face world. You can't merely re-create offline judicial mechanisms online and expect them to work, with e-judges making e-rulings enforced by e-police running e-jails. The model doesn't work, on a fundamental level, when participants in the system can change their identity as easily as they change their email address. It might work to hunt down the odd international criminal who shuts down the stock exchange with a virus, but there's no way law enforcement is going to be able to get every fraudulent seller on eBay, especially when they may be on the other side of the planet.

The delays of face-to-face processes also hamper their applicability to online transactions. Over the web, consumers and businesses expect that any service they need should be available online, 24 hours a day. Courts, in contrast, have long been designed to involve delays, ornate filing requirements, and strict procedural rules, to deter potential users from being cavalier in their decision to file new cases. If two businesses engage in a trans-boundary transaction that goes awry they have no interest in waiting months for an offline dispute resolution body to initiate a process to resolve the dispute. They want to get the matter resolved as quickly as possible so that they can get back to doing business.

Simply put, offline courts do not work for online disputes. Courts can operate as an effective safety net for those cases that involve criminal wrongdoing, or where the parties are unwilling to use a non-public forum, or when they put the highest priority on due process and precedent. But for a huge number of cases that are cropping up online, where the value under dispute is less than likely legal bills, or where both parties truly participated in the transaction in good faith, online dispute resolution is the best solution.

In response to these conclusions, the consensus behind online dispute resolution is growing rapidly. International organizations (The OECD, The Hague Conference on Private International Law, the European Union), consumer groups, governmental bodies, professional associations and business organizations have all issued recommendations calling for online dispute resolution. While there is some debate about how to ensure that online dispute resolution services are fair to consumers, or how best to oversee online dispute resolution service providers, there is no debate over whether or not online dispute resolution is the best option for providing redress on the Internet.

Online dispute resolution is the future. Businesses that integrate it into the way they do business will reap rewards in the form of greater efficiency, cost savings, happier employees, protection from liability, and more loyal customers. Those businesses that ignore it will continue to be drawn into expensive and inefficient legal proceedings that breed ill will and sap competitive strength.

L. YVES FORTIER, INTERNATIONAL "E-COMMERCIAL" DISPUTE RESOLUTION

19 Alternatives 23 (January 2001)

There is no doubt that the advent and proliferation of electronic means of conducting commercial transactions — aka "E-commerce" — have forced a reassessment of how business is carried out. Electronic commerce also has greatly accelerated the convergence of national and regional market forces toward a truly international, indeed global, economy. Globalization influences all aspects of modern life, transforming our perceptions, ideas and expectations of the world we inhabit. In the view of some, globalization implies the end of human history; others, see it in a more benign fashion: merely as the end of geography. . . .

However one approaches the subject, it is undeniable that these developments have engendered a new generation of commercial practices, and hence of commercial issues, which, if they are not entirely unique to the world of E-commerce, nonetheless require solutions tailored to fit this new mode of doing business.

Whether the question is the protection of domain names or other property, transactional security, or any other issue arising in the context of electronic commercial transactions, the need for efficient and effective dispute resolution cannot be overstated. This is all the more true in light of the fact that the march of technology continues to compress not only the time that is actually — or more accurately, "virtually" — required to conclude agreements and effect transactions but, significantly, our perceptions and expectations regarding what are, and are not, acceptable delays.

Clearly, this phenomenon of "time compression" applies equally to the concept and the means of resolution of electronic-commercial disputes. One need look no further (or further back) than the first Internet Corporation for Assigned Names and Numbers (ICANN) award, which was rendered within a few days of the appointment of the arbitral panel and, excluding attorneys' fees, cost a mere $1,000. M. Scott Donahey, *The First ICANN Decision and Some Thoughts on the Future, www.disputes.net/cyberweek2000/donahey.htm*. Nor is this sort of process unique. Increasingly, when it comes to adjudicating conflicting claims to electronic identity and domain, it reflects the norm.

For international arbitrators, mediators and other dispute resolution providers — providers of services being the key to the success of this or any commercial age — the challenge to remain in step with rapid change is particularly important. It is a challenge that goes to the heart of what we do. It is also a challenge that defines what we have been doing for centuries. . . .

As a longtime practitioner and arbitrator of international commercial disputes, I believe E-commerce and, more generally, information technology, may change the way some of the business of dispute resolution is conducted, for example, by imposing specialized techniques such as online arbitration. They will likely generate increased demands for quicker justice and foster greater use of so-called fast-track methods of dispute resolution. They will certainly add to the type of dispute requiring expert adjudication. But they have not, and will not, fundamentally alter the job of the international commercial arbitrator or mediator — any more than the transition from the ancient law merchant to the modern Uniform Commercial Code, or from steam- to electric-powered transportation fundamentally altered the mediator's or arbitrator's job.

Of course, the arbitrator or mediator — if he or she is to remain an expert purveyor of a justice that is uniquely attuned to the interests of parties in a particular industry — will necessarily be required to learn new tricks. He or she must understand the changing environments within which new enterprises incubate, operate and compete. He or she will be required to adapt traditional notions regarding such concepts as "assets" or "value" to the intangible realm in which untold billions of dollars worth of business is transacted today. And of course, he or she will have to become comfortable with new technologies. Yet it was not that long ago that the VCR was a mystery, the fax a miracle, and the original Macintosh the epitome of both style and speed. Time compression notwithstanding, it is not so long since the Internet was the exclusive domain of academics and military scientists.

None of the changes wrought by such innovations has fundamentally altered the nature of the mediator's or arbitrator's role, which has always required an appreciation of the legal, commercial, practical and — even — technological realities of the world within which a particular dispute has arisen. The issues that we are called upon to resolve, and the business contexts that give rise to such issues and in which any solution is to be implemented, may be different than they were just a few years ago. Yet, such changes go more to the question of the "how" — rather than the more basic "what" or "why" — of the mediator's or arbitrator's task. Nor is it at all self-evident that the need for fair, efficient, speedy and appropriate dispute resolution is any more pressing today than it was when Venice or Genoa were centers of global trade and commerce.

In 1622, Gerard Malynes published his treatise: "Consuedo, vel, Lex Mercatoria." Malyne's ambitious text contains one of the first legal commentaries on international commercial arbitration in England, and remains, in many respects (spelling and pronunciation aside), as relevant today as then. Malynes wrote:

> The second Mean or rather ordinarie course to end the questions and controversies arising between Merchants [the first being negotiation], is by way of Arbitrement, when both parties do make choice of honest men to end their causes, which is voluntary and in their own power, and therefore called Arbitrium, or Free will, whence the name Arbitrator is derived: and these men (by some called good men) give their judgements by Awards, according to equity and good conscience, observing the Custome of Merchants, and ought to be void of all partiality more or less to the one and to the other; having only care that right may take place according to the truth, and that the difference be ended with brevity and expedition.

Malynes presumably never contemplated the possibility of online arbitration. Doubtless, he could not have imagined such a phenomenon as electronic commerce. What he could, however, and did, comprehend, was the singular importance in a mercantile world of a system of justice derived from the will of the parties and reposing on the diligence, good faith, impartiality, legal skill and commercial sense of private dispute resolution providers selected by the parties to resolve their differences. . . .

Dispute resolution, a millennia-old practice, has always demanded innovation. It has always required arbitrators and mediators to be both aware of and responsive to the needs of parties, as these have changed over time. Today, the development and ubiquity of information technology, generally, and electronic commerce in particular, represent a new challenge. Yet, information technology and E-commerce also open the door to new opportunities for practitioners of international dispute resolution, to advocate and market their uniquely flexible and well-established brand of service to a new generation of E-business people.

---

2.   An Online Exercise

If you encounter a problem with goods purchased through the "eBay" Website, a few clicks of a computer key direct you to "A Simple 4-Step Process to Resolve Disputes" — a process that, like the underlying transaction, is all online. Here is eBay's description of the process:

STEP 1: FILE A CASE.

> On the SquareTrade website, a buyer or seller clicks "File a Case" and fills out a short online form designed to identify the problem and its possible resolutions.

STEP 2: SQUARETRADE NOTIFIES THE OTHER PARTY.

SquareTrade contacts the other party via an automatically generated email and provides instruction on responding to the case. The case and all related responses appear on a password-protected Case Page on the SquareTrade website.

STEP 3: THE PARTIES DISCUSS THEIR ISSUES DIRECTLY IN DIRECT NEGOTIATION.

Once each party is aware of the issues, they first try to reach an agreement using SquareTrade's Direct Negotiation tool. This initial phase of the service is a completely automated web-based communications tool and is currently free of charge to all users. Using SquareTrade's secure Case Page, the parties try to reach an agreement by communicating directly with each other.

THE OTHER OPTION IS TO HAVE A SQUARETRADE MEDIATOR GUIDE THE PROCESS.

If the parties cannot resolve the case through Direct Negotiation, they can request the assistance of the mediator in developing a fair, mutually agreeable solution. **The mediator's role is to facilitate positive, solution-oriented discussion between the parties**. He or she does NOT act as a judge or arbitrator. The mediator will only recommend a resolution if the parties request it.

STEP 4: THE CASE IS RESOLVED.

The parties may either reach a Settlement Agreement independently during Direct Negotiation, or with the assistance of a SquareTrade Mediator.

Throughout the "ODR" process, SquareTrade gives buyers and sellers an innovative way to establish confidence and trust in one another. By building our services around these ideals, SquareTrade brings buyers and sellers the confidence they need to do business freely online.

In this exercise, you will assume the role of an online mediator for eBay. In order to receive your case assignment from *www.OnlineMediators.com* you should follow the instructions provided by your instructor. After you have gone online you will receive specific instructions regarding your role, and then review a thread of messages between a Complainant and Respondent who were parties to a mock sales transaction on eBay.

After posting your own responses, you will have an opportunity to compare your approach with those of other student "mediators" online.

D. CHALLENGES FACING LAWYERS AS NEUTRALS

In recent years, many lawyers have become increasingly active as mediators and arbitrators. Their activities are a natural outgrowth of the expanding use of ADR in the management of conflict in many different settings — trends that have fueled a growing debate over the need for credentialing mechanisms for those offering ADR services in public and private contexts. In the following excerpt, Linda Singer, a long-time leader in the ADR field, offers personal reflections on issues such as licensing, certification, and regulation.

LINDA R. SINGER, THE LAWYER AS NEUTRAL
19 Alternatives 40 (January 2001)

For lawyers, a refreshing outcome of the increased use of ADR is the diversity of roles now available. From the role of zealous advocate in negotiation or litigation have evolved the roles of settlement counsel and advocate in a variety of forums. But what has most captured the imagination and enthusiasm of many lawyers is the role of neutral dispute resolver.

In the 1960s and 1970s, lawyers serving as neutrals were a fairly new phenomenon, and those of us who did had to struggle for acceptance. Most lawyers and judges then did not even know the difference between mediation and arbitration. Gradually, we caught the attention of a few courts, legislatures and agencies that were brave enough to experiment with alternative processes. Now, primarily as mediators, but possibly as arbitrators or case evaluators, neutral lawyers are likely to be a permanent fixture of the legal landscape.

The increased popularity of this field, however, means that it has attracted a large number of unevenly qualified entrants. As a result, a number of experienced practitioners have become concerned about whether the increased number of persons calling themselves ADR professionals have the necessary training and experience to do the job well. Legislators worry about the dearth of standards to protect the public from inferior services. Legal academics and bar associations question whether mediation or case evaluation constitutes the practice of law and thus, by implication, should be engaged in only by lawyers. Ethicists raise questions about rules — or the lack of all but the most primitive guidelines — and practitioners worry about ensuring the quality of services into the 21st century.

As a result of these often competing pressures, over the next 20 years the field will receive greater emphasis on credentialing, regulation, specialization and commercialization. At the same time, the use of neutrals will continue to expand into ever more widespread and significant disputes, and greater numbers of lawyers will be attracted to the practice.

For years, many of us have resisted credentialing, particularly in the form of licensing or certification, in the belief that the premature imposition of standards would stifle innovation and entrench random qualifications, such as academic degrees in disciplines related only tangentially to the reality of dispute resolution. When I chaired the first Commission on Qualifications of the Society of Professionals in Dispute Resolution in the 1980s, we opted against general licensing or certification requirements for neutrals, recommending, instead, that mandatory qualifications apply only when disputants are required to use a particular process or provider.

Our early opposition to credentialing may have allowed this issue to mature. Institutional users of dispute resolution services seem to be moving toward the imposition of qualifications in particular, often specialized, substantive areas. A roster to mediate multiparty environmental cases, for example, may require that the neutral have certain specialized training, years of experience or number of environmental cases mediated. The World Bank recently published a requirement that mediators wishing to handle its employment disputes have experience mediating at least five other employment cases. Similarly, a growing number of states, following Florida's lead, condition admission to court panels upon demonstration of a myriad of qualifications, which may include law or mental health degrees, specific training and apprenticeships.

It will not be surprising to expect greater regulation of neutral practice in the years to come. It seems inevitable that, at some point, bar associations, courts, or legislatures will examine the extent to which mediating constitutes the practice of law. Such discussions probably will involve determining who may mediate and the standards of care for those who do. It strains credulity to expect that mediation in some contexts, such as school or child custody cases, will be solely the province of lawyers. In other situations, particularly those involving some level of case evaluation, the subject of regulation is less clear cut. The organized bar ignores the crucial role of the lawyer as neutral at its peril. . . .

In addition to enhanced credibility, one positive effect of specialization is the neutral's ability to ask probing questions and assist in developing sophisticated solutions in disputes in his or her specialized field.

The negative effect is more subtle. Lost may be the freshness, the tendency to question broadly and the lack of attachment to any particular option that a generalist can bring to a particular dispute because of his or her distance and objectivity. There also is the concern that substantive experts' knowledge can overwhelm the parties' ability to make their own choices, a feature that always has been a source of enhanced public confidence in the ADR process. Despite these concerns, retired judges may be the only group of generalists that remains into the next generation. I, for one, would consider such a swing toward specialization a loss.

Another result of a maturing profession is bound to be greater commercialization. As with the legal profession as a whole, some dispute resolution practices are being run like the businesses they have become. Advertisements and marketing seminars no longer are a rarity. For those of us who consider the profession a calling, this is a difficult adjustment. Although there still remain think tanks and nonprofits that are oriented toward community and public policy conflicts, the dominant mode of professional practice is likely to become a commercial enterprise. We must be on alert that a trend toward commercialization does not detract from the public's and institutions' confidence in the process.

Some lawyer-neutrals increasingly are applying their skills to streams of disputes, rather than to individual cases. Increasingly, our task is to design systems to resolve the multiple conflicts of large organizations and to resolve class actions by separating individual claims from issues of more general applicability and creating claims processes to negotiate, mediate and/or arbitrate each claim when needed. Examples include the recently mediated settlements of employees' litigation against Amtrak and Merrill Lynch & Co., and the African American farmers' suit against the U.S. Department of Agriculture. Some of us have begun to focus on the issues such processes raise, such as benchmarking, or creating settlement standards, while balancing the goal of efficiency (sometimes needing to resolve thousands of longstanding claims) against the goal of providing access to meaningful processes for people who are one-time players in a system in which everyone else (attorneys, institutional representatives, and mediators) is a repeat player.

From peace in the Middle East and Northern Ireland to huge class actions and the Microsoft Corp.'s antitrust suit, judges and politicians, as well as disputants, are growing ever more ready to consider settlement negotiations assisted by neutrals. This development, together with the teaching of conflict resolution in the schools, should lead to greater public awareness of what we do. The use of mediators in disputes of increased visibility together with pressure from groups like CPR also may continue to provide the counter-vailing force to credentialing. Public figures who are likely to be the most acceptable intervenors in disputes with the highest profile are unlikely to meet any established qualifications for the work. Although the use of well-known judges and politicians (sometimes assisted by experienced mediators) in the most visible conflicts continues to attract debate within the profession, who would say that George Mitchell should have been replaced in Northern Ireland with someone who had been through 40 hours of mediation training or had mediated 1,000 cases? Was his legal training helpful or beside the point?

Now that the lawyer's role as neutral is gaining wider acceptance, we can be optimistic about most developments. Despite concerns about the potential costs of institutionalization to the creativity and freshness of the field, and the lingering lack of recognition of what a good mediator does and can do, those of us who are lucky enough to do this work full-time have maintained vibrant and enviable professional lives. The use of mediation is spreading exponentially and, even more important, is becoming accepted as a way to resolve major disputes with global implications, as well as entire categories of disputes. As students are exposed to mediation at all levels of their education, these trends can be expected to accelerate. My greatest hope is that we find ways of retaining some of the energy and idealism that prompted us to shape the field in its infancy as the profession continues to mature. We will need to be vigilant in demanding services of the highest quality if we are to surmount the pressures to obtain ever faster and cheaper (but not necessarily more creative or lasting) settlements.

Efficiency remains the value that accounts for much of the interest of advocates, the courts and the general public in our processes. At the same time the values of access, preserving relationships, individualizing processes and solutions, party participation, and the opportunities for us to apply our own creativity are what attracted most of us to neutral lawyering in the first place and what will keep our practices vibrant in the coming years.

QUESTIONS

1. What are the arguments supporting regulation of ADR services? What concerns does regulation raise?
2. Besides licensing or certification of individuals, what kinds of regulation might be contemplated? What do you think is appropriate? Does your answer vary depending on whether you are talking about services under a major commercial contract, a court-ordered mediation, or some other scenario? Explain.

E. TRANSFORMING THE COMMUNITY

HON. JANET RENO, PROMOTING PROBLEM SOLVING AND PEACEMAKING AS ENDURING VALUES IN OUR SOCIETY

19 Alternatives 16 (January 2001)

[T]here is an understandable sense of accomplishment and pride within the dispute resolution community. We have witnessed significant growth in the use of dispute resolution by courts, corporations, government bodies, schools and communities. There is much to celebrate. There is also vast, untapped potential for appropriate dispute resolution in so many aspects of society. There are so many ways that dispute resolution can help to improve society's response to conflict. We must all learn how to be effective dispute resolvers and peacemakers. Indeed, our challenge for the 21st century is to make certain that dispute resolution becomes an enduring, ingrained value that is promoted and endorsed in all aspects of our society.

We begin this task by shedding the notion that "cookie-cutter" justice is sufficient, that one size or one process fits all when we deal with disputes. It is neither possible nor appropriate for the courts to serve as the single mechanism for resolving the many kinds of disputes that arise in this complex, busy age. Instead, we need to establish a range of options and processes to resolve disputes.

Recently, the Society of Professionals in Dispute Resolution adopted guidelines for organizations wishing to design integrated conflict management systems. These guidelines emphasize two important points. First, effective integrated systems provide multiple options for addressing conflict, including some processes that are rights based and others that are interest-based. Second, the goal of these systems is to empower people by making them more competent to resolve their own disputes and to offer assistance, rather than decision-making, when direct negotiations are difficult.

I think we need to build on this splendid work by committing ourselves to create an integrated conflict management system for society as a whole. At one end of the spectrum, we must make sure that people have the skills to negotiate disputes one-on-one without intermediaries. In the middle, we need more skilled people to provide an entire spectrum of dispute resolution processes. Here, people can tailor the process to suit the dispute. Finally, we need to ensure that there is adequate access to courts and that our judiciary has the resources to resolve disputes that they are best suited to address. In a sense, this means that we must encourage all elements in our society to identify the best process to resolve their dispute, before moving to the substance of the dispute. This would allow us to be less adversarial at the outset. By using the techniques and skills of the mediator, we can be better listeners, more creative problem solvers and better able to have those difficult conversations with one another. In this manner, we can avoid some disputes and resolve others much earlier.

Our challenge, then, is to engage all sectors of the public in dispute resolution, and to obtain society's recognition that dispute resolution is a necessary life skill at which we should all be proficient, just like math, reading, and spelling. To reach this goal, there are several steps that we must take. First, we must begin with the formal, structured means for resolving conflict in our society, and make sure that the courts have programs to divert those cases into dispute resolution that can and should benefit from facilitated negotiation. We must make the Multidoor Courthouse a reality to ensure appropriate access for all and greater respect for our system of justice.

Second, governments, law firms, and frequent litigants should have programs in place to avoid litigation by using dispute resolution at the earliest possible time. . . . I hope that the efforts now being made by the federal government also will contribute to the growing recognition that dispute resolution is a vital skill every lawyer and senior manager must have.

Third, we need to do more with our law schools to promote problem solving in legal education. Our young lawyers need to be educated to recognize that even if the outcome of litigation is relatively certain, there is not always just one right answer to a problem. Our lawyers need to be educated in how not only to root out the facts of a problem, but to understand the context in which the problem arose. We should work with law schools to encourage curricula that include an expanded approach to traditional casebook study of appellate decisions, exposure to interdisciplinary insights, as well as academic courses and clinics that promote crosscutting skills such as negotiation, mediation, and collaborative practices.

Fourth, the use of these skills should not be limited to a select segment of our society. Our schools should teach our children skills in dispute resolution. Through such training, our children can participate in peer mediation programs and, we hope, carry these skills with them to use through later life. It is my vision that every teacher, every school administrator, and every community police officer who comes in contact with young people will be trained in mediation skills to deal with disputes that involve our youth. It is so exciting to see what is going on in schools all across the country when young people gain insight and confidence into genuine, nonviolent problem solving. It truly makes a difference in their lives.

Fifth, we should make use of dispute resolution concepts in creating community courts where justice is approached from a problem-solving perspective, and all relevant players participate in the resolution of a dispute. At the Midtown Community Court in Manhattan, the building contains not only courtrooms but also a social services center, a community service program with mediators, community probation officers, and other services. Local residents, community prosecutors, businesses, and social service providers collaborate with the criminal justice system to provide swift, visible justice that is augmented by drug treatment, health care, employment counseling, education, and other services. By holding defendants immediately accountable for their crimes while, at the same time, addressing the underlying problems that contribute to crime, we improve the community and free other courts to prosecute more serious crime.

Sixth, we must work hard at developing mechanisms that address the impact of technology in conflict resolution. We are communicating ever so rapidly; our economy is truly global, and the possibilities for new types of disputes have expanded exponentially. We must find ways to use these technologies to resolve conflict and to address those types of conflicts that would not have occurred in an earlier age. Each of these steps represents a formidable undertaking. But we know the way, because substantial progress has been made in every one of these areas. What is needed now is the commitment to see all of this as integrated and effective conflict management for our society, where dispute resolution skills for everyone — participants, neutrals, and bystanders — are valued because of their contribution to the overall health of our institutions, organizations, and communities.

CONCLUSION

As this final chapter has revealed, the revolution in the management of conflict that inspired the writing of this book continues apace. While the future remains uncertain, it is likely that it will become more important for lawyers to provide their clients with the full benefit of a wide and expanding range of tools for managing and resolving disputes — which requires a thorough appreciation of their appropriate uses as well as their limitations and drawbacks. This is true for attorneys who advise or advocate on behalf of businesses and government institutions as well as those representing domestic partners, employees, or consumers. The authors hope that his volume has provided you with the fundamental understanding of process choices essential to modern law practice. If we have not led you to all of the answers, we hope to have equipped you to ask the right questions.

CONCLUSION

APPENDIX

The Appendix to this book is entirely Web based. This makes it possible for students and teachers to download and edit materials to meet their individual needs. To access the Appendix, enter the following URL:

http://www.law.suffolk.edu/pubs/ResolvingDisputes

The contents of the Appendix, which will be updated from time to time, are as follows:

Negotiation

- Ethical Guidelines for Settlement Negotiations (ABA)
- Federal Rule of Civil Procedure 68
- Model Rules of Professional Conduct (ABA)

Mediation

- Legislation
  - ADR Act of 1998
  - Uniform Mediation Act (NCCUSL)
- Rules
  - Commercial Mediation Procedures (AAA)
  - CPR Mediation Procedure (CPR)
  - Ethics 2000 ("E2K") Report (ABA)
  - Model Rule of Professional Conduct for the Lawyer as Third-Party Neutral (CPR-Georgetown)
  - Model Standards of Conduct for Mediators (AAA, ABA, and SPIDR)
  - Model Standards of Practice for Family and Divorce Mediators (ACR)
- Sample Mediation Agreements

Arbitration

- Legislation
  - Federal Arbitration Act
  - Convention on the Recognition and Enforcement of Foreign Arbitral Awards
- Rules
  - Code of Ethics for Arbitrators in Commercial Disputes (AAA and ABA)
  - Commercial Arbitration Rules and Mediation Procedures (AAA)

- Comprehensive Arbitration Rules (JAMS)
- Optional Appeal Procedure (JAMS)
- Principles for ADR Provider Organizations (CPR-Georgetown)
- Rules of Arbitration (ICC)
- Rules for Non-Administered Arbitration (CPR)
- Streamlined Arbitration Rules (JAMS)
- Protocols
  - Consumer Due Process Protocol (AAA)
  - Employment Minimum Standards (JAMS)

BIBLIOGRAPHY AND REFERENCES

Chapter 1 and Part I, Negotiation

BOOKS

Abel, Richard L., ed. (1982) *The Politics of Informal Justice: The American Experience* (2 vols.). New York: Academic Press.

Adler, Warren (1981) *The War of the Roses*. Stonehouse Press.

Albrecht, Karl, & Steve Albrecht (1993) *Added Value Negotiating: The Breakthrough Method for Building Balanced Deals*. Homewood, Ill.: Irwin.

Arrow, Kenneth J., et al., eds. (1995) *Barriers to Conflict Resolution*. New York: W.W. Norton.

Austin, Elizabeth, & Leslie Whitaker (2001) *The Good Girl's Guide to Negotiating: How to Get What You Want at the Bargaining Table*. Boston: Little, Brown.

Axelrod, Robert M. (1984) *The Evolution of Cooperation*. New York: Basic Books.

Babcock, Linda, & Sara Laschever (2003) *Women Don't Ask: Negotiation and the Gender Divide*. Princeton, N.J.: Princeton University Press.

Baird, Douglas G., Robert H. Gertner, & Randal C. Picker (2002) *Game Theory and the Law*. Cambridge, Mass.: Harvard University Press.

Bazerman, Max H., & Roy J. Lewicki, eds. (1983) *Negotiating in Organizations*. Beverly Hills, Calif.: Sage.

Bazerman, Max H., & Margaret A. Neale (1992) *Negotiating Rationally*. New York: Free Press.

Bentham, Jeremy (1996) *An Introduction to the Principles of Morals and Legislation*. Oxford: Oxford University Press.

Bernard, Phyllis, & Bryant Garth, eds. (2002) *Dispute Resolution Ethics: A Comprehensive Guide*. Washington, D.C.: ABA Section of Dispute Resolution.

Brams, Steven J., & Alan D. Taylor (1996) *Fair Division: From Cake-Cutting to Dispute Resolution*. Cambridge: Cambridge University Press.

Brams, Steven J., & Alan D. Taylor (2000) *The Win-Win Solution: Guaranteeing Fair Share to Everybody*. New York: W.W. Norton.

Brazil, Wayne D. (1988) *Effective Approaches to Settlement: A Handbook for Lawyers and Judges*. Clifton, N.J.: Prentice Hall Law and Business.

Breslin, J. William, & Jeffrey Z. Rubin, eds. (1991) *Negotiation Theory and Practice*. Cambridge, Mass.: Program on Negotiation Books.

Bunker, Barbara Benedict, & Jeffrey Z. Rubin, eds. (1995) *Conflict Cooperation & Justice: Essays Inspired by the Work of Morton Deutsch*. San Francisco: Jossey-Bass.

Camp, Jim (2002) *Start With No*. New York: Crown Business.

Carter, Jimmy (1982) *Keeping Faith: Memoirs of a President*. New York: Bantam Books.

Carter, Jimmy (2003) *Negotiation: The Alternative to Hostility*. Macon, GA: Mercer University Press.

Chew, Pat K., ed. (2001) *The Conflict & Culture Reader*. New York: New York University Press.

Cialdini, Robert B. (2001) *Influence: Science and Practice* (4th ed.). Boston: Allyn & Bacon.

Cohen, Herb (2003) *Negotiate This!: By Caring, But Not That Much*. New York: Warner Business Books.

Cohen, Raymond (1999) *Negotiating Across Cultures: International Communication in an Interdependent World*. Washington, D.C.: United States Institute of Peace.

Colosi, Thomas R. (2001) *On and Off the Record: Colosi on Negotiation* (2d ed.). New York: American Arbitration Association.

Craver, Charles B. (2001) *Effective Legal Negotiation and Settlement* (4th ed.). Danvers, Mass.: LEXIS.

Dauer, Edward A. (1994) *Manual of Dispute Resolution*. San Francisco: Shepard's/McGraw-Hill.

Davis, Morton D. (1997) *Game Theory: A Nontechnical Introduction*. Mineola, N.Y.: Dover.

Dawson, Roger (2001) *Secrets of Power Negotiating* (2d ed.). Franklin Lakes, N.J.: Career Press.

Deutsch, Morton (1973) *The Resolution of Conflict*. New Haven, Conn.: Yale University Press.

Deutsch, Morton, & Peter T. Coleman, eds. (2000) *The Handbook of Conflict Resolution*. San Francisco: Jossey-Bass.

Dixit, Avinash K., & Barry J. Nalebuff (1991) *Thinking Strategically: The Competitive Edge in Business, Politics, and Everyday Life*. New York: W.W. Norton.

Dunnette, Marvin D., ed. (1976) *Handbook of Industrial and Organizational Psychology*. Palo Alto, Calif.: Consulting Psychologists Press.

Edwards, Harry, & James J. White (1977) *The Lawyer as Negotiator*. St. Paul, Minn.: West Publishing.

Ellickson, Robert C. (1991) *Order Without Law: How Neighbors Settle Disputes*. Cambridge, Mass.: Harvard University Press.

Fairhurst, Gail T., & Robert A. Sarr (1996) *The Art of Framing*. San Francisco: Jossey-Bass.

Felder, Raoul (2004) *Bare-Knuckle Negotiation*. Hoboken, N.J.: John Wiley.

Fisher, Roger, & Scott Brown (1988) *Getting Together: Building a Relationship that Gets to Yes.* Boston: Houghton Mifflin.

Fisher, Roger, & Danny Ertel (1995) *Getting Ready to Negotiate: The Getting to Yes Workbook.* New York: Penguin.

Fisher, Roger, & William J. Ury, with Bruce Patton (1991) *Getting to Yes* (2d ed.). New York: Penguin.

Fisher, Roger, et al. (1994) *Beyond Machiavelli: Tools for Coping with Conflict.* Cambridge, Mass.: Harvard University Press.

Frascogna, Jr., X.M., & H. Lee Hetherington (2001) *The Lawyer's Guide to Negotiation: A Strategic Approach to Better Contracts and Settlements.* Chicago: American Bar Association.

Freund, James (1975) *Anatomy of a Merger: Strategies for Negotiating Corporate Acquisitions.* New York: Law Journal Seminars Press.

Freund, James C. (1992) *Smart Negotiating: How to Make Good Deals in the Real World.* New York: Simon & Schuster.

Galanter, Marc, & Joel Rogers (1991) *The Transformation of American Business Disputing: Some Preliminary Observation.* Madison, Wis.: University of Wisconsin Law School.

Gifford, Donald G. (1989) *Legal Negotiation: Theory and Applications.* St. Paul, Minn.: West Publishing.

Gilligan, Carol (1982) *In a Different Voice: Psychological Theory and Women's Development.* Cambridge, Mass.: Harvard University Press.

Goleman, Daniel (1996) *Emotional Intelligence.* Vancouver, B.C.: Raincoast.

Goodpaster, Gary (1997) *A Guide to Negotiation and Mediation.* Irvington-on-Hudson, N.Y.: Transnational.

Guernsey, Thomas F. (1996) *A Practical Guide to Negotiation.* South Bend, Ind.: NITA.

Hall, Lavinia, ed. (1993) *Negotiation: Strategies for Mutual Gain.* Newbury Park, Calif.: Sage.

Hammond, John S., Ralph L. Keenney, & Howard Raiffa (1999) *Smart Choices: A Practical Guide to Making Better Decisions.* Cambridge, Mass.: Harvard University Business School.

Harr, Jonathan (1996) *A Civil Action.* New York: Vintage Books.

Haydock, Roger S., et al. (1996) *Lawyering: Practice and Planning.* St. Paul, Minn.: West Publishing.

Hindrey, Leo, & Leslie Cauley (2003) *The Biggest Game of All: The Inside Strategies, Tactics, and Temperaments that Make Great Dealmakers Great.* New York: Free Press.

Illich, John (1973) *The Art and Skill of Successful Negotiation.* Englewood Cliffs, N.J.: Prentice Hall.

Issacs, William (1999) *Dialogue and the Art of Thinking Together.* New York: Doubleday.

Jandt, Fred E., with Paul Gillette (1985) *Win-Win Negotiating: Turning Conflict into Agreement.* New York: John Wiley.

Kahneman, Daniel, Paul Sovic, & Amos Tversky (1982) *Judgment Under Uncertainty: Heuristics and Biases.* Cambridge: Cambridge University Press.

Kaplow, Louis, & Steven Shavell (2004) *Decision Analysis, Game Theory, and Information.* New York: Foundation Press.

Kennedy, Gavin (1994) *Field Guide to Negotiation: A Glossary of Essential Tools and Concepts for Today's Manager.* Boston: Harvard Business School Press.

Kerr, Baine (2000) *Harmful Intent.* New York: Jove Books.

Kheel, Theodore W. (1999) *The Keys to Conflict Resolution. Proven Methods of Settling Disputes Voluntarily.* New York: Four Walls Eight Windows.

Knight, Warren, et al. (2004) *Alternative Dispute Resolution.* Encino, Calif.: The Rutter Group.

Kolb, Deborah (2001) *Shadow Negotiation.* New York: Simon & Schuster.

Kolb, Deborah M., & Judith Williams (2000) *The Shadow Negotiation: How Women Can Master the Hidden Agendas that Determine Bargaining Success.* New York: Simon & Schuster.

Korobkin, Russell (2002) *Negotiation Theory and Strategy.* New York: Aspen.

Kremenyuk, Victor A., ed. (1991) *International Negotiation: Analysis, Approaches, Issues.* San Francisco: Jossey-Bass.

Kritek, Phyllis Beck (2002) *Negotiating at an Uneven Table: Developing Moral Courage in Resolving Our Conflicts* (2d ed.). San Francisco: Jossey-Bass.

Kritzer, Herbert M. (1991) *Let's Make a Deal: Understanding the Negotiation Process in Ordinary Litigation.* Madison: University of Wisconsin Press.

Laborde, Genie Z. (1987) *Influencing with Integrity.* Palo Alto, Calif.: Syntony.

Lax, David A., & James K. Sebenius (1986) *The Manager as Negotiator: Bargaining for Cooperation and Competitive Gain.* New York: Free Press.

Levinson, Jay Conrad, Mark S. A. Smith, & Orvel Ray Wilson (1999) *Guerilla Negotiating: Unconventional Weapons and Tactics to Get What You Want.* New York: John Wiley.

Lewicki, Roy J., David M. Saunders, & John W. Minton (1999) *Negotiation* (3d ed.). New York: McGraw-Hill Higher Education.

Lewicki, Roy J., et al. (2003) *Negotiation: Readings, Exercises, and Cases* (4th ed.). New York: McGraw-Hill Higher Education.

Lewicki, Roy J., et al. (2004) *Essentials of Negotiation* (3d ed.). Chicago Ill.: McGraw-Hill/Irwin.

Lieberman, Jethro K. (1991) *The Litigious Society.* New York: Basic Books.

Locke, Edwin A., & Gary P. Latham (1990) *A Theory of Goal Setting and Task Performance.* Englewood Cliffs, N.J.: Prentice Hall.

Luce, R. Duncan, & Howard Raiffa (1989) *Games and Decisions: Introduction and Critical Survey.* Mineola, N.Y.: Dover.

Lynch, Hon. Eugene F., et al. (1992) *California Negotiation and Settlement Handbook.* San Francisco: Bancroft-Whitney.

Maccoby, Eleanor Emmons, & Carol Jacklin (1974) *The Psychology of Sex Differences.* Palo Alto, Calif.: Stanford University Press.

McKean, David, & Douglas Frantz (1995) *Friends in High Places: The Rise and Fall of Clark Clifford.* Boston: Little, Brown.

Menkel-Meadow, Carrie (2003) *Dispute Processing and Conflict Resolution*. Burlington, Vt.: Ashgate.

Miller, Lee E., & Jessica Miller (2002) *A Woman's Guide to Successful Negotiating: How to Convince, Collaborate, & Create Your Way to Agreement*. New York: McGraw-Hill.

Milton, John (1909) *The Complete Poems of John Milton*. New York: P. F. Collier & Son.

Mnookin, Robert H., Scott R. Peppet, & Andrew S. Tulumello (2000) *Beyond Winning: Negotiating to Create Value in Deals and Disputes*. Cambridge, Mass.: Harvard University Press.

Mnookin, Robert H., & Lawrence E. Susskind, eds. (1999) *Negotiating on Behalf of Others*. Thousand Oaks, Calif.: Sage.

Murnighan, J. Keith (1992) *Bargaining Games*. New York: Wm. Morrow.

Nelken, Melissa L. (2001) *Understanding Negotiation*. Cincinnati, Ohio: Anderson.

Nierenberg, Gerald I. (1981) *The Art of Negotiating*. New York: Pocket Books.

O'Connor, Theron (2003) *Planning and Executing an Effective Concession Strategy*. Bay Group International.

Olson, Walter (1991) *The Litigation Explosion*. New York: Penguin Books.

Perry, Linda A.M., et al., eds. (1992) *Constructing and Reconstructing Gender*. Albany: State University of New York Press.

Poswall, John M. (2003) *The Lawyers: Class of '69*. Sacramento, Calif.: Jullundur Press.

Raiffa, Howard (1982) *The Art and Science of Negotiation*. Cambridge, Mass.: Harvard University Press.

Raiffa, Howard (2002) *Negotiation Analysis: The Science and Art of Collaborative Decision Making*. Cambridge, Mass.: Harvard University Press.

Reed, Barry (1980) *The Verdict*. New York: Simon & Schuster.

Ringer, Robert J. (1974) *Winning Through Intimidation*. New York: Fawcett Crest.

Riskin, Leonard L., & James E. Westbrook (1998) *Dispute Resolution and Lawyers* (2d ed.). St. Paul, Minn.: West Publishing.

Roth, Bette J., Randall W. Wulff, & Charles A. Cooper (1993) *The Alternative Dispute Resolution Practice Guide*. Scarborough, Ont.: Carswell.

Rubin, Jeffrey Z., & Bert R. Brown (1975) *The Social Psychology of Bargaining and Negotiation*. New York: Academic Press.

Rummel, R.J. (1991) *The Conflict Helix*. New Brunswick, N.J.: Transaction Publishers.

Salacuse, Jeswald W. (2003) *The Global Negotiator: Making, Managing, and Mending Deals Around the World in the Twenty-First Century*. Hampshire, U.K.: Palgrave Macmillan.

Saperstein, Guy T. (2003) *Civil Warrior: Memoirs of a Civil Rights Attorney*. Berkeley, Calif.: Berkeley Hills Books.

Schelling, Thomas C. (1960) *The Strategy of Conflict*. Cambridge, Mass.: Harvard University Press.

Schon, Donald (1983) *The Reflective Practitioner*. New York: Basic Books.

Shapiro, Ronald M., & Mark A. Jankowski, with James Dale (2001) *The Power of Nice* (2d ed.). New York: John Wiley.

Shell, G. Richard (1999) *Bargaining for Advantage: Negotiation Strategies for Reasonable People*. New York: Viking.

Sjöstedt, Gunnar (2003) *Professional Cultures in International Negotiation: Bridge or Rift?* Lanham, Md.: Lexington Books.

Sochynsky, Yaroslav, et al. (1992) *California ADR Practice Guide*. Miamisburg, Ohio: LEXIS.

Spegel, Nadja M., Bernadette Rogers, & Ross P. Buckley (1998) *Negotiation: Theory and Techniques*. Sydney, Australia: Butterworths.

Sperber, Philip (1985) *Attorney's Practice Guide to Negotiations*. Wilmette, Ill.: Callaghan.

Stone, Douglas, Bruce Patton, & Sheila Heen (1999) *Difficult Conversations: How to Discuss What Matters Most*. New York: Penguin Books.

Stone, Katharine V.W. (2000) *Private Justice: The Law of Alternative Dispute Resolution*. New York: Foundation Press.

Tesler, Pauline H. (2001) *Collaborative Law*. Chicago: ABA Section on Family Law.

Thompson, Leigh (2001) *The Mind and Heart of the Negotiator* (2d ed.). Upper Saddle River, N.J.: Prentice Hall.

Trachte-Huber, E. Wendy, & Stephen K. Huber (1996) *Alternative Dispute Resolution: Strategies for Law and Business*. Cincinnati, Ohio: Anderson.

Ury, William L. (1991) *Getting Past No: Negotiating with Difficult People*. New York: Bantam Books.

Ury, William (1993) *Getting Past No: Negotiating Your Way from Confrontation to Cooperation*. New York: Bantam Books.

Walton, Richard E., Joel E. Cutcher-Gershenfeld, & Robert B. McKersie (2000) *Strategic Negotiations: A Theory of Change in Labor-Management Relations*. Ithaca, N.Y.: Cornell University Press.

Ware, Stephen J. (2001) *Alternative Dispute Resolution*. St. Paul, Minn.: West Publishing.

Watkins, Michael, & Susan Rosengrant (2001) *Breakthrough International Negotiations*. San Francisco: Jossey-Bass.

Wilkinson, John H., ed. (1990 and annual supplements) *Donovan Leisure Newton & Irvine ADR Practice Book*. New York: Wiley Law Publications.

Williams, Gerald R. (1983) *Legal Negotiation and Settlement*. St. Paul, Minn.: West Publishing.

Zitrin, Richard, & Carol M. Langford (1999) *The Moral Compass of the American Lawyer*. New York: Ballantine Books.

ARTICLES AND CHAPTERS

Aaron, Marjorie Corman, & Hoffer, David P. (1996) "Decision Analysis as a Method of Evaluating the Trial Alternative," in Golann, ed., *Mediating Legal Disputes*. New York: Aspen.

Adamowicz, Viktor L., et al. (1999) "Experiments on the Difference Between Willingness to Pay and Willingness to Accept," 69 *Land Econ.* 86.

Adler, Robert S., & Elliot M. Silverstein (2000) "When David Meets Goliath: Dealing with Power Differentials in Negotiations," 5 *Harv. Negot. L. Rev.* 1 (Spring).

Alfini, James J. (1999) "Settlement Ethics and Lawyering in ADR Proceedings: A Proposal to Revise Rule 4.1," 19 *N. Ill. U. L. Rev.* 255.

Austin, William (1980) "Friendship and Fairness: Effects of Type of Relationship and Task Performance on Choice of Distribution Rules," 6 *Pers. Soc. Psychol. Bull.* 402.

Ayres, Ian (1991) "Fair Driving: Gender and Race Discrimination in Retail Car Negotiations," 104 *Harv. L. Rev.* 817.

Ayres, Ian, & Barry J. Nalebuff (1995) "The Role of Fairness Considerations and Relationships in a Judgmental Perspective of Negotiation," in Kenneth Arrow, et al., eds., *Barriers to Conflict Resolution*. New York: W.W. Norton.

Ayres, Ian, & Barry J. Nalebuff (1997) "Common Knowledge as a Barrier to Negotiation," 44 *UCLA L. Rev.* 1631.

Bartos, Otomar (1978) "Simple Model of Negotiation," in William Zartman, ed., *The Negotiation Process*. Thousand Oaks, Calif.: Sage.

Baruch Bush, Robert A. (1984) "Dispute Resolution Alternatives and the Goals of Civil Justice: Jurisdictional Principles for Process Choice," 1984 *Wis. L. Rev.* 893.

Berger, Marilyn (1998) "Clark Clifford, Key Advisor to Four Presidents, Dies," *New York Times* (October 11).

Berryman-Fink, Cynthia, & Claire C. Brunner (1987) "The Effects of Sex of Source and Target on Interpersonal Conflict Management Styles," 53 *So. Speech Comm. J.* 38.

Birke, Richard (1999) "Reconciling Loss Aversion and Guilty Pleas," 1999 *Utah L. Rev.* 205.

Birke, Richard (2000) "Settlement Psychology: When Decision-Making Processes Fail," 18 *Alternatives* 203 (December).

Birke, Richard, & Craig R. Fox (1999) "Psychological Principles in Negotiating Civil Settlements," 4 *Harv. Negot. L. Rev.* 1 (Spring).

Bohnet, Iris, & Bruno S. Frey (1999) "The Sound of Silence in Prisoner's Dilemma and Dictator Games," 38 *J. Econ. Behav. Organ.* 43.

Bordone, Robert C. (1998) "Electronic Online Dispute Resolution: A Systems Approach — Potential, Problems, and a Proposal," 3 *Harv. Negot. L. Rev.* 175 (Spring).

Brett, Jeanne M. (2000) "Culture and Negotiation," 35 *Int. J. Psychol.* 97, 273, Collected References.

Brett, Jeanne M., et al. (1996) "The Effectiveness of Mediation: An Independent Analysis of Cases Handled by Four Major Service Providers," 12 *Negot. J.* 259.

Brown, Jennifer Gerarda (1997) "The Role of Hope in Negotiation," 44 *UCLA L. Rev.* 1661.

Carlton, Jim (1994) "Microsoft, Stac End Battle With Pact, A 'Win-Win' Cross-Licensing Agreement" *Wall St. J.* (June 22).

Chernick, Richard (2004) "ADR Comes of Age: What Can We Expect in the Future?" 4 *Pepp. Disp. Resol. L.J.* 187.

Cochran, Robert F., Jr. (1999) "ADR, the ABA, and Client Control: A Proposal that the Model Rules Require Lawyers to Present ADR Options to Clients," 41 *S. Tex. L. Rev.* 183 (Winter).

Cohen, Jonathan R. (2000) "Apologizing for Errors," 6 *Disp. Res. Mag.* 4 (Summer).

Cohen, Jonathan (2001) "When People are the Means: Negotiating with Respect," 14 *Geo. J. Legal Ethics* 739.

Condlin, Robert J. (1992) "Bargaining in the Dark: The Normative Incoherence of Lawyer Dispute Bargaining Role," 51 *Md. L. Rev.* 1.

Cooter, Robert, et al. (1982) "Bargaining in the Shadow of the Law: A Testable Model of Strategic Behavior," 11 *J. Legal Stud.* 225.

Craver, Charles B. (1997) "Negotiation Ethics: How to Be Deceptive Without Being Dishonest/ How to Be Assertive Without Being Offensive," 38 *Tex. L. Rev.* 713.

Craver, Charles B., & David W. Barnes (1999) "Gender, Risk Taking, and Negotiation Performance," 5 *Mich. J. Gender & Law* 299.

Croson, Rachel, & Nancy Buchan (1999) "Gender and Culture: International Experimental Evidence from Trust Games," 89 *Am. Econ. Rev.* 386.

Crystal, Nathan M. (1998) "The Lawyer's Duty to Disclose Material Facts in Contract or Settlement Negotiations," 87 *Ky. L.J.* 1055.

Dauer, Edward A. (2000) "Justice Irrelevant: Speculations on the Causes of ADR," 74 *So. Cal. L. Rev.* 83.

Delgado, Richard, et al. (1985) "Fairness and Formality: Minimizing the Risk of Prejudice in Alternative Dispute," 1985 *Wis. L. Rev.* 1359.

Diener, Ed, & Marissa Diener (1995) "Cross-Cultural Correlates of Life Satisfaction and Self-Esteem," 68 *J. Pers. Soc. Psychol.* 653.

Doré, Laurie Kratky (1999) "Secrecy by Consent: The Use and Limits of Confidentiality in the Pursuit of Settlement," 74 *Notre Dame L. Rev.* 283.

Eckel, Catherine, & Philip Grossman (1996) "The Relative Price of Fairness: Gender Differences in a Punishment Game," 30 *J. Econ. Behav. Organ.* 143.

Eckel, Catherine, & Philip Grossman (1998) "Are Women Less Selfish Than Men?: Evidence from Dictator Experiments," 108 *Econ. J.* 726.

Epstein, Lynn A. (1997) "Post-Settlement Malpractice: Undoing the Done Deal," 43 *Cath. U. L. Rev.* 459 (Winter).

Fehr, Ernst, & Simon Gachter (2000) "Fairness and Retaliation: The Economics of Reciprocity," 14 *J. Econ. Perspect.* 159.

Fisher, Roger (1984) "Comments on White's Review of 'Getting to Yes'," 31 *J. Legal Educ.* 128.

Fisher, Roger (1991) "Negotiating Power: Getting and Using Influence," in J. William Breslin & Jeffrey Z. Rubin, eds. *Negotiation Theory and Practice*.

Fiss, Owen (1984) "Against Settlement," 93 *Yale L.J.* 1073.

Fobia, Cynthia S., & Jay J. Christensen-Szalanski (1993) "Ambiguity and Liability Negotiations: The Effects of the Negotiator's Role and the Sensitivity Zone," 54 *Org. Behav. Hum. Decis. Proc.* 277.

Folberg, Jay (2003) "The Continuing History of Conflict Resolution Practice," *AC Resolution*.

Folberg, Jay (1983) "A Mediation Overview: History and Dimensions of Practice," 1 *Mediation Quarterly* 3.

Folberg, Jay, Joshua Rosenberg, & Robert
Barrett (1992) "Use of ADR in California
Courts: Findings and Proposals," 26 *U.S.F. L.
Rev.* 343.

Frey, Martin A. (1997) "Representing Clients
Effectively in an ADR Environment," 33 *Tulsa
L.J.* 443 (Fall).

Fuller, Lon (1978) "The Forms and Limits of
Adjudication," 92 *Harv. L. Rev.* 353.

Galanter, Marc (1974) "Why the 'Haves' Come
Out Ahead: Speculations, or the Limits of Legal
Change," 9 *L. & Socy. Rev.* 95.

Galanter, Marc (1981) "Justice in Many Rooms:
Courts, Private Ordering, and Indigenous
Law," 19 *J. Legal Pluralism & Unofficial L.* 1.

Galanter, Marc (1983) "Reading the Landscape
of Disputes: What We Know and Don't Know
(And Think We Know) About Our Allegedly
Contentious and Litigious Society," 31 *UCLA L.
Rev.* 4.

Galanter, Marc, & Mia Cahill (1994) "Most
Cases Settle: Judicial Promotion and
Regulation of Settlements," 46 *Stan. L. Rev.*
1339.

Garth, Bryant G. (1992) "Privatization and the
New Market for Disputes: A Framework for
Analysis and a Preliminary Assessment," 12
Stud. L. Pol. & Socy. 367.

Gelfand, Michele J., & Sophia Christakopoulou
(1999) "Culture and Negotiator Cognition:
Judgment Accuracy and Negotiation
Processes in Individualistic and Collectivistic
Cultures," 79 *Org. Behav. Hum. Decis.
Processes* 248.

Gilson, Ronald J. (1984) "Value Creation by
Business Lawyers: Legal Skills and Asset
Pricing," 94 *Yale L.J.* 239.

Gilson, Ronald J., & Robert H. Mnookin (1994)
"Disputing Through Agents: Cooperation and
Conflict Between Lawyers in Litigation," 94
Colum. L. Rev. 509.

Goh, Bee Chen (1998) "Sino-Western Negotiating
Styles," 7 *Canterbury L. Rev.* 82.

Golann, Dwight (2001) "Cognitive Barriers to
Effective Negotiation," 6 *ADR Currents* 6
(September).

Goodpaster, Gary (1993) "Rational Decision-
Making in Problem-Solving Negotiation:
Compromise, Interest-Valuation, and
Cognitive Error," 8 *Ohio St. J. on Disp. Resol.*
299.

Grant, Malcolm J., & Vello Sermat (1969) "Status
and Sex of Other as Determinants of Behavior
in a Mixed-Motive Game," 12 *J. Pers. Soc.
Psychol.* 151.

Gross, Samuel R., & Kent D. Syverud (1991)
"Getting to No: A Study of Settlement
Negotiations and the Selection of Cases for
Trial," 90 *Mich. L. Rev.* 319.

Guernsey, Thomas F. (1982) "Truthfulness in
Negotiation," 17 *U. Rich. L. Rev.* 99.

Guthrie, Chris (2003) "Panacea or Pandora's
Box?: The Costs of Options in Negotiation," 88
Iowa L. Rev. 601.

Halpern, Richard G. (1998) "Settlement
Negotiations: Taking Control," 34 *Trial* 64
(February).

Hartman, Raymond S., et al. (1991) "Consumer
Rationality and the Status Quo," 106 *Quart. J.
Econ.* 141.

Hartwell, Steven, et al. (1992) "Women
Negotiating: Assertiveness and Relatedness," in
Linda A.M. Perry, et al., eds., *Constructing and
Reconstructing Gender*. Albany: State University
of New York Press.

Hensler, Deborah R. (2003) "Our Courts,
Ourselves: How the Alternative Dispute
Resolution Movement Is Reshaping
Our Legal System," 108 *Penn St. L. Rev.*
165.

Hetherington, H. Lee (2001) "The Wizard and
Dorothy, Patton and Rommel: Negotiation
Parables in Fiction and Fact," 28 *Pepperdine L.
Rev.* 289.

Hirshleifer, Jack (2001) "Game-Theoretic
Interpretations of Commitment," in Randolph
Nesse, ed., *Evolution and the Capacity for
Commitment*. New York: Russell Sage
Foundation.

Hoffman, Elizabeth, & Matthew L. Spitzer (1985)
"Entitlements, Rights, and Fairness: An
Experimental Examination of Subjects'
Concepts of Distributive Justice," 14 *J. Legal
Stud.* 259.

Hoffman, Elizabeth, et al. (1994) "Preferences,
Property Rights, and Anonymity in Bargaining
Games," 7 *Games Econ. Behav.* 346.

Howell, Benjamin, & Jeanna Steele (2000) "Going
Private: Where Have All the Judges Gone?" *Cal.
Lawyer* 39 (May).

Judicial Council of California (1999) "Report of
the Task Force on the Quality of Justice,
Subcommittee on ADR and the Judicial
System," Jay Folberg, Chair,
*http://www.courtinfo.ca.gov/reference/documents.
adrreport.pdf* (August).

Kahneman, Daniel, & Amos Tversky (1979)
"Prospect Theory: An Analysis of a Decision
Under Risk," 47 *Econometrica* 263.

Kahneman, Daniel, & Amos Tversky (1984)
"Choices, Values, and Frames," 39 *Am. Psychol.*
341.

Kahneman, Daniel, Jack L. Knetsch, & Richard H.
Thaler (1990) "Experimental Tests of the
Endowment Effect and the Coase Theorem," 98
J. Polit. Economy 1325.

Kahneman, Daniel, & Dale T. Miller (1986)
"Norm Theory: Comparing Reality to Its
Alternatives," 93 *Psychol. Rev.* 136.

Kimmel, Melvin J., et al. (1980) "Effects of Trust,
Aspiration and Gender on Negotiating
Tactics," 38 *J. Pers. Soc. Psychol.* 9.

Kimmel, Paul R. (1994) "Cultural Perspectives on
International Negotiations," 50 *J. Social Issues*
179.

Knetsch, Jack L., & J.A. Sinden (1984)
"Willingness to Pay and Compensation
Demanded: Experimental Evidence of an
Unexpected Disparity in Measures of Value,"
99 *Quart. J. Econ.* 507.

Korobkin, Russell (1998) "Inertia and Preference
in Contract Negotiation: The Psychological
Power of Default Rules and Form Terms," 51
Vand. L. Rev. 1583.

Korobkin, Russell (2000) "A Positive Theory of Legal Negotiation," 88 *Georgetown L.J.* 1789.

Korobkin, Russell (2002) "Aspirations and Settlement," 88 *Cornell L. Rev.* 1.

Korobkin, Russell, & Chris Guthrie (1994a) "Opening Offers and Out of Court Settlement: A Little Moderation Might Not Go a Long Way," 10 *Ohio St. J. on Disp. Resol.* 1.

Korobkin, Russell, & Chris Guthrie (1994b) "Psychological Barriers to Litigation Settlement: An Experimental Approach," 93 *Mich. L. Rev.* 107.

Korobkin, Russell, & Chris Guthrie (1997) "Psychology, Economics, and Settlement: A New Look at the Role of the Lawyer," 76 *Tex. L. Rev.* 77.

Korobkin, Russell, Michael Moffett, & Nancy Welch (2004) "The Law of Bargaining," 87 *Marq. L. Rev.* 839.

Kramer, Roderick M., et al. (1993) "Self-Enhancement Biases and Negotiator Judgment: Effects of Self-Esteem and Mood," 56 *Org. Behav. Hum. Decis. Processes* 110.

Kritzer, Herbert M. (1987) "Fee Arrangements and Negotiation," 21 *L. & Socy. Rev.* 341.

Lawrence, James K.L. (2003) "Collaborative Lawyering: A New Development in Conflict Resolution," 17 *Ohio St. J. on Disp. Resol.* 431.

Lax, David, & James Sebenius (1992) "Thinking Coalitionally: Party Arithmetic, Process Opportunism, and Strategic Sequencing," in H. Peyton Young, ed., *Negotiation Analysis.* Ann Arbor: University of Michigan Press.

Loder, Reed Elizabeth (1994) "Moral Truthseeking and the Virtuous Negotiator," 8 *Geo. J. Legal Ethics* 45.

Loewenstein, George F., et al. (1989) "Social Utility and Decision Making in Interpersonal Contexts," 57 *J. Pers. Soc. Psychol.* 426.

Loewenstein, George, et al. (1993) "Self-Serving Assessments of Fairness and Pretrial Bargaining," 22 *J. Legal Stud.* 135.

Longan, Patrick (2001) "Ethics in Settlement Negotiations: Foreword," 52 *Mercer L. Rev.* 810.

Lubet, Steven (1996) "Notes on the Bedouin Horse Trade or 'Why Won't the Market Clear, Daddy?' " 74 *Tex. L. Rev.* 1039.

Luskin, Frederic, & Dana Curtis (2000) "The Power of Forgiveness," *Cal. Lawyer* (December).

McCarthy, William (1985) "The Role of Power and Principle in Getting to Yes," 1 *Negot. J.* 59.

McGuire, James E., & Frank E.A. Sander (2004) "Some Questions About 'The Vanishing Trial,'" 2004 *Disp. Res. Mag.* (Winter).

Menkel-Meadow, Carrie (1984) "Toward Another View of Legal Negotiation: The Structure of Problem-Solving," 31 *UCLA L. Rev.* 754.

Menkel-Meadow, Carrie (1991) "Pursuing Settlement in an Adversary Culture: A Tale of Innovation Co-Opted of 'the Law of ADR,' " 19 *Fla. St. U. L. Rev.* 1.

Menkel-Meadow, Carrie (2000) "When Winning Isn't Everything: The Lawyer as Problem Solver," 28 *Hofstra L. Rev.* 905.

Miller, Geoffrey P. (1987) "Some Agency Problems in Settlement," 16 *J. Legal Stud.* 189.

Mnookin, Robert H. (1993) "Why Negotiations Fail: An Exploration of Barriers to the Resolution of Conflict," 8 *Ohio St. J. Disp. Resol.* 235.

Mnookin, Robert H. (2003) "Strategic Barriers to Dispute Resolution: A Comparison of Bilateral and Multilateral Negotiations," 8 *Harv. Negot. L. Rev.* 1 (Spring).

Mnookin, Robert H., & Ronald J. Gilson (1994) "Disputing Through Agents: Cooperation and Conflict Between Lawyers in Litigation," 94 *Colum. L. Rev.* 509.

Mnookin, Robert H., & Lewis Kornhauser (1979) "Bargaining in the Shadow of the Law: The Case *for* Divorce," 88 *Yale L.J.* 950.

Mnookin, Robert H., Scott R. Peppet, & Andrew S. Tulumello (1996) "The Tension Between Empathy and Assertiveness," 12 *Negot. J.* 217.

Murray, John S. (1986) "Understanding Competing Theories of Negotiation," 2 *Negot. J.* 179.

Murray, John S. (1997) "What Will We Do When Adjudication Ends? A Brief Intellectual History of ADR," 44 *UCLA L. Rev.* 1613 (August).

Nolan-Haley, Jacqueline, moderator (2001) "Symposium: ADR and the Professional Responsibility of Lawyers," 28 *Fordham Urban L.J.* 4 (April).

Ochs, Jack, & Alvin E. Roth (1989) "An Experimental Study of Sequential Bargaining," 79 *Amer. Econ. Rev.* 335.

O'Connor, Kathleen M., & Peter J. Carnevale (1997) "A Nasty but Effective Negotiation Strategy: Misrepresentation of a Common-Value Issue," 23 *Pers. Soc. Psychol. Bull.* 504.

O'Hara, Erin Anne, & Douglas Yarn (2002) "On Apology and Concilience," 77 *Wash. L. Rev.* 1121.

Parks, McLean, et al. (1996) "Distributing Adventitious Outcomes: Social Norms, Egocentric Martyrs, and the Effects of Future Relationships," 67 *Org. Behav. Hum. Decis. Processes* 181.

Peppet, Scott R. (2002) "Mindfulness in the Law and ADR: Can Saints Negotiate?" 7 *Harv. Negot. L. Rev.* 83 (Spring).

Perschbacher, Rex R. (1985) "Regulating Lawyers' Negotiations," 27 *Ariz. L. Rev.* 75.

Peters, Geoffrey M. (1987) "The Use of Lies in Negotiation," 48 *Ohio St. L.J.* 1.

Picker, Bennett G. (1999) "New Roles: Problem Solving ADR: New Challenges, New Roles, and New Opportunities," 72 *Temp. L. Rev.* 883 (Winter).

Pinkley, Robin L., et al. (1994) "The Impact of Alternatives to Settlement in Dyadic Negotiation," 57 *Org. Behav. Hum. Decis. Processes* 97.

Polythress, Norman G. (1994) "Procedural Preferences, Perceptions of Fairness and Compliance with Outcomes: A Study of Alternatives to the Standard Adversary Trial Procedure," 18 *Law Hum. Behav.* 361.

Polzer, Jeffrey T., et al. (1993) "The Effects of Relationship and Justification in an Interdependent Allocation," 2 *Group Decis. Negot.* 135.

Priest, George, & Benjamin Klein (1984) "The Selection of Disputes for Litigation," 13 *J. Legal Stud.* 1.

Rachlinski, Jeffrey J. (1996) "Gains, Losses, and the Psychology of Litigation," 70 *S. Cal. L. Rev.* 113.

Raiffa, Howard (1985) "Post-Settlement Settlements," 1 *Negot. J.* 9.

Resnik, Judith (1995) "Many Doors? Closing Doors? Alternative Dispute Resolution and Adjudication," 10 *Ohio St. J. on Disp. Resol.* 211.

Rhode, Deborah L. (1993) "Missing Questions: Feminist Perspectives on Legal Education," 45 *Stan. L. Rev.* 1547.

Robinson, Robert J. (1995) "Defusing the Exploding Offer: The Farpoint Gambit," 11 *Negot. J.* 277.

Rose, Carol (1995) "Bargaining and Gender," 18 *Harv. J.L. & Pub. Pol'y* 547.

Rosenberg, Joshua, & Jay Folberg (1994) "Alternative Dispute Resolution: An Empirical Analysis," 46 *Stan L. Rev.* 1487.

Ross, Lee (1995) "Reactive Devaluation in Negotiation and Conflict Resolution," in Kenneth Arrow, et al., eds, *Barriers to Conflict Resolution*. New York: W.W. Norton.

Ross, Lee, & Andrew Ward (1995) "Psychological Barriers to Dispute Resolution," 27 *Advances in Experimental Soc. Psychol.* 255.

Rubin, Jeffrey Z. (1991) "Some Wise and Mistaken Assumptions About Conflict and Negotiation," in William Breslin & Jeffrey Z. Rubin, eds., *Negotiation Theory and Practice*. Cambridge, Mass.: Program on Negotiation Books.

Rubin, Jeffrey Z., & Frank E.A. Sander (1991) "Culture, Negotiation, and the Eye of the Beholder," 7 *Negot. J.* 249.

Rubin, Michael H. (1995) "The Ethics of Negotiation: Are There Any?" 56 *La. L. Rev.* 447.

Salacuse, Jeswald W. (1988) "Making Deals in Strange Places: A Beginner's Guide to International Business Negotiations," 4 *Negot. J.* 5.

Salacuse, Jeswald W. (1998) "Ten Ways That Culture Affects Negotiating Style: Some Survey Results," 14 *Negot. J.* 221.

Sander, Frank E.A. (1976) "Varieties of Dispute Processing," 70 *F.R.D.* 111.

Sander, Frank E.A. (1994) "Fitting the Forum of the Fuss: A User-Friendly Guide to Selecting an ADR Procedure," 10 *Negot. J.* 49.

Schneider, Andrea Kupfer (2000a) "Building a Pedagogy of Problem-Solving: Learning to Choose Among ADR Processes," 5 *Harv. Negot. L. Rev.* 113 (Spring).

Schneider, Andrea Kupfer (2000b) "Perception, Reputation and Reality: An Empirical Study of Negotiation Skills," 6 *Disp. Res. Mag.* 24 (Summer).

Schneider, Andrea Kupfer (2002) "Shattering Negotiation Myths: Empirical Evidence on the Effectiveness of Negotiation Style," 7 *Harv. Negot. L. Rev.* 143 (Spring).

Sebenius, James K. (2002) "Caveats for Cross-Border Negotiations," 18 *Negot. J.* 122.

Shavell, Steven (1995) "Alternative Dispute Resolution: An Economic Analysis," 24 *J. Legal Stud.* 1.

Shell, G. Richard (1988) "Substituting Ethical Standards for Common Law Rules in Commercial Cases: An Emerging Statutory Trend," 82 *Nw. U. L. Rev.* 1198.

Shell, G. Richard (1991) "Opportunism and Trust in Negotiation of Commercial Contracts: Toward a New Cause of Action," 44 *Vand. L. Rev.* 221 (1991)

Sherman, Edward F. (1988) "From 'Loser Pays' to Modified Offer of Judgment Rules: Reconciling Incentives to Settle with Access to Justice," 76 *Tex. L. Rev.* 1863.

Simon, William H. (1988) "Ethical Discretion in Lawyering," 101 *Harv. L. Rev.* 1083.

Starr, V. Hale (1999) "The Simple Math of Negotiating," 22 *The Trial Lawyer* 5 (January–February).

Stempel, Jeffrey W. (1996) "Reflections on Judicial ADR and the Multi-Door Courthouse at Twenty: Fait Accompli, Failed Overture, or Fledgling Adulthood?" 11 *Ohio St. J. on Disp. Resol.* 297.

Sternberg, Robert J., & Diane M. Dobson (1987) "Resolving Interpersonal Conflicts: An Analysis of Stylistic Consistency," 52 *J. Pers. Soc. Psychol.* 794.

Sternberg, Robert J., & Lawrence J. Soriano (1984) "Styles of Conflict Resolution," 47 *J. Pers. Soc. Psychol.* 115.

Sternlight, Jean R. (2000) "Is Binding Arbitration a Form of ADR?: An Argument That the Term 'ADR' Has Begun to Outlive its Usefulness," 2000 *J. Disp. Resol.* 97.

Stipanowich, Thomas J. (1998) The Multi-Door Contract and Other Possibilities, 13 *Ohio St. J. on Disp. Resol.* 303.

Stipanowich, Thomas J. (2004) "ADR and 'The Vanishing Trial': What We Know — and What We Don't," *Disp. Res. Mag.* (Summer).

Strudler, Alan (1998) "Incommensurable Goods, Rightful Lies, and the Wrongness of Fraud," 146 *U. Pa. L. Rev.* 1529.

Sumner, Anna Aven (2003) "Is the Gummy Rule of Today Truly Better Than the Toothy Rule of Tomorrow? How Federal Rule 68 Should Be Modified," 52 *Duke L.J.* 1055.

Tesler, Pauline H. (2003) "Collaborative Law Neutrals Produce Better Resolutions," 21 *Alternatives* 1.

Thaler, Richard H. (1988) "Anomalies: The Ultimatum Game," 2 *J. Econ. Perspect* 195.

Thomas, K.W., & Pondy, L.R. (1977) "Toward an Intent Model of Conflict Management Among Principal Parties," 30 *Human Relations* 1089.

Thompson, Leigh, & Reid Hastie (1990) "Social Perception in Negotiation," 47 *Org. Behav. Hum. Decis. Processes* 98.

Thompson, Leigh L., et al. (1999) "Some Like It Hot: The Case for the Emotional Negotiator," in Leigh L. Thompson, et al., eds., *Shared Cognition in Organizations: The Management of Knowledge*. Mahwah, N.J.: LEA.

Tversky, Amos, & Daniel Kahneman (1992) "Advances in Prospect Theory: Cumulative Representation of Uncertainty," 5 *J. Risk Uncertainty* 297.

Uelmen, Gerald F. (1990) "Playing 'Godfather' in Settlement Negotiations: The Ethics of Using Threats," *Cal. Litigation* 3 (Fall).

Ukishima, Allyson (2003) "Women and Legal Negotiation: Moving Beyond Gender Stereotypes and Adopting a 'Yin and Yang' Paradigm," USF Student Paper.

van Dijk, Eric, & Daan van Knippenberg (1996) "Buying and Selling Exchange Goods: Loss Aversion and the Endowment Effect," 17 *J. Econ. Psych.* 517.

Wangerin, Paul T. (1994) "The Political and Economic Roots of the 'Adversary System' of Justice and Alternative Dispute Resolution," 9 *Ohio St. J. on Disp. Resol.* 203.

Ware, Stephen J., & Sarah Rudolph Cole (2000) "Introduction: ADR in Cyberspace," 15 *Ohio St. J. on Disp. Resol.* 589.

Watkins, Normal J. (1999) "Negotiating the Complex Case," 41 *For the Defense* 36 (July).

Watson, Carol (1994) "Gender versus Power as a Predictor of Negotiation Behavior and Outcome," 10 *Negot. J.* 117.

Wetlaufer, Gerald B. (1990) "The Ethics of Lying in Negotiation," 76 *Iowa L. Rev.* 1219.

Wetlaufer, Gerald B. (1996) "The Limits of Integrative Bargaining," 85 *Georgetown L.J.* 369.

White, James J. (1980) "Machiavelli and the Bar: Ethical Limitation on Lying in Negotiation," 1980 *Am. B. Found. Res. J.* 926.

White, James J. (1984) "Essay Review: The Pros and Cons of 'Getting to Yes'," 31 *J. Legal Educ.* 115.

Williams, Gerald R. (1996) "Negotiation as a Healing Process," *J. Disp. Resol.* 1.

Zitrin, Richard A. (1999) "The Case Against Secret Settlements" 2 *J. Inst. for Study Legal Ethics* 115.

WEB SITES

Alternative Dispute Resolution Section of the Association of American Law Schools, *http://www.law.missouri.edu/aalsadr/index.htm.*

American Bar Association Section of Dispute Resolution, *http://www.abanet.org/dispute.*

Art of Negotiating, *http://www.projectkickstart.com.*

Center for Dispute Resolution, Willamette University College of Law, *http://www.willamette.edu/law/wlo/dis-res.*

Collaborative Practice, *http://www.collaborativepractice.com.*

Conflict Research Consortium, A Comprehensive Gateway to the Websites of the University of Colorado Conflict Research Consortium, *http://conflict.colorado.edu.*

Corporate Counsel Litigation Trends Survey Results, *http://www.fulbright.com.*

Indiana Conflict Resolution Institute, *http://www.spea.indiana.edu/icri/condataexp.htm.*

Information, Education, and Web Development for Mediation and Mediators, *http://www.mediate.com.*

Negotiator Pro, *http://www.negotiatorpro.com.*

The Association for Conflict Resolution, *http://www.acrnet.org.*

The Center for Information Technology and Dispute Resolution, *http://www.odr.info.*

The Conflict Resolution Information Source, *http://www.crinfo.com.*

The Mediator, Software for Mediation, *http://www.mcn.org/c/rsurratt/conflict.html.*

The Negotiator Assistant, *www.icasit.org/negotiator.*

Treeage Software, Software for Decision Analysis, Cost Effectiveness, Decision Trees, Markov Models, Influence Diagrams, and Monte Carlo Simulation, *http://www.treeage.com.*

Win Squared: Simple Software for Power Persuasion, *http://www.winxwin.com.*

CASES AND ETHICS OPINIONS

ABA Commission on Ethics and Professional Responsibility, Formal Op. 363 (1992).

Abbot Ford, Inc. v. The Superior Court of Los Angeles County; Ford Motor Co., 43 Cal. 3d 858 (1987).

Alcala Co., Inc. v. Sup. Ct., 57 Cal. 2d 349 (1996).

Booth v. Mary Carter Paint Company, 202 So. 2d 8 (Fla. App. 1967).

BMW of North America, Inc. v. Krathen, 471 So. 2d 585 (1985).

City of Tucson v. Gallagher, 14 Ariz. App. 385, 483 P.2d 798 (1971).

Evans v. Jeff D., 475 U.S. 717 (1986).

Kentucky Bar Assn. v. Geisler, 938 S.W. 578 (Ky. 1997).

Kinnamon v. Staiman & Snyder, 66 Cal. App. 3d 893 (1977).

Marek v. Chesny, 473 U.S. 105 (1985).

Nicolet Instrument Corp. v. Lindquest & Vennum, 34 F.3d 453 (7th Cir. 1994).

Silberg v. Anderson, 50 Cal. 3d 205 (1990).

Spaulding v. Zimmerman, 263 Minn. 346, 116 N.W.2d 704 (1961).

Ziegelheim v. Apollo, 128 N.J. 250 (1992).

Part II, Mediation

BOOKS

Abramson, Harold I. (2004) *Mediation Representation: Advocating in a Problem-Solving Process*. Notre Dame, Ind.: NITA.

Alfini, James J., & Eric R. Galton, eds. (1998) *ADR Personalities and Practice Tips*. Washington, D.C.: ABA Section of Dispute Resolution.

Ambrose, Stephen E. (1996) *Undaunted Courage*. New York: Touchstone Books.

Bennett, Mark D., & Michele S.G. Hermann (1996) *The Art of Mediation*. Notre Dame, Ind.: NITA.

Bercovitch, Jacob (2002) *Studies in International Mediation*. New York: Palgrave Macmillan.

Bernard, Phyllis, & Bryant Garth, eds. (2002) *Dispute Resolution Ethics: A Comprehensive Guide*. Washington, D.C.: ABA Section of Dispute Resolution.

Bowling, Daniel, & David Hoffman, eds. (2003) *Bringing Peace into the Room*. San Francisco: Jossey-Bass.

Buhring-Uhle, Christian (1996) *Arbitration and Mediation in International Business*. Boston: Kluwer Law International.

Bush, Robert A. Baruch, & Joseph P. Folger (2004) *The Promise of Mediation: The Transformative Approach to Conflict*. San Francisco: Jossey-Bass.

Carroll, Eileen, & Karl Mackie (2000) *International Mediation — The Art of Business Diplomacy*. The Hague: Kluwer Law International.

Cloke, Kenneth (2000) *Mediating Dangerously*. San Francisco: Jossey-Bass.

Cole, Sarah R., Craig McEwen, & Nancy H. Rogers (2001) *Mediation: Law, Policy & Practice*. St. Paul, Minn.: West Publishing..

Cooley, John W. (2000) *The Mediator's Handbook*. Notre Dame, Ind.: NITA.

Cooley, John W. (2002) *Mediation Advocacy*. Notre Dame, Ind.: NITA.

CPR Institute of Dispute Resolution (2001) *Into the 21st Century: Thought Pieces on Lawyering, Problem Solving, and ADR*. New York: CPR Institute.

Erickson, Stephen K., & Marilyn S. McKnight (2001) *The Practitioner's Guide to Mediation: A Client Centered Approach*. San Francisco: Jossey-Bass.

Folberg, Jay, & Alison Taylor (1984) *Mediation: A Comprehensive Guide to Resolving Conflicts Without Litigation*. San Francisco: Jossey-Bass.

Folberg, Jay, Ann L. Milne, & Peter Salem (eds.) (2004) *Divorce and Family Mediation — Models, Techniques and Applications*. New York: Guilford Press.

Galton, Eric (1994) *Representing Clients in Mediation*. Dallas, Tex.: American Lawyer Mediation.

Golann, Dwight (1996) *Mediating Legal Disputes: Effective Strategies for Lawyers and Mediators*. Boston: Little, Brown.

Haynes, John (1989) *Mediating Divorce: Casebook of Strategies for Successful Family Negotiations*. San Francisco: Jossey-Bass.

Kolb, Deborah M., & Associates (1994) *When Talk Works — Profiles of Mediators*. San Francisco: Jossey-Bass.

Kressel, Kenneth, & Dean G. Pruitt, eds. (1989) *Mediation Research: The Power and Effectiveness of Third-Party Intervention*. San Francisco: Jossey-Bass.

Lang, Michael D., & Alison Taylor (2000) *The Making of a Mediator: Developing Artistry in Practice*. San Francisco: Jossey-Bass.

Moore, Christopher (2004) *The Mediation Process: Practical Strategies for Resolving Conflict*. San Francisco: Jossey-Bass.

Mosten, Forrest S. (1996) *The Complete Guide to Mediation: The Cutting-Edge Approach to Family Law Practice*. Chicago: ABA Section of Family Law.

Niemic, Robert J., Donna Stienstra, & Randall E. Ravitz (2001) *Guide to Judicial Management of Cases in ADR*. Washington, D.C.: Federal Judicial Center.

Ordover, Abraham P., & Andrea Doneff (2002) *Alternatives to Litigation: Mediation, Arbitration, and the Art of Dispute Resolution*. Notre Dame, Ind.: NITA.

Picker, Bennett G. (2003) *Mediation Practice Guide: A Handbook for Resolving Business Disputes*. Washington, D.C.: ABA Section of Dispute Resolution.

Scanlon, Kathleen, ed. (1999) *Mediator's Deskbook*. New York: CPR Institute.

Senger, Jeffrey M. (2004) *Federal Dispute Resolution: Using Alternative Dispute Resolution with the United States Government*. San Francisco: Jossey-Bass.

Singer, Linda (1994) *Settling Disputes: Conflict Resolution in Business, Families, and the Legal System*. Boulder, Colo.: Westview.

Slaikeu, Karl A. (1996) *When Push Comes to Shove: A Practical Guide to Mediating Disputes*. San Francisco: Jossey-Bass.

Susskind, Lawrence, Sarah McKearnan, & Jennifer Thomas Larmer, eds. (1999) *The Consensus Building Handbook: A Comprehensive Guide to Reaching Agreement*. Thousand Oaks, Calif.: Sage.

ARTICLES AND MONOGRAPHS

Aaron, Marjorie Corman (1995) "The Value of Decision Analysis in Mediation Practice," 11 *Negot. J.* 123.

Aaron, Marjorie Corman (2004) "Mediation Practice Do's and Don'ts."

Alfini, James J. (2001) "Ethics 2000 Leaves Mediation in Ethics 'Black Hole,' " 7 *Disp. Resol. Mag.* 3 (Spring).

Amis, Mike, et al. (1998) "The Texas ADR Experience," in Edward J. Bergman & John G. Bickerman, eds., *Court-Annexed Mediation: Critical Perspective on State and Federal Programs*. Washington, D.C.: American Bar Association.

Arnold, Tom (1995) "Twenty Common Errors in Mediation Advocacy,"13 *Alternatives* 69.

Arnold, Tom (1999) "Client Preparation for Mediation," 15 *Corporate Counsel's Q.* 52 (April).

Bahadoran, Sina (2000) "A Red Flag: Mediator Cultural Bias in Divorce," 18 *Mass. Fam. L.J.* 69.

Berger, Vivian (2003) "Employment Mediation in the Twenty-First Century: Challenges in a Changing Environment," 5 *U. Pa. J. Lab. & Empl. L.* 487 (Spring).

Bingham, Gail (2002) "The Environment in the Balance: Mediators Are Making a Difference," 2 *ACResolution* 21 (Summer).

Bingham, Lisa (2002) "REDRESS™ at the USPS: A Breakthrough Mediation Program," 1 *ACResolution* 34 (Spring).

Birkoff, Juliana, & Robert Rack, with Judith M. Filner (2001) "Points of View: Is Mediation Really a Profession?" 8 *Disp. Res. Mag.* 10 (Fall).

Bowling, Daniel, & David Hoffman (2000) "Bringing Peace into the Room: The Personal Qualities of the Mediator and Their Impact on the Mediation," 16 *Negot. J.* 5.

Brazil, Wayne D. (1998) "Why Should Courts Offer Non-binding ADR Services?" 16 *Alternatives* 65.

Brett, Jeanne M., Zoe I. Barsness, & Stephen B. Goldberg (1996) "The Effectiveness of Mediation: An Independent Analysis of Cases Handled by Four Major Service Providers," 12 *Negot. J.* 259 (July).

Bush, Robert A. Baruch (1996) "What Do We Need a Mediator For?: Mediation's 'Value-Added' for Negotiators," 12 *Ohio St. J. on Disp. Resol.* 1.

Bush, Robert A. Baruch, & Sally Ganong Pope (2004) "Transformative Mediation: Principles and Practice in Divorce Mediation," in J. Folberg, et al., eds., *Divorce and Family Mediation*. New York: Guilford Press.

Chester, Ronald (1999) "Less Law, But More Justice?: Jury Trials and Mediation as Means of Resolving Will Contests," 37 *Duq. L. Rev.* 173 (Winter).

Cobb, Sarah, & Janet Rifkin (1991) "Practice and Paradox: Deconstructing Neutrality in Mediation," 16 *Law & Soc. Inquiry* 35.

Cohen, Jonathan R. (1999) "Advising Clients to Apologize," 72 *S. Cal. L. Rev.* 1009.

Cole, Sarah Rudolph (2000) "Managerial Litigants? The Overlooked Problem of Party Autonomy in Dispute Resolution," 51 *Hastings L.J.* 1199.

Contuzzi, Peter (2000) "Should Parties Tell Mediators Their Bottom Line?" 8 *Disp. Res. Mag.* 30 (Spring).

Cooley, John W. (1997) "Mediation Magic: Its Use and Abuse," 29 *Loy. L. Rev.* 1 (Fall).

Cooper, Christopher (2000) "Police Mediators: Rethinking the Role of Law Enforcement in the New Millennium," 7 *Disp. Res. Mag.* 17 (Fall).

Creo, Robert A. (2001) "Emerging from No Man's Land to Establish a Bargaining Model," 19 *Alternatives* 191 (September).

Curtis, Dana (1998) "Reconciliation and the Role of Empathy," in J. Alfini & E. Galton, eds., *ADR Personalities and Practice Tips*. Washington, D.C.: ABA Section of Dispute Resolution.

Curtis, Dana, & John Toker (2000) "Representing Clients in Appellate Mediation: The Last Frontier," 1 *JAMS Alert.* 3 (December).

Deason, Ellen E. (2001) "Enforcing Mediated Settlement Agreements: Contract Law Collides with Confidentiality," 35 *U.C. Davis L. Rev.* 33 (November).

Deason, Ellen E. (2002) "Predictable Mediation Confidentiality in the U.S. Federal System," 17 *Ohio. St. J. on Disp. Resol.* 239.

Delgado, Richard (1988) "ADR and the Dispossessed: Recent Books About the Deformalization Movement," 13 *Law & Soc. Inquiry* 145.

Donahey, M. Scott (1995) "The Asian Concept of Conciliator/Arbitrator: Is It Translatable to the Western World?" 10 *Foreign Inv. L.J.* 120.

Dunnigan, Alana (2003) "Comment—Restoring Power to the Powerless: The Need to Reform California's Mandatory Mediation for Victims of Domestic Violence," 37 *U.S.F. L. Rev.* 1031.

Edwards, T. Harry (1986) "Alternative Dispute Resolution: Panacea or Anathema?" 99 *Harv. L. Rev.* 668 (January).

Folberg, Jay (1982) "Divorce Mediation: The Emerging American Model," paper presented at the Fourth Ann. Conf. of the Int'l Socy. for Family Law, Harv. U (June).

Folberg, Jay (1985) "Mediation of Child Custody Disputes," 19 *Colum. J.L. Soc. Probs.* 413.

Folberg, Jay (1996) "Certification of Mediators in California: An Introduction," 30 *U.S.F. L. Rev.* 609 (Spring).

Freedman, Lawrence R., & Michael L. Prigoff (1986) "Confidentiality in Mediation: The Need for Protection," 2 *Ohio St. J. on Disp. Resol.* 37.

Fuller, Lon (1971) "Mediation: Its Forms and Functions," 44 *S. Cal. L. Rev.* 305 (February).

Galanter, Marc (1983) "Reading the Landscape of Disputes: What We Know and Don't Know (and Think We Know) About Our Allegedly Contentious and Litigious Society," 31 *UCLA L. Rev.* 4 (October).

Geronemus, David (2001) "The Changing Face of Commercial Mediation," 19 *Alternatives* 38 (January).

Golann, Dwight (1989) "Making Alternative Dispute Resolution Mandatory: The Constitutional Issues," 68 *Or. L. Rev.* 487.

Golann, Dwight (2000) "Variations in Style: How—and Why—Legal Mediators Change Style in the Course of a Case," 2000 *J. Disp. Resol.* 40.

Golann, Dwight (2002) "Is Legal Mediation a Process of Reconciliation—Or Separation? An Empirical Study, and Its Implications," 7 *Harv. Negot. L. Rev.* 301.

Golann, Dwight (2004) "Death of a Claim: The Impact of Loss Reactions on Bargaining," 20 *Negot. J.* 539.

Golann, Dwight (2004) "How to Borrow a Mediator's Powers," 30 *Litig.* 41 (Spring).

Golann, Helaine, & Dwight Golann (2003) "Why Is It Hard for Lawyers to Deal with Emotional Issues?" 9 *Disp. Res. Mag.* 26 (Winter).

Green, Eric (1986) "A Heretical View of the Mediation Privilege," 2 *Ohio St. J. on Disp. Resol.* 1.

Green, Eric, & Jonathan Marks (2001) "How We Mediated the Microsoft Case," *The Boston Globe* A23 (November 15).

Grillo, Trina (1991) "The Mediation Alternative: Process Dangers for Women," 100 *Yale L.J.* 1545 (April).

Guthrie, Chris, & James Levin (1998) "A 'Party Satisfaction' Perspective on a Comprehensive Mediation Statute," 13 *Ohio St. J. on Disp. Resol.* 885.

Hermann, Michele (1994) "New Mexico Research Examines Impact of Gender and Ethnicity in Mediation," 1 *Disp. Res. Mag.* 10 (Fall).

Honeyman, Christopher (1990) "On Evaluating Mediators," 6 *Negot. J.* 23.

Hughes, Scott H. (1998) "A Closer Look: The Case for a Mediation Confidentiality Privilege Still Has Not Been Made," 5 *Disp. Res. Mag.* 14 (Winter).

Kakalik, James, et al. (1996) *An Evaluation of Mediation and Early Neutral Evaluation Under the Civil Justice Reform Act*. Santa Monica, Calif.: RAND Corp.

Keating, Michael (1996) "Mediating In the Dance For Dollars," 14 *Alternatives* 71 (September).

Kichaven, Jeffrey G. (1999) "How Advocacy Fits In Effective Mediation," 17 *Alternatives* 60.

Kirtley, Alan (1995) "The Mediation Privilege's Transition from Theory to Implementation: Designing a Mediation Privilege Standard to Protect Mediation Participants, the Process and the Public Interest," 1995 *J. Disp. Resol.* 1.

Kloppenberg, Lisa A. (2002) "Implementation of Court-Annexed Environmental Mediation: The District of Oregon Pilot Project," 17 *Ohio St. J. on Disp. Resol.* 559.

Kovach, Kimberlee K. (1997) "Good Faith in Mediation — Requested, Recommended, or Required? A New Ethic," 38 *S. Tex. L. Rev.* 38.

Kovach, Kimberlee K., & Lela P. Love (1998) "Mapping Mediation: The Risks of Riskin's Grid," 3 *Harv. Negot. L. Rev.* 71.

Laflin, James, & Robert Werth (2001) "Unfinished Business: Another Look at the Microsoft Mediation," 12 *California Tort Reporter No. 3*, 88 (May).

Lande, John (2002) "Using Dispute Systems Design Methods to Promote Good-Faith Participation in Court-Connected Mediation Programs," 50 *UCLA Law Rev.* 69 (October).

Levi, Deborah (1997) "The Role of Apology in Mediation," 72 *N.Y.U. L. Rev.* 1165.

Lewis, Michael (1995) "Advocacy in Mediation: One Mediator's View," 2 *Disp. Res. Mag.* 7 (Fall).

Lipsky, David A., & Ronald L. Seeber (1999) "Patterns of ADR Use in Corporate Disputes," 54 *Disp. Res. J.* 66 (February).

Love, Lela P. (1997) "The Top Ten Reasons Why Mediators Should Not Evaluate," 24 *Fla. St. U. L. Rev.* 937.

Lowry, L. Randolph (1997) "To Evaluate or Not — That Is Not the Question!" 2 *Resolutions* 2 (Pepperdine University School of Law).

Madoff, Ray D. (2002) "Lurking in the Shadow: The Unseen Hand of Doctrine in Dispute Resolution," 76 *S. Cal. L. Rev.* 161.

Matz, David E. (1999) "Ignorance and Interests," 4 *Harv. Negot. L. Rev.* 59.

Max, Rodney A. (1999) "Multiparty Mediation," 23 *Am. J. Trial Advoc.* 269.

McEwen, Craig (1998) "Managing Corporate Disputing: Overcoming Barriers to the Effective Use of Mediation for Reducing the Cost and Time of Litigation," 14 *Ohio St. J. on Disp. Resol.* 1.

McGuire, James E. (2004) "Certification: An Idea Whose Time Has Come," 10 *Disp. Res. Mag.* 22 (Summer).

Menkel-Meadow, Carrie (1999) "Do the 'Haves' Come out Ahead in Alternative Judicial Systems?: Repeat Players in ADR," 15 *Ohio St. J. on Disp. Resol.* 19.

Menkel-Meadow, Carrie (2001) "Ethics in ADR: The Many 'Cs' of Professional Responsibility and Dispute Resolution," 28 *Fordham Urban L.J.* 979.

Menkel-Meadow, Carrie, & Elizabeth Plapinger (1999) "Model Rules Would Clarify Lawyer Conduct When Serving as a Neutral," 6 *Disp. Res. Mag.* 20 (Summer).

Milne, Ann L. (2004) "Mediation and Domestic Abuse," in J. Folberg, et al., eds., *Divorce and Family Mediation*. New York: Guilford Press.

Mnookin, Robert H. (1993) "Why Negotiations Fail: An Exploration of Barriers to the Resolution of Conflict," 8 *Ohio St. J. Disp. Res.* 235.

Moffit, Michael (2003a) "Suing Mediators," 83 *B.U. L. Rev.* 147.

Moffit, Michael (2003b) "Ten Ways to Get Sued: A Guide for Mediators," 8 *Harv. Negot. L. Rev.* 81.

Nadler, Janice (2001) "In Practice: Electronically Mediated Dispute Resolution and E-Commerce," 17 *Negot. J.* 333.

Nolan-Haley, Jacqueline (1996) "Court Mediation and the Search for Justice Through Law," 74 *Wash. Univ. L.Q.* 47.

Nolan-Haley, Jacqueline (1998) "Lawyers, Clients, and Mediation," 73 *Notre Dame L. Rev.* 1369.

Press, Sharon (1998) "Florida's Court-Connected State Mediation Program," in Edward J. Bergman & John G. Bickerman, eds., *Court-Annexed Mediation: Critical Perspectives on State and Federal Programs*. Washington, D.C.: ABA Section of Dispute Resolution.

Price, Marty (2000) "Personalizing Crime: Mediation Produces Restorative Justice for Victims and Offenders," 7 *Disp. Res. Mag.* 8 (Fall).

Raitt, Susan E., et al. (1993) "The Use of Mediation in Small Claims Courts," 9 *Ohio St. J. on Disp. Resol.* 55.

Riskin, Leonard (1993) "Mediator Orientations, Strategies and Techniques," 12 *Alternatives* 111.

Riskin, Leonard (1996) "Understanding Mediator's Orientations, Strategies, and Techniques: A Grid for the Perplexed," 1 *Harv. Negot. L. Rev.* 7 (Spring).

Riskin, Leonard (2003a) "Decision-Making in Mediation: The New Old Grid and the New New Grid System," 79 *Notre Dame L. Rev.* 1 (December).

Riskin, Leonard (2003b) "Retiring and Replacing the Grid of Mediator Orientations," 21 *Alternatives* 69.

Robinson, Peter (1998) "Contending With Wolves in Sheep's Clothing: A Cautiously Cooperative Approach to Mediation Advocacy," 50 *Baylor L. Rev.* 963.

Rosenberg, Joshua D., & Jay Folberg (1994) "Alternative Dispute Resolution: An Empirical Analysis," 46 *Stan. L. Rev.* 1487.

Ross, David (2000) "Strategic Considerations in Choosing a Mediator: A Mediator's Perspective," 2 *J. Alt. Disp. Res. in Empl.* 7 (Spring).

Salacuse, Jeswald (2002) "Mediation in International Business," in J. Bercovitch, ed., *Studies in International Mediation*. New York: Palgrave Macmillan.

Salem, Richard (2003) "The Benefits of Empathic Listening," Conflict Research Consortium, University of Colorado, *http://www.crinfo.org*.

Schmitz, Suzanne J. (2001) "What Should We Teach in ADR Courses?: Concepts and Skills for Lawyers Representing Clients in Mediation," 6 *Harv. Negot. L. Rev.* 189.

Senger, Jeffrey M. (2002) "In Practice: Tales of the Bazaar—Interest-Based Negotiation Across Cultures," 18 *Negot. J.* 233 (July).

Seul, Jeffrey R. (1999) "How Transformative Is Transformative Mediation?: A Constructive-Developmental Assessment," 15 *Ohio St. J. on Disp. Resol.* 135.

Silbey, Susan S. (2002) "The Emperor's New Clothes: Mediation Mythology and Markets," 2002 *J. Disp. Resol.* 171.

Smith, Robert M. (2000) "Advocacy in Mediation: A Dozen Suggestions," 26 *S.F. Att'y* 14 (June/July).

Spolter, Jerry (2000) "A Mediator's Tip: Talk to Me!," *The Recorder* 4 (March 8).

Stempel, Jeffrey W. (1997) "Beyond Formalism and False Dichotomies: The Need for Institutionalizing a Flexible Concept of the Mediator's Role," 24 *Fla. St. U. L. Rev.* 949.

Stern, David M. (1998) "Mediation: An Old Dog with Some New Tricks," 24 *Litigation* 31 (Summer).

Stienstra, Donna, Molly Johnson, & Patricia Lombard (1997) "Report to the Judicial Conference Committee on Court Administration and Case Management: A Study of the Five Demonstration Programs Established Under the Civil Justice Reform Act of 1990." Washington, D.C.: Federal Judicial Center.

Stipanowich, Thomas J. (1998) "The Multi-Door Contract and Other Possibilities," 13 *Ohio St. J. on Disp. Resol.* 3.

Stipanowich, Thomas J. (2001) "Contracts Symposium: Contract and Conflict Managment," 2001 *Wis. L. Rev.* 831.

Stulberg, Joseph (1981) "The Theory and Practice of Mediation: A Reply to Professor Susskind," 6 *Vt. L. Rev.* 85.

Stulberg, Joseph (1997) "Facilitative Versus Evaluative Mediator Orientations: Piercing the 'Grid' Lock," 24 *Fla. St. U. L. Rev.* 985.

Susskind, Lawrence (1981) "Environmental Mediation and the Accountability Problem," 6 *Vt. L. Rev.* 1.

"Symposium: Dispute Resolution Ethics," *Disp. Resol. Mag.*(Spring 2001).

Technology Mediation Services (2004) "High Tech and Intellectual Property Disputes," *www.technologymediation.com/hightech.htm*.

Thompson, Leigh, & Janice Nadler (2002) "Negotiating Via Information Technology: Theory and Application," 58 *J. Soc. Issues* 109.

Weinstein, John (1996) "Advocacy in Mediation," 32 *Trial* 31.

Welsh, Nancy A. (2001) "Making Deals in Court-Connected Mediation: What's Justice Got to Do With It?," 79 *Wash. Univ. L.Q.* 787 (Fall).

Welsh, Nancy A., & Barbara McAdoo (1998) "Alternative Dispute Resolution in Minnesota—An Update on Rule 114," in Edward J. Bergman & John G. Bickerman, eds., *Court-Annexed Mediation: Critical Perspectives on State and Federal Programs*. Washington, D.C.: ABA Section of Dispute Resolution.

Wissler, Roselle L. (2001) "To Evaluate or Facilitate? Parties' Perceptions of Mediation Affected by Mediator Style," 7 *Disp. Res. Mag.* 35 (Winter).

Wissler, Roselle L. (2002) "Court-Connected Mediation in General Civil Cases: What We Know from Empirical Research," 17 *Ohio St. J. on Disp. Resol.* 641.

Wittenberg, Carol, Susan Mackenzie, & Margaret Shaw (1996) "Employment Disputes," in D. Golann, ed., *Mediating Legal Disputes: Effective Strategies for Lawyers and Mediators*. Boston: Little, Brown.

WEB SITES

American Bar Association Section of Dispute Resolution, *http://www.abanet.org/dispute/home* (Professional association of lawyers and law students interested in mediation and other forms of ADR).

Association for Conflict Resolution, *http://www.spidr.org* (Professional association for lawyers, law students, and nonlawyers interested in mediation and other forms of ADR).

Center for Analysis of Alternative Dispute Resolution Systems, *http://www.caadrs.org* (Abstracts of empirical studies of court-related ADR programs).

Center for the Study of Dispute Resolution, University of Missouri, *http://www.law.missouri.edu/csdr/adr* (References to information and other academic ADR Web sites).

Centre for Effective Dispute Resolution, *http://www.cedr.co.uk* (Information on British and European use of ADR in commercial disputes).

Conflict Resolution Information Source, Conflict Research Consortium, University of Colorado, *http://www.crinfo.org* (Information and referral sources on a wide variety of ADR issues).

CPR Institute of Dispute Resolution, *http://www.cpradr.org* (Information concerning use of ADR in commercial disputes).

Federal ADR Network, *http://www.adr.af.mil./general/guide_adr.doc* (a comprehensive list of ADR Web sites).

CASES

Byrd v. The State, 367 S.E.2d 300 (Ga. App. 1988).

Christian Cooper v. Melodie Austin, 750 So. 2d 711 (Fla. App. 2000).

Olam v. Congress Mortgage Co., 68 F. Supp. 2d 1110 (N.D. Cal. 1999).

Rojas v. Superior Court of Los Angeles County, 33 Cal. 4th 407.

VIDEOTAPES AND DVDS (ALL ARE VIDEOTAPES, UNLESS OTHERWISE NOTED)

Representing Clients

Golann, Dwight (2000) "Representing Clients in Mediation: How Advocates Can Share a Mediator's Powers," *http://www.abanet.org/cle* (Unscripted examples of advocates using mediators to advance bargaining goals).

Phillips, John (2003) "Mediation Madness," *http:// www.abanet.org/dispute/videos.html* (Examples of good and bad mediation advocacy).

Mediation Skills

Aaron, Marjorie Corman, & Dwight Golann (2004) "Mediators at Work: A Case of Discrimination?" *http://www.pon.org* (Unscripted mediation of an age discrimination case).

CPR Institute for Dispute Resolution (1994) "Mediation in Action," *http://www.cpradr.org* (Mediation of international contract dispute).

CPR Institute for Dispute Resolution (2003) "Resolution Through Mediation," *http:// www.cpradr.org* (Mediation of international trademark case).

Golann, Dwight, & Marjorie Corman Aaron (1999) "Mediators at Work: Breach of Warranty?" *http://www.pon.org* (Unscripted mediation of commercial contract dispute).

Himmelstein, Jack, & Gary Friedman (2001) "Saving the Last Dance: Mediation Through Understanding," *http://www.pon.org* (No-caucus mediation of a manager-organization dispute).

JAMS Foundation (2003) (DVD) "Mediating A Sexual Harassment Case: What Would You Do?" *http://www.jamsadr.com* (Vignettes of challenging situations for a mediator).

Part III, Arbitration

BOOKS AND TREATISES

Abrams, Roger I. (1998) *Legal Bases: Baseball and the Law*. Philadelphia: Temple Univ. Press.

American Arbitration Association (2000) *Drafting Dispute Resolution Clauses—A Practical Guide, http://www.adr.org/index2.1.jsp?JSPssid=15727 &JSPsrc=upload\LIVESITE\Rules_Procedures\ ADR_Guides\clausebook.html*.

American Arbitration Association Department of Neutrals' Education & Development (1999) *Role of the Panel Chair: Understanding Panel Dynamics*. New York: American Arbitration Association.

Bergsten, Eric (1980, with updates) *International Commercial Arbitration* (4 vols.). Dobbs Ferry, N.Y.: Oceana Publications.

Born, Gary B. (1994) *International Commercial Arbitration in the United States*. Boston: Kluwer Law and Taxation.

Buhring-Uhle, Christian (1996) *Arbitration and Mediation in International Business*. The Hague: Kluwer Law International.

Chemerinsky, Erwin (2003) *Federal Jurisdiction*. New York: Aspen.

Cronin-Harris, Catherine (1997) *Building ADR into the Corporate Law Department: ADR Systems Design*. New York: CPR Institute.

Dezalay, Yves, & Bryant G. Garth (1996) *Dealing in Virtue: International Commercial Arbitration and the Construction of a Transnational Legal Order*. Chicago: University of Chicago Press.

Kloppenberg, Lisa A. (2001) *Playing it Safe: How the Supreme Court Sidesteps Hard Cases and Stunts the Development of Law*. New York: New York University Press.

Lipsky, David B., & Ronald L. Seeber (1998) *The Appropriate Resolution of Corporate Disputes: A Report on the Growing Use of ADR by U.S. Corporations*. Ithaca, N.Y.: Cornell/PERC Institute on Conflict Resolution.

Macneil, Ian R., Richard E. Speidel, & Thomas J. Stipanowich (Supp. 1997) *Federal Arbitration Law: Agreements, Awards and Remedies Under the Federal Arbitration Act*. Boston: Little, Brown

Noonan, John T., Jr. (2002) *Narrowing the Nation's Power: The Supreme Court Sides with the States*. Berkeley, Calif.: University of California Press.

Nordham, George Washington (1982) *George Washington and the Law*.

Paulsson, Jan, Nigel Rawding, Lucy Reed, & Eric Schwartz (2d ed. 1999) *The Freshfields Guide to Arbitration and ADR: Clauses in International Contracts*. Boston: Kluwer Law International.

Perino, Michael A. (2002) *Report to the Securities and Exchange Commission Regarding Arbitrator Conflict Disclosure Requirements in NASD and NYSE Securities Arbitrations*. Washington, D.C.: SEC.

Redfern, Alan, Martin Hunter, & Murray Smith (2d ed. 1991) *Law and Practice of International Commercial Arbitration*. London: Sweet & Maxwell.

Reisman, Michael W., W. Laurence Craig, William W. Park, & Jan Paulsson (1997) *International Commerce Arbitration*. Westbury, N.Y.: Foundation Press.

Sanders, Pieter, ed. (1984) *International Handbook on Commercial Arbitration*. International Council for Commercial Arbitration. Boston: Kluwer Law International.

Stipanowich, Thomas J., & Peter Kaskell, eds. (2001) *Commercial Arbitration at Its Best: Successful Strategies for Business Users*. Chicago: American Bar Association.

Uff, John, & Elizabeth Jones, eds. (1990) *International and ICC Arbitration: Conference Papers and Source Materials*. London: King's College London, Centre of Construction Law and Management.

Van der Berg, Albert Jan, ed. (1999) *Improving the Efficiency of Arbitration Agreements and Awards: 40 Years of Application of the New York Convention*, International Chamber of Commerce Arbitration Congress series no. 9. Boston: Kluwer Law International.

ARTICLES

(1995) "The ABCs of ADR: A Dispute Resolution Glossary," 13 *Alternatives* 147.

Arnold, Tom (1992) "Contracts to Arbitrate Patent and Other Commercial Disputes," 10 *Alternatives* 191 (December).

Arnold, Tom (1999) "Setting Up the Preliminary Administration Conference, The First Arbitrator-Party Communications" (unpublished manuscript).

Bingham, Lisa (2003) "Self-Determination in a Dispute System Design and Mandatory Commercial Arbitration, 67 *Law & Contemp. Probs.*

Bingham, Lisa B., & Shimon Sharaf (2004) "Employment Arbitration Before and After the Due Process Protocol for Mediation and Arbitration of Statutory Disputes Arising Out of Employment: Preliminary Evidence That Self-Regulation Makes a Difference," in Samuel Estreicher & David Sherwyn, eds., *Alternative Dispute Resolution in the Employment Arena, Proceedings of New York University 53rd Annual Conference on Labor*. The Hague: Kluwer Law International.

Brennan, Lisa (1999) "What Lawyers Like: Mediation," 22 *Nat'l L.J.* A1 (November 15th).

Brunet, Edward (2002) "Seeking Optimal Dispute Resolution Clauses in High Stakes Employment Contracts," 23 *Berkeley J. Empl. & Lab. L.* 107.

Carrington, Paul D., & Paul H. Haagen (1997) "Contract and Jurisdiction," 1996 *Sup. C. Rev.* 331.

Carter, James H. (1996/1997) "The Attorney-Client Privilege in Arbitration," *ADR Currents* 1 (Winter).

Chernick, Richard (2003) "Developments Affect Arbitrator Disclosure and Contractual ADR," *Dispute Resolution Alert* (March/April) 1.

Cole, Sarah Rudolph (1996) "Incentives and Arbitration: The Case Against Enforcement of Executory Arbitration Agreements Between Employers and Employees," 64 *UMKC L. Rev.* 449 (Spring).

Delikat, Michael, & Morris M. Kleiner (2003) "Arbitration Awards Better than Lawsuits," *Insurance Times*, vol. XXIII, no. 9 (April 9).

Eisenberg, Theodore, & Elizabeth Hill (2003-2004) "Arbitration and Litigation of Employment Claims: An Empirical Comparison," 58 *Disp. Res. J.* 44 (November-January).

Gorske, Robert H. (1990) "An Arbitrator Looks at Expediting the Large, Complex Case," 5 *Ohio St. J. on Disp. Resol.* 381.

Harding, Margaret (2004) "The Limits of Due Process Protocols," 19 *Ohio St. J. on Disp. Resol.* 369.

Hayford, Stephen L. (1996) "Law in Disarray: Judicial Standards for Vacatur of Arbitration Awards," 30 *Ga. L. Rev.* 731.

Hayford, Stephen L. (1998) "A New Paradigm for Commercial Arbitration: Rethinking the Relationship Between Reasoned Awards and the Judicial Standards for Vacatur," 66 *Geo. Wash. L. Rev.* 443 (March).

Hayford, Stephen L. (2000) "The Federal Arbitration Act: Key to Stabilizing and Strengthening the Law of Labor Arbitration," 21 *Berkeley J. Empl. & Lab. L.* 521.

Hayford, Stephen (2000) "Unification of the Law of Labor Arbitration and Commercial Arbitration: An Idea Whose Time Has Come," 52 *Baylor L. Rev.* 781.

Hayford, Stephen (2002) "A Response to RUAA Critics," *Disp. Res. Mag.* (Summer).

Hochman, Stephen A. (1999) "Model Dispute Resolution Provisions for Use in Commercial Agreements Between Parties with Equal Bargaining Power," in Paul H. Haagen, ed., *Arbitration Now: Opportunities for Fairness, Process Renewal and Invigoration*. Newark, N.J.: The Alternative Newsletter.

Hoellering, Michael, & Peter Goetz (1992) "Piercing the Veil: Document Discovery in Arbitration Hearings," 47 *Arb. J.* 58 (September).

(1984) "IBM & Gartner Group Settle Trade Secret Suit by Creating Future Arbitration Panel," 2 *Alternatives* 8 (September).

Kaplan, Jarril F. (1996) "ADR Clauses Must Anticipate Contingencies," 14 *Alternatives* 16 (February).

Katsoris, Constantine N. (1996) "SICA: The First Twenty Years," 23 *Fordham Urb. L.J.* 483.

Love, Carl G. (1995) "9th Circuit Gives Lesson about ADR Clauses: Very Narrow Wording Defeats the Purpose," 13 *Alternatives* 87 (July).

Matthews, Donna Meredith (1997) "Employment Law After *Gilmer*: Compulsory Arbitration of Statutory Antidiscrimination Rights," 18 *Berkeley J. Empl. & Lab. L.* 347.

Meth, Elissa M. "Final Offer Arbitration: A Model for Dispute Resolution in Domestic and International Disputes," 10 *Am. Rev. Int'l Arb.* 383.

(1994) "Model Agreement Between Parties, Neutral," 12 *Alternatives* 83 (June).

Moses, Margaret (2004) "Can Parties Tell Courts What to Do? Expanded Judicial Review of Arbitral Awards," 52 *U. Kan. L. Rev.* 429.

Myers, James J. (1996) "Ten Techniques for Managing Arbitration Hearings," 51 *Disp. Res. J.* 28 (January-March).

Offenkrantz, Ronald J. (1997) "Arbitrating RICO: Ten Years After *McMahon*," 1997 *Colum. Bus. L. Rev.* 45.

Poppleton, Allen (1981) "The Arbitrator's Role in Expediting the Large and Complex Commercial Case," 36 *Arb. J.* 6 (December).

Randall, Bret F. (1992) "The History, Application and Policy of the Judicially Created Standards of Review for Arbitration Awards," 1992 *B.Y.U. L. Rev.* 759.

Resnik, Judith (1995) "Many Doors? Closing Doors? Alternative Dispute Resolution and Adjudication," 10 *Ohio St. J. on Disp. Resol.* 211.

Rome, Donald Lee (1997) "Writing Rules: Eliminate the Boilerplate, and Draft According to the Terms of the Deal (Part II of II)," 15 *Alternatives* 159 (December).

Rome, Donald Lee (1998a) "A New Approach to ADR for the Financial Services Industry," 54 *Secured Lender* 23 (May-June).

Rome, Donald Lee (1998b) "Preserving Rights — and ADR — by Knowing When to Use a 'Carve Out' (Part III of III)," 16 *Alternatives* 6 (January).

Sant, John T. (1997) "How Contract Clauses Can Ensure ADR (Part I of III)," 15 *Alternatives* 146 (November).

Schaller, William L. (2000) "Protecting Trade Secrets During Litigation: Policies and Procedures," 88 *Ill. B. J.* 260 (May).

Schwartz, David S. (1997) "Enforcing Small Print to Protect Big Business: Employee and Consumer Rights Claims in an Age of Compelled Arbitration," 1997 *Wis. L. Rev.* 33.

Schwartz, David S. (2003) "Understanding Remedy-Stripping Arbitration Clauses: Validity, Arbitrability, and Preclusion Principles," 38 *U.S.F. L. Rev.* 49 (Fall).

Smit, Hans (1997) "Contractual Modification of the Scope of Judicial Review of Arbitral Awards," 8 *Am. Rev. Int'l Arb.* 147.

Sternlight, Jean R. (1996) "Panacea or Corporate Tool? Debunking the Supreme Court's Preference for Binding Arbitration," 74 *Wash. U. L.Q.* 637.

Sternlight, Jean R. (2002) "As Mandatory Binding Arbitration Meets the Class Action, Will the Class Action Survive? 42 *Wm. & Mary L. Rev.* 1.

Stipanowich, Thomas J. (1988) "Rethinking American Arbitration," 63 *Ind. L.J.* 425.

Stipanowich, Thomas J. (1997) "Punitive Damages and the Consumerization of Arbitration," 92 *Nw. U. L. Rev.* 1.

Stipanowich, Thomas J. (2001) "Contract and Conflict Management," *Wis. L. Rev.* 831.

Stipanowich, Thomas J. (2004a) "ADR and 'The Vanishing Trial': The Growth and Impact of 'Alternative Dispute Resolution,' " — *J. Empirical Leg. Research* — (forthcoming).

Stipanowich, Thomas J. (2004b) "ADR and 'The Vanishing Trial': What We Know — and What We Don't," 10 *Disp. Res. Mag.* 7 (Summer).

Stone, Katherine Van Wezel (1996) "Mandatory Arbitration of Individual Employment Rights: The Yellow Dog Contract of the 1990s," 73 *Denv. U. L. Rev.* 1017.

Ware, Stephen J. (2003) "Contractual Arbitration, Mandatory Arbitration, and State Constitutional Jury-Trial Rights," 38 *U.S.F. L. Rev.* 39.

Williams Walsh, Mary (2001) "Fired Workers Fire Back, Then Fall Hard," *New York Times* G1 (May 9).

Younger, Stephen P. (1999) "Agreements to Expand the Scope of Judicial Review of Arbitration Awards," 63 *Alb. L. Rev.* 241.

CLAUSES, PROCEDURES, AND RULES

American Arbitration Association (2003) *Commercial Arbitration Rules and Mediation Procedures (Including Procedures for Large, Complex Commercial Disputes),* http://www.adr.org/index2.1.jsp?JSPssid= 15747&JSPsrc=upload\LIVESITE\Rules_ Procedures\National_International\..\..\focusArea\ commercial\AAA235current.htm.

American Arbitration Association (1998) *Consumer Due Process Protocol,* http://www.adr.org/ index2.1.jsp?JSPssid=16235&JSPsrc=upload/ livesite/Resources/EduResources/consumer_ protocol.html.

American Arbitration Association/American Bar Association (1977) *Code of Ethics for Arbitrators in Commercial Disputes.*

American Arbitration Association/American Bar Association (2004) *2004 Revised Code of Ethics for Arbitrators in Commercial Disputes,* http://www.abanet.org/dispute/commercial_disputes. pdf.

American Bar Association (1995) *A Due Process Protocol for Mediation and Arbitration of Statutory Disputes Arising Out of the Employment Relationship,* 91 Daily Lab. Rep. (BNA) A-8, E-11 (May 11).

CPR Institute for Dispute Resolution (2000) *CPR Dispute Resolution Clauses,* CPR MAPP Series, vol. I.

CPR Institute for Dispute Resolution (2000) *ADR Suitability Screen,* CPR MAPP Series, vol. 1.

CPR Institute for Dispute Resolution (1999) *Arbitration Appeal Procedure.*

CPR Institute for Dispute Resolution (1994) *CPR Non-Administered Arbitration of Patent and Trade Secret Disputes Rules.*

CPR-Georgetown Commission on Ethics and Standards in ADR (1999) *Proposed Model Rule of Professional Conduct for the Lawyer as Third Party Neutral.*

International Chamber of Commerce International Court of Arbitration (1998) *Rules of Arbitration,* http://www.iccwbo.org/court/english/ arbitration/rules.asp.

JAMS (Rev. 2002) *Comprehensive Arbitration Rules and Procedures* (Aug.).

London Court of International Arbitration (1998) *Arbitration Rules,* http://www.lcia-arbitration.com/ arb/uk.htm.

National Association of Securities Dealers (2004) *Code of Arbitration Procedure,* http:// www.nasdadr.com/arb_code/arb_code.asp.

Simpson Thacher & Bartlett, (1998) *A Chart Comparing International Commercial Arbitration Rules.* Huntington, N. Y.: Juris Publishing.

UNCITRAL Notes on Organizing Arbitral Proceedings, U.N. Doc. V.96-84935 (1996) http://www.transdata.ro/drept/Uncitral/ arbnotes.htm.

**VIDEOS AND OTHER RESOURCES
(ALL ARE VIDEOTAPES, UNLESS
OTHERWISE NOTED)**

Parker School of Foreign and Comparative Law,
Columbia University (1993) *Commercial
Arbitration: An International Bibliography*.
*Report of the Arbitration Policy Task Force to the Board
of Governors National Association of Securities
Dealers, Inc.* (January 1996).

Part IV, Mixing, Matching, and Moving Forward

BOOKS AND TREATISES

ABA Sub-Committee on Alternative Means of
Dispute Resolution (1986) *The Effectiveness of the
Mini-Trial in Resolving Complex Commercial
Disputes: A Survey*. Chicago: American Bar
Association.
Chernick, Richard, et al., eds. (1997) *Private
Judging: Privatizing Civil Justice*. Washington,
D.C.: National Legal Center for the Public
Interest.
Costantino, Cathy A., & Christina S. Merchant
(1996) *Designing Conflict Management Systems*.
San Francisco: Jossey-Bass.
CPR Institute for Dispute Resolution (2003) *How
Companies Manage Employment Disputes*.
New York: CPR Institute.
Dispute Prevention Through Partnering (1998) CPR
Institute for Dispute Resolution MAPP Series.
Goldberg, Stephen B., et al. (1997 Supp.) in
John Wilkinson, et al., eds., *Donovan Leisure
Newton & Irvine ADR Practice Book*. New York:
John Wiley.
Katsh, Ethan, & Janet Rivkin (2001) *Online Dispute
Resolution — Resolving Conflicts in Cyberspace*. San
Francisco: Jossey-Bass.
Maryland Mediation and Conflict Resolution
Office (2004) "The Use of Alternative Dispute
Resolution (ADR) in Maryland Business: A
Benchmarking Study." Annapolis, Md.: MACRO.
Plapinger, Elizabeth, & Donna Stienstra (1996)
*ADR and Settlement in the Federal District Courts: A
Sourcebook for Judges & Lawyers*.
Rule, Colin (2002) *Online Dispute Resolution for
Business: B2B, Ecommerce, Consumer, Employment,
Insurance, and Other Commercial Conflicts*. San
Francisco: Jossey-Bass.
Scanlon, Kathleen (Supp. 2003) *Drafter's
Deskbook — Dispute Resolution Clauses*. New York:
CPR Institutes.
Stipanowich, Thomas J., & Peter Kaskell, eds.
(2001) *Commercial Arbitration at Its Best:
Successful Strategies for Business Users*. Chicago:
American Bar Association.

ARTICLES

Arnold, Tom (1996) "MEDALOA, The Dispute
Resolution Process of Choice," December 27
(unpublished manuscript).

Bartel, Barry C. (1991) "Comment, Med-Arb as a
Distinct Method of Dispute Resolution: History,
Analysis, and Potential," 27 *Willamette L. Rev.*
661.
Brazil, Hon. Wayne (2001) "A Judge's Perspective
on Lawyering and ADR," 19 *Alternatives* 44
(January).
Elliott, David C. (1995) "Med/Arb: Fraught with
Danger or Ripe with Opportunity?" 34 *Alberta
L. Rev.* 163.
Enix-Ross, Deborah, & Thomas D. Halket (1999)
"ADR and On-Line Dispute Resolution," in
Paul H. Haagen, ed., *Arbitration Now:
Opportunities for Fairness, Process Renewal and
Invigoration*. New York: American Bar
Association.
Feinberg, Kenneth R. (2001) "One-Stop
Shopping: Using ADR to Resolve Disputes and
Implement a Settlement," 19 *Alternatives* 59
(January).
Field, Robert C., & Robert W. Robertson (1993)
"The Hearing," in Bette J. Roth, et al., eds., *The
Alternative Dispute Resolution Practice Guide*.
Scarborough, Ont.: Carswell.
Flaherty, Francis (1987) "Neutrals Deployed
Several Kinds of ADR to Solve IBM-Fujitsu
Copyright Dispute," 5 *Alternatives* 187
(November).
Flake, Richard P. (1998) "Nuances of Med/Arb: A
Neutral's Perspective," 3 *ADR Currents* 8 (June).
Fortier, L. Yves (2001) "International
'E-commercial' Dispute Resolution,"
19 *Alternatives* 23 (January).
Green, Tristin K. (2003) "Targeting Workplace
Context: Title VII as a Tool for Institutional
Reform," 72 *Fordham L. Rev.* 659.
Howard, William (1995) "Arbitrating Claims of
Employment Discrimination," 50 *Disp. Res. J.*
40 (October–December).
McEwen, Craig A. (1998) "Managing Corporate
Disputing: Overcoming Barriers to the
Effective Use of Mediation for Reducing the
Cost and Time of Litigation," 14 *Ohio St. J. on
Disp. Resol.* 1.
Nelson, Hon. Dorothy W. (2001) "ADR in the New
Era," 19 *Alternatives* 65 (January).
Niemic, Robert J., et al. (2001) "Descriptions
of the Principal Court-Based ADR Processes,"
in *Guide to Judicial Management of Cases in ADR*.
Washington, D.C.: Federal Judicial Center.
Niemic, Robert J., et al. (2001) "Matching the
ADR Process to the Case," in *Guide to Judicial
Management of Cases in ADR*. Washington, D.C.:
Federal Judicial Center.
Peppet, Scott R. (2004) "Contract Formation in
Imperfect Markets: Should We Use Mediators
in Deals?" 38 *Ohio St. J. on Disp. Resol.* 283.
Peter, James T. (1997) "Note & Comment: Med-
Arb in International Arbitration," 8 *Am. J. Int'l
Arb.* 83.
Plant, David W. (2000) "The Arbitrator as
Settlement Facilitator," 17 *J. Int'l Arb.* 143.
Reno, Hon. Janet (2001) "The Federal
Government and Appropriate Dispute
Resolution: Promoting Problem Solving and
Peacemaking as Enduring Values in Our
Society," 19 *Alternatives* 16 (January).

Sanders, Frank (1976) "Varieties of Dispute Processing," 70 *F.R.D.* 111.

Singer, Linda R. (2001) "The Lawyer as Neutral," 19 *Alternatives* 40 (January)

Stallworth, Lamont E., et al. (2001) "Discrimination in the Workplace: How Mediation Can Help," *Disp. Res. J.* 35 (February-April).

Stipanowich, Thomas J. (1996) "Beyond Arbitration: Innovation and Evolution in the United States Construction Industry," 31 *Wake Forest L. Rev.* 65.

Stipanowich, Thomas J. (1998) "The Multi-Door Contract and Other Possibilities," 13 *Ohio St. J. on Disp. Resol.* 303.

Stipanowich, Thomas J. (2001) "Contract and Conflict Management," *Wis. L. Rev.* 831.

Stipanowich, Thomas J. (forthcoming 2004) "ADR and the 'Vanishing Trial': The Growth and Impact of 'Alternative Dispute Resolution,'" __ *J. Empirical Legal Res.* __.

Trantina, Terry L. (2001) "How to Design ADR Clauses That Satisfy Clients' Needs and Minimize Litigation Risk," 19 *Alternatives* 137 (May).

Warshauer, Irene C. (1999) "The Neutral in Multiple Roles: Practical and Ethical Issues," in Paul H. Haagen, ed., *Arbitration Now: Opportunities for Fairness, Process Renewal and Invigoration*. New York: American Bar Association.

CLAUSES, PROCEDURE, AND RULES

American Chemistry Council, *Chemical Industry Dispute Resolution Commitment*.

CPR Corporate Policy Statement on Alternatives to Litigation (2004).

eBay, *Simple 4-Step Process to Resolve Disputes* (2004).

VIDEOS AND OTHER RESOURCES

CPR Institute for Dispute Resolution (1987) *Out of Court: The Minitrial*, Videotape and Videotape Study Guide. New York: CPR Institute.

TABLE OF CASES

Principal cases are indicated by italics.

INDEX